LABOR RELATIONS LAW
Cases and Materials

Sixth Edition

CONTEMPORARY LEGAL EDUCATION SERIES

Labor Relations Law

CASES AND MATERIALS

Sixth Edition

Russell A. Smith
Professor Emeritus of Law
University of Michigan

Leroy S. Merrifield
Lobingier Professor of Jurisprudence
and Comparative Law
The George Washington University

Theodore J. St. Antoine
Professor of Law
University of Michigan

THE BOBBS-MERRILL COMPANY, INC.
PUBLISHERS

INDIANAPOLIS • NEW YORK • CHARLOTTESVILLE, VIRGINIA

Preface to Sixth Edition

The experience of the editors in teaching from the most recent editions of this casebook is that its structure is essentially sound and workable. Our assessment seems to be confirmed by the kind words of many readers, both faculty members and students. We are deeply grateful to them, not only for their endorsement of our basic design but also for their thoughtful and helpful suggestions for improving the details of our treatment. The aims of this revision are thus to bring LABOR RELATIONS LAW up to date and to adjust the focus to present realities.

As in the past, we have tried to respond generously to the most significant current developments in labor law while at the same time providing a set of materials that will be truly manageable in the usual three- or four-hour introductory course. In 1979 this means, concretely, a substantial expansion in the coverage of equal employment opportunity law, because it has assumed a central role in industrial relations and because it has given rise to certain key new concepts (*e.g.,* the "disparate impact" theory of discrimination) that may have profound implications for the evolution of all American law. Conversely, our approach has led to the deletion of the section on public employee unionism. We believe that adequate treatment of this important and timely (but not indispensable) subject now requires a separate course, along with a comprehensive body of materials like that supplied by the newly revised casebook in the Contemporary Legal Education Series, Edwards, Clark & Craver, LABOR RELATIONS LAW IN THE PUBLIC SECTOR.

For this Sixth Edition we shall continue our practice of publishing an annual softbound supplement so that the book will be up-to-date at the beginning of each school year.

Once again we are pleased to thank those students whose capable, conscientious work as research assistants contributed so much to this revision: Steven Fetter, Kenneth J. Kryvoruka, and Anita Schoomaker.

Ann Arbor, Michigan
Washington, D.C.
July 1979

Russell A. Smith
Leroy S. Merrifield
Theodore J. St. Antoine

Preface to Fourth Edition

The present casebook is a stem-to-stern overhaul of the previous edition. Restructuring, rather than merely updating, the subject matter has enabled us to take better account of shifts in emphasis from one area to another in the fast-moving world of labor law. In recent years, for example, much attention has focused on the emerging body of federal law governing labor contracts; on the rights of individual employees, both in collective bargaining and within unions; and on the resurgence of union organizational efforts, especially among such former "unorganizables" as public employees. Our revision reflects these and other new developments. For the future, we plan to provide annual softbound supplements so that the work will be up-to-date at the beginning of each school year.

To make the interrelationship of the various parts of the course more readily comprehensible, we have abandoned our refined decimal breakdown of sections and have grouped the materials under broader headings. These correspond generally to large chronological units in the union-employer relation, from the organizing drive through contract enforcement. The last part of the volume, which could be the nucleus of a second short course, deals with internal union affairs.

All major substantive parts of the book, and a number of subdivisions, are introduced by short excerpts from labor economists, industrial relations experts, practicing attorneys, and other nondecisional sources. We hope these items will shed fresh light on the subjects covered by the more traditional statutory and case selections, and will stimulate further reading in relevant extralegal materials.

A key assumption underlies this casebook. We believe the field of "labor law" is now so vast that a basic course should confine itself primarily to the law of labor-management relations, with perhaps a brief look at the law of union-member relations. To avoid undue dilution, we feel that the more practical aspects of negotiating and administering labor agreements (including arbitration) should be left for separate treatment—preferably where the "problem" method can be employed. In dealing with collective bargaining, therefore, we concentrate on the legal framework and not on specific contract clauses or the way arbitrators resolve day-to-day disputes.

There is more in this casebook than can be handled in the usual three-hour course, although one editor covers the highlights in an intensive two-hour summer session. We think any teacher worth his salt would want the opportunity for personal selection. One man may wish to stress the rules of union-employer combat, and another the rules of diplomacy. Both should find here ample room for choice.

Our thanks go to the following students who served as research assistants during the preparation of this volume: Terry Fenzl, Peter Hoffman, Cornelius W. Keane, Paul Lieberman, Stanley Lubin, Steven W. Martineau, Lawrence J. Sherman, Gerald Sommer, and Robert M. Vercruysse.

The original footnote numbers in quoted materials have generally been retained. The editors' notes are numbered consecutively within each section. Any deviations from this practice are indicated.

Ann Arbor, Michigan
Washington, D. C.
May 1968

Russell A. Smith
Leroy S. Merrifield
Theodore J. St. Antoine

Preface to First Edition

The development of an adequate course in labor law presents peculiarly difficult problems of organization and method, as every teacher in the field knows. In part, this is because of the convolutions of the subject matter which have resulted from society's confused groping for principles to govern this area of human relations; in part, it is because so many of the important aspects of the labor-management problem are nonlegal, at least in the strict sense. The individual teacher must attempt, within the time allocated by his curriculum committee, to provide his students with the kind of treatment of the subject which he considers best adapted to serve the major objectives of the course.

The selection of these objectives is the critical threshold problem, and in the reasonable differences in judgment on this matter lies a sufficient justification, quite apart from any other, for independent experimentation in the preparation of teaching media. Obviously, the student who expects to practice labor law should be provided with a minimum foundation of knowledge of the materials relating to labor-management relations which he will be called upon to use professionally. In addition, I believe that the course should be of interest to the student who contemplates little, if any, labor law practice, in giving him, as a future lawyer-citizen, an informed awareness of what may loosely be called "the labor-management problem." Each objective, of course, calls for a treatment of the technical structure of the relevant law, and, beyond that, enough of an introduction to the relevant nonlegal considerations to stimulate, if not fully to inform.

Even the attempt to present the strictly legal aspects, however, involves some necessary choices. A complete coverage of the subject would require a treatment of myriad statutes, ordinances, judicial decisions and other materials ranging all the way from regulations of plant sanitary and safety conditions (including workmen's compensation) through child labor, wage-hour and social security legislation and on to all the law pertaining to unionism and collective bargaining. Any such attempt would prove to be abortive in a single course. Some phases of the subject must be omitted or at least given less emphasis than others. It is commonly agreed that the law relating to trade unionism and collective bargaining is to be given priority in the introductory or only course, and I have accordingly emphasized this branch of the law. At the same time I have provided (in Appendix I) a syllabus treatment of the most important statutes representing the policy of legislative regulation of employment conditions. Some knowledge of these statutes is part of the essential informational equipment of the collective bargainer, and is thus amply justified, if not required, in a course devoted primarily to union-management relations. In addition, its inclusion helps to develop a more adequate appreciation of the general architecture of labor law. Ultimately, two law school courses will probably be necessary, if, as seems likely, there is increasing resort to political solutions of the problem of employment standards.

Among the strictly nonlegal materials which are included in this volume are various aspects of the subject of collective bargaining and dispute settlement. I consider these to have a mandatory place in the labor law course, in view of their general significance and their practical importance to the labor lawyer. Indeed, some law teachers would make collective bargaining (including the administration of collective agreements) the main body of the course, since they conceive of this "constructive" aspect of labor-management relations as being far more important than the "pathological" and sporadic instances of improper conduct or of resort to collective action which receive primary attention in a study emphasizing "the law" of labor relations. I share this view of the relative importance of the subject of bargaining, and have devoted to it Part III of the book—which constitutes a substantial portion of the whole. Yet I do not agree that the problems of employer antiunionism, or of union collective action, should be watered down in the law school course, ostrich-like, to the point that they will seem not to exist. And certainly the legal procedures, existing and proposed, for handling the so-called "critical" disputes, and what may be referred to as the "institutional" legal relations of unionism, are independently worthy of treatment.

To undertake this much has resulted in a volume of substantial size. Looked at in terms of the customary law school daily work assignment of straight case material, there is more here than can be covered in a two or three hour course. However, a considerable part of the material (*e.g.*, Chapters I-III) is background. Many of the rather extensive notes develop secondary and collateral considerations. In this as in other public law fields, the student should not consider that there is a "vested interest" in a 10-30 page assignment, as in the traditional private law courses. Even so an instructor may have to make some selections of the materials which he considers most important. If he wishes to emphasize the law of labor-managment relations, he will probably omit substantial parts of Chapter IX, dealing with critical disputes, Chapter X, dealing with collective bargaining, and perhaps all of Chapter XI, dealing with arbitration. If he wishes to give special attention to problems of collective bargaining and dispute settlement, he will skeletonize Chapters IV, VI, VII, VIII, and XII, and emphasize Chapters V, IX, X, and XI. Such an opportunity for variation and selection in treatment seems to me to be desirable in this field.

I have attempted to develop an outline of the subject matter on a topical basis, such that the value of the book will not depend upon the vagaries of a particular session of Congress. Thus, the labor relations acts are not treated separately, with the exception of the special problems considered in Chapter VIII. The chapters commencing with Chapter IV (which really begins the substantive material) deal with the several large problems which are going to be with us in the foreseeable future, regardless of the content of a given statute.

The somewhat complicated numerical system identifying heads and subheads was adopted in order to facilitate the annual preparation of supplementary material. This supplementary material will either be "fed" directly into the book, in the case of the looseleaf edition, or published as a separate addendum in the case of the permanently bound edition. I am myself convinced that in this and other public law fields where the law is changing rapidly there is much to be said for the looseleaf type of publication.

I wish to acknowledge my special indebtedness to the following: Professor William C. Soule of Wake Forest College of Law, who, while a graduate student at Michigan, assisted me, especially in the preparation of some of the materials for Chapter IX; Eleanor Kimball, who, while a research associate at Michigan, did much of the work on the historical materials presented in Chapter I; Frank Elkouri and Sylvester Petro, who, while graduate fellows and research assistants at Michigan, contributed substantially in the development of Chapters XI and XII, respectively; Irving J. Levy, Esq., of the Washington, D. C. bar, who made valuable suggestions concerning the content of the syllabus on the Fair Labor Standards Act, which appears as part of Appendix I; Professor William Haber, of the University of Michigan Department of Economics, who very graciously performed a similar service with respect to the syllabus on social security legislation, which appears as part of Appendix I; Albert Meder, Esq., of the Detroit Bar, for his permission to print in Chapter X portions of his address on the collective bargaining process; the various book publishers, authors, and law reviews and other publications whose consents were given to the quotation of materials used; and K. Douglas Mann, Jerry McCroskey, George Cholack, C. L. Mann, Harold Yamada, and Jean Rudesill, who, while students at Michigan, performed valuable service as research assistants and in other capacities.

Ann Arbor, Michigan   *Russell A. Smith*
February 10, 1950

Summary Table of Contents

Table of Contents

Table of Cases

Principal cases are those with page references in italics.

A

B

C

G

I

J

M

S

Y

PART ONE
HISTORICAL BACKGROUND AND INTRODUCTION

FOREWORD

Labor relations law is dynamic, philosophically divisive, and highly sensitive both to last November's elections and to this morning's headlines. For adequate understanding, the student and the lawyer must examine much more than the law itself. The perspective of history, as well as some knowledge of the economic, social, and political aspects of unionism, all are essential aids in evaluating the efforts of courts and legislatures to create suitable legal standards.

Most of the information presented below concerning American labor organizations is to be found in the literature produced by the labor historians and economists, and there is no pretense of originality in any of it. The objective has been to reduce a mass of material to fairly comfortable dimensions and to make it easily available for immediate consultation as the student begins to work in this field.[1]

SECTION I. Historical Background

A. THE PRE-CIVIL WAR PERIOD

1. EARLY DEVELOPMENT OF LABOR UNIONS

In the early years of this country's history there were comparatively few free workers. The great majority of laborers were either Negro slaves or indentured servants who, to secure passage to America, had bound themselves in servitude for a term of years. As trade and commerce increased, however, there was an increased demand for free workers. The skilled craftsmen, as they began to open small shops and use helpers, soon found it to their advantage to employ free workers whom they could dismiss when business was poor and for whose maintenance they had no responsibility. Other factors such as the seasonal nature of many trades and the danger of loss of a large investment in runaway slaves made free labor desirable. As the terms of the bondsmen expired, and as craftsmen immigrated from Europe in large numbers, lured by the comparatively high prices paid for skilled labor and the glowing accounts of a laborer's life in America, the group of free wage earners steadily increased.

---

[1] Principal sources used in preparing this summary are as follows:

A. BLUM, A HISTORY OF THE AMERICAN LABOR MOVEMENT (1972);

D. BOK & J. DUNLOP, LABOR AND THE AMERICAN COMMUNITY (1970);

J. COMMONS & ASSOCIATES, HISTORY OF LABOR IN THE UNITED STATES (1918);

F. DULLES, LABOR IN AMERICA (3d ed. 1966);

A. FAULKNER & M. STARR, LABOR IN AMERICA (rev. ed. 1957);

A. GOLDBERG, AFL-CIO: LABOR UNITED (1956);

In these times the master worked side by side with his journeymen and apprentices, and there was as yet no well-defined distinction between the interests of master and workmen. Journeymen looked forward to the time when they would become master craftsmen. The market was local and the master bargained directly with his customers for the price of his product. Because of the scarcity of skilled labor and because the master could set his prices noncompetitively, wage rates were generally high, as compared, for example, with wages paid in England. This, however, did not necessarily mean that the Colonial worker's lot as a whole was an enviable one; in some colonies there was maximum wage legislation; workers had to compete with slave labor and, during the winter months, with farmers who sought temporary employment in town. When work was slack, the jails were filled with workers who could not meet their debts, and poverty was widespread. The worker had not yet conceived the idea that he could improve his lot through self-organization.

There were, it is true, labor organizations of a sort existing in America as early as the seventeenth century, but they were not trade unions in the modern sense — that is, permanent organizations of workers created to achieve, by concerted action, improvements in wages, hours, and other terms and conditions of employment. Rather, they were primarily guilds of artisans who marketed their own products. They sought to maintain working standards by regulation of apprenticeship requirements and to exert control over wage rates and prices. The few so-called "strikes" which occurred in the Colonial period were not strikes by workers against their masters for increased wages, but for the most part were protests by master craftsmen against local government regulations relaxing apprenticeship requirements or setting ceilings on prices.

The Philadelphia printers who "turned out" in 1786 for a minimum wage of $6.00 per week are credited with having called the first genuine labor strike. However, it was not until 1792 that any continuous organization of wage earners appeared. In that year the Philadelphia shoemakers formed an organization, which existed for about a year. In 1794 the shoemakers created the Federal Society of Journeymen Cordwainers, which survived until 1806. Other localized craft unions

S. Gompers, Seventy Years of Life and Labor (1925) (P. Taft & J. Sessions abr. ed. 1957);

R. Morris, Government and Labor in Early America (1946);

H. Pelling, American Labor (1960);

S. Perlman, A History of Trade Unionism in the United States (1937);

S. Perlman & P. Taft, History of Labor in the United States, 1896-1932 (1935);

J. Rayback, A History of American Labor (1966);

P. Taft, Organized Labor in American History (1964);

P. Taft, The AF of L from the Death of Gompers to the Merger (1959);

P. Taft, The AF of L in the Time of Gompers (1957);

L. Ulman, The Rise of the National Trade Union (1956);

U.S. Department of Labor, Brief History of the American Labor Movement (1964);

U.S. Department of Labor, Bicentennial History of the American Worker (R. Morris, ed. 1976).

quickly sprang up throughout the country. Besides providing the customary services of fraternal societies, their usual aims were to achieve shorter hours, higher wages, the enforcement of apprenticeship regulations, and the closed shop.

2. THE "CRIMINAL CONSPIRACY" DOCTRINE

Judicial reaction to these early attempts of labor to organize in order to improve working conditions was highly unfavorable. Applying the doctrine as established in England in the early eighteenth century, the courts in this country began to condemn the concerted activities of workers' associations as "criminal conspiracies." The following case, digested from the full report which appears in the monumental documentary history compiled by John R. Commons and associates, is a classic in the history of labor law. It is fully analyzed in its social setting in Nelles, *The First American Labor Case,* 41 YALE L.J. 165 (1931).

PHILADELPHIA CORDWAINERS' CASE
[COMMONWEALTH v. PULLIS]

Philadelphia Mayor's Court (1806)
3 Doc. Hist. of Am. Ind. Soc. 59 (2d ed. Commons 1910)

Indictment for common law conspiracy, tried before a jury consisting of two inn-keepers, a tavern-keeper, three grocers, a merchant, a hatter, a tobacconist, a watchmaker, a tailor, a bottler.

The indictment charged in substance: (1) That defendants conspired and agreed that none of them would work at the shoemaking craft except at certain specified prices higher than prices which had theretofore customarily been paid; (2) that defendants conspired and agreed that they would endeavor to prevent "by threats, menaces, and other unlawful means" other craftsmen from working except at said specified rates; and (3) that defendants, having formed themselves into an association, conspired and agreed that none of them would work for any master who should employ a cordwainer who had broken any rule or bylaw of the association, and that defendants, in accordance with such agreement refused to work at the usual rates and prices.

Counsel for the prosecution were Jared Ingersol and Joseph Hopkinson. Counsel for the defendants were Caesar A. Rodney and Walter Franklin.

During his address to the jury, Mr. Joseph Hopkinson, for the prosecution, stated, among other things, the following:

"If the court and jury shall decide, that journeymen may associate together, and determine that none shall work under certain prices; then, when orders arrive for considerable quantities of any article, the association may determine to raise the wages, and reduce the contracts to diminish their profit; to sustain a loss, or to abandon the execution of the orders, as was done in Bedford's case, who told you he could have afforded to execute the orders he obtained at the southward, had wages remained the same as when he left Philadelphia. When they found he had a contract, they took advantage of his necessity. What was done by the journeymen shoemakers, may be done by those of every other trade, or manufacturer in the city. . . . A few more things of this sort, and you will break up the manufactories; the masters will be afraid to make a contract, therefore he must relinquish the export trade, and depend altogether upon the profits of the work of Philadelphia, and confine his supplies altogether to the city. The last turn-out had liked to have produced that effect: Mr. Ryan told you he had intended to confine himself to bespoke work.

"It must be plain to you, that the master employers have no particular interest in the thing . . . if they pay higher wages, you must pay higher for the articles. They, in truth, are protecting the community. Nor is it merely the advance of wages that encreases the price to the consumer, the master must have some compensation for the advance of his cash, and the credit he frequently gives. They have no interest to serve in the prosecution; they have no vindictive passions to gratify . . . they merely stand as the guardians of the community from imposition and rapacity." (pp. 137-8).

"If this conspiracy was to be confined to the persons themselves, it would not be an offense against the law, but they go further. There are two counts in the indictment; you are to consider each, and give your verdict on each. The first is for contriving, and intending, unjustly and oppressively, to encrease and augment the wages usually allowed them. The other for endeavouring to prevent, by threats, menaces, and other unlawful means, other journeymen from working at the usual prices, and that they compelled others to join them.

"If these persons claim the right to put the price on their own work, if they say their labour is their own, and they are the judges of its value, why not admit the same right to others? If it is the right of Dubois, and the other defendants, is it not equally the right of Harrison and Cummings? We stand up for the right of the journeymen, as well as of the masters. The last turn-out was carried by a small majority . . . 60 against 50, or thereabout: shall 60 unreasonable men, perhaps single men, having no one to provide for but themselves, distress and bring to destruction, 50 married men with their families? Let the 60 put what price they please on their own work; but the others are free agents also: leave them free, or talk no more of equal rights, of independence, or of liberty.

"It may be answered, that when men enter into a society they are bound to conform to its rules; they may say, the majority ought to govern the minority . . . granted . . . but they ought to leave a man free to join, or not to join the society. If I go into a country I am bound to submit to its laws, but surely I may judge, whether or not I will go there. The society has no right to force you into its body, and then say you shall obey its rules under severe penalties. By their constitution you find, and from their own lips I must take the words, that though a man wants no more wages than he gets, he must join in a turn-out. The man who seeks an asylum in this country, from the arbitrary laws of other nations, is coerced into this society, though he does not work in the article intended to be raised; he must leave his seat and join the turn-out." (pp. 138-9.)

Recorder Levy, in his charge to the jury, made the following statements, among others:

"It is proper to consider, is such a combination consistent with the principles of our law, and injurious to the public welfare? The usual means by which the prices of work are regulated, are the demand for the article and the excellence of its fabric. Where the work is well done, and the demand is considerable, the prices will necessarily be high. Where the work is ill done, and the demand is inconsiderable, they will unquestionably be low. If there are many to consume, and few to work, the price of the article will be high; but if there are few to consume, and many to work, the article must be low. Much will depend, too, upon these circumstances, whether the materials are plenty or scarce; the price of the commodity, will in consequence be higher or lower. These are the means by which prices are regulated in the natural course of things. To make an artificial regulation, is not to regard the excellence of the work or quality of the material, but to fix a positive and arbitrary price, governed by no standard, controlled by no impartial person, but dependent on the will of the few who are interested; this is the unnatural way of raising the price of goods or work. This is independent of the number who are to do the work. It is an unnatural, artificial means of raising the price of work beyond its standard, and taking an undue advantage of the public. Is the rule of law bottomed upon such principles, as to permit or protect such conduct? Consider it on the footing of the general commerce of the city. Is there any man who can calculate (if this is tolerated) at what price he may safely contract to deliver articles, for which he may receive orders, if he is to be regulated by the journeymen in an arbitrary jump from one price to another? It renders it impossible for a man, making a contract for a large quantity of such goods, to know whether he shall lose or gain by it. If he makes a large contract for goods today, for delivery at three, six or nine months hence, can he calculate what the prices will be then, if the journeymen in the intermediate time, are permitted to meet and raise their prices, according to their caprice or pleasure? Can he fix the price of his commodity for a future day? It is impossible that any man can carry on commerce in this way. There cannot be a large contract entered into, but what the contractor will make at his peril. He may be ruined by the difference of prices made by the journeymen in the intermediate time. What then is the operation of this kind of conduct upon the commerce of the city? It exposes it to inconveniences, if not to ruin; therefore, it is against the public welfare. . . .

"What is the case now before us? . . . . A combination of workmen to raise their wages may be considered in a two fold point of view; one is to benefit themselves . . . the other is to injure those who do not join their society. The rule of law condemns both. If the rule be clear, we are bound to conform to it even though we do not comprehend the principle upon which it is founded. We are not to reject it because we do not see the reason of it. It is enough, that is the will of the majority. It is law because it is their will — if it is law, there may be good reasons for it though we cannot find them out. But the rule in this case is pregnant with sound sense and all the authorities are clear upon the subject. Hawkins, the greatest authority on the criminal law, has laid it down, that a combination to maintaining one another, carrying a particular object, whether true or false, is criminal ... the authority cited from 8 Mod. Rep. does not rest merely upon the reputation of that book. He gives you other authorities to which he refers. It is adopted by Blackstone, and laid down as the law by Lord Mansfield 1793, that an act innocent in an individual, is rendered criminal by a confederacy to effect it. . . .

"One man determines not to work under a certain price and it may be individually the opinion of all; in such a case it would be lawful in each to refuse to do so, for if each stands, alone, either may extract from his determination when he pleases. In the turn-out of last fall, if each member of the body had stood alone, fettered by no promises to the rest, many of them might have changed their opinion as to the price of wages and gone to work; but it has been given to you in evidence, that they were bound down by their agreement, and pledged by mutual engagements, to persist in it, however contrary to their own judgment. The continuance in improper conduct may therefore well be attributed to the combination. The good sense of those individuals was prevented by this agreement, from having its free exercise." . . .

The defendants were found guilty and were fined eight dollars each plus costs.

It wasn't until the decision in *Commonwealth v. Hunt* [2] in 1842 that the first break in the doctrine of criminal conspiracy occurred, enabling labor to shift its emphasis from political action towards "business unionism" (which seeks improvement through collective bargaining). In that case certain workmen had been found guilty of criminal conspiracy. On appeal, however, exceptions to the indictment were sustained and the conviction was reversed. The opinion of Chief Judge Shaw is confusing as to its rationale, and therefore difficult to dissect, but in some respects it seemed to be in disagreement with the prevailing views concerning the legality of trade union activities. For example, allegations in the indictment that defendants had agreed not to work for any employer who should employ a nonunion workman were held to be insufficient, at least on the assumption that defendants were not under contractual obligations to the employer. The court also ruled that a conspiracy to impoverish another workman, who was alleged to have lost his employment because he was not a union member, was not in itself unlawful; that illegality would depend upon the means used. "If it is to be carried into effect by fair or honorable and lawful means, it is, to say the least, innocent; if by falsehood or force, it may be stamped with the character of conspiracy." [3]

---

[2] 45 Mass. (4 Met.) 111, 38 Am. Dec. 346 (1842).

[3] For a detailed examination of the case, see Nelles, *Commonwealth v. Hunt*, 32 COLUM. L. REV. 1128 (1932).

B. THE POST-CIVIL WAR ERA

1. THE GROWTH OF NATIONAL UNIONS AND LABOR UNREST

Several present-day unions — the typographers, hatters, machinists, and molders — had their origins in the 1850's, but they suffered setbacks in the depression of 1857. During the years of the Civil War there was a heavy demand for labor due to the shortage of manpower. Prices were high, wages lagged behind, and hours were long. As the size of the business unit increased, the impersonalized employer-employee relationship introduced by the factory system became more evident. With improved transportation conditions workers tended to move about more freely in search of suitable employment so that standardized working conditions became increasingly important. Workers came to realize the need for broader organization of their unions. Local units were federated into local trades' associations and many crafts were organized nationally. There were thirty-two national and international (so-called because of affiliates in Canada) unions in 1866. Among the more important of these were organizations of locomotive engineers, bricklayers and masons, carpenters and joiners, cigar makers and shoemakers. The shoemakers, one of the first of the groups to feel the effects of the factory system, organized in 1867 under the designation of the Order of Knights of St. Crispin. The purpose of the union was to protect its members against unemployment occasioned by the introduction of machinery and the attendant use of unskilled labor. By 1868 the Order had chartered 600 chapters, numbered 50,000 members, and was the largest craft union then in existence.

In 1866 the National Labor Union was formed under the leadership of William H. Silvis, a leader in the iron molders' union. This was a loosely-built federation of national trades unions, city trades assemblies, local trade unions, and reform organizations of various kinds. Among the contributions of this union to the development of the trade union movement in the United States was its leadership in the movement for an eight-hour day, its insistence upon organization of women and Negro workers, and its emphasis upon equal pay for equal work for these two categories of workers most frequently and flagrantly discriminated against. Various reasons have been advanced to explain the ultimate failure of the Union: internal dissension which divided the organization when it became involved in politics; the failure of its commercial enterprises, causing many to lose confidence in its leaders; the fact that many of its members, who were primarily interested in local and craft matters, thought its aims too broad; and the loss of the outstanding leadership of Silvis by reason of his death in 1869. By 1872 it had virtually disappeared.

The panic of 1873 began a six-year period of hard times for the worker and with the depression came a severe weakening of labor organization which frustrated plans for further federation. Only a few of the national craft unions survived and these were depleted in membership and financial strength. It was a period of turbulence in management-union relationships. The railroad strikes in the summer of 1877 on the three main trunk lines running west, which were precipitated by reductions in wages, were particularly violent. Federal troops and state militia were called out to "restore order."

One of the two important survivors among the labor unions of the depression years of 1873-1879 was the Noble Order of the Knights of Labor, which was organized in 1869 by the tailors of Philadelphia. The sponsors of this union conceived that the weaknesses which the trade unions had shown in the depression period were in part attributable to lack of unity, and that strength would come from a consolidation in one organization of all labor groups, including the unskilled as well as the skilled. They therefore welcomed into their ranks all who worked, even some employers and members of the professions.

The "Knights" was thus an attempt at amalgamation of local unions into a nationwide organization. The union was highly organized, each local union being subordinate to a district organization which, in turn, was directly responsible to a central supreme council. Since the local assemblies were mixed in craft and industrial character, the sympathetic strike became a powerful weapon in their hands with the bargaining power of the skilled workers reinforcing that of the unskilled. On the other hand, opposing points of view of the constituent groups became the basis for serious internal dissension later on. The general aims of the organization were to oppose the accumulation of wealth in the hands of a few and in other ways to secure for workers a fuller enjoyment of the wealth they created. These aims were to be achieved by legislation and education rather than by strikes and other forms of economic action.

This idealistic program for a co-operative society found its most ardent supporter in Terence V. Powderly who became president (Master Workman) of the Knights in 1878. But despite the philosophy which was written into the Preamble of the Order and was referred to as the "First Principles" — that improvement of the worker's condition should be sought through political action and not by means of the militant methods of industrial warfare — a more pragmatic element in the union ultimately got control and turned to typical economic action in an effort to achieve immediate results. Threats of strikes became common and the fear of a general strike made even such a powerful capitalist as Jay Gould seek terms with the union.[4] In 1886 the Order reached its peak membership of 700,000.

---

[4] In 1885 strikes had been called on Gould-controlled railroads because of a reduction in wages. These strikes were successful, largely because engineers, firemen, brakemen, and conductors all along the lines joined with the strikers. Shortly thereafter another strike was called because of a reduction in labor force on one of the roads. Even though the operating employees did not support the strikers this time, Gould, fearing a general strike, held a conference with members of the executive board of the Order and the receivers of his railroads at which time he threw his influence in favor of the union. This was the first time a great capitalist had discussed the workers' problems with a labor organization. The Order received a great deal of publicity for this achievement and the masses of the laboring

The year 1886 has sometimes been called the period of "the great upheaval." It was a period of nationwide strikes, sympathetic strikes which were set in motion on the least provocation, violence and turbulence including the famous "Haymarket" riots in Chicago,[5] the widespread use of the boycott, and the rise of a strong feeling of labor class consciousness, particularly among the unskilled. During the latter half of 1886, however, the strikes ended, for the most part disastrously for labor.

From 1886 on, the Knights of Labor declined in popularity and membership. One of the reasons for this was the presence of conflicting interests within the Order. Other causes of the disintegration of the organization were the weak, utopian, vacillating leadership of Powderly, the persistent efforts of the newspapers to link the Knights with the famous Haymarket incident, and the efficient spy and blacklist system of the Pinkerton agency, much used by employers. Whatever the reasons, the Knights were practically defunct by the early nineties.

The ideology of the Knights of Labor was in direct contrast with that of the trade unions, one of which, the Cigar Makers' International Union, was the other important survivor of the labor movement of the sixties. Both Adolph Strasser, president of this union in 1877, and Samuel Gompers, then president of its New York local, had been influenced by men trained in the Marxist school, some of whom, formerly workers in the revolutionary labor movements of Europe, were leaders in the cigar makers' unions in New York. Both Strasser and Gompers eventually turned away from the philosophies of the more radical element in the union in support of a program which they believed would bring more immediate benefits to the worker. "The philosophy which these new leaders developed might be termed a philosophy of pure wage consciousness. It signified a labor movement reduced to an opportunistic basis, accepting the existence of capitalism and having for its object the enlarging of the bargaining power of the wage earner in the sale of his labor." [6]

Gompers and other leaders also stood for craft union autonomy and accused the Knights of Labor of trying to make the craft unions subservient to the interest of the less skilled workers. This bitter rivalry

population rushed to join up. S. PERLMAN, HISTORY OF TRADE UNIONISM IN THE UNITED STATES 87 (1937). But Powderly did not on this occasion even ask for union recognition, bargaining machinery, or other conventional union objectives, so that victory was not enduring. See H. HARRIS, AMERICAN LABOR, A HISTORY 78-79 (1939).

[5] A meeting of strikers was held in Haymarket Square, Chicago, in May, 1886, to protest against the killing of four strikers the day before by police who had attacked strikers at the McCormick reaper works. As police advanced to disperse the meeting, a bomb was thrown into their midst, killing many. Although this action was blamed on anarchists, Chicago citizens were thrown into panic and the incident turned many former sympathizers against the strikers. H. HARRIS, AMERICAN LABOR, A HISTORY 85-89 (1939). It has been asserted that the conviction of the "Haymarket Martyrs" followed one of the most unfair trials in history. See generally, H. DAVID, HISTORY OF THE HAYMARKET AFFAIR (1936).

[6] S. PERLMAN, A HISTORY OF TRADE UNIONISM IN THE UNITED STATES 78 (1937).

eventually led to the reorganization of the Federation of Organized Trades and Labor Unions which had been impotent since its birth in 1881. The reorganization occurred in 1886, at which time the name of the organization was changed to "The American Federation of Labor." The AFL placed its emphasis upon business unionism rather than upon reform through legislation, relegating to subordinate state federations its legislative interests. Said Samuel Gompers in his autobiography: "The secret of this continuous progress [of the AFL] has been understanding of the nature and possibilities of economic power and concentration on mobilization of that power. The Federation has maintained that economic organization is adequate to deal with all of the problems of wage earners. Its political action is simply to utilize the functions of the trade union in another field." [7]

While an officer of the Cigar Makers' Union, Gompers had recognized the need for union organization on a business-like basis. He saw that there should be sustained office work and paid union administrators. He believed that financial strength was the foundation of stable unionism and that dues should be paid regularly. In searching for something to make it worthwhile for the worker to maintain continuous membership in the union, he adopted the plan of unemployment benefits and sickness and death provisions from the program of the British trades unions. Another policy adopted from the British was equalization of funds. Under this plan, the central office retained for operating expenses a certain sum from the dues and fees collected, and each local union kept for itself a certain sum proportionate to its membership. Any excess over and above these deductions was used to build up the treasury of any locals whose funds had been depleted by strike or other unusual expenditures.

Originally, the AFL was a federation of national and international craft unions and such locals as were not organized in nationals or internationals. The national and international organizations retained their autonomy. They chartered their locals, determined membership requirements, disciplined their members, conducted strikes, negotiated with employers, and otherwise acted as independent unions with respect to their particular craft problems. The function of the federation was to act in those matters which were of general interest to all. It arbitrated jurisdictional matters, maintained the craft autonomy of its affiliates, and gave financial aid and moral encouragement during strikes.

After 1893 business was depressed, but the AFL and other trade unions were able to maintain their organizations and ride out hard times despite membership losses. Later in the decade business conditions improved but the federation had many obstacles to overcome, the most important of which was the problem of coping with the expansion of corporate power. Giant corporations such as the Carnegie Steel Company and the Pullman Company succeeded in smashing important strikes in 1892 and 1894.[8] But

---

[7] 2 S. GOMPERS, SEVENTY YEARS OF LIFE AND LABOR 268 (1925).

[8] When negotiations failed to end in an agreement, a strike was called on June 29, 1892, by the Amalgamated Iron and Steelworkers against the Carnegie Steel Company in protest against a wage reduction. Pinkerton detective agents had been hired by the company to

by 1898 the AFL had proved its stability, and had even managed to keep out of the violent political campaign of 1896 when, despite the seductive allure of Bryan and "free silver," Gompers' nonpartisan "reward your friends and punish your enemies" policy was approved and supported. By 1904 there were no less than ninety stable national and international unions, most of which, excepting the railroad and postal unions, were affiliated with the AFL.

Employers at this time began to adopt numerous new anti-union tactics. During the depression of 1907 they disregarded collective agreements made when business had been good and labor had been in demand. "Scientific management" and "efficiency" (speed-up) systems were introduced in plants which forced the workers to work harder and faster for the same wages. Vigilante groups and citizens' committees were fostered by employers to resist union activities. Employer associations took a hand. The National Founders' Association and the National Metal Trades Association, for example, each maintained a "labor bureau," which kept a card index of every man in the employ of its members, and facilitated the use of the "black list" against unionists. These associations also furnished workers when needed, so that resort to the unions for employees was unnecessary, and they furnished strikebreakers upon request. There was also the National Association of Manufacturers, whose chief effort lay in the legislative field where it attempted, through lobbying, to nullify labor's political influence.

2. JUDICIAL REACTION AND THE LABOR INJUNCTION

Opposition to the trade union movement came not only from employers. The courts began to issue injunctions against strikes and picketing. This form of remedy, with its obvious advantages of speed and flexibility, especially when issued ex parte, quickly became standard in this country almost to the exclusion of criminal prosecutions, except insofar as such prosecutions were based on statutes such as the antitrust laws or miscellaneous local statutes and ordinances. In consequence, the

---

serve as guards. When they arrived by boat at Homestead, Pennsylvania, a battle with the strikers ensued. At least half a dozen men were killed and many were seriously wounded. The Pinkerton men were defeated and left, but the state militia was called and remained in Homestead for several months, with the result that the strike was eventually broken and the union dismembered. *See* S. PERLMAN, A HISTORY OF TRADE UNIONISM IN THE UNITED STATES 134 (1937).

The American Railway Union, formed in 1893 by Eugene V. Debs, supported a strike of its members at the paternalistic company town of Pullman, Illinois, by refusing to handle trains containing Pullman cars. This sympathetic boycott by railroad employees was accompanied by considerable violence, despite Debs' warnings against it. Upon petition of the United States Attorney General, a federal court issued a sweeping injunction against interfering with the railroads or inducing railroad employees to refrain from doing their work. Debs was found guilty of contempt and sentenced to six months in jail. *In re* Debs, 158 U.S. 564 (1895). The report of the United States Strike Commission which investigated the Pullman strike is important as an early expression of public concern with a national labor policy recognizing collective bargaining.

development of the common law concerning trade unionism has been substantially the work of the equity judges proceeding, by easy transition, from the inheritance of the early common law of criminal conspiracy to the creation of a body of tort law dealing with the propriety of labor union objectives and means.

The majority opinion in the following landmark case exemplifies the prevailing judicial approach around the turn of the century, and the dissent of Judge Oliver Wendell Holmes, Jr., is a forerunner of later developments in labor law.

VEGELAHN v. GUNTNER

Supreme Judicial Court of Massachusetts
167 Mass. 92, 44 N.E. 1077 (1896)

. . . The following decree was entered at a preliminary hearing upon the bill: "This cause came on to be heard upon the plaintiff's motion for a temporary injunction; and after due hearing, at which the several defendants were represented by counsel, it is ordered, adjudged, and decreed that an injunction issue *pendente lite,* to remain in force until the further order of this court, or of some justice thereof, restraining the respondents and each and every one of them, their agents and servants, from interfering with the plaintiff's business by patrolling the sidewalk or street in front or in the vicinity of the premises occupied by him, for the purpose of preventing any person or persons, who now are or may hereafter be in his employment, or desirous of entering the same, from entering it, or continuing in it; or by obstructing or interfering with such persons, or any others, in entering or leaving the plaintiff's said premises; or by intimidating, by threats or otherwise, any person or persons who now are or may hereafter be in the employment of the plaintiff, or desirous of entering the same, from entering it, or continuing in it; or by any scheme or conspiracy among themselves or with others, organized for the purpose of annoying, hindering, interfering with, or preventing any person or persons who now are, or may hereafter be, in the employment of the plaintiff, or desirous of entering the same, from entering it, or from continuing therein."

Hearing upon the bill and the answers before Holmes, J., who reported the case for the consideration of the full court, as follows:

"The facts admitted or proved are that, following upon a strike of the plaintiff's workmen, the defendants have conspired to prevent the plaintiff from getting workmen, and thereby to prevent him from carrying on his business unless and until he will adopt a schedule of prices which has been exhibited to him, and for the purpose of compelling him to accede to that schedule, but for no other purpose. If he adopts that schedule, he will not be interfered with further. The means adopted for preventing the plaintiff from getting workmen are (1) in the first place, persuasion and social pressure. And these means are sufficient to affect the plaintiff disadvantageously, although it does not appear, if that be material, that they are sufficient to crush him. I ruled that the employment of these means for the said purpose was lawful, and for that reason refused an injunction against the employment of them. If the ruling was wrong, I find that an injunction ought to be granted.

"(2) I find also, that, as a further means for accomplishing the desired end, threats of personal injury or unlawful harm were conveyed to persons seeking employment or employed, although no actual violence was used beyond a technical battery, and although the threats were a good deal disguised, and express words were avoided. It appeared to me that there was danger of similar acts in the future. I ruled that conduct of this kind should be enjoined.

"The defendants established a patrol of two men in front of the plaintiff's factory, as one of the instrumentalities of their plan. The patrol was changed every hour, and continued from half-past six in the morning until half-past five in the afternoon, on one of the busy streets of Boston. The number of men was greater at times, and at times showed some little inclination to stop the plaintiff's door, which was not serious, but seemed to me proper to be enjoined. The patrol proper at times went further than simple advice, not obtruded beyond the point where the other person was willing to listen, and conduct of that sort is covered by (2) above, but its main purpose was in aid of the plan held lawful in (1) above. I was satisfied that there was probability of the patrol being continued if not enjoined. I ruled that the patrol, so far as it confined itself to persuasion and giving notice of the strike, was not unlawful, and limited the injunction accordingly.

"There was some evidence of persuasion to break existing contracts. I ruled that this was unlawful, and should be enjoined.

"I made the final decree appended hereto. If, on the foregoing facts, it ought to be reversed, or modified, such decree is to be entered as the full court may think proper; otherwise, the decree is to stand."

The final decree was as follows: "This cause came on to be heard, and was argued by counsel; and thereupon, on consideration thereof, it is ordered, adjudged, and decreed that the defendants, and each and every of them, their agents and servants, be restrained and enjoined from interfering with the plaintiff's business by obstructing or physically interfering with any persons in entering or leaving the plaintiff's premises numbered 141, 143, 145, 147 North Street in said Boston, or by intimidating, by threats, express or implied, of violence or physical harm to body or property, any person or persons who now are or hereafter may be in the employment of the plaintiff, or desirous of entering the same, from entering or continuing in it, or by in any way hindering, interfering with, or preventing any person or persons who now are in the employment of the plaintiff from continuing therein, so long as they may be bound so to do by lawful contract. . . ."

ALLEN, J. The principal question in this case is whether the defendants should be enjoined against maintaining the patrol. The report shows that, following upon a strike of the plaintiff's workmen, the defendants conspired to prevent him from getting workmen, and thereby to prevent him from carrying on his business, unless and until he should adopt a certain schedule of prices. The means adopted were persuasion and social pressure, threats of personal injury, or unlawful harm, conveyed to persons employed or seeking employment, and a patrol of two men in front of the plaintiff's factory, maintained from half-past six in the morning till half-past five in the afternoon, on one of the busiest streets in Boston. The number of men was greater at times, and at times showed some little disposition to stop the plaintiff's door. The patrol proper at times went further than simple advice, not obtruded beyond the point where the other person was willing to listen; and it was found that the patrol would probably be continued, if not enjoined. There was also some evidence of persuasion to break existing contracts.

The patrol was maintained as one of the means of carrying out the defendants' plan, and it was used in combination with social pressure, threats of personal injury or unlawful harm, and persuasion to break existing contracts. It was thus one means of intimidation indirectly to the plaintiff, and directly to persons actually employed, or seeking to be employed, by the plaintiff, and of rendering such employment unpleasant or intolerable to such persons. Such an act is an unlawful interference with the rights both of employer and of employed. An employer has a right to engage all persons who are willing to work for him, at such prices as may be mutually agreed upon; and persons employed or seeking employment have a corresponding right to enter into, or remain in, the employment of any person or corporation willing to employ them. These rights are secured by the constitution itself [citing cases]. No one can lawfully interfere by force or intimidation to prevent employers or persons employed or wishing to be employed from the exercise of these rights. In Massachusetts, as in some other states, it is even made a criminal offense for one by intimidation or force to prevent or seek to prevent a person from entering into or continuing in the employment of a person or corporation. Pub. Sts. c. 74, Section 2. Intimidation is not limited to threats of violence or of physical injury to person or property. It has a broader signification, and there also may be a moral intimidation which is illegal. Patrolling or picketing, under the circumstances stated in the report, has elements of intimidation like those which were found to exist in Sherry v. Perkins, 147 Mass. 212. It was declared to be unlawful in Regina v. Druitt, 10 Cox C.C. 592; Regina v. Hibbert, 13 Cox C.C. 82, and Regina v. Bauld, 13 Cox C.C. 282. It was assumed to be unlawful in Trollope v. London Building Trades Federation, 11 T.L.R. 228, though in that case the pickets were withdrawn before the bringing of the bill. The patrol was an unlawful interference both with the plaintiff and with the workmen, within the principle of many cases, and, when instituted for the purpose of interfering with his business, it became a private nuisance. . . .

The defendants contend that these acts were justifiable, because they were only seeking to secure better wages for themselves by compelling the plaintiff to accept their schedule of wages. This motive or purpose does not justify maintaining a patrol in front of the plaintiff's premises, as a means of carrying out their conspiracy. A combination among persons merely to regulate their own conduct is within allowable competition, and is lawful, although others may be indirectly affected thereby. But a combination to do injurious acts expressly directed to another, by way of intimidation or constraint, either of himself or of persons employed or seeking to be employed by him, is outside of allowable competition, and is unlawful. . . .

Nor does the fact that the defendants' acts might subject them to an indictment prevent a court of equity from issuing an injunction. It is true that ordinarily a court of equity will decline to issue an injunction to restrain the commission of a crime; but a continuing injury to property or business may be enjoined, although it may also be punishable as a nuisance or other crime. . . .

A question is also presented whether the court should enjoin such interference with persons in the employment of the plaintiff who are not bound by contract to remain with him, or with persons who are not under any existing contract, but who are seeking or intending to enter into his employment. A conspiracy to interfere with the plaintiff's business by means of threats and intimidation, and by maintaining a patrol in front of his premises in order to prevent persons who are in his employment from continuing therein, is unlawful, even though such persons are not bound by contract to enter into or to continue in his employment; and the injunction should not be so limited as to relate only to persons who are bound by existing contracts. Walker v. Cronin, 107 Mass. 555, 565; Carew v. Rutherford, 106 Mass. 1; Sherry v. Perkins, 147 Mass. 212; Temperton v. Russell [1893] 1 Q.B. 715, 728, 731; Flood v. Jackson, 11 T.L.R. 276.

In the opinion of a majority of the court the injunction should be in the form originally issued.

So ordered. . . .

HOLMES, J. In a case like the present, it seems to me that, whatever the true result may be, it will be of advantage to sound thinking to have the less popular view of the law stated, and therefore, although when I have been unable to bring my brethren to share my convictions my almost invariable practice is to defer to them in silence, I depart from that practice in this case, notwithstanding my unwillingness to do so in support of an already rendered judgment of my own.

In the first place, a word or two should be said as to the meaning of the report. I assume that my brethren construe it as I meant it to be construed, and that, if they were not prepared to do so, they would give an opportunity to the defendants to have it amended in accordance with what I state my meanings to be. There was no proof of any threat or danger of a patrol exceeding two men, and as of course an injunction is not granted except with reference to what there is reason to expect in its absence, the question on that point is whether a patrol of two men should be enjoined. Again, the defendants are enjoined by the final decree from intimidating by threats, express or implied, of physical harm to body or property, any person who may be desirous of entering into the employment of the plaintiff so far as to prevent him from entering the same. In order to test the correctness of the refusal to go further, it must be assumed that the defendants obey the express prohibition of the decree. If they do not, they fall within the injunction as it now stands, and are liable to summary punishment. The important difference between the preliminary and the final injunction is that the former goes further, and forbids the defendants to interfere with the plaintiff's business "by any scheme . . . organized for the purpose of . . . preventing any person or persons who now are or may hereafter be . . . desirous of entering the [plaintiff's employment] from entering it." I quote only a part, and the part which seems to me most objectionable. This includes refusal of social intercourse, and even organized persuasion or argument, although free from any threat of violence, either express or implied. And this is with reference to persons who have a legal right to contract or not to contract with the plaintiff, as they may see fit. Interference with existing contracts is forbidden by the final decree. I wish to insist a little that the only point of difference which involves a difference of principle between the final decree and the preliminary injunction which it is proposed to restore, is what I have mentioned, in order that it may be seen exactly what we are to discuss. It appears to me that the judgment of the majority turns, in part, on the assumption that the patrol necessarily carries with it a threat of bodily harm. That assumption I think unwarranted, for the reasons which I have given. Furthermore, it cannot be said, I think, that two men walking together up and down a sidewalk and speaking to those who enter a certain shop do necessarily and always thereby convey a threat of force. I do not think it possible to discriminate, and to say that two workmen, or even two representatives of an organization of workmen, do, — especially when they are, and are known to be, under the injunction of this court not to do so. See Stimson, "Handbook to Labor Law," Section 60, esp. pp. 290, 298, 299, 300; Regina v. Shepherd, 11 Cox C.C. 325. I may add, that I think the more intelligent workingmen believe as fully as I do that they no more can be permitted to usurp the State's prerogative of force than can their opponents in their controversies. But if I am wrong, then the decree as it stands reaches the patrol, since it applies to all threats of force. With this I pass to the real difference between the interlocutory and the final decree.

I agree, whatever may be the law in the case of a single defendant, Rice v. Albee, 164 Mass. 88, that when plaintiff proves that several persons have combined and conspired to injure his business, and have done acts producing that effect, he shows temporal damage and a cause of action, unless the facts disclose, or the defendants prove, some ground of excuse or justification. And I take it to be settled, and rightly settled, that doing that damage by combined persuasion is actionable, as well as doing it by falsehood or by force. Walker v. Cronin, 107 Mass. 555; Morasse v. Brochu, 151 Mass. 567; Tasker v. Stanley, 153 Mass. 148.

Nevertheless, in numberless instances, the law warrants the intentional infliction of temporal damage because it regards it as justified. It is on the question of what shall amount to a justification, and more especially on the nature of the consideration which really determine or ought to determine the answer to that question, that judicial reasoning seems to me often to be inadequate. The true grounds of decision are considerations of policy and of social advantage, and it is vain to suppose that solutions can be attained merely by logic and the general propositions of law which nobody disputes. Propositions as to public policy rarely are unanimously accepted, and still more rarely, if ever, are capable of unanswerable proof. They require a special training to enable any one even to form an intelligent opinion about them. In the early stages of law, at least, they generally are acted on rather as inarticulate instincts than as definite ideas for which a rational defense is ready.

To illustrate what I have said in the last paragraph, it has been the law for centuries that a man may set up a business in a country town too small to support more than one, although he expects and intends thereby to ruin some one already there, and succeeds in his intent. In such a case, he is not held to act "unlawfully and without justifiable cause," as was alleged in *Walker v. Cronin* and *Rice v. Albee*. The reason, of course, is that the doctrine generally has been accepted that free competition is worth more to society than it costs, and that on this ground the infliction of the damage is privileged. Commonwealth v. Hunt, 4 Met. 111, 134. Yet even this proposition nowadays is disputed by a considerable body of persons, including many whose intelligence is not to be denied, little as we may agree with them.

I have chosen this illustration partly with reference to what I have to say next. It shows without the need of further authority that the policy of allowing free competition justifies the intentional inflicting of temporal damage, including the damage of interference with a man's business, by some means, when the damage is done, not for its own sake, but as an instrumentality in reaching the end of victory in the battle of trade. In such a case it cannot matter whether the plaintiff is the only rival of the defendant, and so is aimed at specifically, or is one of a class all of whom are hit. The only debatable ground is the nature of the means by which such damage may be inflicted. We all agree that it cannot be done by force or threats of force. We all agree, I presume, that it may be done by persuasion to leave a rival's shop and come to the defendant's. It may be done by the refusal or withdrawal of various pecuniary advantages which, apart from this consequence, are within the defendant's lawful control. It may be done by the withdrawal, or threat to withdraw, such advantages from third persons who have a right to deal or not to deal with the plaintiff, as a means of inducing them not to deal with him either as customers or servants [citing cases].

I pause here to remark that the word "threats" often is used as if, when it appeared that threats had been made, it appeared that unlawful conduct had begun. But it depends on what you threaten. As a general rule, even if subject to some exceptions, what you may do in a certain event you may threaten to do, that is, give warning of your intention to do in that event, and thus allow the other person the chance of avoiding the consequences. So as to "compulsion," it depends on how you "compel." Commonwealth v. Hunt, 4 Met. 111, 133. So as to "annoyance" or "intimidation." Connor

v. Kent, Curran v. Treleaven, 17 Cox C.C. 354, 367, 368, 370. In Sherry v. Perkins, 147 Mass. 212, it was found as a fact that the display of banners which was enjoined was part of a scheme to prevent workmen from entering or remaining in the plaintiff's employment, "by threats and intimidation." The context showed that the words as there used meant threats of personal violence, and intimidation by causing fear of it.

I have seen the suggestion made that the conflict between employers and employed is not competition. But I venture to assume that none of my brethren would rely on that suggestion. If the policy on which our law is founded is too narrowly expressed in the term free competition, we may substitute free struggle for life. Certainly the policy is not limited to struggles between persons of the same class competing for the same end. It applies to all conflicts of temporal interests.

So far, I suppose, we are agreed. But there is a notion which latterly has been insisted on a good deal, that a combination of persons to do what any one of them lawfully might do by himself will make the otherwise lawful conduct unlawful. It would be rash to say that some as yet unformulated truth may not be hidden under this proposition. But in the general form in which it has been presented and accepted by many courts, I think it plainly untrue, both on authority and on principle. Commonwealth v. Hunt, 4 Met. 111; Randall v. Hazleton, 12 Allen 412, 414. There was combination of the most flagrant and dominant kind in *Bowen v. Matheson* and in the *Mogul Steamship Company's* case, and combination was essential to the success achieved. But it is not necessary to cite cases; it is plain from the slightest consideration of practical affairs, or the most superficial reading of industrial history, that free competition means combination, and that the organization of the world, now going on so fast, means an ever increasing might and scope of combination. It seems to me futile to set our faces against this tendency. Whether beneficial on the whole, as I think it, or detrimental, it is inevitable, unless the fundamental axioms of society, and even the fundamental conditions of life, are to be changed.

One of the eternal conflicts out of which life is made up is that between the effort of every man to get the most he can for his services, and that of society, disguised under the name of capital, to get his services for the least possible return. Combination on the one side is patent and powerful. Combination on the other is the necessary and desirable counterpart, if the battle is to be carried on in a fair and equal way. I am unable to reconcile Temperton v. Russell [1893] 1 Q.B. 715, and the cases which follow it, with the *Mogul Steamship Company* case. But *Temperton v. Russell* is not a binding authority here, and therefore I do not think it necessary to discuss it.

If it be true that workingmen may combine with a view, among other things, to getting as much as they can for their labor, just as capital may combine with a view to getting the greatest possible return, it must be true that when combined they have the same liberty that combined capital has to support their interests by argument, persuasion, and the bestowal or refusal of those advantages which they otherwise lawfully control. I can remember when many people thought that, apart from violence or breach of contract, strikes were wicked, as organized refusals to work. I suppose that intelligent economists and legislators have given up that notion today. I feel pretty confident that they equally will abandon the idea that an organized refusal by workmen of social intercourse with a man who shall enter their antagonist's employ is wrong, if it is dissociated from any threat of violence, and is made for the sole object of prevailing, if possible, in a contest with their employer about the rate of wages. The fact, that the immediate object of the act by which the benefit to themselves is to be gained is to injure their antagonist, does not necessarily make it unlawful, any more than when a great house lowers the price of certain goods for the purpose, and with the effect, of driving a smaller antagonist from the business. Indeed, the question seems to me to have been decided as long ago as 1842 by the good sense of Chief Justice Shaw, in Commonwealth v. Hunt, 4 Met. 111. I repeat at the end, as I said at the beginning, that this is the point of difference in principle, and the only one, between the interlocutory and the final decree. See Regina v. Shepherd, 11 Cox C.C. 325; Connor v. Kent, Gibson v. Lawson, Curran v. Treleaven, 17 Cox C.C. 354.

The general question of the propriety of dealing with this kind of case by injunction I say nothing about, because I understand that the defendants have no objection to the final decree if it goes no further and that both parties wish a decision upon the matters which I have discussed.

It would require no particular omniscience to speculate that American courts would be conservative in their approach to the problems thrown up by unionism, even after the atrophy of the doctrine of criminal conspiracy. A judiciary nurtured in the culture of contract and property, and recruited largely from the middle and upper classes of society, would very naturally have moved slowly in the adaptation of its legal system to accommodate and privilege the injuries to recognized interests which collective action in its typical forms necessarily inflicts. It was to be anticipated that organized labor would face an uphill struggle in gaining legal acceptance of its normal modes of conduct in the absence of legislative approbation, and so it has been.

There were, it is true, occasional judicial pronouncements exhibiting tolerance and understanding of the labor movement. Examples are the opinion (in dissent) of Judge Holmes in 1900 in *Plant v. Woods* [9] decided by the Massachusetts Supreme Judicial Court, and the earlier opinion of Judge Macomber of the New York Supreme Court in *The Johnston Harvester Co. v. Meinhardt*.[10] And it is also true that there was a gradual amelioration of the harsh standards of the common law as unions slowly gained ground in numbers and acceptability, a movement in which the New York Court of Appeals played a leading role. But the progress of organized labor at the hands of the courts was slow and halting; employers

---

[9] 176 Mass. 492, 57 N.E. 1011 (1900).
[10] 60 How. Pr. 168 (N.Y. 1880).

had easy access to the courts, especially in equity; by and large the judges were quite ready to supply the policy standards by which to condemn many forms of collective action, and they were able to find in the common law an extraordinarily rich supply of doctrine with which to rationalize the results reached.

A sampling of the common-law torts cases dealing with collective action would disclose that the following are some of the principles of law that have been used:

(1) Although economic injuries inflicted for the purpose of promoting some legitimate interest are privileged, they are actionable if inflicted without justification, maliciously, in bad faith, or where the primary object is to harm others and not to benefit the actors. Thus, in National Fireproofing Co. v. Mason Builders' Ass'n, 169 F. 259, 265 (2d Cir. 1909), the court held that "laborers and builders may combine for mutual advantage, and, so long as the motive is not malicious, the object not unlawful, nor oppressive and the means neither deceitful nor fraudulent, the result is not a conspiracy, although it may necessarily work injury to other persons."

(2) Combinations in restraint of trade are illegal. The use of this theory is illustrated in Berry v. Donovan, 188 Mass. 353, 74 N.E. 603 (1905), where it was held that a contract whereby an employer agrees to hire only members of the Boot and Shoe Workers' Union was not within the ambit of fair competition.

(3) Acts which are privileged if done by individuals may be actionable if done in combination. This view is reflected by Justice Harlan's majority opinion in Arthur v. Oakes, 63 F. 310, 322 (7th Cir. 1894), where he stated:

An intent upon the part of a single person to injure the rights of others or of the public is not in itself a wrong of which the law will take cognizance, unless some injurious act be done in execution of the unlawful intent. But a combination of two or more persons with such an intent, and under circumstances that give them, when so combined, a power to do an injury they would not possess as individuals acting singly, has always been recognized as in itself wrongful and illegal.

(4) An action will lie for a nonprivileged interference in business and contractual relations. Hitchman Coal & Coke Co. v. Mitchell, 245 U.S. 229 (1917), is the leading case in this country on the application of this doctrine to union-management relations. In it the "inducement of breach of contract" principle of law was used to found union liability for interfering with a "yellow-dog" contractual arrangement under which the company had exacted of each employee a warranty that he would not, while employed, become a member of a union.

(5) Concerted action subjects the actors to liability for injuries inflicted if either the object sought or the means used is improper. This theory was adopted by the RESTATEMENT OF TORTS in § 775 where it was stated:

Workers are privileged intentionally to cause harm to another by concerted action if the object and the means of their concerted action are proper; they are subject to liability to the other for harm so caused if either the object or the means of their concerted action is improper.

Probably the most frequently cited doctrine, and certainly the most potent, is the so-called "ends-means" or civil conspiracy test. This has all the flexibility of the older law of criminal conspiracy. It has permitted the judges, in the light of the mores of the times, to pass judgment on the entire gamut of union objectives and methods of collective action. In passing on the propriety of union "methods" the test has been the more effective because the common inquiry has been whether the action taken was "coercive," and this in turn has been a standard so broad and indefinite as to have enabled some courts to condemn even picketing of the most peaceful kind.

Writers have sometimes referred to the various traditional legal standards of union liability as if they were well defined and clearly differentiated. The fact, however, is that they have frequently been confusingly scrambled in judicial opinions. The doctrine of civil conspiracy, for example, has often been used in conjunction with inducement of breach of contractual relations and with restraint of trade, the illegality of the conspiracy being made to rest on the commission of acts which would presumably be independently tortious under some one of the other cited theories. On occasion, when a given objective has been present which the court has felt obliged to uphold under the ends-means test (as, for example, inducing workers to join the union, or pressing for higher wages for a class of workers), illegality has been predicated on a finding that such objective was only "secondary" or that the union was motivated by malice rather than self-interest.

We would discover quickly enough, upon examining the cases, that the plethora of legal principle has not made decisions either easy or automatic, and that, however the rule for the particular case has been phrased, the primary problem has really been to what extent, in the light of the various competing interests involved, the action of the unionists carried a privilege to inflict economic or other injury upon others. Unfortunately the courts have not always recognized this. Many opinions are doctrinaire in the extreme, and hence are useless except in cataloging legal formulae. A famous observation of Justice Holmes is peculiarly apt in the field of labor law: [11]

But whether, and how far, a privilege shall be allowed is a question of policy. Questions of policy are legislative questions, and judges shy of reasoning from such grounds. Therefore, decisions for or against the privilege, which really can stand only upon such grounds, often are presented as hollow deductions from empty general propositions like sic utere tuo ut alienum non laedas, which teaches nothing but a benevolent yearning, or else are put as if they themselves embodied a postulate of the law and admitted of no further deduction, as when it is said that, although there is temporal damage, there is no wrong;

---

[11] Holmes, *Privilege, Malice, and Intent*. 8 HARV. L. REV. 1, 3, 7 (1894).

whereas, the very thing to be found out is whether there is a wrong or not, and if not, why not. . . .

Perhaps one of the reasons why judges do not like to discuss questions of policy, or put a decision in terms upon their views as law-makers, is that the moment you leave the path of merely logical deduction you lose the illusion of certainty which makes legal reasoning seem like mathematics. Views of policy are taught by experience of the interests of life. Those interests are fields of battle. Whatever decisions are made must be against the wishes and opinion of one party, and the distinctions on which they go will be distinctions of degree.

3. EARLY LEGISLATIVE REACTION

During the period after the Civil War, there were sporadic state and federal legislative efforts to correct some of the inequities in the law with respect to trade unionism. These included attempts to outlaw the use of "yellow-dog" contracts, to limit the use of labor injunctions, to abolish the crime of conspiracy as applied to labor combinations, to exempt labor organizations from the antitrust laws, to protect union labels, to outlaw employer "blacklisting" of employees for union activity, and to provide for the mediation and arbitration of labor disputes.

Sooner or later it was inevitable not only that worker organizations should be tolerated under the law, but that they should be regarded as necessary and desirable institutions in promoting an effective democracy and as having commensurate legal privileges and responsibilities. So it was natural, if not inevitable, that ultimately the legislative "bit" treatment should give way to something more positive and comprehensive, and that responsibility for social policies with respect to unionism should gradually be withdrawn from the courts and assumed by the legislative branch of government.

Railway Labor Legislation

In view of the rail strikes of 1886, 1892, and 1894, and the close relation between railroad transportation and the public welfare, it was to be expected that the first legislative efforts directed toward establishing a federal labor policy should be in the railroad field.

The first major pieces of legislation to be passed were the Arbitration Act of 1888 and the Erdman Act of 1898.[12] They provided for voluntary arbitration, and the latter inaugurated the policy of government mediation and conciliation. Also included was a provision outlawing "yellow-dog" contracts, which was later nullified by the Supreme Court in *Adair v. United States*.[13]

The Erdman Act was followed by the Newlands Act of 1913,[14] which established a permanent Board of Mediation and Conciliation, and the Adamson Act of 1916,[15] which established the eight-hour-day principle.

---

[12] 25 Stat. 501 (1888); 30 Stat. 424 (1898).

[13] 208 U.S. 161 (1908).

[14] 38 Stat. 103 (1913).

[15] 39 Stat. 721 (1916), *upheld in* Wilson v. New, 243 U.S. 332 (1917).

During the war-time period of federal operation of the railroads, from 1917 to 1920, the government under the urgent necessity of maintaining efficient transportation service first formulated the policy of protecting the workers' right to unionize, a policy somewhat foreshadowed by the earlier attempt to outlaw the "yellow-dog" contract. General Order No. 8 of the Director General of the railroads provided for the right of self-organization of workers without discrimination.[16] A bipartisan Board of Railroad Wages and Working Conditions was established with advisory duties with respect to wages and other working conditions. The Director General entered into several nationwide agreements with labor organizations, in which wage awards made by the board were incorporated.[17] Disputes arising out of these agreements were required to be referred, after local adjustment machinery failed, to boards of adjustment set up by agreement of the regional directors and the labor organizations to function with respect to the various crafts.[18] This system marked a distinct advance toward a solution of the problem of interpretation of collective agreements, which had proved to be a source of friction under the earlier legislation.

The next phase in the development of railroad labor legislation occurred in connection with the return of the roads to their owners in 1920. Out of a welter of conflicting ideas,[19] Title III of the Transportation Act of 1920 [20] (the Esch-Cummins law) emerged. In substance, this statute provided with respect to labor relations (1) that all disputes should be considered first in conference between representatives of the carriers and of the employees, and (2) that failing of disposition in such conferences, they should be referred to a bipartisan board of adjustment, if one had been created and if the dispute concerned "grievances, rules or working conditions," otherwise to the Railroad Labor Board, created by the act, for "hearing and decision." The principle of mediation which had been the main forte of the earlier statutes was completely abandoned. A basic premise of the legislation was that an agency on which the carriers, labor, and the public were equally represented could settle basic nongrievance disputes simply by decision, as if they were justiciable matters. Its decisions were not legally enforceable, the thought being that public opinion would provide sufficient sanction. The act contained no provisions concerning the right of workers to self-organization, although the Railroad Labor Board did in one of its decisions espouse the right to self-organization without interference and the principle of "majority rule" in labor representation.[21] From the point of view of labor this had the anomalous, and perhaps intended, result of encouraging the formation of

---

[16] TWENTIETH CENTURY FUND, LABOR AND THE GOVERNMENT 177 (1935).

[17] NATIONAL MEDIATION BOARD, FIRST ANNUAL REPORT, App. B at 63 (1935).

[18] *Id.*

[19] TWENTIETH CENTURY FUND, LABOR AND THE GOVERNMENT 178 (1935); NATIONAL MEDIATION BOARD, FIRST ANNUAL REPORT, App. B at 63 (1935).

[20] 41 Stat. 456 (1920).

[21] Decision No. 119, April 14, 1921.

company unions. An important innovation was the provision in the act placing upon the parties a duty to bargain, but no penalties or other means of enforcement were provided. The weaknesses of the statute made new legislation imperative.

The Railway Labor Act of 1926[22] represented an attempt to incorporate into law the best features of all preceding legislation, and was supported both by the railroads and by the railroad unions. The policy of mediation was again brought to the fore, with the creation of a nonpartisan Board of Mediation whose primary duty was to mediate, and, failing in that, to urge arbitration. Arbitration procedures were specified and awards were made enforceable. Bipartite boards of adjustment could be set up to consider secondary disputes involving questions of interpretation of collective agreements, as under the act of 1920. An additional feature was that, if mediation failed and if the parties to a dispute were unwilling to arbitrate, an emergency board of investigation could be named by the President upon the recommendation of the Board of Mediation, whereupon no strike nor change in the terms or conditions of employment could be undertaken until thirty days after the emergency board's report to the President, such report to be made within thirty days after the board's appointment. Finally, the statute reincorporated, in substance, a provision of the act of 1920 placing a duty upon carriers and employees to make reasonable efforts to make and maintain agreements, and also included a declaration of the right of employers and employees to designate representatives without interference, influence, or coercion. No penalties or other means of enforcement of any of the obligations imposed by the act were provided, however. Reliance was to be placed upon collective bargaining through real representatives, and upon the processes of mediation and voluntary arbitration and the avoidance of hasty action in an effort to effectuate the peaceful settlement of disputes.

The Railway Labor Act of 1926 remains the basic labor legislation for the railroads, but it has been amended on several occasions. In 1934, the act was modified in the following main respects: (1) by creating the National Railroad Adjustment Board, which was to function in four divisions, to decide grievances arising under collective agreements; (2) by creating the National Mediation Board, in lieu of the Board of Mediation, which was to mediate disputes other than those arising out of existing agreements and was also to decide representation disputes; and (3) by clarifying the right to organize and to bargain collectively, the principle of "majority rule" with respect to representation being expressly adopted. Penalties were added for violation of certain of the obligations declared.

In 1936, most of the provisions of the act were extended to cover interstate air carriers. In 1951, the act was further amended to authorize the union shop and the check-off, under certain conditions. And in 1966,

---

[22] 44 Stat. 577 (1926), 45 U.S.C. §§ 151-63. *See* THE RAILWAY LABOR ACT AT FIFTY: COLLECTIVE BARGAINING IN THE RAILROAD AND AIRLINE INDUSTRIES (C. Rehmus, ed. 1976).

the act was amended to provide for special boards of adjustment to decide grievances. The Railway Labor Act, as amended, is found in the *Statutory Appendix.*

The Clayton Act

In the noncarrier field the initial effort of the national government toward the creation of a statutory labor relations policy consisted of an attempt to free unions of some of the curse of the labor injunction and of the application of the antitrust laws, which had been a prolific source of federal court jurisdiction to deal with union activities. The Clayton Act, enacted in 1914, declared "that the labor of a human being is not a commodity or article of commerce," that the antitrust laws were not to be construed to forbid the existence and operation of labor organizations, that courts of the United States were not to grant injunctions restraining certain specified types of conduct in cases involving labor disputes, and that such nonenjoinable conduct was not to be held to violate any law of the United States, including, of course, the Sherman Act.[23]

The high hopes of organized labor generated by this legislation were not realized because of a combination of legislative obscurantism and a reactionary judicial approach, which largely nullified the statute and left both the Sherman Act and the federal court injunction substantially intact as important legal tools for shaping labor law as administered in the federal courts. Not until some twenty years later were the alleged evils of the labor injunction again the subject of congressional attention.

4. LABOR UNIONS FROM 1900 TO 1932

After 1898 the membership of the AFL increased considerably and by 1913 it was almost 2,000,000. There was extensive organization in previously unorganized trades, as well as expansion into the South and West, with continued concentration on the skilled and semiskilled groups. For a time some competition came from the Industrial Workers of the World, or "Wobblies," a movement of militant syndicalists that aimed at bringing all workers, without regard to craft or skill, into "One Big Union." Although the IWW was never a serious rival of the AFL, its espousal of the cause of the unskilled brought these workers' problems to the attention of the federation's leaders, who were finally forced to alter the organizational structure of the AFL so as to give the unskilled at least limited recognition.

In 1912 Congress created the United States Commission on Industrial Relations to conduct public hearings on labor problems, which had been accentuated in the public mind because of increased industrial unrest

---

[23] 38 Stat. 730 (1914), §§ 6, 20, 15 U.S.C. § 17, 29 U.S.C. § 52.

throughout the country and numerous acts of violence in connection with strikes. These hearings popularized the labor cause, and with the passage in 1914 of the Clayton Act, organized labor began to exert a more important influence in the government.

The period of World War I resembled that of the Civil War in that the usual peacetime considerations were forced to yield to the exigencies of war. A code of rules was drawn up by the Taft-Walsh War Labor Conference Board, created by President Wilson, for the guidance of management and labor during wartime. This code recognized the basic eight-hour day and the right to a living wage. The *status quo* with respect to the union or closed shop was to be maintained for the duration and although no penalties were provided if strikes and lockouts were employed, the principle was recognized that such tactics should be suspended for the duration. The National Council of Defense appointed by President Wilson included Samuel Gompers, president of the AFL, as one of the seven members comprising the advisory commission which was in charge of government labor policies. It insisted that standards previously won by organized labor be maintained. Such government recognition was a stimulus to union membership, which increased phenomenally. In 1920, the AFL had a total membership of over 4,000,000.

At the end of the war, however, organized labor began to realize it had been living in a false paradise of government concessions. Many employers withdrew union recognition and countered union efforts with personnel management plans, profit-sharing arrangements and company unions. Union demands and strikes were played up in the press as "un-American" and "Bolshevistic." The big coal and steel strikes of 1919 . reflected the results of this reaction. The steel strike, in which 300,000 workers participated, was lost because the craft unions failed to co-operate fully with each other and because "an almost hysterical public opinion" turned against the strikers in favor of the corporations. The use of a federal court injunction in the coal strike convinced the unions that they were again face-to-face with unsympathetic courts.

In 1921, after production had caught up with the demand for goods which had not been available during the war, a two-year recession set in. During this interval total union membership declined to approximately 3,600,000. The next eight years saw little union progress. Various factors contributed toward worker apathy about unionism. Real wages were high. Management was finding it necessary to combat high labor turnover. The wider use by employers of welfare and pension plans, group life insurance and medical services, and personnel department grievance procedures helped to reduce labor discontent. Company unions flourished. By 1929 total union membership had declined to less than 3,500,000, and during the ensuing depression of the early "thirties," it was reduced another 500,000.

5. THE NORRIS-LA GUARDIA ACT

Judicial intervention in labor disputes came under increasing criticism, not only from the labor movement but also from those who were concerned for the prestige of the courts. Federal Judge Amidon, in *Great Northern Ry. v. Brosseau,*[24] commented at length on a number of the abusive aspects of the labor injunction, and Professor Felix Frankfurter of the Harvard Law School wrote a book in 1930 with Nathan Greene, entitled THE LABOR INJUNCTION, which was very influential in calling for reform. Criticisms which were aired at this time were:

(1) temporary restraining orders against union conduct in strikes and picketing were usually issued ex parte;

(2) they were frequently based upon affidavits submitted on behalf of the employers by guards or private detectives — "an untrustworthy guide for judicial action";

(3) the complaints and accompanying affidavits were in stereotyped form, raising "more than a suspicion that conformity to legal formula rather than accuracy of narrative guides oaths";

(4) the temporary restraining order or temporary injunction, while in theory providing merely interlocutory relief, was actually in many instances the means of breaking the union's strike;

(5) the injunction was often phrased in complex terminology, so that the ordinary workman would not be able to know clearly what he had been enjoined from doing;

(6) the armed guards supplied by private detective agencies, who had given the affidavits, were often sworn in as deputy marshals to enforce the decree; and

(7) if violence or breaches of the peace occurred, the unionists did not have the safeguards of ordinary criminal prosecutions before a jury, but were subject to contempt of court proceedings before the judge who had issued the injunction.

All of this led to a widespread feeling that the labor injunction was impairing public confidence in the judicial system. In addition, the point was made that the weight of the law was being thrown into labor disputes on one side, and that the injunctions were not making any contribution to the solution of the industrial relations problems which had caused the disputes.

The continued application of the antitrust laws to labor unions during the 1920's in such cases as Duplex Printing Press Co. v. Deering, 254 U.S. 443 (1921), and Bedford Cut Stone Co. v. Journeymen Stone Cutters' Ass'n, 274 U.S. 37 (1927), where injunctions were issued against secondary boycotts, contributed greatly to the increasing agitation for a stronger federal anti-injunction law.

In 1932, Congress passed the Norris-La Guardia Act,[25] which made sweeping reforms in federal court labor injunction procedure, forbade

---

[24] 286 F. 414 (D.N.D. 1923).
[25] 47 Stat. 70 (1932), 29 U.S.C. §§ 101-15.

injunctions altogether that would prohibit what might be described as peaceful collective action, and repudiated the "yellow-dog" contract as the basis for legal or equitable relief in the federal courts. Perhaps most important as a portent of legislative policy was the preamble of the act, which recognized the impotence of the individual unorganized employee in establishing the terms and conditions of employment in industry, and declared that he should have "full freedom of association, self-organization, and designation of representatives of his own choosing, to negotiate the terms and conditions of his employment" and that he should be "free from the interference, restraint, or coercion of employers of labor, or their agents, in the designation of such representatives or in self-organization or in other concerted activities for the purpose of collective bargaining or other mutual aid or protection." [26] This statute remains in force today, and constitutes an important part of present day labor law, which must later be examined in some detail, particularly in its interrelation with other federal statutes. But, for now, the student should read the act itself, as it appears in the *Statutory Appendix.*

One knowledgeable observer assessed Norris-La Guardia this way:

> The Norris-La Guardia Act had practical economic origins. It was enacted at the bottom of the Great Depression. Employees were weak, ill-paid, and working under deplorable conditions. Its sponsors believed that the workers' bargaining power could be enhanced and their earnings and working conditions improved by concerted action. Labor injunctions were obstacles; therefore they deprived the courts of power to issue injunctions.
>
> Perhaps these economic forces were alone sufficient to carry the day, but the Norris-La Guardia Act also rested upon closely reasoned theory. The central proposition was that law served no useful purpose in labor disputes, save possibly to protect tangible property and preserve public order. Its philosophical underpinning was the belief that the government should not resolve labor disputes or substitute its wage or price determinations for private contracts in a free market. Union organization, strikes, boycotts, and picketing were held to be part of the competitive struggle for life, which society tolerates because the freedom is worth more than it costs. . . . The Norris-La Guardia Act introduced the only period of unqualified laissez faire in labor relations.[27]

C. THE PERIOD SINCE 1933

1. THE INITIAL NEW DEAL LABOR POLICIES

The Roosevelt administration attempted to make effective a national labor policy favorable to trade unionism. An effort in this direction was

---

[26] Section 2 of the act, 29 U.S.C. § 102.

[27] A. Cox, LAW AND THE NATIONAL LABOR POLICY 5, 8 (1960).

made in the ill-starred National Industrial Recovery Act,[28] § 7a of which provided as follows:

> Every code of fair competition, agreement, and license approved, prescribed, or issued under this title shall contain the following conditions: (1) That employees shall have the right to organize and bargain collectively through representatives of their own choosing, and shall be free from the interference, restraint, or coercion of employers of labor, or their agents, in the designation of such representatives or in self-organization or in other concerted activities for the purpose of collective bargaining; (2) that no employee and no one seeking employment shall be required as a condition of employment to join any company union or to refrain from joining, organizing, or assisting a labor organization of his own choosing; and (3) that employers shall comply with the maximum hours of labor, minimum rates of pay, and other conditions of employment, approved or prescribed by the President.

Even prior to the adoption of codes of fair competition under the act, the principles stated in § 7a had been incorporated into the "President's Re-Employment Agreement." Then, in order to compose differences that might arise under such agreement, the President, on August 5, 1933, created the National Labor Board, with Senator Robert F. Wagner as chairman, which subsequently assumed jurisdiction also of labor disputes arising under the codes of fair competition. When the board's authority was questioned, the President issued executive orders on February 1 and 23, 1934, purporting to give the board the right to conduct employee representation elections and to report its findings and recommendations concerning violations of § 7a to the Attorney General for possible prosecution, or to the Compliance Division of the National Recovery Administration for appropriate action.

After a period of considerable activity the National Labor Board was superseded, on July 9, 1934, by the (first) National Labor Relations Board, which was established pursuant to a joint resolution of Congress approved June 19, 1934.[29] This resolution authorized the designation by the President of one or more boards to investigate the facts in labor controversies arising under § 7a with power to conduct elections among employees to determine their collective bargaining representatives, any orders issued in connection therewith to be reviewable by the circuit courts of appeal. The Board adopted procedures of "investigation" similar to the method of complaint, hearing and decision later prescribed under the National Labor Relations Act. As in the case of the National Labor Board, however, its authority was definitely limited, since its orders could merely take the form of advisory recommendations to the Attorney General and to the Compliance Division of NRA.

The Board functioned until the decision of the Supreme Court in the *Schechter* case invalidated the NIRA on May 27, 1935.[30] It had an active

---

[28] 48 Stat. 198 (1933).

[29] 48 Stat. 1183 (1934).

[30] Schechter Poultry Corp. v. United States, 295 U.S. 495 (1935).

life while it lasted, however. Possibly its most important contribution consisted of a total of 202 formal decisions in which an attempt was made to build up a body of labor law involving the principles of § 7a [31] which were later of material assistance in interpreting and applying similar principles set out in the National Labor Relations Act.

2. THE NATIONAL LABOR RELATIONS ACT (WAGNER ACT), 1935

The Roosevelt administration was determined that the labor relations policies, at least, of the NIRA should not be sacrificed but, indeed, should be reinforced, if possible. In little more than two months following the demise of the NIRA, the original National Labor Relations Act was enacted on July 5, 1935. This statute declared it to be "the policy of the United States" to encourage the practice of collective bargaining and full freedom of worker self-organization, as a means of facilitating the free flow of interstate commerce. Employees covered by the act were given the "right" to organize and to bargain collectively and this right was made effective by proscribing as "unfair labor practices," five kinds of employer conduct vis-à-vis unionism. The principle of "majority rule" among employees in selecting union representatives was adopted, and a three-member National Labor Relations Board was created with authority to settle representation questions and to prosecute violations of the unfair labor practice provisions of the act.[32] This Board, in accordance with the then prevailing vogue as to administrative agencies, combined the functions of prosecutor and judge, although its orders had no binding force until "enforced" by a circuit court of appeals upon petition. All employers whose labor practices might "affect" interstate commerce were subject to the act, with the exception of those covered by the Railway Labor Act, and the United States and states or political subdivisions thereof.

This, then, was the statute which placed the full power and influence of the national government behind trade unionism. A detailed study of the principles embodied in this legislation will constitute an important part of this course; hence, their exposition will not be undertaken as a part of this introductory survey. It is noteworthy at this point, however, that the statute was partisan legislation in that restraints were placed upon employers but not upon unions. Moreover, it had a relatively narrow compass, as compared, for example, with the Railway Labor Act. The right of self-organization was secured and collective bargaining was made compulsory, but there was no attempt to deal with the problems of disputes persisting despite good faith bargaining or arising out of collective agreements, although it should be mentioned that facilities for voluntary mediation and arbitration of such disputes continued to be

---

[31] NATIONAL LABOR RELATIONS BOARD, FIRST ANNUAL REPORT 7 (1936).

[32] 49 Stat. 449 (1935), 29 U.S.C. §§ 151-68.

made available through the Conciliation Service of the Department of Labor.

The constitutionality of the Wagner Act was in doubt until the following landmark case in 1937, together with its associated cases.[33]

NLRB v. JONES & LAUGHLIN STEEL CORP.

Supreme Court of the United States
301 U.S. 1, 57 S. Ct. 615, 81 L. Ed. 893 (1937)

[The corporation was engaged in the manufacture of steel in Pennsylvania, importing iron ore from Michigan and Minnesota and shipping steel products to many states. The NLRB found that the corporation had committed an unfair labor practice by discharging ten men because of their union activities. The court of appeals declined to enforce the Board's order to cease and desist. The Supreme Court granted certiorari.]

MR. CHIEF JUSTICE HUGHES delivered the opinion of the Court (four justices dissenting): . . . .

The scheme of the National Labor Relations Act — which is too long to be quoted in full — may be briefly stated. The first section sets forth findings with respect to the injury to commerce resulting from the denial by employers of the right to organize and from the refusal of employers to accept the procedure of collective bargaining. There follows a declaration that it is the policy of the United States to eliminate these causes of obstruction to the free flow of commerce. The act then defines the terms it uses, including the terms "commerce" and "affecting commerce." § 2. It creates the National Labor Relations Board and prescribes its organization. §§ 3-6. It sets forth the right of employees to self-organization and to bargain collectively through representatives of their own choosing. § 7. It defines "unfair labor practices." § 8. It lays down rules as to the representation of employees for the purpose of collective bargaining. § 9. The Board is empowered to prevent the described unfair labor practices affecting commerce and the act prescribes the procedure to that end. The Board is authorized to petition designated courts to secure the enforcement of its orders. . . . Any person aggrieved by a final order of the Board may obtain a review in the designated courts with the same procedure as in the case of an application by the Board for the enforcement of its order. . . .

The Scope of the Act. — The act is challenged in its entirety as an attempt to regulate all industry, thus invading the reserved powers of the States over their local concerns. It is asserted that the references in the Act to interstate and foreign commerce are colorable at best; that the Act is not a true regulation of such commerce or of matters which directly affect it but on the contrary has the fundamental object of placing under

---

[33] NLRB v. Freuhauf Trailer Co., 301 U.S. 49 (1937); NLRB v. Friedman-Harry Marks Clothing Co., 301 U.S. 58 (1937); NLRB v. Associated Press, 301 U.S. 103 (1937); NLRB

the compulsory supervision of the federal government all industrial labor relations within the nation.

.... We think it clear that the National Labor Relations Act may be construed so as to operate within the sphere of constitutional authority.... The grant of authority to the Board does not purport to extend to the relationship between all industrial employees and employers. Its terms do not impose collective bargaining upon all industry regardless of effects upon interstate or foreign commerce. It purports to reach only what may be deemed to burden or obstruct that commerce and, thus qualified, it must be construed as contemplating the exercise of control within constitutional bounds. It is a familiar principle that acts which directly burden or obstruct interstate or foreign commerce, or its free flow, are within the reach of the congressional power. Acts having that effect are not rendered immune because they grow out of labor disputes. See Texas & N.O.R. Co. v. Railway Clerks, 281 U.S. 548, 570 (1930); A.L.A. Schechter Corp. v. United States, 295 U.S. 495 (1935); Virginian Railway Co. v. System Federation, No. 40, R.E.D., 300 U.S. 515 (1937). It is the effect upon commerce, not the source of the injury, which is the criterion. Second Employers' Liability Cases, 223 U.S. 1 (1912). Whether or not particular action does affect commerce in such a close and intimate fashion as to be subject to federal control, and hence to lie within the authority conferred upon the Board, is left by the statute to be determined as individual cases arise. We are thus to inquire whether in the instant case the constitutional boundary has been passed. . . .

[I]n its present application, the statute goes no further than to safeguard the right of employees to self-organization and to select representatives of their own choosing for collective bargaining or other mutual protection without restraint or coercion by their employer.

That is a fundamental right. Employees have as clear a right to organize and select their representatives for lawful purposes as the respondent has to organize its business and select its own officers and agents. Discrimination and coercion to prevent free exercise of the right of employees to self-organization and representation is a proper subject for condemnation by competent legislative authority. Long ago we stated the reason for labor organizations. We said that they were organized out of the necessities of the situation; that a single employee was helpless in dealing with an employer; that he was dependent ordinarily on his daily wage for the maintenance of himself and family; that if the employer refused to pay him the wages that he thought fair, he was nevertheless unable to leave the employ and resist arbitrary and unfair treatment; that union was essential to give laborers opportunity to deal on an equality with their employer. American Steel Foundaries v. Tri-City Central Trades Council, 257 U.S. 184, 209 (1921). We reiterated these views when we had under consideration the Railway Labor Act of 1926. Fully recognizing the legality of collective action on the part of employees in order to safeguard their proper interests, we said that Congress was not

---

v. Washington, V. & M. Coach Co., 301 U.S. 142 (1937). For a discussion of this litigation in its historical context, *see* CORTNER, THE WAGNER ACT CASES (1964).

required to ignore this right but could safeguard it. Congress could seek to make appropriate collective action of employees an instrument of peace rather than of strife. We said that such collective action would be a mockery if representation were made futile by interference with freedom of choice. Hence the prohibition by Congress of interference with the selection of representatives for the purpose of negotiation and conference between employers and employees, "instead of being an invasion of the constitutional rights of either, was based on the recognition of the rights of both." Texas & N.O.R. Co. v. Railway Clerks, *supra*. We have reasserted the same principle in sustaining the application of the Railway Labor Act as amended in 1934. Virginian Railway Co. v. System Federation, No. 40, R.E.D., *supra*. . . .

Experience has abundantly demonstrated that the recognition of the right of employees to self-organization and to have representatives of their own choosing for the purpose of collective bargaining is often an essential condition of industrial peace. Refusal to confer and negotiate has been one of the most prolific causes of strife. This is such an outstanding fact in the history of labor disturbances that it is a proper subject of judicial notice and requires no citation of instances. The opinion in the case of Virginian Railway Co. v. System Federation, No. 40, R.E.D., *supra*, points out that, in the case of carriers, experience has shown that before the amendment, of 1934, of the Railway Labor Act "when there was no dispute as to the organizations authorized to represent the employees and when there was a willingness of the employer to meet such representative for a discussion of their grievances, amicable adjustment of differences had generally followed and strikes had been avoided." That, on the other hand, "a prolific source of dispute had been the maintenance by the railroad of company unions and the denial by railway management of the authority of representatives chosen by their employees." The opinion in that case also points to the large measure of success of the labor policy embodied in the Railway Labor Act. But with respect to the appropriateness of the recognition of self-organization and representation in the promotion of peace, the question is not essentially different in the case of employees in industries of such a character that interstate commerce is put in jeopardy from the case of employees of transportation companies. And of what avail is it to protect the facility of transportation, if interstate commerce is throttled with respect to the commodities to be transported!

These questions have frequently engaged the attention of Congress and have been the subject of many inquiries. The steel industry is one of the great basic industries of the United States, with ramifying activities affecting interstate commerce at every point. The Government aptly refers to the steel strike of 1919-1920 with its far-reaching consequences. The fact that there appears to have been no major disturbance in that industry in the more recent period did not dispose of the possibilities of future and like dangers to interstate commerce which Congress was entitled to foresee and to exercise its protective power to forestall. It is not necessary again to detail the facts as to respondent's enterprise.

Instead of being beyond the pale, we think that it presents in a most striking way the close and intimate relation which a manufacturing industry may have to interstate commerce and we have no doubt that Congress had constitutional authority to safeguard the right of respondent's employees to self-organization and freedom in the choice of representatives for collective bargaining. . . .

Questions under the due process clause and other constitutional restrictions. — Respondent asserts its right to conduct its business in an orderly manner without being subjected to arbitrary restraints. What we have said points to the fallacy in the argument. Employees have their correlative right to organize for the purpose of securing the redress of grievances and to promote agreements with employers relating to rates of pay and conditions of work. Texas & N.O.R. Co. v. Railway Clerks, *supra;* Virginian Railway Co. v. System Federation, No. 40, R.E.D. Restraint for the purpose of preventing an unjust interference with that right cannot be considered arbitrary or capricious. . . .

3. UNION GROWTH UNDER THE WAGNER ACT; THE CIO AND INDUSTRIAL UNIONS

Both the NIRA and the NLRA, with their guarantees of the right to self-organization without employer interference, gave a tremendous impetus to the organization of the millions of unskilled and semiskilled workers in the mass production industries. As a result there came to a head within the AFL the issue of industrial unionism, which had been all but forgotten since the demise of the Knights of Labor in the nineties. The AFL Convention of 1934 recognized that these potential new recruits to the ranks of organized labor would not fit very well into the traditional pattern of craft unionism, but took an equivocal stand as to just what was to be done.

In the 1934 convention a resolution to organize new industrial type unions within the AFL was decisively defeated. The leading craft unionists took the position that the problem could be handled by using local federal unions within plants already partially organized by craft unions and by enlarging the jurisdiction of the established craft unions. Chartering industrial type unions would have precluded the expansion of the craft unions into certain industries, and the Carpenters, Teamsters, Machinists, Plumbers, and other unions could not face this result with equanimity, nor could they, in fact, easily have resolved the competitive problems which would have attended an attempt to enlarge their respective jurisdictions so as to bring in groups of hitherto unorganized employees. On the other hand, the industrial union partisans maintained that to split up workers within an industry among the various craft unions would weaken the bargaining position of such workers by preventing timely and concerted action.

Personal animosity and rivalry for power and control, unfortunately, also loomed large in AFL conclaves. Certain of the federation's affiliates, such as the United Mine Workers, the Ladies Garment Workers and the

Amalgamated Clothing Workers, had become very strong and had successfully used the industrial type of organization. Few of the affiliated craft unions had done so well in rate or extent of growth and the successful pro-industrialist union leaders were impatient with the craft unionists who were dominant in high federation councils. The convention of 1935 was a scene of bitterness and some violence. "Big Bill" Hutcheson, head of the Carpenters union, objected to UMW President John L. Lewis's vociferations in favor of industrial unionism, and harsh words between them ended in fisticuffs. Finally, the industrial union protagonists decided to undertake organizing campaigns in mass production industries on their own, and in November, 1935, the presidents of eight AFL unions created the Committee for Industrial Organization, the purpose of which was stated to be "encouragement and promotion of organization of unorganized workers in mass production and other industries on an industrial basis." John L. Lewis was chosen chairman.

In June, 1936, a drive was undertaken by this group through the "Steelworkers Organizing Committee" to organize the iron and steel industry. It met with great success the following year when the United States Steel Corporation capitulated and entered into an agreement with the committee. Many other steel companies followed suit. There were also important membership gains in other fields, especially in the automobile, electrical manufacturing, and textile industries.

The Committee for Industrial Organization had stated its purpose was purely "educational" and "advisory" to convince the rank and file of the federation of the need of organizing the millions of workers in the mass production industries. However, the Executive Committee of the AFL considered the committee a "dual" organization and ordered its dissolution. When the ultimatum was disregarded, the member unions of the committee were suspended from the federation. Thereafter many attempts were made to reunite the two groups in the interest of labor harmony, but no agreement could be reached on the question of jurisdiction. At meetings of the AFL Executive Council in January and April, 1938, it was decided to revoke the charters of the offending unions, which action was endorsed at the convention that fall.

In November, 1938, the various groups then forming the Committee for Industrial Organization broke away completely from the AFL and changed the name of the organization to the "Congress of Industrial Organizations" (CIO). Its avowed purpose was to promote union organization, to extend the benefits of collective bargaining, and to obtain legislation safeguarding the economic security and social welfare of the workers of America. John L. Lewis was the organization's first president. When he resigned in 1940, Philip Murray, president of the CIO's United Steelworkers and a vice-president of the CIO, became president. For years he had handled difficult organizational assignments, and he was welcomed to the presidency of the CIO as a brilliant organizer and a skillful negotiator.

Both the CIO and the AFL had undertaken very active organizational campaigns which were accompanied by an unprecedented number of strikes, and union membership rose to over 7,000,000 in 1937. The business recession in 1937 and the public reaction against the aggressive organizing tactics of the unions, especially the "sit-down" strikes, led to a temporary decrease in membership, but with returning prosperity the uptrend was resumed. Both federations became active in organizing industries which previously had been substantially neglected. This was true particularly in such war production industries as shipbuilding, aircraft production, and aluminum.

The period following the passage of the NLRA was not, therefore, one of tranquillity in labor relations. Coupled with the AFL-CIO rift was the fact that countless employers, who had neither the desire nor the experience which makes for successful collective bargaining, were forced to deal with unions. And the fact that many of them had to negotiate with young, militant, and inexperienced unions did not improve the opportunity for good relations. The result was a sharp increase, over the previous decade, in the number of strikes and in the number of production man-days lost as a result of labor disputes.[34] The short range consequence of the enactment of the statute was certainly not to mitigate, but rather to increase, those "substantial obstructions to the free flow of commerce" to which the preamble of the act referred. Indeed, any other result could hardly have been anticipated. Amicable labor relations through unionism could only be viewed as a long range objective to be achieved after the organizational stage was completed and both employers and unions had learned the art of collective bargaining.

4. LABOR STANDARDS AND SOCIAL SECURITY LEGISLATION

The Norris-La Guardia Act, the Railway Labor Act, and the National Labor Relations Act were directed toward the problems of trade unionism as such. In addition to these and to certain other federal statutes dealing with specific union-management relations problems [35] there is an important body of federal legislation which represents the quite different policy of direct intervention in the determination of terms and conditions of employment.

Of the statutes in this area, one of the most important is the Fair Labor Standards Act of 1938.[36] Enacted as a humanitarian and "spread the work" depression measure, this act prescribes minimum wage rates, discourages "overtime" employment by requiring premium rates for

---

[34] *See* 62 MONTHLY LAB. REV. 720 (1946).

[35] Section 1231 of the United States Code, Title 18 (Crimes and Criminal Procedure) prohibits the interstate transportation of strike-breakers; § 1951 makes it a felony to obstruct interstate commerce by robbery or extortion; the "Lea Act" of 1946 makes it unlawful, by use of threats, force, or other means to compel a broadcasting company to hire more employees than it needs. 60 Stat. 89 (1946); 47 U.S.C. § 506.

[36] 52 Stat. 1060 (1938); 29 U.S.C. §§ 201-19.
In National League of Cities v. Usery, 426 U.S. 833 (1976), the Supreme Court held (5-4) that the 1974 amendments to the Fair Labor Standards Act that extended the Act's minimum wage and maximum hour provisions to nearly all state and local government employees interfere with governmental functions typically performed by states and their

overtime work, and prohibits the use of child labor — all with respect to employees engaged in interstate commerce or in the production of goods for such commerce. Other federal statutes setting employment standards of one kind or another are listed in the note.[37]

The federal government has also made a major effort toward the equitable adjustment of the problems of superannuation and unemployment in industry. Again, the railroad industry was the subject of initial consideration, when the Railroad Retirement Act of 1934 [38] was enacted, to be followed by the acts of 1935 [39] and 1937.[40] Of most importance, however, is the "social security" legislation, which began with the Social Security Act of 1935.[41] This statute and its amendments are the foundation for a comprehensive system of old-age and survivors' insurance benefits, and unemployment compensation, carried financially by means of payroll taxes on employers and employees.

5. THE WORLD WAR II PERIOD

During World War II unions cooperated with management in converting to war production, and offered their services in supplying

---

local governments in their capacities as sovereign governments and are accordingly not within the authority granted to Congress by the commerce clause. The Court overruled Maryland v. Wirtz, 392 U.S. 183 (1968), which had upheld the application of the FLSA to state hospitals, institutions, and schools. The Court said: "One undoubted attribute of state sovereignty is the States' power to determine the wages which shall be paid to those whom they employ in order to carry out their governmental functions, what hours those persons will work, and what compensation will be provided where these employees may be called upon to work overtime." The Court held that Congress may not abrogate the States' otherwise plenary authority to make these determinations.

Notwithstanding *National League of Cities,* courts of appeals have held that the Equal Pay Act, although an integral part of the FLSA, may be viewed as an anti-discrimination measure and thus may constitutionally be applied to employees of a county school or institution district and to all state employees. Usery v. Charleston County School District, 558 F.2d 1169 (4th Cir. 1977); Usery v. Allegheny County Institution District, 544 F.2d 148, *cert. denied,* 97 S. Ct. 1582 (U.S. 1977).

The Third Circuit refused to invalidate a judgment requiring a school board's payment of past overtime compensation which had become final before the *National League* decision. The court observed that a judgment is not void simply because it is erroneous or based on precedent that is later deemed incorrect or unconstitutional. Having chosen not to appeal its case to the Supreme Court, the school board must live with its decision. Marshall v. Board of Education, 575 F.2d 417 (3d Cir. 1978).

[37] The Public Contracts (Walsh-Healey) Act of 1936 requires contractors with the government to meet specified wage, hour, and child-labor standards, 49 Stat. 2036 (1936); 41 U.S.C. §§ 35-45; the Davis-Bacon Act of 1931 sets minimum wage standards on public projects, 46 Stat. 1494 (1931); 40 U.S.C. § 276a; the Selective Training and Service Act of 1940 and the Universal Military Training and Service Act give reemployment right to veterans, 54 Stat. 885 (1940), as amended, 50 U.S.C. App. §§ 301-18; 62 Stat. 604 (1948), as amended, 50 U.S.C. App. §§ 451-71.

[38] 48 Stat. 1283 (1938), declared unconstitutional in Railroad Retirement Bd. v. Alton R.R., 295 U.S. 330 (1935).

[39] 49 Stat. 967 (1935).

[40] 50 Stat. 307 (1937), 45 U.S.C. §§ 228a-s.

[41] 49 Stat. 620 (1935), 42 U.S.C. §§ 301-1307.

skilled workers as instructors in training centers. In numerous plants labor-management committees were established under the auspices of the War Production Board for the purpose of meeting such problems as the maximum use of equipment and manpower, the spreading of war orders, and the production of strategic war materials. A "no-strike" pledge had been given at a conference of representatives of industry and labor which had been called by the President in December, 1941, to consider the problems of labor relations and the war effort. The group agreed that, following the precedent of World War I, a federal agency should be established "for the peaceful adjustment" of labor disputes. Accordingly, by Executive Order, the President on January 12, 1942, created a "National War Labor Board" of twelve members, tripartite in composition, with authority to "finally determine" labor disputes certified to it by the Secretary of Labor or brought before it on its own motion.

The board had to function for a time without benefit of statutory sanction or guidance, and even after the enactment of the Stabilization Act of 1942 and the War Labor Disputes Act of 1943 the board continued, as a practical matter, to have the basic policy responsibility for wage stabilization and the settlement of labor disputes. Its policy with respect to wage issues was to establish a stabilization front, without, however, attempting a wage freeze. Its cost of living "Little Steel" formula, and companion doctrines relating to "inequalities" and "substandard" wages, were directed to this end, as was its resort to "industry or area practice" in passing on nonwage issues. Among its more famous policies was the "maintenance of membership" compromise solution of the union security issue.

During the first part of the war the "no-strike" pledge was substantially observed. However, after the early flush of patriotism had subsided, irritation at the settlement delays produced by the elaborate procedures of the War Labor Board and its tremendous case load resulted in a fairly large number of work stoppages, most of them "wildcat." There were also stoppages in protest against the "hold the line" policies of the administration. On the whole, however, giving due consideration to the unprecedented power of organized labor, and to the fact that many of the unions were young and undisciplined, the record of union devotion to war production must be regarded as good. The board's decisions with relatively few exceptions were respected. While they were without legal force, they were effectively supported by the possibility, and in some cases the actuality, of plant seizure by presidential directive.

6. THE LABOR MANAGEMENT RELATIONS ACT (TAFT-HARTLEY ACT), 1947

After VJ Day (August 14, 1945), labor-management relations took a turn for the worse. The no-strike, no-lockout pledges were considered as no longer operative. Restraint born of patriotic and emotional impulses, so effective during the war years, lost its force as workers and management faced reconversion problems.

In November, 1945, President Truman called a Labor Management Conference on Industrial Relations. It proved fruitless in so far as the reaching of agreement on specific issues is concerned; but, in contrast to the situation after World War I, the principle of collective bargaining was firmly established. Perhaps the most significant outcome of the conference was the recommendation by both labor and management that disputes involving the application of collective agreements should be settled under a grievance procedure with arbitration as a final step and without resorting to work stoppages. This recognition was followed during the post-war period by a phenomenal growth in voluntary arbitration of grievances.

The process of reconversion during late 1945 and 1946 from a wartime to a peacetime economy was accompanied by a wave of strikes in many vital industries, including steel, coal, oil, automobiles, meat packing, and electrical products. In contrast to the post-World War I situation, the unions, particularly in the mass production industries, demonstrated their cohesiveness and strength of organization. The strikes involved a loss of 116,000,000 man-days — an all-time record.

A reaction to this showing of union power became evident in 1947 when the Eightieth Congress enacted the Labor Management Relations Act (Taft-Hartley Act) [42] over President Truman's veto.

Title I of this statute amended the original National Labor Relations Act in numerous ways, the significance of which will become apparent as each of the topics of labor relations law are taken up in succeeding chapters. Before launching into this detailed study, however, the student should take time now to read through the amended National Labor Relations Act (Title I of LMRA, 1947), especially §§ 7, 8, 9 and 10, which are the heart of the act. Title I of LMRA is set out in the *Statutory Appendix* in a manner which highlights the changes which were made in 1947.

In § 7, a basic change in emphasis can be seen in the addition of the right to refrain from organization and concerted activities. This was implemented in § 8(b)(1) by the prohibition of union restraint and coercion against employees exercising such rights.

In § 8(a), the various employer unfair labor practices were retained, but § 8(c) made it clear that employers may express their opinions about unionism unless they threaten reprisal or wrongfully promise benefits. Under § 8(a)(3), the closed shop was no longer authorized and the union shop was subjected to limitations.

Most important, the Taft-Hartley Act noted in § 1 that certain union practices obstruct commerce, and § 8(b) outlawed a number of them, including secondary boycotts (§ 8(b)(4)(A) and (B)) and jurisdictional strikes (§ 8(b)(4)(D)).

The changes in § 9 placed various restrictions on the NLRB in conducting representation proceedings, and those in § 10 tightened up procedures in unfair labor practice cases.

---

[42] 61 Stat. 136 (1947), 29 U.S.C. §§ 141-97.

The NLRB was increased from three to five members, and the final authority to investigate charges, issue complaints, and present them before the Board was placed in the hands of the General Counsel, in order to avoid casting the Board in the role of both prosecutor and judge.

In addition to these and many other amendments to the Wagner Act, the Taft-Hartley Act contained much entirely new material. In Title II, the Federal Mediation and Conciliation Service was set up as an independent agency, and an elaborate procedure was outlined for the handling of national emergency disputes. Various important matters were dealt with in Title III of the LMRA, including a provision for suits in federal courts to enforce collective agreements (§ 301), restrictions on payments to employee representatives and on health and welfare funds (§ 302), damage suits in federal courts for secondary boycotts (§ 303), restrictions on political contributions (§ 304), and the outlawing of strikes by government employees (§ 305).

7. LABOR UNIONS FROM 1947 TO 1959; THE AFL-CIO MERGER

This statute became a political issue of the first magnitude in connection with the national elections of 1948, in which President Truman defeated Governor Dewey. The repeal of the act was promptly attempted by administration forces, but a coalition of Republicans and conservative Democrats successfully resisted this effort.

In spite of their inability to obtain the repeal of the Taft-Hartley Act, and their signal lack of success in organizing the unorganized, labor unions have remained strong and have won substantial wage increases and fringe benefits through collective bargaining during the post-World War II period.

Union membership had continued to grow steadily during World War II, passing the 15,000,000 mark by 1947. After 1947, however, the rate of growth in union membership leveled off, about 2,000,000 members being added during the following decade. During that period, the ratio of union members to the total labor force remained fairly constant at about twenty-five percent.[43]

In 1949 and 1950, as the "cold war" tightened and the conflict with the Communists in Korea drew near, a major effort was made to remove Communists from positions of power in the labor unions. The CIO Convention in November, 1949, voted to expel the United Electrical, Radio and Machine Workers (UE), and within a year ten other unions were expelled from the CIO on charges of pursuing Communist policies. New unions, such as the International Union of Electrical Workers (IUE), were chartered by the CIO to take the place of the expelled unions.

The Korean crisis from mid-1950 to the end of 1952 presented the labor unions with the problems attendant upon a wage and price

---

[43] U.S. Bureau of Labor Statistics, Dep't of Labor, Directory of National and International Unions in the United States (Bull. No. 1222, 1957). It should be noted that the "labor force" includes many "unorganizables."

stabilization program. The AFL and the CIO cooperated in setting up a United Labor Policy Committee to advise the administration on labor policies. Early in 1951, the labor representatives on the Wage Stabilization Board and other defense agencies withdrew in protest against unduly rigid wage controls and the alleged failure of the administration to give weight to labor's views. The issues were eventually settled and labor representatives returned to a reorganized Wage Stabilization Board and a new Advisory Board on Mobilization. The United Labor Policy Committee was dissolved in August, 1951.

In November, 1952, Philip Murray, President of the CIO since 1940, and William Green, President of the AFL for nearly thirty years, both died. They were succeeded, respectively, by Walter Reuther and George Meany, both men of vigor and wide outlook and interests. As the original issues in the split in the labor movement had faded into history and the areas of economic and political cooperation between the two federations had grown, the time seemed auspicious for the long-thought-of merger.

In June, 1953, a no-raiding agreement was negotiated, which was gradually ratified by a large majority of the constituent unions in the AFL and the CIO. Its purpose was to minimize the fruitless and costly efforts to claim jurisdiction over workers already organized by another union. A forerunner of the actual merger of the AFL and CIO, it went into effect in June, 1954, for the sixty-five AFL and twenty-nine CIO affiliates which had ratified it.

In February, 1955, a joint committee announced that full agreement had been reached for the merger of the two organizations. In December, 1955, the merger became an accomplished fact. The new AFL-CIO, with about 15,000,000 members, was headed by George Meany, and Walter Reuther became head of the Industrial Union Department.

Beginning in 1957, the Senate Select Committee on Improper Activities in the Labor or Management Field (McClellan Committee) held a series of hearings lasting over two years, in the course of which instances were brought into public view of misuse of union funds; lack of democratic procedures in internal union affairs; improper imposition of trusteeships over locals by parent unions; collusive dealings between management and union officials, resulting in "sweetheart" contracts and payoffs to union officials; improper use of "middlemen" to discourage genuine union organization; infiltration of certain unions by gangsters and racketeers; laxity in local law enforcement dealing with violence and racketeering; misuse of picketing and secondary boycotting as an instrument of power, sometimes for extortion; and the existence of a "no-man's land," under which employers and employees were without either a federal or a state forum to hear and determine their complaints.

The McClellan Committee, in its first interim report in 1958 urged legislation to deal with a number of these abuses, and the Kennedy-Ives bill, S. 3974, 85th Cong., 2d Sess., designed to accomplish such objectives, passed the Senate but died in the House of Representatives. Congress did pass legislation requiring disclosure of the operations of welfare and pension plans, the Welfare and Pension Plans Disclosure Act.

8. THE LABOR-MANAGEMENT REPORTING AND DISCLOSURE ACT (LANDRUM-GRIFFIN ACT), 1959

In the first session of the Eighty-Sixth Congress, Senator Kennedy introduced a revised version (S. 505) of the 1958 bill. The Senate Labor Committee, after extensive hearings, reported out a "clean bill," S. 1555, incorporating a number of changes. In April, 1959, the Senate debated the bill at length, finally passing it with a number of amendments, including a modified version of a "bill of rights" for union members which had been introduced by Senator McClellan. The House Labor Committee held its own lengthy hearings and finally reported out a bill (the Elliott bill, H.R. 8342), which was somewhat less restrictive of labor unions than the Senate bill. In August, 1959, the House debated this bill, along with the Shelley bill (H.R. 8490), which was favored by most unions, and the Landrum-Griffin bill (H.R. 8400), which was the "toughest" or most restrictive of union power of the three bills. Following an intensive effort on all sides to mobilize public opinion, including a radio-television appeal for "an effective labor reform bill" by President Eisenhower, the Landrum-Griffin bill was passed by the House of Representatives.

Senate-House conferees labored for twelve days, finally emerging with a compromise measure, basically following the House Landrum-Griffin bill, but with a number of important amendments. In early September, the resulting Labor-Management Reporting and Disclosure Act of 1959 [44] was accepted by both Houses; it was signed into law by the President, September 14, 1959.

The full text is found in the *Statutory Appendix,* and the various provisions are taken up in the appropriate chapters of this volume. Briefly, the 1959 labor reform legislation implements the recommendations of the McClellan Committee by establishing a "bill of rights" for union members; requiring periodic financial and other reports from unions and their officers and employees, employers and labor relations consultants; regulating trusteeships over local unions; regulating union election procedures; regulating misappropriation of union funds and loans from union treasuries; and prohibiting Communists and persons convicted of certain crimes within the preceding five years from holding union office.

In addition, a number of important amendments were made to the Labor Management Relations Act of 1947 (Taft-Hartley Act): in order to fill the "no-man's land," states were permitted to handle cases declined by the NLRB, but the Board was prohibited from further restricting its jurisdiction; economic strikers, though permanently replaced, were given limited voting rights in NLRB elections; the secondary boycott prohibitions of the Taft-Hartley Act were tightened up so as to prevent direct pressure upon secondary employers; hot cargo clauses were outlawed, with certain exceptions for the garment and construction industries; and organizational and recognition picketing was placed under explicit restrictions.

---

[44] 73 Stat. 519 (1959), 24 U.S.C. §§ 401-531.

9. LABOR DEVELOPMENT SINCE 1959

A wide range of social legislation was enacted by the Congress in the sixties as part of President Johnson's "Great Society" program, including increases in the minimum wage and greatly expanded coverage of the Fair Labor Standards Act, improvement of Social Security benefits and the introduction of Medicare for the aged. As part of a broad-scale attack on poverty, Congress enacted legislation dealing with area redevelopment, manpower development and training, and economic opportunity for disadvantaged portions of the population.

(a) Equal Employment Opportunity Laws

Most directly related to labor relations law is Title VII of the Civil Rights Act of 1964,[45] declaring that it is an unfair employment practice for any employer, employment agency, or labor organization to discriminate against any individual because of race, color, religion, sex, or national origin, and creating the Equal Employment Opportunity Commission (EEOC) to investigate and conciliate charges of discrimination filed by the public. The EEOC received huge numbers of charges and was able to conciliate many of them, but its effectiveness was limited by the lack of full enforcement powers. In the Equal Employment Opportunity Act of 1972, Congress gave the EEOC power to institute suits in the federal courts and substantially expanded the Commission's jurisdiction. Congress continues, however, to withhold from the agency the authority to issue its own enforcement orders. Nevertheless, Title VII already has had an enormous impact on hiring, promotions, wage rate differentials, job application forms, want ads, employment testing and record keeping. This is due in part to the attorney's fees provisions in the Act which have made it possible for those who allege discrimination, who are often poor, to obtain representation by the private bar on an individual or class-wide basis. The text of Title VII, as amended by the Equal Employment Opportunity Act of 1972, is reproduced in the *Statutory Appendix.*

Noting that it is not only minority and women employees who find themselves disadvantaged in the face of rising productivity and affluence, Congress in 1967 passed the Age Discrimination in Employment Act.[46] The Act gives the Secretary of Labor authority to investigate, conciliate and prosecute age discrimination complaints against employers, unions, and employment agencies under the procedures of the Fair Labor Standards Act.

In the spirit of such equal employment legislation, President Johnson in 1965 issued Executive Order 11246 [47] requiring nondiscrimination in

---

[45] 78 Stat. 241, 253-66 as amended by Pub. L. No. 92-261 (1972), 86 Stat. 103, 42 U.S.C. §§ 2000e — 2000e-15. Discrimination on the basis of sex in the payment of wages is also prohibited by the Equal Pay Act of 1963. 77 Stat. 56, 29 U.S.C. § 206(d).

[46] 81 Stat. 602 (1967), 29 U.S.C. 621-634. The Act was substantially amended in 1978 by P.L. 95-256.

[47] 30 Fed. Reg. 12319 (1965), amended by E.O. 11375, 32 Fed. Reg. 14303 (1967).

federal government employment and in employment by government contractors. The Office of Federal Contract Compliance in the Department of Labor worked out affirmative action plans to increase minority employment on federally financed projects. Employers were required to set goals and timetables for their accomplishment in those trades where minority groups were not adequately represented.[48]

(b) Job Safety Laws

A 1968 coal mine explosion in Farmington, W. Va. killed 78 men and thrust the issue of job safety to the head of labor's list of legislative concerns. A total of three job safety acts soon emerged from Congress. The Construction Safety Act of 1969 [49] sets safety standards that the construction industry must meet on all federal and federally financed projects. The Act is enforced by way of a three-year blacklisting of any contractor found guilty of noncompliance. The Coal Mine Health and Safety Act of 1969 [50] codifies strict standards designed to prevent coal mine disasters, provides for compensation for victims of coal miners' "black lung" disease, and authorizes a study of ways of improving coal mine health and safety. The Act establishes fines of up to $10,000 for mine operators found not in compliance.

The third and most comprehensive statute is the Occupational Safety and Health Act of 1970.[51] This important statute, passed as a compromise measure, gives the Secretary of Labor broad authority to promulgate safety and health standards for the millions of workers in businesses affecting interstate commerce. The discretion of the Secretary is generally limited by the various procedural safeguards expected in the administrative rule-making process, including notice and public hearings. The enforcement power is lodged in an independent three-member Commission appointed by the President. In contrast to the wide discretion granted to the Secretary to set standards, the Act provides a highly structured set of rules governing penalties. In the event of imminent danger to workers, the Secretary of Labor can petition a district court for an injunction to stop employee exposure to the danger.

---

[48] See 41 C.F.R. Part 60 (1973).

[49] 83 Stat. 96 (1969), 40 U.S.C. § 333.

[50] 83 Stat. 742 (1969), 30 U.S.C. §§ 801-960.

[51] 84 Stat. 1590 (1970), 29 U.S.C. §§ 651-678.

In Marshall v. Barlow's, Inc., 436 U.S. 307 (1978), the Supreme Court declared § 8(a) of the Occupational Safety and Health Act of 1970 violative of the Fourth Amendment insofar as it authorizes warrantless inspections of employment facilities within the Act's jurisdiction. The majority stated, however, that a showing that a particular business had been chosen for an OSHA search on the basis of a general enforcement plan derived from neutral sources would justify the issuance of a warrant even in the absence of "probable cause" that violations existed. Justices Stevens, Blackmun, and Rehnquist dissented, insisting that the ultimate question was whether the category of warrantless searches authorized by the statute was "unreasonable" within the meaning of the first clause of the Fourth Amendment.

(c) Public Employee Unionism

One area of increasing interest and significance for labor is the development of collective bargaining for federal, state, and local government employees. Public employee unions more than doubled their membership during the decade of the sixties.[52] Organizational activity among federal employees was spurred by the report of a Task Force headed by Secretary of Labor Arthur Goldberg. This report was followed by President Kennedy's issuance of Executive Order 10988 [53] in 1962, which established an executive policy favorable to the organization of federal workers and the recognition of those organizations for collective negotiations. By 1969 President Nixon had fleshed out the Kennedy policy with an elaborate statement of recognition and grievance procedures in Executive Order 11491.[54] A number of states enacted legislation to deal with the problem of labor relations for government employees at the state and local level, and a coalition of public employee unions pledged in 1973 to seek federal legislation to govern public employee-management relations at all levels of government. Strikes by local government employees, particularly teachers, presented an increasingly difficult problem, and legislators and administrators turned their attention to devising procedures for resolving collective bargaining impasses.

(d) Economic Controls

The problems of inflation assumed center stage in public debate during the 1970's. President Nixon imposed wage and price controls on the economy, and thereafter the economic controls program went through a series of "phases" between 1971 and 1974. Labor leaders were critical of the controls as weighing most heavily on wages. President Carter found it necessary to institute a program of "voluntary" wage-price guidelines in 1978.

(e) Emergency Strike Problems

Economic problems brought into sharper focus the dilemma of those critical strikes which seem to harm the public more than they do the parties. Many people have long felt that the national emergency provisions of the Taft-Hartley Act (§§ 206-10) are imperfect, but it appears to be extremely difficult to find a solution which would not be destructive of the collective bargaining process. Lacking a consensus as to

---

[52] U.S. Department of Labor, Bureau of Labor Statistics, Handbook of Labor Statistics 328-330 (1972).

[53] 27 Fed. Reg. 551 (1962).

[54] 34 Fed. Reg. 17605 (1969), amended by E.O. 11616, 36 Fed. Reg. 17319 (1971). Statutory status was given to the federal program in 1978 with the enactment of a new Federal Service Labor Management and Employee Relations Law as Title VII of the Civil Service Reform Act of 1978. P.L. 95-454, effective January, 1979.

improved procedures generally, the President and the Congress face each major dispute as a separate problem. Special legislation was enacted as a last resort in 1963, 1967, 1970, and 1971 for the resolution of railroad labor disputes. In 1971, President Nixon proposed legislation to block strikes in the transportation industry and to force settlement by permitting a special board to choose between the last best offer of either labor or management. The plan encountered serious opposition and it was not enacted into law.

(f) Organized Labor in the 1970's

Union membership in the United States passed the 20 million mark in 1970, much of the growth in recent years coming in the public sector. However, the labor force expanded faster than unionization; the percentage of the labor force which was made up of union members declined from a high of 25.5 percent in 1953 to 21.7 percent in 1974.[55] This decline resulted, at least in part, from the shift in employment away from industrial production, the traditional center of strength of organized labor.

A number of problems confronted labor unions early in the decade of the seventies, as indicated by a large number of rejections of negotiated settlements by the rank and file, apparent feelings on the part of skilled workers that their interests were not being adequately represented, and coolness on the part of members living in middle-class suburbs to the traditional social legislation goals of the AFL-CIO.

Having achieved a high level of success in collective bargaining for their members, unions faced increasing pressure from minorities and women for a greater recognition of their distinct interests.

As an established and powerful force in American society, the labor movement was confronted with the challenge of changed conditions. The traditional goal of winning more and bigger "gains" in bargaining may have to be supplemented with new goals concerned with improving the quality of life, both on the job and in the communities surrounding the work place.

SECTION II. Introductory Materials

A. COVERAGE OF THE NATIONAL LABOR RELATIONS ACT

1. SCOPE OF THE CONCEPT "AFFECTING COMMERCE"

In the *Jones & Laughlin* case the Supreme Court approved the interpretation by the NLRB (see First Annual Report 195 (1936)) that Congress had given the Board jurisdiction coextensive with congressional

---

[55] U.S. Department of Labor, Bureau of Labor Statistics, Handbook of Labor Statistics 293 (1977).

power to legislate under the commerce clause of the Constitution. As stated in § 10(a) of the National Labor Relations Act, the NLRB is empowered "to prevent any person from engaging in any unfair labor practice (listed in § 8) affecting commerce."

A long series of later cases have made it clear that federal power (and hence the jurisdiction of the NLRB) over industries in which a labor dispute would "affect commerce" is very broad. As we shall see later, the NLRB has, in its discretion, chosen not to exercise its jurisdiction to the full in some cases; but the power remains in the Board to exercise its jurisdiction to the fullest extent to which the courts have expanded the concept, "affecting commerce."

In general, the NLRA applies to:

    (a) employers producing goods which are destined directly or indirectly to go out into interstate commerce;

    (b) employers receiving goods from out-of-state, directly or indirectly, so that a labor dispute would tend to slow down the flow of goods in interstate commerce;

    (c) employers engaged in commerce — communications, transportation, etc. — or performing services for such industries, so that a labor dispute would interfere with the movement of commerce.

The company need not do a majority of its business across state lines, and the company may do a very small percentage of the total business in its industry. It is immaterial whether the same goods or services could be obtained from another company in the event of a labor dispute.[1]

As the Supreme Court said in *NLRB v. Fainblatt:*[2]

> The power of Congress to regulate interstate commerce is plenary and extends to all such commerce be it great or small. . . . The amount of commerce regulated is of special significance only to the extent that Congress may be taken to have excluded commerce of small volume from the operation of its regulatory measure by express provision or fair implication. . . . Examining the Act in the light of its purpose and of the circumstances in which it must be applied we can perceive no basis for inferring any intention of Congress to make the operation of the Act depend upon any particular volume of commerce affected more than that to which courts would apply the maxim *de minimis.*

And in *Polish National Alliance v. NLRB,*[3] the Court said:

> Whether or not practices may be deemed by Congress to affect interstate commerce is not to be determined by confining judgment to the effect of the activities immediately before the Board.

---

[1] NLRB v. Bradford Dyeing Ass'n, 310 U.S. 318 (1940).

[2] 306 U.S. 601, 605-07 (1939).

[3] 322 U.S. 643, 648 (1944).

Appropriate for judgment is the fact that the immediate situation is representative of many others throughout the country, the total incidence of which if left unchecked may well become far-reaching in its harm to commerce.

The Supreme Court has shown no tendency since the NLRA was amended by the Taft-Hartley Act to narrow its concept of the range of businesses in which a labor dispute would be regarded as "affecting commerce." [4]

2. NLRB EXERCISE OF ITS JURISDICTION

NLRB, A GUIDE TO BASIC LAW AND PROCEDURES UNDER THE NATIONAL LABOR RELATIONS ACT (1976)

Although the National Labor Relations Board could exercise its powers to enforce the Act in all cases involving enterprises whose operations affect commerce, the Board does not act in all such cases. In its discretion it limits the exercise of its power to cases involving enterprises whose effect on commerce is substantial. The Board's requirements for exercising its power or jurisdiction are called "jurisdictional standards." These standards are based on the yearly amount of business done by the enterprise, or on the yearly amount of its sales or of its purchases. They are stated in terms of total dollar volume of business and are different for different kinds of enterprises. The Board's standards in effect on July 1, 1976, are as follows:

1. *Nonretail business:* Direct sales of goods to consumers in other States, or indirect sales through others (called outflow), of at least $50,000 a year; or direct purchases of goods from suppliers in other States, or indirect purchases through others (called inflow), of at least $50,000 a year.

2. *Office buildings:* Total annual revenue of $100,000 of which $25,000 or more is derived from organizations which meet any of the standards except the indirect outflow and indirect inflow standards established for nonretail enterprises.

3. *Retail enterprises:* At least $500,000 total annual volume of business.

4. *Public utilities:* At least $250,000 total annual volume of business, or $50,000 direct or indirect outflow or inflow.

5. *Newspapers:* At least $200,000 total annual volume of business.

6. *Radio, telegraph, television, and telephone enterprises:* At least $100,000 total annual volume of business.

7. *Hotels, motels, and residential apartment houses:* At least $500,000 total annual volume of business.

---

[4] *See* NLRB v. Reliance Fuel Oil Corp., 371 U.S. 224 (1963); Amalgamated Meat Cutters v. Fairlawn Meats, Inc., 353 U.S. 20 (1957); Howell Chevrolet Co. v. NLRB, 346 U.S. 482 (1953); NLRB v. Denver Bldg. & Constr. Trades Council, 341 U.S. 675 (1951).

8. *Privately operated health care institutions:* At least $250,000 total annual volume of business for hospitals; at least $100,000 for nursing homes, visiting nurses associations, and related facilities; at least $250,000 for all other types of private health care institutions defined in the 1974 amendments to the Act. The statutory definition includes: "any hospital, convalescent hospital, health maintenance organization, health clinic, nursing home, extended care facility, or other institution devoted to the care of the sick, infirm, or aged person." Public hospitals are excluded from NLRB jurisdiction by Section 2(2) of the Act.

9. *Transportation enterprises, links and channels of interstate commerce:* At least $50,000 total annual income from furnishing interstate passenger and freight transportation services; also performing services valued at $50,000 or more for businesses which meet any of the jurisdictional standards except the indirect outflow and indirect inflow standards established for nonretail enterprises.

10. *Transit systems:* At least $250,000 total annual volume of business.

11. *Taxicab companies:* At least $500,000 total annual volume of business.

12. *Associations:* These are regarded as a single employer in that the annual business of all association members is totaled to determine whether any of the standards apply.

13. *Enterprises in the Territories and the District of Columbia:* The jurisdictional standards apply in the Territories; all businesses in the District of Columbia come under NLRB jurisdiction.

14. *National defense:* Jurisdiction is asserted over all enterprises affecting commerce when their operations have a substantial impact on national defense, whether or not the enterprises satisfy any other standard.

15. *Private universities and colleges:* At least $1 million gross annual revenue from all sources (excluding contributions not available for operating expenses because of limitations imposed by the grantor).

16. *Symphony orchestras:* At least $1 million gross annual revenue from all sources (excluding contributions not available for operating expenses because of limitations imposed by the grantor).

Through enactment of the 1970 Postal Reorganization Act, jurisdiction of the NLRB was extended to the United States Postal Service, effective July 1, 1971.

Ordinarily if an enterprise does the total annual volume of business listed in the standard, it will necessarily be engaged in activities that "affect" commerce. The Board must find, however, based on evidence, that the enterprise does in fact "affect" commerce.

The Board has established the policy that where an employer whose operations "affect" commerce refuses to supply the Board with information concerning total annual business, etc., the Board may dispense with this requirement and exercise jurisdiction.

Finally, Section 14(c)(1) authorizes the Board, in its discretion, to decline to exercise jurisdiction over any class or category of employers where a labor dispute involving such employees is not sufficiently substantial to warrant the exercise of jurisdiction, provided that it cannot refuse to exercise jurisdiction over any labor dispute over which it would have asserted jurisdiction under the standards it had in effect on August 1, 1959. In accordance with this provision the Board has determined that it will not exercise jurisdiction over racetracks, owners, breeders, and trainers of racehorses, and real estate brokers.

NOTE

The NLRB will assert jurisdiction over the following types of employers, if they meet the Board's appropriate jurisdictional standard: charitable institutions, St. Aloysius Home, 224 N.L.R.B. 1344 (1976); law firms, Foley, Hoag & Eliot, 229 N.L.R.B. 456 (1977); agencies or instrumentalities of a foreign state engaged in commercial activity within the United States, Bank of India, 229 N.L.R.B. 838 (1977).

The NLRB announced that jurisdiction will be asserted over law firms that have at least $250,000 in gross annual revenues. Camden Regional Legal Services, 231 N.L.R.B. 224 (1977).

3. EXCLUSIONS FROM COVERAGE

(a) Independent Contractors

The Wagner Act did not contain any specific exclusion of independent contractors, and the Supreme Court in *NLRB v. Hearst Publications, Inc.* [5] sustained the NLRB in its finding that the newsmen selling papers at fixed spots on the streets were employees entitled to the protection of the act. The Court reasoned:

> The mischief at which the Act is aimed and the remedies it offers are not confined exclusively to "employees" within the traditional legal distinctions separating them from "independent contractors." . . .

> Unless the common-law tests are to be imported and made exclusively controlling, without regard to the statute's purposes, it cannot be irrelevant that the particular workers in these cases are subject, as a matter of economic fact, to the evils the statute was designed to eradicate and that the remedies it affords are appropriate for preventing them or curing their harmful effects in the special situation. Interruption of commerce through strikes and unrest may stem as well from labor disputes between some who, for other purposes, are technically "independent contractors" and their

[5] 322 U.S. 111, 126-28 (1944).

employers as from disputes between persons who, for those purposes, are "employees" and their employers. Cf. Milk Drivers' Union v. Lake Valley Farm Products, 311 U.S. 91. Inequality of bargaining power in controversies over wages, hours and working conditions may as well characterize the status of the one group as of the other. The former, when acting alone, may be as "helpless in dealing with an employer," as "dependent . . . on his daily wage" and as "unable to leave the employ and to resist arbitrary and unfair treatment" as the latter. For each, "union . . . [may be] essential to give . . . opportunity to deal on equality with their employer." And for each, collective bargaining may be appropriate and effective for the "friendly adjustment of industrial disputes arising out of differences as to wages, hours, or other working conditions." 49 Stat. 449. In short, when the particular situation of employment combines these characteristics, so that the economic facts of the relation make it more nearly one of employment than of independent business enterprise with respect to the ends sought to be accomplished by the legislation, those characteristics may outweigh technical legal classification for purposes unrelated to the statute's objectives and bring the relation within its protections.

The Court took the position, moreover, that the task of making "a completely definitive limitation around the term 'employee' " had been assigned primarily to the NLRB to perform, since the everyday experience of the Board equips it with knowledge as to the circumstances and backgrounds of employment relationships in various industries, and of the abilities and needs of the workers for self-organization and collective bargaining. "Resolving that question, like determining whether unfair labor practices have been committed, 'belongs to the usual administrative routine' of the Board," and under the act, according to Justice Rutledge, the reviewing function of the Court was limited.

The Eightieth Congress reacted strongly in 1947, as the following committee report indicates.

HOUSE COMMITTEE ON EDUCATION AND LABOR, H.R. Rep. No. 245 on H.R. 3020, 80th Cong., 1st Sess. 18 (1947)

An "employee," according to all standard dictionaries, according to the law as the courts have stated it, and according to the understanding of almost everyone, with the exception of members of the National Labor Relations Board, means someone who works for another for hire. But in the case of NLRB v. Hearst Publications, Inc., 322 U.S. 111 (1944), the Board expanded the definition of the term "employee" beyond anything that it ever had included before, and the Supreme Court, relying upon the theoretic "expertness" of the Board, upheld the Board. In this case the Board held independent merchants who bought newspapers from the publisher and hired people to sell them to be "employees." The people the merchants hired to sell the papers were "employees" of the merchants, but holding the merchants to be "employees" of the publisher of the papers was most far reaching. It must be presumed that when Congress passed the Labor Act, it intended words it used to have the meanings that they had when Congress passed the Act, not new meanings that, nine years later, the Labor Board might think up. In the law there always has been a difference, and a big difference, between "employees" and "independent contractors." "Employees" work for wages or salaries under direct supervision. "Independent contractors" undertake to do a job for a price, decide how the work will be done, usually hire others to do the work, and depend for their income not upon wages, but upon the difference between what they pay for goods, materials, and labor and what they receive for the end result, that is, upon profits. It is inconceivable that Congress, when it passed the Act, authorized the Board to give to every word in the Act whatever meaning it wished. On the contrary, Congress intended them, and it intends now, the Board to give to words not farfetched meanings but ordinary meanings. To correct what the Board has done, and what the Supreme Court, putting misplaced reliance upon the Board's expertness, has approved, the bill excludes "independent contractors" from the definition of "employee."

—————

The NLRB subsequently explained its understanding of the distinction as follows:

The Board has consistently held that the act requires that the question whether an individual is an independent contractor be determined by applying the "right-of-control" test. Under this test an independent contractor relationship will be found where the record shows that the person for whom services are performed reserves control only as to the result sought. On the other hand, where the record shows that control is retained over the manner and means by which the result is to be accomplished, an employer-employee relationship will be found.[6]

(b) Supervisory Employees

The status of supervisory employees presented one of the most troublesome problems to confront the NLRB under the original NLRA. The question was to what extent, if at all, supervisory groups were to be accorded the rights of "employees" under the statute. It was early and consistently held by the Board with judicial support that supervisory

———

[6] NLRB, TWENTY-THIRD ANNUAL REPORT 40 (1958). For cases illustrating the ordinary tests of the law of agency as required by the Taft-Hartley Act, see Brown v. NLRB, 462 F.2d 699 (9th Cir. 1972); Herald Co. v. NLRB, 444 F.2d 430 (2d Cir. 1971); NLRB v. United Ins. Co., 390 U.S. 254 (1968); National Van Lines, Inc. v. NLRB, 273 F.2d 402 (7th Cir. 1960); NLRB v. Nu-Car Carriers, Inc., 189 F.2d 756 (3d Cir. 1951); Seven-Up Bottling Co. v. NLRB, 506 F.2d 596 (1st Cir. 1974); Seafarers Local 777 v. NLRB [Yellow Cab Co.], 99 L.R.R.M. 2903 (D.C. Cir. 1978). *See also,* Comment, *Employees and Independent Contractors under the NLRA,* 2 IND. REL. L.J. 278 (1977).

employees were protected against acts of discrimination under § 8(3) of the act.

The next question was whether, as employees protected in some respects under the act, supervisors also had bargaining rights, and, if so, in what form of bargaining unit. After considerable difference of opinion among members of the NLRB, the Board certified the Foreman's Association of America as representative of a bargaining unit of foremen, and the Supreme Court enforced an order to bargain in *Packard Motor Car Co. v. NLRB.*[7] In *Jones & Laughlin Steel Corp.,*[8] the Board held that District 50 of the United Mine Workers could represent mine foremen even though the UMW also represented the rank and file miners.

The Board's policy of according to supervisory personnel the full status of employees under the original act was the subject of bitter attack by employers, with the result that in the Taft-Hartley Act of 1947 Congress expressly excluded from the definition of "employee" "any individual employed as a supervisor" (§ 2(3)), and adopted an apparently broad definition of "supervisors" (§ 2(11)). At the same time it was provided in § 14(a) that "Nothing herein shall prohibit any individual employed as a supervisor from becoming or remaining a member of a labor organization, but no employer subject to this act shall be compelled to deem individuals defined herein as supervisors as employees for the purpose of any law, either national or local, relating to collective bargaining." While the act thus established a new national policy with respect to the status of such employees, the debate on the merits will doubtless continue, especially since supervisors remain free of any legislative prohibition against unionization.

The NLRB has commented:

> The supervisory status of an employee under the act depends on whether he possesses authority to act in the interest of his employer in the matters and the manner specified in Section 2(11) which defines the term "supervisors." Generally, it is the existence rather than the exercise of authority within the meaning of Section 2(11) that determines an employee's supervisory status.

> In determining the existence of supervisory authority in contested cases, the Board has continued to take into consideration such record facts as the ratio of supervisory to supervised employees in the particular department or plant. . . . Manner and rate of pay is also considered relevant in ascertaining the status of employees.

> Employees who possess some supervisory authority may be included in a bargaining unit if the exercise of their supervisory functions is only sporadic or occasional. On the other hand, employees who substitute regularly and periodically for their superior during his absence are generally excluded from bargaining units.[9]

---

[7] 330 U.S. 485 (1947).

[8] 66 N.L.R.B. 386 (1946).

[9] NLRB TWENTY-THIRD ANNUAL REPORT 40-41 (1958). Managerial employees (those who are in a position to formulate and effectuate management policies) are excluded from

(c) Other Exclusions

Other categories of persons who are excluded from the coverage of the Taft-Hartley Act by virtue of the definition of "employee" in § 2(3) include agricultural laborers and domestic servants. The NLRB has held, with respect to workers whose duties are partly agricultural and partly not, that "employees who perform any regular amounts of non-agricultural work are covered by the Act with respect to that portion of the work which is non-agricultural." [10] Other workers are excluded from the coverage of the act by virtue of the exclusion of their employers under § 2(2) of the act. In this category of employees not covered by the National Labor Relations Act are employees of federal, state, and local governments and employers subject to the Railway Labor Act.

The Taft-Hartley exemption for nonprofit hospitals was removed in 1974. Are interns and residents in such hospitals employees within the meaning of the Act? The NLRB, with Member Fanning dissenting, held that they were primarily students and not employees. Therefore, their house staff association is not a labor organization, and a bargaining unit composed of interns, residents, and clinical fellows is inappropriate. The Board reasoned that they participate in these programs, not for the purpose of making a living, but to pursue the graduate medical education that is a requirement for the practice of medicine. Member Fanning took the position that the fact that they are students did not preclude them from being considered employees within the meaning of the Act. Cedars-Sinai Medical Center, 223 N.L.R.B. 251 (1976). In March 1978 the House Labor Committee approved H.R. 2222, which would amend the NLRA to include medical interns and residents within the definition of professional employees covered by the Act. The intent of such a bill would be to overturn the Board's decision in *Cedars-Sinai.* 97 L.R.R. 205 (1978).

For a further explanation of the *Cedars-Sinai* decision, *see* St. Clare's Hospital, 229 N.L.R.B. 1000 (1977), pointing out the Board's policy of refusing to allow union representation for students performing services at their educational institutions which are directly related to their educational programs. Relying heavily on the legislative history of the 1974 amendments, a divided panel of the District of Columbia Circuit reversed the Board and held that house staff physicians are employees under the Act. House Staff Ass'n v. Murphy, 100 L.R.R.M. 3055 (D.C. Cir. 1979). *See also* NLRB v. Committee of Interns and Residents, 566 F.2d 810 (2d Cir. 1977), *cert. denied,* 98 S. Ct. 1449 (1978), where the court reversed a district court finding and held that the NLRB had not ceded its jurisdiction over house staff physicians and that the State Labor Relations Board did not have jurisdiction over disputes involving them.

---

the coverage of the Act, even though they are neither supervisors nor persons involved with labor relations policies. NLRB v. Textron, Inc., 416 U.S. 267 (1974). Are full-time faculty members of a private university either supervisors or managerial employees? *See* NLRB v. Yeshiva University, 582 F.2d 686 (2d Cir. 1978) and cases and articles discussed therein.

[10] Olaa Sugar Co., 118 N.L.R.B. 1442 (1957).

The Supreme Court held (5-4) that the NLRB's assertion of jurisdiction over secondary schools operated by the Roman Catholic Church was not authorized by the NLRA, thus avoiding a First Amendment question concerning the separation of church and state. NLRB v. Catholic Bishop of Chicago, 99 S. Ct. 1313 (U.S. 1979).

4. STATE LABOR RELATIONS ACTS

About fifteen states have labor relations statutes with procedures for settling questions as to representation and unfair labor practices.[11] Three of these states have "little Wagner Acts," listing unfair practices of employers only.[12] The rest designate unlawful practices by both employers and unions.

In addition to the labor relations acts, many states have laws limiting the labor injunction, regulating picketing and boycotts, outlawing the union shop (so-called "right-to-work" laws), regulating internal union affairs and welfare and pension funds, and providing procedures for the settlement of labor disputes in public utilities.[13]

The looseleaf services in the labor law field bring together the state laws in one or two volumes, with useful all-state charts. The student would be well advised to consult the state law volumes of a labor service at this point, in order to get a quick view of the types of statutes which prevail in his or her state.

In a business which does not "affect" interstate commerce, these state laws are clearly applicable. Where the industry is one in which a labor dispute would "affect" interstate commerce, however, and Congress has legislated on the matter, the states may be ousted from jurisdiction. The extent to which this "federal preemption" has occurred or should occur is one of the most controversial and complex issues in the labor law field, and it will be considered in detail after we have become more familiar with the federal labor relations law.[14]

B. ORGANIZATION AND PROCEDURE OF THE NATIONAL LABOR RELATIONS BOARD

The functions of the NLRB in implementing the general policy of the NLRA are mainly two-fold: (1) the prevention of unfair labor practices, known as complaint or "C" proceedings; and (2) the settling of

---

[11] Colorado, Connecticut, Hawaii, Kansas, Massachusetts, Michigan, Minnesota, New York, North Dakota, Oregon, Pennsylvania, Rhode Island, Utah, Vermont, and Wisconsin.

[12] Connecticut, New York, and Rhode Island.

[13] For analyses of state labor laws, see C. KILLINGSWORTH, STATE LABOR RELATIONS ACTS (1948); Katz, *Two Decades of State Legislation: 1937-1957,* 25 U. CHI. L. REV. 109 (1957), 8 LAB. L.J. 747 (1957); Merrifield, *State Labor Relations Legislation,* in SYMPOSIUM ON THE LABOR-MANAGEMENT REPORTING AND DISCLOSURE ACT (Slovenko ed. 1961); Smith & Clark, *Reappraisal of the Role of the States in Shaping Labor Relations Law,* 1965 WIS. L. REV. 411.

[14] Note § 14(c)(2) of the NLRA, as amended.

representation questions including the conduct of elections, known as representation or "R" proceedings. The Board's procedure in representation cases will be discussed later.

Before looking at the procedure in unfair labor practice cases, a word about Board organization may be helpful. The Board itself in Washington consists of five members, appointed by the President for staggered five-year terms, and, in deciding cases, it may sit in panels of three. Each Board member has a sizable staff of legal assistants.

The Administrative Law Judges, also located in Washington, with a local office in San Francisco, travel throughout the country to hold hearings. Although selected by the Board, they are independent and may not be removed except for cause after a hearing by the Civil Service Commission.[15]

The General Counsel, appointed by the President for a four-year term, has final authority, under § 3(d) of the NLRA, over the investigation and prosecution of unfair labor practice charges. The forty-odd regional and sub-regional offices of the NLRB are under the supervision of the General Counsel. Each regional office is under the direction of a Regional Director, assisted by a Regional Attorney. Field examiners investigate charges and conduct elections, and field attorneys prosecute complaints before the Administrative Law Judges who come out from Washington or San Francisco.

Our attention will be focused on the difficult, controversial cases which go to the Board and the courts. Consequently, it is well to take note of the fact that the vast bulk of the cases are disposed of at the regional office level and that most of them are disposed of without any formal proceedings. For example, in the fiscal year 1977, out of a total of 37,602 unfair labor practice cases closed, 68.7% were disposed of without the issuance of a formal complaint, and another 25% were settled or adjusted prior to a decision of an Administrative Law Judge. Only 3.8% of the cases closed were decided by the Board in contested cases, and only about 1% reach the court of appeals via petitions for enforcement or review.[16]

An unfair labor practice case begins when some person writes or comes into a Regional Office of the NLRB and makes a charge against an employer (or, after Taft-Hartley, against a union or its agents). The Board has no power to initiate proceedings; a charge is required to set the wheels in motion. Indeed, the charging party may elect, where both the employer and the union are involved in an alleged unfair practice, to bring his charges against one or the other or both.

---

[15] The Administrative Law Judges were called Trial Examiners until 1972. There are currently about 100 of them. In 1979 the Board announced its intention to establish more local offices for ALJs, starting with New York City.

[16] NLRB, FORTY-SECOND ANNUAL REPORT (1977); Miller, *The Role of the NLRB in Settling Industrial Disputes*, NLRB Release R-1308, October 19, 1973; Silverberg, *Informal Procedures of the National Labor Relations Board*, 6 SYRACUSE L. REV. 72 (1954); Weyand & Zarky, *Informal Procedure Before the National Labor Relations Board*, PRAC. LAW. 31 (Jan. 1955).

The act contains a six-month statute of limitations; that is, the charge must be filed with the Board's office and served on the charged party within six months of the date on which the alleged unfair practices occurred.

Under § 10(*l*) and (m) of the NLRA, as amended by the Labor-Management Reporting and Disclosure Act of 1959, priority handling must be given to cases involving secondary boycotts, hot cargo contracts, organizational or recognition picketing, and discrimination against individual employees.

After the case is assigned to a Board agent in the Regional Office, the charging party is usually asked to submit whatever evidence he has to support the charge, including the names and addresses of witnesses.

Then the charged party is asked to submit his version of the facts and circumstances surrounding the alleged unfair labor practices. The Board agent makes an investigation, interviews witnesses, and prepares a report with recommendations. The Regional Director decides whether to issue a complaint.

Short of issuance of a complaint, a charge may be disposed of in three ways:

(1) withdrawal (32.9% of the cases in 1977);

(2) dismissal (35.8% of the cases in 1977); or

(3) settled or adjusted (25% of the cases in 1977; about one-fourth of these were adjusted after issuance of a complaint).

An adjustment means that the Regional Office has reached a settlement of the case, accomplishing the purposes of the act; it may be either informal, in which the charged party agrees to remedy his unfair practices, or formal, in which a consent decree is issued by the NLRB and a U. S. court of appeals.[17]

If the Regional Director decides to dismiss the charge, an appeal may be taken to the General Counsel (not the Board) in Washington. His decision as to whether a complaint should be issued is final, and the courts have refused to review his exercise of discretion.[18]

---

[17] A charging party is entitled to a hearing on its objections to a proposed settlement between the regional director and the respondent once a complaint has been issued, but not before. *Compare* Concrete Materials of Georgia, Inc. v. NLRB, 440 F.2d 61 (5th Cir. 1971), *with* Terminal Freight Cooperative Ass'n v. NLRB, 447 F.2d 1099 (3d Cir. 1971), *cert. denied,* 409 U.S. 1063 (1972).

[18] Division 1267, Amalgamated Ass'n of Street, Elec. Ry. & Motor Coach Employees v. Ordman, 116 U.S. App. D.C. 7, 320 F.2d 729 (1963); Hourihan v. NLRB, 91 U.S. App. D.C. 316, 201 F.2d 187 (1952); Lincourt v. NLRB, 170 F.2d 306 (1st Cir. 1948).

When the General Counsel decides not to issue a complaint, the Freedom of Information Act requires the disclosure of his office's explanatory advice and appeals memorandum as a "final opinion" made in the adjudication of the case. Advice and appeals memoranda explaining decisions by the General Counsel to issue complaints are not "final opinions," however, falling instead within the Act's exemption for "intra-agency memoranda," and thus they need not be disclosed. NLRB v. Sears, Roebuck & Co., 421 U.S. 132 (1975).

In Kent Corp. v. NLRB, 530 F.2d 612 (5th Cir. 1976), the Regional Director decided to issue a complaint against the Kent Corporation on some charges of unfair labor practices and to dismiss other charges. The company sought to obtain under the FOIA

After the formal complaint has been issued, the Board has the power, under § 10(j) of the act, to seek a temporary injunction or restraining order against the unfair labor practice in a U. S. district court, but this is seldom done. Section 10*(l)* *requires* that an injunction be sought where there is reasonable cause to believe that a charge of certain union unfair labor practices is true.

The respondent is given time to file an answer to the complaint, and then the case proceeds to a hearing before an Administrative Law Judge sent out from Washington. The case is presented by an attorney from the Regional Office, representing the General Counsel. The respondent may cross-examine witnesses, and may obtain, for this purpose, a copy of any written pretrial statement of the witness.[19] The charging party is permitted to participate in the hearing.

The Administrative Law Judge is fully responsible for the conduct of the hearing, ruling upon applications for subpoenas and depositions and other motions. He may call witnesses and cross-examine witnesses of the parties. Under § 10(b), he is required to conduct the proceedings in accordance with the rules of evidence applicable in the U. S. district courts, so far as practicable.

Parties may make an oral argument at the conclusion of the testimony and may file a brief with the Administrative Law Judge. The Administrative Law Judge then returns to his office with a transcript of the record and prepares his decision, which includes findings of fact, conclusions of law, and recommended order.

After receiving a copy of the Administrative Law Judge's decision, parties are given an opportunity to file exceptions with the Board within twenty days. If no exceptions are filed, the Board adopts the decision of the Administrative Law Judge as its own. If exceptions are filed, parties may file briefs in support of their exceptions, and the Board will consider

---

certain "final investigative reports" prepared by regional office attorneys which were used by these staff members and the Regional Director in discussion on which charges, if any, a complaint would issue. The court held that these pre-decisional materials are not "final opinions" within the meaning of the *Sears* case *supra* and are exempt from disclosure under FOIA as intra-agency memoranda and attorney's work-products.

[19] Ra-Rich Mfg. Corp., 121 N.L.R.B. 700 (1958).

Exemption 7(A) of the Freedom of Information Act, covering investigatory records whose disclosure would "interfere with enforcement proceedings," does not require a case-by-case showing of particularized risk to each individual proceeding but may be invoked in specific types of enforcement proceedings. Thus, the statements of both employee and nonemployee witnesses are exempt from disclosure prior to an unfair labor practice hearing under the NLRA, since the risks posed by a prehearing release of statements, such as witness intimidation or coercion, would "interfere with enforcement proceedings." NLRB v. Robbins Tire & Rubber Co., 437 U.S. 214 (1978). Justices Powell and Brennan concurred with regard to witnesses who were current employees, but would have required a particularized showing of likely interference with regard to others.

A seemingly new wrinkle in the line of FOIA cases appeared in Deering Milliken, Inc. v. Irving, 548 F.2d 1131 (4th Cir. 1977). The court rejected the NLRB's argument that certain documents concerning a *back pay* proceeding should not be disclosed to the employer on the basis of the "investigatory records compiled for law enforcement purposes" exemption.

the case on the record. Application may be made for oral argument before the NLRB in Washington, but it is seldom granted except where the Board wishes to examine or reexamine a basic policy question.

Although subject to change from time to time, the decisional process when the case goes to the Board has recently been approximately as follows. The Executive Secretary assigns the case to one of the five Board members, and the record is read and analyzed by one of his legal assistants. This assistant meets with his supervisor and the chief counsel of the Board member, and if the case is a simple one, an affirmance of the Administrative Law Judge's decision is prepared for the approval of the three Board members on the panel.

If more difficult questions are involved, the matter goes to a "sub-panel," consisting of the chief counsels of the Board members on the panel, who meet with the legal assistant and his supervisor and analyze the case. A draft of decision and order then goes to the three Board members for approval of changes. When necessary, the Board members hold a conference on it.

If the case involves novel issues or important questions of policy, it is sent to an "agenda" of the full Board. The legal assistant assigned to the case prepares a full memorandum for the consideration of the Board, and he attends the session. After discussion, a tentative decision is reached, and the legal assistant prepares a draft of the Board's decision. This is circulated to the members for approval or modification, and it may be discussed further at a later agenda. Finally, the decision is approved and issued by the Board.

Where the Board finds, upon a "preponderance of the testimony" (§ 10(c) of the act), that an unfair labor practice had been committed, it makes findings of fact and issues a cease and desist order which may be accompanied by an order for affirmative action, such as reinstatement.[20]

If the party against whom the order is issued does not comply, the Board can seek an enforcement order from a U. S. court of appeals. An aggrieved party need not wait for Board enforcement; he may ask the appropriate court of appeals to review the Board's order. In either case, the test for judicial review of factual questions is whether the Board's findings are supported by "substantial evidence on the record considered as a whole" (§ 10(e) of the act).

If the party against whom the court's enforcement order is issued does not comply, he runs the risk of being held in contempt of court.

The final possibility for review is to the U. S. Supreme Court upon petition for writ of certiorari, but the Supreme Court has warned: "Whether on the record as a whole there is substantial evidence to

---

[20] According to the Sixth Circuit, the Board cannot refuse to rule on a complaint charging an unfair labor practice properly brought before it; the NLRA vests discretion solely in the General Counsel to determine whether complaints are sufficiently meritorious to bring to the Board. Moreover, if the Board finds a violation, it must issue a remedial order, even though it believes an order would serve no useful purpose. UAW v. NLRB [Omni Spectra, Inc.], 427 F.2d 1330 (6th Cir. 1970).

support agency findings is a question which Congress has placed in the Courts of Appeals. This Court will intervene only in what ought to be the rare instance when the standard appears to have been misapprehended or grossly misapplied." [21]

The following table, compiled from the NLRB Annual Reports, affords some indication of the trends in cases filed.[22]

NLRB CASES FILED DURING THE FISCAL YEARS
1950-1977

Fiscal Year	Total Cases	% Tot. Cases		Total ULP Cs.	% Tot. Cases	
		Rep. Cases	ULP Cases		R-ULP Cases	U-ULP Cases
1950	15,088	61.5	38.5	5,809	29.6	8.9
1960	21,527	47.2	52.8	11,357	35.9	16.8
1970	33,581	37.4	62.6	21,038	40.5	21.8
1975	44,923	30.5	69.5	31,253	45.2	24.3
1976	49,335	30.1	69.9	34,509	47.6	22.3
1977	52,943	28.6	71.4	37,828	49.3	22.1

Code:
    Rep. cases: Representation cases.
    ULP cases: Unfair Labor Practice cases.
    R-ULP cases: Unfair Labor Practice cases against employers.
    U-ULP cases: Unfair Labor Practice cases against unions.

C. PROPOSALS FOR CHANGE IN DECISION-MAKING UNDER THE NATIONAL LABOR RELATIONS ACT

ROUTES TO REFORM, Remarks of Edward B. Miller, Chairman, National Labor Relations Board Before the Labor Relations Law Section, American Bar Association, August 7, 1973, NLRB Release R-1297

. . . I honestly do not see how it will be physically possible for five Board Members to handle many more cases than are projected for the current fiscal year. We already have too little time adequately to consider our present cases, and any substantial further caseload will either make us rubber stamps for whatever decisions our Administrative Law Judges

---

[21] Universal Camera Corp. v. NLRB, 340 U.S. 474, 491 (1951).

[22] For more detailed information as to NLRB procedure, see Statements of Procedures and Rules and Regulations of the National Labor Relations Board, 29 C.F.R. §§ 101-02; K. McGUINESS, HOW TO TAKE A CASE BEFORE THE NATIONAL LABOR RELATIONS BOARD (4th ed. 1976); F. McCULLOCH & T. BORNSTEIN, THE NATIONAL LABOR RELATIONS BOARD (1974).

make, or we will gradually develop a hopelessly insurmountable backlog. . . . The debatable issue no longer is one of whether some change ought to be made, but rather what kind of change do you want?

The first question which I believe must be squarely answered is this: "How long a road do you want to enforceable decisions?"

As all of you practitioners know, under the present law there are three steps to an enforceable decision: first, a trial before one of our Administrative Law Judges; secondly, an appeal to the five-man Board; and third, enforcement or review proceedings in a court of appeals. Only the court of appeals decision has any legal authority or teeth. . . .

There is a growing consensus that the present three-step procedure is too long and too cumbersome. The simple fact is that with a three-step procedure it is virtually impossible, if due process at all stages is to be properly observed, for anyone to get an enforceable decision in less than about two years. For some time now the median number of days from the filing of a charge to Board decision has hovered around the one-year mark. We have cut a few days off of that and we may be able to cut a few more, but there is no way I can see that it can be drastically reduced. . . .

Then, if you are going to go on from there to a court decision before enforceability arrives, you have to add on just about another year. We have dramatically shortened the time it takes us to initiate court enforcement — from 255 days in 1970 to about 30 days currently. The total median time to get from Board decision to court decision — which ran some 611 days in 1969-70 — is now down to around 355 days. Several of the circuits are making new efforts to expedite their crowded calendars. These new administrative improvements may bring down the current median from Board decision to court opinion, but to hope for as low as six months sometime in the future would be highly optimistic.

So, if we stay with a three-step process, it would take almost a miracle to cut the median time from filing a charge to court decision down to even a total of a year and a half. That, I suggest, would not be regarded by any concerned citizen as prompt justice. That is why most persons who have given serious attention to a revised structure have concluded that the present three-step procedure is too cumbersome and too long.

My own view is that we ought to have only a one-step process, like most all other judicial determinations. When you have a non-labor case in your state courts or in the Federal District Courts, the very first decision you get is an enforceable one. I do not really see why it should be any different in labor cases. You already have it in suits for breach of collective-bargaining agreements; you already have it in most wage hour cases; and you now have it in EEOC cases. One step in all of those labor cases — why three with respect to decisions involving alleged violations of the National Labor Relations Act? . . .

The second question I think you need to answer is, "Who shall the judges be?" . . . How would you select the initial corps of trial judges? How would you select trial judges for the future? Who should serve as appellate judges — an NLRB? A specialized Court of Appeals? The present Courts of Appeal? Or who? And how large and how centralized should any appellate review judiciary be?

My third heading or subject area is: "How separate should labor judiciaries be?" . . . Would it be desirable to have one specialized labor judiciary in which all of these kinds of cases — all EEOC matters, all Labor Board matters, all Railway Labor Act matters, all wage-hour matters, and the like should be brought, so that any cases involving a single set of facts but a combination of issues could be consolidated and heard in a single forum? Is it time to perhaps preserve separate public prosecutors and administrative agencies, each specializing in its own statute, but to require that all litigation initiated by private persons or such public agencies be brought in a single specialized employment relations judiciary?

The Bar has traditionally been reluctant to accept the idea of specialized judiciaries. But times are changing. Is this the time to take a new and bold step in this connection? [23] . . .

REPORT OF THE SENATE COMMITTEE ON HUMAN RESOURCES ON THE PROPOSED LABOR LAW REFORM ACT OF 1978, Report No. 95-628, 95th Congress, 2d Session, Jan. 31, 1978

EXPEDITING THE PROCESSING OF UNFAIR LABOR PRACTICES

If there is a single problem which has contributed most to the breakdown in enforcement of the national labor policy, it has been the inability of the enforcing agency to provide expeditious relief and case disposition. In contested cases an unfair labor practice charge filed in 1975 took a median time of 315 days for disposition by the National Labor Relations Board. In 1976, it took 358 days and in the first quarter of 1977 it was up to 374 days.

To enable the Board to reverse this trend, S.2467 proposes five changes designed to reduce case handling time at every point from the issuance of the complaint until the petition for court review.

A. *Expansion of the Board*

Since 1947 when the Board was expanded from 3 members to its present 5 members, the number of contested unfair labor practice

---

[23] For other statements by Chairman Miller in his campaign to re-structure the decision-making process in labor cases, see Miller, *The NLRB — Past, Present and Future,* 1970 LABOR RELATIONS YEARBOOK 183; Miller, *Toward an Improved Labor Judiciary,* 1972 LABOR RELATIONS YEARBOOK 97; Miller, *The Administrative Law Judge — Who, Where, How, When?,* 1972 LABOR RELATIONS YEARBOOK 71. *See also,* Bartosic, *Labor Law Reform — The NLRB and a Labor Court,* 4 GA. L. REV. 647 (1970); Fields, *Proposal for Five Regional Boards,* 1971 LABOR RELATIONS YEARBOOK 252; Fanning, *Proposals to Speed Disposition of Taft-Hartley Act Cases,* 1970 LABOR RELATIONS YEARBOOK 157; Harris, *The Choice Before Us: Labor Board, Labor Court or District Court,* SOUTHWESTERN LEGAL FOUNDATION, LABOR LAW DEVELOPMENTS, PROCEEDING OF THE 17TH ANNUAL INSTITUTE 331 (1971); Morris, *Labor Court: A New Perspective,* N.Y.U. TWENTY-FOURTH ANNUAL CONFERENCE ON LABOR 27 (1972); Murphy, *The National Labor Relations Board — An Appraisal,* SOUTHWESTERN LEGAL FOUNDATION, LABOR LAW DEVELOPMENTS, PROCEEDINGS OF THE 14TH ANNUAL INSTITUTE 113 (1968).

decisions issued by the agency has increased from 115 to over 1100 in fiscal 1977, with an expected increase to 1400 by fiscal 1979. The result is substantial delay. An increase in Board membership from 5 to 7, as originally proposed by the late Senator Robert Taft, will enable the Board to handle more cases and reduce the time it presently takes to dispose of cases at that level.

Board panels of three members decide the overwhelming number of unfair labor practice cases. The purpose of expanding the Board is to make it possible to process these cases far more promptly. Enlarging the Board to seven members will enable it to establish additional panels (seven instead of the present five) and to distribute to a larger number of people the initial study of the record and the drafting of opinions.

. . . . .

In addition, since a seven-man Board, each of whose members will serve a seven-year rather than five-year term, will have greater stability, it is believed that the Board's decisions in precedent-making cases will be accorded a greater degree of respect by the affected parties. Finally, at present the practice is that no more than three members of the Board shall be members of the same political party. To assure continued balance on the Board, the bill expressly provides that no more than a simple majority of the Board's membership shall be drawn from one party.

B. *Requiring ALJ's to Issue Short Form Decisions in Uncomplicated Cases and Providing Law Clerks to ALJ's*

. . . . .

The median time from the issuance of an unfair labor practice complaint to the issuance of an ALJ decision is 185 days and it presently takes a median of 111 days from the close of an unfair labor practice hearing until the ALJ issues a written opinion. . . . The proper functional approach is to provide that the ALJs shall set out their findings of fact and conclusions of law in brief conclusionary paragraphs commenting only briefly on the method they used in resolving conflicts and the basis for their legal conclusions, and to leave it to the Board to explore and settle open legal questions as necessary. Section 8 of the bill amends Section 10 of the Act to provide precisely that division of responsibility.

. . . . .

[T]he Act does not provide legal assistance or law clerks for the Administrative Law Judges. Just as legal assistants have proved invaluable to the Board members and law clerks have long assisted Federal judges, the proper administration of the Act would be enhanced by providing law clerks to the Administrative Law Judges.

. . . . .

Section 3 of the bill gives the Board authority to hire such law clerks.

C. *Summary Affirmance Procedure for Uncomplicated Cases*

. . . . .

[T]he Committee bill provides that three-member panels should consider summary cases. In addition, the bill spells out that motions for summary affirmance are to be filed by the prevailing party within 10 days after the Administrative Law Judge's decision and that the responding party has 20 days in which to reply. . . . The Board in issuing its rules would determine the types of cases which would be subject to the summary affirmance procedure and establish the particular conditions applicable to the procedure.

. . . . .

The Committee bill . . . amends Section 10(f) to require any party aggrieved by a Board decision to file an appeal in the appropriate Court of Appeals within 30 days. If no petition for review was filed within that time, the Board could, by filing a petition for enforcement, obtain a final decree from the Court without further delay.

[The House of Representatives passed its version of the bill, H.R. 8410, in October 1977 by a vote of 257-163, but the Senate bill was returned to committee in June 1978 after six efforts to invoke cloture failed to end a prolonged filibuster. The bill died when the session ended without further Senate action.]

NOTE ON NLRB PROCEDURE

The NLRB generally adjudicates on a case-by-case basis. Occasionally, especially in setting guidelines for representation elections, it operates through its rule-making power. In NLRB v. Wyman-Gordon Co., 394 U.S. 759 (1969), the Supreme Court declared that the Board had promulgated a rule in violation of the rule-making requirements of the Administrative Procedure Act, 5 U.S.C. § 551, when it decided a case by announcing a rule for prospective application only. Since the rule was not applied to the parties immediately involved, the Board's decision was held not to be an "adjudication," which would have made it exempt from the procedural requirements of the APA. Relying on *Wyman-Gordon,* a court of appeals held that the Board must proceed by rule-making, not adjudication, when it proposes to "reverse a long-standing and oft-repeated policy" in representation cases. Textron, Inc. v. NLRB, 475 F.2d 485 (2d Cir. 1973). The Supreme Court, however, held that the Board has the discretion to proceed either by adjudication or by rule-making in effecting a change in policy so long as the Board's holding does not amount to an abuse of discretion. Adjudication was found to be especially appropriate where the multiplicity and variety of possible applications made it ". . . doubtful whether any generalized standard could be framed which would have more than marginal utility." NLRB v. Textron, Inc., 416 U.S. 267 (1974).

What are the advantages and disadvantages of having the Board rely more on rule-making than on case-by-case adjudication?

See Bernstein, *NLRB's Excelsior Rule: Adjudication or Rule-Making,* 1969 LABOR RELATIONS YEARBOOK 129; Bernstein, *The NLRB's Adjudication — Rule Making Dilemma Under the Administrative Procedure Act,* 79 YALE L.J. 571 (1970); Peck, *The Atrophied Rule Making Powers of the National Labor Relations Board,* 70 YALE L.J. 729 (1961); Peck, *A Critique of the National Labor Relations Board Performance in Policy Formation: Adjudication and Rule Making,* 117 U. OF PA. L. REV. 254 (1968); Shapiro, *The Choice of Rule Making or Adjudication in the Development of Administrative Policy,* 78 HARV. L. REV. 921 (1965); Williams, *The NLRB and Administrative Rulemaking,* in SOUTHWESTERN LEGAL FOUNDATION, LABOR LAW DEVELOPMENTS 1970, PROCEEDINGS OF THE SIXTEENTH ANNUAL INSTITUTE ON LABOR LAW 209.

PART TWO

ORGANIZATION AND REPRESENTATION

OF EMPLOYEES

SEMINAR ON FREE SPEECH AND PREELECTION CONDUCT in SOUTHWESTERN LEGAL FOUNDATION, LABOR LAW DEVELOPMENTS, PROCEEDINGS OF THE ELEVENTH ANNUAL INSTITUTE ON LABOR LAW 239-46 (1965) *

A MANAGEMENT LAWYER: [T]he limitation of free speech in this area of the National Labor Relations Act primarily restricts the employer. Especially is this true of the inexperienced employer who finds out, frequently too late, that speech which comes instinctively is not permitted and, therefore, not free as far as he understands that term. His frustration is aggravated when he discovers the election process bears little resemblance to the democratic process which he understands as a fundamental part of American society.

Thus, the inexperienced employer is astounded to find that his employees are rugged and intelligent enough in a bitter presidential campaign to cast a ballot freely, based on their own judgment — or utter lack of it — for the man who in the next four years will have a life and death atomic choice over their destinies. Yet, the same employees' judgment must be protected by an untrammelled free choice, akin to "laboratory conditions," in the election determining whether or not he wants a union to represent him in dealing with his employer.

Also — and I cannot emphasize this point too much as we get into the area of the so-called great debate — the employer quickly discovers the basic fundamental that probably is the main issue in most elections: "Promise of future benefits" cannot be discussed by him but can be discussed by the union. Picture what would happen if, in the presidential campaign, they could take away all promises of future benefits. . . .

A UNION LAWYER: [E]mployee fear . . . takes this whole question completely outside the area with which we are used to dealing in political elections. . . . Think of a man whose whole livelihood is dependent upon a particular job. That is the loss he faces. This factor may vary. I can imagine that in the city of Pittsburgh an employer could make a certain kind of speech, using the language a lawyer has taken out of a book as being approved in past NLRB elections. He might not cause the least bit of fear in the employees listening to that speech. . . . But there are other places in our country where the identical speech would have a totally different impact. Out on the Great Plains, for example, you can get into a little town where one proprietary employer holds sway as economic emperor. In that little town the banker, the newspaper, the sheriff, and the

---

entire community dance to the tune that employer calls. There, fear can be pervasive. . . .

A much different problem is presented when you are trying to give everyone "equal time" and are trying to provide, as the union people urge, for a fair balance in the right to communicate with the employees. . . . We are not now talking about employee fear; we are talking about a chance to get your point of view across. Here the political analogy holds very well. As far as the unions are concerned, it is almost as if the Republican or the Democratic Party owned the television networks and prevented the opposition from appearing on them to address the voters. . . .

BERNARD KARSH, DIARY OF A STRIKE 47, 117, 119-20 (1958) *

A UNION ORGANIZER: I organized a union and I ran a strike. When you have a job to do, you do it. If anyone tells you that there's a fixed way of running a strike, that you can plan it, they're insane. You build it from day to day, just like you build a union from day to day. There's nothing you can plan ahead. Sure, you can plan pickets, you can plan picket signs and songs, you can plan a kitchen and benefits. But your behavior, it varies from moment to moment according to the needs of the situation, and the important thing is to be there and be ready to do it, whatever it is, and go ahead and do it.

AN EMPLOYER: The management of this Company does not want a union, because we feel that our employees will not benefit by belonging to the union. . . . With the cooperation of our employees and without the interference of any outsiders, we have made the _____ Company a good place in which to work. Our wages, hours and working conditions compare favorably with those of other plants in this area and with the plants of others with whom we are in competition. You have received the benefits of this high standard without having to pay initiation fees, union dues and various special union assessments. . . .

What the intervention of these strangers would mean in our relationship, no one can foretell. All of us know that unions engage in business interruptions and strikes and that frequently these cause substantial financial loss to the employees and their families. . . .

AN EMPLOYEE: I was for it, but at the same time I didn't feel good about it. I had worked there so long, and I felt it wasn't right to strike. The Company had been very nice to me, and sometimes when I didn't feel well, they would let me come to work any time I felt like it and I appreciated that. But I felt we had to strike. We just weren't treated right in a lot of ways. I voted for the strike in the end.

SECTION I. The Right of Self-Organization; Protection Against Employer Unfair Labor Practices

FOREWORD

Labor relations law deals with legal rights and duties. At the same time the student should not overlook the fact that we are dealing with a phase of human relations in which the parties — management and organized labor — through force of circumstances have come to have a relationship which implies responsibilities greatly transcending those minimum standards which the law imposes. The labor union which establishes itself firmly in a plant acquires a status which, even without jural recognition, necessitates important changes in management's conception of its function. Even accepting the narrowest definition of this function, it must be obvious that the presence of a union possessing the power both to interfere with and to promote the processes of production, calls for the adoption of management policies which will enlist the union's interest in continuous and efficient plant operation. The keynote of a desirable relationship between the parties will be their mutual acceptance of the fact that each has a status in the enterprise. When they have accepted this elemental fact, the rudimentary legal obligations which the law may impose upon them will be of minor significance. Just as in the case of the citizen in the community, or the spouse in the family, so here the necessity of continuing relations calls for a code of conduct much above and beyond the call of legal duty.

This conception of management-union relations presupposes the existence of an established union and management acceptance of the "right" of employee self-organization. As shown in Part I, however, and as might be expected in a land in which much emphasis has been placed upon individual initiative and self-determinism, unionism has had to struggle hard against management resistance to gain a place for itself.

In this section we shall survey the statutes which have given to unions and workers the legal protection against employer antiunion tactics which they now enjoy. The cases and other materials in this field are so voluminous that the entire course could easily be devoted to them. The reports of the National Labor Relations Board alone run over 200 volumes. Our aim has been to select materials which will reveal some of the basic principles and approaches developed by the Congress, the NLRB, and the courts over the last forty-odd years and to highlight the problems of pressing current importance. For supplementary reading, *see* THE DEVELOPING LABOR LAW (1971, with annual supplements), edited by Charles J. Morris on behalf of the ABA Section of Labor Relations Law; R. GORMAN, BASIC TEXT ON LABOR LAW (1976); F. BARTOSIC & R. HARTLEY, LABOR RELATIONS LAW IN THE PRIVATE SECTOR (1977).

A. EMPLOYER INTERFERENCE, RESTRAINT OR COERCION

Section 8(a)(1) of the National Labor Relations Act is a broad, general provision. It may be violated by conduct which is contrary to any of the four following subsections. For example, a discharge on account of union activity would violate both §§ 8(a)(1) and 8(a)(3).

We shall deal first, however, with employer conduct which violates § 8(a)(1) independently of any other specific unfair labor practice. Such conduct ranges all the way from the crude and obvious to the ingenious and subtle. A glance at the annual reports of the NLRB or at one of the looseleaf labor services will afford a view of the variety of forms of employer interference, only a few of which can feasibly be treated here.

It is not necessary, for proof of a violation, to show by direct evidence that any particular persons were in fact successfully restrained or coerced; it is enough if it is shown that the employer's conduct has a natural tendency to do so.[1]

The Railway Labor Act, in § 2 (Third and Fourth), also makes it unlawful for a carrier to interfere with, influence or coerce employees in organizing. Since the RLA does not provide an administrative procedure for the prevention of such practices, enforcement must be had through either criminal proceedings or petition for injunctive relief in the courts.[2]

There has been very little litigation under these provisions of the RLA, probably because unionism had reached a fairly mature state in the railroad industry by the time these provisions were written into the law.

1. LIMITING ORGANIZATIONAL ACTIVITIES ON EMPLOYER'S PREMISES

NLRB v. BABCOCK & WILCOX CO.

Supreme Court of the United States
351 U.S. 105, 76 S. Ct. 679, 100 L. Ed. 975 (1956)

MR. JUSTICE REED delivered the opinion of the Court.

In each of these cases the employer refused to permit distribution of union literature by nonemployee union organizers on company-owned parking lots. The National Labor Relations Board, in separate and unrelated proceedings, found in each case that it was unreasonably difficult for the union organizer to reach the employees off company property and held that, in refusing the unions access to parking lots, the employers had unreasonably impeded their employees' right to self-organization in violation of section 8(a)(1) of the National Labor

---

[1] Time-O-Matic, Inc. v. NLRB, 264 F.2d 96 (7th Cir. 1959); NLRB v. Ford, 170 F.2d 735 (6th Cir. 1948); Drennon Food Prod. Co., 122 N.L.R.B. 1353 (1959), *enforced in part*, 272 F.2d 23 (5th Cir. 1959).

[2] Virginian Ry. v. System Federation 40, Railway Employees, 300 U.S. 515 (1937); Texas N.O.R.R. v. Brotherhood of Ry. & S.S. Clerks, 281 U.S. 548 (1930).

Relations Act. Babcock & Wilcox Co., 109 N.L.R.B. 485, 494; Ranco, Inc., id., 998, 1007, and Seamprufe, Inc., id. at 24, 32.

The plant involved in No. 250, NLRB v. Babcock & Wilcox Co., is a company engaged in the manufacture of tubular products such as boilers and accessories, located on a 100-acre tract about one mile from a community of 21,000 people. Approximately 40% of the 500 employees live in that town and the remainder live within a 30-mile radius. More than 90% of them drive to work in private automobiles and park on a company lot that adjoins the fenced in plant area. The parking lot is reached only by a driveway 100 yards long which is entirely on company property excepting for a public right-of-way that extends 31 feet from the metal of the highway to the plant's property. Thus, the only public place in the immediate vicinity of the plant area at which leaflets can be effectively distributed to employees is that place where this driveway crosses the public right-of-way. Because of the traffic conditions at that place the Board found it practically impossible for union organizers to distribute leaflets safely to employees in motors as they enter or leave the lot. The Board noted that the company's policy on such distribution had not discriminated against labor organizations and that other means of communication, such as the mail and telephones, as well as the homes of the workers, were open to the union. The employer justified its refusal to allow distribution of literature on company property on the ground that it had maintained a consistent policy of refusing access to all kinds of pamphleteering and that such distribution of leaflets would litter its property.

The Board found that the parking lot and the walkway from it to the gatehouse, where employees punched in for work, were the only "safe and practicable" places for distribution of union literature. The Board viewed the place of work as so much more effective a place for communication of information that it held the employer guilty of an unfair labor practice for refusing limited access to company property to union organizers. It therefore ordered the employer to rescind its no-distribution order for the parking lot and walkway, subject to reasonable and nondiscriminating regulations "in the interest of plant efficiency and discipline, but not as to deny access to union representatives for the purpose of effecting such distribution." 109 N.L.R.B. at 486.

The Board petitioned the Court of Appeals for the Fifth Circuit for enforcement. That court refused enforcement on the ground the statute did not authorize the Board to impose a servitude on the employer's property where no employee was involved. NLRB v. Babcock & Wilcox Co., 222 F.2d 316 (5th Cir. 1955).

The conditions and circumstances involved in No. 251, *NLRB v. Seamprufe, Inc.,* and No. 422, *Ranco, Inc. v. NLRB,* are not materially different, except that *Seamprufe* involves a plant employing approximately 200 persons and in the *Ranco* case it appears that union organizers had a better opportunity to pass out literature off company property. The Board likewise ordered these employers to allow union organizers limited access to company lots. The orders were in substantially similar form as that in the *Babcock & Wilcox* case. Enforcement of the orders was sought in the Court of Appeals. The Court of Appeals for the Tenth Circuit in No. 251, NLRB v. Seamprufe, Inc., 222 F.2d 858 (10th Cir. 1955), refused enforcement on the ground that a nonemployee can justify his presence on company property only "as it bears a cogent relationship to the exercise of the employees' guaranteed right of self-organization." These "solicitors were therefore strangers to the right of self-organization, absent a showing of non-accessiblity amounting to a handicap to self-organization." Id. at 861. The Court of Appeals for the Sixth Circuit in No. 422 granted enforcement. NLRB v. Ranco, Inc., 222 F.2d 543 (6th Cir. 1955). The *per curiam* opinion depended upon its decision in NLRB v. Monarch Tool Co., 210 F.2d 183 (6th Cir. 1954), a case in which only employees were involved; NLRB v. Lake Superior Lumber Corp., 167 F.2d 147 (6th Cir. 1948), an isolated lumber camp case; and our Republic Aviation Corp. v. NLRB, 324 U.S. 793. It apparently considered, as held in the Monarch Tool case, *supra* at 186, that the attitude of the employer in the *Ranco* case was an "unreasonable impediment to the freedom of communication essential to the exercise of its employees' rights to self-organization." Because of the conflicting decisions on a recurring phase of enforcement of the National Labor Relations Act, we granted certiorari. 350 U.S. 818, 894.

In each of these cases the Board found that the employer violated § 8(a)(1) of the National Labor Relations Act, 61 Stat. 140, making it an unfair labor practice for an employer to interfere with employees in the exercise of rights guaranteed in § 7 of that Act. . . . These holdings were placed on the Labor Board's determination in LeTourneau Company of Georgia, 54 N.L.R.B. 1253. In the *LeTourneau* case the Board balanced the conflicting interests of employees to receive information on self-organization on the company's property from fellow employees during nonworking time, with the employer's right to control the use of his property and found the former more essential in the circumstances of that case. Recognizing that the employer could restrict employees' union activities when necessary to maintain plant discipline or production, the Board said: "Upon all the above considerations, we are convinced, and find, that the respondent, in applying its 'no-distributing' rule to the distribution of union literature by its employees on its parking lots has placed an unreasonable impediment on the freedom of communication essential to the exercise of its employees' right to self-organization," LeTourneau Company of Georgia, 54 N.L.R.B. at 1262. This Court affirmed the Board. Republic Aviation Corp. v. NLRB, 324 U.S. 793, 801 *et seq.* The same rule had been earlier and more fully stated in Peyton Packing Co., 49 N.L.R.B. 828-844.

The Board has applied its reasoning in the *LeTourneau* case without distinction to situations where the distribution was made, as here, by nonemployees. Carolina Mills, 92 N.L.R.B. 1141, 1149, 1168-1169. The fact that our *LeTourneau* case ruled only as to employees had been noted by the courts of appeals in NLRB v. Lake Superior Lumber Corp., 167 F.2d 147, 150 (6th Cir. 1948), and NLRB v. Seamprufe, Inc., 222 F.2d, at 860 (10th Cir. 1955). Cf. NLRB v. American Furnace Co., 158 F.2d 376, 380 (7th Cir. 1946).

In these present cases the Board has set out the facts that support its conclusions as to the necessity for allowing nonemployee union organizers to distribute union literature on the company's property. In essence they are that nonemployee union representatives, if barred, would have to use personal contacts on streets or at home, telephones, letters or advertised meetings to get in touch with the employees. The force of this position in respect to employees isolated from normal contacts has been recognized by this Court and by others. See Republic Aviation Corp. v. NLRB, *supra* at 799, note 3; NLRB v. Lake Superior Lumber Corp., *supra* at 150. We recognize, too, that the Board has the responsibility of "applying the Act's general prohibitory language in the light of the infinite combinations of events which might be charged as violative of its terms." NLRB v. Stowe Spinning Co., 336 U.S. 226, 231 (1949). We are slow to overturn an administrative decision.

It is our judgment, however, that an employer may validly post his property against nonemployee distribution of union literature if reasonable efforts by the union through other available channels of communication will enable it to reach the employees with its message and if the employer's notice or order does not discriminate against the union by allowing other distribution. In these circumstances the employer may not be compelled to allow distribution even under such reasonable regulations as the orders in these cases permit.

This is not a problem of always open or always closed doors for union organization on company property. Organization rights are granted to workers by the same authority, the National Government, that preserves property rights. Accommodation between the two must be obtained with as little destruction of one as is consistent with the maintenance of the other. The employer may not affirmatively interfere with organization; the union may not always insist that the employer aid organization. But when the inaccessibility of employees makes ineffective the reasonable attempts by nonemployees to communicate with them through the usual channels, the right to exclude from property has been required to yield to the extent needed to permit communication of information on the right to organize.

The determination of the proper adjustments rests with the Board. Its rulings, when reached on findings of fact supported by substantial evidence on the record as a whole, should be sustained by the courts unless its conclusions rest on erroneous legal foundations. Here the Board failed to make a distinction between rules of law applicable to employees and those applicable to nonemployees.

The distinction is one of substance. No restriction may be placed on the employees' right to discuss self-organization among themselves, unless the employer can demonstrate that a restriction is necessary to maintain production or discipline. Republic Aviation Corp. v. NLRB, 324 U.S. 793, 803 (1945). But no such obligation is owed nonemployee organizers. Their access to company property is governed by a different consideration. The right of self-organization depends in some measure on the ability of employees to learn the advantages of self-organization from others. Consequently, if the location of a plant and the living quarters of the employees place the employees beyond the reach of reasonable union efforts to communicate with them, the employer must allow the union to approach his employees on his property. No such conditions are shown in these records.

The plants are close to small well-settled communities where a large percentage of the employees live. The usual methods of imparting information are available. . . . The various instruments of publicity are at hand. Though the quarters of the employees are scattered they are in reasonable reach. The Act requires only that the employer refrain from interference, discrimination, restraint or coercion in the employees' exercise of their own rights. It does not require that the employer permit the use of its facilities for organization when other means are readily available.

NOTES

1. This case indicates the law with respect to the validity of employer rules against solicitation and distribution of union literature by *nonemployee* organizers. *See also* S. & H. Grossinger's, 156 N.L.R.B. 233 (1965), *enforced as modified,* 372 F.2d 26 (2d Cir. 1967) (denial of union access to company premises violates § 8(a)(1) if it virtually insulates employees from the efforts of union organizers to reach them). *But cf.* NLRB v. New Pines, Inc., 468 F.2d 427 (2d Cir. 1972) (a resort hotel in the Catskill Mountains did not violate § 8(a)(1) by refusing access to the hotel by nonemployee union organizers, where the union had not first made reasonable attempts to communicate with the employees through usual channels).

In Solo Cup Co., 172 N.L.R.B. 1110 (1968), the Labor Board held it was a violation of § 8(a)(1) for a manufacturer and the owner of an industrial park in which the manufacturer's plant was located to exclude nonemployee union organizers from the park premises and to prevent their distribution of literature to the manufacturer's employees. The Board emphasized that 99 percent of the manufacturer's employees entered the park at a very busy intersection where it was "virtually impossible" to stand safely and pass out literature. Unlike the small town situation in *Babcock & Wilcox,* the employees here lived in Chicago and environs, with a population exceeding four million. This made effective solicitation through home visits, radio, television, or newspapers "virtually impossible." As an additional ground for its decision, the Board concluded that the rules limiting access and the distribution of literature were discriminatorily applied only against unions.

The Board's order was modified in NLRB v. Solo Cup Co., 422 F.2d 1149 (7th Cir. 1970). The court found no substantial evidence that the industrial park was open to the general public or that the union organizers were discriminated against. Moreover, the owner of the industrial park had complied with the Board's order and consented to union solicitation on a street belonging to the park. Since there was now available a reasonable alternative method of solicitation, the court concluded the manufacturer should not be required to allow union organizers to solicit employees on its steps or parking lot, or on other portions of its leased premises.

A 3-2 Board majority declined in Monogram Models, Inc., 192 N.L.R.B 705 (1971), to adopt a "big city rule" and a different "smalltown rule" in applying *Babcock & Wilcox*. A plant's location in a metropolitan area is not enough in itself to open an employer's premises to nonemployee union organizers. The test is "not one of relative convenience, but rather whether the location of a plant and the living quarters of the employees place the employees beyond the reach of reasonable union efforts to communicate" by such conventional methods as mail, telephone, and home visits. In a companion case, Scholle Chemical Corp., 192 N.L.R.B. 724 (1971), another 3-2 Board majority relied heavily on *Solo Cup* to find an employer in violation of § 8(a)(1) for excluding nonemployee union solicitors and handbillers from the company's parking lots. The plant was located in an industrial tract shared by other employers, and the employees' residences were widely dispersed. *Scholle* was enforced in 82 L.R.R.M. 2410 (7th Cir. 1972), *cert. denied*, 94 S. Ct. 229 (1973).

See also Central Hardware Co. v. NLRB, 468 F.2d 252 (8th Cir. 1972); Falk Corp., 192 N.L.R.B. 716 (1971).

2. The law as to nondiscriminatory employer rules against solicitation and distribution of literature on company property by employees may be summarized as follows:

a. *Solicitation:*

(1) During working time — no violation of § 8(a)(1), Peyton Packing Co., 49 N.L.R.B. 828, 843 (1943); Essex International, Inc., 211 N.L.R.B. 749 (1974);

(2) During nonworking time — a violation, Republic Aviation Corp. v. NLRB, 324 U.S. 793 (1945), unless employer can show some special circumstances which make rules necessary to maintain production or discipline; for example, retail stores may generally ban solicitation in public areas of the store even during employees' off-hours, in order to avoid confusion for customers. Marshall Field & Co. v. NLRB, 200 F.2d 375 (7th Cir. 1952); May Dep't Stores Co., 59 N.L.R.B. 976 (1944).

b. *Distribution of literature:*

An employer may usually ban this in working areas of the plant even during off-working time, because of his legitimate interest in keeping the plant free of litter, but he may not ban employee distribution in nonworking areas without a showing of special considerations. Stoddard-Quirk Mfg. Co., 138 N.L.R.B. 615 (1962).

An employer may prevent the distribution of literature which occurs in such a manner as actually to cause litter, even in nonwork areas. Erie Marine, Inc., 192 N.L.R.B. 793 (1971); Genesee Merchants Bank & Trust Co., 206 N.L.R.B. 274 (1973).

Health care facilities must permit employee solicitation and distribution during nonworking time in nonworking areas, where the facility has not

justified prohibitions as necessary to avoid disruption of health care
operations or disturbance of patients. A hospital violated § 8(a)(1) when
it threatened an employee with dismissal for distributing a union
newsletter in a hospital cafeteria largely patronized by employees,
although a few patients and visitors also used it. The hospital had
previously permitted nonunion solicitation and distribution in the
cafeteria. Beth Israel Hospital v. NLRB, 437 U.S. 483 (1978). See also,
NLRB v. St. Joseph Hospital, 99 L.R.R.M. 3404 (10th Cir. 1978); NLRB
v. Baptist Hospital, Inc., 576 F.2d 107 (6th Cir. 1978), *cert. granted*, 99
S. Ct. 829 (U.S. 1979).

An employer may not ban distribution of union literature opposing a
right-to-work law and supporting a higher minimum wage law. Eastex,
Inc. v. NLRB, 98 S. Ct. 2505 (U.S. 1978). Two justices dissented on the
ground the material was political in nature rather than organizational.

Should it make any difference whether an employer phrases his
limitation on solicitation and distribution in terms of "working time" or
"working hours"? *See* Essex International, Inc., 211 N.L.R.B. 749 (1974)
(Members Fanning and Jenkins dissenting).

A retail store's no-solicitation rule must be limited to the selling areas
of the store. McBrides of Naylor Road, 229 N.L.R.B. No. 120, 95 L.R.R.M.
1196 (1977).

See generally, Fanning, *Union Solicitation and Distribution of
Literature on the Job — Balancing the Rights of Employers and
Employees,* 9 GA. L. REV. 367 (1975).

c. *Discrimination:*

Where an employer applies his rules in a manner which discriminates
against union solicitation and distribution — or against one union as
compared with another union — an unfair labor practice is usually found.
The Supreme Court, in NLRB v. Stowe Spinning Co., 336 U.S. 226
(1949), carried this principle to the extent that an employer was found to
have violated § 8(a)(1) when he refused to rent a company-owned
meeting hall to the union, when it was the only available hall in the
company town and evidence indicated that the company was willing to let
other groups use it.

3. PROBLEMS: a. Suppose the employer bans solicitation by employees
during the lunch hour, which is time paid for by the employer but during
which employees are not working. *See* Olin Industries, Inc., Winchester
Repeating Arms Co. Division v. NLRB, 191 F.2d 613 (5th Cir. 1951), *cert.
denied,* 343 U.S. 919 (1952).

b. May an employer enforce a rule that off-duty employees are not
privileged to stay on company property after their shifts to solicit for the
union? See GTE Lenkurt, Inc., 204 N.L.R.B. 921 (1973).

Could a defense contractor rely on national security interests to justify
more stringent no-solicitation rules? See McDonnell Douglas Corp. v.
NLRB, 472 F.2d 539 (8th Cir. 1973) and on remand, 204 N.L.R.B. 1110
(1973).

But cf. McDonnell Douglas Corp., 210 N.L.R.B. 280 (1974).

A rule denying off-duty employees access to the employer's premises is valid only if it (1) limits access solely with respect to the interior of the plant and other working areas, (2) is clearly disseminated to all employees, and (3) applies to off-duty employees seeking access to the plant for any purpose and not just to those employees engaging in union activity. Unless justified by business reasons, a rule which denies off-duty employees entry to parking lots, gates, and other outside non-working areas is invalid. The *GTE Lenkurt* case must be narrowly construed to prevent undue interference with the right of employees to freely communicate their interest in union activity to those who work on different shifts. Tri-County Medical Center, 222 N.L.R.B. 1089 (1976).

c. *Waiver of right to solicit.* Would an employer commit an unfair labor practice if he enforced a no-solicitation rule during nonworking time or a no-distribution rule in nonworking areas of the premises, where the incumbent union has made a collective agreement with him providing that there shall be no such solicitation? Would it make any difference whether the rule is enforced against an employee who opposes the union or one who supports the union? *See* NLRB v. Magnavox Co., 415 U.S. 322 (1974). *Compare,* Comment, *Contractual Waiver by Labor Unions of Employees' Solicitation-Distribution Rights: Time for a Resolution,* 49 NOTRE DAME LAW. 920 (1974) *with,* Note, *Employee's Solicitation-Distribution Rights Supersede Contract Waiver,* 26 U. FLA. L. REV. 908 (1974); Comment, *Protecting Employee Solicitation-Distribution Rights From Union Waiver,* 9 U. MICH. J. L. REFORM 571 (1976).

4. *See generally,* Gould, *The Question of Union Activity on Company Property,* 18 VAND. L. REV. 73 (1964); Hanley, *Union Organization on Company Property — A Discussion of Property Rights,* 47 GEO. L.J. 266 (1958); Vanderheyden, *Employee Solicitation and Distribution — A Second Look,* 14 LAB. L.J. 781 (1963).

The Board and the courts, in this area of the law, are attempting to find the proper accommodation of the employees' statutory right of self-organization with various employer interests — in determining who can come on his property, in obtaining efficient production, and in maintaining discipline and order. In the next case and the following section, we face a further clash of interests — between the employees' statutory right of self-organization, free of employer interference, restraint, or coercion, and the employer's constitutional (and, since Taft-Hartley, statutory) right to express his views and opinions.

NLRB v. UNITED STEELWORKERS
[NUTONE, INC.] [3]

Supreme Court of the United States
357 U.S. 357, 78 S. Ct. 1268, 2 L. Ed. 2d 1383 (1958)

MR. JUSTICE FRANKFURTER delivered the opinion of the Court.

. . . .

In April of 1953 the respondent Steelworkers instituted a campaign to organize the employees of respondent NuTone, Inc., a manufacturer of electrical devices. . . . In June the company began to distribute, through its supervisory personnel, literature that, although not coercive, was clearly anti-union in tenor. In August, while continuing to distribute such material, the company announced its intention of enforcing its rule against employees posting signs or distributing literature on company property or soliciting or campaigning on company time. The rule, according to these posted announcements, applied to "all employees — whether they are for or against the union." . . .

In a proceeding before the Board commenced at the instance of the Steelworkers, the company was charged with a number of violations of the Act . . . including the discriminatory application of the no-solicitation rule. . . . The Board dismissed the allegation that the company had discriminatorily enforced its no-solicitation rule. 112 N.L.R.B. 1153. The Steelworkers sought review of this dismissal in the United States Court of Appeals for the District of Columbia Circuit. . . . The Court of Appeals concluded that it was an unfair labor practice for the company to prohibit the distribution of organizational literature on company property during working hours while the company was itself distributing antiunion literature. . . .

Employer rules prohibiting organizational solicitation are not in and of themselves violative of the Act, for they may duly serve production, order and discipline. See Republic Aviation Corp. v. NLRB, 324 U.S. 793 (1945); NLRB v. Babcock & Wilcox Co., 351 U.S. 105 (1956). In neither of the cases before us did the party attacking the enforcement of the no-solicitation rule contest its validity. Nor is the claim made that an employer may not, under proper circumstances, engage in noncoercive antiunion solicitation; indeed, his right to do so is protected by the so-called "employer free speech" provision of § 8(c) of the Act. Contrariwise, as both cases before us show, coercive antiunion solicitation and other similar conduct run afoul of the Act and constitute unfair labor practices irrespective of the bearing of such practices on enforcement of a no-solicitation rule. The very narrow and almost abstract question here derives from the claim that, when the employer himself engages in antiunion solicitation that if engaged in by employees would constitute a

---

[3] The Supreme Court's discussion of a companion case involving Avondale Mills has not been included in this excerpt from the Court's opinion. [— Eds.]

violation of the rule — particularly when his solicitation is coercive or accompanied by other unfair labor practices — his enforcement of an otherwise valid no-solicitation rule against the employees is itself an unfair labor practice. We are asked to rule that the coincidence of these circumstances necessarily violates the Act, regardless of the way in which the particular controversy arose or whether the employer's conduct to any considerable degree created an imbalance in the opportunities for organizational communication. For us to lay down such a rule of law would show indifference to the responsibilities imposed by the Act primarily on the Board to appraise carefully the interests of both sides of any labor-management controversy in the diverse circumstances of particular cases and in light of the Board's special understanding of these industrial situations. . . .

No attempt was made in either of these cases to make a showing that the no-solicitation rules truly diminished the ability of the labor organizations involved to carry their message to the employees. Just as that is a vital consideration in determining the validity of a no-solicitation rule, see Republic Aviation Corp. v. NLRB, *supra* at 797-798; NLRB v. Babcock & Wilcox Co., *supra* at 112, it is highly relevant in determining whether a valid rule has been fairly applied. Of course the rules had the effect of closing off one channel of communication; but the Taft-Hartley Act does not command that labor organizations as a matter of abstract law, under all circumstances, be protected in the use of every possible means of reaching the minds of individual workers, nor that they are entitled to use a medium of communication simply because the employer is using it. Cf. Bonwit Teller, Inc. v. NLRB, 197 F.2d 640, 646 (2d Cir. 1952); NLRB v. F. W. Woolworth Co., 214 F.2d 78, 84 (6th Cir. 1954) (concurring opinion). No such mechanical answers will avail for the solution of this non-mechanical, complex problem in labor-management relations. If, by virtue of the location of the plant and of the facilities and resources available to the union, the opportunities for effectively reaching the employees with a pro-union message, in spite of a no-solicitation rule, is at least as great as the employer's ability to promote the legally authorized expression of his antiunion message, there is no basis for invalidating these "otherwise valid" rules. The Board, in determining whether or not the enforcement of such a rule in the circumstances of an individual case is an unfair labor practice, may find relevant alternative channels available for communications on the right to organize. When this important issue is not even raised before the Board and no evidence bearing on it adduced, the concrete basis for appraising the significance of the employer's conduct is wanting.

We do not at all imply that the enforcement of a valid no-solicitation rule by an employer who is at the same time engaging in antiunion solicitation may not constitute an unfair labor practice. All we hold is that there must be some basis, in the actualities of industrial relations, for such a finding. . . .

CHIEF JUSTICE WARREN ... concurring in part.

....

In *United Steelworkers,* I concur in the result. The National Labor Relations Board declined to hold that the enforcement of an employer's no-distribution rule against a union was an unfair labor practice even though it was coupled with an antiunion campaign. The Court of Appeals reversed the Board on this point, modifying the Board's order accordingly. This Court sustains the Board. It is conceded that the enforcement of this no-distribution rule against the union is not by itself an unfair labor practice. The Board determined that the employer's expressions of his antiunion views were noncoercive in nature. ... Being noncoercive in nature, the employer's expressions were protected by § 8(c) of the National Labor Relations Act and so cannot be used to show that the contemporaneous enforcement of the no-distribution rule was an unfair labor practice.

JUSTICES BLACK and DOUGLAS dissented for the reasons set forth in the opinion of the Court of Appeals.

NOTES

1. In what kinds of cases does the reasoning in *Babcock & Wilcox* and in *NuTone* require the NLRB to make findings that "reasonable efforts by the union through other available channels of communication will not enable it to reach the employees with its message" or that the employer's conduct has "created an imbalance in opportunities for organizational communication" or "truly diminished the ability of the labor organizations involved to carry their message to the employees" ?

2. In Time-O-Matic, Inc. v. NLRB, 264 F.2d 96 (7th Cir. 1959), the employer issued a no-distribution of literature rule, applicable only to union literature — hence discriminatory. The employer argued that, under the Supreme Court's decision in the above *Steelworkers'* case, the NLRB must prove that alternate channels of communication were not reasonably available to the union. The court said in rejecting this argument (264 F.2d at 100-01): "However, the Steelworkers' case involved an admittedly valid no-solicitation rule and a very narrow question whether an employer who actively engaged in antiunion solicitation could properly enforce an otherwise valid no-solicitation rule against the union. The Court indicated that findings by the Board on the question of alternate channels of communication were vital to such a question. Similarly, such findings were considered essential in determining the validity of a rule prohibiting the solicitation by nonemployees on company property. NLRB v. Babcock & Wilcox Co. (1956), 351 U.S. 105, 113. But the Court also pointed out in *Babcock & Wilcox* that different considerations may be controlling when employees are involved: 'No restriction may be placed on the employees' rights to discuss self-organization among themselves unless the employer can demonstrate that a restriction is necessary to maintain production and discipline.' "

3. In NLRB v. United Aircraft Corp., 324 F.2d 128 (2d Cir. 1963), *cert. denied,* 376 U.S. 951 (1964), the employer argued that the NLRB could not properly find a no-distribution rule as to nonworking areas to be an unfair labor practice where alternative means of communication with employees were readily available. The court said that the suggested requirement "would simply be an incitement to litigation and casuistry" and that "no such showing was required where employees alone were involved." The court commented: "It is inevitable that the thrust of an organizational drive would be blunted by rules which cut into a worker's use of his own time and made his association and expression subject to management limitations. Clearly the existence of available alternatives would not mitigate this deleterious effect or insure the employee the organization freedom which the Act seeks to give him." *Contra,* NLRB v. Rockwell Mfg. Co., 271 F.2d 109 (3d Cir. 1959).

4. We have included the *NuTone* case above at this point because of the no-solicitation and no-distribution issues involved. However, the references to § 8(c) and employer free speech cannot be fully understood until the history and development of the law as to the employer's freedom to express his views and opinions is studied in the next section.

2. ANTIUNION SPEECHES AND PUBLICATIONS

In a broad sense, any expression of antiunion opinion by the employer has a tendency to "interfere with, restrain or coerce" employees in the exercise of their right of self-organization. The attitude of the NLRB in the early days of the Wagner Act was that the employer should remain neutral so that the employees could exercise a free choice as to organization. The Board said in its FIRST ANNUAL REPORT, at 73 (1936):

[A]part from discrimination against union members ... the most common form of interference with self-organization engaged in by employers is to spread propaganda against unions and thus not only poison the minds of workers against them but also indicate to them that the employers are antagonistic to unions and are prepared to make this antagonism effective.

The ideas expressed in J. Rosenfarb, THE NATIONAL LABOR POLICY AND HOW IT WORKS 79 (1940), had a wide acceptance:

An employer's "opinion" about unionism expressed to his employees is not the same as his opinion on what doctor to use or about the international situation.... When an employer addresses his antagonism toward unionism, however devoid his words may be of direct threats, there is always implicit the threat of economic compulsion if his wishes are not heeded.... Freedom of speech is possible only among those who approximate each other in equality of position.

As Judge Learned Hand put it, in *NLRB v. Federbush Co.:* [4]

> What to an outsider will be no more than the vigorous presentation
> of a conviction, to an employee may be the manifestation of a
> determination which it is not safe to thwart.

The Supreme Court said, in *International Ass'n of Machinists v.
NLRB:* [5]

> Slight suggestions as to the employer's choice between unions may
> have telling effect among men who know the consequences of incurring
> that employer's strong displeasure.

However, against these considerations must be weighed the public
policy — indeed the constitutional right — of freedom of speech. The
Supreme Court faced up to the problem in *NLRB v. Virginia Elec. &
Power Co.,* [6] in an opinion by Mr. Justice Murphy (who had written the
Court's opinion in 1940 enunciating employee rights of free speech
through picketing). The *Virginia Electric* case established the proposition
that an employer's statements of opinion about unions should not be
regarded as, or be evidence of, unfair labor practices unless, viewed
against the "totality of conduct" of the employer, they appeared to be
coercive. The Court said:

> The employer in this case is as free now as ever to take any side
> it may choose on this controversial issue. But, certainly, conduct,
> though evidenced in part by speech, may amount, in connection
> with other circumstances, to coercion, within the meaning of the
> Act.

There is some evidence that the Board did not at once construe the
Supreme Court's decision in the *Virginia Electric* case as requiring a
marked departure from the Board's previous position with respect to
employer publications. Thus, in *American Tube Bending Co.,* [7] the
publications consisted of letters sent to each employee and a speech made
by the president to employees who were assembled for the purpose in the
plant during working hours. There was no attempt to vilify the union, but
the company did make clear that it thought the best interests of the
employees would be served by voting against the union in the impending
election. In the election the "no-union" choice received 280 out of 413
votes counted. However, on petition of the losing AFL union the Board
held that the company had interfered with rights guaranteed to employees
by § 7 of the Act, although there were in the case no other alleged unfair
labor practices. It stated in its opinion: [8]

---

[4] 121 F.2d 954, 957 (2d Cir. 1941).
[5] 311 U.S. 72, 78 (1940).
[6] 314 U.S. 469 (1941).
[7] 44 N.L.R.B. 121 (1942).
[8] 44 N.L.R.B. at 133.

Because of the relationship existing between the author of the utterances and the employees, as well as the circumstances under which the communications were delivered, they attained a force stronger than their intrinsic connotation, and beyond that of persuasion. They achieved a coercive effect that could not possibly be dissipated by the deft suggestion of Jones [the Company President] that the election would be "conducted in a fair and impartial manner . . . give you absolute freedom to express your choice without any coercion."

However, enforcement of the Board's order was refused on the authority of the *Virginia Electric* case.[9]

It was against this background that Congress enacted § 8(c) of the Taft-Hartley Act in 1947, the legislative history of which will now be examined.

The Senate Bill (S. 1126) introduced April 17, 1947, contained the following provision:

The Board shall not base any finding of unfair labor practice upon any statement of views or arguments, either written or oral, if such statement contains under all the circumstances no threat, express or implied, of reprisal or force, or offer, express or implied, of benefit.

As to this the Senate Committee on Labor and Public Welfare stated:

Section 8(c): Another amendment to this section would insure both to employers and labor organizations full freedom to express their views to employees on labor matters, refrain from threats of violence, intimation of economic reprisal, or offers of benefit [*sic*]. The Supreme Court in Thomas v. Collins (323 U.S. 516) held, contrary to some earlier decisions of the Labor Board, that the Constitution guarantees freedom of speech on either side in labor controversies and approved the doctrine of the *American Tube Bending* case.

The Board has placed a limited construction upon these decisions by holding such speeches by employers to be coercive if the employer was found guilty of some other unfair labor practice even though severable or unrelated (Monumental Life Insurance, 69 N.L.R.B. 247) or if the speech was made in the plant on working time (Clark Brothers, 70 N.L.R.B. 60). The committee believes these decisions to be too restrictive and, in this section, provides that if, under all the circumstances, there is neither an expressed or implied threat of reprisal, force, or offer of benefit, the Board shall not predicate any finding of unfair labor practice upon the statement. The Board, of course, will not be precluded from considering such statements as evidence.[10]

---

[9] NLRB v. American Tube Bending Co., 134 F.2d 993 (2d Cir. 1943), *cert. denied,* 320 U.S. 768 (1943).

[10] S. REP. No. 105, 80th Cong., 1st Sess. 23 (1947).

Section 8(d) of the House Bill (H.R. 3020) contained the following provision:

The following shall not constitute or be evidence of unfair labor practice under any of the provisions of the Act:

(1) Expressing any views, argument, or opinion, or the dissemination thereof, whether in written, printed, graphic, or visual form, if it does not by its own terms threaten force or economic reprisal. . . .

With reference to this provision the House Committee on Education and Labor said:

Section 8(d)(1). — This guarantees free speech to employers, to employees, and to unions. Although the Labor Board says it does not limit free speech, its decisions show that it uses against people what the Constitution says they can say freely. Thus, if an employer criticizes a union, and later a foreman discharges a union official for gross misconduct, the Board may say that the official's misconduct warranted his being discharged, but "infer," from what the employer said, perhaps long before, that the discharge was for union activity, and reinstate the official with back pay. It has similarly abused the right of free speech in abolishing and penalizing unions of which it disapproved but which workers wished as their bargaining agents. The bill corrects this, providing that nothing that anyone says shall constitute or be evidence of an unfair labor practice unless it, by its own express terms, threatens force or economic reprisal. This means that a statement may not be used against the person making it unless it, standing alone, is unfair within the express terms of Sections 7 and 8 of the amended act.[11]

As to the final version the Conference Report stated:

Section 8(d)(5). Both the House bill and the Senate amendment contained provisions designed to protect the right of both employers and labor organizations to free speech. The conference agreement adopts the provisions of the House bill in this respect with one change derived from the Senate amendment. It is provided that expressing any views, argument, or opinion or the dissemination thereof, whether in written, printed, graphic, or visual form, is not to constitute or be evidence of an unfair labor practice if such expression contains no threat of force or reprisal or promise of benefit. The practice which the Board has had in the past of using speeches and publications of employers concerning labor organizations and collective bargaining arrangements as evidence, no matter how irrelevant or immaterial, that some later act of the employer had an illegal purpose gave rise to the necessity for this change in the law. The purpose is to protect the right of free speech when what the employer says or writes is not of a threatening nature or does not promise a prohibited favorable discrimination.[12]

---

[11] H.R. REP. No. 245, 80th Cong., 1st Sess. 33 (1947).

[12] H.R. REP. No. 510, 80th Cong., 1st Sess. 45 (1947).

NOTE

In the light of this legislative history, did Congress intend that the coercive nature of an employer's communications to his employees should be judged "on the face" of the communication or as viewed in the "totality of conduct of the employer"?

The Court of Appeals for the Seventh Circuit said in NLRB v. Kropp Forge Co., 178 F.2d 822 (7th Cir. 1949), *cert. denied,* 340 U.S. 810 (1950):

"As this court said in NLRB v. LaSalle Steel Company, 178 F.2d 829 (7th Cir. 1949), the language of Section 8(c) 'seems to us no more than a restatement of the principles embodied in the First Amendment. . . .'

"It also seems clear to us that in considering whether such statements or expressions are protected by Section 8(c) of the Act, they cannot be considered as isolated words cut off from the relevant circumstances and background in which they are spoken. A statement considered only as to the words it contains might seem a perfectly innocent statement, including neither a threat nor a promise. But, when the same statement is made by an employer to his employees, and we consider the relation of the parties, the surrounding circumstances, related statements and events and the background of the employer's actions, we may find that the statement is part of a general pattern which discloses action by the employer so coercive as to entirely destroy his employees' freedom of choice and action. To permit statements or expressions to be so used on the theory that they are protected either by the First Amendment or by Section 8(c) of the Act, would be in violation of Section 7 and contrary to the expressed purpose of the Act. Therefore, in determining whether such statements and expressions constitute, or are evidence of unfair labor practice, they must be considered in connection with the positions of the parties, with the background and circumstances under which they are made, and with the general conduct of the parties. If, when so considered, such statements form a part of a general pattern or course of conduct which constitutes coercion and deprives the employees of their free choice guaranteed by Section 7, such statements must still be considered as a basis for a finding of unfair labor practice. To hold otherwise, would nullify the guaranty of employees' freedom of action and choice which Section 7 of the Act expressly provides. Congress, in enacting Section 8(c), could not have intended that result." *Accord,* Irving Air Chute Co. v. NLRB, 350 F.2d 176 (2d Cir. 1965).

In J.P. Stevens & Co. v. NLRB, 380 F.2d 292 (2d Cir. 1967), the court considered an employer statement that "if this Union were to get in here, it would not work to your benefit but, in the long run, would itself operate to your serious harm." The court found that this statement was made in context of "massive" unfair labor practices. The court said: "Apparently the Board has frequently characterized a substantially similar notice as an instrument of coercion. *E.g.,* Greensboro Hosiery Mills, Inc., 162 N.L.R.B. 1275 (1967); White Oak Acres, Inc., 134 N.L.R.B. 1145, 1149-50 (1961). However, the Fourth and Sixth Circuits have disagreed with the

Board, *see* Wellington Mill Division, West Point Mfg. Co. v. NLRB, 330 F.2d 579, 583 (4th Cir. 1964), *cert. denied,* 379 U.S. 882 (1964); Surprenant Mfg. Co. v. NLRB, 341 F.2d 756, 758-60 (6th Cir. 1965). So has the District of Columbia, with the important qualification that the notice may take a different coloration by virtue of the accompanying circumstances, Amalgamated Clothing Workers v. NLRB, 365 F.2d 898, 909-10 (D.C. Cir. 1966) (2-1 decision) . . . there can hardly be disagreement with the view of the District of Columbia Court of Appeals that the words of a notice should not be so regarded [*in vacuo*], but may take on a darker hue when viewed in the perspective of the particular setting." The court proceeded to find that the setting in the *J.P. Stevens* case was of a sufficiently dark hue to warrant finding the "serious harm" statement as coercive and illegal under § 8(a)(1).

In Daniel Constr. Co. v. NLRB, 341 F.2d 805, 811 (4th Cir. 1965), *cert. denied,* 382 U.S. 831 (1965), the court said: "Even if we assume that each of the key statements in the Daniel speeches considered separately would be lawful . . . it still does not follow that we must accept the position pressed upon us by the company [that the whole cannot be greater than the sum of its parts]. Daniel may have accurately stated an accepted rule of mathematics, but words and speech are not governed entirely by mechanical mathematical concepts. Words and phrases, each lawful when considered alone, can be united in such a fashion as to yield an improper end product."

NLRB v. GISSEL PACKING CO.

Supreme Court of the United States
395 U.S. 575, 89 S. Ct. 1918, 23 L. Ed. 2d 547 (1969)

[The main part of the opinion in this case, dealing with the validity of bargaining orders based on authorization cards, is set out, *infra* at 237. However, one of the four employers whose cases were consolidated before the Supreme Court — the Sinclair Company — raised the issue of "employer free speech," and the portion of the Court's opinion which passed upon that point is reproduced below.]

MR. CHIEF JUSTICE WARREN delivered the opinion of the Court.

. . . The petitioner, a producer of mill rolls, wire, and related products at two plants in Holyoke, Massachusetts, was shut down for some three months in 1952 as the result of a strike over contract negotiations with the American Wire Weavers Protective Association (AWWPA), the representative of petitioner's journeymen and apprentice wire weavers from 1933 to 1952. The Company subsequently reopened without a union contract, and its employees remained unrepresented through 1964, when the Company was acquired by an Ohio corporation, with the Company's former president continuing as head of the Holyoke, Massachusetts, division. In July 1965, the International Brotherhood of Teamsters, Local Union No. 404, began an organizing campaign among petitioner's Holyoke employees and by the end of the summer had obtained authorization cards from 11 of the Company's 14 journeymen wire weavers choosing the Union as their bargaining agent. On September 20, the Union notified petitioner that it represented a majority of its wire weavers, requested that the Company bargain with it, and offered to submit the signed cards to a neutral third party for authentication. After petitioner's president declined the Union's request a week later, claiming, *inter alia,* that he had a good faith doubt of majority status because of the cards' inherent unreliability, the Union petitioned, on November 8, for an election that was ultimately set for December 8.

When petitioner's president first learned of the Union's drive in July, he talked with all of his employees in an effort to dissuade them from joining a union. He particularly emphasized the results of the long 1952 strike, which he claimed "almost put our company out of business," and expressed worry that the employees were forgetting the "lessons of the past." He emphasized secondly that the Company was still on "thin ice" financially, that the Union's "only weapon is to strike," and that a strike "could lead to closing the plant," since the parent company had ample manufacturing facilities elsewhere. He noted thirdly that because of their age and the limited usefulness of their skills outside their craft, the employees might not be able to find re-employment if they lost their jobs as a result of a strike. Finally, he warned those who did not believe that the plant could go out of business to "look around Holyoke and see a lot of them out of business." The president sent letters to the same effect to the employees in early November, emphasizing that the parent company had no reason to stay in Massachusetts if profits went down.

During the two or three weeks immediately prior to the election on December 9, the president sent the employees a pamphlet captioned "Do you want another 13-week strike?" stating, *inter alia,* that "We have no doubt that the Teamsters Union can again close the Wire Weaving Department and the entire plant by a strike. We have no hopes that the Teamsters Union bosses will not call a strike. . . . The Teamsters Union is a strike happy outfit." Similar communications followed in late November, including one stressing the Teamsters' "hoodlum control." Two days before the election, the Company sent out another pamphlet that was entitled "Let's Look at the Record," and that purported to be an obituary of companies in the Holyoke-Springfield, Massachusetts, area that had allegedly gone out of business because of union demands, eliminating some 3,500 jobs; the first page carried a large cartoon showing the preparation of a grave for the Sinclair Company and other headstones containing the names of other plants allegedly victimized by the unions. Finally, on the day before the election, the president made another personal appeal to his employees to reject the Union. He repeated that the Company's financial condition was precarious; that a possible strike would jeopardize the continued operation of the plant; and that age and lack of education would make re-employment difficult. The Union lost the election 7-6, and then filed both objections to the election and unfair labor practice charges which were consolidated for hearing before the trial examiner.

The Board agreed with the trial examiner that the president's communications with the employees, when considered as a whole, "reasonably tended to convey to the employees the belief or impression that selection of the Union in the forthcoming election could lead [the Company] to close its plant, or to the transfer of the weaving production, with the resultant loss of jobs to the wire weavers." Thus, the Board found that under the "totality of the circumstances" petitioner's activities constituted a violation of § 8(a)(1) of the Act.

On appeal, the Court of Appeals for the First Circuit sustained the Board's findings and conclusions and enforced its order in full. 397 F.2d 157. . . .

We consider finally petitioner Sinclair's First Amendment challenge to the holding of the Board and the Court of Appeals for the First Circuit. At the outset we note that the question raised here most often arises in the context of a nascent union organizational drive, where employers must be careful in waging their antiunion campaign. As to conduct generally, the above noted gradations of unfair labor practices, with their varying consequences, create certain hazards for employers when they seek to estimate or resist unionization efforts. But so long as the differences involve conduct easily avoided, such as discharge, surveillance, and coercive interrogation, we do not think that employers can complain that the distinctions are unreasonably difficult to follow. Where an employer's antiunion efforts consist of speech alone, however, the difficulties raised are not so easily resolved. The Board has eliminated some of the problem areas by no longer requiring an employer to show affirmative reasons for insisting on an election and by permitting him to make reasonable inquiries. We do not decide, of course, whether these allowances are mandatory. But we do note that an employer's free speech right to communicate his views to his employees is firmly established and cannot be infringed by a union or the Board. Thus, § 8(c) . . . merely implements the First Amendment. . . .

Any assessment of the precise scope of employer expression, of course, must be made in the context of its labor relations setting. Thus, an employer's rights cannot outweigh the equal rights of the employees to associate freely, as those rights are embodied in § 7 and protected by § 8(a)(1) and the proviso to § 8(c). And any balancing of those rights must take into account the economic dependence of the employees on their employers, and the necessary tendency of the former, because of that relationship, to pick up intended implications of the latter that might be more readily dismissed by a more disinterested ear. Stating these obvious principles is but another way of recognizing that what is basically at stake is the establishment of a nonpermanent, limited relationship between the employer, his economically dependent employee and his union agent, not the election of legislators or the enactment of legislation whereby that relationship is ultimately defined and where the independent voter may be freer to listen more objectively and employers as a class freer to talk. Compare New York Times Co. v. Sullivan, 376 U.S. 254 (1964).

Within this framework, we must reject the Company's challenge to the decision below and the findings of the Board on which it was based. The standards used below for evaluating the impact of an employer's statements are not seriously questioned by petitioner and we see no need to tamper with them here. Thus, an employer is free to communicate to his employees any of his general views about unionism or any of his specific views about a particular union, so long as the communications do not contain a "threat of reprisal or force or promise of benefit." He may even make a prediction as to the precise effects he believes unionization will have on his company. In such a case, however, the prediction must be carefully phrased on the basis of objective fact to convey an employer's belief as to demonstrably probable consequences beyond his control or to convey a management decision already arrived at to close the plant in case of unionization. See Textile Workers v. Darlington Mfg. Co., 380 U.S. 263, 274, n.20 (1965). If there is any implication that an employer may or may not take action solely on his own initiative for reasons unrelated to economic necessities and known only to him, the statement is no longer a reasonable prediction based on available facts but a threat of retaliation based on misrepresentation and coercion, and as such without the protection of the First Amendment. We therefore agree with the court below that "conveyance of the employer's belief, even though sincere, that unionization will or may result in the closing of the plant is not a statement of fact unless, which is most improbable, the eventuality of closing is capable of proof." 397 F.2d, at 160. As stated elsewhere, an employer is free only to tell "what he reasonably believes will be the likely economic consequences of unionization that are outside his control," and not "threats of economic reprisal to be taken solely on his own volition." NLRB v. River Togs, Inc., 382 F.2d 198, 202 (2d Cir. 1967). . . .

Equally valid was the finding by the court and the Board that petitioner's statements and communications were not cast as a prediction of "demonstrable economic consequences," 397 F.2d, at 160, but rather as a threat of retaliatory action. The Board found that petitioner's speeches, pamphlets, leaflets, and letters conveyed the following message: that the company was in a precarious financial condition; that the "strike-happy" union would in all likelihood have to obtain its potentially unreasonable demands by striking, the probable result of which would be a plant shut-down, as the past history of labor relations in the area indicated; and that the employees in such a case would have great difficulty finding employment elsewhere. In carrying out its duty to focus on the question "what did the speaker intend and the listener understand," Cox, Law and the National Labor Policy 44 (1960), the Board could reasonably conclude that the intended and understood import of that message was not to predict that unionization would inevitably cause the plant to close but to threaten to throw employees out of work regardless of the economic realities. In this connection, we need go no further than to point out (1) that petitioner had no support for his basic assumption that the union, which had not yet even presented any demands, would have to strike to be heard, and that he admitted at the hearing that he had no basis for attributing other plant closings in the area to unionism; and (2) that the Board has often found that employees, who are particularly sensitive to rumors of plant closings, take such hints as coercive threats rather than honest forecasts.

Petitioner argues that the line between so-called permitted predictions and proscribed threats is too vague to stand up under traditional First Amendment analysis and that the Board's discretion to curtail free speech rights is correspondingly too uncontrolled. It is true that a reviewing court must recognize the Board's competence in the first instance to judge the impact of utterances made in the context of the employer-employee relationship, see NLRB v. Virginia Electric & Power Co., 314 U.S. 469, 479, (1941). But an employer, who has control over that relationship and therefore knows it best, cannot be heard to complain that he is without an adequate guide for his behavior. He can easily make his views known without engaging in " 'brinkmanship' " when it becomes all too easy to "overstep and tumble into the brink," Wausau Steel Corp. v. NLRB, 377 F.2d 369, 372 (7th Cir. 1967). At the least he can avoid coercive speech simply by avoiding conscious overstatements he has reason to believe will mislead his employees.

For the foregoing reasons, we affirm the judgment of the Court of Appeals for the First Circuit.

NOTES

1. The line between a permissible prediction or statement of legal position and an illegal threat has been a difficult one for the Board and the courts to draw.

In NLRB v. Herman Wilson Lumber Co., 355 F.2d 426 (8th Cir. 1966), the employer's speeches included the following remarks: "I will fight the Union in every legal way possible. . . . If the Union calls an economic strike, you place your job on the line. You can be permanently replaced. You can lose your job. . . . In dealing with the Union I'll deal hard with it — I'll deal cold with it — I'll deal at arm's length with it." The NLRB held (2-1) that these statements violated § 8(a)(1), but the court of appeals denied enforcement (2-1).

In Conolon Corp., 191 N.L.R.B. 254 (1971), the central portion of an employer's pre-election speech consisted of selected excerpts from the decision of the court of appeals in *Herman Wilson Lumber Co.* Even though the employer mistakenly identified the quoted remarks as part of an NLRB decision, his speech as a whole was held to be protected by § 8(c), and was neither a violation of § 8(a)(1) nor a basis for setting aside the election.

For later examples of the Labor Board's continuing struggles with the problem of employer speech, *compare* Tommy's Spanish Foods, Inc., 187 N.L.R.B. 235 (1970), *enforced in pertinent part,* 463 F.2d 116 (9th Cir. 1972), *with* Cain Co., 190 N.L.R.B. 109 (1971), *and* ADCO Advertising, Inc., 206 N.L.R.B. 497 (1973). *See also* Birdsall Construction Co., 198 N.L.R.B. 163 (1972) (employer's speeches were lawful since they only amounted to "objective statement of the financial problems which it would face in the event of unionization followed by a prediction that such problems could make relocation . . . an economic necessity"; one Board member dissented).

The Labor Board remains divided over the allowable forcefulness of an employer's language in urging employees not to sign union authorization cards. In Airporter Inn Hotel, 215 N.L.R.B. 824 (1974), the Board held (3-2) that a letter could lawfully conclude: "[A]void a lot of unnecessary turmoil. . . . [A] union . . . can't and won't do anything for you except jeopardize your jobs." With two members again dissenting, the Board ruled in Munro Co., 217 N.L.R.B. 1011 (1975), that an employer did not violate the NLRA when its president and two employer representatives told assembled employees that signing union cards could be "fatal." May an employer urge employees to withdraw authorization cards already signed? See NLRB v. Monroe Tube Co., 545 F.2d 1320 (2d Cir. 1976).

Could an employer tell its employees (truthfully) that its parent company once had to shut down a facility and put 1,200 employees out of work because of unreasonable union demands? Hanover House Industries, Inc., 233 N.L.R.B. No. 36, 96 L.R.R.M. 1463 (1977).

2. The NLRB has taken the position that § 8(c) is limited to unfair labor practice cases and has no application in representation cases. "Conduct that creates an atmosphere which renders improbable a free choice will sometimes warrant invalidating an election even though the conduct may not constitute an unfair labor practice." General Shoe Corp., 77 N.L.R.B. 124 (1948). Thus, some employer statements, which may not constitute a "threat of reprisal" under § 8(c), may so cloud up the atmosphere as to warrant the Board in setting aside an election. The work of the NLRB in conducting representation elections under § 9 of the act will be examined in some detail in section II of Part Two, beginning at 201.

3. See generally, S. SCHLOSSBERG & F. SHERMAN, ORGANIZING AND THE LAW (rev. ed. 1971).

MAY DEPARTMENT STORES CO.

National Labor Relations Board
136 N.L.R.B. 797 (1962)

CHAIRMAN McCULLOCH and MEMBERS BROWN and FANNING:
. . . The Respondent owns and operates two department stores in the Greater Cleveland, Ohio, area. During the years 1959 and 1960, the Joint Petitioners campaigned to organize the Respondent. During this time the Respondent had in effect and enforced a broad no-solicitation rule which prohibited, inter alia, union solicitation in the selling areas of the store during the employees' working and nonworking time. The Respondent's enforcement of this rule, as such, is not alleged by the General Counsel as a violation or as interference with the election. Just prior to the election held on April 28, 1960, at a time when it was enforcing its no-solicitation

rule, the Respondent made noncoercive antiunion speeches to massed assemblies of employees on company property and thereafter denied the Union's request for equal opportunity and time to address the same employees. It is the theory of the General Counsel that the refusal to grant the Union's request to reply, on these uncontested facts, constitutes a violation of § 8(a)(1) of the Act and also warrants setting aside the election. We agree with position taken by the General Counsel.[4]

In the *Bonwit Teller* case, the employer had in effect a no-solicitation rule which forbade solicitation during working and nonworking time on the selling floors of the department store. The employer made preelection antiunion speeches to the employees in the selling areas but refused the Union's request for an opportunity to reply on equal terms. The Board found that such refusal interfered with the employees' organizational rights guaranteed by § 7, in violation of § 8(a)(1), and ordered the employer to cease and desist from such refusals. The Court of Appeals for the Second Circuit upheld the Board's finding of the violation.[6] In substance the Second Circuit reasoned as follows:

> The Board, however, has allowed retail department stores the privilege of prohibiting all solicitation within selling areas of the store during both working and nonworking hours [citations and footnote omitted]. Bonwit Teller chose to avail itself of that privilege and, having done so, was in our opinion required to abstain from campaigning against the Union on the same premises to which the Union was denied access; if it should be otherwise, the practical advantage to the employer who was opposed to unionization would constitute a serious interference with the rights of his employees to organize.[7]

In our opinion, the Board and court holding in the *Bonwit Teller* case, which we consider to be legally sound, squarely controls the issue in the present case.

Each of the contending parties herein relies upon *Livingston Shirt Corporation*[8] as supporting its respective position. The *Bonwit Teller* case itself, as noted, dealt with department store situations. Thereafter,

---

[4] The no-solicitation rule in the instant case is of the broad but privileged type. Generally, in manufacturing industries, for example, a no-solicitation rule which interferes with the right of employees to solicit on nonworking time violates § 8(a)(1) of the Act. See, Republic Aviation Corp. v. NLRB, 324 U.S. 793 (1945). However, department stores have long been exempted from the application of the rule because the nature of the business is such that solicitation, even on nonworking time, in selling areas, would unduly interfere with the retail store operations. See, e.g., Marshall Field & Co., 98 N.L.R.B. 88 and Great A & P Co., 123 N.L.R.B. 747. See also, Walton Mfg. Co., 126 N.L.R.B. 697.

[6] Bonwit Teller, Inc. v. NLRB, 197 F.2d 640 (2d Cir. 1952), *cert. denied,* 345 U.S. 905 (1953).

[7] *Id.* at 645. See also, NLRB v. American Tube Bending Co., 205 F.2d 45 (2d Cir. enfg. 102 N.L.R.B. 735, 1953), wherein the Second Circuit made it clear that its decision in Bonwit Teller gave the union a right of reply precisely *because* the broad rule was permitted.

[8] 107 N.L.R.B. 400 (1953).

for a time, the Board also applied the doctrine of *Bonwit Teller* to establishments other than retail department stores.[9] However, in the *Livingston Shirt* case, the Board modified its approach to the problem in the following terms:

"Accordingly, we are convinced that absent special circumstances as hereinafter indicated, there is nothing improper in an employer refusing to grant to the union a right equal to his own in his plant. We rule therefore that, *in the absence of either an unlawful broad no-solicitation rule (prohibiting union access to company premises on other than working time) or a privileged no-solicitation rule (broad, but not unlawful because of the character of the business)* [citing Marshall Field & Co., 98 N.L.R.B. 887] an employer does not commit an unfair labor practice if he makes a preelection speech on company time and premises to his employees and denies the union's request for an opportunity to reply. . . .

"Our holding here finds support in the recent decision of Second Circuit Court of Appeals in *American Tube Bending* case [citation omitted] in which it explicated its views of permissible employer conduct within the scope of the *Bonwit Teller* doctrine [citation omitted]."

We find no basis for the Respondent's contention that in *Livingston Shirt* the Board overruled the *Bonwit Teller* doctrine as it applies to department stores with broad but privilged no-solicitation rules.[11] It is clear that this latter situation was expressly excluded from the statement of allowable employer conduct and was particularly identified with the citation of the *Marshall Field* case and the explicit reliance upon the court opinions in *Bonwit Teller* and *American Tube Bending, supra.*[12]

However, the Respondent, in the alternative, maintains that certain decisions of the Supreme Court control and resolve the instant case. The Respondent contends in record argument and brief that the *NuTone*[13] and *Babcock & Wilcox*[14] cases stand for the proposition that retail store employer's may: (1) enforce a broad but privileged rule; (2) make antiunion speeches to massed assemblies of employees; and (3) at the same time deny to organizing unions a similar right of reply.

We do not agree. Indeed, we believe that those decisions delineating the extent to which an employer can restrict the organizational activities of employees and nonemployees on its premises, require the result we have reached herein. The no-solicitation rule enforced by Respondent is one which seriously impaired the right of employees to discuss union

---

[9] E.g., Metropolitan Auto Parts, 102 N.L.R.B. 1634 (unfair labor practices found); Gruen Watch Co., 103 N.L.R.B. 3 (objections to election sustained).

[11] It is not necessary to, and we do not, pass upon the Livingston Shirt case insofar as it affects nondepartment store situations.

[12] In both cases, the Second Circuit indicated that enforcement of the Board's order would be confined to the specific situations, i.e., the employer's application of a "broad but privileged" no-solicitation rule while "availing itself of the privilege by campaigning against the union on the same premises, to which the union was denied access."

[13] NLRB v. United Steelworkers (NuTone, Inc.), 357 U.S. 357 (1958).

[14] NLRB v. Babcock & Wilcox, 351 U.S. 105 (1956).

organization on company premises during nonworking as well as working time and thus created an imbalance in the opportunities for organizational communication. Respondent's rule is broader than the valid rule involved in the *NuTone* case, which restricted employees' discussion of such matters only during their working time, but left them free to discuss and evaluate such matters during their nonworking time. Thus Respondent's rule, albeit privileged,[15] involved a significantly greater restriction on employees' self-organization rights than did the rule involved in *NuTone.*

In *NuTone,* the Supreme Court discussed the right of an employer to enforce against its employees a no-solicitation rule relating only to working time, while itself engaging in an antiunion campaign during such time. It noted that the question at issue in such cases was whether such "conduct to any considerable degree created an imbalance in the opportunities for organizational communication." While holding that no such imbalance was shown therein, the Court indicated that the result might have been different had "the employees, or the union on their behalf, requested the employer, himself, engaging in antiunion solicitation, to make an exception to the rule for pro-union solicitation." Further, it indicated that even absent such a request, the employer's conduct might properly have been deemed unlawful, had it "truly diminished the ability of the labor organizations involved to carry their messages to the employees. *Just as that is a vital consideration in determining the validity of a no-solicitation rule, see Republic Aviation Corp. v. NLRB, supra* [324 U.S.] *at 797-798; NLRB v. Babcock & Wilcox Co., supra* [351 U.S.] *at 112, it is highly relevant in determining whether a valid rule has been fairly applied.*" (Emphasis supplied.)

Applying these principles, we find that a glaring "imbalance in opportunities for organizational communication" was created by Respondent's enforcement of the broad rule against union discussion during nonworking time as well as during working time, while it was engaged in utilizing such time to bring its antiunion message to the employees. By such conduct, Respondent seized for itself the most advantageous circumstances in which to present to employees its side of the organizational question. It spoke to them in massed assemblies during working time, thus gaining the not inconsiderable benefit flowing from the utilization of the employment relationship for such purposes, and insuring that its message would reach all of its employees in the most

---

[15] This rule, if promulgated by a nonretail store employer, would be presumptively invalid because it applies to nonworking time. The employer would have the burden of showing that factors relating to production, discipline and order at its particular plant made such additional restriction of employees' organizational activities necessary, thus overcoming the presumption of invalidity. See Walton Mfg. Co., 126 N.L.R.B. 747. In effect the Board's rule for department stores eliminates this latter requirement and permits such employers to promulgate such a rule without a specific showing of such factors. Of course, Respondent's rule also precluded nonemployee organizers from coming on its premises for purposes of distributing literature and soliciting employees. On this point we perceive no difference in the latitude allowed retail store employers and other employers.

carefully thought out and coherent form of maximum effectiveness. At the same time, it relegated the union and its employee supporters to relatively catch-as-catch-can methods of rebuttal, such as home visits, advertised meetings on the employees' own time, telephone calls, letters, and the various mass media of communication. While it is true that the Supreme Court in *Babcock & Wilcox* held that an employer may normally put a union to the task of organizing employees through such channels, it indicated that such right was not absolute, but was limited to those circumstances, where the effectiveness of such channels of communication was not diminished by employer conduct, or by other circumstances.

The normal effectiveness of such channels stems not alone from the ability of a union to make contact with employees, away from their place of work, but also from the availibility of normal opportunities to employees who have been contacted to discuss the matter with their fellow employees at their place of work. The place of work is the one place where all employees involved are sure to be together. Thus it is the one place where they can all discuss with each other the advantages and disadvantages of organization, and lend each other support and encouragement. Such full discussion lies at the very heart of the organizational rights guaranteed by the Act, and is not to be restricted, except as the exigencies of production, discipline and order demand.[16] It is only where opportunities for such discussion are available, limited, of course, by the need to maintain production, order and discipline, that the election procedures established in the Act can be expected to produce the peaceful resolution of representation questions on the basis of a free and informed choice. Where such discussion is not allowed, the normal channels of communication become clogged and lose their effectiveness. In such circumstances, the balance in "opportunities for organizational communication" is destroyed by an employer's utilization of working time and place for its antiunion campaign. Accordingly, while Respondent was under no obligation to forego utilizing such time and place for its antiunion campaign, we find that it was under an obligation to accede to the Union's request to address the employees under similar circumstances. Only by such action could it maintain the balance which the Supreme Court deemed so important a factor in this area. Respondent's failure to accede to the Union's request seriously impaired the employees' ability to learn of the advantages of union organization from others, and to discuss such advantages among themselves. It thereby interfered with their rights of self-organization as guaranteed in § 7 of the Act.

Accordingly, we find that Respondent's conduct as discussed above, violated § 8(a)(1) of the Act, and interfered with the conduct of the election of April 28, 1961. We shall therefore set aside that election and direct a new election. . . .

---

[16] NLRB v. Babcock & Wilcox Co., *supra*.

MEMBER LEEDOM dissenting.

Under the principles established in the *NuTone* case,[31] which I deem dispositive of the issues in this case,[32] the enforcement of a valid no-solicitation rule by an employer who is at the same time engaging in antiunion solicitation may not constitute an unfair labor practice in the absence of substantial evidence that, when all alternative reasonably available channels of communication are considered, the ability of the Union to carry its message to the employees has been truly diminished.[33] Unlike the majority, I do not think such a true diminution can be established merely by showing that as a general proposition department store employees can be more easily reached through the avenues of communication open to their employer than through the avenues open to a union. As I find in this record no evidence of true diminution, I would find that the complaint should be dismissed and the objections to the election should be overruled.[34]

[MEMBER RODGERS dissented in an opinion which is omitted.]

NOTES

1. The Court of Appeals for the Sixth Circuit refused to enforce the Board's order in the *May Department Stores* case, reasoning along lines similar to Member Leedom's dissent. May Dep't Stores Co. v. NLRB, 316 F.2d 797 (6th Cir. 1963). Compare Montgomery Ward & Co. v. NLRB, 339 F.2d 889 (6th Cir. 1965), in which case the court upheld the Board in finding a violation of § 8(a)(1) where the employer who refused the union a chance to reply to his "captive audience" speech had banned all union solicitation on company property and had threatened employees with discharge if they solicited union memberships on their own time away from company property. The Sixth Circuit agreed that this situation created "an imbalance in organizational communication."

2. Suppose the NLRB, in the exercise of its expertise and after considering empirical evidence and oral argument, decided to reverse the *Livingston Shirt* doctrine, on the ground that permitting factory employers to make captive audience speeches and to deny the union a chance to reply creates an imbalance in organizational communication. Would the Supreme Court uphold the Board?

---

[31] NLRB v. United Steelworkers (NuTone, Inc.), 357 U.S. 357 (1958); see also NLRB v. Babcock & Wilcox Co., 351 U.S. 105 (1956).

[32] Although NuTone involved the rights of employees, its principles, insofar as they preclude a finding of violation, apply a *fortiori* to nonemployees; see NLRB v. Babcock & Wilcox Co., *supra.*

[33] To this extent I agree with Member Rodgers that a finding of violation cannot be predicated on Bonwit Teller, Inc., 96 N.L.R.B. 608. In view of the *NuTone* and *Babcock* decisions, the question of the extent to which Livingston Shirt Corp., 107 N.L.R.B. 400, overruled *Bonwit Teller* is largely academic and I see no need to join in the debate on that issue at this late date.

[34] As I find no violation on the facts in this case, I have not considered the impact, if any, which § 8(c) of the Act would have in other factual contexts.

3. May an employer discharge an employee who insists on asking a question following the employer's non-coercive, antiunion speech in an industrial plant? See Prescott Industrial Products Co., 205 N.L.R.B. 51 (1973). The Board held (3-2) that, although the employer had no duty to give a chance to reply, the employee was protected against discharge.

4. *See generally* Barbash, *Employer "Free Speech" and Employee Rights,* 14 LAB. L.J. 313 (1963); Bloom, *Freedom of Communication Under the Labor Relations Act,* in N.Y.U. EIGHTH ANNUAL CONFERENCE ON LABOR 219 (1955); Bok, *The Regulation of Campaign Tactics in Representation Elections Under the National Labor Relations Act,* 78 HARV. L. REV. 38 (1964); Christensen, *Free Speech, Propaganda and the NLRA,* 38 N.Y.U.L. REV. 243 (1963); Drotning, *Employer Free Speech: Two Basic Questions Considered by the NLRB and Courts,* 16 LAB. L.J. 131 (1965); Koretz, *Employer Free Speech Under the Taft-Hartley Act,* 6 SYRACUSE L. REV. 82 (1954); Pokempner, *Employer Free Speech Under the National Labor Relations Act,* 25 MD. L. REV. 111 (1965); Wollett & Rowen, *Employer Speech and Related Issues,* 16 OHIO ST. L.J. 380 (1955).

3. INTERROGATION

BLUE FLASH EXPRESS, INC.

National Labor Relations Board
109 N.L.R.B. 591 (1954)

[Respondent, an interstate motor carrier, received a letter on May 19, 1953, from the union stating that it represented a majority of respondent's employees, that it was prepared to submit proof thereof, and that it desired to enter into collective bargaining negotiations. Before replying, respondent's general manager, Golden, interviewed each employee individually in his office, stating that he had received a letter from the union and that it was immaterial to him whether or not employees were union members, but that he desired to know whether they had joined so that he might know how to answer the letter. Each employee denied to Golden that he had signed any union card, although a majority of them had done so, designating the union as their representative, on or about May 17, 1953. Golden testified that this was the entire conversation. Several employees testified that Golden also stated on this occasion that the company was too small to operate with a union and that it would be impelled to sell out or reduce operations should the business be unionized. The Trial Examiner found that, since the witnesses appeared to be equally credible, the General Counsel had failed to establish the alleged threats of shutdown by a preponderance of the evidence and that the facts as to the interviews were as testified to by Golden.]

. . . .

[W]e are . . . of the opinion that Golden's interrogation of the employees was not violative of the Act. At the time of the interrogation, the Respondent had just received a communication from the Union claiming majority status and the right to represent the Respondent's employees in collective bargaining. Golden so informed the employees. He further gave them assurances that the Respondent would not resort to economic reprisals and advised them that he wished to know whether they had signed union authorization cards in order to enable him to reply to the Union's request for collective bargaining. As found above, there is no credible evidence that the Respondent at any time made any threats or promises violative of the Act, resorted to any reprisals, or exhibited any antiunion animus. Although the employees who had signed union authorization cards gave false answers to Golden's inquiries, the Respondent did nothing to afford them a reasonable basis for believing that the Respondent might resort to reprisals because of their union membership or activity. The facts here are similar to those presented in Atlas Life Ins. Co. v. NLRB, 195 F.2d 136 (10th Cir. 1952), where the Employer tried to find out whether a union represented a majority of the employees so that he would know whether he was obligated to bargain with the union. In that case, the Court of Appeals for the Tenth Circuit held that such interrogation was proper. When such interrogation is conducted under proper safeguards, as was the situation in the instant case, the fact that the interrogation is systematic does not, in itself, impart a coercive character to the interrogation. The purpose of such interrogation could not be achieved without systematic inquiry.

Contrary to the assertion of our dissenting colleagues, we are not holding in this decision that interrogation must be accompanied by other unfair labor practices before it can violate the Act. We are merely holding that interrogation of employees by an employer as to such matters as their union membership or union activities, which, when viewed in the context in which the interrogation occurred, falls short of interference or coercion, is not unlawful.

Our dissenting colleagues rely upon the rationale of Standard-Coosa-Thatcher, 85 N.L.R.B. 1358, in which the Board held that interrogation *per se* is unlawful. They appear to overlook cases, for the most part of recent date, in which the courts of at least six circuits have explicitly or by necessary implication condemned the rationale of *Standard-Coosa-Thatcher*. We hereby repudiate the notion that interrogation *per se* is unlawful and overrule *Standard-Coosa-Thatcher* and the line of cases following it to the extent that they are inconsistent with our decision today.

In our view, the test is whether, under all the circumstances, the interrogation reasonably tends to restrain or interfere with the employees in the exercise of rights guaranteed by the Act. The fact that the employees gave false answers when questioned, although relevant, is not controlling. The Respondent communicated its purpose in questioning the employees—a purpose which was legitimate in nature—to the employees and assured them that no reprisal would take place. Moreover, the questioning occurred in a background free of employer hostility to union organization. These circumstances convince us that the

Respondent's interrogation did not reasonably lead the employees to believe that economic reprisal might be visited upon them by Respondent.

The instant case is thus distinguishable from such cases as Syracuse Color Press, 103 N.L.R.B. 377, *enforced* by the Court of Appeals for the Second Circuit, 209 F.2d 596 (2d Cir. 1954), where the employer called the employees to the superintendent's office a week before a scheduled Board election, advocated adherence to 1 of 2 rival unions, and questioned them concerning their union membership and activities, as well as the membership and activities of other employees, without giving any legitimate explanation for the interrogation or any assurance against reprisal. In such cases, unlike the situation in the instant case, the surrounding circumstances together with the nature of the interrogation itself imparted a coercive character to the interrogation.

This decision does not by any means grant employers a license to engage in interrogation of their employees as to union affiliation or activity. We agree with and adopt the test laid down by the Court of Appeals for the Second Circuit in the *Syracuse Color Press* case which we construe to be that the answer to whether particular interrogation interferes with, restrains, and coerces employees must be found in the record as a whole. And, as the court states "The time, the place, the personnel involved, the information sought and the employer's conceded preference [as in that case] must be considered. . . . " Members of the majority have participated in a number of recent decisions in which we have joined in holding that certain acts of interrogation were violative of the Act, and we reaffirm that position here. Therefore, any employer who engages in interrogation does so with notice that he risks a finding of unfair labor practices if the circumstances are such that his interrogation restrains or interferes with employees in the exercise of their rights under the Act.

The rule which we adopt will require the Trial Examiners and the Board to carefully weigh and evaluate the evidence in such case, but that is what we believe the statute requires us to do. The only alternatives, both of which we reject, are either to find all interrogation *per se* unlawful, or to find that interrogation under all circumstances is permissible under the statute.

Our dissenting colleagues express disagreement with our decision, but do not make it clear precisely what rule they would follow. There is the strong implication that the dissenting members would hold interrogation to be coercive *per se,* which, of course, means wholly without regard to the circumstances in which it occurs. This would mean that a casual, friendly, isolated instance of interrogation by a minor supervisor would subject the employer to a finding that he had committed an unfair labor practice and result in the issuance of a cease and desist order, which, if enforced by the court, would subject the employer to punishment for contempt of court if the same or another minor supervisor repeated the question to the same or another employee. If this is not the position of our colleagues, and they agree that the Board is required to determine the significance of particular acts of interrogation in the light of the entire record in the case, the difference between their view and ours merely reflects disagreement as to the conclusion to be drawn from the particular facts of the case.

Hence, we conclude that the Respondent's interrogation of the employees under the circumstances of this case did not carry an implied threat of reprisal or in any other way interfere with, restrain, or coerce the employees in the exercise of the rights guaranteed in § 7 of the Act. Accordingly, we find that such conduct is not violative of § 8(a)(1) of the Act. . . .

MEMBERS MURDOCK and PETERSON, dissenting:. . . .

The exact meaning and extent of the majority decision is not certain. Apparently, however, the majority has decided that interrogation unaccompanied by other unfair labor practices is not conduct which violates the Act. We cannot agree.

From the very beginning of the administration of this Act the Board has, with court approval, found that interrogation by an employer prevents employees from exercising freely their right to engage in concerted activities. After a substantial period of administrative experience and after amendment of the Act, the Board reaffirmed its position that when an employer questions his employees concerning any aspect of concerted activity he violates § 8(a)(1) of the Act. We believe that the carefully considered position on interrogation taken by the Board in previous cases is well founded, and we are aware of no recent development which warrants a departure from such precedent.

The rationale for finding interrogation violative of the Act is simple. . . . Employees can exercise fully their right to engage in or refrain from self-organizational and other concerted activities only if they are free from employer prying and investigation. When an employer inquires into organizational activity whether by espionage, surveillance, polling, or direct questioning, he invades the privacy in which employees are entitled to exercise the rights given them by the Act. When he questions an employee about union organization or any concerted activities he forces the employee to take a stand on such issues whether or not the employee desires to take a position or has had full opportunity to consider the various arguments offered on the subject. And the employer compels the employee to take this stand alone, without the anonymity and support of group action. Moreover, employer interrogation tends to implant in the mind of the employee the apprehension that the employer is seeking information in order to affect his job security and the fear that economic reprisal will follow the questioning. The fear induced by an employer's questions is illustrated by the fact that employees, as in this case, often give untruthful or evasive answers to such questions. The many cases in the Board's experience in which interrogation was the prelude to discrimination demonstrate the reasonableness of such fear. Interrogation thus serves as an implied threat or a warning to employees of the adverse consequences of organization and dissuades them from participating in concerted activity. It thereby undermines the bargaining agent chosen by the employees, thwarts self-organization, and frustrates employee attempts to bargain collectively. Such conduct tends to interfere with, restrain, or coerce employees in the exercise of the rights guaranteed by § 7 as prohibited by § 8(a)(1). Board condemnation of interrogation, which we believe is required by the Act, protects the right of employees to privacy in their organizational activities, removes the restraint and coercion resulting from the threat implicit in interrogation, and deters the commission of further unfair labor practices.

For these reasons the Board in its expert judgment and in the light of its administrative experience is warranted in concluding, as it has in the past, that interrogation generally inhibits employee self-organization and is violative of § 8(a)(1) whether or not other unfair labor practices are committed. This does not mean that all interrogation is automatically unlawful or requires remedial action by the Board. There are, of course, instances of interrogation which can be properly regarded as isolated, casual, and too inconsequential in their impact to constitute a violation of the Act or to warrant a Board remedy. In such situations we have participated in dismissing the allegations of illegal interrogation.

The test for determining the legality of interrogation—as the members of the majority profess to recognize—is whether the interrogation, reasonably interpreted, tends to impair the free exercise by employees of their rights under the Act. In applying this test in interrogation cases, the Board must, of course, carefully weigh and evaluate the evidence as it must in all cases. And it must do so in the light of its administrative experience and specialized knowledge. Viewing the interrogation in this case with these considerations in mind, we fail to see how the Respondent's questioning of its employees can be considered lawful. Certainly § 8(c) of the Act when it recognizes that an employer's expression of opinion is not an unfair labor practice does not privilege an employer to ferret out the views of his employees and to pry into their organizational activities. We see no circumstances in this case which would make unreasonable the fear which questions such as those of the Respondent usually tend to engender. Here a high managerial representative, the general manager, was the interrogator; all employees in the bargaining unit were subjected to the questioning; each employee was interviewed separately; the place of the interviews was the general manager's office. While the general manager did state to the employees that it was immaterial to him whether they were union members and explained that he was seeking information for the purpose of answering the Union's letter, his assurances were ineffective when the entire situation belied them. As the majority states, the interrogation was not accompanied by express threats or promises and was not followed by reprisals. The interrogation alone, however, we conclude, tended to create fear in the employees and to thwart organization. The facts demonstrate clearly the soundness of our conclusion: The employees obviously did not accept the assertions of the general manager and felt it necessary to misrepresent their union position. Each of the employees questioned denied that he had signed a union card although each had in fact signed a card only about 5 days before. The employees' denial of union adherence through fear furnished the Respondent grounds for refusing to bargain; the Union which had in fact represented all employees in the bargaining unit was deprived of the recognition to which it was entitled by reason of its actual majority status and was incapacitated as bargaining agent; and the employees were deprived of the opportunity for collective bargaining. The majority apparently believes, however, that the employees here, in concealing their union adherence in the face of the general manager's assurances and explanation, behaved in an unreasonable manner. But these employees acted in a manner typical of employees subjected to interrogation. . . .

In addition to arriving at the unsound conclusion that the Respondent's interrogation did not reasonably tend to interfere with, restrain, or coerce its employees, the members of the majority encourage employers to engage in interrogation as a means of determining whether a labor organization represents a majority of their employees. They emphasize that the Respondent here questioned its employees to enable it to reply to the Union's request for recognition and that this purpose was legitimate in nature. An employer's purpose for inquiring into the union activities of his employees, we must point out, is not a significant or mitigating consideration in determining the legality of such conduct under § 8(a)(1). This section is concerned with the *effect* of the employer's conduct upon his employees' exercise of their statutory rights regardless of what motivates the conduct. The Act protects employees from an innocent or ignorant invasion of their rights as well as from an intended invasion. And the remedy for the invasion does not penalize the employer but merely restores freedom of activity to employees by requiring the employer to refrain from the conduct which impairs that freedom and to notify the employees that he will do so. Yet the majority sanctions interrogation, with its attendant discouraging effects upon collective bargaining, when engaged in for the purpose of resolving the question of a labor organization's majority status. We cannot understand this position nor can we see how our colleagues can approve such a method of determining a question concerning representation, a statutory function of the Board. This method places in the hands of an interested party, with obvious capacity to resort to economic reprisal against the voters, complete control over the timing, means of inquiry, the phrasing of the question, and compilation of results of the polling of employees, and it offers none of the traditional safeguards of voting such as a secret ballot and conduct of the poll by an impartial agency. The fallibility of such a method for testing a majority claim and the inaccuracy of the results it obtains is demonstrated in this case where all employees in the bargaining unit when subjected to individual interrogation by the Respondent denied the union adherence which they had earlier adopted.

Several approved methods of determining whether a labor organization represents a majority of his employees are available to an employer. He may ask the labor organization to offer proof of its majority; he may request the organization to file a petition for a Board determination by election; or he may file a similar petition himself. He may agree with the labor organization to submit authorization cards to an impartial third party for a check; and we note that in making its bargaining request the Union here stated its willingness to agree to such a check. Finally, if an employer has a *genuine* doubt as to the labor organization's majority status, he may simply refuse to recognize the organization, and his good-faith doubt is a defense to a charge of a violation of the duty to bargain. With all these avenues open to an employer, plainly there is no need for him to utilize interrogation, with its coercive effect, in order to reply to a union's request for recognition, and the Board should not approve such conduct. . . .

NOTES

1. Although the above case marks an important departure from previous Board practice in rejecting the doctrine that interrogation is per se unlawful, and adopting the principle that it is privileged (1) when the purpose is legitimate, (2) when accompanied by assurances against reprisal, and (3) when unaccompanied by other unfair labor practices, later cases indicate that *Blue Flash* does not give carte blanche license to questioning of employees. Violations of § 8(a)(1) were found, for example, in NLRB v. Associated Naval Architects, 355 F.2d 788 (4th Cir. 1966) (persistent interrogation as to what happened at union meetings and identity of men who were active in the organizing campaign); Montgomery Ward & Co., 115 N.L.R.B. 645 (1956) (questioning in a context of discriminatory discharges); Union News Co., 112 N.L.R.B. 420 (1955) (no claim for recognition; hence no legitimate purpose to ascertain whether majority existed; and technique used tended to intimidate); Clinton Foods, Inc., 237 N.L.R.B. No. 92, 99 L.R.R.M. 1043 (1978) (questioning of a single employee as to reasons for seeking union assistance).

2. In NLRB v. Lorben Corp., 345 F.2d 346 (2d Cir. 1965), the court held that coercion may not be inferred simply from the employer's failure (1) to explain the purpose of a poll and (2) to assure employees against reprisal. *See also* Bon-R Reproductions, Inc. v. NLRB, 309 F.2d 898 (2d Cir. 1962).

3. In Bourne v. NLRB, 332 F.2d 47, 48 (2d Cir. 1964), the court said: "Under our decisions interrogation, not itself threatening, is not held to be an unfair labor practice unless it meets certain fairly severe standards. . . . These include: (1) The background, *i.e.,* is there a history of employer hostility and discrimination? (2) The nature of the information sought, *e.g.,* did the interrogator appear to be seeking information on which to base taking action against individual employees? (3) The identity of the questioner, *i.e.,* how high was he in the company hierarchy? (4) Place and method of interrogation, *e.g.,* was employee called from work to the boss's office? Was there an atmosphere of 'unnatural formality' ? (5) Truthfulness of the reply."

Is it a violation of § 8(a)(1) for an employer to request employees to give him or get him copies of written statements which they had made to

NLRB agents who were investigating alleged unfair labor practices by the employer? The Board, with the approval of some circuits, has regarded this as a *per se* violation because of the inherently coercive effect of the request upon employees. However, the court, in NLRB v. Martin A. Gleason, Inc., 534 F.2d 466 (2d Cir. 1976), refused to apply a *per se* rule and found no violation where the employer asked the employees "if they would mind" supplying copies of their statements and indicated that he was not requiring them to do so, the employees willingly complied, and the information was relevant to the employer's preparation of his defense.

4. In response to a directive from the Court of Appeals for the District of Columbia Circuit in Operating Engineers Local 49 v. NLRB [Struksnes Constr. Co.], 353 F.2d 852 (D.C. Cir. 1965), the Board revised the *Blue Flash* tests and announced standards which may be used as guidelines to determine whether a "poll" by the employer is lawful.

"Absent unusual circumstances, the polling of employees by an employer will be violative of § 8(a)(1) of the Act unless the following safeguards are observed: (1) the purpose of the poll is to determine the truth of a union's claim of majority, (2) this purpose is communicated to the employees, (3) assurances against reprisal are given, (4) *the employees are polled by secret ballot* [emphasis added], and (5) the employer has not engaged in unfair labor practices or otherwise created a coercive atmosphere.

"The purpose of the polling in these circumstances is clearly relevant to an issue raised by a union's claim for recognition and is therefore lawful. The requirement that the lawful purpose be communicated to the employees, along with assurances against reprisal, is designed to allay any fear of discrimination which might otherwise arise from the polling, and any tendency to interfere with employees' § 7 rights. Secrecy of the ballot will give further assurance that reprisals cannot be taken against employees because the views of each individual will not be known. And the absence of employer unfair labor practices or other conduct creating coercive atmosphere will serve as a further warranty to the employees that the poll does not have some unlawful object, contrary to the lawful purpose stated by the employer. In accord with presumptive rules applied by the Board with court approval in other situations, this rule is designed to effectuate the purposes of the Act by maintaining a reasonable balance between the protection of employee rights and legitimate interests of employers.

"On the other hand, a poll taken while a petition for a Board election is pending does not, in our view, serve any legitimate interest of the employer that would not be better served by the forthcoming Board election. In accord with long-established Board policy, therefore, such polls will continue to be found violative of § 8(a)(1) of the Act." Struksnes Constr. Co., 165 N.L.R.B. 1062 (1967).

5. The *Struksnes* standards have generally been followed by the Board, Northeastern Dye Works, 203 N.L.R.B. 1222 (1973), and by the courts of appeals, NLRB v. Super Toys, Inc., 458 F.2d 180 (9th Cir. 1972).

However, the Eighth Circuit, which had previously accepted the *Struksnes* safeguards, stated in General Mercantile & Hardware Co. v. NLRB, 461 F.2d 952 (8th Cir. 1972), that in the absence of antiunion animus, an employer's quizzing of employees concerning their signing of union authorization cards did not violate the Act when the employer did not even imply an opinion against the union or hint at reprisal. See also B.F. Goodrich Footwear Co., 201 N.L.R.B. 353 (1972), where no violation was found from a few instances of questioning.

In Bushnell's Kitchens, 222 N.L.R.B. 110 (1976), where the employer's polling was done at a meeting of the employees upon the suggestion of the union business agent, no violation was found. The Board said that the *Struksnes* requirements were "not a straight-jacket to be applied in any and all circumstances."

4. ECONOMIC COERCION AND INDUCEMENT

NLRB v. EXCHANGE PARTS CO.

Supreme Court of the United States
375 U.S. 405, 84 S. Ct. 457, 11 L. Ed. 2d 435 (1964)

[Respondent was engaged in the business of rebuilding automobiles and its employees were not represented by a union prior to 1959. On November 9, 1959, the Boilermakers Union announced that it was conducting an organizational campaign and on November 16 it petitioned the Board for a representation election which was ordered for March 18, 1960.]

MR. JUSTICE HARLAN delivered the opinion of the Court.

This case presents a question concerning the limitations which § 8(a)(1) of the National Labor Relations Act, 49 Stat. 452 (1935), as amended, 29 U.S.C. § 158(a)(1), places on the right of an employer to confer economic benefits on his employees shortly before a representation election. The precise issue is whether that section prohibits the conferral of such benefits, without more, where the employer's purpose is to affect the outcome of the election. . . .

At two meetings on November 4 and 5, 1959, C. V. McDonald, the Vice-President and General Manager of Exchange Parts, announced to the employees that their "floating holiday" in 1959 would fall on December 26 and that there would be an additional "floating holiday" in 1960. On February 25, six days after the Board issued its election order, Exchange Parts held a dinner for employees at which Vice-President McDonald told the employees that they could decide whether the extra day of vacation in 1960 would be a "floating holiday" or would be taken on their birthdays. The employees voted for the latter. McDonald also referred to the forthcoming representation election as one in which, in the words of the trial examiner, the employees would "determine whether . . . [they] wished to hand over their right to speak and act for themselves." He stated that the union had distorted some of the facts and pointed out the benefits obtained by the employees without a union. He urged all the employees to vote in the election.

On March 4 Exchange Parts sent its employees a letter which spoke of "the *Empty Promises* of the Union" and "the *fact* that *it is the Company that puts things in your envelope* . . . . " After mentioning a number of benefits, the letter said: "The Union can't put any of those things in your envelope—*only the Company can do that.*" [The italics appear in the original letter.] Further on, the letter stated: " . . . [I]t didn't take a Union to get any of those things and . . . it won't take a Union to get additional improvements in the future." Accompanying the letter was a detailed statement of the benefits granted by the company since 1949 and an estimate of the monetary value of such benefits to the employees. Included in the statement of benefits granted by the company for 1960 were the birthday holiday, a new system for computing overtime during holiday weeks which had the effect of increasing wages for those weeks, and a new vacation schedule which enabled employees to extend their vacations by sandwiching them between two weekends. Although Exchange Parts asserts that the policy behind the latter two benefits was established earlier, it is clear that the letter of March 4 was the first general announcement of the changes to the employees. In the ensuing election the union lost.

The Board, affirming the findings of the trial examiner, found that the announcement of the birthday holiday and the grant and announcement of overtime and vacation benefits were arranged by Exchange Parts with the intention of inducing the employees to vote against the union. It found that this conduct violated § 8(a)(1) of the National Labor Relations Act and issued an appropriate order. On the Board's petition for enforcement of the order, the Court of Appeals rejected the finding that the announcement of the birthday holiday was timed to influence the outcome of the election. It accepted the Board's findings with respect to the overtime and vacation benefits, and the propriety of those findings is not in controversy here. However, noting that "the benefits were put into effect unconditionally on a permanent basis, and no one has suggested that there was any implication the benefits would be withdrawn if the workers voted for the union," 304 F.2d 368, 375, the court denied enforcement of the Board's order. It believed that it was not an unfair labor practice under § 8(a)(1) for an employer to grant benefits to its employees in these circumstances.

. . . We think the Court of Appeals was mistaken in concluding that the conferral of employee benefits while a representation election is pending, for the purpose of inducing employees to vote against the union, does not "interfere with" the protected right to organize.

. . . The danger inherent in well-timed increases in benefits is the suggestion of a fist inside the velvet glove. Employees are not likely to miss the inference that the source of benefits now conferred is also the source from which future benefits must flow and which may dry up if it is not obliged. The danger may be diminished if, as in this case, the benefits are conferred permanently and unconditionally. But the absence of conditions or threats pertaining to the particular benefits conferred would be of controlling significance only if it could be presumed that no question of additional benefits or renegotiation of existing benefits would arise in the future; and, of course, no such presumption is tenable.

. . . Other unlawful conduct may often be an indication of the motive behind a grant of benefits while an election is pending, and to that extent it is relevant to the legality of the grant; but when as here the motive is otherwise established, an employer is not free to violate § 8(a)(1) by conferrring benefits simply because it refrains from other, more obvious violations. We cannot agree with the Court of Appeals that enforcement of the Board's order will have the "ironic" result of "discouraging benefits for labor." 304 F.2d, at 376. The beneficence of an employer is likely to be ephemeral if prompted by a threat of unionization which is subsequently removed. Insulating the right of collective organization from calculated good will of this sort deprives employees of little that has lasting value.

Reversed.

NOTES

1. The pertinent part of the Board's order in the *Exchange Parts* case reads: "Cease and desist from interfering with, restraining, or coercing its employees in the exercise of rights guaranteed in § 7 of the Act by granting them economic benefits or by changing the terms and conditions of their employment; provided, however, that *nothing in this recommended order shall be construed as requiring the Respondent to vary or abandon any economic benefit or any term or condition of employment which it has heretofore established.*" 131 N.L.R.B. at 807 (1961) (Emphasis added).

2. Employer statements containing threats of reprisal or promises of benefits constitute unlawful interference, restraint, and coercion. If the employer actually puts into effect such reprisals or benefits for the purpose of defeating unionization, this, too, is an unfair labor practice. "The Act does not preclude an employer from introducing benefits during an organizational period. But when an employer uses proposed benefits as an inducement not to join the union, his activity bears no shield of privilege." Joy Silk Mills, Inc. v. NLRB, 185 F.2d 732, 739 (D.C. Cir. 1950), *cert. denied,* 341 U.S. 914 (1951). What elements in the factual situation would be relevant and important in determining whether the employer had a wrongful purpose? *Cf.* Imco Container Co. v. NLRB, 346 F.2d 178 (4th Cir. 1965; Delchamps, Inc. v. NLRB, 100 L.R.R.M. 2555 (5th Cir. 1979). Suppose the employer customarily changed wages at this time of the year?

Three female welders were rehired by a company in June 1973 after new management assumed control in April. Following their reinstatement, the women protested a pay differential between them and male welders which had been a source of complaint since 1970. No action was taken on their grievance, however, until after a union filed an election petition in October 1973. In mid-October they were advised the pay discrimination would be corrected, and at the end of the month they received rate increases and back pay. Could the timing of the correction of this admittedly inequitable and probably unlawful pay policy make it a violation of § 8(a)(1)? *See* Rupp Industries, Inc., 217 N.L.R.B. 385 (1975). *Cf.* Styletek, 214 N.L.R.B. 736 (1974), *enforcement granted,* 520 F.2d 275 (1st Cir. 1975).

The implicit or explicit solicitation of grievances at preelection meetings creates a rebuttable presumption that the employer is impliedly promising to correct the inequities it discovers through its inquiries. The inference may be rebutted by evidence that the employer emphasized it could not make any promises concerning the grievances raised. Uarco Inc., 216 N.L.R.B. 1 (1974).

An employer did not violate the NLRA when it told an employee that it was willing to spend $20,000 to keep a union out of its shop. An employer may spend whatever sums it deems advisable in opposing union activity, and the statement at issue was unaccompanied by any threats that expenditures would be used to finance unlawful activities. Jeffries Truck Parts & Equipment, Inc., 216 N.L.R.B. 147 (1975).

3. What if an employer *withholds* a customary wage increase pending an election? *See* Gates Rubber Co., 182 N.L.R.B. 95 (1970); NLRB v. Hendel Mfg. Co., 483 F.2d 350 (2d Cir. 1973). *But cf.* Newberry Co. v. NLRB, 442 F.2d 897 (2d Cir. 1971); Great A & P Tea Co., 192 N.L.R.B. 645 (1971).

4. For a consideration of employer reprisal, such as closing or moving the plant, *see* NLRB v. Darlington Mfg. Co., *infra* at 182, and accompanying materials.

5. *Economic inducement of individual employees.* Outright bribery of individual employees to stay out of unions is, of course, a clear violation of the duty of noninterference. Examples: Reliance Mfg. Co., 28 N.L.R.B. 1051 (1941) — advising an employee interested in unionism that he had a "good chance of going places" with the company if he "would get on the right side of the fence"; Sterling Cabinet Corp., 109 N.L.R.B. 6 (1954) — telling employee that he would get a wage increase if he got rid of representation petition.

Use of the "blacklist." Obviously, threats and acts of economic retaliation against individual employees who persist in union activities are unlawful under the labor relations acts. *See, e.g.,* Reeves-Ely Laboratories, Inc., 76 N.L.R.B. 728 (1948), where it was held that the threat of a company vice-president to "blacklist" an employee because of his union proclivities, made in the course of his testimony in an open Board hearing, itself constituted a violation of the NLRA. "A long experience had shown that one of the most provocative and effective means by which employers sought to impede the organization of workers was the blacklisting of union men, thereby denying them opportunities for employment." Magruder, J., in NLRB v. Waumbec Mills, Inc., 114 F.2d

226, 232 (1st Cir. 1940). Statutes in many states specifically outlaw such practices. In some instances the prohibition is contained in the state labor relations act; in others, the matter is covered by special statute.

5. VIOLENCE, INTIMIDATION, ESPIONAGE, AND SURVEILLANCE

Violence and Intimidation. Violence and threats of violence to deter union organization are clearly unlawful. Examples were fairly common during the early days of the Wagner Act: an overseer offered to buy an employee a gallon of whiskey if he would "stamp hell out of" a union organizer — Mansfield Mills, Inc., 3 N.L.R.B. 901 (1937); a forelady supplemented her attempt to dissuade employees from accepting union pamphlets by suggesting, with reference to the union organizer, "What do you say, girls, we give her a beating?" — Tiny Town Togs, Inc., 7 N.L.R.B. 54 (1938); a reign of terror was conducted by an employer association, of which the company was a member, with union organizers ordered out of the county at gun point by private police hired by the association — Clover Fork Coal Co., 4 N.L.R.B. 202 (1937). The use of such crude tactics has declined considerably. *But see Hearings on Labor-Management Relations in the Southern Textile Industry,* 82d Cong., 1st Sess. (1951); Dan River Mills, Inc., 121 N.L.R.B. 645 (1958). The difficult problems concern whether the employer should be held responsible for the actions of nonunion employees, supervisors, and other persons, discussed in the next section.

The Byrnes Act, 18 U.S.C. § 1231, makes unlawful and criminal the interstate transportation of persons employed for the purpose of obstructing, by force or threats, "(1) peaceful picketing by employees during any labor controversy affecting wages, hours or conditions of labor; or (2) the exercise by employees of any of the rights of self-organization, or collective bargaining."

A number of states have statutes specifically dealing with the use of professional strikebreakers. See the state law volumes of the looseleaf labor services.

More subtle forms of strikebreaking may be seen in the famous "Mohawk Valley Formula," described in Remington Rand, Inc., 2 N.L.R.B. 626 (1937), *order enforced, with modifications,* NLRB v. Remington Rand, Inc., 94 F.2d 862 (2d Cir. 1938), *cert. denied,* 304 U.S. 576 (1938), and discussed in R. BROOKS, WHEN LABOR ORGANIZES, ch. V (1937).

Espionage and Surveillance. In the period prior to the Wagner Act, the use of labor spies, often hired from detective agencies, to infiltrate union organizations and report on the "ringleaders" who were then discharged and blacklisted, received considerable publicity, and such practices were obviously included in the abuses aimed at in § 8(1). An early example may be seen in Baldwin Locomotive Works, 20 N.L.R.B. 1100 (1940).

It is not necessary to prove that employees had knowledge that they were being spied upon, NLRB v. Grower-Shipper Vegetable Ass'n, 122

F.2d 368 (9th Cir. 1941). On the other hand, it is enough to show that the employer fostered the impression that employees were being subjected to surveillance. Idaho Egg Producers, 111 N.L.R.B. 93 (1955); Filler Prod., Inc. v. NLRB, 376 F.2d 369 (4th Cir. 1967).

6. EMPLOYER RESPONSIBILITY FOR ANTIUNION CONDUCT OF SUBORDINATES AND OTHERS

The Wagner Act contained no test or standard of employer responsibility except that the term "employer" was defined in § 2(2) to include "any person acting in the interest of an employer, directly or indirectly."

Section 2(2) as amended substituted the language of agency for "interest" in defining "employer." According to the House Committee, it was intended by the change in § 2(2) to make "employers responsible for what people say and do only when it is within the *actual* or *apparent* scope of their authority" and thus to make the "ordinary rules of the law of agency equally applicable to employers and to unions." H.R. REP. No. 245, 80th Cong., 1st Sess. 11 (1947). The dissenters on the committee objected to this change. "It would make necessary proof that an employer had specifically authorized his foremen or superintendents to engage in unfair labor practices; matters which are easily concealed. In modern industrial enterprises foremen and superintendents *are* management to the workers under them and employers should be held responsible for their actions." H.R. REP. No. 245, 80th Cong., 1st Sess. 68 (1947). Later the conference report recommended both the change proposed in the House bill *and* a new provision, § 2(13), providing: "In determining whether any person is acting as an 'agent' of another person so as to make such other person responsible for his acts, the question of whether the specific acts performed were actually authorized or subsequently ratified shall not be controlling." According to the report, this means that "both employers and labor organizations will be responsible for the acts of their agents in accordance with the ordinary common law rules of agency (and only ordinary evidence will be required to establish the agent's authority)." H.R. CONF. REP. No. 510, 80th Cong., 1st Sess. 36 (1947).

(a) *Supervisors* — An employer is generally held responsible for the statements and acts of foremen and supervisors, since it can usually be said that they have apparent authority to speak for the employer.

Even where the employer has instructed his supervisors not to interfere with the employees' organizational activities, he may still be responsible if he has not communicated these instructions to the rank-and-file employees. Otis L. Broyhill Furniture Co., 94 N.L.R.B. 1452 (1951).

Isolated or sporadic instances of coercive statements by a supervisor do not give rise to employer responsibility, where the circumstances are indicative of no authorization by the employer. Pittsburgh S.S. Co. v. NLRB, 180 F.2d 731 (6th Cir. 1950), aff'd, 340 U.S. 498 (1951).

(b) *Nonsupervisory employees* — The employer will be held responsible for acts of his nonsupervisory employees where it is shown that the employee was acting as agent of the employer. This may be shown where the employee was acting within the general scope of his employment, regardless of whether the specific act was authorized or even forbidden. National Paper Co., 102 N.L.R.B. 1569 (1953) (armed guard made threatening and abusive phone calls to the union secretary, in a context of other coercive conduct by the employer).

Where an employee, although not a supervisor, is clothed with apparent authority to speak for the employer, the employer is held responsible for his acts. NLRB v. Mississippi Prod., Inc., 213 F.2d 670 (5th Cir. 1954). The necessary agency relationship may also be found on the basis of implied authority or implied ratification, where the employer condones and countenances violence by rank-and-file employees. In J. D. Jewell, Inc., 99 N.L.R.B. 61 (1952), an employee asked a manager what would happen if they whipped the union representative; the manager replied, "As long as you stick to personal affairs — don't involve me or the Company whatever — it is plumb all right with me." The company made no investigation when a mob of employees later beat up an organizer.

(c) *Nonemployees* — Whether an employer will be held responsible for threatening speeches and publications of local businessmen and town officials depends upon evidence of some connection showing an agency relationship, such as employer instigation, participation, express, implied, or apparent authority, or express or implied ratification. Southland Mfg. Co., 94 N.L.R.B. 813 (1951) (a supervisor urged employees to attend a meeting addressed by the mayor and a bank official, was present at the meeting and failed to disavow threats). But where the employer refrains from "aiding, abetting, assisting, or co-operating" with the local citizens, coercive statements and conduct by them are not an unfair labor practice. Clarke Mills, 109 N.L.R.B. 666 (1954).

Note that the NLRB may set an election aside, without proof of agency, where citizens in the community have so inflamed the atmosphere with threats and appeals to passion and prejudice that employee free choice is prevented. Universal Mfg. Co., 156 N.L.R.B. 1459 (1966).

In Marlowe Mfg. Co., 213 N.L.R.B. 278 (1974), the Labor Board held it would not set aside an election lost by a union where certain rank-and-file employees had distributed a leaflet containing threats that the plant would close if the union won. There was no indication that the employer was involved in any way in the preparation or distribution of the leaflet. Chairman Miller and Member Fanning dissented, arguing that the leaflet was plainly a last-minute appeal to fear, and contending that the Board should not validate elections conducted in an atmosphere of fear, no matter who creates that atmosphere.

B. EMPLOYER DOMINATION OR SUPPORT

During the 1920's and the early 1930's, "company unions" or "employee representation plans" flourished.[13] With the Railway Labor

---

[13] *See* H. PELLING, AMERICAN LABOR 146, 160 (1960).

Act as a precedent, prohibiting in § 2, Fourth, a carrier from interfering with the organization of its employees or using its funds in maintaining or assisting any labor organization, the "Wagner Act" Congress in 1935 attacked the company union problem by making it an unfair labor practice for an employer to dominate or interfere with the formation or administration of any labor organization or to contribute financial or other support to it. The prohibition is now embodied in § 8(a)(2) of the NLRA.

During the early days of the NLRB, there was a heavy volume of litigation against company unions. For example, in *NLRB v. Pennsylvania Greyhound Lines, Inc.,*[14] the Supreme Court sustained the Board's findings of an unfair labor practice, based on evidence that company representatives were active in promoting the plan, in urging employees to join, in the preparation of the details of organization, including the bylaws, in presiding over organization meetings, and in selecting the employee representatives of the organization. The bylaws, themselves, indicated that the company had control of its functioning. In a companion case, *NLRB v. Pacific Greyhound Lines, Inc.,*[15] although the formal provisions to show company domination were lacking in the bylaws, the evidence showed that the employer's control was nonetheless effective.

The problem as to "successor" unions. Employer-dominated unions have customarily been ordered "disestablished" as employee representatives, which means that they have lost, at least for a time, their capacity to represent employees for statutory purposes. Sometimes another unaffiliated or company union has been organized to replace the disestablished union, and the question has arisen whether the legal disability of the latter attached to the successor.

The Board has taken the position that an organization is tainted with the illegality of its predecessor unless the employer, prior to the formation of the successor organization, has established a clear line of fracture between the two organizations, by publicly and unequivocally disestablishing the old organization and by assuring the employees of their freedom from further employer interference with their choice of bargaining representatives.[16]

Remedies for (a) domination or (b) illegal assistance or support not amounting to domination. During the Wagner Act period, the NLRB had a tendency to order unaffiliated dominated unions to be completely disestablished, but in the case of affiliated dominated unions, only to order the employer to withdraw recognition until such time as the affiliated union's majority status could be established by a secret Board election. The "Taft-Hartley" Congress, however, in 1947 amended § 10(c) of the act to put an end to this disparity of treatment. The NLRB's reasoning had been that the affiliated union could probably shake off the effects of the employer's illegal practices, but the Congress thought this

----

[14] 303 U.S. 261 (1938).
[15] 303 U.S. 272 (1938).
[16] NLRB, Sixteenth Annual Report 102 (1951).

was unfair to independent unions, which might also free themselves from employer control.

After examining the above history, the Board concluded in *Carpenter Steel Co.*,[17] that it may no longer concern itself with the affiliation of a union, or the lack thereof, in framing a remedy for violations of § 8(a)(2). The Board said:

> So plain a mandate must be carried out without reservation or purpose of evasion, no matter how great the practical difficulties. Upon similar facts, the Board will hereafter apply the same remedy to both affiliated and unaffiliated labor organizations. Similarity of facts must be the test.
>
> Henceforth the Board's policy will be as follows: In all cases in which we find that an employer has dominated, or interfered with, or contributed support to a labor organization, or has committed any of these proscribed acts, we will find such conduct a violation of Section 8(a)(2) of the Act, as amended in 1947, regardless of whether the organization involved is affiliated. Where we find that an employer's unfair labor practices have been so extensive as to constitute *domination* of the organization, we shall order its disestablishment, whether or not it be affiliated. The Board believes that disestablishment is still necessary as a remedy, in order effectively to remove the consequences of an employer's unfair labor practices and to make possible a free choice of representatives, in those cases, perhaps few in number, in which an employer's control of *any* labor organization has extended to the point of actual domination.

Cases in which the Board has found domination, and hence ordered disestablishment of an affiliated local union are extremely rare.[18]

Indeed, cases in which unaffiliated unions have been found to be dominated, and hence disestablished, have been few in number in recent years, as compared with the flourishing of such "company unions" in the 1930's.[19] Domination is found only where the employer has interfered with the formation of the organization and has assisted and supported its administration to such an extent that it must be regarded as his own creation and subject to his control.

Cases often refuse to find domination, but find the lesser offense of assistance and support.[20]

Employer co-operation with and aid to independent unions or employee committees has been found to constitute insufficient evidence of either domination or the lesser offense of assistance and support.[21]

---

[17] 76 N.L.R.B. 670 (1948).

[18] *See* Jack Smith Beverages, Inc., 94 N.L.R.B. 1401 (1951), *enforced,* 202 F.2d 100 (6th Cir. 1953), *cert. denied,* 345 U.S. 995 (1953).

[19] *See* NLRB v. O.E. Szekely & Associates, Inc., 259 F.2d 652 (5th Cir. 1958).

[20] NLRB v. Wemyss, 212 F.2d 465 (9th Cir. 1954).

[21] Modern Plastics Corp. v. NLRB, 379 F.2d 201 (6th Cir. 1967). For an argument in favor of permissibly assisted employee organizations "which would fill the need for more

During World War II, in order to increase efficiency and productivity, the War Labor Board encouraged the formation of employee committees, which also handled grievances in plants without unions. The employer paid the expenses of these committees. After the War Labor Board authorization ceased, some of these committees lingered on. The Supreme Court held in *NLRB v. Cabot Carbon Co.,*[22] that such committees are "labor organizations," within the meaning of § 8(a)(2), and the employer must disestablish them, if they "deal with him concerning grievances." *See* § 2(5) of the act. Presentation to management of employee "views" and information, without specific recommendations as to what action is needed to accommodate those views, constitutes dealing with management under § 2(5) if the purpose of the management-employee discussion is the correction of grievances.[23]

INTERNATIONAL LADIES GARMENT WORKERS' UNION v. NLRB

[BERNHARD-ALTMANN TEXAS CORP.]

Supreme Court of the United States
366 U.S. 731, 81 S. Ct. 1603, 6 L. Ed. 2d 762 (1961)

Mr. Justice Clark delivered the opinion of the Court.

We are asked to decide in this case whether it was an unfair labor practice for both an employer and a union to enter into an agreement under which the employer recognized the union as exclusive bargaining representative of certain of his employees, although in fact only a minority of those employees had authorized the union to represent their interests. The Board found that by extending such recognition, even though done in the good-faith belief that the union had the consent of a majority of employees in the appropriate bargaining unit, the employer interfered with the organizational rights of his employees in violation of § 8(a)(1) of the National Labor Relations Act and that such recognition also constituted unlawful support to a labor organization in violation of § 8(a)(2). In addition, the Board found that the union violated § 8(b)(1)(A) by its acceptance of exclusive bargaining authority at a time when in fact it did not have the support of a majority of the employees, and this in spite of its bona fide belief that it did. Accordingly, the Board ordered the unfair labor practices discontinued and directed the holding of a representation election. The Court of Appeals, by a divided vote, granted enforcement, 108 U.S. App. D.C. 68, 280 F.2d 616. We granted certiorari. 364 U.S. 811. We agree with the Board and the Court of Appeals that such extension and acceptance of recognition constitute unfair labor practices, and that the remedy provided was appropriate.

---

innovative labor-management structures," *see* Note, *New Standards for Domination and Support Under Section 8(a)(2),* 82 YALE L.J. 510 (1973).

[22] 360 U.S. 203 (1959).

[23] NLRB v. Thompson Ramo Wooldridge, Inc., 305 F.2d 807 (7th Cir. 1962).

In October 1956 the petitioner union initiated an organizational campaign at Bernhard-Altmann Texas Corporation's knitwear manufacturing plant in San Antonio, Texas. No other labor organization was similarly engaged at that time. During the course of that campaign, on July 29, 1957, certain of the company's Topping Department employees went on strike in protest against a wage reduction. That dispute was in no way related to the union campaign, however, and the organizational efforts were continued during the strike. Some of the striking employees had signed authorization cards solicited by the union during its drive, and, while the strike was in progress, the union entered upon a course of negotiations with the employer. As a result of those negotiations, held in New York City where the home offices of both were located, on August 30, 1957, the employer and union signed a "memorandum of understanding." In that memorandum the company recognized the union as exclusive bargaining representative of "all production and shipping employees." The union representative asserted that the union's comparison of the employee authorization cards in its possession with the number of eligible employees representatives of the company furnished it indicated that the union had in fact secured such cards from a majority of employees in the unit. Neither employer nor union made any effort at that time to check the cards in the union's possession against the employee roll, or otherwise, to ascertain with any degree of certainty that the union's assertion, later found by the Board to be erroneous, was founded on fact rather than upon good-faith assumption. The agreement, containing no union security provisions, called for the ending of the strike and for certain improved wages and conditions of employment. It also provided that a "formal agreement containing these terms" would "be promptly drafted . . . and signed by both parties within the next two weeks."

Thereafter, on October 10, 1957, a formal collective bargaining agreement, embodying the terms of the August 30 memorandum, was signed by the parties. The bargaining unit description set out in the formal contract, although more specific, conformed to that contained in the prior memorandum. It is not disputed that as of execution of the formal contract the union in fact represented a clear majority of employees in the appropriate unit. In upholding the complaints filed against the employer and union by the General Counsel, the Board decided that the employer's good-faith belief that the union in fact represented a majority of employees in the unit on the critical date of the memorandum of understanding was not a defense, "particularly where, as here, the Company made no effort to check the authorization cards against its payroll records." 122 N.L.R.B. 1289, 1292. Noting that the union was "actively seeking recognition at the time such recognition was granted," and that "the Union was [not] the passive recipient of an unsolicited gift bestowed by the Company," the Board found that the union's execution of the August 30 agreement was a "direct deprivation" of the nonconsenting majority employees' organizational and bargaining rights. At pp. 1292, 1293, note 9. Accordingly, the Board ordered the employer to withhold all recognition from the union and to cease giving effect to agreements entered into with the union; the union was ordered to cease acting as bargaining representative of any of the employees until such time as a Board-conducted election demonstrated its majority status, and to refrain from seeking to enforce the agreements previously entered. . . .

At the outset, we reject as without relevance to our decision the fact that, as of the execution date of the formal agreement on October 10, petitioner represented a majority of the employees. As the Court of Appeals indicated, the recognition of the minority union on August 30, 1957, was "a *fait accompli* depriving the majority of the employees of their guaranteed right to choose their own representative." 280 F.2d, at 621. It is, therefore, of no consequence that petitioner may have acquired by October 10 the necessary majority if, during the interim, it was acting unlawfully. Indeed, such acquisition of majority status itself might indicate that the recognition secured by the August 30 agreement afforded petitioner a deceptive cloak of authority with which to persuasively elicit additional employee support.

Nor does this case directly involve a strike. The strike which occurred was in protest against a wage reduction and had nothing to do with petitioner's quest for recognition. Likewise, no question of picketing is presented. Lastly, the violation which the Board found was the grant by the employer of exclusive representation status to a minority union, as distinguished from an employer's bargaining with a minority union for its members only. Therefore, the exclusive representation provision is the vice in the agreement, and discussion of "collective bargaining," as distinguished from "exclusive recognition," is pointless. Moreover, the insistence that we hold the agreement valid and enforceable as to those employees who consented to it must be rejected. On the facts shown, the agreement must fail in its entirety. It was obtained under the erroneous claim of majority representation. Perhaps the employer would not have entered into it if he had known the facts. Quite apart from other conceivable situations, the unlawful genesis of this agreement precludes its partial validity.

In their selection of a bargaining representative, § 9(a) of the Wagner Act guarantees employees freedom of choice and majority rule. J. I. Case Co. v. NLRB, 321 U.S. 332, 339 (1944). In short, as we said in Brooks v. NLRB, 348 U.S. 96, 103 (1954), the Act placed "a nonconsenting minority under the bargaining responsibility of an agency selected by a majority of the workers." Here, however, the reverse has been shown to be the case. Bernhard-Altmann granted exclusive bargaining status to an agency selected by a minority of its employees, thereby impressing that agent upon the nonconsenting majority. There could be no clearer abridgement of § 7 of the Act, assuring employees the right "to bargain collectively through representatives of their own choosing" or "to refrain from" such activity. It follows, without need of further demonstration, that the employer activity found present here violated § 8(a)(1) of the Act which prohibits employer interference with, and restraint of, employee exercise of § 7 rights. Section 8(a)(2) of the Act makes it an unfair labor practice for an employer to "contribute . . . support" to a labor organization. The law has long been settled that a grant of exclusive recognition to a minority union constitutes unlawful support in violation of that section, because the union so favored is given "a marked advantage over any other in securing the adherence of employees," NLRB v. Pennsylvania Greyhound Lines, 303 U.S. 261, 267 (1938). In the Taft-Hartley Law, Congress added § 8(b)(1)(A) to the Wagner Act, prohibiting, as the Court of Appeals held, "unions from invading the rights of employees under § 7 in a fashion comparable to the activities of employers prohibited under § 8(a)(1)." 280 F.2d at 620. It was the intent of Congress to impose upon unions the same restrictions which the Wagner Act imposed on employers with respect to violations of employee rights.

The petitioner, while taking no issue with the fact of its minority status on the critical date, maintains that both Bernhard-Altmann's and its own good-faith beliefs in petitioner's majority status are a complete defense. To countenance such an excuse would place in permissibly careless employer and union hands the power to completely frustrate employee realization of the premise of the Act — that its prohibitions will go far to assure freedom of choice and majority rule in employee selection of representatives. We find nothing in the statutory language prescribing *scienter* as an element of the unfair labor practices here involved. The act made unlawful by § 8(a)(2) is employer support of a minority union. Here that support is an accomplished fact. More need not be shown, for, even if mistakenly, the employees' rights have been invaded. It follows that prohibited conduct cannot be excused by a showing of good faith.

This conclusion, while giving the employee only the protection assured him by the Act, places no particular hardship on the employer or the union. It merely requires that recognition be withheld until the Board-conducted election results in majority selection of a representative. The Board's order here, as we might infer from the employer's failure to resist its enforcement, would apparently result in similarly slight hardship upon it. We do not share petitioner's apprehension that holding such conduct unlawful will somehow induce a breakdown, or seriously impede the progress of collective bargaining. If an employer takes reasonable steps to verify union claims, themselves advanced only after careful estimate — precisely what Bernhard-Altmann and petitioner failed to do here — he can readily ascertain their validity and obviate a Board election. We fail to see any onerous burden involved in requiring responsible negotiators to be careful, by cross-checking, for example, well-analyzed employer records with union listings or authorization cards. Individual and collective employee rights may not be trampled upon merely because it is inconvenient to avoid doing so. Moreover, no penalty is attached to the violation. Assuming that an employer in good faith accepts or rejects a union claim of majority status, the validity of his decision may be tested in an unfair labor practice proceeding. If he is found to have erred in extending or withholding recognition, he is subject only to a remedial order requiring him to conform his conduct to the norms set out in the

Act, as was the case here. No further penalty results. We believe the Board's remedial order is the proper one in such cases. NLRB v. District 50, U.M.W., 355 U.S. 453 (1958).

Affirmed.

[MR. JUSTICE DOUGLAS and MR. JUSTICE BLACK dissented in part.]

NOTES

1. Suppose the employer negotiates, with a minority union, an agreement purporting to bind all employees, but conditioned upon the union's obtaining majority status before actual execution of the agreement. The NLRB permitted such conditional negotiation in Julius Resnick, Inc., 86 N.L.R.B. 38 (1949), but found it to be an unfair labor practice in Majestic Weaving Co., 147 N.L.R.B. 859 (1964). The Court of Appeals for the Second Circuit denied enforcement on a procedural ground, but Judge Friendly had this to say:

"We can begin by narrowing the area of debate. The Board no longer maintains that its overruling of the long-standing Resnick decision permitting such conditional negotiation ... was compelled by the Supreme Court's holding that the execution of an agreement recognizing as the exclusive bargaining representative a minority union, mistakenly believed to represent a majority, is an unfair labor practice. . . . Its position is rather, as it has stated elsewhere, that 'the premature grant of exclusive bargaining status to a union,' even if conditioned on attainment of a majority before execution of a contract, is similar to formal recognition 'with respect to the deleterious effect upon employee rights.' 29 NLRB ANN. REP. 69 (1964).

"On our part, we would entertain no difficulty if the Board, after appropriate proceedings, should fashion for prospective application a principle along the general lines of that adopted here; rational basis exists for some such specification of the language of Section 8(a)(2) even in cases like this where no other union was on the scene when the negotiations occurred. The problem arises from the Board's attempt to achieve its desire by a shorter road and in a more summary fashion. . . . In this case, we might well conclude that where for fifteen years the Board considered conditional negotiation consistent with the statutory design 'the ill effect of the retroactive application of a new standard' so far outweighs any demonstrated need for immediate application to past conduct . . . as to render the action 'arbitrary.' APA Section 10(e), 5 U.S.C. Section 1009(e). However, we do not need to decide that serious substantive issue, since we deny enforcement on a procedural ground." NLRB v. Majestic Weaving Co., 355 F.2d 854, 859-61 (2d Cir. 1966).

The NLRB again held it to be an unfair labor practice for an employer to reach an agreement with a union not yet representing a majority, subject to the union's securing signed authorization cards of a majority, in Wickes Corp., 197 N.L.R.B. 128, 80 L.R.R.M. 1458 (1972).

2. This is the first occasion we have had, other than in the historical introduction in Part One at 39, to observe the enforcement of Taft-Hartley prohibitions against *union* unfair labor practices. Detailed materials on the various union unfair practices will appear at appropriate places throughout the book. Unions causing an employer to discriminate will be noted in the next section. Most of the regulation of union collection act, such as strikes, picketing, and secondary boycotts, will be studied in Part Four, and union fines for crossing picket lines will be studied in Part Five, dealing with union-member relations.
with union-member relations.

3. Taft-Hartley amended § 7 to provide that employees have the right to *refrain* from joining unions and engaging in concerted activities, and § 8(b)(1)(A) made it unlawful for a union or its agents to restrain or coerce employees in their exercise of that § 7 right. The basic principle is employee freedom of choice — free from employer coercion under § 8(a)(1) and from union coercion under § 8(b)(1)(A). The point of the principal case is that both the employer and the union interfered with the individual employee's freedom of choice by making an agreement recognizing the union as exclusive bargaining representative before it in fact had a majority of the employees as members. What about their good faith — their lack of wrongful motive? Notice that frequently under § 8(b)(1) and § 8(a)(1), you can have an unfair labor practice without proof of wrongful motive. For example, an employer's nondiscriminatory rule against all forms of solicitation on his property, which may have been in existence and impartially enforced against various kinds of solicitors long before the union ever came upon the scene, violates the act as applied to employee self-organization during nonworking time. Republic Aviation Corp. v. NLRB, 324 U.S. 793 (1945). The reason is that the statutory policy favoring employee self-organization and employee freedom of choice needs to be protected regardless of the respondent's motivation.

4. What are some other forms of union restraint and coercion?

(a) Violence, threats of violence, physical blocking of ingress and egress, and intimidation by following employees through the town. Longshoremen's Local 6, and Sunset Line & Twine Co., 79 N.L.R.B. 1487 (1948).

(b) Threats to individual employees of discharge or other job discrimination. Seamprufe, Inc. (ILGWU), 82 N.L.R.B. 892 (1949), *enforced,* 186 F.2d 671 (10th Cir. 1951), *cert. denied,* 342 U.S. 813 (1951) ("those who do not join the union will eventually lose their jobs").

C. EMPLOYER DISCRIMINATION
1. GENERAL CONSIDERATIONS; PROBLEMS OF PROOF

STATUTORY REFERENCES

RLA § 2, Third, Fourth, Fifth and Eleventh;
NLRA §§ 8(a)(3) and 10(c)

These provisions of the federal acts and their state counterparts are, of course, directed against the most potent antiunion weapon possessed by the employer at common law, namely, his absolute legal control of the job in his plant. He was free to hire, fire, transfer, promote, demote, prefer, layoff, or otherwise deal with employees, subject only to the general pressures of the labor market. The labor relations acts have taken away some of this freedom by forbidding discriminatory treatment for the purpose of encouraging or discouraging union membership. The RLA does not expressly proscribe such discrimination, but the practice is easily encompassed by the broad language of § 2, Fourth and contractual discrimination of the "yellow-dog" variety is outlawed by § 2, Fifth.

It should be apparent at once that the possible kinds of prohibited discrimination are legion. No attempt will be made here to list or catalog them. A reference to any of the labor relations service annotations is suggested for those who are curious as to the varieties of ways in which discrimination has been practiced. For the most part the cases have presented simply questions of fact. But the use of the word "simply" should not be misunderstood as indicating the absence of substantial problems. Perhaps the most troublesome aspect of these cases lies in the fact that overt acts of the kind which are part of every day business management are laid open to interpretation as to motive and effect. It is not an exaggeration to say that *whenever* the employer makes a decision affecting adversely the employment situation of an employee who happens to belong to or to be interested in a union, and some other employee who happens not to belong to or to be interested in a union is not similarly treated, a charge of discrimination *may be made* with the possibility that it will be sustained. And it is important again to remember that the fact question is one which will be decided not by the courts (except under the RLA) but by an administrative tribunal. The lawyer and law student will therefore be interested in the manner in which the labor tribunals approach such questions.

Put yourself in the position of the Administrative Law Judge as you read the following problem cases and think about what factors seem most significant in deciding the employer's real reason for the discharges. In 1972, there were 11,164 charges of discrimination filed — 63% of the total filings against employers.[24]

---

[24] NLRB, THIRTY-SEVENTH ANNUAL REPORT 225 (1972).

PROBLEM I

Mr. James was a trucker for ABC Corp. (engaged in interstate commerce) and had 30 years unblemished service with the company. Late in 1971, however, his performance at his position became somewhat erratic. He began arriving to work a little late, and leaving work a little early. He also began to pick up hitchhikers along his truck route, thereby violating a seldom enforced regulation of the company. His supervisor, Mr. Langland, expressed displeasure with Mr. James' tardiness on several occasions, but dismissal was never recommended because of Mr. James' longstanding excellent record and because the infractions appeared to be minor and easily remedied by docking Mr. James' pay.

In January 1972, Mr. James began to wear a rather inconspicuous union button to work and pasted a union decal onto the cab window of the truck which he regularly drove, again contrary to a seldom enforced regulation against decals on trucks. Mr. Langland noticed the button and decal and called Mr. James into his office for a talk. There, Mr. Langland requested Mr. James to remove the decal from his truck, and Mr. James refused, countering with the argument that all the drivers had decals on their trucks' windows. Mr. Langland insisted on the point, and also criticized Mr. James' tardiness, concluding with a threat of firing if the situation did not improve. Mr. James replied that he could not be fired because he was working with a union and was thereby protected against any discharge.

The next day, Mr. James was told by Mr. Langland that he was immediately discharged and that his pay would be forwarded to him at the end of the pay period. The reasons for the discharge were given as repeated infractions of the company regulations, chronic tardiness, and insubordination.

PROBLEM II

Mr. Larson was a probationary employee for the XYZ Corp., a large manufacturing company engaged in interstate commerce, and as such had the lowest seniority in his 42-man plant section. In early May of 1972, Mr. Larson began to actively advocate unionization of the plant among the other employees during lunch breaks. Mr. Miller, the supervisor, was told of Mr. Larson's organizational activities by a Mr. Sydney, an employee who had been specially recruited by Mr. Miller to keep management informed of such activities. Mr. Miller consequently called Mr. Larson into his office to review the latter's probationary period report, which was, by all accounts, unsatisfactory. Mr. Miller also lectured Mr. Larson on the evils of unionization, but asked Mr. Larson no questions about his own union activities.

On May 25, without any prior warnings, Mr. Larson was told by Mr. Miller that he need not report in at his job the next morning because the XYZ Corp. was being forced to cut back on employees due to an economic slowdown and Mr. Larson, having the least seniority, would be the first employee laid off. Mr. Larson complained that his probationary period was not yet over, and then accused Mr. Miller of antiunion bias in the discharge, to which Mr. Miller replied only that "I have my orders."

The XYZ Corp. retained all other employees, including several other union advocates. Proof was later offered which tended to show that May was a very poor month for the XYZ Corp., but that business in the months both before and after May was above the normal. A new employee was hired on June 15 to perform substantially the same job as Mr. Larson had performed.

NOTES

1. *Burden of proof.* Since the General Counsel is the moving party, he has the burden of proving a violation of the act. Miller Elec. Mfg. Co. v. NLRB, 265 F.2d 225 (7th Cir. 1959).

2. *Preponderance of the testimony taken.* Before the Board may find a violation of the act, it must find, under § 10(c) of the Taft-Hartley Act, that a preponderance of the testimony taken shows that the employer committed an unfair labor practice. In other words, in the "run-of-the-mill" case where a discriminatory discharge is alleged, when the Board looks at all the evidence, it must decide whether a preponderance (more than 50-50 weight) of the testimony shows that the employer's real reason was to discourage union activity, regardless of the stated reason for the discharge. NLRB v. West Point Mfg. Co., 245 F.2d 783 (5th Cir. 1957).

Suppose the employer testifies that his real reason for discharging an employee was some infraction of the company rules. What kind of proof would be required to constitute a "preponderance of the testimony" from which the Board could draw the inference that his real reason was to discourage union activity? *Compare* Edward G. Budd Mfg. Co. v. NLRB, 138 F.2d 86 (3d Cir. 1943), *cert. denied,* 321 U.S. 778 (1943); I. C. Sutton Handle Factory v. NLRB, 255 F.2d 697 (8th Cir. 1958); Wellington Mill Division, West Point Mfg. Co., 141 N.L.R.B. 819 (1963), *enforcement denied in part,* 330 F.2d 579 (4th Cir. 1964), *cert. denied,* 379 U.S. 882 (1964).

Suppose the employer denies that he knew that the discharged employee had been engaging in union activities. What kind of proof is needed to overcome this statement? *See* NLRB, SIXTEENTH ANNUAL REPORT 163 (1952); Bituminous Material & Supply Co., 124 N.L.R.B. 945 (1959); Stokely Foods, Inc., 91 N.L.R.B. 1267, *enforced,* 193 F.2d 736 (5th Cir. 1952); Long Island Airport Limousine Service Corp., 191 N.L.R.B. 94 (1971).

3. *Effect of "for cause" provision of the Taft-Hartley Act, § 10(c).* The conference report (H.R. REP. No. 510 on H.R. 3020, 80th Cong., 1st Sess. 55 (1974)), explained the provision as follows:

"The House bill also included, in Section 10(c) of the amended Act, a provision forbidding the Board to order reinstatement or back pay for any employee who had been suspended or discharged, unless the weight of the evidence showed that the employee was not suspended or discharged for cause. The Senate amendment contained no corresponding provision. The conference agreement omits the 'weight of evidence' language, since the Board, under the general provisions of Section 10, must act on a preponderance of the evidence. . . . Thus employees who are discharged or suspended for interfering with other employees at work, whether or not in order to transact union business, or for engaging in activities, whether or not union activities, contrary to shop rules, or for Communist activities, or for other cause . . . will not be entitled to reinstatement."

NLRB General Counsel, Robert N. Denham, put it this way in an address delivered November 3, 1947, before the St. Louis Bar Ass'n (21 L.R.R.M. 55):

"As I see it, 'good cause,' as the basis of a discharge, must be just as good under the provisions of this Act as it ever has been. . . . If a man is entitled to be discharged and the offenses he has committed are not offenses that customarily have been condoned in other employees, that constitutes good cause. On the other hand, where the offenses are relatively minor and are of a character that have been more or less common within the plant and have been passed over without disciplinary action, but the employee involved is one who has been an active union leader in an atmosphere of some degree of antagonism on the part of the employer, everyone is entitled to look at such a discharge with much questioning. We still are not only entitled, but are obligated to, weigh the bona fides of the so-called 'good cause' and to reject the 'good cause' theory if it has all the earmarks of nothing but a subterfuge."

Thus the question still remains, what was the employer's real reason for discharge?

4. *Employer antiunion statements as evidence.* In the light of § 8(c), may an antiunion statement of an employer be used as evidence that his reason for discharging an employee was to discourage union activity? In this connection, note the following exchange in Congress in the debate on the act (93 CONG. REC. 6604 (1947)):

Senator Pepper. ". . . If an employer were to say on Monday, 'I hate labor unions, and I think they are a menace to this country,' and if he fired a man on Thursday and the question was whether that man was fired for cause or fired because he was agitating for a union in the plant, would the statement made on Monday . . . be admissible in evidence as bearing on the question of the reason for the discharge?"

Senator Taft. "It would depend upon the facts. Under the facts generally stated by the Senator, I think that statement would not be evidence of any threat. There would have to be some other circumstances to tie in with the act of the employer. If the act of discharging is illegal and an unfair labor practice, consideration of such a statement would be proper. But it would not be proper to consider as evidence in such a case a speech which in itself contained no threat express or implied."

See also, Pittsburgh S.S. Co. v. NLRB, 180 F.2d 731, 735 (6th Cir. 1950), *aff'd,* 340 U.S. 498 (1951); and Indiana Metal Prod. Corp. v. NLRB, 202 F.2d 613 (7th Cir. 1953), in which it was held that unless the antiunion statements of the employer contained threats of reprisal or promises of benefit, they were not admissible as evidence of wrongful motivation as regards a discharge.

The cases are legion, however, in which employer statements which *did* contain threats or were otherwise coercive have constituted important evidence of employer hostility relevant for proof of motivation. Senator Taft said in this regard, "It should be noted that this subsection [8(c)] is limited to 'views, argument or opinion' and does not cover instructions, directions or other statements which might be deemed admissions under ordinary rules of evidence. In other words, this section does not make incompetent, evidence which would ordinarily be deemed relevant and admissible in courts of law." 93 CONG. REC. 6601 (1947).

5. *Scope of judicial review.* Prior to the Taft-Hartley Act, the findings of fact of the Board (on such issues as the employer's real reason for a discharge) were conclusive if supported "by evidence," and this was construed by the courts to mean "substantial evidence." The Taft-Hartley Act substituted the language "substantial evidence on the record considered as a whole." What did this add?

The authoritative case in which the Supreme Court dealt with the scope of judicial review under the National Labor Relations Act was Universal Camera Corp. v. NLRB, 340 U.S. 474 (1951). This case should be read in full by every lawyer and student concerned with the work of the NLRB. It is not set out in full here, however, because the student will doubtless deal with it in the course in administrative law.

On the point of immediate interest here Mr. Justice Frankfurter said:

"Whether or not it was ever permissible for courts to determine the substantiality of evidence supporting a Labor Board decision merely on the basis of evidence which in and of itself justified it, without taking into account contradictory evidence or evidence from which conflicting inferences could be drawn, the new legislation definitely precludes such a theory of review and bars its practice. The substantiality of evidence must take into account whatever in the record fairly detracts from its weight. This is clearly the significance of the requirement . . . that courts consider the whole record. . . .

"To be sure, the requirement for canvassing 'the whole record' in order to ascertain substantiality does not furnish a calculus of value by which a reviewing court can assess the evidence. Nor was it intended to negative the function of the Labor Board as one of those agencies presumably equipped or informed by experience to deal with a specialized field of knowledge, whose findings within that field carry the authority of an expertness which courts do not possess and therefore must respect. Nor does it mean that even as to matters not requiring expertise a court may displace the Board's choice between two fairly conflicting views, even though the court would justifiably have made a different choice had the matter been before it *de novo.* Congress has merely made it clear that a reviewing court is not barred from setting aside a Board decision when it cannot conscientiously find that the evidence supporting that decision is substantial, when viewed in the light of evidence that the record in its entirety furnishes, including the body of evidence opposed to the Board's view."

See Jaffe, *Judicial Review: "Substantial Evidence on the Whole Record,"* 64 HARV. L. REV. 1233 (1951).

6. *Where Trial Examiner and NLRB disagree.* Mr. Justice Frankfurter also wrote in *Universal Camera Corp. v. NLRB, supra*:

"We do not require that the examiner's findings be given more weight than in reason and in the light of judicial experience they deserve. The 'substantial evidence' standard is not modified in any way when the Board and its examiner disagree. We intend only to recognize that evidence supporting a conclusion may be less substantial when an impartial, experienced examiner who has observed the witnesses and lived with the case has drawn conclusions different from the Board's than when he has reached the same conclusion. The findings of the examiner are to be considered along with the consistency and inherent probability of testimony. The significance of his report, of course, depends largely on the importance of credibility in the particular case. To give it this significance does not seem to us materially more difficult than to heed the other factors which in sum determine whether evidence is 'substantial.' " 340 U.S. at 496-97.

See Gibson, *The Trial Examiner's Intermediate Report and Its Role in Unfair Labor Practice Cases,* 19 GEO. WASH. L. REV. 23 (1950); *cf.* NLRB v. Pyne Molding Corp., 226 F.2d 818 (2d Cir. 1955).

7. In reviewing discrimination cases, the courts of appeals ordinarily give great weight to the Administrative Law Judge's findings on credibility. MPC Restaurant Corp. v. NLRB, 481 F.2d 75 (2d Cir. 1973); NLRB v. A. & S. Electronics Die Corp., 423 F.2d 218 (2d Cir. 1970), *cert. denied,* 400 U.S. 833 (1970). *But cf.* NLRB v. Elias Bros. Big Boy, 327 F.2d 421 (6th Cir. 1964).

8. Suppose the employer, in discharging an employee who was a union adherent, acts out of mixed motives. Is it sufficient for the Board to show that the discharge was improperly motivated "at least in part"? Berland Paint City, Inc. v. NLRB, 478 F.2d 1405 (7th Cir. 1973), *cert. denied,* 94 S. Ct. 158 (1973); or must the Board show that the improper motive was "dominant"? NLRB v. Fibers International Corp., 439 F.2d 1311 (1st Cir. 1971); Liberty Mutual Ins. Co. v. NLRB, 100 L.R.R.M. 2776 (1st Cir. 1979); or that "the employee would not have been fired *but for* the anti-union animus of the employee"? NLRB v. Whitfield Pickle Co., 374 F.2d 576 (5th Cir. 1967).

9. In NLRB v. Walton Mfg. Co., 369 U.S. 404 (1962), the Fifth Circuit Court of Appeals attempted to apply a special, more onerous rule for review of cases where the remedy would be reinstatement and back pay, since these remedies "may impoverish or break an employer." If the discharger swears that the true reason for the discharge was "not union membership or activity but something else which in fact existed as a ground, his oath cannot be disregarded because of suspicion that he may be lying. There must be impeachment of him, or substantial contradiction, or, if circumstances raise doubts, they must be inconsistent with the positive sworn evidence on the exact point."

However, the Supreme Court reversed and remanded, saying "There is no place in the statutory scheme for one test of the substantiality of evidence in reinstatement cases and another test in other cases."

10. *Intervention by successful party in enforcement and review proceedings.* In UAW Local 283 v. Scofield, and UAW Local 133 v. Fafnir Bearing Co., 382 U.S. 205 (1965), the Court held that parties who are successful in unfair labor practice proceedings before the Board — a charged party when the complaint is dismissed and a charging party when the complaint is sustained in its entirety — have a right to intervene in court of appeals proceedings to review or enforce the Board's order.

Note that giving the successful party before the NLRB the right to intervene in the court of appeals carries with it the right to petition the Supreme Court for a writ of certiorari, which the NLRB and the Solicitor General might not choose to do.

2. DISCRIMINATION TO ENCOURAGE UNION MEMBERSHIP

INTERNATIONAL BROTHERHOOD OF TEAMSTERS, LOCAL 357 v. NLRB

Supreme Court of the United States
365 U.S. 667, 81 S. Ct. 835, 6 L. Ed. 2d 11 (1961)

MR. JUSTICE DOUGLAS delivered the opinion of the Court.

Petitioner union (along with the International Brotherhood of Teamsters and a number of other affiliated local unions) executed a three-year collective bargaining agreement with California Trucking Associations which represented a group of motor truck operators in California. The provisions of the contract relating to hiring of casual or temporary employees were as follows:

"Casual employees shall, wherever the Union maintains a dispatching service, be employed only on a seniority basis in the Industry whenever such senior employees are available. An available list with seniority status will be kept by the Unions, and employees requested will be dispatched upon call to any employer who is a party to this Agreement. Seniority rating of such employees shall begin with a minimum of three months service in the Industry, *irrespective of whether such employee is or is not a member of the Union.*

"Discharge of any employee by any employer shall be grounds for removal of any employee from seniority status. No casual employee shall be employed by any employer who is a party to this Agreement in violation of seniority status if such employees are available and if the dispatching service for such employees is available. The employer shall first call the Union or the dispatching hall designated by the Union for such help. In the event the employer is notified that such help is not available, or in the event the employees called for do not appear for work at the time designated by the employer, the employer may hire from any other available source." (Emphasis added.)

Accordingly the union maintained a hiring hall for casual employees. One Slater was a member of the union and had customarily used the hiring hall. But in August 1955 he obtained casual employment with an employer who was a party to the hiring-hall agreement without being dispatched by the union. He worked until sometime in November of that year, when he was discharged by the employer on complaint of the union that he had not been referred through the hiring-hall arrangement.

Slater made charges against the union and the employer. Though, as plain from the terms of the contract, there was an express provision that employees would not be discriminated against because they were or were not union members, the Board found that the hiring-hall provision was unlawful *per se* and that the discharge of Slater on the union's request constituted a violation by the employer of § 8(a)(1) and § 8(a)(3) and a violation by the union of § 8(b)(2) and § 8(b)(1)(A) of the National Labor Relations Act, as amended by the Taft-Hartley Act, 61 Stat. 140-141, as amended, 29 U.S.C. § 158. The Board ordered, *inter alia*, that the company and the union cease giving any effect to the hiring-hall agreement; that they jointly and severally reimburse Slater for any loss sustained by him as a result of his discharge; and that they jointly and severally reimburse all casual employees for fees and dues paid by them to the union beginning six months prior to the date of the filing of the charge. 121 N.L.R.B. 1629.

The union petitioned the Court of Appeals for review of the Board's action, and the Board made a cross-application for enforcement. That court set aside the portion of the order requiring a general reimbursement of dues and fees. By a divided vote it upheld the Board in ruling that the hiring-hall agreement was illegal *per se*. 107 App. D.C. 188, 275 F.2d 646 (1960). Those rulings are here on certiorari, 363 U.S. 837, one on the petition of the union, the other on petition of the Board.

Our decision in *Carpenters Local 60 v. NLRB*, decided this day, *supra* at 651, is dispositive of the petition of the Board that asks us to direct enforcement of the order of reimbursement. The judgment of the Court of Appeals on that phase of the matter is affirmed.

The other aspect of the case goes back to the Board's ruling in Mountain Pacific Chapter, 119 N.L.R.B. 883. That decision, rendered in 1958, departed from earlier rulings and held, Abe Murdock dissenting, that the hiring-hall agreement, despite the inclusion of a nondiscrimination clause, was illegal, *per se*:

"Here the very grant of work at all depends solely upon union sponsorship, and it is reasonable to infer that the arrangement displays and enhances the Union's power and control over the employment status. Here all that appears is unilateral union determination and subservient employer action with no above-board explanation as to the reason for it, and it is reasonable to infer that the Union will be guided in its concession by an eye towards winning compliance with a membership obligation or union fealty in some other respect. The Employers here have surrendered all hiring authority to the Union and have given advance notice via the established hiring hall to the world at large that the Union is arbitrary master and is contractually guaranteed to remain so. From the final authority over hiring vested in the Respondent Union by the three AGC chapters, the inference of the encouragement of union membership is inescapable." *Id.* 896.

The Board went on to say that a hiring-hall arrangement to be lawful must contain protective provisions. Its views were stated as follows:

"We believe, however, that the inherent and unlawful encouragement of union membership that stems from unfettered union control over the hiring process would be negated, and we would find an agreement to be nondiscriminatory on its face, only if the agreement explicitly provided that:

"(1) Selection of applicants for referral to jobs shall be on a nondiscriminatory basis and shall not be based on, or in any way affected by, union membership, bylaws, rules, regulations, constitutional provisions, or any other aspect or obligation of union membership, policies, or requirements.

"(2) The employer retains the right to reject any job applicant referred by the union.

"(3) The parties to the agreement post in places where notices to employees and applicants for employment are customarily posted, all provisions relating to the functioning of the hiring arrangement, including the safeguards that we deem essential to the legality of an exclusive hiring agreement." *Id.* 897.

The Board recognizes that the hiring hall came into being "to eliminate wasteful, time-consuming, and repetitive scouting for jobs by individual workmen and haphazard uneconomical searches by employers." *Id.* 896, note 8. The hiring hall at times has been a useful adjunct to the closed shop. But Congress may have thought that it need not serve that cause, that in fact it has served well both labor and management — particularly in the maritime field and in the building and construction industry. In the latter the contractor who frequently is a stranger to the area where the work is done requires a "central source" for his employment needs; and a man looking for a job finds in the hiring hall "at least a minimum guarantee of continued employment."

Congress has not outlawed the hiring hall, though it has outlawed the closed shop except within the limits prescribed in the *provisos* to § 8(a)(3). Senator Taft made clear his views that hiring halls are useful, that they are not illegal *per se,* that unions should be able to operate them so long as they are not used to create a closed shop:

"In order to make clear the real intention of Congress, it should be clearly stated that the hiring hall is not necessarily illegal. The employer should be able to make a contract with the union as an employment agency. The union frequently is the best employment agency. The employer should be able to give notice of vacancies, and in the normal course of events to accept men sent to him by the hiring hall. He should not be able to bind himself, however, to reject nonunion men if they apply to him; nor should he be able to contract to accept men on a rotary-hiring basis. . . .

". . . The National Labor Relations Board and the courts did not find hiring halls as such illegal, but merely certain practices under them. The Board and the court found that the manner in which the hiring halls operated created in effect a closed shop in violation of the law. Neither the law nor these decisions forbid hiring halls, even hiring halls operated by the unions as long as they are not so operated as to create a closed shop with all of the abuses possible under such arrangement, including discrimination against employees, prospective employees, members of union minority groups, and operation of a closed union." S. Rep. No. 1827, 81st Cong., 2d Sess., pp. 13, 14.

There being no express ban of hiring halls in any provisions of the Act, those who add one, whether it be the Board or the courts, engage in a legislative act. The Act deals with discrimination either by the employers or unions that encourages or discourages union membership. As respects § 8(a)(3) we said in Radio Officers' Union v. NLRB, 347 U.S. 17, 42, 43 (1954):

"The language of § 8(a)(3) is not ambiguous. The unfair labor practice is for an employer to encourage or discourage membership by means of discrimination. Thus this section does not outlaw all encouragement or discouragement of membership in labor organizations; only such as is accomplished by discrimination is prohibited. Nor does this section outlaw discrimination in employment as such; only such discrimination as encourages or discourages membership in a labor organization is proscribed."

It is the "true purpose" or "real motive" in hiring or firing that constitutes the test. Id. 347 U.S. 43. Some conduct may by its very nature contain the implications of the required intent; the natural foreseeable consequences of certain action may warrant the inference. Id. 347 U.S. 45. And see Republic Aviation Corp. v. NLRB, 324 U.S. 793 (1945). The existence of discrimination may at times be inferred by the Board, for "it is permissble to draw on experience in factual inquiries." Radio Officers' Union v. NLRB, *supra*, 49.

But surely discrimination cannot be inferred from the face of the instrument when the instrument specifically provides that there will be no discrimination against "casual employees" because of the presence or absence of union membership. The only complaint in the case was by Slater, a union member, who sought to circumvent the hiring-hall agreement. When an employer and the union enforce the agreement against union members, we cannot say without more that either indulges in the kind of discrimination to which the Act is addressed.

It may be that the very existence of the hiring hall encourages union membership. We may assume that it does. The very existence of the union has the same influence. When a union engages in collective bargaining and obtains increased wages and improved working conditions, its prestige doubtless rises and, one may assume, more workers are drawn to it. When a union negotiates collective bargaining agreements that include arbitration clauses and supervises the functioning of those provisions so as to get equitable adjustments of grievances, union membership may also be encouraged. The truth is that the union is a service agency that probably encourages membership whenever it does its job well. But as we said in Radio Officers' Union v. NLRB, *supra*, the only encouragement or discouragement of union membership banned by the Act is that which is "accomplished by discrimination." P. 43.

Nothing is inferable from the present hiring-hall provision except that employer and union alike sought to route "casual employees" through the union hiring hall and required a union member who circumvented it to adhere to it.

It may be that hiring halls need more regulation than the Act presently affords. As we have seen, the Act aims at every practice, act, source or institution which in fact is used to encourage and discourage union membership by discrimination in regard to hire or tenure, term or condition of employment. Perhaps the conditions which the Board attaches to hiring-hall arrangements will in time appeal to the Congress. Yet where Congress has adopted a selective system for dealing with evils, the Board is confined to that system. NLRB v. Drivers Local Union, 362 U.S. 274, 284-290 (1960). Where, as here, Congress has aimed its sanctions only at specific discriminatory practices, the Board cannot go farther and establish a broader, more pervasive regulatory scheme.

The present agreement for a union hiring hall has a protective clause in it, as we have said; and there is no evidence that it was in fact used unlawfully. We cannot assume that a union conducts its operations in violation of law or that the parties to this contract did not intend to adhere to its express language. Yet we would have to make those assumptions to agree with the Board that it is reasonable to infer the union will act discriminatorily.

Moreover, the hiring hall, under the law as it stands, is a matter of negotiation between the parties. The Board has no power to compel directly or indirectly that the hiring hall be included or excluded in collective agreements. Cf. NLRB v. American Nat. Ins. Co., 343 U.S. 395, 404 (1952). Its power, so far as here relevant, is restricted to the elimination of discrimination. Since the present agreement contains such a prohibition, the Board is confined to determining whether discrimination has in fact been practiced. If hiring halls are to be subjected to regulation that is less selective and more pervasive, Congress not the Board is the agency to do it.

Affirmed in part and reversed in part.

Mr. Justice Frankfurter took no part in the consideration or decision of this case.

[The concurring opinion of Mr. Justice Harlan, joined in by Mr. Justice Stewart, and the dissenting opinion of Mr. Justice Clark, joined in by Mr. Justice Whittaker, are omitted.]

NOTES

1. The problem in this type of case is somewhat different from the problem in the cases involving the discharge of a union adherent. There the problem was largely a matter of proof on a question of fact — what was the employer's real reason for a discharge: the employee's union activity or something else? Here, however, there is little factual dispute: the employer has discharged an employee or otherwise discriminated against him for some reason connected with his union or nonunion status in a way which encourages union membership, usually under pressure from a union. Both the employer and the union may be guilty of an unfair labor practice — the union for causing or attempting to cause the discrimination (§ 8(b)(2)), and the employer for acquiescing (§ 8(a)(3)). The aggrieved employees may bring their charges against either the union or the employer — or both; but the Board can proceed only against the charged parties.

If the charge is brought only against the union, it is not necessary that the employer be a party; and a back-pay order can run against the union without an order of reinstatement against an employer.

2. In the leading *Radio Officers'* case, cited in the principal case, the Supreme Court held the following to constitute unlawful encouragement of union membership by discrimination: (a) reducing a truck driver's seniority standing because he did not keep up his union dues; (b) causing a ship's radio officer to be refused employment because he did not obtain union clearance, where there was no valid hiring-hall agreement; (c) granting a retroactive wage increase to union members and refusing such benefits to other employees because they were not union members.

3. Consider the following excerpts from the opinion of Mr. Justice Reed in the *Radio Officers'* case:

"Necessity for Proving Employer's Motive.

"The language of § 8(a)(3) is not ambiguous. The unfair labor practice is for an employer to encourage or discourage membership by means of discrimination. Thus this section does not outlaw all encouragement or discouragement of membership in labor organizations; only such as is accomplished by discrimination is prohibited. Nor does this section outlaw discrimination in employment as such; only such discrimination as encourages or discourages membership in a labor organization is proscribed.

"The relevance of the motivation of the employer in such discrimination has been consistently recognized under both § 8(a)(3) and its predecessor. . . .

"That Congress intended the employer's purpose in discriminating to be controlling is clear. The Senate Report on the Wagner Act said: 'Of course nothing in the bill prevents an employer from discharging a man for incompetence; from advancing him for special aptitude; or from demoting him for failure to perform. . . .'

"Proof of Motive.

"But it is also clear that specific evidence of intent to encourage or discourage is not an indispensable element of proof of violation of § 8(a)(3). . . . [A]n employer's protestation that he did not intend to encourage or discourage must be unavailing where a natural consequence of his action was such encouragement or discouragement. Concluding that encouragement or discouragement will result, it is presumed that he intended such consequence. In such circumstances intent to encourage is sufficiently established. . . .

"Power of Board to Draw Inferences.

. . . .

"There is nothing in the language of the amendment itself that suggests denial to the Board of power to draw reasonable inferences. It is inconceivable that the authors of the reports intended such a result for a fact-finding body must have some power to decide which inferences to draw and which to reject. We therefore conclude that insofar as the power to draw reasonable inferences is concerned, Taft-Hartley did not alter prior law. . . ." 347 U.S. at 42-45, 50.

4. Where the charge is brought against the employer for discriminating against an employee, at the union's request, the test is not whether the employer subjectively wanted to encourage union membership (or the adherence to union rules or policies), but whether he must have known that his actions would tend to have that consequence. He will then be held to have intended the natural consequences of his acts. *See* Printz Leather Co., 94 N.L.R.B. 1312 (1951) (employer complied with union demand to discharge employee who refused to cooperate in the concerted effort of his fellow employees to limit production).

5. Under a valid hiring-hall agreement, such as the contract in the *Local 357* case, what kind of evidence would be required to prove that it functioned in actual practice to encourage union membership by discrimination? *See* Lummus Co. v. NLRB, 339 F.2d 728 (D.C. Cir. 1964) (union refused to refer out a member of another local who had given "a hard time" to a member of the union executive committee); NLRB v. Southern Stevedoring & Contr. Co., 332 F.2d 1017 (5th Cir. 1964) (union hiring hall gave direct preference to ILA members over IBL members); NLRB v. Houston Maritime Ass'n, 337 F.2d 333 (5th Cir. 1964) (union hiring hall selected members first and referred nonmembers only if members were not available); Longshoremen Local 13 [Pacific Maritime Ass'n], 192 N.L.R.B. 260 (1971) (hiring hall referred only men sponsored by union members); NLRB v. Plumbers Local 725 [Powers Regulation Co.], 572 F.2d 550 (5th Cir. 1978) (refusal to refer union member for supervisory position even though, as an expectant foreman, member was not a statutory employee).

6. What should be the response of a union operating an exclusive hiring hall when a job referral is demanded by an employee who was discharged from his previous employment for refusing to join the union in accordance with a valid union security agreement? See Asbestos Workers Local 5 (Insulation Specialties Corp.), 191 N.L.R.B. 220 (1971), *enforced,* 464 F.2d 1394 (9th Cir. 1972).

7. Detailed consideration of the provisos to § 8(a)(3), dealing with the union shop and other union security arrangements, will be made in Part Five, *infra* beginning at 851.

———

CARPENTERS LOCAL 60 v. NLRB, 365 U.S. 651, 81 S. Ct. 875, 6 L. Ed. 2d 1 (1961). A company and a union maintained an illegal closed-shop preferential hiring system. Two job applicants were denied employment by the company because they could not obtain referrals from the union. The Labor Board included among other relief its so-called *"Brown-Olds"* remedy [see 115 N.L.R.B. 594 (1956)], requiring the reimbursement to *all* employees of all dues and fees collected by the union under the illegal contract during the six-months' period prior to the filing of the charges. The Supreme Court rejected the Board's refund order. "[T]he power of the Board 'to command affirmative action is remedial, not punitive. . . .' Where no membership in the union was shown to be influenced or compelled by reason of any unfair practice, no 'consequences of violation' are removed by the order compelling the union to return all dues and fees collected from the members. . . ." [Prior to this Supreme Court decision, the NLRB applied the *"Brown-Olds"* remedy against both unions and employers found guilty of unlawful union security arrangements. Often the remedy was used in conjunction with the "Mountain Pacific" hiring hall standards, at issue in *Teamsters Local 357 v. NLRB.*]

NOTE

The enforcement of a clause in a collective bargaining agreement giving union stewards superseniority for purposes other than layoff and recall, such as choice of lucrative delivery routes, violates § 8(a)(3) and (b)(2) in the absence of proof by the union that alternate union inducements would be insufficient to encourage capable workers to become stewards. The NLRB was within the bounds of fairness and reasonableness in drawing the inference that such job preferences would encourage "good, enthusiastic" union membership by discrimination against employees who had worked for the employer longer than the person chosen by the union to be shop steward. NLRB v. Teamsters, Local 338 [Dairylea Cooperative, Inc.], 531 F.2d 1162 (2d Cir. 1976). *But cf.* NLRB v. Auto Warehousers, Inc., 571 F.2d 860 (5th Cir. 1978), where the Fifth Circuit held that a contract clause permitting union stewards to exercise superseniority for purposes beyond layoff and recall is not *per se* invalid. In rejecting NLRB's contention that the clause was unlawful, the court concluded that the legality of including the clause in a collective bargaining contract depended upon the existence of an adequate business justification for such a clause at the time of its execution. As to the application of a contract clause allowing a union to appoint shop stewards on construction sites, see Painters District Council 2, 239 N.L.R.B. No. 192, 100 L.R.R.M. 1152 (1979).

Superseniority for purpose of *layoffs* is presumptively valid in the case of shop stewards in the interest of insuring that there will be someone at the work place to handle grievances and administer the collective agreement. What should be the rule as to union officials other than shop stewards? *See* UE Local 623 [Limpco Mfg.], 230 N.L.R.B. 406 (1977); Otis Elevator Co., 231 N.L.R.B. 1128 (1977); American Can Co., 235 N.L.R.B. No. 102, 98 L.R.R.M. 1013 (1978).

3. PROTECTED CONCERTED ACTIVITIES AND EMPLOYER RESPONSE

"To support a finding that § 8(a)(3) has been violated, the record in the case must show that the complaining employees were in fact discriminated against because of activities protected by § 7 of the Act and that the discrimination tended to encourage or discourage union membership. Section 7 of the Act protects the right of employees to organize for collective bargaining purposes, and to engage in other concerted activities for the purpose of collective bargaining or other mutual aid or protection." [25]

Some concerted activities such as striking for higher wages are obviously protected by § 7 against employer reprisal. (See the *Mackay Radio* case in this section). But even informal action without union organization may be protected, as long as it is "concerted" and "for mutual aid and protection." For example, in *Ohio Oil Co.,*[26] an informal protest against the elimination of overtime work was held protected, although the employees had no authorization from other employees. And in *Root-Carlin, Inc.,*[27] the Board said, where "one employee discusses with another the need for union organization, their action is 'concerted' . . . for it involves more than one employee, even though one be in the role of speaker and the other of listener." Similarly, concerted activity may take place where only one person is seeking to induce action from a group. *Salt River Valley Water Users' Ass'n v. NLRB.*[28]

On the other hand, in *Joanna Cotton Mills Co. v. NLRB,*[29] the court held that circulating a petition for removal of a foreman was not protected where a particular individual was nursing a grudge against a particular foreman and it was not truly being circulated "for mutual aid and protection." And in *NLRB v. Office Towel Supply Co.,*[30] the court held

---

[25] NLRB, Twenty-Third Annual Report 63-64 (1959).

[26] 92 N.L.R.B. 1597 (1951).

[27] 92 N.L.R.B. 1313 (1951).

[28] 206 F.2d 325 (9th Cir. 1953) (circulating a petition for back wages).

[29] 176 F.2d 749 (4th Cir. 1949).

[30] 201 F.2d 838 (2d Cir. 1953).

that mere griping ("This is a hell of a place to work. They expect one girl to do the work of five and a girl doesn't get time to go to the ladies' room") is too inchoate a form of concerted activity to be protected, where the employer had no knowledge that the employee had also discussed with other employees the need for a union.

NOTES

1. In NLRB v. Washington Aluminum Co., 370 U.S. 9 (1962), the Supreme Court held that a group of seven wholly unorganized employees were engaged in protected concerted activity when they walked out of the machine shop where they worked to protest the bitter cold conditions in the shop. They had previously complained about the cold, and they were protected against employer discharge when they took this concerted action, in spite of a company rule which forbade employees to leave their work without permission.

2. In NLRB v. Weingarten, Inc., 420 U.S. 251 (1975), the Supreme Court held that an employer's denial of an employee's request that her union representative be present at an investigatory interview which the employee reasonably believed might result in disciplinary action violated § 8(a)(1) of the NLRA because it interfered with the rights of the employee under § 7 of the Act. The Court agreed with the NLRB that the right to union representation at such interviews falls within the guarantee in § 7 of the right of employees to act in concert for mutual aid and protection. Mr. Justice Powell, dissenting, thought that this was not concerted activity within the meaning of the Act and that the matter is better left to collective bargaining. *See also* Amax, Inc., 227 N.L.R.B. 798 (1977); Coca-Cola Bottling Co., 227 N.L.R.B. 1276 (1977); NLRB v. Columbia University, 541 F.2d 922 (2d Cir. 1976); Mt. Vernon Tanker Co. v. NLRB, 549 F.2d 571 (9th Cir. 1977).

In Glomac Plastics, Inc., 234 N.L.R.B. No. 199, 97 L.R.R.M. 1441 (1978), the Board decided that an employee has a right to representation at an investigative interview even in the absence of a recognized union, where the employer has unlawfully refused to bargain with a certified union. What if there is not a certified union?

3. The NLRB has found protected concerted activity in various situations in which an employee speaks up and seeks to enforce statutory provisions designed for the benefit of all employees; in the absence of any evidence that fellow employees disavow such representation, the Board will infer consent and deem such activity to be concerted. Alleluia Cushion Co., Inc., 221 N.L.R.B. 999 (1975) (occupational safety); Dawson Cabinet Company, 228 N.L.R.B. 290 (1977) (equal pay for women); Self Cycle & Marine Distributor, 237 N.L.R.B. No. 9, 98 L.R.R.M. 1517 (1978) (unemployment compensation appeal).

———

Assuming that the activity is "concerted" and that it is for "the purpose of collective bargaining or other mutual aid or protection," it still may not be protected against employer interference (§ 8(a)(1)) and discrimination (§ 8(a)(3)). Not all concerted activities are protected by § 7. The problem is how to draw the line. In general, it may be said, as the NLRB indicates in its Annual Reports (*see, e.g.,* Twenty-Third Annual Report 64 (1959)), that the activities must have a lawful objective and must be carried on in a lawful manner. But what is meant by the term "lawful" in this connection?

Compare the process that was carried on by the courts at common law in determining what union activities were "lawful," and hence not tortious and enjoinable, according to the objectives-means tests.

Fairly clear are the cases in which the concerted activities are for an objective which is outlawed by the Taft-Hartley Act itself as a union unfair labor practice. It would not effectuate the policies of the act to afford relief against employer reprisal to employees who were themselves violating the act. "For example, the act expressly prohibits jurisdictional strikes, secondary boycotts, and strikes for recognition in defiance of a certified union." *See* Local 1229, Electrical Workers v. NLRB, 202 F.2d 186, 187 (D.C. Cir. 1952). Employees who engage in recognition picketing in violation of § 8(b)(7) lose their protected status under the Act, and an employer may lawfully refuse to reinstate them. Claremont Polychemical Corp., 196 N.L.R.B. 613 (1972) (one member dissenting).

The principal problem in this kind of a case would be whether the illegal conduct of the union and its agents can be attributed to the individual employee.

Other forms of concerted activity which are unprotected because the objective is illegal include:

a. A strike to force the employer to grant a wage increase in violation of a wartime wage stabilization statute, requiring approval by the War Labor Board of all wage increases. NLRB v. Indiana Desk Co., 149 F.2d 987 (7th Cir. 1945); American News Co., 55 N.L.R.B. 1302 (1944).

b. A strike or a boycott to compel an employer to commit an employer unfair labor practice. Hoover Co. v. NLRB, 191 F.2d 380 (6th Cir. 1951); Thompson Prod., Inc., 72 N.L.R.B. 886 (1947).

Even though the objective is legal, the protection of the NLRA is withdrawn if the concerted activity is tortious or criminal in nature. For example, action involving sitdown strikes (forcible seizure of property), NLRB v. Fansteel Metallurgical Corp., 306 U.S. 240 (1939), or mutiny in violation of the federal criminal code, Southern S.S. Co. v. NLRB, 316 U.S. 31 (1942).

The most difficult cases are those in which the concerted activities are not illegal in the strict sense but in which, for various considerations of public policy, including regard for the employer's basic rights, the concerted activity appears to be questionable, indefensible, and not the sort of thing which the members of Congress, had they thought about it, probably would have intended to protect against employer reprisals.

ELK LUMBER CO.

National Labor Relations Board
91 N.L.R.B. 333 (1950)

[The General Counsel's complaint alleged that the respondent Elk Lumber Company had violated §§ 8(a)(1) and 8(a)(3) of the act by discharging five employees because they engaged in protected concerted activity to protest a change in the method of wage payment.]

The Respondent contends, and the Trial Examiner apparently found, that the five carloaders were discharged, not for having engaged in concerted activities, as alleged in the complaint, but because their production was not satisfactory. It is clear, however, that their failure to produce was the result of an agreement to slow down. In our opinion, therefore, the only question presented is whether this conduct was a form of concerted activity protected by the act. We believe, contrary to the contention of the General Counsel, that it was not.

Section 7 of the act guarantees to employees the right to engage in concerted activities for the purpose of collective bargaining or other mutual aid or protection. However, both the Board and the courts have recognized that not every form of activity that falls within the letter of this provision is protected. The test, as laid down by the Board in the *Harnischfeger Corporation* case, and referred to with apparent approval by the Supreme Court in the recent *Wisconsin* case [UAWA-AFL v. WERB, 336 U.S. 245], is whether the particular activity involved is so indefensible as to warrant the employer in discharging the participating employees. Either an unlawful objective or the adoption of improper means of achieving it may deprive employees engaged in concerted activities of the protection of the act.

Here, the objective of the carloaders' concerted activity — to induce the Respondent to increase their hourly rate of pay or to return to the piecework rate — was a lawful one. To achieve this objective, however, they adopted the plan of decreasing their production to the amount they considered adequate for the pay they were then receiving. In effect, this constituted a refusal on their part to accept the terms of employment set by their employer without engaging in a stoppage, but to continue rather to work on their own terms. The courts, in somewhat similar situations, have held that such conduct is justifiable cause for discharge. Thus, in the *Conn* case [108 F.2d 390], the Court of Appeals for the Seventh Circuit found that the employer was justified in discharging employees who refused to work overtime, saying:

"We are aware of no law or logic that gives the employee the right to work upon terms prescribed solely by him. That is plainly what was sought to be done in this instance. It is not a situation in which employees ceased work in protest against conditions imposed by the employer, but one in which the employees sought and intended to work upon their own notion of the terms which should prevail. If they had a right to fix the hours of their employment, it would follow that a similar right existed by which they could prescribe all conditions and regulations affecting their employment."

And in the *Montgomery Ward* case [157 F.2d 486], in which employees at one of the employer's plants refused to process orders from another plant where a strike was in progress, the Court of Appeals for the Eighth Circuit said:

"It was implied in the contract of hiring that these employees would do the work assigned to them in a careful and workmanlike manner; that they would comply with all reasonable orders and conduct themselves so as not to work injury to the employer's business; that they would serve faithfully and be regardful of the interests of the employer during the term of their service, and carefully discharge their duties to the extent reasonably required. . . . Any employee may, of course, be lawfully discharged for disobedience of the employer's directions in breach of his contract. . . . While these employees had the undoubted right to go on a strike and quit their employment, they could not continue to work and remain at their positions, accept the wages paid them, and at the same time select what part of their allotted tasks they cared to perform of their own volition, or refuse openly or secretly to the employer's damage, to do other work."

We believe that the principle of these decisions is applicable to the situation before us, and that, under the circumstances, the carloaders' conduct justified their discharge.

The General Counsel contends, however, that "if such activity [a slowdown] is to be condemned by the Board, it should only be done after there has been a deliberate refusal to do the Employer's bidding," and that here, "at the time of discharge there still had been no failure to comply with any command of management." In support of this contention, he asserts that "after the outset of this slowdown, the Employer obviously acquiesced in it and made no protest"; that it "did not set a definite rate [of production], nor did it make any statement as to what rate of production was considered accurate"; and that it discharged the men "without any warning or reason being given."

On the record before us, however, we find no convincing evidence that the Respondent at any time acquiesced in the slowdown. . . .

Furthermore, although the Respondent admittedly did not tell the carloaders how many cars a day they were expected to load, and, so far as the present record shows, did not warn them that they would be discharged if they did not increase their production, it is clear that the men knew that the rate they had adopted was not satisfactory. Despite this knowledge, they continued to load fewer cars a day than they could have loaded, or than they would have loaded for more money. Under these particular circumstances, we regard it as immaterial that the Respondent had given them no express order as to the amount of work required, or any warning that they would be discharged if they failed to meet the requirement.

We therefore find that the Respondent did not violate the act by discharging the five carloaders named in the complaint. As no other unfair labor practices are alleged, we affirm and adopt the Trial Examiner's ruling dismissing the complaint in its entirety. . . .

NOTES

1. *See also* Raleigh Water Heater Mfg. Co., 136 N.L.R.B. 76 (1962) (slowdown); Scott Lumber Co., Inc., 117 N.L.R.B. 1790, 1824 (1957) (concerted refusal to do certain assigned work held unprotected as insubordination).

2. "Partial" strikes of various varieties have been held to constitute unprotected concerted activity. Some of the leading cases were discussed in the *Elk Lumber* case above. *See also* Honolulu Rapid Transit Co., 110 N.L.R.B. 1806 (1954) (weekend and intermittent strikes); Pacific Tel. & Tel. Co., 107 N.L.R.B. 1547 (1954) ("hit-and-run" unannounced work stoppages); Valley City Furniture Co., 110 N.L.R.B. 1589 (1954), *enforced,* 230 F.2d 947 (6th Cir. 1956) (one-hour a day strikes).

3. In Hoover Co. v. NLRB, 191 F.2d 380 (6th Cir. 1951), after holding that a consumer boycott was unprotected because it was for an unlawful purpose — forcing the employer to recognize and deal with a union at a time when an NLRB election was pending, which would be an employer unfair labor practice — the court further stated, at 389-90:

"But even if the purpose of the boycott had changed, the employees in question would not, in that case, be entitled to be reinstated. It is held that the right to strike requires that strikers who exercise it must thereby cease to work and draw their pay. NLRB v. Montgomery Ward & Co., Inc., 8 Cir., 157 F.2d 486. An employee cannot work and strike at the same time. He cannot continue in his employment and openly or secretly refuse to do his work. He cannot collect wages for his employment, and, at the same time, engage in activities to injure or destroy his employer's business. . . .

"Of course, an employee can engage in 'concerted activity for mutual aid and protection' even though it may be highly prejudicial to his employer, and results in his customers' refusal to deal with him, just as long as such activity is not a wrong done to the company. NLRB v. Peter Cailler Kohler Swiss Chocolates Co., Inc., 2 Cir., 130 F.2d 503. In the instant case, it appears, however, that not only were the members of the Local and International, and other unions, asked to boycott the company's products, but, in the strike bulletin of the Local which was distributed to the company's employees, it was stated: 'SALESMEN HELP — Salesmen for rival cleaners have contacted Local 709 for literature about the Hoover Company's Union-busting activities. Apparently, these salesmen intend to help our boycott campaign against Hoovers in order to promote the sale of their own products.' It is a wrong done to the company for employees, while being employed and paid wages by a company, to engage in a boycott to prevent others from purchasing what their employer is engaged in selling and which is the very thing their employer is paying them to produce. An employer is not required, under the Act, to finance a boycott against himself."

4. The Court of Appeals for the District of Columbia Circuit was critical of this rather loose test of unprotected concerted activity and suggested a somewhat tighter test — whether the activity was "unlawful," as explained in the following quotation:

"Protection under § 7 of the Act, then, is withdrawn only from those concerted activities which contravene either (a) specific provisions or basic policies of the Act or of related federal statutes, or (b) specific rules of other federal or local law that is not incompatible with the Board's governing statute. . . . More recently, the Board in the *Hoover Co.* case reiterated the correct rule when it declared that it is 'not free . . . to measure concerted activity in terms of whether the conduct is wise or fair, or satisfies standards which we think desirable.' 90 N.L.R.B. 1614, 1621 (1950), *rev'd* on another ground, i.e., that the concerted action intended to force the employer to violate the Act, Hoover Co. v. NLRB, 191 F.2d 380 (6th Cir. 1951). We disagree with the court's suggestion by way of dictum that even if the objectives as well as the means of the boycott were lawful, the protection of the Act could be withdrawn. 191 F.2d at page 389 et seq." IBEW Local 1229 v. NLRB, 202 F.2d 186, 188 n.11 (D.C. Cir. 1952).

The Supreme Court granted certiorari in the *Local 1229* case and resolved the problem by resorting to still another test: whether the employees' conduct was such that their discharge could be found to be "for cause" within the meaning of § 10(c) of the Taft-Hartley Act. "Cause," in turn, was found to depend upon whether the employees' conduct was "disloyal." On the facts of the case, the Supreme Court found such disloyalty. During the course of a collective bargaining dispute, the TV technicians, while remaining on the job, distributed handbills in their off-hours to the public criticizing the TV station for failing to purchase the equipment needed to present live programs and suggesting that the company was treating "Charlotte as a second-class city" by putting on only programs which were on film. The handbills made no reference to the union, to a labor controversy or to collective bargaining. The Court found that this "sharp, public disparaging attack upon the quality of the Company's product and its business policies, in a manner reasonably calculated to harm the Company's reputation and reduce its income," was a demonstration of such detrimental disloyalty as to provide cause for the company's refusal to continue in its employ the perpetrators of the attack. NLRB v. IBEW Local 1229 [Jefferson Standard Broadcasting Co.], 346 U.S. 464 (1953). (Justices Frankfurter, Black, and Douglas dissented.)

5. Suppose that (a) the handbill, in the *Local 1229* case, had been distributed while the employees were on strike, and (b) the handbill had stated an appeal for public support in the union's current labor dispute with the company? *Cf.* Patterson-Sargent Co., 115 N.L.R.B. 1627 (1956), where several employees were discharged for distributing the following handbill to consumers during a strike at a paint company:

"Beware Paint Substitute"

"The employees of the Patterson-Sargent Company in Cleveland who manufacture paint under the brand of B.P.S., were forced on strike by the Company. As a result, there is not being manufactured any paint at the Patterson-Sargent Company in Cleveland by the well-trained, experienced employees who have made the paint you have always bought.

"This is a warning that you should make certain that any B.P.S. paint you buy is made by the regular employees who know the formulas and the exact amount of ingredients to put into paint. If you should happen to get paint which is made by any other than the regular, well-trained experienced workers, it might not do for you what you want it to do. It could peel, crack, blister, scale or any one of many undesirable things that would cause you inconvenience, lost time and money.

"Stop! Think! Is it worth your while to risk spending your good money for a product which might not be what you are accustomed to using? You will be informed when you can again buy B.P.S. paint which is made by the regular employees in Cleveland."

The NLRB split 3-2, the majority holding this conduct to be a disloyal disparagement of the employer's product and hence unprotected and good cause for discharge under the principles of the *Local 1229* case. The minority argued that since the handbill was distributed during a strike and its contents showed a direct relation to a current labor dispute, its distribution should be regarded as protected concerted activity. *Compare* Boeing Airplane Co. v. NLRB, 238 F.2d 188 (9th Cir. 1956).

6. PROBLEM: A Trial Examiner of the NLRB found National Furniture Mfg. Co. guilty of unfair labor practices and recommended that it be ordered to reinstate six employees who had been discriminatorily discharged and to bargain with the union. Upon request, the company did reinstate the six employees, but bargaining had not begun, and the company was challenging the Trial Examiner's conclusions before the NLRB. As was customary, the company closed down from December 23 to January 15 for inventory, and employees were laid off. The company executives went to the annual Furniture Mart in Chicago to meet buyers. The above six employees went too, handing out handbills at the entrance of the mart stating that National had been found guilty of unfair labor practices and that the company still had not fulfilled the remedy which the Trial Examiner had recommended. The handbill asked for help and support in inducing National to do the right thing and stop undermining the labor conditions of fair-minded furniture manufacturers who had union contracts. National promptly discharged the men. Was there "protected concerted activity" or "discharge for cause"? *See* NLRB v. National Furniture Mfg. Co., 315 F.2d 280 (7th Cir. 1963).

7. Concerted activities which contravene a basic policy of the National Labor Relations Act, such as the promotion of stable collective bargaining

relationships and the sanctity of collective agreements, have also been held to be unprotected, and hence employees who engage in such activities cannot complain about employer discharges for such activity. Examples are "wildcat" strikes in derogation of the authority of the recognized collective bargaining representative, NLRB v. Sunbeam Lighting Co., 318 F.2d 661 (7th Cir. 1963); Harnischfeger Corp. v. NLRB, 207 F.2d 575 (7th Cir. 1953); NLRB v. Draper Corp., 145 F.2d 199 (4th Cir. 1944). *But see,* NLRB v. R.C. Can Co., 328 F.2d 974 (5th Cir. 1964). An interesting discussion of the problem is found in Gould, *The Status of Unauthorized and "Wildcat" Strikes Under the National Labor Relations Act,* 52 CORNELL L.Q. 672 (1967).

Expressing doubts about the continued validity of its *R.C. Can* decision, the Fifth Circuit decided that an employer which was engaged in bargaining with a newly certified union did not violate the NLRA when it discharged a minority of its employees for participating in an unauthorized strike. NLRB v. Shop Rite Foods, Inc., 430 F.2d 786 (5th Cir. 1970). The Labor Board had found the strike to be protected, since the minority action was in support of an apparent union goal, the protection of a discharged employee. The court concluded, however, that the *R.C. Can* reasoning followed by the Board should be restricted: "*R.C. Can* concerned a very narrow set of circumstances in which the minority action was directed toward a specific, previously considered and articulated union objective. If union objectives are characterized in general terms — such as wages, job security, conditions of employment and the like — one can assume that in a great majority of instances minority action will be consistent with one or more of these objectives. If *R.C. Can* is not applied with great care, it would allow minority action in a broad range of circumstances and permit unrestrained undercutting of collective bargaining." Here the minority action occurred spontaneously, before the union had acted on the issue in question. *See also* Lee A. Consaul Co., 469 F.2d 84 (9th Cir., 1972), declining to follow the *R.C. Can* approach and holding that wildcat strikers were unprotected.

8. Another example of concerted activity which was held to be unprotected because it was in derogation of the authority of the exclusive bargaining representative occurred in Emporium Capwell Co. v. Western Addition Community Organization, 420 U.S. 50 (1975). The union was in the process of taking employee complaints of racial discrimination in job assignments through the contractual grievance procedure. Two black employees, feeling that procedure inadequate, picketed the store and demanded to deal directly with the company president. The company warned the employees that they might be fired for their activities. They refused to desist, and the company discharged them. The company was charged with a violation of § 8(a)(1), but the NLRB and the Supreme Court held that this bypassing of the grievance procedure in favor of attempting to bargain separately with the employer for a minority group was not protected by § 7 of the Act. For a full report of the case, *see* p. 489, *infra. And see,* Cantor, *Dissident Worker Action, After the Emporium,* 29 RUTGERS L. REV. 35 (1975).

What if the minority picketers protesting alleged racial discrimination had not tried to go through the exclusive bargaining representative at all? *See* NLRB v. Tanner Motor Livery, Ltd., 419 F.2d 216 (9th Cir. 1969).

MASTRO PLASTICS CORP. v. NLRB

Supreme Court of the United States
350 U.S. 270, 76 S. Ct. 349, 100 L. Ed. 309 (1956)

[The petitioners were in the plastics manufacturing business in New York, and were working under a one-year collective bargaining agreement with the Carpenters Union governing wages, hours, and working conditions. The agreement provided for arbitration of disputes and contained a clause outlawing strikes. The agreement was due to expire on November 30, 1950. The Carpenters Union gave notice of a desire to negotiate new conditions of employment on October 10, 1950. Therefore, the 60-day "cooling-off" period prescribed in § 8(d)(4) would end on December 8, 1950.

[During the life of this agreement the Wholesale and Warehouse Workers Union sought to displace the Carpenters as the bargaining representative of petitioner's employees. In an effort to keep the Warehouse Workers out of their plant, petitioners, not believing the Carpenters strong enough for the task, enlisted the aid of a third union, the Pulp, Sulphite and Paper Mill Workers. Petitioners unlawfully assisted the Pulp, Sulphite and Paper Mill Workers in its organizational activities, causing the Carpenters to file unfair labor practice charges with the Board. Some members of the incumbent Carpenters Union tried to counteract the influence of petitioners upon the employees, and one of these, Ciccone, was discharged for his activities on November 10.

[The discharge of Ciccone, in conjunction with the antecedent employer unfair labor practices, precipitated a plant-wide strike accompanied by peaceful picketing, although neither the contract nor the 60-day waiting period had expired. The strikers made no demands relating to contract negotiations but offered to return to work if Ciccone were reinstated. The request was rejected by petitioner who notified the strikers of their discharge.

[In the ensuing unfair labor practice proceedings petitioner opposed reinstatement of the strikers upon two grounds: (1) because they had struck in breach of contract; and (2) because they lost their status as employees when they struck during the 60-day waiting period required by § 8(d) of the Taft-Hartley Act.]

MR. JUSTICE BURTON delivered the opinion of the Court:

. . . .

In the absence of some contractual or statutory provision to the contrary, petitioners' unfair labor practices provide adequate ground for the orderly strike that occurred here. Under those circumstances, the striking employees do not lose their status and are entitled to reinstatement with back pay, even if replacements for them have been made. Failure of the Board to enjoin petitioners' illegal conduct or failure of the Board to sustain the right to strike against that conduct would seriously undermine the primary objectives of the Labor Act. See NLRB v. [International] Rice Milling Co., 341 U.S. 665, 673. While we assume that the employees, by explicit contractual provision, could have waived their right to strike against such unfair labor practices and that Congress, by explicit statutory provision, could have deprived strikers, under the circumstances of this case, of their status as employees, the questions before us are whether or not such a waiver was made by the Carpenters in their 1949-1950 contract and whether or not such a deprivation of status was enacted by Congress in § 8(d) of the act, as amended in 1947.

I. *Does the collective-bargaining contract waive the employees' right to strike against the unfair labor practices committed by their employers?* The answer turns upon the proper interpretation of the particular contract before us. Like other contracts, it must be read as a whole and in the light of the law relating to it when made. . . .

On the premise of fair representation, collective-bargaining contracts frequently have included certain waivers of the employees' right to strike and of the employers' right to lockout to enforce their respective economic demands during the term of those contracts. *Provided the selection of the bargaining representative remains free,* such waivers contribute to the normal flow of commerce and to the maintenance of regular production schedules. Individuals violating such clauses appropriately lose their status as employees.

The waiver in the contract before us, upon which petitioners rely, is as follows:

"5. The Union agrees that during the term of this agreement, there shall be no interference of any kind with the operations of the Employers, or any interruptions or slackening of production of work by any of its members. The Union further agrees to refrain from engaging in any strike or work stoppage during the term of this agreement."

That clause expresses concern for the continued operation of the plant and has a natural application to strikes and work stoppages involving the subject matter of the contract. . . .

Petitioners argue that the words "any strike" leave no room for interpretation and necessarily include all strikes, even those against unlawful practices destructive of the foundation on which collective bargaining must rest. We disagree. We believe that the contract, taken as a whole, deals solely with the economic relationship between the employers and their employees. It is a typical collective-bargaining contract dealing with terms of employment and the normal operations of the plant. It is for one year and assumes the existence of a lawfully designated bargaining representative. Its strike and lockout clauses are natural adjuncts of an operating policy aimed at avoiding interruptions of production prompted by efforts to change existing economic relationships. The main function of arbitration under the contract is to provide a mechanism for avoiding similar stoppages due to disputes over the meaning and application of the various contractual provisions.

To adopt petitioners' all-inclusive interpretation of the clause is quite a different matter. That interpretation would eliminate, for the whole year, the employees' right to strike, even if petitioners, by coercion, ousted the employees' lawful bargaining representative and, by threats of discharge, caused the employees to sign membership cards in a new union. Whatever may be said of the legality of such a waiver when explicitly stated, there is no adequate basis for implying its existence without a more compelling expression of it than appears in § 5 of this contract. . . .

II. *Does § 8(d) of the National Labor Relations Act, as amended, deprive individuals of their status as employees if, within the waiting period prescribed by § 8(d)(4), they engage in a strike solely against unfair labor practices of their employers?* . . . .

The language in § 8(d) especially relied upon by petitioners is as follows: "Any employee who engages in a strike within the sixty-day period specified in this subsection shall lose his status as an employee of the employer engaged in the particular labor dispute, for the purposes of §§ 8, 9, and 10 of this Act, as amended. . . ."

Petitioners contend that the above words must be so read that employees who engage in any strike, regardless of its purpose, within the 60-day waiting period, thereby lose their status as employees. That interpretation would deprive Ciccone and his fellow strikers of their rights to reinstatement and would require the reversal of the judgment of the Court of Appeals. If the above words are read in complete isolation from their context in the Act, such an interpretation is possible. However, "In expounding a statute, we must not be guided by a single sentence or member of a sentence, but look to the provisions of the whole law, and its object and policy." United States v. Boisdore's Heirs, 8 How. 113, 122. . . .

Reading the clause in conjunction with the rest of § 8, the Board points out that "the sixty-day period" referred to is the period mentioned in paragraph (4) of § 8(d). That pargraph requires the party giving notice of a desire to *"terminate or modify"* such a contract, as part of its obligation to bargain under § 8(a)(5) or § 8(b)(3), to continue "in full force and effect, without resorting to strike or lockout, all the terms and conditions of the existing contract for a period of sixty days after such notice is given or until the expiration date of such contract, whichever occurs later." Section 8(d) thus seeks, during this natural renegotiation period, to relieve the parties from the economic pressure of a strike or lockout in relation to the subjects of negotiation. The final clause of § 8(d) also warns employees that, if they join a proscribed strike, they shall thereby lose their status as employees and, consequently, their right to reinstatement.

The Board reasons that the words which provide the key to a proper interpretation of § 8(d) with respect to this problem are "termination or modification." Since the Board expressly found that the instant strike was *not to terminate or modify* the contract, but was designed instead to protest the unfair labor practices of petitioners, the loss-of-status provision of § 8(d) is not applicable. We sustain that interpretation. Petitioners' construction would produce incongruous results. It concedes that prior to the 60-day negotiating period, employees have a right to strike against unfair labor practices designed to oust the employees' bargaining representative, yet petitioners' interpretation of § 8(d) means that if the employees give the 60-day notice of their desire to modify the contract, they are penalized for exercising that right to strike. This would deprive them of their most effective weapon at a time when their need for it is obvious. Although the employees' request to modify the contract would demonstrate their need for the services of their freely chosen representative, petitioners' interpretation would have the incongruous effect of cutting off the employees' freedom to strike against unfair labor practices aimed at that representative. This would relegate the employees to filing charges under a procedure too slow to be effective. The result would unduly favor the employers and handicap the employees during negotiation periods contrary to the purpose of the act. There also is inherent inequity in any interpretation that penalizes one party to a contract for conduct induced solely by the unlawful conduct of the other, thus giving advantage to the wrongdoer.

Petitioners contend that, unless the loss-of-status clause is applicable to unfair labor practice strikes, as well as to economic strikes, it adds nothing to the existing law relating to loss of status. Assuming that to be so, the clause is justifiable as a clarification of the law and as a warning to employees against engaging in economic strikes during the statutory waiting period. Moreover, in the face of the affirmative emphasis that is placed by the act upon freedom of concerted action and freedom of choice of representatives, any limitation on the employees' right to strike against violations of §§ 7 and 8(a), protecting those freedoms, must be more explicit and clear than it is here in order to restrict them at the very time they may be most needed. . . .

As neither the collective-bargaining contract nor § 8(d) of the National Labor Relations Act, as amended, stands in the way, the judgment of the Court of Appeals is

Affirmed.

Mr. Justice Frankfurter, whom Mr. Justice Minton and Mr. Justice Harlan join, dissenting.

. . . .

. . . The Board and the Court of Appeals rightly held that the "no-strike" clause in the contract does not cover a work stoppage provoked by the petitioners' unfair labor practices. . . . Petitioners contend that the discharged workers lost their status as employees by reason of the 60-day "cooling-off" period provided by § 8(d) of the act. . . .

. . . Section 8 of the Wagner Act was amended [by the Taft-Hartley Act] and duties were placed upon unions. Collective action which violates any of these duties is, of course, activity unprotected by § 7. See Cox, The Right to Engage in Concerted Activities, 26 Ind. L.J. 319, 325-333 (1951). One of these new union duties, and an important one, is contained in § 8(d): unions may not strike to enforce their demands during the 60-day "cooling-off" period.

By reason of this new enactment, participating workers would not be engaged in a protected activity under § 7 by striking for the most legitimate economic reasons during the 60-day period. The strike would be in violation of the provision of that section which says that during the period there shall be no resort to a strike. The employer could discharge such strikers without violating § 8. This would be so if § 8 were without the loss-of-status provision. The Board would be powerless to order reinstatement under § 10. The loss-of-status provision in § 8(d) does not curtail the Board's power, since it did not have power to order reinstatement where a strike is resorted to for economic reasons before the 60-day period has expired. In such a situation the striker has no rights under §§ 8 and 10. Yet the Board would have us construe the loss-of-status provision as applicable only to the economic striker and qualifying a power which the Board does not have.

It is with respect to the unfair-labor-practice striker that the provision serves a purpose. This becomes clear if we assume that there were no such provision and examine the consequences of its absence. On such an assumption, a strike based on an unfair labor practice by the employer during the 60-day period may or may not be a protected activity under § 7. If it is, obviously discharged strikers would be entitled to reinstatement. The strike would not be a § 7 activity, however, if, for example, it were in breach of a no-strike clause in the contract which extends to a work stoppage provoked by an employer unfair labor practice, cf. NLRB v. Sands Mfg. Co., 306 U.S. 332, 344 (1939), or if the no-strike clause in § 8(d)(4) (not to be confused with the loss-of-status provision) extends to such a work stoppage. However, even if the strike is not a § 7 activity, the Board in the unfair-labor-practice strike situation as distinguished from the economic strike situation, may in its discretion order the discharged participants reinstated. This is so because of the antecedent employer unfair practice which caused the strike, and which gave employees rights under § 8. If the Board finds that reinstatement of such strikers is a remedy that would effectuate the policies of the act, it has the power under § 10(c) to issue the necessary order.

This would not be the case, however, if the loss-of-status provision were held applicable to unfair-labor-practice strikes, because participating workers would lose their rights as "employees" for the purposes of §§ 8 and 10. Under the act only "employees" are eligible for reinstatement. The unfair-labor-practice strike, then, is the one situation where loss of status for the purposes of §§ 8 and 10 is of significance. At any rate, we have not been advised of any other situation to which the provision would apply.

We are therefore confronted with the demonstrable fact that if the provision stripping strikers of their status as employees during the 60-day period is to have any usefulness at all and not be an idle collection of words, the fact that a strike during that period is induced by the employer's unfair labor practice is immaterial.[1] Even though this might on first impression seem an undesirable result, it is so only by rejecting the important considerations in promoting peaceful industrial relations which might well have determined the action of Congress. In the first place, the Congress may have set a very high value on peaceful adjustments, *i.e.,* the absence of strikes. One may take judicial notice of the fact that this consideration was at the very forefront of the thinking and feeling of the Eightieth Congress. And there is another consideration not unrelated to this. While in a particular case the cause of a strike may be clear, and in a particular case there may be no controversy regarding the circumstances which prove that an employer committed an unfair labor practice, as a matter of experience that is not always true, indeed often it is not true. One of the sharpest controversies, one of the issues most difficult of determination, is the very question of what precipitated a work stoppage. This is especially true where a new contract is being negotiated. It is not at all unreasonable, therefore, to find a congressional desire to preclude litigation over what all too often is a contentious subject and to deter all strikes during the crucial period of negotiation. . . .

. . . Since the loss-of-status provision has an effect only in an unfair-labor-practice strike, the judgment of the Court of Appeals should be reversed.

NOTES

1. A walkout in good faith because of abnormally dangerous conditions for work is specifically protected under § 502 of the LMRA. Therefore, it is not considered a strike within the meaning of a "no-strike" clause. NLRB v. Knight Morley Co., 251 F.2d 753 (6th Cir. 1957), *cert. denied,* 357 U.S. 927 (1958).

2. Does the reasoning of the *Mastro Plastics* case to the effect that a "no-strike" clause, properly interpreted, does not mean a promise not to

---

[1] It may be noted that the opponents of the Taft-Hartley Act objected to the loss-of-status provision for just this reason:

"[T]he section is silent as to the Board's authority to accommodate conflicting issues such as provocation on the part of the employer. Under this section an employer desirous of ridding himself either of the employees or their representative can engage in the most provocative conduct without fear of redress except by way of a lengthy hearing before the Board and a subsequent admonition to thereafter 'cease and desist' from such practices. In striking contrast to the relatively delicate treatment provided for such action by an employer, employees unwilling idly to countenance abuse, who resort to self-help under the circumstances are removed from the protection of the statute and lose 'employee' status. An employer is at liberty under such circumstances freely to replace any employee bold enough to insist upon justice. The provision denies to the Board the exercise of any discretion to accommodate the equitable doctrine of 'clean hands.' The provisions of the section are conclusive — the employee is subject to summary dismissal irrespective of the employer's conduct." S. Rep. No. 105 (Minority), Part 2, 80th Cong., 1st Sess. 21-22 (1947).

strike over employer unfair practices, apply to a clause that only provides for no strikes over grievances until all steps in the grievance procedure have been exhausted? The NLRB held "no" in Mid-West Metallic Prod., Inc., 121 N.L.R.B. 1317, 1319-20 (1958), reasoning that the Supreme Court had required an explicit waiver of the right to strike against the employer's unfair labor practices in *Mastro Plastics* because the waiver of the right to strike for any cause for the entire term of the contract found in that case was so broad that a literal construction could have jeopardized the union's very existence. In the instant case, the limitation of the right to strike was very narrow, only requiring the exhaustion of the grievance procedure which could be completed in five days. Therefore, the Board held that the protective function of an explicit waiver was not required in the contract and that the employer did not violate § 8(a)(3) and (1) by discharging employees who did strike without first exhausting the grievance procedure.

3. Depending on their particular terms, no-strike clauses may waive some rights of the parties and not others. Thus, the NLRB has declared that a strike ban may forbid work stoppages over disputes arising under a union's own contract, but not forbid individual employees to honor a picket line out of sympathy for another union's strike. Kellogg Co., 189 N.L.R.B. 948 (1971), *enforced,* 457 F.2d 519 (6th Cir. 1972).

A union must clearly and unequivocally waive its right to engage in a sympathy strike where another union in the same plant is on strike. There is no waiver if the no-strike clause is limited to disputes arising under the contract and subject to the grievance procedure, since the employer's dispute with the other union is not resolvable under the first union's contract. Gary-Hobart Water Corp., 210 N.L.R.B. 742 (1974) *enforcement granted,* 511 F.2d 284 (7th Cir. 1975). *See also* Laconia Shoe Co., 215 N.L.R.B. 573 (1974) (sympathetic walkout in response to unfair labor practice strike).

4. *Compare* Arlan's Dep't Store, 133 N.L.R.B. 802 (1961), where a majority of a Board panel held that only strikes in protest against *serious* unfair labor practices should be held immune from general no-strike clauses. Member Fanning dissented, taking the position that all unfair labor practices are serious.

In Steelworkers Local 14055 v. NLRB (Dow Chemical Co.), 530 F.2d 266 (3d Cir. 1976), *cert. denied,* 429 U.S. 807 (1976), the employer unilaterally announced certain shift changes and the union struck in protest without completing the grievance procedure. The court agreed with the NLRB that the employer's action was an unfair labor practice, but refused to resolve the case by "simply pigeonholing it as within the rule of *Mastro Plastics* or that of *Arlan's.*" The Board panel had held (2-1, Member Fanning dissenting) that the employer's conduct, although an unfair labor practice, was not of such a serious nature as to be destructive of the foundation on which collective bargaining must rest. The strike was, therefore, unprotected and the employer was free to discharge the strikers. Judge Aldisert, for the court of appeals, observed that fundamental development had occurred in national labor policy since

Mastro Plastics (in 1956) and *Arlan's* (in 1961) that should have commanded the Board's attention. He summarized numerous Supreme Court decisions favoring arbitration as the preferred means of settling labor disputes; and, even though the collective agreement did not have a mandatory arbitration clause, the court held that the employer's failure to utilize all available means, such as consensual arbitration, precluded the Board's conclusion that the strikers were unprotected.

Once the decision is reached that certain conduct is protected concerted activity (such as a strike for higher wages or a strike to protest the employer's unfair labor practices), a number of important questions remain as to how much it is protected. For example, is the employer free to hire replacements for the strikers? Can he offer the replacements superseniority in order to induce them to come? To what extent can the employer make distinctions between strikers and nonstrikers on such matters as accrued vacations with pay? Finally, under what circumstances, is the employer free to lock out or close the plant in response to union concerted activity? The following cases explore these problems, beginning with *Mackay Radio* which is the early landmark case on the employer's freedom to replace economic strikers.

NLRB v. MACKAY RADIO & TELEGRAPH CO.

Supreme Court of the United States
304 U.S. 333, 58 S. Ct. 904, 82 L. Ed. 1381 (1938)

[The Mackay Company, which was engaged in the communication business, maintained an office in San Francisco, where it employed some sixty supervisors, operators, and clerks, many of whom were members of Local No. 3 of the American Radio Telegraphists Association. In an attempt to force the company to enter into a collective agreement covering marine and point-to-point operators the ARTA called a strike on October 4, 1935, in which Local No. 3 participated. In order to maintain service, the company brought employees from its Los Angeles and Chicago offices to fill the San Francisco strikers' places. The strike was unsuccessful, and on October 7 overtures to return to work were made in San Francisco. Company representatives advised the strikers that they could return to work, but subject to the qualification that eleven of the replacements had been promised permanent employment in San Francisco if they so desired. Accordingly, the strikers were told that they could return to work in a body, with the exception of eleven men who were told they would have to file applications for reinstatement, to be passed upon by a New York executive of the company. Thereafter, it appeared that only five of the replacements desired to remain with the company in San Francisco, and six of the eleven strikers who had been told to file formal applications for reinstatement were allowed to return to their jobs, along with the other strikers. The five strikers who were denied reinstatement were prominent in the activities of the union, and filed charges with the NLRB that the company had violated §§ 8(1) and 8(3) of the original NLRA in denying them reinstatement. An NLRB complaint issued, and in due course the NLRB held the company guilty as charged, and issued a cease and desist order, and an order requiring the company to offer the five men immediate and full reinstatement. After refusal by the circuit court of appeals to enforce this order, the case was taken by the Supreme Court on certiorari. *Held,* reversed and remanded. The strikers remained "employees" under § 2(3) of the act. While there was no unfair labor practice by the company prior to or during the strike, the Board's finding of discrimination in excluding the five strikers from reinstatement was supported by the evidence.]

MR. JUSTICE ROBERTS delivered the opinion of the Court.

. . . .

. . . Nor was it an unfair labor practice to replace the striking employees with others in an effort to carry on the business. Although § 13 provides, "Nothing in this Act shall be construed so as to interfere with or impede or diminish in any way the right to strike," it does not follow that an employer, guilty of no act denounced by the statute, has lost the right to protect and continue his business by supplying places left vacant by strikers. And he is not bound to discharge those hired to fill the places of strikers, upon the election of the latter to resume their employment, in order to create places for them. The assurance by respondent to those who accepted employment during the strike that if they so desired their places might be permanent was not an unfair labor practice nor was it such to reinstate only so many of the strikers as there were vacant places to be filled. But the claim put forward is that the unfair labor practice indulged by the respondent was discrimination in reinstating striking employees by keeping out certain of them for the sole reason that they had been active in the union. As we have said, the strikers retained, under the Act, the status of employees. Any such discrimination in putting them back to work is, therefore, prohibited by § 8. . . .

As we have said, the respondent was not bound to displace men hired to take the strikers' places in order to provide positions for them. It might have refused reinstatement on the grounds of skill or ability, but the Board found that it did not do so. It might have resorted to any one of a number of methods of determining which of its striking employees would have to wait because five men had taken permanent positions during the strike, but it is found that the preparation and use of the list [*i.e.,* the list of the names of the eleven men originally selected for exclusion], and the action taken by the respondent, were with the purpose to discriminate against those most active in the union. There is evidence to support these findings.

NOTES

1. *Economic strikes* — Since the decision in the principal case it has been considered as settled that where the employer is "guilty of no act

denounced by the statute," he has a right, in order to keep his plant in operation, to hire permanent replacements for strikers, and thus to deprive such replaced strikers of an immediate right of reinstatement. "If employees go out on strike for economic reasons and not because of any unfair labor practices on the part of their employer, the latter may replace them in order to keep his business running, and the strikers thereafter have no absolute right of reinstatement to their old jobs. After the termination of a strike, however, an employer may not discriminatorily refuse to reinstate or reemploy the strikers merely because of their union membership or concerted activity." NLRB, EIGHTH ANNUAL REPORT 32 (1943).

In order to take advantage of their reinstatement rights, unreplaced economic strikers must make an unconditional application for reinstatement, either personally or through their union.

In Laidlaw Corp., 171 N.L.R.B. 1366 (1968), the Labor Board declared that "economic strikers who unconditionally apply for reinstatement at a time when their positions are filled by permanent replacements: (1) remain employees; (2) are entitled to full reinstatement upon the departure of replacements unless they have in the meantime acquired regular and substantially equivalent employment, or the employer can sustain his burden of proof that the failure to offer full reinstatement was for legitimate and substantial business reasons." Left unresolved was the extent of an employer's duty to seek out employees who have applied for reinstatement. *Laidlaw* was enforced in 414 F.2d 99 (7th Cir. 1969), *cert. denied,* 397 U.S. 920 (1970).

In its *Laidlaw* decision, the NLRB relied heavily on NLRB v. Fleetwood Trailer Co., 389 U.S. 375 (1967), which held that an employer, who refused to reinstate unreplaced economic strikers at the time of their unconditional application due to temporary cutbacks in production resulting from the strike, was under an obligation to offer them reinstatement when full production resumed two months later. He violated the act in hiring some new employees instead of offering reinstatement to the strikers. What if the strikers' jobs had been eliminated during the strike through a change in production methods, such as the introduction of new machinery? The Court said that the employer has the burden to show "legitimate and substantial business justifications."

Could a union and an employer, as part of a strike settlement, place time limits on the reinstatement rights of economic strikers? What are the factors that should be considered in evaluating such an agreement? See United Aircraft Corp., 192 N.L.R.B. 382 (1971). In Brooks Research & Mfg., Inc., 202 N.L.R.B. 634 (1973), the Labor Board held that there is no time limit on an employer's obligation to reinstate economic strikers who have made an unconditional application for reinstatement. An employer may not unilaterally terminate their seniority and recall rights without bargaining with the union.

Under *Laidlaw,* unreinstated strikers have no statutory right to recall in accordance with a collective bargaining agreement's provision covering recall from layoff, where the parties have not agreed to the application of that provision to the reinstatement of economic strikers. An employer's unilateral imposition of a preferential reinstatement plan was not an unlawful refusal to bargain, since an impasse had been reached when the employer declined to terminate the permanent replacements, pursuant to the *Mackay Radio* doctrine. Bio-Science Laboratories, 209 N.L.R.B. 796 (1974).

For a discussion of the extent of an employee's obligation to pursue reinstatement, see NLRB v. Pepsi Cola Co., 496 F.2d 226 (4th Cir. 1974).

2. *Unfair labor practice strikes* — It is well established that where a strike has been called because of the employer's unfair labor practices (e.g., a refusal to bargain with a certified union), the employer is not legally free to hire permanent replacements and he is obligated to reinstate the strikers upon their request. Collins & Aikman Corp., 165 N.L.R.B. 678 (1967).

3. *Economic strikes converted to unfair labor practice strikes* — If the employer first commits unfair labor practices during the course of an economic strike, thereby prolonging it, the strike at that point becomes an unfair practice strike, and strikers who are replaced after that point are entitled to reinstatement upon request. NLRB v. Pecheur Lozenge Co., 209 F.2d 393 (2d Cir. 1953); American Cyanamid Co. v. NLRB, 100 L.R.R.M. 2640 (7th Cir. 1979).

In NLRB v. International Van Lines, 409 U.S. 48 (1972), the Supreme Court held that an employer had to offer unconditional reinstatement to striking employees whom it had fired before hiring permanent replacements, regardless of whether or not the discharges converted the strike from an economic to an unfair labor practice strike. The discharges themselves were unfair labor practices sufficient to justify the Labor Board's reinstatement order.

See generally, Comment, *Reconversion of Unfair Labor Practice Strikes to Economic Strikes,* 64 GEO. L.J. 1143 (1976).

4. Is an employer free to replace an employee who refuses to cross a picket line at the premises of another employer where there is a labor dispute in progress, but where the employee in the normal course of his work, would be expected to go (such as to make deliveries)? *See* NLRB v. Rockaway News Supply Co., 197 F.2d 111 (2d Cir. 1952), *aff'd on other grounds,* 345 U.S. 71 (1953); Auto Parts Co., 107 N.L.R.B. 242 (1953); *cf.* Cyril de Cordova & Bro., 91 N.L.R.B. 1121 (1950). Consider the relevance of the proviso at the end of § 8(b)(4) of the Taft-Hartley Act.

In Redwing Carriers, Inc., 137 N.L.R.B. 1545 (1962), *enforced,* 325 F.2d 1011 (D.C. Cir. 1963), *cert. denied,* 377 U.S. 905 (1964), the NLRB held that employees who refuse to cross a picket line at another employer's premises are protected to the extent that their employer may not discharge or discipline them as a reprisal; however, the employer is free to discharge them solely for business reasons, where necessary to preserve the efficient operation of his business by replacement by others who will cross the picket line.

See also L. G. Everist, Inc., 142 N.L.R.B. 193 (1963), where the Board held that the employer had committed an unfair labor practice by refusing to reinstate, upon their unconditional application, four drivers who had been discharged for refusing to cross a picket line. Such employees are regarded as similar to economic strikers, who may be replaced to permit continued operation of the business, but who, if not permanently replaced, are entitled to reinstatement upon unconditional application. Members Rodgers and Leedom dissented on the ground that the refusal to cross the picket line was unprotected activity. Enforcement on this point was denied in NLRB v. L. G. Everist, Inc., 334 F.2d 312 (8th Cir. 1964). The court refused to equate these drivers with economic strikers.

In Torrington Construction Co., 235 N.L.R.B. No. 211, 98 L.R.R.M. 1135 (1978), the Board reaffirmed the *Redwing Carriers* doctrine that an employer may replace, but may not discharge, an employee who refuses to make deliveries across a lawful primary picket line.

For a comprehensive discussion, *see* Haggard, *Picket Line Observance as a Protected Concerted Activity,* 53 N.C. L. REV. 43 (1974).

5. The validity of employer agreements not to discipline employees for refusing to cross picket lines will be taken up in Truck Drivers Local 413 v. NLRB, 334 F.2d 539 (D.C. Cir. 1964), *infra* at 384.

NLRB v. ERIE RESISTOR CORP.

Supreme Court of the United States
373 U.S. 221, 83 S. Ct. 1139, 10 L. Ed. 2d 308 (1963)

MR. JUSTICE WHITE delivered the opinion of the Court.

The question before us is whether an employer commits an unfair labor practice under § 8(a) of the National Labor Relations Act . . . when he extends a 20-year seniority credit to strike replacements and strikers who leave the strike and return to work. . . .

Erie Resistor Corporation and Local 613 of the International Union of Electrical, Radio and Machine Workers were bound by a collective-bargaining agreement which was due to expire on March 31, 1959. In January 1959, both parties met to negotiate new terms but, after extensive bargaining, they were unable to reach agreement. Upon expiration of the contract, the union, in support of its contract demands, called a strike which was joined by all of the 478 employees in the unit.[2]

The company, under intense competition and subject to insistent demands from its customers to maintain deliveries, decided to continue production operations. Transferring clerks, engineers and other nonunit employees to production jobs, the company managed to keep production at about 15% to 30% of normal during the month of April. On May 3, however, the company notified the union members that it intended to begin hiring replacements and that strikers would retain their jobs until replaced. The plant was located in an area classified by the United States

---

[2] In addition to these employees, 450 employees in the unit were on layoff status.

Department of Labor as one of severe unemployment and the company had in fact received applications for employment as early as a week or two after the strike began.

Replacements were told that they would not be laid off or discharged at the end of the strike. To implement that assurance, particularly in view of the 450 employees already laid off on March 31, the company notified the union that it intended to accord the replacements some form of super-seniority. At regular bargaining sessions between the company and union, the union made it clear that, in its view, no matter what form the super-seniority plan might take, it would necessarily work an illegal discrimination against the strikers. As negotiations advanced on other issues, it became evident that super-seniority was fast becoming the focal point of disagreement. On May 28, the company informed the union that it had decided to award 20 years'[3] additional seniority both to replacements and to strikers who returned to work, which would be available only for credit against future layoffs and which could not be used for other employee benefits based on years of service. The strikers, at a union meeting the next day, unanimously resolved to continue striking now in protest against the proposed plan as well.

The company made its first official announcement of the super-seniority plan on June 10, and by June 14, 34 new employees, 47 employees recalled from layoff status and 23 returning strikers had accepted production jobs. The union, now under great pressure, offered to give up some of its contract demands if the company would abandon super-seniority or go to arbitration on the question, but the company refused. In the following week, 64 strikers returned to work and 21 replacements took jobs, bringing the total to 102 replacements and recalled workers and 87 returned strikers. When the number of returning strikers went up to 125 during the following week, the union capitulated. A new labor agreement on the remaining economic issues was executed on July 17, and an accompanying settlement agreement was signed providing that the company's replacement and job assurance policy should be resolved by the National Labor Relations Board and the federal courts but was to remain in effect pending final disposition.

Following the strike's termination, the company reinstated those strikers whose jobs had not been filled (all but 129 were returned to their jobs). At about the same time, the union received some 173 resignations from membership. By September of 1959, the production unit work force had reached a high of 442 employees but by May of 1960, the work force had gradually slipped back to 240. Many employees laid off during this cutback period were reinstated strikers whose seniority was insufficient to retain their jobs as a consequence of the company's super-seniority policy.

The union filed a charge with the National Labor Relations Board alleging that awarding super-seniority during the course of the strike

---

[3] The figure of 20 years was developed from a projection, on the basis of expected orders, of what the company's work force would be following the strike. As of March 31, the beginning of the strike, a male employee needed seven years' seniority to avoid layoff and a female employee nine years.

constituted an unfair labor practice and that the subsequent layoff of the recalled strikers pursuant to such a plan was unlawful. The Trial Examiner found that the policy was promulgated for legitimate economic reasons, not for illegal or discriminatory purposes, and recommended that the union's complaint be dismissed. The Board could not agree with the Trial Examiner's conclusion that specific evidence of subjective intent to discriminate against the union was necessary to finding that super-seniority granted during a strike is an unfair labor practice. Its consistent view, the Board said, had always been that super-seniority, in circumstances such as these, was an unfair labor practice. . . .

The Court of Appeals rejected as unsupportable the rationale of the Board that a preferential seniority policy is illegal however motivated. . . .

It consequently denied the Board's petition for enforcement and remanded the case for further findings.

We think the Court of Appeals erred in holding that, in the absence of a finding of specific illegal intent, a legitimate business purpose is always a defense to an unfair labor practice charge. Cases in this Court dealing with unfair labor practices have recognized the relevance and importance of showing the employer's intent or motive to discriminate or to interfere with union rights. But specific evidence of such subjective intent is "not an indispensable element of proof of violation." Radio Officers' Union v. NLRB, 347 U.S. 17, 44 (1954). "Some conduct may by its very nature contain the implications of the required intent; the natural foreseeable consequences of certain action may warrant the inference. . . . The existence of discrimination may at times be inferred by the Board, for 'it is permissible to draw on experience in factual inquiries.' " Teamsters Local 357 v. NLRB, 365 U.S. 667, 675 (1961).

Though the intent necessary for an unfair labor practice may be shown in different ways, proving it in one manner may have far different weight and far different consequences than proving it in another. When specific evidence of a subjective intent to discriminate or to encourage or discourage union membership is shown, and found, many otherwise innocent or ambiguous actions which are normally incident to the conduct of a business may, without more, be converted into unfair labor practices. NLRB v. Jones & Laughlin Steel Corp., 301 U.S. 1, 46 (1937) (discharging employees); The Associated Press v. NLRB, 301 U.S. 103, 132 (1937) (discharging employees); Phelps Dodge Corp. v. NLRB, 313 U.S. 177 (1941) (hiring employees). Compare NLRB v. Brown-Dunkin Co., 287 F.2d 17 (10th Cir. 1961), with NLRB v. Houston Chronicle Publishing Co., 211 F.2d 848 (5th Cir. 1954) (subcontracting union work); and Fiss Corp., 43 N.L.R.B. 125, with Jacob H. Klotz, 13 N.L.R.B. 746 (movement of plant to another town). Such proof itself is normally sufficient to destroy the employer's claim of a legitimate business purpose, if one is made, and provides strong support to a finding that there is interference with union rights or that union membership will be discouraged. Conduct which on its face appears to serve legitimate business ends in these cases is wholly impeached by the showing of an intent to encroach upon protected rights. The employer's claim of legitimacy is totally dispelled.[6]

The outcome may well be the same when intent is founded upon the inherently discriminatory or destructive nature of the conduct itself. The employer in such cases must be held to intend the very consequences which foreseeably and inescapably flow from his actions and if he fails to explain away, to justify or to characterize his actions as something different than they appear on their face, an unfair labor practice charge is made out. Radio Officers' Union v. NLRB, *supra.* But, as often happens, the employer may counter by claiming that his actions were taken in the pursuit of legitimate business ends and that his dominant purpose was not to discriminate or to invade union rights but to accomplish business objectives acceptable under the act. Nevertheless, his conduct *does* speak for itself — it *is* discriminatory and it *does* discourage union membership and whatever the claimed overriding justification may be, it carries with it unavoidable consequences which the employer not only foresaw but which he must have intended. As is not uncommon in human experience, such situations present a complex of motives and preferring one motive to another is in reality the far more delicate task, reflected in part in decisions of this Court,[7] of weighing the interests of employees in concerted activity against the interest of the employer in operating his business in a particular manner and of balancing in the light of the act and its policy the intended consequences upon employee rights against the business ends to be served by the employer's conduct.[8] This essentially is the teaching of the Court's prior cases dealing with this problem and, in our view, the Board did not depart from it.

The Board made a detailed assessment of super-seniority and, to its experienced eye, such a plan had the following characteristics:

(1) Super-seniority affects the tenure of all strikers whereas permanent replacement, proper under *Mackay,* affects only those who are, in actuality, replaced. It is one thing to say that a striker is subject to loss of his job at the strike's end but quite another to hold that in addition to the threat of replacement, all strikers will at best return to their jobs with seniority inferior to that of the replacements and of those who left the strike.

---

[6] Accordingly, those cases holding unlawful a super-seniority plan prompted by a desire on the part of the employer to penalize or discriminate against striking employees, Ballas Egg Products, Inc. v. NLRB, 283 F.2d 871 (6th Cir. 1960); NLRB v. California Date Growers Ass'n, 259 F.2d 587 (9th Cir. 1958); Olin Mathieson Chem. Corp. v. NLRB, 232 F.2d 158 (4th Cir. 1956), *aff'd per curiam,* 352 U.S. 1020 (1957), are explainable without reaching the considerations present here.

[7] See, e.g., NLRB v. Mackay Radio & Tel. Co., 304 U.S. 333 (1938); Republic Aviation Corp. v. NLRB, 324 U.S. 793 (1945); NLRB v. Babcock & Wilcox Co., 351 U.S. 105 (1956); NLRB v. Truck Drivers Local Union No. 449, 353 U.S. 87 (1957).

[8] In a variety of situations, the lower courts have dealt with and rejected the approach urged here that conduct otherwise unlawful is automatically excused upon a showing that it was motivated by business exigencies. Thus, it has been held that an employer cannot justify the discriminatory discharge of union members upon the ground that such conduct

(2) A super-seniority award necessarily operates to the detriment of those who participated in the strike as compared to nonstrikers.

(3) Super-seniority made available to striking bargaining unit employees as well as to new employees is in effect offering individuals benefits to the strikers to induce them to abandon the strike.

(4) Extending the benefits of super-seniority to striking bargaining unit employees as well as to new employees is in effect offering individual strike effort. At one stroke, those with low seniority have the opportunity to obtain the job security which ordinarily only long years of service can bring, while conversely, the accumulated seniority of older employees is seriously diluted. This combination of threat and promise could be expected to undermine the strikers' mutual interest and place the entire strike effort in jeopardy. The history of this strike and its virtual collapse following the announcement of the plan emphasize the grave repercussions of super-seniority.

(5) Super-seniority renders future bargaining difficult, if not impossible, for the collective bargaining representative. Unlike the replacement granted in *Mackay* which ceases to be an issue once the strike is over, the plan here creates a cleavage in the plant continuing long after the strike is ended. Employees are henceforth divided into two camps: those who stayed with the union and those who returned before the end of the strike and thereby gained extra seniority. This breach is re-emphasized with each subsequent layoff and stands as an ever-present reminder of the dangers connected with striking and with union activities in general.

In the light of this analysis, super-seniority by its very terms operates to discriminate between strikers and nonstrikers, both during and after a strike, and its destructive impact upon the strike and union activity cannot be doubted. The origin of the plan, as respondent insists, may have been to keep production going and it may have been necessary to offer super-seniority to attract replacements and induce union members to leave the strike. But if this is true, accomplishment of respondent's business purpose inexorably was contingent upon attracting sufficient replacements and strikers by offering preferential inducements to those who worked as opposed to those who struck. We think the Board was entitled to treat this case as involving conduct which carried its own indicia of intent and which is barred by the act unless saved from illegality by an overriding business purpose justifying the invasion of union rights. The Board concluded that the business purpose asserted was insufficient to insulate the super-seniority plan from the reach of § 8(a)(1) and (3), and we turn now to a review of that conclusion.

The Court of Appeals and respondent rely upon *Mackay* as precluding the result reached by the Board but we are not persuaded. Under the decision in that case an employer may operate his plant during a strike and at its conclusion need not discharge those who worked during the strike in order to make way for returning strikers. It may be as the Court of

---

is the only way to induce a rival union to remove a picket line and permit the resumption of business, NLRB v. Star Publishing Co., 97 F.2d 465 (9th Cir. 1938).

Appeals said that "such a replacement policy is obviously discriminatory and may tend to discourage union membership." But *Mackay* did not deal with super-seniority, with its effects upon all strikers, whether replaced or not, or with its powerful impact upon a strike itself. Because the employer's interest must be deemed to outweigh the damage to concerted activities caused by permanently replacing strikers does not mean it also outweighs the far greater encroachment resulting from super-seniority in addition to permanent replacement.

We have no intention of questioning the continuing vitality of the *Mackay* rule but we are not prepared to extend it to the situation we have here. To do so would require us to set aside the Board's considered judgment that the act and its underlying policy require, in the present context, giving more weight to the harm wrought by super-seniority than to the interest of the employer in operating its plant during the strike by utilizing this particular means of attracting replacements. We find nothing in the act or its legislative history to indicate that super-seniority is necessarily an acceptable method of resisting the economic impact of a strike nor do we find anything inconsistent with the result which the Board reached. On the contrary, these sources are wholly consistent with, and lend full support to, the conclusion of the Board.

Section 7 guarantees, and § 8(a)(1) protects from employer interference, the rights of employees to engage in concerted activities, which as Congress has indicated, H.R. Rep. No. 245, 80th Cong., 1st Sess. 26, includes the right to strike. Under § 8(a)(3), it is unlawful for an employer by discrimination in terms of employment to discourage "membership in any labor organization," which includes discouraging participation in concerted activities, such as a legitimate strike. NLRB v. Wheeling Pipe Line, Inc., 229 F.2d 391 (8th Cir. 1956); Republic Steel Corp. v. NLRB, 114 F.2d 820 (3d Cir. 1940). Section 13 makes clear that although the strike weapon is not an unqualified right, nothing in the act except as specifically provided is to be construed to interfere with this means of redress, H.R. Conf. Rep. No. 510, 80th Cong., 1st Sess. 59, and § 2(3) preserves to strikers their unfilled positions and status as employees during the pendency of a strike. S. Rep. No. 573, 74th Cong., 1st Sess. 6. This repeated solicitude for the right to strike is predicated upon the conclusion that a strike when legitimately employed is an economic weapon which in great measure implements and supports the principles of the collective bargaining system.

While Congress has from time to time revamped and redirected national labor policy, its concern for the integrity of the strike weapon has remained constant. Thus when Congress chose to qualify the use of the strike, it did so by prescribing the limits and conditions of the abridgment in exacting detail, *e.g.,* §§ 8(b)(4), 8(d), by indicating the precise procedures to be followed in effecting the interference, *e.g.,* § 10(j), (k), (*l*); §§ 206-210, Labor-Management Relations Act, and by preserving the positive command of § 13 that the right to strike is to be given a generous interpretation within the scope of the labor act. . . .

Accordingly, in view of the deferences paid the strike weapon by the federal labor laws and the devastating consequences upon it which the Board found was and would be precipitated by respondent's inherently discriminatory super-seniority plan, we cannot say the Board erred in the balance which it struck here. . . . The matter before the Board lay well within the mainstream of its duties. It was attempting to deal with an issue which Congress had placed in its hands and ". . . Where Congress has in the statute given the Board a question to answer, the courts will give respect to that answer. . . ." NLRB v. Insurance Agents, *supra,* 361 U.S. at 499. Here as in other cases, we must recognize the Board's special function of applying the general provisions of the act to the complexities of industrial life, Republic Aviation Corp. v. NLRB, 324 U.S. 793 (1945); Phelps Dodge Corp. v. NLRB, *supra,* at 194, and of "[appraising] carefully the interests of both sides of any labor-management controversy in the diverse circumstances of particular cases" from its special understanding of "the actualities of industrial situations." NLRB v. United Steelworkers, *supra,* 357 U.S., at 362, 363. "The ultimate problem is the balancing of conflicting legitimate interests. The function of striking that balance to effectuate national labor policy is often a difficult and delicate responsibility, which the Congress committed primarily to the National Labor Relations Board, subject to limited judicial review." NLRB v. Truck Drivers Local Union No. 449, 353 U.S. 87 (1957).

Consequently, because the Board's judgment was that the claimed business purpose would not outweigh the necessary harm to employee rights — a judgment which we sustained, it could properly put aside evidence of respondent's motive and decline to find whether the conduct was or was not prompted by the claimed business purpose. We reverse the judgment of the Court of Appeals and remand the case to that court since its review was a limited one and it must now reach the remaining questions before it, including the propriety of the remedy which at least in part turns upon the Board's construction of the settlement agreement as being no barrier to an award not only of reinstatement but of back pay as well.

Reversed and remanded.

Mr. Justice Harlan, concurring.

I agree with the Court that the Board's conclusions respecting this 20-year "super-seniority" plan were justified without inquiry into the respondents' motives. However, I do not think that the same thing would necessarily be true in all circumstances, as for example with a plan providing for a much shorter period of extra seniority. Being unsure whether the Court intends to hold that the Board has power to outlaw *all* such plans, irrespective of the employer's motives and other circumstances, or only to sustain its action in the particular circumstances of *this* case, I concur in the judgment.

4. LOCKOUTS, PLANT CLOSINGS, AND "RUNAWAY SHOPS"

NLRB v. TRUCK DRIVERS, LOCAL 449
INTERNATIONAL BROTHERHOOD OF TEAMSTERS
[BUFFALO LINEN CASE]

Supreme Court of the United States
353 U.S. 87, 77 S. Ct. 643, 1 L. Ed. 2d 676 (1957)

[The union, engaged in collective bargaining on a multiemployer basis with an employers association representing eight linen supply companies in Buffalo, put into effect a "whipsaw" plan by striking one of the companies. The other seven employers locked out their employees and ceased operating. Multiemployer negotiations continued, and, after one week, a new contract was signed and employees returned to work. The union charged the seven employers with violations of §§ 8(a)(1) and (3). The NLRB held no violation, since the lockout was defensive. The court of appeals found a violation, holding the lockout not privileged in the absence of unusual economic hardship.]

MR. JUSTICE BRENNAN delivered the opinion of the Court.

. . . .

We are not concerned here with the cases in which the lockout has been held unlawful because designed to frustrate organizational efforts, to destroy or undermine bargaining representation, or to evade the duty to bargain. Nor are we called upon to define the limits of the legitimate use of the lockout.[19] The narrow question to be decided is whether a temporary lockout may lawfully be used as a defense to a union strike tactic which threatens the destruction of the employers' interest in bargaining on a group basis.

. . . .

Although the act protects the right of the employees to strike in support of their demands, this protection is not so absolute as to deny self-help by employers when legitimate interests of employees and employers collide. Conflict may arise, for example, between the right to strike and the interest of small employers in preserving multiemployer bargaining as a means of bargaining on an equal basis with a large union and avoiding the competitive disadvantages resulting from nonuniform contractual terms. The ultimate problem is the balancing of the conflicting legitimate interests. The function of striking that balance to effectuate national labor policy is often a difficult and delicate responsibility, which the Congress committed primarily to the National Labor Relations Board, subject to limited judicial review.

The Court of Appeals recognized that the National Labor Relations Board has legitimately balanced conflicting interests by permitting

---

[19] We thus find it unnecessary to pass upon the question whether, as a general proposition, the employer lockout is the corollary of the employees' statutory right to strike.

lockouts where economic hardship was shown. The court erred, however, in too narrowly confining the exercise of Board discretion to the cases of economic hardship. We hold that in the circumstances of the case the Board correctly balanced the conflicting interests in deciding that a temporary lockout to preserve the multiemployer bargaining basis from the disintegration threatened by the Union's strike action was lawful.

Reversed.

NLRB v. BROWN

Supreme Court of the United States
380 U.S. 278, 85 S. Ct. 980, 13 L. Ed. 2d 839 (1965)

[The union, engaged in collective bargaining on a multiemployer basis with a group of six retail food stores in Carlsbad, New Mexico, put into effect a "whipsaw" plan by striking one of the stores, Food Jet. Food Jet continued operations with management personnel and their relatives and with a few temporary replacements. The other five stores laid off their union employees, regarding "the strike against one as a strike against all." However, in contrast to the *Buffalo Linen* situation, the five stores continued operations with management personnel, relatives, and temporary replacements, who were told that their employment would end when the "whipsaw" strike ended. Group bargaining continued; an agreement was reached after about a month; and the employers immediately released the temporary employees and recalled the strikers and locked-out employees. The NLRB (3-2) found a violation of §§ 8(a)(1) and (3), inferring that the employers acted not merely to protect the integrity of their multiemployer unit, but for the purpose of inhibiting a lawful strike. The court of appeals refused to enforce the Board's order.]

MR. JUSTICE BRENNAN delivered the opinion of the Court.

. . . .

The Board's decision does not rest upon independent evidence that the respondents acted either out of hostility toward the Local or in reprisal for the whipsaw strike. It rests upon the Board's appraisal that the respondents' conduct carried its own indicia of unlawful intent, thereby establishing, without more, that the conduct constituted an unfair labor practice. It was disagreement with this appraisal, which we share, that led the Court of Appeals to refuse to enforce the Board's order. . . .

In the circumstances of this case, we do not see how the continued operations of respondents and their use of temporary replacements any more implies hostile motivation, nor how it is inherently more destructive of employee rights, than the lockout itself. Rather, the compelling inference is that this was all part and parcel of respondents' defensive measure to preserve the multiemployer group in the face of the whipsaw strike. Since Food Jet legitimately continued business operations, it is only reasonable to regard respondents' action as evincing concern that the integrity of the employer group was threatened unless they also managed to stay open for business during the lockout. For with Food Jet open for business and respondents' stores closed, the prospect that the whipsaw strike would succeed in breaking up the employer association was not at all fanciful. The retail food industry is very competitive and repetitive patronage is highly important. Faced with the prospect of a loss of patronage to Food Jet, it is logical that respondents should have been concerned that one or more of their number might bolt the group and come to terms with the Local, thus destroying the common front essential to multiemployer bargaining. The Court of Appeals correctly pictured the respondents' dilemma in saying, "If . . . the struck employer does choose to operate with replacements and the other employers cannot replace after lockout, the economic advantage passes to the struck member, the non-struck members are deterred in exercising the defensive lockout, and the whipsaw strike . . . enjoys an almost inescapable prospect of success." 319 F.2d, at 11. Clearly respondents' continued operations with the use of temporary replacements following the lockout was wholly consistent with a legitimate business purpose.

Nor are we persuaded by the Board's argument that justification for the inference of hostile motivation appears in the respondents' use of temporary employees rather than some of the regular employees. It is not common sense, we think, to say that the regular employees were "willing to work at the employers' terms." 137 N.L.R.B., at 76. It seems probable that this "willingness" was motivated as much by their understandable desire to further the objective of the whipsaw strike — to break through the employers' united front by forcing Food Jet to accept the Local's terms — as it was by a desire to work for the employers under the existing unacceptable terms. As the Board's dissenting members put it, "These employees are willing only to receive wages while their brethren in the rest of the association-wide unit are exerting whipsaw pressure on one employer to gain benefits that will ultimately accrue to all employees in the association-wide unit, including those here locked out." 137 N.L.R.B., at 78. Moreover, the course of action to which the Board would limit the respondents would force them into the position of aiding and abetting the success of the whipsaw strike and consequently would render "largely illusory," 137 N.L.R.B., at 78-79, the right of lockout recognized by *Buffalo Linen*; the right would be meaningless if barred to nonstruck stores that find it necessary to operate because the struck store does so.

The Board's finding of a § 8(a)(1) violation emphasized the impact of respondents' conduct upon the effectiveness of the whipsaw strike. It is no doubt true that the collective strength of the stores to resist that strike is maintained, and even increased, when all stores stay open with temporary replacements. The pressures on the employees are necessarily greater when none of the union employees is working and the stores remain open. But these pressures are no more than the result of the Local's inability to make effective use of the whipsaw tactic. Moreover, these effects are no different from those that result from the legitimate use of any economic weapon by an employer. Continued operations with the use of temporary replacements may result in the failure of the whipsaw strike, but this does not mean that the employers' conduct is demonstrably so destructive of employee rights or so devoid of significant service to any legitimate business end that it cannot be tolerated consistently with the act. Certainly then, in the absence of evidentiary findings of hostile motive, there is no support for the conclusion that respondents violated § 8(a)(1). . . .

We recognize that, analogous to the determination of unfair practices under § 8(a)(1), when an employer practice is inherently destructive of employee rights and is not justified by the service of important business ends, no specific evidence of intent to discourage union membership is necessary to establish a violation of § 8(a)(3). This principle, we have said, is "but an application of the common-law rule that a man is held to intend the foreseeable consequences of his conduct." Radio Officers Union v. NLRB, *supra,* 347 U.S. at 45 (1954). For example, in NLRB v. Erie Resistor Corp., *supra,* we held that an employer's action in awarding superseniority to employees who worked during a strike was discriminatory conduct that carried with it its own indicia of improper intent. The only reasonable inference that could be drawn by the Board from the award of superseniority — balancing the prejudicial effect upon the employees against any asserted business purpose — was that it was directed against the striking employees because of their union membership; conduct so inherently destructive of employee interests could not be saved from illegality by an asserted overriding business purpose pursued in good faith. But where, as here, the tendency to discourage union membership is comparatively slight, and the employer's conduct is reasonably adapted to achieve legitimate business ends or to deal with business exigencies, we enter into an area where the improper motivation of the employer must be established by independent evidence. When so established, antiunion motivation will convert an otherwise ordinary business act into an unfair labor practice. NLRB v. Erie Resistor Corp., *supra,* 373 U.S. at 227 (1963), and cases there cited.

We agree with the Court of Appeals that respondents' conduct here clearly fits into the latter category, where actual subjective intent is determinative, and where the Board must find from evidence independent of the mere conduct involved that the conduct was primarily motivated by an antiunion animus. While the use of temporary nonunion personnel in preference to the locked-out union members is discriminatory, we think that any resulting tendency to discourage union membership is comparatively remote, and that this use of temporary personnel constitutes a measure reasonably adapted to the effectuation of a legitimate business end. Here discontent on the part of the Local's membership in all likelihood is attributable largely to the fact that the membership was locked out as a result of the Local's whipsaw stratagem. But the lockout itself is concededly within the rule of *Buffalo Linen.* We think that the added dissatisfaction and resultant pressure on membership attributable to the fact that the nonstruck employers remain in business with temporary replacements is comparatively insubstantial. First, the replacements were expressly used for the duration of the labor dispute only; thus, the displaced employees could not have looked upon the replacements as threatening their jobs. At most the union would be forced to capitulate and return its members to work on terms which, while not as desirable as hoped for, were still better than under the old contract. Second, the membership, through its control of union policy, could end the dispute and terminate the lockout at any time simply by agreeing to the employers' terms and returning to work on a regular basis. Third, in light of the union-shop provision that had been carried forward into the new contract from the old collective agreement, it would appear that a union member would have nothing to gain, and much to lose, by quitting the union. Under all these circumstances, we cannot say that the employers' conduct had any great tendency to discourage union membership. Not only was the prospect of discouragement of membership comparatively remote, but the respondents' attempt to remain open for business with the help of temporary replacements was a measure reasonably adapted to the achievement of a legitimate end — preserving the integrity of the multiemployer bargaining unit. . . .

It is argued, finally, that the Board's decision is within the area of its expert judgment and that, in setting it aside, the Courts of Appeals exceeded the authorized scope of judicial review. This proposition rests upon our statement in *Buffalo Linen* that in reconciling the conflicting interests of labor and management the Board's determination is to be subjected to "limited judicial review." 353 U.S., at 96. When we used the phrase "limited judicial review" we did not mean that the balance struck by the Board is immune from judicial examination and reversal in proper cases. Courts are expressly empowered to enforce, modify or set aside, in whole or in part, the Board's orders, except that the findings of the Board with respect to questions of fact, if supported by substantial evidence on the record considered as a whole, shall be conclusive. . . . Reviewing courts are not obliged to stand aside and rubber-stamp their affirmance of administrative decisions that they deem inconsistent with a statutory mandate or that frustrate the congressional policy underlying a statute. Not only is such review always properly within the judicial province, but courts would abdicate their responsibility if they did not fully review such administrative decisions. Of course, due deference is to be rendered to agency determinations of fact, so long as there is substantial evidence to be found in the record as a whole. But where, as here, the review is not of a question of fact, but of a judgment as to the proper balance to be struck between conflicting interests, "[t]he deference owed to an expert tribunal cannot be allowed to slip into a judicial inertia which results in the unauthorized assumption by an agency of major policy decisions properly made by Congress." American Ship Building Co. v. NLRB, 380 U.S. at 318 (1965).

Courts must, of course, set aside Board decisions which rest on "an erroneous legal foundation." NLRB v. Babcock & Wilcox, *supra*, 351 U.S. at 112-113. Congress has not given the Board untrammeled authority to catalogue which economic devices shall be deemed freighted with indicia of unlawful intent. NLRB v. Insurance Agents, *supra*, 361 U.S. at 498. In determining here that the respondents' conduct carried its own badge of improper motive, the Board's decision, for the reasons stated, misapplied the criteria governing the application of §§ 8(a)(1) and (3). Since the order therefore rested on "an erroneous legal foundation," the Court of Appeals properly refused to enforce it.[6]

Affirmed.

MR. JUSTICE GOLDBERG, whom THE CHIEF JUSTICE joins, concurring.

. . . There would be grave doubts as to whether locking out and hiring permanent replacements is justified by any legitimate interest of the nonstruck employers, for *Buffalo Linen* makes clear that the test in such a situation is not whether parity is achieved between struck and nonstruck employers, but, rather, whether the nonstruck employer's actions are necessary to counteract the whipsaw effects of the strike and to preserve the employer bargaining unit. Since in this case the nonstruck employers did nothing more than hire temporary replacements, an activity necessary to counter whipsawing by the union and to preserve the bargaining unit, I agree that, applying *Buffalo Linen,* the judgment of the Court of Appeals should be affirmed.

MR. JUSTICE WHITE, dissenting.

. . . This decision represents a departure from the many decisions in this Court holding that the Board has primary responsibility to weigh the interest of employees in concerted activities against that of the employer in operating his business. . . .

The Court reasons that *Buffalo Linen* gave the nonstruck employer in a multiemployer unit a "right" to lockout whenever a member of the unit is struck so that a parity of economic advantage or disadvantage between the struck and nonstruck employers can be maintained. In order to maintain parity where the struck employer hires replacements, the nonstruck employers must also be free to hire replacements, lest the right to lockout to protect the unit be illusory. And they need not offer these jobs to the locked-out employees desiring to work, lest the parity between the struck and nonstruck employers be lost and the right to lockout be meaningless. If this reasoning is sound, the nonstruck employers can not only lock out employees who belong to the union because of their union membership but also hire permanent as well as temporary nonunion replacements whenever the struck employer hires such replacements, for parity may well so require. But I cannot accept this reasoning.

One, *Buffalo Linen* established no unqualified "right" of employers in a multiemployer unit to lockout. . . .

---

[6] We do not here decide whether the case would be the same had the struck employer exercised its prerogative to hire permanent replacements for the strikers under our rule in NLRB v. Mackay Radio & Tel. Co., 304 U.S. 333 (1938), and the nonstruck employers had then hired permanent replacements for their locked-out employees.

Two, the threat to the integrity of the multiemployer unit, the consideration that was decisive in *Buffalo Linen,* is obviously very different where the struck employer continues operations with replacements; it certainly cannot be assumed that the struck employer operating with replacements is at the same disadvantage vis-à-vis the nonstruck employers as the employer in *Buffalo Linen* whose operations were totally shut down by the union. Indeed, there was no showing here that the struck employer was substantially disadvantaged at all, and the Board found that there was "no economic necessity for the other members shutting down. . . ."

Three, the disparity between the struck employer who resumes operations and the nonstruck employers who choose to lockout to maintain a united front is caused by the unilateral action of one of the employer members of the unit and not by the union's whipsawing tactic. The integrity of the multiemployer unit may be important, but surely that consideration cannot justify employer tandem action destructive of concerted activity.

Four, the Court asserts that the right of nonstruck employers to hire temporary replacements, and to refuse to hire union men, is but a concomitant of the right to lockout to preserve the multiemployer group. This sanctification of the multiemployer unit ignores the fundamental rule that an employer may not displace union members with nonunion members solely on account of union membership, the prototype of discrimination under § 8(a)(3), NLRB v. Mackay Radio & Telegraph Co., 304 U.S. 333 (1938), and may not maintain operations and refuse to retain or hire nonstriking union members, notwithstanding that most of the union members and most of the workers at that very plant are on strike. The struck employer need not continue operations, but if he does, he may not give a preference to employees not affiliated with the striking union, no more than he may do so after the strike, for § 7 explicitly and unequivocally protects the right of employees to engage and not to engage in a concerted activity and § 8(a)(3) clearly prohibits discrimination which discourages union membership. . . .

Finally, I cannot agree with the Court's fundamental premise on which its balance of rights is founded: that a lockout followed by the hiring of nonunion men to operate the plant has but a "slight" tendency to discourage union membership, which includes participation in union activities, Radio Officers' Union v. NLRB, 347 U.S. 17 (1954), and to impinge on concerted activity generally. This proposition overturns the Board's longheld views on the effect of lockouts and dismissal of union members. Moreover, it is difficult to fathom the logic or industrial experience which on the one hand dictates that a guarantee to strike replacements that they will not be laid off after a strike is "inherently destructive of employee interests," although based on a legitimate and important business justification, Erie Resistor, 373 U.S. 221 (1963), and yet at the same time dictates that the dismissal of and refusal to hire nonstriking union members who desire to work because other union members working for a different employer have struck have but a slight unimportant inhibiting effect on affiliation with the union and on concerted activities. I think the Board's finding that this activity substantially burdens concerted activities and discourages union membership is far more consistent with *Erie Resistor* and industrial realities. . . .

NOTE

Where the union strikes some members of a multiemployer bargaining unit, the other employers lockout (as they are entitled to do under the *Buffalo Linen* case), and some of the employees inquire whether they can work despite the lockout, may an employer tell them they can only if they resign from the union? *See* NLRB v. Martin A. Gleason, Inc., 534 F.2d 466 (2d Cir. 1976).

AMERICAN SHIP BUILDING CO. v. NLRB

Supreme Court of the United States
380 U.S. 300, 85 S. Ct. 955, 13 L. Ed. 2d 855 (1965)

[After two months of negotiating sessions, the American Ship Building Co. and a group of eight unions bargaining jointly reached an impasse on August 9, 1961. The company had made five previous contracts with the unions since 1952, each one preceded by a strike. The company operated four shipyards on the Great Lakes, most of their work coming in the winter months when the lakes are icebound. What limited business was obtained in the summer months was frequently such that speed of execution was of the utmost importance to minimize immobilization of the ships. Despite union protestations to the contrary, the company feared a strike would be called as soon as a ship should enter the Chicago yard or that there would be a delay in negotiations into the winter to increase strike leverage. In light of the failure to reach agreement and the lack of available work, the company gradually laid off almost all employees, sending each one a notice, "Because of the labor dispute which has been unresolved . . . you are laid off until further notice." Negotiations resumed; an agreement was signed October 27; and employees were recalled the following day.

[The trial examiner found that the employer could reasonably anticipate a strike in spite of the unions' assurances to the contrary, and concluded that the employer was economically motivated and justified in laying off its employees when it did. The Board (3-2) rejected the trial examiner's conclusions and found that the layoff was motivated solely by a desire to bring economic pressure and secure settlement of the dispute on favorable terms. It was agreed that the layoff had not occurred until after a bargaining impasse had been reached.]

MR. JUSTICE STEWART delivered the opinion of the Court.

. . . .

The difference between the Board and the trial examiner is thus a narrow one turning on their differing assessments of the circumstances which the employer claims gave him reason to anticipate a strike. Both the Board and the examiner assumed, within the established pattern of Board analysis, that if the employer had shut down his yard and laid off his workers solely for the purpose of bringing to bear economic pressure to break an impasse and secure more favorable contract terms, an unfair labor practice would be made out. . . .

The Board has, however, exempted certain classes of lockouts from proscription. "Accordingly, it has held that lockouts are permissible to safeguard against loss where there is reasonable ground for believing that a strike was threatened or imminent." [Quaker State Oil Refining Co., 121 N.L.R.B. 334, 337.] Developing this distinction in its rulings, the Board has approved lockouts designed to prevent seizure of a plant by a sitdown strike, Link-Belt Co., 26 N.L.R.B. 227; to forestall repetitive disruptions of an integrated operation by quickie strikes, International Shoe Co., 93 N.L.R.B. 907; to avoid spoilage of materials which would result from a sudden work stoppage, Duluth Bottling Assn., 48 N.L.R.B. 1335; and to avert the immobilization of automobiles brought in for repair, Betts Cadillac-Olds, 96 N.L.R.B. 268. . . .

In analyzing the status of the bargaining lockout under §§ 8(a)(1) and 8(a)(3) of the National Labor Relations Act, it is important that the practice with which we are here concerned be distinguished from other forms of temporary separation from employment. No one would deny that an employer is free to shut down his enterprise temporarily for reasons of renovation or lack of profitable work unrelated to his collective bargaining situation. Similarly, we put to one side cases where the Board has concluded on the basis of substantial evidence that the employer has used a lockout as a means to injure a labor organization or to evade his duty to bargain collectively. Hopwood Retinning Co., 4 N.L.R.B. 922; Scott Paper Box Co., 81 N.L.R.B. 535. What we are here concerned with is the use of a temporary layoff of employees solely as a means to bring economic pressure to bear in support of the employer's bargaining position, after an impasse has been reached. This is the only issue before us, and all that we decide.[8]

To establish that this practice is a violation of § 8(a)(1), it must be shown that the employer has interfered with, restrained, or coerced employees in the exercise of some right protected by § 7 of the act. The Board's position is premised on the view that the lockout interferes with two of the rights guaranteed by § 7: the right to bargain collectively and the right to strike. In the Board's view, the use of the lockout "punishes" employees for the presentation of and adherence to demands made by their bargaining representatives and so coerces them in the exercise of their right to bargain collectively. It is important to note that there is here no allegation that the employer used the lockout in the service of designs

---

[8] Contrary to the view expressed in a concurring opinion filed in this case, we intimate no view whatever as to the consequences which would follow had the employer replaced his employees with permanent replacements or even temporary help. Cf. NLRB v. Mackay Radio & Telegraph Co., 304 U.S. 333 (1938).

inimical to the process of collective bargaining. There was no evidence and no finding that the employer was hostile to his employees banding together for collective bargaining or that the lockout was designed to discipline them for doing so. It is therefore inaccurate to say that the employer's intention was to destroy or frustrate the process of collective bargaining. What can be said is that he intended to resist the demands made of him in the negotiations and to secure modification of these demands. We cannot see that this intention is in any way inconsistent with the employees' rights to bargain collectively.

Moreover, there is no indication, either as a general matter or in this specific case, that the lockout will necessarily destroy the unions' capacity for effective and responsible representation. The unions here involved have vigorously represented the employees since 1952, and there is nothing to show that their ability to do so has been impaired by the lockout. Nor is the lockout one of those acts which is demonstrably so destructive of collective bargaining that the Board need not inquire into employer motivation, as might be the case, for example, if an employer permanently discharged his unionized staff and replaced them with employees known to be possessed of a violent antiunion animus. Cf. NLRB v. Erie Resistor Corp., 373 U.S. 221 (1963). The lockout may well dissuade employees from adhering to the position which they initially adopted in the bargaining, but the right to bargain collectively does not entail any "right" to insist on one's position free from economic disadvantage. Proper analysis of the problem demands that the simple intention to support the employer's bargaining position as to compensation and the like be distinguished from a hostility to the process of collective bargaining which could suffice to render a lockout unlawful. See NLRB v. Brown [380 U.S. 278 (1965)].

The Board has taken the complementary view that the lockout interferes with the right to strike protected under §§ 7 and 13 of the act in that it allows the employer to pre-empt the possibility of a strike and thus leave the union with "nothing to strike against." Insofar as this means that once employees are locked out, they are deprived of their right to call a strike against the employer because he is already shut down, the argument is wholly specious, for the work stoppage which would have been the object of the strike has in fact occurred. It is true that recognition of the lockout deprives the union of exclusive control of the timing and duration of work stoppages calculated to influence the result of collective bargaining negotiations, but there is nothing in the statute which would imply that the right to strike "carries with it" the right exclusively to determine the timing and duration of all work stoppages. The right to strike as commonly understood is the right to cease work — nothing more. No doubt a union's bargaining power would be enhanced if it possessed not only the simple right to strike but also the power exclusively to determine when work stoppages shall occur, but the act's provisions are not indefinitely elastic, content-free forms to be shaped in whatever manner the Board might think best conforms to the proper balance of bargaining power.

Thus, we cannot see that the employer's use of a lockout solely in support of a legitimate bargaining position is in any way inconsistent with the right to bargain collectively or with the right to strike. Accordingly, we conclude that on the basis of the findings made by the Board in this case, there has been no violation of § 8(a)(1).

Section 8(a)(3) prohibits discrimination in regard to tenure or other conditions of employment to discourage union membership. Under the words of the statute there must be both discrimination and a resulting discouragement of union membership. It has long been established that a finding of violation under this section will normally turn on the employer's motivation. . . .

This is not to deny that there are some practices which are inherently so prejudicial to union interests and so devoid of significant economic justification that no specific evidence of intent to discourage union membership or other antiunion animus is required. In some cases, it may be that the employer's conduct carries with it an inference of unlawful intention so compelling that it is justifiable to disbelieve the employer's protestations of innocent purpose. Radio Officers' Union v. NLRB, *supra*, 347 U.S. at 44-45; NLRB v. Erie Resistor Corp., *supra*. Thus where many have broken a shop rule, but only union leaders have been discharged, the Board need not listen too long to the plea that shop discipline was simply being enforced. In other situations, we have described the process as the "far more delicate task . . . of weighing the interests of employees in concerted activity against the interest of the employer in operating his business in a particular manner. . . ." NLRB v. Erie Resistor Corp., *supra*, 373 U.S. at 229 (1965).

But this lockout does not fall into that category of cases arising under § 8(a)(3) in which the Board may truncate its inquiry into employer motivation. As this case well shows, use of the lockout does not carry with it any necessary implication that the employer acted to discourage union membership or otherwise discriminate against union members as such. The purpose and effect of the lockout was only to bring pressure upon the union to modify its demands. Similarly, it does not appear that the natural tendency of the lockout is severely to discourage union membership while serving no significant employer interest. In fact, it is difficult to understand what tendency to discourage union membership or otherwise discriminate against union members was perceived by the Board. There is no claim that the employer locked out only union members, or locked out any employee simply because he was a union member; nor is it alleged that the employer conditioned rehiring upon resignation from the union. It is true that the employees suffered economic disadvantage because of their union's insistence on demands unacceptable to the employer, but this is also true of many steps which an employer may take during a bargaining conflict, and the existence of an arguable possibility that someone may feel himself discouraged in his union membership or discriminated against by reason of that membership cannot suffice to label them violations of § 8(a)(3) absent some unlawful intention. The employer's permanent replacement of strikers (NLRB v.

Mackay Radio & Telegraph Co., *supra*), his unilateral imposition of terms (Labor Board v. Tex-Tan, Inc., 318 F.2d 472, 479-482), or his simple refusal to make a concession which would terminate a strike — all impose economic disadvantage during a bargaining conflict, but none is necessarily a violation of § 8(a)(3).

To find a violation of § 8(a)(3) then, the Board must find that the employer acted for a proscribed purpose. Indeed, the Board itself has always recognized that certain "operative" or "economic" purposes would justify a lockout. But the Board has erred in ruling that only these purposes will remove a lockout from the ambit of § 8(a)(3), for that section requires an intention to discourage union membership or otherwise discriminate against the union. There was not the slightest evidence and there was no finding, that the employer was actuated by a desire to discourage membership in the union as distinguished from a desire to affect the outcome of the particular negotiations in which he was involved. We recognize that the "union membership" which is not to be discouraged refers to more than the payment of dues and that measures taken to discourage participation in protected union activities may be found to come within the proscription. Radio Officers' Union v. NLRB, *supra*, 347 U.S. at 39-40. However, there is nothing in the act which gives employees the right to insist on their contract demands, free from the sort of economic disadvantage which frequently attends bargaining disputes. Therefore, we conclude that where the intention proven is merely to bring about a settlement of a labor dispute on favorable terms, no violation of § 8(a)(3) is shown.

The conclusions which we draw from analysis of §§ 8(a)(1) and 8(a)(3) are consonant with what little of relevance can be drawn from the balance of the statute and its legislative history. In the original version of the act, the predecessor of § 8(a)(1) declared it an unfair labor practice "[t]o attempt, by interference, influence, restraint, favor, coercion, or lockout, or by any other means, to impair the right of employees guaranteed in section 4." [11] Prominent in the criticism leveled at the bill in the Senate Committee hearings was the charge that it did not accord evenhanded treatment to employers and employees because it prohibited the lockout while protecting the strike.[12] In the face of such criticism, the Committee added a provision prohibiting employee interference with employer

---

[11] 1 Legislative History of the Labor Management Relations Act, 1935, 3 (hereafter L.M.R.A.). Section 4 of the bill provided:

"Employees shall have the right to organize and join labor organizations, and to engage in concerted activities, either in labor organizations or otherwise, for the purposes of organizing and bargaining collectively through representatives of their own choosing or for other purposes of mutual aid or protection." *Ibid.*

[12] 1 L.M.R.A. 406, 545, 570, 946.

bargaining activities [13] and deleted the reference to the lockout.[14] A plausible inference to be drawn from this history is that the language was defeated to mollify those who saw in the bill an inequitable denial of resort to the lockout, and to remove any language which might give rise to fears that the lockout was being proscribed *per se.* It is in any event clear that the Committee was concerned with the status of the lockout and that the bill, as reported and as finally enacted, contained no prohibition on the use of the lockout as such.

Although neither § 8(a)(1) nor § 8(a)(3) refers specifically to the lockout, various other provisions of the Labor Management Relations Act do refer to the lockout, and these references can be interpreted as a recognition of the legitimacy of the device as a means of applying economic pressure in support of bargaining positions. Thus 29 U.S.C. § 158(d)(4) (1958 ed.) prohibits the use of strike or lockout unless requisite notice procedures have been complied with; 29 U.S.C. § 173(c) (1958 ed.) directs the Federal Mediation and Conciliation Service to seek voluntary resolution of labor disputes without resort to strikes or lockouts; and 29 U.S.C. §§ 176, 178 (1958 ed.), authorize procedures whereby the President can institute a board of inquiry to forestall certain strikes or lockouts. The correlative use of the terms "strike" and "lockout" in these sections contemplates that lockouts will be used in the bargaining process in some fashion. This is not to say that these provisions serve to define the permissible scope of a lockout by an employer. That, in the context of the present case, is a question ultimately to be resolved by analysis of §§ 8(a)(1) and 8(a)(3).

The Board has justified its ruling in this case and its general approach to the legality of lockouts on the basis of its special competence to weigh the competing interests of employers and employees and to accommodate these interests according to its expert judgment. "The Board has reasonably concluded that the availability of such a weapon would so substantially tip the scales in the employer's favor as to defeat the Congressional purpose of placing employees on a par with their adversaries at the bargaining table." [15] To buttress its decision as to the balance struck in this particular case, the Board points out that the employer has been given other weapons to counterbalance the employees' power of strike. The employer may permanently replace workers who

---

[13] S. 2926, § 3 (2):

"It shall be an unfair labor practice [f]or employees to attempt, by interference or coercion, to impair the exercise by employers of the right to join or form employer organizations and to designate representatives of their own choosing for the purpose of collective bargaining." 1 L.M.R.A. 1087.

[14] S. 2926, § 3 (1):

"It shall be an unfair labor practice [f]or an employer to attempt, by interference or coercion, to impair the exercise by employees of the right to form or join labor organizations, to designate representatives of their own choosing, and to engage in concerted activities for the purpose of collective bargaining or other mutual aid or protection." 1 L.M.R.A. 1087.

[15] Respondent's Brief 17.

have gone out on strike, or by stockpiling and subcontracting, maintain his commercial operations while the strikers bear the economic brunt of the work stoppage. Similarly, the employer can institute unilaterally the working conditions which he desires once his contract with the union has expired. Given these economic weapons, it is argued, the employer has been adequately equipped with tools of economic self-help.

There is, of course, no question that the Board is entitled to the greatest deference in recognition of its special competence in dealing with labor problems. In many areas its evaluation of the competing interests of employer and employee should unquestionably be given conclusive effect in determining the application of §§ 8(a)(1), (a)(3), and (a)(5). However, we think that the Board construes its functions too expansively when it claims general authority to define national labor policy by balancing the competing interests of labor and management.

While a primary purpose of the National Labor Relations Act was to redress the perceived imbalance of economic power between labor and management, it sought to accomplish that result by conferring certain affirmative rights on employees and by placing certain enumerated restrictions on the activities of employers. . . . Having protected employee organization in countervailance to the employers' bargaining power, and having established a system of collective bargaining whereby the newly coequal adversaries might resolve their disputes, the act also contemplated resort to economic weapons should more peaceful measures not avail. Sections 8(a)(1) and 8(a)(3) do not give the Board a general authority to assess the relative economic power of the adversaries in the bargaining process and to deny weapons to one party or the other because of its assessment of that party's bargaining power. NLRB v. Brown [380 U.S. 278 (1965)]. In this case the Board has, in essence, denied the use of the bargaining lockout to the employer because of its conviction that use of this device would give the employer "too much power." In so doing, the Board has stretched §§ 8(a)(1) and 8(a)(3) far beyond their functions of protecting the rights of employee organization and collective bargaining. What we have recently said in a closely related context is equally applicable here:

"[W]hen the Board moves in this area . . . it is functioning as an arbiter of the sort of economic weapons the parties can use in seeking to gain acceptance of their bargaining demands. It has sought to introduce some standard of properly 'balanced' bargaining power, or some new distinction of justifiable and unjustifiable, proper and 'abusive' economic weapons into . . . the Act. . . . We have expressed our belief that this amounts to the Board's entrance into the substantive aspect of the bargaining process to an extent Congress has not countenanced." NLRB v. Insurance Agents' International Union, 361 U.S. 477, 497-498 (1960).

We are unable to find that any fair construction of the provisions relied on by the Board in this case can support its finding of an unfair labor practice. Indeed, the role assumed by the Board in this area is fundamentally inconsistent with the structure of the act and the function of the sections relied upon. The deference owed to an expert tribunal cannot be allowed to slip into a judicial inertia which results in the unauthorized assumption by an agency of major policy decisions properly made by Congress. Accordingly, we hold that an employer violates neither § 8(a)(1) nor § 8(a)(3) when, after a bargaining impasse has been reached, he temporarily shuts down his plant and lays off his employees for the sole purpose of bringing economic pressure to bear in support of his legitimate bargaining position.

Reversed.

MR. JUSTICE WHITE, concurring in the result.

. . . .

In my view the issue posed in this case is whether an employer who in fact anticipates a strike may inform customers of this belief to protect his commercial relationship with customers and to safeguard their property, thereby discouraging business, and then lay off employees for whom there is no available work. I, like the trial examiner, think he may, and do not think this conduct can be impeached under §§ 8(a)(1) and 8(a)(3) by merely asserting that the employer and his customers were erroneous in believing a strike was imminent. . . .

. . . Since I think an employer's decision to lay off employees because of lack of work is not ordinarily barred by the act, and since neither the Board nor the Court properly can ignore this claim, I would reverse the Board's order, but without reaching out to decide an issue not at all presented by this case. . . .

MR. JUSTICE GOLDBERG, with whom THE CHIEF JUSTICE joins, concurring in the result.

I concur in the Court's conclusion that the employer's lockout in this case was not a violation of either § 8(a)(1) or § 8(a)(3) of the National Labor Relations Act, 49 Stat. 453, as amended, 29 U.S.C. §§ 158(a)(1) and (3) (1958 ed.), and I therefore join in the judgment reversing the Court of Appeals. I reach this result not for the Court's reasons, but because, from the plain facts revealed by the record, it is crystal clear that the employer's lockout here was justified. The very facts recited by the Court in its opinion show that this employer locked out his employees in the face of a threatened strike under circumstances where, had the choice of timing been left solely to the unions, the employer and his customers would have been subject to economic injury over and beyond the loss of business normally incident to a strike upon the termination of the collective bargaining agreement. A lockout under these circumstances has been recognized by the Board itself to be justifiable and not a violation of the labor statutes. Betts Cadillac-Olds, Inc., 96 N.L.R.B. 268. . . .

My view of this case would make it unnecessary to deal with the broad question of whether an employer may lock out his employees solely to bring economic pressure to bear in support of his bargaining position. The question of which types of lockout are compatible with the labor statute is a complex one as this decision and the other cases decided today illustrate. See Textile Workers Union v. Darlington Mfg. Co., *supra* at 263; NLRB v. Brown, *supra* at 278. This Court has said that the problem of the legality of certain types of strike activity must be "revealed by unfolding variant situations" and requires "an evolutionary process for its rational response, not a quick, definitive formula as a comprehensive answer." Electrical Workers, Local 761 v. NLRB, 366 U.S. 667, 674 (1961); see also NLRB v. Steelworkers, *supra,* 357 U.S. 362-363 (1958). The same is true of lockouts.

The types of situation in which an employer might seek to lock out his employees differ considerably one from the other. This case presents the situation of an employer with a long history of union recognition and collective bargaining, confronted with a history of past strikes, who locks out only after considerable good-faith negotiation involving agreement and compromise on numerous issues, after a bargaining impasse has been reached, more than a week after the prior contract has expired, and when faced with the threat of a strike at a time when he and the property of his customers can suffer unusual harm. Other cases in which the Board has held a lockout illegal have presented far different situations. For example, in Quaker State Oil Refining Corp., *supra,* an employer locked out his employees the day after his contract with the union expired although no impasse had been reached in the bargaining still in progress, no strike had been threatened by the unions, which had never called a sudden strike during the 13 years they had bargained with the employer, and the unions had offered to resubmit the employer's proposals to his employees for a vote. See also Utah Plumbing and Heating Contractors Assn., 126 N.L.R.B. 973. These decisions of the Labor Board properly take into account, in determining the legality of lockouts under the labor statutes, such factors as the length, character, and history of the collective bargaining relation between the union and the employer, as well as whether a bargaining impasse has been reached. Indeed, the Court itself seems to recognize that there is a difference between locking out before a bargaining impasse has been reached and locking out after collective bargaining has been exhausted, for it limits its holding to lockouts in the latter type of situation without deciding the question of the legality of locking out before bargaining is exhausted. Since the examples of different lockout situations could be multiplied, the logic of the Court's limitation of its holding should lead it to recognize that the problem of lockouts requires "an evolutionary process," not "a quick, definitive formula," for its answer.

The Court should be chary of sweeping generalizations in this complex area. When we deal with the lockout and the strike, we are dealing with weapons of industrial warfare. While the parties generally have their choice of economic weapons, see NLRB v. Insurance Agents, 361 U.S. 477 (1960), this choice, both with respect to the strike and the lockout, is not unrestricted. While we have recognized "the deference paid the strike weapon by the federal labor laws," NLRB v. Erie Resistor, *supra* at 235, not all forms of economically motivated strikes are protected nor even permissible under the labor statutes or the prior decisions of this Court. Moreover, a lockout prompted by an antiunion motive is plainly illegal under the National Labor Relations Act, though no similar restrictions as to motive operate to limit the legality of a strike. See NLRB v. Somerset

Shoe Co., 111 F.2d 681 (1st Cir. 1940); NLRB v. Stremel, 141 F.2d 317 (10th Cir. 1944); NLRB v. Somerset Classics, Inc., 193 F.2d 613 (2d Cir. (1952). The varieties of restriction imposed upon strikes and lockouts reflect the complexities presented by variant factual situations.

The Court not only overlooks the factual diversity among different types of lockout, but its statement of the rules governing unfair labor practices under §§ 8(a)(1) and (3) does not give proper recognition to the fact that "[t]he ultimate problem [in this area] is the balancing of the conflicting legitimate interests." NLRB v. Truck Drivers Union, 353 U.S. 87, 96 (1957). The Court states that employer conduct, not actually motivated by antiunion bias, does not violate §§ 8(a)(1) or (3) unless it is "demonstrably so destructive of collective bargaining," or "so prejudicial to union interests and so devoid of significant economic justification," that no antiunion animus need be shown. This rule departs substantially from both the letter and the spirit of numerous prior decisions of the Court. *See, e.g.,* NLRB v. Truck Drivers Union, *supra,* 353 U.S. at 96; Republic Aviation Corp. v. NLRB, 324 U.S. 793 (1945); NLRB v. Babcock & Wilcox Co., 351 U.S. 105 (1956); NLRB v. Burnup & Sims, Inc., 379 U.S. 21 (1964).

These decisions demonstrate that the correct test for determining whether § 8(a)(1) has been violated in cases not involving an employer antiunion motive is whether the business justification for the employer's action outweighs the interference with § 7 rights involved. In Republic Aviation Corp. v. NLRB, *supra,* for example, the Court affirmed a Board holding that a company "no-solicitation" rule was invalid as applied to prevent solicitation of employees on company property during periods when employees were free to do as they pleased, not because such a rule was "demonstrably . . . destructive of collective bargaining," but simply because there was no significant employer justification for the rule and there was a showing of union interest, though far short of a necessity, in its abolition. See also, NLRB v. Burnup & Sims, Inc., *supra.*

A similar test is applicable in § 8(a)(3) cases where no antiunion motive is shown. The Court misreads Radio Officers' Union v. NLRB, 347 U.S. 17, and NLRB v. Erie Resistor Corp., *supra,* in stating that the test in such cases under § 8(a)(3) is whether practices "are inherently so prejudicial to union interests and so devoid of significant economic justification that no specific evidence of intent to discourage union membership or other antiunion animus is required." *Supra,* at pp. 863, 864. *Radio Officers* did not restrict the application of § 8(a)(3) in cases devoid of antiunion motive to the extreme situations encompassed by the Court's test. Rather, in holding applicable the common-law rule that a man is presumed to intend the foreseeable consequences of his own actions, the Court extended the reach of § 8(a)(3) to all cases in which a significant antiunion effect is foreseeable regardless of the employer's motive. In such cases the Court, in *Erie Resistor Corp.,* held that conduct might be determined by the Board to violate § 8(a)(3) where the Board's determination resulted from a reasonable "weighing [of] the interests of employees in concerted activity against the interests of the employer in operating his business in a particular manner and . . . [from] balancing in the light of the Act and its policy the intended consequences upon employee rights against the business ends to be served by the employer's conduct." 373 U.S. at 229.

These cases show that the tests as to whether an employer's conduct violates § 8(a)(1) or violates § 8(a)(3) without a showing of antiunion motive come down to substantially the same thing: whether the legitimate ecomomic interests of the employer justify his interference with the rights of his employees—a test involving "the balancing of the conflicting legitimate interests." NLRB v. Truck Drivers Union, *supra*, 353 U.S. at 96. As the prior decisions of this Court have held, "[t]he function of striking . . . [such a] balance, . . . often a difficult and delicate responsibility, . . . Congress committed primarily to the National Labor * Relations Board, subject to limited judicial review." *ibid.*

This, of course, does not mean that reviewing courts are to abdicate their function of determining whether, giving due deference to the Board, the Board has struck the balance consistently with the language and policy of the act. See NLRB v. Brown, *supra;* NLRB v. Truck Drivers Union, *supra.* Nor does it mean that reviewing courts are to rubberstamp decisions of the Board where the application of principles in a particular case is irrational or not supported by substantial evidence on the record as a whole. Applying these principles to the factual situation here presented, I would accept the Board's carefully limited rule, fashioned by the Board after weighing the "conflicting legitimate interests" of employers and unions, that a lockout does not violate the act where used to "safeguard against unusual operational problems or hazards or economic loss where there is reasonable ground for believing that a strike [is] . . . threatened or imminent." Quaker State Oil Refining Corp., *supra* at 337. This rule is consistent with the policies of the act and based upon the actualities of industrial relations. I would, however, reject the determination of the Board refusing to apply this rule to this case, for the undisputed facts revealed by the record bring this case clearly within the rule.

In view of the necessity for, and the desirability of, weighing the legitimate conflicting interests in variant lockout situations, there is not and cannot be any simple formula which readily demarks the permissible from the impermissible lockout. This being so, I would not reach out in this case to announce principles which are determinative of the legality of all economically motivated lockouts whether before or after a bargaining impasse has been reached. In my view both the Court and the Board, in reaching their opposite conclusions, have inadvisably and unnecessarily done so here. Rather, I would confine our decision to the simple holding, supported both by the record and the actualities of industrial relations, that the employer's fear of a strike was reasonable, and therefore, under the settled decisions of the Board, which I would approve, the lockout of his employees was justified.

NOTES

1. Suppose six employers are bargaining jointly with a union, although they do not have a formally established multiemployer unit. An impasse is reached in the bargaining, and the union strikes two of the employers, advising its members that this device would be the most effective method to obtain a satisfactory industry-wide settlement. May the other four employers lock out without committing an unfair labor practice? Weyerhaeuser Co., 166 N.L.R.B. 299 (1967) (*Held:* Yes).

2. Suppose two newspapers in a city bargain on a multiemployer basis with most of the fourteen unions which represent various groups of their employees. But for twenty years, each paper has bargained separately with the Teamsters as the representative of its distribution employees. The two papers confer on three common issues, and the News agrees that if the union strikes the Free Press on these issues, the News will not publish. The Free Press is struck and the News locks out. Union President Hoffa had said that he regarded the News' latest proposal as a final offer, and had threatened the News with a strike. Is the News' lockout lawful? Evening News Ass'n, 166 N.L.R.B. 219 (1967) (*Held:* Yes). The Board said: "There is no question but that the Supreme Court's American Ship decision has obliterated, as a matter of law the line previously drawn by the Board between offensive and defensive lockouts. . . . The Court stated that the test of a lockout's legality, assuming no motive to discourage union activity or to evade bargaining exists, is whether the lockout 'is inherently so prejudicial to union interest and so devoid of significant economic justification' that no evidence of intent is necessary. That test affords the basis for our determination here."

3. How essential is it that the negotiations have reached an impasse before the employer would be privileged to lock out?

A preimpasse lockout to support an employer's bargaining position and to forestall a strike during its busy shipping season was held not violative of §§ 8(a)(3) or (1) in Darling & Co., 171 N.L.R.B. 801 (1968). The Board stated that the absence of an impasse did not render the *American Ship* tests per se inapplicable, although "the finding of an impasse in negotiations may be a factor supporting the determination that a particular lockout is lawful." The determination must be made on a case-by-case basis. Here there had been extensive good faith bargaining on all subjects and accord on many issues, but continuing disagreement on certain key items, including a work assignment clause. Strikes had occurred during the parties' twenty-year relationship, and work assignments were a major issue in a crippling strike about four years earlier. *Darling & Co.* was affirmed *sub nom.* Lane v. NLRB, 418 F.2d 1208 (D.C. Cir. 1969).

4. Even though three employers could lawfully lock out their employees following the expiration of their separate collective bargaining agreements with a union, the hiring of temporary replacements was ruled a violation of §§ 8(a)(1) and (3) by the Labor Board in the absence of a showing of a substantial business justification for the employers' conduct.

Inland Trucking Co., 179 N.L.R.B. 350 (1969). In enforcing the Board's order, the Seventh Circuit observed that the use of replacements by an employer during an offensive, as distinguished from a defensive, lockout "would not merely pit the employer's ability to withstand a shut down of its business against the employees' ability to endure cessation of their jobs, but would permit the employer to impose on his employees the pressure of being out of work while obtaining for himself the returns of continued operation. Employees would be forced, at the initiative of the employer, not only to forego their job earnings, but, in addition, to watch other workers enjoy the earning opportunities over which the locked-out employees were endeavoring to bargain." Inland Trucking Co. v. NLRB, 440 F.2d 562 (7th Cir. 1971), *cert. denied*, 404 U.S. 858 (1971).

However, in Ottawa Silica Co., Inc., 197 N.L.R.B. 449 (1972), *aff'd,* 482 F.2d 945 (6th Cir. 1973), and Inter-Collegiate Press, 199 N.L.R.B. 177 (1972), *aff'd,* 84 L.R.R.M. 2562 (8th Cir. 1973), *cert. denied,* 416 U.S. 938 (1974), the Board majority found no violation where the employer showed legitimate and substantial business justification for using temporary replacements during an otherwise lawful lockout and there was no wrongful motivation.

5. The Fifth Circuit reversed a Board order and held that sabotage by employees during contract negotiations amounted to an in-plant strike, justifying a lockout of the employees and their subsequent *permanent* replacement without notification to their union. Judge Wisdom dissented and said he would follow previous decisions that action may not be taken against in-plant strikers until the participants are identified. Johns-Manville Products v. NLRB, 557 F.2d 1126 (5th Cir. 1977).

For critiques of *Johns-Manville, see* Comment, 10 St. MARY'S L. REV. 179 (1978) and Note, 46 GEO. WASH. L. REV. 638 (1978).

6. A lockout which is, in part, for the purpose of compelling the union to submit the employer's final offer for ratification by a mail ballot referendum procedure is a violation of § 8(a)(3) and § 8(a)(5). Movers & Warehousemen's Ass'n v. NLRB, 550 F.2d 962 (4th Cir. 1977), *cert. denied,* 98 S. Ct. 75 (U.S. 1977).

7. See Baird, *Lockout Law: The Supreme Court and the NLRB,* 38 GEO. WASH. L. REV. 396 (1970); Bernhardt, *Lockouts: An Analysis of Board and Court Decisions Since Brown and American Ship,* 57 CORNELL L. REV. 211 (1972); Feldesman & Koretz, *Lockouts,* 46 BOSTON U.L. REV. 329 (1966); Oberer, *Lockouts and the Law: The Impact of American Ship Building and Brown Food,* 51 CORNELL L.Q. 193 (1966); Note, *An Employer Who Locks Out His Employees Solely as a Means of Applying Economic Pressure May Not Hire Temporary Replacements,* 23 SYRACUSE L. REV. 179 (1972).

Proof of Motive in Cases Involving Violations of §§ 8(a)(3) and (1)

The Supreme Court in NLRB v. Great Dane Trailers Inc., 388 U.S. 26 (1967), further developed its requirements on the extent to which *scienter* must be proved in order to find a violation of § 8(a)(3). In that case, an employer was held by the NLRB to have violated § 8(a)(3) by refusing to pay striking employees vacation benefits which had accrued under a terminated collective bargaining agreement while at the same time announcing an intent to pay such benefits to those individuals who had worked on a certain day during the strike. The court of appeals, at 363 F.2d 130 (5th Cir. 1966) refused enforcement because it found no affirmative showing of an unlawful employer motivation to discourage union membership.

The Supreme Court overturned the appeals court decision. It divided employers' conduct into two categories: that which is "inherently destructive" of employee rights, and that which has a "comparatively slight" effect on those rights. In both situations, "once it had been proved that the employer engaged in discriminatory conduct which could have adversely affected employee rights to some extent, the burden is upon the employer to establish that it was motivated by legitimate objectives. . . ." The court held that a violation of § 8(a)(3) can be found without proof of improper motivation in instances in which "inherently destructive" conduct is present even though the employer does introduce evidence of justification; as to conduct which has "comparatively slight" effect, if the employer comes forward with exculpatory evidence which outweighs the interference with the employees' exercise of their § 7 rights, a violation can be found only if antiunion motivation is proved.

NOTES

1. In Molders Local 155 v. NLRB [U.S. Pipe & Foundry Co.], 442 F.2d 742 (D.C. Cir. 1971), the court of appeals agreed (2-1) with the Labor Board that an employer had violated the Act by withdrawing employee benefits following an impasse in bargaining. The court found that the employer's conduct was designed in part to provoke the employees into striking, and was therefore "of a character to undermine the Union's protected control of its right to strike." Section 7 protects not only the right to strike, but also the right to refrain from striking, and here the employer had sought to control the strike initiative, which under the Act resides with the employees. One judge dissented on the ground that "the Company properly exercised legitimate means after the impasse in bargaining had been reached to so effect the timing of the strike, which was inevitable, as to place it in a period of minimum production demands upon the Company. The utilization of legal economic pressures must, as a matter of fairness, be as available to management as it is to unions." The dissenting judge also emphasized that the record evidenced no antiunion motivation on the part of the employer.

2. Relying on *Great Dane Trailers,* the NLRB held that it would be "inherently destructive of employee interests" for an employer, upon the resumption of operations following an economic layoff, to hire a whole new work force represented by one union to the exclusion of its laid-off employees who were represented by another union. Rushton & Mercier Woodworking Co., 203 N.L.R.B. 123 (1973).

3. In NLRB v. Burnup & Sims, Inc., 379 U.S. 21 (1964), the Supreme Court held that an employer violated § 8(a)(1) when he discharged two employees who were engaged in protected organizing activities, even though he had no wrongful motive. In this case, the employer had discharged the two employees on the information that they were planning to use violence in the union's organizing campaign; the information later proved to be untrue. The Court held that the policy behind § 8(a)(1) dictated the reinstatement of the employees, "Otherwise, the protected activity would lose some of its immunity, since the example of employees who are discharged on false charges would or might have a deterrent effect on other employees." Employer good faith in the discharges was deemed irrelevant.

4. See Christensen and Svanoe, *Motive and Intent in the Commission of Unfair Labor Practices*, 77 YALE L.J. 1269 (1968); Getman, *Section 8(a)(3) of the NLRA and the Effort to Insulate Free Employee Choice*, 32 U. CHI. L. REV. 735 (1965); Oberer, *The Scienter Factor in Sections 8(a)(1) and (3) of the Labor Act; Of Balancing, Hostile Motive, Dogs and Tails*, 52 CORNELL L.Q. 491 (1967); Shieber, *Section 8(a)(1) of the NLRA: A Rationale, Part I, Discrimination*, 29 LA. L. REV. 46 (1968); Shieber and Moore, *Part II, Encouragement and Discouragement of Membership in Any Labor Organization and the Significance of Employer Motive*, 33 LA. L. REV. 1 (1972); Note, *Employer Motive and § 8(a)(3) Violations*, 48 B.U. L. REV. 142 (1968); Note, *Intent, Effect, Purpose, and Motive as Applicable Elements to §§ 8(a)(1) and (3) Violations of the NLRA*, 7 WAKE FOREST L. REV. 616 (1971).

TEXTİLE WORKERS UNION v. DARLINGTON MFG. CO. NLRB v. DARLINGTON MFG. CO.

Supreme Court of the United States
380 U.S. 263, 85 S. Ct. 994, 13 L. Ed. 2d 827 (1965)

MR. JUSTICE HARLAN delivered the opinion of the Court.

We here review judgments of the Court of Appeals setting aside and refusing to enforce an order of the National Labor Relations Board which found respondent Darlington guilty of an unfair labor practice by reason of having permanently closed its plant following petitioner union's election as the bargaining representative of Darlington's employees.

Darlington Manufacturing Company was a South Carolina corporation operating one textile mill. A majority of Darlington's stock was held by Deering Milliken, a New York "selling house" marketing textiles produced by others.[1] Deering Milliken in turn was controlled by Roger Milliken, president of Darlington, and by other members of the Milliken

---

[1] Deering Milliken & Co. owned 41% of the Darlington stock. Cotwool Manufacturing Co., another textile manufacturer, owned 18% of the stock. In 1960 Deering Milliken & Co. was merged into Cotwool, the survivor being named Deering Milliken, Inc.

family.[2] The National Labor Relations Board found that the Milliken family, through Deering Milliken, operated 17 textile manufacturers, including Darlington, whose products, manufactured in 27 different mills, were marketed through Deering Milliken.

In March 1956 petitioner Textile Workers Union initiated an organizational campaign at Darlington which the company resisted vigorously in various ways, including threats to close the mill if the union won a representation election.[3] On September 6, 1956, the union won an election by a narrow margin. When Roger Milliken was advised of the union victory, he decided to call a meeting of the Darlington board of directors to consider closing the mill. Milliken testified before the Labor Board:

"I felt that as a result of the campaign that had been conducted and the promises and statements made in these letters that had been distributed [favoring unionization], that if before we had had some hope, possible hope of achieving competitive [costs] . . . by taking advantage of new machinery that was being put in, that this hope had diminished as a result of the election because a majority of the employees had voted in favor of the union. . . ." (R. 457).

The board of directors met on September 12 and voted to liquidate the corporation, action which was approved by the stockholders on October 17. The plant ceased operations entirely in November, and all plant machinery and equipment was sold piecemeal at auction in December.

The union filed charges with the Labor Board claiming that Darlington had violated §§ 8(a)(1) and 8(a)(3) of the National Labor Relations Act by closing its plant, and § 8(a)(5) by refusing to bargain with the union after the election.[5] The Board, by a divided vote, found that Darlington had been closed because of the antiunion animus of Roger Milliken, and held that to be a violation of § 8(a)(3).[6] The Board also found Darlington

---

[2] The Milliken family owned only 6% of the Darlington stock, but held a majority stock interest in both Deering Milliken & Co. and Cotwool, see note 1, *supra*.

[3] The Board found that Darlington had interrogated employees and threatened to close the mill if the union won the election. After the decision to liquidate was made (see *infra*), Darlington employees were told that the decision to close was caused by the election, and they were encouraged to sign a petition disavowing the union. These practices were held to violate § 8(a)(1) of the National Labor Relations Act, and that part of the Board decision is not challenged here.

[5] The union asked for a bargaining conference on September 12, 1956 (the day that the board of directors voted to liquidate), but was told to await certification by the Board. The union was certified on October 24, and did meet with Darlington officials in November, but no actual bargaining took place. The Board found this to be a violation of § 8(a)(5). Such a finding was in part based on the determination that the plant closing was an unfair labor practice, and no argument is made that § 8(a)(5) requires an employer to bargain concerning a purely business decision to terminate his enterprise. *Cf.* Fibreboard Paper Prod. Corp. v. NLRB, 379 U.S. 203 (1964).

[6] Since the closing was held to be illegal, the Board found that the gradual discharges of all employees during November and December constituted § 8(a)(1) violations. The propriety of this determination depends entirely on whether the decision to close the plant violated § 8(a)(3).

to be part of a single integrated employer group controlled by the Milliken family through Deering Milliken; therefore Deering Milliken could be held liable for the unfair labor practices of Darlington.[7] Alternatively, since Darlington was a part of the Deering Milliken enterprise, Deering Milliken had violated the Act by closing part of its business for a discriminatory purpose. The Board ordered back pay for all Darlington employees until they obtained substantially equivalent work or were put on preferential hiring lists at the other Deering Milliken mills. Respondent Deering Milliken was ordered to bargain with the union in regard to details of compliance with the Board order. 139 N.L.R.B. 241.

On review, the Court of Appeals sitting *en banc,* set aside the order and denied enforcement by a divided vote. 325 F.2d 682. The Court of Appeals held that even accepting arguendo the Board's determination that Deering Milliken had the status of a single employer, a company has the absolute right to close out a part or all of its business regardless of antiunion motives. The court therefore did not review the Board's finding that Deering Milliken was a single integrated employer. . . . We hold that so far as the Labor Act is concerned, an employer has the absolute right to terminate his entire business for any reason he pleases, but disagree with the Court of Appeals that such right includes the ability to close part of a business no matter what the reason. We conclude that the cause must be remanded to the Board for further proceedings.

Preliminarily it should be observed that both petitioners argue that the Darlington closing violated § 8(a)(1) as well as § 8(a)(3) of the Act. We think, however, that the Board was correct in treating the closing only under § 8(a)(3).[8] Section 8(a)(1) provides that it is an unfair labor practice for an employer "to interfere with, restrain, or coerce employees in the exercise of" § 7 rights. Naturally, certain business decisions will, to some degree, interfere with concerted activities by employees. But it is only when the interference with § 7 rights outweighs the business justification for the employer's action that § 8(a)(1) is violated. See, *e.g.,* NLRB v. Steelworkers, 357 U.S. 357 (1958); Republic Aviation Corp. v. NLRB, 324 U.S. 793 (1945). A violation of § 8(a)(1) alone therefore presupposes an act which is unlawful even absent a discriminatory motive. Whatever may be the limits of § 8(a)(1), some employer decisions are so peculiarly matters of management prerogative that they would never constitute violations of § 8(a)(1), whether or not they involved sound business judgment, unless they also violated § 8(a)(3). Thus it is not questioned in this case that an employer has the right to terminate his business, whatever the impact of such action on concerted activities, if the decision to close is motivated by other than discriminatory reasons.[10] But such

_____

[7] Members Leedom and Rodgers agreed with the trial examiner that Deering Milliken was not a single employer. Member Rodgers dissented in arguing that Darlington had not violated § 8(a)(3) by closing.

[8] The Board did find that Darlington's discharge of employees following the decision to close violated § 8(a)(1). See note 6, *supra.*

[10] It is also clear that the ambiguous act of closing a plant following the election of a union is not, absent an inquiry into the employer's motive, inherently discriminatory. We

action, if discriminatorily motivated, is encompassed within the literal language of § 8(a)(3). We therefore deal with the Darlington closing under that section.

I. We consider first the argument, advanced by the petitioner union but not by the Board, and rejected by the Court of Appeals, that an employer may not go completely out of business without running afoul of the Labor Act if such action is prompted by a desire to avoid unionization.[11] Given the Board's findings on the issue of motive, acceptance of this contention would carry the day for the Board's conclusion that the closing of this plant was an unfair labor practice, even on the assumption that Darlington is to be regarded as an independent unrelated employer. A proposition that a single businessman cannot choose to go out of business if he wants to would represent such a startling innovation that it should not be entertained without the clearest manifestation of legislative intent or unequivocal judicial precedent so construing the Labor Act. We find neither.

So far as legislative manifestation is concerned, it is sufficient to say that there is not the slightest indication in the history of the Wagner Act or of the Taft-Hartley Act that Congress envisaged any such result under either statute.

As for judicial precedent, the Board recognized that "[t]here is no decided case directly dispositive of Darlington's claim that it had an absolute right to close its mill, irrespective of motive." 139 N.L.R.B., at 250. The only language by this Court in any way adverting to this problem is found in Southport Petroleum Co. v. NLRB, 315 U.S. 100, 106 (1942), where it was stated:

"Whether there was a bona fide discontinuance and a true change of ownership — which would terminate the duty of reinstatement created by the Board's order — or merely a disguised continuance of the old employer, does not clearly appear. . . ."

The courts of appeals have generally assumed that a complete cessation of business will remove an employer from future coverage by the Act. Thus the Court of Appeals said in these cases: The Act "does not compel a person to become or remain an employee. It does not compel one to become or remain an employer. Either may withdraw from that status with immunity, so long as the obligations of an employment contract have been met." 325 F.2d, at 685. The Eighth Circuit, in NLRB v. New Madrid Mfg. Co., 215 F.2d 908, 914 (8th Cir. 1954), was equally explicit:

"But none of this can be taken to mean that an employer does not have the absolute right, at all times, to permanently close and go out of

---

are thus not confronted with a situation where the employer "must be held to intend the very consequences which foreseeably and inescapably flow from his actions. . . ." (NLRB v. Erie Resistor Corp., 373 U.S. 221, 228 (1963)), in which the Board could find a violation of § 8(a)(3) without an examination into motive. See Radio Officers v. NLRB, 347 U.S. 17, 42-43 (1954); Teamsters Local v. NLRB, 365 U.S. 667, 674-676 (1961).

[11] The Board predicates its argument on the finding that Deering Milliken was an integrated enterprise, and does not consider it necessary to argue that an employer may not go completely out of business for antiunion reasons. Brief for National Labor Relations Board, at 3, n. 2.

business . . . for whatever reason he may choose, whether union animosity or anything else, and without his being thereby left subject to a remedial liability under the Labor Management Relations Act for such unfair labor practices as he may have committed in the enterprise, except up to the time that such actual and permanent closing . . . has occurred." [12]

The AFL-CIO suggests in its *amicus* brief that Darlington's action was similar to a discriminatory lockout, which is prohibited " 'because designed to frustrate organizational efforts, to destroy or undermine bargaining representation, or to evade the duty to bargain.' " [13] One of the purposes of the Labor Act is to prohibit the discriminatory use of economic weapons in an effort to obtain future benefits. The discriminatory lockout designed to destroy a union like a "runaway shop," is a lever which has been used to discourage collective employee activities in the future. But a complete liquidation of a business yields no such future benefit for the employer, if the termination is bona fide.[14] It may be motivated more by spite against the union than by business reasons, but it is not the type of discrimination which is prohibited by the Act. The personal satisfaction that such an employer may derive from standing on his beliefs or the mere possibility that other employers will follow his example are surely too remote to be considered dangers at which the labor statutes were aimed.[15] Although employees may be prohibited from engaging in a strike under certain conditions, no one would consider it a violation of the Act for the same employees to quit their employment *en masse,* even if motivated by a desire to ruin the employer. The very permanence of such action would negate any future economic benefit to the employees. The employer's right to go out of business is no different.

We are not presented here with the case of a "runaway shop," [16] whereby Darlington would transfer its work to another plant or open a

---

[12] In *New Madrid* the business was transferred to a new employer, which was held liable for the unfair labor practices committed by its predecessor before closing. The closing itself was not found to be an unfair labor practice.

[13] Brief for AFL-CIO, at 7, quoting from NLRB v. Truck Drivers Local, 353 U.S. 87, 93 (1957). This brief was incorporated by reference as Point I of the petitioner union's brief in this Court.

[14] The Darlington property and equipment could not be sold as a unit, and were eventually auctioned off piecemeal. We therefore are not confronted with a sale of a going concern, which might present different considerations under §§ 8(a)(3) and 8(a)(5). Cf. John Wiley & Sons v. Livingston, 376 U.S. 543 (1964); NLRB v. Deena Artware, Inc., 361 U.S. 398 (1960).

[15] Cf. NLRB § 8(c), 29 U.S.C. § 158(c) (1958 ed.). Different considerations would arise were it made to appear that the closing employer was acting pursuant to some arrangement or understanding with other employers to discourage employee organizational activities in their businesses.

[16] *E.g.,* NLRB v. Preston Feed Corp., 309 F.2d 346 (4th Cir. 1962); NLRB v. Wallick, 198 F.2d 477 (3d Cir. 1952). An analogous problem is presented where a department is closed for antiunion reasons but the work is continued by independent contractors. See, *e.g.,* NLRB v. Kelly & Picerne, Inc., 298 F.2d 895 (1st Cir. 1962); Jays Foods, Inc. v. NLRB, 292 F.2d 317 (7th Cir. 1961); NLRB v. R. C. Mahon Co., 269 F.2d 44 (6th Cir. 1959); NLRB v. Bank of America, 130 F.2d 624 (9th Cir. 1942); Williams Motor Co. v. NLRB, 128 F.2d 960 (8th Cir. 1942).

new plant in another locality to replace its closed plant.[17] Nor are we concerned with a shutdown where the employees, by renouncing the union, could cause the plant to reopen.[18] Such cases would involve discriminatory employer action for the purpose of obtaining some benefit from the employees in the future.[19] We hold here only that when an employer closes his entire business, even if the liquidation is motivated by vindictiveness toward the union, such action is not an unfair labor practice.[20]

II. While we thus agree with the Court of Appeals that viewing Darlington as an independent employer the liquidation of its business was

---

[17] After the decision to close the plant, Darlington accepted no new orders, and merely continued operations for a time to fill pending orders. 139 N.L.R.B., at 244.

[18] *E.g.,* NLRB v. Norma Mining Corp., 206 F.2d 38 (4th Cir. 1963). Similarly, if all employees are discharged but the work continues with new personnel, the effect is to discourage any future union activities. See NLRB v. Waterman S.S. Corp., 309 U.S. 206 (1940); NLRB v. National Garment Co., 166 F.2d 233 (8th Cir. 1948); NLRB v. Stremel, 141 F.2d 317 (10th Cir. 1944).

[19] All of the cases to which we have been cited involved closings found to have been motivated, at least in part, by the expectation of achieving future benefits. See cases cited notes 16, 18 *supra*. The two cases which are urged as indistinguishable from Darlington are NLRB v. Savoy Laundry, 237 F.2d 370 (9th Cir. 1956), and NLRB v. Missouri Transit Co., 250 F.2d 261 (8th Cir. 1957). In Savoy Laundry the employer operated one laundry plant where he processed both retail laundry pickups and wholesale laundering. Once that laundry was marked, all of it was processed together. After some of the employees organized, the employer discontinued most of the wholesale service, and thereafter discharged some of his employees. There was no separate wholesale department, and the discriminatory motive was obviously to discourage unionization in the entire plant. Missouri Transit presents a similar situation. A bus company operated an interstate line and intrastate shuttle service connecting a military base with the interstate terminal. When the union attempted to organize all of the drivers, the shuttle service was sold and the shuttle drivers discharged. Although the two services were treated as separate departments, it is clear from the facts of the case that the union was attempting to organize all of the drivers, and the discriminatory motive of the employer was to discourage unionization in the interstate service as well as the shuttle service.

[20] Nothing we have said in this opinion would justify an employer interfering with employee organizational activities by threatening to close his plant, as distinguished from announcing a decision to close already reached by the board of directors or other management authority empowered to make such a decision. We recognize that this safeguard does not wholly remove the possibility that our holding may result in some deterrent effect on organizational activities independent of that arising from the closing itself. An employer may be encouraged to make a definite decision to close on the theory that its mere announcement before a representation election will discourage the employees from voting for the union, and thus his decision may not have to be implemented. Such a possibility is not likely to occur, however, except in a marginal business; a solidly successful employer is not apt to hazard the possibility that the employees will call his bluff by voting to organize. We see no practical way of eliminating this possible consequence of our holding short of allowing the Board to order an employer who chooses so to gamble with his employees not to carry out his announced intention to close. We do not consider the matter of sufficient significance in the over-all labor-management relations picture to require or justify a decision different from the one we have made.

not an unfair labor practice, we cannot accept the lower court's view that the same conclusion necessarily follows if Darlington is regarded as an integral part of the Deering Milliken enterprise.

The closing of an entire business, even though discriminatory, ends the employer-employee relationship; the force of such a closing is entirely spent as to that business when termination of the enterprise takes place. On the other hand, a discriminatory partial closing may have repercussions on what remains of the business, affording employer leverage for discouraging the free exercise of § 7 rights among remaining employees of much the same kind as that found to exist in the "runaway shop" and "temporary closing" cases. Moreover, a possible remedy open to the Board in such a case, like the remedies available in the "runaway shop" and "temporary closing" cases, is to order reinstatement of the discharged employees in the other parts of the business.[21] No such remedy is available when an entire business has been terminated. By analogy to those cases involving a continuing enterprise we are constrained to hold, in disagreement with the Court of Appeals, that a partial closing is an unfair labor practice under § 8(a)(3) if motivated by a purpose to chill unionism in any of the remaining plants of the single employer and if the employer may reasonably have foreseen that such closing will likely have that effect.

While we have spoken in terms of a "partial closing" in the context of the Board's finding that Darlington was part of a larger single enterprise controlled by the Milliken family, we do not mean to suggest that an organizational integration of plants or corporations is a necessary prerequisite to the establishment of such a violation of § 8(a)(3). If the persons exercising control over a plant that is being closed for antiunion reasons (1) have an interest in another business, whether or not affiliated with or engaged in the same line of commercial activity as the closed plant, of sufficient substantiality to give promise of their reaping a benefit from the discouragement of unionization in that business; (2) act to close their plant with the purpose of producing such a result; and (3) occupy a relationship to the other business which makes it realistically foreseeable that its employees will fear that such business will also be closed down if they persist in organizational activities, we think that an unfair labor practice has been made out.

Although the Board's single employer finding necessarily embraced findings as to Roger Milliken and the Milliken family which, if sustained by the Court of Appeals, would satisfy the elements of "interest" and "relationship" with respect to other parts of the Deering Milliken enterprise, that and the other Board findings fall short of establishing the factors of "purpose" and "effect" which are vital requisites of the general principles that govern a case of this kind.

Thus, the Board's findings as to the purpose and foreseeable effect of the Darlington closing pertained *only* to its impact on the Darlington employees. No findings were made as to the purpose and effect of the

---

[21] In the view we take of these cases we do not reach any of the challenges made to the Board's remedy afforded here.

closing with respect to the employees in the other plants comprising the Deering Milliken group. It does not suffice to establish the unfair labor practice charged here to argue that the Darlington closing necessarily had an adverse impact upon unionization in such other plants. We have heretofore observed that employer action which has a foreseeable consequence of discouraging concerted activities generally [22] does not amount to a violation of § 8(a)(3) in the absence of a showing of motivation which is aimed at achieving the prohibited effect. See Teamsters Local v. NLRB, 365 U.S. 667 (1961), and the concurring opinion therein, at 677. In an area which trenches so closely upon otherwise legitimate employer prerogatives, we consider the absence of Board findings on this score a fatal defect in its decision. The Court of Appeals for its part did not deal with the question of purpose and effect at all, since it concluded that an employer's right to close down his entire business because of distaste for unionism, also embraced a partial closing so motivated.

Apart from this, the Board's holding should not be accepted or rejected without court review of its single employer finding, judged, however, in accordance with the general principles set forth above. Review of that finding, which the lower court found unnecessary on its view of the cause, now becomes necessary in light of our holding in this part of our opinion, and is a task that devolves upon the Court of Appeals in the first instance. Universal Camera Corp. v. NLRB, 340 U.S. 474 (1951).

In these circumstances, we think the proper disposition of this cause is to require that it be remanded to the Board so as to afford the Board the opportunity to make further findings on the issue of purpose and effect. See, e.g., NLRB v. Virginia Elec. & Power Co., 314 U.S. 469, 479-480 (1941). This is particularly appropriate here since the cases involve issues of first impression. If such findings are made, the cases will then be in a posture for further review by the Court of Appeals on all issues. Accordingly, without intimating any view as to how any of these matters should eventuate, we vacate the judgments of the Court of Appeals and remand the cases to that court with instructions to remand them to the Board for further proceedings consistent with this opinion.

It is so ordered.

Mr. Justice Stewart took no part in the decision of these cases.

Mr. Justice Goldberg took no part in the consideration or decision of these cases.

NOTES

1. On remand, the Trial Examiner concluded, after hearing additional testimony, that there was no preponderance of evidence to show a purpose to chill unionism at the other plants or a foreseeable effect of such chilling. However, the NLRB disagreed with the Trial Examiner and

---

[22] See n. 10 *supra.*

reached the conclusion that the record indicated, at least in part, an illegal "purpose" and "foreseeable effect." Darlington Mfg. Co., 165 N.L.R.B. 1074 (1967), *enforced,* 397 F.2d 760 (4th Cir. 1968), *cert. denied,* 393 U.S. 1023 (1968).

Evidence which the Board found telling included the following:

(a) Roger Milliken made speeches to South Carolina government and business leaders before the Darlington organization drive, indicating his intense concern with what he regarded as a threat to the Southern industrial community posed by unionism and the need to preserve "cooperation between management and labor . . . at all costs." Section 8(c) does not preclude the Board from using such speeches as evidence of motivation, the Board said, because "this Section left unrestricted the Board's right to consider employer statements for purposes for which they would be admissible in courts of law."

(b) Milliken sent officials of all other Deering Milliken mills reprints of a trade magazine article headlined, "Darlington Situation Becomes Object Lesson to All Concerned," urging the other mill officials to undertake a "public relations" program to make the community leaders understand the consequences of unionization. "The only way the community leaders could make use of this information would be by impressing upon employees the risks of unionism."

(c) The dispatch with which Milliken closed the plant and auctioned off the machinery led the Board to infer that "he saw the opportunity to convey to all his employees an object lesson of the folly of selecting the Union."

(d) There was evidence that news of the Darlington closing spread rapidly to other Deering Milliken plants and was much discussed, frequently in terms of "Mr. Milliken would not operate a plant under a union." From such evidence, the Board inferred a "foreseeable chilling effect." Proof of actual effect, according to the NLRB, is not an essential element.

For other cases applying the Supreme Court's *Darlington* tests, see A. C. Rochat Co., 163 N.L.R.B. 421 (1967), and Motor Repair, Inc., 168 N.L.R.B. 1082 (1968); Frito-Lay v. NLRB, 99 L.R.R.M. 2658 (3d Cir. 1978).

2. For an example of the "runaway shop," which the Supreme Court mentioned in *Darlington* at note 16, as an unfair labor practice, see Garwin Corp., 153 N.L.R.B. 664 (1965), *enforced in part,* 374 F.2d 295 (D.C. Cir. 1967). In this case, the employer's motivation for the move was found to be antiunion hostility — not economic necessity. However, where the employer has sufficient economic reasons for the plant removal, there may be a failure of adequate proof of wrongful purpose. NLRB v. Rapid Bindery, Inc., 293 F.2d 170 (2d Cir. 1961); NLRB v. Adkins Transfer Co., 226 F.2d 324 (6th Cir. 1955); Mount Hope Finishing Co. v. NLRB, 211 F.2d 365 (4th Cir. 1954).

3. Where a violation is found, there is the problem of a proper remedy. The Board does not order the employer to move the "runaway" plant back to the old location. *See* Note, *Applicable Remedies When an Employer Transfers to a New Location to Avoid Dealing With a Union,* 53 MICH. L. REV. 627 (1955). But the Board sometimes orders an employer to reestablish a department which had been replaced by a "contracting-out system," *see* Drennon Food Prod. Co., 122 N.L.R.B. 1353 (1959); R.C. McMahon Co., 118 N.L.R.B. 1537 (1957), *enforcement denied,* 269 F.2d 44 (6th Cir. 1959) (on ground that employer had good economic reasons for setting up an independent contractor system); The Houston Chronicle Pub. Co., 101 N.L.R.B. 1208 (1952), *enforcement denied,* 211 F.2d 848 (5th Cir. 1954) (same reason).

In the case of the "runaway plant," the Board has ordered back pay, together with reinstatement at either the old or the new location, and, where appropriate, reimbursement of expenses of moving to the new location. Industrial Fabricating, Inc., 119 N.L.R.B. 162 (1957), *enforced,* 272 F.2d 184 (6th Cir. 1959); Rome Prod. Co., 77 N.L.R.B. 1217 (1948); Schieber Millinery Co., 26 N.L.R.B. 937 (1940), *enforced,* 116 F.2d 281 (8th Cir. 1940).

In Jacob H. Klotz, 13 N.L.R.B. 746 (1939), the alternative order included a provision for the payment of the employee's expenses of commuting biweekly to the new location, but the Board refused this type of remedy in New Madrid Mfg. Co., 104 N.L.R.B. 117 (1953), *enforced in part,* 215 F.2d 908 (8th Cir. 1954), where the commuting involved would have been daily.

4. The question whether the employer can be ordered to bargain with the old union at the new location will be discussed in Part Four, *infra* at 584.

5. REMEDIAL PROBLEMS

KOHLER CO.

National Labor Relations Board
148 N.L.R.B. 1434 (1964)
Aff'd, 345 F.2d 748 (D.C. Cir. 1965), *cert. denied,* 382 U.S. 836 (1965)

. . . .

[T]he record shows that Respondent failed and refused to bargain collectively with the Union in good faith at all times material herein, and that this unfair labor practice caused the strike which began on April 5, 1954. It was an unfair labor practice strike from its inception.

Discharge of the 77 Strikers

In remanding this aspect of the case, the court directed the Board to follow the doctrine of the *Thayer* case in determining whether the conduct of the 77 dischargees was sufficient to disqualify them for reinstatement. Specifically, the court stated:

"... [W]here an employer who has committed unfair labor practices discharges employees for unprotected acts of misconduct, the Board must consider both the seriousness of the employer's unlawful acts and the seriousness of the employees' misconduct in determining whether reinstatement would effectuate the policies of the Act. Those policies inevitably come into conflict when both labor and management are at fault. To hold that employee "misconduct" automatically precludes compulsory reinstatement ignores two considerations which we think important. First, the employer's antecedent unfair labor practices may have been so blatant that they provoked employees to resort to unprotected action. Second, reinstatement is the only sanction which prevents an employer from benefiting from his unfair labor practices through discharges which may weaken or destroy a union. In the Matter of H. N. Thayer Co., 115 N.L.R.B. 1591, 1605-06 (1956) (dissenting opinion). But sanctions other than discharge — criminal prosecutions, civil suits, union unfair labor practice proceedings and the *possibility* of discharge — are available to prevent or remedy certain employee misconduct. Hart & Pritchard, The Fansteel Case: Employee Misconduct and the Remedial Powers of the National Labor Relations Board, 52 HARV. L. REV. 1275, 1319 (1939). See also Berkshire Knitting Mills, 46 N.L.R.B. 955, 1001-03 (1943), *enforced,* 139 F.2d 134 (3d Cir. 1943), *cert. denied,* 322 U.S. 747 (1944). Hence automatic denial of reinstatement prevents the Board from protecting the rights of employees, but may not be essential to the protection of legitimate interests of employers and the public. We conclude that the teaching of the Thayer case is sound and must be followed in order to assure the Board's compliance with the statutory command that its remedial orders effectuate the policies of the Act." [Footnotes omitted.]

We shall consider the discharges in the light of these court-enunciated principles.

Turning to the facts of the discharges, the record shows that the unprotected activities for which the 77 strikers were discharged fall into four broad categories: (1) mass picketing; (2) presence at or participation in home demonstrations or employment office picketing; (3) organizational responsibility by the 13 strike leaders for their direction and control of the strike from April 5 through May 28, 1954; and (4) individual acts of assault, threats, or other misconduct. The record also shows that all of the misconduct occurred in a context of flagrant antecedent and concurrent unfair labor practices on the part of the Respondent.

We have already found that as a direct result of the Respondent's willful evasion of its bargaining obligations, and its continuous, open provocations of their collective-bargaining agent, the employees commenced their strike on April 5, 1954. It is clear that this strike came as no surprise to the Respondent, for indeed, the Respondent had persevered in a course of conduct calculated ultimately to destroy the Union and had openly prepared watchtowers and armed itself with an arsenal for which "there [was] no possible justification." [18]

---

[18] Indeed, the fact that the employees remained at work for several weeks after the expiration of their contract and in the face of Respondent's open hostility to the Union and the principles of collective bargaining was a remarkable demonstration of self-control.

Moreover, even after the strike began, the Respondent continued to provoke the strikers by maintaining its blatantly illegal course of repeated violations of the Act. Thus, as judicially determined, the Respondent refused to bargain in good faith at any time after contract negotiations resumed on June 1, rejected all efforts at mediation and conciliation, unilaterally instituted two wage increases, discharged striking shell department employees and transferred nonstrikers in that department without notifying or consulting with the Union, delayed and refused to furnish vital wage information to the Union, evicted strikers from company-owned dwellings, discriminated against reinstated shell department strikers, initiated extensive surveillance and espionage of union activities and of union leaders, and unlawfully solicited strikers to return to work.

In view of these unremitting calculated provocations, it is not surprising that the strikers themselves felt compelled to seek both economic survival and the survival of their collective-bargaining agent by a massive and sustained demonstration of solidarity.[19] Nor is it surprising that in the face of such provocative conduct by the Respondent, the union leaders urged and directed mass picketing as the only means of union survival. While we do not condone the mass picketing of the strikers or the planning and direction of such picketing by the union leaders, we must conclude that such activity is attributable no less to the Respondent which provoked that behavior, than to the strikers and union leaders who accepted the challenge presented by the Respondent's open preparations and its complete disregard for its employees' statutory rights.

It also appears that, just as the Respondent's prestrike provocations created the climate of desperation and fear among its employees which produced the mass picketing, so too the Respondent's continuing violations after June 1 induced the home demonstrations and the employment office picketing. While striker participation in these latter forms of retaliation may not be specifically attributable to any individual instance of Respondent's numerous unfair labor practices perpetrated during that period, the total causative effect of Respondent's illegal acts is unquestionable.

Thus, having found that the Respondent engaged in many serious and deliberate violations of the Act for the purpose of ridding itself of the Union and reasserting unilateral control of matters properly subject to collective bargaining, and having found that this unlawful conduct of the Respondent provoked or contributed to the strike and the resultant mass picketing, home demonstrations, and employment office picketing, we next consider whether it would effectuate the policies of the Act to order

---

[19] In this regard, we note that a great many of the Kohler workers participating in this strike had also been employed by Kohler in 1934 at the time of the bloody strike where employee efforts to obtain a forceful independent bargaining agent were crushed. Many others had witnessed, as employees of Respondent, those "20 years of labor peace" during which the Respondent continually displayed its disdain for their rights guaranteed by law and later by a collective-bargaining contract.

reinstatement to those employees who were discharged for directing or engaging in such unprotected conduct. In this regard, we are mindful of the court's notice to the Board that "reinstatement is the only sanction which prevents an employer from benefitting from his unfair labor practices through discharges which may weaken or destroy a union," while "sanctions other than discharge . . . are available to prevent or remedy certain employee misconduct."

As the court directed, we have carefully balanced or weighed the dischargees' participation in the mass picketing, home demonstrations, and employment office picketing, and the union strike committee's direction and control of the mass picketing, against the Respondent's unfair labor practices. We conclude that the latter outweighs the former. Viewing the Respondent's violations of its employees' rights and the provocations with which it thereby confronted its employees both before and after the commencement of the strike, it is clear that now to permit the Respondent to discharge with impunity those strikers who succumbed to its provocations would be to permit the Respondent to take advantage of its own wrongdoing.[20] We have also carefully considered the fact that the Respondent, since 1933, has consistently refused to honor its collective-bargaining obligations, and it is plain that the restoration of the jobs of those dischargees set forth below, including the strike committee members, is essential if Respondent is to be brought to conform to the fundamental requirements of the Act.

Accordingly, having considered all the foregoing factors in the light of those guidelines set forth by the court, we conclude that the policies of the Act would best be effectuated by ordering reinstatement to all those dischargees now in issue who were discharged only for engaging in or directing and controlling the mass picketing, for participating in the home demonstrations, for participating in the employment office picketing, or for a combination of such activities.

However, as noted above, the Respondent contended that several of the discharged strikers had also participated in still other unprotected activities in connection with the strike, before or after being discharged, which would bar a remedial order of reinstatement. It was unnecessary for

---

[20] As the Respondent provoked that conduct of the strikers which we are herein considering, it cannot now validly argue that such provoked conduct constituted "cause" for discharge within the meaning of § 10(c). See NLRB v. Thayer Co., 213 F.2d 748, 753 (1st Cir. 1954), where the First Circuit Court of Appeals noted ". . . a determination that an employee is not engaged in a § 7 activity does not necessarily mean that, if he is discharged for his participation in the unprotected action, the discharge is 'for cause.' That depends on the surrounding circumstances. What is cause in one situation may not be in another." Thus, while directing or engaging in mass picketing and other coercive demonstrations might indicate, in some circumstances, unfitness for further employment, in the instant case it revealed only that employees can be goaded into excesses after many years of flagrant disregard of their lawful rights. Moreover, we do not believe that the above-described conduct has any bearing upon future job performance or would render those participants now under consideration unfit for future service. Indeed, we note that the Respondent reinstated or offered reinstatement to other strikers who engaged in the mass picketing, home demonstrations, and employment office picketing.

the Board to consider these allegations in the earlier Decision and Order.[21] Now, however, in view of our determination that those strikers who were discharged only for engaging in or directing and controlling the mass picketing, participating in the home demonstrations, and participating in the employment office picketing are entitled to reinstatement, it is necessary for us to determine whether or not still other unprotected conduct of some of the strikers, when weighed against the Respondent's unfair labor practices, was sufficient to bar their reinstatement.

In this regard, the Trial Examiner has set forth in the Intermediate Report attached to the Board's earlier Decision substantially all of the incidents relied on by the Respondent, as well as the evidence pertaining thereto. Accordingly, we shall not herein recount all of those numerous incidents and related evidence of striker misconduct. Suffice it to say that in general, most of these incidents involved the following types of action by some of the strikers: (1) actively engaging in halting, encircling, blocking, shouldering, and bumping of nonstrikers or job applicants during the mass picketing or employment office picketing; (2) verbally harassing, insulting, and abusing nonstrikers at the picket line, their homes, business establishments, or places of amusement; (3) participating in inspecting railroad cars leaving Respondent's plant or attempting temporarily to halt certain trucks leaving Respondent's plant; and (4) physically and violently assaulting nonstrikers or threatening members of nonstrikers' families.

As to those numerous incidents included in (1), (2), and (3), above, we have carefully balanced or weighed the individual striker's participation therein against the Respondent's unfair labor practices. However, even apart from the Respondent's conduct, we do not believe that the conduct of some of the employees involved was so flagrant as to warrant depriving them of the protection of the Act. And, with respect to some of the other conduct, for the reasons we expressed in connection with the mass picketing, employment office picketing, and home demonstrations, we conclude that the Respondent's flagrant unfair practices outweigh the strikers' misconduct. Accordingly, we find that the policies of the Act would best be effectuated by ordering reinstatement to those individual strikers who were discharged for engaging in that conduct described in (1), (2), and (3), above.

We now turn to those remaining incidents where the evidence clearly establishes that certain strikers assaulted nonstrikers or threatened members of nonstrikers' families, and the Respondent, in part, either relied on such misconduct as grounds for discharging the striker, or

---

[21] There, a majority of the Board found that all of the discharged strikers had participated in the mass picketing, had directed and controlled such picketing, had participated in the home demonstrations, or had participated in the employment office picketing. As the majority of the Board found that such conduct constituted valid grounds for discharge, the Board did not consider still other conduct on which the Respondent had relied in discharging or refusing to reinstate some of those dischargees now in issue.

contended that such misconduct occurring after the discharge bars reinstatement. . . .

[W]e have carefully considered the above-described incidents of flagrant and deliberate assaults upon nonstrikers and job applicants and the clear threat of violence directed towards the family of a nonstriker, in conjunction with the Respondent's unfair labor practices. Also, as directed by the court, we have carefully weighed one against the other. However, here, unlike other aspects of misconduct we have heretofore considered, we must conclude that the foregoing acts of violence or threats of violence engaged in or uttered by the above-named strikers outweigh the Respondent's unfair labor practices. In arriving at this conclusion, we are persuaded that unlike the unprotected conduct hereinbefore considered, the above-described individual, violent attacks upon certain nonstrikers and job applicants as well as the threat of violence directed toward the family of a nonstriker, though probably in part provoked by the Respondent's flagrant unfair labor practices, were also in part the product of personal vindictiveness or grievances. This misconduct we consider more severe and serious than the previously described bumping, shoving, vituperation, and the like. By engaging in such violent conduct, the strikers have rendered questionable their ability or fitness for future satisfactory service at the Respondent's plant. We recognize that to bar reinstatement to those strikers will permit the Respondent to benefit to some extent from its own unfair labor practices. However, we consider that this is more than offset by the encouragement such misconduct would receive, with the possible disorder and instability which such encouragement might induce in collective bargaining, were we to order them reinstated. Accordingly, we find that it would not effectuate the policies of the Act to reinstate those strikers who engaged in the above-described acts of violence or threats of physical harm.

NOTES

1. What if the misconduct occurred during an economic strike instead of a strike caused by the employer's unfair labor practices? In the leading case of NLRB v. Thayer Co., 213 F.2d 748, 752-53 (1st Cir. 1954), Judge Magruder said: "If an economic strike as conducted is not concerted activity within the protection of § 7, then the employer is free to discharge the participating employees for the strike activity and the Board is powerless to order their reinstatement. . . . This is so because, if the particular collective action is not a protected § 7 activity, the employer commits no unfair labor practice by thus terminating the employment relation. He has not interfered with, restrained or coerced employees in the exercise of their rights guaranteed in § 7. . . . Therefore, since the power of the Board to order reinstatement under § 10(c) is dependent upon its finding that an unfair labor practice has been committed, and since by hypothesis the economic strike was not caused by an unfair labor practice, it becomes crucial to the question of reinstatement of an economic striker to inquire whether the strike as conducted constituted

concerted activity within the protection of § 7. On the other hand, where, as in the instant case, the strike was caused by an unfair labor practice, the power of the Board to order reinstatement is not necessarily dependent upon a determination that the strike activity was a 'concerted activity' within the protection of § 7. Even if it was not, the National Labor Relations Board has power under § 10(c) to order reinstatement if the discharges were not 'for cause' and if such an order would effectuate the policies of the Act."

2. *See* Cox, *The Right to Engage in Concerted Activities*, 26 IND. L.J. (1951); Lipton, *Misconduct in Concerted Activities*, 8 LABOR L.J. 299 (1957); Schatzki, *Some Observations and Suggestions Concerning a Misnomer* — *"Protected" Concerted Activities*, 47 TEXAS L. REV. 378 (1969); Note, *Strike Misconduct as Grounds for Denial of Reinstatement,* 32 N.Y.U.L. REV. 839 (1957).

3. Where a striker substantially insulted a *customer* during an economic strike, the employer was not required to reinstate her. Montgomery Ward & Co. v. NLRB, 374 F.2d 606 (10th Cir. 1967).

4. In balancing the misconduct of unfair labor practice strikers against the seriousness of the employer's misconduct in causing or prolonging the strike, the Board may not reinstate strikers who were guilty of violent intimidation of nonstrikers. Oneita Knitting Mills v. NLRB, 375 F.2d 385 (4th Cir. 1967); Kayser-Roth Hosiery Co., 187 N.L.R.B. 562 (1970), *modified,* 447 F.2d 396 (6th Cir. 1971).

PHELPS DODGE CORP. v. NLRB, 313 U.S. 177, 61 S. Ct. 845, 85 L. Ed. 1271 (1941). In this landmark case, the Supreme Court interpreted the National Labor Relations Act as giving the Board broad and flexible powers to fashion remedies to effectuate the purposes of the act. The Court held that the Board has the power to order the hiring of applicants for employment who were discriminated against because of their union membership. Would you have any problems with this, in the light of the language of § 10(c) — "affirmative action, including reinstatement of employees with or without back pay"? The Court also indicated that the Board may order reinstatement of an employee who had been discriminated against, even though he had obtained substantially equivalent employment. Would you have any difficulty on this, in the light of the language in § 2(3) of the act? Finally, the Court held that, in calculating back pay, a deduction should be made, not only for actual earnings of the worker, but also for amounts which he failed without excuse to earn. However the Board has within its discretion the power to keep the matter within reasonable bounds by flexible procedural devices. The Court said generally:

"A statute expressive of such large public policy as that on which the National Labor Relations Board is based must be broadly phrased and necessarily carries with it the task of administrative application. There is an area plainly covered by the language of the act and an area no less plainly without it. But in the nature of things Congress could not catalogue all the devices or stratagems for circumventing the policies of the act. Nor could it define the whole gamut of remedies to effectuate these policies in an infinite variety of specific situations. Congress met these difficulties by leaving the adaptation of means to end to the empiric process of administration. The exercise of the process was committed to the Board, subject to limited judicial review. Because the relation of remedy to policy is peculiarly a matter for administrative competence, courts must not enter the allowable area of the Board's discretion and must guard against the danger of sliding unconsciously from the narrow confines of law into the more spacious domain of policy. On the other hand, the power with which Congress invested the Board implies responsibility — the responsibility of exercising its judgment in employing the statutory powers. The act does not create rights for individuals which must be vindicated according to a rigid scheme of remedies. It entrusts to an expert agency the maintenance and promotion of industrial peace." 313 U.S. at 194.

NOTES

1. Unemployment compensation benefits are not deducted from back pay. Does this make the employee "more than whole"? What would be the rationale? *See* NLRB v. Gullett Gin Co., 340 U.S. 361 (1951).

2. *Period of computation.* In F.W. Woolworth Co., 90 N.L.R.B. 289 (1950), the Board significantly revised its policy with respect to the manner of computation of back-pay awards to take account of interim earnings of the discharged employee. Prior thereto the practice was to compute such awards "by calculating the difference between what an employee would have earned, during the whole period of discrimination, absent discrimination against him, and what he actually earned in other employment during this period." NLRB, Fifteenth Annual Report 155-56 (1950). In *Woolworth,* the policy adopted was to compute the difference between "(1) the earnings the employee would have received in each separate calendar quarter or portion thereof, but for the employer's discrimination against him and (2) the quarterly earnings from other employment in each quarte. during the period of discrimination," so that "earnings of one particular quarter shall have no effect upon the back-pay liability for any other quarter." *Id.* at 156. This method of computation on a quarterly basis was approved by the Supreme Court as being within the authority of the Board even where applied to a seasonal business. NLRB v. Seven-Up Bottling Co., 344 U.S. 344 (1953); NLRB v. Operating Engineers Local 138, 380 F.2d 244 (2d Cir. 1967).

3. In 1962, the NLRB commenced the practice of requiring the payment of six percent interest on back pay due to discriminatorily discharged employees, Members Rodgers and Leedom dissenting. Isis Plumbing & Heating Co., 138 N.L.R.B. 716 (1962). The practice was approved in Philip Carey Mfg. Co. v. NLRB, 331 F.2d 720 (6th Cir. 1964), *cert. denied,* 379 U.S. 888 (1964). In Florida Steel Co., 231 N.L.R.B. 651

(1977), the Board decided to follow the interest rates charged by the Internal Revenue Service for underpayment of federal taxes.

Also in 1962, the Board discontinued its practice of tolling back-pay awards from the date of a Trial Examiner's report to the date of a Board order in those cases in which the examiner found no violation but the Board later reversed his recommendation and held that a discriminatory discharge had occurred. The Board noted that the sole reason for the practice of tolling was that the respondent could not have been expected to reinstate the discharged men after it received the Trial Examiner's report and therefore it should not be required to pay back pay from that time to the date of the Board decision. The Board decided to discontinue this practice because "the blameless discriminatees are not made whole for their monetary loss for the full period of the discrimination and are to that extent punished for exercising their statutory rights under § 7, solely because of the erroneous conclusion reached by the Trial Examiner." A.P.W. Prod. Co., 137 N.L.R.B. 25 (1962). Members Rodgers and Leedom dissented. *Enforcement granted,* 316 F.2d 899 (2d Cir. 1963).

4. In cases in which the Board finds "massive" unfair labor practices, it will often order novel remedies. Among these are the remedies found in the numerous cases involving J.P. Stevens and Co., Inc. The Board has ordered, and the courts have upheld, the following remedies: requiring that the employer post notice of the Board's order not only in the plant in which the unfair labor practice occurred, but in all the employer's forty-three plants, and requiring the employer to mail the order to each of the employees in the forty-three plants, 380 F.2d 292 (2d Cir. 1967); requiring that the employer give the union, upon request, reasonable access to plant bulletin boards for a period of one year, and requiring that the Board order be read to employees during working time, 441 F.2d 514 (5th Cir. 1971), 461 F.2d 490 (4th Cir. 1972); requiring that the employer give a list of the names and addresses of all the employees in all its plants to the union, 406 F.2d 1017 (4th Cir. 1968), 417 F.2d 533 (5th Cir. 1969). In finding J.P. Stevens to be in civil contempt, the court in 464 F.2d 1326 (2d Cir. 1972), *cert. denied,* 410 U.S. 926 (1973) ordered the company to pay to the NLRB all costs and expenses, including counsel fees and salaries, incurred by the Board as a result of the contempt proceedings.

In still another case involving J.P. Stevens, the court regarded the Board's traditional remedies for discriminatory discharge as insufficient. Textile Workers Union of America v. NLRB [J.P. Stevens], 475 F.2d 973 (D.C. Cir. 1973). Recognizing that the Board had already issued eleven orders concerning the company, the court remanded the case to the Board with orders to consider the history of the violating employer, not simply the immediate unfair labor practice. The Board reconsidered and ordered that notice of the order be given to all employees in all J.P. Stevens plants. 205 N.L.R.B. 1032 (1973). *See also* 240 N.L.R.B. No. 35, 100 L.R.R.M. 1342 (1979).

The courts continue to have conflicts with J.P. Stevens & Co. The Second Circuit broadened the scope of its remedy to include corrective action at all of the Stevens plants, as well as substantial compliance fines which had been urged by the NLRB. Additionally, the court added that it was prepared to consider even more drastic sanctions should Stevens continue in direct violation of its orders. NLRB v. J.P. Stevens & Co., 563 F.2d 8 (2d Cir. 1977), *cert. denied,* 434 U.S. 1064 (1978). Stevens has begun to show some willingness to comply with the NLRB, however; a settlement agreement was reached in which the Board was to drop a § 10(j) injunction action in exchange for voluntary remedial action by Stevens. 98 L.R.R.M. 36 (1978).

5. In Baptist Memorial Hospital, 229 N.L.R.B. 45 (1977), an employer that discriminatorily discharged an employee after having him arrested and convicted for disorderly conduct in connection with his handbilling in its lobby during his lunch break not only must reinstate him with back pay, and reimburse him for a $25 fine, but it must pay the legal fees and expenses he incurred. Also, the employer must, at his request, join him in petitioning the police department that arrested him and the court that convicted him to expunge their records.

Another remedy fashioned by the Board in a case of massive unfair labor practices was to require the employer to permit employees to have access to union organizers on plant parking lots and plant approaches during nonworking time for a six-month period. Marlene Industries Corp., 166 N.L.R.B. 703 (1967).

6. The proposed Labor Reform Act of 1978, which failed to pass in the 95th Congress, would have provided stiff new remedies in cases of discrimination against employees during an organizing campaign or before the signing of an initial contract. These would have included use of § 10(*1*)'s mandatory injunction procedures and the award of either double back pay (House bill) or an amount equal to one and a half times back pay (Senate bill) to the victims of discrimination. In addition, "willful" violators of final Board or court orders would have been subject to debarment from federal contracts for up to three years.

7. Suppose an employer who has been found guilty of discriminatory discharges sells his business to a bona fide purchaser (not just an alter ego of the employer) who has knowledge of the unfair labor practices? The Board concluded that such a purchaser who continues to operate the business without significant change may be held jointly and severally liable with the seller for remedying the unfair labor practices. Perma Vinyl Corp., 164 N.L.R.B. 968 (1967), reversing the previous practice of the Board. *Accord,* Golden State Bottling Co. v. NLRB, 467 F.2d 164 (9th Cir. 1972), *aff'd,* 414 U.S. 168 (1973).

SECTION II. Representation Questions

A. ESTABLISHING REPRESENTATIVE STATUS THROUGH NLRB ELECTIONS

STATUTORY REFERENCES
RLA § 2, Fourth and Ninth; NLRA § 9

FOREWORD

Problems with respect to the representation of employees arise at the moment the process of organization begins, and continue until a given union achieves a secure position as bargaining representative. The labor relations acts have accented these problems by according a special status to the union which succeeds in organizing a "majority" of the employees in a defined group. At the same time, the statutes have provided procedures which may be utilized for the purpose of determining whether a given union has achieved this status. In this section we are concerned with these procedures and the questions which arise in connection with their use. Problems with respect to the use by unions of collective action for organizational purposes are to be treated in Part Three. Presumptively, the availability and use of the labor relations act procedures has tended to reduce the resort to self-help.

It would be difficult to overemphasize the importance of the legislative efforts to deal with representation matters. The tremendous practical significance of these procedures to the parties involved is obvious. In addition, these procedures are an experiment with the use of quasi-judicial processes in resolving some kinds of labor disputes, and, as such, may be significant as an indication of future developments on a broader scale. Finally, the use by the statutes of the machinery of popular expression undoubtedly has real educational values in stimulating rank-and-file worker participation in the solution of group problems.

The procedure in representation cases has been summarized by the NLRB in its "Statements of Procedure, Subpart C — Representation Cases Under Section 9(c) of the Act." This statement is reproduced in the *Statutory Appendix,* and it should be read at this point.

NLRB, TWENTY-SIXTH ANNUAL REPORT 3, 4 (1961)

In fiscal 1961, the National Labor Relations Board delegated its decisional powers with respect to employee collective bargaining election cases to its 28 regional directors. This was a new procedural step — and one of the most important in Board history — made possible by the 1959 amendments to the Act. The principal effect of this delegation was to permit regional directors to decide in their regions election cases that before the 1959 amendments had been ruled on only by the five-man Board in Washington.

This delegation includes decisions as to whether a question concerning representation exists, determination of appropriate bargaining unit, directions of elections to determine whether employees wish union representation for collective-bargaining purposes, and rulings on other matters such as challenged ballots and objections to elections.

Announcing the delegation, Chairman McCulloch said:

"This delegation of decision making and other powers by the Board to its regional directors promises to be one of the most far-reaching steps the Board has ever taken with respect to its election cases. It should provide a major speed up in NLRB case handling in line with the policy of President Kennedy for the independent regulatory agencies."

Actions taken by regional directors under the delegation are final, subject to discretionary review by the Board in Washington on restricted grounds. The Board's delegation covers not only employee petitions to select collective-bargaining representatives, but also employer petitions questioning representation, employee petitions to decertify unions, and petitions to rescind union-security authorizations.

In the delegation the Board provided that review of regional directors' decisions could be sought on these four grounds:

1. Where a substantial question of law or policy is raised because of (a) the absence of, or (b) the departure from, officially reported precedent.

2. Where a regional director's decision on a substantial factual issue is clearly erroneous, and such error prejudicially affects the rights of a party.

3. Where the conduct of the hearing in an election case or any ruling made in connection with the proceeding has resulted in prejudicial error.

4. Where there are compelling reasons for reconsideration of an important Board rule or policy.

NLRB, FORTY-SECOND ANNUAL REPORT 47 (1977)

The Act requires that an employer bargain with the representative designated by a majority of his employees in a unit appropriate for collective bargaining. But it does not require that the representative be designated by any particular procedure as long as the representative is clearly the choice of a majority of the employees. As one method for employees to select a majority representative, the Act authorizes the Board to conduct representation elections. The Board may conduct such an election after a petition has been filed by or on behalf of the employees, or by an employer who has been confronted with a claim for recognition from an individual or a labor organization. Incident to its authority to conduct elections, the Board has the power to determine the unit of employees appropriate for collective bargaining, and formally to certify a collective-bargaining representative upon the basis of the results of the election. Once certified by the Board, the bargaining agent is the exclusive representative of all employees in the appropriate unit for collective bargaining in respect to rates of pay, wages, hours of employment, or other conditions of employment. The Act also empowers the Board to conduct elections to decertify incumbent bargaining agents which have been previously certified, or which are being currently recognized by the employer. Decertification petitions may be filed by employees, or individuals other than management representatives, or by labor organizations acting on behalf of employees.

1. BARS TO CONDUCTING AN ELECTION

NLRB, THIRTY-SEVENTH ANNUAL REPORT 50-52 (1972)

In certain situations the Board, in the interest of promoting the stability of labor relations, will conclude that circumstances appropriately preclude the raising of a question concerning representation. Thus, under the Board's contract-bar rules, a present election among employees currently covered by a valid collective-bargaining agreement may, with certain exceptions, be barred by an outstanding contract. Generally, these rules require that to operate as a bar, the contract must be in writing, properly executed, and binding on the parties; it must be of definite duration and in effect for no more than 3 years; and it must also contain substantive terms and conditions of employment which in turn must be consistent with the policies of the Act.

The period during the contract term when a petition may be timely filed is ordinarily calculated from the expiration date of the agreement. A petition is timely when filed not more than 90 nor less than 60 days before the terminal date of an outstanding contract. Thus, a petition which is filed during the last 60 days of a valid contract will be considered untimely and will be dismissed. During this 60-day "insulated" period, the parties to the existing contract are free to execute a new or amended agreement without the intrusion of a rival petition, but if no agreement is reached or if the agreement which is reached does not constitute a bar itself, then a petition filed after the expiration of the old valid contract will be timely and entertained. In addition, the Board's contract-bar rules do not permit the parties to an existing collective-bargaining relationship to avoid this filing period by executing an amendment or new contract term which prematurely extends the date of expiration of that contract. In the event of such premature extension, the new contract ordinarily will not bar an election.

NOTES

1. The statutory objective of stability in labor relations is also promoted by the longstanding, judicially approved Board practice under which the certification of a representative by the Board ordinarily will be held binding for at least 1 year, barring all representation petitions filed within the 1-year period. Under some circumstances where the employer frustrates the union's bargaining efforts for a significant portion of the certification year, however, the Board may extend the period for a commensurate time.

2. "The Board has decided to adopt the rule that a contract does not bar an election if executed (1) before any employees had been hired or (2) prior to a substantial increase in personnel. When the question of a substantial increase in personnel is in issue, a contract will bar an election only if at least 30 percent of the complement employed at the time of the hearing had been employed at the time the contract was executed, *and* 50

percent of the job classifications in existence at the time of the hearing were in existence at the time the contract was executed." General Extrusion Co., 121 N.L.R.B. 1165 (1958).

3. In Paragon Prod. Corp., 134 N.L.R.B. 662, 666 (1961), the Board overruled Keystone Coat, Apron & Towel Supply Co., 121 N.L.R.B. 880 (1958), and said: "[W]e now hold that only those contracts containing a union-security provision which is clearly unlawful on its face, or which has been found to be unlawful in an unfair labor practice proceeding, may not bar a representation petition. A clearly unlawful union-security provision for this purpose is one which by its express terms clearly and unequivocally goes beyond the limited form of union-security permitted by § 8(a)(3) of the act, and is therefore incapable of a lawful interpretation. Such unlawful provisions include (1) those which expressly and unambiguously require the employer to give preference to union members (a) in hiring, (b) in laying off, or (c) for purpose of seniority; (2) those which specifically withhold from incumbent nonmembers and/or new employees the statutory 30-day grace period; and (3) those which expressly require as a condition of continued employment the payment of sums of money other than periodic dues and initiation fees uniformly required." Detailed examination of union security arrangements will be made in Part Five, beginning at 862.

4. In Food Haulers, Inc., 136 N.L.R.B. 394 (1962), the NLRB overruled Pilgrim Furniture Co., 128 N.L.R.B. 910 (1960), and held that a contract stands as a bar to an election, even though it contains an illegal "hot-cargo" clause. The majority reasoned that the clause, though unlawful, does not interfere with the employees' choice of bargaining representative or with any other objective of contract-bar rules, and the setting aside of the entire contract as an election bar on a finding of an unlawful hot-cargo clause constitutes a more drastic sanction in the representation proceeding than is permitted under the statute in unfair labor practice proceedings. See § 8(e) and the material in Part Three on "hot-cargo" contracts, beginning at 377.

5. In Pioneer Bus Co., 140 N.L.R.B. 54 (1962), the Board held that where an employer met separately with representatives of white and black workers and executed separate contracts with each, although the terms were substantially the same, this separate representational treatment along racial lines which appeared in the contracts asserted as bars prevented the contracts from standing as a bar to a new election. The Board stated, "Consistent with clear court decisions in other contexts which condemn government sanctioning of racially separate groupings as inherently discriminatory, the Board will not permit its contract bar rules to be utilized to shield contracts such as those here involved from the challenge of otherwise appropriate election petitions." See also the Miranda Fuel case, infra at 760, on the duty of fair representation. And compare NLRB v. Mansion House Corp., 473 F.2d 471 (8th Cir. 1973), with the Board's Handy Andy decision, infra at 229.

6. If a union is defunct, its contract will not be a bar. A union is defunct if it is unable or unwilling to represent the employees. However, loss of all members in the unit does not constitute defunctness if the representative otherwise continues in existence and is willing and able to represent the employees. Hershey Chocolate Corp., 121 N.L.R.B. 901 (1958).

7. The *Hershey* case also dealt with the situation where a schism develops in the union which made the contract. The Board held that the contract will not bar an election where a local union has voted in open meeting after notice to disaffiliate from its parent union because of a basic intra-union conflict over policy existing at the highest level of the parent union. On the other hand, the Board will not find a schism where there is only a local faction fight. The schism doctrine was very important in two periods of labor history: (1) when the CIO expelled a number of unions on grounds of alleged Communist domination, setting up rival unions to compete for their members, and (2) when the AFL-CIO expelled a number of unions on charges of corruption and misuse of members' funds, again setting up rival unions to attempt to take their place.

2. DEFINING THE APPROPRIATE UNIT

NLRB, THIRTEENTH ANNUAL REPORT 35-36 (1948)

Under § 9(a) of the amended act, as before, the collective bargaining representative designated by the majority of the employees *in an appropriate unit,* is the exclusive representative of all the employees in that unit, "for the purposes of collective bargaining in respect to rates of pay, wages, hours of employment, or other conditions of employment." And it is the Board's responsibility under § 9(b) of the act to "decide in each case whether, in order to assure to employees the fullest freedom in exercising the rights guaranteed by this act, the unit appropriate for the purposes of collective bargaining shall be the employer unit, craft unit, plant unit, or subdivision thereof. . . ." Guided by this general statement of statutory purposes and standards, the opening part of which was slightly rephrased but not substantially changed by the amendments, the Board, over a period of years, has formulated certain criteria which are applicable to the determination of all questions concerning the appropriate bargaining unit. Except in the particular and important situations discussed below, the 1947 amendments of the act have left unchanged these familiar basic tests of appropriateness. Chief among them is the rule, restated by the Board this year in *Matter of Chrysler Corp.* [76 N.L.R.B. 55] that "employees with similar interests shall be placed in the same bargaining unit." This factor of mutuality of interest, together with the history of collective bargaining in the particular plant or industry involved, is given great weight by the Board in deciding any unit controversy, whether the dispute concerns the geographical scope of the proper bargaining unit, or its general character (for example, whether craft or industrial), or questions as to the inclusion of particular occupational categories of employees.

In deciding each case on its own facts, as it must do, the Board is vested with broad discretion, but its discretion in certain instances is now limited by provisions of the amended act. In brief outline, the innovations are as follows: "Professional employees," "guards," and "supervisors," respectively, are now defined in the statute; and supervisors, as well as "independent contractors" are expressly excluded from the definition of "employees" covered by the act. Two new provisos added to § 9(b) dictate conditions affecting the unit placement of professional employees and guards. Another proviso, § 9(b)(2), affects the Board's consideration of certain cases involving the familiar controversy over craft versus industrial units. Finally, § 9(c)(5) prescribes that the extent of employee organization shall not be "controlling" in unit determinations.

NOTES

1. *Professional Employees. See Leedom* v. *Kyne, infra* at 230.

2. *Plant Guards.* What is the rationale for the special treatment of plant guards in § 9(b)(3)?

3. *Extent of Organization.* Although the statute directs that the extent of organization shall not be controlling, this does not preclude the Board from determining a unit which coincides with extent of organization where such unit is found to be appropriate according to other considerations. NLRB v. Morganton Full Fashioned Hosiery Co., 241 F.2d 913 (4th Cir. 1957); NLRB v. Smythe, 212 F.2d 664 (5th Cir. 1954). The extent of organization may be a contributing factor in the determination of the unit so long as it is not the controlling factor. Westinghouse Elec. Corp. v. NLRB, 236 F.2d 939 (3d Cir. 1956); Foreman & Clark, Inc. v. NLRB, 215 F.2d 396 (9th Cir. 1954). *But cf.* NLRB v. Glen Raven Knitting Mills, Inc., 235 F.2d 413 (4th Cir. 1956). *And see,* NLRB v. Metropolitan Life Ins. Co., 380 U.S. 438 (1965).

4. *Railway Labor Act.* What is the nature of the National Mediation Board's authority under § 2, Fourth and Ninth, of the RLA to define the "craft or class" for bargaining purposes? Compare § 9(b) of the NLRA. Is the mediation board's task that of merely *identifying* existing crafts and classes? Is there a difference between the process of identification and that of determining what is an "appropriate" bargaining unit of employees? Why does the RLA stress the "craft or class" as the unit for bargaining purposes?

See generally, Krislov, *Representation Disputes in the Railroad and Airline Industries,* 7 LAB. L.J. 98 (1956); Northrup, *The Appropriate Bargaining Unit Question Under the Railway Labor Act,* 60 QUARTERLY J. ECON. 250 (1946); Eischen, *Representation Disputes and Their Resolution in the Railroad and Airline Industries,* in THE RAILWAY LABOR ACT AT FIFTY (1976).

5. The proposed Labor Reform Act of 1978 would have directed the NLRB to use its rule-making authority to define appropriate bargaining units.

CRAFT AND INDUSTRIAL UNITS

GLOBE MACHINE & STAMPING CO., 3 N.L.R.B. 294 (1937). Three AFL unions — the Metal Polishers Union (claiming to represent the polishers and buffers), the Machinists Union (claiming to represent the punch press operators) and Federal Labor Union No. 18788 (claiming to represent the rest of the production and maintenance workers in the plant) — filed representation petitions with the NLRB. The UAW-CIO intervened, claiming to represent *all* the production and maintenance workers. For some years, prior to 1937, most of the employees involved had belonged to some one of the AFL unions, or its predecessor. The UAW had undertaken a strenuous organizational campaign in 1937, and claimed that it had organized most of the plant. There was some evidence that there had been a swing back to the AFL unions in some of the skilled groups, but the membership rolls of the four unions were in such confusion that no accurate finding was possible as to the preference of the various contended-for-groups. The Board found that the polishing and the punch press work at the plant was done in separate, clearly defined areas, and was differentiated as to skill from other classifications, but that the actual production at the plant was highly integrated. It further found that the history of bargaining in the plant was inconclusive to show any clear pattern of preference or clear appropriateness of either plant-wide or separate units. The Board concluded as follows with respect to the problem of defining the appropriate unit or units (3 N.L.R.B. at 299-300):

"In view of the facts described above, it appears that the Company's production workers can be considered either as a single unit appropriate for the purposes of collective bargaining, as claimed by the UAWA, or as three such units, as claimed by the petitioning unions. The history of successful separate negotiations at the Company's plant, and also the essential separateness of polishing and punch press work at that plant, and the existence of a requirement of a certain amount of skill for that work, are proof of the feasibility of the latter approach. The successful negotiation of a plant-wide agreement on May 20, 1937, as well as the interrelation and interdependence of the various departments at the Company's plant, are proof of the feasibility of the former.

"In such a case where the considerations are so evenly balanced, the determining factor is the desire of the men themselves. On this point, the record affords no help. There has been a swing toward the UAW and then away from it. The only documentary proof is completely contradictory. We will therefore order elections to be held separately for the men engaged in polishing and those engaged in punch press work. We will also order an election for the employees of the Company engaged in production and maintenance, exclusive of the polishers and punch press workers and of clerical and supervisory employees.

"On the results of these elections will depend the determination of the appropriate unit for the purposes of collective bargaining. Such of the groups as do not choose the UAWA will constitute separate and distinct appropriate units, and such as do choose the UAWA will, together, constitute a single appropriate unit."

NOTE

The Board's practice of holding "Globe" elections was upheld in NLRB v. Underwood Mach. Co., 179 F.2d 118 (1st Cir. 1949), against the employer's claim that the Board had improperly delegated to the employees themselves the determination of what should be the appropriate unit. The Board having made a determination that either a single unit or several units in the plant would be "appropriate," the Board could properly come to the conclusion that the single factor that would tip the scales was the preference of the employees.

However, where a craft or other subordinate group sought to sever itself off from a larger bargaining unit, the Board did not always grant a self-determination election, as appears from the leading *American Can* case.

In this case, the Steel Workers Organizing Committee, CIO, had been certified in 1937 as collective bargaining representative for the approximately 800 nonsupervisory, nonclerical, production and maintenance workers employed in the American Can Company's Brooklyn plant. Collective bargaining relations between SWOC and the company ensued. In August, 1938, shortly before the consummation of a new contract between these parties, two AFL craft unions sought separate recognition for four oilers and firemen and four engineers (as one unit) and twelve electricians (as another unit). Such recognition was refused, whereupon the AFL unions instituted representation proceedings under the original NLRA. The Board dismissed the petition, finding that such separate bargaining units would not be appropriate, American Can Co., 13 N.L.R.B. 1252, 1256-57 (1939), saying:

"We are of the opinion that the Board is not authorized by the act to split the appropriate unit thus established by collective bargaining and embodied in a valid, exclusive bargaining contract. In any appropriate unit it is to be presumed that there will be dissatisfied groups from time to time. To permit such small groups to break up an appropriate unit established and maintained by a bona fide collective bargaining contract against the will of the majority of the employees who are bound by the contract would make stability and responsibility in collective bargaining impossible. Neither craft, plant, nor industrial units could maintain any unity in bargaining if any subordinate parts of established appropriate units were free to disregard contractual obligations and claim separate representation with separate contracts."

The congressional reaction in the 1947 amendments and subsequent developments are analyzed in the following case.

MALLINCKRODT CHEMICAL WORKS

National Labor Relations Board
162 N.L.R.B. 387 (1966)

[The petitioner (IBEW) sought a separate unit composed of certain skilled instrument mechanics in a chemical plant.]

. . . .

Reconsideration of the American Potash Doctrine.

Petitioner, relying on its showing that the instrument mechanics are craftsmen and on its claim that it qualifies as a traditional representative of such craftsmen, contends it has met the requirements set forth in the *American Potash* decision [4] for obtaining a craft severance election. On the other hand, the Employer, though not receding from its contention that the instrument mechanics are not true craftsmen and that the Petitioner is not, in any event, the traditional representative of such mechanics, argues that the *American Potash* decision improperly makes the question of severance turn solely on affirmative findings with respect to the above issues, ignoring many other relevant and weighty considerations. In this latter respect, the Employer places particular emphasis on the fact that the *American Potash* decision precludes, for all practical purposes, consideration of the duration and character of the representation which craft employees have received while being represented in a more inclusive unit, and completely rules out any consideration of the effect that integration of the functions of the craft employees involved in the proceeding with the overall production processes of the employer may have on the Board's unit determination. With respect to both points, the Employer urges that to the extent the *American Potash* decision forbids realistic consideration of bargaining history and integration of the craft employees' functions in the production process unless the case involves one of the so-called *National Tube* industries,[5] it is plainly discriminatory in application and requires reversal.

We believe there is much force to the Employer's arguments and contentions, and we have undertaken in this and other cases a review of our present policies regarding severance elections.

At the outset, it is appropriate to set forth the nature of the issue confronting the Board in making unit determinations in severance cases. Underlying such determinations is the need to balance the interest of the employer and the total employee complement in maintaining the industrial stability and resulting benefits of an historical plant-wide bargaining unit as against the interest of a portion of such complement in having an opportunity to break away from the historical unit by a vote for separate representation. The Board does not exercise its judgment lightly in these difficult areas. Each such case involves a resolution of "what would best serve the working man in his effort to bargain collectively with his employer, and what would best serve the interest of the country as a whole." [6] It is within the context of this declared

---

[4] American Potash & Chemical Corp., 107 N.L.R.B. 1418.

[5] National Tube Co., 76 N.L.R.B. 1199; Permanente Metals Co., 89 N.L.R.B. 804; Corn Prod. Ref. Co., 80 N.L.R.B. 362; Weyerhaeuser Timber Co., 87 N.L.R.B. 1076. See also, American Potash & Chemical Corp., *supra* at 1422.

[6] NLRB v. Pittsburgh Plate Glass Co., 270 F.2d 167, 173 (4th Cir. 1959), *cert. denied,* 361 U.S. 943.

legislative purpose that Congress has delegated to the Board the obligation to determine appropriate bargaining units. We do not believe that the Board can properly, or perhaps even lawfully, discharge its statutory duties by delegating the performance ot so important a function to a segment of the affected employee body. Thus, we accept the Court's view in *Pittsburgh Plate Glass* that "the Board was not authorized by . . . [the act] to surrender to anyone else its statutory duty to determine in each case the appropriate unit for collective bargaining." *(Ibid.)*

The cohesiveness and special interest of a craft or departmental group seeking severance may indicate the appropriateness of a bargaining unit limited to that group. However, the interests of all employees in continuing to bargain together in order to maintain their collective strength, as well as the public interest and the interests of the employer and the plant union in maintaining overall plant stability in labor relations and uninterrupted operation of integrated industrial or commercial facilities, may favor adherence to the established patterns of bargaining.

The problem of striking a balance has been the subject of Board and Congressional concern since the early days in the administration of the Wagner Act. In the *American Can* decision,[7] the Board refused to allow craft severance in the face of a bargaining history on a broader basis. This so-called *American Can* doctrine was not, however, rigidly applied to rule out all opportunities for craft severance.[8] Nevertheless, when Congress amended the Wagner Act in 1947 by enactment of the Taft-Hartley Act, it added a proviso to § 9(b), stating in pertinent part:

"The Board shall . . . not decide that any craft unit is inappropriate on the ground that a different unit has been established by a prior Board determination, unless a majority of the employees in the proposed craft unit vote against separate representation."

Though the legislative history indicates that this proviso grew out of Congressional concern that the *American Can* doctrine unduly restricted the rights of craft employees to seek a separate representation, it is equally clear that Congress did not intend to take away the Board's discretionary authority to find craft units to be inappropriate for collective-bargaining purposes if a review of *all* the facts, both *pro* and *con* severance, led to such result. Thus, as stated in *Senate Report No. 105 on S. 1126,* submitted by Senator Taft:

"Since the decision in the *American Can* case (13 N.L.R.B. 1252), where the Board refused to permit craft units to be "carved out" from a broader bargaining unit already established, the Board, except under unusual circumstances, has virtually compelled skilled artisans to remain part of

---

[7] American Can Co., 13 N.L.R.B. 1252. See also, Pressed Steel Car Co., 69 N.L.R.B. 629.

[8] See, for example, Bendix Aviation Corp., 39 N.L.R.B. 81; Aluminum Corp. of America, 42 N.L.R.B. 772; General Elec. Co., Lynn River Works & Everett Plant, 58 N.L.R.B. 57; Remington Rand, Inc., 62 N.L.R.B. 1419; United States Potash Co., 63 N.L.R.B. 1379; International Minerals & Chemical Corp., 71 N.L.R.B. 878; Food Machinery Corp., 72 N.L.R.B. 918. Sometimes severance was denied because of bargaining history and other factors. See, for example, Packard Motor Car Co., 63 N.L.R.B. 317; Tamiami Trail Tours, Inc., 74 N.L.R.B. 918.

a comprehensive plant unit. The committee regards the application of this doctrine as inequitable. *Our bill still leaves to the Board discretion to review all the facts in determining the appropriate unit,* but it may not decide that any craft unit is inappropriate on the ground that a different unit has been established by a prior Board determination." [9] [Emphasis supplied.]

This conclusion is further buttressed by the fact that the House Bill provisions [10] making the granting of severance mandatory were rejected by Congress in favor of the present provision which, as Senator Taft described it above, requires the Board to exercise its "discretion to review all the facts."

Shortly after the enactment of § 9(b)(2), the Board, in the *National Tube* case, dismissed a craft severance petition filed on behalf of a group of bricklayer craftsmen who were employed in the basic steel industry. After an exhaustive analysis of the section and its legislative history, the Board concluded that: "(1) the only restriction imposed by § 9(b)(2) is that a prior Board determination cannot be the basis for denying separate representation to a craft group; (2) under the language of the statute there is nothing to bar the Board from considering either a prior determination or the bargaining history of a particular employer as a factor, even if not controlling, in determining the appropriateness of a proposed craft unit; (3) there is nothing in either statute or legislative history to preclude the Board from considering or giving such weight as it deems necessary to the factors of bargaining history in an industry, the basic nature of the duties performed by the craft employees in relation to those of the production employees, the integration of craft functions with the overall production processes of the employer, and many other circumstances upon which the Board has customarily based its determination as to the appropriateness or inappropriateness of a proposed unit." The bricklayer unit was there found to be inappropriate because of the existence of such a pattern and history of bargaining in the basic steel industry and because the functions of the craft bricklayers were intimately connected with the basic steel production process which was highly integrated in nature.[11] In

---

[9] 1 Leg. Hist. 417-418. A statement by Senator Taft on the floor of the Senate is to the same effect: "In effect I think it (§ 9(b)(2)) gives greater power to the craft units to organize separately. It does not go the full way of giving them the absolute right in every case; it simply provides that the Board shall have discretion and shall not bind itself by previous decision, but that the subject shall always be open for further consideration." 93 Cong. Rec. 3952; 2 Leg. Hist. 1009.

[10] See H.R. 3020, § 9(f)(2), 1 Leg. Hist. 188-9. See, also, Hearings before the Senate Committee on S. 55, 80th Cong., 1st Sess. 1007 et seq. (1947), for a proposal by the President of the American Federation of Labor which would have made the establishment of craft units mandatory unless the craft employees rejected separate representation.

[11] This decision was basically an affirmation of earlier decisions in Geneva Steel Co., 57 N.L.R.B. 50; 67 N.L.R.B. 1159, and Tennessee Coal, Iron & R.R., 39 N.L.R.B. 617. Similarly, the *Corn Products Refining* decision reaffirmed an earlier decision involving the same company, reported at 60 N.L.R.B. 92. Thus, the doctrine known as the *National Tube* doctrine had its origin in decisions decided prior to the amendments. The doctrine applies to new plants as well as old plants in the industries involved, and precludes the initial

subsequent cases,[12] the same grounds were relied upon for denying the formation of craft units in the wet milling, basic aluminum, and lumbering industries.

In the *American Potash* decision, the Board, in effect, reversed the *National Tube* decision as to both the proper construction of § 9(b)(2) and the propriety of denying craft severance on the basis of integrated production processes in an industry where the prevailing pattern of bargaining is industrial in character.

As to the first, the Board stated:

". . . [W]e find that the intent of Congress will best be effectuated by a finding, and we so find, that a craft group will be appropriate for severance purposes in cases where a true craft group is sought and where, in addition, the union is one which traditionally represents that craft.

". . . All that we are considering here is whether true craft groups should have an opportunity to decide the issue for themselves. We conclude that we *must* afford them that choice in order to give effect to the statute. [Emphasis supplied.]

As to the second, the Board stated:

". . . [W]e feel that the right of separate representation should not be denied members of a craft group merely because they are employed in an industry which involves highly integrated production processes and in which the prevailing pattern of bargaining is industrial in character. We shall, therefore, not extend the practice of denying craft severance on an industry-wide basis."

It is apparent that the decision in *American Potash* was predicated in substantial part on the view that § 9(b)(2) virtually forecloses discretion and compels the Board to grant craft severance. This view represented an almost diametrically opposite construction of the statute from that adopted by the Board in *National Tube.* On the basis of what has already been indicated herein respecting the legislative history of the section, we believe the revised construction of the statute adopted in *American Potash* was erroneous, a belief apparently shared by the Court of Appeals for the Fourth Circuit: [13]

"The Board was right . . . [in the *National Tube* decision] in reaching the conclusion that the addition of subsection 2 of § 9(b) created no ambiguity. As amended, § 9(b) does not strip the Board of its original power and duty to decide in each case what bargaining unit is most appropriate. . . . In effect it frees the Board from the domination of its past decisions and directs it to reexamine each case on its merits and leaves it free to select that unit which it deems best suited to accomplish the statutory purposes. . . . Congress clearly did not command the Board, as it could have done, to establish a craft bargaining unit whenever requested by a qualified craft union, or relieve the Board of its duty to consider the

---

establishment of craft units as well as the severance of such units. See Kaiser Aluminum & Chemical Corp., 119 N.L.R.B. 695.

[12] See cases cited in note 5.

[13] NLRB v. Pittsburgh Plate Glass Co., 270 F.2d 26, 167, 172-73 (4th Cir. 1959).

interests of the plant unions and wishes of the employees who desire to bargain on a plantwide basis. The amended section expressly requires the Board to decide *in each case* what unit would be most appropriate to effectuate the overall purpose of the Act to preserve industrial peace."

Rejecting, as we do, the statutory interpretation on which the *American Potash* decision is premised, and recognizing that *American Potash* itself constituted a change in the applicable criteria, we now consider whether the tests laid down in the *American Potash* case nevertheless permit a satisfactory resolution of the issues posed in severance cases. We find that they do not. *American Potash* established two basic tests: (1) the employees involved must constitute a true craft or departmental group, and (2) the union seeking to carve out a craft or departmental unit must be one which has traditionally devoted itself to the special problems of the group involved. These tests do serve to identify and define those employee groups which normally have the necessary cohesiveness and special interests to distinguish them from the generality of production and maintenance employees, and place in the scales of judgment the interests of the craft employees. However, they do not consider the interests of the other employees and thus do not permit a weighing of the craft group against the competing interests favoring continuance of the established relationship. Thus, by confining consideration solely to the interests favoring severance, the *American Potash* tests preclude the Board from discharging its statutory responsibility to make its unit determinations on the basis of all relevant factors, including those factors which weigh against severance. In short, application of these mechanistic tests leads always to the conclusion that the interests of craft employees always prevail. It does this, moreover, without affording a voice in the decision to the other employees, whose unity of association is broken and whose collective strength is weakened by the success of the craft or departmental group in pressing its own special interests.

Furthermore, the *American Potash* decision makes arbitrary distinctions between industries by forbidding the application of the *National Tube* doctrine to other industries whose operations are as highly integrated, and whose plantwide bargaining patterns are as well established, as is the case in the so-called *"National Tube"* industries. In fact, the *American Potash* decision is inherently inconsistent in asserting that ". . . it is not the province of this Board to dictate the course and pattern of labor organization in our vast industrial complex," while, at the same time, establishing rules which have that very effect. Thus, *American Potash* clearly "dictate[s] the course and pattern of labor organization" by establishing rigid qualifications for unions seeking craft units and by automatically precluding severance of all such units in *National Tube* industries.

It is patent, from the foregoing, that the *American Potash* tests do not effectuate the policies of the act. We shall, therefore, no longer allow our inquiry to be limited by them. Rather, we shall, as the Board did prior to *American Potash*, broaden our inquiry to permit evaluation of all considerations relevant to an informed decision in this area. The following areas of inquiry are illustrative of those we deem relevant:

1. Whether or not the proposed unit consists of a distinct and homogeneous group of skilled journeymen craftsmen performing the functions of their craft on a nonrepetitive basis, or of employees constituting a functionally distinct department, working in trades or occupations for which a tradition of separate representation exists.[14]

2. The history of collective bargaining of the employees sought and at the plant involved, and at other plants of the employer, with emphasis on whether the existing patterns of bargaining are productive of stability in labor relations, and whether such stability will be unduly disrupted by the destruction of the existing patterns of representation.

3. The extent to which the employees in the proposed unit have established and maintained their separate identity during the period of inclusion in a broader unit, and the extent of their participation or lack of participation in the establishment and maintenance of the existing pattern of representation and the prior opportunities, if any, afforded them to obtain separate representation.

4. The history and pattern of collective bargaining in the industry involved.

5. The degree of integration of the employer's production processes, including the extent to which the continued normal operation of the production processes is dependent upon the performance of the assigned functions of the employees in the proposed unit.

6. The qualifications of the union seeking to "carve out" a separate unit, including that union's experience in representing employees like those involved in the severance action.[15]

In view of the nature of the issue posed by a petition for severance, the foregoing should not be taken as a hard and fast definition or an inclusive or exclusive listing of the various considerations involved in making unit determinations in this area. No doubt other factors worthy of consideration will appear in the course of litigation.[16] We emphasize the foregoing to demonstrate our intention to free ourselves from the restrictive effect of rigid and inflexible rules in making our unit determinations. Our determinations will be made only after a weighing of

---

[14] We are not in disagreement with the emphasis the *American Potash* decision placed on the importance of limiting severance to true craft or traditional departmental groups, nor do we disagree with the admonitions contained in that decision as to the need for strict adherence to these requirements. Our dissatisfaction with the Board's existing policy in this area stems not only from the overriding importance given to a finding that a proposed unit is composed of such employees, but also to the loose definition of a true craft or traditional department which may be derived from the decisions directing severance elections pursuant to the *American Potash* decision.

[15] With respect to this factor, we shall no longer require, as a *sine qua non* for severance, that the petitioning union qualify as a "traditional representative" in the *American Potash* sense. The fact that a union may or may not have devoted itself to representing the special interests of a particular craft or traditional departmental group of employees is a factor which will be considered in making our unit determinations in this area.

all relevant factors on a case-by-case basis, and we will apply the same principles and standards to all industries.[17]

Turning to the facts of this case, we conclude that it will not effectuate the policies of the act to permit the disruption of the production and maintenance unit by permitting Petitioner to "carve out" a unit of instrument mechanics. Our conclusion is predicated on the following considerations.

The Employer is engaged in the production of uranium metal. It is the only enterprise in the country which is engaged in all phases of such production. All of its finished product is sold to the Atomic Energy Commission. Continued stability in labor relations at such facilities is vital to our national defense.

The Employer produces uranium metal by means of a highly integrated continuous flow production system which the record herein shows is beyond doubt as highly integrated as are the production processes of the basic steel, basic aluminum, wet milling, and lumbering industries. The process itself is largely dependent upon the proper functioning of a wide variety of instrument controls which channel the raw materials through the closed pipe system and regulate the speed of flow of the materials as well as the temperatures within different parts of the system. These controls are an integral part of the production system. The instrument mechanics' work on such controls is therefore intimately related to the production process itself. Indeed, in performing such work, they must do so in tandem with the operators of the controls to insure that the system continues to function while new controls are installed, and existing controls are calibrated, maintained, and repaired.

The instrument mechanics have been represented as part of a production and maintenance unit for the last 25 years. The record does not demonstrate that their interests have been neglected by their bargaining representative. In fact, the record shows that their pay rates are comparable to those received by the skilled electricians who are currently represented by the Petitioner, and that such rates are among the highest in the plant. The instrument mechanics have their own seniority system

---

[16] We are in a period of industrial progress and change which so profoundly affect the product, process, operational technology, and organization of industry that a concomitant upheaval is reflected in the types and standards of skills, the working arrangements, job requirements, and community of interests of employees. Through modern technological development, a merging and overlapping of old crafts is taking place and new crafts are emerging. Highly skilled workers are, in some situations, required to devote those skills wholly to the production process itself, so that old departmental lines no longer reflect a homogeneous grouping of employees.

[17] To the extent that *American Potash* forecloses inquiry into all relevant factors, and to the extent that it limits consideration of the factors of industry bargaining history and integration of operations to cases arising in the so-called *National Tube* industries, it is overruled. To the extent that the decisions in National Tube Company, *supra*, Permanente Metals Co., *supra*, Corn Products Refining Company, *supra*, Weyerhaeuser Timber Company, *supra*, and decisions relying thereon, may be read as automatically foreclosing craft or departmental severance or the initial formation of such units in unorganized plants in the industries involved, they are hereby overruled.

for purposes of transfer, layoff, and recall. Viewing this long lack of concern for maintaining and preserving a separate group identity for bargaining purposes, together with the fact that Petitioner has not traditionally represented the instrument mechanic craft, we find that the interests served by maintenance of stability in the existing bargaining unit of approximately 280 production and maintenance employees outweigh the interests served by affording the 12 instrument mechanics an opportunity to change their mode of representation.

We conclude that the foregoing circumstances present a compelling argument in support of the continued appropriateness of the existing production and maintenance unit for purposes of collective bargaining, and against the appropriateness of a separate unit of instrument mechanics. In reaching this conclusion, we have not overlooked the fact that the instrument mechanics do constitute an identifiable group of skilled journeymen mechanics, similar to groups the Board heretofore has found entitled to severance from an overall unit. However, it appears that the separate community of interests which these employees enjoy by reason of their skills and training has been largely submerged in the broader community of interests which they share with other employees by reason of long and uninterrupted association in the existing bargaining unit, the high degree of integration of the employer's production processes, and the intimate connection of the work of these employees with the actual uranium metal-making process itself. We find, accordingly, that the unit sought by the Petitioner is inappropriate for the purposes of collective bargaining. We shall, therefore, dismiss the petition.

MEMBER FANNING dissented.

NOTES

1. For other cases applying the tests stated in the principal case, *see* E. I. Du Pont Co., 162 N.L.R.B. 413 (1966); Holmberg, Inc., 162 N.L.R.B. 407 (1966); Eaton Yale & Towne, Inc., 191 N.L.R.B. 217 (1971); Pueblo International Inc., d/b/a Supermercados Pueblo, 203 N.L.R.B. 629 (1973).

2. In General Motors Corp., 120 N.L.R.B. 1215 (1958), several organizations of skilled workers in the automobile industry petitioned for craft severance elections. The NLRB, in a rather unusual proceeding, heard oral argument in Detroit. The UAW, intervening, argued that these organizations did not meet the "traditional" craft representative test of the *American Potash* case and that the Board ought not to establish any craft or "smaller-than-plant-wide" bargaining units in the automobile industry generally. The Board did not find it necessary to rule on these important issues, dismissing the petition on the ground that the units requested were not appropriate in that they were not coextensive with the existing bargaining unit. The Board found that although originally the UAW was certified by the Board as bargaining representative in each GM plant as a separate bargaining unit, there now exists a single company-wide bargaining unit as a result of a long multiplant bargaining history in which national agreements were negotiated. Accordingly, since the organizations of skilled craftsmen had requested elections in single plants, these requested units were inappropriate because not coextensive with the existing company-wide bargaining unit.

3. See Cohen, *Two Years Under Mallinckrodt: A Review of the Board's Latest Craft Unit Policy,* 20 Lab. L.J. 195 (1969); Sharp, *Craft Certification: New Expansion of an Old Concept,* 33 Ohio St. L.J. 102 (1972); Note, *Unit Determination and the Problem of Craft Severance,* 19 Case W. Res. L. Rev. 327 (1968).

4. For some insight into the problems of determining appropriate bargaining units in a newly covered industry (nonprofit hospitals), *see* Barnett Memorial Hospital Center, 217 N.L.R.B. 775 (1975); Mercy Hospital of Sacramento, 217 N.L.R.B. 765 (1975); Allegheny General Hospital, 239 N.L.R.B. No. 104, 100 L.R.R.M. 1030 (1978). *See also* Menard, *Exploding Representation Areas: Colleges and Universities,* 17 B.C. Ind. & Com. L. Rev. 931 (1976).

MULTIPLE PLANT UNITS

NLRB, SEVENTEENTH ANNUAL REPORT 68-69 (1952)

When dealing with employees of companies which operate more than one plant, the Board must frequently determine whether an employer-wide unit, or a less comprehensive one, is appropriate. In making such determinations, the Board must take into consideration all relevant factors, but it is precluded by the act from determining the scope of the unit solely on the basis of the extent to which the company's employees have organized. This statutory limitation sometimes is invoked in opposition to a less than company-wide unit. On this point, the Board has repeatedly held that it is precluded only from giving *controlling* weight to extent of organization, but not from taking the present extent of the employees' organization into consideration together with other pertinent circumstances. In cases where extent of organization was the only basis for the proposed unit, the Board has consistently rejected the unit.

Principal factors considered in cases where multiplant units are proposed include: (1) Bargaining history, (2) the extent of interchange and contacts between employees in the various plants, (3) the extent of functional integration of operations between the plants, (4) differences in the products of the plants or in the skills and types of work required, (5) the centralization, or lack of centralization, of management and supervision, particularly in regard to labor relations and the power to hire and discharge, and (6) the physical or geographical location of the plants in relation to each other.

In most cases, several of these factors are present; some pointing to the appropriateness of a multiplant unit, others pointing to the appropriateness of a narrower unit. In each case, the Board must weigh all the factors present, one against the other, in deciding the proper scope of the unit. However, in certain industries, company-wide or multiplant units are generally favored. Foremost among such industries are public utilities, such as power, telephone, and gas companies, where it has long been the Board's policy to establish system-wide or multiplant units whenever feasible. This policy is based upon the highly integrated and interdependent character of public utility operations and the high degree of coordination among the employees required by the type of service rendered.

The Board similarly favors system-wide and division-wide units of employees in the transportation industry.

NOTES

1. Until recently, the Board seemed to favor multiplant and other broadly-based bargaining units. However, during the early 1960's, the Board appeared to become more receptive to petitions from single stores, plants, or offices.

"[P]roduct integration is becoming a less significant factor in determining an appropriate unit because modern manufacturing techniques combined with the increased speed and ease of transport make it possible for plants located in different states to have a high degree of product integration and still maintain a separate identity for bargaining purposes." Black & Decker Mfg. Co., 147 N.L.R.B. 825 (1964).

Have any of the other factors listed above been made obsolete by modern industrial methods?

2. *Chain Stores.* In Sav-On Drugs, 138 N.L.R.B. 1032 (1962), the Board modified its bargaining unit policy with regard to chain store operations so that the same unit policy which now applies to multiplant operations will be determinative of the appropriate bargaining unit for chain stores. Here the Board allowed a single store in the chain to be an appropriate bargaining unit where there was (1) geographical separation of the store in question, (2) substantial authority of store manager, (3) minimal interchange of employees between this store and other stores, (4) absence of bargaining history for any employees in the division, and (5) fact that no union was seeking to represent employees on a broader basis.

For court rejections of single-store units, see NLRB v. Purity Food Stores, Inc., 376 F.2d 497 (1st Cir. 1967); NLRB v. Frisch's Big Boy Ill-Mar, Inc., 356 F.2d 895 (7th Cir. 1966). *Cf.* NLRB v. Sun Drug Co., 359 F.2d 408 (3d Cir. 1966), where a single-store unit was approved.

A 3-2 majority in Gray Drug Stores, Inc., 197 N.L.R.B. No. 105, 80 L.R.R.M. 1449 (1972), rejected a union's petition for separate units at each store of a drug-store chain in one county, or for one unit covering the eleven stores in that county. Instead, an election was directed in a unit comprising all the stores in two adjacent counties. The majority felt this reflected the employees' community of interest, based upon common supervision and geographical proximity.

3. *See* Note, *The Board and § 9(c)(5): Multi-Location and Single-Location Bargaining Units in the Insurance and Retail Industries,* 79 HARV. L. REV. 811 (1966); Note, *Effects of the NLRB's Unit Policies* *in the Retail Chain Store Industry,* 23 LAB. L.J. 80 (1972); Vladek, *Nixon Board and Retail Bargaining Units,* 61 CORNELL L. REV. 416 (1976).

MULTIPLE EMPLOYER UNITS

NLRB, TWENTY-THIRD ANNUAL REPORT 36-37 (1958)

In dealing with requests for multi-employer units, the Board is primarily guided by the rule that a single-employer unit is presumptively appropriate and that to establish a contested claim for a broader unit a controlling history of collective bargaining on such a basis by the employers and the union involved must be shown. But no controlling weight was given to multi-employer bargaining which was preceded by a long history of single-employer bargaining, was of brief duration, did not result in a written contract of substantial duration, and was not based on any Board unit finding.

The existence of a controlling multi-employer bargaining history may also depend on whether the employer group has in fact bargained jointly or on an individual basis. Generally, the Board will find that joint bargaining is established where the employers involved have for a substantial period directly participated in joint bargaining or delegated the power to bind them in collective bargaining to a joint agent, have executed the resulting contract, and have not negotiated on an individual basis. Execution of the contract by each employer separately does not preclude a finding of a multi-employer bargaining history where the employers are clearly shown to have participated in a pattern of joint bargaining.

(1) Scope of Multi-employer Unit

A multi-employer unit may include only employers who have participated in and are bound by joint negotiations. The mere adoption of a group contract by an employer who has not participated in joint bargaining directly or through an agent, or has indicated his intention not to be bound by future group negotiations, is insufficient to permit his inclusion in a proposed multi-employer unit.

(2) Withdrawal From Multi-employer Unit

A petition for a single-employer unit, in the face of a multi-employer bargaining history, will be granted if it appears that the employer involved has effectively withdrawn from the multi-employer group and has abandoned group bargaining. In order for withdrawal from multi-employer bargaining to be effective, the withdrawing party must unequivocally indicate at an appropriate time that it desires to abandon such bargaining. Pointing out in one case that the necessary stability in bargaining relations requires reasonable limits on the time and manner for withdrawal from an established multi-employer bargaining unit, the Board held that —

> The decision to withdraw must contemplate a sincere abandonment, with relative permanency, of the multi-employer unit and the embracement of a different course of bargaining on an individual-employer basis. The element of good faith is a necessary

requirement in any such decision to withdraw, because of the unstabilizing and disrupting effect on multi-employer collective bargaining which would result if such withdrawal were permitted to be lightly made.

A majority of the Board also believed that the issues raised in this case justified establishment of "specific ground rules" governing the withdrawal from multi-employer bargaining units in future cases. Noting particularly that insurance of stability in multi-employer bargaining relationships requires limitations on the timing of withdrawals, the majority announced that hereafter —

[The Board] would ... refuse to permit the withdrawal of an employer or a union from a duly established multi-employer bargaining unit, except upon adequate written notice given prior to the date set by the contract for modification, or to the agreed-upon date to begin the multi-employer negotiations. Where actual bargaining negotiations based on the existing multi-employer unit have begun, we would not permit, except on mutual consent, an abandonment of the unit upon which each side has committed itself to the other, absent unusual circumstances. [Retail Associates, Inc., 120 N.L.R.B. 388 (1958).] *See also* Charles D. Bonanno Linen Serv., 229 N.L.R.B. 629 (1977).

But see NLRB v. Hi-Way Billboards, Inc., 500 F.2d 181 (5th Cir. 1974); NLRB v. Associated Shower Door Co., 512 F.2d 230 (9th Cir. 1975); NLRB v. Beck Engraving Co., 522 F.2d 475 (3d Cir. 1975); NLRB v. Independent Ass'n of Steel Fabricators, 582 F.2d 135 (2d Cir. 1978), indicating that a negotiating impasse justifies an employer in withdrawing from a multi-employer unit. *And see,* Note, 44 FORDHAM L. REV. 1256 (1976) and Comment, *Effect of Negotiating Impasse on Employer's Right to Withdraw from a Multi-employer Bargaining Association,* 17 B.C. IND. & COM. L. REV. 525 (1976).

NOTES

1. "Multi-employer bargaining long antedated the Wagner Act, both in industries like the garment industry, characterized by numerous employers of small work forces, and in industries like longshoring and building construction, where workers change employers from day to day or week to week. This basis of bargaining has had its greatest expansion since enactment of the Wagner Act because employers have sought through group bargaining to match increased union strength. Approximately four million employees are now governed by collective bargaining agreements signed by unions with thousands of employer associations. At the time of the debates on the Taft-Hartley amendments, proposals were made to limit or outlaw multi-employer bargaining. These proposals failed of enactment. They were met with a storm of protest that their adoption would tend to weaken and not strengthen the process of collective bargaining and would conflict with the national labor policy of promoting industrial peace through effective collective bargaining." Mr.

Justice Brennan in NLRB v. Truck Drivers, Local 449 [Buffalo Linen], 353 U.S. 87, 94-95 (1957), *supra* at 161.

2. The courts of appeals have given approval to the Board's rigid "specific ground rules" governing employer withdrawal from a multi-employer association. *See* Universal Insulation Corp. v. NLRB, 361 F.2d 406 (6th Cir. 1966); NLRB v. Sheridan Creations, Inc., 357 F.2d 245 (2d Cir. 1966), *cert. denied,* 385 U.S. 1005 (1967); NLRB v. Unelko Corp., 478 F.2d 1404 (7th Cir. 1973); NLRB v. Johnson Sheet Metal, Inc., 442 F.2d 1056 (10th Cir. 1971).

Rules governing employer withdrawal are equally applicable to unions. Since the multi-employer unit depends for its existence upon the continuing consent of both parties, if either party indicates in a timely and unequivocal fashion a preference for bargaining as a single-employer unit, the Board will give effect to such a preference. Detroit Newspaper Publishers Ass'n v. NLRB, 372 F.2d 569 (6th Cir. 1967); Publishers Ass'n of New York City v. NLRB, 364 F.2d 293 (2d Cir. 1966), *cert. denied,* 385 U.S. 971 (1966); Evening News Ass'n, 154 N.L.R.B. 1482 (1965). The Board has gone one step further and allowed a union to withdraw from the multi-employer unit with respect to some of the employers, while continuing multi-employer bargaining with the others. Pacific Coast Ass'n of Pulp & Paper Mfrs., 163 N.L.R.B. 892 (1967). The Board noted that if the employer had made a timely bid to withdraw, he would be allowed to do so, and the union may be allowed no less a right to withdraw.

3. What are the advantages and disadvantages of multi-employer bargaining from (1) the employers' point of view, (2) the union's point of view, (3) the point of view of the general public?

See C. REHMUS, MULTIEMPLOYER BARGAINING (1965); Freidin, *The Taft-Hartley Act and Multi-Employer Bargaining,* and Pollock, *Social Implications of Industry-Wide Bargaining,* in INDUSTRY-WIDE COLLECTIVE BARGAINING SERIES, LABOR RELATIONS COUNCIL, WHARTON SCHOOL OF FINANCE AND COMMERCE (1948-1949).

3. THE CONDUCT OF REPRESENTATION ELECTIONS

NLRB, THIRTY-FIRST ANNUAL REPORT 59, 61-65 (1966)

Section 9(c)(1) of the act provides that if, upon a petition filed, a question of representation exists, the Board must resolve it through an election by secret ballot. The election details are left to the Board. Such matters as voting eligibility, timing of elections, and standards of election conduct are subject to rules laid down in the Board's Rules and Regulations and in its decisions. Board elections are conducted in accordance with strict standards designed to assure that the participating employees have an opportunity to determine, and to register a free and untrammeled choice in the selection of, a bargaining representative. Any party to an election who believes that the standards have not been met may file timely objections to the election with the regional director under whose supervision it was held. In that event, the regional director may, as the situation warrants, either make an administrative investigation of the objections or hold a formal hearing to develop a record as the basis for decision. If the election was held pursuant to a consent-election agreement authorizing a determination by the regional director, the regional director will then issue a decision on the objections which is final. If the election was held pursuant to a consent agreement authorizing a determination by the Board, the regional director will then issue a report on objections which is then subject to exceptions by the parties and decision by the Board. However, if the election was one directed by the Board, the regional director may (1) either make a report on the objections, subject to exceptions with the decision to be made by the Board, or (2) dispose of the issues by issuing a decision, which is then subject to limited review by the Board.

Disclosure of Names and Addresses of Eligible Employees

In fulfillment of "the Board's function to conduct elections in which employees have the opportunity to cast their ballots for or against representation under circumstances that are free not only from interference, restraint, or coercion violative of the act, but also from other elements that prevent or impede a free and reasoned choice," the Board, in the *Excelsior Underwear* case,[67] promulgated an employee name and address disclosure rule designed to facilitate campaign communications with the eligible voters and thereby assure an informed electorate. It established as a requirement applicable prospectively to all election cases [68] that within 7 days after the election has been directed or agreed upon, "the employer must file with the Regional Director an election eligibility list, containing the names and addresses of all the eligible voters. The Regional Director, in turn, shall make this information available to all parties in the case. Failure to comply with this requirement shall be grounds for setting aside the election whenever proper objections are filed." . . . .

In rejecting the contention that disclosure could only be required if the union would otherwise be unable to reach the employees with its message, the Board distinguished court cases [69] which limit a union's access to employer's premises to those situations where alternative channels of communication are unavailable. It viewed those decisions as being predicated upon protection of property rights, a significant employer interest, whereas in the situation presented the employer has no such significant interest in the secrecy of employee names and addresses.

---

[67] 156 N.L.R.B. 1236 (1966).

[68] The requirement not only applies to petitions for certification or decertification of representatives under § 9(c)(1) of the act, but also to deauthorization elections under § 9(e)(1). Due to the expedited procedure it does not apply to elections conducted pursuant to § 8(b)(7)(C). It became applicable only to elections directed or consented to subsequent to 30 days from the date of the *Excelsior* decision.

[69] NLRB v. Babcock & Wilcox Co., 351 U.S. 105 (1956); NLRB v. United Steelworkers (NuTone, Inc.), 357 U.S. 357 (1958).

NOTES

1. In General Elec. Co. and in McCulloch Corp., 156 N.L.R.B. 1247 (1966), the union asked that elections which it had lost be set aside because the employer had made an antiunion speech on company premises during working time a few days before the election and had refused the union's request for a chance to reply. The Board took occasion to hear oral argument (on the same day as *Excelsior Underwear*) on the following question: "Can a fair and free election be held where an employer makes an antiunion speech on company time and premises, in the period immediately preceding an election, and the union involved is not afforded the opportunity, which it seeks, to reply under similar circumstances?"

The Board decided not to set the elections aside and said: "In light of the increased opportunities for employees' access to communications which should flow from *Excelsior,* but with which we have, as yet, no experience, and because we are not persuaded on the basis of our current experience that other fundamental changes in Board policy are necessary to make possible that free and reasoned choice for or against unionization which the National Labor Relations Act contemplates and which it is our function to insure we prefer to defer any reconsideration of Board doctrine in the area of plant access until after the effects of *Excelsior* become known." 156 N.L.R.B. at 1251.

2. Do you think that the Board members were worried about *Babcock & Wilcox* and *NuTone*? Should they have been? Do you think that those cases would stand in the way of the NLRB making a rule, under its power to conduct elections, that when an employer chooses to make a "captive audience" speech, he must give the union a chance to reply?

3. If the Board members decided to make such a rule to be applied in representation proceedings (setting elections aside), could they and should they also change the *Livingston Shirt* doctrine in unfair labor practice proceedings (that an employer does not violate § 8(a)(1) when he refuses the union "equal time")?

4. In thinking about the above two questions, consider the Board's reasoning in the *Excelsior* case: "The argument is also made . . . that under the decisions of the Supreme Court in *Babcock & Wilcox* and *[Nu Tone]. . .,* the Board may not require employer disclosure of employee names and addresses unless, in the particular case involved the union would otherwise be unable to reach the employees with its message. We disagree. . . . [B]oth *Babcock* and *NuTone* dealt with the circumstances under which the Board might find an employer to have committed an unfair labor practice in violation of § 8 of the Act, whereas the instant cases pose the substantially distinguishable issue of the circumstances under which the Board may set aside an election. '[T]he test of conduct which may interfere with the "laboratory conditions" for an election is considerably more restrictive than the test of conduct which amounts to interference, restraint, or coercion which violates § 8(a)(1)'. Dal-Tex Optical Co., 137 N.L.R.B. 1782 (1962). Whether or not an employer's refusal to disclose employee names and addresses after an election is directed would constitute 'interference, restraint, or coercion' within the meaning of § 8(a)(1) of the Act, despite the existence of alternative channels of communication open to the union, is a question on which we express no view because it is not before us. However, we are persuaded, for the reasons previously stated, that disclosure is one of the 'safeguards necessary to insure the fair and free choice of bargaining representative by employees' and that an employer's refusal to disclose, regardless of the existence of alternative channels of communication, tends to interfere with a fair and free election. Thus *Babcock* and *NuTone,* which dealt with the substantially different issue of whether the employers' conduct violated § 8(a)(1), are, for this reason also, inapposite." Excelsior Underwear, Inc., 156 N.L.R.B. 1236, 1244-46 (1966).

5. The proposed Labor Reform Act of 1978 would direct the Labor Board to use its rule-making authority to establish guidelines providing unions an equal opportunity to reply to an employer's antiunion speeches on company premises during an organizing drive.

6. The validity of the *Excelsior Underwear* "names-and-addresses" rule was sustained by the Supreme Court in NLRB v. Wyman-Gordon Co., 394 U.S. 759 (1969).

7. See Sandler, *Labor Board's "Name and Address" Rule in Action,* 27 RECORD OF N.Y.C.B.A. 153 (1972); Note, *The Judicial Role in the Enforcement of the "Excelsior" Rule,* 66 MICH. L. REV. 1292 (1968).

8. In an effort to speed up the process, the proposed Labor Reform Act of 1978 would prescribe set timetables for the conduct of representation elections in various circumstances. In most instances where a union has the initial backing of a majority of the employees, the election would be ordered held between 21 days and 30 days of the filing of the petition.

NLRB, THIRTY-FIRST ANNUAL REPORT 66-68 (1966)

Conduct Affecting Elections—Election Propaganda

Threats of adverse economic consequences as well as appeals to racism were alleged as a basis for objections to the election in the *Universal Mfg. Corp.* case.[80] There, the Board was called upon to evaluate the impact of antiunion election campaign propaganda originating with community groups which injected themselves into the campaign. The community members and groups, not shown to be acting as agents of the employer, were responsible for newspaper editorials, advertisements, and handbills containing appeals to racist sentiment, charges of Communist control over unions and the civil rights movement, and warnings of economic disaster to the community in the event of unionization of the plant. Applying its established standards [81] that racial propaganda will not be tolerated unless the statements are "truthful, temperate, and germane to a party's position," and do not "deliberately seek to overstress and

---

[80] 156 N.L.R.B. 1459 (1966).

[81] Sewell Mfg. Co., 138 N.L.R.B. 66, Twenty-eighth Annual Report 58-59 (1963).

exacerbate racial feelings by irrelevant, inflammatory appeals," the Board found that permissible bounds had been exceeded by handbills, cartoons, and newspaper editorials concerning actions and attitudes of union leaders and supporters. The matters commented on were, at best, irrelevant to the campaign and inflammatory in nature and intent. In some instances the handbills were distributed by methods which also established that "the sponsoring parties intended, not to educate or inform the employees about an issue germane to the election, but to prompt them to vote against the union 'on racial grounds alone.' "

The newspaper editorials, full-page advertisements, and handbills reiterated the themes that success of the union might cause the plant to close and would squelch any chance for industrial expansion in the area, thereby impairing employment opportunities and causing higher taxes, and in general could spell out economic hardship for employees, their families, and neighbors. The newspaper communications also contained threats of blacklisting, along with statements which linked unions, civil rights, and communism as if they were aspects of a single pernicious entity, implying that union dues would end up in Communist Party coffers. The Board found that "By appealing to the employees' sentiments as civic minded individuals, injecting the fear of personal economic loss, and playing on racial prejudice, the full-page ads, the editorials, the cartoon, and the handbill were calculated to convince the employees that a vote for the union meant the betrayal of the community's best interests. Faced with pressures of this sort, the employees in our opinion were inhibited from freely exercising their choice in the election." The election was therefore set aside.

Employer Talks to Employee Groups

In determining whether preelection propaganda has interfered with the holding of a free election, the Board looks not only to the content of the propaganda but also at the circumstances under which it was disseminated. One means of dissemination which may overstep permissible bounds is employer talks to groups of employees brought together in some "locus of final authority in the plant," [82] such as a supervisor's office, under circumstances where statements made may be expected to have greater impact. In one case,[83] decided during the year, the Board overruled an objection to an election based upon the fact that the employer had held a series of meetings in the plant cafeteria attended by groups of from 10 to 14 employees to propagandize against union representation. The meetings, all held more than 24 hours before the election, were addressed by the company president and its attorney with comments limited to legitimate campaign propaganda. The Board noted that the plant cafeteria had been used for other employee meetings and activities in the past and that about 90 percent of the 400 unit employees, eligible and ineligible, were at different times called to the meetings in

---

[82] General Shoe Corp., 97 N.L.R.B. 499.
[83] Dempster Brothers, Inc., 154 N.L.R.B. 688.

question. Under these circumstances, it found "insufficient basis for concluding that the Employer's action in holding group meetings constituted an isolation of a few from among the many at a locus of managerial authority in order to create an aura of special treatment to individuals, as distinguished from employees as a whole, so as to bring . . . [that] conduct within the prohibition of the *General Shoe* doctrine."

Another limitation upon the circumstances under which propaganda is disseminated is the *Peerless Plywood*[84] rule prohibiting either party from making election speeches on company time to massed assemblies of employees within 24 hours before the election, even though such speeches may not be otherwise objectionable.

NOTES

1. In Dal-Tex Optical Co., 137 N.L.R.B. 1782 (1962), the employer delivered speeches to employees which were found to be grounds for setting aside the election. The Board in its decision held that conduct which is violative of § 8(a)(1) also automatically interferes with the exercise of a free election "because the test of conduct which may interfere with the 'laboratory conditions' for an election is considerably more restrictive than the test of conduct which amounts to interference, restraint, or coercion which violates § 8(a)(1)." The Board found that "Congress specifically limited § 8(c) to the adversary proceedings involved in unfair labor practice cases and it has no application to representation cases. . . . The strictures of the first amendment, to be sure, must be considered in all cases."

See also Trane Co., 137 N.L.R.B. 1506 (1962); Lord Baltimore Press, 142 N.L.R.B. 308 (1963); Oak Mfg. Co., 141 N.L.R.B. 1323 (1963).

2. A 3-2 Board majority in NVF Co., 210 N.L.R.B. 663 (1974), restated the rules governing employer talks to employees, individually or in small groups, in company offices. The majority rejected any per se approach, and declared that elections would be set aside only when interference could reasonably be inferred from such particular facts as the small size of the groups interviewed, the locus of the interview, the position of the interviewer in the employer's hierarchy, and the tenor of the speaker's remarks.

3. *Misleading Statements.* The Board has adopted the policy to set aside an election where it appears that (1) there has been a material misrepresentation of fact, (2) this misrepresentation comes from a party who had special knowledge or was in an authoritative position to know the true facts, and (3) no other party had sufficient opportunity to correct the misrepresentations before the election. Celanese Corp. v. NLRB, 291 F.2d 244 (7th Cir. 1961). *See also* Hollywood Ceramics Co., 140 N.L.R.B. 221 (1962).

In Shopping Kart Food Market, 228 N.L.R.B. 1311 (1977) a 3-2 Board majority abandoned the *Hollywood Ceramics* tests and stated that the

---

[84] Peerless Plywood Co., 107 N.L.R.B. 427, Nineteenth Annual Report 65 (1954).

Board will no longer set elections aside on the basis of misleading statements. Member Murphy concurred, but would set an election aside where there has been "an egregious mistake of fact." Members Fanning and Jenkins filed a vigorous dissent.

The Board said that it will still set elections aside where a party has engaged in coercive tactics such as threats of reprisal or deceptive practices such as the use of forged documents, but will no longer probe into the truth or falsity of campaign statements. The majority asserted that Board rules "must be based on a view of employees as mature individuals who are capable of recognizing campaign propaganda for what it is and discounting it."

However, in General Knit of California, Inc., 239 N.L.R.B. No. 101, 99 L.R.R.M. 1687 (1978), a new 3-2 Board majority overruled the *Shopping Kart* case and indicated its intention to return to the *Hollywood Ceramics* standard that "an election should be set aside only where there has been a misrepresentation or other similar campaign trickery, which involves a substantial departure from the truth, at a time which prevents the party or parties from making an effective reply, so that the misrepresentation, whether deliberate or not, may reasonably be expected to have a significant impact on the election." The Board majority also stated its "firm belief that employees should be afforded a degree of protection from overzealous campaigners who distort the issues by substantial misstatements of relevant and material facts within the special knowledge of the campaigner, so shortly before the election that there is no effective time for reply." In their dissent, Members Penello and Murphy argued strongly that the *Hollywood Ceramics* tests had proved extremely difficult to apply and that their revival would encourage parties to challenge the results of Board elections as a delaying tactic, thereby clogging up the Board's election proceedings. Both *Shopping Kart* and *General Knit* also involved a conflict within the Board as to the proper inferences to be drawn from an empirical study of voters' behavior in 31 NLRB elections as to effect of the parties' electioneering upon how the employees voted. See Getman & Goldberg, *The Behavioral Assumptions Underlying NLRB Regulation of Campaign Misrepresentations: An Empirical Evaluation,* 28 STAN. L. REV. 263 (1976); J. GETMAN, S. GOLDBERG & J. HERMAN, UNION REPRESENTATION ELECTIONS: LAW AND REALITY (1976).

4. Should the NLRB set aside an election where the employer, shortly before the day of the election, shows the antiunion movie, "And Women Must Weep," telling the dramatic story of a strike which resulted in violence, fear and hatred? *Compare* Plochman & Harrison — Cherry Lane Foods, 140 N.L.R.B. 130 (1962) *and* Carl T. Mason, Inc., 142 N.L.R.B. 480 (1963) *with* Litho Press of San Antonio, 211 N.L.R.B. 1014 (1974).

5. For a concise summary of NLRB rules as to preelection propaganda, see K. McGUINESS, HOW TO TAKE A CASE BEFORE THE NLRB (4th ed. 1976). *See* Bok, *The Regulation of Campaign Tactics in Representation Elections Under the NLRA,* 78 HARV. L. REV. 38 (1964); Pollitt, *The National Labor Relations Board and Race Hate Propaganda in Union Organization Drives,* 17 STAN. L. REV. 373 (1965); Note, *Labor Representation Elections and the Constitutional Right to Campaign*

Vigorously — The Use of Racial Propaganda, 23 S.C.L.Q. 400 (1971); Symposium: *Four Perspectives on Union Representation Elections: Law and Reality, The Getman, Goldberg and Herman Questions,* 28 STAN. L. REV. 1161 (1976); Roomkin & Abrams, *Using Behavioral Evidence in NLRB Regulation: A Proposal,* 90 HARV. L. REV. 1441 (1977); King, *Pre-election Conduct, Expanding Employer Rights and Some New and Renewed Perspectives,* 2 IND. REL. L.J. 185 (1977).

6. Should an election be set aside where a union offered to waive the initiation fee, if the union won the election, for all employees who executed authorization cards prior to the election? *See* NLRB v. Savair Mfg. Co., 414 U.S. 27 (1973).

A union interfered with an election by a preelection offer to waive initiation fees for "charter members," since the term "charter member" was not defined and employees could have been induced to become early card signers on the reasonable belief that only those signing prior to the election would be eligible for the waiver. Inland Shoe Mfg. Co., 211 N.L.R.B. 724 (1974). *Compare* Aladdin Hotel Corp., 229 N.L.R.B. No. 73, 95 L.R.R.M. 1150 (1977).

7. *What Constitutes a Majority Choice?* It has been held that the outcome of an NLRB election depends on "a majority of those voting in the election" rather than "a majority of those eligible to vote." R.C.A. Mfg. Co., 2 N.L.R.B. 168 (1936).

An employee is normally entitled to vote if he was employed on the eligibility date (usually the pay day preceding direction of election) and on election day.

8. *Runoff Elections.* Where two or more unions are competing for the votes of employees in an election, and no union receives a majority of the votes cast, § 9(c)(3) of the Taft-Hartley Act requires that "a run-off shall be conducted, the ballot providing for a selection between the two choices receiving the largest number of valid votes cast in the election." Thus, if 100 employees vote in the original election as follows: 45 for Union One, 30 for No Union, and 25 for Union Two, the runoff will be between Union One and No Union.

9. *Eligibility to Vote During a Strike.* During the Wagner Act period, strikers were allowed to vote, but a Taft-Hartley amendment deprived economic strikers who had been replaced of a right to vote. Experience demonstrated that this could be used as a "union-busting" device, so Congress passed a compromise amendment in 1959 providing in § 9(c)(3) that "employees engaged in an economic strike who are not entitled to reinstatement shall be eligible to vote under such regulations as the Board shall find are consistent with the purposes and provisions of the National Labor Relations Act, as amended, in any election conducted within twelve months after the commencement of the strike."

In Pacific Tile & Porcelain Co., 137 N.L.R.B. 1358 (1962), the NLRB clarified its rules concerning the status of strikers and replacements in elections. The Board held that in order to challenge an economic striker's vote, the challenger must affirmatively show that the striker has "no further interest in his struck job." To challenge the vote of a replacement, the challenger must show that he was not employed on a struck job on a permanent basis. In this connection the Board places the burden of proving disqualification upon the party who challenges the vote. *Accord,* Q-T Tool Co., Inc., 199 N.L.R.B. 500 (1972).

Even though an employer that had lost business during an economic strike did not know when it would have enough work to take back the strikers, they were eligible to vote in a representation election. They could not be disqualified because they had no "reasonable expectancy of recall." Globe Molded Plastics Co., 200 N.L.R.B. 377 (1972).

In Gulf States Paper Corp., 219 N.L.R.B. 806 (1975), the Board held that economic strikers who have been on strike for more than one year and have been permanently replaced are ineligible to vote in an NLRB election. However, unreplaced economic strikers are eligible to vote if their jobs have not been permanently eliminated, they have not found permanent employment elsewhere, and the employer has not refused to reinstate them for misconduct rendering them unsuitable for reemployement.

10. The Court of Appeals for the Eighth Circuit held, in NLRB v. Mansion House Center Management Corp., 473 F.2d 471 (1973), that racial discrimination by the union may be set up as a defense to an NLRB bargaining order. The Court said that "we hold the remedial machinery of the National Labor Relations Act cannot be made available to a union which is unwilling to correct past practices of racial discrimination. Federal complicity through recognition of a discriminating union serves not only to condone the discrimination, but in effect legitimizes and perpetuates such invidious practices. Certainly such a degree of federal participation in the maintenance of racially discriminatory practices violates basic constitutional tenets."

In response to the *Mansion House* case, the Board announced in Bekins Moving & Storage Co., 211 N.L.R.B. 138 (1974), that it would consider claims of invidious discrimination by a union in a representation proceeding, but only after the election is over and the union has won.

However, in Handy Andy, Inc., 228 N.L.R.B. 447 (1977), the Board reversed the *Bekins* case, which had held that the Board is constitutionally required to consider issues raised by an objection grounded on alleged invidious discrimination prior to issuance of a Board certification of a union as exclusive bargaining representative. In *Handy Andy,* the NLRB concluded that neither the Fifth Amendment to the Constitution nor the Act requires the Board to resolve such questions before certifying a union. "Indeed, it appears to us that the contrary is true; namely, that the Board is not authorized to withhold certification of a labor organization duly selected by a majority of the unit employees." The Board stated that claims of invidious discrimination will be considered in appropriate unfair labor practice proceedings, particularly where charges are filed that the union is failing to carry out its duty of fair representation. *See infra* at 760.

On reconsideration, the NLRB reaffirmed its decision that an employer violated the NLRA by refusing to bargain with a newly certified union, notwithstanding a contention that certification was invalidly issued because the Board refused to conduct a precertification investigation and hearing on the issue of whether the union discriminated against women.

Bell & Howell, 230 N.L.R.B. No. 57, 95 L.R.R.M. 1333 (1977), *enforced,*
100 L.R.R.M. 2192 (D.C. Cir. 1979). But could a bargaining order be
entered against a union if there were allegations that an employer
discriminates on the basis of race or nationality? Yes, since there exist
"appropriate means of redress and relief designed to eliminate the
offensive practices while preserving a collective bargaining relationship."
Graphic Arts Union Local 280 (James H. Barry Co.), 235 N.L.R.B. No.
139, 98 L.R.R.M. 1188 (1978). *See also* Grede Foundries, Inc., 235
N.L.R.B. No. 40, 97 L.R.R.M. 1510 (1978), where the Board ruled that
issuance of a bargaining order against an employer that refused to bargain
with a union while committing serious violations of the Taft-Hartley Act
is appropriate, even though the union engaged in serious misconduct
during a strike. The Board weighed the union's misconduct against that
of the employer and concluded that it was "clearly insufficient" to justify
denial of a bargaining order. One member dissented.

See generally, Axelrod and Kaufman, *Mansion House — Bekins —
Handy Andy: The National Labor Relations Board's Role in Racial
Discrimination Cases,* 45 GEO. WASH. L. REV. 675 (1977).

4. COURT REVIEW OF REPRESENTATION PROCEEDINGS

LEEDOM v. KYNE

Supreme Court of the United States
358 U.S. 184, 79 S. Ct. 180, 3 L. Ed. 2d 210 (1958)

MR. JUSTICE WHITTAKER delivered the opinion of the Court.

Section 9(b)(1) of the National Labor Relations Act, § 9, 49 Stat. 453,
61 Stat. 143, 29 U.S.C. § 159(b)(1), provides that, in determining the unit
appropriate for collective bargaining purposes, "the Board shall not (1)
decide that any unit is appropriate for such purposes if such unit includes
both professional employees and employees who are not professional
employees unless a majority of such professional employees vote for
inclusion in such unit." The Board, after refusing to take a vote among
the professional employees to determine whether a majority of them
would "vote for inclusion in such unit," included both professional and
nonprofessional employees in the bargaining unit that it found
appropriate. The sole and narrow question presented is whether a Federal
District Court has jurisdiction of an original suit to vacate that
determination of the Board because made in excess of its powers.

The facts are undisputed. Buffalo Section, Westinghouse Engineers
Association, Engineers and Scientists of America, a voluntary
unincorporated labor organization, hereafter called the Association, was
created for the purpose of promoting the economic and professional
status of the nonsupervisory professional employees of Westinghouse
Electric Corporation at its plant in Cheektowaga, New York, through
collective bargaining with their employer. In October, 1955, the
Association petitioned the National Labor Relations Board for
certification as the exclusive collective bargaining agent of all

nonsupervisory professional employees, being then 233 in number, of the Westinghouse Company at its Cheektowaga plant, pursuant to the provisions of § 9 of the act, 29 U.S.C. § 159. A hearing was held by the board upon that petition. A competing labor organization was permitted by the Board to intervene. It asked the Board to expand the unit to include employees in five other categories who performed technical work and were thought by it to be "professional employees" within the meaning of § 2(12) of the act, 29 U.S.C. § 152(12). The Board found that they were not professional employees within the meaning of the act. However, it found that nine employees in three of those categories should nevertheless be included in the unit because they "share a close community of employment interests with [the professional employees, and their inclusion would not] destroy the predominantly professional character of such a unit." The Board, after denying the Association's request to take a vote among the professional employees to determine whether a majority of them favored "inclusion in such unit," included the 233 professional employees and the nine nonprofessional employees in the unit and directed an election to determine whether they desired to be represented by the Association, by the other labor organization, or by neither. The Association moved the Board to stay the election and to amend its decision by excluding the nonprofessional employees from the unit. The Board denied that motion and went ahead with the election at which the Association received a majority of the valid votes cast and was thereafter certified by the Board as the collective bargaining agent for the unit.

Thereafter respondent, individually, and as president of the Association, brought this suit in the District Court against the members of the Board, alleging the foregoing facts and asserting that the Board had exceeded its statutory power in including the professional employees, without their consent, in a unit with nonprofessional employees in violation of § 9(b)(1) which commands that the Board "shall not" do so, and praying, among other things, that the Board's action be set aside. The defendants, members of the Board moved to dismiss for want of jurisdiction and, in the alternative, for a summary judgment. The plaintiff also moved for summary judgment. The trial court found that the Board had disobeyed the express command of § 9(b)(1) in including nonprofessional employees and professional employees in the same unit without the latter's consent, and in doing so had acted in excess of its powers to the injury of the professional employees, and that the court had jurisdiction to grant the relief prayed. It accordingly denied the Board's motion and granted the plaintiff's motion and entered judgment setting aside the Board's determination of the bargaining unit and also the election and the Board's certification.

On the Board's appeal it did not contest the trial court's conclusion that the Board, in commingling professional with nonprofessional employees in the unit, had acted in excess of its powers and had thereby worked injury to the statutory rights of the professional employees. Instead, it contended only that the District Court lacked jurisdiction to entertain the suit. The Court of Appeals held that the District Court did have jurisdiction and affirmed the judgment. 101 App. D.C. 398, 249 F.2d 490. . . .

Petitioners, members of the Board, concede here that the District Court had jurisdiction of the suit under § 24(8) of the Judicial Code, 28 U.S.C. § 1337, unless the review provisions of the National Labor Relations Act destroyed it. In American Federation of Labor v. NLRB, 308 U.S. 401 (1940), this Court held that a Board order in certification proceedings under § 9 is not "a final order" and therefore is not subject to judicial review except as it may be drawn in question by a petition for enforcement or review of an order, made under § 10(c) of the act, restraining an unfair labor practice. But the Court was at pains to point out in that case "[t]he question [there presented was] distinct from . . . whether petitioners are precluded by the provisions of the Wagner Act from maintaining an independent suit in a district court to set aside the Board's action because contrary to the statute. . . ." Id. at 404. The Board argued there, as it does here, that the provisions of the act, particularly § 9(d), have foreclosed review of its action by an original suit in a District Court. This Court said: "But that question is not presented for decision by the record before us. Its answer involves a determination whether the Wagner Act, in so far as it has given legally enforceable rights, has deprived the district courts of some portion of their original jurisdiction conferred by § 24 of the Judicial Code. It can be appropriately answered only upon a showing in such a suit that unlawful action of the Board has inflicted an injury on the petitioners for which the law, *apart from the review provisions of the Wagner Act,* affords a remedy. This question can be properly and adequately considered only when it is brought to us for review upon a suitable record." Id. at 412. (Emphasis added.)

The record in this case squarely presents the question found not to have been presented by the record in American Federation of Labor v. NLRB, *supra.* This case, in its posture before us, involves "unlawful action of the Board [which] has inflicted an injury on the [respondent]." Does the law, "apart from the review provisions of the . . . act," afford a remedy? We think the answer surely must be yes. This suit is not one to "review," in the sense of that term as used in the act, a decision of the Board made within its jurisdiction. Rather it is one to strike down an order of the Board made in excess of its delegated powers and contrary to a specific prohibition in the act. Section 9(b)(1) is clear and mandatory. It says that, in determining the unit appropriate for the purposes of collective bargaining, "the Board *shall not* (1) decide that any unit is appropriate for such purposes if such unit includes both professional employees and employees who are not professional employees unless a majority of such professional employees vote for inclusion in such unit." (Emphasis added.) Yet, the Board included in the unit employees whom it found were not professional employees, after refusing to determine whether a majority of the professional employees would "vote for inclusion in such unit." Plainly, this was an attempted exercise of power that had been specifically withheld. It deprived the professional employees of a "right" assured to them by Congress. Surely, in these circumstances, a Federal District Court has jurisdiction of an original suit to prevent deprivation of a right so given.

In Texas & New Orleans R. Co. v. Railway Clerks, 281 U.S. 548 (1930), it was contended that, because no remedy had been expressly given for redress of the congressionally created right in suit, the act conferred "merely an abstract right which was not intended to be enforced by legal proceedings." *Id.* at 558. This Court rejected that contention. It said: "While an affirmative declaration of duty contained in a legislative enactment may be of imperfect obligation because not enforceable in terms, a definite statutory prohibition of conduct which would thwart the declared purpose of the legislation cannot be disregarded. . . . If Congress intended that the prohibition, as thus construed, should be enforced, the courts would encounter no difficulty in fulfilling its purpose. . . . The definite prohibition which Congress inserted in the act cannot therefore be overridden in the view that Congress intended it to be ignored. As the prohibition was appropriate to the aim of Congress, and is capable of enforcement, the conclusion must be that enforcement was contemplated." *Id.* at 568, 569. And compare Virginian R. Co. v. System Federation, 300 U.S. 515.

In Switchmen's Union v. National Mediation Board, 320 U.S. 297, this Court held that the District Court did not have jurisdiction of an original suit to review an order of the National Mediation Board determining that all yardmen of the rail lines operated by the New York Central system constituted an appropriate bargaining unit, because the Railway Labor Board had acted within its delegated powers. But in the course of that opinion the Court announced principles that are controlling here. "If the absence of jurisdiction of the federal courts meant a sacrifice or obliteration of a right which Congress had created, the inference would be strong that Congress intended the statutory provisions governing the general jurisdiction of those courts to control. That was the purport of the decisions of this Court in Texas & New Orleans R. Co. v. Brotherhood of Clerks, 281 U.S. 548 (1930), and Virginian R. Co. v. System Federation, 300 U.S. 515 (1937). In those cases it was apparent that but for the general jurisdiction of the federal courts there would be no remedy to enforce the statutory commands which Congress had written into the Railway Labor Act. The result would have been that the 'right' of collective bargaining was unsupported by any legal sanction. That would have robbed the act of its vitality and thwarted its purpose." *Id.* at 300.

Here, differently from *Switchmen's* case, "absence of jurisdiction of the federal courts" would mean "a sacrifice or obliteration of a right which Congress" has given professional employees, for there is no other means within their control (American Federation of Labor v. NLRB, *supra*), to protect and enforce that right. And "the inference [is] strong that Congress intended the statutory provisions governing the general jurisdiction of those courts to control." 320 U.S. at 300. This Court cannot lightly infer that Congress does not intend judicial protection of rights it confers against agency action taken in excess of delegated powers.

Cf. Harmon v. Brucker, 355 U.S. 579 (1958); Stark v. Wickard, 321 U.S. 288 (1944); School of Magnetic Healing v. McAnnulty, 187 U.S. 94 (1902).

Where, as here, Congress has given a "right" to the professional employees it must be held that it intended that right to be enforced, and the "courts . . . encounter no difficulty in fulfilling its purpose." Texas & New Orleans R. Co. v. Railway Clerks, *supra* at 568.

The Court of Appeals was right in holding, in the circumstances of this case, that the District Court had jurisdiction of this suit, and its judgment is

Affirmed.

MR. JUSTICE BRENNAN, whom MR. JUSTICE FRANKFURTER joins, dissenting.

The legislative history of the Wagner Act, and of the Taft-Hartley amendments, shows a considered congressional purpose to restrict judicial review of National Labor Relations Board representation certifications to review in the Courts of Appeals in the circumstances specified in § 9(d), 29 U.S.C. § 159(d). The question was extensively debated when both acts were being considered, and on both occasions Congress concluded that, unless drastically limited, time-consuming court procedures would seriously threaten to frustrate the basic national policy of preventing industrial strife and achieving industrial peace by promoting collective bargaining. . . .

The Court today opens a gaping hole in this congressional wall against direct resort to the courts. The Court holds that a party alleging that the Board was guilty of "unlawful action" in making an investigation and certification of representatives need not await judicial review until the situation specified in § 9(d) arises, but has a case immediately cognizable by a District Court under the "original jurisdiction" granted by 28 U.S.C. § 1337 of "any civil action or proceeding arising under any Act of Congress regulating commerce." The Court, borrowing a statement from Switchmen's Union v. National Mediation Board, 320 U.S. 297, 300 (1943), finds that, in such case "the inference [is] strong that Congress intended the statutory provisions governing the general jurisdiction of those [District] courts to control." . . .

I daresay that the ingenuity of counsel will, after today's decision, be entirely adequate to the task of finding some alleged "unlawful action," whether in statutory interpretation or otherwise, sufficient to get a foot in a District Court door under 28 U.S.C. § 1337. Even when the Board wins such a case on the merits, . . . while the case is dragging through the courts the threat will be ever present of the industrial strife sought to be averted by Congress in providing only drastically limited judicial review under § 9(d). Both union and management will be able to use the tactic of litigation to delay the initiation of collective bargaining when it suits their purposes. . . .

It is no support for the Court's decision that the respondent union may suffer hardship if review under 28 U.S.C. § 1337 is not open to it. The Congress was fully aware of the disadvantages and possible unfairness which could result from the limitation on judicial review enacted in § 9(d). The House proposal for direct review of Board certifications in the Taft-Hartley amendments was based in part upon the fact that, under the Wagner Act, the operation of § 9(d) was "unfair to . . . the union that loses, which has no appeal at all no matter how wrong the certification may be; [and to] the employees, who have no appeal. . . ." Congress nevertheless continued the limited judicial review provided by § 9(d) because Congress believed the disadvantages of broader review to be more serious than the difficulties which limited review posed for the parties. Furthermore, Congress felt that the Board procedures and the limited review provided in § 9(d) were adequate to protect the parties.

. . .

I would reverse and remand the case to the District Court with instructions to dismiss the complaint for lack of jurisdiction of the subject matter.

NOTES

1. What kinds of alleged errors by the NLRB in representation proceedings may be challenged by direct suit in equity in the district courts under the doctrine of *Leedom v. Kyne?*

2. Direct challenges were made in federal district court of the NLRB's holding that a contract of a union in which there is a schism resulting from the union's expulsion from the AFL-CIO will not be regarded as a bar to an election. (See the *Hershey* case, noted at 205.) The argument, resting on *Leedom v. Kyne,* was that this was in violation of § 9(c)(2) — "In determining whether or not a question of representation affecting commerce exists, the same regulations and rules of decision shall apply irrespective of the identity of the persons filing the petition or the kind of relief sought." Held: No violation of § 9(c)(2); the NLRB acted within the allowable limits of its discretion. National Biscuit Div. v. Leedom, 265 F.2d 101 (D.C. Cir. 1959), *cert. denied,* 359 U.S. 1011 (1959).

3. A district court may enjoin the NLRB from holding an election among seamen on foreign-flag ships even though the Board did not violate any specific prohibition in the NLRA, in view of the fact that the Board's assertion of power to determine representation of foreign seamen aboard vessels under foreign flags had aroused vigorous protests from foreign governments and created international problems for the United States, the presence of which was a uniquely compelling justification for prompt judicial resolution of the controversy over the Board's power. McCulloch v. Sociedad Nacional de Marineros de Honduras, 372 U.S. 10 (1963).

4. May a federal district court enjoin the NLRB from continuing with its representation proceedings where the employer challenges the application of the NLRA on First Amendment religious freedom grounds?

Compare Grutka v. Barbour, 549 F.2d 5 (7th Cir. 1977) *with* Caulfield v. Hirsch, 95 L.R.R.M. 3164 (E.D. Pa. 1977), *and* McCormick v. Hirsch, 99 L.R.R.M. 3342 (M.D. Pa. 1978).

5. A federal district court ordered the NLRB to conduct a decertification election involving employees of an employer against which unfair labor practice charges were pending, where the employees' concededly valid decertification petition had been on file for more than two years. The Board's refusal to hold the election was based on its "blocking charge" rule, under which election petitions are held in abeyance until outstanding unfair labor practice charges are disposed of. The court found the rule invalid as applied to a situation where the petition is filed by employees and the Board unreasonably delays action. The court also noted that the blocking rule was only an "instruction" in the Board's Field Manual. Templeton v. Dixie Color Printing Co., 313 F. Supp. 105 (N.D. Ala. 1970), *vacated and remanded,* 444 F.2d 1064 (5th Cir. 1971) (Board instructed to process decertification petition).

6. In Boire v. Greyhound Corp., 376 U.S. 473 (1964), the Supreme Court declared that "the *Kyne* exception is a narrow one, not to be extended to permit plenary district court review of Board orders in certification proceedings whenever it can be said that an erroneous assessment of the particular facts before the Board has led it to a conclusion which does not comport with the law." Accordingly, the Court held that a federal district court erred when it enjoined the Board from conducting an election among maintenance and service workers at a bus company's terminals. The district court had stated that the Board misapplied the act in holding the bus company and the maintenance company to be joint employers.

Accord: Kingsport Press, Inc. v. McCulloch, 118 App. D.C. 365, 336 F.2d 753 (1964), *cert. denied,* 379 U.S. 931 (1964) (the district court had no jurisdiction over an employer's suit to enjoin a representation election directed by the Board, after a hearing, but without waiting for the parties to file briefs); Boire v. Miami Herald Pub. Co., 343 F.2d 17 (5th Cir. 1965), *cert. denied,* 382 U.S. 824 (1965) (the district court was not warranted in enjoining an election where the Board failed to issue regulations concerning the voting eligibility of economic strikers who were replaced); and Teamsters Local 714 v. Madden, 343 F.2d 497 (7th Cir. 1965), *cert. denied,* 382 U.S. 822 (1965) (the court of appeals affirmed the district court's holding that it lacked jurisdiction over a union's action to enjoin a union shop deauthorization election which was held without a formal hearing); New York University v. NLRB, 364 F. Supp. 161 (S.D.N.Y. 1973) (various issues in university election); Board of Trustees v. NLRB, 523 F.2d 845 (10th Cir. 1975) (the district court erred in enjoining the Board from holding an election in a hospital on grounds that it was not an "employer" because allegedly exempt).

7. The Supreme Court stated in Railway Clerks v. Non-Contract Employees, 380 U.S. 650, 659 (1965): "It is sometimes said that in Leedom v. Kyne, 358 U.S. 184 (1958), the Court created an 'exception' to the doctrine of *Switchmen's Union.* In *Kyne,* it was held that the law afforded a remedy in the courts when unlawful action by the National Labor Relations Board inflicted injury on one of the parties to a bargaining dispute. But this was no exception to *Switchmen's Union.* Rather the Court was careful to note that '[t]his suit is not one to "review," in the sense of that term as used in the act, a decision of the Board made within its jurisdiction. Rather it is one to strike down an order of the Board made in excess of its delegated powers and contrary to a *specific prohibition in the act.'* Leedom v. Kyne, 358 U.S. 184, 188 (1958). (Emphasis supplied.) The limited nature of this holding was reemphasized only last Term where we referred to the 'narrow limits' and 'painstakingly delineated procedural boundaries of *Kyne.'* Boire v. Greyhound Corp., 376 U.S. 473, 481 (1964)."

8. How does an employer ordinarily obtain judicial review of an NLRB ruling in a representation case? *See, e.g.,* NLRB v. Pittsburgh Plate Glass Co., 270 F.2d 167 (4th Cir. 1959), *cert. denied,* 361 U.S. 943 (1960).

9. How would a union do it? See discussion of this question in House Staff Ass'n v. Murphy, 100 L.R.R.M. 3055 (D.C. Cir. 1979).

B. ESTABLISHING REPRESENTATIVE STATUS THROUGH UNFAIR LABOR PRACTICE PROCEEDINGS

We have been concerned thus far in this section with formal representation proceedings before the NLRB, which result, if the union wins the secret ballot election, in a certification of the union as exclusive bargaining representative.

It is also commonplace for the collective bargaining relationship to become established simply by the union showing the employer that it has a majority of his employees, usually by a "card check" of authorization cards signed by the employees, and by his consenting voluntarily to bargain with it.

If the employer refuses to recognize the union, another procedure by which the union can get the NLRB to order the employer to bargain with it and thus establish a representative status, is to bring unfair labor practice proceedings.

NLRB v. GISSEL PACKING CO.

Supreme Court of the United States
395 U.S. 575, 89 S. Ct. 1918, 23 L. Ed. 2d 547 (1969)

MR. CHIEF JUSTICE WARREN delivered the opinion of the Court.

These cases involve the extent of an employer's duty under the National Labor Relations Act to recognize a union that bases its claim to representative status solely on the possession of union authorization cards, and the steps an employer may take, particularly with regard to the scope and content of statements he may make, in legitimately resisting such card-based recognition. The specific questions facing us here are whether the duty to bargain can arise without a Board election under the

Act; whether union authorization cards, if obtained from a majority of employees without misrepresentation or coercion, are reliable enough generally to provide a valid, alternate route to majority status; whether a bargaining order is an appropriate and authorized remedy where an employer rejects a card majority while at the same time committing unfair labor practices that tend to undermine the union's majority and make a fair election an unlikely possibility; and whether certain specific statements made by an employer to his employees constituted such an election-voiding unfair labor practice and thus fell outside the protection of the First Amendment and § 8(c) of the Act. For reasons given below, we answer each of these questions in the affirmative.

I. . . . In each of the cases from the Fourth Circuit, the course of action followed by the Union and the employer and the Board's response were similar. In each case, the union waged an organizational campaign, obtained authorization cards from a majority of employees in the appropriate bargaining unit, and then on the basis of the cards, demanded recognition by the employer. All three employers refused to bargain on the ground that authorization cards were inherently unreliable indicators of employee desires; and they either embarked on, or continued, vigorous antiunion campaigns that gave rise to numerous unfair labor practice charges. In *Gissel,* where the employer's campaign began almost at the outset of the Union's organizational drive, the Union (petitioner in No. 691), did not seek an election, but instead filed three unfair labor practice charges against the employer, for refusing to bargain in violation of § 8(a)(5), for coercion and intimidation of employees in violation of § 8(a)(1), and for discharge of union adherents in violation of § 8(a)(3). In *Heck's* an election sought by the Union was never held because of nearly identical unfair labor practice charges later filed by the Union as a result of the employer's antiunion campaign, initiated after the Union's recognition demand. And in *General Steel,* an election petitioned for by the Union and won by the employer was set aside by the Board because of the unfair labor practices committed by the employer in the pre-election period.

In each case, the Board's primary response was an order to bargain directed at the employers, despite the absence of an election in *Gissel* and *Heck's* and the employer's victory in *General Steel.* More specifically the Board found in each case that (1) the union had obtained valid authorization cards [4] from a majority of the employees in the bargaining unit and was thus entitled to represent the employees for collective bargaining purposes; and (2) that the employers' refusal to bargain with the unions in violation of § 8(a)(5) was motivated not by a "good faith" doubt of the unions' majority status, but by a desire to gain time to dissipate that status. The Board based its conclusion as to the lack of good faith doubt on the fact that the employers had committed substantial unfair labor practices during their antiunion campaign efforts to resist recognition. Thus, the Board found that all three employers had engaged in restraint and coercion of employees in violation of § 8(a)(1) — in *Gissel,* for coercively interrogating employees about union activities, threatening them with discharge and promising them benefits; in *Heck's,* for coercively interrogating employees, threatening reprisals, creating the appearance of surveillance, and offering benefits for opposing the Union; and in *General Steel,* for coercive interrogation and threats of reprisals, including discharge. In addition, the Board found that the employers in *Gissel* and *Heck's* had wrongfully discharged employees for engaging in union activities in violation of § 8(a)(3). And, because the employers had rejected the card-based bargaining demand in bad faith, the Board found that all three had refused to recognize the unions in violation of § 8(a)(5).

Only in *General Steel* was there any objection by an employer to the validity of the cards and the manner in which they had been solicited, and the doubt raised by the evidence was resolved in the following manner. The customary approach of the Board in dealing with allegations of misrepresentation by the union and misunderstanding by the employees of the purpose for which the cards were being solicited has been set out in Cumberland Shoe Corp., 144 N.L.R.B. 1268 (1964), and reaffirmed in Levi Strauss & Co., 172 N.L.R.B. No. 57, 68 L.R.R.M. 1338 (1968). Under the *Cumberland Shoe* doctrine, if the card itself is unambiguous (*i.e.,* states on its face that the signer authorizes the union to represent the employee for collective bargaining purposes and not to seek an election), it will be counted unless it is proved that the employee was told that the card was to be used *solely* for the purpose of obtaining an election. In *General Steel,* the trial examiner considered the allegations of misrepresentation at length and, applying the Board's customary analysis, rejected the claims with findings that were adopted by the Board and are reprinted in the margin.

Consequently, the Board ordered the companies to cease and desist from their unfair labor practices, to offer reinstatement and back pay to the employees who had been discriminatorily discharged, to bargain with the Union on request, and to post the appropriate notices.

On appeal, the Court of Appeals for the Fourth Circuit, in *per curiam* opinions in each of the three cases (398 F.2d 336, 337, 339), sustained the Board's findings as to the §§ 8(a)(1) and (3) violations, but rejected the Board's findings that the employers' refusal to bargain violated § 8(a)(5) and declined to enforce those portions of the Board's orders directing the respondent companies to bargain in good faith. The court based its § 8(a)(5) rulings on its 1967 decisions raising the same fundamental issues, Crawford Mfg. Co. v. NLRB, 386 F.2d 367 (C.A. 4th Cir. 1967),

---

4 The cards used in all four campaigns in Nos. 573 and 691 and in the one drive in No. 585 unambiguously authorized the Union to represent the signing employee for collective bargaining purposes; there was no reference to elections. Typical of the cards was the one used in the Charleston campaign in *Heck's,* and it stated in relevant part:

"Desiring to become a member of the above Union of the International Brotherhood of Teamsters, Chauffeurs, Warehousemen and Helpers of America, I hereby make application for admission to membership. I hereby authorize you, or your agents or representatives to act for me as collective bargaining agent on all matters pertaining to rates of pay, hours or any other condition of employment."

cert. denied, 390 U.S. 1028 (1968); NLRB v. Logan Packing Co., 386 F.2d 562 (C.A. 4th Cir. 1967); NLRB v. Sehon Stevenson & Co., Inc., 386 F.2d 551 (C.A. 4th Cir. 1967). The court in those cases held that the 1947 Taft-Hartley amendments to the Act, which permitted the Board to resolve representation disputes by certification under § 9(c) only by secret ballot election, withdrew from the Board the authority to order an employer to bargain under § 8(a)(5) on the basis of cards, in the absence of NLRB certification, unless the employer knows independently of the cards that there is in fact no representation dispute. The court held that the cards themselves were so inherently unreliable that their use gave an employer virtually an automatic, good faith claim that such a dispute existed, for which a secret election was necessary. Thus, these rulings established that a company could not be ordered to bargain unless (1) there was no question about a union's majority status (either because the employer agreed the cards were valid or had conducted his own poll so indicating), or (2) the employer's §§ 8(a)(1) and (3) unfair labor practices committed during the representation campaign were so extensive and pervasive that a bargaining order was the only available Board remedy irrespective of a card majority. . . .

II. In urging us to reverse the Fourth Circuit and to affirm the First Circuit, the National Labor Relations Board contends that we should approve its interpretation and administration of the duties and obligations imposed by the Act in authorization card cases. The Board argues (1) that unions have never been limited under § 9(c) of either the Wagner Act or the 1947 amendments to certified elections as the sole route to attaining representative status. Unions may, the Board contends, impose a duty to bargain on the employer under § 8(a)(5) by reliance on other evidence of majority employee support, such as authorization cards. Contrary to the Fourth Circuit's holding, the Board asserts, the 1947 amendments did not eliminate the alternative routes to majority status. The Board contends (2) that the cards themselves, when solicited in accordance with Board standards which adequately insure against union misrepresentation, are sufficiently reliable indicators of employee desires to support a bargaining order against an employer who refuses to recognize a card majority in violation of § 8(a)(5). The Board argues (3) that a bargaining order is the appropriate remedy for the § 8(a)(5) violation, where the employer commits other unfair labor practices that tend to undermine union support and render a fair election improbable.

Relying on these three assertions, the Board asks us to approve its current practice, which is briefly as follows. When confronted by a recognition demand based on possession of cards allegedly signed by a majority of his employees, an employer need not grant recognition immediately, but may, unless he has knowledge independently of the cards that the union has a majority, decline the union's request and insist on an election, either by requesting the union to file an election petition or by filing such a petition himself under § 9(c)(1)(B). If, however, the employer commits independent and substantial unfair labor practices disruptive of election conditions, the Board may withhold the election or set it aside, and issue instead a bargaining order as a remedy for the various violations. A bargaining order will not issue, of course, if the union obtained the cards through misrepresentation or coercion or if the employer's unfair labor practices are unrelated generally to the representation campaign. Conversely, the employers in these cases urge us to adopt the views of the Fourth Circuit. . . .

The traditional approach utilized by the Board for many years has been known as the *Joy Silk* doctrine. Joy Silk Mills, Inc. v. NLRB, 85 N.L.R.B. 1263 (1949), *enforced* 87 U.S. App. D.C. 360, 185 F.2d 732 (C.A.D.C. Cir. 1950). Under that rule, an employer could lawfully refuse to bargain with a union claiming representative status through possession of authorization cards if he had a "good faith doubt" as to the union's majority status; instead of bargaining, he could insist that the union seek an election in order to test out his doubts. The Board, then, could find a lack of good faith doubt and enter a bargaining order in one of two ways. It could find (1) that the employer's independent unfair labor practices were evidence of bad faith, showing that the employer was seeking time to dissipate the union's majority. Or the Board could find (2) that the employer had come forward with no reasons for entertaining any doubt and therefore that he must have rejected the bargaining demand in bad faith. An example of the second category was Snow & Sons, 134 N.L.R.B. 709 (1961), *enforced* 308 F.2d 687 (C.A. 9th Cir. 1962), where the employer reneged on his agreement to bargain after a third party checked the validity of the card signatures and insisted on an election because he doubted that the employees truly desired representation. The Board entered a bargaining order with very broad language to the effect that an employer could not refuse a bargaining demand and seek an election instead "without valid ground therefor," 134 N.L.R.B. at 710-711. See also Dixon Ford Shoe Co., Inc., 150 N.L.R.B. 861 (1965); Kellogg Mills, 147 N.L.R.B. 342, 346 (1964), *enforced* 347 F.2d 219 (C.A. 9th Cir. 1965).

The leading case codifying modifications to the *Joy Silk* doctrine was Aaron Brothers, 158 N.L.R.B. 1077 (1966). There the Board made it clear that it had shifted the burden to the General Counsel to show bad faith and that an employer "will not be held to have violated his bargaining obligation . . . simply because he refuses to rely on cards, rather than an election, as the method for determining the union's majority." 158 N.L.R.B., at 1078. Two significant consequences were emphasized. The Board noted (1) that not every unfair labor practice would automatically result in a finding of bad faith and therefore a bargaining order; the Board implied that it would find bad faith only if the unfair labor practice was serious enough to have the tendency to dissipate the union's majority. The Board noted (2) that an employer no longer needed to come forward with reasons for rejecting a bargaining demand. The Board pointed out, however, that a bargaining order would issue if it could prove that an employer's "course of conduct" gave indications as to the employer's bad faith. As examples of such a "course of conduct," the Board cited Snow & Sons, *supra*; Dixon Ford Shoe Co., Inc., *supra*, and Kellogg Mills, *supra*, thereby reaffirming the John P. Serpa, Inc., 155 N.L.R.B. No. 12 (1965), where the Board had limited *Snow & Sons* to its facts.

Although the Board's brief before this Court generally followed the approach as set out in Aaron Brothers, *supra,* the Board announced at oral argument that it had virtually abandoned the *Joy Silk* doctrine altogether. Under the Board's current practice, an employer's good faith doubt is largely irrelevant, and the key to the issuance of a bargaining order is the commission of serious unfair labor practices that interfere with the election processes and tend to preclude the holding of a fair election. Thus, an employer can insist that a union go to an election, regardless of his subjective motivation, so long as he is not guilty of misconduct; he need give no affirmative reasons for rejecting a recognition request, and he can demand an election with a simple "no comment" to the union. The Board pointed out, however, (1) that an employer could not refuse to bargain if he *knew,* through a personal poll for instance, that a majority of his employees supported the union, and (2) that an employer could not refuse recognition initially because of questions as to the appropriateness of the unit and then later claim, as an afterthought, that he doubted the union's strength.

The union argues here that an employer's right to insist on an election in the absence of unfair labor practices should be more circumscribed, and a union's right to rely on cards correspondingly more expanded, than the Board would have us rule. The union's contention is that an employer, when confronted with a card-based bargaining demand, can insist on an election only by filing the election petition himself immediately under § 9(c)(1)(B) and not by insisting that the union file the election petition, whereby the election can be subjected to considerable delay. If the employer does not himself petition for an election, the union argues, he must recognize the union regardless of his good or bad faith and regardless of his other unfair labor practices, and should be ordered to bargain if the cards were in fact validly obtained. And if this Court should continue to utilize the good faith doubt rule, the union contends that at the least we should put the burden on the employer to make an affirmative showing of his reasons for entertaining such doubt.

Because the employers' refusal to bargain in each of these cases was accompanied in each instance by independent unfair labor practices which tend to preclude the holding of a fair election, we need not decide whether a bargaining order is ever appropriate in cases where there is no interference with the election processes. . . .

III. A. The first issue facing us is whether a union can establish a bargaining obligation by means other than a Board election and whether the validity of alternate routes to majority status, such as cards, was affected by the 1947 Taft-Hartley amendments. The most commonly traveled route for a union to obtain recognition as the exclusive bargaining representative of an unorganized group of employees is through the Board's election and certification procedures under § 9(c) of the Act (29 U.S.C. § 159(c) (1964 ed.)); it is also, from the Board's point of view, the preferred route. A union is not limited to a Board election, however, for, in addition to § 9, the present Act provides in § 8(a)(5) . . ., as did the Wagner Act in § 8(5), that "it shall be an unfair labor practice for an employer ... to refuse to bargain collectively with the representatives of his employees, subject to the provisions of section 9(a)." Since § 9(a), in both the Wagner Act and the present Act, refers to the representative as the one "designated or selected" by a majority of the employees without specifying precisely how that representative is to be chosen, it was early recognized that an employer had a duty to bargain whenever the union representative presented "convincing evidence of majority support." Almost from the inception of the Act, then, it was recognized that a union did not have to be certified as the winner of a Board election to invoke a bargaining obligation; it could establish majority status by other means under the unfair labor practice provision of § 8(a)(5) — by showing convincing support, for instance, by a union-called strike or strike vote, or, as here, by possession of cards signed by a majority of the employees authorizing the union to represent them for collective bargaining purposes. . . .

... Indeed, the 1947 amendments weaken rather than strengthen the position taken by the employers here and the Fourth Circuit below. An early version of the bill in the House would have amended § 8(5) of the Wagner Act to permit the Board to find a refusal to bargain violation only where an employer had failed to bargain with a union "currently recognized by the employer or certified as such [through an election] under section 9." Section 8(a)(5) of H.R. 3020, 80th Cong., 1st Sess. (1947). The proposed change, which would have eliminated the use of cards, was rejected in Conference (H.R. Conf. Rep. No. 510, 80th Cong., 1st Sess., 41 (1947)), however, and we cannot make a similar change in the Act simply because, as the employers assert, Congress did not expressly approve the use of cards in rejecting the House amendment. Nor can we accept the Fourth Circuit's conclusion that the change was wrought when Congress amended § 9(c) to make election the sole basis for *certification* by eliminating the phrase "any other suitable method to ascertain such representatives," under which the Board had occasionally used cards as a certification basis. A certified union has the benefit of numerous special privileges which are not accorded unions recognized voluntarily or under a bargaining order and which, Congress could determine, should not be dispensed unless a union has survived the crucible of a secret ballot election.

The employers rely finally on the addition to § 9(c) of subparagraph (B), which allows an employer to petition for an election whenever "one or more individuals or labor organizations have presented to him a claim to be recognized as the representative defined in section 9(a)." That provision was not added, as the employers assert, to give them an absolute right to an election at any time; rather, it was intended, as the legislative history indicates, to allow them, after asked to bargain, to test out their doubts as to a union's majority in a secret election which they would then presumably not cause to be set aside by illegal antiunion activity. We agree with the Board's assertion here that there is no suggestion that Congress intended § 9(c)(1)(B) to relieve any employer of his § 8(a)(5) bargaining obligation where, without good faith, he engaged in unfair labor practices disruptive of the Board's election machinery. And we agree that the policies reflected in § 9(c)(1)(B) fully support the Board's present administration of the Act . . .; for an employer can insist on a secret ballot election, unless, in the words of the Board, he engages "in contemporaneous unfair labor practices likely to destroy the union's majority and seriously impede the election." . . .

In short, we hold that the 1947 amendments did not restrict an employer's duty to bargain under § 8(a)(5) solely to those unions whose representative status is certified after a Board election.

B. We next consider the question whether authorization cards are such inherently unreliable indicators of employee desires that whatever the validity of other alternate routes to representative status, the cards themselves may never be used to determine a union's majority and to support an order to bargain. In this context, the employers urge us to take the step the 1947 amendments and their legislative history indicate Congress did not take, namely, to rule out completely the use of cards in the bargaining arena. Even if we do not unhesitatingly accept the Fourth Circuit's view in the matter, the employers argue, at the very least we should overrule the *Cumberland Shoe* doctrine . . . and establish stricter controls over the solicitation of the cards by union representatives. . . .

That the cards, though admittedly inferior to the election process, can adequately reflect employee sentiment when that process has been impeded, needs no extended discussion, for the employers' contentions cannot withstand close examination. The employers argue that their employees cannot make an informed choice because the card drive will be over before the employer has had a chance to present his side of the unionization issues. Normally, however, the union will inform the employer of its organization drive early in order to subject the employer to the unfair labor practice provisions of the Act; the union must be able to show the employer's awareness of the drive in order to prove that his contemporaneous conduct constituted unfair labor practices on which a bargaining order can be based if the drive is ultimately successful. See, *e.g.,* Hunt Oil Co., 157 N.L.R.B. 282 (1966); Don Swart Trucking Co., 154 N.L.R.B. 1345 (1965). Thus, in all of the cases here but the Charleston campaign in *Heck's* the employer, whether informed by the union or not, was aware of the union's organizing drive almost at the outset and began his antiunion campaign at that time; and even in the *Heck's-Charleston* case, where the recognition demand came about a week after the solicitation began, the employer was able to deliver a speech before the union obtained a majority. Further, the employers argue that without a secret ballot an employee may, in a card drive, succumb to group pressures or sign simply to get the union "off his back" and then be unable to change his mind as he would be free to do once inside a voting booth. But the same pressures are likely to be equally present in an election, for election cases arise most often with small bargaining units where virtually every voter's sentiments can be carefully and individually canvassed. And no voter, of course, can change his mind after casting a ballot in an election even though he may think better of his choice shortly thereafter.

The employers' second complaint, that the cards are too often obtained through misrepresentation and coercion, must be rejected also in view of the Board's present rules for controlling card solicitation, which we view as adequate to the task where the cards involved state their purpose clearly and unambiguously on their face. We would be closing our eyes to obvious difficulties, of course, if we did not recognize that there have been abuses, primarily arising out of misrepresentations by union organizers as to whether the effect of signing a card was to designate the union to represent the employee for collective bargaining purposes or merely to authorize it to seek an election to determine that issue. And we would be equally blind if we did not recognize that various courts of appeals and commentators have differed significantly as to the effectiveness of the Board's *Cumberland Shoe* doctrine . . . to cure such abuses. . . .

We need make no decision as to the conflicting approaches used with regard to dual-purpose cards, for in each of the five organization campaigns in the four cases before us the cards used were single-purpose cards, stating clearly and unambiguously on their face that the signer designated the union as his representative. And even the view forcefully voiced by the Fourth Circuit below that unambiguous cards as well present too many opportunities for misrepresentation comes before us somewhat weakened in view of the fact that there were no allegations of irregularities in four of those five campaigns (*Gissel,* the two *Heck's* campaigns, and *Sinclair*). Only in *General Steel* did the employer challenge the cards on the basis of misrepresentations. There, the trial examiner, after hearing testimony from over 100 employees and applying the traditional Board approach . . . concluded that "all of these employees not only intended, but were fully aware that they were designating the union as their representative." Thus, the sole question before us, raised in only one of the four cases here, is whether the *Cumberland Shoe* doctrine is an adequate rule under the Act for assuring employee free choice.

In resolving the conflict among the circuits in favor of approving the Board's *Cumberland* rule, we think it sufficient to point out that employees should be bound by the clear language of what they sign unless that language is deliberately and clearly canceled by a union adherent with words calculated to direct the signer to disregard and forget the language above his signature. There is nothing inconsistent in handing an employee a card that says the signer authorizes the union to represent him and then telling him that the card will probably be used first to get an election. Elections have been, after all, and will continue to be, held in the vast majority of cases; the union will still have to have the signatures of 30% of the employees when an employer rejects a bargaining demand and insists that the union seek an election. We cannot agree with the employers here that employees as a rule are too unsophisticated to be bound by what they sign unless expressly told that their act of signing represents something else. In addition to approving the use of cards, of course, Congress has expressly authorized reliance on employee signatures alone in other areas of labor relations, even where criminal sanctions hang in the balance, and we should not act hastily in disregarding congressional judgments that employees can be counted on to take responsibility for their acts.

We agree, however, with the Board's own warnings in Levi Strauss, 172 N.L.R.B. No. 57, 68 L.R.R.M. 1338, 1341, and n.7 (1968), that in hearing testimony concerning a card challenge, trial examiners should not neglect their obligation to ensure employee free choice by a too easy mechanical application of the *Cumberland* rule. We also accept the observation that employees are more likely than not, many months after a card drive and in response to questions by company counsel, to give testimony damaging to the union, particularly where company officials have previously threatened reprisals for union activity in violation of § 8(a)(1). We therefore reject any rule that requires a probe of an employee's subjective motivations as involving an endless and unreliable inquiry. . . .

C. Remaining before us is the propriety of a bargaining order as a remedy for a § 8(a)(5) refusal to bargain where an employer has committed independent unfair labor practices which have made the holding of a fair election unlikely or which have in fact undermined a union's majority and caused an election to be set aside. We have long held that the Board is not limited to a cease-and-desist order in such cases, but has the authority to issue a bargaining order without first requiring the union to show that it has been able to maintain its majority status. See NLRB v. Katz, 369 U.S. 736, 748, n.16 (1962); NLRB v. P. Lorillard Co., 314 U.S. 512 (1942). And we have held that the Board has the same authority even where it is clear that the union, which once had possession of cards from a majority of the employees, represents only a minority when the bargaining order is entered. Franks Bros. Co. v. NLRB, 321 U.S. 702 (1943). We see no reason now to withdraw this authority from the Board. If the Board could enter only a cease-and-desist order and direct an election or a rerun, it would in effect be rewarding the employer and allowing him "to profit from [his] own wrongful refusal to bargain." Franks Bros., *supra*, at 704, while at the same time severely curtailing the employees' right freely to determine whether they desire a representative. The employer could continue to delay or disrupt the election processes and put off indefinitely his obligation to bargain; and any election held under these circumstances would not be likely to demonstrate the employees' true, undistorted desires. . . .

Before considering whether the bargaining orders were appropriately entered in these cases, we should summarize the factors that go into such a determination. Despite our reversal of the Fourth Circuit below in Nos. 573 and 691 on all major issues, the actual area of disagreement between our position here and that of the Fourth Circuit is not large as a practical matter. While refusing to validate the general use of a bargaining order in reliance on cards, the Fourth Circuit nevertheless left open the possibility of imposing a bargaining order, without need of inquiry into majority status on the basis of cards or otherwise, in "exceptional" cases marked by "outrageous" and "pervasive" unfair labor practices. Such an order would be an appropriate remedy for those practices, the court noted, if they are of "such a nature that their coercive effects cannot be eliminated by the application of traditional remedies, with the result that a fair and reliable election cannot be had." NLRB v. Logan Packing Co., 386 F.2d 562, 570 (C.A. 4th Cir. 1967); see also NLRB v. Heck's, *supra,* 308 F.2d, at 338. The Board itself, we should add, has long had a similar policy of issuing a bargaining order, in the absence of a § 8(a)(5) violation or even a bargaining demand, when that was the only available, effective remedy for substantial unfair labor practices. . . .

The only effect of our holding here is to approve the Board's use of the bargaining order in less extraordinary cases marked by less pervasive practices which nonetheless still have the tendency to undermine majority strength and impede the election processes. The Board's authority to issue such an order on a lesser showing of employer misconduct is appropriate, we should reemphasize, where there is also a showing that at one point the union had a majority; in such a case, of course, effectuating ascertainable employee free choice becomes as important a goal as deterring employer misbehaviour. In fashioning a remedy in the exercise of its discretion, then, the Board can properly take into consideration the extensiveness of an employer's unfair practices in terms of their past effect on election conditions and the likelihood of their recurrence in the future. If the Board finds that the possibility of erasing the effects of past practices and of ensuring a fair election (or a fair rerun) by the use of traditional remedies, though present, is slight and that employee sentiment once expressed through cards would, on balance, be better protected by a bargaining order, then such an order should issue. . . .

We emphasize that under the Board's remedial power there is still a third category of minor or less extensive unfair labor practices, which, because of their minimal impact on the election machinery, will not sustain a bargaining order. There is, the Board says, no *per se* rule that the commission of any unfair practice will automatically result in a § 8(a)(5) violation and the issuance of an order to bargain. See *Aaron Brothers, supra.*

With these considerations in mind, we turn to an examination of the orders in these cases. In *Sinclair*, No. 585, the Board made a finding, left undisturbed by the First Circuit, that the employer's threats of reprisal were so coercive that, even in the absence of a § 8(a)(5) violation, a bargaining order would have been necessary to repair the unlawful effect of those threats. The Board therefore did not have to make the determination called for in the intermediate situation above that the risks that a fair rerun election might not be possible were too great to disregard the desires of the employees already expressed through the cards. . . .

In the three cases in Nos. 573 and 691 from the Fourth Circuit, on the other hand, the Board did not make a similar finding that a bargaining order would have been necessary in the absence of an unlawful refusal to bargain. Nor did it make a finding that, even though traditional remedies might be able to ensure a fair election, there was insufficient indication that an election (or a rerun in *General Steel*) would definitely be a more reliable test of the employees' desires than the card count taken before the unfair labor practices occurred. The employees [employers] argue that such findings would not be warranted, and the court below ruled in *General Steel* that available remedies short of a bargaining order could guarantee a fair election. . . . We think it possible that the requisite findings were implicit in the Board's decisions below to issue bargaining orders (and to set aside the election in *General Steel*); and we think it clearly inappropriate for the court below to make any contrary finding on its own. . . . Because the Board's current practice at the time required it to phrase its findings in terms of an employer's good- or bad-faith doubts (see Part II, *supra*), however, the precise analysis the Board now puts forth was not employed below, and we therefore remand these cases to the Board for proper findings. . . .

NOTES

1. In the first reported federal appellate court decision on the point, the Second Circuit held that in *Gissel*-type cases, an NLRB regional director may be entitled to a bargaining order against an employer under § 10(j) of the NLRA, pending a final determination by the Board concerning the union's status as bargaining representative of the employer's employees. Seeler v. Trading Port, Inc., 517 F.2d 33 (2d Cir. 1975). The injunction was denied in Boire v. Pilot Freight Carriers, 515 F.2d 1185 (5th Cir. 1977). *See* Pettibone, *Section 10(j) Bargaining Order in Gissel-Type Cases,* 27 LAB. L. J. 648 (1976); Comment, *The Use of Section 10(j) of the Labor-Management Relations Act in Employer Refusal to Bargain Cases,* 1976 U. ILL. L. F. 845.

2. On remand in *Gissel,* the Board upheld the issuance of the bargaining order, since it found that the employer's unfair labor practices, both before and after the denial of the union's request for recognition on the basis of the authorization cards, were so pervasive as to preclude the holding of a fair election. Gissel Packing Co., 180 N.L.R.B. 54 (1969), *enforced,* 76 L.R.R.M. 2175, 64 CCH Lab. Cas. ¶ 11,333 (4th Cir. 1970). Does this suggest that in most post-*Gissel* decisions, the same types of unfair labor practices which formerly were used to show the employer's lack of a "good faith doubt" under the *Joy Silk* doctrine will now be used to demonstrate the unlikelihood of holding a fair and reliable election? See, *e.g.,* Garland Knitting Mills, 178 N.L.R.B. 396 (1969); J.H. Rutter-Rex Mfg. Co., 180 N.L.R.B. 878 (1970), *enforced,* 434 F.2d 1318 (6th Cir. 1970).

The *Gissel* tests apply even where the union possessed only a "bare majority" of authorization cards. NLRB v. Empire Corp., 518 F.2d 860 (6th Cir. 1975).

3. The Labor Board believes that *Gissel* "contemplated that the propriety of a bargaining order would be judged as of the time of the commission of the unfair labor practices and not in the light of subsequent events." Otherwise, the Board argues, an employer could profit from its wrongdoing by preventing a union whose majority has been undermined from securing a bargaining order. Gibson Products Co., 185 N.L.R.B. 362 (1970), *supplemented,* 199 N.L.R.B. 794 (1972), *enforcement denied,* 494 F.2d 762 (5th Cir. 1974). This approach has been followed by the Seventh Circuit in New Alaska Development Corp. v. NLRB, 441 F.2d 491 (7th Cir. 1971) (bargaining order valid even though turnover of employees and their lack of knowledge of threats had changed situation so that fair election could now be had) and by the Ninth Circuit in NLRB v. L.B. Foster Co., 418 F.2d 1 (9th Cir. 1969) (court of appeals cannot set aside the Board's bargaining order only because there was a possibility that not one employee remained who had been at the plant during the original election). The Fifth Circuit disagreed, declaring that no bargaining order should issue unless *at the time such an order is directed* the Board "finds the electoral atmosphere unlikely to produce a fair election." NLRB v. American Cable Systems, Inc., 427 F.2d 446 (5th Cir. 1970), *cert. denied,* 400 U.S. 957 (1970). This approach was followed by General Steel Products, Inc. v. NLRB, 445 F.2d 1350 (4th Cir. 1971) (on remand from circuit court which denied enforcement of bargaining order, and in the absence of outrageous unfair labor practices, Board should hear material facts on whether or not a fair election could now be held).

In NLRB v. Armcor Industries, 535 F.2d 239 (3d Cir. 1976), the court refused to enforce the bargaining order in a *Gissel*-type situation and remanded the case to the Board for further analysis of the reasons why the Board concluded that the employer's unfair labor practices would make a fair election unlikely. The court also indicated that the Board should consider whether conditions at the plant are still so contaminated as to warrant a bargaining order.

In remanding the case for a second time, the Third Circuit restated that when a court remands a bargaining order to the NLRB for want of substantiation, the Board cannot issue a new order unless it fully considers changed circumstances in the plant at the time of the remand. NLRB v. Armcor Industries, Inc., 98 L.R.R.M. 2441 (3d Cir. 1978). *See also* NLRB v. Craw, 96 L.R.R.M. 3188 (3d Cir. 1977); Note, *"After All, Tomorrow is Another Day": Should Subsequent Events Affect the Validity of Bargaining Orders?* 31 STAN. L. REV. 505 (1979).

4. In J.P. Stevens Co. v. NLRB, 441 F.2d 514 (5th Cir. 1971), *cert. denied,* 404 U.S. 830 (1971), the court interpreted *Gissel* as authorizing the issuance of a bargaining order regardless of whether a union has ever established its majority status, where an employer's unfair labor practices are so "outrageous" and "pervasive" that their coercive effects cannot be overcome by traditional remedies. Although finding in the *Stevens* case that the union at one point did in fact represent a majority of the employees, the court said that the employer's "full scale war against unionization" made it unnecessary for the union to demonstrate its majority status. The company had discharged three leading union adherents and had engaged in a campaign of blatant surveillance, interrogation, and threats.

5. In Marie Phillips, Inc., 178 N.L.R.B. 340 (1969), the Board rejected an employer's contention that 26 unequivocal authorization cards which helped establish a union's majority were invalid because the union had solicited them by misrepresenting that a majority of the employees had already signed. But the Board said it would no longer adhere to the view suggested in G & A Truck Line, 168 N.L.R.B. 846 (1967), that reliance upon a misrepresentation is wholly irrelevant in determining the validity of a card. Instead, declared the Board: "Where the objective facts, as evidenced by events contemporaneous with the signing, clearly demonstrate that the misrepresentation was the decisive factor in causing an employee to sign a card, we shall not count such a card in determining a union's majority. However, . . . where the only indication of reliance is a signer's subsequent testimony as to his subjective state of mind when signing the card, such showing is insufficient to invalidate the card." The Board's order was enforced in Garment Workers Local 153 v. NLRB, 443 F.2d 667 (D.C. Cir. 1970).

6. Authorization cards which are either ambiguous as to their effect, or are "dual purpose" cards (authorizing the union to represent the employees and to obtain an election) have often been denied validity in representation matters, particularly if their purpose is not made clear to the signer. Dayco Corp. v. NLRB, 382 F.2d 577 (6th Cir. 1967); NLRB v. Peterson Bros., Inc., 342 F.2d 221 (5th Cir. 1965).

7. Bernel Foam Products Co., 146 N.L.R.B. 1277 (1964), was an important pre-*Gissel* case which held that when an employer refused to bargain on the basis of a majority of authorization cards and committed unfair labor practices during the election campaign, with the result that the union lost the election, the election would be set aside and the union could file unfair labor practice charges based on the refusal to bargain and receive a bargaining order. Prior to this case, the rule had been that the union's participation in an election after the employer had refused to bargain on the basis of authorization cards waived the union's right to file § 8(a)(5) unfair labor practice charges.

In Irving Air Chute Co., 149 N.L.R.B. 627 (1964), *enforced*, 350 F.2d 176 (2d Cir. 1965), the Board applied the *Bernel Foam* doctrine and issued a bargaining order after the union had lost an election following employer unfair labor practices. The Board said: "We will not grant such relief, however, unless the election be set aside on the basis of meritorious objections filed in the representation case."

The Board explained in Photobell Co., Inc., 158 N.L.R.B. 738 (1966): "The basic premise underlying this type of case is that there is no outstanding valid election. If there is a valid election outstanding, no bargaining order can issue."

Even though a union's specific objection to an election was overruled, the Board issued a bargaining order where the regional director in his postelection investigation discovered various employer unfair labor practices that had interfered with the fairness of the election. Pure Chem. Corp., 192 N.L.R.B. 681 (1971). Member Kennedy dissented on the ground this was contrary to *Irving Air Chute*.

8. For pre-*Gissel* discussions, see Bok, Phillips & St. Antoine, *Seminar on Free Speech and Preelection Conduct*, in SOUTHWESTERN LEGAL

FOUNDATION, LABOR LAW DEVELOPMENTS, PROCEEDINGS OF 11TH ANNUAL INSTITUTE ON LABOR LAW 239 (1964); Lesnick, *Establishment of Collective Bargaining Rights Without an Election*, 65 MICH. L. REV. 851 (1967); Lewis, *The Use and Abuse of Authorization Cards in Determining Union Majority*, 16 LAB. L.J. 434 (1965); Rains, *Authorization Cards as an Indefensible Basis for Board Directed Union Representation Status: Fact and Fancy*, 18 LAB. L.J. 226 (1967); Note, *Refusal-to-Recognize Charges Under § 8(a)(5) of the NLRA: Card Checks and Employee Free Choice*, 33 U. CHI. L. REV. 389 (1966); Note, *Union Authorization Cards*, 75 YALE L.J. 805 (1966).

9. Post-*Gissel* discussions include Christensen & Christensen, *Gissel Packing and "Good Faith Doubt": The Gestalt of Required Recognition of Unions Under the NLRA*, 37 U. CHI. L. REV. 411 (1970); Lewis, *Gissel Packing: Was the Supreme Court Right?*, 56 A.B.A.J. 877 (1970); Platt, *Supreme Court Looks at Bargaining Orders Based on Authorization Cards*, 4 GA. L. REV. 779 (1970); Pogrebin, *NLRB Bargaining Orders Since Gissel: Wanderings From a Landmark*, 46 ST. JOHN'S L. REV. 193 (1971); Note, *NLRB v. Gissel Packing: Bargaining Orders and Employee Free Choice*, 45 N.Y.U.L. REV. 318 (1970).

10. In a *Gissel*-type situation, where the Board is issuing a bargaining order to remedy the employer's serious violations of §§ 8(a)(1) and (3), should the Board also find a violation of § 8(a)(5)? *See* Steel-Fab, Inc., 212 N.L.R.B. 363 (1974).

In Trading Port, Inc., 219 N.L.R.B. 298 (1975), the Board reconsidered its *Steel-Fab* decision and held that "an employer's obligation under a bargaining order remedy should commence as of the time the employer has embarked on a clear course of unlawful conduct or has engaged in sufficient unfair labor practices to undermine the union's majority status." The Board amplified this holding by stating that where an employer fatally impedes the election process, he forfeits his right to a Board election and "must bargain with the union on the basis of other clear indications of employees' desires. It is at this point that the employer's unlawful refusal to bargain has taken place." *See also* American Map Co., 219 N.L.R.B. 1174 (1975), where the Board issued a bargaining order to remedy the employer's serious unfair labor practices and made it retroactive to the date of the union's demand for recognition on the basis of authorization cards from a majority of the employees. From a practical standpoint, why has the Board made the bargaining order retroactive? *See also* Brown Group, Inc., 223 N.L.R.B. 1409 (1976); Curtin Matheson Scientific, Inc., 228 N.L.R.B. 996 (1977).

In Drug Package, Inc. v. NLRB, 570 F.2d 1340 (8th Cir. 1978), a court of appeals denied enforcement of a retroactive bargaining order that was based on conduct occurring prior to the *Trading Port* decision. The court found that retroactive application of the *Trading Port* decision was unfair to an employer that had acted in reliance upon the Board's earlier ruling in *Steel-Fab*. But on remand the Board fashioned an unusual reinstatement remedy for replaced economic strikers in order to make its bargaining order fully effective. 241 N.L.R.B. No. 44, 100 L.R.R.M. 1601 (1979).

LINDEN LUMBER DIV., SUMMER & CO. v. NLRB

Supreme Court of the United States
419 U.S. 817, 95 S. Ct. 429, 42 L. Ed. 2d 465 (1974)

MR. JUSTICE DOUGLAS delivered the opinion of the Court.

These cases present a question expressly reserved in National Labor Relations Board v. Gissel Packing Co., 395 U. S. 575, 595, 601, n. 18 (1969).

In *Linden* respondent union obtained authorization cards from a majority of petitioner's employees and demanded that it be recognized as the collective-bargaining representative of those employees. Linden said it doubted the union's claimed majority status and suggested the union petition the Board for an election. The union filed such a petition with the Board but later withdrew it when Linden declined to enter a consent election agreement or abide by an election on the ground that respondent union's organizational campaign had been improperly assisted by company supervisors. Respondent union thereupon renewed its demand for collective bargaining; and again Linden declined, saying that the union's claimed membership had been improperly influenced by supervisors. Thereupon respondent union struck for recognition as the bargaining representative and shortly filed a charge of unfair labor practice against Linden based on its refusal to bargain.

There is no charge that Linden engaged in an unfair labor practice apart from its refusal to bargain. The Board held that Linden should not be guilty of an unfair labor practice solely on the basis "of its refusal to accept evidence of majority status other than the results of a Board election." . . .

In *Wilder* there apparently were 30 employees in the plant and the union with 11 signed and two unsigned authorization cards requested recognition as the bargaining agent for the company's production and maintenance employees. Of the 30 employees 18 were in the production and maintenance unit which the Board found to be appropriate for collective bargaining. No answer was given by Wilder, and recognitional picketing began. The request was renewed when the two unsigned cards were signed, but Wilder denied recognition. Thereupon the union filed unfair labor practice charges against Wilder. A series of Board decisions and judicial decisions, not necessary to recapitulate here, consumed about seven years until the present decision by the Court of Appeals. The Board made the same ruling as respects Wilder as it did in Linden's case. . . . On petitions for review the Court of Appeals reversed. 487 F.2d 1099 (1973). We reverse the Court of Appeals.

In *Gissel* we held that an employer who engages in "unfair" labor practices "likely to destroy the union's majority and seriously impede the election" may not insist that before it bargains the union get a secret ballot election. 395 U. S. at 600. There were no such unfair labor practices here, nor had the employer in either case agreed to a voluntary settlement of the dispute and then reneged. As noted, we reserved in *Gissel* the questions "whether, absent election interference by an employer's unfair labor practices, he may obtain an election only if he petitions for one himself; whether, if he does not, he must bargain with a card majority if the union chooses not to seek an election; and whether, in the latter situation, he is bound by the Board's ultimate determination of the card results regardless of his earlier good faith doubts, or whether he can still insist on a Union-sought election if he makes an affirmative showing of his positive reasons for believing there is a representation dispute." *Id.* at 601, n. 18.

We recognized in *Gissel* that while the election process had acknowledged superiority in ascertaining whether a union has majority support, cards may "adequately reflect employee sentiment." *Id.* at 603.

Generalizations are difficult; and it is urged by the unions that only the precise facts should dispose of concrete cases. As we said, however, in *Gissel*, the Board had largely abandoned its earlier test that the employer's refusal to bargain was warranted, if he had a good-faith doubt that the union represented a majority. . . .

In the present cases the Board found that the employers "should not be found guilty of a violation of Section 8(a)(5) solely upon the basis of [their] refusal to accept evidence of majority status other than the results of a Board election." . . . The question whether the employers had good reasons or poor reasons was not deemed relevant to the inquiry. The Court of Appeals concluded that if the employer had doubts as to a union's majority status, it could and should test out its doubts by petitioning for an election. . . .

To take the Board's position is not to say that authorization cards are wholly unreliable as an indication of employee support of the union. An employer concededly may have valid objections to recognizing a union on that basis. His objection to cards may, of course, mask his opposition to unions. On the other hand he may have rational, good-faith grounds for distrusting authorization cards in a given situation. He may be convinced that the fact that a majority of the employees strike and picket does not necessarily establish that they desire the particular union as their representative. Fear may indeed prevent some from crossing a picket line; or sympathy for strikers, not the desire to have the particular union in the saddle, may influence others. These factors make difficult an examination of the employer's motive to ascertain whether it was in good faith. To enter that domain is to reject the approval by *Gissel* of the retreat which the Board took from its "good faith" inquiries.

The union which is faced with an unwilling employer has two alternative remedies under the Board's decision in the instant case. It can file for an election; or it can press unfair labor practices against the employer under *Gissel*. The latter alternative promises to consume much time. In *Linden* the time between filing the charge and the Board's ruling was about 4½ years; in *Wilder*, about 6½ years. The Board's experience indicates that the median time in a contested case is 388 days. *Gissel*, 395 U. S. at 611, n. 30. On the other hand the median time between the filing of the petition for an election and the decision of the regional director is about 45 days. In terms of getting on with the problems of inaugurating regimes of industrial peace, the policy of encouraging secret elections under the Act is favored. The question remains — should the burden be on the union to ask for an election or should it be the responsibility of the employer?

The Court of Appeals concluded that since Congress in 1947 authorized employers to file their own representation petitions by enacting § 9(c)(1)(B), the burden was on them. But the history of that provision indicates it was aimed at eliminating the discrimination against employers which had previously existed under the Board's prior rules, permitting employers to petition for an election only when confronted with claims by two or more unions. There is no suggestion that Congress wanted to place the burden of getting a secret election on the employer.

> "Today an employer is faced with this situation. A man comes into his office and says, 'I represent your employees. Sign this agreement or we strike tomorrow.' Such instances have occurred all over the United States. The employer has no way in which to determine whether this man really does represent his employees or does not. The bill gives him the right to go to the Board under those circumstances, and say, 'I want an election. I want to know who is the bargaining agent for my employees.' " 93 Cong. Rec. 3838 (1947) (remarks of Senator Taft).

Our problem is not one of picking favorites but of trying to find the congressional purpose by examining the statutory and administrative interpretations that squint one way or another. Large issues ride on who takes the initiative. A common issue is, what should be the representative unit? In *Wilder* the employer at first took the position that the unit should be one of 30 employees. If it were 18, as the union claimed (or even 25 as the employer later argued), the union with its 13 authorization cards (assuming them to be valid) would have a majority. If the unit were 30, the union would be out of business.

Section 9(c)(1)(B) visualizes an employer faced with a claim by individuals or unions "to be recognized as the representative defined in § 9(a)." That question of representation is raised only by a claim that the applicant represents a majority of employees, "in a unit appropriate for such purposes." § 9(a). If there is a significant discrepancy between the unit which the employer wants and the unit for which the union asked recognition, the Board will dismiss the employer's petition. [Citing cases.] In that event the union, if it desired the smaller unit, would have to file its own petition, leaving the employer free to contest the appropriateness of that unit. The Court of Appeals thought that if the employer were required to petition the Board for an election, the litigable issues would be reduced. The recurring conflict over what should be the appropriate bargaining unit coupled with the fact that if the employer asks for a unit which the union opposes, his election petition is dismissed is answer enough.

The Board has at least some expertise in these matters and its judgment is that an employer's petition for an election, though permissible, is not the required course. It points out in its brief here that an employer wanting to gain delay can draw a petition to elicit protests by the union, and the thought that an employer petition would obviate litigation over the sufficiency of the union's showing of interest is in its purview apparently not well taken. A union petition to be sure must be backed by a 30% showing of employee interest. But the sufficiency of such a showing is not litigable by the parties.

In light of the statutory scheme and the practical administrative procedural questions involved, we cannot say that the Board's decision that the union should go forward and ask for an election on the employer's refusal to recognize the authorization cards was arbitrary and capricious or an abuse of discretion.

In sum, we sustain the Board in holding that, unless an employer has engaged in an unfair labor practice that impairs the electoral process, a union with authorization cards purporting to represent a majority of the employees, which is refused recognition, has the burden of taking the next step in invoking the Board's election procedure.

Reversed.

MR. JUSTICE STEWART, with whom MR. JUSTICE WHITE, MR. JUSTICE MARSHALL, and MR. JUSTICE POWELL join, dissenting.

. . . .

Section 9(a) expressly provides that the employees' exclusive bargaining representative shall be the union "designated or selected" by a majority of the employees in an appropriate unit. Neither § 9(a) nor § 8(a)(5), which makes it an unfair labor practice for an employer to refuse to bargain with the representative of his employees, specifies how that representative is to be chosen. The language of the Act thus seems purposefully designed to impose a duty upon an employer to bargain whenever the union representative presents convincing evidence of majority support, regardless of the method by which that support is demonstrated. And both the Board and this Court have in the past consistently interpreted §§ 8(a)(5) and 9(a) to mean exactly that. . . .

As the Court recognized in *Gissel*, the 1947 Taft-Hartley amendments strengthen this interpretation of the Act. One early version of the House bill would have amended the Act to permit the Board to find an employer unfair labor practice for refusing to bargain with a union only if the union was "currently recognized by the employer or certified as such [through an election] under section 9." Section 8(a)(5) of H. R. 3020, 80th Cong., 1st Sess. The proposed change, which would have eliminated any method of requiring employer recognition of a union other than a Board-supervised election, was rejected in Conference. H. R. Conf. Rep. No. 510, 80th Cong., 1st Sess., 41. After rejection of the proposed House amendment, the House Conference Report explicitly stated that § 8(a)(5) was intended to follow the provisions of "existing law." *Ibid.* And "existing law" unequivocally recognized that a union could establish majority status and thereby impose a bargaining obligation on an unwilling employer by means other than petitioning for and winning a Board-supervised election. NLRB v. Gissel Packing Co., *supra*, at 596-598.

The 1947 amendments, however, did provide an alternative to immediate union recognition for an employer faced with a union demand to bargain on behalf of his employees. Section 9(c)(1)(B), added to the Act in 1947, provides that an employer, alleging that one or more individuals or labor organizations have presented a claim to be recognized as the exclusive representative of his employees, may file a petition for a Board-supervised representation election.

This section, together with §§ 8(a)(5) and 9(a), provides clear congressional direction as to the proper approach to the situation before us. When an employer is faced with a demand for recognition by a union that has presented convincing evidence of majority support, he may elect to follow one of four alternatives. First, he is free to recognize the union and thereby satisfy his § 8(a)(5) obligation to bargain with the representatives "designated or selected" by his employees. Second, he may petition for a Board-supervised election, pursuant to § 9(c)(1)(B). NLRB v. Gissel Packing Co., *supra*, at 599. Third, rather than file his own election petition, the employer can agree to be bound by the results of an expedited consent election ordered after the filing of a union election petition. See 29 CFR § 102.62. Finally, the employer can refuse to recognize the union, despite its convincing evidence of majority support, and also refuse either to petition for an election or to consent to a union-requested election. In this event, however, the Act clearly provides that the union may charge the employer with an unfair labor practice under § 8(a)(5) for refusing to bargain collectively with the representatives of his employees. If the General Counsel issues a complaint and the Board determines that the union in fact represents a majority of the employees, the Board must issue an order directing the employer to bargain with the union. See, *e.g.*, NLRB v. Dahlstrom Metallic Door Co., 112 F.2d 756; cf. NLRB v. Gissel Packing Co., 395 U. S., at 595-600.

The Court offers two justifications for its approval of the new Board practice which, disregarding the clear language of §§ 8(a)(5) and 9(a), requires an employer to bargain only with a union certified as bargaining representative after a Board-supervised election conducted upon the petition of the union.

First, it is suggested that to require the Board under some circumstances to find a § 8(a)(5) violation when an employer refuses to bargain with the noncertified union supported by a majority of his employees would compel the Board to re-enter the domain of subjective "good faith" inquiries. *Ante*, at slip op. 5. This fear is unwarranted. . . .

Within broad limits imposed by the Act itself, the Board may use its understanding of the policies and practical considerations of the Act's administration to determine the circumstances under which an employer must take evidence of majority support as "convincing." Cf. NLRB v. Insurance Agents' International Union, 361 U. S. 477, 499; NLRB v. Local 449, Teamsters, 353 U. S. 87, 96. The Act in no way requires the Board to define "convincing evidence" in a manner that reintroduces a subjective test of the employer's good faith in refusing to bargain with the union. If the Board continues to believe, as it has in the recent past, that it is unworkable to adopt any standard for determining when an employer has breached his duty to bargain that incorporates a subjective element, see NLRB v. Gissel Packing Co., 395 U. S. at 592-594, it may define "convincing evidence of majority support" solely by reference to objective criteria — for example, by reference to "a union-called strike or strike vote, or, as here, by possession of cards signed by a majority of the employees. . . ." *Id.* at 597.

Even with adoption of such an objective standard for measuring "convincing evidence of majority support," the employer's "subjective" doubts would be adequately safeguarded by § 9(c)(1)(B)'s assurance of the right to file his own petition for an election. Despite the Board's broad discretion in this area, however, the Act simply does not permit the Board to adopt a rule that avoids *subjective* inquiries by eliminating entirely *all* inquiries into an employer's obligation to bargain with a noncertified union selected by a majority of his employees.

The second ground upon which the Court justifies its approval of the Board's new practice is that it serves to remove from the employer the burden of obtaining a Board-supervised election. . . . Although I agree with the Court that it would be improper to impose such an obligation on an employer, the Board's new policy is not necessary to eliminate such a burden.

The only employer obligation relevant to this case, apart from the requirement that the employer not commit independent unfair labor practices that would prejudice the holding of a fair election, is the one imposed by §§ 8(a)(5) and 9(a) of the Act: an employer has a duty to bargain collectively with the representative designated or selected by his employees. When an employer is confronted with "convincing evidence of majority support," he has the *option* of petitioning for an election or consenting to an expedited union-petitioned election. As the Court explains, § 9 (c)(1)(B) does not require the employer to exercise this option. If he does not, however, and if he does not voluntarily recognize the union, he must take the risk that his conduct will be found by the Board to constitute a violation of his § 8(a)(5) duty to bargain. In short, petitioning for an election is not an employer obligation; it is a device created by Congress for the employer's self-protection, much as Congress gave unions the right to petition for elections to establish their majority status but deliberately chose not to require a union to seek an election before it could impose a bargaining obligation on an unwilling employer. NLRB v. Gissel Packing Co., 395 U. S. at 598-599.

The language and history of the Act clearly indicate that Congress intended to impose upon an employer the duty to bargain with a union that has presented convincing evidence of majority support, even though the union has not petitioned for and won a Board-supervised election. "It is not necessary for us to justify the policy of Congress. It is enough that we find it in the statute. That policy cannot be defeated by the Board's policy." Colgate-Palmolive-Peet Co. v. NLRB, 388 U. S. 355, 363. Accordingly, I would affirm the judgment of the Court of Appeals remanding the case to the Board, but for further proceedings consistent with the views expressed in this opinion.

NOTE

In Retail Clerks Local 455 v. NLRB [Kroger Co.], 510 F.2d 802 (D.C. Cir. 1975), a court of appeals held, contrary to the NLRB, that an employer could waive its right to petition for an election by signing a so-called "additional store clause," under which the employer agrees to recognize the union as bargaining agent for the employees in any store added to the original unit. In this particular case, the union had also proffered concededly valid authorization cards from a majority of the employees in the store in dispute.

PART THREE

UNION COLLECTIVE ACTION

SELIG PERLMAN, A THEORY OF THE LABOR MOVEMENT 238-42 (1928)

In an economic community, there is a separation between those who prefer a secure, though modest return — that is to say, a mere livelihood — and those who play for big stakes and are willing to assume risk in proportion. The first compose the great bulk of manual workers of every description . . . while the latter are, of course, the entrepreneurs and the big business men. The limited or unlimited purpose is, in either case, the product of a simple survey of accessible economic opportunity and of a psychic self-appraisal. The manual worker is convinced by experience that he is living in a world of limited opportunity. He sees, to be sure, how others, for instance business men, are finding the same world a storehouse of apparently unlimited opportunity. Yet he decisively discounts that, so far as he is himself concerned. The business man, on the contrary, is an eternal optimist. To him the world is brimful of opportunities that are only waiting to be made his own. . . .

The economic pessimism of the manual group is at the bottom of its characteristic manner of adjusting the relation of the individual to the whole group. It prompts also the attitude of exclusion which manual groups assume towards those regarded as "outsiders." Again the manualist's psychology can best be brought out by contrast with that of the fully developed business man. Basically the business man is an economic individualist, a competitor *par excellence.* If opportunity is plentiful, if the enterprising person can create his own opportunity, what sane object can there be in collectively controlling the extent of the individual's appropriation of opportunity, or in drastically excluding those from other localities? Nor will this type of individual submit to group control, for he is confident of his ability to make good bargains for himself. If, on the contrary, opportunity is believed to be limited, as in the experience of the manual worker, it then becomes the duty of the group to prevent the individual from appropriating more than his rightful share, while at the same time protecting him against oppressive bargains. *The group then asserts its collective ownership over the whole amount of opportunity,* and, having determined who are entitled to claim a share in that opportunity, undertakes to parcel it out fairly, directly or indirectly, among its recognized members, permitting them to avail themselves of such opportunities, job or market, only on the basis of a "common rule." Free competition becomes a sin against one's fellows, anti-social, like a self-indulgent consumption of the stores of a beleaguered city, and obviously detrimental to the individual as well. A collective disposal of opportunity, including the power to keep out undesirables, and a "common rule" in making bargains are as natural to the manual group as *"laissez-faire"* is to the business man.

NEIL W. CHAMBERLAIN, THE PHILOSOPHY OF AMERICAN MANAGEMENT TOWARD LABOR, in LABOR IN A CHANGING AMERICA 181-82 (W. Haber ed. 1966)*

When a businessman strives for cost reduction, quality control, an improved rate of output, he is simply conforming to the institutional role which has been written for him by the society of which he is a part. But inescapably, that role brings him into conflict with organized labor, whose own institutional role is bound up with preserving the income continuity of its members, protecting the value of their learned skills, relaxing disciplinary and production pressures. It is not a matter of one of these groups being right and the other wrong, or of one being narrowly preoccupied with money values and the other more broadly concerned with human values. It is simply that American society has written different scripts for these two sets of economic performers, and the roles in which they are respectively cast *call* for a clash of objectives on the economic stage. . . .

. . . The consequence of this continuing encounter is readily predictable. In terms of management's philosophical disposition toward organized labor, it leads to a state of mind where unions are identified with efforts to interfere with that efficient performance which society expects of business — to interfere by such tactics as fighting for the retention of outworn work rules and customs, opposing new technologies, insisting on rewards for long service rather than ability. One can hardly expect managers to look benignly on those who are impeding it in doing its job, however sincere or well motivated they may be.

LLOYD G. REYNOLDS, LABOR ECONOMICS AND LABOR RELATIONS 441, 442, 447, 449 (7th ed. 1978)**

In an average year during the period 1970-75, about 2.5 million workers were involved in strikes. This was about 13 percent of union members, and 3 percent of all employed workers. The average length of strikes was about three weeks. The amount of time lost through strikes, as a proportion of total working time in the economy, varied from about 0.37 percent in 1970 to 0.14 percent in 1973. . . .

To discover [what] was responsible for a particular strike requires careful analysis of the circumstances. The union normally makes the first overt move, and the public therefore tends to regard it as the aggressor. The employer can cause a strike by doing nothing; the union has to take the positive step of calling out the workers. But all one can conclude from the fact of a strike is that there was a failure to reach agreement. The reasons for the failure can be learned from an inside knowledge of the people and issues involved. . . .

The costs of a shutdown are a key factor in the power relation between the parties. In part, these costs depend on the nature of the product and the industry. If the company is producing a service or a perishable commodity, sales lost during a strike can never be regained. In an industry that produces a durable good and that normally operates below capacity, such as coal mining, what is not produced during the strike will be produced later on. . . .

A shutdown brings losses to workers and the union as well as to the employer. Striking members are usually excused from dues payments and entitled to draw strike benefits, so that a long strike drains the union treasury. On this score, union bargaining power fluctuates over time. A union that has just been through an expensive strike has reduced bargaining power because the treasury is low and the memory of lost paychecks is fresh in the members' minds. As time passes, the union's ability to strike recovers and its bargaining power rises.

The prospective losses are usually serious enough to serve as a substantial deterrent to both sides. . . .

SECTION I. Introduction

It is apparent that labor organizations are not mere fraternal societies having polite social functions. They are militant groups formed for the primary purpose of advancing what are conceived to be the economic interests of their members, and they have not been content to rely exclusively on the art of persuasion through exhortation either in gaining members or in wresting concessions from employers. From the beginning they have made use also of economic and political action to gain their ends. Economic action has typically taken the form of the strike, the picket line, and the boycott, and with the legality of these methods of "industrial warfare" we are now concerned. It is perhaps unfortunate, yet true, that our labor relations have not yet developed (matured?) to the point that the use of economic force is so unusual as to be regarded as "pathological."

A. COLLECTIVE ACTION AT COMMON LAW

There was presented, in Part One, a brief treatment of the early antecedents of American labor law and an outline of the principles, in variety and contrariety, which courts have used, or at least have said they used, in deciding cases involving collective action by labor groups. It was suggested that the concept most frequently to be found in the cases (although there are plenty of others), is that union activities which inflict injury are to be tested by the propriety of the objective sought and the means used, and this is the general principle which, in 1938, was considered by Professor Shulman and his assisting experts to be appropriate for inclusion in the *Torts Restatement* of the law of labor disputes. The principle was implemented in the *Restatement* by a rather elaborate attempt to set out the appropriate tests for evaluating both the objects and methods of collective action. These will be given due consideration as we proceed. It is a fact, however, that the rules stated in the *Restatement* were by no means universally accepted by the courts, and there is a real question whether anything purporting to be an actual "restatement" could reasonably be attempted.

We have, of course, now come a long way from the views represented in the old criminal conspiracy cases of the early part of the nineteenth century. The individual's right to quit his job is considered to be inviolate, at least as against injunctive or other official restraint, and the peaceful strike is privileged at common law, at least as long as the objective is "proper" and it does not go beyond the "proper" area for economic action (of which more later). Picketing has had more difficulty in gaining recognition as an accepted method of collective action, because, as we shall see, it has carried in the minds of some judges connotations of violence regardless of its actual physical characteristics, and many courts have been quick to seize upon the slightest manifestation of violence or abuse (*e.g.,* numbers of picketers, minor breaches of peace, rough and tumble and frequently "unnice" language) as a pretext for granting relief despite lip service to the doctrine, now generally established, that peaceful and nonfraudulent picketing for a proper objective is lawful. The boycott has fared least well, particularly where it has been found to be "secondary."

Labor law with respect to union collective action can be thought of as consisting of four layers. The common law, which we have been discussing, is the underlying layer. It is essentially tort law, and most of the cases involved the equity remedy of an injunction. Supposing that the union activity would be characterized as tortious, either because of its wrongful objective or its wrongful means, the next question to be considered by a court would be whether there is an anti-injunction statute which prevents issuance of the decree. This may be thought of as the second layer of labor law.

B. ANTI-INJUNCTION STATUTES

An attempt was made in 1914 to get the federal courts out of the business of issuing injunctions in labor disputes by the passage of the Clayton Act. However, this legislative effort was not fully effective. One frequent basis for an injunction in the federal courts was the Sherman Antitrust Act; and, during the decade of the 1920's, in such cases as Duplex Printing Press Co. v. Deering, 254 U.S. 443 (1921), and Bedford Cut Stone Co. v. Journeymen Stone Cutters' Ass'n, 274 U.S. 37 (1927), the federal courts continued to issue injunctions against secondary boycotts as violations of the antitrust laws.

Public dissatisfaction with the labor injunction grew in the late 1920's and early 1930's, with agitation for reform coming not only from representatives of the labor movement, but also from persons in the legal profession who were concerned about the reputation of the judicial system. The particularized evils of the labor injunction which were highly publicized at this time have been set out in the historical introduction (Part One at 27), and it would be useful to review them now.[1]

The Norris-La Guardia Act, enacted in 1932, operates as a restriction upon the equity jurisdiction of the federal courts in cases involving or growing out of labor disputes. The act is set out in the *Statutory Appendix*. Its incidence is twofold: (1) It lays down certain definite requirements of procedure and proof (which we shall refer to as "procedural" requirements) which must be met before injunction may issue (see §§ 6, 7, 8, 9, 10, 11 and 12); (2) it removes from the federal courts all "jurisdiction" to restrain certain specified kinds of acts, even though the procedural requirements are met (see § 4). Note also that the statute does not apply at all unless the particular case involves or grows out of a labor dispute, and in this connection, see § 13.

The Norris Act has now been substantially duplicated by state legislation in a considerable group of states, in some instances with more or less important variations designed to meet specific problems considered important. Another substantial group of states have statutes more limited in scope, some of which are of the Clayton Act variety.[2]

The constitutionality of the Wisconsin anti-injunction act was sustained in *Senn v. Tile Layers Protection Union*.[3] The validity of the Norris-La Guardia Act was sustained in *Lauf v. E.G. Shinner & Co.*[4]

The Norris-La Guardia Act has been remarkably effective in removing the jurisdiction of the federal courts to issue injunctions in labor disputes, as the following case illustrates.

MARINE COOKS & STEWARDS v. PANAMA S.S. Co.

Supreme Court of the United States
362 U.S. 365, 80 S. Ct. 779, 4 L. Ed. 2d 797 (1960)

MR. JUSTICE BLACK delivered the opinion of the Court.

The respondents, who are the owner, time charterer, and master of the Liberian registered vessel, S.S. Nikolos, brought this action in a United States District Court against the petitioner union and its members praying for temporary and permanent injunctions to restrain, and for damages allegedly suffered from, the union's peaceful picketing of the ship in

---

[1] For an able treatment of the background of anti-injunction legislation, see F. FRANKFURTER & N. GREENE, THE LABOR INJUNCTION (1930).

[2] For a summary of the legislative pattern, see Smith & Delancey, *The State Legislatures and Unionism,* 38 MICH. L. REV. 987, 1013-20 (1940). For the current status of anti-injunction acts in particular states, see the state labor law volume of one of the looseleaf labor law services.

[3] 301 U.S. 468 (1937).

[4] 303 U.S. 323 (1938).

American waters and its threats to picket shore consignees of the ship's cargo should they accept delivery. The union's sole contention was that the District Court was without jurisdiction to restrain the picketing because of the Norris-LaGuardia Act which states in § 1:

"That no court of the United States, as herein defined, shall have jurisdiction to issue any restraining order or temporary or permanent injunction in a case involving or growing out of a labor dispute, except in a strict conformity with the provisions of this Act; nor shall any such restraining order or temporary or permanent injunction be issued contrary to the public policy declared in this Act."

Section 4 of that same law specifically denies jurisdiction to District Courts to issue any restraining order or temporary or permanent injunction to prohibit unions from:

"(e) Giving publicity to the existence of, or the facts involved in, any labor dispute, whether by advertising, speaking, patrolling, or by any other method not involving fraud or violence; . . . ."

Notwithstanding these provisions of the Norris-LaGuardia Act and despite an express finding that the union and its members had not been guilty of fraud, or threatened or committed any acts of physical violence to any person or any property, the District Court issued a temporary injunction to restrain the picketing. The injunction prohibited picketing by the petitioner union of "the S.S. 'Nikolos' or any other vessel registered under a foreign flag and manned by an alien crew and owned, operated or chartered by" respondents, in the Puget Sound area. This action of the court was based on its conclusions that (a) the case did not involve or grow out of any labor dispute within the meaning of the Norris-LaGuardia Act and (b) even if there were a labor dispute within the meaning of that Act, the court had jurisdiction to restrain the picketing because it interfered in the internal economy of a vessel registered under the flag of a friendly foreign power and amounted to "an unlawful interference with foreign commerce." The court's conclusion rested on the following facts, about which there was no substantial dispute.

The petitioner and other national labor organizations act as bargaining representatives for most of the unlicensed personnel of vessels that fly the American flag on the Pacific Coast. Petitioner alone, pursuant to National Labor Relations Board certification, represents employees of the stewards department on a large majority of those vessels. The S.S. Nikolos is owned by a Liberian corporation, was time-chartered for this trip by another Liberian corporation, and all members of its crew were aliens working under employment contracts made outside this country. There was no labor dispute between the ship's employees and the ship. The Nikolos picked up a cargo of salt in Mexico and carried it to the harbor of the port of Tacoma, Washington, for delivery to an American consignee there. After the ship entered the Tacoma harbor it was met by the union's boat which began to circle around the Nikolos displaying signs marked "PICKET BOAT." Later an additional sign was put on the boat reading: "AFL-CIO seamen protest loss of their livelihood to foreign flag ships with sub-standard wages or sub-standard conditions." The union threatened to extend its picketing to the consignee of the salt should an attempt be made to berth and unload that cargo. Although the picketing was peaceful and there was no fraud, the result was that the ship could not deliver its cargo.

On appeal from the temporary injunction to the Court of Appeals the petitioner argued that the injunction granted by the District Court was beyond the jurisdiction of that court because of the provisions of § 4 of the Norris-LaGuardia Act, but the Court of Appeals rejected that contention and upheld the injunction.... Certiorari was granted to consider the question of the applicability of the Norris-LaGuardia Act here.

That Act's language is broad. The language is broad because Congress was intent upon taking the federal courts out of the labor injunction business except in the very limited circumstances left open for federal jurisdiction under the Norris-LaGuardia Act. The history and background that led Congress to take this view have been adverted to in a number of prior opinions of this Court in which we refused to give the Act narrow interpretations that would have restored many labor dispute controversies to the courts.[7]

It is difficult to see how this controversy could be thought to spring from anything except one "concerning terms or conditions of employment," and hence a labor dispute within the meaning of the Norris-LaGuardia Act. The protest stated by the pickets concerned "sub-standard wages or sub-standard conditions." The controversy does involve, as the Act requires, "persons who are engaged in the same industry, trade, craft or occupation." And it is immaterial under the Act that the unions and the ship and the consignees did not "stand in a proximate relation of employer and employee." This case clearly does grow out of a labor dispute within the meaning of the Norris-LaGuardia Act.

The District Court held, however, that even if this case involved a labor dispute under the Norris-LaGuardia Act the court had jurisdiction to issue the injunction because the picketing was an "unlawful interference with foreign commerce" and interfered "in the internal economy of a vessel registered under the flag of a friendly foreign power" and prevented "such a vessel from lawfully loading or discharging cargo at ports in the United States." The Court of Appeals adopted this position, but cited no

---

[7] ... "The underlying aim of the Norris-LaGuardia Act was to restore the broad purpose which Congress thought it had formulated in the Clayton Act but which was frustrated, so Congress believed, by unduly restrictive judicial construction." United States v. Hutcheson, 312 U.S. 219, 236.

This congressional purpose, as is well known, was prompted by a desire to protect the rights of laboring men to organize and bargain collectively and to withdraw federal courts from a type of controversy for which many believed they were ill-suited and from participation in which, it was feared, judicial prestige might suffer. See Frankfurter and Greene, The Labor Injunction (1930), at 200; Gregory, Labor and the Law (1958), at 184-199.

authority for its statement that the picketing was "unlawful," nor have the respondents in this Court pointed to any statute or persuasive authority proving that petitioner's conduct was unlawful. Compare § 20 of the Clayton Act, 15 U.S.C. § 20. And even if unlawful, it would not follow that the federal court would have jurisdiction to enjoin the particular conduct which § 4 of the Norris-LaGuardia Act declared shall not be enjoined. Nor does the language of the Norris-LaGuardia Act leave room to hold that jurisdiction it denies a District Court to issue a particular type of restraining order can be restored to it by a finding that the nonenjoinable conduct may "interfere in the internal economy of a vessel registered under the flag of a friendly foreign power."

Congress passed the Norris-LaGuardia Act to curtail and regulate the jurisdiction of courts, not, as they passed the Taft-Hartley Act, to regulate the conduct of people engaged in labor disputes. . . . [T]he ship that voluntarily enters the territorial limits of this country subjects itself to our laws and jurisdiction as they exist. The fact that a foreign ship enters a United States court as a plaintiff cannot enlarge the jurisdiction of that court. There is not presented to us here, and we do not decide, whether the picketing of petitioner was tortious under state or federal law. All we decide is that the Norris-LaGuardia Act deprives the United States court of jurisdiction to issue the injunction it did under the circumstances shown.

The judgment of the Court of Appeals is reversed and the case is remanded to the District Court with directions to dismiss the petition for injunction.

It is so ordered.

NOTES

1. In New Negro Alliance v. Sanitary Grocery Co., 303 U.S. 552 (1938), the Supreme Court reversed the granting of an injunction against the New Negro Alliance, an incorporated association (not a labor union) which was boycotting and picketing a grocery store, demanding that the store hire blacks. The Supreme Court applied the Norris-La Guardia Act, reasoning that the parties in a labor dispute need not have the relationship of employer and employee, and that the Alliance had a direct interest in the labor dispute. The Court also emphasized that the Act is not concerned with the motives for the dispute.

2. In Bakery Sales Drivers' Local 33 v. Wagshal, 333 U.S. 437 (1948), it was held that no "labor dispute" was involved where a delicatessen proprietor, plaintiff in the case, had discontinued purchase of goods from a certain bakery due to inability to obtain a convenient delivery hour, and the defendant union, of which the bakery's employee who had delivered goods to plaintiff was a member, had objected to the basis of settling plaintiff's accrued account with the bakery, and in connection therewith picketed and threatened to boycott plaintiff's store. "To hold that, under such circumstances, a failure of two businessmen to come to terms created a labor dispute merely because what one of them sought might have affected the work of a particular employee of the other, would be to turn almost every controversy between sellers and buyers over price, quantity, quality, delivery, payment, credit, or any other business transaction into a 'labor dispute.' " 333 U.S. at 443.

3. Under §§ 10(j) and (*l*) of the National Labor Relations Act, the NLRB is empowered, and in the case of some union unfair labor practices, directed, to petition a federal district court for a temporary restraining order. Also, in order to enforce its orders, the NLRB is authorized under § 10(e) to petition a federal court of appeals for an enforcement order.

Accordingly, § 10(h) of the Act provides:

"(h) When granting appropriate temporary relief or a restraining order, or making and entering a decree enforcing, modifying, and enforcing as so modified, or setting aside in whole or in part an order of the Board, as provided in this section, the jurisdiction of courts sitting in equity shall not be limited by the Act entitled 'An Act to amend the Judicial Code and to define and limit the jurisdiction of courts sitting in equity, and for other purposes,' approved March 23, 1932 (29 U.S.C. §§ 101-15) [Norris-La Guardia Act]."

Thus the Norris-La Guardia Act does not stand in the way of injunctions against unfair labor practices when they are sought by the NLRB. But this does not mean that a private party is permitted to obtain an injunction against an unfair labor practice. For example, the Supreme Court said in Bakery Sales Drivers, Local 33 v. Wagshal, 333 U.S. 437 (1948), "The short answer to the argument that the Labor Management Relations Act of 1947 . . . has removed the limitations of the Norris-La Guardia Act upon the power to issue injunctions against what are known as secondary boycotts is that the law has been changed only where an injunction is sought by the National Labor Relations Board, not where proceedings are instituted by a private party." The statutory scheme, as shown by the legislative history, is to vest paramount authority in the NLRB. *See also* Aetna Freight Lines v. Clayton, 228 F.2d 384 (2d Cir. 1955); Amalgamated Ass'n of Street, Elec. Ry. & Motor Coach Employees v. Dixie Motor Coach Co., 170 F.2d 902 (8th Cir. 1948); Amazon Cotton Mill Co. v. Textile Workers, 167 F.2d 183 (4th Cir. 1948).

The power to initiate or maintain an injunction action under § 10(*l*) has been held restricted to the NLRB. Thus, charging parties were denied permission even to intervene in proceedings brought by a Board regional director against a union under § 10(*l*). Solien v. Miscellaneous Drivers & Helpers Union, Local 610 [Sears, Roebuck & Co.], 440 F.2d 124 (8th Cir. 1971), *cert. denied,* 403 U.S. 905 (1971). At the same time, a regional director's discretion under the mandatory injunction provisions of § 10(*l*) is limited, and an employer charging a union with an unlawful secondary boycott is entitled to go into federal district court for an order compelling the regional director to seek a temporary injunction against the union's activity. Terminal Freight Handling Co. v. Solien, 444 F.2d 699 (8th Cir. 1971), *cert. denied,* 405 U.S. 996 (1972).

A union or an individual is not entitled to a jury trial under 18 U.S.C. § 3692 when charged with criminal contempt for violating an injunction issued pursuant to § 10(*l*) of the NLRA. Muniz v. Hoffman, 422 U.S. 454 (1975).

4. In Brotherhood of R.R. Trainmen v. Atlantic Coast Line R. Co., the Court of Appeals for the Fifth Circuit held that the Norris-La Guardia Act required the vacating of an injunction issued against striking employees of the Florida East Coast Railroad who picketed the premises of the Jacksonville Terminal Co. in order to get its employees to cease performing certain essential services for FEC trains coming into the terminal. Any "unlawfulness under nonlabor legislation such as the Interstate Commerce Act did not remove the restrictions of the Norris-LaGuardia Act upon the jurisdiction of federal courts." 362 F.2d 649 (1966), *aff'd by equally divided Court,* 385 U.S. 20 (1966).

5. The applicability of the Norris-La Guardia Act will be considered further in a number of other cases involving its relationship to the antitrust laws, the Railway Labor Act, and the Taft-Hartley Act. These include Boys Markets, Inc. v. Retail Clerks Local 770, 398 U.S. 235 (1970) (federal court may enjoin strike in breach of contract in action under § 301), *infra* at 674; Order of Railroad Telegraphers v. Chicago & N.W.R.R., 362 U.S. 330 (1960) (strike to prevent elimination of railroad stations and certain jobs therein nonenjoinable as arising out of a "labor dispute"), *infra* at 564; Brotherhood of R.R. Trainmen v. Chicago River & Indiana R.R., 353 U.S. 30 (1957) (strike over grievances arising under existing collective agreement enjoinable where disputes are subject to final and binding arbitration before the National Railroad Adjustment Board); Textile Workers v. Lincoln Mills, 353 U.S. 448 (1957) (federal court may decree specific performance of agreement to arbitrate under § 301 of Taft-Hartley), *infra* at 651; Allen Bradley Co. v. IBEW, Local 3, 325 U.S. 797 (1945) (union participation in businessmen's combination to restrain trade not within the exemptions of the Norris-La Guardia and Sherman Acts), *infra* at 603; Steele v. Louisville & Nashville R.R., 323 U.S. 192 (1944) (federal court may issue injunction to enforce union's duty of fair representation), *infra* at 739; United States v. Hutcheson, 312 U.S. 219 (1941) (union conduct nonenjoinable under Norris-La Guardia, also immune to Sherman Act prosecution), *infra* at 598.

6. *Compare* Windward Shipping Ltd. v. American Radio Ass'n, 415 U.S. 104 (1974), and American Radio Ass'n v. Mobile S.S. Ass'n, 419 U.S. 215 (1974), where the Supreme Court upheld the power of a *state* court to enjoin picketing of foreign flag ships.

C. LABOR RELATIONS ACTS AND OTHER STATUTES

A third layer of law, overlaying the common law and interacting with the anti-injunction legislation, is now to be found in federal and state labor relations statutes and other miscellaneous regulations of labor union collective action. Undoubtedly the most important development in this field was the proscription of union unfair labor practices in the Taft-Hartley Act of 1947, with the additions and refinements made in the Landrum-Griffin Act of 1959.

Most of Part Three of this book will be devoted to a detailed consideration of how this modern labor legislation regulates the most important and controversial aspects of union collective action, such as organizational and recognition picketing, secondary boycotts, hot cargo agreements, jurisdictional strikes and featherbedding.

But first we shall take a brief look at the fourth and highest layer of law — constitutional protection. This is largely a matter of civil rights under the Constitution, such as freedom of speech. However, to the extent that Congress has either outlawed or protected certain collective action by unions, the federal law has taken on additional importance because of the doctrine of federal preemption. This federal-state problem will be examined in detail in the last section of Part Three. The materials in this next section dealing with state regulation of various union practices must all be read, as far as industries affecting interstate commerce are concerned, with the qualification in mind that some state action may now be precluded under the federal preemption doctrine.

SECTION II. Constitutional Protection

INTERNATIONAL BROTHERHOOD OF TEAMSTERS, LOCAL 695, A.F.L. v. VOGT, INC.

Supreme Court of the United States
354 U.S. 284, 77 S. Ct. 1166, 1 L. Ed. 2d 1347 (1957)

MR. JUSTICE FRANKFURTER delivered the opinion of the Court.

This is one more in the long series of cases in which this Court has been required to consider the limits imposed by the Fourteenth Amendment on the power of a State to enjoin picketing. The case was heard below on the pleadings and affidavits, the parties stipulating that the record contained "all of the facts and evidence that would be adduced upon a trial on the merits. . . ." Respondent owns and operates a gravel pit in Oconomowoc, Wisconsin, where it employs 15 to 20 men. Petitioner unions sought unsuccessfully to induce some of respondent's employees to join the unions and commenced to picket the entrance to respondent's business with signs reading, "The men on this job are not 100% affiliated with the AFL." "In consequence," drivers of several trucking companies refused to deliver and haul goods to and from respondent's plant, causing substantial damage to respondent. Respondent thereupon sought an injunction to restrain the picketing.

The trial court did not make the finding, requested by respondent, "That the picketing of plaintiff's premises has been engaged in for the purpose of coercing, intimidating and inducing the employer to force, compel, or induce its employees to become members of defendant labor organizations, and for the purpose of injuring the plaintiff in its business because of its refusal to in any way interfere with the rights of its employees to join or not to join a labor organization." It nevertheless held that by virtue of Wis. Stat. § 103.535, prohibiting picketing in the absence of a "labor dispute," the petitioners must be enjoined from maintaining any pickets near respondent's place of business, from displaying at any place near respondent's place of business signs indicating that there was a labor dispute between respondent and its employees or between respondent and any of the petitioners, and from inducing others to decline to transport goods to and from respondent's business establishment.

On appeal, the Wisconsin Supreme Court at first reversed, relying largely on AFL v. Swing, 312 U.S. 321 (1941), to hold § 103.535 unconstitutional, on the ground that picketing could not constitutionally be enjoined merely because of the absence of a "labor dispute." 270 Wis. 315, 71 N.W.2d 359 (1955).

Upon reargument [270 Wis. 315, 74 N.W.2d 749, 753 (1956)], however, the court withdrew its original opinion. Although the trial court had refused to make the finding requested by respondent, the Supreme Court, noting that the facts as to which the request was made were undisputed, drew the inference from the undisputed facts and itself made the finding. It canvassed the whole circumstances surrounding the picketing and held that "One would be credulous indeed to believe under the circumstances that the Union had no thought of coercing the employer to interfere with its employees in their right to join or refuse to join the defendant union." Such picketing, the court held, was for "an unlawful purpose," since Wis. Stat. § 111.06(2)(b) made it an unfair labor practice for an employee individually or in concert with others to "coerce, intimidate or induce any employer to interfere with any of his employes in the enjoyment of their legal rights . . . or to engage in any practice with regard to his employees which would constitute an unfair labor practice if undertaken by him on his own initiative." Relying on Building Service Employees v. Gazzam, 339 U.S. 532 (1950), and Pappas v. Stacey, 151 Me. 36, 116 A.2d 497 (1955), the Wisconsin Supreme Court therefore affirmed the granting of the injunction on this different ground. 270 Wis. 315, 74 N.W.2d 749 (1956).

We are asked to reverse the judgment of the Wisconsin Supreme Court, which to a large extent rested its decision on that of the Supreme Judicial Court of Maine in Pappas v. Stacey, *supra*. When an appeal from that decision was filed here, this Court granted appellee's motion to dismiss for lack of a substantial federal question. 350 U.S. 870 (1955). Since the present case presents a similar question, we might well have denied certiorari on the strength of our decision in that case. In view of the recurrence of the question, we thought it advisable to grant certiorari, 352 U.S. 817, and to restate the principles governing this type of case.

It is inherent in the concept embodied in the Due Process Clause that its scope be determined by a "gradual process of judicial inclusion and exclusion," Davidson v. New Orleans, 96 U.S. 97, 104 (1878). Inevitably, therefore, the doctrine of a particular case "is not allowed to end with its enunciation, and . . . an expression in an opinion yields later to the impact of facts unforeseen." Jaybird Mining Co. v. Weir, 271 U.S. 609, 619 (1926)

(Brandeis, J., dissenting). It is not too surprising that the response of States — legislative and judicial — to use of the injunction in labor controversies should have given rise to a series of adjudications in this Court relating to the limitations on state action contained in the provisions of the Due Process Clause of the Fourteenth Amendment. It is also not too surprising that examination of these adjudications should disclose an evolving, not a static, course of decision.

The series begins with Truax v. Corrigan, 257 U.S. 312 (1921), in which a closely divided Court found it to be violative of the Equal Protection Clause — not of the Due Process Clause — for a State to deny use of the injunction in the special class of cases arising out of the labor conflicts. The considerations that underlay that case soon had to yield, through legislation and later through litigation, to the persuasiveness of undermining facts. Thus, to remedy the abusive use of the injunction in the federal courts (see Frankfurter and Greene, The Labor Injunction), the Norris-La Guardia Act, 47 Stat. 70, 29 U.S.C. § 101, withdrew, subject to qualifications, jurisdiction from the federal courts to issue injunctions in labor disputes to prohibit certain acts. Its example was widely followed by state enactments.

Apart from remedying the abuses of the injunction in this general type of litigation, legislatures and courts began to find in one of the aims of picketing an aspect of communication. This view came to the fore in Senn v. Tile Layers Union, 301 U.S. 468 (1937), where the Court held that the Fourteenth Amendment did not prohibit Wisconsin from authorizing peaceful stranger picketing by a union that was attempting to unionize a shop and to induce an employer to refrain from working in his business as a laborer.

Although the Court had been closely divided in the *Senn* case, three years later, in passing on a restrictive instead of a permissive state statute, the Court made sweeping pronouncements about the right to picket in holding unconstitutional a statute that had been applied to ban all picketing, with "no exceptions based upon either the number of persons engaged in the proscribed activity, the peaceful character of their demeanor, the nature of their dispute with an employer, or the restrained character and the accurateness of the terminology used in notifying the public of the facts of the dispute." Thornhill v. Alabama, 310 U.S. 88, 99 (1940). As the statute dealt at large with all picketing, so the Court broadly assimilated peaceful picketing in general to freedom of speech, and as such protected against abridgement by the Fourteenth Amendment.

These principles were applied by the Court in AFL v. Swing, 312 U.S. 321 (1941), to hold unconstitutional an injunction against peaceful picketing, based on a State's common-law policy against picketing when there was no immediate dispute between employer and employee. On the same day, however, the Court upheld a generalized injunction against picketing where there had been violence because "it could justifiably be concluded that the momentum of fear generated by past violence would survive even though future picketing might be wholly peaceful." Milk Wagon Drivers Union v. Meadowmoor Dairies, 312 U.S. 287, 294 (1941).

Soon, however, the Court came to realize that the broad pronouncements, but not the specific holding, of *Thornhill* had to yield "to the impact of facts unforeseen," or at least not sufficiently appreciated. Cf. People v. Charles Schweinler Press, 214 N.Y. 395, 108 N.E. 639 (1915), 28 Harv. L. Rev. 790. Cases reached the Court in which a State had designed a remedy to meet a specific situation or to accomplish a particular social policy. These cases made manifest that picketing, even though "peaceful," involved more than just communication of ideas and could not be immune from all state regulation. "Picketing by an organized group is more than free speech, since it involves patrol of a particular locality and since the very presence of a picket line may induce action of one kind or another, quite irrespective of the nature of the ideas which are being disseminated." Bakery and Pastry Drivers Local v. Wohl, 315 U.S. 769, 776 (1942) (concurring opinion); see Carpenters and Joiners Union v. Ritter's Cafe, 315 U.S. 722, 725-728 (1942).

These latter two cases required the Court to review a choice made by two States between the competing interests of unions, employers, their employees, and the public at large. In the *Ritter's Cafe* case, Texas had enjoined as a violation of its antitrust law picketing of a restaurant by unions to bring pressure on its owner with respect to the use of nonunion labor by a contractor of the restaurant owner in the construction of a building having nothing to do with the restaurant. The Court held that Texas could, consistent with the Fourteenth Amendment, insulate from the dispute a neutral establishment that industrially had no connection with it. This type of picketing certainly involved little, if any, "communication."

In Bakery and Pastry Drivers Local v. Wohl, 315 U.S. 769 (1942), in a very narrowly restricted decision, the Court held that because of the impossibility of otherwise publicizing a legitimate grievance and because of the slight effect on "strangers" to the dispute, a State could not constitutionally prohibit a union from picketing bakeries in its efforts to have independent peddlers, buying from bakers and selling to small stores, conform to certain union requests. Although the Court in *Ritter's Cafe* and *Wohl* did not question the holding of *Thornhill,* the strong reliance on the particular facts in each case demonstrated a growing awareness that these cases involved not so much questions of free speech as review of the balance struck by a State between picketing that involved more than "publicity" and competing interests of state policy. (See also Cafeteria Employees Union v. Angelos, 320 U.S. 293 (1943), where the Court reviewed a New York injunction against picketing by a union of a restaurant that was run by the owners without employees. The New York court appeared to have justified an injunction on the alternate grounds that there was no "labor dispute" under the New York statute or that use of untruthful placards justified the injunction. We held, in a brief opinion, that the abuses alleged did not justify an injunction against all picketing and that *AFL v. Swing* governed the alternate ground for decision.)

The implied reassessments of the broad language of the *Thornhill* case were finally generalized in a series of cases sustaining injunctions against peaceful picketing, even when arising in the course of a labor controversy, when such picketing was counter to valid state policy in a domain open to state regulation. The decisive reconsideration comes in Giboney v. Empire Storage & Ice Co., 336 U.S. 490 (1949). A union, seeking to organize peddlers, picketed a wholesale dealer to induce it to refrain from selling to nonunion peddlers. The state courts, finding that such an agreement would constitute a conspiracy in restraint of trade in violation of the state antitrust laws, enjoined the picketing. This Court affirmed unanimously.... The Court ... concluded that it was "clear that appellants were doing more than exercising a right of free speech or press.... They were exercising their economic power together with that of their allies to compel Empire to abide by union rather than by state regulation of trade." Id. 336 U.S. at page 503.

The following Term, the Court decided a group of cases applying and elaborating on the theory of Giboney. In Hughes v. Superior Court, 339 U.S. 460 (1950), the Court held that the Fourteenth Amendment did not bar use of the injunction to prohibit picketing of a place of business solely to secure compliance with a demand that its employees be hired in percentage to the racial origin of its customers. "We cannot construe the Due Process Clause as prohibiting California from securing respect for its policy against involuntary employment on racial lines by prohibiting systematic picketing that would subvert such policy." Id. 339 U.S. at page 466. The Court also found it immaterial that the state policy had been expressed by the judiciary rather than by the legislature.

On the same day, the Court decided International Brotherhood of Teamsters Union v. Hanke, 339 U.S. 470 (1950), holding that a State was not restrained by the Fourteenth Amendment from enjoining picketing of a business, conducted by the owner himself without employees, in order to secure compliance with a demand to become a union shop. Although there was no one opinion for the Court, its decision was another instance of the affirmance of an injunction against picketing because directed against a valid public policy of the State.

A third case, Building Service Employees v. Gazzam, 339 U.S. 532 (1950), was decided the same day. Following an unsuccessful attempt at unionization of a small hotel and refusal by the owner to sign a contract with the union as bargaining agent, the union began to picket the hotel with signs stating that the owner was unfair to organized labor. The State, finding that the object of the picketing was in violation of its statutory policy against employer coercion of employees' choice of bargaining representative, enjoined picketing for such purpose. This Court affirmed, rejecting the argument that "the Swing case, supra, is controlling.... In that case this Court struck down the State's restraint of picketing based solely on the absence of an employer-employee relationship. An adequate basis for the instant decree is the unlawful objective of the picketing, namely, coercion by the employer of the employees' selection of a bargaining representative. Peaceful picketing for any lawful purpose is not prohibited by the decree under review." Id. 339 U.S. at page 539.

A similar problem was involved in Plumbers Union, Local 10 v. Graham, 345 U.S. 192 (1953), where a state court had enjoined, as a violation of its "Right to Work" law, picketing that advertised that nonunion men were being employed on a building job. This Court found that there was evidence in the record supporting a conclusion that a substantial purpose of the picketing was to put pressure on the general contractor to eliminate nonunion men from the job and, on the reasoning of the cases that we have just discussed, held that the injunction was not in conflict with the Fourteenth Amendment.

This series of cases, then, established a broad field in which a State, in enforcing some public policy, whether of its criminal or its civil law, and whether announced by its legislature or its courts, could constitutionally enjoin peaceful picketing aimed at preventing effectuation of that policy.

In the light of this background, the Maine Supreme Judicial Court in 1955 decided, on an agreed statement of facts, the case of Pappas v. Stacey, 151 Me. 36, 116 A.2d 497, 498 (1955). From the statement, it appeared that three union employees went on strike, and picketed a restaurant peacefully "for the sole purpose of seeking to organize other employees of the Plaintiff, ultimately to have the Plaintiff enter into collective bargaining and negotiations with the Union. . . ." Maine had a statute providing that workers should have full liberty of self-organization, free from restraint by employers or other persons. [R.S. 1954, ch. 30, § 15] The Maine Supreme Judicial Court drew the inference from the agreed statement of facts that "there is a steady and exacting pressure upon the employer to interfere with the free choice of the employees in the matter of organization. To say that the picketing is not designed to bring about such action is to forget an obvious purpose of the picketing — to cause economic loss to the business during noncompliance by the employees with the requests of the union." 151 Me. at 42, 116 A.2d at 500. It therefore enjoined the picketing, and an appeal was taken to this Court.

The whole series of cases discussed above allowing, as they did, wide discretion to a State in the formulation of domestic policy, and not involving a curtailment of free speech in its obvious and accepted scope, led this Court without the need of further argument, to grant appellee's motion to dismiss the appeal in that it no longer presented a substantial federal question. 350 U.S. 870.

The *Stacey* case is this case. As in *Stacey,* the present case was tried without oral testimony. As in *Stacey,* the highest state court drew the inference from the facts that the picketing was to coerce the employer to put pressure on his employees to join the union, in violation of the declared policy of the State. (For a declaration of similar congressional policy, see § 8 of the Taft-Hartley Act, 61 Stat. 140, 29 U.S.C. § 158). The cases discussed above all hold that, consistent with the Fourteenth Amendment, a State may enjoin such conduct.

Of course, the mere fact that there is "picketing" does not automatically justify its restraint without an investigation into its conduct and purposes. State courts, no more than state legislatures, can enact blanket prohibitions against picketing. Thornhill v. Alabama and AFL v. Swing, *supra.* The series of cases following *Thornhill* and *Swing* demonstrate that the policy of Wisconsin enforced by the prohibition of this picketing is a valid one. In this case, the circumstances set forth in the opinion of the Wisconsin Supreme Court afford a rational basis for the inference it drew concerning the purpose of the picketing. No question was raised here concerning the breadth of the injunction, but of course its terms must be read in the light of the opinion of the Wisconsin Supreme Court, which justified it on the ground that the picketing was for the purpose of coercing the employer to coerce his employees. "If astuteness may discover argumentative excess in the scope of the [injunction] beyond what we constitutionally justify by this opinion, it will be open to petitioners to raise the matter, which they have not raised here, when the [case] on remand [reaches] the [Wisconsin] court." Teamsters Union v. Hanke, 399 U.S. at 480-481.

Therefore, having deemed it appropriate to elaborate on the issues in the case, we affirm.

Affirmed.

MR. JUSTICE WHITTAKER took no part in the consideration or decision of this case.

MR. JUSTICE DOUGLAS, with whom THE CHIEF JUSTICE and MR. JUSTICE BLACK concur, dissenting.

The Court has now come full circle. In Thornhill v. Alabama, 310 U.S. 88, 102 (1940), we struck down a state ban on picketing on the ground that "the dissemination of information concerning the facts of a labor dispute must be regarded as within that area of free discussion that is guaranteed by the Constitution." Less than one year later, we held that the First Amendment protected organizational picketing on a factual record which cannot be distinguished from the one now before us. AFL v. Swing, 312 U.S. 321 (1941). Of course, we have always recognized that picketing has aspects which make it more than speech. Bakery Drivers Local v. Wohl, 315 U.S. 769, 776-777 (1942) (concurring opinion). That difference underlies our decision in Giboney v. Empire Storage & Ice Co., 336 U.S. 490 (1949). There, picketing was an essential part of "a single and integrated course of conduct, which was in violation of Missouri's valid law." *Id.* 336 U.S. at page 498. And see NLRB v. Virginia Power Co., 314 U.S. 469, 477-478 (1941). We emphasized that "there was clear danger, imminent and immediate, that unless restrained, appellants would succeed in making [the state] policy a dead letter. . . ." 336 U.S. at page 503. Speech there was enjoined because it was an inseparable part of conduct which the State constitutionally could and did regulate.

But where, as here, there is no rioting, no mass picketing, no violence, no disorder, no fisticuffs, no coercion — indeed nothing but speech — the principles announced in *Thornhill* and *Swing* should give the advocacy of one side of a dispute First Amendment protection.

The retreat began when, in Teamsters Union v. Hanke, 339 U.S. 470 (1950), four members of the Court announced that all picketing could be prohibited if a state court decided that that picketing violated the State's public policy. The retreat became a rout in Plumbers Union, Local 10 v. Graham, 345 U.S. 192 (1953). It was only the "purpose" of the picketing which was relevant. The state court's characterization of the picketers' "purpose" had been made well-nigh conclusive. Considerations of the proximity of picketing to conduct which the State could control or prevent were abandoned, and no longer was it necessary for the state court's decree to be narrowly drawn to prescribe a specific evil. *Id.* 345 U.S. at pages 201-205 (dissenting opinion).

Today, the Court signs the formal surrender. State courts and state legislatures cannot fashion blanket prohibitions on all picketing. But, for practical purposes, the situation now is as it was when Senn v. Tile Layers Union, 301 U.S. 468 (1937), was decided. State courts and state legislatures are free to decide whether to permit or suppress any particular picket line for any reason other than a blanket policy against all picketing. I would adhere to the principle announced in *Thornhill.* I would adhere to the result reached in *Swing.* I would return to the test enunciated in *Giboney* — that this form of expression can be regulated or prohibited only to the extent that it forms an essential part of a course of conduct which the State can regulate or prohibit. I would reverse the judgment below.

NOTES

1. For discussions of the *Vogt* case and its predecessors, see Cox, *Strikes, Picketing, and the Constitution,* 4 VAND. L. REV. 574 (1951); Gregory, *Peaceful Picketing and Freedom of Speech,* 26 A.B.A.J. 709 (1940); Farmer & Williamson, *Picketing and the Injunctive Power of State Courts — From Thornhill to Vogt,* 35 U. DET. L.J. 431 (1958); Samoff, *Picketing and the First Amendment: "Full Circle" and "Formal Surrender,"* 9 LAB. L.J. 889 (1958); Note, *Stranger Picketing and the Vogt Case,* 1958 WIS. L. REV. 154. For two excellent but contradictory analyses of the problem of picketing and free speech, see Gregory, *Constitutional Limitations on the Regulation of Union and Employer Conduct,* 49 MICH. L. REV. 191 (1950); and Jones, *Free Speech: Pickets on the Grass, Alas!, Amidst Confusion, a Consistent Principle,* 29 S. CAL. L. REV. 137 (1956).

2. "It is now, of course, obvious that the Supreme Court has found room, despite *Thornhill,* for the application to picketing of the venerable, if sometimes maligned, common law and legislative ends-means test. One may wonder, in retrospect, why the Court in 1940 elected to use the 'free speech' analysis as a means of circumscribing regulatory action. That which, in the *Thornhill* opinion of Justice Murphy was regarded as the most practicable and effective means of publicizing a labor dispute now is said to contain but an 'element' or 'ingredient' of 'communication,' and to embody 'inherent' 'compulsive features' which make it subject to regulation. The communication aspect of picketing appears to have been so subordinated that the civil rights and 'substantive due process' constitutional tests have become fairly indistinguishable, and thus negligible, in their impact. As in the case of the problem of emergency disputes, the influence of this current attitude of the Court is to force attention upon the totality of policy considerations which should, in balance, determine the extent and nature of the legal privilege to picket.

"Like many if not most other observers, I have tended to regard as sound the Court's more recent emphasis, for constitutional purposes, upon the coercive aspects of picketing. Yet, I have the uncomfortable feeling that we have not fully thought through or seen the implications of this approach. That which makes peaceful picketing possibly objectionable, hence actionable, is not the picketing, itself, provided it is peaceful, but the responses of others (employees of the picketed employer or of other employers or, for example, customers) to the picket line. The Court seems even today to assume that the unions have a constitutional right to use the ordinary media of communication (radio, press pamphlets, etc.) to advertise the existence of a dispute; yet it is obvious that, depending upon the sympathies and *mores* of the community, such publicity may result in responses of the kind elicited by picketing. Will the Court ultimately, then, be driven to conclude that these non-picketing means of publicizing a union aim or complaint may be enjoined if the objective is reasonably deemed to be improper?" Smith, *The Supreme Court and Labor, 1950-1953,* 8 Sw. L.J. 1, 9-11 (1954).

3. It should be emphasized that, although the Supreme Court made sweeping pronouncements about the right to picket in the landmark *Thornhill* case, the holding was a narrow one. The Alabama courts had made it clear that they would apply their criminal statute to prohibit a single individual from walking slowly back and forth on the public sidewalk in front of the premises of an employer, without speaking to anyone, carrying a sign or placard on a staff above his head, stating only the fact that the employer did not employ union men. Since the statute, as authoritatively construed and applied, left no room for exceptions, the Court held it to be invalid on its face.

4. *The Constitutional Status of Strikes* — The right to strike has never had its *Thornhill* case. In other words, the Supreme Court has never held state or federal regulation of strikes unconstitutional on "civil rights" grounds. Yet, it can hardly be doubted that, in the union hierarchy of values the "right" to strike ranks higher than the "right" to picket.

In Stapleton v. Mitchell, 60 F. Supp. 51 (D. Kan. 1945), a three-judge court held invalid a Kansas statute which imposed the requirement of a majority vote for a strike, and the court referred to "the right to peaceably strike" as among the "fundamental human liberties."

But in UAW-AFL, Local 232 v. WERB, 336 U.S. 245 (1949), the Supreme Court upheld a state order against intermittent, unannounced work stoppages (quickie strikes) against constitutional challenge under the fourteenth amendment. Mr. Justice Jackson in discussing § 13 of the NLRA, commented:

"This Court less than a decade earlier [than the Wagner Act] had stated that law to be that the state constitutionally could prohibit strikes and make a violation criminal. It had unanimously adopted the language of Mr. Justice Brandeis that 'Neither the common law, nor the Fourteenth

Amendment, confers the absolute right to strike,' Dorchy v. Kansas, 272 U.S. 306, 311. Dissenting views most favorable to labor in other cases had conceded the right of the state legislature to mark the limits of tolerable industrial conflict in the public interest. Duplex Co. v. Deering, 254 U.S. 443, 488. This court has adhered to that view. Thornhill v. Alabama, 310 U.S. 88, 103. The right to strike, because of its more serious impact upon the public interest, is more vulnerable to regulation than the right to organize and select representatives for lawful purposes of collective bargaining which this Court has characterized as a 'fundamental right.' " 336 U.S. at 259.

5. Would an injunction or a statute outlawing strikes run afoul of the thirteenth amendment which prohibits involuntary servitude? The Supreme Court considered this question in the *UAW-AFL* case above, saying:

"The Union contends that the statute, as thus applied, violates the Thirteenth Amendment in that it imposes a form of compulsory service or involuntary servitude. However, nothing in the statute or the order makes it a crime to abandon work individually (Compare Pollock v. Williams, 322 U.S. 4), or collectively. Nor does either undertake to prohibit or restrict any employee from leaving the service of the employer, either for reason or without reason, either with or without notice. The facts afford no foundation for the contention that any action of the State has the purpose or effect of imposing any form of involuntary servitude." 336 U.S. at 251.

6. In Postal Clerks v. Blount, 325 F. Supp. 879 (D.D.C. 1971), a three-judge federal court said: "At common law no employee, whether public or private, had a constitutional right to strike in concert with his fellow workers. Indeed, such collective action on the part of employees was often held to be a conspiracy. When the right of private employees to strike finally received full protection, it was by statute, Section 7 of the National Labor Relations Act, which 'took this conspiracy weapon away from the employer in employment relations which affect interstate commerce' and guaranteed to employees in the private sector the right to engage in concerted activities for the purpose of collective bargaining. . . . It seems clear that public employees stand on no stronger footing in this regard than private employees and that in the absence of a statute, they too do not possess the right to strike. . . . Given the fact that there is no constitutional right to strike, it is not irrational or arbitrary for the Government to . . . prohibit strikes by those in public employment. . . ."

Judge J. Skelly Wright concurred in the result. However, he stated that the question is a very difficult one and that "it is by no means clear to me that the right to strike is not fundamental. The right to strike seems intimately related to the right to form labor organizations, a right which the majority recognizes as fundamental and which, more importantly, is generally thought to be constitutionally protected under the First Amendment — even for public employees. . . . If the inherent purpose of a labor organization is to bring the workers' interests to bear on management, the right to strike is, historically and practically, an important means of effectuating that purpose. A union that never strikes, or which can make no credible threat to strike, may wither away in ineffectiveness. That fact is not irrelevant to the constitutional calculations. . . . I do believe that the right to strike is, at least, within constitutional concern. . . ."

The Supreme Court affirmed the decision and upheld a ban on strikes by federal employees without hearing argument or writing an opinion. 404 U.S. 802 (1971). Mr. Justice Douglas thought the case should be set for oral argument.

A federal government order against all picketing during a labor controversy between the Internal Revenue Service and its employees was held to violate the First Amendment. National Treasury Employees Union v. Fasser, 428 F. Supp. 295 (D.D.C. 1976). The court concluded that confined, informational picketing "does not in all situations create the probability of interference with Government functions sufficient to justify the limitation on free speech involved here."

7. State legislation requiring strike votes and prohibiting strikes in public utilities has been held unconstitutional by the Supreme Court on the ground that it conflicted with the Taft-Hartley Act. Amalgamated Ass'n of Street, Elec. Ry. & Motor Coach Employees, Div. 1287 v. Missouri, 374 U.S. 74 (1963) (statute forbidding strikes after seizure by the state); Amalgamated Ass'n of Street Elec. Ry. & Motor Coach Employees, Div. 998 v. WERB, 340 U.S. 383 (1951); International Union of UAW-CIO v. O'Brien, 339 U.S. 454 (1950). This federal-state problem will be considered further, *infra* at 438.

HUDGENS v. NLRB

Supreme Court of the United States
424 U.S. 507, 96 S. Ct. 1029, 47 L. Ed. 2d 128 (1976)

MR. JUSTICE STEWART delivered the opinion of the Court.

A group of labor union members who engaged in peaceful primary picketing within the confines of a privately owned shopping center were threatened by an agent of the owner with arrest for criminal trespass if they did not depart. The question presented is whether this threat violated the National Labor Relations Act, as amended 61 Stat. 136, 29 U. S. C. § 151 *et seq.* The National Labor Relations Board concluded that it did, 205 N.L.R.B. 628, and the Court of Appeals for the Fifth Circuit agreed. 501 F.2d 161. We granted certiorari because of the seemingly important questions of federal law presented. 420 U. S. 971.

I. The petitioner, Scott Hudgens, is the owner of the North DeKalb Shopping Center, located in suburban Atlanta, Ga. The center consists of a single large building with an enclosed mall. Surrounding the building is a parking area which can accommodate 2,640 automobiles. The shopping center houses 60 retail stores leased to various businesses. One of the lessees is the Butler Shoe Company. Most of the stores, including Butler's, can be entered only from the interior mall.

In January 1971, warehouse employees of the Butler Shoe Company went on strike to protest the company's failure to agree to demands made by their union in contract negotiations.[1] The strikers decided to picket not only Butler's warehouse but its nine retail stores in the Atlanta area as well, including the store in the North DeKalb Shopping Center. On January 22, 1971, four of the striking warehouse employees entered the center's enclosed mall carrying placards which read, "Butler Shoe Warehouse on Strike, AFL-CIO, Local 315." The general manager of the shopping center informed the employees that they could not picket within the mall or on the parking lot and threatened them with arrest if they did not leave. The employees departed but returned a short time later and began picketing in an area of the mall immediately adjacent to the entrances of the Butler store. After the picketing had continued for approximately 30 minutes, the shopping center manager again informed the picketers that if they did not leave they would be arrested for trespassing. The picketers departed.

The union subsequently filed with the Board an unfair labor practice charge against Hudgens, alleging interference with rights protected by § 7 of the Act, 29 U. S. C. § 157. Relying on this Court's decision in Amalgamated Food Employees Union, Local 590 v. Logan Valley Plaza, Inc., 391 U. S. 308, the Board entered a cease-and-desist order against Hudgens, reasoning that because the warehouse employees enjoyed a First Amendment right to picket on the shopping center property, the owner's threat of arrest violated § 8(a)(1) of the Act.[3] Hudgens filed a petition for review in the Court of Appeals for the Fifth Circuit. Soon thereafter this Court decided Lloyd Corp. v. Tanner, 407 U. S. 551, and Central Hardware Co. v. NLRB, 407 U. S. 539, and the Court of Appeals remanded the case to the Board for reconsideration in the light of those two decisions.

The Board, in turn, remanded to an administrative law judge, who made findings of fact, recommendations and conclusions to the effect that Hudgens had committed an unfair labor practice by excluding the picketers. This result was ostensibly reached under the statutory criteria set forth in NLRB v. Babcock & Wilcox Co., 351 U. S. 105, a case which held that union organizers who seek to solicit for union membership may intrude on an employer's private property if no alternative means exist for communicating with the employees. But the administrative law judge's opinion also relied on this Court's constitutional decision in *Logan Valley*

---

[1] The Butler warehouse was not located within the North DeKalb Shopping Center.

[3] Hudgens v. Local 315, Retail, Wholesale and Department Store Union, 192 N. L. R. B. 671 (1971). . . . While Hudgens was not the employer of the employees involved in this case, it seems to be undisputed that he was an employer engaged in commerce within the meaning of § 2(6) and (7) of the Act. The Board has held that a statutory "employer" may violate § 8(a)(1) with respect to employees other than his own. See *Austin Co.,* 101 N. L. R. B. 1257, 1258-1259. See also § 2(13) of the Act.

for a "realistic view of the facts." The Board agreed with the findings and recommendation of the administrative law judge, but departed somewhat from his reasoning. It concluded that the picketers were within the scope of Hudgens' invitation to members of the public to do business at the shopping center, and that it was, therefore, immaterial whether or not there existed an alternative means of communicating with the customers and employees of the Butler store.[4]

Hudgens again petitioned for review in the Court of Appeals for the Fifth Circuit, and there the Board changed its tack and urged that the case was controlled not by *Babcock & Wilcox,* but by Republic Aviation Corp. v. NLRB, 324 U. S. 793, a case which held that an employer commits an unfair labor practice if he enforces a no-solicitation rule against employees on his premises who are also union organizers, unless he can prove that the rule is necessitated by special circumstances. The Court of Appeals enforced the Board's cease-and-desist order but on the basis of yet another theory. While acknowledging that the source of the picketers' rights was § 7 of the Act, the Court of Appeals held that the competing constitutional and property right considerations discussed in *Lloyd Corp. v. Tanner, supra,* "burde[n] the General Counsel with the duty to prove that other locations less intrusive upon Hudgens' property rights than picketing inside the mall were either unavailable or ineffective," 501 F.2d, at 169, and that the Board's General Counsel had met that burden in this case.

In this Court the petitioner Hudgens continues to urge that *Babcock & Wilcox Co.* is the controlling precedent, and that under the criteria of that case the judgment of the Court of Appeals should be reversed. The respondent union agrees that a statutory standard governs, but insists that, since the § 7 activity here was not organizational as in *Babcock* but picketing in support of a lawful economic strike, an appropriate accommodation of the competing interests must lead to an affirmance of the Court of Appeals' judgment. The respondent Board now contends that the conflict between employee picketing rights and employer property rights in a case like this must be measured in accord with the commands of the First Amendment, pursuant to the Board's asserted understanding of *Lloyd Corp. v. Tanner, supra,* and that the judgment of the Court of Appeals should be affirmed on the basis of that standard.

II. As the above recital discloses, the history of this litigation has been a history of shifting positions on the part of the litigants, the Board, and the Court of Appeals. It has been a history, in short, of considerable confusion, engendered at least in part by decisions of this Court that intervened during the course of the litigation. In the present posture of the case the most basic question is whether the respective rights and liabilities of the parties are to be decided under the criteria of the National Labor Relations Act alone, under a First Amendment standard, or under

---

[4] Hudgens v. Local 315, Retail, Wholesale and Department Store Union, 205 N. L. R. B. 628 (1973).

some combination of the two. It is to that question, accordingly, that we now turn.

It is, of course, a commonplace that the constitutional guarantee of free speech is a guarantee only against abridgment by government, federal or state. *See* Columbia Broadcasting System, Inc. v. Democratic National Committee, 412 U. S. 94. Thus, while statutory or common law may in some situations extend protection or provide redress against a private corporation or person who seeks to abridge the free expression of others, no such protection or redress is provided by the Constitution itself.

This elementary proposition is little more than a truism. But even truisms are not always unexceptionably true, and an exception to this one was recognized almost 30 years ago in the case Marsh v. Alabama, 326 U. S. 501. In *Marsh,* a Jehovah's Witness who had distributed literature without a license on a sidewalk in Chickasaw, Ala., was convicted of criminal trespass. Chickasaw was a so-called company town, wholly owned by the Gulf Shipbuilding Corporation. It was described in the Court's opinion as follows:

> "Except for [ownership by a private corporation] it has all the characteristics of any American town. The property consists of residential buildings, streets, a system of sewers, a sewage disposal plant and a 'business block' on which business places are situated. A deputy of the Mobile County Sheriff, paid by the company, serves as the town's policeman. Merchants and service establishments have rented the stores and business places on the business block and the United States uses one of the places as a post office from which six carriers deliver mail to the people of Chickasaw and the adjacent area. The town and the surrounding neighborhood, which can not be distinguished from the Gulf property by anyone not familiar with the property lines, are thickly settled, and according to all indications the residents use the business block as their regular shopping center. To do so, they now, as they have for many years, make use of a company-owned paved street and sidewalk located alongside the store fronts in order to enter and leave the stores and the post office. Intersecting company-owned roads at each end of the business block lead into a four-lane public highway which runs parallel to the business block at a distance of thirty feet. There is nothing to stop highway traffic from coming onto the business block and upon arrival a traveler may make free use of the facilities available there. In short the town and its shopping district are accessible to and freely used by the public in general and there is nothing to distinguish them from any other town and shopping center except the fact that the title to the property belongs to a private corporation." 326 U. S., at 502-503.

The Court pointed out that if the "title" to Chickasaw had "belonged not to a private but to a municipal corporation and had appellant been arrested for violating a municipal ordinance rather than a ruling by those appointed by the corporation to manage a company town it would have been clear that appellant's conviction must be reversed." 326 U. S., at 504.

Concluding that Gulf's "property interests" should not be allowed to lead to a different result in Chickasaw, which did "not function differently from any other town," 326 U. S., at 506-508, the Court invoked the First and Fourteenth Amendments to reverse the appellant's conviction.

It was the *Marsh* case that in 1968 provided the foundation for the Court's decision in Amalgamated Food Employees Union Local 590 v. Logan Valley Plaza, Inc., 391 U. S. 308. That case involved peaceful picketing within a large shopping center near Altoona, Pa. One of the tenants of the shopping center was a retail store that employed a wholly nonunion staff. Members of a local union picketed the store, carrying signs proclaiming that it was nonunion and that its employees were not receiving union wages or other union benefits. The picketing took place on the shopping center's property in the immediate vicinity of the store. A Pennsylvania court issued an injunction that required all picketing to be confined to public areas outside the shopping center, and the Supreme Court of Pennsylvania affirmed the issuance of this injunction. This Court held that the doctrine of the *Marsh* case required reversal of that judgment.

The Court's opinion pointed out that the First and Fourteenth Amendments would clearly have protected the picketing if it had taken place on a public sidewalk:

> "It is clear that if the shopping center premises were not privately owned but instead constituted the business area of a municipality, which they to a large extent resemble, petitioners could not be barred from exercising their First Amendment rights there on the sole ground that title to the property was in the municipality. Lovell v. Griffin, 303 U. S. 444 (1938); Hague v. CIO, 307 U. S. 496 (1939); Schneider v. State, 308 U. S. 147 (1939); Jamison v. Texas, 318 U. S. 413 (1943). The essence of those opinions is that streets, sidewalks, parks, and other similar public places are so historically associated with the exercise of First Amendment rights that access to them for the purpose of exercising such rights cannot constitutionally be denied broadly and absolutely." 391 U. S., at 315.

The Court's opinion then reviewed the *Marsh* case in detail, emphasized the similarities between the business block in Chickasaw, Ala., and the Logan Valley shopping center, and unambiguously concluded:

> "The shopping center here is clearly the functional equivalent of the business district of Chickasaw involved in *Marsh.*" 391 U. S., at 318.

Upon the basis of that conclusion, the Court held that the First and Fourteenth Amendments required reversal of the judgment of the Pennsylvania Supreme Court.

There were three dissenting opinions in the *Logan Valley* case, one of them by the author of the Court's opinion in *Marsh,* Mr. Justice Black. His disagreement with the Court's reasoning was total:

"In affirming petitioners' contentions the majority opinion relies on *Marsh v. Alabama, supra,* and holds that respondents' property has been transformed to some type of public property. But *Marsh* was never intended to apply to this kind of situation. *Marsh* dealt with the very special situation of a company-owned town, complete with streets, alleys, sewers, stores, residences, and everything else that goes to make a town. . . . I can find very little resemblance between the shopping center involved in this case and Chickasaw, Alabama. There are no homes, there is no sewage disposal plant, there is not even a post office on this private property which the Court now considers the equivalent of a 'town'." 391 U. S., at 330-331 (footnote omitted).

. . . .

"The question is, Under what circumstances can private property be treated as though it were public? The answer that *Marsh* gives is when that property has taken on *all* the attributes of a town, *i.e.,* 'residential buildings, streets, a system of sewers, a sewage disposal plant and a "business block" on which business places are situated.' 326 U. S., at 502. I can find nothing in *Marsh* which indicates that if one of these features is present, *e.g.,* a business district, this is sufficient for the Court to confiscate a part of an owner's private property and give its use to people who want to picket on it." 391 U. S., at 332.

. . . .

"To hold that store owners are compelled by law to supply picketing areas for pickets to drive store customers away is to create a court-made law wholly disregarding the constitutional basis on which private ownership of property rests in this country. . . ." 391 U. S., at 332-333.

Four years later the Court had occasion to reconsider the *Logan Valley* doctrine in Lloyd Corp. v. Tanner, 407 U. S. 551. That case involved a shopping center covering some 50 acres in downtown Portland, Ore. On a November day in 1968 five young people entered the mall of the shopping center and distributed handbills protesting the then ongoing American military operations in Vietnam. Security guards told them to leave, and they did so, "to avoid arrest." 407 U. S., at 556. They subsequently brought suit in a federal district court, seeking declaratory and injunctive relief. The trial court ruled in their favor, holding that the distribution of handbills on the shopping center's property was protected by the First and Fourteenth Amendments. The Court of Appeals for the Ninth Circuit affirmed the judgment, 446 F. 2d 545, expressly relying on this Court's *Marsh* and *Logan Valley* decisions. This Court reversed the judgment of the Court of Appeals.

The Court in its *Lloyd* opinion did not say that it was overruling the *Logan Valley* decision. Indeed, a substantial portion of the Court's opinion in *Lloyd* was devoted to pointing out the differences between the two cases, noting particularly that, in contrast to the handbilling in *Lloyd,* the picketing in *Logan Valley* had been specifically directed to a store in the shopping center and the picketers had had no other reasonable opportunity to reach their intended audience. 407 U. S., at 561-567. But the fact is that the reasoning of the Court's opinion in *Lloyd* cannot be squared with the reasoning of the Court's opinion in *Logan Valley.*

It matters not that some members of the Court may continue to believe that the *Logan Valley* case was rightly decided. Our institutional duty is to follow until changed the law as it now is, not as some members of the Court might wish it to be. And in the performance of that duty *we make clear now,* if it was not clear before, *that the rationale of Logan Valley did not survive the Court's decision in the Lloyd case.* Not only did the *Lloyd* opinion incorporate lengthy excerpts from two of the dissenting opinions in *Logan Valley,* 407 U. S., at 562-563, 565; the ultimate holding in *Lloyd* amounted to a total rejection of the holding in *Logan Valley.*

> "The basic issue in this case is whether respondents, in the exercise of asserted First Amendment rights, may distribute handbills on Lloyd's private property contrary to its wishes and contrary to a policy enforced against *all* handbilling. In addressing this issue, it must be remembered that the First and Fourteenth Amendments safeguard the rights of free speech and assembly by limitations on *state* action, not on action by the owner of private property used nondiscriminatorily for private purposes only. . . ." 407 U. S., at 567.

> . . . .

> "Respondents contend . . . that the property of a large shopping center is 'open to the public,' serves the same purposes as a 'business district' of a municipality, and therefore has been dedicated to certain types of public use. The argument is that such a center has sidewalks, streets, and parking areas which are functionally similar to facilities customarily provided by municipalities. It is then asserted that all members of the public, whether invited as customers or not, have the same right of free speech as they would have on the similar public facilities in the streets of a city or town.

> "The argument reaches too far. The Constitution by no means requires such an attenuated doctrine of dedication of private property to public use. The closest decision in theory, *Marsh v. Alabama, supra,* involved the assumption by a private enterprise of all of the attributes of a state-created municipality and the exercise by that enterprise of semi-official municipal functions as a delegate of the State. In effect, the owner of the company town was performing the full spectrum of municipal powers and stood in the shoes of the State. In the instant case there is no comparable assumption or exercise of municipal functions or power." 407 U. S., at 568-569 (footnote omitted).

> . . . .

> "We hold that there has been no such dedication of Lloyd's privately owned and operated shopping center to public use as to entitle respondents to exercise therein the asserted First Amendment rights. . . ." 407 U. S., at 570.

If a large self-contained shopping center *is* the functional equivalent of a municipality, as *Logan Valley* held, then the First and Fourteenth Amendments would not permit control of speech within such a center to depend upon the speech's content. For while a municipality may constitutionally impose reasonable time, place, and manner regulations on the use of its streets and sidewalks for First Amendment purposes, see Cox v. New Hampshire, 312 U. S. 569; Poulos v. New Hampshire, 345 U. S. 395, and may even forbid altogether such use of some of its facilities, see Adderley v. Florida, 385 U. S. 39, what a municipality may *not* do under the First and Fourteenth Amendments is to discriminate in the regulation of expression on the basis of the content of that expression. Erznoznik v. City of Jacksonville, 422 U. S. 205. "[A]bove all else, the First Amendment means that government has no power to restrict expression because of its message, its ideas, its subject matter, or its content." Police Department of Chicago v. Mosley, 408 U. S. 92, 95. It conversely follows, therefore, that if the respondents in the *Lloyd* case did not have a First Amendment right to enter that shopping center to distribute handbills concerning Vietnam, then the respondents in the present case did not have a First Amendment right to enter this shopping center for the purpose of advertising their strike against the Butler Shoe Company.

We conclude, in short, that under the present state of the law the constitutional guarantee of free expression has no part to play in a case such as this.

III. From what has been said it follows that the rights and liabilities of the parties in this case are dependent exclusively upon the National Labor Relations Act. Under the Act the task of the Board, subject to review by the courts, is to resolve conflicts between § 7 rights and private property rights, "and to seek a proper accommodation between the two." Central Hardware Co. v. NLRB, 407 U. S. 539, 543. What is "a proper accommodation" in any situation may largely depend upon the content and the context of the § 7 rights being asserted. The task of the Board and the reviewing courts under the Act, therefore, stands in conspicuous contrast to the duty of a court in applying the standards of the First Amendment, which requires "above all else" that expression must not be restricted by government "because of its message, its ideas, its subject matter, or its content."

In the *Central Hardware* case, and earlier in the case of NLRB v. Babcock & Wilcox Co., 351 U. S. 105, the Court considered the nature of the Board's task in this area under the Act. Accommodation between employees' § 7 rights and employers' property rights, the Court said in *Babcock & Wilcox,* "must be obtained with as little destruction of one as is consistent with the maintenance of the other." 351 U. S., at 112.

Both *Central Hardware* and *Babcock & Wilcox* involved organizational activity carried on by nonemployees on the employers' property.[10] The

---

[10] A wholly different balance was struck when the organizational activity was carried on by employees already rightfully on the employer's property, since the employer's management interests rather than his property interests were there involved. Republic

context of the § 7 activity in the present case was different in several respects which may or may not be relevant in striking the proper balance. First, it involved lawful economic strike activity rather than organizational activity. See United Steelworkers v. NLRB (Carrier Corp.), 376 U. S. 492, 499; Bus Employees v. Missouri, 374 U. S. 74, 82; *NLRB v. Erie Resistor Corp.,* 373 U. S. 221, 234. Cf. Houston Insulation Contractors Assn. v. NLRB, 386 U. S. 664, 668-669. Second, the § 7 activity here was carried on by Butler's employees (albeit not employees of its shopping center store), not by outsiders. See NLRB v. Babcock & Wilcox Co., 351 U. S., at 111-113. Third, the property interests impinged upon in this case were not those of the employer against whom the § 7 activity was directed, but of another.[11]

The *Babcock & Wilcox* opinion established the basic objective under the Act: accommodation of § 7 rights and private property rights "with as little destruction of one as is consistent with the maintenance of the other." [12] The locus of that accommodation, however, may fall at differing points along the spectrum depending on the nature and strength of the respective § 7 rights and private property rights asserted in any given context. In each generic situation, the primary responsibility for making this accommodation must rest with the Board in the first instance. See NLRB v. Babcock & Wilcox, 351 U. S., at 112; cf. NLRB v. Erie Resistor Corp., 373 U. S. 221, 235-236; NLRB v. Truckdrivers Union, 353 U. S. 87, 97. "The responsibility to adapt the Act to changing patterns of industrial life is entrusted to the Board." NLRB v. Weingarten, Inc., 420 U. S. 251, 266.

For the reasons stated in this opinion, the judgment is vacated and the case is remanded to the Court of Appeals with directions to remand to the National Labor Relations Board, so that the case may be there considered under the statutory criteria of the National Labor Relations Act alone.

It is so ordered.

MR. JUSTICE STEVENS took no part in the consideration or decision of this case.

MR. JUSTICE POWELL, with whom THE CHIEF JUSTICE joins, concurring.

Although I agree with MR. JUSTICE WHITE's concurring view that Lloyd Corp. v. Tanner, 407 U. S. 551 (1972), did not overrule Amalgamated Food Employees Union v. Logan Valley Plaza, 391 U. S. 308 (1968), and that the present case can be distinguished narrowly from *Logan Valley,* I nevertheless have joined the opinion of the Court today.

Aviation Corp. v. NLRB, 324 U. S. 793. This difference is "one of substance." NLRB v. Babcock & Wilcox Co., 351 U. S., at 113.

[11] This is not to say that Hudgens was not a statutory "employer" under the Act. See n. 3, *supra.*

[12] 351 U. S., at 112. This language was explicitly reaffirmed as stating "the guiding principle" in Central Hardware Co. v. NLRB, 407 U. S., at 544.

The law in this area, particularly with respect to whether First Amendment or labor law principles are applicable, has been less than clear since *Logan Valley* analogized a shopping center to the "company town" in Marsh v. Alabama, 326 U. S. 501 (1946). Mr. Justice Black, the author of the Court's opinion in *Marsh,* thought the decisions were irreconcilable. I now agree with Mr. Justice Black that the opinions in these cases cannot be harmonized in a principled way. Upon more mature thought, I have concluded that we would have been wiser in *Lloyd Corp.* to have confronted this disharmony rather than draw distinctions based upon rather attenuated factual differences.

The Court's opinion today clarifies the confusion engendered by these cases by accepting Mr. Justice Black's reading of *Marsh* and by recognizing more sharply the distinction between the First Amendment and labor law issues that may arise in cases of this kind. It seems to me that this clarification of the law is desirable.

MR. JUSTICE WHITE, concurring in the judgment.

While I concur in the result reached by the Court, I find it unnecessary to inter Amalgamated Food Employees Union Local 590 v. Logan Valley Plaza, Inc., 391 U. S. 308 (1968), and therefore do not join the Court's opinion. I agree that "the constitutional guarantee of free expression has no part to play in a case such as this," *ante,* p. 13; but Lloyd Corp. v. Tanner, 407 U. S. 551 (1972), did not overrule *Logan Valley,* either expressly or implicitly, and I would not, somewhat after the fact, say that it did.

One need go no further than *Logan Valley* itself, for the First Amendment protection established by *Logan Valley* was expressly limited to the picketing of a specific store for the purpose of conveying information with respect to the operation in the shopping center of *that* store:

> "The picketing carried on by petitioners was directed specifically at patrons of the Weis Market located within the shopping center and the message sought to be conveyed to the public concerned the manner in which that particular market was being operated. We are, therefore, not called upon to consider whether respondents' property rights could, consistently with the First Amendment, justify a bar on picketing which was not thus directly related in its purpose to the use to which the shopping center property was being put." 391 U. S., at 320 n. 9.

On its face, *Logan Valley* does not cover the facts of this case. The pickets of the Butler Shoe Company store in the North DeKalb Shopping Center were not purporting to convey information about the "manner in which that particular [store] was being operated" but rather about the operation of a warehouse not located on the Center's premises. The picketing was thus not "directly related in its purpose to the use to which the shopping center property was being put."

The First Amendment question in this case was left open in *Logan Valley.* I dissented in *Logan Valley,* 391 U. S., at 337, and I see no reason to extend it further. Without such extension, the First Amendment provides no protection for the picketing here in issue and the Court need say no more. *Lloyd* v. *Tanner* is wholly consistent with this view. There is no need belatedly to overrule *Logan Valley,* only to follow it as is.

MR. JUSTICE MARSHALL, with whom MR. JUSTICE BRENNAN joins, dissenting.

The Court today holds that the First Amendment poses no bar to a shopping center owner's prohibiting speech within his shopping center. After deciding this far-reaching constitutional question, and overruling Food Employees Local 590 v. Logan Valley, 391 U. S. 308 (1968), in the process, the Court proceeds to remand for consideration of the statutory question whether the shopping center owner in this case unlawfully interfered with the Butler Shoe Company employees' rights under § 7 of the National Labor Relations Act, 29 U. S. C. § 157.

In explaining why it addresses any constitutional issue at all, the Court observes simply that the history of the litigation has been one of "shifting positions on the part of the litigants, the Board, and the Court of Appeals," *ante,* at 5, as to whether relief was being sought, or granted, under the First Amendment, under § 7 of the Act, or under some combination of the two. On my reading, the Court of Appeals' decision and, even more clearly, the Board's decision here for review, were based solely on § 7, not on the First Amendment; and this Court ought initially consider the statutory question without reference to the First Amendment — the question on which the Court remands. But even under the Court's reading of the opinions of the Board and the Court of Appeals, the statutory question on which it remands is now before the Court. By bypassing that question and reaching out to overrule a constitutionally based decision, the Court surely departs from traditional modes of adjudication.

I would affirm the judgment of the Court of Appeals on purely statutory grounds. And on the merits of the only question that the Court decides, I dissent from the overruling of *Logan Valley.*

. . . .

II. On the merits of the purely statutory question that I believe is presented to the Court, I would affirm the judgment of the Court of Appeals. To do so, one need not consider whether consumer picketing by employees is subject to a more permissive test under § 7 than the test articulated in *Babcock & Wilcox* for organizational activity by nonemployees. In *Babcock & Wilcox* we stated that an employer "must allow the union to approach his employees on his property" [5] if the employees are "beyond the reach of reasonable efforts to communicate with them," 351 U. S., at 113 — that is, if "other means" of

---

[5] It is irrelevant, in my view, that the property in this case was owned by the shopping center owner rather than by the employer. The nature of the property interest is the same in either case.

communication are not "readily available." *Id.,* at 114. Thus the general standard that emerges from *Babcock & Wilcox* is the ready availability of reasonably effective alternative means of communication with the intended audience.

In *Babcock & Wilcox* itself, the intended audience was the employees of a particular employer, a limited identifiable group; and it was thought that such an audience could be reached effectively by means other than entrance onto the employer's property — for example, personal contact at the employees' living quarters, which were "in reasonable reach." *Id.,* at 113. In this case, of course, the intended audience was different, and what constitutes reasonably effective alternative means of communication also differs. As the Court of Appeals noted, the intended audience in this case "was only identifiable as part of the citizenry of greater Atlanta until it approached the store, and thus for the picketing to be effective, the location chosen was crucial unless the audience could be known and reached by other means." 501 F.2d 2d, at 168. Petitioner contends that the employees could have utilized the newspapers, radio, television, direct mail, handbills, and billboards to reach the citizenry of Atlanta. But none of those means is likely to be as effective as on-location picketing: the initial impact of communication by those means would likely be less dramatic, and the potential for dilution of impact significantly greater. As this Court has observed:

> "Publication in a newspaper, or by distribution of circulars, may convey the same information or make the same charge as do those patrolling a picket line. But the very purpose of a picket line is to exert influences, and it produces consequences, different from other modes of communication. The loyalties and responses evoked and exacted by picket lines are unlike those flowing from appeals by printed word." Hughes v. Superior Court, 339 U. S. 460, 465 (1950).

In addition, all of the alternatives suggested by petitioner are considerably more expensive than on-site picketing. Certainly *Babcock & Wilcox* did not require resort to the mass media,[6] or to more individualized efforts on a scale comparable to that which would be required to reach the intended audience in this case.

Petitioner also contends that the employees could have picketed on the public rights-of-way, where vehicles entered the shopping center. Quite apart from considerations of safety, that alternative was clearly inadequate: prospective customers would have had to read the picketers' placards while driving by in their vehicles — a difficult task indeed. Moreover, as both the Board and the Court of Appeals recognized, picketing at an entrance used by customers of all retail establishments in the shopping center, rather than simply customers of the Butler Shoe Company store, may well have invited undesirable secondary effects.

---

[6] The only alternative means of communication referred to in *Babcock & Wilcox* were "personal contacts on streets or at home, telephones, letters or advertised meetings to get in touch with the employees." 351 U.S., at 111.

In short, I believe the Court of Appeals was clearly correct in concluding that "alternatives to picketing inside the mall were either unavailable or inadequate." 501 F.2d, at 169. Under *Babcock & Wilcox,* then, the picketing in this case was protected by § 7. I would affirm the judgment of the Court of Appeals on that basis.

III. Turning to the constitutional issue resolved by the Court, I cannot escape the feeling that *Logan Valley* has been laid to rest without ever having been accorded a proper burial. The Court today announces that "the ultimate holding in *Lloyd* amounted to a total rejection of the holding in *Logan Valley." Ante,* at 11. To be sure, some Members of the Court, myself included, believed that *Logan Valley* called for a different result in *Lloyd* and alluded in dissent to the possibility that "it is *Logan Valley* itself that the Court finds bothersome." 407 U. S., at 570, 584 (MARSHALL, J., dissenting). But the fact remains that *Logan Valley* explicitly reserved the question later decided in *Lloyd,* and *Lloyd* carefully preserved the holding of *Logan Valley.* And upon reflection, I am of the view that the two decisions are reconcilable.

. . . .

It is inescapable that after *Lloyd, Logan Valley* remained "good law," binding on the state and federal courts. Our institutional duty in this case, if we consider the constitutional question at all, is to examine whether *Lloyd* and *Logan Valley* can continue to stand side-by-side, and, if they cannot, to decide which one must fall. I continue to believe that the First Amendment principles underlying *Logan Valley* are sound, and were unduly limited in *Lloyd.* But accepting *Lloyd,* I am not convinced that *Logan Valley* must be overruled.

The foundation of *Logan Valley* consisted of this Court's decisions recognizing a right of access to streets, sidewalks, parks, and other public places historically associated with the exercise of First Amendment rights. *E.g.,* Hague v. CIO, 307 U. S. 496, 515-516 (1939); Schneider v. State, 308 U. S. 147 (1939); Cantwell v. Connecticut, 310 U. S. 296, 308 (1940); Cox v. New Hampshire, 312 U. S. 569, 574 (1941); Jamison v. Texas, 318 U. S. 413 (1943); Saia v. New York, 334 U. S. 558 (1948). Thus, the Court in *Logan Valley* observed that access to such forums "cannot constitutionally be denied broadly and absolutely." 391 U. S., at 315. The importance of access to such places for speech-related purposes is clear, for they are often the only places for effective speech and assembly.

Marsh v. Alabama, 326 U. S. 501 (1946), which the Court purports to leave untouched, made clear that in applying those cases granting a right of access to streets, sidewalks and other public places, courts ought not let the formalities of title put an end to analysis. The Court in *Marsh* observed that "the town and its shopping district are accessible to and freely used by the public in general and there is nothing to distinguish them from any other town and shopping center except the fact that the title to the property belongs to a private corporation." *Id.,* at 503. That distinction was not determinative:

"Ownership does not always mean absolute dominion. The more an owner, for his advantage, opens up his property for use by the public in general, the more do his rights become circumscribed by the statutory and constitutional rights of those who use it." *Id.*, at 506.

Regardless of who owned or possessed the town in *Marsh,* the Court noted, "the public . . . has an identical interest in the functioning of the community in such manner that the channels of communication remain free," *id.*, at 507, and that interest was held to prevail.

The Court adopts the view that *Marsh* has no bearing on this case because the privately owned property in *Marsh* involved all the characteristics of a typical town. But there is nothing in *Marsh* to suggest that its general approach was limited to the particular facts of that case. The underlying concern in *Marsh* was that traditional public channels of communication remain free, regardless of the incidence of ownership. Given that concern, the crucial fact in *Marsh* was that the company owned the traditional forums essential for effective communication; it was immaterial that the company also owned a sewer system and that its property in other respects resembled a town.

In *Logan Valley* we recognized what the Court today refuses to recognize — that the owner of the modern shopping center complex, by dedicating his property to public use as a business district, to some extent displaces the "state" from control of historical First Amendment forums, and may acquire a virtual monopoly of places suitable for effective communication. The roadways, parking lots and walkways of the modern shopping center may be as essential for effective speech as the streets and sidewalks in the municipal or company-owned town.[7] I simply cannot reconcile the Court's denial of any role for the First Amendment in the shopping center with *Marsh's* recognition of a full role for the First Amendment on the streets and sidewalks of the company-owned town.

My reading of *Marsh* admittedly carried me farther than the Court in *Lloyd,* but the *Lloyd* Court remained responsive in its own way to the concerns underlying *Marsh. Lloyd* retained the availability of First Amendment protection when the picketing is related to the function of the shopping center, and when there is no other reasonable opportunity to convey the message to the intended audience. Preserving *Logan Valley* subject to *Lloyd's* two related criteria guaranteed that the First Amendment would have application in those situations in which the shopping center owner had most clearly monopolized the forums essential for effective communication. This result, although not the optimal one in my view, Lloyd Corp. v. Tanner, 407 U. S. 551, 570, 579-583 (MARSHALL, J., dissenting), is nonetheless defensible.

---

[7] No point would be served by adding to the observations in *Logan Valley* and my dissent in *Lloyd* with respect to the growth of suburban shopping centers and the proliferation of activities taking place in such centers. See *Logan Valley,* 391 U. S., at 324; *Lloyd,* 407 U. S., at 580, 585-586. See also *Lloyd Corp.* v. *Tanner:* The Demise of Logan Valley and the Disguise of Marsh, 61 Geo. L. J. 1187, 1216-1219 (1973).

In *Marsh,* the private entity had displaced the "state" from control of all the places to which the public had historically enjoyed access for First Amendment purposes, and the First Amendment was accordingly held fully applicable to the private entity's conduct. The shopping center owner, on the other hand, controls only a portion of such places, leaving other traditional public forums available to the citizen. But the shopping center owner may nevertheless control all places essential for the effective undertaking of some speech-related activities — namely, those related to the activities of the shopping center. As for those activities, then, the First Amendment ought to have application under the reasoning of *Marsh,* and that was precisely the state of the law after *Lloyd.*

The Court's only apparent objection to this analysis is that it makes the applicability of the First Amendment turn to some degree on the subject matter of the speech. But that in itself is no objection, and the cases cited by the Court to the effect that government may not "restrict expression because of its message, its ideas, its subject matter, or its content," Police Department of Chicago v. Mosley, 408 U. S. 92, 95 (1972), are simply inapposite. In those cases, it was clearly the government that was acting, and the First Amendment's bar against infringing speech was unquestionably applicable; the Court simply held that the government, faced with a general command to permit speech, cannot choose to forbid some speech because of its message. The shopping center cases are quite different; in these cases the primary regulator is a private entity whose property has "assume[d] to some significant degree the functional attributes of public property devoted to public use." Central Hardware Co. v. NLRB, *supra,* 407 U. S. at 547. The very question in these cases is whether, and under what circumstances, the First Amendment has any application at all. The answer to that question, under the view of *Marsh* described above, depends to some extent on the subject of the speech the private entity seeks to regulate, because the degree to which the private entity monopolizes the effective channels of communication may depend upon what subject is involved.[8] This limited reference to the subject matter of the speech poses none of the dangers of government suppression or censorship that lay at the heart of the cases cited by the Court. See, *e.g.,* Police Department of Chicago v. Mosley, 408 U. S. 92, 95-96 (1972). It is indeed ironic that those cases, whose obvious concern was the promotion of free speech, are cited today to require its surrender.

In the final analysis, the Court's rejection of any role for the First Amendment in the privately owned shopping center complex stems, I believe, from an overly formalistic view of the relationship between the institution of private ownership of property and the First Amendment's guarantee of freedom of speech. No one would seriously question the legitimacy of the values of privacy and individual autonomy traditionally associated with privately owned property. But property that is privately owned is not always held for private use, and when a property owner

---

[8] See The Supreme Court, 1967 Term, 82 Harv. L. Rev. 63, 135-138 (1968).

opens his property to public use the force of those values diminishes. A degree of privacy is necessarily surrendered; thus, the privacy interest that petitioner retains when he leases space to 60 retail businesses and invites the public onto his land for the transaction of business and other members of the public is small indeed. Cf. Paris Adult Theatre I v. Slaton, 413 U. S. 49, 65-67 (1973). And while the owner of property open to public use may not automatically surrender any of his autonomy interest in managing the property as he sees fit, there is nothing new about the notion that that autonomy interest must be accommodated with the interests of the public. As this Court noted some time ago, albeit in another context:

> "Property does become clothed with a public interest when used in a manner to make it of public consequence, and affect the community at large. When, therefore, one devotes his property to a use in which the public has an interest, he, in effect, grants to the public an interest in that use, and must submit to be controlled by the public for the common good, to the extent of the interest he has thus created." Munn v. Illinois, 94 U. S. 113, 126 (1876).

The interest of members of the public in communicating with one another on subjects relating to the businesses that occupy a modern shopping center is substantial. Not only employees with a labor dispute, but also consumers with complaints against business establishments, may look to the location of a retail store as the only reasonable avenue for effective communication with the public. As far as these groups are concerned, the shopping center owner has assumed the traditional role of the state in its control of historical First Amendment forums. *Lloyd* and *Logan Valley* recognized the vital role the First Amendment has to play in such cases, and I believe that this Court errs when it holds otherwise.

NOTE

On remand pursuant to the decision of the Supreme Court, the Board reaffirmed its conclusion that the owner of the mall violated the NLRA by threatening to cause the arrest of the retail store's warehouse employees who picketed the retail store located within the owner's enclosed shopping mall. Scott Hudgens, 230 N.L.R.B. 414 (1977). *See also* Giant Food Markets, 241 N.L.R.B. No. 105, 100 L.R.R.M. 1598 (1979) (area standards picketing in a shopping center).

In People v. Bush, 39 N.Y.2d 529, 92 L.R.R.M. 3269 (N.Y. Ct. App. 1976), the court followed *Hudgens* and held that picketing in a shopping center was not protected by the First Amendment from the application of the New York criminal trespass statute.

See generally, Etelson, *Picketing and Freedom of Speech: Comes the Evolution,* 10 JOHN MARSHALL J. OF PRAC. & PROC. 1 (1976); Comment, *Hudgens v. NLRB: A Final Definition of the Public Forum?* 13 WAKE FOREST L. REV. 139 (1977).

SECTION III. Picketing

A. REGULATION OF COERCIVE METHODS IN PICKETING

Picketing and its attendant representations and verbal onslaughts have presented courts and legislators with difficult problems. The general shift to a test of physical coercion gradually led most courts to give at least lip service to the doctrine that "peaceful" and noncoercive picketing for a lawful purpose is privileged, but it was easy, in most cases, to discover nonpeaceful and coercive incidents with which to characterize the entire situation; then the question, if the case arose in equity, was whether to enjoin all picketing or only the continuance of acts of coercion. Very often picketing has been accompanied by the bitter invective of highly aroused men, and the courts have pondered whether and to what extent to have regard for the sensibilities of others by holding the picketers to certain minimum standards of propriety in their use of language. Frequently the publications of picketers have contained misrepresentations of fact, and the question has been whether to impose a requirement of fairness.

VEGELAHN v. GUNTNER

Supreme Judicial Court of Massachusetts
167 Mass. 92, 44 N.E. 1077 (1896)

[Read the case again as reproduced *supra* at 12.]

NOTES

1. Judicial attitudes toward picketing, usually finding expression in cases where an injunction was sought, have varied considerably since the *Vegelahn* case. At one end of the spectrum are such statements as that of McPherson, J., in Atchison, Topeka & Santa Fe Ry. v. Gee, 139 Fed. 582, 584 (S.D. Ia. 1905): "There is and can be no such thing as peaceful picketing, any more than there can be chaste vulgarity, or peaceful mobbing or lawful lynching." *See also* Pierce v. Stablemen's, Local 8760, 156 Cal. 70, 103 Pac. 324 (1909). Hardly more sympathetic toward picketing was the approach of Berry, V.C. in Gevas v. Greek Restaurant Worker's Club, 99 N.J. Eq. 770, 134 Atl. 309, 313 (1926): "Obviously, the line of demarcation between peaceful picketing, if there is any such thing, and that which is threatening, intimidating, and coercive, is so finely drawn as to be imperceptible."

On the other hand, some judges came to adopt the approach of Holmes, J. in the *Vegelahn* case, that only the abuses of picketing should be enjoined — violence, threats, obstruction of entrances, fraud, and misrepresentation. This was the view taken by the draftsmen of the RESTATEMENT OF TORTS §§ 775, 798-99 (1939).

2. Assuming that violence has already occurred in the course of picketing, and that the court will enjoin any further violence, should the court issue a broad injunction against all further picketing, as a matter of practical policy? What considerations are involved?

a. Where there is an anti-injunction statute like the Norris-La Guardia Act (note especially § 4), would such a broad injunction be proper? *Cf.* Wilson & Co. v. Birl, 105 F.2d 948 (3d Cir. 1939); May's Furs and Ready to Wear, Inc. v. Bauer, 282 N.Y. 331, 26 N.E.2d 279 (1940) (no finding that peaceful picketing was out of the question); Busch Jewelry Co. v. United Retail Employees, Local 830, 281 N.Y. 150, 22 N.E.2d 320 (1939) (court found that violence "will continue" unless picketing enjoined).

b. Assuming the picketing is for a proper objective, but violence has occurred, would a broad injunction against all further picketing violate the Federal Constitution? See the following case.

MILK WAGON DRIVERS, LOCAL 753 v. MEADOWMOOR DAIRIES, INC.

Supreme Court of the United States
312 U.S. 287, 61 S. Ct. 552, 85 L. Ed. 836 (1941)

MR. JUSTICE FRANKFURTER delivered the opinion of the Court.

The supreme court of Illinois sustained an injunction against the Milk Wagon Drivers Union over the latter's claim that it involved an infringement of the freedom of speech guaranteed by the Fourteenth Amendment. . . . The present respondent, Meadowmoor Dairies, Inc., brought suit against the Union and its officials to stop interference with the distribution of its products. A preliminary injunction restraining all union conduct, violent and peaceful, promptly issued, and the case was referred to a master for report. Besides peaceful picketing of the stores handling Meadowmoor's products, the master found that there had been violence on a considerable scale. . . . In the light of his findings, the master recommended that all picketing, and not merely violent acts, should be enjoined. The trial court, however, accepted the recommendations only as to acts of violence and permitted peaceful picketing. The reversal of this ruling by the supreme court, 371 Ill. 377, 21 N.E.2d 308, directing a permanent injunction as recommended by the master, is now before us.

The question, which thus emerges, is whether a state can choose to authorize its courts to enjoin acts of picketing in themselves peaceful when they are enmeshed with contemporaneously violent conduct, which is concededly outlawed. . . .

In this case, the master found "intimidation of the customers of the plaintiff's vendors by the commission of the acts of violence," and the supreme court justified its decision because picketing, "in connection with or following a series of assaults or destruction of property, could not help but have the effect of intimidating the persons in front of whose premises such picketing occurred, and of causing them to believe that non-compliance would possibly be followed by acts of an unlawful character." It is not for us to make an independent valuation of the testimony before the master. We have not only his findings but his findings authenticated by the state of Illinois speaking through her supreme court. We can reject such a determination only if we can say that it is so without warrant as to be a palpable evasion of the constitutional guarantee here invoked. The place to resolve conflicts in the testimony and in its interpretation was in the Illinois courts and not here. To substitute our judgment for that of the state court is to transcend the limits of our authority. And to do so, in the name of the Fourteenth Amendment in a matter peculiarly touching the local policy of a state regarding violence, tends to discredit the great immunities of the Bill of Rights. No one will doubt that Illinois can protect its storekeepers from being coerced by fear of window-smashings or burnings or bombings. And acts which, in isolation, are peaceful may be part of a coercive thrust when entangled with acts of violence. The picketing in this case was set in a background of violence. In such a setting it could justifiably be concluded that the momentum of fear generated by past violence would survive even though future picketing might be wholly peaceful. So the supreme court of Illinois found. We cannot say that such a finding so contradicted experience as to warrant our rejection. Nor can we say that it was written into the Fourteenth Amendment that a state, through its courts, cannot base protection against future coercion on an inference of the continuing threat of past misconduct. . . .

NOTES

1. What findings must the trial court make, in order validly to issue a broad injunction under the *Meadowmoor* case? In Ellingsen v. Milk Wagon Drivers, Local 753, 377 Ill. 76, 35 N.E.2d 349 (1941), it was held that minatory action (threats by picketers who sought to coerce deliverymen and others to stay out of retail stores which were being picketed), and blocking of a store entrance, while enjoinable, could not found a sweeping injunction under the *Meadowmoor* case. *Compare* Washington Post Co. v. Local 6, 92 L.R.R.M. 2961 (D.C. Super. Ct. 1976).

2. In Youngdahl v. Rainfair, 355 U.S. 131, 139 (1957), the Supreme Court held:

"Though the state court was within its discretionary power in enjoining future acts of violence, intimidation and threats of violence by the strikers and the union, yet it is equally clear that such court entered the pre-empted domain of the National Labor Relations Board insofar as it enjoined peaceful picketing by petitioners. The picketing proper, as contrasted with the activities around the headquarters, was peaceful. There was little, if any, conduct designed to exclude those who desired to return to work. Nor can we say that a pattern of violence was established which would inevitably reappear in the event picketing were later resumed. *Cf.* Milk Wagon Drivers Union v. Meadowmoor Dairies, Inc., 312 U.S. 287. What violence there was was scattered in time and much of it was unconnected with the picketing. There is nothing in the record to indicate that an injunction against such conduct would be ineffective if picketing were resumed. Accordingly, insofar as the injunction before us prohibits petitioners and others cooperating with them from threatening violence against, or provoking violence on the part of, any of the officers, agents or employees of respondent and prohibits them from obstructing or attempting to obstruct the free use of the streets adjacent to respondent's place of business, and the free ingress and egress to and from that property, it is affirmed. On the other hand, to the extent the injunction prohibits all other picketing and patrolling of respondent's premises and in particular prohibits peaceful picketing, it is set aside."

Although the *Meadowmoor* criteria were employed by the Court, the ground for partially setting aside the injunction was federal preemption rather than "free speech." The federal preemption issue will be taken up in section VIII of Part Three.

That there is still life in the "picketing as free speech" doctrine, however, may be seen from Teamsters, Local 795 v. Newell, 356 U.S. 341 (1958). In this case, the Supreme Court reversed the Kansas Supreme Court, *per curiam,* merely citing "Thornhill v. Alabama, 310 U.S. 88, 98." The Kansas court had issued a broad injunction against all further picketing in a situation where pickets had taken pictures of persons who crossed the picket line and the court had found this conduct to be "intimidation," "coercion," and "an invasion of privacy." Newell v. Teamsters, Local 795, 181 Kan. 898, 317 P.2d 817 (1957). Note also the free speech implications of NLRB v. Fruit & Vegetable Packers [Tree Fruits], 377 U.S. 58 (1964), *infra* at 362.

3. *Mass Picketing.* Even where no actual violence has occurred, the courts have enjoined that form of picketing in which the pickets march so closely together as to block free ingress and egress. As the New Jersey court put it, "a picket fence is not the legitimate child of a picket line." Westinghouse Elec. Corp. v. UE, Local 410, 139 N.J. Eq. 97, 49 A.2d 896 (1946).

Consider the following dicta by the members of the United States Supreme Court: "We do not doubt the right of the state to impose . . . many restrictions upon peaceful picketing. Reasonable numbers, quietness, truthful placards, open ingress and egress, suitable hours or other proper limitations, not destructive of the right to tell of labor difficulties, may be required." Reed, J., dissenting in Carpenters & Joiners Union, Local 213 v. Ritter's Cafe, 315 U.S. 722, 738-39 (1942), in which the majority upheld a Texas injunction against secondary, not mass, picketing. In *Thornhill v. Alabama, supra,* Justice Murphy for the Court said: "We are not now concerned with picketing *en masse* or otherwise conducted which might occasion such imminent and aggravated danger to these interests as to justify a statute narrowly drawn to cover the precise situation giving rise to the danger."

Is it simply *mass* picketing that is enjoinable (if such be the case), despite constitutional doctrine and the anti-injunction acts, or is it mass picketing which *in fact* denies access to the plant or blocks the use of the streets? And what *is* "mass" picketing — 200, 100, or ten pickets? *Cf.* American Steel Foundries v. Tri-City Central Trades Council, 257 U.S. 184 (1921) (violence found; injunction limited pickets to one at each gate and all others enjoined from congregating nearby); Westinghouse Elec. Corp. v. UE, Local 107, 383 Pa. 297, 118 A.2d 180 (1955) (no violence found, but mass picketing enjoined; pickets limited to three at each gate, spaced not less than ten feet apart, and others enjoined from congregating in large numbers nearby; *see* dissent by Musmanno, J.).

Should the assemblage of large numbers of strikers near the struck plant be privileged in order to demonstrate solidarity and maintain morale? Or is it so conducive to a breach of the peace as to be enjoinable?

4. *Standards Applied to Language Used by Pickets.* The courts have traditionally enjoined the use of language which constitutes fraud, libel, misrepresentation, or inciting to a breach of the peace. Consider, however, some of the problems involved in the application of such general standards.

a. Does the statement, "Employer is unfair to organized labor," constitute misrepresentation or fraud, when he has no labor dispute *with his employees*? Does "unfair" wrongfully imply that his workers are on strike — or does it simply mean that his place of business is nonunion? *Cf.* Cafeteria Employees, Local 302 v. Angelos, 320 U.S. 293 (1943) ("To use loose language or undefined slogans that are part of the conventional give and take of our political and economic controversies — like 'unfair' and 'Fascist' — is not to falsify fact"); Paducah Newspapers, Inc. v. Wise, 247 S.W.2d 989 (Ky. 1951), *cert. denied,* 343 U.S. 942 (1952) (libel); Dinny & Robbins, Inc. v. Davis, 290 N.Y. 101, 48 N.E.2d 280 (1943) (enjoinable).

b. May pickets properly be enjoined from calling persons working during a strike "scabs"? *Compare* United States v. Taliaferro, 290 F. 214, 218 (W.D. Va. 1922), *with* Walter A. Wood Mowing & Repairing Mach. Co. v. Toohey, 114 Misc. 185, 190, 191, 186 N.Y.S. 95, 99 (1921) *and* Youngdahl v. Rainfair, 355 U.S. 131, 134-35 (1957).

c. What about "silent" forms of alleged intimidation, such as the visible writing down of license numbers of automobiles entering a place of business being picketed?

In Wallace Co. v. Machinists, Local 1005, 155 Ore. 652, 63 P.2d 1090 (1936), the court said, "We disapprove of taking the license numbers of automobiles belonging to customers of the plaintiffs, as it may reasonably be interpreted by such customers as an implied threat to do them injury and thereby interfere with the right of the plaintiffs to transact business." But in Loder Bros. Co. v. Machinists, Local 1506, 209 Ore. 305, 306 P.2d 411 (1957), where the union followed the taking of license numbers with a letter to the car owners moderately stating the issues in the labor dispute and requesting support, the court refused an injunction. *See* Jones, *The Loder Letter — Have Union Picketers Finally Found the Formula?* 4 U.C.L.A. L. Rev. 370 (1957).

In Associated Grocers of New England v. NLRB, 562 F.2d 1333 (1st Cir. 1977), the First Circuit reversed the Labor Board and ruled that a striker who verbally threatened the lives of three job applicants in the presence of 40 or 50 pickets was not engaging in protected activity under § 7 of the NLRA. Rejecting the Board's standard that verbal threats lose the protection of § 7 only when "accompanied by . . . physical acts or gestures that would provide added emphasis or meaning to [the] words. . .," the court stated that such a standard is too inelastic to provide a reliable means for distinguishing serious misconduct or threats from protected activity. Since a serious threat may draw its credibility from the totality of circumstances and not from the physical gestures of the speaker, a better test is whether the misconduct under the circumstances reasonably tends to coerce or intimidate employees in the exercise of their protected rights.

5. The following material deals with union coercive methods under the Taft-Hartley Act.

TEAMSTERS, LOCAL 901 (LOCK JOINT PIPE & CO.)

National Labor Relations Board
202 N.L.R.B. No. 43, 82 L.R.R.M. 1525 (1973)

[During a strike, three officials of the union, designated as being agents of the union, threatened nonstriking employees with physical harm and damaged some cars. They also threatened truck drivers who handled the employer's product with physical harm to themselves and their trucks, and attempted to wreck one truck while it was being driven. The Administrative Law Judge found that the union was guilty of restraint and coercion within § 8(b)(1) and recommended as a remedy, in addition to the usual cease and desist order and mailing of the Board order to all employees, that the union be ordered to give backpay to the employees who were unable to work because of the union's unfair labor practices.]

We agree with the Administrative Law Judge that Respondent Union violated Section 8(b)(1)(A) by engaging in threats and picket line violence at the Lock Joint Plant in Puerto Rico beginning on August 9, 1971.

We do not, however, agree with his further recommendation that the proper remedy in this case, contrary to Board precedent, is an order directing the Union to give backpay to all employees who did not work as a result of these unfair labor practices. From the very earliest days of the Taft-Hartley Act the desirability of such a remedy has been argued to the Board. In each case the Board has refused to enlarge the scope of its traditional remedies for picket line misconduct. The latest Board decision, Long Construction Company, 145 NLRB 554, involved physical injury to employees attempting to cross the picket line. The Board reiterated its view that a backpay order was not appropriate where the union's unfair labor practices involved solely interference with an employee's right of ingress to his place of employment.

These important decisions have stood the test of 24 years of court litigation and Congressional scrutiny. They have not been reversed or nullified and we do not believe the time has come for the Board itself to take that step. National Cash Register Co., et al. v. N.L.R.B., 466 F.2d 945, on which our dissenting colleagues rely, stands only for the well-established principle that where an employer unlawfully prevents an employee from working at the insistence of a union both are jointly and severally liable for the employee's loss of pay.[4]

---

[4] See also Stuart Wilson, Inc., 200 NLRB No. 83, 82 LRRM 1165, which is likewise distinguishable as there the employer discriminated against the employees by sending them home because of the union's unlawful threats and violence.

In exercising its broad discretionary powers under Section 10(c) of the Act the Board has always been careful to balance the effectiveness of a particular remedy against its consequences. Thus, the Board has refrained from directing an otherwise appropriate remedy where practical and economic considerations dictated a lesser deterrent. . . . The extension of backpay liability to a situation where, as here, only picket line misconduct has occurred involves important considerations going to the heart of the right to strike under Sections 7 and 13 of the Act. Those sections of the Act have been called the safety valves of labor management relations. Emotions run high among those for and those against the union. Regrettably, sometimes there is violence and the threat of violence. This we deplore and in no way condone. However, adequate remedies under the Act other than backpay exist to prevent the occurrence of violence without interfering with the right to strike.[5] Where union agents, including pickets, engage in conduct violative of Section 8(b)(1)(A) the Board enjoins the continuation of such conduct and may, if warranted seek an immediate court injunction under Section 10(j) of the Act. If such judicially directed injunctive relief is ignored effective contempt action is available. Finally, when a union resorts to or encourages the use of violent tactics to enforce its representation rights the Board may decline to issue a bargaining order to remedy an employer's unfair labor practices and instead may direct an election to determine whether or not the union is the recognized representative.

To do more, in our opinion, runs the risk of inhibiting the right of employees to strike to such an extent as to substantially diminish that right. For the misconduct of a few pickets may be sufficient to find the union in violation of Section 8(b)(1)(A) and enough to intimidate many employees. The Board would then be required, under the logic of our dissenting colleagues, to seek backpay for all intimidated employees. Faced with this financial responsibility, few unions would be in a position to establish a picket line. In our opinion, union misconduct of this nature, while serious, does not warrant the adoption of a remedy so severe as to risk the diminution of the right to strike, a fundamental right guaranteed by Sections 7 and 13 of the Act. Rather, we believe, the availability to the General Counsel of Section 10(j) of the Act, implemented by contempt action, if necessary, as well as the withholding of an otherwise appropriate bargaining order and the direction of an election are the preferred methods of deterring picket line misconduct violative of Section 8(b)(1)(A).

_____

[5] As we noted in Long, *supra,* the lack of a Board order awarding backpay to employees unable to work because of injuries resulting from a union's unlawful conduct will not leave such employees without redress against those responsible for their injuries. These individuals will still have available those private remedies traditionally used to process claims resulting from another's tortious conduct. In fact they may be better served by pursuing such remedies as the employee's pay may be only a small part of the total required to make him whole, such as medical expenses as well as compensation for physical injury and pain and suffering.

MILLER, Chairman, and KENNEDY, Member, dissenting in part:

We agree with our colleagues that by engaging in acts of violence against nonstriking employees, by damaging the property of nonstriking employees, and by threatening injury to other employees, the Union has, in violation of Section 8(b)(1)(A), engaged in coercive activity designed to prevent nonstriking employees from working and to deter striking employees from returning to work. However, we dissent from our colleagues' refusal to adopt the Administrative Law Judge's recommended remedy to make the employees whole for the loss of wages suffered when they were prevented from working by the Union's unlawful conduct.

We are unable to perceive the basis of our colleagues' conclusion that backpay remedy herein would unnecessarily "risk the diminution of the right to strike," and their reliance on the existence of "adequate remedies . . . other than backpay . . . to prevent the occurrence of violence without interfering with the right to strike." Section 10(c)'s concern is not with preventing or deterring violence but with eliminating and remedying the effects of that violence. Hence, any incidental deterrent or penal effect of backpay is irrelevant in our determination of an adequate remedy for the violation found herein. Indeed, it is difficult to comprehend how making an employee whole for loss of wages suffered because of the union's unlawful activity in preventing employees from working is any less remedial or any more punitive or deterrent in effect than making an employee whole for loss of wages suffered when the employer would not allow him to work because of the union's unlawful activity.

In our view, a backpay order herein is no more penal or deterring in effect than any other backpay order issued by the Board. Indeed, a backpay remedy in the instant case is necessary to remove the effect of the Union's unlawful conduct and thereby effectuate the policies of the Act.

NOTES

1. "The Board has held that it can award back pay where a union has wrongfully caused a termination in the employee status, but not in a case such as this when a union merely interferes with access to work by one who remains at all times an employee. United Furn. Workers, 84 N.L.R.B. 563, 565. That view was acknowledged in Progressive Mine Workers v. NLRB, 187 F.2d 298, 306-307 (7th Cir. 1951), and has been adhered to by the Board in subsequent cases. *E.g.,* Local 983, 115 N.L.R.B. 1123. Petitioners contend that the Board's above interpretation of its own power conflicts with the rationale of Phelps Dodge Corp. v. NLRB, 313 U.S. 177. . . . As the decision of this question is not essential in the instant case, we do not pass upon it." UAW v. Russell, 356 U.S. 634, 641 n.5 (1958).

2. The NLRA, as amended in 1947, prohibits unions and their agents from restraining and coercing employees in the exercise of § 7 rights, which include the right to refrain from concerted activities. "The legislative history of the act shows that, by this particular section, Congress primarily intended to proscribe the *coercive conduct* which

sometimes accompanies a strike, but not the strike itself. By § 8(b)(1)(A), Congress sought to fix the rules of the game, to insure that strikes and other organizational activities of employees were conducted peaceably by persuasion and propaganda and not by physical force, or threats of force, or of economic reprisal. In that section, Congress was aiming at means, not at ends." Perry Norvell Co., 80 N.L.R.B. 225, 239 (1948). *See also* National Maritime Union, 78 N.L.R.B. 971 (1948). As to the question whether peaceful picketing for recognition constitutes a violation of § 8(b)(1)(A) see the *Curtis Brothers* case, the Supreme Court opinion which follows at 308.

3. In International Longshoremen's & Warehousemen's Union, CIO, Local 6 (Sunset Line & Twine Co.), 79 N.L.R.B. 1487 (1948), the NLRB discussed the responsibility of a union for the acts of individuals:

"[T]he Board has a clear statutory mandate to apply the 'ordinary law of agency.' The act, as amended, envisages that the Board shall now hold labor organizations responsible for conduct of their agents which is proscribed by § 8(b) of the statute, just as it has always held employers responsible for the acts of their agents which were violative of § 8(a). For this purpose we are to treat labor organizations as legal entities, like corporations, which act, and can only act, through their duly appointed agents, as distinguished from their individual members.[41] Hence, our task of determining the responsibility of unions in cases arising under § 8(b) of the act is not essentially new, for the Board has been deciding similar questions in cases involving corporate employers, ever since the statute was enacted in 1935. The fact patterns in § 8(b) cases, however, are a novel study in the administration of the act. We have rarely had occasion to examine the relationships between a labor organization and its officers or other persons allegedly representing it, especially for the purpose of deciding whether or not the officer or other person was acting, in a particular instance, as the agent of the labor organization. Because this is a case of first impression in that sense, we shall set forth, in abstract, those fundamental rules of the law of agency which we believe must control our decision of the issue of responsibility in this and similar cases:

"1. The burden of proof is on the party asserting an agency relationship, both as to the existence of the relationship and as to the nature and extent of the agent's authority. In this case, for example, it was incumbent upon the General Counsel to prove, not only that the acts of restraint and coercion alleged in the complaint were committed, but also that those acts were committed by agents of the Respondent Unions, acting in their representative capacity. The Respondents' failure to introduce evidence *negating* the imputations in the complaint did not relieve the General Counsel of that burden.

---

[41] Proponents of the 1947 Amendments stated emphatically, in the Senate debates, that a member of a labor union is not *per se* an agent of the union. *See* 93 CONG. REC. 4561 (May 2, 1947); *Id.* 4142 (April 25, 1947). *See also,* United States v. White, 322 U.S. 694, 702 (1944); Hill v. Eagle Glass & Mfg. Co., 219 F. 719 (4th Cir. 1915), *rev'd on other grounds,* 245 U.S. 275 (1917).

"2. Agency is a *contractual relationship,* deriving from the mutual consent of principal and agent that the agent shall act for the principal. But the principal's consent, technically called authorization or ratification, may be manifested by conduct, sometimes even passive acquiescence, as well as by words. Authority to act as agent in a given manner will be implied whenever the conduct of the principal is such as to show that he actually intended to confer that authority.

"3. A principal may be responsible for the act of his agent within the scope of the agent's general authority, or the 'scope of his employment' if the agent is a servant, even though the principal has not specifically authorized or indeed may have specifically forbidden the act in question. It is enough if the principal empowered the agent to represent him in the general area within which the agent acted."

4. Applying the above principles, under what circumstances, "according to the ordinary law of agency," should a union be held to have committed an unfair labor practice because of violence by a picket who is not a union officer or business agent? *See* International Woodworkers (W.T. Smith Lumber Co.), 116 N.L.R.B. 507 (1956).

5. Under what circumstances would the International Union, as well as the Local Union, be held in violation of § 8(b)(1)(A) when threats and violence occur on the picket line? See the *Sunset Line & Twine* case, *supra,* note 3.

6. Contrast § 2(13) of the National Labor Relations Act with § 6 of the Norris-La Guardia Act.

7. Suppose union agents assault an employee who is striking and picketing in violation of a no-strike clause in a collective agreement. Has the union violated § 8(b)(1)(A)? *Compare* NLRB v. Furriers Joint Council, 224 F.2d 78 (2d Cir. 1955) *with* Teamsters Local 729 (Penntruck Co.), 189 N.L.R.B. 696 (1971).

8. The Supreme Court held in NLRB v. Allis-Chalmers Mfg. Co., 388 U.S. 175 (1967), that a union did not violate § 8(b)(1)(A) when it fined members for crossing a picket line during a strike. This case and related problems under § 8(b)(1)(A) dealing with union discipline will be taken up in Part Five.

9. *State labor relations acts and other state legislation regulating union methods.* Most of the state labor relations acts now deal with union or employee misconduct, or both. In addition, there exists a wide variety of statutes and ordinances, some general and others specific, which have frequently been called into use in attempts to deal with labor strife. Examples are statutes concerning riots, unlawful assembly, disturbing the peace, criminal syndicalism, enticing away employees, mass picketing, and interference with employment. For general reviews of the state legislation, see Katz, *Two Decades of State Labor Legislation: 1937-1957,* 8 LAB. L.J. 747 (1957), 25 U. CHI. L. REV. 109 (1957); Millis & Katz, *A Decade of State Labor Legislation: 1937-1947,* 15 U. CHI. L. REV. 282, 295-300 (1948); Smith & Clark, *Reappraisal of the Role of the States in Shaping Labor Relations Law,* 1965 WIS. L. REV. 411; Smith & Delancey, *The State Legislatures and Unionism; A Survey of State Legislation Relating to*

Problems of Unionization and Collective Bargaining, 38 MICH. L. REV. 987, 1006-13 (1940).

B. ORGANIZATIONAL AND RECOGNITION PICKETING

The use of collective action to induce persons to affiliate with a labor organization raises important questions of principle. Insofar as the union's appeal is confined to oral or written solicitation, there could be no basis for legal complaint by employer or solicited employees except where such solicitation disturbs some existing contractual status (as in former "yellow-dog" contract situations). On the other hand, when the union's appeal is accompanied by or takes the form of economic pressure through any of the traditional modes of collective action, both employer and employee affected may raise the question whether the coercive element is a legal wrong.

The basic question was nicely raised in 1900 in *Plant v. Woods*,[1] which involved a contest between two craft unions. Defendant union, in an effort to force members of the plaintiff union to change their affiliation, threatened to strike and boycott employers of members of the latter union. This action was enjoined. The basis for the decision appears in the following excerpt from the opinion by Judge Hammond:

". . . The purpose of these defendants was to force the plaintiffs to join the defendant association, and to that end they injured the plaintiffs in their business, and molested and disturbed them in their efforts to work at their trade. It is true they committed no acts of personal violence, or of physical injury to property, although they threatened to do something which might reasonably be expected to lead to such results. In their threat, however, there was plainly that which was coercive in its effect upon the will. It is not necessary that the liberty of the body should be restrained. Restraint of the mind, provided it would be such as would be likely to force a man against his will to grant the thing demanded, and actually has that effect, is sufficient in cases like this. . . . The necessity that the plaintiffs should join this association is not so great, nor is its relation to the rights of the defendants, as compared with the right of the plaintiffs to be free from molestation, such as to bring the acts of the defendants under the shelter of the principles of trade competition. Such acts are without justification, and therefore are malicious and unlawful, and the conspiracy thus to force the plaintiffs was unlawful. Such conduct is intolerable, and inconsistent with the spirit of our laws." [2]

In a memorable dissenting opinion, Chief Judge Holmes remarked:

". . . I infer that a majority of my brethren would admit that a boycott or strike intended to raise wages directly might be lawful, if it did not embrace in its scheme or intent violence, breach of contract, or other conduct unlawful on grounds independent of the mere fact that the action

---

[1] 176 Mass. 492, 57 N.E. 1011 (1900).

[2] *Id.* at 502, 57 N.E. at 1015.

of the defendants was combined. .... To come directly to the point, the issue is narrowed to the question whether, assuming that some purposes would be a justification, the purpose in this case of the threatened boycotts and strikes was such as to justify the threats. That purpose was not directly concerned with wages. It was one degree more remote. The immediate object and motive was to strengthen the defendants' society as a preliminary and means to enable it to make a better fight on questions of wages or other matters of clashing interests. I differ from my brethren in thinking that the threats were as lawful for this preliminary purpose as for the final one to which strengthening the union was a means. I think that unity of organization is necessary to make the contest of labor effectual, and that societies of laborers lawfully may employ in their preparation the means which they might use in the final contest. ...." [3]

Which was the sounder view? If plaintiff workers had not been members of *any* union, would their case have been stronger or weaker?

Compare the more liberal approach of the New York Court of Appeals, as indicated by the following from the opinion of Judge Andrews in *Exchange Bakery & Restaurant, Inc. v. Rifkin:* [4]

The purpose of a labor union to improve the conditions under which its members do their work; to increase their wages; to assist them in other ways may justify what would otherwise be a wrong. So would an effort to increase its numbers and to unionize an entire trade or business. It may be as interested in the wages of those not members, or in the conditions under which they work as in its own members because of the influence of one upon the other. All engaged in a trade are affected by the prevailing rate of wages. All, by the principle of collective bargaining. Economic organization today is not based on the single shop. Unions believe that wages may be increased, collective bargaining maintained only if union conditions prevail, not in some single factory but generally. That they may prevail, it may call a strike and picket the premises of an employer with the intent of inducing him to employ only union labor. And it may adopt either method separately. Picketing without a strike is no more unlawful than a strike without picketing. Both are based upon a lawful purpose. Resulting injury is incidental and must be endured.

State court consideration under the common law of the use of collective action to organize new shops may be complicated by (1) state anti-injunction statutes, (2) state labor relations statutes, (3) constitutional "free speech" issues (*see* the *Vogt* case at 269), and (4), in industries affecting commerce, the doctrine of federal preemption (see section VIII of Part Three).

---

[3] *Id.* at 504-05, 57 N.E. at 1016.

[4] 245 N.Y. 260, 263, 157 N.E. 130, 132-33 (1927).

NOTES

1. The basic problem is to reach some kind of an accommodation between the employees' interest in being free of economic pressure in the selection or rejection of a union as bargaining representative and the organized employees' interest in extending their organization and in protecting their labor standards won by collective bargaining from the competition of unorganized firms. Also to be considered is the employer's interest in being free from economic injury.

2. Situations in which organizational or recognition picketing has been enjoined by the state courts include the following:

(a) Where an election under governmental auspices was pending and picketing for the purpose of obtaining immediate recognition occurred;

(b) Where another union had been certified and picketing for recognition occurred;

(c) Where the employer had a collective agreement in effect with a union representing a majority of his employees, and picketing for recognition occurred;

(d) Where the union had lost an election, but picketing for recognition still continued;

(e) Where picketing occurred for the purpose of compelling the employer, who had no labor dispute with his own employees, to sign a contract which would require his employees to join the union;

(f) Where picketing occurred for the purpose of forcing the employer to recognize the union at a time when it did not represent a majority of his employees; or where the picketing was found to be for the purpose of forcing the employer to force his employees to join the union. (*See* the *Vogt* case, for example, *supra* at 269.)

3. On the other hand, a number of state courts have refused to enjoin the picketing where the purpose was found to be "organizational," thus giving weight to the unionized workers' interest in extending organization to nonunion businesses, or where the union's purpose was to publicize the fact that a place of business was nonunion or not operating under union standards of working conditions. *See* Wood v. O'Grady, 307 N.Y. 532, 122 N.E.2d 386 (1954).

4. Is the distinction between "organizational" and "recognition" picketing a tenable and realistic basis for decision? If the union's purpose is to be the test, what evidence would be crucial: (a) whether the union asked the employer for recognition; (b) whether the signs read, "Employer unfair," "This store is nonunion," or "We urge nonunion employees to join"; (c) whether the effect of the picketing was to cause customers and employees of other employers to refuse to enter; or (d) the duration of the picketing?

5. It should be noted that the approach which is taken in any particular state may be influenced by the existence, language, and interpretation of a state labor relations law or a state anti-injunction act.

6. With the development of the doctrine of federal preemption in the labor field in recent years (*see* section VIII of Part Three) attention has been increasingly drawn to the status of picketing for organizational or recognition purposes under the National Labor Relations Act, as amended in 1947, which is discussed in the following case. It will then be necessary to consider the 1959 amendments contained in the Labor-Management Reporting and Disclosure Act, in which Congress legislated specifically with reference to organizational and recognition picketing.

NLRB v. DRIVERS, CHAUFFEURS, HELPERS, LOCAL 639 [CURTIS BROS., INC.]

Supreme Court of the United States
362 U.S. 274, 80 S. Ct. 706, 4 L. Ed. 2d 710 (1960)

[The union was certified by the Board in 1953 as the exclusive bargaining representative of Curtis Brothers' drivers, helpers, warehousemen, and furniture finishers. An impasse was reached in the resultant bargaining and the union started picketing the company's premises early in 1954. This picketing continued for about two years, during which time the company replaced the strikers.

[On February 1, 1955, the company filed a representation petition, in which it questioned the union's continued majority status and asked for an election. About two weeks later, on February 16, 1955, the union filed a statement purportedly disavowing any current intention to represent the employees in their dealings with the company. Before such disclaimer, the union's picket signs read: "CURTIS BROTHERS ON STRIKE. UNFAIR TO ORGANIZED LABOR. DRIVERS, HELPERS, AND WAREHOUSEMEN OF LOCAL 639 (AF of L)." Thereafter, they read on one side "CURTIS BROS. EMPLOYS Non-Union drivers, helpers, warehousemen, etc. Unfair to Teamsters Union No. 639 AFL," and on the other side "Teamsters Union No. 639 AFL wants employees of Curtis Bros. to join them to gain union wages, hours and working conditions."

[In September 1955, the Board directed an election in the representation case, finding that the union was still seeking to win immediate recognition by the company. The Board reasoned:

["[T]hat the Union's current picketing activities cannot be reconciled with its disclaimer of interest in representing the employees in question. In the light of all the material facts of this case, including the certification of the Petitioner, the circumstances preceding the strike, the nature of the first signs carried by the pickets, the brief discontinuance of picketing, and its early resumption, we are convinced that the current picketing is not for the sole purpose of getting employees to join the Union, as the more recent picket signs indicate, but is tantamount to a present demand that the Employer enter into a contract with the Union without regard to the question of its majority status among the employees concerned. [Citing cases.]"

[Twenty-eight employees voted against Local 639, and only one for it. As stated, the union never altered its picketing activities. It is conceded that at no time after February, 1955, did the union represent a majority of the employees.

[The NLRB held that the picketing violated § 8(b)(1)(A). The court of appeals set the Board's order aside.]

MR. JUSTICE BRENNAN delivered the opinion of the Court.

The question in this case is whether peaceful picketing by a union, which does not represent a majority of the employees, to compel immediate recognition as the employees' exclusive bargaining agent, is conduct of the union "to restrain or coerce" the employees in the exercise of rights guaranteed in § 7, and thus an unfair labor practice under § 8(b)(1)(A) of the Taft-Hartley Act. . . .

After we granted certiorari, the Congress enacted the Labor-Management Reporting and Disclosure Act of 1959, which, among other things, adds a new § 8(b)(7) to the National Labor Relations Act. It was stated by the Board on oral argument that if this case arose under the 1959 Act, the Board might have proceeded against the Local under § 8(b)(7). This does not, however, relegate this litigation to the status of an unimportant controversy over the meaning of a statute which has been significantly changed. For the Board contends that new § 8(b)(7) does not displace § 8(b)(1)(A) but merely "supplements the power already conferred by § 8(b)(1)(A)." It argues that the Board may proceed against peaceful "recognitional" picketing conducted by a minority union in more situations than are specified in § 8(b)(7) and without regard to the limitations of § 8(b)(7)(C). . . .

We conclude that the Board's interpretation of § 8(b)(1)(A) finds support neither in the way Congress structured § 8(b) nor in the legislative history of § 8(b)(1)(A). Rather it seems clear, and we hold, that Congress in the Taft-Hartley Act authorized the Board to regulate peaceful "recognitional" picketing only when it is employed to accomplish objectives specified in § 8(b)(4); and that § 8(b)(1)(A) is a grant of power to the Board limited to authority to proceed against union tactics involving violence, intimidation, and reprisal or threats thereof — conduct involving more than the general pressures upon persons employed by the affected employers implicit in economic strikes.

The Board's own interpretation for nearly a decade after the passage of the Taft-Hartley Act gave § 8(b)(1)(A) this limited application. . . .

We are confirmed in our view by the action of Congress in passing the Labor-Management Reporting and Disclosure Act of 1959. That act goes beyond the Taft-Hartley Act to legislate a comprehensive code governing organizational strikes and picketing and draws no distinction between "organizational" and "recognitional" picketing. While proscribing peaceful organizational strikes in many situations, it also establishes safeguards against the Board's inference with legitimate picketing activity. See § 8(b)(7)(C). Were § 8(b)(1)(A) to have the sweep contended for by the Board, the Board might proceed against peaceful picketing in disregard of these safeguards. To be sure, what Congress did in 1959 does not establish what it meant in 1947. However, as another major step in an evolving pattern of regulation of union conduct, the 1959 Act is a relevant consideration. Courts may properly take into account the later act when asked to extend the reach of the earlier act's vague language to the limits which, read literally, the words might permit. We avoid the incongruous result implicit in the Board's construction, by reading § 8(b)(1)(A) which is only one of many interwoven sections in a complex act mindful of the manifest purpose of the Congress to fashion a coherent national labor policy.

Affirmed.

NOTE

Provisions of the Labor-Management Reporting and Disclosure Act of 1959 dealing with organizational and recognition picketing.

As can readily be observed in the *Curtis Bros.* case, there was considerable confusion in 1958 and 1959 as to the applicability of § 8(b)(1) of the NLRA to organizational and recognition picketing. During the same period, the McClellan Committee hearings were revealing instances in which certain unions, particularly the Teamsters, were employing such economic weapons under circumstances that were widely regarded as abusive. President Eisenhower, in his radio-television appeal for "an effective labor reform law" dramatized the problem in this manner:

"Chief among the abuses from which Americans need protection are the oppressive practices of coercion.

"Take a company in the average American town — your town. A union official comes into the office, presents the company with a proposed labor contract, and demands that the company either sign or be picketed. The company refuses, because its employees don't want to join that union.

"And remember, the law definitely gives employees the right to have or not to have a union — clearly a basic American right of choice.

"Now what happens? The union official carries out the threat and puts a picket line outside the plant, to drive away customers, to cut off deliveries. In short, to force the employees into a union they do not want. This is one example of what has been called blackmail picketing. It is unfair and unjust. This could force the company out of business and result in the loss of all the jobs in the plant.

"I want that sort of thing stopped. So does America." N.Y. Times, Aug. 7, 1959, at 8, col. 6.

Congressman Griffin, in explaining the Landrum-Griffin bill to the House, similarly described the need for legislation:

"It is intended to prohibit blackmail recognition picketing by unions which do not represent the employees. Under the National Labor Relations Act elaborate election machinery is provided for ascertaining the wishes of employees in selecting or rejecting bargaining representatives. The act contains provisions for giving employees an opportunity to vote by secret ballot. In recent years the safeguards intended by these election provisions have been thwarted by unions which have lost elections and unions which do not have enough employee support to petition for an election but yet insist upon compelling employers to sign contracts with them — irrespective of the sentiment of the employees.

"The customary method employed to force employers to do this is to place picket lines around their plants or shops. Such picketing, even when peaceful, will frequently cause small employers to capitulate. The picket line is a signal for truckers not to pick up or deliver goods to employees of maintenance contractors. Pickets also deter many customers from entering retail or service establishments. In the face of such tactics employees whose jobs are in jeopardy as they see their employer's business choked off are soon coerced into joining the picketing union — even though they might prefer another union. In many such cases their employer forces them in a particular union by signing a compulsory membership agreement with the picketing union.

"The NLRB has attempted to give some relief to employers and employees victimized in such situations by holding it an unfair labor practice for a union to picket for recognition after it has lost an election. While such relief seems called for, nevertheless the courts of appeal are in conflict as to whether the Board has even this limited power." 105 CONG. REC. 14347 (1959).

George Meany, President of the AFL-CIO argued, however, that the Landrum-Griffin bill would "prohibit any union from advertising to the public that an employer is unfair to labor, pays substandard wages or operates a sweatshop." N.Y. Times, Aug. 7, 1959, at 8, col. 6.

The House of Representatives passed the Landrum-Griffin bill, embodying essentially the administration's proposals; the final enactment drafted by the conference committee of the House and Senate followed the Landrum-Griffin bill in general as to organizational and recognition picketing, but with certain mitigating modifications exacted by Senator Kennedy and others in the effort to arrive at a compromise.

SMITLEY, d/b/a CROWN CAFETERIA v. NLRB

United States Court of Appeals, Ninth Circuit
327 F.2d 351 (1964)

[The NLRB dismissed a complaint that the union had engaged in unlawful recognition picketing under § 8(b)(7)(C).]

DUNIWAY, Circuit Judge. . . . The findings of the Board as to the facts are not attacked. It found, in substance, that the unions picketed the cafeteria for more than thirty days before filing a representation petition under § 9(c) of the act (29 U.S.C. § 159(c)), that an object of the picketing was to secure recognition, that the purpose of the picketing was truthfully to advise the public that petitioners employed nonunion employees or had no contract with the unions, and that the picketing did not have the effect of inducing any stoppage of deliveries or services to the cafeteria by employees of any other employer. The matter was twice heard by the

Board, which first concluded, by a majority of 3 to 2, that the picketing did violate the statute in question (130 N.L.R.B. 570), and then held, following a change in its membership, and by a majority of 3 to 2, that the picketing did not violate the statute (135 N.L.R.B. 1183). We conclude that the views of the Board, as stated after its second consideration of the matter, are correct, and that the statute has not been violated.

The Board states its interpretation of the section, including the proviso quoted above, as follows:

"Congress framed a general rule covering all organizational or recognitional picketing carried on for more than 30 days without the filing of a representation petition. Then, Congress excepted from that rule picketing which, although it had an organizational or recognitional objective, was addressed primarily to the public, was truthful in nature, and did not interfere to any significant extent with deliveries or the rendition of services by the employees of any other employer."

We think that this is the correct interpretation. It will be noted that subdivision (7) of subsection (b), § 8, quoted above, starts with the general prohibition of picketing "where an object thereof is forcing or requiring an employer to recognize or bargain with a labor organization" (This is often called recognitional picketing) ". . . or forcing or requiring the employees of an employer to accept or select such labor organization. . . ." (This is often called organizational picketing), ". . . unless such labor organization is currently certified as the representative of such employees: . . . ." This is followed by three subparagraphs, (A), (B) and (C). Each begins with the same word, "where." (A) deals with the situation "where" the employer has lawfully recognized another labor organization and a question of representation cannot be raised under § 9(c). (B) refers to the situation "where," within the preceding 12 months, a valid election under § 9(c) has been conducted. (C), with which we are concerned, refers to a situation "where" there has been no petition for an election under § 9(c) filed within a reasonable period of time, not to exceed thirty days, from the commencement of the picketing. Thus, § 8(b)(7) does not purport to prohibit all picketing having the named "object" of recognitional or organizational picketing. It limits the prohibition of such picketing to three specific situations.

There are no exceptions or provisos in subparagraphs (A) and (B), which describe two of those situations. There are, however, two provisos in subparagraph (C). The first sets up a special procedure for an expedited election under § 9(c). The second is the one with which we are concerned. It is an exception to the prohibition of "such picketing," *i.e.,* recognitional or organizational picketing, being a proviso to a prohibition of such picketing "where" certain conditions exist. It can only mean, indeed, it says, that "such picketing," which otherwise falls within subparagraph (C), is not prohibited if it falls within the terms of the proviso. That proviso says that subparagraph (C) is not to be construed to prohibit "any picketing" for "the purpose" of truthfully advising the public (including consumers) that an employer does not employ members of, or have a contract with, a labor organization. To this exception there is an exception, stated in the last "unless" clause, namely, that "such picketing," *i.e.,* picketing where "an object" is recognitional or organizational, but which has "the" excepting "purpose," would still be illegal if an effect were to induce any individual employee of other persons not to pick up, deliver, or transport any goods, or not to perform any services. Admittedly, the picketing here does not fall within the "unless" clause in the second proviso to subparagraph (C). It does, however, fall within the proviso, since it does have "the purpose" that brings it within the proviso. It also has "an object" that brings it within the first sentence of subsection (b) and the first clause of subdivision (7), and within the circumstances stated in the opening clause of subparagraph (C). If it did not have "an object" bringing it within subdivision (7), it would not be prohibited at all. Moreover, if it did have that "object," it still would not be prohibited at all, unless it occurred in circumstances described in subparagraph (A), (B) or (C). Here, neither (A) or (B) applies; (C) does. But, unlike (A) or (B), it has an excepting proviso. Unless that proviso refers to picketing having as "an object" either recognition or organization, it can have no meaning, for it would not be an exception or proviso to anything. It would be referring to conduct not prohibited in § 8(b) at all.

Petitioners urge that if the picketing has as "an object" recognition or organization, then it is still illegal, even though it has "the purpose" of truthfully advising the public, etc., within the meaning of the second proviso to subparagraph (C). It seems to us, as it did to the Board, that to so construe the statute would make the proviso meaningless. The hard realities of union-employer relations are such that it is difficult, indeed almost impossible, for us to conceive of picketing falling within the terms of the proviso that did not also have as "an object" obtaining a contract with the employer. This is normally the ultimate objective of any union in relation to an employer who has employees whose jobs fall within the categories of employment that are within the jurisdiction of the union, which is admittedly the situation here.

We note that the Court of Appeals for the Second Circuit has reached a similar conclusion. In NLRB v. Local 3, International Bhd. of Electrical Workers, 317 F.2d 193 (2d Cir. 1963), that court considered the section at some length, and said:

"It seems, however, much more realistic to suppose that Congress framed a general rule covering the field of recognitional and organizational picketing, conducted under alternate sets of circumstances described in subparagraphs (A), (B), and (C), and then excepted from the operation of the rule, as it applied to the circumstances set forth in subparagraph (C), a comparatively innocuous species of picketing having the immediate purpose of informing or advising the public, even though its ultimate object was success in recognition and organization. . . .

"One of the principal difficulties in construing and applying subparagraph (C) is that § 8(b)(7) contains the partially synonymous words, 'object' and 'purpose,' used in two distinct contexts but to which much of the same evidence is relevant. These are: 'where an object thereof is forcing or requiring an employer to recognize or bargain . . .' and 'for the purpose of truthfully advising the public. . . .' It does not necessarily follow that, where an object of the picketing is forcing or requiring an employer to recognize or bargain, the purpose of the picketing, in the context of the second proviso, is not truthfully to advise the public, etc. The union may legitimately have a long range or strategic objective of getting the employer to bargain with or recognize the union and still the picketing may be permissive. This proviso gives the union freedom to appeal to the unorganized public for spontaneous popular pressure upon an employer; it is intended, however, to exclude the invocation of pressure by organized labor groups or members of unions, as such.

"The permissible picketing is, therefore, that which through the dissemination of certain allowed representations, is designed to influence members of the unorganized public, as individuals, because the impact upon the employer by way of such individuals is weaker, more indirect and less coercive."

We agree. See also Getreu v. Bartenders and Hotel & Restaurant Employees Union Local 58, 181 F.Supp. 738 (N.D. Ind. 1960).

Both sides have reviewed legislative history. We think this unnecessary, because we think that the meaning of the statute is clear. We also find the history inconclusive, but it seems to us to point somewhat more strongly toward the view that we here adopt than to the contrary view. Petitioners rely on language used by Senator Kennedy, who was one of the sponsors of the bill in the Senate and one of the Senate Conferees, in which he referred to the second proviso as permitting "purely informational" picketing. Counsel for petitioners frankly conceded, however, at oral argument, that most of the legislative history is against the view that he urged, and we agree. A discussion of legislative history appears in the dissent to the Board's first opinion (130 N.L.R.B. 576-77) and we therefore do not repeat it here. We think that even Senator Kennedy's comment, upon which petitioners most heavily rely, taken in context, was not intended to have the limiting effect which petitioners would give it. Senator Kennedy was more concerned, on the one hand, with the economic pressure involved in recognitional and organizational picketing, and on the other hand, with the right of labor truthfully to advise the public that the employer was nonunion, or that the employer did not have a contract with the union, than he was with whether or not, in addition to having an informational purpose described in the proviso, there was also a recognitional or organizational object. See 105 Cong. Rec. 17898 (1959). See also Cox, The Landrum-Griffin Amendments to the National Labor Relations Act, 44 Minn. L. Rev. 257, 267. Mr. Cox, now the Solicitor General, was then Senator Kennedy's chief advisor on the bill.

We think that, in substance, the effect of the second proviso to subparagraph (C) is to allow recognitional or organizational picketing to continue if it meets two important restrictions: (1) it must be addressed to the public and be truthful and (2) it must not induce other unions to stop deliveries or services. The picketing here met those criteria.

NOTES

1. In other decisions interpreting § 8(b)(7), the NLRB and the courts have declared:

a. Section 8(b)(7)(C) applies to a majority union which has not been certified. Hod Carriers, Local 840 (Blinne Constr. Co.), 135 N.L.R.B. 1153 (1962).

b. The fact that organization or recognition picketing is also for the purpose of protesting an employer unfair labor practice does not prevent violation of § 8(b)(7)(C). However, a union may continue organization or recognition picketing, without filing a petition for an election, if it files a refusal-to-bargain charge and the General Counsel finds it meritorious and issues a complaint. Hod Carriers, Local 840 (Blinne Constr. Co.), *supra.*

Compare Retail Clerks, Local 1557 (Giant Foods of Chattanooga), 217 N.L.R.B. 4 (1975).

c. Picketing solely to protest an employee's discharge and not for union recognition does not violate § 8(b)(7)(C). UAW, Local 259 (Fanelli Ford Sales, Inc.), 133 N.L.R.B. 1468 (1961).

d. Where the union's picketing is solely to compel the employer to comply with an existing valid collective agreement it is not unlawful picketing for recognition within the meaning of § 8(b)(7)(C) of the NLRA. Building & Constr. Trades Council (Sullivan Elec. Co.), 146 N.L.R.B. 1086 (1964).

e. Employees who engage in recognition picketing in violation of § 8(b)(7) lose their protected status under the Act, and an employer may lawfully refuse to reinstate them. Claremont Polychemical Corp., 196 N.L.R.B. 613 (1972) (one member dissenting).

f. In NLRB v. Iron Workers Local 103, 98 S. Ct. 651 (1978), the Supreme Court held that it was a violation of § 8(b)(7)(C) for an uncertified union, not representing a majority of construction employees, to engage in extended picketing to enforce a § 8(f) prehire agreement, since such picketing was legally equivalent to picketing for organizational purposes.

g. Although § 8(b)(7)(C) refers to "picketing" that "has been conducted," *threats to picket* are proscribed by the same provision if the union is barred from being certified as a collective bargaining representative. Service Employees, Local 73 v. NLRB [A-1 Security Service Co.], 578 F.2d 361 (D.C. Cir. 1978).

2. In defining the term "effect" in the proviso to § 8(b)(7)(C), the Board has looked to the "actual impact" on the employer's business, rather than to a quantitative test based solely on the number of deliveries not made or services not performed, when determining whether to remove the informational picketing from the proviso's protection. The presence or absence of a violation depends upon whether the picketing disrupted, interfered with or curtailed employer's business. This is a question of fact to be resolved in the light of the facts in each case. In Retail Clerks, Local 324 (Barker Bros. Corp. & Golds, Inc.), 138 N.L.R.B.

478 (1962), where the union picketed eighteen stores over a period of twelve weeks, taking active measures to insure no interruption of service, the Board held that three delivery stoppages, two work delays, and several delivery delays were insufficient to constitute the "effect" contemplated by the proviso. The Board's decision was enforced in Barker Bros. Corporation v. NLRB, 328 F.2d 431 (9th Cir. 1964). However, in San Diego County Waiters & Bartenders (Joe Hunt's Restaurant), 138 N.L.R.B. 470 (1962), where all trucks refused to deliver, the Board found "sufficient impact" to remove the picketing from the protection of the § 8(b)(7)(C) proviso.

HOUSTON BUILDING & CONSTRUCTION TRADES COUNCIL (CLAUDE EVERETT CONSTRUCTION CO.)

National Labor Relations Board
136 N.L.R.B. 321 (1962)

. . . The Respondent, a council of local unions in the building and construction industry in the Houston, Texas, area, inquired on March 8, 1961, about the wage rates of Claude Everett Construction Company, a general construction contractor in that area. The Respondent's representative was told by Wilson, the Company's construction superintendent, that it operated an "open shop," and that its wage rates were lower than those negotiated in the area by the local unions which were members of the Respondent. On March 10, 1961, the Respondent wrote to the Company protesting its "substandard" wages and threatening to picket its construction site on March 13, unless "prevailing" rates were paid. When this letter had not been answered by March 16, the Respondent began picketing the Company's jobsite with a sign which read as follows:

"Houston Building and Construction Trades Council, AFL-CIO protests substandard wages and conditions being paid on this job by Claude Everett Company. Houston Building and Construction Trades Council does not intend by this picket line to induce or encourage the employees of any other employer to engage in a strike or a concerted refusal to work."

Such picketing continued for more than 30 days without the filing of a petition under § 9(c) of the act. The Respondent has never been certified as the representative of the Company's employees. The parties stipulated at the hearing that the picketing interfered with deliveries and services by inducing individuals employed by suppliers, service companies, and common carriers not to make pickups or deliveries or to perform services for the Company.

The Trial Examiner found that the Respondent picketed the Company to require it to conform its wage rates to those paid by employers having union contracts. Relying on the original Board decision in the *Calumet Contractors* case,[2] he concluded that such picketing violated § 8(b)(7)(C)

---

[2] Hod Carriers, Local 41 (Calumet Contractors Ass'n), 130 N.L.R.B. 78.

of the act. Subsequent to the issuance of his Intermediate Report, however, the Board, having reconsidered the *Calumet Contractors* case,[3] found the picketing there involved not unlawful, and stated that:

". . . Respondent's admitted objective to require the Association . . . to conform standards of employment to those prevailing in the area, is not tantamount to, nor does it have an objective of, recognition or bargaining. A union may legitimately be concerned that a particular employer is undermining area standards of employment by maintaining lower standards. It may be willing to forego recognition and bargaining provided subnormal working conditions are eliminated from area considerations."

While the *Calumet Contractors* case arose under § 8(b)(4)(C) of the act, which prohibits only recognitional picketing, whereas the instant case arose under § 8(b)(7)(C), which proscribes both recognitional and organizational picketing, the language of both subsections is similar, and the rationale in that case is equally applicable herein. The Respondent in the present case did not, in its conversation with the Company, its letter to the Company, or its picket sign, claim to represent the Company's employees, request recognition by the Company, or solicit employees of the Company to become members of any of the locals which are members of the Respondent. Moreover, the undisputed testimony of Executive Secretary Graham reveals that the Respondent Union has on numerous occasions in the past made similar protests against substandard wages paid by other employers without ever requesting recognition as the bargaining representative of their employees. Thus, it is clear, from the entire record, that the objective of the Respondent's picketing was to induce the Company to raise its wage rates to the union scale prevailing in the area. We cannot, as do our dissenting colleagues, equate this attempt to maintain area wage standards with conduct "forcing or requiring an employer to recognize or bargain with a labor organization as the representative of his employees, or forcing or requiring the employees . . . to accept or select such labor organization as their collective bargaining representative," the conduct proscribed by § 8(b)(7).[4]

Nor do we agree with our dissenting colleagues that the fact that the picketing interfered with deliveries and services in itself constitutes a violation of § 8(b)(7)(C). To determine the effect of § 8(b)(7)(C), we must look at the section in its entirety, in accord with the long-established principle of statutory construction that a legislative enactment is to be read in its entirety, not in bits and pieces. It is clear that this section, read as a whole, declares picketing by an uncertified union unlawful if it has a

---

[3] Hod Carriers, Local 41 (Calumet Contractors Ass'n), 133 N.L.R.B. 512 (Members Rodgers and Leedom dissenting).

[4] See Cox, The Landrum-Griffin Amendments to the National Labor Relations Act, 44 Minn. L. Rev. 257, 266-267 (1959).

recognitional or organizational objective and if a petition has not been filed within a reasonable time, and that the interruption-of-deliveries clause does not enter into the picture unless the picketing can first be shown to have such a prohibited objective. As we stated in the *Blinne* case [135 N.L.R.B. 1153]:

"[S]tructurally, as well as grammatically, subparagraphs (A), (B), and (C) are subordinate to and controlled by the opening phrases of § 8(b)(7). In other words, the thrust of all the § 8(b)(7) provisions is only upon picketing for an object of recognition or organization, and not upon picketing for other objects. Similarly, both structurally and grammatically, the two provisos in subparagraph (C) appertain only to the situation defined in the principal clause of that subparagraph."

Our dissenting colleagues interpret the second proviso of subparagraph (C) as though it creates a completely independent unfair labor practice, without reference to the fact that it is a subsidiary clause in a section which initially prohibits picketing with a recognitional or organizational objective. Such a reading would remove the proviso from its statutory setting, an interpretive result we feel constrained to avoid.

Accordingly, on the basis of the facts in the present case and of "the thrust of all the § 8(b)(7) provisions," we find that the Respondent's picketing did not have a recognitional or organizational objective, and, therefore, that it did not violate the act even though the picketing interfered with deliveries and services. Accordingly, we shall dismiss the complaint.

[The Board dismissed the complaint.]

[MEMBERS RODGERS and LEEDOM, dissented.]

NOTES

1. Compare, however, Centralia Bldg. Trades Council (Pacific Sign & Steel Bldg. Co.) v. NLRB, 363 F.2d 699 (D.C. Cir. 1966). The Board and the court held that the union's picketing was not "standards" picketing but that an object was recognitional, where the union, without inquiring whether Pacific's wages were in fact substandard, demanded that it sign an agreement to pay its employees "wages and fringe benefits equal to such allowances then being received by comparable employees working under the Union Agreement. If [the Union's] industry agreements were so negotiated as to provide increases or decreases, Pacific's total 'economic package' was to be increased or decreased by an equivalent amount." The union also demanded that its accountants be permitted to make monthly inspection of Pacific's records as to the economic benefits being paid to its employees. It was held that the net effect of this would be to establish the union as negotiator of wages and benefits, tantamount to recognition, the union's disclaimers to the contrary notwithstanding. *See also* Culinary Workers (McDonald's System of California), 203 N.L.R.B. 719 (1973).

2. In Retail Clerks, Local 899 (State-Mart, Inc.), 166 N.L.R.B. 818 (1967), the Board held that, although a union may picket for "area

standards" by demanding that the nonunion employer pay his employees an economic package equal in total cost to what unionized employers pay, the picketing becomes illegal "recognition" picketing, when it insists that the package include specific benefits, such as a welfare and pension plan.

3. See Rosen, *Area Standards Picketing,* 23 LAB. L.J. 67 (1972); Note, *Picketing for Area Standards: An Exception to Section 8(b)(7),* 1968 DUKE L.J. 767.

SECTION IV. Secondary Pressure

No problem of labor law is more acute, complex, or confused than the attempt to restrict, within "legitimate" areas, the use by unions of the power which they exert by means of the strike, picketing, and the boycott. The difficulty arises out of the fact that, even when conducted peacefully, these methods involve economic coercion. A strike of employees in order to force their employer to accede to some demand is the simplest example, but we are not here concerned with this kind of coercion, since, subject to the propriety of the object sought and to such statutory prerequisites as may be applicable, the legal privilege to engage in such a strike is no longer doubted. Nor is it doubted any longer that picketing in support of such a strike is permissible so long as it is peaceable. But when such picketing goes beyond the bounds of "fair persuasion," to use the language of the *Restatement of Torts,* in the sense that it involves an attempt to induce, by economic threats, non-dealing with the employer, or when the strike is sought to be supported by "secondary" or "sympathetic" action by other labor groups or is itself secondary or sympathetic, or when the strikers or their union agents seek to organize in their support an economic "bloc" of consumers or others against an employer, there arises the problem with which we are here concerned.

The primary question is how far and on what principle the state should intervene to attempt to limit such use of economic force. Other questions of first magnitude are (1), whether such intervention should come by way of common-law (judge-made) determinations of the policy issues involved, or, on the other hand, by specific action of the legislative body, and (2), what types of legal controls to use. Historically, our courts have not hesitated to assume the responsibilities of policy making in this area, although, as might be supposed, there has been a profound lack of agreement among them, as among legislators, as to the proper solutions.

A general concept of the range of judicial opinion regarding the use of "secondary" pressures may be gained from the following summaries of some well-known common-law cases. Notice the tendency toward branding as "secondary" — and hence wrongful — economic sanctions directed at "neutral" employers in order to force them to cease dealing with the primary employer with whom the union had its dispute. On the other hand, notice that some respect was paid to the traditional freedom of union men to refrain from conduct which would aid a nonunion employer or an employer engaged in a labor dispute.

BOSSERT V. DHUY, 221 N.Y. 342, 117 N.E. 582 (1917). The Carpenters notified building contractors that their members would refuse to work on woodwork made by nonunion manufacturers. Plaintiff, who operated an open shop woodworking mill sought an injunction. *Held:* Denied. The method — announcement of a concerted refusal to work — was proper, and the objective was the legitimate advancement of working conditions in the workers' own industry in which they had a direct interest. *Accord,* Kingston Trap Rock Co. v. Operating Engineers, Local 825, 129 N.J. Eq. 570, 19 A.2d 661 (1941).

AUBURN DRAYING CO. V. WARDELL, 227 N.Y. 1, 124 N.E. 97 (1919). In an effort to organize the plaintiff trucking company, the teamsters had plaintiff placed on the "unfair list" of the Central Labor Union, an association of all the unions in the city of Auburn. *Held:* Injunction granted. This was an illegal combination of all the union men in the city for the purpose of injuring the plaintiff's business unless he compelled his employees to join the union, accomplished by coercion of third persons to refrain from doing business with him.

GOLDFINGER V. FEINTUCH, 276 N.Y. 281, 11 N.E.2d 910 (1937). Defendant union, in attempting to obtain a collective agreement with the manufacturer of kosher meats, picketed the product at plaintiff's delicatessen store. The signs indicated that the store sold nonunion made meat and urged consumers not to buy the nonunion product. *Held:* Picketing of the product sold by one in "unity of interest" with the manufacturer permitted. "Where a manufacturer pays less than union wages, both it and the retailers who sell its products are in a position to undersell competitors who pay the higher scale, and this may result in unfair reduction of the wages of union members." The union may follow the product and ask the public not to buy it, at the place where it is sold to the public. *Cf.* People v. Bellows, 281 N.Y. 67, 22 N.E.2d 238 (1939) (there is no right to picket a store which purchased a neon sign from a company employing members of a rival union; there is no such unity of interest as was developed in the *Goldfinger* case). *And see* Feldman v. Weiner, 173 Misc. 461, 17 N.Y.S.2d 730 (1940) (injunction granted against picketing of a supplier of raw materials to a manufacturer with whom the union had a dispute; no such unity of interest exists as to justify picketing).

PACIFIC TYPESETTING CO. V. INTERNATIONAL TYPOGRAPHICAL UNION, 125 Wash. 273, 216 P. 358 (1923). Plaintiff did linotyping for other printing companies with whom the union had a dispute. The union called a strike of plaintiff's employees to force plaintiff to cease dealing with the other establishments. *Held:* In an action for damages, defendant's demurrer overruled. This was an effort to "conscript a neutral" — an impartial bystander — and make him a weapon in the hands of the union. Also, a third party is liable in tort for his persuasion of one to break his contract with another. Lumley v. Guy, 2 El. & Bl. 216 (Q.B. 1853). *Accord,* Bricklayers' Int'l Union v. Seymour Ruff & Sons, Inc., 160 Md. 483, 154 A. 52 (1931).

NOTES

1. Should a distinction be drawn between the situation where an embattled union simply *asks* for the support (by boycott) of other unions and of the consuming public without being able to *command* such support and that in which the union is able, by virtue of binding obligations, as through a central trades council, to command at least a labor boycott? If either such procedure is thought to be undesirable, what is the legal remedy — to enjoin the request for public support, in the first case, and the request for the aid of affiliates in the second? What if the action of affiliates is unsolicited, and comes automatically whenever a member union itself resorts to collective action, such as a strike? It is well known that many unions, either by formulated policy or by custom, "respect" another union's picket line, even that of a non-affiliated union. The result is that, in some cases, an employer who is fighting it out with his own union suddenly finds, for example, that he can't get supplies because members of a teamsters' or drivers' union will not deliver goods to him across the picket line.

2. For useful general discussions *see* C. GREGORY, LABOR AND THE LAW, chs. V, VI (2d rev. ed. 1961); L. TELLER, LABOR DISPUTES AND COLLECTIVE BARGAINING, ch. 9 (1940); Barnard & Graham, *Labor and the Secondary Boycott,* 15 WASH. L. REV. 137 (1940); Feinberg, *Analysis of the New York Law of Secondary Boycott,* 6 BROOKLYN L. REV. 209 (1936); Gromfine, *Labor's Use of Secondary Boycotts,* 15 GEO. WASH. L. REV. 327 (1947); Hellerstein, *Secondary Boycotts in Labor Disputes,* 47 YALE L.J. 341 (1938); Smith, *Coercion of Third Parties in Labor Disputes — The Secondary Boycott,* 1 LA. L. REV. 277 (1939).

3. The common law as to secondary activity is still involved in some cases, but its importance is much diminished by several factors:

a. Anti-injunction acts, such as the Norris-La Guardia Act, may preclude resort to the most effective remedy. The Norris-La Guardia Act has been interpreted to prevent the federal courts from issuing injunctions on the petition of a private party against illegal secondary boycotts, peacefully conducted. *See* Bakery Sales Drivers, Local 33 v. Wagshal, 333 U.S. 437 (1948); Brotherhood of Railroad Trainmen v. Atlantic Coast Line R.R., 362 F.2d 649 (5th Cir. 1966), *aff'd by equally divided Court,* 385 U.S. 20 (1966). However, not all state anti-injunction acts are so phrased or interpreted.

b. For a time, it appeared as though certain peaceful secondary picketing within the employees' own industry might be constitutionally protected as a form of free speech. *See* Bakery & Pastry Drivers, Local 802 (Teamsters Union) v. Wohl, 315 U.S. 769 (1942); *cf.* Carpenters, Local 213 v. Ritter's Cafe, 315 U.S. 722 (1942). But later cases have made it clear that there is no such constitutional protection where the picketing is found to be contrary to a valid state or federal policy. *See* IBEW, Local 501 v. NLRB, 341 U.S. 694 (1951); Giboney v. Empire Storage & Ice Co., 336 U.S. 490 (1949).

c. Many states and the federal government have statutes dealing specifically with the subject, which, as a practical matter, may leave little room for common-law doctrine.

d. To the extent that Congress has legislated in the field and the NLRB will exercise jurisdiction, states are ousted from jurisdiction over secondary boycotts in industries affecting interstate commerce by the doctrine of federal preemption. Weber v. Anheuser-Busch, Inc., 348 U.S. 468 (1955). *See* section VIII of Part Three.

Consequently, the focus of attention in recent years has been largely upon the rather complex enactments of Congress dealing with the problem. As Mr. Justice Frankfurter said:

"Whatever may have been said in Congress preceding the passage of the Taft-Hartley Act concerning the evil of all forms of 'secondary boycotts' and the desirability of outlawing them, it is clear that no such sweeping prohibition was in fact enacted in § 8(b)(4)(A). The section does not speak generally of secondary boycotts. It describes and condemns specific union conduct directed to specific objectives." Local 1976, United Brotherhood of Carpenters & Joiners v. NLRB, 357 U.S. 93, 98 (1958).

As the result of a widespread feeling that there were "loopholes" in the provisions of the LMRA dealing with secondary boycotts, and particularly as the result of the McClellan Committee's dramatization of the power of James R. Hoffa and the Teamsters Union, Congress acted in the Labor-Management Reporting and Disclosure Act of 1959 to tighten up the secondary boycott provisions. Some cases decided under the Taft-Hartley Act have been retained in this edition in order to show the background of the 1959 legislation. The following charts may be of assistance in analyzing § 8(b)(4)(A) and (B) before and after the 1959 amendments. In reading the cases prior to the 1959 amendments, it should be noted that the lettering of the clauses of § 8(b)(4) was modified in 1959, *e.g.*, § 8(b)(4)(A) becomes § 8(b)(4)(B).

4. For helpful general discussions of secondary boycotts under the federal statutes, see Farmer, *Secondary Boycotts — Loopholes Closed or Reopened?*, GEO. L.J. 392 (1964); Goetz, *Secondary Boycotts and the LMRA: A Path Through the Swamp,* 19 KAN. L. REV. 651 (1971); Koretz, *Federal Regulation of Secondary Strikes and Boycotts — Another Chapter,* 59 COLUM. L. REV. 125 (1959); Lesnick, *Job Security and Secondary Boycotts: The Reach of NLRA §§ 8(b)(4) and 8(e),* 113 U. PA. L. REV. 1000 (1965); Lesnick, *The Gravamen of the Secondary Boycott,* 62 COLUM. L. REV. 1363 (1962); Ross, *Assessment of the Landrum-Griffin Act's Secondary Boycott Amendments to the Taft-Hartley Act,* 22 LAB. L.J. 675 (1971); St. Antoine, *What Makes Secondary Boycotts Secondary?,* SOUTHWESTERN LEGAL FOUNDATION, LABOR LAW DEVELOPMENTS, PROCEEDINGS OF THE ELEVENTH ANNUAL INSTITUTE ON LABOR LAW 5 (1965); St. Antoine, *Secondary Boycotts and Hot Cargo: A Study in Balance of Power,* 40 U. DET. L.J. 189 (1962); Shalov, *The Landrum-Griffin Amendments: Labor's Use of the Secondary Boycott,* 45 CORNELL L.Q. 724 (1960).

ANALYSIS OF §§ 8(b)(4)(A) and (B) PRIOR TO
1959 AMENDMENTS
§ 8(b)(4)

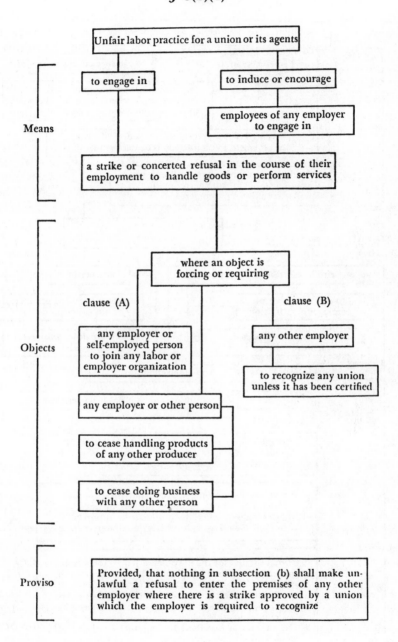

Means

Unfair labor practice for a union or its agents

to engage in

to induce or encourage

employees of any employer to engage in

a strike or concerted refusal in the course of their employment to handle goods or perform services

Objects

where an object is forcing or requiring

clause (A)

clause (B)

any employer or self-employed person to join any labor or employer organization

any other employer

to recognize any union unless it has been certified

any employer or other person

to cease handling products of any other producer

to cease doing business with any other person

Proviso

Provided, that nothing in subsection (b) shall make unlawful a refusal to enter the premises of any other employer where there is a strike approved by a union which the employer is required to recognize

ANALYSIS OF §§ 8(b)(4)(A) and (B) AS AMENDED IN 1959
§ 8(b)(4)

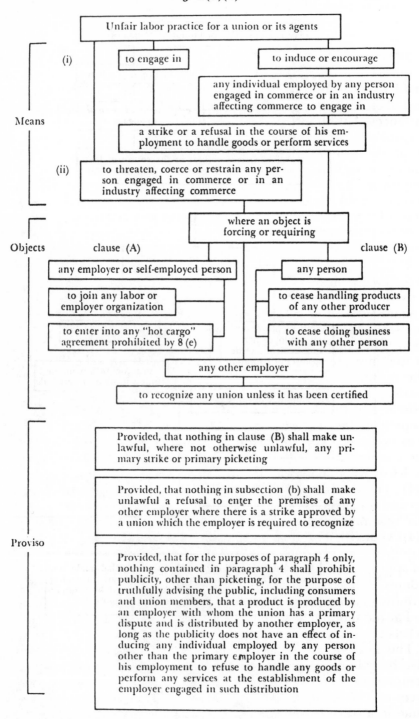

Means

Unfair labor practice for a union or its agents

(i) to engage in | to induce or encourage

any individual employed by any person engaged in commerce or in an industry affecting commerce to engage in

a strike or a refusal in the course of his employment to handle goods or perform services

(ii) to threaten, coerce or restrain any person engaged in commerce or in an industry affecting commerce

Objects

where an object is forcing or requiring

clause (A)

any employer or self-employed person

to join any labor or employer organization

to enter into any "hot cargo" agreement prohibited by 8 (e)

clause (B)

any person

to cease handling products of any other producer

to cease doing business with any other person

any other employer

to recognize any union unless it has been certified

Proviso

Provided, that nothing in clause (B) shall make unlawful, where not otherwise unlawful, any primary strike or primary picketing

Provided, that nothing in subsection (b) shall make unlawful a refusal to enter the premises of any other employer where there is a strike approved by a union which the employer is required to recognize

Provided, that for the purposes of paragraph 4 only, nothing contained in paragraph 4 shall prohibit publicity, other than picketing, for the purpose of truthfully advising the public, including consumers and union members, that a product is produced by an employer with whom the union has a primary dispute and is distributed by another employer, as long as the publicity does not have an effect of inducing any individual employed by any person other than the primary employer in the course of his employment to refuse to handle any goods or perform any services at the establishment of the employer engaged in such distribution

A. PRIMARY-SECONDARY DISTINCTION

NLRB v. INTERNATIONAL RICE MILLING CO.

Supreme Court of the United States
341 U.S. 665, 71 S. Ct. 961, 95 L. Ed. 1277 (1951)

MR. JUSTICE BURTON delivered the opinion of the Court.

The question presented is whether a union violated § 8(b)(4) of the National Labor Relations Act, 49 Stat. 449, 29 U.S.C. § 151, as amended by the Labor Management Relations Act, 1947, under the following circumstances: Although not certified or recognized as the representative of the employees of a certain mill engaged in interstate commerce, the agents of the union picketed the mill with the object of securing recognition of the union as the collective bargaining representative of the mill employees. In the course of their picketing, the agents sought to influence, or in the language of the statute they "encouraged," two men in charge of a truck of a neutral customer of the mill to refuse, in the course of their employment, to go to the mill for an order of goods. For the reasons hereinafter stated, we hold that such conduct did not violate § 8(b)(4). . . .

This review is confined to the single incident described in the complaint issued by the Acting Regional Director of the National Labor Relations Board against the International Brotherhood of Teamsters, Chauffeurs, Warehousemen and Helpers of America, Local 201, AFL, herein called the union. The complaint originally was based upon four charges made against the union by several rice mills engaged in interstate commerce near the center of the Louisiana rice industry. The mills included the International Rice Milling Company, Inc., which gives its name to this proceeding, and the Kaplan Rice Mills, Inc., a Louisiana corporation, which operated the mill at Kaplan, Louisiana, where the incident now before us occurred. The complaint charged that the union or its agents, by their conduct toward two employees of a neutral customer of the Kaplan Rice Mills, engaged in an unfair labor practice contrary to § 8(b)(4). The Board, with one member not participating, adopted the findings and conclusions of its trial examiner as to the facts but disagreed with his recommendation that those facts constituted a violation of § 8(b)(4)(A) or (B). The Board dismissed the complaint but attached the trial examiner's intermediate reports to its decision. 84 N.L.R.B. 360. The court of appeals set aside the dismissal and remanded the case for further proceedings. 183 F.2d 21. . . .

The findings adopted by the Board show that the incident before us occurred at the union's picket line near the Kaplan Mill, October, 1947. The pickets generally carried signs, one being "This job is unfair to" the union. The goal of the pickets was recognition of the union as the collective bargaining representative of the mill employees, but none of those employees took part in the picketing. Late one afternoon two employees of The Sales and Service House, which was a customer of the mill, came in a truck to the Kaplan Mill to obtain rice or bran for their employer. The union had no grievance against the customer and the latter was a neutral in the dispute between the union and the mill. The pickets formed a line across the road and walked toward the truck. When the truck stopped, the pickets told its occupants there was a strike on and that the truck would have to go back. Those on the truck agreed, went back to the highway and stopped. There one got out and went to the mill across the street. At that time a vice president of the Kaplan Mill came out and asked whether the truck was on its way to the mill and whether its occupants wanted to get the order they came for. The man on the truck explained that he was not the driver and that he would have to see the driver. On the driver's return, the truck proceeded, with the vice president, to the mill by a short detour. The pickets ran toward the truck and threw stones at it. The truck entered the mill, but the findings do not disclose whether the articles sought there were obtained. The Board adopted the finding that "the stopping of the Sales House truck drivers and the use of force in connection with the stoppage were within the 'scope of the employment' of the pickets as agents of the respondent [union] and that such activities are attributable to the respondent." 84 N.L.R.B. 360, 372.

The most that can be concluded from the foregoing, to establish a violation of § 8(b)(4), is that the union, in the course of picketing the Kaplan Mill, did encourage two employees of a neutral customer to turn back from an intended trip to the mill and thus to refuse, in the course of their employment, to transport articles or perform certain services for their employer. We may assume, without the necessity of adopting the Board's findings to that effect, that the objects of such conduct on the part of the union and its agents were (1) to force Kaplan's customer to cease handling, transporting or otherwise dealing in products of the mill or to cease doing business with Kaplan, at that time and place, and (2) to add to the pressure on Kaplan to recognize the union as the bargaining representative of the mill employees.

A sufficient answer to this claimed violation of the section is that the union's picketing and its encouragement of the men on the truck did not amount to such an inducement or encouragement to "concerted" activity as the section proscribes. While each case must be considered in the light of its surrounding circumstances, yet the applicable proscriptions of § 8(b)(4) are expressly limited to the inducement or encouragement of *concerted* conduct by the employees of the neutral employer. That language contemplates inducement or encouragement to some concert of action greater than is evidenced by the pickets' request to a driver of a single truck to discontinue a pending trip to a picketed mill. There was no attempt by the union to induce any action by the employees of the neutral customer which would be more widespread than that already described. There were no inducements or encouragements applied elsewhere than on the picket line. The limitation of the complaint to an incident in the geographically restricted area near the mill is significant, although not necessarily conclusive. The picketing was directed at the Kaplan employees and at their employer in a manner traditional in labor disputes. Clearly, that, in itself, was not proscribed by § 8(b)(4). Insofar as the union's efforts were directed beyond that and toward the employees of anyone other than Kaplan, there is no suggestion that the union sought *concerted* conduct by such other employees. Such efforts also fall short of the proscriptions in § 8(b)(4). In this case, therefore, we need not determine the specific objects toward which a union's encouragement of concerted conduct must be directed in order to amount to an unfair labor practice under subsection (A) or (B) of § 8(b)(4). A union's inducements or encouragements reaching individual employees of neutral employers only as they happen to approach the picketed place of business generally are not aimed at concerted, as distinguished from individual, conduct by such employees. Generally, therefore, such actions do not come within the proscription of § 8(b)(4), and they do not here.

In the instant case the violence on the picket line is not material. The complaint was not based upon that violence, as such. To reach it, the complaint more properly would have relied upon § 8(b)(1)(A) or would have addressed itself to local authorities. The substitution of violent coercion in place of peaceful persuasion would not in itself bring the complained-of conduct into conflict with § 8(b)(4). It is the object of union encouragement that is proscribed by that section, rather than the means adopted to make it felt.

That Congress did not seek, by § 8(b)(4), to interfere with the ordinary strike has been indicated recently by this Court. This is emphasized in § 13 as follows:

"Nothing in this Act, except as specifically provided for herein, shall be construed so as either to interfere with or impede or diminish in any way the right to strike, or to affect the limitations or qualifications on that right." 61 Stat. 151, 29 U.S.C. (Supp. III) § 163.

By § 13, Congress has made it clear that § 8(b)(4), and all other parts of the act which otherwise might be read so as to interfere with, impede or diminish the union's traditional right to strike, may be so read only if such interference, impediment or diminution is "specifically provided for" in the act. No such specific provision in § 8(b)(4) reaches the incident here. The material legislative history supports this view.

On the single issue before us, we sustain the action of the Board and the judgment of the court of appeals, accordingly is

Reversed.

NOTES

1. *Inducement of "concerted" activity.* The 1959 amendments removed the requirement of an inducement of a *"concerted"* refusal to work on the part of employees of secondary employers. Congressman Griffin, in his analysis of this provision of the Landrum-Griffin bill, explained it as follows:

"As the present act forbids inducing 'employees' to engage in a strike or 'concerted' refusal to do their work, the courts have held that unions may induce employees one at a time to engage in secondary boycotts (citing NLRB v. International Rice Milling Co., 341 U.S. 665). By changing 'employees' to 'any individual' and omitting the word 'concerted,' the proposed revision . . . closes this loophole." 105 CONG. REC. 14347 (1959).

2. *"Primary" picketing.* Was the fundamental basis for the decision in the *Rice Milling* case the fact that the picketing was "primary" in the sense that it was done at the primary employer's premises?

Consider the following quotation from Local 618, Automotive, Petroleum & Allied Industries Employees Union, AFL-CIO v. NLRB, 249 F.2d 332, 334 (8th Cir. 1957):

"In National Labor Relations Board v. International Rice Milling Co., 341 U.S. 665 (1951), the Court found picketing at the primary employer's premises did not exceed conduct, traditional and permissible in a primary strike, and hence that the picketing there involved did not constitute an unfair labor practice violative of 8(b)(4)(A)."

When the 1959 amendments to the LMRA were passed, the conference committee inserted a new proviso to the secondary boycott provisions of the Landrum-Griffin bill: "[N]othing contained in clause (B) of this paragraph (4) shall be construed to make unlawful, where not otherwise unlawful, any primary strike or primary picketing." The House managers explained:

"The purpose of this provision is to make it clear that the changes in § 8(b)(4) do not overrule or qualify the present rules of law permitting picketing at the site of a primary labor dispute. This provision does not eliminate, restrict, or modify the limitations on picketing at the site of a primary labor dispute that are in existing law. See for example, NLRB v. Denver Building & Construction Trades Council (341 U.S. 675 (1951)); Brotherhood of Painters, Decorators, & Paper Hangers, and Pittsburgh Plate Glass Co., (110 N.L.R.B. 455 (1954)); Moore Dry Dock Co., (81 N.L.R.B. 1108); Washington Coca-Cola Bottling Works, Inc., (107 N.L.R.B. [299] (1953))." H.R. REP. No. 1147, 86th Cong., 1st Sess. 38 (1959).

B. COMMON SITUS PROBLEMS

SAILORS' UNION OF THE PACIFIC AND MOORE DRY DOCK CO.

National Labor Relations Board
92 N.L.R.B. 547 (1950)

[Samsoc, a Greek-owned shipping company made a contract with Kaiser Gypsum to carry gypsum from Mexico in the Samsoc ship *Phopho.* This meant replacement of an American crew for the Greek ship with a Greek crew. To convert the *Phopho* for this job, it was placed in the Moore Dry Dock Co. shipyard. Moore Dry Dock agreed that two weeks before completion Samsoc could put its crew on board for training purposes. In January, 1950, while the boat was in the shipyard, the union learned of the arrangement. It demanded bargaining rights on the ship, but on February 16, this demand was refused. On the next day it placed pickets at the entrance to the shipyard. The union also informed the bargaining representatives of Moore's employees that the *Phopho* was "hot" and requested cooperation. On February 21, all of Moore's employees refused to work on the *Phopho*, but continued on other work.]

. . . .

Section 8(b)(4)(A) is aimed at secondary boycotts and secondary strike activities. It was not intended to proscribe primary action by a union having a legitimate labor dispute with an employer. Picketing at the premises of a primary employer is traditionally recognized as primary action, even though it is "necessarily designed to induce and encourage third persons to cease doing business with the picketed employer. . . ." [3]

Hence, if Samsoc, the owner of the *S.S. Phopho*, had had a dock of its own in California to which the *Phopho* had been tied up while undergoing conversion by Moore Dry Dock employees, picketing by the Respondent at the dock site would unquestionably have constituted *primary* action even though the Respondent might have expected that the picketing would be more effective in persuading Moore employees not to work on the ship than to persuade the seamen aboard the *Phopho* to quit that vessel. The difficulty in the present case arises therefore, not because of any difference in picketing objectives,[5] but from the fact that the *Phopho* was not tied up at its own dock, but at that of Moore, while the picketing was going on in front of the Moore premises.

In the usual case, the *situs* of a labor dispute is the premises of the primary employer. Picketing of the premises is also picketing of the *situs;* the test of legality of picketing is that enunciated by the Board in the *Pure Oil* [7] and *Ryan Construction* [8] cases. But in some cases the *situs* of the dispute may not be limited to a fixed location; it may be ambulatory. Thus, in the *Schultz* [9] case, a majority of the Board held that the truck upon which a truck driver worked was the *situs* of a labor dispute between him and the owner of the truck. Similarly, we hold in the present case that, as the *Phopho* was the place of employment of the seamen, it was the *situs* of the dispute between Samsoc and the Respondent over working conditions aboard the vessel.

---

[3] Oil Workers Local 346 (Pure Oil Co.) [84 N.L.R.B. 315, 318].

[5] "Plainly, the object of all picketing at all times is to influence third persons to withhold their business or services from the struck employer. In this respect there is no distinction between lawful primary picketing and unlawful secondary picketing proscribed by § 8(b)(4)(A)." Teamsters Local 807 (Schultz Refrigerated Service, Inc.) [87 N.L.R.B. 502].

[7] [*Supra* note 3.]

[8] [United Electrical, Radio & Machine Workers (Ryan Constr. Co.), 85 N.L.R.B. 417.]

[9] [*Supra* note 5.]

When the *situs* is ambulatory, it may come to rest temporarily at the premises of another employer. The perplexing question is: Does the right to picket follow the *situs* while it is stationed at the premises of a secondary employer, when the only way to picket that *situs* is in front of the secondary employer's premises? Admittedly, no easy answer is possible. Essentially the problem is one of balancing the right of a union to picket at the site of its dispute as against the right of a secondary employer to be free from picketing in a controversy in which it is not directly involved.

When a secondary employer is harboring the *situs* of a dispute between a union and a primary employer, the right of neither the union to picket nor of the secondary employer to be free from picketing can be absolute. The enmeshing of premises and *situs* qualifies both rights. In the kind of situation that exists in this case, we believe that picketing of the premises of a secondary employer is primary if it meets the following conditions: (a) The picketing is strictly limited to times when the *situs* of dispute is located on the secondary employer's premises; (b) at the time of the picketing the primary employer is engaged in its normal business at the *situs;* (c) the picketing is limited to places reasonably close to the location of the *situs;* (d) the picketing discloses clearly that the dispute is with the primary employer. All these conditions were met in the present case.

(a) During the entire period of the picketing the *Phopho* was tied up at a dock in the Moore shipyard.

(b) Under its contract with Samsoc, Moore agreed to permit the former to put a crew on board the *Phopho* for training purposes during the last two weeks before the vessel's delivery to Samsoc. At the time the picketing started on February 17, 1950, 90 per cent of the conversion job had been completed, practically the entire crew had been hired, the ship's oil bunkers had been filled and other stores were shortly to be put aboard. The various members of the crew commenced work as soon as they reported aboard the *Phopho.* Those in the deck compartment did painting and cleaning up; those in the steward's department, cooking and cleaning up; and those in the engine department, oiling and cleaning up. The crew were thus getting the ship ready for sea. They were on board to serve the purposes of Samsoc, the *Phopho's* owners, and not Moore. The normal business of a ship does not only begin with its departure on a scheduled voyage. The multitudinous steps of preparation, including hiring and training a crew and putting stores aboard, are as much a part of the normal business of a ship as the voyage itself. We find, therefore, that the *Phopho* was engaged in its normal business.

(c) Before placing its pickets outside the entrance to the Moore shipyard, the Respondent Union asked, but was refused, permission to place its pickets at the dock where the *Phopho* was tied up. The Respondent, therefore, posted its pickets at the yard entrance which, as the parties stipulated, was as close to the *Phopho* as they could get under the circumstances.

(d) Finally, by its picketing and other conduct the Respondent was scrupulously careful to indicate that its dispute was solely with the primary employer, the owners of the *Phopho.* Thus the signs carried by the pickets said only that the *Phopho* was unfair to the Respondent. The *Phopho* and not Moore was declared "hot." Similarly, in asking co-operation of other unions, the Respondent clearly revealed that its dispute was with the *Phopho*. Finally, Moore's own witnesses admitted that no attempt was made to interfere with other work in progress in the Moore yard.

We believe that our dissenting colleagues' expressions of alarm are based on a misunderstanding of our decision. We are not holding, as the dissenters seem to think, that a union which has a dispute with a shipowner over working conditions of seamen aboard a ship may lawfully picket the premises of an independent shipyard to which the shipowner has delivered his vessel for overhaul and repair. We are only holding that, if a shipyard permits the owner of a vessel to use its dock for the purpose of readying and training a crew and putting stores aboard a ship, a union representing seamen may then, within the careful limitations laid down in this decision, lawfully picket the front of the shipyard premises to advertise its dispute with the shipowner. . . .

NOTES

1. Suppose the owner of the ship (primary employer with whom the union has its dispute) removes all of the employees from the ship while it is in dry dock undergoing repairs. May the union still picket legally, assuming that it indicates that the dispute is only with the shipowner? *Cf.* Seafarers International Union v. NLRB, 265 F.2d 585 (D.C. Cir. 1959) *(Held:* Yes. In response to the argument that "an object" must have been to induce employees of the dry dock company concertedly to refuse to work on the ship, the court reasoned that the *"situs"* of the dispute was at the ship, the picketing was "primary," and the employer should not be permitted to make the picketing illegal by removing his employees from the ship; the fact that the dry dock employees refused to work on the ship was "incidental.")

But where a nonunion subcontractor responded to a union's picketing by arranging with the general contractor to work only on weekends and after 4:30 P.M. on weekdays, and the union was duly notified of this change, it was unlawful for the union to continue to picket the site during the regular weekday hours. Plumbers Local 519 v. NLRB (H. L. Robertson & Associates), 416 F.2d 1120 (D.C. Cir. 1969). The *Seafarers* case was distinguished on the ground that there the primary employees were removed from the job situs *without* notice to the union, and the purpose was to eliminate the union's picketing entirely.

For a sharp clash over the still unresolved issue of when lawful primary picketing can take place at a construction site in the absence of the primary employees, see Operating Engineers Local 675 (Industrial Contracting Co.), 192 N.L.R.B. 1188 (1971) (3-2 majority included Board member whose term has since expired).

Where a reserved time is set up for a subcontractor to work only in the evenings but the subcontractor's foreman is visible inside during the day receiving and arranging materials for the evening work, a union which has a dispute with the subcontractor can picket during the day without a violation. Operating Engineers Local 450 (Linbeck Construction Co.), 219 N.L.R.B. 997 (1975), *aff'd,* 550 F.2d 311 (5th Cir. 1977).

2. Even though a union complied with the *Moore Dry Dock* standards for common situs picketing (including picketing only at the gate reserved for a nonunion subcontractor), and used signs stating that the sub was not paying area wage rates, the evidence established that the union's real purpose was to force the general contractor to replace the sub and so the picketing violated § 8(b)(4)(B) of the NLRA. Among the damaging evidence were the union's lack of concern about the fact of the sub's compliance or noncompliance with area standards, instructions to pickets not to tell persons whether they should cross the lines, and the temporary removal of the pickets in the mistaken belief that the general contractor had replaced the nonunion sub with a union sub. IBEW Local 480 v. NLRB, 413 F.2d 1085 (D.C. Cir. 1969). *See also* Teamsters Local 126 (Ready Mixed Concrete, Inc.), 200 N.L.R.B. 253 (1972).

Compare IBEW, Local 441 (Rollins Communications), 222 N.L.R.B. 99 (1976); IBEW, Local 369 (Garst-Receuveur Constr. Co.), 229 N.L.R.B. No. 17, 95 L.R.R.M. 1001 (1977).

3. In Steelworkers Local 6991 (Auburndale Freezer Corp.), 177 N.L.R.B. 791 (1969), the Labor Board held (3-2) that an independently owned and operated warehouse in which a struck employer stored citrus concentrate was a common situs, thus enabling a union to picket in compliance with the *Moore Dry Dock* tests. The Board found the continuous "presence of the primary" at the warehouse was established because it maintained effective control of the stored concentrate and because storage was an "integral part" of its operations, even though no primary employees worked there or made deliveries during the picketing. The majority emphasized that the struck employer's employees had delivered the concentrate to the warehouse for storage in an area leased by the primary, and that the concentrate was shipped from the warehouse by common carriers in accordance with the primary's instructions. The Board's decision was reversed in Auburndale Freezer Corp. v. NLRB, 434 F.2d 1219 (5th Cir. 1970), *cert. denied,* 402 U.S. 1013 (1971). The court rejected (2-1) the Board's "continuous presence" theory as an unwarranted extension of the common situs doctrine. The mere presence of a primary employer's goods on a neutral employer's premises, pursuant to an established business relationship, was not considered sufficient to enable picketing of the neutral premises.

4. Suppose the primary employer has a place of business at which the union could publicize the dispute by picketing. But he also sends trucks out to the premises of secondary employers making deliveries. May the union legally picket the trucks while they are at the secondary employer's premises, if the four *Moore Dry Dock* tests are met? The NLRB once held that the existence of a place of business of the primary employer at which adequate publicity of the dispute could be given to *his employees,* is strong evidence that an object of the picketing while the trucks were at the secondary employer's premises was to induce a concerted refusal to work by the secondary employer's employees, and hence a violation of the act. *See* Brewery & Beverage Drivers Local 67 (Washington Coca-Cola Bottling Works), 107 N.L.R.B. 299 (1953), *enforced,* 220 F.2d 380 (D.C. Cir. 1955).

However, the Board, in reversing the *Washington Coca-Cola* rule in IBEW, Local 861 (Plauche Electric, Inc.), 135 N.L.R.B. 250 (1962), said that the fact that a struck employer has a separate place of business in the area at which the union can picket is merely one of the circumstances to be considered in determining the legality of picketing of a common situs. The Board said that the *Moore Dry Dock* standards "are not to be applied on an indiscriminate 'per se' basis, but are to be regarded merely as aids in determining the underlying question of statutory violation."

In Teamsters Local 83 (Allied Concrete), 231 N.L.R.B. 1097 (1977), the Board held that a union lawfully picketed "between the headlights" of a struck employer's ready-mix concrete trucks that were making deliveries at a construction site, even though the struck employer had established a reserved gate for the use of its employees and suppliers and the picketing caused neutral employees to walk off the job. Peaceful primary picketing at any location is explicitly protected by the Taft-Hartley Act regardless of its effect on the operations of neutral employers, and primary picketing remains primary picketing even if there are other locations at which it might have been carried on without affecting neutral employees. Two members dissented.

NLRB v. DENVER BUILDING & CONSTRUCTION TRADES COUNCIL

Supreme Court of the United States
341 U.S. 675, 71 S. Ct. 943, 95 L. Ed. 1284 (1951)

MR. JUSTICE BURTON delivered the opinion of the Court.

The principal question here is whether a labor organization committed an unfair labor practice, within the meaning of § 8(b)(4)(A) of the National Labor Relations Act, ... as amended by the Labor Management Relations Act, 1947, by engaging in a strike, an object of which was to force the general contractor on a construction project to terminate its contract with a certain subcontractor on that project. For the reasons hereafter stated, we hold that such an unfair labor practice was committed.

In September, 1947, Doose & Lintner was the general contractor for the construction of a commercial building in Denver, Colorado. It awarded a subcontract for electrical work on the building, in an estimated amount of $2,300, to Gould & Preisner, a firm which for 20 years had employed nonunion workmen on construction work in that city. The latter's employees proved to be the only nonunion workmen on the project. Those of the general contractor and of the other subcontractors were members of unions affiliated with the respondent Denver Building and Construction Trades Council (here called the Council). In November a representative of one of those unions told Gould that he did not see how the job could progress with Gould's nonunion men on it. Gould insisted that they would complete the electrical work unless bodily put off. The representative replied that the situation would be difficult for both Gould & Preisner and Doose & Lintner.

January 8, 1948, the Council's Board of Business Agents instructed the Council's representative "to place a picket on the job stating that the job was unfair" to it. In keeping with the Council's practice, each affiliate was notified of that decision. That notice was a signal in the nature of an order to the members of the affiliated unions to leave the job and remain away until otherwise ordered. Representatives of the Council and each of the respondent unions visited the project and reminded the contractor that Gould & Preisner employed nonunion workmen and said that union men could not work on the job with nonunion men. They further advised that if Gould & Preisner's men did work on the job, the Council and its affiliates would put a picket on it to notify their members that nonunion men were working on it and that the job was unfair. All parties stood their ground.

January 9, the Council posted a picket at the project carrying a placard stating "This Job Unfair to Denver Building and Construction Trades Council." He was paid by the Council and his picketing continued from January 9 through January 22. During that time the only persons who reported for work were the nonunion electricians of Gould & Preisner. January 22, before Gould & Preisner had completed its subcontract, the general contractor notified it to get off the job so that Doose & Lintner could continue with the project. January 23, the Council removed its picket and shortly thereafter the union employees resumed work on the project. Gould & Preisner protested this treatment but its workmen were denied entrance to the job.

On charges filed by Gould & Preisner, the Regional Director of the National Labor Relations Board issued the complaint in this case against the Council and the respondent unions. It alleged that they had engaged in a strike or had caused strike action to be taken on the project by employees of the general contractor and of other subcontractors, an object of which was to force the general contractor to cease doing business with Gould & Preisner on that project.

Between the Board's receipt of the charges and the filing of the complaint based upon them, the Regional Director of the Board petitioned the United States District Court for the District of Colorado for injunctive relief. That petition was dismissed on the jurisdictional ground that the activities complained of did not affect interstate commerce. Sperry v. Denver Building Trades Council, 77 F. Supp. 321 (1958). Such action will be discussed later under the heading of *res judicata*. Hearings were held by the Board's trial examiner on the merits of the complaint. The Board adopted its examiner's findings, conclusions and recommendations, with minor additions and modifications not here material. It attached the examiner's intermediate report to its decision and ordered respondents to cease and desist from engaging in the activities charged. 82 N.L.R.B. 1195. Respondents petitioned the United States

Court of Appeals for the District of Columbia Circuit for a review under
§ 10(f). The Board answered and asked for enforcement of its order. That
court held, with one judge dissenting, that the conduct complained of
affected interstate commerce sufficiently to give the Board jurisdiction
over it, but the court unanimously set aside the order of the Board and
said: "Convinced that the action in the circumstances of this case is
primary and not secondary we are obliged to refuse to enforce the order
based on § 8(b)(4)(A)." 87 App. D.C. 293, 304, 186 F.2d 326, 337. . . .

III. *The Secondary Boycott.* — We now reach the merits. They require
a study of the objectives of the strike and a determination whether the
strike came within the definition of an unfair labor practice stated in
§ 8(b)(4)(A).

The language of that section which is here essential is as follows:

"(b) It shall be an unfair labor practice for a labor organization. . . .

"(4) to engage in . . . a strike . . . where an object thereof is: (A) forcing
or requiring . . . any employer or other person . . . to cease doing business
with any other person; . . . ." 61 Stat. 141, 29 U.S.C. (Supp. III)
§ 158(b)(4)(A).

While § 8(b)(4) does not expressly mention "primary" or "secondary"
disputes, strikes or boycotts, that section often is referred to in the act's
legislative history as one of the act's "secondary boycott sections." The
other is § 303, 61 Stat. 158, 29 U.S.C. (Supp. III) § 187, which uses the
same language in defining the basis for private actions for damages caused
by these proscribed activities.

Senator Taft, who was the sponsor of the bill in the Senate and was the
Chairman of the Senate Committee on Labor and Public Welfare in
charge of the bill, said, in discussing this section:

". . . [U]nder the provisions of the Norris-La Guardia Act, it became
impossible to stop a secondary boycott or any other kind of a strike, no
matter how unlawful it may have been at common law. All this provision
of the bill does is to reverse the effect of the law as to secondary boycotts.
It has been set forth that there are good secondary boycotts and bad
secondary boycotts. Our committee heard evidence for weeks and never
succeeded in having anyone tell us any difference between different kinds
of secondary boycotts. So we have so broadened the provision dealing
with secondary boycotts as to make them an unfair labor practice." 93
Cong. Rec. 4198.

The Conference Report to the House of Representatives said:

"Under clause (A) [of § 8(b)(4)] strikes or boycotts, or attempts to
induce or encourage such action, were made unfair labor practices if the
purpose was to force an employer or other person to cease using, selling,
handling, transporting, or otherwise dealing in the products of another,
or to cease doing business with any other person. Thus it was made an
unfair labor practice for a union to engage in a strike against employer A
for the purpose of forcing that employer to cease doing business with
employer B. Similarly it would not be lawful for a union to boycott
employer A because employer A uses or otherwise deals in the goods of,
or does business with, employer B." H.R. Rep. No. 510, 80th Cong., 1st
Sess. 43.

At the same time that §§ 7 and 13 safeguard collective bargaining, concerted activities and strikes between the primary parties to a labor dispute, § 8(b)(4) restricts a labor organization and its agents in the use of economic pressure where an object of it is to force an employer or other person to boycott someone else.

A. We must first determine whether the strike in this case had a proscribed object. The conduct which the Board here condemned is readily distinguishable from that which it declined to condemn in the *Rice Milling* case, *supra* at 665. There the accused union sought merely to obtain its own recognition by the operator of a mill, and the union's pickets near the mill sought to influence two employees of a customer of the mill not to cross the picket line. In that case we supported the Board in its conclusion that such conduct was no more than was traditional and permissible in a primary strike. The union did not engage in a strike against the customer. It did not encourage concerted action by the customer's employees to force the customer to boycott the mill. It did not commit any unfair labor practice proscribed by § 8(b)(4).

In the background of the instant case there was a long-standing labor dispute between the Council and Gould & Preisner due to the latter's practice of employing nonunion workmen on construction jobs in Denver. The respondent labor organizations contend that they engaged in a primary dispute with Doose & Lintner alone, and that they sought simply to force Doose & Lintner to make the project an all-union job. If there had been no contract between Doose & Lintner and Gould & Preisner there might be substance in their contention that the dispute involved no boycott. If, for example, Doose & Lintner had been doing all the electrical work on this project through its own nonunion employees, it could have replaced them with union men and thus disposed of the dispute. However, the existence of the Gould & Preisner subcontract presented a materially different situation. The nonunion employees were employees of Gould & Preisner. The only way that respondents could attain their purpose was to force Gould & Preisner itself off the job. This, in turn, could be done only through Doose & Lintner's termination of Gould & Preisner's subcontract. The result is that the Council's strike, in order to attain its ultimate purpose, must have included among its objects that of forcing Doose & Lintner to terminate that subcontract. On that point, the Board adopted the following finding:

"That *an* object, if not the only object, of what transpired with respect to ... Doose & Lintner was to force or require them to cease doing business with Gould & Preisner seems scarcely open to question, in view of all of the facts. And it is clear, at least as to Doose & Lintner, that that purpose was achieved." (Emphasis supplied.) 82 N.L.R.B. at 1212.

We accept this crucial finding. It was an object of the strike to force the contractor to terminate Gould & Preisner's subcontract.

B. We hold also that a strike with such an object was an unfair labor practice within the meaning of § 8(b)(4)(A).

It is not necessary to find that the *sole* object of the strike was that of forcing the contractor to terminate the subcontractor's contract. This is emphasized in the legislative history of the section. See also, NLRB v. Wine, Liquor & Distillery Workers Union, 178 F.2d 584, 586 (2d Cir. 1949).

We agree with the Board also in its conclusion that the fact that the contractor and subcontractor were engaged on the same construction project, and that the contractor had some supervision over the subcontractor's work, did not eliminate the status of each as an independent contractor or make the employees of one the employees of the other. The business relationship between independent contractors is too well established in the law to be overridden without clear language doing so. The Board found that the relationship between Doose & Lintner and Gould & Preisner was one of "doing business" and we find no adequate reason for upsetting that conclusion.

Finally, § 8(c) safeguarding freedom of speech has no significant application to the picket's placard in this case. Section 8(c) does not apply to a mere signal by a labor organization to its members, or to the members of its affiliates, to engage in an unfair labor practice such as a strike proscribed by § 8(b)(4)(A). That the placard was merely such a signal, tantamount to a direction to strike, was found by the Board.

". . . [T]he issues in this case turn upon acts by labor organizations which are tantamount to directions and instructions to their members to engage in strike action. The protection afforded by § 8(c) of the Act to the expression of 'any views, arguments or opinion' does not pertain where, as here, the issues raised under § 8(b)(4)(A) turn on official directions or instructions to a union's own members." 82 N.L.R.B. at 1213.

The further conclusion that § 8(c) does not immunize action against the specific provisions of § 8(b)(4)(A) has been announced in other cases. See IBEW, Local 108 v. NLRB, *infra* at 694.

Not only are the findings of the Board conclusive with respect to questions of fact in this field when supported by substantial evidence on the record as a whole, but the Board's interpretation of the act and the Board's application of it in doubtful situations are entitled to weight. In the views of the Board as applied to this case we find conformity with the dual congressional objectives of preserving the right of labor organizations to bring pressure to bear on offending employers in primary labor disputes and of shielding unoffending employers and others from pressures in controversies not their own.

For these reasons we conclude that the conduct of respondents constituted an unfair labor practice within the meaning of § 8 (b)(4)(A). The judgment of the Court of Appeals accordingly is reversed and the case is remanded to it for procedure not inconsistent with this opinion.

It is so ordered.

MR. JUSTICE JACKSON would affirm the judgment of the Court of Appeals.

MR. JUSTICE DOUGLAS, with whom MR. JUSTICE REED joins, dissenting.

The employment of union and nonunion men on the same job is a basic protest in trade union history. That was the protest here. The union was not out to destroy the contractor because of his antiunion attitude. The union was not pursuing the contractor to other jobs. All the union asked was that union men not be compelled to work alongside nonunion men on the same job. As Judge Rifkind stated in an analogous case, "the union was not extending its activity to a front remote from the immediate dispute but to one intimately and indeed inextricably united to it."

The picketing would undoubtedly have been legal if there had been no subcontractor involved — if the general contractor had put nonunion men on the job. The presence of a subcontractor does not alter one whit the realities of the situation; the protest of the union is precisely the same. In each the union was trying to protect the job on which union men were employed. If that is forbidden, the Taft-Hartley Act makes the right to strike, guaranteed by § 13, dependent on fortuitous business arrangements that have no significance so far as the evils of the secondary boycott are concerned. I would give scope to both § 8(b)(4) and § 13 by reading the restrictions of § 8(b)(4) to reach the case where an industrial dispute spreads from the job to another front.

NOTE

Are there circumstances under which a general contractor on a construction project assumes such substantial control over the subcontractors' employees that it would no longer be regarded as a neutral, but instead as a primary employer along with the subcontractors, and thus subject to picketing by a union without recourse under § 8(b)(4)(B) of the NLRA? *See* Teamsters Local 363 (Roslyn Americana Corp.), 214 N.L.R.B. 868 (1974).

INTERNATIONAL UNION OF ELECTRICAL, RADIO & MACHINE WORKERS, LOCAL 761, AFL-CIO v. NLRB [GENERAL ELECTRIC CO.]

Supreme Court of the United States
366 U.S. 667, 81 S. Ct. 1285, 6 L. Ed. 2d 592 (1961)

Mr. Justice Frankfurter delivered the opinion of the Court.

Local 761 of International Union of Electrical, Radio and Machine Workers, AFL-CIO was charged with a violation of § 8(b)(4)(A) of the National Labor Relations Act, as amended by the Taft-Hartley Act, 61 Stat. 136, 141, upon the following facts.

General Electric Corporation operates a plant outside of Louisville, Kentucky, where it manufactures washers, dryers, and other electrical household appliances. The square-shaped, thousand-acre, unfenced plant is known as Appliance Park. A large drainage ditch makes ingress and egress impossible except over five roadways across culverts, designated as gates.

Since 1954, General Electric sought to confine the employees of independent contractors, described hereafter, who work on the premises of the Park, to the use of Gate 3-A and confine its use to them. The undisputed reason for doing so was to insulate General Electric employees from the frequent labor disputes in which the contractors were involved. Gate 3-A is 550 feet away from the nearest entrance available for General Electric employees, suppliers, and deliverymen. Although anyone can pass the gate without challenge, the roadway leads to a guardhouse where identification must be presented. Vehicle stickers of various shapes and colors enable a guard to check on sight whether a vehicle is authorized to use Gate 3-A. Since January 1958, a prominent sign has been posted at the gate which states: "GATE 3-A FOR EMPLOYEES OF CONTRACTORS ONLY — G. E. EMPLOYEES USE OTHER GATES." On rare occasions, it appears, a General Electric employee was allowed to pass the guardhouse, but such occurrence was in violation of company instructions. There was no proof of any unauthorized attempts to pass the gate during the strike in question.

The independent contractors are utilized for a great variety of tasks on the Appliance Park premises. Some do construction work on new buildings; some install and repair ventilation and heating equipment; some engage in retooling and rearranging operations necessary to the manufacture of new models; others do "general maintenance work." These services are contracted to outside employers either because the company's employees lack the necessary skill or manpower, or because the work can be done more economically by independent contractors. The latter reason determined the contracting of maintenance work for which the Central Maintenance department of the company bid competitively with the contractors. While some of the work done by these contractors had on occasion been previously performed by Central Maintenance, the findings do not disclose the number of employees of independent contractors who were performing these routine maintenance services, as compared with those who were doing specialized work of a capital-improvement nature.

The Union, petitioner here, is the certified bargaining representative for the production and maintenance workers who constitute approximately 7,600 of the 10,500 employees of General Electric at Appliance Park. On July 27, 1958, the Union called a strike because of 24 unsettled grievances with the company. Picketing occurred at all gates, including Gate 3-A, and continued until August 9 when an injunction was issued by a Federal District Court. The signs carried by the pickets at all gates read: "LOCAL 761 ON STRIKE G.E. UNFAIR." Because of the picketing, almost all of the employees of independent contractors refused to enter the company premises.

Neither the legality of the strike or of the picketing at any of the gates except 3-A is in dispute, nor that the picketing was other than peaceful in nature. The sole claim was that the picketing before the gate exclusively used by employees of independent contractors was conduct proscribed by § 8(b)(4)(A).

The Trial Examiner recommended that the Board dismiss the complaint. He concluded that the limitations on picketing which the Board had prescribed in so-called "common situs" cases were not applicable to the situation before him, in that the picketing at Gate 3-A represented traditional primary action which necessarily had a secondary effect of inconveniencing those who did business with the struck employer. He reasoned that if a primary employer could limit the area of picketing around his own premises by contructing a separate gate for employees of independent contractors, such a device could also be used to isolate employees of his suppliers and customers, and that such action could not relevantly be distinguished from oral appeals made to secondary employees not to cross a picket line where only a single gate existed.

The Board rejected the Trial Examiner's conclusion, 123 N.L.R.B. 1547. It held that since only the employees of the independent contractors were allowed to use Gate 3-A, the Union's object in picketing there was "to enmesh these employees of the neutral employers in its dispute with the Company" thereby constituting a violation of § 8(b)(4)(A) because the independent employees were encouraged to engage in a concerted refusal to work "with an object of forcing the independent contractors to cease doing business with the Company."

The Court of Appeals for the District of Columbia granted enforcement of the Board's order, 107 App. D.C. 402, 278 F.2d 282. Although noting that a fine line was being drawn, it concluded that the Board was correct in finding that the objective of the Gate 3-A picketing was to encourage the independent-contractor employees to engage in a concerted refusal to perform services for their employers in order to bring pressure on General Electric. . . .

I. Section 8(b)(4)(A) . . . could not be literally construed; otherwise it would ban most strikes historically considered to be lawful, so-called primary activity. "While § 8(b)(4) does not expressly mention 'primary' or 'secondary' disputes, strikes or boycotts, that section often is referred to in the Act's legislative history as one of the Act's 'secondary boycott sections.' " NLRB v. Denver Bldg. & Constr. Trades Council, 341 U.S. 675, 686 (1951). "Congress did not seek by § 8(b)(4), to interfere with the ordinary strike. . . ." NLRB v. International Rice Milling Co., 341 U.S. 665, 672 (1951). The impact of the section was directed toward what is known as the secondary boycott whose "sanctions bear, not upon the employer who alone is a party to the dispute, but upon some third party who has no concern in it." IBEW, Local 501 v. NLRB, 181 F.2d 34, 37 (2d Cir. 1950). Thus the section "left a striking labor organization free to use persuasion, including picketing, not only on the primary employer and his employees but on numerous others. Among these were secondary employers who were customers or suppliers of the primary employer and persons dealing with them . . . and even employees of secondary employers so long as the labor organization did not . . . 'induce or encourage the employees of any employer to engage, in a strike or a concerted refusal in the course of their employment'. . . ." NLRB v. Teamsters Local 294, 284 F.2d 887, 889 (2d Cir. 1960).

But not all so-called secondary boycotts were outlawed in § 8(b)(4)(A). "The section does not speak generally of secondary boycotts. It describes and condemns specific union conduct directed to specific objectives. . . . Employees must be induced; they must be induced to engage in a strike or concerted refusal; an object must be to force or require their employer or another person to cease doing business with a third person. Thus, much that might argumentatively be found to fall within the broad and somewhat vague concept of secondary boycott is not in terms prohibited." Local 1976, United Brotherhood of Carpenters & Joiners v. NLRB, 357 U.S. 93, 98 (1958). See also United Bhd. of Carpenters (Wadsworth Bldg. Co.), 81 N.L.R.B. 802, 805.

Important as is the distinction between legitimate "primary activity" and banned "secondary activity," it does not present a glaringly bright line. The objectives of any picketing include a desire to influence others from withholding from the employer their services or trade. See Sailors' Union of the Pacific (Moore Dry Dock), 92 N.L.R.B. 547. "[I]ntended or not, sought for or not, aimed for or not, employees of neutral employers do take action sympathetic with strikers and do put pressure on their own employers." Seafarers Int'l Union v. NLRB, 105 App. D.C. 211, 265 F.2d 585, 590 (1959). "It is clear that, when a union pickets an employer with whom it has a dispute, it hopes, even if it does not intend, that all persons will honor the picket line, and that hope encompasses the employees of neutral employers who may in the course of their employment (deliverymen and the like) have to enter the premises." Id. at page 591. "Almost all picketing, even at the situs of the primary employer and surely at that of the secondary, hopes to achieve the forbidden objective, whatever other motives there may be and however small the chances of success." Local 294, supra, 284 F.2d at 890. But picketing which induces secondary employees to respect a picket line is not the equivalent of picketing which has an object of inducing those employees to engage in concerted conduct against their employer in order to force him to refuse to deal with the struck employer. NLRB v. International Rice Milling Co., supra.

However difficult the drawing of lines more nice than obvious, the statute compels the task. Accordingly, the Board and the courts have attempted to devise reasonable criteria drawing heavily upon the means to which a union resorts in promoting its cause. Although "[n]o rigid rule which would make . . . [a] few factors conclusive is contained in or deducible from the statute," Sales Drivers v. NLRB, 97 App. D.C. 173, 229 F.2d 514, 517 (1955), "[I]n the absence of admissions by the union of an illegal intent, the nature of acts performed shows the intent." Seafarers Int'l Union, supra at 591.

The nature of the problem, as revealed by unfolding variant situations, inevitably involves an evolutionary process for its rational response, not a quick, definitive formula as a comprehensive answer. And so, it is not surprising that the Board has more or less felt its way during the fourteen years in which it has had to apply § 8(b)(4)(A), and has modified and reformed its standards on the basis of accumulating experience. . . .

II. The early decisions of the Board following the Taft-Hartley amendments involved activity which took place around the secondary employer's premises. For example, in Wadsworth Building Co., *supra*, the union set up a picket line around the situs of a builder who had contracted to purchase prefabricated houses from the primary employer. The Board found this to be illegal secondary activity. See also Printing Specialties Union (Sealbright Pacific), 82 N.L.R.B. 271. In contrast, when picketing took place around the premises of the primary employer, the Board regarded this as valid primary activity. . . .

In United Electrical Workers (Ryan Constr. Corp.), 85 N.L.R.B. 417, Ryan had contracted to perform construction work on a building adjacent to the Bucyrus plant and inside its fence. A separate gate was cut through the fence for Ryan's employees which no employee of Bucyrus ever used. The Board concluded that the union — on strike against Bucyrus — could picket the Ryan gate, even though an object of the picketing was to enlist the aid of Ryan employees, since Congress did not intend to outlaw primary picketing. . . .

However, the impact of the new situations made the Board conscious of the complexity of the problem by reason of the protean forms in which it appeared. This became clear in the "common situs" cases — situations where two employers were performing separate tasks on common premises. The *Moore Dry Dock* case, *supra*, laid out the Board's new standards in this area. . . .

In Local 55 (PBM), 108 N.L.R.B. 363, the Board for the first time applied the *Dry Dock* test although the picketing occurred at premises owned by the primary employer. There, an insurance company owned a tract of land that it was developing, and also served as the general contractor. A neutral subcontractor was also doing work at the site. The union, engaged in a strike against the insurance company, picketed the entire premises, characterizing the entire job as unfair, and the employees of the subcontractor walked off. The Court of Appeals for the Tenth Circuit enforced the Board's order which found the picketing to be illegal on the ground that the picket signs did not measure up to the *Dry Dock* standard that they clearly disclose that the picketing was directed against the struck employer only. 218 F.2d 226.

The Board's application of the *Dry Dock* standards to picketing at the premises of the struck employer was made more explicit in Retail Fruit & Vegetable Clerks (Crystal Palace Market), 116 N.L.R.B. 856. The owner of a large common market operated some of the shops within, and leased out others to independent sellers. The union, although given permission to picket the owner's individual stands, chose to picket outside the entire market. The Board held that this action was violative of § 8(b)(4)(A) in that the union did not attempt to minimize the effect of its picketing, as required in a common-situs case, on the operations of the neutral employers utilizing the market. "We believe . . . that the foregoing principles should apply to all common situs picketing, including cases where, as here, the picketed premises are owned by the primary employer." 116 N.L.R.B., at 859. The *Ryan* case, *supra*, was overruled to the extent it implied the contrary. The Court of Appeals for the Ninth Circuit, in enforcing the Board's order, specifically approved its disavowance of an ownership test. 249 F.2d 591. The Board made clear that its decision did not affect situations where picketing which had effects on neutral third parties who dealt with the employer occurred at premises occupied solely by him. "In such cases, we adhere to the rule established by the Board . . . that more latitude be given to picketing at such separate primary premises than at premises occupied in part (or entirely) by secondary employers." 116 N.L.R.B., at 860, n. 10.

In rejecting the ownership test in situations where two employers were performing work upon a common site, the Board was naturally guided by this Court's opinion in *Rice Milling*, in which we indicated that the location of the picketing at the primary employer's premises was "not necessarily conclusive" of its legality. 341 U.S. at 671. Where the work done by the secondary employees is unrelated to the normal operations of the primary employer, it is difficult to perceive how the pressure of picketing the entire situs is any less on the neutral employer merely because the picketing takes place at property owned by the struck employer. The application of the *Dry Dock* tests to limit the picketing effects to the employees of the employer against whom the dispute is directed carries out the "dual congressional objectives of preserving the right of labor organizations to bring pressure to bear on offending employers in primary labor disputes and of shielding unoffending employers and others from pressures in controversies not their own." NLRB v. Denver Bldg. & Constr. Trades Council, *supra*, 341 U.S. at 692 (1951).

III. From this necessary survey of the course of the Board's treatment of our problem, the precise nature of the issue before us emerges. With due regard to the relation between the Board's function and the scope of judicial review of its ruling, the question is whether the Board may apply the *Dry Dock* criteria so as to make unlawful picketing at a gate utilized exclusively by employees of independent contractors who work on the struck employers' premises. The effect of such a holding would not bar the union from picketing at all gates used by the employees, suppliers, and customers of the struck employer. Of course an employer may not, by removing all his employees from the situs of the strike, bar the union from publicizing its cause, see Automotive, Petroleum, Local 618 v. NLRB, 249 F.2d 332 (8th Cir. 1957). The basis of the Board's decision in this case would not remotely have that effect, nor any such tendency for the future.

The Union claims that if the Board's ruling is upheld, employers will be free to erect separate gates for deliveries, customers, and replacement workers which will be immunized from picketing. This fear is baseless. The key to the problem is found in the type of work that is being performed by those who use the separate gate. It is significant that the Board has since applied its rationale, first stated in the present case, only to situations where the independent workers were performing tasks unconnected to the normal operations of the struck employer — usually construction work on his buildings. In such situations, the indicated limitations on picketing activity respect the balance of competing interests that Congress has required the Board to enforce. On the other hand, if a separate gate were devised for regular plant deliveries, the barring of picketing at that location would make a clear invasion on traditional primary activity of appealing to neutral employees whose tasks aid the employer's everyday operations. . . .

In a case similar to the one now before us, the Court of Appeals for the Second Circuit sustained the Board in its application of § 8(b)(4)(A) to a separate-gate situation. "There must be a separate gate marked and set apart from other gates; the work done by the men who use the gate must be unrelated to the normal operations of the employer, and the work must be of a kind that would not, if done when the plant were engaged in its regular operations, necessitate curtailing those operations." United Steelworkers v. NLRB, 289 F.2d 591, 595 (2d Cir. 1961). These seem to us controlling considerations.

IV. The foregoing course of reasoning would require that the judgment below sustaining the Board's order be affirmed but for one consideration, even though this consideration may turn out not to affect the result. The legal path by which the Board and the Court of Appeals reached their decisions did not take into account that if Gate 3-A was in fact used by employees of independent contractors who performed conventional maintenance work necessary to the normal operations of General Electric, the use of the gate would have been a mingled one outside the bar of § 8(b)(4)(A). In short, such mixed use of this portion of the struck employer's premises would not bar picketing rights of the striking employees. While the record shows some such mingled use, it sheds no light on its extent. It may well turn out to be that the instances of these maintenance tasks were so insubstantial as to be treated by the Board as *de minimis.* We cannot here guess at the quantitative aspects of this problem. It calls for Board determination. For determination of the questions thus raised, the case must be remanded by the Court of Appeals to the Board.

Reversed.

The Chief Justice and Mr. Justice Black concur in the result.

Mr. Justice Douglas.

I did not vote to grant certiorari in this case because it seemed to me that the problem presented was in the keeping of the Courts of Appeals within the meaning of Universal Camera Corp. v. NLRB, 340 U.S. 474, 490 (1951). Since the Court of Appeals followed the guide lines of that case (see 278 F.2d 282, 286), I would leave the decision with it. I cannot say it made any egregious error, though I might have decided the case differently had I sat on the Labor Board or on the Court of Appeals.

NOTES

1. *Compare* Chemical Workers Local 557 (Crest, Inc.), 179 N.L.R.B. 168 (1969), with UAW Local 422 (Crow Constr. Co.), 192 N.L.R.B. 808 (1971).

2. In United Steelworkers v. NLRB [Carrier Corp.], 376 U.S. 492 (1964), the Supreme Court unanimously upheld a union's picketing of a gate through which a railroad entered a fenced-in area alongside the primary employer's plant, the right-of-way being owned by the railroad. The Court stated that its decision was grounded on the doctrine enunciated in the 1961 *General Electric* reserved-gate picketing case, *i.e.,* if the duties of the secondary employees were connected with the normal operations of the struck plant, then the picketing would be primary activity within the protection of the primary-picketing proviso to § 8(b)(4)(B). In noting that "the location of the picketing is an important but not decisive factor," the Court said that in the instant case the "railroad gate adjoined company property and was in fact the railroad entrance gate to the Carrier plant." Therefore, "for the purposes of § 8(b)(4) picketing at a situs so proximate and related to the employer's day-to-day operations is no more illegal than if it had occurred at a gate owned by Carrier." Moreover, the Court held that "under § 8(b)(4) the distinction between primary and secondary picketing carried on at a separate gate maintained on the premises of the primary employer does not rest upon the peaceful or violent nature of the conduct, but upon the type of work being done by the picketed secondary employees." However, the Court cautioned that this did not mean that violent primary picketing is in all respects legal but only that it is not forbidden by the secondary boycott provisions.

3. *See generally,* Cantor, *Separate Gates, Related Work, and Secondary Boycotts,* 27 RUTGERS L. REV. 613 (1974).

BUILDING & CONSTRUCTION TRADES COUNCIL OF NEW ORLEANS (MARKWELL & HARTZ, INC.)

National Labor Relations Board
155 N.L.R.B. 319 (1965)

. . . .

In the period covered by the complaint, M & H was the general contractor on a project for expansion of a filtration plant on the premises of the East Jefferson Water Works, District No. 1, in Jefferson Parish, Louisiana. M & H decided to perform about 80 percent of the project with its own employees while subcontracting the balance. Included in the work contracted out was the piledriving awarded to Binnings, and the electrical work awarded to Barnes. Both Binnings and Barnes employ members of craft unions affiliated with Respondent.

The East Jefferson Water Works is surrounded by a chain-link fence, with two vehicular gates on Jefferson Highway which bounds the property on the north, and two additional gates on Arnoult Road, bounding the premises on the east. The gate on Jefferson Highway closest to Arnoult

Road is the principal gate insofar as the construction project is concerned, and is called the main gate. On Arnoult Road the northern-most gate is the warehouse gate while the southern-most shall be referred to as the rear gate.

At all times material, Respondent has been engaged in a primary labor dispute with M & H, and has had no dispute with either Binnings or Barnes.

On October 17 [1963], in connection with its dispute with M & H, Respondent commenced picketing the gates leading to the jobsite. The picketing took place during normal workhours, with the number of pickets varying from one to three individuals. The picket sign listed both the rates that should be paid on the job and carried the following message:

> MARKWELL AND HARTZ
> GENERAL CONTRACTOR
> DOES NOT HAVE A SIGNED AGREEMENT WITH THE
> BUILDING AND CONSTRUCTION TRADES COUNCIL
> OF NEW ORLEANS
> AFL-CIO

The picketing continued until enjoined in the . . . 10 (*l*) proceeding on January 16, 1964. At no time during the picketing did employees of Binnings or Barnes cross the picket line to perform work in connection with their employers' subcontract.

The validity of Respondent's picketing prior to October 23 is not in issue. However, on that date M & H posted the two gates on Jefferson Highway and the warehouse gate on Arnoult Road, reserving them for use of subcontractors and persons making deliveries to the project, and prohibiting their use by M & H's employees. The rear gate on Arnoult Road was designated for exclusive use of the latter.

That morning, when Respondent's picket encountered the newly marked gates, he moved to the rear gate which was reserved for M & H's employees. As a result, piledriving crews employed by Binnings entered the main gate and began working. About an hour and a half later the picket returned to the main gate, and Binnings' employees walked off. M & H then decided to remove its employees, with the exception of the superintendent and project engineer, in the hope that Binnings would then be able to complete the piledriving work. By 10 o'clock that morning its employees were off the site. Though Respondent was notified of the absence of the primary employees, the picketing continued. When Binnings' crew again honored the picket line, M & H recalled its employees. They reported to work on October 24 at 10 a.m. to complete the piledriving work themselves.

On November 14, M & H changed the signs on the Jefferson Highway gates to indicate that these entrances were not to be used by employees of M & H or carriers and suppliers making deliveries to M & H, and that such persons were to use the rear gate on Arnoult Road. M & H informed Respondent of these changes and notified suppliers to use the rear gate only. Identical changes were made at the warehouse gate on November 16, and on December 6 the rear gate was marked as reserved for use of employees of M & H and suppliers and carriers making deliveries to M & H.

The record does not show that the gates were at any time used in a manner inconsistent with the postings. Excepting a brief period on October 23, and the period between December 16 and 20, Respondent picketed the gates which were posted for exclusive use of subcontractors and which were not used by M & H's employees and suppliers.[3]

B. Discussion

On these facts, we are asked to decide whether a union, in futherance of a primary dispute with a general contractor in the construction industry, may lawfully engage in jobsite picketing at gates reserved and set apart for exclusive use of neutral subcontractors. . . .

Without passing upon whether the subcontractor gates involved herein were established and maintained in accordance with the *General Electric* requirements, we are of the opinion that the principles expressed in that case are inapposite in determining whether a union may lawfully extend its dispute with a general contractor on a construction site by picketing gates reserved for exclusive use of subcontractors also engaged on that project. Rather, we believe that this issue must be resolved in the light of the *Moore Dry Dock* standards, traditionally applied by the Board in determining whether picketing at a common situs is protected primary activity.

Unlike *General Electric* and *Carrier Corp.*, both of which involved picketing *at the premises of a struck manufacturer,* the picketing in the instant case occurred at a construction project on which M & H, the primary employer, was but one of several employers operating on premises owned and operated by a third party, the Jefferson Parish Water Works. Picketing of neutral and primary contractors under such conditions, has been traditionally viewed as presenting a "common situs" problem.[9]

Over the years, the distinction between common situs picketing and that which occurs at premises occupied solely by the struck employer has been a guiding consideration in Board efforts to strike a balance between the competing interests underlying the boycott provisions of the act. Mindful

---

[3] Because M & H, Binnings, Barnes, and suppliers and carriers making deliveries to M & H are the only persons identified as using the four gates, it is assumed that, after November 16, Binnings and Barnes and their employees had exclusive use of all gates save the "rear gate" set aside for M & H, its employees, and persons making deliveries to it.

[9] See . . . Carpenters, Local 55 (Professional & Business Men's Life Ins. Co.), 108 N.L.R.B. 363, *enforced,* 218 F.2d 226 (10th Cir. 1954). The Board, in the *PBM* case, rejected a contention that, where the union's dispute is with the general contractor, the entire project must be viewed as the primary situs, stating at 366, that:

"[T]he Supreme Court has rejected the view that prime contractors and subcontractors working on a construction project constitute for present purposes a single integrated

of the fact that "Congress did not seek, by § 8(b)(4), to interfere with the ordinary strike," [11] the Board has given wide latitude to picketing and related conduct confined to the sole premises of the primary employer. On the other hand, in the interest of shielding "unoffending employers" from disputes not their own, the Board has taken a more restrictive view of common situs picketing, requiring that it be conducted so as "to minimize its impact on neutral employees insofar as this can be done without substantial impairment of the effectiveness of the picketing in reaching the primary employees." [13]

In accordance with the foregoing, the Board, in determining whether a labor organization, when picketing a common situs, has taken all reasonable precaution to prevent enmeshment of neutrals, traditionally applies the limitations set forth in the *Moore Dry Dock* case. In our opinion application of these standards to all common situs situations, including those, which like the instant case, involve picketing of gates reserved exclusively for neutral contractors on a construction project, serves the "dual congressional objectives" underlying the boycott provisions of the act.

The instant facts, when considered in the light of the legislative history and decisional precedent, do not warrant a departure from our long-established policy with respect to common situs picketing. Quite to the contrary, our continued adherence to the *Moore Dry Dock* standards in such cases comports with the clear expression of Congress, in enacting the "primary strike and picketing" proviso, that said proviso ". . . does not eliminate, restrict, or modify the limitations on picketing at the site of a primary dispute that are in existing law." [14] Nor do the Supreme Court's decisions in *General Electric* and *Carrier* detract from our conclusions in this regard; for, the mere fact that picketing of a neutral gate *at premises of a struck employer,* may in proper circumstances be lawful primary action, does not require a like finding when a labor organization applies

---

operation. The Supreme Court has agreed with the Board 'in its conclusion that the fact that the contractor and subcontractor were engaged in the same construction project, and that the contractor had some supervision over the subcontractor's work, did not eliminate the status of each as an independent contractor or make the employees of one the employees of the other.' NLRB v. Denver Bldg. Council, 341 U.S. 675, at 689-690 (1951)."

[11] International Rice Milling Co. v. NLRB, 341 U.S. 665, 672 (1951).

[13] Crystal Palace Market, *supra* at 859.

[14] As indicated by the following statement on the part of the House conferees, the enactment of specific language protecting primary activity was accompanied by express preservation of the *Denver Building Trades* and *Moore Dry Dock* cases:

"[T]he amendment adopted by the committee of conference contains a provision 'that nothing contained in clause (B) of this paragraph (4) shall be construed to make unlawful, where not otherwise unlawful, any primary strike or primary picketing.' The purpose of this provision is to make it clear that the changes in § 8(b)(4) do not overrule or qualify the present rules of law permitting picketing at the site of a primary labor dispute. This provision does not eliminate, restrict, or modify the limitations on picketing at the site of a primary labor dispute that are in existing law. See, for example, NLRB v. Denver Building and Construction Trades Council, et al. (341 U.S. 675 (1951)); . . . Moore Dry Dock Co. (81 N.L.R.B. 1108) [*sic*]; . . ." 1 Leg. Hist. 942 (1959).

direct pressure upon secondary employers engaged on a common situs.[15] That the Supreme Court had no intention of overriding this historic distinction is evidenced by its express approval of the *Moore Dry Dock* standards,[16] and its observation that the *General Electric* case did not present a common situs situation to which the *Moore Dry Dock* standards should apply.[17] It is plain, therefore, that the Court did not seek to interfere with the Board's traditional approach to common situs problems; [18] rather, the Court's decisions in *General Electric* and *Carrier Corp.,* merely represent an implementation of the concomitant policy that lenient treatment be given to strike action taking place at the separate premises of a struck employer.

Applying the *Moore Dry Dock* standards to the instant case requires the timing and location of the picketing and the legends on the picket signs to be tailored to reach the employees of the primary employer, rather than those of the neutral employer, and deviations from these requirements establish the secondary object of the picketing and render it unlawful. Indeed, our dissenting colleagues do not disagree with this principle, but cite the *PBM* decision [20] with apparent approval. If the mere failure, as in *PBM,* to name the general contractor on the picket signs as the sole disputant suffices to demonstrate that a union is seeking to induce employees of the subcontractors not to work, it is self-evident that picketing a gate used solely by the neutral subcontractors demonstrates the same purpose. And if it is unlawful to induce such employees in the indirect, and more subtle, fashion represented by the facts in *PBM,* it is *a fortiori* unlawful in the direct inducement of such employees at a separate gate. *PBM,* in short, stands for the proposition that the relationship of a subcontractor to a general contractor does not make the former's employees fair game in connection with a union's dispute with the latter. The sole difference between *PBM* and the instant case lies in the means used to convey the union's respective messages to the employees of the neutral subcontractors. That this is an irrelevant difference is established by the Supreme Court's holding in *IBEW, Local 501 (Samuel Langer) v. NLRB,*[21] that "The words 'induce and encourage' are broad enough to include in them every form of influence and

---

[15] The diverse inferences to be drawn from economic pressures applied to neutrals at the premises of a struck employer and that applied at a common situs were recognized in early decisions of the Supreme Court interpreting § 8(b)(4). Thus in NLRB v. Carpenters, Local 74 (Ira A. Watson Co., d/b/a Watson's Specialty Store), 341 U.S. 707 (1951), in finding a union's inducement of work stoppages at a common situs to be secondary and unlawful, the Court distinguished International Rice Milling Co., *supra,* pointing out at 712, that picketing at the premises of the struck employer was not involved.

[16] IUE, Local 761 (General Electric Co.) v. NLRB, 366 U.S. 667, 679 (1961).

[17] Steelworkers (Carrier Corp.) v. NLRB, 376 U.S. 492, 497 (1964).

[18] As stated by the Supreme Court in Denver Bldg. & Const. Trades Council, *supra,* 692: "the Board's interpretation of the Act and . . . application of it in doubtful situations are entitled to weight."

[20] *Supra* note 9.

[21] 341 U.S. 694, 701-702 (1951).

persuasion." Since Respondent's picketing at the neutral gates of Binnings and Barnes continued after November 16, we find, in agreement with the General Counsel, that the picketing after that date [22] failed to comply with the *Moore Dry Dock* requirement that such action take place reasonably close to the situs of Respondent's dispute with M & H. We are completely satisfied that Respondent's picketing at the subcontractor gates was to induce strike action by employees of subcontractors with whom Respondent had no dispute. By such conduct, Respondent unlawfully sought to disrupt the operations of the neutral subcontractors and their employees and to enmesh them in the primary dispute in a manner which could not be condoned as an unavoidable by-product of legitimate primary picketing.

The dissent does not persuade us otherwise. The dissent's analysis, although well-stated and on first reading not unreasonable as an application of *General Electric* standards in a construction industry setting, nevertheless runs counter to firmly established principles governing common situs picketing in that industry. Simply because the work of the neutral subcontractors in one sense is "related to M & H's normal operations," our dissenting colleagues would exonerate the pickets' appeals to the secondary employees to honor the picket line aimed at M & H. And notwithstanding their suggestion (in footnote 35) that they would apply the "related work" standard only where the dispute is with a general contractor, the plain logic of their position is equally applicable where the primary dispute is with a building construction *sub-*contractor whose employees are working closely with employees of other subcontractors or those of the general contractors. Given the close relation — which is not only characteristic of but almost inevitable at many stages of a building construction project — of the work duties of the various other employees with those of the primary subcontractor, the principle of the dissent would also permit picket line appeals to the

----

[22] We do not regard, as unlawful, Respondent's picketing prior to November 16, as it was on that date that the respective neutral gates were first marked to preclude use by persons making deliveries to M & H. Although a common situs problem is presented where a gate is reserved for both neutral subcontractors and persons making deliveries to a struck contractor, a balance of the competing interests underlying 8(b)(4)(B) requires our respecting the traditional right of labor organizations to appeal to such deliverymen as a lawful incident of legitimate strike action against the primary employer.

In so finding, we note that, on October 23, M & H withdrew its employees for a 24-hour period in an attempt to prevent any legitimate picketing of the project. It is apparent that the primary employees were removed from the project though work was then available for them, that they could have been recalled at any time, that M & H's superintendent and project engineer remained on the job at all times, and that M & H otherwise continued its duties as general contractor during the 24-hour absence of its employees. In the circumstances, we are satisfied that despite the removal of its workers, M & H was then engaged in its normal business on the project, and that Respondent's continued picketing during this period fully complied with *Moore Dry Dock,* and did not evidence a departure from what at that time constituted lawful primary action. IBEW, Local 3 (New Power Wire & Elec. Corp.), 144 N.L.R.B. 1089; IBEW, Local 861 (Brownfield Electric, Inc.), 145 N.L.R.B. 1163; and Seafarers' Int'l Union (Salt Dome Production Co.) v. NLRB, 265 F.2d 585 (D.C. Cir. 1959).

employees of the neutral general contractor and other subcontractors whatever the situation as to common or separate gates.

But it was precisely this claim, that the *close* working relations of various building construction contractors on a common situs involved them in a common undertaking which destroyed the neutrality and thus the immunity of secondary employers and employees to picket line appeals, that the Supreme Court rejected in *Denver Building Trades*. And there is not the slightest intimation by the Court in *General Electric* or *Carrier* that it was reversing or revising the rule in *Denver*. Although our dissenting colleagues disclaim such a purpose, by applying the "close relation to normal operations" test of *General Electric*, the theory of the dissent, if logically extended, is one that would in effect reverse *Denver* not only where the overarching general contractor on the building site is the primary employer, but also, where the intertwined work of a construction *sub*contractor is the primary target. . . .

For the reasons stated, we conclude that Respondent violated § 8(b)(4)(i) and (ii)(B) of the act by inducing employees of Binnings and Barnes to engage in work stoppages, and by restraining and coercing said Employers, for an object of forcing or requiring them to cease doing business with M & H. . . .

MEMBERS FANNING and JENKINS, dissenting:

We dissent from the majority's conclusion that Respondent violated § 8(b)(4)(B) of the act by picketing, in the course of its primary dispute with Markwell & Hartz, gates reserved for employees of the subcontractors M & H had engaged to aid it in performing the construction work it was obligated to complete. In our view, the majority has inferred that Respondent's picketing was for an unlawful object simply from the fact that the reserved gates were used only by secondary employees, without inquiry into the question of whether the appeals to such employees, were, in the circumstances of this case, permissible primary activity, an inquiry which we believe is required by the Supreme Court's decisions in *General Electric* and *Carrier Corp.* As we believe, for reasons stated below, that the Court in those decisions applied principles of general application, we dissent from the majority's conclusion that the tests announced in *General Electric* for determining whether appeals to employees of neutral contractors constitute legitimate primary activity are not applicable to the building and construction industry. . . .

The *General Electric* case involved appeals to employees of neutral subcontractors and the Court, noting that "the key to the problem is found in the type of work that is being performed by those who use the separate gate," held that, before such appeals may be ruled unlawful under § 8(b)(4)(B),

"There must be a separate gate, marked and set apart from other gates; the work done by the men who use the [separate] gate must be unrelated to the normal operations of the employer, and the work must be of a kind that would not, if done when the plant were engaged in its regular operations, necessitate curtailing those operations."

The crucial consideration regarding this holding is not, as the majority apparently views it, that it was made with respect to conduct occurring in connection with a strike at an industrial plant, but that it held that appeals to respect a picket line made to employees of secondary employers whose operations do not meet the tests stated above constitute legitimate primary activity just as do similar appeals to employees of neutral suppliers and deliverers.

In view of the foregoing, we find, contrary to the majority opinion, that the principles set forth in the *General Electric* decision, and the tests there enunciated by the Court for the application of those principles, govern picketing in the construction industry as well as in other industries. In our view, neither the fact that the Court expressly approved the *Moore Dry Dock* standards, nor its holding that the *General Electric* case did not present a common situs situation to which those standards should be applied, requires a different conclusion. The *Moore Dry Dock* standards were not designed to restrict primary activity at common situs disputes, but rather to assure that banned secondary activity would not be permitted. . . . Furthermore, it is clear that, had the Board concluded in its decision on remand in the *General Electric* case [31] that the work of the neutral contractors was not directly related to General Electric's normal operations, the application of the *Moore Dry Dock* tests to the picketing of the reserved gate in that case would be permissible.

Significantly, Congress has not seen fit to distinguish between industries, by adopting a more narrow definition of the lawful scope of picketing in the construction industry than is permitted in other industries. Certainly, the economic pressure sustained by neutral subcontractors as a consequence of reserved gate picketing on a construction job is no different from that imposed by like conduct upon neutral subcontractors performing work on premises occupied by a struck manufacturer. Nor is it any different from the pressures sustained by neutral suppliers making deliveries to the struck primary employer whether he be a manufacturer or a general contractor in the building and construction industry. Accordingly, it is only by determining the legality of reserved gate picketing by standards generally applicable to all industries that the dual congressional objectives are served and the competing interests of picketing unions and secondary employers protected.

Nor do we regard the Court's decision in *Denver Bldg. & Constr. Trades Council* as precluding application of *General Electric* to the instant

---

[31] 137 N.L.R.B. 1684. In this connection, the Board found that construction operations performed by contractors for General Electric, whose employees also were engaged in similar construction work, were "directly related" to General Electric's operations, thus giving the union engaged in a primary dispute with General Electric the right to make direct appeals to employees of the neutral contractors to honor its picket line. It is ironical, to say the least, for the majority now to hold that the undisputed direct relationship which does exist between the operations of general contractors and their subcontractors in the building and construction industry goes for nought in determining whether a striking union's picket line publication of its primary dispute with the general contractor, with

case. In *Denver,* the Court held that despite their close relationship, the several contractors on a construction job were not allies or a single employer for purposes of the boycott provisions of the act.[35]

The Supreme Court in *General Electric* affirmed the rule stated in *Denver* and, accepting the separate legal status of *General Electric* and its contractors, addressed itself to the question whether the picketing involved had an unlawful secondary objective. Here, too, we accept the proposition that the various contractors at a construction job are separate employers and concern ourselves only with the circumstances under which the Board, absent direct proof or admission, may properly infer that the picketing involved had an unlawful secondary objective.

In applying the *General Electric* standards to the instant case, we find that the work of Binnings and Barnes was related to the normal operations of M & H, the general contractor. In this connection it is relevant that employees of the named subcontractors were scheduled to work during the picketing period together with the employees of M & H in completing the filtration plant expansion job.[38] In addition, during this period, M & H's project engineer and superintendent were to work with the subcontractors to insure that M & H's commitment to the owner was performed in compliance with project specifications. We find that M & H's portion of the work on this job was part of its normal operations, as was completion of the entire project, and that the work of the subcontractors

---

consequent appeals to neutral employees to respect the picket line, constitutes legitimate primary activity.

[35] [341 U.S. 675], 680-690. In *Denver,* the conduct evidencing the union's objective of enmeshing the neutral employer was its demand that the neutral general contractor remove a nonunion subcontractor from the project, which demand was accompanied by picketing which failed to disclose that the Respondent Council's primary dispute was only with a nonunion subcontractor. These facts plus the other factors supporting the finding that the picketing constituted a "signal in the nature of an order to the members of the affiliated unions to leave the job and remain away until otherwise ordered" demonstrated the secondary objectives of the picketing, and distinguishes that case from the instant case. Here, in contrast, the Respondent's primary dispute is with the general contractor and the picketing clearly discloses this fact. . . . We have no quarrel with the requirement that a union's picketing at a common situs must clearly disclose that its dispute is with the primary employer. We in fact insist upon observance of that requirement but, when it and the other *Moore Dry Dock* requirements are observed, we believe that there is no warrant for inferring that the picketing is for an object other than to induce employees to honor the picket line. In view of the *General Electric* decision, we believe that the *Moore Dry Dock* tests cannot be applied in a manner which will bar primary appeals to employees of employers whose operations are directly related to the normal operations of the struck employer. In so finding, we do not imply that simply because a union has a dispute with one subcontractor on a construction project, appeals to employees of other subcontractors using different gates constitute primary appeals within the meaning of the *General Electric* decision. . . . In such situations, the work of the employees of the neutral general contractor and subcontractors, though obviously bearing a close relationship to the work of the primary employees, is nevertheless not work which the primary subcontractor has obligated himself to perform or which lies within his power to control or to assign to whomsoever he sees fit. It is therefore not "related to the normal operations of the [primary] employer" nor does it "otherwise contribut[e] to the operations which the strike is endeavoring to halt" within the meaning of the *General Electric* and *Carrier* decisions. . . .

was related to both M & H's work on the job and its responsibility to complete the project itself, and hence related to M & H's normal operations.[39] We, accordingly, hold that the work of the subcontractors failed to meet the "unrelated work" condition [40] and, on this basis, we find that Respondent had the right to appeal to the employees of the subcontractor to honor its picket line around M & H's operations.

This being the case, the fact that such appeals were addressed to those employees at gates reserved for their exclusive use by M & H furnishes no basis for the majority's conclusion that the picketing after November 16 "failed to comply with the *Moore Dry Dock* requirement that such action take place reasonably close to the situs of Respondent's dispute with M & H." As the Supreme Court indicated in the *General Electric* decision, the barring of picketing through the device of a gate reserved for the exclusive use of secondary employees whose tasks aid the struck employer's everyday operations constitutes a clear invasion of traditional primary activity. Furthermore, the *Moore Dry Dock* tests are utilized by the Board to aid it in determining whether certain kinds of picketing constitute proscribed secondary or protected primary activity whereas the *General Electric* tests are designed to aid in determining whether a union has the right to appeal directly to the secondary employees using a reserved gate. Accordingly, it seems obvious that the former tests must be applied in a manner which will give full effect to the latter tests. As we find that Respondent had the right to appeal to the employees of the neutral subcontractor, we find that the picketing at the reserved gates constituted compliance with the requirement that its picketing be limited to places reasonably close to the situs of Respondent's dispute with M & H. Accordingly, as the picketing also conformed to the other *Moore Dry Dock* tests, we perceive no basis on which to conclude that Respondent's object in picketing the reserved gates was to induce the employees of M & H's subcontractors to engage in a refusal to perform services with the object of forcing their employers to cease dealing with M & H.

Accordingly, we would find that Respondent's picketing did not violate § 8(b)(4)(B), and we would dismiss the complaint.

---

[38] M & H undertook to perform about 80 percent of the project with its own employees, while subcontracting the balance. It also appears that M & H in certain instances could not work until completion of a subcontractor's phase of the job, while in others subcontractors would have to hold up while M & H was performing.

[39] In so finding, we reject the General Counsel's view that the "unrelated work" condition is met unless the work is "identical or substantially similar" to that of the primary employer. The work of those using the reserved gate may be related to the normal operations of the primary employer though not "identical or substantially similar" to that normally performed by the latter. . . .

[40] Having found that the work of those using the reserved gate was directly related to the normal operations of M & H, we need not decide whether, or under what circumstances, the "interruption of operations" test applies to reserved gate picketing in the construction industry.

NOTES

1. The Board's order was enforced in Markwell & Hartz, Inc. v. NLRB, 387 F.2d 79 (5th Cir. 1967), *cert. denied,* 391 U.S. 914 (1968).

The rule in *Markwell & Hartz* was applied even where the general contractor was engaged in building an apartment complex on land that it owned. Carpenters, Local 470 (Mueller-Anderson, Inc.), 224 N.L.R.B. 315 (1976), Members Fanning and Jenkins dissenting. *Mueller-Anderson* was affirmed in 570 F.2d 742 (9th Cir. 1977).

2. A bill authorizing "common-situs" picketing in the construction industry passed both Houses of Congress in 1976, but was vetoed by President Ford and was not passed over his veto. A similar bill was defeated in the House of Representatives in 1977.

3. In NLRB v. Operating Engineers Local 825 [Burns & Roe, Inc.], 400 U.S. 297 (1971), Burns, a general contractor, subcontracted all construction work on a project to three companies, White, Chicago Bridge, and Poirier. All three employed members of an operating engineers union, but White, unlike Chicago Bridge and Poirier, did not have a collective bargaining agreement with the union. White installed an electric welding machine and assigned its operation to members of an ironworkers union. The engineers demanded this work and informed Burns, the general contractor, that they would strike the job unless Burns signed a contract, which would bind all three subcontractors as well as Burns, giving the engineers jurisdiction over the welding equipment. When White and Burns refused to accede to these demands, the engineers struck the project. The NLRB found the union guilty of violating both §§ 8(b)(4)(B) and 8(b)(4)(D) (the latter being the "jurisdictional dispute" provision). A court of appeals approved the 8(b)(4)(D) finding but disapproved the 8(b)(4)(B) finding. On a review limited to the 8(b)(4)(B) issue, the Supreme Court reversed the court of appeals. Declared the Court:

> "The more difficult task is to determine whether one of Local 825's objectives was to force Burns and the other neutrals to 'cease doing business' with White as § 8(b)(4)(B) requires. The Court of Appeals concluded that the union's objective was to force Burns 'to use its influence with the subcontractor to change the subcontractor's conduct, not to terminate their relationship' and that this was not enough. That court read the statute as requiring that the union demand nothing short of a complete termination of the business relationship between the neutral and the primary employer. Such a reading is too narrow.
>
> "Some disruption of business relationships is the necessary consequence of the purest form of primary activity. These foreseeable disruptions are, however, clearly protected. Steelworkers (Carrier), 376 U.S. at 492; Electrical Workers (General Electric), 366 U.S. at 682. Likewise, secondary activity could have such a limited goal and the foreseeable result of the conduct could be, while disruptive, so slight that the 'cease doing business' requirement is not met.

"Local 825's goal was not so limited nor were the foreseeable consequences of its secondary pressure slight. The operating engineers sought to force Burns to bind all the subcontractors on the project to a particular form of job assignments. The clear implication of the demands was that Burns would be required either to force a change in White's policy or to terminate White's contract. The strikes shut down the whole project. If Burns was unable to obtain White's consent, Local 825 was apparently willing to continue disruptive conduct that would bring all the employers to their knees.

"Certainly, the union would have preferred to have the employers capitulate to its demands; it wanted to take the job of operating the welding machines away from the Ironworkers. It was willing, however, to try to obtain this capitulation by forcing neutrals to compel White to meet union demands. To hold that this flagrant secondary conduct with these most serious disruptive effects was not prohibited by § 8(b)(4)(B) would be largely to ignore the original congressional concern. . . ."

C. THE ALLY DOCTRINE

NLRB v. BUSINESS MACHINE & OFFICE APPLIANCE MECHANICS CONFERENCE BOARD, IUE, LOCAL 459 [ROYAL TYPEWRITER CO.]

United States Court of Appeals, Second Circuit
228 F.2d 553 (1955)
Cert. denied, 351 U.S. 962 (1956)

LUMBARD, Circuit Judge. This case arose out of a labor dispute between the Royal Typewriter Company and the Business Machine and Office Appliance Mechanics Conference Board, Local 459, IUE-CIO, the certified bargaining agent of Royal's typewriter mechanics and other service personnel. The National Labor Relations Board now seeks enforcement of an order directing the Union to cease and desist from certain picketing and to post appropriate notices.

The findings of the Board, adequately supported by the record, disclose the following facts, about which there is no significant dispute. On about March 23, 1954, the Union, being unable to reach agreement with Royal on the terms of a contract, called the Royal service personnel out on strike. The service employees customarily repair typewriters either at Royal's branch offices or at its customers' premises. Royal has several arrangements under which it is obligated to render service to its customers. First, Royal's warranty on each new machine obligates it to provide free inspection and repair for one year. Second, for a fixed periodic fee Royal contracts to service machines not under warranty. Finally, Royal is committed to repairing typewriters rented from it or loaned by it to replace machines undergoing repair. Of course, in addition Royal provides repair service on call by non-contract users.

During the strike Royal differentiated between calls from customers to whom it owed a repair obligation and others. Royal's office personnel were instructed to tell the latter to call some independent repair company listed in the telephone directory. Contract customers, however, were advised to select such an independent from the directory, to have the repair made, and to send a receipted invoice to Royal for reimbursement for reasonable repairs within their agreement with Royal. Consequently many of Royal's contract customers had repair services performed by various independent repair companies. In most instances the customer sent Royal the unpaid repair bill and Royal paid the independent company directly. Among the independent companies paid directly by Royal for repairs made for such customers were Typewriter Maintenance and Sales Company and Tytell Typewriter Company. . . .

During May, 1954, the Union picketed four independent typewriter repair companies who had been doing work covered by Royal's contracts pursuant to the arrangement described above. The Board found this picketing unlawful with respect to Typewriter Maintenance and Tytell. Typewriter Maintenance was picketed for about three days and Tytell for several hours on one day. In each instance the picketing, which was peaceful and orderly, took place before entrances used in common by employees, deliverymen and the general public. The signs read substantially as follows (with the appropriate repair company name inserted):

Notice to the Public Only
Employees of Royal Typewriter Company
on Strike
Tytell Typewriter Company Employees
Are Being Used as Strikebreakers

Business Machine & Office Appliance
Mechanics Union, Local 459, IUE-CIO

Both before and after this picketing, which took place in mid-May, Tytell and Typewriter Maintenance did work on Royal accounts and received payment directly from Royal. Royal's records show that Typewriter Maintenance's first voucher was passed for payment by Royal on April 20, 1954, and Tytell's first voucher was passed for payment on May 3, 1954. After these dates each independent serviced various of Royal's customers on numerous occasions and received payment directly from Royal. . . .

On the above facts the Trial Examiner and the Board found that . . . the repair company picketing violated § 8(b)(4) of the National Labor Relations Act, 29 U.S.C. § 158(b)(4). . . .

We are of the opinion that the Board's finding with respect to the repair company picketing cannot be sustained. The independent repair companies were so allied with Royal that the Union's picketing of their premises was not prohibited by § 8(b)(4)(A).

We approve the "ally" doctrine which had its origin in a well reasoned opinion by Judge Rifkind in the *Ebasco* case, Douds v. Architects, Engineers, Chemists & Technicians, Local 231, 75 F. Supp. 672 (S.D.N.Y. 1948). Ebasco, a corporation engaged in the business of providing engineering services, had a close business relationship with Project, a firm providing similar services. Ebasco subcontracted some of its work to Project and when it did so Ebasco supervised the work of Project's employees and paid Project for the time spent by Project's employees on Ebasco's work plus a factor for overhead and profit. When Ebasco's employees went on strike, Ebasco transferred a greater percentage of its work to Project, including some jobs that had already been started by Ebasco's employees. When Project refused to heed the Union's requests to stop doing Ebasco's work, the Union picketed Project and induced some of Project's employees to cease work. On these facts Judge Rifkind found that Project was not "doing business" with Ebasco within the meaning of § 8(b)(4)(A) and that the Union had therefore not committed an unfair labor practice under that Section. He reached this result by looking to the legislative history of the Taft-Hartley Act and to the history of the secondary boycotts which it sought to outlaw. He determined that Project was not a person "wholly unconcerned in the disagreement between an employer and his employees" such as § 8(b)(4)(A) was designed to protect. The result has been described as a proper interpretation of the Act by its principal sponsor, Senator Taft, 95 Cong. Rec. 8709 (1949), and President Eisenhower in his January, 1954, recommendations to Congress for revision of the Act included a suggestion which would make this rule explicit.

Here there was evidence of only one instance where Royal contacted an independent (Manhattan Typewriter Service, not named in the complaint) to see whether it could handle some of Royal's calls. Apart from that incident there is no evidence that Royal made any arrangement with an independent directly. It is obvious, however, that what the independents did would inevitably tend to break the strike. As Judge Rifkind pointed out in the *Ebasco* case:

"The economic effect on Ebasco's employees was precisely that which would flow from Ebasco's hiring strikebreakers to work on its own premises."

And at 95 Cong. Rec. 8709 (1949) Senator Taft said:

"The spirit of the Act is not intended to protect a man who in the last case I mentioned is cooperating with a primary employer and taking his work and doing the work which he is unable to do because of the strike."

President Eisenhower's recommendation referred to above was to make it explicit "that concerted action against (1) an employer who is performing 'farmed-out' work for the account of another employer whose employees are on strike . . . will not be treated as a secondary boycott." Text of President's Message to Congress on Taft-Hartley Amendments, January 11, 1954. At least one commentator has suggested that the enactment of this change would add nothing to existing law. Cushman, Secondary Boycotts and the Taft-Hartley Law, 6 Syracuse L. Rev. 109, 121

(1954). Moreover, there is evidence that the secondary strikes and boycotts sought to be outlawed by § 8(b)(4)(A) were only those which had been unlawful at common law. 93 Cong. Rec. 3950, 4323 (1947) (Senator Taft), 2 Legislative History of Labor Management Relations Act, 1947, 1006, 1106. And although secondary boycotts were generally unlawful, it has been held that the common law does not proscribe union activity designed to prevent employers from doing the farmed-out work of a struck employer. Iron Moulders Union v. Allis-Chalmers Co., 166 Fed. 45, 51 (7th Cir. 1908). Thus the picketing of the independent typewriter companies was not the kind of secondary activity which § 8(b)(4)(A) of the Taft-Hartley Act was designed to outlaw. Where an employer is attempting to avoid the economic impact of a strike by securing the services of others to do his work, the striking union obviously has a great interest, and we think a proper interest, in preventing those services from being rendered. This interest is more fundamental than the interest in bringing pressure on customers of the primary employer. Nor are those who render such services completely uninvolved in the primary strike. By doing the work of the primary employer they secure benefits themselves at the same time that they aid the primary employer. The ally employer may easily extricate himself from the dispute and insulate himself from picketing by refusing to do that work. A case may arise where the ally employer is unable to determine that the work he is doing is "farmed-out." We need not decide whether the picketing of such an employer would be lawful, for that is not the situation here. The existence of the strike, the receipt of checks from Royal, and the picketing itself certainly put the independents on notice that some of the work they were doing might be work farmed-out by Royal. Wherever they worked on new Royal machines they were probably aware that such machines were covered by a Royal warranty. But in any event, before working on a Royal machine they could have inquired of the customer whether it was covered by a Royal contract and refused to work on it if it was. There is no indication that they made any effort to avoid doing Royal's work. The Union was justified in picketing them in order to induce them to make such an effort. We therefore hold that an employer is not within the protection of § 8(b)(4)(A) when he knowingly does work which would otherwise be done by the striking employees of the primary employer and where this work is paid for by the primary employer pursuant to an arrangement devised and originated by him to enable him to meet his contractual obligations. The result must be the same whether or not the primary employer makes any direct arrangement with the employers providing the services. . . .

Enforcement of the Board's order is therefore in all respects denied.

NOTES

1. For cases applying the principles of the *Royal Typewriter* case, *supra,* see General Teamsters, Local 314 (Truck Operators League), 122 N.L.R.B. 25 (1958); United Brewery Workers, Local 366 (Adolph Coors

Co.), 121 N.L.R.B. 271 (1958); San Jacinto Die Sinkers Conference (Gen. Metals Corp.), 120 N.L.R.B. 1227 (1958).

In Graphic Arts Union, Local 277 (S & M Rotogravure Service, Inc.), 222 N.L.R.B. 280 (1976), the Board held (Chairman Murphy dissenting) that the ally doctrine applied, despite the announcement by the struck employer that he had decided to discontinue that part of the business (engraving rotogravure cylinders) which the union had struck and which he had subcontracted out during the strike. Also, the fact that the struck employer has the customer contract for the ally's services does not prevent him from being an ally, where the struck employer "orchestrated" the arrangements and the ally knew he was doing struck work. *See also,* later decisions in this case, 225 N.L.R.B. 1253 (1976), *affirmed,* 545 F.2d 1079 (7th Cir. 1976). An associated case, in accord, is Blackhawk Engraving Co. v. NLRB, 540 F.2d 1296 (7th Cir. 1976).

2. When there is a finding of economic alliance, employees of the secondary employer may be induced to stop work altogether and not merely induced to quit work on "hot" products destined to or from the primary employer. *See* Shopmen's Local 501 (Oliver Whyte Co.), 120 N.L.R.B. 856 (1958).

3. In Teamsters Local 563 (Fox Valley Material Suppliers Ass'n), 176 N.L.R.B. 386 (1969), the Labor Board indicated that a contractor could become an ally of a primary employer by "unknowingly" performing struck work for him. An employer has "the burden of determining whether or not he is engaged in neutral or ally type work." Here, the contractor was hired directly by the primary employer, and had reason to know the latter was involved in a strike.

4. Sears, Roebuck sells carpeting at a price which includes installation, but the customer is informed that Sears will arrange for someone else to install it. Sears maintains a "working relationship" with sixty independent business firms that perform this service. Are Sears and the installers "allies," so that a union seeking to organize the installers may lawfully picket Sears too? *See* Carpet Layers Local 419 (Sears, Roebuck & Co.), 190 N.L.R.B. 143 (1971).

5. Where the jobsite of a supplier of building stone who usually delivered his stone f.o.b. was struck and customers arranged with independent truckers to go get the stone and deliver it, the truckers became allies, subject to picketing while the trucks were unloading. The customers deducted the delivery cost from the contract price of the stone. The court of appeals said, "it is not important how the ally gets that work . . . it makes no difference who makes the telephone call which brings into the dispute those who do the struck work." Laborers International Union Local 859 v. NLRB, 446 F.2d 1319 (D.C. Cir. 1971).

6. *Treatment of "struck work" in the 1959 amendments.* The Landrum-Griffin bill (H.R. 8400, 86th Cong., 1st Sess.) included the following proviso in its section dealing with secondary boycotts:

"*Provided further,* That nothing contained in clause (B) of this paragraph (4) shall be construed to make unlawful where not otherwise unlawful, any strike against, or a refusal to perform services for any person who has contracted or agreed with an employer to perform for such employer work which he is unable to perform because his employees are engaged in a strike not unlawful under this Act or in violation of a collective bargaining agreement, if such strike was ratified or approved by the representatives of such employees whom such employer is required to recognize under this Act, and the refusal is limited to services which would ordinarily be performed by the striking employees."

However, this proviso was not included in the final enactment, and the House managers explained it this way:

"[N]o language has been included with reference to struck work because the committee of conference did not wish to change the existing law as illustrated by such decisions as Douds v. Metropolitan Federation of Architects (75 F. Supp. 672 (S.D.N.Y. 1948)) and NLRB v. Business Machine & Office Appliance Mechanics Bd., 228 F.2d 553 (2d Cir. 1955)." H.R. REP. No. 1147, 86th Cong., 1st Sess. 38 (1959).

7. Under what circumstances will common ownership and control bring two businesses within the "ally doctrine"? *See* J.G. Roy & Sons Co. v. NLRB, 251 F.2d 771 (1st Cir. 1958).

In Miami Newspaper Pressmen's Local 46 v. NLRB, 322 F.2d 405 (D.C. Cir. 1963), the court in enforcing a Board order held that common ownership of two newspapers, each, however, owned by a different corporation, was not alone sufficient to deprive either of them of its neutral status in a labor dispute involving the other. Consequently, the court said that the union could not claim, in defending against a charge that it engaged in an unlawful secondary boycott by picketing a Detroit newspaper in connection with a dispute between the union and a Miami paper, that the Detroit paper was not neutral by reason of its being commonly owned with the Miami newspaper, where the evidence showed that the two papers were independently managed and transacted only a negligible amount of business between each other. *See also* Television & Radio Artists v. NLRB, 462 F.2d 887 (D.C. Cir. 1972).

In Teamsters, Local 391 v. NLRB (Vulcan Materials Co.), 543 F.2d 1373 (D.C. Cir. 1976), the union had a labor dispute with the Mideast division of Vulcan; it then picketed the Chattanooga division of Vulcan, inducing its employees to strike in furtherance of the union's dispute with the Mideast division. The Board found, and the Court of Appeals agreed, that Chattanooga and Mideast were separate "persons" within the meaning of § 8(b)(4), since the divisions were operated as autonomous enterprises; thus the union's picketing was illegal.

In Quick Shop Markets v. Retail Clerks, 98 L.R.R.M. 2082 (D.C. Mo. 1978), the court ruled that an international union and its local violated the secondary boycott prohibitions of the Taft-Hartley Act when, in furtherance of their labor dispute with a corporation that sells foods and grocery-related products, the unions picketed grocery stores that had been franchised by the corporation to individual operators. Inasmuch as the corporation did not retain *de facto* control over the franchisees, they were "neutrals" in the dispute between the corporation and the unions.

8. *See* Levin, *"Wholly Unconcerned": The Scope and Meaning of the Ally Doctrine Under Section 8(b)(4) of the NLRA,* 119 U. Pa. L. Rev. 283 (1970); Irving, *Struck Work Ally Doctrine: Some Issues and Answers,* 9 Ga. L. Rev. 303 (1976).

D. CONSUMER PICKETING

NLRB v. FRUIT & VEGETABLE PACKERS & WAREHOUSEMEN, LOCAL 760 [TREE FRUITS]

Supreme Court of the United States
377 U.S. 58, 84 S. Ct. 1063, 12 L. Ed. 2d 129 (1964)

Mr. Justice Brennan delivered the opinion of the Court.

Under § 8(b)(4)(ii)(B) of the National Labor Relations Act, as amended, it is an unfair labor practice for a union "to threaten, coerce, or restrain any person," with the object of "forcing or requiring any person to cease using, selling, handling, transporting, or otherwise dealing in the products of any other producer . . . or to cease doing business with any other person. . . ." A proviso excepts, however, "publicity *other than picketing,* for the purpose of truthfully advising the public . . . that a product or products are produced by an employer with whom the labor organization has a primary dispute and are distributed by another employer, as long as such publicity does not have an effect of inducing any individual employed by any person other than the primary employer in the course of his employment to refuse to pick up, deliver, or transport any goods, or not to perform any services, at the establishment of the employer engaged in such distribution." (Italics supplied). The question in this case is whether the respondent unions violated this section when they limited their secondary picketing of retail stores to an appeal to the customers of the stores not to buy the products of certain firms against which one of the respondents was on strike.

Respondent Local 760 called a strike against fruit packers and warehousemen doing business in Yakima, Washington.[2] The struck firms sold Washington State apples to the Safeway chain of retail stores in and about Seattle, Washington. Local 760, aided by respondent Joint Council, instituted a consumer boycott against the apples in support of the strike. They placed pickets who walked back and forth before the customers' entrances of 46 Safeway stores in Seattle. The pickets—two at each of 45 stores and three at the 46th store—wore placards and distributed handbills which appealed to Safeway customers, and to the public generally, to refrain from buying Washington State apples, which were

---

[2] The firms, 24 in number, are members of the Tree Fruits Labor Relations Committee, Inc., which acts as the members' agent in labor disputes and in collective bargaining with unions which represent employees of the members. The strike was called in a dispute over the terms of the renewal of a collective bargaining agreement.

only one of numerous food products sold in the stores.[3] Before the pickets appeared at any store, a letter was delivered to the store manager informing him that the picketing was only an appeal to his customers not to buy Washington State apples, and that the pickets were being expressly instructed "to patrol peacefully in front of the consumer entrances of the store, to stay away from the delivery entrances and not to interfere with the work of your employees, or with deliveries to or pickups from your store." A copy of written instructions to the pickets—which included the explicit statement that "you are also forbidden to request that the customers not patronize the store" — was enclosed with the letter. Since it was desired to assure Safeway employees that they were not to cease work, and to avoid any interference with pickups or deliveries, the pickets appeared after stores opened for business and departed before the stores closed. At all times during the picketing, the store employees continued to work, and no deliveries or pickups were obstructed. Washington State apples were handled in normal course by both Safeway employees and the employees of other employers involved. Ingress and egress by customers and others was not interfered with in any manner.

---

[3] The placard worn by each picket stated: "To the Consumer: Non-Union Washington State apples are being sold at this store. Please do not purchase such apples. Thank you. Teamsters Local 760, Yakima, Washington."

A typical handbill read:

"DON'T BUY
WASHINGTON STATE
APPLES

THE 1960 CROP OF WASHINGTON STATE APPLES
IS BEING PACKED BY NON-UNION FIRMS

Included in this non-union operation are twenty-six firms in the Yakima Valley with which there is a labor dispute. These firms are charged with being

UNFAIR

by their employees who, with their union, are on strike and have been *replaced by non-union strikebreaking workers* employed under substandard wage scales and working conditions.

In justice to these striking union workers who are attempting to protect their living standards and their right to engage in good-faith collective bargaining, we request that you

DON'T BUY
WASHINGTON STATE
APPLES

TEAMSTERS UNION LOCAL 760 YAKIMA, WASHINGTON

This is not a strike against any store or market.

(P.S. PACIFIC FRUIT & PRODUCE CO. is the only firm packing Washington State Apples under a union contract.)"

A complaint issued on charges that this conduct violated § 8(b)(4) as amended.[5] The case was submitted directly to the National Labor Relations Board on a stipulation of facts and the waiver of a hearing and proceedings before a Trial Examiner. The Board held, following its construction of the statute in Upholsterers Frame & Bedding Workers Twin City Local No. 61, 132 N.L.R.B. 40, that "by literal wording of the proviso [to § 8(b)(4)] as well as through the interpretive gloss placed thereon by its drafters, consumer picketing in front of a secondary establishment is prohibited." 132 N.L.R.B. 1172, 1177. Upon respondents' petition for review and the Board's cross-petition for enforcement, the Court of Appeals for the District of Columbia Circuit set aside the Board's order and remanded. The court rejected the Board's construction and held that the statutory requirement of a showing that respondents' conduct would "threaten, coerce or restrain" Safeway could only be satisfied by affirmative proof that a substantial economic impact on Safeway had occurred, or was likely to occur as a result of the conduct. Under the remand the Board was left "free to reopen the record to receive evidence upon the issue whether Safeway was in fact threatened, coerced, or restrained." 308 F.2d 311, 318. . . .

The Board's reading of the statute—that the legislative history and the phrase "other than picketing" in the proviso reveal a congressional purpose to outlaw all picketing directed at customers at a secondary site —necessarily rested on the finding that Congress determined that such picketing always threatens, coerces or restrains the secondary employer. We therefore have a special responsiblity to examine the legislative history for confirmation that Congress made that determination. Throughout the history of federal regulation of labor relations, Congress has consistently refused to prohibit peaceful picketing except where it is used as a means to achieve specific ends which experience has shown are undesirable. "In the sensitive area of peaceful picketing Congress has dealt explicitly with isolated evils which experience has established flow from such picketing." NLRB v. Drivers Local Union, 362 U.S. 274, 284 (1960). We have recognized this congressional practice and have not ascribed to Congress a purpose to outlaw peaceful picketing unless "there is the clearest indication in the legislative history," ibid., that Congress intended to do so as regards the particular ends of the picketing under review. Both the congressional policy and our adherence to this principle of interpretation reflect concern that a broad ban against peaceful picketing might collide with the guarantees of the First Amendment.

We have examined the legislative history of the amendments to § 8(b)(4), and conclude that it does not reflect with the requisite clarity

---

[5] The complaint charged violations of both subsections (i) and (ii) of § 8(b)(4). The Board held however that as the evidence indicated "that Respondents' picketing was directed at consumers only, and was not intended to 'induce or encourage' employees of Safeway or of its suppliers to engage in any kind of action, we find that by such picketing Respondents did not violate § 8(b)(4)(i)(B) of the Act." 132 N.L.R.B. at 1177. See also NLRB v. Servette, Inc., supra at 46, decided today.

a congressional plan to proscribe all peaceful consumer picketing at secondary sites, and, particularly, any concern with peaceful picketing when it is limited, as here, to persuading Safeway customers not to buy Washington State apples when they traded in the Safeway stores. All that the legislative history shows in the way of an "isolated evil" believed to require proscription of peaceful consumer picketing at secondary sites, was its use to persuade the customers of the secondary employer to cease trading with him in order to force him to cease dealing with, or to put pressure upon, the primary employer. This narrow focus reflects the difference between such conduct, and peaceful picketing at the secondary site directed only at the struck product. In the latter case, the union's appeal to the public is confined to its dispute with the primary employer, since the public is not asked to withhold its patronage from the secondary employer, but only to boycott the primary employer's goods. On the other hand, a union appeal to the public at the secondary site not to trade at all with the secondary employer goes beyond the goods of the primary employer, and seeks the public's assistance in forcing the secondary employer to cooperate with the union in its primary dispute.[7] This is not to say that this distinction was expressly alluded to in the debates. It is to say, however, that the consumer picketing carried on in this case is not attended by the abuses at which the statute was directed.

The story of the 1959 amendments, which we have detailed at greater length in our opinion filed today in *NLRB v. Servette,* begins with the original § 8(b)(4) of the Taft-Hartley Act. Its prohibition, in pertinent part, was confined to the inducing or encouraging of "the employees of any employer to engage in, a strike or a concerted refusal . . . to handle . . . any goods . . ." of a primary employer. This proved to be inept language. Three major loopholes were revealed. Since only inducement of "employees" was proscribed, direct inducement of a supervisor or the secondary employer by threats of labor trouble was not prohibited. Since only a "strike or concerted refusal" was prohibited, pressure upon a single employee was not forbidden. Finally, railroads, airlines and municipalities were not "employers" under the Act and therefore inducement or encouragement of their employees was not unlawful.

---

[7] The distinction between picketing a secondary employer merely to "follow the struck goods," and picketing designed to result in a generalized loss of patronage, was well established in the state cases by 1940. The distinction was sometimes justified on the ground that the secondary employer, who was presumed to receive a competitive benefit from the primary employer's nonunion, and hence lower, wage scales, was in "unity of interest" with the primary employer, Goldfinger v. Feintuch, 276 N.Y. 281, 286, 11 N.E.2d 910 (1937); Newark Ladder & Bracket Sales Co. v. Furniture Workers, Local 66, 125 N.J. Eq. 99, 4 A.2d 49 (1939); Johnson v. Milk Drivers & Dairy Employees, Local 854, 195 So. 791 (Ct. App. La. 1940), and sometimes on the ground that picketing restricted to the primary employer's product is "a primary boycott against the merchandise." Chiate v. United Cannery Agricultural Packing & Allied Workers, 2 CCH Lab. Cas. 125, 126 (Cal. Sup. Ct.). See I Teller, Labor Disputes and Collective Bargaining § 123 (1940).

When major labor relations legislation was being considered in 1958, the closing of these loopholes was important to the House and to some members of the Senate. But the prevailing Senate sentiment favored new legislation primarily concerned with the redress of other abuses, and neither the Kennedy-Ives bill, which failed of passage in the House in the Eighty-fifth Congress, nor the Kennedy-Ervin bill, adopted by the Senate in the Eighty-sixth Congress, included any revision of § 8(b)(4). Proposed amendments of § 8(b)(4) offered by several Senators to fill the three loopholes were rejected. The Administration introduced such a bill, and it was supported by Senators Dirksen and Goldwater. Senator Goldwater, an insistent proponent of stiff boycott curbs, also proposed his own amendments. We think it is especially significant that neither Senator, nor the Secretary of Labor in testifying in support of the Administration's bill, referred to consumer picketing as making the amendments necessary.[10] Senator McClellan, who also offered a bill to curb boycotts, mentioned consumer picketing but only such as was "pressure in the form of dissuading customers *from dealing with* secondary employers." (Emphasis supplied.) It was the opponents of the amendments who, in expressing fear of their sweep, suggested that they might proscribe consumer picketing. Senator Humphrey first sounded the warning early in April. Many months later, when the Conference bill was before the Senate, Senator Morse, a conferee, would not support the Conference bill on the express ground that it prohibited consumer picketing. But we have often cautioned against the danger, when interpreting a statute, of reliance upon the views of its legislative opponents. In their zeal to defeat a bill, they understandably tend to overstate its reach. "The fears and doubts of the opposition are no authoritative guide to the construction of legislation. It is the sponsor that we look to when the meaning of the statutory words is in doubt." Schwegmann Bros. v. Calvert Distillers Corp., 341 U.S. 384, 394-395 (1951); see also Mastro Plastics Corp. v. Labor Board, 350 U.S. 270, 288 (1956); United States v. Calamaro, 354 U.S. 351, n. 9, at 358 (1957). The silence of the sponsors of amendments is pregnant with significance since they must have been aware that consumer picketing as such had been held to be outside the reach of § 8(b)(4). We are faithful to our practice of respecting the congressional policy of legislating only against clearly identified abuses of peaceful picketing when we conclude that the Senate neither specified the kind of picketing here involved as an abuse, nor indicated any intention of banning all consumer picketing.

---

[10] 105 Cong. Rec. 1283, 6428, II Leg. Hist. 979, 1079 (Senator Goldwater); 105 Cong. Rec. 1729-1730, II Leg. Hist. 993-994 (remarks of the Secretary of Labor, inserted in the record by Senator Dirksen).

It is true that Senator Goldwater referred to consumer picketing when the Conference bill was before the Senate. His full statement reads as follows: "the House bill . . . closed up every loophole in the boycott section of the law including the use of a secondary consumer line, an example of which the President gave in his nationwide TV program on August 6. . . ." 105 Cong. Rec. 17904, II Leg. Hist. 1437. The example given by the President was this: "The employees [of a furniture manufacturer] vote against joining a

The House history is similarly beclouded, but what appears confirms our conclusion. From the outset the House legislation included provisions concerning secondary boycotts. The Landrum-Griffin bill, which was ultimately passed by the House, embodied the Eisenhower Administration's proposals as to secondary boycotts. The initial statement of Congressman Griffin in introducing the bill which bears his name, contains no reference to consumer picketing in the list of abuses which he thought required the secondary boycott amendments. Later in the House debates he did discuss consumer picketing, but only in the context of its abuse when directed against shutting off the patronage of a secondary employer.

In the debates before passage of the House bill he stated that the amendments applied to consumer picketing of customer entrances to retail stores selling goods manufactured by a concern under strike, if the picketing were designed to "coerce or to restrain the employer of [the] second establishment, to get him not to do business with the manufacturer . . .," and further that, "of course, this bill and any other bill is limited by the constitutional right of free speech. If the purpose of the picketing is to *coerce the retailer not to do business* with the manufacturer—then such a boycott could be stopped." [17] (Italics supplied.)

The relevant changes in former § 8(b)(4) made by the House bill substituted "any individual employed by any person" for the Taft-Hartley wording, "the employees of any employer," deleted the requirement of a "concerted" refusal, and made it an unfair labor practice "to threaten, coerce or restrain any person" where an object thereof was an end forbidden by the statute, *e.g.*, forcing or requiring a secondary employer to cease handling the products of, or doing business with, a primary employer. There is thus nothing in the legislative history prior to the convening of the Conference Committee which shows any congressional concern with consumer picketing beyond that with the "isolated evil" of its use to cut off the business of a secondary employer as a means of forcing him to stop doing business with the primary employer. When Congress meant to bar picketing *per se,* it made its meaning clear; for example, § 8(b)(7) makes it an unfair labor practice, "to picket or cause to be picketed . . . any employer. . . ." In contrast, the prohibition of

---

particular union. Instead of picketing the furniture plant itself, unscrupulous organizing officials . . . picket the stores which sell the furniture. . . . How can anyone justify this kind of pressure against stores which are not involved in any dispute? . . . . This kind of action is designed to make the stores bring pressure on the furniture plant and its employees. . . ." 105 Cong. Rec. 19954, II Leg. Hist. 1842. Senator Goldwater's own definition of what he means by a secondary consumer boycott is even more clearly narrow in scope: "A secondary consumer, or customer, boycott involves the refusal of consumers or customers to buy the products or services of one employer in order to force him to stop doing business with another employer." 105 Cong. Rec. 17674, II Leg. Hist. 1386.

[17] 105 Cong. Rec. 15673, II Leg. Hist. 1615. The same concern with direct coercion of secondary employers appears in President Eisenhower's message accompanying the Administration bill. S. Doc., No. 10, I Leg. Hist. 81-82. See also minority report of the Senate Committee on the Kennedy-Ervin bill. S. Rep. No. 187, I Leg. Hist. 474-475.

§ 8(b)(4) is keyed to the coercive nature of the conduct, whether it be picketing or otherwise.

Senator Kennedy presided over the Conference Committee. He and Congressman Thompson prepared a joint analysis of the Senate and House bills. This analysis pointed up the First Amendment implications of the broad language in the House revisions of § 8(b)(4) stating,

"The prohibition [of the House bill] reaches not only picketing but leaflets, radio broadcasts and newspaper advertisements, thereby interfering with freedom of speech.

"[O]ne of the apparent purposes of the amendment is to prevent unions from appealing to the general public as consumers for assistance in a labor dispute. This is a basic infringement upon freedom of expression."

This analysis was the first step in the development of the publicity proviso, but nothing in the legislative history of the proviso alters our conclusion that Congress did not clearly express an intention that amended § 8(b)(4) should prohibit all consumer picketing. Because of the sweeping language of the House bill, and its implications for freedom of speech, the Senate conferees refused to accede to the House proposal without safeguards for the right of unions to appeal to the public, even by some conduct which might be "coercive." The result was the addition of the proviso. But it does not follow from the fact that some coercive conduct was protected by the proviso, that the exception "other than picketing" indicates that Congress had determined that all consumer picketing was coercive.

No Conference Report was before the Senate when it passed the compromise bill, and it had the benefit only of Senator Kennedy's statement of the purpose of the proviso. He said that the proviso preserved "the right to appeal to consumers by methods other than picketing asking them to refrain from buying goods made by nonunion labor *and* to refrain from trading with a retailer who sells such goods. . . . We were not able to persuade the House conferees to permit picketing in front of that secondary shop, but were able to persuade them to agree that the union shall be free to conduct informational activity short of picketing. In other words, the union can hand out handbills at the shop . . . and can carry on all publicity short of having ambulatory picketing. . . ." (Italics supplied.) This explanation does not compel the conclusion that the Conference Agreement contemplated prohibiting any consumer picketing at a secondary site beyond that which urges the public, in Senator Kennedy's words, to "refrain from trading with a retailer who sells such goods." To read into the Conference Agreement, on the basis of a single statement, an intention to prohibit all consumer picketing at a secondary site would depart from our practice of respecting the congressional policy not to prohibit peaceful picketing except to curb "isolated evils" spelled out by the Congress itself.

Peaceful consumer picketing to shut off all trade with the secondary employer unless he aids the union in its dispute with the primary employer, is poles apart from such picketing which only persuades his customers not to buy the struck product. The proviso indicates no more than that the Senate conferees' constitutional doubts led Congress to authorize publicity other than picketing which persuades the customers of a secondary employer to stop all trading with him, but not such publicity which has the effect of cutting off his deliveries or inducing his employees to cease work. On the other hand, picketing which persuades the customers of a secondary employer to stop all trading with him was also to be barred.

In sum, the legislative history does not support the Board's finding that Congress meant to prohibit all consumer picketing at a secondary site, having determined that such picketing necessarily threatened, coerced or restrained the secondary employer. Rather, the history shows that Congress was following its usual practice of legislating against peaceful picketing only to curb "isolated evils."

This distinction is opposed as "unrealistic" because, it is urged, all picketing automatically provokes the public to stay away from the picketed establishment. The public will, it is said, neither read the signs and handbills, nor note the explicit injunction that "This is not a strike against any store or market." Be that as it may, our holding today simply takes note of the fact that a broad condemnation of peaceful picketing, such as that urged upon us by petitioners, has never been adopted by Congress, and an intention to do so is not revealed with that "clearest indication in the legislative history," which we require. NLRB v. Drivers Local Union, *supra.*

We come then to the question whether the picketing in this case, confined as it was to persuading customers to cease buying the product of the primary employer, falls within the area of secondary consumer picketing which Congress did clearly indicate its intention to prohibit under § 8(b)(4)(ii). We hold that it did not fall within that area, and therefore did not "threaten, coerce, or restrain" Safeway. While any diminution in Safeway's purchases of apples due to a drop in consumer demand might be said to be a result which causes respondents' picketing to fall literally within the statutory prohibition, "it is a familiar rule, that a thing may be within the letter of the statute and yet not within the statute, because not within its spirit, nor within the intention of the makers." Holy Trinity Church v. United States, 143 U.S. 457, 459 (1892). See United States v. American Trucking Ass'n, 310 U.S. 534, 543-544 (1940). When consumer picketing is employed only to persuade customers not to buy the struck product, the union's appeal is closely confined to the primary dispute. The site of the appeal is expanded to include the premises of the secondary employer, but if the appeal succeeds, the secondary employers' purchases from the struck firms are decreased only because the public has diminished its purchases of the struck product. On the other hand, when consumer picketing is employed to persuade customers not to trade at all with the secondary employer, the latter stops buying the struck product, not because of a falling demand, but in response to pressure designed to inflict injury on his business generally. In such case, the union does more than merely follow the struck product; it creates a separate dispute with the secondary employer.

We disagree therefore with the Court of Appeals that the test of "to threaten, coerce, or restrain" for the purposes of this case is whether Safeway suffered or was likely to suffer economic loss. A violation of § 8(b)(4)(ii)(B) would not be established, merely because respondents' picketing was effective to reduce Safeway's sales of Washington State apples, even if this led or might lead Safeway to drop the item as a poor seller.

The judgment of the Court of Appeals is vacated and the case is remanded with direction to enter judgment setting aside the Board's order.

It is so ordered.

MR. JUSTICE DOUGLAS took no part in the consideration or decision of this case.

[The concurring opinion of JUSTICE BLACK and the dissenting opinion of JUSTICE HARLAN, joined in by JUSTICE STEWART, are omitted.]

NOTES

1. In Hoffman v. Cement Masons Local 337, 468 F.2d 1187 (9th Cir. 1972), an NLRB finding of a § 8(b)(4)(ii)(B) violation was upheld where a union, in pursuing its dispute with a nonunion general contractor who built homes in a subdivision, picketed to urge customers not to buy the homes, although they were solely owned and sold by a third party. *Tree Fruits* was distinguished on the ground the homes were the owner's sole product at the site, and thus the picketing "necessarily encompassed the entire business of . . . the neutral secondary."

A similar conclusion was reached in Retail Clerks, Local 1001 v. NLRB, 99 L.R.R.M. 3330 (D.C. Cir. 1978). In furtherance of its labor dispute with Safeco Title Insurance Company, the union engaged in picketing calling for a consumer product boycott at five land title insurance companies whose *sole* product was title insurance underwritten by Safeco. The Court held that the *Tree Fruits* holding does not apply to a retailer that sells only the struck product. *Compare* Steelworkers Local 14055 (Dow Chemical Co.), 211 N.L.R.B. 649 (1974) (*Tree Fruits* doctrine not applicable to picketing of gasoline stations urging consumers not to buy gasoline produced by primary employer).

The Board's order in the *Dow* case was denied enforcement. Steelworkers Local 14055 v. NLRB (Dow Chemical Co.), 524 F.2d 853 (D.C. Cir. 1975). Judge Fahy's opinion stated that the *Tree Fruits* decision may not be limited to a factual situation where the struck product constitutes only a small part of the business of the secondary retailer. He noted that the Supreme Court had held in *Tree Fruits* that the District of Columbia Circuit Court had erred in remanding the case to the Board on the theory that the case turned on whether the picketing had a "substantial economic impact" on the secondary retailer. As long as the pickets' appeal is limited to the struck product, the fact that the sale of the product represents *most* of the retailer's gross revenue does not make the picketing unlawful. "We may not hold Congress intended by section 8(b)(4) that the exercise of the arguable First Amendment right should turn for its lawfulness upon a factor extremely difficult to subject to line-drawing, and as to which the union exercising the claimed right might have poor information as to where to draw the line." Petition for *cert. granted; judgment vacated,* with directions to remand for reconsideration in light of intervening circumstances. 429 U.S. 807 (1976). (The "intervening circumstances" apparently were that the union's strike at Dow was unsuccessful; Dow had hired replacements, and the picketing at the gasoline stations had ceased.) Judicial elucidation of the problem in the *Dow* case will apparently have to await later cases.

2. May a union engage in consumer picketing of nonunion bread served in a restaurant? Is the restaurant distributing a primary product, or has that product lost its identity and become fully integrated into the meals prepared by the restaurant? *See* Teamsters Local 327 (American Bread Co.), 170 N.L.R.B. 91 (1968), *enforced,* 411 F.2d 147 (6th Cir. 1969).

The Board found that a union that picketed and distributed handbills at a housing development project did not engage in an unlawful secondary boycott since the union's object was to publicize its area-standards dispute with a subcontractor. It rejected the administrative law judge's overly mechanical application of the "merged product" doctrine since it would be overly restrictive as to the construction industry. One member dissented. Carpenters Local 399 (K & K Constr. Co.), 233 N.L.R.B. No. 99, 96 L.R.R.M. 1575 (1977), *rev'd,* 100 L.R.R.M. 2416 (3d Cir. 1979).

May a union which has a labor dispute with a paper bag company picket a retail store urging consumers not to use bags for their groceries which were made by the company — "bring your own bags or ask for a box"? *See* Paperworkers Local 832 (Duro Paper Bag Mfg. Co.), 236 N.L.R.B. No. 183, 98 L.R.R.M. 1430 (1978).

3. Does the *Tree Fruits* rationale extend to consumer picketing of a secondary employer utilizing a primary employer's services, *e.g.,* advertising, rather than distributing a tangible "struck product"? Should it make any difference if the union confines its appeal to the particular item advertised? What if the secondary's business is such that it can only be advertised in its entirety (*e.g.,* a restaurant)? *See* Honolulu Typographical Union v. NLRB, 401 F.2d 952 (D.C. Cir. 1968); *cf.* NLRB v. Building Serv. Employees, Local 105, 367 F.2d 227 (10th Cir. 1966); NLRB v. San Francisco Typographical Union No. 21 (California Newspapers, Inc.), 465 F.2d 53 (9th Cir. 1972).

4. The Board is not prohibited from looking behind the facade of "consumer picketing" to determine that the true purpose of the union's action is to appeal to employees. In NLRB v. Millmen & Cabinet Makers, Local 550, 367 F.2d 953 (9th Cir. 1966), the court affirmed the Board's finding that union picketing at a construction site to protest builder's use of a particular lumber company's products was unlawful in spite of legends on the placards which read "Consumer picket" and "Directed to Consumers only." The picketing union did not inform the builder or his employees of the intended purpose of the picketing; signs did not explain that there was no dispute with the builder; and signs did not request any specific consumer action. *Cf.* Bedding, Curtain & Drapery Workers, Local 140 (U.S. Mattress Corp.), 390 F.2d 495 (2d Cir. 1968), *cert. denied,* 392 U.S. 905 (1968).

5. *See* Lewis, *Consumer Picketing and the Court — The Questionable Yield of Tree Fruits,* 49 MINN. L. REV. 479 (1965).

E. THREATS AND COERCION OF SECONDARY EMPLOYERS

NLRB v. SERVETTE, INC.

Supreme Court of the United States
377 U.S. 46, 84 S. Ct. 1098, 12 L. Ed. 2d 121 (1964)

MR. JUSTICE BRENNAN delivered the opinion of the Court.

Respondent Servette, Inc., is a wholesale distributor of specialty merchandise stocked by retail food chains in Los Angeles, California. In 1960, during a strike which Local 848 of the Wholesale Delivery Drivers and Salesmen's Union was conducting against Servette, the Local's representative sought to support the strike by asking managers of supermarkets of the food chains to discontinue handling merchandise supplied by Servette. In most instances the representatives warned that handbills asking the public not to buy named items distributed by Servette would be passed out in front of stores which refused to cooperate, and in a few cases handbills were in fact passed out. A complaint was issued on charges by Servette that this conduct violated subsections (i) and (ii) of § 8(b)(4) of the National Labor Relations Act, as amended. . . .

The National Labor Relations Board dismissed the complaint. The Board adopted the finding of the Trial Examiner that "the managers of McDaniels Markets were authorized to decide as they best could whether to continue doing business with Servette in the face of threatened or actual handbilling. This, a policy decision, was one for them to make. The evidence is persuasive that the same authority was vested in the managers of Kory." 133 N.L.R.B. 1506. The Board held that on these facts the Local's efforts to enlist the cooperation of the supermarket managers did not constitute inducement of an "individual" within the meaning of that term in subsection (i); the Board held further that the handbilling, even if constituting conduct which "threaten[s], coerce[s], or restrain[s] any person" under subsection (ii), was protected by the [publicity] proviso to amended § 8(b)(4). 133 N.L.R.B. 1501. The Court of Appeals set aside the Board's order, holding that the term "individual" in subsection (i) was to be read literally, thus including the supermarket managers, and that the distributed products were not "produced" by Servette within the meaning of the proviso, thus rendering its protection unavailable. 310 F.2d 659. We granted certiorari, 374 U.S. 805. We reverse the judgment of the Court of Appeals.

The Court of Appeals correctly read the term "individual" in subsection (i) as including the supermarket managers, but it erred in holding that the Local's attempts to enlist the aid of the managers constituted inducement of the managers in violation of the subsection. The 1959 statute amended § 8(b)(4)(A) of the Taft-Hartley Act, which made it unlawful to induce or encourage "the employees of any employer" to strike or engage in a "concerted" refusal to work. We defined the central thrust of that statute to be to forbid "a union to induce employees to strike against or to refuse to handle goods for their employer when an object is to force him or another person to cease doing business with some third party." Carpenters' Local 1976 v. NLRB, 357 U.S. 93, 98 (1958). In the instant case, however, the Local, in asking the managers not to handle Servette items, was not attempting to induce or encourage them to cease performing their managerial duties in order to force their employers to cease doing business with Servette. Rather, the managers were asked to make a managerial decision which the Board found was within their authority to make. Such an appeal would not have been a violation of § 8(b)(4)(A) before 1959, and we think that the legislative history of the 1959 amendments makes it clear that the amendments were not meant to render such an appeal an unfair labor practice.

The 1959 amendments were designed to close certain loopholes in the application of § 8(b)(4)(A) which had been exposed in Board and court decisions. Thus, it had been held that the term "the employees of any employer" limited the application of the statute to those within the statutory definitions of "employees" and "employer." Section 2(2) of the National Labor Relations Act defines "employer" to exclude the federal and state governments and their agencies or subdivisions, nonprofit hospitals, and employers subject to the Railway Labor Act. 29 U.S.C. § 152(2). The definition of "employee" in § 2(3) excludes agricultural laborers, supervisors, and employees of an employer subject to the Railway Labor Act.[6] 29 U.S.C. § 152(3). Furthermore, since the section proscribed only inducement to engage in a strike or "concerted" refusal to perform services, it had been held that it was violated only if the inducement was directed at two or more employees. To close these loopholes, subsection (i) substituted the phrase "any individual employed by any person" for "the employees of any employer," and deleted the word "concerted." The first change was designed to make the provision applicable to refusals by employees who were not technically "employees" within the statutory definitions, and the second change was intended to make clear that inducement directed to only one individual was proscribed. But these changes did not expand the type of conduct which § 8(b)(4)(A) condemned, that is, union pressures calculated to induce the employees of a secondary employer to withhold their services in order to force their employer to cease dealing with the primary employer.

---

[6] In view of these definitions, it was permissible for a union to induce work stoppages by minor supervisors, and farm, railway or public employees. See Ferro-Co Corp., 102 N.L.R.B. 1660 (supervisors); Arkansas Express, Inc., 92 N.L.R.B. 255 (supervisors);

Moreover, the division of § 8(b)(4)(A) into subsections (i) and (ii) by the 1959 amendments has direct relevance to the issue presented by this case. It had been held that § 8(b)(4)(A) did not reach threats of labor trouble made to the secondary employer himself. Congress decided that such conduct should be made unlawful, but only when it amounted to conduct which "threaten[s], coerce[s] or restrain[s] any person"; hence the addition of subsection (ii). The careful creation of separate standards differentiating the treatment of appeals to the employees of the secondary employer not to perform their employment services, from appeals for other ends which are attended by threats, coercion or restraint, argues conclusively against the interpretation of subsection (i) as reaching the Local's appeals to the supermarket managers in this case. If subsection (i), in addition to prohibiting inducement of employees to withhold employment services, also reaches an appeal that the managers exercise their delegated authority by making a business judgment to cease dealing with the primary employer, subsection (ii) would be almost superfluous. Harmony between (i) and (ii) is best achieved by construing subsection (i), to prohibit inducement of the managers to withhold their services from their employer, and subsection (ii) to condemn an attempt to induce the exercise of discretion only if the inducement would "threaten, coerce, or restrain" that exercise.[12]

We turn finally to the question whether the proviso to amended § 8(b)(4) protected the Local's handbilling. The Court of Appeals, following its decision in Great Western Broadcasting Co. v. NLRB, 310 F.2d 591 (9th Cir. 1962), held that the proviso did not protect the Local's conduct because, as a distributor, Servette was not directly involved in the physical process of creating the products, and thus "does not produce any products." The Board on the other hand followed its ruling in Lohman Sales Co., 132 N.L.R.B. 901, that products "produced by an employer" included products distributed, as here, by a wholesaler with whom the primary dispute exists. We agree with the Board. The proviso was the outgrowth of a profound Senate concern that the unions' freedom to appeal to the public for support of their case be adequately safeguarded.

Conway's Express, 87 N.L.R.B. 972, 980, aff'd, 195 F.2d 906, 911 (2d Cir. 1962) (supervisors); Great Northern R. Co., 122 N.L.R.B. 1403, enforcement denied, 272 F.2d 741 (9th Cir. 1959), and supplemental Board decision, 126 N.L.R.B. 57 (railroad employees); Smith Lumber Co., 116 N.L.R.B. 1756, enforcement denied, 246 F.2d 129, 132 (5th Cir. 1957) (railroad employees); Paper Makers Importing Co., Inc., 116 N.L.R.B. 267 (municipal employees). Compare Di Giorgio Fruit Corp., 87 N.L.R.B. 720, 721, enforced, 191 F.2d 642 (D.C. Cir. 1951), cert. denied, 342 U.S. 869 (1951) (agricultural labor organization).

[12] The Conference Committee in adopting subsection (ii) understood that the subsection would reach only threats, restraints or coercion of the secondary employer and not a mere request to him for voluntary cooperation. Senator Dirksen, one of the conferees, stated that the new amendment "makes it an unfair labor practice for a union to try to coerce or threaten an employer directly (but not to persuade or ask him) in order — . . . to get him to stop doing business with another firm or handling its goods." 105 Cong. Rec. 19849, II Leg. Hist. 1823. (Italics supplied.)

We elaborated the history of the proviso in *NLRB v. Fruit & Vegetable Packers, Local 760*, decided today. It would fall far short of achieving this basic purpose if the proviso applied only in situations where the union's labor dispute is with the manufacturer or processor. Moreover, a primary target of the 1959 amendments was the secondary boycotts conducted by the Teamsters Union, which ordinarily represents employees not of manufacturers, but of motor carriers. There is nothing in the legislative history which suggests that the protection of the proviso was intended to be any narrower in coverage than the prohibition to which it is an exception, and we see no basis for attributing such an incongruous purpose to Congress.

The term "produced" in other labor laws was not unfamiliar to Congress. Under the Fair Labor Standards Act, the term is defined as "produced, manufactured, mined, handled, or in any other manner worked on . . . ," 29 U.S.C. § 203(j), and has always been held to apply to the wholesale distribution of goods. The term "production" in the War Labor Disputes Act has been similarly applied to a general retail department and mail-order business. The Court of Appeals' restrictive reading of "producer" was prompted in part by the language of § 8(b)(4)(B), which names as a proscribed object of the conduct defined in subsections (i) and (ii) "forcing or requiring any person to cease dealing in the products of any other *producer, processor,* or *manufacturer.*" (Italics supplied.) In its decision in Great Western Broadcasting Corp. v. NLRB, *supra*, the Court of Appeals reasoned that since a "processor" and a "manufacturer" are engaged in the physical creation of goods, the word "producer" must be read as limited to one who performs similar functions. On the contrary, we think that "producer" must be given a broader reach, else it is rendered virtually superfluous.

Finally, the warnings that handbills would be distributed in front of noncooperating stores are not prohibited as "threats" within subsection (ii). The statutory protection for the distribution of handbills would be undermined if a threat to engage in protected conduct were not itself protected.

Reversed.

NOTES

1. In applying the publicity proviso, the NLRB draws no distinction between processors, distributors, and those supplying services. *E.g.,* Television & Radio Artists, San Francisco Local (Great Western Broadcasting Corp.), 150 N.L.R.B. 467 (1964), *aff'd,* 356 F.2d 434 (9th Cir. 1966) (union may seek total consumer boycott of firms advertising over television station with which union has dispute).

2. Congressman Griffin, in his analysis of the Landrum-Griffin bill before the House of Representatives, made these comments upon the new § 8(b)(4)(ii):

"The courts also have held that, while a union may not induce employees of a secondary employer to strike for one of the forbidden objects, they may threaten the secondary employer, himself, with a strike or other economic retaliation in order to force him to cease doing business with a primary employer with whom the union has a dispute. The bill makes such coercion unlawful by the insertion of a clause 4(ii) forbidding threats or coercion against 'any person engaged in commerce or an industry affecting commerce.' " 105 Cong. Rec. 14347 (1959).

3. Senator John F. Kennedy, reporting to the Senate from the conference committee on the 1959 amendments, said:

"[T]he union shall be free to conduct informational activity short of picketing. In other words, the union can hand out handbills at the shop, can place advertisements in the newspapers, can make announcements over the radio, and can carry on all publicity short of having ambulatory picketing in front of the secondary site." 105 Cong. Rec. 17899 (1959).

Is there a fundamental difference between picketing and handbilling? *See generally,* Note, *Picketing and Publicity Under Section 8(b)(4) of the LMRA,* 73 Yale L.J. 1265 (1964).

4. Since picketing was expressly excluded from the protection of the publicity proviso to § 8(b)(4), problems have arisen as to whether or not certain union activities should be characterized as picketing. Similar problems exist under § 8(b)(7) since that section contains prohibitions against picketing which has organization or recognition as an object. Consequently, if the union's activities do not constitute picketing, § 8(b)(7)'s proscriptions are inapplicable. In Teamsters, Local 537 (Lohman Sales Co.), 132 N.L.R.B. 901 (1962), the Board held that passing out handbills to consumers did not amount to picketing. The William J. Burns case (Service & Maintenance Employees, Local 399), 136 N.L.R.B. 431 (1962), illustrates the difficulties which the Board sometimes has in characterizing various kinds of union conduct. Two members of the Board, Rodgers and Leedom, were convinced that patrolling by twenty to seventy union members in an elliptical path in front of the main entrance to a sports arena constituted picketing and therefore violated § 8(b)(4)(ii)(B). The patrollers distributed handbills; however, they carried no placards and wore no arm bands. Members Brown and Fanning held that even if the patrolling did not constitute picketing, it did exceed the limits of allowable publicity since the patrollers, by virtue of their numbers and close-knit formation, imposed some element of physical restraint upon patrons of the arena. Chairman McCulloch voted to dismiss the complaint. In United Furniture Workers (Jamestown Sterling Corp.), 146 N.L.R.B. 474 (1964), the Board held that the conduct of union representatives in nailing picket signs to poles and trees in front of an employer's premises and then watching the signs from their cars across the street was picketing within the meaning of the act and that therefore the picketing violated § 8(b)(7)(B) since the union had just lost an NLRB election.

Carrying of placards is not necessarily "picketing." An essential element of picketing, the Board has said, is some form of confrontation between the pickets and employees, customers or suppliers who are trying to enter the picketed premises. Union members patrolling shopping centers and the entrances to public buildings with signs advertising a labor dispute were found to be conducting "publicity other than picketing." Chicago Typographical Union, Local 16, 151 N.L.R.B. 1666 (1965).

In Teamsters Local 688 (Levitz Furniture Co.), 205 N.L.R.B. 1131 (1973), the Board held that the union's handbilling did not constitute picketing for the purposes of § 8(b)(7). The issue recognized by the Board was whether or not the union's conduct was such that it "was not merely engaged in communicating the information set out in its handbills, but was actually seeking in distributing such handbills to convey a 'signal' to induce those confronted by its agents to take the kind of action which traditional picket lines are expected to evoke."

F. HOT CARGO AGREEMENTS

UNITED BROTHERHOOD OF CARPENTERS & JOINERS, LOCAL 1976 v. NLRB
[SAND DOOR]

Supreme Court of the United States
357 U.S. 93, 78 S. Ct. 1011, 2 L. Ed. 2d 1186 (1958)

MR. JUSTICE FRANKFURTER delivered the opinion of the Court.
. . . .

[This case] arises out of a labor dispute between carpenter unions and an employer engaged in the building construction trade in Southern California. The Sand Door and Plywood Company is the exclusive distributor in Southern California of doors manufactured by the Paine Lumber Company of Oshkosh, Wisconsin. Watson and Dreps are millwork contractors who purchase doors from Sand. Havstad and Jensen are the general contractors who were at the time of the dispute involved, engaged in the construction of a hospital in Los Angeles. Havstad and Jensen are parties to a master labor agreement negotiated with the United Brotherhood of Carpenters and Joiners of America on behalf of its affiliated district councils and locals including petitioner unions. This agreement, comprehensively regulating the labor relations of Havstad and Jensen and its carpenter employees, includes a provision that, "workmen shall not be required to handle nonunion material."

In August, 1954, doors manufactured by Paine and purchased by Sand were delivered to the hospital construction site by Watson and Dreps. On the morning of August 17, Fleisher, business agent of petitioner Local 1976, came to the construction site and notified Steinert, Havstad and Jensen's foreman, that the doors were nonunion and could not be hung. Steinert therefore ordered employees to cease handling the doors. When Nicholson, Havstad, and Jensen's general superintendent, appeared on the job and asked Fleisher why the workers had been prevented from handling the doors, he stated that they had been stopped until it could be determined whether the doors were union or nonunion. Subsequent negotiations between officers of Sand and the Union failed to produce an agreement that would permit the doors to be installed. . . .

. . . .

    ... The employees' action may be described as a "strike or concerted refusal," and there is a "forcing or requiring" of the employer, even though there is a hot cargo provision. The realities of coercion are not altered simply because it is said that the employer is forced to carry out a prior engagement rather than forced now to cease doing business with another. A more important consideration, and one peculiarly within the cognizance of the Board because of its closeness to and familiarity with the practicalities of the collective bargaining process, is the possibility that the contractual provision itself may well not have been the result of choice on the employer's part free from the kind of coercion Congress has condemned. It may have been forced upon him by strikes that, if used to bring about a boycott when the union is engaged in a dispute with some primary employer, would clearly be prohibited by the act. Thus, to allow the union to invoke the provision to justify conduct that in the absence of such a provision would be a violation of the statute might give it the means to transmit to the moment of boycott, through the contract, the very pressures from which Congress has determined to relieve secondary employers.

    Thus inducements of employees that are prohibited under § 8(b)(4)(A) in the absence of a hot cargo provision are likewise prohibited when there is such a provision. The Board has concluded that a union may not, on the assumption that the employer will respect his contractual obligation, order its members to cease handling goods, and that any direct appeal to the employees to engage in a strike or concerted refusal to handle goods is proscribed. This conclusion was reached only after considerable experience with the difficulty of determining whether an employer has in fact acquiesced in a boycott, whether he did or did not order his employees to handle the goods, and the significance of an employer's silence. Of course if an employer does intend to observe the contract, and does truly sanction and support the boycott, there is no violation of § 8(b)(4)(A). A voluntary employer boycott does not become prohibited activity simply because a hot cargo clause exists. But there remains the question whether the employer has in fact truly sanctioned and supported the boycott, and whether he has exercised the choice contemplated by the statute. The potentiality of coercion in a situation where the union is free to approach the employees and induce them to enforce their contractual rights by self-help is very great. Faced with a concerted work stoppage already in progress, an employer may find it substantially more difficult than he otherwise would to decide that business should go on as usual and that his employees must handle the goods. His "acquiescence" in the boycott may be anything but free. In order to give effect to the statutory policy, it is not unreasonable to insist, as the Board has done, that even when there is a contractual provision the union must not appeal to the employees or induce them not to handle the goods. Such a rule expresses practical judgment on the effect of union conduct in the framework of actual labor disputes and what is necessary to preserve to the employer the freedom of choice that Congress has decreed. On such a matter the judgment of the Board must be given great weight, and we ought not set against it our estimate of the relevant factors.

There is no occasion to consider the invalidity of hot cargo provisions as such. The sole concern of the Board in the present cases was whether the contractual provision could be used by the unions as a defense to a charge of inducing employees to strike or refuse to handle goods for objectives proscribed by § 8(b)(4)(A). As we have said, it cannot be so used. But the Board has no general commission to police collective bargaining agreements and strike down contractual provisions in which there is no element of an unfair labor practice. Certainly the voluntary observance of a hot cargo provision by an employer does not constitute a violation of § 8(b)(4)(A), and its mere execution is not, contrary to the suggestion of two members of the Board in the *Genuine Parts* case, Truck Drivers, 119 N.L.R.B. No. 53, *prima facie* evidence of prohibited inducement of employees. It does not necessarily follow from the fact that the unions cannot invoke the contractual provision in the manner in which they sought to do so in the present cases that it may not, in some totally different context not now before the Court still have legal radiations affecting the relations between the parties. All we need now say is that the contract cannot be enforced by the means specifically prohibited in § 8(b)(4)(A).

MR. JUSTICE DOUGLAS, with whom THE CHIEF JUSTICE and MR. JUSTICE BLACK concur, dissenting. . . .

The provision of the collective bargaining agreement in the *Carpenters* case is typical of those in issue here:

"Workmen shall not be required to handle non-union material."

That provision was bargained for like every other claim in the collective agreement. It was agreed to by the employer. How important it may have been to the parties — how high or low in their scale of values — we do not know. But on these records it was the product of bargaining, not of coercion. The Court concedes that its inclusion in the contracts may not be called "forcing or requiring" the employer to cease handling other products within the meaning of the act. Enforcing the collective bargaining agreement — standing by its terms — is not one of the coercive practices at which the act was aimed. Enforcement of these agreements is conducive to peace. Disregard of collective agreements — the flouting of them — is disruptive. That was the philosophy of the *Conway's Express* decision of the Labor Board, 87 N.L.R.B. 972, *aff'd sub nom.* Rabouin v. NLRB, 195 F.2d 906 (2d Cir. 1952), and I think it squares with the act.

The present decision is capricious. The boycott is lawful if the employer agrees to abide by this collective bargaining agreement. It is unlawful if the employer reneges.

The hostile attitude of labor against patronizing or handling "unfair" goods goes deep into our history. It is not peculiarly American, though it has found expression in various forms in our history from the refusal of Americans to buy British tea, to the refusal of Abolitionists to buy slave-made products, to the refusal of unions to work on convict-made or on other nonunion goods. Unions have adhered to the practice because of their principle of mutual aid and protection. Section 7 of the act, indeed, recognizes that principle in its guarantee that "Employees shall have the right . . . to engage in . . . concerted activities for the purpose of collective bargaining or other mutual aid or protection." We noticed in Apex Hosiery Co. v. Leader, 310 U.S. 469, 503 (1940), that the elimination of "competition from non-union made goods" was a legitimate labor objective.

The reason an employer may also agree to that phase of union policies, the reason he may acquiesce in the inclusion of such a clause in a particular collective agreement, may only be surmised. Perhaps he sees eye to eye with the union. Perhaps he receives important concessions in exchange for his assistance to the union.

Certain it is that where he voluntarily agrees to the "unfair" goods clause he is not forced or coerced in the statutory sense. . . .

We act today more like a Committee of the Congress than the Court. We strain to outlaw bargaining contracts long accepted, long used. Perhaps these particular provisions have evils in them that should be declared contrary to the public interest. They are, however, so much a part of the very fabric of collective bargaining that we should leave this policy-making to Congress and not rush in to undo what a century or more of experience has imbedded into labor-management agreements. I have not found a word of legislative history which even intimates that these "unfair" goods provisions of collective bargaining agreements are unlawful.

NOTES

1. Congress took drastic action with respect to "hot cargo" agreements in the amendments to the LMRA included in the Labor-Management Reporting and Disclosure Act of 1959. The House members of the conference committee made the following explanation:

"The Senate bill amends § 8 of the National Labor Relations Act, as amended, by adding at the end thereof a new subsection (e) which makes it an unfair labor practice for any labor organization and any employer who is a common carrier subject to part II of the Interstate Commerce Act to enter into any contract or agreement, express or implied, whereby such employer ceases or refrains or agrees to cease or refrain from handling, using, or transporting any of the products of any other employer, or to cease doing business with the same.

"The House amendment amends § 8 of the National Labor Relations Act, as amended, by adding at the end thereof a new subsection (e) to make it an unfair labor practice for any labor organization and any employer to enter into any contract or agreement, express or implied, whereby such employer ceases or refrains or agrees to cease or refrain from handling, using, selling, transporting or otherwise dealing in any of the products of any other employer, or to cease doing business with any other person. The House amendment also makes any such agreement heretofore or hereafter executed unenforcible and void.

"The committee of conference adopted the House amendment but added three provisos. The first proviso specifies—

> that nothing in this subsection (e) shall apply to an agreement between a labor organization and an employer in the construction industry relating to the contracting or subcontracting of work to be done at the site of the construction, alteration, painting, or repair of a building, structure, or other work.

"It should be particularly noted that the proviso relates only and exclusively to the contracting or subcontracting of work to be done at the site of the construction. The proviso does not exempt from § 8(e) agreements relating to supplies or other products or materials shipped or otherwise transported to and delivered on the site of the construction. The committee of conference does not intend that this proviso should be construed so as to change the present state of the law with respect to the validity of this specific type of agreement relating to work to be done at the site of the construction project or to remove the limitations which the present law imposes with respect to such agreements. Picketing to enforce such contracts would be illegal under the *Sand Door* case, Carpenters, Local 1976, AFL v. NLRB, 357 U.S. 93 (1958). To the extent that such agreements are legal today under § 8(b)(4) of the National Labor Relations Act, as amended, the proviso would prevent such legality from being affected by § 8(e). The proviso applies only to § 8(e) and therefore leaves unaffected the law developed under § 8(b)(4). The *Denver Building Trades* case and the *Moore Dry Dock* cases would remain in full force and effect. The proviso is not intended to limit, change, or modify the present state of the law with respect to picketing at the site of a construction project. Restrictions and limitations imposed upon such picketing under present law as interpreted, for example, in the U. S. Supreme Court decision in the *Denver Building Trades* case would remain in full force and effect. It is not intended that the proviso change the existing law with respect to judicial enforcement of these contracts or with respect to the legality of a strike to obtain such a contract.

"The second proviso specifies that for the purposes of this subsection (e) and § 8(b)(4) the terms 'any employer,' 'any person engaged in commerce or an industry affecting commerce,' and 'any person' when used in relation to the terms 'any other producer, processor, or manufacturer,' 'any other employer,' or 'any other person' shall not include persons in the relation of a jobber, manufacturer, contractor, or subcontractor working on the goods or premises of a jobber or manufacturer or performing parts of an integrated process of production in the apparel and clothing industry. This proviso grants a limited exemption in three specific situations in the apparel and clothing industry, but in no other industry regardless of whether similar integrated processes of production may exist between jobbers, manufacturers, contractors, and subcontractors.

"The third proviso applies solely to the apparel and clothing industry."
H.R. Rep. No. 1147, 86th Cong., 1st Sess. 39-40 (1959).

2. It should also be noted that under the 1959 amendments to § 8(b)(4)(A) of the NLRA, a strike for a "hot cargo" clause prohibited by § 8(e) is made a union unfair labor practice. Likewise, to threaten or coerce an employer to enter such an agreement is prohibited.

3. A Board majority has interpreted "any employer," as used in § 8(e), to include an airline, even though airlines are not within the NLRA definition of "employer." Thus, a union and an airline may be liable for entering into an unlawful hot cargo agreement. Machinists Union (Lufthansa German Airlines), 197 N.L.R.B. 232 (1972).

4. The construction industry exemption from § 8(e)'s ban on "hot cargo" clauses allows "an agreement between a labor organization and an employer in the construction industry relating to the contracting or subcontracting of work to be done at the site of the construction. . . ." In construing this exception, the Board took the position that it merely permits voluntary subcontracting restrictions and does not legalize strikes or picketing to obtain or enforce such restrictions. Construction Laborers Local 383 (Colson & Stevens Constr. Co.), 137 N.L.R.B. 1650 (1962). However, the Court of Appeals for the Ninth Circuit, although agreeing with the board that coercive action to enforce such an agreement would be unlawful, held that "picketing to secure an agreement to cease doing business with certain persons is not made unlawful by this section where that agreement is within the construction proviso of § 8(e)." Laborers Local 383 v. NLRB, 323 F.2d 422 (9th Cir. 1963). *Accord,* Essex County & Vicinity Dist. Council of Carpenters v. NLRB, 332 F.2d 636 (3d Cir. 1964); Orange Belt Dist. Council of Painters No. 48, AFL-CIO v. NLRB, 328 F.2d 534 (D.C. Cir. 1964).

In view of this disapproval, the Board acquiesced in Bldg. & Constr. Trades Council (Centlivre Village Apartments), 148 N.L.R.B. 854 (1964), holding that picketing to obtain such an agreement is lawful.

5. Suppose a building contractor agrees that he will not contract with any nonunion contractors for work to be done at the site. May he also agree that he will not discipline any employees who refuse to work if he does bring such people onto the site? May the union strike to enforce the contract? *See* NLRB v. Plumbers Journeymen Local 217 [Carvel Co.], 361 F.2d 160 (1st Cir. 1966); Muskegon Bricklayers, 152 N.L.R.B. 360 (1965), *enforced,* 378 F.2d 859 (6th Cir. 1967).

Compare Bricklayers, Local 2 (Associated General Contractors), 224 N.L.R.B. 1021 (1976). And *see* Grove, *Obtaining and Enforcing Hot-Cargo Contracts in the Construction Industry,* 51 A.B.A.J. 732 (1965).

Suppose there is already a nonunion contractor on the site. May the union strike to obtain the above clause and also to get rid of the nonunion contractor who is already on the job?

6. In Connell Constr. Co. v. Plumbers Local 100, 421 U.S. 616 (1975), the union contended in an antitrust case (see the full report, *infra* at 627) that an agreement, which it had made with a general building contractor, that he would subcontract plumbing work to be done at his job sites only to firms having contracts with Local 100, was explicitly allowed by the construction industry proviso to § 8(e) of the NLRA. The Supreme Court held that the agreement was not protected by the proviso. Connell employed no plumbers himself and Local 100 had no collective bargaining relationship with him. The Court said, "We think [the § 8(e) proviso's] authorization extends only to agreements in the context of collective bargaining relationships and, in light of congressional references to the *Denver Building Trades* problem, possibly to common-situs relationships on particular jobsites as well."

7. After hearing oral argument in February, 1978, the NLRB issued four decisions on November 13, 1978, stating its interpretation of the § 8(e) proviso in the light of the Supreme Court's pronouncement in the *Connell* case.

In Carpenters Local 944 (Woelke & Romero Framing), 239 N.L.R.B. No. 40, 99 L.R.R.M. 1580 (1978), the Board held there was no violation of the Act where a union pickets to obtain, in the context of a collective bargaining relationship, a contract provision permitting the contractor to subcontract jobsite work only to subcontractors that are signatory to a current agreement with the local union. The Board rejected a narrower interpretation of the § 8(e) proviso, suggested by the General Counsel, which would have banned such collectively bargained provisions unless: (1) the clause is operational only at times when the employer has employees represented by the labor organization; (2) the clause applies only to sites at which the employer has employees represented by the labor organization; and (3) the clause does not require that the employer have collective bargaining relationships with particular unions.

In Operating Engineers Local 701 (Pacific Northwest Chapter of Associated Builders) 239 N.L.R.B. No. 43, 99 L.R.R.M. 1589 (1978), the Board held that a subcontracting clause otherwise privileged by the proviso violates § 8(e) if it is enforceable by self-help (concerted economic action, such as strikes and picketing). *See* Muskegon Bricklayers, 152 N.L.R.B. 360 (1965), *enforced,* 378 F.2d 859 (6th Cir. 1967).

In Los Angeles Bldg. v. Constr. Trades Council (Shriver, Inc.), 239 N.L.R.B. No. 42, 99 L.R.R.M. 1593 (1978), the Board held that a § 8(f) prehire agreement is a sufficient collective bargaining relationship to sustain the § 8(e) proviso privilege, and the union need not be a majority representative at the time it makes the agreement.

Finally, in Colorado Bldg. & Constr. Trades Council (Utilities Services Engineering Co.), 239 N.L.R.B. No. 41, 99 L.R.R.M. 1601 (1978), the Board held that a subcontracting provision that is sought *outside* of a bargaining relationship is not protected by the proviso, unless, possibly, the clause is addressed to problems posed by the common situs relationships on a particular jobsite or to the reduction of friction between union and nonunion employees at a jobsite.

TRUCK DRIVERS, LOCAL 413 v. NLRB

United States Court of Appeals, District of Columbia Circuit
334 F.2d 539 (1964)
Cert. denied, 379 U.S. 916 (1964)

J. SKELLY WRIGHT, Circuit Judge. The National Labor Relations Board has found certain Picket Line, Struck Goods, Subcontracting, and Hazardous Work clauses in the collective bargaining agreements of petitioner unions void under § 8(e) of the Labor Act. In their Petition to Review and Set Aside, the unions contend that these provisions are outside the prohibitions of § 8(e) because their aim is benefit to the employees of the bargaining unit, not control of, or interference with, the contracting employer's third-party relationships. The Board cross-petitions for enforcement.

A preliminary issue is whether it is the *object,* the *effect,* or the express or implied *terms* of the challenged clauses which are relevant to the § 8(e) charge. The unions suggest an object test, by parity of reasoning with § 8(b)(4)(B)'s secondary boycott provisions. The Trial Examiner, in one of these companion cases, No. 17,663, considered the effect of the clauses to be relevant to their validity under § 8(e), and took extensive evidence of their effect. The Board, however, at the instance of its General Counsel, held that the implementation of a contract was not relevant to its validity under § 8(e), that extrinsic evidence of object alone was not determinative, and that the contract must be tested by its terms, express or implied. See Mary Feifer, d/b/a American Feed Co., 133 N.L.R.B. 214 (1961). We agree.

The Picket Line Clause

A key provision in the union contracts protects the right of individual employees to refuse to cross picket lines by immunizing them against employer discipline. This picket line clause is broadly worded to achieve maximum application permitted by the law. The Board held that under § 8(e) of the act the clause may validly apply only to certain types of picket lines; the union apparently would apply it to all.

The clause provides:

"It shall not be a violation of this Agreement and it shall not be cause for discharge or disciplinary action in the event an employee refuses to enter upon any property involved in a labor dispute or refuses to go through or work behind any picket line, including the picket line of Unions party to this Agreement and including picket lines at the Employer's place or places of business."

The Board concedes that the contract clause may permissibly operate to protect refusals to cross a picket line where the line is in connection with a *primary* dispute at the *contracting* employer's *own premises.* This seems clearly correct. Employees who refuse to cross such a line are entitled to the same protection as strikers under §§ 7 and 13 of the act. See N.L.R.B. v. John S. Swift Co., 277 F.2d 641, 646 (7th Cir. 1960). The refusal to cross being a protected activity, the union and the employer may provide by contract that such refusal shall not be grounds for discharge. See NLRB v. Rockaway News Co., 345 U.S. 71, 80 (1953).

A different result must be reached where the picket line at the contracting employer's own premises is itself in promotion of a *secondary* strike or boycott. Refusal to cross that line would itself be secondary activity. To the extent that the clause would protect such refusal to cross, it would then be authorizing a secondary strike, and would *pro tanto* be void under § 8(e) of the act. There is no merit to the unions' suggestion that this clause is outside the reach of § 8(e) because it protects *individual* refusals, not *union*-induced refusals. We read our own cases as having rejected this argument. See Los Angeles Mailers Union No. 9 v. NLRB, 114 App. D.C. 72, 311 F.2d 121 (1962).

The Board also held that the clause may validly protect refusals to cross a picket line at the premises of *another* employer if that picket line meets the conditions expressed in the *proviso* to § 8(b)(4) of the act. Clearly this is the law. See NLRB v. Rockaway News Co., *supra*. . . .

The remaining question concerns refusals to cross a picket line at *another* employer's premises where that line does *not* meet the conditions of the § 8(b)(4) *proviso*. The unions maintain that refusal to cross any lawful primary picket line is primary activity under the act and that protection thereof in the bargaining agreement falls outside the ambit of § 8(e). The Board held that refusal to cross a non-*proviso* picket line constitutes secondary activity, and that contractual protection of such activity violates § 8(e).

A useful approach to this question is through the legislative history of the 1959 amendments which incorporated § 8(e) into the act. The House Labor Committee report stated: "It is settled law that the National Labor Relations Act does not require a truck driver to cross a primary picket line. . . . [T]he employer could agree that he would not require the driver to enter the strikebound plant." House Committee Report, 1 LEGISLATIVE HISTORY OF THE LABOR-MANAGEMENT REPORTING AND DISCLOSURE ACT OF 1959 at 779 (1959). It is also clear "that the right to refuse to cross a primary picket line would not be affected by" the hot cargo ban in the bill passed by the Senate. Kennedy-Thompson analysis, 2 *id.* 1708 (2-3). "However, in order to set at rest false apprehensions on this score, the [House] committee appended the disclaimer proviso" which appears in the bill as reported by the House Committee. This disclaimer explicitly protected the right of refusal to cross primary picket lines, and the right to sign contracts immunizing such refusals from employer discipline. The entire House Committee bill, however, including this disclaimer, was replaced by the Landrum-Griffin substitute on the floor of the House. But the Landrum-Griffin substitute was unacceptable to the Senate conferees because: "[T]he House [Landrum-Griffin] bill apparently destroys the right to picket a plant and to honor a picket line even in a strike for higher wages. This change in the present law is entirely unacceptable." 2 *id.* 1708(3). It seems clear that, at least on this point, the Senate viewpoint was adopted in conference, modifying the Landrum-Griffin version. The Senate conferees secured the insertion of the following broad and all-encompassing declaration of congressional policy in the bill: *"Provided,* That nothing contained in this clause (B) shall be construed to make unlawful, where not otherwise unlawful, any primary strike or primary picketing." § 8(b)(4)(B).

The then Senator Kennedy explained the effect of this new provision to the Senate:

". . . The secondary boycott provisions of the House bill would have curtailed legitimate union activities. Accordingly, the Senate conferees insisted that the report secure the following rights:

"(a) The right to engage in primary strikes and primary picketing even though the employees of other employers refused to cross the picket line.

"The fact of the matter is that there is some question under the Landrum-Griffin bill whether employees of another employer could have properly refused not [sic] to cross a picket line in a primary strike. That has been clarified in the conference report." 2 LEGISLATIVE HISTORY OF THE LABOR-MANAGEMENT REPORTING AND DISCLOSURE ACT OF 1959 at 1432-1433.

Senator Kennedy further stated in a report to the Senate on the Conference: "We have protected the right of employees of a secondary employer, in the case of a primary strike, to refuse to cross a primary strike picket line." 2 *id.* 1389(1). This stated effect of the Senate-House Conference action seems to have been generally accepted. . . .

In addition, Professor Cox, now the Solicitor General, who was one of the principal architects of the legislation, has confirmed that the intendment of the act is that "section 8(e) would not prohibit agreements sanctioning refusal to cross a lawful primary picket line."

It would seem that even without this legislative history, a similar conclusion would be demanded by the case law. It has been clear since *Rockaway News* that whenever refusal to cross a picket line is a protected activity, unions and employers may sign contracts providing that the refusal shall not be ground for discharge. In *Rockaway News* the activity in question was within the § 8(b)(4) *proviso,* but the Court did not limit the principle there announced to *proviso* activity. The Board itself recently held in the *Redwing* and *Everist* cases that refusal to cross a primary picket line was indeed a protected activity, without even considering whether the picket lines met the terms of the § 8(b)(4) *proviso.* And, in *Redwing,* we affirmed the Board's holding "that the employees had in fact engaged in *protected* concerted activity when they refused to cross the picket line," also without regard to whether the *proviso* was satisfied. *Sub nom.* Teamsters Local 79 v. NLRB, 117 App D.C. 84, 325 F.2d 1011, 1012 (1963). In fact, we are aware of no case which limits protection of refusal to cross a primary picket line to § 8(b)(4) *proviso* situations.

Similar conclusions are suggested by NLRB v. International Rice Milling Co., *supra,* and Electrical Workers Local 761 v. National Labor Relations Board, 366 U.S. 667 (1961). Since "appealing to neutral employees whose tasks aid the employer's everyday operations" is a traditional primary activity," *id.* at 681 of 366 U.S., primary picketing retains its primary characteristic even though it induces deliverymen to refuse to cross the line. Thus it seems clear that refusal to cross a lawful primary picket line, absent demonstrated secondary intent, is itself primary, and as such falls outside the act's proscriptions against secondary activity. Teamsters, Local 79 v. NLRB, *supra.* Compare Seafarers Int'l Union v. NLRB, 105 App. D.C. 211, 216, 265 F.2d 585, 590 (1959). Since § 8(e) is limited to secondary activity, a provision in the bargaining agreement immunizing the exercise of this protected right against employer discipline does not violate it. See NLRB v. Rockaway News Co., *supra.*

The Struck Goods Clause

A second section of the collective bargaining agreement which is in dispute concerns Struck Goods. It reads:

"Recognizing that many individual employees covered by this contract may have personal convictions against aiding the adversary of other workers, and recognizing the propriety of individual determination by an individual workman as to whether he shall perform work, labor or service which he deems contrary to his best interest, the parties recognize and agree that:

"[(a)] It shall not be a violation of this Agreement and it shall not be a cause for discharge or disciplinary action if any employee refuses to perform any service which, but for the existence of a controversy between a labor union and any other person (whether party to this Agreement or not), would be performed by the employees of such person.

"[(b)] Likewise, it shall not be a violation of the Agreement and it shall not be a cause for discharge or disciplinary action if any employee refuses to handle any goods or equipment transported, interchanged, handled or used by any carrier or other person, whether a party to this Agreement or not, at any of whose terminals or places of business there is a controversy between such carrier, or person, or its employees on the one hand and a labor union on the other hand; and such rights may be exercised where such goods or equipment are being transported, handled or used by the originating, interchanging or succeeding carriers or persons, whether parties to this agreement or not.

"[(c)] The Employer agrees that it will not cease or refrain from handling, using, transporting, or otherwise dealing in any of the products of any other employer or cease doing business with any other person, or fail in any obligation imposed by the Motor Carriers' Act or other applicable law, as a result of individual employees exercising their rights under this Agreement or under law, but the Employer shall, notwithstanding any other provision in this Agreement, when necessary, handle, use, transport or otherwise deal in such products and continue doing such business by use of other employees (including management and representatives), other carriers, or by any other method it deems appropriate or proper."

In considering clause (a) of this section, the Board acknowledged that it may lawfully apply where the relationship between the contracting employer and the employer with a labor dispute is so close as to render them "allies." The present state of the struck work — ally doctrine is outlined in Douds v. Federation of Architects, 75 F. Supp. 672 (S.D.N.Y. 1948), and NLRB v. Business Machine & Office Appliance Mechanics, 228 F.2d 553 (2d Cir. 1955), *cert. denied,* 351 U.S. 962 (1956). These cases are specifically cited in the conference report on the 1959 amendments, as representing the existing law which Congress did not intend to supersede. 1 LEGISLATIVE HISTORY OF THE LABOR-MANAGEMENT REPORTING AND DISCLOSURE ACT OF 1959 at 942. Under these decisions, an employer is characterized as an "ally" of the struck firm "when he knowingly does work which would otherwise be done by the striking employees of the primary employer and where this work is paid for by the primary employer pursuant to an arrangement devised and originated by him to enable him to meet his contractual obligations. The result must be the same whether or not the primary employer makes any direct arrangement with the employers providing the services." NLRB v. Business Machine & Office Appliance Mechanics, *supra* at 559 of 228 F.2d. As Judge Learned Hand phrased the test: "One does not make oneself a party to the dispute with a primary employer by taking over the business that the strike has prevented him from doing. On the other hand if a secondary employer, knowing of the strike, not only accepts the customer of the primary employer but takes his pay, not from the customer but from the primary employer . . . [then he has] made common cause with the primary employer." Concurring opinion, *id.* at 562. This court has adopted the ally doctrine in New York Mailers' Union No. 6 v. NLRB, 114 App. D.C. 370, 371, 316 F.2d 371, 372 (1963).

The Trial Examiner found clause (a) to be limited in scope to the "ally" doctrine, and therefore valid. But the Board read the clause as impermissibly broad, in that under it employees of the contracting employer might refuse to perform services which met the *first* test of *Business Machine, supra* ("otherwise done by the striking employees"), even if the *second* test of that rule were not met ("pursuant to an arrangement"). *But cf.* NLRB v. Amalgamated Lithographers, 309 F.2d 31, 37-38 (9th Cir. 1962), *cert. denied,* 372 U.S. 943 (1963).

We agree with the Board that to the extent clause (a) protects refusals to work beyond the scope of the ally doctrine, it authorizes a secondary boycott, and so is *pro tanto* void under § 8(e) of the Labor Act. We refrain from defining the exact limits of the ally doctrine, however, and do not decide whether the *Business Machine* tests are adequate for all variations in factual situations. Such spelling out is best left for the elucidating process of gradual inclusion and exclusion provided by specific cases.

Clause (b) of the Struck Goods section, set out above, seems to be a typical hot cargo clause, prohibited by § 8(e) of the act. The unions contend, however, that this clause — like others in the contract — is immune from § 8(e)'s prohibition because it protects the freedom of decision of the individual laborer, rather than creates a power of decision in the union itself. Since few workers will exercise their rights under these clauses, the unions argue, there will be no substantial interference with the business of the employer, particularly in view of the provisions of clause (c). The short answer to this contention is that it has already been rejected by this court. See Los Angeles Mailers Union No. 9 v. NLRB, *supra.* . . . Moreover, the legislative history of the 1959 amendments equates these "employee-rights" clauses with other hot cargo clauses. It is clear that § 8(e) was aimed, among other targets, at provisions in contracts under which an employer agrees: he cannot "require his employees to handle any [goods] which . . . came from an employer engaged in a labor dispute," 1 LEGISLATIVE HISTORY OF THE LABOR-MANAGEMENT REPORTING AND DISCLOSURE ACT OF 1959 at 779 (House Report); he cannot "require his employees to handle goods or provide other services for the benefit of an employer who is involved in a labor dispute," 2 *id.* at 1007 (Senator McClellan); "that his employees do not have to handle goods which the union labels as 'hot,' " 2 *id.* at 1197 (Senator Curtis); "his employees do not have to handle or work on goods produced or handled by another employer who happens to be in disfavor with the union," 2 *id.* at 1079 (Senator Goldwater); he will "not . . . carry the goods and not . . . require his employees to handle them," 2 *id.* at 1708 (Kennedy-Thompson analysis).

We must conclude, therefore, as did the Board, that this clause (b) is void under § 8(e) of the act and that clause (c) does not save it.

The Subcontracting Clause

The third major challenged provision of the collective bargaining agreements here concerns Subcontracting:

"The Employer agrees to refrain from using the services of any person who does not observe the wages, hours and conditions of employment established by labor unions having jurisdiction over the type of services performed." [13]

The Board found this clause was secondary, and therefore void under § 8(e) of the act. It reasoned:

"Like the typical hot cargo clause itself, a subcontractor clause is secondary where it limits, *not the fact of subcontracting* — either prohibiting it outright or conditioning it upon, *e.g.,* current full employment in the unit — but the *persons with whom* the signatory employer may subcontract."

This Board position groups together, as secondary, contract clauses which impose boycotts on subcontractors not signatory to union agreements, and those which merely require subcontractors to meet the equivalent of union standards in order to protect the work standards of the employees of the contracting employer. But the distinction between these two types of clauses is vital. Union-signatory subcontracting clauses are secondary, and therefore within the scope of § 8(e), while

---

[13] Since this clause is entitled "Subcontracting," we assume — in the absence of any indication to the contrary — that its scope is limited to the contracting out of work which otherwise would be performed by members of the bargaining unit.

union-standards subcontracting clauses are primary as to the contracting employer. We so held in Building & Construction Trades Council v. NLRB, 117 App. D.C. 239, 328 F.2d 540 (1964)....

This clause would be a union-signatory clause if it required subcontractors to have collective bargaining agreements with petitioner unions or their affiliates, or with unions generally. We interpret it, however, as merely requiring that subcontractors observe the equivalent of union wages, hours, and the like.[14] Since we find that this clause only requires union standards, and not union recognition, we follow the line of cases in this court cited above to rule it primary, and thus outside § 8(e)'s prohibitions....

We therefore conclude that a decree should be drafted condemning the challenged contract clauses only to the extent found unlawful by this court.

Enforced in part and set aside in part.

NOTES

1. *See* St. Antoine, *Secondary Boycotts and Hot Cargo: A Study in Balance of Power*, 40 U. DET. L.J. 189 (1962); Victor, *Hot Cargo Clauses: An Examination of Developments Under Section 8(e) of the LMRDA of 1959*, 15 LAB. L.J. 269 (1964); Note, *Hot Cargo Agreements Under the National Labor Relations Act: An Analysis of Section 8(e)*, 38 N.Y.U.L. REV. 97 (1963); Note, *Hot Cargo Clauses: The Scope of Section 8(e)*, 71 YALE L.J. 158 (1961).

2. In Drivers Local 695 (Madison Employers' Council) v. NLRB, 361 F.2d 547 (D.C. Cir. 1966), a contract clause read, "No employee shall be subject to discipline by the Employer for refusal to cross a picket line or enter upon the premises of another employer if the employees of such other employer are engaged in an authorized strike." *Cf.* the picket line proviso to § 8(b)(4). The Board and the court held this clause violative of § 8(e) insofar as it applies to the crossing of *secondary* picket lines. *See also,* Carney & Florsheim, *Treatment of Refusals to Cross Picket Lines: "By-paths and Crookt Ways,"* 55 CORNELL L.Q. 940 (1970).

NATIONAL WOODWORK MFRS. ASS'N v. NLRB

Supreme Court of the United States
386 U.S. 612, 87 S. Ct. 1250, 18 L. Ed. 2d 357 (1967)

MR. JUSTICE BRENNAN delivered the opinion of the Court.

Under the Landrum-Griffin Act amendments enacted in 1959, § 8(b)(4)(A) of the National Labor Relations Act became § 8(b)(4)(B) and § 8(e) was added. The questions here are whether, in the

---

[14] The Board's processes are adequate, we take it, to insure that substantial compliance with union standards or the equivalent will suffice under such a clause, and that the union will not be allowed to use it as a device to limit subcontracting to union firms.

circumstances of this case, the Metropolitan District Council of Philadelphia and Vicinity of the United Brotherhood of Carpenters and Joiners of America, AFL-CIO (hereafter the Union), committed the unfair labor practices prohibited by §§ 8(e) and 8(b)(4)(B).

Frouge Corporation, a Bridgeport, Connecticut concern, was the general contractor on a housing project in Philadelphia. Frouge had a collective bargaining agreement with the Carpenters' International Union under which Frouge agreed to be bound by the rules and regulations agreed upon by local unions with contractors in areas in which Frouge had jobs. Frouge was therefore subject to the provision of a collective bargaining agreement between the Union and an organization of Philadelphia contractors, the General Building Contractors Association, Inc. A sentence in a provision of that agreement entitled Rule 17 provides that ". . . no member of the District Council will handle . . . any doors . . . which have been fitted prior to being furnished on the job. . . ." [2] Frouge's Philadelphia project called for 3,600 doors. Customarily, before the doors could be hung on such projects, "blank" or "blind" doors would be mortised for the knob, routed for the hinges, and beveled to make them fit between jambs. These are tasks traditionally performed in the Philadelphia area by the carpenters employed on the jobsite. However, precut and prefitted doors ready to hang may be purchased from door manufacturers. Although Frouge's contract and job specifications did not call for premachined doors, and "blank" or "blind" doors could have been ordered, Frouge contracted for the purchase of premachined doors from a Pennsylvania door manufacturer which is a member of the National Woodwork Manufacturers Association, petitioner in No. 110 and respondent in No. 111. The Union ordered its carpenter members not to hang the doors when they arrived at the jobsite. Frouge thereupon withdrew the prefabricated doors and substituted "blank" doors which were fitted and cut by his carpenters on the jobsite.

The National Woodwork Manufacturers Association and another filed charges with the National Labor Relations Board against the Union alleging that by including the "will not handle" sentence of Rule 17 in the collective bargaining agreement the Union committed the unfair labor practice under § 8(e) of entering into an "agreement . . . whereby . . . [the] . . . employer . . . agrees to cease or refrain from handling . . . any of the products of any other employer . . ." and alleging further that in

---

[2] The full text of Rule 17 is as follows:

"No employee shall work on any job on which cabinet work, fixtures, mill work, sash doors, trim or other detailed millwork is used unless the same is Union-made and bears the Union Label of the United Brotherhood of Carpenters and Joiners of America. No member of this District Council will handle material coming from a mill where cutting out and fitting has been done for butts, locks, letter plates, or hardware of any description, nor any doors or transoms which have been fitted prior to being furnished on job, including base, chair, rail, picture moulding, which has been previously fitted. This section to exempt partition work furnished in sections." The National Labor Relations Board determined that the first sentence violated § 8(e), 149 N.L.R.B. 646, 655-656, and the Union did not seek judicial review of that determination.

enforcing the sentence against Frouge, the Union committed the unfair labor practice under § 8(b)(4)(B) of "forcing or requiring any person to cease using . . . the products of any other . . . manufacturer. . . ." The National Labor Relations Board dismissed the charges, 149 N.L.R.B. 646.[3] The Board adopted the findings of the Trial Examiner that the "will not handle" sentence in Rule 17 was language used by the parties to protect and preserve cutting out and fitting as unit work to be performed by the jobsite carpenters. The Board also adopted the holding of the Trial Examiner that both the sentence of Rule 17 itself and its maintenance against Frouge were therefore "primary" activity outside the prohibitions of §§ 8(e) and 8(b)(4)(B). . . .

The Court of Appeals for the Seventh Circuit reversed the Board in this respect. 354 F.2d 594, 599 (1965). The court held that the "will not handle" agreement violated § 8(e) without regard to any "primary" or "secondary" objective, and remanded to the Board with instructions to enter an order accordingly. . . .

The Court of Appeals sustained, however, the dismissal of the § 8(b)(4)(B) charge. The court agreed with the Board that the Union's conduct as to Frouge involved only a primary dispute with him and held that the conduct was therefore not prohibited by that section but expressly protected by the proviso "that nothing contained in this clause (B) shall be construed to make unlawful, where not otherwise unlawful, any primary strike or primary picketing. . . ." *Id.* at 597.

We granted certiorari on the petition of the Woodwork Manufacturers Association in No. 110 and on the petition of the Board in No. 111. 384 U.S. 968. We affirm in No. 110 and reverse in No. 111.

I. Even on the doubtful premise that the words of § 8(e) unambiguously embrace the sentence of Rule 17,[4] this does not end

---

[3] There were also charges of violation of §§ 8(e) and 8(b)(4)(B) arising from the enforcement of the Rule 17 provision against three other contractors whose contracts with the owners of the construction projects involved specified that the contractors should furnish and install precut and prefinished doors. The Union refused to permit its members to hang these doors. The Board held that this refusal violated § 8(b)(4)(B). The Board reasoned that, since these contractors (in contrast to Frouge) did not have "control" over the work that the Union sought to preserve for its members, the Union's objective was secondary — to compel the project owners to stop specifying precut doors in their contracts with the employer-contractors. 149 N.L.R.B., at 658. The Union petitioned the Court of Appeals to set aside the remedial order issued by the Board on this finding, but the court sustained the Board. 354 F.2d 594, 597 (1965). The Union did not seek review of the question here. Not before us, therefore, is the issue argued by the AFL-CIO in its brief *amicus curiae,* namely, whether the Board's "right-to-control doctrine — that employees can never strike against their own employer about a matter over which he lacks the legal power to grant their demand" is an incorrect rule of law inconsistent with the Court's decision in NLRB v. Insurance Agents' Int'l Union, 361 U.S. 477, 497-498 (1960).

[4] The statutory language of § 8(e) is far from unambiguous. It prohibits agreements to "cease . . . from handling . . . any of the products *of any other employer.* . . ." [Emphasis supplied.] Since both the product and its source are mentioned, the provision might be read not to prohibit an agreement relating solely to the nature of the product itself, such as a work preservation agreement, but only to prohibit one arising from an objection to

inquiry into Congress' purpose in enacting the section. It is a "familiar rule, that a thing may be within the letter of the statute and yet not within the statute, because not within its spirit, nor within the intention of its makers." Holy Trinity Church v. United States, 143 U.S. 457, 459 (1892). That principle has particular application in the construction of labor legislation which is "to a marked degree, the result of conflict and compromise between strong contending forces and deeply held views on the role of organized labor in the free economic life of the Nation and the appropriate balance to be struck between the uncontrolled power of management and labor to further their respective interests." Carpenters, Local 1976 v. NLRB, 357 U.S. 93, 99-100 (1958). . . .

Strongly held opposing views have invariably marked controversy over labor's use of the boycott to further its aims by involving an employer in disputes not his own. But congressional action to deal with such conduct has stopped short of proscribing identical activity having the object of pressuring the employer for agreements regulating relations between him and his own employees. That Congress meant §§ 8(e) and 8(b)(4)(B) to prohibit only "secondary" objectives clearly appears from an examination of the history of congressional action on the subject. . . .

[The Court reviewed the history of the treatment of secondary boycotts under the Sherman Act, Clayton Act, Norris-La Guardia Act, and Taft-Hartley Act.]

Judicial decisions interpreting the broad language of § 8(b)(4)(A) of the Taft-Hartley Act uniformly limited its application to such "secondary" situations.[16] This limitation was in "conformity with the dual Congressional objectives of preserving the right of labor organizations to bring pressure to bear on offending employers in primary labor disputes and of shielding unoffending employers and others from pressures in controversies not their own." NLRB v. Denver Bldg. Trades Council, 341 U.S. 675, 692 (1951). This Court accordingly refused to read § 8(b)(4)(A) to ban traditional primary strikes and picketing having an impact on neutral employers even though the activity fell within its sweeping terms. NLRB v. International Rice Milling Co., 341 U.S. 665 (1951); see IUE, Local 761 v. NLRB, 366 U.S. 667 (1961). Thus, however severe the impact of primary activity on neutral employers, it was not thereby transformed into activity with a secondary objective.

----

the other employers or a definable group of employers who are the source of the product, for example, their nonunion status.

[16] [Citations] An oft-cited definition of the conduct banned by § 8(b)(4)(A) was that of Judge Learned Hand in IBEW v. NLRB, 181 F.2d 34, 37 (2d Cir. 1950): "The gravamen of a secondary boycott is that its sanctions bear, not upon the employer who alone is a party to the dispute, but upon some third party who has no concern in it. Its aim is to compel him to stop business with the employer in the hope that this will induce the employer to give in to his employees' demands." For the scholarly acceptance of this primary-secondary dichotomy in the scope of § 8(b)(4)(A), see Koretz, Federal Regulation of Secondary Strikes and Boycotts — A New Chapter, 37 Cornell L.Q. 235 (1952); Tower, A Perspective on Secondary Boycotts, 2 Lab. L.J. 727 (1951); Cushman, Secondary

The literal terms of § 8(b)(4)(A) also were not applied in the so-called "ally doctrine" cases, in which the union's pressure was aimed toward employers performing the work of the primary employer's striking employees. The rationale, again, was the inapplicability of the provision's central theme, the protection of neutrals against secondary pressure, where the secondary employer against whom the union's pressure is directed has entangled himself in the vortex of the primary dispute. "[T]he union was not extending its activity to a front remote from the immediate dispute but to one intimately and indeed inextricably united to it." Douds v. Metropolitan Federation of Architects, 75 F. Supp. 672, 677 (S.D.N.Y. 1948) (Rifkind, J.); see NLRB v. Business Machine & Office Appliance Mechanics, 228 F.2d 553 (2d Cir. 1955). We summarized our reading of § 8(b)(4)(A) just a year before enactment of § 8(e):

"It aimed to restrict the area of industrial conflict insofar as this could be achieved by prohibiting the most obvious, widespread, and, as Congress evidently judged, dangerous practice of unions to widen that conflict: the coercion of neutral employers, themselves not concerned with a primary labor dispute, through the inducement of their employees to engage in strikes or concerted refusals to handle goods." Carpenters, Local 1976 v. NLRB (Sand Door), 357 U.S. 93, 100 (1958). . . .

In effect Congress, in enacting § 8(b)(4)(A) of the Taft-Hartley Act, returned to the regime of *Duplex Printing Press Co.* and *Bedford Stone Cutters, supra,* and barred as a secondary boycott union activity directed against a neutral employer, including the immediate employer when in fact the activity directed against him was carried on for its effect elsewhere.

Indeed, Congress in rewriting § 8(b)(4)(A) as § 8(b)(4)(B) took pains to confirm the limited application of the section to such "secondary" conduct. The word "concerted" in former § 8(b)(4)(A) was deleted to reach secondary conduct directed to only one individual. This was in response to the Court's holding in NLRB v. International Rice Milling Co., 341 U.S. 665 (1951), that "concerted" required proof of inducement of two or more employees. But to make clear that the deletion was not to be read as supporting a construction of the statute as prohibiting the incidental effects of traditional primary activity, Congress added the proviso that nothing in the amended section "shall be construed to make unlawful, where not otherwise unlawful, any primary strike or primary picketing." Many statements and examples proffered in the 1959 debates confirm this congressional acceptance of the distinction between primary and secondary activity.

II. The Landrum-Griffin Act amendments in 1959 were adopted only to close various loopholes in the application of § 8(b)(4)(A) which had been exposed in Board and court decisions. . . .

Boycotts and the Taft-Hartley Law, 6 Syracuse L. Rev. 109 (1954); Lesnick, The Gravamen of the Secondary Boycott, 62 Colum. L. Rev. 1363 (1962); Cox, The Landrum-Griffin Amendments to the National Labor Relations Act, 44 Minn. L. Rev. 257, 271 (1959); Aaron, The Labor-Management Reporting and Disclosure Act of 1959, 73 Harv. L. Rev. 1086, 1112 (1960). For the NLRB's vacillations during the period, see Lesnick, *supra,* 62 Colum. L. Rev., at 1366-1392.

Section 8(e) simply closed still another loophole.[22] In Carpenters, Local 1976 v. NLRB [Sand Door], 357 U.S. 93 (1958), the Court held that it was no defense to an unfair labor practice charge under § 8(b)(4)(A) that the struck employer had agreed, in a contract with the union, not to handle nonunion material. However, the Court emphasized that the mere execution of such a contract provision (known as a "hot cargo" clause because of its prevalence in Teamsters Union contracts), or its voluntary observance by the employer, was not unlawful under § 8(b)(4)(A). Section 8(e) was designed to plug this gap in the legislation by making the "hot cargo" clause itself unlawful. The *Sand Door* decision was believed by Congress not only to create the possibility of damage actions against employers for breaches of "hot cargo" clauses, but also to create a situation in which such clauses might be employed to exert subtle pressures upon employers to engage in "voluntary" boycotts. Hearings in late 1958 before the Senate Select Committee explored seven cases of "hot cargo" clauses in Teamster union contracts, the use of which the Committee found conscripted neutral employers in Teamster organizational campaigns.[24]

This loophole closing measure likewise did not expand the type of conduct which § 8(b)(4)(A) condemned. Although the language of § 8(e) is sweeping, it closely tracks that of § 8(b)(4)(A), and just as the latter and its successor § 8(b)(4)(B) did not reach employees' activity to pressure their employer to preserve for themselves work traditionally done by them, § 8(e) does not prohibit agreements made and maintained for that purpose.

The legislative history of § 8(e) confirms this conclusion. . . .

The only mention of a broader reach for § 8(e) appears in isolated statements by opponents of that provision, expressing fears that work preservation agreements would be banned. These statements have scant probative value against the backdrop of the strong evidence to the contrary. Too, "we have often cautioned against the danger, when interpreting a statute, of reliance upon the views of its legislative opponents. In their zeal to defeat a bill, they understandably tend to overstate its reach." NLRB v. Fruit & Vegetable Packers, 377 U.S. 58, 66 (1964). "It is the sponsors that we look to when the meaning of the statutory words is in doubt." Schwegmann Bros. v. Calvert Distillers Corp., 341 U.S. 384, 394-395 (1951). . . .

---

[22] Throughout the committee reports and debates on § 8(e), it was referred to as a measure designed to close a loophole in § 8(b)(4)(A) of the 1947 Act. See, *e.g.*, S. Rep. No. 187, 86th Cong., 1st Sess. 78-79, I 1959 Leg. Hist. 474-475 (1959) (Minority Views); H.R. Rep. No. 741, 86th Cong., 1st Sess. 20-21, I 1959 Leg. Hist. 778-779.

[24] See Final Report for the Senate Select Committee on Improper Activities in the Labor or Management Field, S. Rep. No. 1139, 86th Cong., 2d Sess. 3 (1960). The Final Report, ordered to be printed after enactment of the LMRDA, defined a "hot cargo" clause as "an agreement between a union and a unionized employer that his employees shall not be required to work on or handle 'hot goods' or 'hot cargo' being manufactured or transferred by another employer with whom the union has a labor dispute or whom the union considers and labels as being unfair to organized labor." Final Report, *supra* at 3.

In addition to all else, "the silence of the sponsors of [the] Amendments is pregnant with significance. . . ." NLRB v. Fruit & Vegetable Packers, *supra* at 66. Before we may say that Congress meant to strike from workers' hands the economic weapons traditionally used against their employers' efforts to abolish their jobs, that meaning should plainly appear. It would . . . be incongruous to interpret § 8(e) to invalidate clauses over which the parties may be mandated to bargain and which have been successfully incorporated through collective bargaining in many of this Nation's major labor agreements.

Finally, important parts of the historic accommodation by Congress of the powers of labor and management are §§ 7 and 13 of the National Labor Relations Act, passed as part of the Wagner Act in 1935 and amended in 1947. The former section assures to labor "the right . . . to bargain collectively through representatives of their own choosing, to engage in other concerted activities for the purpose of collective bargaining or other mutual aid or protection. . . ." Section 13 preserves the right to strike, of which the boycott is a form, except as specifically provided in the Act. In the absence of clear indicia of congressional intent to the contrary, these provisions caution against reading statutory prohibitions as embracing employee activities to pressure their own employers into improving the employees' wages, hours, and working conditions. . . .

The Woodwork Manufacturers Association and *amici* who support its position advance several reasons, grounded in economic and technological factors, why "will not handle" clauses should be invalid in all circumstances. Those arguments are addressed to the wrong branch of government. It may be "that the time has come for re-evaluation of the basic content of collective bargaining as contemplated by the federal legislation. But that is for Congress. Congress has demonstrated its capacity to adjust the Nation's labor legislation to what, in its legislative judgment, constitutes the statutory pattern appropriate to the developing state of labor relations in the country. Major revisions of the basic statute were enacted in 1947 and 1959. To be sure, then, Congress might be of opinion that greater stress should be put on . . . eliminating more and more economic weapons from the . . . [Union's] grasp. . . . But Congress' policy has not yet moved to this point. . . ." Insurance Agents' Int'l Union v. NLRB, 361 U.S. 477, 500 (1960).

III. The determination whether the "will not handle" sentence of Rule 17 and its enforcement violated § 8(e) and § 8(b)(4)(B) cannot be made without an inquiry into whether, under all the surrounding circumstances,[38] the Union's objective was preservation of work for Frouge's employees, or whether the agreements and boycott were tactically calculated to satisfy union objectives elsewhere. Were the latter

---

[38] As a general proposition, such circumstances might include the remoteness of the threat of displacement by the banned product or services, the history of labor relations between the union and the employers who would be boycotted, and the economic personality of the industry. See Comment, 62 Mich. L. Rev. 1176, 1185 *et seq.* (1964).

the case, Frouge, the boycotting employer, would be a neutral bystander, and the agreement or boycott would, within the intent of Congress, become secondary. There need not be an actual dispute with the boycotted employer, here the door manufacturer, for the activity to fall within this category, so long as the tactical object of the agreement and its maintenance is that employer, or benefits to other than the boycotting employees or other employees of the primary employer thus making the agreement or boycott secondary in its aim. The touchstone is whether the agreement or its maintenance is addressed to the labor relations of the contracting employer *vis-à-vis* his own employees. This will not always be a simple test to apply. But "[h]owever difficult the task of drawing lines more nice than obvious, the statute compels the task." IUE, Local 761 v. NLRB, 366 U.S. 667, 674 (1961).

That the "will not handle" provision was not an unfair labor practice in this case is clear. The finding of the Trial Examiner, adopted by the Board, was that the objective of the sentence was preservation of work traditionally performed by the job-site carpenters. This finding is supported by substantial evidence, and therefore the Union's making of the "will not handle" agreement was not a violation of § 8(e).

Similarly, the Union's maintenance of the provision was not a violation of § 8(b)(4)(B). The Union refused to hang prefabricated doors whether or not they bore a union label, and even refused to install prefabricated doors manufactured off the jobsite by members of the Union. This and other substantial evidence supported the finding that the conduct of the Union on the Frouge jobsite related solely to preservation of the traditional tasks of the job-site carpenters.

Memorandum of MR. JUSTICE HARLAN.

In joining the Court's opinion, I am constrained to add these few words by way of underscoring the salient factors which, in my judgment, make for the decision that has been reached in these difficult cases.

1. The facts as found by the Board and the Court of Appeals show that the contractual restrictive-product rule in question, and the boycott in support of its enforcement, had as their sole objective the protection of union members from a diminution of work flowing from changes in technology. Union members traditionally had performed the task of fitting doors on the jobsite, and there is no evidence of any motive for this contract provision and its companion boycott other than the preservation of that work. This, then, is not a case of a union seeking to restrict by contract or boycott an employer with respect to the products he uses, for the purpose of acquiring for its members work that had not previously been theirs.

2. The only question thus to be decided, and which is decided, is whether Congress meant, in enacting §§ 8(b)(4)(ii)(B) and 8(e) of the National Labor Relations Act, to prevent this kind of labor-management arrangement designed to fend against possible adverse effects upon workers arising from changing technology.

3. Because of the possibly profound impacts that the answer to this question may have upon labor-management relations and upon other

aspects of the economy, both sides of today's division in the Court agree that we must be especially careful to eschew a resolution of the issue according to our own economic ideas and to find one in what Congress has done. It is further agreed that in pursuing the search for the true intent of Congress we should not stop with the language of the statute itself, but must look beneath its surface to the legislative history.

4. It is recognized by court and counsel on both sides that the legislative history of § 8(b)(4)(ii)(B), with which § 8(e), it is agreed, is to be taken *pari passu,* contains only the most tangential references to problems connected with changing technology. Also, a circumspect reading of the legislative record evincing Congress' belief that the statutory provisions in question prohibited agreements and conduct of the kind involved in Allen Bradley Co. v. IBEW, Local 3, 325 U.S. 797 (1945), will not support a confident assertion that Congress also had in mind the sort of union-management activity before us here. And although it is arguable that Congress, in the temper of the times, would have readily accepted a proposal to outlaw work-preservation agreements and boycotts, even, as here, in their most limited sense, such a surmise can hardly serve as a basis for the construction of an existing statute.

5. We are thus left with a legislative history which, on the precise point at issue, is essentially negative, which shows with fair conclusiveness only that Congress was not squarely faced with the problem this case presents. In view of Congress' deep commitment to the resolution of matters of vital importance to management and labor through the collective bargaining process, and its recognition of the boycott as a legitimate weapon in that process, it would be unfortunate were this Court to attribute to Congress, on the basis of such an opaque legislative record, a purpose to outlaw the kind of collective bargaining and conduct involved in this case. Especially at a time when Congress is continuing to explore methods for meeting the economic problems increasingly arising in this technological age from scientific advances, this Court should not take such a step until Congress has made unmistakably clear that it wishes wholly to exclude collective bargaining as one avenue of approach to solutions in this elusive aspect of our economy.

Mr. Justice Stewart, whom Mr. Justice Black, Mr. Justice Douglas, and Mr. Justice Clark join, dissenting. . . .

The Court undertakes a protracted review of legislative and decisional history in an effort to show that the clear word of the statute should be disregarded in these cases. But the fact is that the relevant history fully confirms that Congress meant what it said, and I therefore dissent.

The Court concludes that the Union's conduct in these cases falls outside the ambit of § 8(b)(4) because it had an ultimate purpose that the Court characterizes as "primary" in nature — the preservation of work for union members. But § 8(b)(4) is not limited to boycotts that have as their only purpose the forcing of any person to cease using the products of another; it is sufficient if that result is "an object" of the boycott. Legitimate union objectives may not be accomplished through means proscribed by the statute. See NLRB v. Denver Bldg. & Const. Trades

Council, 341 U.S. 675, 688-689. Without question, preventing Frouge from using prefitted doors was "an object" of the Union's conduct here.

It is, of course. true that courts have distinguished "primary" and "secondary" activities, and have found the former permitted despite the literal applicability of the statutory language. But the Court errs in concluding that the product boycott conducted by the Union in these cases was protected primary activity. As the Court points out, a typical form of secondary boycott is the visitation of sanctions on Employer A, with whom the union has no dispute, in order to force him to cease doing business with Employer B, with whom the union does have a dispute. But this is not the only form of secondary boycott that § 8(b)(4) was intended to reach. The Court overlooks the fact that a product boycott for work preservation purposes has consistently been regarded by the courts. and by the Congress that passed the Taft-Hartley Act, as a proscribed "secondary boycott" [citing *Allen Bradley* and earlier labor antitrust decisions].

NOTES

1. In a companion case, Houston Insulation Contractors Ass'n v. NLRB, 386 U.S. 664 (1967), the Supreme Court also found no violation of § 8(b)(4)(B). (No violation of § 8(e) was charged.)

The employer ordered precut steel bands used to fasten asbestos material around pipes to be insulated. The collective agreement reserved the work of cutting the bands from large rolls to the company's employees, as had been customary. Union agents instructed employees not to install the precut bands. Upon charges that this was an illegal secondary boycott, *held*, no violation. This was a primary dispute for the purpose of protecting work which had customarily been done by the company's own employees.

One question in the case was whether a refusal to handle by one local in order to protect the work customarily done by members of a sister local for the same employer constituted an illegal secondary boycott. *Held:* No. "*National Woodwork Mfrs.* holds that collective activity by employees of the primary employer, the object of which is to affect the labor policies of that primary employer, and not engaged in for its effect elsewhere, is protected primary activity. 'Congress was not concerned to protect primary employers against pressures by disinterested unions, but rather to protect disinterested employers against direct pressures by any union.'"

2. If a ship operator agrees with a union not to sell a tanker unless the buyer promises to recognize the union as the crew's bargaining agent, is this a work preservation clause or a hot cargo clause? See National Maritime Union v. Commerce Tankers Corp., 457 F.2d 1127 (2d Cir. 1972); NLRB v. NMU, 486 F.2d 907 (2d Cir. 1973).

3. Is there any statutory basis for treating "work acquisition" clauses differently from "work preservation" clauses? If such a distinction is sustained, how would you classify a union's efforts to obtain the right to perform a new operation that has displaced an operation formerly performed by the union's members?

National Woodwork was read as sustaining a "work *re*acquisition" clause in American Boiler Mfrs. Ass'n v. NLRB, 404 F.2d 547 (8th Cir. 1968), *cert. denied,* 398 U.S. 960 (1970). The employer argued unsuccessfully that the allowable preservation of "traditional work" encompassed only work which is "currently, continuously and exclusively performed by unit employees."

Compare Carrier Air Conditioning Co. v. NLRB, 547 F.2d 1178 (2d Cir. 1976); Plumbers, Local 342 (Conduit Fabricators, Inc.), 225 N.L.R.B. 1364 (1976); Longshoremen, ILA v. NLRB (Consolidated Express, Inc.), 537 F.2d 706 (2d Cir. 1976), *cert. denied,* 429 U.S. 1041 (1977).

4. In Retail Clerks, Local 324 (Federated Dep't Stores, Inc.), 235 N.L.R.B. No. 69, 97 L.R.R.M. 1556 (1978), the Labor Board ruled that a union that has a collective bargaining agreement with a multi-employer association violated the "hot cargo" provisions of the NLRA by bringing an arbitration proceeding to require a member supermarket operator to comply with a contract clause requiring it to retain full control over the labor relations policies of a photo shop lessee of store space, and providing that the lessee's employees must be members of the same bargaining unit as the supermarket workers. It found that the clause exceeds lawful work preservation objectives, is an unlawful unit acquisition clause, and has the effects of an unlawful "union signatory" provision.

For a concise summary of the distinction between valid (union standards) and invalid (union signatory) subcontracting clauses and between valid work preservation clauses and invalid work acquisition clauses, *see* Carpenters Local 944 (Woelke & Romero Framing), 239 N.L.R.B. No. 40, 99 L.R.R.M. 1580 (1978).

See Feldacker, *Subcontracting Restrictions and the Scope of § 8(b)(4)(A) and (B) and of § 8(e) of the NLRA,* 17 LAB. L.J. 170 (1966); Hickey, *Subcontracting Clauses Under § 8(e) of the NLRA,* 40 NOTRE DAME LAW. 377 (1965); Lesnick, *Job Security and Secondary Boycotts: The Reach of NLRA §§ 8(b)(4) and 8(e),* 113 U. PA. L. REV. 1000 (1965); Comment, *Subcontracting Clauses and § 8(e) of the National Labor Relations Act,* 62 MICH. L. REV. 1176 (1964); Note, *Rational Approach to Secondary Boycotts and Work Preservation,* 57 VA. L. REV. 1280 (1971).

5. What is your opinion on the problem mentioned in footnote 3 of the principal case, on which the union did not seek review? Is the practical result that the union cannot block the use of precut doors, if they are called for in the specifications, and the union cannot then "protect" its traditional work?

The Supreme Court dealt with the problem in the following case.

NLRB v. ENTERPRISE ASSOCIATION OF PIPEFITTERS, LOCAL 638

Supreme Court of the United States
429 U.S. 507, 97 S. Ct. 891, 51 L. Ed. 2d 1 (1977)

[The collective bargaining agreement between Respondent Union and Hudik Ross Co. (Hudik), a heating and air conditioning contractor, contained a work preservation clause which provided that Hudik's employees represented by the Union would cut and thread the internal piping in climate control units installed by Hudik. There was no dispute that this work was traditionally performed by the Hudik employees.

Hudik obtained a subcontract from the Austin Company to do certain work at a construction project known as the Norwegian Home for the Aged. The subcontract incorporated Austin's job specifications and provided that Hudik would install prefabricated climate control units manufactured by Slant-Fin Corp., whose employees had already cut and threaded the internal piping before the units were delivered to the jobsite.

The Union then informed both Hudik and Austin that, because of Hudik's alleged breach of the collective bargaining agreement, its members would not install the units. Austin filed a complaint with the NLRB, charging that the Union had committed an unfair labor practice under § 8(b)(4)(B) of the NLRA. The Board found that the Union's refusal to install the units constituted prohibited secondary pressure on Hudik because a Union object was to either force a change in Austin's business practice or to force Hudik to terminate its subcontract with Austin. The Board recognized that the Union based its action on a valid work preservation clause; but it still concluded that the pressure was secondary because it believed the Union's primary dispute was with Austin since it, and not Hudik, controlled the assignment of the internal piping work. Hudik, lacking such control, was a mere neutral in the dispute, the Board found. The Court of Appeals for the District of Columbia, sitting en banc, rejected the Board's ruling. 521 F.2d 885 (1975).]

MR. JUSTICE WHITE delivered the opinion of the Court.

. . . The question now before us is whether a union seeking the kind of work traditionally performed by its members at a construction site violates § 8(b)(4)(B) when it induces its members to engage in a work stoppage against an employer who does not have control over the assignment of the work sought by the union. More specifically, the issue is whether a union-instigated refusal of a subcontractor's employees to handle or install factory-piped climatic control units, which were included in the general contractor's job specifications and delivered to the construction site, was primary activity beyond the reach of § 8(b)(4)(B) or whether it was secondary activity prohibited by the statute. As we shall see, this issue turns on whether the boycott was "addressed to the labor relations of the contracting employer vis-à-vis his own employees," National Woodwork Manufacturers Assn. v. NLRB, 386 U.S. 612 (1967), at 645, and is therefore primary conduct, or whether the boycott was "tactically calculated to satisfy union objectives elsewhere," id., at 644, in which event the boycott would be prohibited secondary activity. . . .

II. In setting aside the Board's order, the Court of Appeals disagreed with the Board on both legal and factual grounds. We deal first with the Court of Appeals' proposition that "an employer who is struck by his own employees for the purpose of requiring him to do what he has lawfully contracted to do to benefit those employees can [n]ever be considered a neutral bystander in a dispute not his own." 521 F.2d, at 903 (footnote omitted). Under this view, a strike or refusal to handle undertaken to enforce such a contract would not itself warrant an inference that the union sought to satisfy secondary, rather than primary, objectives, whatever the impact on the immediate employer or on other employers might be. Thus, where a union seeks to enforce a work preservation agreement by a strike or work stoppage, the existence of the agreement would always provide an adequate defense to a § 8(b)(4) unfair labor practice charge. This approach is untenable under the Act and our cases construing it.

Local 1976, United Brotherhood of Carpenters v. NLRB (Sand Door), 357 U.S. 93 (1958), involved a collective-bargaining contract containing a provision, then quite legal, that "workmen shall not be required to handle non-union material." 357 U.S., at 95. . . .

The union argued that if the statute was aimed at protecting neutral employers from becoming involuntarily involved in the labor disputes of others, "protection should not extend to an employer who has agreed to a hot cargo provision, for such an employer is not in fact involuntarily involved in the dispute," especially "when the employer takes no steps at the time of the boycott to repudiate the contract and to order his employees to handle the goods." In such circumstances, "[t]he union does no more than inform the employees of their contractual rights and urge them to take the only action effective to enforce them." 357 U.S., at 105. These arguments were squarely rejected:

> "Nevertheless, it seems most probable that the freedom of choice for the employer contemplated by § 8(b)(4)(A) is a freedom of choice at the time the question whether to boycott or not arises. . ."

Sand Door's holding that employer promises in a collective-bargaining contract provide no defense to a § 8(b)(4) charge against a union has not been disturbed. In contemplating the 1959 amendments to the Landrum-Griffin Act, Congress viewed that part of Sand Door in which the Court suggested that contractual provisions having secondary objectives were not forbidden by law as creating a loophole in the Act. Section 8(e) was enacted to close that loophole. . . . Section 8(e) does not prohibit agreements made for "primary" purposes, including the purpose of preserving for the contracting employees themselves work traditionally done by them.

By no stretch of the imagination, however, can it be thought, that in enacting § 8(e) Congress intended to disagree with or ease Sand Door's construction of § 8(b)(4), under which a perfectly legal collective bargaining contract may not be enforced by a strike or refusal to handle which in the absence of such a provision would be a violation of the statute. The intention of Congress as to this aspect of *Sand Door* could not be clearer. A proviso to § 8(e) exempted from that section certain agreements in the construction industry that the section would otherwise have prohibited, but the Committee Report explained that the "proviso applies only to section 8(e) and therefore leaves unaffected the law developed under section 8(b)(4)," noting particularly that picketing to enforce agreements saved by the proviso "would be illegal under the *Sand Door* case." H. R. Rep. No. 1147, p. 39, I Leg. Hist. 943. Undoubtedly, Congress embraced the rule then followed by the Board and approved by this Court in *Sand Door* that a contract permitting or justifying the challenged union conduct is no defense to a § 8(b)(4) charge. To hold, as the Court of Appeals did, that a work stoppage is necessarily primary and not an unfair practice when it aims at enforcing a legal promise in a collective bargaining contract is inconsistent with the statute as construed in *Sand Door,* a construction that was accepted and that has never been abandoned by Congress.

Nor did we modify *Sand Door* in *National Woodwork.* . . .

Our rationale was *not* that the work preservation provision was valid under § 8(e) and that *therefore* it could be enforced by striking or picketing without violating § 8(b)(4)(B). Expressly recognizing the continuing validity of the *Sand Door* decision that a valid contract does not immunize conduct otherwise violative of § 8(b)(4), 386 U.S., at 634, we held that neither § 8(b)(4)(B) nor § 8(e) forbade primary activity by employees designed to preserve for themselves work traditionally done by them and that on this basis the union's conduct violated neither section. To determine whether the Frouge employees' refusal to handle was permissible primary activity or was forbidden secondary coercion, we inquired whether,

> "under all the surrounding circumstances, the Union's objective was preservation of work for Frouge's employees, or whether the agreements and boycott were tactically calculated to satisfy union objectives elsewhere. . . . The touchstone is whether the agreement or its maintenance is addressed to the labor relations of the contracting employer *vis-à-vis* his own employees." 386 U.S., at 644-645 (footnotes omitted).

There is thus no doubt that the collective bargaining provision that pipes be cut by hand on the job and that the work be conducted by units of two is not itself a sufficient answer to a § 8(b)(4)(B) charge. The substantial question before us is whether, with or without the collective bargaining contract, the union's conduct at the time it occurred was proscribed secondary activity within the meaning of the section. If it was, the collective bargaining provision does not save it. If it was not, the reason is that § 8(b)(4)(B) did not reach it, not that it was immunized by the contract. Thus, regardless of whether an agreement is valid under § 8(e), it may not be enforced by means that would violate § 8(b)(4).[8]

---

[8] . . . [T]he Board's decision [does not] undermine the collective bargaining process as the Court of Appeals suggests. In appropriate circumstances, the Board has not found the

III. The Court of Appeals was also of the view that the Board's "control" test, under which the union commits an unfair practice under § 8(b)(4)(B) when it coerces an employer in order to obtain work that the employer has no power to assign, is invalid as a matter of law because it fails to comply with the *National Woodwork* standard that the union's conduct be judged in light of all the relevant circumstances. Again, we think the Court of Appeals was in error. . . .

Here, the administrative law judge, cognizant of *National Woodwork* and the Board's own precedents, examined the history both of the relevant jobsite work traditionally done by the steamfitters and of the contractual provision calling for jobsite cutting and threading of pipe, assessed the agreement and refusal to handle in the light of the actual conditions in the New York market, and concluded that "under all the surrounding circumstances," Hudik was "only a means or instrumentality for exerting pressure against Slant/Fin and Austin with whom the Union has its primary dispute." It thus does not appear to us that either the administrative law judge or the Board, in agreeing with him, articulated a different standard from that which this Court recognized as the proper test in *National Woodwork*.[11]

Nor is it the case that the Board, in applying its control standard, failed to consider all of the relevant circumstances. Surely the fact that the Board distinguishes between two otherwise identical cases because in the one the employer has control of the work and in the other he has no power over it does not indicate that the Board has ignored any material circumstance.

---

lack of control to be determinative, Painters District Council No. 20 (Uni-Coat), 185 N.L.R.B. 930 (1970), and the Board has declared its intention to continue to eschew a mechanical application of its control test in order to ascertain whether the struck employer is truly an unoffending employer. See Local Union No. 438, United Association of Journeymen and Apprentices (George Koch Sons, Inc.), 201 N.L.R.B. 59, 64 (1973).

[11] The Board addressed the question in *George Koch Sons, Inc., supra*. The Board recognized that there had been some ambiguity on this issue in earlier decisions.

"Specifically, of late, the Board has characterized its approach simply in terms of a right-of-control test. The test as stated would seem to imply that the Board looked solely at the pressured employer's 'contract right to control' the work at issue at the time of the pressure to determine whether that pressure was primary or secondary. In fact, this is not now the Board's approach nor was it ever.

"Rather, the Board has always proceeded with an analysis of (1) whether under all the surrounding circumstances the union's objective was work preservation and then (2) whether the pressures exerted were directed at the right person, *i.e.*, at the primary in the dispute. . . . In following this approach, however, our analysis has not nor will it ever be a mechanical one, and, in addition to determining, under all the surrounding circumstances, whether the union's objective is truly work preservation, we have studied and shall continue to study not only the situation the pressured employer finds himself in but also how he came to be in that situation. And if we find that the employer is not truly an 'unoffending employer' who merits the Act's protections, we shall find no violation in a union's pressures such as occurred here, even though a purely mechanical or surface look at the case might present an appearance of a parallel situation." 201 N.L.R.B., at 64 (footnotes omitted).

The contrary might more rationally be inferred. Of course, the Board may assign to the presence or absence of control much more weight than would the Court of Appeals, but this far from demonstrates a departure from the totality-of-the-circumstances test recognized in *National Woodwork*.[12] . . .

IV. Wholly apart from its determination that the union's conduct was justified as a measure to enforce its collective bargaining contract and that the Board applied an incorrect standard for determining liability, the Court of Appeals held that since there was "no substantial evidence . . . in this record that the union's purpose was also 'to satisfy union objectives elsewhere,' the Board's decision holding the union guilty of a section 8(b)(4)(B) violation may not stand." 521 F.2d, at 904. We disagree.

That there existed inducement and coercion within the meaning of § 8(b)(4) is not disputed. The issue is whether "an object" of the inducement and the coercion was to cause the cease-doing-business consequences prohibited by § 8(b)(4), the resolution of which in turn depends on whether the product boycott was "addressed to the labor relations of [Hudik] . . . *vis-à-vis* his own employees," *National Woodwork, supra,* 386 U.S., at 645, or whether the union's conduct was "tactically calculated to satisfy [its] objectives elsewhere," *id.,* at 644.[16]

---

[12] The Board also adopted the administrative law judge's discussion of the economic context in which the dispute arose.

The administrative law judge was of the view that union pressure on Austin and other contractors who preferred factory-piped units could effectively foreclose Slant/Fin and similar producers from the market. The Board did not disturb the administrative law judge's findings that "If prepaid units cannot be installed in the large commercial, public, and industrial buildings in the New York area or in other areas effectively organized by the Union and other building trades unions, the manufacture will be materially affected and Austin and other engineers and general contractors will not specify their purchase and use in buildings." 204 N.L.R.B., at 764. . . .

[16] The dissenters now assert a different definition of what constitutes prohibited secondary activity:

"If the purpose of a contract provision, or of economic pressure on an employer, is to secure benefits for that employer's own employees, it is primary; if the object is to affect the policies of some other employer toward his employees, the contract or its enforcement is secondary."

National Woodwork did not, however, adopt this standard for applying the proscriptions of § 8(b) (4) (B). The distinction between primary and secondary activity does not always turn on which group of employees the union seeks to benefit. There are circumstances under which the union's conduct is secondary when one of its purposes is to influence directly the conduct of an employer other than the struck employer. In these situations, a union's efforts to influence the conduct of the nonstruck employer are not rendered primary simply because it seeks to benefit the employees of the struck employer. *National Woodwork* itself embraced the view that the union's conduct would be secondary if its tactical object was to influence another employer:

"There need not be an actual dispute with the boycotted employer, here the door manufacturer, for the activity to fall within this category, *so long as the tactical object of the agreement and its maintenance is that employer,* or benefits to other than the boycotting employees or other employees of the primary employer thus making the agreement or boycott secondary in its aim." (Emphasis added.) . . .

There is ample support in the record for the Board's resolution of this question. The union sought to enforce its contract with Hudik by a jobsite product boycott by which the steamfitters asserted their rights to the cutting and threading work on the Norwegian Home project. It is uncontrovertible that the work at this site could not be secured by pressure on Hudik alone and that the union's work objectives could not be obtained without exerting pressure on Austin as well. That the union may also have been seeking to enforce its contract and to convince Hudik that it should bid on no more jobs where prepiped units were specified does not alter the fact that the union refused to install the Slant/Fin units and asserted that the piping work on the Norwegian Home job belonged to its members.[17] It was not error for the Board to conclude that the union's objectives were not confined to the employment relationship with Hudik but included the object of influencing Austin in a manner prohibited by § 8(b)(4)(B).[18]

The Court of Appeals was of the view that other inferences from the facts were possible. The court, for example, could "clearly see that it was possible for Hudik-Ross to settle the labor dispute which it had" created. The record is void of any suggestion that Hudik-Ross attempted to negotiate a compromise with the union under which the union would have agreed to install the climate control units in exchange for extra pay or other special benefits. 521 F.2d, at 899. How this observation impugns the

---

The *National Woodwork* opinion also noted that the Court then had no occasion "to decide the questions which might arise where the workers carry on a boycott to reach out to monopolize jobs or acquire new job tasks." 386 U. S., at 630-631. That reservation was apparently meaningless, for under the theory of the dissent, seemingly derived from *National Woodwork* itself, striking workers may legally demand that their employer cease doing business with another company even if the union's object is to obtain new work so long as that work is for the benefit of the striking employees. If, for example, Hudik had in the past used prepiped units without opposition from the union, and the union had demanded that Hudik not fulfill its contract with Austin on the Norwegian Home job — all for the benefit of Hudik employees — it would appear that the dissenters' approach would exonerate the union. Respondents take the same view. Tr. of Oral Arg., at 22. We disagree, for the union's object would necessarily be to force Hudik to cease doing business with Austin, not to preserve, but to aggrandize, its own position and that of its members. Such activity is squarely within the statute.

Here, of course, the union not only sought to acquire work that it never had and that its employer had no power to give it, namely, the piping work on units specified by any contractor or developer who prefers and uses prepiped units. By seeking the work at the Norwegian Home, the union's tactical objects necessarily included influencing Austin; this conduct falls squarely within the statement of *National Woodwork* that a union's activity is secondary if its tactical object is to influence the boycotted employer.

[17] "It is not necessary to find that the *sole* object of the strike" was secondary so long as one of the union's objectives was to influence another employer by inducing the struck employer to cease doing business with that other employer. See NLRB v. Denver Building and Construction Trades Council, 341 U. S. 675, 689 (1951). . . .

[18] The dissenters assert that "[n]othing whatever in the record even remotely suggests that the Union had any quarrel with Slant/Fin or Austin." The Court has held, however, that there is no need for the Board to make such a finding in order to conclude that a § 8(b)(4)(B) violation has occurred. *National Woodwork,* 386 U. S., at 645 quoted, at n. 16, *supra.*

Board's finding with respect to the union's object is not clear. The union simply refused to handle the Slant/Fin units and asserted that under the contract the cutting and threading work belonged to them. The common sense inference from these facts is that the product boycott was in part aimed at securing the cutting and threading work at the Norwegian Home job, which could only be obtained by exerting pressure on Austin.

The statutory standard under which the Court of Appeals was obliged to review this case was not whether the Court of Appeals would have arrived at the same result as the Board did, but whether the Board's findings were "supported by substantial evidence on the record considered as a whole."

. . . It appears to us that in reweighing the facts and setting aside the Board's order, the Court of Appeals improperly substituted its own views of the facts for those of the Board.

The judgment of the Court of Appeals is

Reversed.

MR. JUSTICE BRENNAN, with whom MR. JUSTICE STEWART and MR. JUSTICE MARSHALL join, dissenting.

. . . .

II. The Court's result cannot be squared with *National Woodwork Manufacturers Assn.* v. *NLRB, supra,* whose totality-of-the-circumstances test the Court purports to apply. . . .

National Woodwork exemplifies application of the test in precisely the factual context of the instant case: a dispute over the application of a negotiated work-preservation rule to the use of prefabricated materials in the construction industry. The crux of *National Woodwork* is the following passage:

> "The determination whether the 'will not handle' sentence of Rule 17 and its enforcement violated § 8(e) and § 8(b)(4)(B) cannot be made without an inquiry into whether, under all the surrounding circumstances, the Union's objective was preservation of work for Frouge's employees, or whether the agreements and boycott were tactically calculated to satisfy union objectives elsewhere. . . . The touchstone is whether the agreement or its maintenance is addressed to the labor relations of the contracting employer *vis-à-vis* his own employees." 386 U. S., at 644-645 (footnotes omitted).

Two principles follow from this passage. First, § 8 (b) (4) (B) and § 8 (e) prohibit only conduct which is secondary, as that term has generally been understood in American labor law. If the purpose of a contract provision, or of economic pressure on an employer, is to secure benefits for that employer's own employees, it is primary; if the object is to affect the policies of some other employer toward his employees, the contract or its enforcement is secondary. Second, work preservation is necessarily a primary goal. . . . Only if examination of "all the surrounding circumstances" indicated that the purpose of the clause is not work preservation, but rather "to satisfy union objectives elsewhere," would the provision violate § 8(e) and its enforcement by economic pressure violate § 8(b)(4)(B).

III. The Court's acknowledgment that these principles must control the result here rings hollow in the face of its conclusion. For here, as in *National Woodwork,* the Board found that the Union's actions were taken "for the purpose of preserving work [its members] had traditionally performed." 204 N. L. R. B., at 760. Cf. 386 U. S., at 645-646. . . . Nothing whatever in the record even remotely suggests that the Union had any quarrel with Slant/Fin or Austin. Those companies were simply the vehicles used by Hudik to effect the breach which created the primary dispute between it and its own employees and their Union. Nor is there the slightest basis for a suggestion that the true purpose of the work-preservation clause or the pressure applied to enforce it was to benefit employees "other than the boycotting employees or other employees of [Hudik]." 386 U. S., at 645. Rather, the Board found that the purpose of the job action was "preserving work [the boycotting employees] had traditionally performed" for Hudik.[2] Since the purpose of the Union's pressure was, by the Board's own finding, work preservation, and since *National Woodwork* holds that work preservation is a legitimate primary objective, the only possible conclusion on this record is that the pressure here was primary, and not prohibited by § 8 (b)(4)(B).

Nor is *National Woodwork* distinguishable, as contended, because Austin, and not Hudik, had the "right to control" the assignment of the work of cutting and threading the internal piping. Any conclusion from this that the Union's pressure must have been directed at Austin and not Hudik is totally inconsistent with the premises and conclusion of *National Woodwork.* First, Hudik was by no means a "neutral" in the sense contemplated by Congress as warranting or requiring protection. See 386 U. S., at 624-628. Hudik made the agreement with its employees to satisfy their deep concern for work preservation. But in defiance of his obligations voluntarily assumed, Hudik accepted a subcontract knowing that it disabled it from keeping the bargain.

. . . .

Second, it is not true that Hudik was a neutral because it was powerless to deal with the union demands. As the Court of Appeals pointed out, if the Union's purpose is truly work preservation for the benefit of its own members, it presumably would be willing to negotiate some substitute for full compliance, such as premium pay, to replace the lost work. . . .

---

[2] The Court argues, contrary to this finding, that the Union's object was "to acquire work that it never had," because unit members had never done "the piping work on units specified by" a contractor who preferred prefabricated units. The Board's finding that the Union's aim was work preservation, rather than work acquisition, disposes of this argument. At any rate, striking workers in any work preservation dispute have never before done the particular job at issue in the dispute, and are seeking to "acquire" work that has been assigned to other workers, but that is of a *type* that they have traditionally performed for their employer. As the majority correctly points out, the Court in *National Woodwork* had no occasion to decide what implications its analysis might have when a union seeks to acquire tasks not traditionally performed by its members, and since this is not such a situation, I have no occasion to reach that question here.

Third, there is no basis in the record for the conclusion that Austin should be regarded as the "real" target of the Union's pressure. . . .

IV. The Court maintains that the collective bargaining agreement between Enterprise and Hudik is irrelevant to the determination of whether the Union exerted primary or secondary pressure, relying on Local 1976, United Brotherhood of Carpenters v. NLRB (Sand Door), 357 U. S. 93 (1958). With all respect, this totally misapprehends the relevance of the agreement to the issue before us, and misapplies *Sand Door.* . . . *Sand Door* holds that pressure to enforce a *secondary* boycott clause remains secondary, despite the then legality of the clause itself; it is not authority that union pressure to enforce a concededly *primary* work-preservation clause (which, since the enactment of § 8 (e), is legal only because it is primary), is anything but primary pressure. The Union here does not argue, as in *Sand Door,* that pressure otherwise secondary is magically transformed into primary pressure by an employer's prior agreement to support a secondary boycott. . . . In short, the agreement in this case, as the Board found, was for a primary purpose; pressure brought to compel Hudik to agree to it would have been primary; and pressure brought to enforce it when Hudik breached it, whether by ordering prefabricated units himself, as in *National Woodwork,* or by entering a contract that required him to breach it, was no less primary. . . .

NOTES

1. The carpenters union responded to Boise Cascade's effort to start building modular houses by negotiating a valid work-preservation agreement with an employers' association. The union attempted to enforce the agreement by inducing employees of various companies to refuse to erect the modular houses. Following the *Enterprise* case, the Board held that this conduct violated § 8(b)(4), because the companies whose employees were induced to stop work did not have the right of control over the use of the modular houses. Thus it was an illegal attempt to pressure Boise Cascade. The Court of Appeals enforced the Board order, noting that "right of control" was not a *per se* test; but, taking other circumstances into account, the Board had properly found secondary pressure. Chamber of Commerce v. NLRB, 574 F.2d 457 (9th Cir. 1978).

2. In Carpenters Local 742 (J.L. Simmons Co.), 237 N.L.R.B. No. 82, 99 L.R.R.M. 1021 (1978), on remand following the *Enterprise* case, the Board held that a union whose members refused to install pre-machined doors in a hospital violated § 8(b)(4). Their employer did not have the right to control use of the doors, since they were provided for in the hospital's specifications; thus, this work stoppage was not primary, but was designed to influence the hospital. Does it make any difference that the union's attorney suggested that the dispute might be resolved by the negotiation of a wage premium for each precut door installed? The Board held no; that is merely the substitution of one form of economic pressure for another for the same wrongful, secondary objective — to influence the hospital. Could the union legally demand, in the *next* collective bargaining agreement, that if the employer violates the work-preservation agreement, he will pay a premium in return for the union members handling the precut doors? Chairman Fanning added a caveat stating that he does not understand the *Simmons* case to decide that question.

3. *See generally* Leslie, *Right to Control: A Study in Secondary Boycotts and Labor Antitrust,* 89 HARV. L. REV. 904 (1976).

G. DAMAGES FOR UNLAWFUL SECONDARY ACTIVITY

UNITED MINE WORKERS, DISTRICT 28 v. PATTON

United States Court of Appeals, Fourth Circuit
211 F.2d 742 (1954)
Cert. denied, 348 U.S. 824 (1954)

[Plaintiff was a partner in a mining operation in the coal fields of Western Virginia. The basis of the action was that the defendants by a strike at the mines of the Clinchfield Coal Corp. caused that corporation to cease doing business with plaintiff, resulting in the destruction of the partnership business. A jury in the trial court below awarded the partnership actual damages in the sum of $150,000 and punitive damages in the sum of $75,000 under the provisions of § 303 of the LMRA.]

PARKER, Chief Judge. . . . The chief argument of defendants . . . is that there is no evidence that they authorized or ratified the strikes upon which plaintiffs rely for recovery. It is true that there is no evidence of any resolution of either the United Mine Workers or District 28 authorizing or ratifying the strikes. There is evidence, however, that the strikes were called by the Field Representative of the United Mine Workers, who was employed by District 28, and that he was engaged in the organization work that was being carried on by the international union through District 28, which was a mere division of the international union. . . .

Section 301(b) of the Labor Management Relations Act, 29 U.S.C. § 185(b) expressly provides:

"(b) Any labor organization which represents employees in an industry affecting commerce as defined in this chapter and any employer whose activities affect commerce as defined in this chapter shall be bound by the acts of its agents." . . .

[S]ection 301(e), 61 Stat. 156, 157, 29 U.S.C. § 185(e) . . . provides:

"For the purposes of this section, in determining whether any person is acting as an 'agent' of another person so as to make such other person responsible for his acts, the question of whether the specific acts performed were actually authorized or subsequently ratified shall not be controlling." . . .

In his analysis of the bill Senator Taft had the following to say, 93 Cong. Record, p. 7001, Legislative History of Labor Management Relations Act, vol. 2, p. 1622:

"Section 2(2), 2(13), and 301(e):

"The conference agreement in defining the term employer struck out the vague phrase in the Wagner Act 'anyone acting in the interest of an employer' and inserted in lieu thereof the word 'agent.' The term agent is defined in § 2(13) and § 301(e), since it is used throughout the unfair labor practice sections of title I and in §§ 301 and 303 of title III. In defining the term the conference amendment reads 'the question of whether the specific acts performed were actually authorized or subsequently ratified shall not be controlling.' This restores the law of agency as it has been developed at common law." . . .

[W]e think there was error in allowing the jury to award punitive damages. This is not a case brought under the diversity jurisdiction of the federal courts to enforce a common law liability, where we are governed by state decisions and would be bound on the question of punitive damages by the decision of the Supreme Court of Appeals of Virginia in United Constr. Workers v. Laburnum Constr. Corp., *supra,* 194 Va. 872, 75 S.E.2d 694 (1953). There is no diversity of citizenship and the plaintiffs are entitled to invoke the jurisdiction of the federal courts only because they sue on a cause of action created by a federal statute, *i.e.,* on the cause of action created by § 303(b) of the Labor Management Relations Act, 29 U.S.C. § 187(b), heretofore quoted. That section makes no provision for the recovery of punitive damages; but on the contrary provides expressly that the aggrieved party "shall recover *the damages by him sustained* and the cost of the suit." (Italics supplied.) "Punitive damages are damages beyond and above the amount which a plaintiff has really suffered, and they are awarded upon the theory that they are a punishment to the defendant, and not a mere matter of compensation for injuries sustained by plaintiff." Washington Gas Light Co. v. Lansden, 172 U.S. 534, 553 (1899). . . .

In the absence of anything in the act itself or in its history indicating an intention on the part of Congress to authorize the recovery of punitive damages by this highly controversial legislation, the courts would not be justified, we think, in construing it to permit such recovery. . . .

NOTES

1. *Punitive damages.* As indicated in the principal case, punitive damages cannot be awarded under § 303. However, such damages may be given under applicable state law. For an interesting commentary on this divergence, see United Mine Workers v. Meadow Creek Coal Co., 263 F.2d 52 (6th Cir. 1959), in which it was held that the federal courts had jurisdiction to award punitive damages arising under state law of civil conspiracy where primary jurisdiction was obtained through an action under § 303, if both claims constituted "one cause of action." This result followed even though the court found against the plaintiff on the § 303 claim.

However, in Teamsters Local 20 v. Morton, 377 U.S. 252 (1964), the Court unanimously held that "state law has been displaced by § 303 in private damage actions based on peaceful union secondary activity." Consequently, the Court declared that "the district court was without authority to award punitive damages," or "damages proximately caused by lawful, primary activities, even though the petitioner may have contemporaneously engaged in unlawful acts elsewhere." The Court's earlier opinions in UAW v. Russell, 356 U.S. 634 (1958), and United Constr. Workers v. Laburnum Constr. Corp., 347 U.S. 656 (1954), were approved, the Court noting that "in cases involving union violence, state law has been permitted to prevail by reason of controlling considerations which are entirely absent in the present case." However, Justice Goldberg in his concurring opinion said that his concurrence did not indicate approval with the holding in either the *Russell* or *Laburnum* case. With respect to federal-state relations generally, see section VIII of Part Three.

Then, in UMW v. Gibbs, 383 U.S. 715 (1966), a mine superintendent recovered compensatory and punitive damages in a federal district court, where he sued for a violation of § 303 of the Taft-Hartley Act. The district court properly found no violation of the Taft-Hartley Act, but, having taken "pendent" jurisdiction on the state common law claim, the court found that claim meritorious and awarded compensatory and punitive damages. The Supreme Court reversed. The state claim was not preempted, as it was in *Morton,* because in *Gibbs* there was violence, and federal labor law does not preempt state law to remedy violence. The district court properly exercised "pendent" jurisdiction over the state claim in a § 303 suit. But § 6 of the Norris-La Guardia Act applied to the suit in federal court on the state claim, and, under § 6, there was no clear proof of actual participation, authorization, or ratification of violence by the international union.

2. *Parties plaintiff under § 303.* Either primary or secondary employers may sue for damages under § 303. United Brick & Clay Workers v. Deena Artware, 198 F.2d 637 (6th Cir. 1952).

An employer subject to the NLRA may sue for damages under § 303 against a union representing airline workers subject to the Railway Labor Act. Marriott In-Flight Services v. Transport Workers, 557 F.2d 295 (2d Cir. 1977). Although literally the union is not a "labor organization," since its members are not "employees" of an "employer" as defined in the NLRA, the court concluded that the intent of Congress in the 1959 amendments to the Taft-Hartley Act was to prohibit secondary boycotts and picketing and "to end the exemption from this prohibition enjoyed by RLA unions."

3. *Nature of the remedy.* Under § 303 a union may be sued for damages by a private party in a federal district court for engaging in any of the kinds of activity defined in § 8(b)(4). This does not mean that the filing of a damage suit must await a final NLRB order stating that § 8(b)(4) was violated. An action may be brought under § 303 regardless of whether unfair practice charges are filed with the NLRB; or, if unfair practice charges are filed, a damage suit may be brought at the same time. Longshoremen's Union v. Juneau Spruce Corp., 342 U.S. 237 (1952). Damages have been awarded even though there has been a finding that no unfair labor practice was committed. *See* United Brick & Clay Workers v. Deena Artware, *supra.* However, in several cases, a final decision of the NLRB as to an unfair labor practice under § 8(b)(4) has been treated as res judicata or collateral estoppel in a subsequent § 303 action. H. L. Robertson & Associates v. Plumbers Local 519, 429 F.2d 520 (5th Cir. 1970); Paramount Transport Systems v. Teamsters Local 150, 436 F.2d 1064 (9th Cir. 1971); International Wire v. IBEW Local 38, 475 F.2d 1078 (6th Cir. 1973), *cert. denied,* 414 U.S. 867 (1973). *But cf.,* Old Dutch Farms, Inc. v. Milk Drivers Local 584, 281 F. Supp. 971 (E.D.N.Y. 1968). *See* Note, *The Applicability of Res Judicata and Collateral Estoppel to Actions Brought Under Section 8(b)(4) of the National Labor Relations Act,* 67 MICH. L. REV. 824 (1969).

4. Note also the mandatory injunction remedy which § 10(*l*) provides.

SECTION V. Jurisdictional Disputes

NLRB, THIRTY-SEVENTH ANNUAL REPORT 121 (1972)

Section 8(b)(4)(D) prohibits a labor organization from engaging in or inducing strike action for the purpose of forcing any employer to assign particular work to "employees in a particular labor organization or in a particular trade, craft, or class rather than to employees in another labor organization or in another trade, craft, or class, unless such employer is failing to conform to an order or certification of the Board determining the bargaining representative for employees performing such work."

An unfair labor practice charge under this section, however, must be handled differently from a charge alleging any other type of unfair labor practice. Section 10(k) requires that parties to a jurisdictional dispute be given 10 days, after notice of the filing of the charges with the Board, to adjust their dispute. If at the end of that time they are unable to "submit to the Board satisfactory evidence that they have adjusted, or agreed upon methods for the voluntary adjustment of the dispute," the Board is empowered to hear the dispute and make an affirmative assignment of the disputed work.

Section 10(k) further provides that pending 8(b)(4)(D) charges shall be dismissed where the Board's determination of the underlying dispute has been complied with, or the parties have voluntarily adjusted the dispute. An 8(b)(4)(D) complaint issues if the party charged fails to comply with the Board's determination. A complaint may be also issued by the General Counsel in the event recourse to the method agreed upon to adjust the dispute fails to result in an adjustment.

NLRB v. RADIO & TELEVISION BROADCAST ENGINEERS, LOCAL 1212 [CBS]

Supreme Court of the United States
364 U.S. 573, 81 S. Ct. 330, 5 L. Ed. 2d 302 (1961)

MR. JUSTICE BLACK delivered the opinion of the Court.

This case, in which the Court of Appeals refused to enforce a cease-and-desist order of the National Labor Relations Board, grew out of a "jurisdictional dispute" over work assignments between the respondent union, composed of television "technicians," and another union, composed of "stage employees." Both of these unions had collective bargaining agreements in force with the Columbia Broadcasting System and the respondent union was the certified bargaining agent for its members, but neither the certification nor the agreements clearly apportioned between the employees represented by the two unions the work of providing electric lighting for television shows. This led to constant disputes, extending over a number of years, as to the proper assignment of this work, disputes that were particularly acrimonious with reference to "remote lighting" that is, lighting for telecasts away from the home studio. Each union repeatedly urged Columbia to amend its bargaining agreement so as specifically to allocate remote lighting to its members rather than to members of the other union. But, as the Board found, Columbia refused to make such an agreement with either union because "the rival locals had failed to agree on the resolution of this jurisdictional dispute over remote lighting." Thus feeling itself caught "between the devil and the deep blue," Columbia chose to divide the disputed work between the two unions according to criteria improvised apparently for the sole purpose of maintaining peace between the two. But, in trying to satisfy both of the unions, Columbia has apparently not succeeded in satisfying either. During recent years, it has been forced to contend with work stoppages by each of the two unions when a particular assignment was made in favor of the other.

The precise occasion for the present controversy was the decision of Columbia to assign the lighting work for a major telecast from the Waldorf-Astoria Hotel in New York City to the stage employees. When the technicians' protest of this assignment proved unavailing, they refused to operate the cameras for the program and thus forced its cancellation. This caused Columbia to file the unfair labor practice charge which started these proceedings, claiming a violation of § 8(b)(4)(D) of the National Labor Relations Act. That section clearly makes it an unfair labor practice for a labor union to induce a strike or a concerted refusal to work in order to compel an employer to assign particular work to employees represented by it rather than to employees represented by another union, unless the employer's assignment is in violation of "an order or certification of the Board determining the bargaining representative for employees performing such work. . . ." Obviously, if § 8(b)(4)(D) stood alone, what this union did in the absence of a Board order or certification entitling its members to be assigned to these particular jobs would be enough to support a finding of an unfair labor practice in a normal proceeding under § 10(c) of the act. But when Congress created this new type of unfair labor practice by enacting § 8(b)(4)(D) as part of the Taft-Hartley Act in 1947, it also added § 10(k) to the act. Section 10(k), set out below, quite plainly emphasizes the belief of Congress that it is more important to industrial peace that jurisdictional disputes be settled permanently than it is that unfair labor practice sanctions for jurisdictional strikes be imposed upon unions. Accordingly, § 10(k) offers strong inducements to quarrelling unions to settle their differences by directing dismissal of unfair labor practice charges upon voluntary adjustment of jurisdictional disputes. And even where no voluntary adjustment is made, "the Board is empowered and directed," by § 10(k), "to hear and determine the dispute out of which such unfair labor practice shall have arisen," and upon compliance by the disputants with the Board's decision the unfair labor practice charges must be dismissed.

In this case respondent failed to reach a voluntary agreement with the stage employees union so the Board held the § 10(k) hearing as required to "determine the dispute." The result of this hearing was a decision that the respondent union was not entitled to have the work assigned to its members because it had no right to it under either an outstanding Board order or certification, as provided in § 8(b)(4)(D), or a collective bargaining agreement.[12] The Board refused to consider other criteria, such as the employer's prior practices and the custom of the industry, and also refused to make an affirmative award of the work between the employees represented by the two competing unions. The respondent union refused to comply with this decision, contending that the Board's conception of its duty to "determine the dispute" was too narrow in that this duty is not at all limited, as the Board would have it, to strictly legal considerations growing out of prior Board orders, certifications or collective bargaining agreements. It urged, instead, that the Board's duty was to make a final determination, binding on both unions, as to which of the two unions' members were entitled to do the remote lighting work, basing its determination on factors deemed important in arbitration proceedings, such as the nature of the work, the practices and customs of this and other companies and of these and other unions, and upon other factors deemed relevant by the Board in the light of its experience in the field of labor relations. On the basis of its decision in the § 10(k) proceeding and the union's challenge to the validity of that decision, the Board issued an order under § 10(c) directing the union to cease and desist from striking to compel Columbia to assign remote lighting work to its members. The Court of Appeals for the Second Circuit refused to enforce the cease-and-desist order, accepting the respondent's contention that the Board had failed to make the kind of determination that § 10(k) requires. The Third and Seventh Circuits have construed § 10(k) the same way, while the Fifth Circuit has agreed with the Board's narrower conception of its duties. Because of this conflict and the importance of this problem, we granted certiorari.

---

[12] This latter consideration was made necessary because the Board has adopted the position that jurisdictional strikes in support of contract rights do not constitute violations of § 8(b)(4)(D) despite the fact that the language of that section contains no provision for special treatment of such strikes. See Fur Workers, Local 26, 90 N.L.R.B. 1379. The Board has explained this position as resting upon the principle that "to fail to hold as controlling . . . the contractual preemption of the work in dispute would be to encourage disregard for observance of binding obligations under collective bargaining agreements and invite the very jurisdictional disputes § 8(b)(4)(D) is intended to prevent." National Ass'n of Broadcast Engineers [105 N.L.R.B. 355], at 364.

We agree with the Second, Third and Seventh Circuits that § 10(k) requires the Board to decide jurisdictional disputes on their merits and conclude that in this case that requirement means that the Board should affirmatively have decided whether the technicians or the stage employees were entitled to the disputed work. The language of § 10(k), supplementing § 8(b)(4)(D) as it does, sets up a method adopted by Congress to try to get jurisdictional disputes settled. The words "hear and determine the dispute" convey not only the idea of hearing but also the idea of deciding a controversy. And the clause "the dispute out of which such unfair labor practice shall have arisen" can have no other meaning except a jurisdictional dispute under § 8(b)(4)(D) which is a dispute between two or more groups of employees over which is entitled to do certain work for an employer. To determine or settle the dispute as between them would normally require a decision that one or the other is entitled to do the work in dispute. Any decision short of that would obviously not be conducive to quieting a quarrel between two groups which, here as in most instances, is of so little interest to the employer that he seems perfectly willing to assign work to either if the other will just let him alone. This language also indicates a congressional purpose to have the Board do something more than merely look at prior Board orders and certifications or a collective bargaining contract to determine whether one or the other union has a clearly defined statutory or contractual right to have the employees it represents perform certain work tasks. For, in the vast majority of cases, such a narrow determination would leave the broader problem of work assignments in the hands of the employer, exactly where it was before the enactment of § 10(k) — with the same old basic jurisdictional dispute likely continuing to vex him, and the rival unions, short of striking, would still be free to adopt other forms of pressure upon the employer. The § 10(k) hearing would therefore accomplish little but a restoration of the pre-existing situation, a situation already found intolerable by Congress and by all parties concerned. If this newly granted Board power to hear and determine jurisdictional disputes had meant no more than that, Congress certainly would have achieved very little to solve the knotty problem of wasteful work stoppages due to such disputes.

This conclusion reached on the basis of the language of § 10(k) and § 8(b)(4)(D) is reinforced by reference to the history of those provisions. Prior to the enactment of the Taft-Hartley Act, labor, business and the public in general had for a long time joined in hopeful efforts to escape the disruptive consequences of jurisdictional disputes and resulting work stoppages. To this end unions had established union tribunals, employers had established employer tribunals, and both had set up joint tribunals to arbitrate such disputes.[18] Each of these efforts had helped some but none had achieved complete success. The result was a continuing and widely expressed dissatisfaction with jurisdictional strikes. As one of the

---

[18] For a review and criticism of some of these efforts, see Dunlop, Jurisdictional Disputes, N.Y.U.2d Ann. Conference on Labor 477, at 494-504.

forerunners to these very provisions of the act, President Truman told the Congress in 1947 that disputes "involving the question of which labor union is entitled to perform a particular task" should be settled, and that if the "rival unions are unable to settle such disputes themselves, provision must be made for peaceful and binding determination of the issues." [19] And the House Committee report on one of the proposals out of which these sections came recognized the necessity of enacting legislation to protect employers from being "the helpless victims of quarrels that do not concern them at all." [20]

The Taft-Hartley Act as originally offered contained only a section making jurisdictional strikes an unfair labor practice. Section 10(k) came into the measure as the result of an amendment offered by Senator Morse which, in its original form, proposed to supplement this blanket proscription by empowering and directing the Board either "to hear and determine the dispute out of which such unfair labor practice shall have arisen or to appoint an arbitrator to hear and determine such dispute. . . ." [21] That the purpose of this amendment was to set up machinery by which the underlying jurisdictional dispute would be settled is clear and, indeed, even the Board concedes this much. The authority to appoint an arbitrator passed the Senate [22] but was eliminated in conference,[23] leaving it to the Board alone "to hear and determine" the underlying jurisdictional dispute. The Board's position is that this change can be interpreted as an indication that Congress decided against providing for the compulsory determination of jurisdictional disputes. We find this argument unpersuasive, to say the very least. The obvious effect of this change was simply to place the responsibility for compulsory determination of the dispute entirely on the Board, not to eliminate the requirement that there be such a compulsory determination. The Board's view of its powers thus has no more support in the history of § 10(k) than it has in the language of that section. Both show that the section was designed to provide precisely what the Board has disclaimed the power to provide — an effective compulsory method of getting rid of what were deemed to be the bad consequences of jurisdictional disputes.

The Board contends, however, that this interpretation of § 10(k) should be rejected, despite the language and history of that section. In support of this contention, it first points out that § 10(k) sets forth no standards to guide it in determining jurisdictional disputes on their merits. From this fact, the Board argues that § 8(b)(4)(D) makes the employer's assignment decisive unless he is at the time acting in violation

---

[19] 93 Cong. Rec. 136.

[20] H.R. Rep. No. 245, 80th Cong., 1st Sess. 23, I Legislative History of the Labor Management Relations Act, 1947, at 314 (hereinafter cited as Leg. Hist.).

[21] The amendment was contained in a bill (S. 858) offered by Senator Morse, which also contained a number of other proposals. 93 Cong. Rec. 1913, II Leg. Hist. 987.

[22] I Leg. Hist. 241, 258-259. See also the Senate Committee Report on the bill, S. Rep. No. 105, 80th Cong., 1st Sess. 8, I Leg. Hist. 414.

[23] H.R. Conf. Rep. No. 510, 80th Cong., 1st Sess. 57, I Leg. Hist. 561.

of a Board order or certification and that the proper interpretation of
§ 10(k) must take account of this right of the employer. It is true, of
course, that employers normally select and assign their own individual
employees according to their best judgment. But here, as in most
situations where jurisdictional strikes occur, the employer has contracted
with two unions, both of which represent employees capable of doing the
particular tasks involved. The result is that the employer has been placed
in a situation where he finds it impossible to secure the benefits of stability
from either of these contracts, not because he refuses to satisfy the unions,
but because the situation is such that he cannot satisfy them. Thus, it is
the employer here, probably more than anyone else, who has been and
will be damaged by a failure of the Board to make the binding decision
that the employer has not been able to make. We therefore are not
impressed by the Board's solicitude for the employer's right to do that
which he has not been, and most likely will not be, able to do. It is true
that this forces the Board to exercise under § 10(k) powers which are
broad and lacking in rigid standards to govern their application. But
administrative agencies are frequently given rather loosely defined
powers to cope with problems as difficult as those posed by jurisdictional
disputes and strikes. It might have been better, as some persuasively
argued in Congress, to intrust this matter to arbitrators. But Congress,
after discussion and consideration, decided to intrust this decision to the
Board. It has had long experience in hearing and disposing of similar
labor problems. With this experience and a knowledge of the standards
generally used by arbitrators, unions, employers, joint boards and others
in wrestling with this problem, we are confident that the Board need not
disclaim the power given it for lack of standards. Experience and common
sense will supply the grounds for the performance of this job which
Congress has assigned the Board.

The Board also contends that respondent's interpretation of § 10(k)
should be avoided because that interpretation completely vitiates the
purpose of Congress to encourage the private settlement of jurisdictional
disputes. This contention proceeds on the assumption that the parties to
a dispute will have no incentive to reach a private settlement if they are
permitted to adhere to their respective views until the matter is brought
before the Board and then given the same opportunity to prevail which
they would have had in a private settlement. Respondent disagrees with
this contention and attacks the Board's assumption. We find it
unnecessary to resolve this controversy for it turns upon the sort of policy
determination that must be regarded as implicitly settled by Congress
when it chose to enact § 10(k). Even if Congress has chosen the wrong
way to accomplish its aim, that choice is binding both upon the Board and
upon this Court.

The Board's next contention is that respondent's interpretation of
§ 10(k) should be rejected because it is inconsistent with other provisions
of the Taft-Hartley Act. The first such inconsistency urged is with
§§ 8(a)(3) and 8(b)(2) of the act on the ground that the determination of
jurisdictional disputes on their merits by the Board might somehow

enable unions to compel employers to discriminate in regard to employment in order to encourage union membership. The argument here, which is based upon the fact that § 10(k), like § 8(b)(4)(D), extends to jurisdictional disputes between unions and unorganized groups as well as to disputes between two or more unions, appears to be that groups represented by unions would almost always prevail over non-union groups in such a determination because their claim to the work would probably have more basis in custom and tradition than that of unorganized groups. No such danger is present here, however, for both groups of employees are represented by unions. Moreover, we feel entirely confident that the Board, with its many years of experience in guarding against and redressing violations of §§ 8(a)(3) and 8(b)(2), will devise means of discharging its duties under § 10(k) in a manner entirely harmonious with those sections. A second inconsistency is urged with § 303(a)(4) of the Taft-Hartley Act, which authorizes suits for damages suffered because of jurisdictional strikes. The argument here is that since § 303(a)(4) does not permit a union to establish, as a defense to an action for damages under that section, that it is entitled to the work struck for on the basis of such factors as practice or custom, a similar result is required here in order to preserve "the substantive symmetry" between § 303(a)(4) on the one hand and §§ 8(b)(4)(D) and 10(k) on the other. This argument ignores the fact that this Court has recognized the separate and distinct nature of these two approaches to the problem of handling jurisdictional strikes.[26] Since we do not require a "substantive symmetry" between the two, we need not and do not decide what effect a decision of the Board under § 10(k) might have on actions under § 303(a)(4). . . .

We conclude therefore that the Board's interpretation of its duty under § 10(k) is wrong and that under that section it is the Board's responsibility and duty to decide which of two or more employee groups claiming the right to perform certain work tasks is right and then specifically to award such tasks in accordance with its decision. Having failed to meet that responsibility in this case, the Board could not properly proceed under § 10(c) to adjudicate the unfair labor practice charge. The Court of Appeals was therefore correct in refusing to enforce the order which resulted from that proceeding.

Affirmed.

NOTES

1. In Transportation-Communication Employees v. Union Pac. R.R., 385 U.S. 157 (1966), the Supreme Court also directed, in effect, the National Railroad Adjustment Board to resolve railroad work-assignment disputes on the merits. The TCEU (representing the telegraphers) complained to the NRAB that the railroad had given certain automated jobs to the clerks, claiming that the telegraphers were entitled to the work

---

[26] International Longshoremen v. Juneau Spruce Corp., 342 U.S. 237 (1952).

under their contract. The clerks' union, given notice, declined to participate, indicating their readiness to file another proceeding under their contract if the railroad took away their jobs. Without considering the clerks' contract, the NRAB held that the telegraphers were entitled to the work. The telegraphers sued in district court to enforce the Board's order. Holding that the clerks were an indispensable party, the district court dismissed the case and the court of appeals affirmed. The Supreme Court held that the NRAB must exercise its exclusive jurisdiction to settle the entire work-assignment dispute between the competing unions in one proceeding, considering both contracts and "usage, practice and custom." Mr. Justice Fortas and Chief Justice Warren dissented, urging that Congress had not assigned this function to the NRAB, as it had to the NLRB under § 10(k) of the Taft-Hartley Act, which has no counterpart in the Railway Labor Act. "There is nothing in the statute or precedents that permits or justifies this peremptory judicial foray into other people's business. . . . Labor relations are not susceptible of reduction to such simplicities; and with all deference this Court should fear to tread this path."

2. A union that wins a § 10(k) award may use economic pressure to compel the employer's compliance without running afoul of § 8(b)(4)(D), but the union may not rely on § 8(a)(3) even if the employer succumbs to pressure from another union and discharges the winning union's members in order to assign their work to the other union's members. The Labor Board says it cannot "implement our 10(k) determinations via the 8(a)(3) route." Brady-Hamilton Stevedore Co., 198 N.L.R.B. 147 (1972) (two members dissenting).

3. Reversing a court of appeals, the Supreme Court held in NLRB v. Plasterers Local 79, 404 U.S. 116 (1971), that employers with substantial financial stakes in the outcome of § 10(k) proceedings were "parties to the dispute" within the meaning of the section. The NLRB was therefore empowered to determine the jurisdictional dispute under § 10(k), where only the competing unions, and not the employers, had agreed upon a voluntary method of adjustment.

4. The factors which the Board considers relevant in determining who is entitled to the work in dispute are: "the skills and work involved, certifications by the Board, company and industry practice, agreements between unions and between employers and unions, awards of arbitrators, joint boards, and the AFL-CIO in the same or related cases, the assignment made by the employer, and the efficient operation of the employer's business." Machinists Lodge 1743 (J. A. Jones Constr. Co.), 135 N.L.R.B. 1402, 1410-1411 (1962).

For a case in which the NLRB gave great weight to an inter-union arbitration award and to the decisions of the National Joint Board for the Settlement of Jurisdictional Disputes in the Construction Industry, see Millwrights Local 1102 (Don Cartage Co.), 160 N.L.R.B. 1061 (1966).

5. It has been estimated that since the *CBS* case, well over ninety percent of the Labor Board's awards in § 10(k) hearings have confirmed the employer's own assignment of disputed work. Does this raise doubts about the Board's compliance with the mandate of *CBS?* Or is it entirely proper that the employer's assignment should be given major weight in a § 10(k) determination? Insofar as economic considerations are taken into account in an award, is it quite correct to say, as Justice Black said in *CBS,* that the unions' quarrel "is of so little interest to the employer that he seems perfectly willing to assign work to either if the other will just let him alone"?

6. *See generally* Cohen, *The NLRB and Section 10(k): A Study of the Reluctant Dragon,* 14 LAB. L.J. 905 (1963); Hickey, *Government Regulation of Inter-Union Work Assignment Disputes,* 16 S.C. L. REV. 333 (1964); Leslie, *The Role of the NLRB and the Courts in Resolving Union Jurisdictional Disputes,* 75 COLUM. L. REV. 1470 (1975); O'Donoghue, *Jurisdictional Disputes in the Construction Industry Since "CBS,"* 52 GEO. L.J. 314 (1964); Player, *Work Assignment Disputes Under Section 10(k): Putting the Substantive Cart Before the Procedural Horse,* 52 TEXAS L. REV. 417 (1974); Sussman, *Section 10(k): Mandate for Change,* 47 B.U. L. REV. 201 (1967).

7. In Plumbers Local 393 (Hall-Way Contracting Co.), 232 N.L.R.B. No. 83, 97 L.R.R.M. 1153 (1977), the Board held that it is neither constitutionally nor statutorily required to consider evidence of alleged racial discrimination by a union in proceedings for determination of a jurisdictional dispute under § 10(k).

SECTION VI. "Featherbedding"

AMERICAN NEWSPAPER PUBLISHERS ASS'N v. NLRB

Supreme Court of the United States
345 U.S. 100, 73 S. Ct. 552, 97 L. Ed. 852 (1953)

MR. JUSTICE BURTON delivered the opinion of the Court.

The question here is whether a labor organization engages in an unfair labor practice within the meaning of § 8(b)(6) of the National Labor Relations Act, as amended by the Labor Management Relations Act, 1947, when it insists that newspaper publishers pay printers for reproducing advertising matter for which the publishers ordinarily have no use. For the reasons hereafter stated, we hold that it does not. . . .

When a newspaper advertisement was set up in type, it was impressed on a cardboard matrix, or "mat." These mats were used by their makers and also were reproduced and distributed, at little or no cost, to other publishers who used them as molds for metal castings from which to print the same advertisement. This procedure by-passed all compositors except those who made up the original form. Facing this loss of work, ITU secured the agreement of newspaper publishers to permit their respective compositors, at convenient times, to set up duplicate forms for all local advertisements in precisely the same manner as though the mat had not been used. For this reproduction work the printers received their regular pay. The doing of this "made work" came to be known in the trade as "setting bogus." It was a wasteful procedure. Nevertheless, it has become a recognized idiosyncrasy of the trade and a customary feature of the wage structure and work schedule of newspaper printers. . . . On rare occasions the reproduced compositions are used to print the advertisements when rerun, but, ordinarily, they are promptly consigned to the "hell box" and melted down.

However desirable the elimination of all industrial featherbedding practices may have appeared to Congress, the legislative history of the Taft-Hartley Act demonstrates that when the legislation was put in final form Congress decided to limit the practice but little by law.

A restraining influence throughout this congressional consideration of featherbedding was the fact that the constitutionality of the Lea Act penalizing featherbedding in the broadcasting industry was in litigation. . . . The case was pending here on appeal throughout the debate on the Taft-Hartley bill. Not until June 23, 1947, on the day of the passage of the Taft-Hartley bill over the President's veto, was the constitutionality of the Lea Act upheld. United States v. Petrillo, 332 U.S. 1 (1947).

The purpose of the sponsors of the Taft-Hartley bill to avoid the controversial features of the Lea Act is made clear in the written statement which Senator Taft, cosponsor of the bill and Chairman of the Senate Committee on Labor and Public Welfare, caused to be incorporated in the proceedings of the Senate, June 5, 1947. Referring to the substitution of § 8(b)(6) in place of the detailed featherbedding provisions of the House bill, that statement said:

"The provisions in the Lea Act from which the House language was taken are now awaiting determination by the Supreme Court, partly because of the problem arising from the term 'in excess of the number of employees reasonably required.' Therefore, the conferees were of the opinion that general legislation on the subject of featherbedding was not warranted at least until the joint study committee proposed by this bill could give full consideration to the matter." 93 Cong. Rec. 6443.

On the same day this was amplified in the Senator's oral statement on the floor of the Senate:

"There is one further provision which may possibly be of interest which was not in the Senate bill. The House had rather elaborate provisions prohibiting so-called featherbedding practices and making them unlawful labor practices. The Senate conferees, while not approving of featherbedding practices, felt that it was impracticable to give to a board or a court the power to say that so many men are all right, and so many men are too many. It would require a practical application of the law by the courts in hundreds of different industries, and a determination of facts which it seemed to me would be almost impossible. So we declined to adopt the provisions which are now in the Petrillo Act. After all, that statute applies to only one industry. Those provisions are now the subject of court procedure. Their constitutionality has been questioned. We thought that probably we had better wait and see what happened, in any event, even though we are in favor of prohibiting all featherbedding practices. However, we did accept one provision which makes it an unlawful labor practice for a union to accept money for people who do not work. That seemed to be a fairly clear case, easy to determine, and we accepted that additional unfair labor practice on the part of unions, which was not in the Senate bill." 93 Cong. Rec. 6441. See also, his supplementary analysis inserted in the Record June 12, 1947. 93 Cong. Rec. 6859.

As indicated above, the Taft-Hartley bill, H.R. 3020, when it passed in the House, April 17, 1947, contained in §§ 2(17) and 12(a)(3)(B) an explicit condemnation of featherbedding. Its definition of featherbedding was based upon that in the Lea Act. For example, it condemned practices which required an employer to employ "persons in excess of the number of employees reasonably required by such employer to perform actual services," as well as practices which required an employer to pay "for services . . . which are not to be performed."

The substitution of the present § 8(b)(6) for that definition compels the conclusion that § 8(b)(6) means what the court below has said it means. The Act now limits its condemnation to instances where a labor organization or its agents exact pay from an employer in return for services not performed or not to be performed. Thus, where work is done by an employee, with the employer's consent, a labor organization's demand that the employee be compensated for time spent in doing the disputed work does not become an unfair labor practice. The transaction simply does not fall within the kind of featherbedding defined in the statute. ... Section 8(b)(6) leaves to collective bargaining the determination of what, if any, work, including bona fide "made work," shall be included as compensable services and what rate of compensation shall be paid for it.

Accordingly, the judgment of the Court of Appeals sustaining dismissal of the complaint, insofar as it was based upon § 8(b)(6), is

Affirmed.

The dissenting opinions of MR. JUSTICE DOUGLAS and MR. JUSTICE CLARK, with whom THE CHIEF JUSTICE joined, are omitted.

NLRB v. GAMBLE ENTERPRISES, INC., 345 U.S. 117, 73 S. Ct. 560, 97 L. Ed. 864 (1953). The Musicians' Union refused to permit out-of-town orchestras to appear in respondent's theater unless he agreed to employ local musicians for a number of independent performances having a relation to the number of travelling band appearances. This and similar union proposals were declined by respondent on the ground that the local orchestra was neither necessary nor desired. Respondent sought a Board order based on § 8(b)(6). *Held:* "Since we and the Board treat the union's proposals as in good faith contemplating the performance of actual services, we agree that the union has not, on this record, engaged in a practice proscribed by § 8(b)(6). It has remained for respondent to accept or reject the union's offers on their merits in the light of all material circumstances. We do not find it necessary to determine also whether such offers were 'in the nature of an exaction.' We are not dealing here with offers of mere 'token' or nominal services. The proposals before us were appropriately treated by the Board as offers in good faith of substantial performances by competent musicians. There is no reason to think that sham can be substituted for substance under § 8(b)(6) any more than under any other statute. Payments for 'standing-by,' or for the substantial equivalent of 'standing-by,' are not payments for services performed, but when an employer receives a bona fide offer of competent performance of relevant services, it remains for the employer, through free and fair negotiation, to determine whether such offer shall be accepted and what compensation shall be paid for the work done." 345 U.S. at 123-24.

NOTES

1. For discussions of the "featherbedding" problem, see Aaron, *Governmental Restraints on Featherbedding,* 5 STAN. L. REV. 680 (1953); Daykin, *Featherbedding,* 7 LAB. L.J. 699 (1956); Edelman & Kovarsky, *Featherbedding: Law and Arbitration,* 10 LAB. L.J. 233 (1959); Van de Water, *A Fresh Look at Featherbedding,* 7 BAYLOR L. REV. 138 (1955); Wood, *Wisdom of Outlawing Featherbedding,* 6 LAB. L.J. 821 (1955); Note, *Featherbedding and Taft-Hartley,* 52 COLUM. L. REV. 1020 (1952); Note, *Technological Change: Management Prerogative vs. Job Security,* 31 IND. L.J. 389 (1956).

2. *The Lea Act (Anti-Petrillo Act).* The practices of the American Federation of Musicians led to special federal legislation in 1946 (47 U.S.C. § 506), in an amendment to the Communications Act of 1934. The Lea Act made it a criminal offense "by the use or express or implied threat of the use of force, violence, intimidation, or duress, or by the use of express or implied threat of the use of other means, to coerce, compel or constrain a licensee — (1) to employ or agree to employ, in connection with the conduct of the broadcasting business of such licensee, any person or persons in excess of the number of employees needed by such licensee to perform actual services. . . ."

The constitutionality of the Lea Act was challenged on the ground, *inter alia,* that it defines a crime in terms that are so excessively vague and indefinite that a person would not be able to tell when his conduct would be a violation of the law. The Supreme Court upheld the statute. United States v. Petrillo, 332 U.S. 1 (1947).

What is the test as to how many employees are "needed" by an employer? The Supreme Court said, "Certainly, an employer's statements as to the number of employees 'needed' is not conclusive as to that question. It . . . must be decided in the light of all the evidence."

When the case went back to the district court for trial, Petrillo was acquitted, on the ground that there was insufficient proof that he "had knowledge of, or was told that the station had no need" for three additional employees whom he was attempting by strike action to require the station to employ. United States v. Petrillo, 75 F. Supp. 176 (N.D. Ill. 1948). No further criminal prosecutions appear to have been attempted.

However, in General Teleradio, Inc. v. Manuti, 284 App. Div. 400, 131 N.Y.S.2d 365 (1954), the New York courts held that a violation of the Lea Act gives rise to a cause of action in tort. In granting a permanent injunction and damages against picketing of a radio station for the purpose of securing retention of live musicians on all live programs, the trial court relied on both the Lea Act and the common law of New York, as stated in Opera on Tour, Inc. v. Weber, 285 N.Y. 348, 34 N.E.2d 349 (1941), that "for a union to insist that machinery be discarded in order that manual labor may take its place and thus secure additional opportunity of employment is not a lawful labor objective." General Teleradio, Inc. v. Manuti, 133 N.Y.S.2d 362 (Sup. Ct. 1954). For an interesting and exhaustive study of the musicians' union and its problems, see Countryman, *The Organized Musicians,* 16 U. CHI. L. REV. 56 (1948), 239 (1949).

3. Consider, as a problem in legislative drafting, whether language can be devised which would effectuate a desirable public policy with respect to "featherbedding," in the light of experience under the Lea Act and § 8(b)(6) of the Taft-Hartley Act.

4. Compare also National Woodwork Mfrs. Ass'n v. NLRB, *supra* at 443.

SECTION VII. Emergency Disputes

A. INTRODUCTION

A basic tenet of national labor policy is that most labor disputes over the terms and conditions of employment should be settled by free collective bargaining. The possibility of a work stoppage through the exercise of organized labor's right to strike is normally thought to supply the motive power — the incentive to the parties — to bargain out an agreement. Such shutdowns as do occur — and the man-days lost through strikes are always an extremely small percentage of total man-days worked — are generally regarded in peacetime as a reasonable price to pay for the advantages of industrial self-regulation.

Of course, it is recognized that the provision of mediation services is an appropriate part of our labor relations policy, the objective of mediation being to assist the parties in arriving at a negotiated settlement themselves.

However, there are some situations (not easily defined) in which the impact of a work stoppage upon the public interest may be so great that further steps are considered necessary to protect the public. The dilemma is that these steps must be formulated in such a way as to preserve — and not weaken — the basic social institution of collective bargaining.

The material following is designed to sketch briefly our present laws governing such emergency disputes and various proposals which have been made to improve them.

B. NATIONAL EMERGENCY STRIKES UNDER THE LMRA

STATUTORY REFERENCES
LMRA §§ 206-10

Whenever in the opinion of the President there is an actual or threatened strike or lockout affecting all or a substantial part of an entire industry engaged in commerce which if permitted to occur or continue will constitute a threat to the national health or safety, he may invoke the national emergency strike procedures contained in §§ 206 through 210 of the LMRA. Under the terms of those sections, he may delay or suspend such strikes in the following manner:

(i) appoint a board of inquiry to report without recommendation the facts of the dispute;

(ii) on receipt of the board's report, order the Attorney General to seek a federal district court injunction restraining the strike;

(iii) if an injunction is issued, reconvene the board of inquiry which shall report on the current position of the parties in the eventuality that they do not reach an agreement within 60 days;

(iv) publish the board's second report, including the efforts which have been made towards settlement and the employer's last offer of settlement;

(v) within 15 days after publication of the board of inquiry's second report, require the NLRB to conduct a strike vote to determine if the employees will accept the employer's last offer of settlement; and

(vi) if the strike vote rejects the employer's offer, the Attorney General must move to discharge the injunction within five days.

KLEILER, A LEGISLATIVE HISTORY OF THE NATIONAL EMERGENCY PROVISIONS, in EMERGENCY DISPUTES AND NATIONAL POLICY 91, 106-08 (I. Bernstein, H. Enarson, and R. Fleming eds. 1955)*

The important fact about the legislative history is that the emergency provisions survived the Senate Committee and the Senate-House conference in almost the exact form that Senator Taft wanted. In his own committee and in the conference he made numerous compromises in other parts of the bill to gain support, but the emergency section of the law is almost pure Taft. To the extent that it provided for injunctions against strikes, this part of the bill was popular with an overwhelming majority in Congress; but the Taft concept of how to handle emergency disputes was far more sophisticated than that of the average injunction-minded legislator.

Senator Taft recognized that the injunctive process does not deal with the main causes of labor trouble. He regarded injunctions only as a device for enforced delay to give mediation, fact-finding, and energized public opinion an opportunity to produce a settlement. He wanted no recommendations from the fact-finding board simply because he believed

---

* Copyright © 1955. Reprinted by permission of Harper & Row, Inc.

that government boards with power to recommend settlements come dangerously close to compulsory arbitration. He opposed compulsory arbitration as vigorously as he opposed seizure. If compulsory arbitration were available as a routine remedy, Taft contended, there would always be pressure to resort to it by whichever party thought it would receive better treatment through such a process than it would receive in collective bargaining. If a national emergency dispute could not be settled during the delay process, Taft believed, then no authority lower than the Congress should deal with it. He felt strongly that if the safety and health of the people were finally threatened, an emergency law should be designed to deal with the particular emergency. . . .

The record-breaking wave of large strikes created the need. The imminent expiration of wartime legislation made the need more imperative. The antilabor sentiment found in the 1946 election returns fixed the attitude. The distrust in Congress of the President eliminated any possibility of increasing the chief executive's authority to handle labor disputes.

Uniquely designed to emphasize the paramountcy of Congress over the President in emergencies while simultaneously providing a method for prompt government action to delay strikes, the virtues of the Taft bill were readily apparent. Not even the supporters of the Hartley bill were much dismayed when the House conferees went along with the Senate on the emergency provisions. As a product of its times, Senator Taft's proposal for handling the troublesome strike problem looked good enough to Congress, and Congress did not want to take the time to shop for anything better.

NOTES

1. The national emergency provisions of the LMRA were invoked 35 times between 1947 and 1978. On 9 occasions (all involving maritime or longshoring disputes), there were serious strikes after the 80-day injunction was dissolved. On one occasion, the United Mine Workers and John L. Lewis were fined large sums for contempt of court. United Mine Workers v. United States, 85 App. D.C. 149, 177 F.2d 29 (1949), *cert. denied,* 338 U.S. 871 (1949).

2. A detailed summary of each of the disputes in which the national emergency procedures of the Taft-Hartley Act were utilized is found in FEDERAL LEGISLATION TO END STRIKES: A DOCUMENTARY HISTORY, prepared for the Subcommittee on Labor of the Committee on Labor and Public Welfare of the U.S. Senate by the Legislative Reference Service of the Library of Congress, at 575-609 (1967).

3. For thorough critical examinations of the operation of the Taft-Hartley procedures, see Jones, *The National Emergency Disputes Provisions of the Taft-Hartley Act: A View From a Legislative Draftsman's Desk,* 17 W. RES. L. REV. 133 (1965); Jones, *Toward a Definition of "National Emergency Dispute,"* 1971 WIS. L. REV. 700; Rehmus, *The Operation of the National Emergency Provisions of the LMRA of 1947,* 62 YALE L.J. 1047 (1953).

4. Some use has been made of extra-statutory procedures; for example, the use by President Truman of a fact-finding board which made recommendations in the steel dispute of 1949. Also, in the steel dispute of 1952, President Truman did not use the Taft-Hartley procedures, resorting instead to the use of the Wage Stabilization Board for recommendations, and ultimately to seizure. However, the Supreme Court held that the President had exceeded his powers in seizing the steel mills in the absence of legislation authorizing it. Youngstown Sheet & Tube Co. v. Sawyer, 343 U.S. 579 (1952). Some idea of the complexity of the political factors that come into play during a national emergency dispute may be gained from reading Enarson, *The Politics of an Emergency Dispute,* in EMERGENCY DISPUTES AND NATIONAL POLICY 46-74 (I. Bernstein, H. Enarson & R. Fleming eds. 1955), which tells the story of the 1952 steel case.

5. The constitutionality of the Taft-Hartley national emergency dispute provisions was sustained by the Supreme Court in United Steelworkers v. United States, 361 U.S. 39 (1959).

6. Before issuing an injunction, the court must find that all or a substantial part of an industry engaged in commerce will be affected, and that the strike if permitted to occur or continue will endanger the national health or safety. It is not necessary, however, that there be a finding that the strike is industry-wide. United States v. United Steelworkers, 202 F.2d 132 (2d Cir. 1953). In fact, a strike at a single plant which manufactures vital equipment for the atomic energy industry may threaten national health or safety. United States v. American Locomotive Co., 109 F. Supp. 78 (W.D.N.Y. 1952).

In a precedent-making decision, a federal district court refused an injunction requested by the Government under the national emergency provisions of the Taft-Hartley Act. United States v. International Longshoremen's Local 418, 335 F. Supp. 501 (N.D. Ill. 1971), *stay denied,* 78 L.R.R.M. 2801 (STEVENS, J., 7th Cir. 1971). The court ruled that a strike at most of the grain elevators in Chicago did not affect an entire industry or a substantial part thereof, and that the continuation of the strike would not imperil the national health or safety.

7. Some of the criticisms which have been made of the Taft-Hartley emergency dispute procedures include the following: (a) the burden of the 80-day injunction falls too heavily upon the workers, since they must continue to work under the existing working conditions; (b) the 80-day injunction period merely delays the strike deadline date and it is difficult to get the parties down to serious bargaining during this time; (c) the ballot on the employer's last offer has proved to be futile, since the employees invariably vote to back up their union's position, and it actually constitutes an obstacle to genuine bargaining near the end of the period; and (d) the board of inquiry, not being empowered to make recommendations, fails to serve its potentially most useful function — focusing public attention on and rallying public opinion pressure behind a basis for settlement.

8. As to the last point, however, it may be observed that the emergency boards under the Railway Labor Act do make recommendations, and experience with them in recent years has not been signally successful.

C. EMERGENCY RAILROAD AND AIRLINE DISPUTES

STATUTORY REFERENCES
RLA §§ 5, 6, 10

Under the Railway Labor Act (which applies to railroads and airlines) the procedure is as follows: the parties are required to give 30 days' notice of an intended change in the existing agreement; the National Mediation Board attempts to mediate the dispute; if mediation fails, the NMB suggests voluntary arbitration; if arbitration is declined, the NMB gives notice that its efforts have failed, and for 30 days thereafter no change may be made in rates of pay, rules, or working conditions; if the NMB believes that the dispute "threatens substantially to interrupt interstate commerce to a degree such as to deprive any section of the country of essential transportation service," it notifies the President, who may appoint a board to investigate and report within 30 days; after the creation of such a board and for 30 days after it has made its report to the President, no change may be made in existing conditions.

For many years, the Railway Labor Act procedures appeared to be realizing their objectives. However, since the beginning of World War II, the situation has progressively deteriorated. In the words of an emergency board in 1952: "[D]irect collective bargaining failed to settle a growing number of cases. More and more cases came to the Mediation Board. Mediation itself came to be increasingly difficult, except in the smaller cases. More and more Emergency Boards had to be appointed, mainly for the big national cases involving over-all wage rate, hours, and rules. . . . The term 'emergency,' in the sense of limitation to rare cases, was becoming outmoded. Nor were the recommendations of these Boards being accepted, if distasteful to the organizations. . . . The post-recommendation strikes led to further government intervention — White House conferences. . . ."

In 1963 and in 1967, certain railroad labor disputes proved so intractable that the President found it necessary to lay the dispute before Congress, and the Congress enacted special legislation to dispose of the particular dispute. See Public Law 88-108, 77 Stat. 132 (1963); Public Law 90-54, 81 Stat. 122 (1967).

The detailed story of the so-called "work rules" or "fireman-on-the-diesel" dispute, running from 1959 to 1964 may be found in Kaufman, *The Railroad Labor Dispute: A Marathon of Maneuver and Improvisation*, 18 IND. & LAB. REL. REV. 196 (1965); Levinson, *The Locomotive Firemen's Dispute*, 17 LAB. L.J. 671 (1966); and *Hearings Before the Senate Committee on Commerce, Railroad Work Rules Dispute*, 89th Cong., 1st Sess. (1966).

For an overall assessment of experience in the railroad and airline industries, *see* Cullen, *Emergency Boards Under the Railway Labor Act*

and *Strike Experience Under the Railway Labor Act,* in THE RAILWAY
LABOR ACT AT FIFTY (C. Rehmus, ed. 1976).

D. STATE EMERGENCY DISPUTE LEGISLATION

A number of states have enacted legislation placing limitations on
strikes in public utilities or other essential industries. Those statutes
prohibiting strikes and providing for systems of compulsory arbitration
have been invalidated, as to employers and employees subject to the
National Labor Relations Act, on the ground of federal preemption by the
Supreme Court's decision in Amalgamated Ass'n of Street, Elec. Ry. &
Motor Coach Employees Div. 998 v. WERB, 340 U.S. 383 (1951).

A similar fate befell the Missouri statute providing for seizure of a public
utility whose operation is threatened by a strike. *See* Amalgamated Ass'n
of Street, Elec. Ry. & Motor Coach Employees Div. 1287 v. Missouri, 374
U.S. 74 (1963).

A field of growing importance concerns regulation of collective
bargaining disputes involving state and local government employees,
which are not covered by the National Labor Relations Act.

E. ALTERNATIVE APPROACHES AND PROPOSALS

**WILLIAMS, SETTLEMENT OF LABOR DISPUTES IN INDUSTRIES
AFFECTED WITH A NATIONAL INTEREST, 49 A.B.A.J. 862, 867-68
(1963) ***

Critical labor disputes differ. Each has its own stumbling-blocks to
settlement. The impact upon the public differs. Sometimes the public can
tolerate a work stoppage for quite a while, even though in a critical
industry. At other times a strike for one minute, as in the case of electric
power, could be disastrous. These considerations indicate that there
should be a choice of procedures for use in resolving critical work
stoppages.

There might well be concern that the choice-of-procedures approach
leaves too much to the discretion of the President. But power must be
lodged somewhere, and it cannot be lodged in a more responsible place
than in the executive. To have these procedures available is not to give
the President a bludgeon consisting of threats of many different kinds of
procedures. The power should be given to the President, instead, because
of the need for flexibility, since the disputes differ so much in their
attributes.

Variety of Procedures Should Be Available

The remaining issue, is the nature of the procedures which should be
available in handling critical labor disputes. Properly, the most usually
recommended procedure is the development and refinement of the
process of fact finding by an independent board, coupled with the

additional power of that board to suggest terms of settlement. The theory is that there will be strong pressures upon the parties to settle in close conformity to the recommendations, if the recommendations are reasonable. Public opinion, reacting to a sensible proposal for settlement, could make it quite difficult for the parties to refuse to accept it.

One serious need is for the fact-finding boards to be activated before the emergency develops. The investigation should be made and the recommendation should be ready before the strike occurs. Earlier governmental intervention is receiving increasing acceptance, as is shown through its approval by the President's Labor-Management Committee. We should experiment with the operation of fact-finding boards, and the details need not be explored here.

From time to time the government has used the device of seizing businesses to bring about the end of critical strikes. But seizure as the sole governmental intervention disregards the rights of employees. It takes away the source of bargaining strength, the right to strike, and gives nothing to take its place. Seizure should be used only as an enforcement device to aid in effectively carrying out other procedures, such as fact finding with recommendations. Seizure was used merely as an enforcing device during World War II.

It is necessary to accept the need to have available additional means for governmental intervention more stringent than fact finding. There are some work stoppages in which, because of the nature of the goods withdrawn from the market, the public automatically opposes those who strike, regardless of the merits of the dispute. In these situations employers would be enabled effectively to hold out against any board-recommended settlement properly favorable to the workers. It follows that when necessary the government should have the power to introduce a fact-finding board's recommendations as the work conditions actually to be used for a temporary period. It is true this device would tend strongly to establish the recommended settlement as the final settlement of the dispute, since the parties would be forced to operate under these conditions for a time. Yet where the strike cannot be tolerated, some such procedure is justified. It must be stressed again that in this kind of situation collective bargaining in the usual sense cannot exist. Since it cannot, wages and working conditions must ultimately be established in another way if the parties fail to reach agreement under the threat of governmental intervention.

Compulsory Arbitration May Be Justified

Even the final step, so bitterly opposed both by management and labor, is justified by the analysis here set forth. The compulsory arbitration of wages and working conditions to settle a dispute in an industry in which a work stoppage would be disastrous to the national interest is a proper procedure to have available. We used compulsory arbitration in wartime because we could not tolerate strikes. It needs to be an available ultimate weapon in those instances in which the right to strike simply cannot exist.

Compulsory settlement procedures should not ever be the only available procedures in a given industry, no matter how critical. Often mechanisms short of compulsory settlement could bring the parties to a resolution of the labor dispute. It must be frankly realized that the availability and use of compulsory arbitration tends seriously to weaken bargaining; the party most likely to benefit from a forced settlement may negoiate only perfunctorily. But the premise here stated is that at least sometimes there cannot be a right to strike. When this is so, bargaining is not available as the ultimate solution to the dispute, and the fact that compulsory settlement seriously weakens the bargaining does not outweigh the necessity that a means of settlement without stoppage must be ready for use, although only in the most extreme situations. If the right to strike is gone, something else must take its place.

The most common objection stated both to compulsory arbitration and to fact finding with recommendations is that they put the government in the business of fixing wages, leading inevitably to a managed economy. We already have enough experience to show that this is not necessarily so. We have had a number of past instances of fact finding with recommendations forming the basis of settlement. There is a clear distinction to be made. The wage settlement proposed with regularity by a government agency is a far greater intrusion by the government than is the recommendation of an *ad hoc* fact-finding board or board of arbitration which has been chosen to bring about settlement of one particular dispute. Insofar as the independent board can approximate the settlement that the parties themselves would have reached if the strike had been allowed to run its course, the settlement has no more effect upon the economy than would the settlement of the parties themselves. Of course, just what the settlement of the parties would have been can never be known exactly. But there is enough experience with collective bargaining settlements and voluntary arbitrations of wage disputes to know that, given the facts, the economic pattern which should be followed can be ascertained.

Collective Bargaining Is Absolute Requisite

The key to the resolution of the emergency dispute problem is therefore revealed. The matter of pressure in settlements by governmental intervention through emergency-dispute processes will not disrupt the role of collective bargaining so long as the settlements brought about follow collective bargaining patterns rather than establish them. The maintaining and strengthening of effective collective bargaining then becomes the absolute requisite to the keeping of emergency procedures in narrow bounds. If the basic labor-cost decisions in the American economy are made by collective bargaining, we have little to fear from the occasional emergency settlement dictated by *ad hoc* governmental intervention. The dictated settlements can follow the pattern established by bargaining.

So it is that the newly awakened emphasis on improving collective bargaining is as significant a part of the solution to the emergency strike problem as are the techniques for dealing with such strikes. Governmental intervention in emergency work stoppages need not bring about governmental management of the economic bargains in our society if collective bargaining is strengthened to maintain its proper role in making these economic decisions.

We must endeavor to reach this balanced approach. Realistically speaking, we cannot continue to hold a false belief that the right to strike is unlimited. We cannot insist that all bargains must be made through the collective bargaining process. We can and must make every effort to hone the keen edge of collective bargaining so that it is an effective tool in all but the very hardest of cases. But we must be courageous enough to handle the hardest cases another way.

The alternative is facing the resolution of each crisis after the crisis occurs. Drastic measures which will destroy the process of collective bargaining seem the inevitable outgrowth of such a passive approach when the spectrum of the kinds of crises which can arise is viewed. Advance preparation for emergencies by creating the structures to meet them is needed to preserve our economic freedom. Freedom does not flourish in chaos, but in enlightened order.

NOTES

1. For other expositions of the "choice of procedures" or "arsenal of weapons" approach, *see* A. Cox, Law and the National Labor Policy (1960); Fleming, *Emergency Strikes and National Policy*, 11 Lab. L.J. 267, 336 (1960); Wirtz, *The "Choice of Procedures" Approach to National Emergency Disputes,* in Emergency Disputes and National Policy (I. Bernstein, H. Enarson & R. Fleming eds. 1955).

2. Problems attendant upon seizure are discussed in Cox, *Seizure in Emergency Disputes,* in Emergency Disputes and National Policy, *supra,* and in Teller, *Government Seizure in Labor Disputes,* 60 Harv. L. Rev. 1017 (1947).

3. Compulsory arbitration is analyzed in Jones, Farmer & Feller, *Compulsory Arbitration: Three Views,* 51 Va. L. Rev. 369, 396, 410 (1965) (three separate papers); *see also* Aaron, Landis & Katz, *Emergency Dispute Settlement,* in Southwestern Legal Foundation, Labor Law Developments 1967, Proceedings of the 13th Annual Institute on Labor Law 185, 209, 223 (1967) (three separate papers).

4. New approaches to "creative bargaining" are summarized by Wirtz, *The Challenge to Free Collective Bargaining,* in Labor Arbitration and Industrial Change, Proceedings of the 16th Annual Meeting, National Academy of Arbitrators 297 (1963).

5. The American Bar Association appointed a special committee, headed by retired Chief Judge Desmond of the New York Court of Appeals, to study means of avoiding national strikes in transportation industries. For a discussion of its report, see Curtin, *Transportation Strikes and the Public Interest: The Recommendations of the ABA's Special Committee,* 58 Geo. L.J. 243 (1969).

6. In 1971, the Nixon administration endorsed an emergency disputes bill containing a provision for "final offer selection" as an alternative procedure. If the President chose this option, each party would submit one or two final offers to the Secretary of Labor. Each offer would be a complete collective bargaining agreement resolving all issues in dispute. A special Board would then choose the most "reasonable" final offer, which would become the final contract. The Board would not mediate, and it could not alter in any way the offer it selects. The proponents of this plan argued that it would have the effect of forcing the positions of the parties closer together, since it requires the selection of the more reasonable offer. See Moskow, *National Emergency Strikes: The Final Offer Selection Procedure and Other Options,* in N.Y.U. TWENTY-FOURTH ANNUAL CONFERENCE ON LABOR 1 (1972); Silberman, *National Emergency Disputes — The Considerations Behind a Legislative Proposal,* 4 GA. L. REV. 673 (1970). For critical comments, see Aaron, *National Emergency Disputes: Some Current Proposals,* 22 LAB. L.J. 461 (1971); Lewis, *Proposals for Change in the Taft-Hartley Emergency Procedures: A Critical Appraisal,* 40 TENN. L. REV. 689 (1973).

SECTION VIII. Federal Preemption

To what extent does federal labor legislation "preempt" the regulatory power of the states? This perplexing and persistent question has produced over three dozen leading decisions by the United States Supreme Court since 1945, and recent major efforts have deeply divided the Court.

All of the following materials on federal preemption are concerned with industries "affecting commerce." In those small and local trades in which there is no direct or indirect connection with interstate commerce, state power remains unaffected by the federal preemption doctrine. Furthermore, under the amendments contained in the Labor-Management Reporting and Disclosure Act of 1959, the states may take jurisdiction of cases in industries affecting interstate commerce over which the NLRB declines to assert jurisdiction.

Ever since its original enactment, the National Labor Relations Act has provided in § 10(a) that the NLRB may, by agreement, cede to a state agency jurisdiction over labor disputes affecting commerce unless the applicable state statute "is inconsistent with the corresponding provision of this act or has received a construction inconsistent therewith." No cession agreements are currently in effect.

The "No-Man's-Land" and the 1959 Amendments. The Supreme Court in Guss v. Utah Labor Relations Bd., 353 U.S. 1 (1957), created a legal "no-man's-land" by holding that the states were preempted from acting even in those areas where the NLRB declined to exercise its jurisdiction. Although the NLRB expanded its jurisdictional standards in 1958, this was only a partial solution, since about four-fifths of the cases previously consigned to the "no-man's-land" still remained there.

Congress considered several alternative proposals during its deliberations on the 1959 amendments to the Taft-Hartley Act. The bill reported out by the House Labor Committee was the "most federal." It would have required the NLRB to assert jurisdiction over all labor disputes subject to the commerce power. The bill originally passed by the Senate would have allowed state agencies (not courts) to take jurisdiction over cases in the "no-man's-land," but federal substantive law would have governed. The Landrum-Griffin bill, as originally passed by the House, gave the widest scope to state action. Both state agencies and state courts could assume jurisdiction, and there was no requirement that federal law be applied.

The bill which ultimately emerged from the Senate-House conference essentially adopted the House approach, with an important modification. Section 14(c), as added to the National Labor Relations Act, permitted the states to assert jurisdiction where the Labor Board declined. It also provided, however, that the NLRB could not narrow its jurisdiction beyond the point set by the discretionary standards in effect on August 1, 1959. The bill did not say whether the states were to apply federal or state law, but Senator Kennedy, the conference chairman, was more explicit: "It was the opinion of the Senate that the Federal law should prevail with respect to interstate commerce, and, in order to compromise that feature, it was agreed that State law could prevail, but only in those areas in which the National Labor Relations Board does not now assume jurisdiction." 105 CONG. REC. 17720 (1959). State courts have generally assumed that local law is applicable. *See, e.g.,* Cooper v. Nutley Sun Printing Co., 36 N.J. 189, 175 A.2d 639 (1961); Kempf v. Carpenters Local 1273, 229 Ore. 337, 367 P.2d 436 (1961).

If state law controls in the former "no-man's-land," are employers on the borderline of federal jurisdiction (and the unions dealing with them) faced with the threat that what seems today a legitimate act may become an unfair labor practice at the close of the fiscal year? What happens if the NLRB revises its standards to enlarge the area of its jurisdiction? Would the Senate bill have supplied a more practical solution by requiring the states to apply federal law? What obstacles would that approach have encountered? Are state administrative agencies authorized to enforce anything but local law? Was the congressional silence in § 14(c) on the issue of applicable law a sound legislative technique? *See generally* Beeson, *Boundaries of State-Federal Jurisdiction in Labor-Management Relations Under the New Labor Law — A Federal View,* in N.Y.U. THIRTEENTH ANNUAL CONFERENCE ON LABOR 51, 58-61 (1960); Cohen, *Congress Clears the Labor No Man's Land: A Long-Awaited Solution Spawns a Host of New Problems,* 56 Nw. U.L. REV. 333, 371-77 (1961); McCoid, *State Regulation of Labor-Management Relations: The Impact of Garmon and Landrum-Griffin,* 48 IOWA L. REV. 578, 618-20 (1963). A few commentators think that § 14(c) calls for the application of federal substantive law. *See* Hanley, *Federal-State Jurisdiction in Labor's No Man's Land: 1960,* 48 GEO. L.J. 709, 721-35 (1960).

SAN DIEGO BUILDING TRADES COUNCIL v. GARMON

Supreme Court of the United States
359 U.S. 236, 79 S. Ct. 773, 3 L. Ed. 2d 775 (1959)

[In the *Garmon* case, which has become the leading case setting out the general principles of federal preemption, the issue on certiorari was whether the State of California had jurisdiction to award damages for a tort under state law against a union for engaging in peaceful picketing. The purpose of the picketing was in dispute, the union claiming that the only purpose was to educate the workers and persuade them to become members and the employer claiming that the sole purpose was to compel the employer to execute a union shop agreement.]

MR. JUSTICE FRANKFURTER delivered the opinion of the Court. . . .

Administration is more than a means of regulation; administration is regulation. We have been concerned with conflict in its broadest sense; conflict with a complex and interrelated federal scheme of law, remedy, and administration. Thus, judicial concern has necessarily focused on the nature of the activities which the States have sought to regulate, rather than on the method of regulation adopted. When the exercise of state power over a particular area of activity threatened interference with the clearly indicated policy of industrial relations, it has been judicially necessary to preclude the States from acting. However, due regard for the presuppositions of our embracing federal system, including the principle of diffusion of power not as a matter of doctrinaire localism but as a promoter of democracy, has required us not to find withdrawal from the States of power to regulate where the activity regulated was a merely peripheral concern of the Labor Management Relations Act. See IAM v. Gonzales, 356 U.S. 617 (1958). Or where the regulated conduct touched interests so deeply rooted in local feeling and responsibility that, in the absence of compelling congressional direction, we could not infer that Congress had deprived the States of the power to act.

When it is clear or may fairly be assumed that the activities which a State purports to regulate are protected by § 7 of the Taft-Hartley Act, or constitute an unfair labor practice under § 8, due regard for the federal enactment requires that state jurisdiction must yield. To leave the States free to regulate conduct so plainly within the central aim of federal regulation involves too great a danger of conflict between power asserted by Congress and requirements imposed by state law. Nor has it mattered whether the States have acted through laws of broad general application rather than laws specifically directed towards the governance of industrial relations. Regardless of the mode adopted, to allow the States to control conduct which is the subject of national regulation would create potential frustration of national purposes.

At times it has not been clear whether the particular activity regulated by the States was governed by § 7 or § 8 or was, perhaps, outside both these sections. But courts are not primary tribunals to adjudicate such issues. It is essential to the administration of the Act that these determinations be left in the first instance to the National Labor Relations

Board. What is outside the scope of this Court's authority cannot remain within a State's power and state jurisdiction too must yield to the exclusive primary competence of the Board. *See, e.g.,* Garner v. Teamsters, 346 U.S. 485 (1953), especially at 489-491; Weber v. Anheuser-Busch, Inc., 348 U.S. 468 (1955).

The case before us is such a case. The adjudication in California has throughout been based on the assumption that the behavior of the petitioning unions constituted an unfair labor practice. This conclusion was derived by the California courts from the facts as well as from their view of the Act. It is not for us to decide whether the National Labor Relations Board would have, or should have, decided these questions in the same manner. When an activity is arguably subject to § 7 or § 8 of the Act, the States as well as the federal courts must defer to the exclusive competence of the National Labor Relations Board if the danger of state interference with national policy is to be averted.

To require the States to yield to the primary jurisdiction of the National Board does not ensure Board adjudication of the status of a disputed activity. If the Board decides, subject to appropriate federal judicial review, that conduct is protected by § 7, or prohibited by § 8, then the matter is at an end, and the States are ousted of all jurisdiction. Or the Board may decide that an activity is neither protected nor prohibited, and thereby raise the question whether such activity may be regulated by the States.[4] . . . In the absence of the Board's clear determination that an activity is neither protected nor prohibited or of compelling precedent applied to essentially undisputed facts, it is not for this Court to decide whether such activities are subject to state jurisdiction. . . . The governing consideration is that to allow the States to control activities that are potentially subject to federal regulation involves too great a danger of conflict with national labor policy.[5]

In the light of these principles the case before us is clear. Since the National Labor Relations Board has not adjudicated the status of the conduct for which the State of California seeks to give a remedy in damages, and since such activity is arguably within the compass of § 7 or § 8 of the Act, the State's jurisdiction is displaced.

Nor is it significant that California asserted its power to give damages rather than to enjoin what the Board may restrain though it could not compensate. Our concern is with delimiting areas of conduct which must be free from state regulation if national policy is to be left unhampered. Such regulation can be as effectively exerted through an award of damages as through some form of preventive relief. The obligation to pay compensation can be, indeed is designed to be, a potent method of

---

[4] See UAW v. WERB, 336 U.S. 245 (1949). The approach taken in that case, in which the Court undertook for itself to determine the status of the disputed activity, has not been followed in later decisions, and is no longer of general application.

[5] "When Congress has taken the particular subject matter in hand coincidence is as ineffective as opposition. . . ." Charleston & West. Carolina R. Co. v. Varnville Furniture Co., 237 U.S. 597, 601 (1915).

governing conduct and controlling policy. Even the States' salutary effort to redress private wrongs or grant compensation for past harm cannot be exerted to regulate activities that are potentially subject to the exclusive federal regulatory scheme. See Garner v. Teamsters, 346 U.S. 485, 492-497 (1953). It may be that an award of damages in a particular situation will not, in fact, conflict with the active assertion of federal authority. The same may be true of the incidence of a particular state injunction. To sanction either involves a conflict with federal policy in that it involves allowing two law-making sources to govern. In fact, since remedies form an ingredient of any integrated scheme of regulation, to allow the State to grant a remedy here which has been withheld from the National Labor Relations Board only accentuates the danger of conflict.

It is true that we have allowed the States to grant compensation for the consequences, as defined by the traditional law of torts, of conduct marked by violence and imminent threats to the public order. UAW v. Russell, 356 U.S. 634 (1958); United Constr. Workers v. Laburnum, 347 U.S. 656 (1954). We have also allowed the States to enjoin such conduct. Youngdahl v. Rainfair, 355 U.S. 131 (1957); UAW v. WERB, 351 U.S. 266 (1956). State jurisdiction has prevailed in these situations because the compelling state interest, in the scheme of our federalism, in the maintenance of domestic peace is not overridden in the absence of clearly expressed congressional direction. We recognize that the opinion in United Constr. Workers v. Laburnum, 347 U.S. 656 (1954), found support in the fact that the state remedy had no federal counterpart. But that decision was determined, as is demonstrated by the question to which review was restricted by the "type of conduct" involved, *i.e.,* "intimidation and threats of violence." In the present case there is no such compelling state interest.

[The concurring opinion of MR. JUSTICE HARLAN, with whom JUSTICES CLARK, WHITTAKER, AND STEWART joined, is omitted.]

NOTES

1. Since the 1959 Landrum-Griffin amendments settled the no-man's-land problem by giving it to the states, the principal federal preemption problems have concerned the situation where the National Labor Relations Act applies and the NLRB would take the case under its jurisdictional yardsticks. The question then is: to what extent does the fact that Congress has undertaken to regulate labor relations and entrust the administration to the NLRB oust the states from power to regulate?

2. Under the "federal supremacy" clause of Article VI of the U.S. Constitution, it is clear that a state prohibition or limitation which is in conflict with a federally protected right must fall. For example, the Supreme Court has struck down a number of state laws limiting the right to strike on the part of the employees of privately owned utilities. UAW v. O'Brien, 339 U.S. 383 (1950); Street, Elec. Ry. & Motor Coach Employees, Div. 998 v. WERB, 340 U.S. 383 (1951); Street, Elec. Ry. & Motor Coach Employees, Div. 1287 v. Missouri, 374 U.S. 74 (1963) (statute forbidding strikes after seizure by the state).

3. *Scope and review of state court injunctions.* In Youngdahl v. Rainfair, Inc., 355 U.S. 131 (1957), the Supreme Court held that a state may enjoin threats of violence, obstruction of the streets and of entrances to a plant, and massed name-calling, calculated to provoke violence, but that the state may not at the same time enjoin all other picketing at the plant, because the regulation of peaceful picketing is within the preempted domain of the NLRB.

Where a state court has issued an injunction against union collective action which appears to be within the exclusive jurisdiction of the NLRB, the federal courts will not enjoin enforcement of the state court injunction upon petition of the union. Amalgamated Clothing Workers v. Richman Bros., 348 U.S 511 (1955). The reason is that, under 28 U.S.C. § 2283, "a court of the United States may not grant an injunction to stay proceedings in a State court except as expressly authorized by Act of Congress, or where necessary in aid of its jurisdiction, or to protect or effectuate its judgments."

Ordinarily, therefore, a union must litigate an injunction action by appealing to the highest state court and to the United States Supreme Court. A union's burden in contesting a state court injunction has been considerably eased, however, by Supreme Court decisions modifying the general rule as follows:

a. If an unfair labor practice charge has been filed with the NLRB and the Board has sought an injunction in a federal court, then the federal court, "in aid of its jurisdiction," may enjoin the enforcement of the state court injunction. Capital Serv., Inc. v. NLRB, 347 U.S. 501 (1954). Even in the absence of unfair labor practice charges before it, the NLRB may now seek federal injunctive relief against preempted state court action. In NLRB v. Nash-Finch Co., 404 U.S. 138 (1971), the Supreme Court sustained the power of the Board to ask a federal court to enjoin a state court injunction against peaceful picketing, despite the usual prohibitions of 28 U.S.C. § 2283 against federal injunctions to stay state court proceedings, and despite the failure of the company involved to file § 8(b)(4) or § 8(b)(7) charges against the union. Since the Board had no basis for requesting a § 10(j) or § 10(*l*) injunction, the express exception in § 2283 permitting a federal court to enjoin state proceedings "in aid of its jurisdiction" was not applicable. But in order "to prevent frustration of the policies of the Act," the Board was held to have "an implied authority," as a federal agency, "to enjoin state action where its federal power preempts the field."

Following the policies of the *Nash-Finch* case, a federal district court entertained a suit by the NLRB to enjoin a union from attempting to require the New York State Labor Relations Board to assert jurisdiction over housestaff in nonprofit hospitals. On the merits, the court held that there was no federal preemption since there is no national labor policy that housestaff be completely unregulated, but the Second Circuit reversed on this point. NLRB v. Committee of Interns and Residents, 426 F.Supp. 483 (D.C.N.Y. 1977), *rev'd,* 566 F.2d 810 (2d Cir. 1977).

b. The United States Supreme Court has jurisdiction to review a state supreme court's authorization of the entry of a *temporary* injunction in a controversy within the exclusive competence of the NLRB, even though the Supreme Court's jurisdiction is limited to the review of "final" judgments of state courts under 28 U.S.C. § 1257. Construction & General Laborers, Local 438 v. Curry, 371 U.S. 542 (1963). Said the Court: "The truth is that authorizing the issuance of a temporary injunction, as is frequently true of temporary injunctions in labor disputes, may effectively dispose of petitioner's rights and render entirely illusory his right to review here as well as his right to a hearing before the Labor Board."

c. The Supreme Court is not bound by a state court's ruling that a case has been rendered moot by the completion of the job which was the object of the picketing, since "the question of mootness is itself a question of federal law upon which we must pronounce final judgment." Liner v. Jafco, Inc., 375 U.S. 301 (1964). *See also* Allee v. Medrano, 94 S. Ct. 2191 (U.S. 1974).

d. A state court has no power to hold a person in contempt for violating an injunction entered by a court lacking jurisdiction because of federal preemption. It is a denial of due process to convict a man of contempt without a hearing and an opportunity to establish that the state court was trenching on an exclusive federal domain. *In re* Green, 369 U.S. 689 (1962). *See also Ex parte* George, 371 U.S. 72 (1962). *Compare* United States v. United Mine Workers, 330 U.S. 258 (1947).

AMALGAMATED ASSOCIATION OF STREET, ELECTRIC RAILWAY & MOTOR COACH EMPLOYEES OF AMERICA v. LOCKRIDGE

Supreme Court of the United States
403 U.S. 274, 91 S. Ct. 1909, 29 L. Ed. 2d 473 (1971)

[In this case, a union member had recovered damages against his union in a state court on a breach of contract theory for causing the employer to discharge him under a union shop agreement. Lockridge had failed to pay his union dues one month, and the question whether the union had properly sought his job termination involved interpretation of both the union's constitution and the collective bargaining agreement. The Supreme Court reversed the judgment on the basis of federal preemption, and the Court's opinion explains more fully the rationale of *Garmon*.]

MR. JUSTICE HARLAN delivered the opinion of the Court. . . .

A . . . [I]n San Diego Building Trades Council v. Garmon, 359 U.S. 236, 245 (1959), we held that the National Labor Relations Act preempts the jurisdiction of state and federal courts to regulate conduct "arguably subject to § 7 or § 8 of the Act." On their face, [§§ 8(b)(2), 8(b)(1)(A), and 8(a)(3)] of the Act at least arguably either permit or forbid the union conduct dealt with by the judgment below. For the evident thrust of this aspect of the federal statutory scheme is to permit the enforcement of union security clauses, by dismissal from employment, only for failure to pay dues. Whatever other sanctions may be employed to exact compliance with those internal union rules unrelated to dues payment, the Act seems generally to exclude dismissal from employment. See Radio Officers' Union v. National Labor Relations Bd., 347 U.S. 17 (1954). Indeed, in the course of rejecting petitioner's preemption argument, the Idaho Supreme Court stated that, in its opinion, the Union "did most certainly violate 8(b)(1)(A), did most certainly violate 8(b)(2) . . . and probably caused the employer to violate 8(a)(3)." 93 Idaho at 299, 460 P.2d at 724. Thus, given the broad preemption principle enunciated in *Garmon,* the want of state court power to resolve Lockridge's complaint might well seem to follow as a matter of course.

The Idaho Supreme Court, however, concluded that it nevertheless possessed jurisdiction in these circumstances. That determination, as we understand it, rested upon three separate propositions, all of which are urged here by respondent. The first is that the Union's conduct was not only an unfair labor practice, but a breach of its contract with Lockridge as well. "Preemption is not established simply by showing that the same facts will establish two different legal wrongs." 93 Idaho at 300, 460 P.2d at 725. In other words *Garmon,* the state court and respondent assert, states a principle applicable only where the state law invoked is designed specifically to regulate labor relations; it has no force where the State applies its general common law of contracts to resolve disputes between a union and its members. Secondly, it is urged that the facts that might be shown to vindicate Lockridge's claim in the Idaho state courts differ from those relevant to proceedings governed by the National Labor Relations Act. It is said that the conduct regulated by the Act is union and employer discrimination; general contract law takes into account only the correctness of competing interpretations of the language embodied in agreements. 93 Idaho at 303-304, 460 P.2d at 728-729. Finally, there recurs throughout the state court opinion, and the arguments of respondent here, the theme that the facts of the instant case render it virtually indistinguishable from Association of Machinists v. Gonzales, 356 U.S. 617 (1959), where this Court upheld the exercise of state court jurisdiction in an opinion written only one Term prior to *Garmon,* by the author of *Garmon* and which was approvingly cited in the *Garmon* opinion itself.

We do not believe that any of these arguments suffice to overcome the plain purport of *Garmon* as applied to the facts of this case. However, we have determined to treat these considerations at some length because of the understandable confusion, perhaps in a measure attributable to the previous opinions of this Court, they reflect over the jurisprudential bases upon which the *Garmon* doctrine rests.

B. The constitutional principles of preemption, in whatever particular field of law they operate, are designed with a common end in view: to avoid conflicting regulation of conduct by various official bodies which might have some authority over the subject matter. A full understanding of the particular preemption rule set forth in *Garmon* especially requires, we think, appreciation of the precise nature and extent of the potential for injurious conflict that would inhere in a system unaffected by such a doctrine, and also the setting in which the general problem of accommodating conflicting claims of competence to resolve disputes touching upon labor relations has been presented to this Court. . . .

The rationale for preemption, then, rests in large measure upon our determination that when it set down a federal labor policy Congress plainly meant to do more than simply to alter the then prevailing substantive law. It sought as well to restructure fundamentally the processes for effectuating that policy, deliberately placing the responsibility for applying and developing this comprehensive legal system in the hands of an expert administrative body rather than the federalized judicial system. Thus, that a local court, while adjudicating a labor dispute also within the jurisdiction of the NLRB, may purport to apply legal rules identical to those prescribed in the federal Act or may eschew the authority to define or apply principles specifically developed to regulate labor relations does not mean that all relevant potential for debilitating conflict is absent.

A second factor that has played an important role in our shaping of the preemption doctrine has been the necessity to act without specific congressional direction. The precise extent to which state law must be displaced to achieve those unifying ends sought by the national legislature has never been determined by the Congress. This has, quite frankly, left the Court with few available options. We cannot declare preempted all local regulation that touches or concerns in any way the complex interrelationships between employees, employers, and unions; obviously, much of this is left to the States. Nor can we proceed on a case-by-case basis to determine whether each particular final judicial pronouncement does, or might reasonably be thought to, conflict in some relevant manner with federal labor policy. This Court is ill-equipped to play such a role and the federal system dictates that this problem be solved with a rule capable of relatively easy application, so that lower courts may largely police themselves in this regard. Equally important, such a principle would fail to take account of the fact, as discussed above, that simple congruity of legal rules does not, in this area, prove the absence of untenable conflict. Further, it is surely not possible for this Court to treat the National Labor Relations Act section by section, committing enforcement of some of its provisions wholly to the NLRB and others to the concurrent domain of local law. Nothing in the language or underlying purposes of the Act suggests any basis for such distinctions. Finally, treating differently judicial power to deal with conduct protected by the Act from that prohibited by it would likewise be unsatisfactory. Both areas equally involve conduct whose legality is governed by federal law, the application of which Congress committed to the Board, not courts.

This is not to say, however, that these inherent limitations on this Court's ability to state a workable rule that comports reasonably with apparent congressional objectives are necessarily self-evident. In fact, varying approaches were taken by the Court in initially grappling with this preemption problem. Thus, for example, some early cases suggested the true distinction lay between judicial application of general common law, which was permissible, as opposed to state rules specifically designed to regulate labor relations, which were preempted. See, *e.g.,* Automobile Workers v. Russell, 356 U.S. 634, 645 (1958). Others made preemption turn on whether the States purported to apply a remedy not provided for by the federal scheme, *e.g.,* Weber v. Anheuser-Busch, Inc., 348 U.S. 468, 479-480 (1955), while in still others the Court undertook a thorough scrutiny of the federal Act to ascertain whether the state courts had, in fact, arrived at conclusions inconsistent with its provisions, *e.g.,* Automobile Workers v. Wisconsin Employment Relations Bd., 336 U.S. 245 (1949). For the reasons outlined above none of these approaches proved satisfactory, however, and each was ultimately abandoned. It was, in short, experience — not pure logic — which initially taught that each of these methods sacrificed important federal interests in a uniform law of labor relations centrally administered by an expert agency without yielding anything in return by way of predictability or ease of judicial application.

The failure of alternative analyses and the interplay of the foregoing policy considerations, then, led this Court to hold in *Garmon,* 359 U.S. at 244:

> When it is clear or may fairly be assumed that the activities which a State purports to regulate are protected by § 7 of the National Labor Relations Act, or constitute an unfair labor practice under § 8, due regard for the federal enactment requires that state jurisdiction must yield. To leave the States free to regulate conduct so plainly within the central aim of federal regulation involves too great a danger of conflict between power asserted by Congress and requirements imposed by state law.

C. Upon these premises, we think that *Garmon* rather clearly dictates reversal of the judgment below. None of the propositions asserted to support that judgment can withstand an application, in light of those factors that compelled its promulgation, of the *Garmon* rule.

Assuredly the proposition that Lockridge's complaint was not subject to the exclusive jurisdiction of the NLRB because it charged a breach of contract rather than an unfair labor practice is not tenable. Preemption, as shown above, is designed to shield the system from conflicting regulation of conduct. It is the conduct being regulated, not the formal description of governing legal standards, that is the proper focus of concern. Indeed, the notion that a relevant distinction exists for such purposes between particularized and generalized labor law was explicitly rejected in *Garmon* itself. 359 U.S. at 244.

The second argument, closely related to the first, is that the state courts in resolving this controversy, did deal with different conduct, *i.e.,* interpretation of contractual terms, than would the NLRB which would be required to decide whether the Union discriminated against Lockridge. At bottom, of course, the Union's action in procuring Lockridge's dismissal from employment is the conduct which Idaho courts have sought to regulate. Thus, this second point demonstrates at best that Idaho defines differently what sorts of such union conduct may permissibly be proscribed. This is to say either that the regulatory schemes, state and federal, conflict (in which case preemption is clearly called for) or that Idaho is dealing with conduct to which the federal Act does not speak. If the latter assertion was intended, it is not accurate. As pointed out in Part II A, *supra,* the relevant portions of the Act operate to prohibit a union from causing or attempting to cause an employer to discriminate against an employee because his membership in the union has been terminated "on some ground other than" his failure to pay those dues requisite to membership. This has led the Board routinely and frequently to inquire into the proper construction of union regulations in order to ascertain whether the union properly found an employee to have been derelict in his dues-paying responsibilities, where his discharge was procured on the asserted grounds of nonmembership in the union. . . . That a union may in good faith have misconstrued its own rules has not been treated by the Board as a defense to a claimed violation of § 8(b)(2). In the Board's view, it is the fact of misapplication by a union of its rules, not the motivation for that discrimination, that constitutes an unfair labor practice. . . .

From the foregoing, then, it would seem that this case indeed represents one of the clearest instances where the *Garmon* principle, properly understood, should operate to oust state court jurisdiction. There being no doubt that the conduct here involved was arguably protected by § 7 or prohibited by § 8 of the Act, the full range of very substantial interests the preemption doctrine seeks to protect are directly implicated here.

However, a final strand of analysis underlies the opinion of the Idaho Supreme Court, and the position of respondent, in this case. Our decision in Association of Machinists v. Gonzales, 356 U.S. 617 (1958), it is argued, fully survived the subsequent reorientation of preemption doctrine effected by the *Garmon* decision, providing, in effect, an express exception for the exercise of judicial jurisdiction in cases such as this. . . .

Although it was decided only one Term subsequent to *Gonzales, Garmon* clearly did not fully embrace the technique of the prior case. It was precisely the realization that disparities in remedies and administration could produce substantial conflict, in the practical sense of the term, between the relevant state and federal regulatory schemes and that this Court could not effectively and responsibly superintend on a case-by-case basis the exertion of state power over matters arguably governed by the National Labor Relations Act that impelled the somewhat broader formulation of the preemption doctrine in *Garmon.* It seems evident that the full-blown rationale of *Gonzales* could not survive the rule of *Garmon.* Nevertheless, *Garmon* did not cast doubt upon the result reached in *Gonzales,* but cited it approvingly as an example of the fact that state court jurisdiction is not preempted "where the activity regulated was a merely peripheral concern of the . . . Act." 359 U.S. at 243.

Against this background, we attempted to define more precisely the reach of *Gonzales* within the more comprehensive framework *Garmon* provided in the companion cases of Plumbers Union v. Borden, 373 U.S. 690 (1963), and Iron Workers v. Perko, 373 U.S. 701 (1963).

Borden had sued his union in state courts, alleging that the union had arbitrarily refused to refer him to a particular job which he had lined up. He recovered damages, based on lost wages, on the grounds that this conduct constituted both tortious interference with his right to contract for employment and a breach of promise, implicit in his membership arrangement with the union, not to discriminate unfairly against any member or deny him the right to work. Perko had obtained a large money judgment in the Ohio courts on proof that the union had conspired, without cause, to deprive him of employment as a foreman by demanding his discharge from one such position he had held and representing to others that his foreman's rights had been suspended. We held both Perko's and Borden's judgments inconsistent with the *Garmon* rule essentially for the same reasons we have concluded that Lockridge could not, consistently with the *Garmon* decision, maintain his lawsuit in the state courts. We further held there was no necessity to "consider the present vitality of [the *Gonzales*] rationale in the light of more recent decisions," because in those cases, unlike *Gonzales,* "the crux of the action[s] . . . concerned alleged interference with the plaintiff's existing or prospective employment relations and was not directed to internal union matters." Because no specific claim for restoration of membership rights had been advanced, "there was no permissible state remedy to which the award of consequential damages for loss of earnings might be subordinated." Perko, 373 U.S. at 705. See also Borden, 373 U.S. at 697.

In sum, what distinguished *Gonzales* from *Borden* and *Perko* was that the former lawsuit "was focused on purely internal union matters," *Borden, supra,* at 697, a subject the National Labor Relations Act leaves principally to other processes of law. The possibility that, in defining the scope of the union's duty to Gonzales, the state courts would directly and consciously implicate principles of federal law was at best tangential and remote. In the instant case, however, this possibility was real and immediate. To assess the legality of his union's conduct toward Gonzales the California courts needed only to focus upon the union's constitution and by-laws. Here, however, Lockridge's entire case turned upon the construction of the applicable union security clause, a matter as to which, as shown above, federal concern is pervasive and its regulation complex. The reasons for Gonzales' deprivation of union membership had nothing to do with matters of employment, while Lockridge's cause of action and claim for damages was based solely upon the procurement of his discharge from employment. It cannot plausibly be argued, in any meaningful sense, that Lockridge's lawsuit "was focused upon purely internal matters." Although nothing said in *Garmon* necessarily suggests that States cannot regulate the general conditions which unions may impose on their membership, it surely makes crystal clear that *Gonzales* does not stand for the proposition that resolution of any union-member conflict is within state competence so long as one of the remedies provided is restoration of union membership. This much was settled by *Borden* and *Perko,* and it is only upon such an unwarrantably broad interpretation of *Gonzales* that the judgment below could be sustained.

III. The preemption doctrine we apply today is, like any other purposefully administered legal principle, not without exception. Those same considerations that underlie *Garmon* have led this Court to permit the exercise of judicial power over conduct arguably protected or prohibited by the Act where Congress has affirmatively indicated that such power should exist, Smith v. Evening News, 371 U.S. 195 (1962); Teamsters v. Morton, 377 U.S. 252 (1964), where this Court cannot, in spite of the force of the policies *Garmon* seeks to promote, conscientiously presume that Congress meant to intrude so deeply into areas traditionally left to local law, *e.g.,* Linn v. Plant Guard Workers, 383 U.S. 53 (1966); Automobile Workers v. Russell, 356 U.S. 634 (1958), and where the particular rule of law sought to be invoked before another tribunal is so structured and administered that, in virtually all instances, it is safe to presume that judicial supervision will not disserve the interests promoted by the federal labor statutes, Vaca v. Sipes, 386 U.S. 171 (1967).

In his brief before this Court, respondent has argued for the first time since this lawsuit was started that two of these exceptions to the *Garmon* principle independently justify the Idaho courts' exercise of jurisdiction over this controversy. First, Lockridge contends that his action, properly viewed, is one to enforce a collective bargaining agreement. Alternatively, he asserts the suit, in essence, was one to redress petitioner's breach of its duty of fair representation. As will be seen, these contentions are somewhat intertwined.

In § 301 of the Taft-Hartley Act, Congress authorized federal courts to exercise jurisdiction over suits brought to enforce collective bargaining agreements. We have held that such actions are judicially cognizable, even where the conduct alleged was arguably protected or prohibited by the National Labor Relations Act because the history of the enactment of § 301 reveals that "Congress deliberately chose to leave the enforcement of collective agreements 'to the usual processes of law.' " Charles Dowd Box Co. v. Courtney, 368 U.S. 502, 513 (1962). It is firmly established, further, that state courts retain concurrent jurisdiction to adjudicate such claims, Charles Dowd Box Co., *supra,* and that individual employees have standing to protect rights conferred upon them by such agreements, Smith v. Evening News, *supra;* Humphrey v. Moore, 375 U.S. 335 (1964).

Our cases also clearly establish that individual union members may sue their employers under § 301 for breach of a promise embedded in the collective bargaining agreement that was intended to confer a benefit upon the individual. Smith v. Evening News, *supra.* Plainly, however, this is not such a lawsuit. Lockridge specifically dropped Greyhound as a named party from his initial complaint and has never reasserted a right to redress from his former employer.

This Court has further held in Humphrey v. Moore, 375 U.S. 335 (1964), that § 301 will support, regardless of otherwise applicable preemption considerations, a suit in the state courts by a union member against his union that seeks to redress union interference with rights conferred on individual employees by the employer's promises in the collective-bargaining agreement, where it is proved that such interference constituted a breach of the duty of fair representation. Indeed, in Vaca v. Sipes, 386 U.S. 171 (1967), we held that an action seeking damages for injury inflicted by a breach of a union's duty of fair representation was judicially cognizable in any event, that is, even if the conduct complained of was arguably protected or prohibited by the National Labor Relations Act and whether or not the lawsuit was bottomed on a collective agreement. Perhaps Count One of Lockridge's second amended complaint could be construed to assert either or both of these theories of recovery. However, it is unnecessary to pass upon the extent to which *Garmon* would be inapplicable if it were shown that in these circumstances petitioner not only breached its contractual obligations to respondent, but did so in a manner that constituted a breach of the duty of fair representation. For such a claim to be made out, Lockridge must have proved "arbitrary or bad faith conduct on the part of the union." Vaca v. Sipes, *supra,* at 193. There must be "substantial evidence of fraud, deceitful action or dishonest conduct." Humphrey v. Moore, *supra,* at 348. Whether these requisite elements have been proved is a matter of federal law. Quite obviously, they were not even asserted to be relevant in the proceedings below. As the Idaho Supreme Court stated in affirming the verdict for Lockridge, "[t]his was a misinterpretation of a contract. Whatever the underlying motive for expulsion might have been, this case has been submitted and tried on the interpretation of the contract, not on a theory of discrimination." Thus, the trial judge's conclusion of law in sustaining Lockridge's claim specifically incorporates the assumption that the Union's "acts . . . were predicated solely upon the ground that [Lockridge] had failed to tender periodic dues in conformance with the requirements of the union Constitution and employment contract as they interpreted [it]. . . ." App., 66. Further, the trial court excluded as irrelevant petitioner's proffer of evidence designed to show that the Union's interpretation of the contract was reasonably based upon its understanding of prior collective bargaining agreements negotiated with Greyhound. Transcript of Trial, at 259-260. . . .

For the reasons stated above, the judgment below is

Reversed.

MR. JUSTICE WHITE, with whom THE CHIEF JUSTICE joins, dissenting.
. . . .

. . . I cannot agree with the opinion of the Court because it reaffirms the *Garmon* doctrine as applied to conduct arguably protected under § 7, as well as to that arguably prohibited under § 8. The essential difference, for present purposes, between activity which is arguably prohibited and that which is arguably protected is that a hearing on the latter activity is virtually impossible unless one deliberately commits an unfair labor practice. In a typical unfair practice case, by alleging conduct arguably prohibited by § 8 the charging party can at least present the General Counsel with the facts, and if the General Counsel issues a complaint, the charging party can present the Board with the facts and arguments to support the claim. But for activity which is arguably protected, there is no provision for an authoritative decision by the Board in the first instance; yet the *Garmon* rule blindly preempts other tribunals. . . .

Though the most natural arena for this conflict occurs when picketers trespass on private property, see Taggart v. Weinacker's, Inc., 397 U.S. 223, 227 (1970) (Burger, C.J., concurring), . . . other instances include "quickie" strikes or slowdowns, see NLRB v. Holcombe, 325 F.2d 508 (5th Cir. 1963), or employees' inaccurate complaints to state officials about sanitary conditions in the plant, Walls Mfg. Co. v. NLRB, 116 U.S. App. D.C. 140, 321 F.2d 753 (1963), or collective activity designed to persuade the employer to hire Negroes, NLRB v. Tanner Motor Livery, Ltd., 349 F.2d 1 (9th Cir. 1965), or failure to participate in a union check-off, Radio Officers' Union v. NLRB, 347 U.S. 17, 24-28 (1954).

There seems little point in a doctrine which, in the name of national policy, encourages the commission of unfair labor practices, the evils which above all else were the object of the Act. Surely the policy of seeking uniformity in the regulation of labor practices must be given closer scrutiny when it leads to the alternative "solutions" of denying the aggrieved party a hearing or encouraging the commission of a putative unfair labor practice as the price of that hearing. . . .

Congress found the no-man's land created by *Guss* unacceptable precisely because there was no way to have rights determined. In terms of congressional intention I find it unsupportable to hold that one threatened by conduct illegal under state law may not proceed against it because it is arguably protected by federal law when he has absolutely no lawful method for determining whether that is actually, as well as arguably, the case. Particularly is this true where the dispute is between a union and its members and the latter are asserting claims under state law based on the union constitution. I would permit the state court to entertain the action and if the union defends on the ground that its conduct is protected by federal law, to pass on that claim at the outset of the proceeding. If the federal law immunizes the challenged union action, the case is terminated; but if not, the case is adjudicated under state law.

[The dissenting opinion of MR. JUSTICE DOUGLAS and the dissenting statement of MR. JUSTICE BLACKMUN are omitted.]

NOTES

1. *See generally* Come, *Federal Preemption of Labor-Management Relations: Current Problems with the Application of Garmon,* 56 VA. L. REV. 1435 (1970); Cox, *Labor Law Preemption Revisited,* 85 HARV. L. REV. 1337 (1972); Lesnick, *Preemption Reconsidered: The Apparent Reaffirmation of Garmon,* 72 COLUM. L. REV. 469 (1972). *See also* Bryson, *A Matter of Wooden Logic: Labor Law Preemption and Individual Rights,* 51 TEXAS L. REV. 1037 (1973).

2. When is an employed person excluded from the operation of federal law and subject instead to state jurisdiction? In a companion case to *Borden,* International Ass'n of Bridge Workers, Local 207 v. Perko, 373 U.S. 701 (1963), a state damage action was brought against a union for allegedly conspiring to deprive a member of his job "as a foreman." The plaintiff argued against preemption on the ground he was a "supervisor"

and thus outside the National Labor Relations Act's definition of "employee." The Supreme Court held that the plaintiff's duties made him at least arguably an "employee" within the meaning of the act, thereby precluding state jurisdiction. Similarly, in Marine Engineers Beneficial Ass'n v. Interlake S.S. Co., 370 U.S. 173 (1962), the Supreme Court ruled that since a union of marine engineers was arguably a "labor organization" as defined by the federal act, the NLRB had exclusive primary jurisdiction to determine the union's status. Despite the contention that the MEBA was composed entirely of supervisors, therefore, a state court could not enjoin the MEBA's picketing of a ship employing nonunion marine engineers.

On the other hand, a state is not foreclosed from acting once the NLRB has concluded, through the dismissal of a representation petition and of unfair labor practice charges, that there is no federal jurisdiction because the union consists exclusively of supervisors. In such circumstances a state court may enjoin peaceful organizational picketing by the supervisors' union. Hanna Mining Co. v. District 2, Marine Engineers, 382 U.S. 181 (1965).

A state may assume jurisdiction over organizational picketing or "standards" picketing by an American labor organization aimed at foreign seamen on vessels of foreign registry, since the maritime operations of foreign flag ships employing alien seamen are not in "commerce" within the meaning of the NLRA. Incres S.S. Co. v. International Maritime Workers, 372 U.S. 24 (1963); Windward Shipping, Ltd. v. American Radio Ass'n, 415 U.S. 104 (U.S. 1974).

The Supreme Court held (5-4) that a state court was not preempted from issuing an injunction, at the behest of shippers and stevedoring companies, against picketing of a foreign flag ship by maritime unions. The majority concluded that since in *Windward* the foreign flag ship was not considered as being "in commerce," it would be inconsistent to consider the shippers and stevedoring firms servicing such a ship as being "in commerce." American Radio Ass'n v. Mobile S.S. Ass'n, 419 U.S. 215 (1974).

Cf. McCulloch v. Sociedad Nacional de Marineros de Honduras, 372 U.S. 10 (1963).

MACHINISTS, LODGE 76 v. WISCONSIN EMPLOYMENT RELATIONS COMMISSION

Supreme Court of the United States
427 U.S. 132, 96 S. Ct. 2548, 49 L. Ed. 2d 396 (1976)

MR. JUSTICE BRENNAN delivered the opinion of the Court.

The question to be decided in this case is whether federal labor policy preempts the authority of a state labor relations board to grant an employer covered by the National Labor Relations Act an order enjoining a union and its members from continuing to refuse to work overtime pursuant to a union policy to put economic pressure on the employer in negotiations for renewal of an expired collective bargaining agreement.

A collective bargaining agreement between petitioner Local 76 (the Union) and respondent, Kearney and Trecker Corporation (the employer) was terminated by the employer pursuant to the terms of the agreement on June 19, 1971. Good-faith bargaining over the terms of a renewal agreement continued for over a year thereafter, finally resulting in the signing of a new agreement effective July 23, 1972. A particularly controverted issue during negotiations was the employer's demand that the provision of the expired agreement under which, as for the prior 17 years, the basic workday was seven and one-half hours, Monday through Friday, and the basic workweek was 37½ hours, be replaced with a new provision providing a basic workday of eight hours and a basic workweek of 40 hours, and that the terms on which overtime rates of pay were payable be changed accordingly.

A few days after the old agreement was terminated the employer unilaterally began to make changes in some conditions of employment provided in the expired contract, e.g., eliminating the checkoff of Union dues, eliminating the Union's office in the plant and eliminating Union lost time. No immediate change was made in the basic workweek or workday, but in March 1972, the employer announced that it would unilaterally implement, as of March 13, 1972, its proposal for a 40-hour week and eight-hour day. The Union response was a membership meeting on March 7 at which strike action was authorized and a resolution was adopted binding union members to refuse to work any overtime, defined as work in excess of seven and one-half hours in any day or 37½ hours in any week. Following the strike vote, the employer offered to "defer the implementation" of its workweek proposal if the Union would agree to call off the concerted refusal to work overtime. The Union, however, refused the offer and indicated its intent to continue the concerted ban on overtime. Thereafter, the employer did not make effective the proposed changes in the workday and workweek before the new agreement became effective on July 23, 1972. Although all but a very few employees complied with the Union's resolution against acceptance of overtime work during the negotiations, the employer did not discipline, or attempt to discipline, any employee for refusing to work overtime.

Instead, while negotiations continued, the employer filed a charge with the National Labor Relations Board that the Union's resolution violated § 8(b)(3) of the National Labor Relations Act. The Regional Director dismissed the charge on the ground that the "policy prohibiting overtime work by its member employees does not appear to be in violation of the Act" and therefore was not conduct cognizable by the Board under NLRB v. Insurance Agents Intern'l Union, 361 U. S. 477 (1960). However, the employer also filed a complaint before the Wisconsin Employment Relations Commission charging that the refusal to work overtime constituted an unfair labor practice under state law. The Union filed a motion before the Commission to dismiss the complaint for want of "jurisdiction over the subject matter" in that jurisdiction over "the activity of the [union] complained of [is] preempted by" the National Labor

Relations Act. The motion was denied and the Commission adopted the Conclusion of Law of its Examiner that "the concerted refusal to work overtime is not an activity which is arguably protected under Section 7 or arguably prohibited under Section 8 of the National Labor Relations Act, as amended and . . . therefore the . . . Commission is not preempted from asserting its jurisdiction to regulate said conduct." The Commission also adopted the further Conclusion of Law that the Union "by authorizing . . . the concerted refusal to work overtime . . . engaged in a concerted effort to interfere with production and . . . committed an unfair labor practice within the meaning of Section 111.06(2)(h). . . ." [1] The Commission thereupon entered an order that the Union, *inter alia,* "[i]mmediately cease and desist from authorizing, encouraging or condoning any concerted refusal to accept overtime assignments . . . ." The Wisconsin Circuit Court affirmed and entered judgment enforcing the Commission's order. The Wisconsin Supreme Court affirmed the Circuit Court. 67 Wis. 2d 13, 226 N. W. 2d 203 (1975). We granted certiorari, 423 U. S. 890 (1975). We reverse.

I. "The national . . . Act . . . leaves much to the states, though Congress has refrained from telling us how much. We must spell out from conflicting indications of congressional will the area in which state action is still permissible." Garner v. Teamsters Union, 346 U. S. 485, 488 (1953). Federal labor policy as reflected in the National Labor Relations Act as amended has been construed not to preclude the States from regulating aspects of labor relations that involve "conduct touch[ing] interests so deeply rooted in local feeling and responsibility that . . . we could not infer that Congress had deprived the States of the power to act." San Diego Unions v. Garmon, 359 U. S. 236, 244 (1959). Policing of actual or threatened violence to persons or destruction of property has been held most clearly a matter for the States. Similarly, the federal law governing labor relations does not withdraw "from the States . . . power to regulate where the activity regulated [is] a merely peripheral concern of the Labor Management Relations Act." *San Diego Unions* v. *Garmon, supra,* at 243.

Cases that have held state authority to be preempted by federal law tend to fall into one of two categories: (1) those that reflect the concern that "one forum would enjoin, as illegal, conduct which the other forum would find legal" and (2) those that reflect the concern "that the [application of state law by] state courts would restrict the exercise of rights guaranteed

---

[1] Wis. Stat. § 116.06 (2) provides:

"It shall be an unfair labor practice for an employee individually or in concert with others:

. . . .

"(h) To take unauthorized possession of the property of the employer or to engage in any concerted effort to interfere with production except by leaving the premises in an orderly manner for the purpose of going on strike."

by the Federal Acts." Automobile Workers v. Russell, 356 U. S. 634, 644 (1958). "[I]n referring to decisions holding state laws preempted by the NLRA, care must be taken to distinguish preemption based on federal protection of the conduct in question . . . from that based predominantly on the primary jurisdiction of the National Labor Relations Board . . . , although the two are often not easily separable." Railroad Trainmen v. Jacksonville Terminal Co., 394 U. S. 369, 383 n. 19 (1969). Each of these distinct aspects of labor law preemption has had its own history in our decisions to which we now turn.

We consider first pre-emption based predominantly on the primary jurisdiction of the Board. This line of preemption analysis was developed in San Diego Unions v. Garmon, 359 U. S. 236, and its history was recently summarized in Motor Coach Employees v. Lockridge, 403 U. S. 274, 290-291 (1971). . . .

However, a second line of pre-emption analysis has been developed in cases focusing upon the crucial inquiry whether Congress intended that the conduct involved be unregulated because left "to be controlled by the free play of economic forces." NLRB v. Nash-Finch Co., 404 U. S. 138, 144 (1971). Concededly this inquiry was not made in 1949 in the so-called *Briggs-Stratton* case. Automobile Workers v. Wisconsin Board, 336 U. S. 245 (1949), the decision of this Court heavily relied upon by the court below in reaching its decision that state regulation of the conduct at issue is not pre-empted by national labor law. In *Briggs-Stratton,* the union, in order to bring pressure on the employer during negotiations, adopted a plan whereby union meetings were called at irregular times during working hours without advance notice to the employer or any notice as to whether or when the workers would return. In a proceeding under the Wisconsin Employment Peace Act, the Wisconsin Employment Relations Board issued an order forbidding the union and its members from engaging in concerted efforts to interfere with production by those methods. This Court did not inquire whether Congress meant that such methods should be reserved to the union "to be controlled by the free play of economic forces." Rather, because these methods were "neither made a right under federal law nor a violation of it" the Court held that there "was no basis for denying to Wisconsin the power, in governing her internal affairs, to regulate" such conduct. *Id.,* at 265.

However, the *Briggs-Stratton* holding that state power is not preempted as to peaceful conduct neither protected by § 7 nor prohibited by § 8 of the federal Act, a holding premised on the statement that "[t]his conduct is either governable by the State or it is entirely ungoverned," *id.,* at 254, was undercut by subsequent decisions of this Court. For the Court soon recognized that a particular activity might be "protected" by federal law not only where it fell within § 7, but also when it was an activity that Congress intended to be "unrestricted by *any* governmental power to regulate" because it was among the permissible "economic weapons in reserve . . . actual exercise [of which] on occasion by the parties is part and parcel of the system that the Wagner and Taft-Hartley Acts have recognized." *NLRB* v. *Insurance Agents,* 361 U. S., at 488, 489 (emphasis added). "[T]he legislative purpose may ... dictate that certain activity 'neither protected nor prohibited' be privileged against state regulation." *Hanna Mining Co.* v. *Marine Engineers,* 382 U. S., at 187.

II. *Insurance Agents, supra,* involved a charge of a refusal by the union to bargain in good faith in violation of § 8(b)(3) of the Act. The charge was based on union activities that occurred during good-faith bargaining over the terms of a collective bargaining agreement. During the negotiations, the union directed concerted on-the-job activities by its members of a harassing nature designed to interfere with the conduct of the employer's business, for the avowed purpose of putting economic pressure on the employer to accede to the union's bargaining demands. ... We held that such tactics would not support a finding by NLRB that the union had failed to bargain in good faith as required by § 8(b)(3) and rejected the *per se* rule applied by the Board that use of "economically harassing activities" alone sufficed to prove a violation of that section. The Court assumed "that the activities in question were not 'protected' under § 7 of the Act," *id.,* at 483 n. 6, but held that the *per se* rule was beyond the authority of NLRB to apply. ... We noted further that "Congress has been rather specific when it has come to outlaw particular economic weapons on the part of unions" and "the activities here involved have never been specifically outlawed by Congress." *Id.,* at 498. Accordingly, the Board's claim "to power ... to distinguish among various economic pressure tactics and brand the ones at bar inconsistent with good-faith collective bargaining," *id.,* at 492, was simply inconsistent with the design of the federal scheme in which "the use of economic pressure by the parties to a labor dispute is ... part and parcel of the process of collective bargaining." *Id.,* at 495.

The Court had earlier recognized in pre-emption cases that Congress meant to leave some activities unregulated and to be controlled by the free play of economic forces. Garner v. Teamsters Union, 346 U. S. 485. ... Moreover, San Diego Unions v. Garmon, 359 U. S. 236, expressly recognized "the Board may decide that an activity is neither protected nor prohibited, and thereby raise the question whether such activity may be regulated by the States." *Id.,* at 245.

It is true, however, that many decisions fleshing out the concept of activities "protected" because Congress meant them to be "unrestricted by any governmental power to regulate," *Insurance Agents,* 361 U. S., at 488, involved review of *per se* NLRB rules applied in the regulation of the bargaining process. *E.g.,* NLRB v. American National Insurance Co., 343 U. S. 395 (1952); NLRB v. Insurance Agents, 361 U. S. 477; NLRB v. Drivers Union, 362 U. S. 274 (1960); NLRB v. Brown, 380 U. S. 378 (1965); American Ship Building Co. v. NLRB, 380 U. S. 300 (1965) ... But the analysis of *Garner* and *Insurance Agents* came full bloom in the pre-emption area in Teamsters Union v. Morton, 377 U. S. 252 (1964), which held pre-empted the application of state law to award damages for peaceful union secondary picketing. Although *Morton* involved conduct neither "protected nor prohibited" by § 7 or § 8 of the NLRA, we recognized the necessity of an inquiry whether " 'Congress occupied the field and closed it to state regulation.' " *Id.,* at 258. Central to *Morton's* analysis was the observation that "[i]n selecting which forms of economic pressure should be prohibited ..., Congress struck the 'balance ... between the uncontrolled power of management and labor to further their respective interests,' " *id.,* at 258-259, and that:

> "This weapon of self-help, permitted by federal law, formed an integral part of the petitioner's effort to achieve its bargaining goals during negotiations with the respondent. Allowing its use is a part of the balance struck by Congress between the conflicting interests of the union, the employees, the employer and the community. . . . If the Ohio law of secondary boycott can be applied to proscribe the same type of conduct which Congress focused upon but did not proscribe when it enacted § 303, the inevitable result would be to frustrate the congressional determination to leave this weapon of self-help available, and to upset the balance of power between labor and management expressed in our national labor policy. 'For a state to impinge on the area of labor combat designed to be free is quite as much an obstruction of federal policy as if the state were to declare picketing free for purposes or by methods which the federal Act prohibits.' Garner v. Teamsters Union, 346 U. S. 485, 500." *Morton, supra,* at 259-260.

Although many of our past decisions concerning conduct left by Congress to the free play of economic forces address the question in the context of union and employee activities, self-help is of course also the prerogative of the employer because he too may properly employ economic weapons Congress meant to be unregulable. . . . "[R]esort to economic weapons should more peaceful measures not avail" is the right of the employer as well as the employee, *American Ship Building Co.* v. *NLRB,* 380 U. S., at 317, and the State may not prohibit the use of such weapons or "add to an employer's federal legal obligations in collective bargaining" any more than in the case of employees. Cox, Labor Law Preemption Revisited, 85 Harv. L. Rev. 1337, 1365 (1972). See, *e.g.,* Beasley v. Food Fair, Inc., 416 U. S. 653 (1974). Whether self-help economic activities are employed by employer or union, the crucial inquiry regarding preemption is the same; whether "the exercise of plenary state authority to curtail or entirely prohibit self-help would frustrate effective implementation of the Act's processes." *Railroad Trainmen* v. *Jacksonville Terminal Co.,* 394 U. S., at 380.

III. There is simply no question that the Act's processes would be frustrated in the instant case were the State's ruling permitted to stand. The employer in this case invoked the Wisconsin law because unable to overcome the union tactic with its own economic self-help means. Although it did employ economic weapons putting pressure on the union when it terminated the previous agreement, it apparently lacked sufficient economic strength to secure its bargaining demands under "the balance of power between labor and management expressed in our national labor policy," *Teamsters Union* v. *Morton,* 377 U. S., at 260. But the economic weakness of the affected party cannot justify state aid contrary to federal law for, "as we have developed, the use of economic pressure by the parties to a labor dispute is not a grudging exception [under] . . . the [federal] Act; it is part and parcel of the process of collective bargaining." *Insurance Agents,* 361 U. S., at 495. The state action in this case is not filling "a regulatory void which Congress plainly assumed would not exist," *Hanna Mining Co.* v. *Marine Engineers,* 382 U. S., at 196 (BRENNAN, J., concurring). Rather, it is clear beyond question that Wisconsin "[entered] into the substantive aspects of the bargaining process to an extent Congress has not countenanced." *NLRB* v. *Insurance Agents, supra,* at 498.

Our decisions hold that Congress meant that these activities, whether of employer or employees, were not to be regulable by States any more than by the NLRB, for neither States nor the Board are "afforded flexibility in picking and choosing which economic devices of labor and management would be branded as unlawful." *Ibid.* Rather, both are without authority to attempt to "introduce some standard of properly 'balanced' bargaining power," *id.,* at 497, or to define "what economic sanctions might be permitted negotiating parties in an 'ideal' or 'balanced' state of collective bargaining." *Id.,* at 500. To sanction state regulation of such economic pressure deemed by the federal Act "desirabl[y] . . . left for the free play of contending economic forces, . . . is not merely [to fill] a gap [by] outlaw[ing] what federal law fails to outlaw; it is denying to one party to an economic contest a weapon that Congress meant him to have available." Lesnick, Preemption Reconsidered: The Apparent Reaffirmation of *Garmon,* 72 Col. L. Rev. 469, 478 (1972). Accordingly, such regulation by the State is impermissible because it " 'stands as an obstacle to the accomplishment and execution of the full purposes and objectives of Congress.' " Hill v. Florida, 325 U. S. 538, 542 (1945).

IV. There remains the question of the continuing vitality of *Briggs-Stratton. San Diego Unions* v. *Garmon,* 359 U. S., at 245 n. 4, made clear that the *Briggs-Stratton* approach to pre-emption is "no longer of general application." See also *Insurance Agents,* 361 U. S., at 493 n. 23. We hold today that the ruling of *Briggs-Stratton,* permitting state regulation of partial strike activities such as are involved in this case is likewise "no longer of general application."

Briggs-Stratton assumed "management . . . would be disabled from any kind of self-help to cope with these coercive tactics of the union" and could not "take any steps to resist or combat them without incurring the sanctions of the Act." 336 U. S., at 264. But as *Insurance Agents* held, where the union activity complained of is "protected," not because it is within § 7, but only because it is an activity Congress meant to leave unregulated, "the employer could have discharged or taken other appropriate disciplinary action against the employees participating." 361 U. S., at 493. Moreover, even were the activity presented in the instant case "protected" activity within the meaning of § 7,[14] economic weapons

---

[14] The assumption, *arguendo,* in *Insurance Agents* that the union activities involved were "unprotected" by § 7 reflected the fact that those activities included some bearing

were available to counter the union's refusal to work overtime, *e.g.,* a lockout, American Ship Building Co. v. NLRB, 380 U. S. 300, and the hiring of permanent replacements under NLRB v. Mackay Radio & Tel. Co., 304 U. S. 333 (1938). See Prince Lithograph Co., 205 N.L.R.B. 110, 115 (1973).

Although we are not unmindful of the demands of *stare decisis* and the "important policy considerations militat[ing] in favor of continuity and predictability in the law," Boys Markets, Inc. v. Retail Clerks, 398 U. S. 235, 240 (1970), *Briggs-Stratton* "stands as a significant departure from our . . . emphasis upon the congressional policy" central to the statutory scheme it has enacted, and since our later decisions make plain that *Briggs-Stratton* "does not further but rather frustrates realization of an important goal of our national labor policy," *Boys Markets, supra,* at 241, *Briggs-Stratton* is expressly overruled. Its authority "has been 'so restricted by our later decisions' . . . that [it] must be regarded as having 'been worn away by the erosion of time' . . . and of contrary authority" United States v. Raines, 362 U. S. 17, 26 (1960).

V. This survey of the extent to which federal labor policy and the federal Act have preempted state regulatory authority to police the use by employees and employers of peaceful methods of putting economic pressure upon one another compels the conclusion that the judgment of the Wisconsin Supreme Court must be reversed. It is not contended, and on the record could not be contended, that the union policy against overtime work was enforced by violence or threats of intimidation or injury to property. Workers simply left the plant at the end of their work shift and refused to volunteer for or accept overtime or Saturday work. In sustaining the order of the Wisconsin Commission, the Wisconsin Supreme Court relied on *Briggs-Stratton* as dispositive against the union's claim of preemption, 67 Wis. 2d, at 19; 226 N. W. 2d, at 206. The court held further that the refusal to work overtime was neither arguably protected under § 7 nor arguably prohibited under § 8 of the federal Act, 68 Wis. 2d, at 23-24, 226 N. W. 2d, at 208, an analysis which, as developed, is largely inapplicable to the circumstances of this case. *NLRB v. Insurance Agents* was distinguished on the ground that that case dealt only with NLRB power "to regulate . . . strike tactics" and left such "regulation . . . to the states." 67 Wis. 2d, at 22, 226 N. W. 2d, at 207.

---

at least a resemblance to the "sit-down" strike held unprotected in NLRB v. Fansteel Metallurgical Corp., 306 U. S. 240 (1939), and the "disloyal" activities held unprotected in NLRB v. Electrical Workers, 346 U. S. 464 (1953). See *Insurance Agents,* 361 U. S., at 492-494. The concerted refusal to work overtime presented in this case, however, is wholly free of such overtones.

It may be that case-by-case adjudication by the federal Board will ultimately result in the conclusion that some partial strike activities such as the concerted ban on overtime in the instant case, when unaccompanied by other aspects of conduct such as those present in *Insurance Agents* or those in *Briggs-Stratton* (overtones of threats and violence, 336 U. S., at 250 n. 8, and a refusal to specify bargaining demands, *id.,* at 249; see also *Insurance Agents, supra,* at 487 & n. 13), are "protected" activities within the meaning of § 7, although not so protected as to preclude the use of available countervailing economic weapons by the employer. . . .

Finally, the court rejected the union's argument relying on *Teamsters Union v. Morton* that the refusal to work overtime was affirmatively "permitted" under federal law, stating, "Congress has not 'focused upon' partial . . . strikes," and therefore "[p]olicing of such conduct is left wholly to the states." 67 Wis. 2d, at 26, 226 N. W. 2d, at 209.

Since *Briggs-Stratton* is today overruled, and as we hold further that the Union's refusal to work overtime is peaceful conduct constituting activity which must be free of regulation by the States if the congressional intent in enacting the comprehensive federal law of labor relations is not to be frustrated, the judgment of the Wisconsin Supreme Court is

Reversed.

MR. JUSTICE POWELL, with whom THE CHIEF JUSTICE joins, concurring. . . . I agree with the Court that the Wisconsin law, as applied in this case, is preempted since it directly curtails the self-help capability of the union and its members, resulting in a significant shift in the balance of free economic bargaining power struck by Congress. I write to make clear my understanding that the Court's opinion does not, however, preclude the States from enforcing, in the context of a labor dispute, "neutral" state statutes or rules of decision: state laws that are not directed toward altering the bargaining positions of employers or unions but which may have an incidental effect on relative bargaining strength. Except where Congress has specifically provided otherwise, the States generally should remain free to enforce, for example, their law of torts or of contracts, and other laws reflecting neutral public policy.* See Cox, Labor Law Preemption Revisited, 85 Harv. L. Rev. 1337, 1355-1356 (1972).

With this understanding, I join the opinion of the Court.

MR. JUSTICE STEVENS, with whom MR. JUSTICE STEWART and MR. JUSTICE REHNQUIST join, dissenting.

If the partial strike activity in this case were protected, or even arguably protected by § 7 of the National Labor Relations Act, the Court's conclusion would be supported by San Diego Unions v. Garmon, 359 U. S. 236. But in Automobile Workers v. Wisconsin Board (Briggs-Stratton), 336 U. S. 245, the Court rejected the argument that comparable activity was protected by § 7. And as I understand the Court's holding today, it assumes that this activity remains unprotected.[1] Moreover, if such activity

---

* State laws should not be regarded as neutral if they reflect an accommodation of the special interests of employers, unions, or the public in areas such as employee self-organization, labor disputes, or collective bargaining.

[1] I recognize that there is some ambiguity in the Court's discussion, *ante,* at 20-21, which first implies that the employer may take any appropriate disciplinary action, including discharge, since the union activity is unprotected by § 7, and then immediately casts doubt on this assurance to the employer by indicating that some economic weapons may be used in reprisal even if the activity is protected. The ambiguity of the Court's rationale is inconsistent with its assumption that the employer is wholly free to use economic self-help without fear of committing an unfair labor practice. In all events, while I recognize that

were prohibited or arguably prohibited by § 8 of the Act, the Court's conclusion would also be supported by *Garmon.* But ever since NLRB v. Insurance Agents, 361 U. S. 477, it has been clear that this activity is not even arguably prohibited.

If Congress had focused on the problems presented by partial strike activity, and enacted special legislation dealing with this subject matter, but left the form of the activity disclosed by this record unregulated, the Court's conclusion would be supported by Teamsters Union v. Morton, 377 U. S. 252. But this is not such a case. Despite the numerous statements in the Court's opinion about Congress' intent to leave partial strike activity wholly unregulated, I have found no legislative expression of any such intent nor any evidence that Congress has scrutinized such activity.[2]
. . .

If adherence to the rule of *Briggs-Stratton* would permit the States substantially to disrupt the balance Congress has struck between union and employer, I would readily join in overruling it. But I am not persuaded that partial strike activity is so essential to the bargaining process that the States should not be free to make it illegal.

Stability and predictability in the law are enhanced when the Court resists the temptation to overrule its prior decisions. It is particularly inappropriate to do so when the Court is purporting to implement the intent of Congress with respect to an issue that Congress has yet to address. Edelman v. Jordan, 415 U. S. 651, 671 n. 14. Finally, I am not nearly as sanguine as the Court about the likelihood that this decision will clarify or harmonize a fairly confused area of the law. In sum, I would adhere to prior precedent which is directly in point.

I may be misreading the Court's opinion, I assume that its holding rests on the predicate that the concerted refusal to work overtime in this case, like the partial strike activity in *Briggs-Stratton,* is unprotected by § 7.

[2] A scholar who has criticized *Briggs-Stratton* has observed: "The omission of a federal prohibition against 'quickie' strikes certainly could not have implied a desire that unions be free to embrace the tactic without restraint; congressional silence almost surely is attributable to the happy circumstance that no prohibition is urgently required because American labor unions have almost unanimously rejected such tactics." Cox, Labor Law Preemption Revisited, 85 Harv. L. Rev. 1337, 1347 (1972).

The Union argues that Congress focused upon partial strike activity during passage of the Taft-Hartley Act, 61 Stat. 136, relying upon a provision passed by the House, but rejected in the conference committee, that declared unlawful "any sit-down strike or other concerted interference with an employer's operations conducted by remaining on the employer's premises." H. R. 3020, 80th Cong., 1st Sess., § 12(a)(3)(A) (1947). See H. R. Rep. No. 245, 80th Cong., 1st Sess., 27-28, 43-44 (1947); H. R. Rep. No. 510, 80th Cong., 1st Sess., 38-39, 42-43, 58-59 (1947). The concerted refusal to work overtime in this case does not involve "concerted interference with an employer's operations conducted by remaining on the employer's premises."

TEAMSTERS LOCAL 24 v. OLIVER, 358 U.S. 283, 79 S. Ct. 297, 3 L. Ed. 2d 312 (1959). Teamster locals entered into a collective bargaining agreement with motor carriers operating in twelve midwestern states, including Ohio. The contract included a provision prescribing the minimum rental fee and other terms of the lease when a motor vehicle was leased to a carrier by an owner who drove his own vehicle for the carrier. At the suit of one owner driver, the Ohio courts enjoined a local and several carriers from giving effect to this provision, on the ground it violated the Ohio antitrust law as a form of price-fixing. The United States Supreme Court held that the provision in dispute dealt with a subject matter within the scope of "collective bargaining" under federal law, and that the Ohio antitrust law could not be applied to prevent the parties from carrying out their agreement on a matter "as to which federal law directs them to bargain." The Court reasoned that the purpose of the questioned clause was to protect the negotiated wage scale for employees driving carrier-owned vehicles. If owner drivers accepted inadequate rentals for their trucks, they would have to make up the excess operating costs from their compensation as drivers. This in effect would undercut the union's wage scale, and might invite a progressive curtailment of jobs through the gradual withdrawal of carrier-owned vehicles from service. Concluded the Court: "Of course, the paramount force of federal law remains even though it is expressed in the details of a contract federal law empowers the parties to make, rather than in terms of an enactment of Congress. . . . Clearly it is immaterial that the conflict is between federal labor law and the application of what the State characterizes as an anti-trust law. . . . [T]he conflict here is between the federally sanctioned agreement and state policy which seeks specifically to adjust relationships in the world of commerce."

NOTES

1. In Weber v. Anheuser-Busch, Inc., 348 U.S. 468 (1955), the Supreme Court set aside a state court injunction against a strike to force an employer to agree to assign certain repair work to machinists rather than carpenters. The strike had been found to violate Missouri's restraint of trade statute, after the NLRB had ruled it did not violate § 8(b)(4)(D) of the National Labor Relations Act. The Board had not passed on possible violations of subsections (A) or (B). The Supreme Court commented that if the union conduct did not fall within the prohibition of § 8 of the NLRA, it might fall within the protection of § 7, and rejected the employer's attempt to distinguish the *Garner* preemption decision on the ground that there the state was trying to regulate "labor relations as such."

2. Do *Weber* and *Oliver* mean that a state may not regulate, under laws of general application, union conduct arguably protected or prohibited by the NLRA, or matters contained in collective bargaining agreements? *See* Locomotive Engineers v. Chicago, Rock Island & Pac. R.R., 382 U.S. 423

(1966) (state "full-crew" laws not preempted by federal statute providing for binding arbitration of dispute over firemen). *See generally* Cox, *Federalism in the Law of Labor Relations,* 67 HARV. L. REV. 1297, 1324-31 (1954); Meltzer, *The Supreme Court, Congress, and State Jurisdiction Over Labor Relations,* 59 COLUM. L. REV. 6, 47-55 (1959).

3. Questions continue to arise as to whether various kinds of state regulations and actions interfere with the national labor policy and are accordingly preempted.

A court of appeals sitting *en banc* held (5-4) that a union had failed to state a cause of action in alleging that New Jersey officials had wrongfully interfered in collective bargaining between the union and several transit companies by threatening to halt state subsidies for any transit company that agreed to an "uncapped" cost-of-living clause or to a wage increase greater than that given to state employees. Amalgamated Transit Union v. Byrne, 568 F.2d 1025 (3d Cir. 1977).

In New York Telephone Co. v. New York State Dep't of Labor, 99 S. Ct. 1328 (U.S. 1979), the Supreme Court held that the federal preemption doctrine does not invalidate the New York unemployment compensation statute, which gives benefits to strikers after eight weeks. Three dissenting justices (Justice Powell, joined by Chief Justice Burger and Justice Stewart) thought that such payments were preempted because they substantially altered the economic balance of free collective bargaining, contrary to the policy of the national labor laws. However, the majority found that the legislative history of the National Labor Relations Act and the Social Security Act showed that Congress intended that the states be free to authorize or prohibit the payment of unemployment benefits to strikers. It is not clear what the impact of the *New York Telephone* case will be upon general federal preemption theory, since Justices Brennan, Blackmun, and Marshall only concurred in the result and did not agree with the reasoning process employed in the opinion of Justice Stevens, in which Justices White and Rehnquist joined.

Consider the following excerpts from the lead opinion of Mr. Justice Stevens:

I. The doctrine of labor law preemption concerns the extent to which Congress has placed implicit limits on "the permissible scope of state regulation of activity touching upon labor-management relations." . . . Although this case involves the exploration of those limits in a somewhat novel setting, it soon becomes apparent that much of that doctrine is of limited relevance in the present context.

There is general agreement on the proposition that the "animating force" behind the doctrine is a recognition that the purposes of the federal statute would be defeated if state and federal courts were free, without limitation, to exercise jurisdiction over activities that are subject to regulation by the National Labor Relations Board. . . The overriding interest in a uniform, nationwide interpretation of the federal statute by the centralized expert agency created by Congress not only demands that the NLRB's primary jurisdiction be protected; it also forecloses overlapping state enforcement of the prohibitions in § 8 of the Act, . . . as well as state interference with the exercise of rights protected by § 7 of the Act. . . . Consequently, almost all of the Court's labor law decisions in which state regulatory schemes have been found to be preempted have involved state efforts to regulate or to prohibit private conduct that was either protected by § 7, prohibited by § 8, or at least arguably so protected or prohibited.

In contrast to those decisions, there is no claim in this case that New York has sought to regulate or prohibit any conduct subject to the regulatory jurisdiction of the Labor Board under § 8. Nor are the petitioning employers pursuing any claim of interference with employee rights protected by § 7. The State simply authorized striking employees to receive unemployment benefits, and assessed a tax against the struck employers to pay for some of those benefits, once the economic welfare between the two groups reached its ninth week. Accordingly, beyond identifying the interest in national uniformity underlying the doctrine, the cases comprising the main body of labor preemption law are of little relevance in deciding this case.

There is, however, a pair of decisions in which the Court has held that Congress intended to forbid state regulation of economic warfare between labor and management, even though it was clear that none of the regulated conduct on either side was covered by the federal statute. In Teamsters Union v. Morton, 377 U. S. 252, the Court held that an Ohio court could not award damages against a union for peaceful secondary picketing even though the union's conduct was neither protected by § 7 nor prohibited by § 8. Because Congress had focused upon this type of conduct and elected not to proscribe it when § 303 of the Labor Management Relations Act was enacted, the Court inferred a deliberate legislative intent to preserve this means of economic warfare for use during the bargaining process.

More recently, in Lodge 76 v. Wisconsin Employment Relations Comm'n, 427 U. S. 132, the Court held that the state commission could not prohibit a union's concerted refusal to work overtime. Although this type of partial strike activity had not been the subject of special congressional consideration, as had the secondary picketing involved in Morton, the Court nevertheless concluded that it was a form of economic self-help that was "part and parcel of the process of collective bargaining" . . . that Congress implicitly intended to be governed only by the free play of economic forces. The Court identified the crucial inquiry in its preemption analysis in Lodge 76 as whether the exercise of state authority to curtail or entirely prohibit self-help would frustrate effective implementation of the policies of the National Labor Relations Act.

The economic weapons employed by labor and management in Morton, Lodge 76, and the present case are similar, and petitioners rely heavily on the statutory policy, emphasized in the former two cases, of allowing the free policy of economic forces to operate during the bargaining process. Moreover, because of the two-fold impact of § 592.1, which not only provides financial support to striking employees but also adds to the burdens of the struck employers, . . . we must accept the District Court's finding that New York's law, like the state action involved in *Morton* and *Lodge 76*, has altered the economic balance between labor and management.

But there is not a complete unity of state regulation in the three cases. Unlike *Morton* and *Lodge 76*, as well as the main body of labor preemption cases, the case before us today does not involve any attempt by the State to regulate or prohibit private conduct in the labor-management field. It involves a state program for the distribution of benefits to certain members of the public. Although the class benefited is primarily made up of employees in the State and the class providing the benefits is primarily made up of employers in the State, and although some of the members of each class are occasionally engaged in labor disputes, the general purport of the program is not to regulate the bargaining relationships between the two classes but instead to provide an efficient means of insuring employment security in the State. It is therefore clear that even though the statutory policy underlying *Morton* and *Lodge 76* lends support to petitioners' claim, the holdings in those cases are not controlling. The Court is being asked to extend the doctrine of labor law preemption into a new area. . . .

Section 591.1 is not a "State law . . . regulating the relations between employees, their union and their employer," as to which the reasons underlying the preemption doctrine have their "greatest force". . . . Instead, as discussed below, the statute is a law of general applicability. Although that is not a sufficient reason to exempt it from preemption, . . . our cases have consistently recognized that a congressional intent to deprive the States of their power to enforce such general laws is more difficult to infer than an intent to preempt laws directed specifically at concerted activity. . . .

Because New York's program, like those in other States, is financed in part by taxes assessed against employers, it is not strictly speaking a public welfare program. It nevertheless remains true that the payments to the strikers implement a broad state policy that does not primarily concern labor-management relations, but is implicated whenever members of the labor force become unemployed. Unlike most States, New York has concluded that the community interest in the security of persons directly affected by a strike outweighs the interest in avoiding any impact on a particular labor dispute. . . .

Congress has been sensitive to the importance of the States' interest in fashioning their own unemployment compensation programs and especially their own eligibility criteria. It is therefore appropriate to treat New York's statute with the same deference that we have afforded analogous state laws of general applicability that protect interests "deeply rooted in local feeling and responsibility." With respect to such laws, we have stated "that, in the absence of compelling congressional direction, we could not infer that Congress had deprived the States of the power to act." San Diego Building Trades Council v. Garmon, 359 U. S. 236, 244.

SEARS, ROEBUCK & CO. v. SAN DIEGO COUNTY DISTRICT COUNCIL OF CARPENTERS

Supreme Court of the United States
436 U.S. 180, 98 S. Ct. 1745, 56 L. Ed. 2d 209 (1978)

MR. JUSTICE STEVENS delivered the opinion of the Court.

The question in this case is whether the National Labor Relations Act, as amended, deprives a state court of the power to entertain an action by an employer to enforce state trespass laws against picketing which is arguably — but not definitely — prohibited or protected by federal law.

I. On October 24, 1973, two business representatives of respondent Union visited the department store operated by petitioner (Sears) in Chula Vista, Cal., and determined that certain carpentry work was being performed by men who had not been dispatched from the Union hiring hall. Later that day, the Union agents met with the store manager and requested that Sears either arrange to have the work performed by a contractor who employed dispatched carpenters or agree in writing to abide by the terms of the Union's master labor agreement with respect to the dispatch and use of carpenters. The Sears manager stated that he would consider the request, but he never accepted or rejected it.

Two days later the Union established picket lines on Sears' property. The store is located in the center of a large rectangular lot. The building is surrounded by walkways and a large parking area. A concrete wall at one end separates the lot from residential property; the other three sides adjoin public sidewalks which are adjacent to the public streets. The pickets patrolled either on the privately owned walkways next to the building or in the parking area a few feet away. They carried signs indicating that they were sanctioned by the "Carpenters Trade Union." The picketing was peaceful and orderly.

Sears' security manager demanded that the Union remove the pickets from Sears' property. The Union refused, stating that the pickets would not leave unless forced to do so by legal action. On October 29, Sears filed a verified complaint in the Superior Court of California seeking an injunction against the continuing trespass; the court entered a temporary restraining order enjoining the Union from picketing on Sears' property. The Union promptly removed the pickets to the public sidewalks. On November 21, 1973, after hearing argument on the question whether the Union's picketing on Sears' property was protected by state or federal law, the court entered a preliminary injunction. The California Court of Appeals affirmed. While acknowledging the preemption guidelines set forth in San Diego Union v. Garmon, 359 U. S. 236, the court held that the Union's continuing trespass fell within the longstanding exception for conduct which touched interests so deeply rooted in local feeling and responsibility that preemption could not be inferred in the absence of clear evidence of congressional intent.

The Supreme Court of California reversed. It concluded that the picketing was arguably protected by § 7 because it was intended to secure work for Union members and to publicize Sears' undercutting of the prevailing area standards for the employment of carpenters. The court reasoned that the trespassory character of the picketing did not disqualify it from arguable protection, but was merely a factor which the National Labor Relations Board would consider in determining whether or not it was in fact protected. The court also considered it "arguable" that the Union had engaged in recognitional picketing subject to § 8(b)(7)(C) of the Act which could not continue for more than 30 days without petitioning for a representation election. Because the picketing was both arguably protected by § 7 and arguably prohibited by § 8, the court held that state jurisdiction was preempted under the *Garmon* guidelines.

Since the Wagner Act was passed in 1935, this Court has not decided whether, or under what circumstances, a state court has power to enforce local trespass laws against a union's peaceful picketing. The obvious importance of this problem led us to grant certiorari in this case. . . .

II. We start from the premise that the Union's picketing on Sears' property after the request to leave was a continuing trespass in violation of state law. We note, however, that the scope of the controversy in the state court was limited. Sears asserted no claim that the picketing itself violated any state or federal law. It sought simply to remove the pickets from its property to the public walkways, and the injunction issued by the state court was strictly confined to the relief sought. Thus, as a matter of state law, the location of the picketing was illegal but the picketing itself was unobjectionable.

As a matter of federal law, the legality of the picketing was unclear. Two separate theories would support an argument by Sears that the picketing was prohibited by § 8 of the NLRA and a third theory would support an argument by the Union that the picketing was protected by § 7. Under each of these theories the Union's purpose would be of critical importance.

If an object of the picketing was to force Sears into assigning the carpentry work away from its employees to Union members dispatched from the hiring hall, the picketing may have been prohibited by § 8(b)(4)(D). Alternatively, if an object of the picketing was to coerce Sears into signing a prehire or members-only type agreement with the Union, the picketing was at least arguably subject to the prohibition on recognitional picketing contained in § 8(b)(7)(C). Hence, if Sears had filed an unfair labor practice charge against the Union, the Board's concern would have been limited to the question whether the Union's picketing had an objective proscribed by the Act; the location of the picketing would have been irrelevant.

On the other hand, the Union contends that the sole objective of its action was to secure compliance by Sears with area standards, and therefore the picketing was protected by § 7. Longshoremen v. Ariadne Co., 397 U. S. 195. Thus, if the Union had filed an unfair labor practice charge under § 8(a)(1) when Sears made a demand that the pickets leave its property, it is at least arguable that the Board would have found Sears guilty of an unfair labor practice.

Our second premise, therefore, is that the picketing was both arguably prohibited and arguably protected by federal law. The case is not, however, one in which "it is clear or may fairly be assumed" that the subject matter which the state court sought to regulate — that is, the location of the picketing — is either prohibited or protected by the Federal Act.

III. In San Diego Building Trades Council v. Garmon, 359 U. S. 236, the Court made two statements which have come to be accepted as the general guidelines for deciphering the unexpressed intent of Congress regarding the permissible scope of state regulation of activity touching upon labor-management relations. The first related to activity which is clearly protected or prohibited by the federal statute. The second articulated a more sweeping prophylactic rule:

"When an activity is arguably subject to § 7 or § 8 of the Act, the States as well as the federal courts must defer to the exclusive competence of the National Labor Relations Board if the danger of state interference with national policy is to be averted." Id., at 245.

While the Garmon formulation accurately reflects the basic federal concern with potential state interference with national labor policy, the history of the labor preemption doctrine in this Court does not support an approach which sweeps away state-court jurisdiction over conduct traditionally subject to state regulation without careful consideration of the relative impact of such a jurisdictional bar on the various interests affected. As the Court noted last Term:

"Our cases indicate . . . that inflexible application of the doctrine is to be avoided, especially where the State has a substantial interest in regulation of the conduct at issue and the State's interest is one that does not threaten undue interference with the federal regulatory scheme." Farmer v. Carpenters, 430 U. S. 290, 302.

Thus the Court has refused to apply the Garmon guidelines in a literal, mechanical fashion. This refusal demonstrates that "the decision to preempt . . . state court jurisdiction over a given class of cases must depend upon the nature of the particular interests being asserted and the effect upon the administration of national labor policies" of permitting the state court to proceed. Vaca v. Sipes, 386 U. S. 171, 180.

With this limitation in mind, we turn to the question whether preemption is justified in a case of this kind under either the arguably protected or the arguably prohibited branch of the Garmon doctrine.

While the considerations underlying the two categories overlap, they differ in significant respects and therefore it is useful to review them separately. We therefore first consider whether the arguable illegality of the picketing as a matter of federal law should oust the state court of jurisdiction to enjoin its trespassory aspects. Thereafter, we consider whether the arguably protected character of the picketing should have that effect.

IV. The leading case holding that when an employer grievance against a union may be presented to the National Labor Relations Board it is not subject to litigation in a state tribunal is Garner v. Teamsters Union, 346 U. S. 485. *Garner* involved peaceful organizational picketing which arguably violated § 8(b)(2) of the Federal Act. A Pennsylvania equity court held that the picketing violated the Pennsylvania Labor Relations Act and therefore should be enjoined. The State Supreme Court reversed because the union conduct fell within the jurisdiction of the National Labor Relations Board to prevent unfair labor practices.

This Court affirmed because Congress had "taken in hand this particular type of controversy . . . [i]n language almost identical to parts of the Pennsylvania statute." 346 U. S. at 488. Accordingly, the State, through its courts, was without power to "adjudge the same controversy and extend its own form of relief." *Id.,* at 489. This conclusion did not depend on any surmise as to "how the National Labor Relations Board might have decided this controversy had petitioners presented it to that body." *Ibid.* The precise conduct in controversy was arguably prohibited by federal law and therefore state jurisdiction was preempted. The reason for preemption was clearly articulated:

> . . . "A multiplicity of tribunals and a diversity of procedures are quite as apt to produce incompatible or conflicting adjudications as are different rules of substantive law. The same reasoning which prohibits federal courts from intervening in such cases, except by way of review or on application of the federal Board, precludes state courts from doing so." . . . 346 U. S., at 490-491 (footnote omitted). "The conflict lies in remedies . . . . [W]hen two separate remedies are brought to bear on the same activity, a conflict is imminent." *Id.,* at 498-499.

This reasoning has its greatest force when applied to state laws regulating the relations between employees, their union, and their employer. It may also apply to certain laws of general applicability which are occasionally invoked in connection with a labor dispute. Thus, a State's antitrust law may not be invoked to enjoin collective activity which is also arguably prohibited by the Federal Act. Capital Service, Inc. v. Labor Board, 347 U. S. 501; Weber v. Anheuser Busch, Inc., 348 U. S. 468. In each case, the pertinent inquiry is whether the two potentially conflicting statutes were "brought to bear on precisely the same conduct." *Id.,* at 479.

On the other hand, the Court has allowed a State to enforce certain laws of general applicability even though aspects of the challenged conduct were arguably prohibited by § 8 of the Taft-Hartley Act. Thus, for example, the Court has upheld state-court jurisdiction over conduct that touches "interests so deeply rooted in local feeling and responsibility that, in the absence of compelling congressional direction, we could not infer that Congress had deprived the States of the power to act." San Diego Building Trades Council v. Garmon, 359 U. S. 236, 244. See United Construction Workers v. Laburnum Construction Corp., 347 U. S. 656 (threats of violence); Youngdahl v. Rainfair, 335 U. S. 131 (violence); Automobile Workers v. Russell, 356 U. S. 634 (violence); Linn v. Plant Guard Workers, 383 U. S. 53 (libel); Farmer v. Carpenters, 430 U. S. 290 (intentional infliction of mental distress).

In *Farmer,* the Court held that a union member, who alleged that his union had engaged in a campaign of personal abuse and harassment against him, could maintain an action for damages against the union and its officers for the intentional infliction of emotional distress. One aspect of the alleged campaign was discrimination by the union in hiring hall referrals. Although such discrimination was arguably prohibited by §§ 8(b)(1)(A) and 8(b)(2) of the NLRA and therefore an unfair labor practice charge could have been filed with the Board, the Court permitted the state action to proceed.

The Court identified those factors which warranted a departure from the general preemption guidelines in the "local interest" cases. Two are relevant to the arguably *prohibited* branch of the *Garmon* doctrine.[25] First, there existed a significant state interest in protecting the citizen from the challenged conduct. Second, although the challenged conduct occurred in the course of a labor dispute and an unfair labor practice charge could have been filed, the exercise of state jurisdiction over the tort claim entailed little risk of interference with the regulatory jurisdiction of the Labor Board. Although the arguable federal violation and the state tort arose in the same factual setting, the respective controversies presented to the state and federal forums would not have been the same.[26]

---

[25] One of the factors identified by the Court was that the conduct giving rise to the state cause of action (*e.g.,* violence, libel or intentional infliction of emotional distress), if proven, would not be protected by § 7 of the NLRA, and therefore there existed no risk that state regulation of the conduct *alleged in the complaint* would result in prohibition of conduct protected by the Federal Act. To this extent, the instant case is not controlled by the decision in *Farmer.* Sears' state cause of action was for trespass, and some trespassory union activity may be protected under the Federal Act. See Part V, *infra.* However, two points must be made regarding the apparent distinction between *Farmer* and the case at bar. First, *Farmer* itself involved some risk that protected conduct would be regulated; for, while the complaint *alleged* outrageous conduct, there remained a possibility that the plaintiff would only have been able to *prove* a robust intra-union dispute and that the state tribunal would have found that sufficient to support recovery. Second, the distinction between this case and *Farmer,* to the extent that it exists, has significance only with respect to the arguably *protected* branch of the *Garmon* doctrine, which we discuss in Part V, it does not detract from the support *Farmer* provides for our conclusion with respect to preemption under the arguably *prohibited* branch of the doctrine.

[26] As the Court explained:
"If the charges in Hill's complaint were filed with the Board, the focus of any unfair labor practice proceeding would be on whether the statements or conduct on the part of union

The critical inquiry, therefore, is not whether the State is enforcing a law relating specifically to labor relations or one of general application but whether the controversy presented to the state court is identical to (as in *Garner*) or different from (as in *Farmer*) that which could have been, but was not, presented to the Labor Board. For it is only in the former situation that a state court's exercise of jurisdiction necessarily involves a risk of interference with the unfair labor practice jurisdiction of the Board which the arguably prohibited branch of the *Garmon* doctrine was designed to avoid.

In the present case, the controversy which Sears might have presented to the Labor Board is not the same as the controversy presented to the state court. If Sears had filed a charge, the federal issue would have been whether the picketing had a recognitional or work reassignment objective; decision of that issue would have entailed relatively complex factual and legal determinations completely unrelated to the simple question whether a trespass had occurred. Conversely, in the state action, Sears only challenged the location of the picketing; whether the picketing had an objective proscribed by federal law was irrelevant to the state claim. Accordingly, permitting the state court to adjudicate Sears' trespass claim would create no realistic risk of interference with the Labor Board's primary jurisdiction to enforce the statutory prohibition against unfair labor practices.

The reasons why preemption of state jurisdiction is normally appropriate when union activity is arguably prohibited by federal law plainly do not apply to this situation; they therefore are insufficient to preclude a State from exercising jurisdiction limited to the trespassory aspects of that activity.

V. The question whether the arguably protected character of the Union's trespassory picketing provides a sufficient justification for preemption of the state court's jurisdiction over Sears' trespass claim involves somewhat different considerations.

Apart from notions of "primary jurisdiction," there would be no objection to state courts and the NLRB exercising concurrent jurisdiction

---

officials discriminated or threatened discrimination against him in employment referrals for reasons other than failure to pay union dues. . . . Whether the statements or conduct of the respondents also caused Hill severe emotional distress and physical injury would play no role in the Board's disposition of the case, and the Board could not award Hill damages for pain, suffering, or medical expenses. Conversely, the state court tort action can be adjudicated without resolution of the 'merits' of the underlying labor dispute. Recovery for the tort of emotional distress under California law requires proof that the defendant intentionally engaged in outrageous conduct causing the plaintiff to sustain mental distress. . . . The state court need not consider, much less resolve, whether a union discriminated or threatened to discriminate against an employee in terms of employment opportunities. To the contrary, the tort action can be resolved without reference to any accommodation of the special interests of unions and members in the hiring hall context.

"On balance, we cannot conclude that Congress intended to oust state court jurisdiction over actions for tortious activity such as that alleged in this case. At the same time, we reiterate that concurrent state court jurisdiction cannot be permitted where there is a realistic threat of interference with the federal regulatory scheme." 430 U. S., at 304-305.

over conduct prohibited by the Federal Act. But there is a constitutional objection to state court interference with conduct actually protected by the Act. Considerations of federal supremacy, therefore, are implicated to a greater extent when labor-related activity is protected than when it is prohibited. Nevertheless, several considerations persuade us that the mere fact that the Union's trespass was *arguably* protected is insufficient to deprive the state court of jurisdiction in this case.

The first is the relative unimportance in this context of the "primary jurisdiction" rationale articulated in *Garmon.* In theory, of course, that rationale supports preemption regardless of which section of the NLRA is critical to resolving a controversy which may be subject to the regulatory jurisdiction of the NLRB. Indeed, at first blush, the primary jurisdiction rationale provides stronger support for preemption in this case when the analysis is focused upon the arguably protected, rather than the arguably prohibited, character of the Union's conduct. For to the extent that the Union's picketing was arguably protected, there existed a potential overlap between the controversy presented to the state court and that which the Union might have brought before the NLRB. Prior to granting any relief from the Union's continuing trespass, the state court was obligated to decide that the trespass was not actually protected by federal law, a determination which might entail an accommodation of Sears' property rights and the Union's § 7 rights. In an unfair labor practice proceeding initiated by the Union, the Board might have been required to make the same accommodation.

Although it was theoretically possible for the accommodation issue to be decided either by the state court or by the Labor Board, there was in fact no risk of overlapping jurisdiction in this case. The primary jurisdiction rationale justifies preemption only in situations in which an aggrieved party has a reasonable opportunity either to invoke the Board's jurisdiction himself or else to induce his adversary to do so. In this case, Sears could not directly obtain a Board ruling on the question whether the Union's trespass was federally protected. Such a Board determination could have been obtained only if the Union had filed an unfair labor practice charge alleging that Sears had interfered with the Union's § 7 right to engage in peaceful picketing on Sears' property. By demanding that the Union remove its pickets from the store's property, Sears in fact pursued a course of action which gave the Union the opportunity to file such a charge. But the Union's response to Sears' demand foreclosed the possibility of having the accommodation of § 7 and property rights made by the Labor Board; instead of filing a charge with the Board, the Union advised Sears that the pickets would only depart under compulsion of legal process.

In the face of the Union's intransigence, Sears had only three options: permit the pickets to remain on its property; forcefully evict the pickets; or seek the protection of the State's trespass laws. Since the Union's conduct violated state law, Sears legitimately rejected the first option. Since the second option involved a risk of violence, Sears surely had the right — perhaps even the duty — to reject it. Only by proceeding in state court, therefore, could Sears obtain an orderly resolution of the question whether the Union had a federal right to remain on its property.

The primary jurisdiction rationale unquestionably requires that when the same controversy may be presented to the state court or the NLRB, it must be presented to the Board. But that rationale does not extend to cases in which an employer has no acceptable method of invoking, or inducing the Union to invoke, the jurisdiction of the Board. We are therefore persuaded that the primary jurisdiction rationale does not provide a *sufficient* justification for preempting state jurisdiction over arguably protected conduct when the party who could have presented the protection issue to the Board has not done so and the other party to the dispute has no acceptable means of doing so.

This conclusion does not, however, necessarily foreclose the possibility that preemption may be appropriate. The danger of state interference with federally protected conduct is the principal concern of the second branch of the *Garmon* doctrine. To allow the exercise of state jurisdiction in certain contexts might create a significant risk of misinterpretation of federal law and the consequent prohibition of protected conduct. In those circumstances, it might be reasonable to infer that Congress preferred the costs inherent in a jurisdictional hiatus to the frustration of national labor policy which might accompany the exercise of state jurisdiction. Thus, the acceptability of "arguable protection" as a justification for preemption in a given class of cases is, at least in part, a function of the strength of the argument that § 7 does in fact protect the disputed conduct.

The Court has held that state jurisdiction to enforce its laws prohibiting violence, defamation, the intentional infliction of emotional distress, or obstruction of access to property, is not preempted by the NLRA. But none of those violations of state law involves protected conduct. In contrast, some violations of state trespass laws may be actually protected by § 7 of the Federal Act.

In NLRB v. Babcock & Wilcox, 351 U. S. 105, for example, the Court recognized that in certain circumstances nonemployee union organizers may have a limited right of access to an employer's premises for the purpose of engaging in organization solicitation. And the Court has indicated that *Babcock* extends to § 7 rights other than organizational activity, though the "locus" of the "accommodation of § 7 rights and the private property rights . . . may fall at differing points along the spectrum depending on the nature and strength of the respective § 7 rights and private property rights asserted in any given context." Hudgens v. NLRB, 424 U. S. 507.

For purpose of analysis we must assume that the Union could have proved that its picketing was, at least in the absence of a trespass, protected by § 7. The remaining question is whether under *Babcock* the trespassory nature of the picketing caused it to forfeit its protected status. Since it cannot be said with certainty that, if the Union had filed an unfair labor practice charge against Sears, the Board would have fixed the locus of the accommodation at the unprotected end of the spectrum, it is indeed "arguable" that the Union's peaceful picketing, though trespassory, was protected. Nevertheless, permitting state courts to evaluate the merits of an argument that certain trespassory activity is protected does not create an unacceptable risk of interference with conduct which the Board, and a court reviewing the Board's decision, would find protected. For while there are unquestionably examples of trespassory union activity in which the question whether it is protected is fairly debatable, experience under the Act teaches that such situations are rare and that a trespass is far more likely to be unprotected than protected.

Experience with trespassory organizational solicitation by nonemployees is instructive in this regard. While *Babcock* indicates that an employer may not always bar nonemployee union organizers from his property, his right to do so remains the general rule. To gain access, the union has the burden of showing that no other reasonable means of communicating its organizational message to the employees exists or that the employer's access rules discriminate against union solicitation. That the burden imposed on the Union is a heavy one is evidenced by the fact that the balance struck by the Board and the courts under the *Babcock* accommodation principle has rarely been in favor of trespassory organizational activity.

Even on the assumption that picketing to enforce area standards is entitled to the same deference in the *Babcock* accommodation analysis as organizational solicitation, it would be unprotected in most instances. While there does exist some risk that state courts will on occasion enjoin a trespass that the Board would have protected, the significance of this risk is minimized by the fact that in the cases in which the argument in favor of protection is the strongest, the union is likely to invoke the Board's jurisdiction and thereby avoid the state forum. Whatever risk of an erroneous state court adjudication does exist is outweighed by the anomalous consequence of a rule which would deny the employer access to any forum in which to litigate either the trespass issue or the protection issue in those cases in which the disputed conduct is least likely to be protected by § 7.

If there is a strong argument that the trespass is protected in a particular case, a union can be expected to respond to an employer demand to depart by filing an unfair labor practice charge; the protection question would then be decided by the agency experienced in accommodating the § 7 rights of unions and the property rights of employers in the context of a labor dispute. But if the argument for protection is so weak that it has virtually no chance of prevailing, a trespassing union would be well advised to avoid the jurisdiction of the Board and to argue that the protected character of its conduct deprives the state court of jurisdiction.

As long as the union has a fair opportunity to present the protection issue to the Labor Board, it retains meaningful protection against the risk of error in a state tribunal. In this case the Union failed to invoke the jurisdiction of the Labor Board, and Sears had no right to invoke that jurisdiction and could not even precipitate its exercise without resort to self-help. Because the assertion of state jurisdiction in a case of this kind does not create a significant risk of prohibition of protected conduct, we are unwilling to presume that Congress intended the arguably protected character of the Union's conduct to deprive the California courts of jurisdiction to entertain Sears' trespass action.

The judgment of the Supreme Court of California is therefore reversed and the case is remanded to that court for further proceedings not inconsistent with this opinion.

MR. JUSTICE BLACKMUN, concurring.

I join the Court's opinion, but add three observations:

1. The problem of a no-man's land in regard to trespassory picketing has been a troubling one in the past because employers have been unable to secure a Labor Board adjudication whether the picketing was "actually protected" under § 7 of the National Labor Relations Act except by resorting to self-help to expel the pickets and thereby inducing the union to file an unfair labor practice charge. The unacceptable possibility of precipitating violence in such a situation called into serious question the practicability there of the *Garmon* preemption test, see International Longshoremen's Association v. Ariadne Shipping Co., 397 U. S. 195, 202 (1970) (WHITE, J., concurring), despite the virtues of the *Garmon* test in ensuring uniform application of the standards of the NLRA.

In this case, however, the NLRB as *amicus curiae* has taken a position that narrows the no-man's land in regard to trespassory picketing, namely, that an employer's mere act of informing nonemployee pickets that they are not permitted on his property "would constitute a sufficient interference with rights arguably protected by Section 7 to warrant the General Counsel, had a charge been filed by the Union, in issuing a Section 8(a)(1) complaint" against the employer. Brief for NLRB as *Amicus Curiae* 18. Hence, if the union, once asked to leave the property, files a § 8(a)(1) charge, there is a practicable means of getting the issue of trespassory picketing before the Board in a timely fashion without danger of violence.

In this case, as the Court notes, the union failed to file an unfair labor practice charge after being asked to leave. In such a situation preemption cannot sensibly obtain because the "risk of an erroneous state court adjudication . . . is outweighed by the anomalous consequence of a rule which would deny the employer access to any forum in which to litigate either the trespass issue or the protection issue." *Ante,* at 26. It should be made clear, however, that the logical corollary of the Court's reasoning is that if the union *does* file a charge upon being asked by the employer to leave the employer's property and continues to process the charge expeditiously, state court jurisdiction is preempted until such time as the General Counsel declines to issue a complaint or the Board, applying the standards of NLRB v. Babcock & Wilcox Co., 351 U. S. 105 (1956), rules against the union and holds the picketing to be unprotected. . . .

2. The opinion correctly observes, . . . that in implementing this Court's decision in *Babcock* the NLRB only occasionally has found trespassory picketing to be protected under § 7. That observation is important, as is noted, . . . in that even the existence of a no-man's land

may not justify departure from *Garmon's* preemption standard if the exercise of state court jurisdiction portends frequent interference with actually protected conduct. But in its conclusion that trespassory picketing has been found in "experience under the Act" to be only "rare[ly]" protected and "far more likely to be unprotected than protected," . . . I take the opinion merely to be observing what the Board's past experience has been, not as glossing how the Board must treat the *Babcock* test in the future, either in regard to organizational picketing or other sorts of protected picketing. . . .

3. The acceptability of permitting state court jurisdiction over "arguably protected" activities where there is a jurisdictional no-man's land depends, as the Court notes, on whether the exercise of state court jurisdiction is likely to interfere frequently with actually protected conduct. The likelihood of such interference will depend in large part on whether the state courts take care to provide an adversary hearing *before* issuing any restraint against union picketing activities. In this case, Sears filed a verified complaint seeking an injunction against the picketing on October 29, 1973. The Superior Court of California entered a temporary restraining order that day. So far as the record reveals, the union was not accorded a hearing until November 16, on the order to show cause why a preliminary injunction should not be entered. The issue of a prompt hearing was apparently not raised before the Superior Court and was not raised on appeal, and hence does not enter into our judgment here approving the exercise of state court jurisdiction. But it may be remiss not to observe that in labor-management relations, where *ex parte* proceedings historically were abused, see F. Frankfurter and N. Greene, The Labor Injunction 60, 64-66 (1930), it is critical that the state courts provide a prompt adversary hearing, preferably before any restraint issues and in all events within a few days thereafter, on the merits of the § 7 protection question. Labor disputes are frequently short-lived, and a temporary restraining order issued upon *ex parte* application may, if in error, render the eventual finding of § 7 protection a hollow vindication.

Mr. Justice Powell, concurring.

Although I join the Court's opinion, Mr. Justice Blackmun's concurrence prompts me to add a word as to the "no-man's land" discussion with respect to trespassory picketing. Mr. Justice Blackmun, relying on the *amicus brief* of the National Labor Relations Board (Board), observes that "there is a practicable means of getting the issue of trespassory picketing before the Board in a timely fashion without danger of violence," . . . if the union — having been requested to leave the property — files a § 8(a)(1) charge. . . .

If a § 8(a)(1) charge is filed, nothing is likely to happen "in a timely fashion." The Board cannot issue, or obtain from the federal courts, a restraining order directed at the picketing. And it may take weeks for the General Counsel to decide whether to issue a complaint. Meanwhile, the "no-man's land" prevents all recourse to the courts, and is an open invitation to self-help. I am unwilling to believe that Congress intended, by its silence in the Act, to create a situation where there is no forum to which the parties may turn for orderly interim relief in the face of a potentially explosive situation. . . .

In sum, I do not agree with MR. JUSTICE BLACKMUN that "the logical corollary of the Court's reasoning" in its opinion today is that state-court jurisdiction is preempted forthwith upon the filing of a charge by the union. I would not join the Court's opinion if I thought it fairly could be read to that effect.

MR. JUSTICE BRENNAN, with whom MR. JUSTICE STEWART and MR. JUSTICE MARSHALL join, dissenting.

The Court concedes that both the objective and the location of the Union's peaceful, nonobstructive picketing of Sears' store may have been protected under the National Labor Relations Act. Therefore, despite the Court's transparent effort to disguise it, faithful application of the principles of labor law preemption established in San Diego Trades Council v. Garmon, 359 U. S. 236 (1959), would compel the conclusion that the California Superior Court was powerless to enjoin the Union from picketing on Sears' property: that the trespass was arguably protected is determinative of the state court's lack of jurisdiction, whether or not preemption limits an employer's remedies. . . .

By holding that the arguably protected character of union activity will no longer be sufficient to preempt state court jurisdiction, the Court creates an exception of indeterminate dimensions to a principle of labor law preemption that has been followed for at least two decades. Now, when the employer lacks a "reasonable opportunity" to have the Board consider whether the challenged *aspect* of the employee conduct is protected and when employees having that opportunity have not invoked the Board's jurisdiction, a state court will have jurisdiction to enjoin arguably protected activity if "the risk of erroneous adjudication by it does not outweigh the anomalous consequence [of denying a remedy to the employer]." . . . In making this rather amorphous determination, the lower courts apparently are to consider the strength of the argument that § 7 in fact protects the arguably protected activity, their own assessments of their ability correctly to determine the underlying labor law issue, and the strength of the state interest in affording the employer an opportunity to have a state court restrain the arguably protected conduct.

This drastic abridgement of established principles is unjustified and unjustifiable. The *Garmon* test, itself fashioned after some 15 years of judicial experience with jurisdictional conflicts that threatened national labor policy, see Motor Coach Employees v. Lockridge, 403 U. S. 270, 290-291 (1971), has provided stability and predictability to a particularly complex area of the law for nearly 20 years. Thus, the most elementary notions of *stare decisis* dictate that the test be reconsidered only upon a compelling showing, based on actual experience, that the test disserves important interests. Emphatically, that showing has not been and cannot be made. Rather, the *Garmon* test has proved to embody an entirely acceptable, and probably the best possible, accommodation of the competing state-federal interests. That an employer's remedies in consequence may be limited, while anomalous to the Court, produces no positive social harm; on the contrary, the limitation on employer remedies is fully justified both by the ease of application of the test by thousands of state and federal judges and by its effect of averting the danger that state courts may interfere with national labor policy. In sharp contrast, today's decision creates the certain prospect of state-court interference that may seriously erode § 7's protections of labor activities. Indeed, the most serious objection to the decision today is not that it is contrary to the teachings of *stare decisis* but rather that the Court's attempt to create a narrow exception to the principles of *Garmon* promises to be applied by the lower courts so as to disserve the interests protected by the national labor laws.

I. The Act's treatment of picketing illustrates the nature of the generic problem, and at the same time highlights the issue in this case. While this Court has never held that the prescription of detailed procedures for the restraint of specific types of picketing and the provision that other types of picketing are protected implies that picketing is to be free from all restraint under state law, see, *e. g.,* Automobile Workers v. Russell, 356 U. S. 634 (1958) (state courts may restrain violent conduct on picket lines), it by the same token necessarily is true that to permit local adjudications, without limitation, of the legality of picketing would threaten intolerable interference with the interests protected by the Act. As the Court recognizes, the nature of the threatened interference differs depending on whether the picketing implicates the Act's prohibitions or its protections. . . . As to arguably prohibited picketing, there is a risk that the state court might misinterpret or misapply the federal prohibition and restrain conduct that Congress may have intended to be free from governmental restraint. But, even when state courts can be depended upon accurately to determine whether conduct is in fact prohibited, local adjudication may disrupt the congressional scheme by resulting in different forms of relief than would adjudication by the NLRB. By providing that an expert, centralized agency would administer the Act, Congress quite plainly evidenced an intention that, ordinarily at least, this expert agency should, on the basis of its experience with labor matters, determine the remedial implications of violations of the Act. If state courts were permitted to administer all the Act's prohibitions, the divergencies in relief would add up to significant departures from federal policy. These considerations led the Court to fashion the rule, announced in *Garmon, supra,* at 245, that state courts have no jurisdiction over "arguably prohibited" conduct.

This aspect of *Garmon* has never operated as a flat prohibition. There are circumstances in which state courts can be depended upon accurately to determine whether the underlying conduct is prohibited and in which Congress cannot be assumed to have intended to oust state-court jurisdiction. Illustrative are decisions holding that States may regulate mass picketing, obstructive picketing, or picketing that threatens or results in violence. . . . Because violent tortious conduct on a picket line is prohibited by § 8(b) and because state courts can reliably determine whether such conduct has occurred without considering the merits of the underlying labor dispute, allowing local adjudications of these tort actions could neither fetter the exercise of rights protected by the Act nor otherwise interfere with the effective administration of the federal scheme. And the possible inconsistency of remedy is not alone a sufficient reason for preempting state-court jurisdiction. In view of the historic state interest in "such traditionally local matters as public safety and order," Allen-Bradley Local v. Wisconsin Empl. Rel. Bd., [315 U. S. 740] at 749, the Act could not, in the absence of a clear statement to the contrary, be construed as precluding the imposition of different, even harsher, state remedies in such cases. See *Automobile Workers* v. *Russell, supra,* at 641-642. Indeed, in view of the delay attendant upon resort to the Board, it could well produce positive harm to prohibit state jurisdiction in these circumstances. Our decisions leave no doubt that exceptions to the *Garmon* principle are to be recognized only in comparable circumstances. See Farmer v. Carpenters, 430 U. S. 290, 297-301 (1977); Vaca v. Sipes, 386 U. S. 171 (1967); Linn v. Plant Guard Workers, 383 U. S. 53 (1966).

When, on the other hand, the underlying conduct may be *protected* by the Act, the risk of interference with the federal scheme is of a different character. The danger of permitting local adjudications is not that timing or form of relief might be different than the Board would administer, but rather that the local court might restrain conduct that is in fact protected by the Act. This might result not merely from attitudinal differences but even more from unfair procedures or lack of expertise in labor relations matters. The present case illustrates both the nature and magnitude of the danger. Because the location of employee picketing is often determinative of the meaningfulness of the employees' ability to engage in effective communication with their intended audience, employees often have the right to engage in picketing at particular locations, including the private property of another. See Hudgens v. NLRB, 424 U. S. 507 (1975); Scott Hudgens, 230 N.L.R.B. No. 73 (1977); *cf. NLRB v. Babcock & Wilcox Co., supra.* The California Superior Court here entered an order, *ex parte,* broad enough to prohibit all effective picketing of Sears' store for a period of 35 days. See opinion of my Brother BLACKMUN. . . . Since labor disputes are usually short lived, see *ibid.,* this possibly erroneous order may well have irreparably altered the balance of the competing economic forces by prohibiting the Union's use of a permissible economic weapon at a crucial time. Obviously it is not lightly to be inferred that a Congress that provided elaborate procedures for restraint of prohibited picketing and that failed to provide an employer with a remedy against otherwise unprotected picketing could have contemplated that local tribunals with histories of insensitivity to the organizational interests of employees be permitted effectively to enjoin protected picketing.

In recognition of this fact, this Court's efforts in the area of labor law preemption have been largely directed to developing durable principles to ensure that local tribunals not be in a position to restrain protected conduct. Because the Court today appears to have forgotten some of the lessons of history, it is appropriate to summarize this Court's efforts. The first approach to be tried — and abandoned — was for this Court to proceed on a case by case basis and determine whether each particular final state-court ruling "does, or might reasonably be thought to, conflict, in some relevant manner with federal policy." *Motor Coach Employees* v. *Lockridge, supra,* at 290-291; see Automobile Workers v. Wisconsin Empl. Rel. Bd., 336 U. S. 245 (1949). Not surprisingly, such an effort proved institutionally impossible. Because of the infinite combinations of events that implicate the central protections of the Act, this Court could not, without largely abdicating its other responsibilities, hope to determine on an ad hoc, generic situation by generic situation, basis whether applications of state laws threatened national labor policy. In any case, such an approach necessarily disserved national labor policy because decision by this Court came too late to repair the damage that an erroneous decision would do to the congressionally established balance of power and was no substitute for decision in the first instance by the Board. The Court soon concluded that protecting national labor policy from disruption or defeat by conflicting local adjudications demanded broad principles of labor law preemption, easily administered by state and federal courts throughout the Nation, that would minimize, if not eliminate entirely, the possibility of decisions of local tribunals that irreparably injure interests protected by § 7. The only rule [6] satisfying these dual requirements was *Garmon*'s flat prohibition: "[w]hen an activity is arguably protected by § 7 of the Act . . . the State as well as the federal courts must defer to the exclusive competence of the Board." *Garmon, supra,* at 245.

While there is some unavoidable uncertainty concerning the arguably *prohibited* prong of *Garmon,* I emphasize that it has heretofore been absolutely clear that there is no state power to deal with conduct that is a central concern of the Act and arguably *protected* by it, see *Longshoremen* v. *Ariadne Co., supra; Garmon, supra; Fairlawn Meat, supra; Guss, supra.* As the Court itself recognizes, . . . none of the *Garmon* exceptions have ever been or could ever be applied to local attempts to restrain such conduct. But the *Garmon* approach to "arguably protected" activity does not "sweep [. . .] away state-court jurisdiction over conduct traditionally subject to state regulation without careful consideration of the relative impact of such a jurisdictional bar on the various interests affected." . . . Quite the contrary such careful consideration is subsumed by the determination whether the underlying conduct may be protected by § 7. By enacting § 7, Congress necessarily intended to preempt certain state laws: *e.g.,* those prohibiting concerted activities as conspiracies or unlawful restraints of trade. In any instance in which it can

---

[6] A second approach was suggested and rejected by *Garmon* itself: that state-court jurisdiction be preempted only when "it is clear or fairly may be assumed that the activities which a State purports to regulate are protected by § 7 of the Act." *Id.,* at 244. This Court recognized that state and federal courts, quite simply, lack the familiarity and requisite sensitivity to labor law matters to be counted on accurately to determine which combinations of facts could "fairly be assumed" to fall within the ambit of § 7.

seriously be maintained that the congressionally established scheme protects the employee activity, the assessment of the relative weight of the competing state and federal interests has to be regarded as having been made by Congress. By drafting the statute so as to permit a Board determination that the underlying conduct is in fact within the ambit of § 7's protections, Congress necessarily indicated its view that the historic state interest in regulating the conduct, however defined, may have to yield to the attainment of other objectives and that the State interest thus must be regarded as less than compelling. And, of course, there is necessarily a possibility that to permit state-court jurisdiction over arguably protected conduct could fetter the exercise of rights protected by the Act and otherwise interfere with the congressional scheme. A local tribunal could recognize an activity as arguably protected, yet, given its attitude towards organized labor, lack of expertise in labor matters, and insensitive procedures, misapply or misconceive the Board's decisional criteria and restrain conduct that is within the ambit of § 7. . . .

IV. But what is far more disturbing than the specific holding in this case is its implications for different generic situations. Whatever the shortcomings of *Garmon,* none can deny the necessity for a rule in this complex area that is capable of uniform application by the lower courts. The Court's new exception to *Garmon* cannot be expected to be correctly applied by those courts and thus most inevitably will threaten erosion of the goal of uniform administration of the national labor laws. Even though the Court apparently intends to create only a very narrow exception to *Garmon* — largely if not entirely limited to situations in which the employer first requested the nonemployees engaged in area standards picketing on the employer's property to remove the pickets from the employer's land and the union did not respond by filing § 8(a)(1) unfair labor practice charges — the approach the Court today adopts cannot be so easily cabined and thus threatens intolerable disruption of national labor policy.

Because § 8(b) only affords an employer a remedy against certain types of unprotected employee activity, there necessarily will be a myriad of circumstances in which an employer will be confronted with possibly unprotected employee or union conduct, and yet be unable directly to invoke the Board's processes to receive a determination of the protected character of the conduct. Today's decision certainly opens the door to a conclusion by state and federal courts that the Court's new exception applies in any situation where the employer has requested that the labor organization cease what the employer claims is unprotected conduct and the union has not responded by filing a § 8(a)(1) charge. In that circumstance, today's decision sanctions a three-step process by the state or federal court.

First, the court must inquire whether the employer had a "reasonable opportunity" to force a Board determination. What constitutes a "reasonable opportunity"? I have to assume from today's decision that the employer can never be deemed to have an acceptable opportunity when nonemployees are engaged in the arguably protected activity. But what if employees are involved? Will the fact that the employer can provoke the filing of an unfair labor practice charge by disciplining the employee always constitute an acceptable alternative? Perhaps so, but the Court provides no guidance that can help the local judges. Some may believe that the fact that any discipline will enhance the seriousness of the unfair labor practice renders that course unacceptable. Similarly, what of the instances in which employer discipline might not, under the circumstances, provoke the filing of a charge: e. g., if an economic strike were in progress?

Second, if the lower court concludes that the employer did not have an acceptable means of placing the protection issue before the Board, it must then proceed to inquire whether, in light of its assessment of the strength of the argument that § 7 might protect the generic type of conduct involved, there is a substantial likelihood that its adjudication will be incompatible with national labor policy. This is a particularly onerous task to assign to judges having no special expertise or specialized sensitivity in the application of the federal labor laws, and it is not clairvoyant to predict that many local tribunals will misconceive the relevant criteria and erroneously conclude that they are capable of correctly applying the labor laws. With all respect, the Court's opinion proves my point. As I have already observed, in concluding that peaceful picketing upon Sears' walkway was more likely to be unprotected than protected, the Court makes an entirely unfounded assumption concerning the approach the Board is likely to apply to the organizational activities of nonemployees at shopping centers. Since the great majority of state and federal judges around the Nation rarely if ever have this Court's exposure to the federal labor laws, local tribunals surely will commit far more grievous errors in assessing the likelihood that its adjudication will subvert national labor policy. But the final step in the Court's new preemption inquiry is the most troublesome: the range of circumstances in which local tribunals might conclude that the anomaly of denying an employer a remedy outweighs the risk of erroneous determinations by the state courts is limitless. Many erroneous determinations of nonpreemption are certain to occur, and the local adjudications of the protection issues will inevitably often be inconsistent and contrary to national policy. . . .

NOTES

1. In Farmer v. Carpenters, 430 U.S. 290 (1977), discussed in *Sears, Roebuck,* the Supreme Court held that the NLRA does not preempt a state court tort action by a union member against the union and its officials to recover damages for the intentional infliction of emotional distress through "frequent public ridicule" and "incessant verbal abuse." But a verdict could not be based on evidence of a discriminatory refusal to dispatch him to any but the briefest and least desirable jobs.

2. In Linn v. Plant Guard Workers, 383 U.S. 53 (1966), also mentioned in the *Sears* case, the Supreme Court held that state libel suits based on defamatory statements made in the course of a union organizing campaign are not preempted. The Court noted the compelling state interest involved — a matter so deeply rooted in local feeling and responsibility that it cannot be assumed that Congress had deprived the states of the power to act. However, the Court limited the availability of state remedies for libel to those instances in which the complainant can show that the defamatory statements were circulated with malice and caused him damage. "The standards enunciated in New York Times v. Sullivan, 376 U.S. 254 (1964), are adopted by analogy rather than by constitutional compulsion. We apply the malice test to effectuate the statutory design with respect to preemption. Construing the Act to permit recovery of damages in a state cause of action only for defamatory statements published with knowledge of their falsity or with reckless disregard of whether they were true or false guards against abuse of libel actions and unwarranted intrusion upon free discussion envisioned by the Act."

In Letter Carriers Branch 496 v. Austin, 418 U.S. 264 (1974), decided under E. O. 11491, applicable to federal employees, the Supreme Court held that the *Linn* partial preemption doctrine requires a state court to instruct on "malice" in terms of the reckless-or-knowing falsehood test of *New York Times* rather than in common-law terms. The Court concluded that a union was protected by the federal labor laws in listing plaintiffs as scabs under a heading containing Jack London's colorful definition of "The Scab," which includes such epithets as "tumor of rotten principles" and "traitor."

Would the *Linn* standards apply to a libel committed in a collective bargaining session or in the processing of a contract grievance, or should union and employer statements in such circumstances be regarded as "unqualifiedly privileged"? *See* General Motors Corp. v. Mendicki, 367 F.2d 66 (10th Cir. 1966). *See generally* Currier, *Defamation in Labor Disputes: Preemption and the New Federal Common Law,* 53 VA. L. REV. 1 (1967).

3. Does the *Sears* case represent just another narrow exception to the general principles of *Garmon* — or does it indicate a major new approach, giving greater access to state courts? *See* Goetz, *Labor Law Decisions of The Supreme Court, 1977-78 Term,* 98 L.R.R. 325 (1978) ("takes the law of federal preemption down a strange new path . . . could significantly alter the relationship between state and federal regulation of labor relations"); Williams, *Supreme Court's Labor Law Decisions, 1977-78 Term,* 99 L.R.R. 204 (1978) (*Sears* appears to be not as broad as it first seems).

Has the preemption doctrine, as developed by the Supreme Court, achieved a proper balance of national and local interests? Has it been too conceptualistic? Do decisions like *Sears, Farmer,* and *Linn* afford the states too great an opportunity to interfere with national labor policy? Have the states been overly restricted in dealing with matters of vital local concern, for example, strikes in public utilities? Have the states, in the area of labor relations, been unwisely deprived of their traditional function as "laboratories" for social experimentation? Is there a need for more congressional involvement in fixing the boundaries of federal-state jurisdiction?

A few of the leading articles on federal-state relations in labor law are Cox, *Federalism in the Law of Labor Relations,* 67 HARV. L. REV. 1297 (1954); Cox, *Labor Law Preemption Revisited,* 85 HARV. L. REV. 1337 (1972); Kirby, *Constitutional Issues in Labor Law: Federal Preemption in Labor Relations,* 63 NW. U.L. REV. 1 (1968); Lesnick, *Preemption Reconsidered: The Apparent Reaffirmation of Garmon,* 72 COLUM. L. REV. 469 (1972); Meltzer, *The Supreme Court, Congress, and State Jurisdiction Over Labor Relations* (pts. 1 & 2), 59 COLUM. L. REV. 6, 269 (1959); Michelman, *State Power to Govern Concerted Employee Activities,* 74 HARV. L. REV. 641 (1961); Smith & Clark, *Reappraisal of the Role of the States in Shaping Labor Relations Law,* 1965 WIS. L. REV. 411; Updegraff, *Preemption, Predictability and Progress in Labor Law,* 17 HASTINGS L.J. 473 (1966); Wellington, *Labor and the Federal System,* 26 U. CHI. L. REV. 542 (1959).

Preemption problems raised by the enforcement of collective bargaining agreements, the union duty of fair representation, and state right-to-work laws are covered in the later sections dealing with those particular topics.

PART FOUR
COLLECTIVE BARGAINING

ALBERT REES, THE ECONOMICS OF TRADE UNIONS 79, 94-96, 194-95 (1962)*

My own best guess of the average effects of all American unions on the wages of their members in recent years would lie somewhere between 10 and 15 per cent. . . .

Many people view trade unions as a device for increasing the worker's share in the distribution of income at the expense of capital; that is, at the expense of the receivers of rent, interest, and profits. Attempts to test this view, which is often expressed by the unions themselves, have led to a number of studies of the effect of unions on labor's share. The studies to date must be regarded as highly inconclusive; no union effect on labor's share can be discovered with any consistency. . . .

It may seem very strange that statistical studies can find a considerable effect of unions on wages and none on labor's share. On further consideration, however, this result is quite reasonable. . . . [A] successful union will not necessarily raise labor's share even in its own industry. The wage bill will rise following a wage increase if the demand for labor is inelastic (that is, if the percentage reduction in employment is smaller than the percentage increase in wages) and this will raise labor's share in the short run. But as time passes the employer will tend to substitute capital for labor. . . . In extreme cases, total wage payments may fall as employment contracts so that they are smaller than they were before the wage increase. . . . It is thus entirely possible for a union simultaneously to raise the relative wages of its members and to reduce their aggregate share of income arising in their industry. . . .

If the union is viewed solely in terms of its effect on the economy, it must in my opinion be considered an obstacle to the optimum performance of our economic system. It alters the wage structure in a way that impedes the growth of employment in sectors of the economy where productivity and income are naturally high and that leaves too much labor in low-income sectors of the economy like southern agriculture and the least skilled service trades. It benefits most those workers who would in any case be relatively well off, and while some of this gain may be at the expense of the owners of capital, most of it must be at the expense of consumers and the lower-paid workers. Unions interfere blatantly with the use of the most productive techniques in some industries, and this effect is probably not offset by the stimulus to higher productivity furnished by some other unions.

Many of my fellow economists would stop at this point and conclude that unions are harmful and that their power should be curbed. I do not agree that one can judge the value of a complex institution from so narrow

---

* Reprinted with the permission of the University of Chicago Press.

a point of view. Other aspects of unions must also be considered. The protection against the abuse of managerial authority given by seniority systems and grievance procedures seems to me to be a union accomplishment of the greatest importance. So too is the organized representation in public affairs given the worker by the political activities of unions. . . . If the job rights won for workers by unions are not conceded by the rest of society simply because they are just, they should be conceded because they help to protect the minimum consensus that keeps our society stable. In my judgment, the economic losses imposed by unions are not too high a price to pay for their successful performance of this role.[1]

JOHN T. DUNLOP, THE SOCIAL UTILITY OF COLLECTIVE BARGAINING, in CHALLENGES TO COLLECTIVE BARGAINING 172-79 (Ulman ed. 1967)*

My own summary appraisal would state that our collective bargaining system must be classified as one of the more successful distinctive American institutions along with the family farm, our higher educational system and constitutional government of checks and balances. The industrial working class has been assimilated into the mainstream of the community, and has altered to a degree the values and direction of the community, without disruptive conflict or alienation and with a stimulus to economic efficiency. This is no mean achievement in an industrial society. The institution faces, however, new challenges in the generation ahead. . . .

The public vision of collective bargaining highlights the large strike, the public debate and invective and the legislative investigation. The routine negotiations, the smaller scale and local relationships, the parties who shun publicity, and technical developments escape all but the specialists. Moreover, the press does not report or interpret, and the public does not understand, many of the most significant functions which collective bargaining performs. It would be remiss not to call attention to a few of these unappreciated contributions.

1. One of the major activities of collective bargaining involves the determination of priorities *within* each side in the bargaining process. The view that a homogeneous union negotiates with a homogeneous management or association is erroneous and mischievous. A great deal of the complexity and beauty of collective bargaining involves the process of compromise and assessment of priorities within each side. In an important sense collective bargaining typically involves three coincidental bargains — the rejection of some claims and the assignment of priorities to others within the union, an analogous process of assessing priorities and

---

[1] For other views, see R. Lester, Economics of Labor 292-330, 597-602 (2d ed. 1964); L. Reynolds, Labor Economics and Labor Relations 228-50, 519-31 (7th ed. 1978); S. Slichter, J. Healey & E. Livernash, The Impact of Collective Bargaining on Management 954-61 (1960).—[Eds.]

trade-offs within a single management or association, and the bargaining across the table. The same processes are involved in the administration and application of the agreement. . . .

2. It is strange indeed that public opinion in an industrial society would appear to understand so little of the problems and opportunities of the immediate work place — the factory machine, office desk, airplane cockpit, the construction site, the truck cab, etc. The handling of grievances is decisive both to labor costs and earnings or income; it is basic to morale and efficiency. The day-to-day administration of incentive systems and job evaluation, the flow of workers in the internal labor market by promotions, transfers, layoffs and retirements, the adjustment to technological and market changes and thousands of other types of questions arise each day. These processes have little public glamour but they are vital to management, workers and labor organizations; they are decisive to an industrial society. . . .

3. At the market or industry level collective bargaining also performs a variety of functions. (Some of these points may apply in some cases to the plant level as well.) The method of wage payment is a significant problem which may seem unimportant. The joint development of the job evaluation plan in basic steel, for instance, and its continued revision, is central to orderly operations. The review and revisions of methods of wage payment have fundamental consequences for labor costs and earnings as experience with any demoralized incentive plan will indicate. The development and administration of apprenticeship and training programs is typically a locality or nation-wide function of collective bargaining in an industry or a sector. The establishment of health and welfare and pension plans has often been at the industry level. The development and spread of supplementary unemployment benefits and other approaches to more stable earnings is a contribution of collective bargaining above the level of plant administration. Any approach to decasualization and seasonality in industries such as longshoring and construction requires a market-wide or industry-wide approach. . . .

In recent years the community has placed new obligations on collective bargaining, and recent public criticism of collective bargaining basically involves the issue whether still additional constraints and obligations are to be imposed upon this institution. Beyond the central purposes of collective bargaining noted at the outset of this paper — rule making at the work place, compensation setting, and disputes settlement — an expectation is being developed for imposing four new qualities of performance and new purposes on collective bargaining: (a) Collective bargaining is now to be conducted by labor organizations which are expected to adhere to new standards of democratic procedures to insure more immediate response of officers to the rank-and-file. (b) The results of collective bargaining are expected to meet new standards of efficient performance. The test of long-term market survival is not enough; regardless of the preference or power of workers and their unions, excessive manning and inefficiencies are to be rooted out. As Professor Taylor has commented: "Featherbedding, which once upon a time had such happy connotations, has been remade into a general call to arms not simply against preferred treatment but for denial to labor of some kinds of leisure and job security which is treasured by so many of us in managements and the professions." (c) The results of collective bargaining are to conform further to stabilization guideposts promulgated by government without consultation and without labor and management assent. (d) Not only should the public health and safety be protected in industrial conflict, but the public convenience should not be disrupted. The reaction to recent airline and newspaper stoppages is illustrative. . . .

In the inter-relations between collective bargaining and the community, not all of the adjustments are on the side of collective bargaining. The community has some tough choices to make. The community must learn that it cannot expect all good things; it must learn to give up desired, but second ranked, objectives. Free collective bargaining, democratic unions, industrial peace, full employment, improvement in the position of the disadvantaged, price stability, balance in the international accounts, the present price of gold, freedom from governmental controls etc. are simply not fully compatible. The relative priorities and preferences the community assigns to these objectives will be crucial for the future of collective bargaining.

SECTION I. The Duty to Bargain Collectively

A. EXCLUSIVE REPRESENTATION AND MAJORITY RULE

J. I. CASE CO. v. NLRB

Supreme Court of the United States
321 U.S. 332, 64 S. Ct. 576, 88 L. Ed. 762 (1944)

MR. JUSTICE JACKSON delivered the opinion of the Court.

This cause was heard by the National Labor Relations Board on stipulated facts which so far as concern present issues are as follows:

The petitioner, J. I. Case Company, at its Rock Island, Illinois, plant, from 1937 offered each employee an individual contract of employment. The contracts were uniform and for a term of one year. The Company agreed to furnish employment as steadily as conditions permitted, to pay a specified rate, which the Company might redetermine if the job changed, and to maintain certain hospital facilities. The employee agreed to accept the provisions, to serve faithfully and honestly for the term, to comply with factory rules, and that defective work should not be paid for. About 75% of the employees accepted and worked under these agreements. . . .

While the individual contracts executed August 1, 1941, were in effect, a CIO union petitioned the Board for certification as the exclusive bargaining representative of the production and maintenance employees. On December 17, 1941, a hearing was held, at which the Company urged the individual contracts as a bar to representation proceedings. The Board, however, directed an election, which was won by the union. The union was thereupon certified as the exclusive bargaining representative of the employees in question in respect to wages, hours, and other conditions of employment.

The union then asked the Company to bargain. It refused, declaring that it could not deal with the union in any manner affecting rights and obligations under the individual contracts while they remained in effect. It offered to negotiate on matters which did not affect rights under the individual contracts, and said that upon the expiration of the contracts it would bargain as to all matters. Twice the Company sent circulars to its employees asserting the validity of the individual contracts and stating the position that it took before the Board in reference to them.

The Board held that the Company had refused to bargain collectively, in violation of § 8(5) of the National Labor Relations Act. . . .

Individual contracts, no matter what the circumstances that justify their execution or what their terms, may not be availed of to defeat or delay the procedures prescribed by the National Labor Relations Act looking to collective bargaining, nor to exclude the contracting employee from a duly ascertained bargaining unit; nor may they be used to forestall bargaining or to limit or condition the terms of the collective agreement. "The Board asserts a public right vested in it as a public body, charged in the public interest with the duty of preventing unfair labor practices." National Licorice Co. v. NLRB, 309 U.S. 350, 364 (1940). Wherever private contracts conflict with its functions, they obviously must yield or the Act would be reduced to a futility.

It is equally clear since the collective trade agreement is to serve the purpose contemplated by the Act, the individual contract cannot be effective as a waiver of any benefit to which the employee otherwise would be entitled under the trade agreement. The very purpose of providing by statute for the collective agreement is to supersede the terms of separate agreements of employees with terms which reflect the strength and bargaining power and serve the welfare of the group. Its benefits and advantages are open to every employee of the represented unit, whatever the type or terms of his pre-existing contract of employment.

But it is urged that some employees may lose by the collective agreement, that an individual workman may sometimes have, or be capable of getting, better terms than those obtainable by the group and that his freedom of contract must be respected on that account. We are not called upon to say that under no circumstances can an individual enforce an agreement more advantageous than a collective agreement, but we find the mere possibility that such agreements might be made no ground for holding generally that individual contracts may survive or surmount collective ones. The practice and philosophy of collective bargaining looks with suspicion on such individual advantages. Of course, where there is a great variation in circumstances of employment or capacity of employees, it is possible for the collective bargain to prescribe only minimum rates or maximum hours or expressly to leave certain areas open to individual bargaining. But except as so provided, advantages to individuals may prove as disruptive of industrial peace as disadvantages. They are a fruitful way of interfering with organization and choice of representative; increased compensation, if individually deserved, is often earned at the cost of breaking down some other standard thought to be for the welfare of the group, and always creates the suspicion of being paid at the long-range expense of the group as a whole. Such discriminations not infrequently amount to unfair labor practices. The workman is free, if he values his own bargaining position more than that of the group, to vote against representation; but the majority rules, and if it collectivizes the employment bargain, individual advantages or favors will generally in practice go in as a contribution to the collective result. We cannot except individual contracts generally from the operation of collective ones because some may be more individually advantageous. Individual contracts cannot subtract from collective ones, and whether under some circumstances they may add to them in matters covered by the collective bargain, we leave to be determined by appropriate forums under the laws of contracts applicable, and to the Labor Board if they constitute unfair labor practices.

It also is urged that such individual contracts may embody matters that are not necessarily included within the statutory scope of collective bargaining, such as stock purchase, group insurance, hospitalization, or medical attention. We know of nothing to prevent the employee's, because he is an employee, making any contract provided it is not inconsistent with a collective agreement or does not amount to or result from or is not part of an unfair labor practice. But in so doing the employer may not incidentally exact or obtain any diminution of his own obligation or any increase of those of employees in the matters covered by collective agreement. Hence we find that the contentions of the Company that the individual contracts precluded a choice of representatives and warranted refusal to bargain during their duration were properly overruled. It follows that representation to the employees by circular letter that they had such legal effect was improper and could properly be prohibited by the Board. . . .

NOTE

In Order of Railroad Telegraphers v. Railway Express Agency, 321 U.S. 342 (1944), the Supreme Court held that individual contracts made after the collective agreement did not supersede the collective provisions. Under the collective agreement, unexpectedly high rates were payable to a few specially situated station agents. To correct this situation, the company made individual contracts with those agents, but without getting the union's approval or modifying the collective agreement. Under the principle of exclusive representation, the Court held that the union was entitled to be consulted about "the exceptional as well as the routine rates, rules and working conditions."

The power of exclusive representation enables unions to bind dissenters, within certain limits, on the wages they will receive, the hours they will work, and nearly every other facet of their industrial existence. Is this a far more significant encroachment on "individual rights" than the union shop, under which employees may be required to contribute to the financial support of their bargaining representative? Should the doctrine of majority rule be the proper target of those concerned about excessive union power? Or is exclusive representation indispensable to the effective functioning of collective bargaining? *See generally* Weyand, *Majority Rule in Collective Bargaining,* 45 COLUM. L. REV. 556 (1945); Schatzki, *Majority Rule, Exclusive Representation, and the Interests of Individual Workers: Should Exclusivity Be Abolished?* 123 U. PA. L. REV. 897 (1975). For consideration of exclusivity in a broader context, see Bok, *Reflections on the Distinctive Character of American Labor Laws,* 84 HARV. L. REV. 1394, 1426-27 (1971).

In societies with a more feudalistic structure, such as Japan, exclusive representation has not been a characteristic of collective bargaining. *See* C. KERR, ET AL., INDUSTRIALISM AND INDUSTRIAL MAN 196-98 (2d ed. 1964). But in these countries the detailed administration of the work place is the prerogative of a paternalistic management. There is little connection between the plant level and the industry level of workers' organizations, and their functions tend to be more social and political than economic. Does this experience shed any light on the problem of exclusive representation?

EMPORIUM CAPWELL CO. v. WESTERN ADDITION COMMUNITY ORGANIZATION

Supreme Court of the United States
420 U.S. 50, 95 S. Ct. 977, 43 L. Ed. 2d 12 (1975)

Opinion of the Court by MR. JUSTICE MARSHALL. . . .
This litigation presents the question whether, in light of the national policy against racial discrimination in employment, the National Labor Relations Act protects concerted activity by a group of minority employees to bargain with their employer over issues of employment discrimination. The National Labor Relations Board held that the employees could not circumvent their elected representative to engage in such bargaining. The Court of Appeals for the District of Columbia Circuit reversed and remanded, holding that in certain circumstances the activity would be protected. . . . We now reverse.

I. The Emporium Capwell Co. (Company) operates a department store in San Francisco. At all times relevant to this litigation it was a party to the collective bargaining agreement negotiated by the San Francisco Retailer's Council, of which it was a member, and the Department Store Employees Union (Union) which represented all stock and marking area employees of the Company. The agreement, in which the Union was recognized as the sole collective bargaining agency for all covered employees, prohibited employment discrimination by reason of race, color, creed, national origin, age, or sex, as well as union activity. It had a no-strike or lockout clause, and it established grievance and arbitration machinery for processing any claimed violation of the contract, including a violation of the antidiscrimination clause.

On April 3, 1968, a group of Company employees covered by the agreement met with the Secretary-Treasurer of the Union, Walter

Johnson, to present a list of grievances including a claim that the Company was discriminating on the basis of race in making assignments and promotions. The union official agreed to take certain of the grievances and to investigate the charge of racial discrimination. He appointed an investigating committee and prepared a report on the employees' grievances, which he submitted to the Retailer's Council and which the Council in turn referred to the Company. The report described "the possibility of racial discrimination" as perhaps the most important issue raised by the employees and termed the situation at the Company as potentially explosive if corrective action were not taken. It offered as an example of the problem the Company's failure to promote a Negro stock employee regarded by other employees as an outstanding candidate but a victim of racial discrimination.

Shortly after receiving the report, the Company's labor relations director met with Union representatives and agreed to "look into the matter" of discrimination and see what needed to be done. Apparently unsatisfied with these representations, the Union held a meeting in September attended by Union officials, Company employees, and representatives of the California Fair Employment Practices Committee (FEPC) and the local antipoverty agency. The Secretary-Treasurer of the Union announced that the Union had concluded that the Company was discriminating, and that it would process every such grievance through to arbitration if necessary. Testimony about the Company's practices was taken and transcribed by a court reporter, and the next day the Union notified the Company of its formal charge and demanded that the joint union-management Adjustment Board be convened "to hear the entire case."

At the September meeting some of the Company's employees had expressed their view that the contract procedures were inadequate to handle a systemic grievance of this sort; they suggested that the Union instead begin picketing the store in protest. Johnson explained that the collective agreement bound the Union to its processes and expressed his view that successful grievants would be helping not only themselves but all others who might be the victims of invidious discrimination as well. The FEPC and antipoverty agency representatives offered the same advice. Nonetheless, when the Adjustment Board meeting convened on October 16, James Joseph Hollins, Tom Hawkins, and two other employees whose testimony the Union had intended to elicit refused to participate in the grievance procedure. Instead, Hollins read a statement objecting to reliance on correction of individual inequities as an approach to the problem of discrimination at the store and demanding that the president of the Company meet with the four protestants to work out a broader agreement for dealing with the issue as they saw it. The four employees then walked out of the hearing.

Hollins attempted to discuss the question of racial discrimination with the Company president shortly after the incidents of October 16. The president refused to be drawn into such a discussion but suggested to Hollins that he see the personnel director about the matter. Hollins, who had spoken to the personnel director before, made no effort to do so again. Rather, he and Hawkins and several other dissident employees held a press conference on October 22 at which they denounced the store's employment policy as racist, reiterated their desire to deal directly with "the top management" of the Company over minority employment conditions, and announced their intention to picket and institute a boycott of the store. On Saturday, November 2, Hollins, Hawkins, and at least two other employees picketed the store throughout the day and distributed at the entrance handbills urging consumers not to patronize the store.[2] Johnson encountered the picketing employees, again urged them to rely on the grievance process, and warned that they might be fired for their activities. The picketers, however, were not dissuaded, and they continued to press their demand to deal directly with the Company president.

On November 7, Hollins and Hawkins were given written warnings that a repetition of the picketing or public statements about the Company could lead to their discharge. When the conduct was repeated the following Saturday, the two employees were fired.

Respondent Western Addition Community Organization, a local civil rights association of which Hollins and Hawkins were members, filed a charge against the Company with the National Labor Relations Board. The Board's General Counsel subsequently issued a complaint alleging that in discharging the two the Company had violated § 8 (a)(1) of the National Labor Relations Act.... After a hearing the NLRB Trial Examiner found that the discharged employees had believed in good faith that the Company was discriminating against minority employees, and that they had resorted to concerted activity on the basis of that belief. He concluded, however, that their activity was not protected by § 7 of the Act and that their discharges did not, therefore, violate § 8 (a)(1).

The Board, after oral argument, adopted the findings and conclusions of its Trial Examiner and dismissed the complaint. 192 N. L. R. B. 173. Among the findings adopted by the Board was that the discharged employees' course of conduct

---

[2] The full text of the handbill read:

"* * BEWARE * * * * BEWARE * * * * BEWARE * *
"EMPORIUM SHOPPERS
" 'Boycott Is On' 'Boycott Is On' 'Boycott Is On'

"For years at The Emporium black, brown, yellow and red people have worked at the lowest jobs at the lowest levels. Time and time again we have seen intelligent, hard working brothers and sisters denied promotions and respect.

"The Emporium is a 20th Century colonial plantation. The brothers and sisters are being treated the same way as our brothers are being treated in the slave mines of Africa.

"Whenever the racist pig at The Emporium injures or harms a black sister or brother, they injure and insult all black people. THE EMPORIUM MUST PAY FOR THESE INSULTS. Therefore, we encourage all of our people to take their money out of this racist store, until black people have full employment and are promoted justly through out The Emporium.

"We welcome the support of our brothers and sisters from the churches, unions, sororities, fraternities, social clubs, Afro-American Institute, Black Panther Party, W. A. C. O. and the Poor Peoples Institute."

"was no mere presentation of a grievance, but nothing short of a demand that the [Company] bargain with the picketing employees for the entire group of minority employees."

The Board concluded that protection of such an attempt to bargain would undermine the statutory system of bargaining through an exclusive, elected representative, impede elected unions' efforts at bettering the working conditions of minority employees "and place on the Employer an unreasonable burden of attempting to placate self-designated representatives of minority groups while abiding by the terms of a valid bargaining agreement and attempting in good faith to meet whatever demands the bargaining representative put forth under that agreement."

On respondent's petition for review the Court of Appeals reversed and remanded. The court was of the view that concerted activity directed against racial discrimination enjoys a "unique status" by virtue of the national labor policy against discrimination, as expressed in both the NLRA, see United Packinghouse Workers Union v. NLRB, 416 F. 2d 1126, cert. denied, 396 U. S. 903 (1969), and in Title VII of the Civil Rights Act of 1964, 42 U. S. C. § 2000e et seq., and that the Board had not adequately taken account of the necessity to accommodate the exclusive bargaining principle of the NLRA to the national policy of protecting action taken in opposition to discrimination from employer retaliation. The court recognized that protection of the minority group concerted activity involved in this case would interfere to some extent with the orderly collective bargaining process, but it considered the disruptive effect on that process to be outweighed where protection of minority activity is necessary to full and immediate realization of the policy against discrimination. In formulating a standard for distinguishing between protected and unprotected activity, the majority held that the "Board should inquire, in cases such as this, whether the union was actually remedying the discrimination to the *fullest extent possible by the most expedient and efficacious means.* Where the union's efforts fall short of this high standard, the minority group's concerted activity cannot lose its section 7 protection." Accordingly, the court remanded the case for the Board to make this determination and, if it found in favor of the employees, to consider whether their particular tactics were so disloyal to their employer as to deprive them of § 7 protection under our decision in NLRB v. Local Union No. 1229, 346 U. S. 464 (1953).

II. Before turning to the central question of labor policy raised by this case, it is important to have firmly in mind the character of the underlying conduct to which we apply them. As stated, the Trial Examiner and the Board found that the employees were discharged for attempting to bargain with the Company over the terms and conditions of employment as they affected racial minorities. Although the Court of Appeals expressly declined to set aside this finding, respondent has devoted considerable effort to attacking it in this Court, on the theory that the employees were attempting only to present a grievance to their employer within the meaning of the first proviso to § 9(a). We see no occasion to disturb the finding of the Board. Universal Camera Corp. v. NLRB, 340 U. S. 474, 491 (1951). The issue, then, is whether such attempts to engage in separate bargaining are protected by § 7 of the Act or proscribed by § 9 (a).

A. Section 7 affirmatively guarantees employees the most basic rights of industrial self-determination.... These are, for the most part, collective rights, rights to act in concert with one's fellow employees; they are protected not for their own sake but as an instrument of the national labor policy of minimizing industrial strife "by encouraging the practice and procedure of collective bargaining." 29 U. S. C. § 151.

Central to the policy of fostering collective bargaining, where the employees elect that course, is the principle of majority rule. See NLRB v. Jones & Laughlin Steel Corp., 301 U. S. 1 (1937). If the majority of a unit chooses union representation, the NLRA permits them to bargain with their employer to make union membership a condition of employment, thereby imposing their choice upon the minority.... In establishing a regime of majority rule, Congress sought to secure to all members of the unit the benefits of their collective strength and bargaining power, in full awareness that the superior strength of some individuals or groups might be subordinated to the interest of the majority. Vaca v. Sipes, 386 U. S. 171, 182 (1967); J. I. Case Co. v. NLRB, 321 U. S. 332, 338-339 (1944); H. R. Rep. No. 972, 74th Cong., 1st Sess., 18, II Leg. Hist. of the NLRA 2974 (1935). As a result, "[t]he complete satisfaction of all who are represented is hardly to be expected." Ford Motor Co. v. Huffman, 345 U. S. 330, 338 (1953)....

In vesting the representatives of the majority with this broad power Congress did not, of course, authorize a tyranny of the majority over minority interests. First, it confined the exercise of these powers to the context of a "unit appropriate for the purposes of collective bargaining," i.e., a group of employees with a sufficient commonality of circumstances to ensure against the submergence of a minority with distinctively different interests in the terms and conditions of their employment. See Allied Chemical Workers v. Pittsburgh Plate Glass Co., 404 U. S. 157, 171 (1971). Second, it undertook in the 1959 Landrum-Griffin amendments, 73 Stat. 519, to assure that minority voices are heard as they are in the functioning of a democratic institution. Third, we have held, by the very nature of the exclusive bargaining representative's status as representative of all unit employees, Congress implicitly imposed upon it a duty fairly and in good faith to represent the interests of minorities within the unit. Vaca v. Sipes, supra; Wallace Corp. v. NLRB, 323 U. S. 248 (1948); cf. Steele v. Louisville & N. R. Co., 323 U. S. 192 (1944). And the Board has taken the position that a union's refusal to process grievances against racial discrimination, in violation of that duty, is an unfair labor practice. Hughes Tool Co., 147 N. L. R. B. 1573 (1964); see Miranda Fuel Co., 140 N. L. R. B. 181 (1962), enforcement denied, 326 F. 2d 172 (2d Cir. 1962). Indeed, the Board has ordered a union implicated by a collective bargaining agreement in discrimination with an employer to propose specific contractual provisions to prohibit racial discrimination. See Local Union No. 12, United Rubber Workers of

America v. NLRB, 368 F. 2d 12 (5th Cir. 1966) (enforcement granted).

B. Against this background of long and consistent adherence to the principle of exclusive representation tempered by safeguards for the protection of minority interests, respondent urges this Court to fashion a limited exception to that principle: employees who seek to bargain separately with their employer as to the elimination of racially discriminatory employment practices peculiarly affecting them, should be free from the constraints of the exclusivity principle of § 9 (a). Essentially because established procedures under Title VII or, as in this case, a grievance machinery, are too time-consuming, the national labor policy against discrimination requires this exception, respondent argues, and its adoption would not unduly compromise the legitimate interests of either unions or employers.

Plainly, national labor policy embodies the principles of nondiscrimination as a matter of highest priority, Alexander v. Gardner-Denver Co., 415 U. S. 36, 47 (1974), and it is a common-place that we must construe the NLRA in light of the broad national labor policy of which it is a part. See Textile Workers v. Lincoln Mills, 353 U. S. 448, 456-458 (1958). These general principles do not aid respondent, however, as it is far from clear that separate bargaining is necessary to help eliminate discrimination. Indeed, as the facts of this case demonstrate, the proposed remedy might have just the opposite effect. The collective bargaining agreement in this case prohibited without qualification all manner of invidious discrimination and made any claimed violation a grievable issue. The grievance procedure is directed precisely at determining whether discrimination has occurred. That orderly determination, if affirmative, could lead to an arbitral award enforceable in court. Nor is there any reason to believe that the processing of grievances is inherently limited to the correction of individual cases of discrimination. Quite apart from the essentially contractual question of whether the Union could grieve against a "pattern or practice" it deems inconsistent with the nondiscrimination clause of the contract, one would hardly expect an employer to continue in effect an employment practice that routinely results in adverse arbitral decisions.

The decision by a handful of employees to bypass the grievance procedure in favor of attempting to bargain with their employer, by contrast, may or may not be predicated upon the actual existence of discrimination. An employer confronted with bargaining demands from each of several minority groups would not necessarily, or even probably, be able to agree to remedial steps satisfactory to all at once. Competing claims on the employer's ability to accommodate each group's demands, e.g., for reassignments and promotions to a limited number of positions, could only set one group against the other even if it is not the employer's intention to divide and overcome them. Having divided themselves, the minority employees will not be in position to advance their cause unless it be by recourse seriatim to economic coercion, which can only have the effect of further dividing them along racial or other lines. Nor is the situation materially different where, as apparently happened here, self-designated representatives purport to speak for all groups that might consider themselves to be victims of discrimination. Even if in actual bargaining the various groups did not perceive their interests as divergent and further subdivide themselves, the employer would be bound to bargain with them in a field largely preempted by the current collective bargaining agreement with the elected bargaining representatives. . . .

What has been said here in evaluating respondent's claim that the policy against discrimination requires § 7 protection for concerted efforts at minority bargaining has obvious implications for the related claim that legitimate employer and union interests would not be unduly compromised thereby. The court below minimized the impact on the Union in this case by noting that it was not working at cross-purposes with the dissidents, and that indeed it could not do so consistent with its duty of fair representation and perhaps its obligations under Title VII. As to the Company, its obligations under Title VII are cited for the proposition that it could have no legitimate objection to bargaining with the dissidents in order to achieve full compliance with that law.

This argument confuses the employees' substantive right to be free of racial discrimination with the procedures available under the NLRA for securing these rights. Whether they are thought to depend upon Title VII or have an independent source in the NLRA, they cannot be pursued at the expense of the orderly collective bargaining process contemplated by the NLRA. The elimination of discrimination and its vestiges is an appropriate subject of bargaining, and an employer may have no objection to incorporating into a collective agreement the substance of his obligation not to discriminate in personnel decisions; the Company here has done as much, making any claimed dereliction a matter subject to the grievance-arbitration machinery as well as to the processes of Title VII. But that does not mean that he may not have strong and legitimate objections to bargaining on several fronts over the implementation of the right to be free of discrimination for some of the reasons set forth above. Similarly, while a union cannot lawfully bargain for the establishment or continuation of discriminatory practices, see Steele v. Louisville & N. R. Co., *supra,* 42 U. S. C. § 2000-2(c)(3), it has legitimate interest in presenting a united front on this as on other issues and in not seeing its strength dissipated and its stature denigrated by subgroups within the unit separately pursuing what they see as separate interests. When union and employer are not responsive to their legal obligations, the bargain they have struck must yield *pro tanto* to the law, whether by means of conciliation through the offices of the EEOC, or by means of federal court enforcement at the instance of either that agency or the party claiming to be aggrieved.

Accordingly, we think neither aspect of respondent's contention in support of a right to short-circuit orderly, established processes for eliminating discrimination in employment is well-founded. The policy of industrial self-determination as expressed in § 7 does not require fragmentation of the bargaining unit along racial or other lines in order to consist with the national labor policy against discrimination. And in the face of such fragmentation, whatever its effect on discriminatory practices, the bargaining process that the principle of exclusive representation is meant to lubricate could not endure unhampered.

III. . . . Even assuming that § 704(a) [of Title VII] protects employees' picketing and instituting a consumer boycott of their employer, the same conduct is not necessarily entitled to affirmative protection from the NLRA. Under the scheme of that Act, conduct which is not protected concerted activity may lawfully form the basis for the participants' discharge. That does not mean that the discharge is immune from attack on other statutory grounds in an appropriate case. . . .

Respondent objects that reliance on the remedies provided by Title VII is inadequate effectively to secure the rights conferred by Title VII.. . . [W]e are told that relief is typically available to the party filing a charge with the NLRB in a significantly shorter time, and with less risk, than obtains for one filing a charge with the EEOC.

Whatever its factual merit, this argument is properly addressed to the Congress and not to this Court or the NLRB. In order to hold that employer conduct violates § 8(a)(1) of the NLRA *because* it violates § 704(a) of Title VII, we would have to override a host of consciously made decisions well within the exclusive competence of the Legislature. This obviously, we cannot do.

Reversed.

[The dissenting opinion of MR. JUSTICE DOUGLAS is omitted.]

NOTE

The First and Fourteenth Amendments protect the right of a public school teacher to oppose, at a public school board meeting, a position advanced by the teacher's union. The principle of exclusivity cannot be used to muzzle a public employee who, like any other citizen, might wish to express his view about governmental decisions concerning labor relations. City of Madison School District No. 8 v. Wisconsin Employment Relations Commission, 429 U.S. 167 (1976). *See also* Cantor, *Dissident Worker Action after The Emporium,* 29 RUTGERS L. REV. 35 (1975).

B. THE NATURE OF THE DUTY TO BARGAIN

The obligation to "bargain collectively" is generally, though not universally, included in federal and state labor relations acts. The original NLRA imposed the duty on the employer as a means of implementing the right to organize and to bargain collectively which was declared in § 7. The "Wagner Act" type of statute exacted no requirements of unions. The later "Taft-Hartley" type of statute made the bargaining obligation mutual.

The legal duty which the original NLRA and the RLA created was not defined by Congress. Section 2, First, of the RLA requires that the parties exert "every reasonable effort to make and maintain agreements concerning rates of pay, rules, and working conditions," and § 2, Ninth, obligates the carrier to "treat with" the duly certified employee representative. These provisions, together with the duty "to bargain collectively" specified in the Wagner Act, and corresponding provisions of state acts, had to be given meaning by the courts and the enforcement agencies.

In the first case to come before the Supreme Court under the RLA it was declared that the statute "does not undertake to compel agreement between the employer and employees, but it does command those preliminary steps without which no agreement can be reached," including "reasonable efforts to compose differences." [2] Even prior to this decision there had been some development of the concept of bargaining by the National Labor Board and the old National Labor Relations Board, which had been given advisory adjudicative responsibility regarding § 7a of the National Industrial Recovery Act of 1933. In the much cited *Houde Engineering Corp.* case,[3] the old NLRB interpreted the decisions of the NLB as having established the "incontestably sound principle that the employer is obligated by the statute to negotiate in good faith with his employees' representatives; to match their proposals, if unacceptable, with counter-proposals; and to make every reasonable effort to reach an agreement." In applying § 8(5) of the NLRA of 1935, the NLRB adopted this principle with the full support of the courts. The duty to bargain encompassed an obligation to enter into negotiations with "an open and fair mind" and "a sincere purpose to find a basis of agreement." [4]

Section 8(5) of the NLRA had its origin in a Senate bill (S. 2926) introduced by Senator Wagner in March 1934. One provision, obviously patterned on the Railway Labor Act counterpart, read as follows:

> It shall be an unfair labor practice . . . to refuse to recognize and/or deal with representatives of his [the employer's] employees, or to fail to exert every reasonable effort to make and maintain agreements with such representatives concerning wages, hours, and other conditions of employment.

At the committee hearings on the bill Dr. Slichter of Harvard argued for deletion of the requirement of a "reasonable effort to make and maintain agreements," and so forth, as merely the expression of a pious wish: "You cannot make it a definite duty of a man to try to agree. . . . You might almost enact that the lions and lambs shall not fail to exert every reasonable effort to lie down together." Dr. Leiserson, then Chairman of the Petroleum Labor Policy Board, disagreed: "Now, I think it is exceedingly important that it should stay in the bill. It should not be thrown out on the theory, 'Well, you cannot enforce that anyway.' If we can say, . . . to an employer, 'Now, you really haven't tried to agree with

---

[2] Virginian Ry. v. System Fed'n No. 40, 300 U.S. 515, 548 (1937).

[3] 1 N.L.R.B. (Old) 35 (1934).

[4] *See, e.g.,* NLRB v. Boss Mfg. Co., 118 F.2d 187, 189 (7th Cir. 1941); Globe Cotton Mills v. NLRB, 103 F.2d 91, 94 (5th Cir. 1939); Highland Park Mfg. Co., 12 N.L.R.B. 1238, 1248-49 (1939).

them, so that we will avoid a strike. They have elected their representatives. Now sit down and make an earnest effort, the way the law says.' You will avoid many disputes in that way." [5]

The Senate Committee on Education and Labor, reporting in 1935 on the Wagner-Connery Bill, said regarding § 8(5):

> The committee wishes to dispel any possible false impression that this bill is designed to compel the making of agreements or to permit governmental supervision of their terms. It must be stressed that the duty to bargain collectively does not carry with it the duty to reach an agreement, because the essence of collective bargaining is that either party shall be free to decide whether proposals made to it are satisfactory.[6]

Senator Walsh, Chairman of the Committee on Education and Labor, summed up one prominent legislative attitude in these terms:

> The bill indicates the method and manner in which employees may organize, the method and manner of selecting their representatives or spokesmen, and leads them to the office door of their employer with the legal authority to negotiate for their fellow employees. The bill does not go beyond the office door. It leaves the discussion between the employer and the employee, and the agreements which they may or may not make, voluntary and with that sacredness and solemnity to a voluntary agreement with which both parties to an agreement should be enshrouded.[7]

When Congress passed the LMRA in 1947, § 8(d) was written into the law, spelling out to some extent the duty to bargain collectively.

The Senate bill (S. 1126), in its proposed amendment of the NLRA, included a § 8(d) substantially similar to this section as eventually enacted, but lacking its final paragraph. The Senate Committee on Labor and Public Welfare stated:

> Section 8(d) contains a definition of the duty to bargain collectively and, consequently, relates both to the duties of employers to bargain and labor organizations to bargain under Sections 8(a)(5) and 8(b)(3), respectively. The definition makes it clear that the duty to bargain collectively does not require either party to agree to a particular demand or to make a concession. It should be noted that

---

[5] Smith, *The Evolution of the "Duty to Bargain" Concept in American Law,* 39 MICH. L. REV. 1065, 1083-84 (1941).

[6] *Id.* at 1085.

[7] *Id.* at 1087. *See also* Latham, *Legislative Purpose and Administrative Policy Under the National Labor Relations Act,* 4 GEO. WASH. L. REV. 433 (1936). For contrasting views, see W. SPENCER, THE NATIONAL LABOR RELATIONS ACT 24 (1935); Rheinstein, *Methods of Wage Policy,* 6 U. CHI. L. REV. 552, 576 (1939).

the word "concession" was used rather than "counterproposal" to meet an objection raised by the Chairman of the Board to a corresponding provision in one of the early drafts of the bill.[8]

The Conference Committee reported concerning the version of § 8(d) as finally enacted:

This mutual obligation was not to compel either party to agree to a proposal or require the making of any concession. Hence, the Senate amendment, while it did not prescribe a purely objective test of what constituted collective bargaining, as did the House bill, had, to a very substantial extent, the same effect as the House bill in this regard, since it rejected, as a factor in determining good faith, the test of making a concession and thus prevented the Board from determining the merits of the positions of the parties.[9]

1. GOOD FAITH

LABOR STUDY GROUP,* THE PUBLIC INTEREST IN NATIONAL LABOR POLICY 82 (Committee for Economic Development 1961)

Parties have been told that they must bargain in good faith, and elaborate tests have been devised in an attempt to determine "objectively" whether the proper subjective attitude prevails. The limitations and artificiality of such tests are apparent, and the possibilities of evasion are almost limitless. . . . Basically, it is unrealistic to expect that, by legislation, "good faith" can be brought to the bargaining table. Indeed, the provisions designed to bring "good faith" have become a tactical weapon used in many situations as a means of harassment.

NLRB v. AMERICAN NATIONAL INSURANCE CO.

Supreme Court of the United States
343 U.S. 395, 72 S. Ct. 824, 96 L. Ed. 1027 (1952)

MR. CHIEF JUSTICE VINSON delivered the opinion of the Court.

This case arises out of a complaint that respondent refused to bargain collectively with the representatives of its employees as required under the National Labor Relations Act, as amended.

The Office Employees International Union, AFL, Local No. 27, certified by the National Labor Relations Board as the exclusive bargaining representative of respondent's office employees, requested a meeting

---

[8] S. REP. No. 105, 80th Cong., 1st Sess. 24 (1947).

[9] H.R. REP. No. 510, 80th Cong., 1st Sess. 34 (1947).

* The members of the Study Group were Clark Kerr, Douglass V. Brown, David L. Cole, John T. Dunlop, William Y. Elliott, Albert Rees, Robert M. Solow, Philip Taft, and George W. Taylor.

with respondent for the purpose of negotiating an agreement governing employment relations. At the first meetings, beginning on November 30, 1948, the Union submitted a proposed contract covering wages, hours, promotions, vacations and other provisions commonly found in collective bargaining agreements, including a clause establishing a procedure for settling grievances arising under the contract by successive appeals to management with ultimate resort to an arbitrator.

On January 10, 1949, following a recess for study of the Union's contract proposals, respondent objected to the provisions calling for unlimited arbitration. To meet this objection, respondent proposed a so-called management functions clause listing matters such as promotions, discipline and work scheduling as the responsibility of management and excluding such matters from arbitration. The Union's representative took the position "as soon as [he] heard [the proposed clause]" that the Union would not agree to such a clause so long as it covered matters subject to the duty to bargain collectively under the Labor Act.

Several further bargaining sessions were held without reaching agreement on the Union's proposal or respondent's counter-proposal to unlimited arbitration. As a result, the management functions clause was "by-passed" for bargaining on other terms of the Union's contract proposal. On January 17, 1949, respondent stated in writing its agreement with some of the terms proposed by the Union and, where there was disagreement, respondent offered counterproposals, including a clause entitled "Functions and Prerogatives of Management" along the lines suggested at the meeting of January 10th. The Union objected to the portion of the clause providing:

"The right to select and hire, to promote to a better position, to discharge, demote or discipline for cause, and to maintain discipline and efficiency of employees and to determine the schedules of work is recognized by both union and company as the proper responsibility and prerogative of management to be held and exercised by the company, and while it is agreed that an employee feeling himself to have been aggrieved by any decision of the company in respect to such matters, or the union in his behalf, shall have the right to have such decision reviewed by top management officials of the company under the grievance machinery hereinafter set forth, it is further agreed that the final decision of the company made by such top management officials shall not be further reviewable by arbitration."

At this stage of the negotiations, the National Labor Relations Board filed a complaint against respondent based on the Union's charge that respondent had refused to bargain as required by the Labor Act and was thereby guilty of interfering with the rights of its employees guaranteed by § 7 of the Act and of unfair labor practices under §§ 8(a)(1) and 8(a)(5) of the Act. While the proceeding was pending, negotiations between the Union and respondent continued with the management functions clause remaining an obstacle to agreement. . . .

On May 19, 1949, a Union representative offered a second contract proposal which included a management functions clause containing much of the language found in respondent's second counterproposal, quoted above, with the vital difference that questions arising under the Union's proposed clause would be subject to arbitration as in the case of other grievances. Finally, on January 13, 1950, after the Trial Examiner had issued his report but before decision by the Board, an agreement between the Union and respondent was signed. The agreement contained a management functions clause that rendered nonarbitrable matters of discipline, work schedules and other matters covered by the clause. The subject of promotions and demotions was deleted from the clause and made the subject of a special clause establishing a union-management committee to pass upon promotion matters.

While these negotiations were in progress, the Board's Trial Examiner conducted hearings on the Union's complaint. The Examiner held that respondent had a right to bargain for inclusion of a management functions clause in a contract. However, upon review of the entire negotiations, including respondent's unilateral action in changing working conditions during the bargaining, the Examiner found that from and after November 30, 1948, respondent had refused to bargain in a good faith effort to reach agreement. The Examiner recommended that respondent be ordered in general terms to bargain collectively with the Union.

The Board agreed with the Trial Examiner that respondent had not bargained in a good faith effort to reach an agreement with the Union. But the Board rejected the Examiner's views on an employer's right to bargain for a management functions clause and held that respondent's action in bargaining for inclusion of any such clause "constituted, quite [apart from] Respondent's demonstrated bad faith, per se violations of § 8(a)(5) and (1)." Accordingly, the Board not only ordered respondent in general terms to bargain collectively with the Union (par. 2(a)), but also included in its order a paragraph designed to prohibit bargaining for any management functions clause covering a condition of employment. (Par. 1(a).) 89 N.L.R.B. 185. . . .

First. The National Labor Relations Act is designed to promote industrial peace by encouraging the making of voluntary agreements governing relations between unions and employers. The Act does not compel any agreement whatsoever between employees and employers. Nor does the Act regulate the substantive terms governing wages, hours and working conditions which are incorporated in an agreement. The theory of the Act is that the making of voluntary labor agreements is encouraged by protecting employees' rights to organize for collective bargaining and by imposing on labor and management the mutual obligation to bargain collectively.

Enforcement of the obligation to bargain collectively is crucial to the statutory scheme. And, as has long been recognized, performance of the duty to bargain requires more than a willingness to enter upon a sterile discussion of union-management differences. Before the enactment of the National Labor Relations Act, it was held that the duty of an employer to bargain collectively required the employer "to negotiate in good faith with his employees' representatives; to match their proposals, if unacceptable, with counterproposals; and to make every reasonable effort to reach an agreement." The duty to bargain collectively, implicit in the Wagner Act as introduced in Congress, was made express by the insertion of the fifth employer unfair labor practice accompanied by an explanation of the purpose and meaning of the phrase "bargain collectively in a good faith effort to reach an agreement." This understanding of the duty to bargain collectively has been accepted and applied throughout the administration of the Wagner Act by the National Labor Relations Board and the Courts of Appeal.

In 1947, the fear was expressed in Congress that the Board "has gone very far, in the guise of determining whether or not employers had bargained in good faith, in setting itself up as the judge of what concessions an employer must make and of the proposals and counterproposals that he may or may not make." Accordingly, the Hartley Bill, passed by the House, eliminated the good faith test and expressly provided that the duty to bargain collectively did not require submission of counterproposals. As amended in the Senate and passed as the Taft-Hartley Act, the good faith test of bargaining was retained and written into § 8(d) of the National Labor Relations Act. That section contains the express provision that the obligation to bargain collectively does not compel either party to agree to a proposal or require the making of a concession.

Thus it is now apparent from the statute itself that the Act does not encourage a party to engage in fruitless marathon discussions at the expense of frank statement and support of his position. And it is equally clear that the Board may not, either directly or indirectly, compel concessions or otherwise sit in judgment upon the substantive terms of collective bargaining agreements.

Second. The Board offers in support of the portion of its order before this Court a theory quite apart from the test of good faith bargaining prescribed in § 8(d) of the Act, a theory that respondent's bargaining for a management functions clause as a counterproposal to the Union's demand for unlimited arbitration was, *"per se,"* a violation of the Act.

Counsel for the Board do not contend that a management functions clause covering some conditions of employment is an illegal contract term. As a matter of fact, a review of typical contract clauses collected for convenience in drafting labor agreements shows that management functions clauses similar in essential detail to the clause proposed by respondent have been included in contracts negotiated by national unions with many employers. The National War Labor Board, empowered during the last war "[t]o decide the dispute, and provide by order the wages and hours and all other terms and conditions (customarily included in collective bargaining agreements)," ordered management functions clauses included in a number of agreements. Several such clauses ordered by the War Labor Board provided for arbitration in case of union dissatisfaction with the exercise of management functions, while others, as in the clause proposed by respondent in this case, provided that management decisions would be final. Without intimating any opinion as to the form of management function clause proposed by respondent in this case or the desirability of including any such clause in a labor agreement, it is manifest that bargaining for management functions clauses is common collective bargaining practice.

If the Board is correct, an employer violates the Act by bargaining for a management functions clause touching any condition of employment without regard to the traditions of bargaining in the particular industry or such other evidence of good faith as the fact in this case that respondent's clause was offered as a counterproposal to the Union's demand for unlimited arbitration. The Board's argument is a technical one for it is conceded that respondent would not be guilty of an unfair labor practice if, instead of proposing a clause that removed some matters from arbitration, it simply refused in good faith to agree to the Union proposal for unlimited arbitration. The argument starts with a finding, not challenged by the court below or by respondent, that at least some of the matters covered by the management functions clause proposed by respondent are "conditions of employment" which are appropriate subjects of collective bargaining under §§ 8(a)(5), 8(d) and 9(a) of the Act. The Board considers that employer bargaining for a clause under which management retains initial responsibility for work scheduling, a "condition of employment," for the duration of the contract is an unfair labor practice because it is "in derogation of" employees' statutory rights to bargain collectively as to conditions of employment.[22]

Conceding that there is nothing unlawful in including a management functions clause in a labor agreement, the Board would permit an employer to "propose" such a clause. But the Board would forbid bargaining for any such clause when the Union declines to accept the proposal, even where the clause is offered as a counterproposal to a Union demand for unlimited arbitration. Ignoring the nature of the Union's demand in this case, the Board takes the position that employers subject to the Act must agree to include in any labor agreement provisions establishing fixed standards for work schedules or any other condition of employment. An employer would be permitted to bargain as to the content of the standard so long as he agrees to freeze a standard into a contract. Bargaining for more flexible treatment of such matters would be denied employers even though the result may be contrary to common collective bargaining practice in the industry. The Board was not empowered so to disrupt collective bargaining practices. On the contrary, the term "bargain collectively" as used in the Act "has been considered

---

[22] The Board's argument would seem to prevent an employer from bargaining for a "no-strike" clause, commonly found in labor agreements, requiring a union to forego for the duration of the contract the right to strike expressly granted by § 7 of the Act. However, the Board has permitted an employer to bargain in good faith for such a clause. Shell Oil Co., 77 N.L.R.B. 1306 (1948). This result is explained by referring to the "salutary objective" of such a clause. Bethlehem Steel Co., 89 N.L.R.B. 341, 345 (1950).

to absorb and give statutory approval to the philosophy of bargaining as worked out in the labor movement in the United States." Order of Railroad Telegraphers v. Railway Express Agency, 321 U.S. 342 (1944).

Congress provided expressly that the Board should not pass upon the desirability of the substantive terms of labor agreements. Whether a contract should contain a clause fixing standards for such matters as work scheduling or should provide for more flexible treatment of such matters is an issue for determination across the bargaining table, not by the Board. If the latter approach is agreed upon, the extent of union and management participation in the administration of such matters is itself a condition of employment to be settled by bargaining.

Accordingly, we reject the Board's holding that bargaining for the management functions clause proposed by respondent was, *per se,* an unfair labor practice. Any fears the Board may entertain that use of management functions clauses will lead to evasion of an employer's duty to bargain collectively as to "rates of pay, wages, hours and conditions of employment" do not justify condemning all bargaining for management functions clauses covering any "condition of employment" as *per se* violations of the Act. The duty to bargain collectively is to be enforced by application of the good faith bargaining standards of § 8(d) to the facts of each case rather than by prohibiting all employers in every industry from bargaining for management functions clauses altogether. . . .

Accepting as we do the finding of the court below that respondent bargained in good faith for the management functions clause proposed by it, we hold that respondent was not in that respect guilty of refusing to bargain collectively as required by the National Labor Relations Act. Accordingly, enforcement of paragraph 1(a) of the Board's order was properly denied.

Affirmed.

MR. JUSTICE MINTON, with whom MR. JUSTICE BLACK and MR. JUSTICE DOUGLAS join, dissenting:

I do not see how this case is solved by telling the National Labor Relations Board that since *some* "management functions" clauses are valid (which the Board freely admits), respondent was not guilty of an unfair labor practice *in this case.* The record is replete with evidence that respondent insisted on a clause which would classify the control over certain conditions of employment as a management prerogative, and that the insistence took the form of a refusal to reach a settlement unless the union accepted the clause. The Court of Appeals agreed that the respondent was "steadfast" in this demand. Therefore, *this case* is one where the employer came into the bargaining room with a demand that certain topics upon which it had a duty to bargain were to be removed from the agenda — that was the price the union had to pay to gain a contract. There is all the difference between the hypothetical "management functions" clauses envisioned by the majority and this "management functions" clause as there is between waiver and coercion. No one suggests that an employer is guilty of an unfair labor practice when it proposes that it be given unilateral control over certain working conditions and the union accepts the proposal in return for various other benefits. But where, as here, the employer tells the union that the only way to obtain a contract as to wages is to agree not to bargain about certain other working conditions, the employer has refused to bargain about those other working conditions. There is more than a semantic difference between a proposal that the union waive certain rights and a demand that the union give up those rights as a condition precedent to enjoying other rights.

I need not and do not take issue with the Court of Appeals' conclusion that there was no absence of good faith. Where there is a refusal to bargain, the Act does not require an inquiry as to whether that refusal was in good faith or bad faith. The duty to bargain about certain subjects is made absolute by the Act. The majority seems to suggest that an employer could be found guilty of bad faith if it used a "management functions" clause to close off bargaining about all topics of discussion. Whether the employer closes off all bargaining or, as in this case, only a certain area of bargaining, he has refused to bargain as to whatever he has closed off, and any discussion of his good faith is pointless.

That portion of § 8(d) of the Act which declares that an employer need not agree to a proposal or make concessions does not dispose of this case. Certainly the Board lacks power to compel concessions as to the substantive terms of labor agreements. But the Board in this case was seeking to compel the employer to bargain about subjects properly within the scope of collective bargaining. That the employer has such a duty to bargain and that the Board is empowered to enforce the duty is clear.

An employer may not stake out an area which is a proper subject for bargaining and say, "As to this we will not bargain." To do so is a plain refusal to bargain in violation of § 8(a)(5) of the Act. If employees' bargaining rights can be cut away so easily, they are indeed illusory. I would reverse.

NOTE

Does *American Nat'l Ins. Co.* justify an employer's insistence on a management functions clause reserving unilateral control over virtually all aspects of the employment relationship, leaving the employees no better off than they would be without any agreement? *Compare* White v. NLRB, 255 F.2d 564 (5th Cir. 1958) ("Yes"), *with* Majure v. NLRB, 198 F.2d 735 (5th Cir. 1952), *and* NLRB v. Reed & Prince Mfg. Co., 205 F.2d 131 (1st Cir. 1953), *cert. denied,* 346 U.S. 887 (1953).

For more recent Board views on employer demands for management rights clauses, *compare* East Texas Steel Casting Co., 154 N.L.R.B. 1080 (1965), *with* Proctor & Gamble Mfg. Co., 160 N.L.R.B. 334 (1966).

NLRB v. INSURANCE AGENTS' INTERNATIONAL UNION, 361 U.S. 477, 80 S. Ct. 419, 4 L.Ed. 2d 454 (1960). In order to put economic pressure on an employer to yield to bargaining demands, a union of insurance agents engaged in concerted on-the-job activities designed to harass the company. These included refusal for a time to solicit new business, refusal to follow reporting procedures, late arrival at work and early departure, failure to attend meetings, and picketing of company offices. Although the union continued to negotiate with the employer in an effort to reach agreement on a new contract, the National Labor Relations Board held that its harassing tactics constituted a refusal to bargain in good faith as required by § 8(b)(3) of the NLRA. The Supreme Court disagreed. Pointing out that Congress did not intend the NLRB to regulate the substantive terms of labor agreements, the Court stated: "[I]f the Board could regulate the choice of economic weapons that may be used as part of collective bargaining, it would be in a position to exercise considerable influence upon the substantive terms on which the parties contract." Even on the assumption the employees' conduct was unprotected, and they could have been discharged for it, it was not inconsistent with good faith bargaining.

GENERAL ELECTRIC CO.

National Labor Relations Board
150 N.L.R.B. 192 (1964)

. . . .

The Trial Examiner found that Respondent had not bargained in good faith with the Union, thereby violating § 8(a)(5) and (1) of the Act, as evidenced by:

(a) Its failure timely to furnish certain information requested by the Union during contract negotiations.

(b) Its attempts, while engaged in national negotiations with the Union, to deal separately with Locals on matters which were properly the subject of national negotiations, and its solicitations of Locals separately to abandon or refrain from supporting the strike.

(c) Its presentation of its personal accident insurance proposal to the Union on a take-it-or-leave-it basis.[3]

(d) Its over-all approach to and conduct of bargaining.

We agree with these findings of the Trial Examiner. Because Respondent's defense of its bargaining conduct raises a fundamental question as to the requirements of the statutory bargaining obligation, we have stated for more particular emphasis the reasons why we agree with the Trial Examiner that Respondent did not bargain in good faith with the Union.

---

[3] For the reasons set forth in his dissent in Equitable Life Ins. Co., 133 N.L.R.B. 1675, 1677, Member Fanning would not find that Respondent's refusal to bargain in regard to the insurance plan was unlawful. However, he believes that Respondent's take-it-or-leave-it position on June 13 can be properly considered in gauging its over-all good faith in negotiations.

In challenging the Trial Examiner's finding that it violated § 8(a)(5), Respondent argues that an employer cannot be found guilty of having violated its statutory bargaining duty where it is desirous of entering into a collective bargaining agreement, where it has met and conferred with the bargaining representative on all required subjects of bargaining as prescribed by statute and has not taken unlawful unilateral action, and where it has not demanded the inclusion in the collective bargaining contract of any illegal clauses or insisted to an impasse upon any nonmandatory bargaining provisions. Given compliance with the above, Respondent further argues that an employer's technique of bargaining is not subject to approval or disapproval by the Board.

Respondent reads the statutory requirements for bargaining collectively too narrowly. It is true that an employer does violate § 8(a)(5) where it enters into bargaining negotiations with a desire not to reach an agreement with the union, or has taken unilateral action with respect to a term or condition of employment, or has adamantly demanded the inclusion of illegal or nonmandatory clauses in the collective bargaining contract. But, having refrained from any of the foregoing conduct, an employer may still have failed to discharge its statutory obligation to bargain in good faith. As the Supreme Court has said: [8]

". . . the Board is authorized to order the cessation of behavior which is in effect a refusal to negotiate, *or* which directly obstructs or inhibits the actual process of discussion, *or* which reflects a cast of mind against reaching agreement." [Emphasis supplied.]

Thus, a party who enters into bargaining negotiations with a "take-it-or-leave-it" attitude violates its duty to bargain although it goes through the forms of bargaining, does not insist on any illegal or nonmandatory bargaining proposals, and wants to sign an agreement.[9] For good-faith bargaining means more than "going through the motions of negotiating." [10] ". . . the essential thing is rather the serious intent to adjust differences and to reach an acceptable common ground. . . ." [11]

Good-faith bargaining thus involves both a procedure for meeting and negotiating, which may be called the externals of collective bargaining, and a bona fide intention, the presence or absence of which must be discerned from the record. It requires recognition by both parties, not merely formal but real, that "collective bargaining" is a shared process in which each party, labor union and employer, has the right to play an active

---

[8] NLRB v. Bennie Katz, etc., d/b/a Williamsburg Steel Prod. Co., *supra* [369 U.S. 736] at 747 (1962).

[9] NLRB v. Insurance Agents' Union, AFL-CIO (Prudential Ins. Co.), 361 U.S. 477, 487 (1960).

[10] NLRB v. Truitt Mfg. Co., 351 U.S. 149, 155 (1956) (Frankfurter, J.).

[11] First Annual Report of the National Labor Relations Board, at 85, quoted with approval by the Supreme Court in NLRB v. Insurance Agents' Union, AFL-CIO (Prudential Ins. Co.), *supra* at 485.

role. On the part of the employer, it requires at a minimum recognition that the statutory representative is the one with whom it must deal in conducting bargaining negotiations, and that it can no longer bargain directly or indirectly with the employees. It is inconsistent with this obligation for an employer to mount a campaign, as Respondent did, both before and during negotiations, for the purpose of disparaging and discrediting the statutory representative in the eyes of its employee constituents, to seek to persuade the employees to exert pressure on the representative to submit to the will of the employer, and to create the impression that the employer rather than the union is the true protector of the employees' interests. As the Trial Examiner phrased it, the employer's statutory obligation is to deal with the employees through the union, and not with the union through the employees.

We do not rely solely on Respondent's campaign among its employees for our finding that it did not deal in good faith with the Union. Respondent's policy of disparaging the Union by means of the communications campaign as fully detailed in the Trial Examiner's Intermediate Report, was implemented and furthered by its conduct at the bargaining table. Thus, the negotiations themselves, although maintaining the form of "collective bargaining," fell short, in a realistic sense, of the concept of meaningful and fruitful "negotiation" envisaged by the Act. As the record in the case reflects, Respondent regards itself as a sort of administrative body which has the unilateral responsibility for determining wages and working conditions for employees, and it regards the union's role as merely that of a kind of advisor for an interested group — the employees. Thus, according to its professed philosophy of "bargaining," Respondent on the basis of its own research and evaluation of union demands, determines what is "right" for its employees, and then makes a "fair and firm offer" to the unions without holding anything back for later trading or compromising. It professes a willingness to make prompt adjustments in its offer, but only if new information or a change in facts indicates that its initial offer is no longer "right." It believes that if its research has been done properly there will be no need to change its offer unless something entirely unforeseen has developed in the meantime. Simultaneously, Respondent emphasizes, especially to employees, that as a matter of policy it will not be induced by a strike or a threat of a strike to make any change in its proposals which it believes to be "wrong." This "bargaining" approach undoubtedly eliminates the "ask-and-bid" or "auction" form of bargaining, but in the process devitalizes negotiations and collective bargaining and robs them of their commonly accepted meaning. "Collective bargaining" as thus practiced is tantamount to mere formality and serves to transform the role of the statutory representative from a joint participant in the bargaining process to that of an advisor. In practical effect, Respondent's "bargaining" position is akin to that of a party who enters into negotiations "with a predetermined resolve not to budge from an initial position," an attitude inconsistent with good-faith bargaining. In fact Respondent here went even further. It consciously placed itself in a position where it could not give unfettered consideration to the merits of any proposals the Union might offer. Thus, Respondent pointed out to the Union, after Respondent's communications to the employees and its "fair and firm offer" to the Union, that "everything we think we should do is in the proposal and we told our employees that, and we would look ridiculous if we changed now."

In short, both major facets of Respondent's 1960 "bargaining" technique, its campaign among the employees and its conduct at the bargaining table, complementing each other, were calculated to disparage the Union and to impose without substantial alteration Respondent's "fair and firm" proposal, rather than to satisfy the true standards of good-faith collective bargaining required by the statute. A course of conduct whose major purpose is so directed scarcely evinces a sincere desire to resolve differences and reach a common ground. For the above reasons, as well as those elaborated at greater length by the Trial Examiner in his Intermediate Report, we adopt his conclusion that Respondent did not bargain in good faith with the Union, thereby violating § 8(a)(5) and (1) of the Act.

Our concurring colleague, Member Jenkins, who joins us in finding certain conduct of the Respondent inconsistent with its bargaining obligation under the statute, misreads the majority opinion, and the Trial Examiner's Intermediate Report which we affirm, in asserting that our decision is not based on an assessment of Respondent's conduct, but only on its approach to or techniques in bargaining.

On the contrary our determination is based upon our review of the Respondent's entire course of conduct, its failure to furnish relevant information, its attempts to deal separately with locals and to bypass the national bargaining representative, the manner of its presentation of the accident insurance proposal, the disparagement of the Union as bargaining representative by the communication program, its conduct of the negotiations themselves, and its attitude or approach as revealed by all these factors.

Nothing in our decision bans fact-gathering or any specific methods of formulating proposals. We prescribe no time-table for negotiators. We lay down no rules as to any required substance or content of agreements. Our decision rests rather upon a consideration of the totality of Respondent's conduct.

In one central point of our colleague's comment, with all respect we believe he is in error. His strictures in relation to our interpretation of the law's restraints on "take-it-or-leave-it" bargaining were decisively answered by the Supreme Court in its review of the nature of the bargaining obligation in *Insurance Agents:* [18]

. . . the legislative history [of Taft-Hartley] makes it plain that Congress was wary of the position of some unions, and wanted to ensure that they would approach the bargaining table with the same attitude of willingness

---

[18] NLRB v. Insurance Agents' Union, AFL-CIO, *supra* at 487.

to reach an agreement as had been enjoined on management earlier. It intended to prevent employee representatives from putting forth the same "take it or leave it" attitude that had been condemned in management.

And in JUSTICE FRANKFURTER'S opinion in *Truitt* [19] upon which our colleague relies, the Justice also wrote:

... [I]t [good faith] is inconsistent with a predetermined resolve not to budge from an initial position.

While we share his objective and that of our dissenting colleague of encouraging a maximum of freedom and experimentation in collective bargaining, when questions are raised under the law as construed by the courts and the Board concerning the conformity of a specific respondent's course of conduct with the requirements of the law, the Board must apply the law to the totality of that conduct in the interest of preserving and fostering collective bargaining itself. That is what we have sought to do here. . . .

MEMBER JENKINS, concurring:

The fundamental issues in this case have been obscured by slogans and shibboleths which have understandably led my colleagues into deciding issues which in my judgment are not presented for decision. Moreover, the Board has undertaken to describe the statutory obligation to bargain in good faith by utilizing conclusionary comments which may be justified by the facts in this case but which have such far-reaching implications as to warrant the expression of my individual views designed to limit the reach of this decision. . . .

. . . This Board has repeatedly held that conduct designed to undermine the Union, or to demonstrate to employees the futility of engaging in collective bargaining through a union, fails to meet the standard of good-faith bargaining. If my colleagues had been content to thus ground their finding in the instant case, I would have no reason to disagree. The record clearly supports their findings with respect to (a) the failure of Respondent to furnish certain information requested by the Union during contract negotiations, (b) the attempts to deal separately with locals on matters which were properly the subject of national negotiations, and (c) the Respondent's importuning of locals to abandon or refrain from supporting the strike authorized by the collective bargaining representative. I share Member Fanning's view that Respondent's presentation of its personal accident insurance proposal to the Union on a take-it-or-leave-it basis was not violative of § 8(a)(5). Within the context of the facts of this case, were the Board to conclude that the foregoing derelictions justify a broad remedial order, I would be able to join and find no fault with the disposition of the case. However, in view of the fact that the majority has gone beyond conduct and indeed concedes that it is not basing its finding of overall bad faith on conduct but rather is basing that finding on an assessment of the Respondent's approach to its duty to bargain in good faith, I am constrained to disavow their comments concerning the employer's bargaining technique.

---

[19] NLRB v. Truitt Mfg. Co., *supra* at 154.

In effect I read the majority opinion to hold that the Act so regulates a party's choice of techniques in collective bargaining as to make unlawful an advance decision, and a frank communication of that decision, concerning the position from which a party is unwilling to retreat. The majority would apparently find that it is unlawful for a union to present a contract proposal on a take-it-or-leave-it basis since I assume the majority would not apply different standards to unions than to employers. The bargaining technique often employed by unions in support of "area standards" contracts is not significantly different from the technique described as the "firm fair offer" by an employer. I would not find a lack of good-faith bargaining where either the employer or the union entered the negotiations with a fixed position from which it proposed not to retreat, engaged in hard bargaining to maintain or protect such position, and made no concessions from that position as a result of bargaining. As one member of the Supreme Court has pointed out, good faith is not necessarily incompatible with stubbornness or even with what to an outsider may seem unreasonableness.

The majority states frankly that the holding of a predetermined resolve not to budge from an initial position is incompatible with good-faith bargaining. That statement seems to ignore the language in § 8(d) of the Act which makes it clear in unequivocal words that "such obligation does not compel either party to agree to a proposal or require the making of a concession." The opinion of my colleagues fails to distinguish between two important concepts, viz., the formulation of a settlement position and the techniques employed in reaching a settlement. The Act does not dictate the methods which a party may choose to utilize in formulating its bargaining position. Indeed, many unions and employers use surveys of one sort or another as a fact-gathering device in advance of bargaining. Moreover, both employers and unions are free from statutory regulation under this Act in formulating the kind of proposal or counter proposal which each will communicate to the other. I know of no decision of this Board which has sought to interpret the statute as requiring either unions or employers to follow a prescribed timetable in communicating the various shifts in position which seem desirable as a matter of self interest. Thus, if either an employer or a union for reasons dictated by self interest chooses to include in a proposal trading items which it is willing later to withdraw or conversely chooses to limit its proposal to items which it will never withdraw voluntarily, the choice is its and not the Board's. . . .

Some portions of my colleagues' opinion may be read as holding that the Act was violated because Respondent chose to decide in advance on the proposal which it was willing to make and from which it was unwilling to retreat unless forced to do so by economic pressure which it apparently regarded as a calculated risk. If such an inference be drawn I disavow it. If free collective bargaining is to survive, both employers and unions must remain free of governmental interference with their right to formulate independently the economic positions which each desires to take and to decide without governmental compulsion whether that position shall be conveyed to the other party at the outset, at some mid point, or at the conclusion of negotiations. To do otherwise maximizes governmental construction of the bargain and minimizes the free flow of independent economic judgment essential to a strong, independent trade union movement and a strong, independent entrepreneurial system, both of which are vital to the kind of economy envisaged by the Act which we administer.

MEMBER LEEDOM, dissenting in part:

My colleagues have found that the Respondent failed to bargain in good faith with the Union in the 1960 negotiations, both in certain specific respects and generally. Although I agree with the specific violations found, I cannot justify the bad-faith finding with respect to the Respondent's overall bargaining conduct.

On the issue as to Respondent's overall good or bad faith it should be conceded that there are various approaches to, and tactics in, negotiations that are wholly consistent with the bargaining obligation imposed by the Act; and it seems to me that both management and labor should not be discouraged from seeking new techniques in dealing with the constantly evolving problems with which they are faced across the bargaining table. Consequently we should take care not to create the impression that we view with suspicion novel approaches to, and techniques of, collective bargaining. . . .

No matter how much we may disclaim any intent to compel bargaining to proceed in some set form, the fact that we closely scrutinize what goes on at the bargaining table will necessarily have the effect of directing bargaining into channels which we have in the past approved, for in such channels will lie security in bargaining, if not success. Whether the substitution of our judgment as to the proper forms and content of bargaining be made directly or indirectly is a difference of no consequence insofar as it interferes with free bargaining and tends to discourage innovation both in tactics and proposals which, as I believe, could be of benefit not only to the parties but to the public as well. Consequently, good policy suggests that we leave the parties to their own devices at the bargaining table unless some compelling facts force us into the area of bargaining . . . .

I do not mean to suggest that the issue of good or bad faith has any clear cut answer here. My position is not dictated so much by strong conviction as by uncertainty. I am not persuaded by the reasons that the majority state for their finding of bad-faith bargaining; and the finding itself and the supporting rationale leave me in the dark as to their practical efficacy. But I am particularly disturbed by the treatment accorded Respondent's communications. Surely the Respondent can lawfully communicate with its employees. Yet here, although the communications are held to be some evidence of bad faith, the majority neither in its decision nor in adopting the Trial Examiner's Recommended Order provides the Respondent with any guides by which it can with reasonable certainty determine what it can lawfully say to its employees. In areas such as this bordering on § 8(c) of the Act and free speech, I believe that the Respondent is entitled to something more by way of clarification than the vague proscription implied in the general bargaining order. But I doubt if the facts and findings indicate what specific limitations can properly be laid down. In any event, the situation with respect to the bad-faith finding is at best ambiguous, and I would, therefore, find that the General Counsel has failed to prove by a preponderance of the evidence that the Respondent did not bargain in good faith during the 1960 negotiations with the Union.

NOTE

The bargaining technique employed by General Electric in the 1960 negotiations is commonly known as "Boulwareism," after Lemuel R. Boulware, a former GE vice-president who first devised it in the late 1940's. It is discussed in detail by its leading academic exponent in H. NORTHRUP, BOULWAREISM (1964). *See also* Cooper, *Boulwareism and the Duty to Bargain in Good Faith,* 20 RUTGERS L. REV. 653 (1966); Gross, Cullen, and Hanslowe, *Good Faith in Labor Negotiations: Tests and Remedies,* 53 CORNELL L. REV. 1009 (1968); Note, *Boulwareism and Good Faith Collective Bargaining,* 63 MICH. L. REV. 1473 (1965).

"Almost ten years after the events that gave rise to this controversy," as the court put it, the Second Circuit in a 2-to-1 decision sustained the Labor Board's condemnation of "Boulewareism." Three judges wrote opinions totaling some 40 pages. Reproduced below are severely edited excerpts from the majority and minority opinions, with the emphasis on those portions dealing with General Electric's "overall approach to bargaining."

NLRB v. GENERAL ELECTRIC CO.

United States Court of Appeals, Second Circuit
418 F.2d 736 (1969), *cert. denied,* 397 U.S. 965 (1970)

IRVING R. KAUFMAN, Circuit Judge . . . .
The new plan ["Boulewareism"] was threefold. GE began by soliciting comments from its local management personnel on the desires of the work force, and the type and level of benefits that they expected. These were then translated into specific proposals, and their cost and effectiveness researched, in order to formulate a "product" that would be attractive to the employees, and within the Company's means. The last step was the most important, most innovative, and most often criticized. GE took its "product" — now a series of fully-formed bargaining proposals — and "sold" it to its employees and the general public. Through a veritable avalanche of publicity, reaching awesome proportions prior to and during negotiations, GE sought to tell its side of the issues to its employees. It described its proposals as a "fair, firm offer," characteristic of its desire to "do right voluntarily," without the need for any union pressure or

strike. In negotiations, GE announced that it would have nothing to do with the "blood-and-threat-and-thunder" approach, in which each side presented patently unreasonable demands, and finally chose a middle ground that both knew would be the probable outcome even before the beginning of the bargaining. The Company believed that such tactics diminished the company's credibility in the eyes of its employees, and at the same time appeared to give the union credit for wringing from the Company what it had been willing to offer all along. Henceforth GE would hold nothing back when it made its offer to the Union; it would take all the facts into consideration, and make that offer it thought right under all the circumstances. Though willing to accept Union suggestions based on facts the Company might have overlooked, once the basic outlines of the proposal had been set, the mere fact that the Union disagreed would be no ground for change. When GE said firm, it meant firm, and it denounced the traditional give and take of the so-called auction bargaining as "flea bitten eastern type of cunning and dishonest but pointless haggling."

To bring its position home to its employees, GE utilized a vast network of plant newspapers, bulletins, letters, television and radio announcements, and personal contacts through management personnel . . . .

We now approach the most troublesome and most vigorously contested of the charges. In addition to the three specific unfair labor practices, GE is also charged with an overall failure to bargain in good faith, compounded like a mosaic of many pieces, but depending not on any one alone. They are together to be understood to comprise the "totality of the circumstances." . . .

Specifically, the Board found that GE's bargaining stance and conduct, considered as a whole, were designed to derogate the Union in the eyes of its members and the public at large. This plan had two major facets: first, a take-it-or-leave-it approach ("firm, fair offer") to negotiations in general which emphasized both the powerlessness and uselessness of the Union to its members, and second, a communications program that pictured the Company as the true defender of the employees' interests, further denigrating the Union, and sharply curbing the Company's ability to change its own position.

The Board relies both on the unfair labor practices already discussed and on several other specific instances to show that GE had developed a pattern of conduct inconsistent with good faith bargaining. It points to GE's proposed personal accident insurance proposal on a take-it-or-leave-it basis as an example of an attempt to bypass the Union, and an attempt to disparage its importance and usefulness in the eyes of its members . . . .

[A]cts not in themselves unfair labor practices may support an inference that a party is acting in bad faith. See NLRB v. Insurance Agents' Union, 361 U.S. 477, 506 (1960) (Frankfurter, J., concurring). While GE may have believed that it was acting within its "rights" in offering a take-it-or-leave-it proposal, doing so may still be some evidence of lack of good faith. Here there was no substantial justification offered for refusing to discuss the matter, other than a niggling — and incorrect — view of the contract and the statute. Cf. NLRB v. Reed & Prince Mfg. Co., 205 F.2d 131 (1st Cir.) (Magruder, J.) ("must make *some* reasonable effort in *some* direction"), *cert. denied,* 346 U.S. 887 (1953). Given the effects of take-it-or-leave-it proposals on the Union, . . . the Board could appropriately infer the presence of anti-Union animus, and in conjunction with other similar conduct could reasonably discern a pattern of illegal activity designed primarily to subvert the Union.

We have already discussed at length the Company's failure to furnish information. As in the instance of the personal accident insurance proposal, GE's attitude on information was characterized by a pettifogging insistence on doing not one whit more than the law absolutely required, an insistence that eventually strayed over into doing considerably less. GE's conduct, as the Board's opinion points out, was all of a piece. It negotiated, to the greatest possible extent, by ignoring the legitimacy and relevance of the Union's position as statutory representative of its members. Thus it is hardly surprising that IUE requests for information were met (at least once negotiations had begun) with less than enthusiasm, for they reflect the Union's contrary belief that it had to know the worth of the Company proposals in order to evaluate them for its members. . . .

When the last act was virtually played out and it had become apparent that the Union would have to end its abortive strike and concede to GE's terms, the Company continued to display a stiff and unbending patriarchal posture hardly consistent with "common willingness among the parties to discuss freely and fully their respective claims and demands and, when these are opposed, to justify them on reason." NLRB v. George P. Pilling & Son Co., 119 F.2d 32, 37 (3d Cir. 1941). With the Union, as it were, "on the ropes," the Company insisted that IUE choose the options that it preferred, and assent to the contract unconditionally, without ever seeing the final contract language. When the Union protested that the memorandum proposed for its signature was too vague, the Company refused to submit more definite language. Four days later, the Union capitulated completely and signed the short form memorandum, still without having seen the final contract to which it was agreeing . . . .

The Company's stand, however, would be utterly inexplicable without the background of its publicity program. Only when viewed in that context does it become meaningful. We have already indicated that one of the central tenets of "the Boulware approach" is that the "product" or "firm, fair offer" must be marketed vigorously to the "consumers" or employees, to convince them that the Company, and not the Union, is their true representative. GE, the Trial Examiner found, chose to rely "entirely" on its communications program to the virtual exclusion of genuine negotiations, which it sought to evade by any means possible. Bypassing the national negotiators in favor of direct settlement dealings with employees and local officials forms another consistent thread in this pattern. The aim, in a word, was to deal with the Union through the employees, rather than with the employees through the Union.

The Company's refusal to withhold publicizing its offer until the Union had had an opportunity to propose suggested modifications is indicative of this attitude. Here two interests diverged. The command of the Boulware approach was clear: employees and the general public must be barraged with communications that emphasized the generosity of the offer, and restated the firmness of GE's position. A genuine desire to reach a mutual accommodation might, on the other hand, have called for GE to await Union comments before taking a stand from which it would be difficult to retreat. GE hardly hesitated. It released the offer the next day without waiting for Union comments on the specific portions.

The most telling effect of GE's marketing campaign was not on the Union, but on GE itself. Having told its employees that it had made a "firm, fair offer," that there was "nothing more to come," and that it would not change its position in the face of "threats" of a strike, GE had in effect rested all on the expectation that it could institute its offer without significant modification. Properly viewed, then, its communications approach determined its take-it-or-leave-it bargaining strategy. Each was the natural complement of the other; if either were substantially changed, the other would in all probability have to be modified as well . . . .

The Company, having created a view of the bargaining process that admitted of no compromise, was trapped by its own creation. It could no longer seek peace without total victory, for it had by its own words and actions branded any compromise a defeat.

GE urges that § 8(c) . . . prohibits the Board from considering its publicity efforts in passing on the legality of its bargaining conduct . . . . GE would have us read that section as a bar to the Board's use of any communications, in any manner, unless the communication itself contained a threat or a promise of benefit. The legislative history, past decisions, and the logic of the statutory framework, however, indicate a contrary conclusion.

The bald prohibition of § 8(c) invited comment when it was enacted, as well as later. Senator Taft replied to some of the criticism of the bill that bears his name:

> "It should be noted that this subsection is limited to 'views, arguments, or opinions' and does not cover instructions, directions, or other statements that would ordinarily be deemed relevant and admissible in courts of law." I Legislative History of the LMRA 1947, at 1541.

The key word is "relevant." The evil at which the section was aimed was the alleged practice of the Board in inferring the existence of an unfair labor practice from a totally unrelated speech or opinion delivered by an employer. Senator Taft later indicated, for example, in the context of a § 8(a)(3) discriminatory firing, that prior statements of the employer would have to be shown to "tie in" with the specific unfair labor practice. I Legislative History of the LMRA 1947, at 1545. Later references to the section described the barred statements at those which were "severable or unrelated," and "irrelevant or immaterial." II Legislative History of the

LMRA 1947, at 429 (Senate Report), 549 (House Conference Report). The objective of 8(c) then, was to impose a rule of relevancy on the Board in evaluating the legality of statements by parties to a labor dispute. Its purpose was hardly to eliminate all communications from the Board's purview, for to do so would be to emasculate a statute whose structure depends heavily on evaluation of motive and intent . . . .

While it is clear that the Board is not to control the substantive terms of a collective bargaining contract, nonetheless the parties must do more than meet. Our brother Friendly makes much of the point that General Electric did bargain and reach an "agreement" with the Union . . . . The statute does not say that any "agreement" reached will validate whatever tactics have been employed to exact it. To imply such a Congressional purpose would be to encourage parties to make their violation so blatant that it would be impossible for the other side to continue to exist without signing. Instead the statute clearly contemplates that to the end of encouraging productive bargaining, the parties must make "a serious attempt to resolve differences and reach a common ground," NLRB v. Insurance Agents' Int'l Union, 361 U.S. 477, 486, 487, 488 (1960), an effort inconsistent with a "predetermined resolve not to budge from an initial position." NLRB v. Truitt Mfg. Co., 351 U.S. 149, 154-155 (1956) (Frankfurter, J., concurring). . . .

The Company and the dissenting opinion seem to take the novel position that the holding in *Insurance Agents'* — that the Board might not forbid a partial strike during bargaining — ousts the Board's control over bargaining tactics. But in NLRB v. Katz, 369 U.S. 736 (1962), the Court held that at least one tactic — instituting unilateral changes during bargaining — was forbidden, for it put a bargainable topic outside the reach of the bargaining process. GE had done no less; it has, if anything, done more. By its communications and bargaining strategy it in effect painted itself into a corner on *all* bargainable matters. . . .

We do not today hold that an employer may not communicate with his employees during negotiations. Nor are we deciding that the "best offer first" bargaining technique is forbidden. Moreover, we do not require an employer to engage in "auction bargaining," or, as the dissent seems to suggest, compel him to make concessions, "minor" or otherwise . . . .

We hold that an employer may not so combine "take-it-or-leave-it" bargaining methods with a widely publicized stance of unbending firmness that he is himself unable to alter a position once taken. It is this specific conduct that GE must avoid in order to comply with the Board's order, and not a carbon copy of every underlying event relied upon by the Board to support its findings. Such conduct, we find, constitutes a refusal to bargain "in fact." NLRB v. Katz, 369 U.S. 736, 743 (1962). It also constitutes, as the facts of this action demonstrate, an absence of subjective good faith, for it implies that the Company can deliberately bargain and communicate as though the Union did not exist, in clear derogation of the Union's status as exclusive representative of its members under § 9(a). . . .

FRIENDLY, Circuit Judge (concurring and dissenting). . . .

The danger of collision with § 8(c) or (d) arises only when the Board makes a finding of violation although the parties have sat down with each other and have not engaged in any proscribed tactic. Still I have no difficulty with the Board's making a finding of bad faith based on an entire course of conduct so long as the standard of bad faith is, in Judge Magruder's well-known phrase, a "desire not to reach an agreement with the Union." NLRB v. Reed & Prince Mfg. Co., 205 F.2d 131, 134 (1st Cir.), *cert. denied,* 346 U.S. 887 (1953). . . .

While the lead opinion makes much use of the "take-it-or-leave-it" phrase, it never defines this. I should suppose it meant a resolve to adhere to a position without even listening to and considering the views of the other side. To go further and say that a party, whether employer or union, who, after listening to and considering such proposals, violates § 8(a)(5) if he rejects them because of confidence in his own bargaining power, would ignore the explicit command of § 8(d). . . .

It surely cannot be, for example, that a union intent on imposing area standards violates § 8(b)(3) if it refuses to heed the well-documented presentation of an employer who insists that acceptance of them will drive him out of business. Neither can it be that a union violates § 8(b)(3) if it insists on its demands because it knows the employer simply cannot stand a strike. It must be equally true that an employer is not to be condemned for "take-it-or-leave-it" bargaining when, after discussing the union's proposals and supporting arguments, he formulates what he considers a sufficiently attractive offer and refuses to alter it unless convinced an alteration is "right." . . .

Once we rid ourselves of the prejudice inevitably engendered by this catch-phrase, we reach the argument that a party violates § 8(a)(5) if he gets himself into a situation where he is "unable to alter a position once taken," even though he would otherwise be willing to do so.

While this sounds fair enough, as does the Board's somewhat similar remark about the continuing duty to give "unfettered consideration," it would seemingly outlaw practices that no one has considered illegal up to this time. A union that has won a favorable contract from one employer and has broadcast that it will take no less from others seems to me to be quite as "unable to alter a position once taken" as GE was here, yet I should not have supposed this violated the Act. So also with an employer who has negotiated a contract with one union and has proclaimed that he will do no better for others. To say that taking such positions violates § 8(b)(3) or 8(a)(5) is steering a collision course with § 8(d). . . .

An essential element to the Board's conclusion of GE's offending was the Company's publicity campaign. "The disparagement of the Union as bargaining representative" is item (5) in the Board's bill of particulars. . . .

I find no warrant for such a holding in the language of the statute, its legislative history or decisions construing it. GE's communications fit snugly under the phrase "views, argument, or opinion" in § 8(c). The very archetypes of what Congress had in mind were communications by an employer to his workers designed to influence their decisions contrary to union views, and communications by unions to workers designed to influence their decisions contrary to employer views. The statute draws no distinctions between communications by an employer in an effort to head off organization and communications after organization intended to show that he is doing right by his employees and will do no more under the threat of a strike. Congress had enough faith in the common sense of the American working man to believe he did not need — or want — to be shielded by a government agency from hearing whatever arguments employers or unions desired to make to him. Freedom of choice by employees after hearing all relevant arguments is the cornerstone of the National Labor Relations Act. . . .

The Examiner coined a phrase, echoed both by the Board and in the lead opinion, . . . namely, that GE's communications program was an attempt "to deal with the Union through the employees rather than with the employees through the Union." . . . Picturesque characterizations of this sort, at such sharp variance with the record, scarcely aid the quest for a right result. Members of Congress would probably be surprised to learn that being "exclusive representatives" means that interested parties may not go to constituents in an endeavor to influence the representatives to depart from positions they have taken. There can be nothing wrong in an employer's urging employees to communicate with their representatives simply because the communication is one the representatives do not want to hear. I thus find it impossible to accept the proposition that, by exercising its § 8(c) right to persuade the employees and by encouraging them to exercise their right to persuade their representatives, GE was somehow "ignoring the legitimacy and relevance of the Union's position as statutory representative of its members." . . .

NOTE

"Hard bargaining" by an employer is not in itself unlawful. Dierks Forests, Inc., 148 N.L.R.B. 923 (1964). At some juncture in the negotiations an employer clearly may make a firm and final offer. In Philip Carey Mfg. Co., 140 N.L.R.B. 1103 (1963), *enforced in part,* 331 F.2d 720 (6th Cir. 1964), *cert. denied,* 379 U.S. 888 (1964), the Board held that an employer did not violate § 8(a)(5) when it made a final offer at the eleventh meeting in a series of give-and-take bargaining sessions.

Occasionally, an employer's substantive proposals have been treated as some evidence of bad faith, when combined with other conduct such as delaying tactics. So classified were refusals to contract without a reduction of the wage rate currently in effect, C & D Coal Co., 93 N.L.R.B. 799 (1951), or without a reduction of vacation benefits, NLRB v. Deena Artware, Inc., 198 F.2d 645 (6th Cir. 1952). *See also* Federal Mogul Corp., 212 N.L.R.B. 950 (1974), *enforced,* 524 F.2d 37 (6th Cir. 1975) (employer refused to discuss economic issues until union agreed to employer's noneconomic proposals); Bartlett-Collins Co., 237 N.L.R.B. No. 106, 99 L.R.R.M. 1034 (1978) (employer insisted on presence of court reporter as precondition to contract negotiations). In the latter two cases the Board apparently applied a *per se* theory of illegality, an approach that was sharply criticized in Modjeska, *Guess Who's Coming to the Bargaining Table?* 39 Ohio St. L.J. 415 (1978).

In a few instances a finding of bad faith has been predicated in part on the employer's rejection of proposals submitted by the union. The proposals at issue included a clause embodying a right guaranteed employees by the labor relations statute, Montgomery Ward & Co., 37 N.L.R.B. 100 (1941), *enforced,* 133 F.2d 676 (9th Cir. 1943); permission for the union to use the company bulletin board, an accepted practice in the industry, Reed & Prince Mfg. Co., 96 N.L.R.B. 850 (1951), *enforced,* 205 F.2d 131 (1st Cir. 1953), *cert. denied,* 346 U.S. 887 (1953); and a checkoff provision, H.K. Porter Co., 153 N.L.R.B. 1370 (1965), *enforced,* 363 F.2d 272 (D.C. Cir. 1966), *cert. denied,* 385 U.S. 851 (1966), and Roanoke Iron & Bridge Works, Inc., 160 N.L.R.B. 175 (1966), *enforced,* 390 F.2d 846 (D.C. Cir. 1967), *cert. denied,* 391 U.S. 904 (1968) (employer intransigent for purpose of undermining union, not for "legitimate" business reasons).

Ordinarily, however, the good faith of the employer is to be judged by the NLRB on the basis of all the circumstances. The inference of bad faith has usually been drawn from a pattern of conduct evidencing a lack of a genuine effort to come to an agreement. In NLRB v. Montgomery Ward & Co., 133 F.2d 676, 687 (9th Cir. 1943), the court said: "Wards was not bound to offer a counterproposal . . . but when one is asked for, it ought to be made, although not indispensable. [I]t is not incumbent upon the employees continually to present new contracts until ultimately one meets the approval of the company." Could one say there is a duty to make counterproposals but no duty to make concessions? What would that mean? *See* Marcus, *The Employer's Duty to Bargain: Counterproposal v. Concession,* 17 Lab. L.J. 541 (1966).

On good faith bargaining in general, see Duvin, *The Duty to Bargain: Law in Search of Policy,* 64 Colum. L. Rev. 248 (1964); Fanning, *The Duty to Bargain in 1962,* 14 Lab. L.J. 18 (1963); Feinsinger, *The National Labor Relations Act and Collective Bargaining,* 57 Mich. L. Rev. 807 (1959); Fleming, *New Challenges for Collective Bargaining,* 1964 Wis. L. Rev. 426; Goldstein, *When and Where Should Be the Limits of NLRB Intervention?* in N.Y.U. Twenty-Third Annual Conference on Labor 55 (1970); Murphy, *Impasse and the Duty to Bargain in Good Faith,* 39 U. Pitt. L. Rev. 1 (1977).

GENERAL ELECTRIC CO. v. NLRB

United States Court of Appeals, Second Circuit
412 F.2d 512 (2d Cir. 1969)

Feinberg, Circuit Judge: — In the spring of 1966, General Electric Company walked out of a meeting with the International Union of Electrical, Radio and Machine Workers, AFL-CIO (IUE), because the Company objected to the presence on the IUE bargaining committee of representatives of other unions.

. . .[T]he IUE and other unions representing the Company's employees had been concerned over the results of their separate efforts to bargain with General Electric. According to the unions, the Company had successfully followed a practice of divide and conquer in the past by making a separate "fair, firm offer" almost simultaneously to each union and then whipsawing one against the other. In any event, dissatisfied with the results of their prior separate efforts, the unions in 1965 formed a Committee on Collective Bargaining (CCB), consisting eventually of the IUE and seven other international unions whose locals also had agreements with General Electric. The avowed purposes of the members of the CCB were to coordinate bargaining in 1966 with General Electric and its chief competitor, Westinghouse Electric Corporation, to formulate national goals, and otherwise to support one another. [The 1963-1966 national contract between GE and the IUE was due to expire on October 2, 1966.]

The CCB made several efforts to persuade the Company to meet with it for joint informal discussions on various matters; presumably, this would have taken the place of preliminary discussions with the IUE alone. The last such CCB proposal was rejected by the Company on March 25, 1966. On the same day, Moore wrote to Callahan of IUE, stating that the Company was "very receptive to appropriate pre-negotiation discussions with IUE, but . . . [did] not intend to participate in any eight-union coalition discussions or in any other steps in the direction of industry-wide bargaining." On April 13, Callahan responded and suggested that a meeting be called to formulate rules for subcommittee meetings. He stated that the IUE had not intended any formal request for joint bargaining and that the IUE would "abandon any suggestions for any such joint meeting or for joint discussions." Thereafter, Moore agreed to a meeting and the date was set for May 4.

The May 4 meeting never took place. When the IUE representatives arrived that morning, the Company for the first time became aware of the addition of seven members to the IUE negotiating committee, one member of each of the other seven unions that comprised the CCB. The Company representatives attended the meeting only long enough to announce that they would meet "only with . . . IUE people." The Company subsequently maintained its position even after it had been told that the seven new members of the IUE committee were non-voting members who were present solely to aid in IUE negotiations and not to represent their own unions.

On May 9, 1966, the IUE filed failure to bargain charges with the Board. . . . On August 2, 1966, the IUE formally requested in writing that the Company open contract talks under the reopener provision of the national agreement. . . . On August 9, Moore replied, accepting an August 15 meeting date but making it quite clear that the Company was agreeing to meet only on the condition that no "representatives of other unions" be present. The Company adhered to this position until August 18 when the district court granted the Board's request for a preliminary injunction compelling the Company to meet with the enlarged IUE committee. . . .

The basic question before us is whether a union's inclusion of members of other unions on its bargaining committee justifies an employer's refusal to bargain. The Company contends that there is more to the case than that, claiming that the IUE was engaged in an illegal attempt to obliterate bargaining unit lines and was, as the Board put it, "'locked in' to a conspiratorial understanding." We discuss that phase of the case below, but turn first to the crucial issue before us.

Section 7 of the National Labor Relations Act, 29 U.S.C. § 157, guarantees certain rights to employees, including the right to join together in labor organizations and "to bargain collectively through representatives of their own choosing." This right of employees and the corresponding right of employers, see § 8(b)(1)(B) of the Act, 29 U.S.C. § 158(b)(1)(B), to choose whomever they wish to represent them in formal labor negotiations is fundamental to the statutory scheme. In general, either side can choose as it sees fit and neither can control the other's selection, a proposition confirmed in a number of opinions, some of fairly ancient vintage. For example, the following asserted objections to bargaining representatives have all been rejected as defenses to charges of refusal to bargain: that a local union president could not act for the international union in grievance handling, see Prudential Insurance Co. of America v. NLRB, 278 F.2d 181, 182-83 (3d Cir. 1960); that an AFL "general organizer," not a member or officer of the union, could not bargain for the latter, see NLRB v. Deena Artware, Inc., 198 F.2d 645, 650-51 (6th Cir. 1952), *cert. denied,* 345 U.S. 906 (1953); that employees could not be represented by a local union, a majority of whose members were employed by a rival industry and which the employees were not eligible to join, see Pueblo Gas & Fuel Co. v. NLRB, 118 F.2d 304, 307-08 (10th Cir. 1941); and that an international union representative could not negotiate for a local, see Oliver Corp., 74 N.L.R.B. 483 (1947).

There have been exceptions to the general rule that either side can choose its bargaining representatives freely, but they have been rare and confined to situations so infected with ill will, usually personal, or conflict of interest as to make good faith bargaining impractical. See, *e.g.,* NLRB v. ILGWU, 274 F.2d 376, 379 (3d Cir. 1960) (ex-union official added to employer committee to "put one over on the union"); Bausch & Lomb Optical Co., 108 N.L.R.B. 1555 (1954) (union established company in direct competition with employer); NLRB v. Kentucky Utilities Co., 182 F.2d 810 (6th Cir. 1950) (union negotiator had expressed great personal animosity towards employer). But cf. NLRB v. Signal Manufacturing Co., 351 F.2d 471 (1st Cir. 1965) (*per curiam), cert. denied,* 382 U.S. 985 (1966) (similar claim of animosity rejected). Thus, the freedom to select representatives is not absolute, but that does not detract from its significance. Rather the narrowness and infrequency of approved exceptions to the general rule emphasizes its importance. Thus, in arguing that employees may not select members of other unions as "representatives of their own choosing" on a negotiating committee, the Company clearly undertakes a considerable burden, characterized in an analogous situation in NLRB v. David Buttrick Co., 399 F.2d 505, 507 (1st

Cir. 1968), as the showing of a "clear and present" danger to the collective bargaining process. . . .

Turning to specific policy reasons for inclusion of members of other unions on a negotiating committee, we are told that a union has an interest in using experts to bargain, whether the expertise be on technical, substantive matters or on the general art of negotiating. In filling that need, no good reason appears why it may not look to "outsiders," just as an employer is free to do. See Detroit Newspaper Publishers Ass'n v. NLRB, 372 F.2d 569, 572 (6th Cir. 1967); NLRB v. Local 294, International Brotherhood of Teamsters, 284 F.2d 893 (2d Cir. 1960). However, the heat generated by this controversy does not arise from that bland consideration. The Company has in the past made effective use of its own ability to plan centralized bargaining strategy in dealing with the various unions representing its employees while keeping the actual bargaining with each union separate. . . .

IUE claims that having members of the other unions on its committee increases communications between all of them and to that extent reduces the ability of the Company to play one off against the other. In any event, the plain facts are that the IUE proposed negotiating technique is a response to the Company's past bargaining practices, that it is designed to strengthen the IUE's bargaining position, and that both sides know it.

The Board held that a mixed-union negotiating committee is not per se improper and that absent a showing of "substantial evidence of ulterior motive or bad faith" an employer commits an unfair labor practice unless it bargains with such a group. The Company and amicus attack the Board rule on a number of grounds. They claim that the rule will inevitably allow the injection of conflicting interests and "outside and extraneous influences" into the bargaining process, will make the always difficult task of determining the motives of the other side an impossibility, is an improper effort by the Board to adjust economic power, and finally is unworkable because an employer confronted with bad faith or ulterior motives can only break off negotiations with the mixed group and file unfair labor practices charges with the Board, an option disruptive of collective bargaining at best and in actuality no remedy at all.

The claim that outside influences and alleged conflicts require an outright ban on mixed-union committees is not weighty in view of the cases discussed above. Equally unpersuasive is the assertion that the Board made an improper effort to adjust economic power. The Board gave no such rationale for its decision. Of course, it would be nonsense to pretend that IUE's purpose was not to increase its bargaining strength, but that goal is a normal one for unions or employers. That Board application of an old policy to a new situation may have such an effect does not vitiate a rule if it is otherwise justified. The possibility that there will be improper attempts to ignore unit boundaries is, of course, real. The Company argues that different unions certified for separate units may not force an employer to bargain with them jointly as to all units on any subject, despite the implications of United States Pipe & Foundry Co. v. NLRB, 298 F.2d 873 (5th Cir.), cert. denied, 370 U.S. 919 (1962), which approved an arrangement whereby three unions conditioned their agreements in separate but substantially simultaneous negotiations upon a joint demand for common contract expiration dates. The Board did not come to grips with this problem, and we similarly do not now consider the extent to which the law permits cooperation in bargaining among unions or employers. . . . The point is that the chance that negotiators may improperly press impermissible subjects is inherent in the bargaining process, and therefore must be taken. As to the increased difficulty in determining motives of the other side, we agree that this may occur. However, although evidence that bargaining for other employees is being attempted may be difficult to obtain, the Board is certainly capable of making such a determination when a case comes before it. . . . Indeed, the dangers foreseen could exist even if there were no members of other unions on a committee if, for example, the unions were to meet together immediately before and after each bargaining session. Surely an employer would not be justified because of that fact alone in refusing to meet even though evidence of an attempt by the unions to merge bargaining units or to obtain a common bargaining agreement would, if anything, be more difficult to produce. We agree that a mixed-union committee could make it easier to press such plans illegally, although not by that much, in view of modern communication techniques. Nevertheless, cooperation between unions is not improper up to a point and it is for the Board in the first instance to determine whether the line has been crossed. In view of the overall policy of encouraging free selection of representatives, we agree with the Board's rejection of a per se rule which bans mixed-union committees.

In sum, we do not think that the Company has demonstrated the type of clear and present danger to the bargaining process that is required to overcome the burden on one who objects to the representatives selected by the other party. We hold that the IUE did have the right to include members of other unions on its negotiating committee, and the Company was not lawfully entitled to refuse to bargain with that committee so long as it sought to bargain solely on behalf of those employees represented by the IUE, a question we discuss further below. . . .

As to the period before the formal contract reopener in August, the Board found that the Company had agreed to a limited reopening of the contract to discuss preliminary matters, that this agreement was unconditional — or at least not conditioned on the presence of a "traditional" IUE negotiating committee — and that having agreed even to this limited reopening the Company was necessarily bound by the traditional requirements of good faith bargaining. The Company strenuously disputes all three propositions.

On this aspect of the case, we agree in substance with the Company [regarding the spring of 1966]. . . .

. . . Thus, we have decided that it was improper for the Company to refuse to bargain in August 1966 on the ground that members of other unions were on the IUE committee. However, we must still deal with the Company's claim that in any event it could refuse to meet with the IUE committee because the CCB was attempting to use it to impose joint bargaining upon the Company and because the IUE was "locked-in" to an agreement whereby it would not accept any offer made by the Company until the other unions did.

The Board rejected these contentions without deciding whether either factor would have justified a refusal to meet. Instead, the Board held that the Company had the duty once the IUE had retreated from its advocacy of joint bargaining, to put the negotiators to the test. . . . [T]he trial examiner found that on May 4 the IUE was neither "locked-in" nor bent on joint bargaining, and the Board found that there was no substantial evidence of the IUE committee's ulterior motive or bad faith. Moreover, if we focus only on the situation in August and thereafter, with which we are specifically concerned, the Board's determination has, if anything, more support. Throughout the proceedings before Judge Frankel the IUE disclaimed any intention to bargain for others and maintained its ability to enter into any agreement that satisfied its demands regardless of the position of other unions. Still, the Company did not offer to test IUE's good faith. Rather it continued to refuse to meet until required to by court order. Moreover, during the period when the Company had to — and did — deal with the mixed IUE committee, the committee neither bargained nor tried to bargain for employees other than those represented by IUE. . . . In sum, we think that the Board's findings on this aspect of the case are supported by substantial evidence and must be upheld.

The Company was thus guilty of a refusal to bargain in violation of sections 8(a)(1) and (5) of the Act. . . . The order of the Board is set aside insofar as it rests on a violation of the Act prior to August 1966. With this modification, the order is enforced.

NOTES

1. Was the IUE's introduction of "coordinated bargaining" in the 1966 negotiations a predictable escalation of the combat following GE's resort to Boulwareism in 1960? Does it seem like an effective technique? *See generally* Northrup, *Boulwareism v. Coalitionism — The 1966 GE Negotiations,* MANAGEMENT OF PERSONNEL QUARTERLY, Summer 1966, at 2; Anker, *Pattern Bargaining, Antitrust Laws and the National Labor Relations Act,* in N.Y.U. NINETEENTH ANNUAL CONFERENCE ON LABOR 81 (1967); Goldberg, *Coordinated Bargaining Tactics of Unions,* 54 CORNELL L. REV. 897 (1969).

2. Should labor organizations representing different bargaining units of the same employer ever be entitled to insist upon joint negotiations? If so, when? In AFL-CIO Joint Negotiating Committee (Phelps Dodge Corp.), 184 N.L.R.B. 754 (1970), the Labor Board held that a group of unions violated § 8(b)(3) by insisting in effect on company-wide bargaining. The unions demanded the simultaneous and satisfactory settlement of contracts in other bargaining units of the company, and struck in support of their demands. The Board said that the integrity of a bargaining unit, whether established by certification or by voluntary

agreement of the parties, may not be unilaterally attacked. Enforcement was denied in AFL-CIO Joint Negotiating Committee v. NLRB, 459 F.2d 374 (3d Cir. 1972), *cert. denied,* 409 U.S. 1059 (1972). The court of appeals pointed out that all the union demands were mandatory subjects of bargaining, and that the parallel action of the units in going to impasse was not evidence of an attempt to merge the bargaining of separate units. "The fact a demand may have extra-unit effects does not alter its status as a mandatory subject of bargaining." *Cf.* Paperworkers Local 1027 (Mead Corp.), 216 N.L.R.B. 486 (1975) (union may insist on bargaining for pensions for seven units represented by seven unions on multiplant basis pursuant to 20-year practice); United Steelworkers (Lynchburg Foundry Co.), 192 N.L.R.B. 773 (1971) (approving "pooled ratification" of company's wage proposals by two locals having close community of interests). *But cf.* Utility Workers (Ohio Power Co.), 203 N.L.R.B. 230 (1973), *enforced,* 490 F.2d 1383 (6th Cir. 1974) (unions representing separate units violated § 8(b)(3) by insisting that several subsidiaries of same parent company bargain for all units jointly, and that the employers submit identical offers for all units, as a condition of agreement). *See also* Oil, Chemical & Atomic Workers v. NLRB [Shell Oil Co.], 486 F.2d 1266 (D.C. Cir. 1973) (employer did not violate § 8(a)(5) by rejecting request of union representing nineteen separate bargaining units for simultaneous bargaining concerning revisions in company-wide fringe benefit plans).

3. An employer may not insist upon joint negotiations with two unions representing separate units of the company's employees. To carry such a demand to impasse is a violation of § 8(a)(5), since only the employees or their representatives have the right to select the members of the union's bargaining team. F. W. Woolworth Co., 179 N.L.R.B. 748 (1969).

4. On a somewhat related point, the NLRB holds that multiemployer bargaining is purely voluntary, and both unions and employers may withdraw by giving timely, unequivocal notice prior to negotiations. Evening News Ass'n, 154 N.L.R.B. 1494 (1965), *enforced,* 372 F.2d 569 (6th Cir. 1967); NLRB v. Ass'n of Steel Fabricators, 582 F.2d 135 (2d Cir. 1978). *See also* McAx Sign Co. v. NLRB, 576 F. 2d 62 (5th Cir. 1978) (authorization for multiemployer bargaining inferred from employer's conduct). Once negotiations have begun, however, withdrawal requires "mutual consent" or "unusual circumstances." A sharp decline in a company's business, or a genuine impasse in bargaining, may not constitute "unusual circumstances" permitting a unilateral employer withdrawal. Serv-All Co., 199 N.L.R.B. 1131 (1972); Hi-Way Billboards, Inc., 206 N.L.R.B. 22 (1973), *enforcement denied,* 500 F.2d 181 (5th Cir. 1974).

5. Uniformity of labor standards in an industry or geographical area is a traditional goal of many unions. After a union has come to terms with the principal employer association in a given area, is it an unlawful refusal to bargain for the union to require an identical contract with every independent employer? Is there any difference between the union's "take-it-or-leave-it" attitude in such circumstances and GE's in the 1960 negotiations with the IUE? Even if the union engaged in the usual give-and-take bargaining with the employer association, what good is this to an independent confronted by a peremptory demand that he sign the standard labor agreement?

2. BARGAINING REMEDIES

H. K. PORTER CO. v. NLRB

Supreme Court of the United States
397 U.S. 99, 90 S. Ct. 821, 26 L. Ed. 2d 146 (1970)

MR. JUSTICE BLACK delivered the opinion of the Court.

After an election respondent United Steelworkers Union was, on October 5, 1961, certified by the National Labor Relations Board as the bargaining agent for the employees at the Danville, Virginia, plant of the petitioner, H. K. Porter Co. Thereafter negotiations commenced for a collective bargaining agreement. Since that time the controversy has seesawed between the Board, the Court of Appeals for the District of Columbia Circuit, and this Court. This delay of over eight years is not because the case is exceedingly complex, but appears to have occurred chiefly because of the skill of the company's negotiators in taking advantage of every opportunity for delay in an Act more noticeable for its generality than for its precise prescriptions. The entire lengthy dispute mainly revolves around the union's desire to have the company agree to "check off" the dues owed to the union by its members, that is, to deduct those dues periodically from the company's wage payments to the employees. The record shows, as the Board found, that the company's objection to a checkoff was not due to any general principle or policy against making deductions from employees' wages. The company does deduct charges for things like insurance, taxes, and contributions to charities, and at some other plants it has a checkoff arrangement for union dues. The evidence shows, and the court below found, that the company's objection was not because of inconvenience, but solely on the ground that the company was "not going to aid and comfort the union." Efforts by the union to obtain some kind of compromise on the checkoff request were all met with the same staccato response to the effect that the collection of union dues was the "union's business" and the company was not going to provide any assistance. Based on this and other evidence the Board found, and the Court of Appeals approved the finding, that the refusal of the company to bargain about the checkoff was not made in good faith, but was done solely to frustrate the making of any collective bargaining agreement. In May 1966, the Court of Appeals upheld the Board's order requiring the company to cease and desist from refusing to bargain in good faith and directing it to engage in further collective bargaining, if requested by the union to do so, over the checkoff. United Steelworkers v. NLRB, 363 F.2d 272, *cert. denied,* 385 U.S. 851.

In the course of that opinion, the Court of Appeals intimated that the Board conceivably might have required petitioner to agree to a checkoff provision as a remedy for the prior bad-faith bargaining, although the order enforced at that time did not contain any such provision. 363 F.2d at 275-276, n. 16. In the ensuing negotiations the company offered to discuss alternative arrangements for collecting the union's dues, but the union insisted that the company was required to agree to the checkoff proposal without modification. Because of this disagreement over the proper interpretation of the court's opinion, the union, in February 1967, filed a motion for clarification of the 1966 opinion. The motion was denied by the court on March 22, 1967, in an order suggesting that contempt proceedings before the Board would be the proper avenue for testing the employer's compliance with the original order. A request for the institution of such proceedings was made by the union, and in June 1967, the Regional Director of the Board declined to prosecute a contempt charge, finding that the employer had "satisfactorily complied with the affirmative requirements of the Order." . . . The union then filed in the Court of Appeals a motion for reconsideration of the earlier motion to clarify the 1966 opinion. The court granted that motion and issued a new opinion in which it held that in certain circumstances a "checkoff may be imposed as a remedy for bad-faith bargaining." United Steelworkers v. NLRB, 389 F.2d 295, 298 (1967). The case was then remanded to the Board and on July 3, 1968, the Board issued a supplemental order requiring the petitioner to "[g]rant to the Union a contract clause providing for the checkoff of union dues." 172 N.L.R.B. No. 72. The Court of Appeals affirmed this order, H. K. Porter Co. v. NLRB, 414 F.2d 1123 (1969). We granted certiorari to consider whether the Board in these circumstances had the power to remedy the unfair labor practice by requiring the company to agree to check off the dues of the workers. . . . For reasons to be stated we hold that while the Board does have power under the Labor Management Relations Act . . . to require employers and employees to negotiate, it is without power to compel a company or a union to agree to any substantive contractual provision of a collective bargaining agreement.

Since 1935 the story of labor relations in this country has largely been a history of governmental regulation of the process of collective bargaining. In that year Congress decided that disturbances in the area of labor relations led to undesirable burdens on and obstructions of interstate commerce, and passed the National Labor Relations Act. . . . Without spelling out the details, the Act provided that it was an unfair labor practice for an employer to refuse to bargain. Thus a general process was established which would ensure that employees as a group could express their opinions and exert their combined influence over the terms and conditions of their employment. The Board would act to see that the process worked.

The object of this Act was not to allow governmental regulation of the terms and conditions of employment, but rather to ensure that employers and their employees could work together to establish mutually satisfactory conditions. The basic theme of the Act was that through collective bargaining the passions, arguments, and struggles of prior years would be channeled into constructive, open discussions leading, hopefully, to mutual agreement. But it was recognized from the beginning that agreement might in some cases be impossible, and it was never intended that the Government would in such cases step in, become a party to the negotiations and impose its own views of a desirable settlement. This fundamental limitation was made abundantly clear in the legislative reports accompanying the 1935 Act. . . . The discussions on the floor of Congress consistently reflect this same understanding.

The Act was passed at a time in our Nation's history when there was considerable legal debate over the constitutionality of any law that required employers to conform their business behavior to any governmentally imposed standards. It was seriously contended that Congress could not constitutionally compel an employer to recognize a union and allow his employees to participate in setting the terms and conditions of employment. In NLRB v. Jones & Laughlin Steel Corp., 301 U.S. 1 (1937), this Court, in a 5-to-4 decision, held that Congress was within the limits of its constitutional powers in passing the Act. In the course of that decision the Court said:

"The Act does not compel agreements between employers and employees. It does not compel any agreement whatever. . . . The theory of the Act is that free opportunity for negotiation with accredited representatives of employees is likely to promote industrial peace and may bring about the adjustments and agreements which the Act in itself does not attempt to compel." *Id.* at 45.

In 1947 Congress reviewed the experience under the Act and concluded that certain amendments were in order. In the House committee report accompanying what eventually became the Labor Management Relations Act of 1947, the committee referred to the above quoted language in *Jones & Laughlin* and said:

"Notwithstanding this language of the Court, the present Board has gone very far, in the guise of determining whether or not employers had bargained in good faith, in setting itself up as the judge of what concessions an employer must make and of the proposals and counterproposals that he may or may not make.

. . . .

"[U]nless Congress writes into the law guides for the Board to follow, the Board may attempt to carry this process still further and seek to control more and more the terms of collective bargaining agreements." [3] Accordingly Congress amended the provisions defining unfair labor practices and said in § 8(d) that: ". . . *such obligation [to bargain collectively] does not compel either party to agree to a proposal or require the making of a concession.*"

In discussing the effect of that amendment, this Court said it is "clear that the Board may not, either directly or indirectly, compel concessions or otherwise sit in judgment upon the substantive terms of collective

---

[3] H.R. Rep. No. 245, 80th Cong., 1st Sess. 19-20 (1947).

bargaining agreements." NLRB v. American Ins. Co., 343 U.S. 395, 404 (1952). Later this Court affirmed that view stating that "it remains clear that § 8(d) was an attempt by Congress to prevent the Board from controlling the settling of the terms of collective bargaining agreements." NLRB v. Insurance Agents, 361 U.S. 477, 487 (1960). The parties to the instant case are agreed that this is the first time in the 35-year history of the Act that the Board has ordered either an employer or a union to agree to a substantive term of a collective bargaining agreement.

Recognizing the fundamental principle "that the National Labor Relations Act is grounded on the premise of freedom of contract," 389 F.2d at 300, the Court of Appeals in this case concluded that nevertheless in the circumstances presented here the Board could properly compel the employer to agree to a proposed checkoff clause. The Board had found that the refusal was based on a desire to frustrate agreement and not on any legitimate business reason. On the basis of that finding the Court of Appeals approved the further finding that the employer had not bargained in good faith, and the validity of that finding is not now before us. Where the record thus revealed repeated refusals by the employer to bargain in good faith on this issue, the Court of Appeals concluded that ordering agreement to the checkoff clause "may be the only means of assuring the Board, and the court, that [the employer] no longer harbors an illegal intent." 389 F.2d at 299.

In reaching this conclusion the Court of Appeals held that § 8(d) did not forbid the Board from compelling agreement. That court felt that "[s]ection 8(d) defines collective bargaining and relates to a determination of *whether* a . . . violation has occurred and not to the *scope* of the remedy which may be necessary to cure violations which have already occurred." 389 F.2d at 299. We may agree with the Court of Appeals that as a matter of strict, literal interpretation of that section it refers only to deciding when a violation has occurred, but we do not agree that that observation justifies the conclusion that the remedial powers of the Board are not also limited by the same considerations that led Congress to enact § 8(d). It is implicit in the entire structure of the Act that the Board acts to oversee and referee the process of collective bargaining, leaving the results of the contest to the bargaining strengths of the parties. It would be anomalous indeed to hold that while § 8(d) prohibits the Board from relying on a refusal to agree as the sole evidence of bad faith bargaining, the Act permits the Board to compel agreement in that same dispute. The Board's remedial powers under § 10 of the Act are broad, but they are limited to carrying out the policies of the Act itself. One of these fundamental policies is freedom of contract. While the parties' freedom of contract is not absolute under the Act, allowing the Board to compel agreement when the parties themselves are unable to do so would violate the fundamental premise on which the Act is based — private bargaining under governmental supervision of the procedure alone, without any official compulsion over the actual terms of the contract.

In reaching its decision the Court of Appeals relied extensively on the equally important policy of the Act that workers' rights to collective bargaining are to be secured. In this case the Court apparently felt that the employer was trying effectively to destroy the union by refusing to agree to what the union may have considered its most important demand. Perhaps the court, fearing that the parties might resort to economic combat, was also trying to maintain the industrial peace which the Act is designed to further. But the Act as presently drawn does not contemplate that unions will always be secure and able to achieve agreement even when their economic position is weak, nor that strikes and lockouts will never result from a bargaining to impasse. It cannot be said that the Act forbids an employer or a union to rely ultimately on its economic strength to try to secure what it cannot obtain through bargaining. It may well be true, as the Court of Appeals felt, that the present remedial powers of the Board are insufficiently broad to cope with important labor problems. But it is the job of Congress, not the Board or the courts, to decide when and if it is necessary to allow governmental review of proposals for collective bargaining agreements and compulsory submission to one side's demands. The present Act does not envision such a process.

The judgment is reversed and the case is remanded to the Court of Appeals for further action consistent with this opinion.

Reversed and remanded.

MR. JUSTICE WHITE took no part in the decision of this case.

MR. JUSTICE MARSHALL took no part in the consideration or decision of this case.

[The concurring opinion of MR. JUSTICE HARLAN and the dissenting opinion of MR. JUSTICE DOUGLAS, in which MR. JUSTICE STEWART concurred, are omitted.]

NOTE

Does *H. K. Porter* undercut the anti-Boulwareism stance of the NLRB and the Second Circuit in the *General Electric* decisions, *supra* at 506 and 513? *See* Goldstein, *When and Where Should Be the Limits of NLRB Intervention?* in N.Y.U. TWENTY-THIRD ANNUAL CONFERENCE ON LABOR 55 (1970). *See also* Comment, *The H. K. Porter Experiment in Bargaining Remedies: A Study in Black and Wright,* 56 VA. L. REV. 530 (1970).

EX-CELL-O CORP.

National Labor Relations Board
185 N.L.R.B. 107 (1970)

This case began with the UAW's request for recognition on August 3, 1964. Ex-Cell-O refused the Union's request on August 10, 1964, and the Union immediately filed a petition for Certification of Representative. After a hearing the Regional Director ordered an election, which was held on October 22, 1964, and a majority of the employees voted for the Union. The Company, however, filed objections to the conduct of the election, alleging that the Union made certain misrepresentations which assertedly interfered therewith, but the Acting Regional Director, in a Supplemental Decision of December 29, 1964, overruled them. The Company then requested review of that decision, which the Board granted, and a hearing was held on May 18 and 19, 1965. The Hearing Officer issued his Report on Objections on July 15, 1965, and recommended that the objections be overruled. The Company filed exceptions thereto, but on October 28, 1965, the Board adopted the Hearing Officer's findings and recommendations and affirmed the Regional Director's certification of the Union.

The day after the Board's certification was issued, the Company advised the Union that it would refuse to bargain in order to secure a court review of the Board's action and later reiterated this position after receiving the Union's request for a bargaining meeting. The Union thereupon filed the 8(a)(1) and (5) charge in this case and the complaint was issued on November 23, 1965. The Respondent's answer admitted the factual allegations of the complaint but denied the violation on the ground that the Board's certification was invalid. The hearing herein, originally scheduled for February 15, 1966, commenced on June 1, 1966; it was adjourned until June 29, 1966, to permit the Union to offer evidence supporting its request for a compensatory remedy for the alleged refusal to bargain; the hearing was postponed again until July 28, 1966. The Company also petitioned the United States District Court for an injunction against the Regional Director and the Trial Examiner to restrain the latter from closing the hearing until the Regional Director had produced the investigative records in the representation case. The court issued a summary judgment denying the injunction on December 13, 1966, and on December 21, 1966, the Trial Examiner formally closed his hearing. On March 2, 1967, the Trial Examiner issued his Decision, finding that the Company had unlawfully refused to bargain in violation of Section 8(a)(5) and (1) of the Act and recommended the standard bargaining order as a remedy. In addition the Trial Examiner ordered the Company to compensate its employees for monetary losses incurred as a result of its unlawful conduct.

It is not disputed that Respondent refused to bargain with the Union, and we hereby affirm the Trial Examiner's conclusion that Respondent thereby violated Section 8(a)(1) and (5) of the Act. The compensatory remedy which he recommends, however, raises important issues concerning the Board's powers and duties to fashion appropriate remedies in its efforts to effectuate the policies of the National Labor Relations Act.

It is argued that such a remedy exceeds the Board's general statutory powers. In addition, it is contended that it cannot be granted because the amount of employee loss, if any, is so speculative that an order to make employees whole would amount to the imposition of a penalty. And the position is advanced that the adoption of this remedy would amount to the writing of a contract for the parties, which is prohibited by Section 8(d).

We have given most serious consideration to the Trial Examiner's recommended financial reparations order, and are in complete agreement with his finding that current remedies of the Board designed to cure violations of Section 8(a)(5) are inadequate. A mere affirmative order that an employer bargain upon request does not eradicate the effects of an unlawful delay of 2 or more years in the fulfillment of a statutory bargaining obligation. It does not put the employees in the position of bargaining strength they would have enjoyed if their employer had immediately recognized and bargained with their chosen representative. It does not dissolve the inevitable employee frustration or protect the Union from a loss of employee support attributable to such delay. The inadequacy of the remedy is all the more egregious where, as in the recent *NLRB v. Tiidee Products Inc.*[6] case, the court found that the employer had raised "frivolous" issues in order to postpone or avoid its lawful obligation to bargain. We have weighed these considerations most carefully. For the reasons stated below, however, we have reluctantly concluded that we cannot approve the Trial Examiner's Recommended Order that Respondent compensate its employees for monetary losses incurred as a consequence of Respondent's determination to refuse to bargain until it had tested in court the validity of the Board's certification.

Section 10(c) of the Act directs the Board to order a person found to have committed an unfair labor practice to cease and desist and "to take such affirmative action including reinstatement of employees with or without back pay, as will effectuate the policies of this Act." This authority, as our colleagues note with full documentation, is extremely broad and was so intended by Congress. It is not so broad, however, as to permit the punishment of a particular respondent or a class of respondents. Nor is the statutory direction to the Board so compelling that the Board is without discretion in exercising the full sweep of its power, for it would defeat the purposes of the Act if the Board imposed an otherwise proper remedy that resulted in irreparable harm to a particular respondent and hampered rather than promoted meaningful collective bargaining. Moreover, as the Supreme Court recently emphasized, the Board's grant of power does not extend to compelling agreement. (H. K. Porter Co., Inc. v. NLRB, 397 U.S. 99.) It is with respect to these three limitations upon the Board's power to remedy a violation of Section 8(a)(5) that we examine the UAW's requested remedy in this case.

The Trial Examiner concluded that the proposed remedy was not punitive, that it merely made the employees partially whole for losses occasioned by the Respondent's refusal to bargain, and was much less harsh than a backpay order for discharged employees, which might require the Respondent to pay wages to these employees as well as their replacements. Viewed solely in the context of an assumption of employee

---

[6] 426 F.2d 1243 (D.C. Cir. 1970), [*cert. denied*, 400 U.S. 950 (1970)].

monetary losses resulting directly from the Respondent's violation of
Section 8(a)(5), as finally determined in court, the Trial Examiner's
conclusion appears reasonable. There are, however, other factors in this
case which provide counter weights to that rationale. In the first place,
there is no contention that this Respondent acted in a manner flagrantly
in defiance of the statutory policy. On the contrary, the record indicates
that this Respondent responsibly fulfills its legally established collective
bargaining obligations. It is clear that Respondent merely sought judicial
affirmance of the Board's decision that the election of October 22, 1964,
should not be set aside on the Respondent's objections. In the past
whenever an employer has sought court intervention in a representation
proceeding the Board has argued forcefully that court intervention would
be premature, that the employer had an unquestioned right under the
statute to seek court review of any Board order before its bargaining
obligation became final. Should this procedural right in 8(a)(5) cases be
tempered by a large monetary liability in the event the employer's position
in the representation case is ultimately found to be without merit? Of
course, an employer or a union, which engages in conduct later found in
violation of the Act, does so at the peril of ultimate conviction and
responsibility for a make-whole remedy.

But the validity of a particular Board election tried in an unfair labor
practice case is not, in our opinion, an issue on the same plane as the
discharge of employees for union activity or other conduct in flagrant
disregard of employee rights. There are wrongdoers and wrongdoers.
Where the wrong in refusing to bargain is, at most, a debatable question,
though ultimately found a wrong, the imposition of a large financial
obligation on such a respondent may come close to a form of punishment
for having elected to pursue a representation question beyond the Board
and to the courts. The desirability of a compensatory remedy in a case
remarkably similar to the instant case was recently considered by the
Court of Appeals for the District of Columbia in United Steelworkers
[Quality Rubber Manufacturing Company, Inc.] v. NLRB, [430 F.2d 519]
(July 10, 1970). There the court, distinguishing *Tiidee Products, supra,*
indicated that the Board was warranted in refusing to grant such a remedy
in an 8(a)(5) case where the employer "desired only to obtain an
authoritative determination of the validity of the Board's decision." It is
not clear whether the court was of the opinion that the requested remedy
was within the Board's discretion or whether it would have struck down
such a remedy as punitive in view of the technical nature of the
respondent's unfair labor practice. In any event, we find ourselves in
disagreement with the Trial Examiner's view that a compensatory remedy
as applied to the Respondent in the instant case is not punitive "in any
sense of the word."

In *Tiidee Products* the court suggested that the Board need not follow
a uniform policy in the application of a compensatory remedy in 8(a)(5)
cases. Indeed, the court noted that such uniformity in this area of the law
would be unfair when applied "to unlike cases." The court was of the
opinion that the remedy was proper where the employer had engaged in

a "manifestly unjustifiable refusal to bargain" and where its position was "palpably without merit." As in *Quality Rubber,* the court in *Tiidee Products* distinguished those cases in which the employer's failure to bargain rested on a "debatable question." With due respect for the opinion of the Court of Appeals for the District of Columbia, we cannot agree that the application of a compensatory remedy in 8(a)(5) cases can be fashioned on the subjective determination that the position of one respondent is "debatable" while that of another is "frivolous." What is debatable to the Board may appear frivolous to a court, and vice versa. Thus, the debatability of the employer's position in an 8(a)(5) case would itself become a matter of intense litigation.

We do not believe that the critical question of the employer's motivation in delaying bargaining should depend so largely on the expertise of counsel, the accident of circumstances, and the exigencies of the moment.

In our opinion, however, the crucial question to be determined in this case relates to the policies which the requested order would effectuate. The statutory policy as embodied in Section 8(a)(5) and (d) of the Act was considered at some length by the Supreme Court in H. K. Porter Co., Inc. v. NLRB, *supra. . . .*

It is argued that the instant case is distinguishable from *H. K. Porter* in that here the requested remedy merely would require an employer to compensate employees for losses they incurred as a consequence of their employer's failure to agree to a contract he would have agreed to if he had bargained in good faith. In our view, the distinction is more illusory than real. The remedy in *H. K. Porter* operates prospectively to bind an employer to a specific contractual term. The remedy in the instant case operates retroactively to impose financial liability upon an employer flowing from a presumed contractual agreement. The Board infers that the latter contract, though it never existed and does not and need not exist, was denied existence by the employer because of his refusal to bargain. In either case the employer has not agreed to the contractual provision for which he must accept full responsibility as though he had agreed to it. Our colleagues contend that a compensatory remedy is not the "writing of a contract" because it does not "specify new or continuing terms of employment and does not prohibit changes in existing terms and conditions." But there is no basis for such a remedy unless the Board finds, as a matter of fact, that a contract would have resulted from bargaining. The fact that the contract, so to speak, is "written in the air" does not diminish its financial impact upon the recalcitrant employer who, willy-nilly, is forced to accede to terms never mutually established by the parties. Despite the admonition of the Supreme Court that Section 8(d) was intended to mean what it says, *i.e.,* that the obligation to bargain "does not compel either party to agree to a proposal or require the making of a concession," one of the parties under this remedy is forced by the Government to submit to the other side's demands.

It does not help to argue that the remedy could not be applied unless there was substantial evidence that the employer would have yielded to these demands during bargaining negotiations. Who is to say in a specific case how much an employer is prepared to give and how much a union is willing to take? Who is to say that a favorable contract would, in any event, result from the negotiations? And it is only the employer of such good will as to whom the Board might conclude that he, at least, would have given his employees a fair increase, who can be made subject to a financial reparations order; should such an employer be singled out for the imposition of such an order? To answer these questions the Board would be required to engage in the most general, if not entirely speculative, inferences to reach the conclusion that employees were deprived of specific benefits as a consequence of their employer's refusal to bargain.

Much as we appreciate the need for more adequate remedies in 8(a)(5) cases, we believe that, as the law now stands, the proposed remedy is a matter for Congress, not the Board. In our opinion, however, substantial relief may be obtained immediately through procedural reform, giving the highest possible priority to 8(a)(5) cases combined with full resort to the injunctive relief provisions of Section 10(j) and (e) of the Act.

MEMBERS McCULLOCH and BROWN, dissenting in part: Although concurring in all other respects in the Decision and Order of the Board, we part company with our colleagues on the majority in that we would grant the compensatory remedy recommended by the Trial Examiner. Unlike our colleagues, we believe that the Board has the statutory authority to direct such relief and that it would effectuate the policies of the Act to do so in this case.

Section 10(c) of the Act directs the Board to remedy unfair labor practices by ordering the persons committing them to cease and desist from their unlawful conduct "and to take such affirmative action including reinstatement of employees with or without back pay, as will effectuate the policies of this Act. . . ." The phrase "affirmative action" is nowhere qualified in the statute, except that such action must "effectuate the policies of this Act," and indicates the intent of Congress to vest the Board with remedial powers coextensive with the underlying policies of the law which is to be enforced. The provision "did not pass the Wagner Act Congress without objection to the uncontrolled breadth of this power."

But the broad language survived the challenge. . . .

Deprivation of an employee's statutory rights is often accompanied by serious financial injury to him. Where this is so, an order which only guarantees the exercise of his rights in the future often falls far short of expunging the effects of the unlawful conduct involved. Therefore, one of the Board's most effective and well-established affirmative remedies for unlawful conduct is an order to make employees financially whole for losses resulting from violations of the Act. Various types of compensatory orders have been upheld by the Supreme Court in the belief that "Making the workers whole for losses suffered on account of an unfair practice is part of the vindication of the public policy which the Board enforces." The most familiar of these is the backpay order used to remedy the effect of employee discharges found to be in violation of Section 8(a)(3) of the Act. . . .

It is clear from the Act that the Board's compensatory remedies need not be limited to the above situations, and the courts have always interpreted the phrase "with or without back pay" as being merely an illustrative example of the general grant of power to award affirmative relief. . . .

The Board has already recognized in certain refusal-to-bargain situations that the usual bargaining order is not sufficient to expunge the effects of an employer's unlawful and protracted denial of its employees' right to bargain. Though the bargaining order serves to remedy the loss of the legal right and protect its exercise in the future, it does not remedy the financial injury which may also have been suffered. In a number of situations the Board has ordered the employer who unlawfully refused to bargain to compensate its employees for their resultant financial losses. Thus, some employers unlawfully refuse to sign after an agreement. The Board has in these cases ordered the employer to execute the agreement previously reached and, according to its terms, to make whole the employees for the monetary losses suffered because of the unlawful delay in its effectuation. . . .

The question now before us is whether a reimbursement order is an appropriate remedy for other types of unlawful refusals to bargain. On the basis of the foregoing analysis regarding Section 10(c), we believe that the Board has the power to order this type of relief. Further, for the reasons set forth herein, we are of the view that the compensatory remedy is appropriate and necessary in this case to effectuate the policies of the Act. . . .

The present remedies for unlawful refusals to bargain often fall short, as in the present case, of adequately protecting the employees' right to bargain. Recent court decisions, congressional investigations, and scholarly studies have concluded that, in the present remedial framework, justice delayed is often justice denied.

In *NLRB v. Tiidee Products, Inc.,* the Court of Appeals for the District of Columbia Circuit recently stated that: "While the Board's usual bargaining remedy may provide some bargaining from the date of the order's enforcement, it operates in a real sense so as to be counterproductive, and actually to reward an employer's refusal to bargain during the critical period following a union's organization of his plant. The obligation of collective bargaining is the core of the Act, and the primary means fashioned by Congress for securing industrial peace. . . .

". . . Employee interest in a union can wane quickly as working conditions remain apparently unaffected by the union or collective bargaining. When the company is finally ordered to bargain with the union some years later, the union may find that it represents only a small fraction of the employees. . . . Thus the employer may reap a second benefit from his original refusal to comply with the law: He may continue to enjoy lower labor expenses after the order to bargain either because the union is gone or because it is too weak to bargain effectively." . . .

The present case is but another example of a situation where a bargaining order by itself is not really adequate to remedy the effects of an unlawful refusal to bargain. The Union herein requested recognition on August 3, 1964, and proved that it represented a majority of employees 2½ months later in a Board-conducted election. Nonetheless, since October 1965 the employer, by unlawfully refusing to bargain with the Union, had deprived its employees of their legal right to collective bargaining through their certified bargaining representative. While a bargaining order at this time, operating prospectively, may insure the exercise of that right in the future, it clearly does not repair the injury to the employees here, caused by the Respondent's denial of their rights during the past 5 years.

In these refusal-to-bargain cases there is at least a legal injury. . . . [W]here the legal injury is accompanied by financial loss, the employees should be compensated for it. The compensatory period would normally run from the date of the employer's unlawful refusal to bargain until it commences to negotiate in good faith, or upon the failure of the Union to commence negotiations within 5 days of the receipt of the Respondent's notice of its desire to bargain with the Union, although here a later starting date could be used because this remedy would be a substantial departure from past practices. Further, the Board could follow its usual procedure of providing a general reimbursement order with the amount, if any, to be determined as part of the compliance procedure.

This type of compensatory remedy is in no way forbidden by section 8(d). It would be designed to compensate employees for injuries incurred by them by virtue of the unfair labor practices and would not require the employer to accept the measure of compensation as a term of any contract which might result from subsequent collective bargaining. The remedy contemplated in no way "writes a contract" between the employer and the union, for it would not specify new or continuing terms of employment and would not prohibit changes in existing terms and conditions. All of these would be left to the outcome of bargaining, the commencement of which would terminate Respondent's liability.

Furthermore, this compensatory remedy is not a punitive measure. It would be designed to do no more than reimburse the employees for the loss occasioned by the deprivation of their right to be represented by their collective bargaining agent during the period of the violation. The amount to be awarded would be only that which would reasonably reflect and be measured by the loss caused by the unlawful denial of the opportunity for collective bargaining. Thus, employees would be compensated for the injury suffered as a result of their employer's unlawful refusal to bargain, and the employer would thereby be prohibited from enjoying the fruits of its forbidden conduct to the end, as embodied in the Act, that collective bargaining be encouraged and the rights of injured employees be protected. . . . [W]here the defendant's wrongful act prevents exact determination of the amount of damage, he cannot plead such uncertainty in order to deny relief to the injured person, but rather must bear the risk of the uncertainty which was created by his own wrong. The Board is often faced with the task of determining the precise amount of a make-whole order where the criteria are less than ideal, and has successfully resolved the questions presented. . . .

A showing at the compliance stage by the General Counsel or Charging Party by acceptable and demonstrable means that the employees could have reasonably expected to gain a certain amount of compensation by bargaining would establish a prima facie loss, and the Respondent would then be afforded an opportunity to rebut such a showing. This might be accomplished, for example by adducing evidence to show that a contract would probably not have been reached, or that there would have been less or no increase in compensation as a result of any contract which might have been signed.

Accordingly, uncertainty as to the amount of loss does not preclude a make-whole order proposed here, and some reasonable method or basis of computation can be worked out as part of the compliance procedure. . . . Thus, if the particular employer and union involved have contracts covering other plants of the employer, possibly in the same or a relevant area, the terms of such agreements may serve to show what the employees could probably have obtained by bargaining. The parties could also make comparisons with compensation patterns achieved through collective bargaining by other employees in the same geographic area and industry. Or the parties might employ the national average percentage changes in straight time hourly wages computed by the Bureau of Labor Statistics. . . .

NOTES

1. The conventional Board remedy for an employer violation of § 8(a)(5) is a cease-and-desist order and an affirmative order for the employer to bargain collectively with the majority representative of its employees. Since the Board cannot compel agreement, is an order to bargain anything more than a pious exhortation? Empirical studies indicate that it is. Thus, one survey revealed that successful bargaining relationships were eventually established in seventy-five percent of the cases sampled which went through to a final Board order, and in ninety percent of the cases which were voluntarily adjusted after the issuance of a complaint. *See* P. Ross, The Government as a Source of Union Power 180-230 (1965); McCulloch, *The Development of Administrative Remedies,* 14 Lab. L.J. 339, 348 (1963). Nonetheless, doubts remain about the efficacy of the Board's traditional remedy, especially where a union is seeking recognition or is trying to negotiate its first contract. This has led to the focusing of attention on innovative Board remedies. *See, e.g.,* McCulloch, *Past, Present and Future Remedies under Section 8(a)(5) of the NLRA,* 19 Lab. L.J. 131 (1968); D. McDowell & K. Huhn, NLRB Remedies for Unfair Labor Practices (1976); Morris, *The Role of the NLRB and the Courts in the Collective Bargaining Process: A Fresh Look at the Conventional Wisdom and Unconventional Remedies,* 30 Vand. L. Rev. 661 (1977); St. Antoine, *A Touchstone for Labor Board Remedies,*

14 WAYNE L. REV. 1039 (1968); Note, *The Use of Section 10(j) of the Labor-Management Relations Act in Employer Refusal to Bargain Cases,* 1976 ILL. L. F. 845.

2. Was the Board majority in *Ex-Cell-O* primarily influenced by theoretical or by practical considerations? Did *H. K. Porter* preclude the "make-whole" remedy sought by the union?

3. As indicated in the *Ex-Cell-O* opinions, a court of appeals has ruled (2-1) that the usual cease-and-desist order is inadequate to remedy an employer's "clear and flagrant" violation of his bargaining duty. IUE v. NLRB [Tiidee Products, Inc.], 426 F.2d 1243 (D.C. Cir. 1970), *cert. denied,* 400 U.S. 950 (1970). The case was remanded to the Board for further consideration of an appropriate remedy, which might include back pay to compensate the employees for the benefits denied them by the employer's refusal to bargain. In reaching this result, the majority stressed that the remand was limited to consideration of past damages, and not to compulsion of a future contract term, thus distinguishing the case from the Supreme Court's decision in *H. K. Porter.* The same court held that the Board had not abused its discretion in refusing to grant make-whole relief, however, where employers declined to bargain in good faith efforts to challenge a union's certification or other representational determinations. United Steelworkers v. NLRB [Quality Rubber Mfg. Co.], 430 F.2d 519 (D.C. Cir. 1970). In keeping with this distinction, the court of appeals sustained the Board's decision in *Ex-Cell-O* on the ground the company's objections to the certification there fell in the "fairly debatable" rather than the "frivolous" or "bad faith" category. Ex-Cell-O Corp. v. NLRB, 449 F.2d 1058 (D.C. Cir. 1971).

The "make-whole" remedy was interred, at least for the foreseeable future, in Tiidee Products, Inc., 194 N.L.R.B. 1234 (1972), *enforced,* 502 F.2d 349 (D.C. Cir. 1974), *cert. denied,* 421 U.S. 991 (1975); *see also* Betra Mfg. Co., 233 N.L.R.B. No. 156, 97 L.R.R.M. 1005 (1977). On the remand in *Tiidee,* a unanimous Board rejected a reimbursement order, even where the employer's refusal to bargain was a "clear and flagrant" violation of law. Nonetheless, the Board thought such a violation did merit a remedy going beyond the customary cease and desist order. It therefore required the employer to reimburse both the NLRB and the union for their litigation expenses, to mail copies of the NLRB's notice to each employee's home, to keep the union supplied with an employee name-and-address list for one year, and to give the union reasonable access to company bulletin boards. The court of appeals in granting enforcement eliminated the award of litigation expenses to the Board, and bowed to the Board's expertise in concluding it was incapable of calculating an appropriate make-whole remedy. *Cf.* United Steelworkers v. NLRB [Metco, Inc.], 496 F.2d 1342 (5th Cir. 1974).

In NLRB v. Food Store Employees Local 347 [Heck's, Inc.], 417 U.S. 1 (1974), the Supreme Court held that a court of appeals exceeded its authority in ordering an employer guilty of "aggravated and pervasive" unfair labor practices to pay a union's litigation expenses and excess organizational costs, since the NLRB had ruled against such a remedy.

The proper procedure was a remand to the Board for reconsideration in light of its 1972 *Tiidee* decision.

4. Under the proposed Labor Reform Act of 1978, an employer would have been subject to a make-whole remedy in favor of its employees if it unlawfully refused to bargain with a union prior to the execution of a first contract.

3. UNILATERAL ACTION

NLRB v. KATZ

Supreme Court of the United States
369 U.S. 736, 82 S. Ct. 1107, 8 L. Ed. 2d 230 (1962)

MR. JUSTICE BRENNAN delivered the opinion of the Court.

Is it a violation of the duty "to bargain collectively" imposed by § 8(a)(5) of the National Labor Relations Act for an employer, without first consulting a union with which it is carrying on bona fide contract negotiations, to institute changes regarding matters which are subjects of mandatory bargaining under § 8(d) and which are in fact under discussion? The National Labor Relations Board answered the question affirmatively in this case, in a decision which expressly disclaimed any finding that the totality of the respondents' conduct manifested bad faith in the pending negotiations. 126 N.L.R.B. 288. A divided panel of the Court of Appeals for the Second Circuit denied enforcement of the Board's cease-and-desist order, finding in our decision in NLRB v. Insurance Agents, 361 U.S. 477 (1960), a broad rule that the statutory duty to bargain cannot be held to be violated, when bargaining is in fact being carried on, without a finding of the respondent's subjective bad faith in negotiating. 289 F.2d 700.... We granted certiorari, 368 U.S. 811, in order to consider whether the Board's decision and order were contrary to *Insurance Agents.* We find nothing in the Board's decision inconsistent with *Insurance Agents* and hold that the Court of Appeals erred in refusing to enforce the Board's order....

As amended and amplified at the hearing and construed by the Board, the complaint's charge of unfair labor practices particularly referred to three acts by the company: unilaterally granting numerous merit increases in October 1956 and January 1957; unilaterally announcing a change in sick-leave policy in March 1957; and unilaterally instituting a new system of automatic wage increases during April 1957. As the ensuing litigation has developed, the company has defended against the charges along two fronts: First, it asserts that the unilateral changes occurred after a bargaining impasse had developed through the union's fault in adopting obstructive tactics. According to the Board, however, "the evidence is clear that the Respondent undertook its unilateral actions before negotiations were discontinued in May 1957, or before, as we find on the record, the existence of any possible impasse." 126 N.L.R.B. at 289-290. There is ample support in the record considered as a whole for this finding of fact, which is consistent with the Examiner's Intermediate Report, 126 N.L.R.B. at 295-296, and which the Court of Appeals did not question.

The second line of defense was that the Board could not hinge a conclusion that § 8(a)(5) had been violated on unilateral actions alone, without making a finding of the employer's subjective bad faith at the bargaining table; and that the unilateral actions were merely evidence relevant to the issue of subjective good faith. This argument prevailed in the Court of Appeals. . . .

The duty "to bargain collectively" enjoined by § 8(a)(5) is defined by § 8(d) as the duty to "meet . . . and confer in good faith with respect to wages, hours, and other terms and conditions of employment." Clearly, the duty thus defined may be violated without a general failure of subjective good faith; for there is no occasion to consider the issue of good faith if a party has refused even to negotiate *in fact* — "to meet . . . and confer" — about any of the mandatory subjects. A refusal to negotiate *in fact* as to any subject which is within § 8(d), and about which the union seeks to negotiate, violates § 8(a)(5) though the employer has every desire to reach agreement with the union upon an over-all collective agreement and earnestly and in all good faith bargains to that end. We hold that an employer's unilateral change in conditions of employment under negotiation is similarly a violation of § 8(a)(5), for it is a circumvention of the duty to negotiate which frustrates the objectives of § 8(a)(5) much as does a flat refusal.[11]

The unilateral actions of the respondent illustrate the policy and practical considerations which support our conclusion.

We consider first the matter of sick leave. A sick-leave plan had been in effect since May 1956, under which employees were allowed ten paid sick-leave days annually and could accumulate half the unused days, or up to five days each year. Changes in the plan were sought and proposals and counterproposals had come up at three bargaining conferences. In March

---

[11] Compare Medo Corp. v. Labor Board, 321 U.S. 678 (1944); May Department Stores v. NLRB, 326 U.S. 376 (1945); NLRB v. Crompton-Highland Mills, 337 U.S. 217 (1949).

In *Medo,* the Court held that the employer interfered with his employees' right to bargain collectively through a chosen representative, in violation of § 8(1), 49 Stat. 452 (now § 8(a)(1)), when it treated directly with employees and granted them a wage increase in return for their promise to repudiate the union they had designated as their representative. It further held that the employer violated the statutory duty to bargain when he refused to negotiate with the union after the employees had carried out their promise.

May held that the employer violated § 8(1) when, after having unequivocally refused to bargain with a certified union on the ground that the unit was inappropriate, it announced that it had applied to the War Labor Board for permission to grant a wage increase to all its employees except those whose wages had been fixed by "closed shop agreements."

Crompton-Highland Mills sustained the Board's conclusion that the employer's unilateral grant of a wage increase substantially greater than any it had offered to the union during negotiations which had ended in impasse clearly manifested bad faith and violated the employer's duty to bargain.

1957, the company, without first notifying or consulting the union, announced changes in the plan, which reduced from ten to five the number of paid sick-leave days per year, but allowed accumulation of twice the unused days, thus increasing to ten the number of days which might be carried over. This action plainly frustrated the statutory objective of establishing working conditions through bargaining. Some employees might view the change to be a diminution of benefits. Others, more interested in accumulating sick-leave days, might regard the change as an improvement. If one view or the other clearly prevailed among the employees, the unilateral action might well mean that the employer had either uselessly dissipated trading material or aggravated the sick-leave issue. On the other hand, if the employees were more evenly divided on the merits of the company's changes, the union negotiators, beset by conflicting factions, might be led to adopt a protective vagueness on the issue of sick leave, which also would inhibit the useful discussion contemplated by Congress in imposing the specific obligation to bargain collectively.

Other considerations appear from consideration of the respondents' unilateral action in increasing wages. At the April 4, 1957, meeting the employers offered, and the union rejected, a three-year contract with an immediate across-the-board increase of $7.50 per week, to be followed at the end of the first year and again at the end of the second by further increases of $5 for employees earning less than $90 at those times. Shortly thereafter, without having advised or consulted with the union, the company announced a new system of automatic wage increases whereby there would be an increase of $5 every three months up to $74.99 per week; an increase of $5 every six months between $75 and $90 per week; and a merit review every six months for employees earning over $90 per week. It is clear at a glance that the automatic wage increase system which was instituted unilaterally was considerably more generous than that which had shortly theretofore been offered to and rejected by the union. Such action conclusively manifested bad faith in the negotiations, NLRB v. Crompton-Highland Mills, 337 U.S. 217 (1949), and so would have violated § 8(a)(5) even on the Court of Appeals' interpretation, though no additional evidence of bad faith appeared. An employer is not required to lead with his best offer; he is free to bargain. But even after an impasse is reached he has no license to grant wage increases greater than any he has ever offered the union at the bargaining table, for such action is necessarily inconsistent with a sincere desire to conclude an agreement with the union.[12]

The respondents' third unilateral action related to merit increases, which are also a subject of mandatory bargaining. NLRB v. Allison & Co., 165 F.2d 766 (6th Cir. 1948). The matter of merit increases had been

_____

[12] Of course, there is no resemblance between this situation and one wherein an employer, after notice and consultation, "unilaterally" institutes a wage increase identical with one which the union has rejected as too low. . . .

raised at three of the conferences during 1956 but no final understanding had been reached. In January 1957, the company, without notice to the union, granted merit increases to 20 employees out of the approximately 50 in the unit, the increases ranging between $2 and $10. This action too must be viewed as tantamount to an outright refusal to negotiate on that subject, and therefore as a violation of § 8(a)(5), unless the fact that the January raises were in line with the company's long-standing practice of granting quarterly or semiannual merit reviews — in effect, were a mere continuation of the status quo — differentiates them from the wage increases and the changes in the sick-leave plan. We do not think it does. Whatever might be the case as to so-called "merit raises" which are in fact simply automatic increases to which the employer has already committed himself, the raises here in question were in no sense automatic, but were informed by a large measure of discretion. There simply is no way in such case for a union to know whether or not there has been a substantial departure from past practice, and therefore the union may properly insist that the company negotiate as to the procedures and criteria for determining such increases.

It is apparent from what we have said why we see nothing in *Insurance Agents* contrary to the Board's decision. The union in that case had not in any way whatever foreclosed discussion of any issue, by unilateral actions or otherwise. The conduct complained of consisted of partial-strike tactics designed to put pressure on the employer to come to terms with the union negotiators. We held that Congress had not, in § 8(b)(3), the counterpart of § 8(a)(5), empowered the Board to pass judgment on the legitimacy of any particular economic weapon used in support of genuine negotiations. But the Board *is* authorized to order the cessation of behavior which is in effect a refusal to negotiate, or which directly obstructs or inhibits the actual process of discussion, or which reflects a cast of mind against reaching agreement. Unilateral action by an employer without prior discussion with the union does amount to a refusal to negotiate about the affected conditions of employment under negotiation, and must of necessity obstruct bargaining, contrary to the congressional policy. It will often disclose an unwillingness to agree with the union. It will rarely be justified by any reason of substance. It follows that the Board may hold such unilateral action to be an unfair labor practice in violation of § 8(a)(5), without also finding the employer guilty of over-all subjective bad faith. While we do not foreclose the possibility that there might be circumstances which the Board could or should accept as excusing or justifying unilateral action, no such case is presented here.

The judgment of the Court of Appeals is reversed and the case is remanded with direction to the court to enforce the Board's order.

It is so ordered.

Mr. Justice Frankfurter took no part in the decision of this case.

Mr. Justice White took no part in the consideration or decision of this case.

NOTES

1. To what extent does *Katz* make an employer's unilateral change in working conditions a refusal to bargain per se? How does the approach differ from that in NLRB v. Crompton-Highland Mills, Inc., 337 U.S. 217 (1949), cited in note 11 of the *Katz* opinion?

2. After an "impasse" in bargaining has been reached, an employer is usually free to initiate changes unilaterally, so long as they are not more favorable than the proposals made to the union. NLRB v. U.S. Sonics Corp., 312 F.2d 610 (1st Cir. 1963); Pacific Gamble Robinson Co. v. NLRB, 186 F.2d 106 (6th Cir. 1950) (strike replacements were offered wages not substantially higher than those offered the union before the strike). The expiration of an existing contract does not in itself allow an employer to take unilateral action. Industrial Union of Marine & Shipbuilding Workers v. NLRB, 320 F.2d 615 (3d Cir. 1963), *cert. denied,* 375 U.S. 984 (1964). Even in the absence of an impasse, business necessity, such as the need to maintain operations during a strike, may enable an employer to institute unilateral changes, provided they are consistent with offers unaccepted by the union. NLRB v. Bradley Washfountain Co., 192 F.2d 144 (7th Cir. 1951); Raleigh Water Heating Mfg. Co., 136 N.L.R.B. 76 (1962).

3. What steps should be taken by an employer, upon entering negotiations for a new contract, to ensure that he will not be precluded from extending such employment benefits as he thinks necessary to keep a satisfied work force, in the event he is unable to conclude an agreement with the union? Suppose the employer has a multiplant operation with various bargaining units and various unions, and with a substantial number of unrepresented employees. What legal and practical considerations must he take into account if he wishes to raise the wage rates and improve the existing health and welfare plan of his employees, both represented and unrepresented? Assume that some of the union contracts are "open" for renegotiation and others are not. *See generally* Stewart & Engeman, *Impasse, Collective Bargaining, and Action,* 39 U. Cin. L. Rev. 233 (1970).

4. An employer's unilateral *decrease* of benefits during negotiations has also been held a violation of § 8(a)(5). Molders Local 155 [United States Pipe & Foundry Co.], 442 F.2d 742 (D.C. Cir. 1971); Borden, Inc., 196 N.L.R.B. 1170 (1972). Is this consistent with the employer lockout (*American Ship*) and union "harassment" (*Insurance Agents*) decisions? See Schatzki, *The Employer's Unilateral Act — A Per Se Violation — Sometimes,* 44 Texas L. Rev. 470, 502-03 (1966).

5. Once a union contract has expired, does an employer's right to institute unilateral changes vary depending on the nature of the particular working conditions involved? For example, should there be different treatment of a union shop and check-off, super-seniority for union officials, wage scales and hours of work, and the grievance or arbitration procedure? *See* Industrial Union of Marine & Shipbuilding Workers v. NLRB, *supra;* NLRB v. Cone Mills Corp., 373 F.2d 595 (4th Cir. 1967);

Hilton-Davis Chem. Co., 185 N.L.R.B. 241 (1970); Note, *Good Faith Grievance Handling as an Aspect of the Duty to Bargain Collectively,* 38 N.Y.U.L. REV. 350 (1963).

6. Unilateral employer action is discussed in Bowman, *An Employer's Unilateral Action — An Unfair Labor Practice?* 9 VAND. L. REV. 487 (1956); Cox, *The Duty to Bargain in Good Faith,* 71 HARV. L. REV. 1401 (1958); Lang, *Unilateral Changes by Management as a Violation of the Duty to Bargain Collectively,* 9 SW. L.J. 276 (1955), 30 TULANE L. REV. 431 (1956); Comment, *Impasse in Collective Bargaining,* 44 TEXAS L. REV. 769 (1966).

7. Could a union violate § 8(b)(3) by unilateral action? How? See Painters Dist. Council 9, 186 N.L.R.B. 964 (1970), *enforced,* 453 F.2d 783 (2d Cir. 1971), *cert. denied,* 408 U.S. 930 (1972) (production ceiling). *But cf.* Scofield v. NLRB, 394 U.S. 423 (1969).

DETROIT & TOLEDO SHORE LINE R.R. v. UNITED TRANSPORTATION UNION, 396 U.S. 142, 90 S. Ct. 294, 24 L. Ed. 2d 325 (1969). Section 6 of the Railway Labor Act provides that "rates of pay, rules, or working conditions shall not be altered" during the period from the first notice of a proposed change in an agreement until the conclusion of any proceedings concerning a "major dispute" before the National Mediation Board. A railroad made certain "outlying work assignments" while a dispute over the issue was pending before the NMB. This meant that railroad employees had to report for work at points elsewhere than at the railroad's principal yard. The railroad contended that § 6 requires a party to preserve the status quo only in those working conditions covered by the parties' existing collective agreement, and insisted that nothing in its contract precluded the railroad from altering the location of work assignments. The Supreme Court disagreed, and upheld an injunction against the railroad's establishing new outlying assignments. According to the Court, the status quo applies to those "actual, objective working conditions and practices, broadly conceived, which were in effect prior to the time the pending dispute arose and which are involved in or related to that dispute." The Court cautioned, however, that "the mere fact that the collective agreement before us does not expressly prohibit outlying assignments would not have barred the railroad from ordering the assignments that gave rise to the present dispute if, apart from the agreement, such assignments had occurred for a sufficient period of time with the knowledge and acquiescence of the employees to become in reality a part of the actual working conditions."

4. SUPPLYING INFORMATION

NLRB v. TRUITT MANUFACTURING CO.

Supreme Court of the United States
351 U.S. 149, 76 S. Ct. 753, 100 L. Ed. 1027 (1956)

MR. JUSTICE BLACK delivered the opinion of the Court.

The National Labor Relations Act makes it an unfair labor practice for an employer to refuse to bargain in good faith with the representative of his employees. The question presented by this case is whether the National Labor Relations Board may find that an employer has not bargained in good faith where the employer claims it cannot afford to pay higher wages but refuses requests to produce information substantiating its claim.

The dispute here arose when a union representing certain of respondent's employees asked for a wage increase of 10 cents per hour. The company answered that it could not afford to pay such an increase, it was undercapitalized, had never paid dividends, and that an increase of more than 2½ cents per hour would put it out of business. The union asked the company to produce some evidence substantiating these statements, requesting permission to have a certified public accountant examine the company's books, financial data, etc. This request being denied, the union asked that the company submit "full and complete information with respect to its financial standing and profits," insisting that such information was pertinent and essential for the employees to determine whether or not they should continue to press their demand for a wage increase. A union official testified before the trial examiner that "[W]e were wanting anything relating to the Company's position, any records or what have you, books, accounting sheets, cost expenditures, what not, anything to back the Company's position that they were unable to give any more money." The company refused all the requests, relying solely on the statement that "the information . . . is not pertinent to this discussion and the company declines to give you such information; You have no legal right to such."

On the basis of these facts the National Labor Relations Board found that the company had "failed to bargain in good faith with respect to wages in violation of Section 8(a)(5) of the Act." 110 N.L.R.B. 856. The Board ordered the company to supply the union with such information as would "substantiate the Respondent's position of its economic inability to pay the requested wage increase." The Court of Appeals refused to enforce the Board's order, agreeing with respondent that it could not be held guilty of an unfair labor practice because of its refusal to furnish the information requested by the union. 224 F.2d 869 (4th Cir. 1955). In NLRB v. Jacobs Mfg. Co., 196 F.2d 680 (2d Cir. 1952), the Second Circuit upheld a Board finding of bad-faith bargaining based on an employer's refusal to supply financial information under circumstances similar to those here. Because of the conflict and the importance of the question we granted certiorari. . . .

The company raised no objection to the Board's order on the ground that the scope of information required was too broad or that disclosure would put an undue burden on the company. Its major argument throughout has been that the information requested was irrelevant to the bargaining process and related to matters exclusively within the province of management. Thus we lay to one side the suggestion by the company here that the Board's order might be unduly burdensome or injurious to its business. In any event, the Board has heretofore taken the position in cases such as this that "It is sufficient if the information is made available in a manner not so burdensome or time-consuming as to impede the process of bargaining." And in this case the Board has held substantiation of the company's position requires no more than "reasonable proof."

We think that in determining whether the obligation of good-faith bargaining has been met the Board has a right to consider an employer's refusal to give information about its financial status. While Congress did not compel agreement between employers and bargaining representatives, it did require collective bargaining in the hope that agreements would result. Section 204(a)(1) of the Act admonishes both employers and employees to "exert every reasonable effort to make and maintain agreements concerning rates of pay, hours, and working conditions. . . ." In their effort to reach an agreement here both the union and the company treated the company's ability to pay increased wages as highly relevant. The ability of an employer to increase wages without injury to his business is a commonly considered factor in wage negotiations. Claims for increased wages have sometimes been abandoned because of an employer's unsatisfactory business condition; employees have even voted to accept wage decreases because of such conditions.

Good-faith bargaining necessarily requires that claims made by either bargainer should be honest claims. This is true about an asserted inability to pay an increase in wages. If such an argument is important enough to present in the give and take of bargaining, it is important enough to require some sort of proof of its accuracy. And it would certainly not be farfetched for a trier of fact to reach the conclusion that bargaining lacks good faith when an employer mechanically repeats a claim of inability to pay without making the slightest effort to substantiate the claim. Such has been the holding of the Labor Board since shortly after the passage of the Wagner Act. In *Pioneer Pearl Button Co.,* decided in 1936, where the employer's representative relied on the company's asserted "poor financial condition," the Board said: "He did no more than take refuge in the assertion that the respondent's financial condition was poor; he refused either to prove his statement, or to permit independent verification. This is not collective bargaining." 1 N.L.R.B. 837, 842-843. This was the position of the Board when the Taft-Hartley Act was passed in 1947 and has been its position ever since. We agree with the Board that a refusal to attempt to substantiate a claim of inability to pay increased wages may support a finding of a failure to bargain in good faith.

The Board concluded that under the facts and circumstances of this case the respondent was guilty of an unfair labor practice in failing to bargain in good faith. We see no reason to disturb the findings of the Board. We do not hold, however, that in every case in which economic inability is raised as an argument against increased wages it automatically follows that the employees are entitled to substantiating evidence. Each case must turn upon its particular facts. The inquiry must always be whether or not under the circumstances of the particular case the statutory obligation to bargain in good faith has been met. Since we conclude that there is support in the record for the conclusion of the Board here that respondent did not bargain in good faith, it was error for the Court of Appeals to set aside the Board's order and deny enforcement.

Reversed.

[MR. JUSTICE FRANKFURTER, whom MR. JUSTICE CLARK and MR. JUSTICE HARLAN joined, concurred in part and dissented in part in an opinion that is omitted.]

———

NLRB v. ACME INDUSTRIAL CO., 385 U.S. 432, 87 S. Ct. 565, 17 L. Ed. 2d 495 (1967). A collective bargaining agreement provided that if plant equipment was moved to another location, employees subject as a result to layoff or reduction in grade could transfer under certain conditions to the new location. The contract also contained a grievance procedure culminating in binding arbitration. When the union discovered that certain machinery was being removed from the employer's plant, it filed contract grievances and requested information about the dates of the move, the destination of the equipment, the amount of machinery involved, the reason for the transfer, and the new use to be made of the equipment. The employer replied it had no duty to furnish this information since no layoffs or reductions had occurred within the five-day time limit for filing grievances. The NLRB ruled the employer had refused to bargain in good faith, observing that the information sought was "necessary in order to enable the Union to evaluate intelligently the grievances filed" and pointing out that the agreement contained no "clause by which the Union waives its statutory right to such information." The Supreme Court upheld the Board's order. The "duty to bargain unquestionably extends beyond the period of contract negotiations and applies to labor-management relations during the term of an agreement." Moreover, the Board did not have to await an arbitrator's determination of the relevancy of the information before enforcing the union's statutory rights under § 8(a)(5). The Board "was not making a binding construction of the labor contract. It was only acting upon the probability that the desired information was relevant, and that it would be of use to the union in carrying out its statutory duties and responsibilities. . . . Thus, the assertion of jurisdiction by the Board in this case in no way threatens the power which the parties have given the arbitrator to make binding interpretations of the labor agreement."

NOTES

1. Under *Truitt* and *Acme,* is an employer's failure to supply relevant information a refusal to bargain per se? Should it be? For contrasting views, see Woodworkers Locals 6-7 & 6-122 v. NLRB, 263 F.2d 483 (D.C. Cir. 1959); Taylor Forge & Pipe Works v. NLRB, 234 F.2d 227 (7th Cir. 1956), *cert. denied,* 352 U.S. 942 (1956).

2. *Wage and financial data.* An employer must furnish all information necessary and relevant to the performance of the union's collective bargaining responsibilities. This applies to the administration as well as the negotiation of the labor agreement. J. I. Case Co. v. NLRB, 253 F.2d 149 (7th Cir. 1958). In determining relevance, the Labor Board and the courts have distinguished between wage data and financial data. Wage data include information concerning all the factors that enter into the computation of wages or other forms of compensation. Generally, an employer has to supply all requested wage data not obviously beyond the needs of the union. Examples of wage data that must be furnished are: job rates and classifications, Taylor Forge & Pipe Works v. NLRB, *supra;* time study data, NLRB v. Otis Elevator Co., 208 F.2d 176 (2d Cir. 1953); merit increases, Otis Elevator Co., 170 N.L.R.B. 395 (1968); pension information, Electric Furnace Co., 137 N.L.R.B. 1077 (1962); group insurance data, Stowe-Woodward, Inc., 123 N.L.R.B. 287 (1959); incentive earnings, Dixie Mfg. Co., 79 N.L.R.B. 645 (1948), *enforced,* 180 F.2d 173 (6th Cir. 1950). But in Sylvania Elec. Prod., Inc. v. NLRB, 291 F.2d 128 (1st Cir. 1961), *cert. denied,* 368 U.S. 926 (1961), the court, in denying enforcement of a Board order, held that premiums paid by the employer for its noncontributory group insurance program were neither wages nor conditions of employment. *Cf.* Sylvania Elec. Prod., Inc., 154 N.L.R.B. 1756 (1965), *enforced,* 358 F.2d 591 (1st Cir. 1966), *cert. denied,* 385 U.S. 852 (1966) (employer must supply cost data on noncontributory plan when it injects cost issue into bargaining). Wage data must ordinarily be made available regardless of employer claims of "confidentiality." General Elec. Co. v. NLRB, 466 F. 2d 1177 (6th Cir. 1972).

Financial data include sales and production figures and other information concerning the employer's ability to meet the union's economic demands. Generally, an employer need not divulge such information unless he makes his financial position an issue in the negotiations by claiming he cannot afford to pay. Empire Terminal Warehouse Co., 151 N.L.R.B. 1359 (1965), *aff'd,* 355 F.2d 842 (D.C. Cir. 1966); Caster Mold & Mach. Co., 148 N.L.R.B. 1614 (1964). Is an employer pleading inability to pay when he asserts that maintaining a "proper balance" in his business does not permit him "to reach the union's numbers"? *See* Milbin Printing, Inc., 218 N.L.R.B. 223 (1975). *See also* Western Massachusetts Elec. Co. v. NLRB, 98 L.R.R.M. 2851 (1st Cir. 1978) (subcontracting costs). Is the difference in the treatment of wage data and financial data justified? Could anything be more "relevant" to a union in formulating its demands in preparation for collective bargaining than knowledge of the employer's capacity to pay?

3. A union whose collective agreement contains a nondiscrimination clause is entitled to information concerning an employer's minority and female employment practices, apparently even including information the EEOC would ordinarily not furnish charging parties. Westinghouse Elec. Corp., 239 N.L.R.B. No. 19, 99 L.R.R.M. 1482 (1978). The Supreme Court has held, however, that an employer has sufficient interest in the secrecy of psychological aptitude test questions and answers to refuse disclosure, and that disclosure of individual scores may be conditioned on the employees' consent. Detroit Edison Co. v. NLRB, 47 U.S.L.W. 4233 (U. S. 1979).

4. *Manner of presentation.* The employer is not obliged to supply information in the exact form requested so long as it is submitted in a manner which is not unduly burdensome to interpret. Westinghouse Elec. Corp., 129 N.L.R.B. 850 (1960); McLean-Arkansas Lumber Co., 109 N.L.R.B. 1022 (1954).

5. Must an employer let a union make its own time studies of disputed operations on the plant premises? *Compare* Fafnir Bearing Co., 146 N.L.R.B. 1582 (1964), *enforced,* 362 F.2d 716 (2d Cir. 1966) ("Yes"), *with* Hercules Motor Corp., 136 N.L.R.B. 1648 (1962). On the need to provide access to the company's books, *compare* Metlox Mfg. Co., 153 N.L.R.B. 1388 (1965), *enforced,* 378 F.2d 728 (9th Cir. 1967) (conclusory profit-and-loss statement inadequate), *with* McLean-Arkansas Lumber Co., *supra.*

6. An exclusive bargaining representative is entitled to a list of the names and addresses of the employees in the unit when this is necessary for the effective negotiation or administration of the collective agreement. Prudential Ins. Co., 173 N.L.R.B. 792 (1968), *enforced,* 412 F.2d 77 (2d Cir. 1969), *cert. denied,* 396 U.S. 928 (1969). *See also* Florida Mach. & Foundry Co., 174 N.L.R.B. 1156 (1969) (names of employees working during strike), *rev'd and remanded on other grounds,* 441 F.2d 1005 (D.C. Cir. 1970). *But cf.* Glazers Wholesale Drug Co., 211 N.L.R.B. 1063 (1974), *enforced,* 523 F.2d 1053 (5th Cir. 1975) (strike replacements' names and addresses not presumed relevant during strike). What about information concerning unit (or non-unit) employees being trained to perform non-unit (or unit) work in the event of a strike? *Compare* Newspaper Guild v. NLRB, 548 F.2d 863 (9th Cir. 1977), *with* A.S. Abell Co., 230 N.L.R.B. No. 161, 95 L.R.R.M. 1493 (1977).

7. The duty to furnish information is discussed in Bartosic & Hartley, *The Employer's Duty to Supply Information to the Union,* 58 CORNELL L. REV. 23 (1972); Fanning, *The Obligation to Furnish Information During the Contract Term,* 9 GA. L. REV. 375 (1975); Huston, *Furnishing Information as an Element of Employer's Good Faith Bargaining,* 35 U. DET. L.J. 471 (1958); Miller, *Employer's Duty to Furnish Economic Data to Unions — Revisited,* 17 LAB. L.J. 272 (1966).

C. THE SUBJECT MATTER OF COLLECTIVE BARGAINING

NEIL CHAMBERLAIN, THE UNION CHALLENGE TO MANAGEMENT CONTROL 8-9 (1948)

The problem is highly charged with an ethical content. Judgments are required as to the moral validity of legal relationships, the justification for economic powers and distributive shares, the degree of weight to be accorded technological efficiency, the philosophical foundations for political arrangements. Here indeed lies the final basis for decision. We should be missing the heart of the problem if we failed to realize that legal and economic arguments, technological and political considerations must give way before widely held moral convictions. What is the ethical basis of the workers' struggle for increasing participation in business decisions? On what standards of justice and rightness does management rest its defensive tactics? Such questions should not produce wry smiles from those recalling union terrorism and intimidation, and management use of *agents provocateurs,* bribery, and tear gas. Such condemned activity reveals the deep roots of ethical persuasions.

S. SLICHTER, J. HEALY & E. LIVERNASH, THE IMPACT OF COLLECTIVE BARGAINING ON MANAGEMENT 958 (1960)*

Management has moved in the direction of concessions to unions, for example, by accepting a narrowing of managerial discretion, most obviously indicated by the expanded scope of labor contracts, by agreeing to extensive reliance on seniority, and by endorsing arbitration of grievances. Managements have also furthered the process of adjustment by the development of management by policy. Unions have made important concessions to the needs of management, for example, in the acceptance of job evaluation, progressive discipline, and discipline for wildcat strikes.

Adjustment of the goals and policies of management and of unions has gone farther in the case of some issues than others. It has gone farthest in the following areas: (1) work-sharing and layoff systems, (2) formal or informal evaluation of particular job rates, (3) administration of the wide range of employee benefit plans and provisions, (4) systems of employee discipline, including the control of wildcats, (5) scheduling of work, (6) development and operation of the grievance procedure, and (7) acceptance of arbitration. Adjustment is less well developed in the following areas: (1) production standards and wage incentives, (2) promotion principles, (3) work assignment, and (4) subcontracting.

NLRB v. WOOSTER DIVISION OF BORG-WARNER CORP.

Supreme Court of the United States
356 U.S. 342, 78 S. Ct. 718, 2 L. Ed. 2d 823 (1958)

MR. JUSTICE BURTON delivered the opinion of the Court.

In these cases an employer insisted that its collective-bargaining contract with certain of its employees include: (1) a "ballot" clause calling for a prestrike secret vote of those employees (union and non-union) as to the employer's last offer, and (2) a "recognition" clause which excluded, as a party to the contract, the International Union which had been certified by the National Labor Relations Board as the employees' exclusive bargaining agent, and substituted for it the agent's uncertified local affiliate. The Board held that the employer's insistence upon either of such clauses amounted to a refusal to bargain, in violation of § 8(a)(5) of the National Labor Relations Act, as amended. The issue turns on whether either of these clauses comes within the scope of mandatory collective bargaining as defined in § 8(d) of the Act. For the reasons hereafter stated, we agree with the Board that neither clause comes within that definition. Therefore, we sustain the Board's order directing the employer to cease insisting upon either clause as a condition precedent to accepting any collective-bargaining contract. . . .

[T]he "ballot" clause . . . provided that, as to all nonarbitrable issues (which eventually included modification, amendment or termination of the contract), there would be a 30-day negotiation period after which, before the union could strike, there would have to be a secret ballot taken among all employees in the unit (union and non-union) on the company's last offer. In the event a majority of the employees rejected the company's last offer, the company would have an opportunity, within 72 hours, of making a new proposal and having a vote on it prior to any strike. The unions' negotiators announced they would not accept this clause "under any conditions."

From the time that the company first proposed these clauses, the employees' representatives thus made it clear that each was wholly unacceptable. The company's representatives made it equally clear that no agreement would be entered into by it unless the agreement contained both clauses. In view of this impasse, there was little further discussion of the clauses, although the parties continued to bargain as to other matters. The company submitted a "package" proposal covering economic issues but made the offer contingent upon the satisfactory settlement of "all other issues. . . ." The "package" included both of the controversial clauses. On March 15, 1953, the unions rejected that proposal and the membership voted to strike on March 20 unless a settlement were reached by then. None was reached and the unions struck. Negotiations, nevertheless, continued. . . .

Read together, [§§ 8(a)(5) and 8(d)] establish the obligation of the employer and the representative of its employees to bargain with each other in good faith with respect to "wages, hours, and other terms and conditions of employment. . . ." The duty is limited to those subjects, and within that area neither party is legally obligated to yield. NLRB v. American National Insurance Co., 343 U.S. 395. As to other matters, however, each party is free to bargain or not to bargain, and to agree or not to agree.

The company's good faith has met the requirements of the statute as to the subjects of mandatory bargaining. But that good faith does not license the employer to refuse to enter into agreements on the ground that they do not include some proposal which is not a mandatory subject of bargaining. We agree with the Board that such conduct is, in substance, a refusal to bargain about the subjects that are within the scope of mandatory bargaining. This does not mean that bargaining is to be confined to the statutory subjects. Each of the two controversial clauses is lawful in itself. Each would be enforceable if agreed to by the unions. But it does not follow that, because the company may propose these clauses, it can lawfully insist upon them as a condition to any agreement.

Since it is lawful to insist upon matters within the scope of mandatory bargaining and unlawful to insist upon matters without, the issue here is whether either the "ballot" or the "recognition" clause is a subject within the phrase "wages, hours, and other terms and conditions of employment" which defines mandatory bargaining. The "ballot" clause is not within that definition. It relates only to the procedure to be followed by the employees among themselves before their representative may call a strike or refuse a final offer. It settles no term or condition of employment — it merely calls for an advisory vote of the employees. It is not a partial "no-strike" clause. A "no-strike" clause prohibits the employees from striking during the life of the contract. It regulates the relations between the employer and the employees. See NLRB v. American National Insurance Co., *supra* at 408, n. 22. The "ballot" clause, on the other hand, deals only with relations between the employees and their unions. It substantially modifies the collective bargaining system provided for in the statute by weakening the independence of the "representative" chosen by the employees. It enables the employer, in effect, to deal with its employees rather than with their statutory representative. Cf. Medo Photo Supply Corp. v. NLRB, 321 U.S. 678 (1944).

The "recognition" clause likewise does not come within the definition of mandatory bargaining. The statute requires the company to bargain with the certified representative of its employees. It is an evasion of that duty to insist that the certified agent not be a party to the collective bargaining contract. The Act does not prohibit the voluntary addition of a party, but that does not authorize the employer to exclude the certified representative from the contract. . . .

MR. JUSTICE FRANKFURTER joins this opinion insofar as it holds that insistence by the company on the "recognition" clause, in conflict with the provisions of the Act requiring an employer to bargain with the representative of his employees, constituted an unfair labor practice. He agrees with the views of MR. JUSTICE HARLAN regarding the "ballot" clause. The subject matter of that clause is not so clearly outside the reasonable range of industrial bargaining as to establish a refusal to bargain in good faith, and is not prohibited simply because not deemed to be within the rather vague scope of the obligatory provisions of § 8(d).

MR. JUSTICE HARLAN, whom MR. JUSTICE CLARK and MR. JUSTICE WHITTAKER join, concurring in part and dissenting in part. . . .

The legislative history behind the Wagner and Taft-Hartley Acts persuasively indicates that the Board was never intended to have power to prevent good faith bargaining as to any subject not violative of the provisions or policies of those Acts. . . .

[E]arly intrusions of the Board into the substantive aspects of the bargaining process became a matter of concern to Congress, and in the 1947 Taft-Hartley amendments to the Wagner Act, Congress took steps to curtail them by writing into § 8(d) the particular fields as to which it considered bargaining *should* be required. . . .

The decision of this Court in 1952 in NLRB v. American National Insurance Co., *supra,* was fully in accord with this legislative background in holding that the Board lacked power to order an employer to cease bargaining over a particular clause because such bargaining under the Board's view, entirely apart from a showing of bad faith, constituted *per se* an unfair labor practice. . . .

I therefore cannot escape the view that today's decision is deeply inconsistent with legislative intention and this Court's precedents. The Act sought to compel management and labor to meet and bargain in good faith as to certain topics. This is the *affirmative* requirement of § 8(d) which the Board is specifically empowered to enforce, but I see no warrant for inferring from it any power in the Board to *prohibit* bargaining in good faith as to lawful matters not included in § 8(d). The Court reasons that such conduct on the part of the employer, when carried to the point of insistence, is in substance equivalent to a refusal to bargain as to the statutory subjects, but I cannot understand how this can be said over the Trial Examiner's unequivocal finding that the employer did in fact bargain in "good faith," not only over the disputed clauses but also over the statutory subjects. . . .

The most cursory view of decisions of the Board and the circuit courts under the National Labor Relations Act reveals the unsettled and evolving character of collective bargaining agreements. Provisions which two decades ago might have been thought to be the exclusive concern of labor or management are today commonplace in such agreements. The bargaining process should be left fluid, free from intervention of the Board leading to premature crystallization of labor agreements into any one pattern of contract provisions, so that these agreements can be adapted through collective bargaining to the changing needs of our society and to the changing concepts of the responsibilities of labor and management. What the Court does today may impede this evolutionary process. Under the facts of this case, an employer is precluded from attempting to limit the likelihood of a strike. But by the same token it would seem to follow that unions which bargain in good faith would be precluded from insisting upon contract clauses which might not be deemed statutory subjects within § 8(d).

As unqualifiedly stated in American National Insurance Co., *supra*, . . . it is through the "good faith" requirement of § 8(d) that the Board is to enforce the bargaining provisions of § 8. A determination that a party bargained as to statutory or non-statutory subjects in good or bad faith must depend upon an evaluation of the total circumstances surrounding any given situation. I do not deny that there may be instances where unyielding insistence on a particular item may be a relevant consideration in the overall picture in determining "good faith," for the demands of a party might in the context of a particular industry be so extreme as to constitute some evidence of an unwillingness to bargain. But no such situation is presented in this instance by the "ballot" clause. "No strike" clauses, and other provisions analogous to the "ballot" clause limiting the right to strike, are hardly novel to labor agreements. And in any event the uncontested finding of "good faith" by the Trial Examiner forecloses that issue here.

Of course, an employer or union cannot insist upon a clause which would be illegal under the Act's provisions, NLRB v. National Maritime Union, 175 F.2d 686 (2d Cir. 1949), or conduct itself so as to contravene specific requirements of the Act. Medo Photo Supply Corp. v. NLRB, 321 U.S. 678 (1944). But here the Court recognizes, as it must, that the clause is lawful under the Act, and I think it clear that the company's insistence upon it violated no statutory duty to which it was subject. . . .

The company's insistence on the "recognition" clause, which had the effect of excluding the International Union as a party signatory to agreement and making Local 1239 the sole contracting party on the union side, presents a different problem. In my opinion the company's action in this regard did constitute an unfair labor practice since it contravened specific requirements of the Act. . . .

NOTES

1. Would unions or employers have benefited the most from a decision in *Borg-Warner* that *all* lawful provisions are "mandatory" subjects, on which bargaining is required and which may be forced to an impasse? Is an employer more likely to be disadvantaged by the obligation to bargain over a "management function," or by his failure to bargain over a decision that the NLRB later rules is a mandatory subject? Does *Borg-Warner* give the Board too great a power to freeze or expand the list of topics on which unions and employers must bargain? *See* Cox, *Labor Decisions of the Supreme Court at the October Term, 1957*, 44 VA. L. REV. 1057, 1075 (1958); Fleming, *The Obligation to Bargain in Good Faith*, 16 Sw. L.J. 43 (1962); Christensen, *New Subjects and New Concepts in Collective Bargaining*, in A.B.A. SECTION OF LABOR RELATIONS LAW PROCEEDINGS 245 (1970). *Borg-Warner* is noted in 11 STAN. L. REV. 188 (1958); 43 MINN. L. REV. 1225 (1959). *See also* Horvitz, *What's Happening in Collective Bargaining*, 29 LAB. L.J. 453 (1978).

2. Employee compensation in a wide variety of forms has been held to be "wages" or "other conditions of employment," and thus a mandatory subject of bargaining. *See, e.g.,* Inland Steel Co. v. NLRB, 170 F.2d 247 (7th Cir. 1948), *cert. denied,* 336 U.S. 960 (1949) (pensions); Richfield Oil Corp. v. NLRB, 231 F.2d 717 (D.C. Cir. 1956), *cert. denied,* 351 U.S. 909 (1956) (stock purchase plan); NLRB v. Wonder State Mfg. Co., 344 F.2d 210 (8th Cir. 1965) (Christmas bonus); Central Illinois Pub. Serv. Co., 139 N.L.R.B. 1407 (1962), *enforced,* 324 F.2d 916 (7th Cir. 1963) (employee discounts). Rental fees in company-owned housing provided for employees who want it may be a mandatory topic of bargaining, depending on such circumstances as the distance to, and the availability of, other accommodations. American Smelting & Ref. Co. v. NLRB, 406 F.2d 552 (9th Cir. 1969), *cert. denied,* 395 U.S. 935 (1969). What about the prices of food in a plant's cafeteria and vending machines? *See* Ford Motor Co. v. NLRB, 47 U.S.L.W. 4498 (U.S. 1979).

3. Provisions governing the employment relation that have been ruled subject to mandatory bargaining include a no-strike clause covering both union and nonunion members of the bargaining unit, Lloyd A. Fry Roofing Co., 123 N.L.R.B. 647 (1959); a nondiscriminatory exclusive hiring hall arrangement in a right-to-work state, Associated Gen. Contractors, 143 N.L.R.B. 409 (1963), *enforced,* 349 F.2d 449 (5th Cir. 1965), *cert. denied,* 382 U.S. 1026 (1966); and a clause providing for the continued accumulation of seniority by employees while in a supervisory status, Mobil Oil Co., 147 N.L.R.B. 337 (1964). What about a union's insistence on an "interest arbitration" clause? *See* Columbus Printing Pressmen (R.W. Page Corp.), 219 N.L.R.B. 268 (1975), *enforced,* 543 F.2d 1161 (5th Cir. 1976); NLRB v. Sheet Metal Workers Local 38 [Elmsford Sheet Metal Works, Inc.], 575 F.2d 394 (2d Cir. 1978); Note, 86 YALE L.J. 715 (1977).

4. On the other hand, matters considered too remote from the employment relationship, or deemed a peculiar prerogative of employer or union, are not mandatory subjects of bargaining. If lawful, such matters are permissible subjects. The parties may bargain by mutual agreement, but neither side may insist on a proposal to an impasse. Examples of nonmandatory topics are performance bonds, NLRB v. American Compress Warehouse Div. of Frost-Whited Co., 350 F.2d 365 (5th Cir. 1965), *cert. denied,* 382 U.S. 982 (1966); a newspaper code of ethics prohibiting acceptance of gifts from news sources, Capital Times Co., 223 N.L.R.B. 651 (1976); contributions to an industry promotion fund, Detroit Resilient Floor Decorators, Local 2265, 136 N.L.R.B. 769 (1962), *enforced,* 317 F.2d 269 (6th Cir. 1963); a requirement for the signatures of individual employees on grievances, Bethlehem Steel Co., 136 N.L.R.B. 1500 (1962), *enforcement denied on other grounds,* 320 F.2d 615 (3d Cir. 1963), *cert. denied,* 375 U.S. 984 (1964); and the rehiring of replaced economic strikers, American Optical Co., 138 N.L.R.B. 681 (1962). How should an employer demand for a clause forbidding a union to discipline members for strike-breaking be classified? *See* Universal Oil Prod. Corp. v. NLRB, 445 F.2d 155 (7th Cir. 1971). What about a union demand for bargaining over the choice of the insurance carrier for an employee health plan? *See* Connecticut Light & Power Co. v. NLRB, 476 F.2d 1079 (2d Cir. 1973); *cf.* Keystone Consol. Indus., 237 N.L.R.B. No. 91, 99 L.R.R.M. 1036 (1978).

5. National policies from outside the field of labor relations may occasionally have to be taken into account in determining the allowable scope of mandatory bargaining. For example, how should the NLRB treat a demand by a contractors' association for a so-called "most favored nation" clause, under which there would be a readjustment in the association's contract if the union subsequently granted more favorable terms to any other employer? Consider the implications of United Mine Workers v. Pennington, 381 U.S. 657 (1965), *infra* at 607 (anticompetitive collective bargaining agreements as antitrust violations). In Dolly Madison Industries, 182 N.L.R.B. 1037 (1970), the Labor Board declared a "most favored nation" clause to be a mandatory subject of bargaining, which an employer could insist upon in the absence of a "predatory purpose." The Board distinguished *Pennington* on the ground the clause sought here did not obligate the union to impose the same standards on competitors of the employer. Is this a realistic assessment of the practicalities of the situation? Should the nature of the clause itself, or the presence of a "predatory purpose," be the critical factor in these cases?

6. Should a labor union be able to demand bargaining over employer practices adversely affecting the public interest, such as pollution of the atmosphere? *See generally* Oldham, *Organized Labor, the Environment, and the Taft-Hartley Act,* 71 MICH. L. REV. 936 (1973); Comment, *A Case for Air Pollution as a Mandatory Bargaining Subject,* 51 ORE. L. REV. 223 (1971).

ALLIED CHEMICAL & ALKALI WORKERS LOCAL 1 v. PITTSBURGH PLATE GLASS CO.

Supreme Court of the United States
404 U.S. 157, 92 S. Ct. 383, 30 L. Ed. 2d 341 (1971)

MR. JUSTICE BRENNAN delivered the opinion of the Court. . . .

I. Since 1949, Local 1, Allied Chemical and Alkali Workers of America, has been the exclusive bargaining representative for the employees "working" on hourly rates of pay at the Barberton, Ohio, facilities of the respondent, Pittsburgh Plate Glass Company. In 1950, the Union and the Company negotiated an employee group health insurance plan, in which, it was orally agreed, retired employees could participate by contributing the required premiums, to be deducted from their pension benefits. This program continued unchanged until 1962, except for an improvement unilaterally instituted by the Company in 1954 and another improvement negotiated in 1959.

In 1962 the Company agreed to contribute two dollars per month toward the cost of insurance premiums of employees who retired in the future and elected to participate in the medical plan. The parties also agreed at this time to make 65 the mandatory retirement age. In 1964 insurance benefits were again negotiated, and the company agreed to increase its monthly contribution from two to four dollars, applicable to employees retiring after that date and also to pensioners who had retired since the effective date of the 1962 contract. It was agreed, however, that the Company might discontinue paying the two-dollar increase if Congress enacted a national health program.

In November 1965, Medicare, a national health program, was enacted. 79 Stat. 291, 42 U.S.C. § 1395 *et seq.* The 1964 contract was still in effect, and the Union sought mid-term bargaining to renegotiate insurance benefits for retired employees. The Company responded in March 1966 that, in its view, Medicare rendered the health insurance program useless because of a non-duplication of benefits provision in the Company's insurance policy, and stated, without negotiating any change, that it was planning to (a) reclaim the additional two-dollar monthly contribution as of the effective date of Medicare; (b) cancel the program for retirees; and (c) substitute the payment of the three-dollar monthly subscription fee for supplemental Medicare coverage for each retired employee.

The Union acknowledged that the Company had the contractual right to reduce its monthly contribution, but challenged its proposal unilaterally to substitute supplemental Medicare coverage for the negotiated health plan. The Company, as it had done during the 1959 negotiations without pressing the point, disputed the Union's right to bargain in behalf of retired employees, but advised the Union that upon further consideration it had decided not to terminate the health plan for pensioners. The Company stated instead that it would write each retired employee, offering to pay the supplemental Medicare premium if the employee would withdraw from the negotiated plan. Despite the Union's objections the Company did circulate its proposal to the retired employees, and 15 of 190 retirees elected to accept it. The Union thereupon filed unfair labor practice charges. . . .

II. . . . This obligation [to bargain under §§ 1, 8(a)(5), 8(d), and 9(a)] extends only to the "terms and conditions of employment" of the employer's "employees" in the "unit appropriate for such purposes" which the union represents. . . . The Board found that benefits of already retired employees fell within these constraints on alternative theories. First, it held that pensioners are themselves "employees" and members of the bargaining unit, so that their benefits are a "term and condition" of their employment. . . .

First. . . . In this cause we hold that the Board's decision is not supported by the law. The Act, after all, as § 1 makes clear, is concerned with the disruption to commerce that arises from interference with the organization and collective bargaining rights of "workers" — not those who have retired from the work force. The inequality of bargaining power that Congress sought to remedy was that of the "working" man, and the labor disputes that it ordered to be subjected to collective bargaining were those of employers and their active employees. Nowhere in the history of the National Labor Relations Act is there any evidence that retired workers are to be considered as within the ambit of the collective bargaining obligations of the statute.

To the contrary, the legislative history of § 2(3) itself indicates that the term "employee" is not to be stretched beyond its plain meaning embracing only those who work for another for hire. . . . In doubtful cases resort must still be had to economic and policy considerations to infuse § 2(3) with meaning. But, as the House comments . . . demonstrate, this is not a doubtful case. The ordinary meaning of "employee" does not include retired workers; retired employees have ceased to work for another for hire.

The decisions on which the Board relied in construing § 2(3) to the contrary are wide of the mark. The Board enumerated "unfair labor practice situations where the statute has been applied to persons who have not been initially hired by an employer or whose employment has terminated." . . . Yet all of these cases involved people who, unlike the pensioners here, were members of the active work force available for hire and at least in that sense could be identified as "employees." No decision under the Act is cited, and none to our knowledge exists, in which an individual who has ceased work without expectation of further employment has been held to be an "employee."

The Board also found support for its position in decisions arising under § 302(c)(5) of the Labor Management Relations Act. . . . Section 302 prohibits, *inter alia,* any payment by an employer to any representative of any of his employees. Subsection (c)(5) provides an exemption for payments to an employee trust fund established "for the sole and exclusive benefit of the employees of such employer" and administered by equal numbers of representatives of the employer and employees. The word "employee," as used in that provision, has been construed to include "current employees and persons who were . . . current employees but are now retired." Blassie v. Kroger Co., 345 F.2d 58, 70 (8th Cir. 1965). . . .

Yet the rationale of *Blassie* is not at all in point. The question there was simply whether under § 302(c)(5) retirees remain eligible for benefits of trust funds established during their active employment. The conclusion that they do was compelled by the fact that the contrary reading of the statute would have made illegal contributions to pension plans, which the statute expressly contemplates in subsections (A) and (C). No comparable situation exists in this case. Furthermore, there is no anomaly in the conclusion that retired workers are "employees" within § 302(c)(5) entitled to the benefits negotiated while they were active employees, but are not "employees" whose ongoing benefits are embraced by the bargaining obligation of § 8(a)(5). Contrary to the Board's assertion, the union's role in the administration of the fund is of a far different order from its duties as collective bargaining agent. To accept the Board's reasoning that the union's § 302(c)(5) responsibilities dictate the scope of the § 8(a)(5) collective bargaining obligation would be to allow the tail to wag the dog.

Second. Section 9(a) of the Labor Relations Act accords representative status only to the labor organization selected or designated by the majority of employees in a "unit appropriate" "for the purposes of collective bargaining." . . .

In this case, in addition to holding that pensioners are not "employees" within the meaning of the collective bargaining obligations of the Act, we hold that they were not and could not be "employees" included in the bargaining unit. The unit determined by the Board to be appropriate was composed of "employees of the Employer's plant . . . working on hourly rates, including group leaders who work on hourly rates of pay. . . ." Apart from whether retirees could be considered "employees" within this language, they obviously were not employees "working" or "who work" on hourly rates of pay. Although those terms may include persons on temporary or limited absence from work, such as employees on military duty, it would utterly destroy the function of language to read them as embracing those whose work has ceased with no expectation of return. . . .

Here, even if, as the Board found, active and retired employees have a common concern in assuring that the latter's benefits remain adequate, they plainly do not share a community of interests broad enough to justify inclusion of the retirees in the bargaining unit. Pensioners' interests extend only to retirement benefits, to the exclusion of wage rates, hours, working conditions, and all other terms of active employment. Incorporation of such a limited-purpose constituency in the bargaining unit would create the potential for severe internal conflicts which would impair the unit's ability to function and would disrupt the processes of collective bargaining. Moreover, the risk cannot be overlooked that union representatives on occasion might see fit to bargain for improved wages or other conditions favoring active employees at the expense of retirees' benefits. . . .

Third. The Board found that bargaining over pensioners' rights has become an established industrial practice. But industrial practice cannot alter the conclusions that retirees are neither "employees" nor bargaining unit members. The parties dispute whether a practice of bargaining over pensioners' benefits exists and, if so, whether it reflects the views of labor and management that the subject is not merely a convenient but a mandatory topic of negotiation. But even if industry commonly regards retirees' benefits as a statutory subject of bargaining, that would at most, as we suggested in Fibreboard Corp. v. NLRB, 379 U.S. 203, 211 (1964), reflect the interests of employers and employees in the subject matter as well as its amenability to the collective bargaining process; it would not be determinative. Common practice cannot change the law and make into bargaining unit "employees" those who are not.

III. Even if pensioners are not bargaining unit "employees," are their benefits, nonetheless, a mandatory subject of collective bargaining as "terms and conditions of employment" of the active employees who remain in the unit? The Board held, alternatively, that they are, on the ground that they "vitally" affect the "terms and conditions of employment" of active employees principally by influencing the value of both their current and future benefits. . . .

Section 8(d) of the Act, of course, does not immutably fix a list of subjects for mandatory bargaining. . . . But it does establish a limitation against which proposed topics must be measured. In general terms, the limitation includes only issues which settle an aspect of the relationship between the employer and employees. See, *e.g., NLRB v. Borg-Warner Corp., supra.* Although normally matters involving individuals outside the employment relationship do not fall within that category, they are not wholly excluded. In Teamsters Union v. Oliver, 358 U.S. 283 (1959), for example, an agreement had been negotiated in the trucking industry, establishing a minimum rental which carriers would pay to truck owners who drove their own vehicles in the carriers' service in place of the latter's employees. Without determining whether the owner-drivers were themselves "employees," we held that the minimum rental was a mandatory subject of bargaining, and hence immune from state antitrust laws, because the term "was integral to the establishment of a stable wage structure for clearly covered employee-drivers." United States v. Drum, 368 U.S. 370, 382-383, n. 26 (1962). Similarly, in *Fibreboard Corp. v. NLRB, supra* at 215, we held that "the type of 'contracting out' involved in this case — the replacement of employees in the existing bargaining unit with those of an independent contractor to do the same work under similar conditions of employment — is a statutory subject of collective bargaining. . . ." . . .

The Board urges that *Oliver* and *Fibreboard* provide the principle governing this case. The Company, on the other hand, would distinguish those decisions on the ground that the unions there sought to protect employees from outside threats, not to represent the interests of third parties. We agree with the Board that the principle of *Oliver* and *Fibreboard* is relevant here; in each case the question is not whether the third-party concern is antagonistic to or compatible with the interests of bargaining unit employees, but whether it vitally affects the "terms and conditions" of their employment. But we disagree with the Board's assessment of the significance of a change in retirees' benefits to the "terms and conditions of employment" of active employees.

The benefits which active workers may reap by including retired employees under the same health insurance contract are speculative and insubstantial at best. As the Board itself acknowledges in its brief, the relationship between the inclusion of retirees and the overall insurance rate is uncertain. Adding individuals increases the group experience and thereby generally tends to lower the rate, but including pensioners, who are likely to have higher medical expenses, may more than offset that effect. In any event, the impact one way or the other on the "terms and conditions of employment" of active employees is hardly comparable to the loss of jobs threatened in *Oliver* and *Fibreboard.* . . . The inclusion of retirees in the same insurance contract surely has even less an impact on the "terms and conditions of employment" of active employees than some of the contracting activities which we excepted from our holding in *Fibreboard.*

The mitigation of future uncertainty and the facilitation of agreement on active employees' retirement plans which the Board said would follow from the union's representation of pensioners are equally problematical. . . . Under the Board's theory, active employees undertake to represent pensioners in order to protect their own retirement benefits, just as if they were bargaining for, say, a cost-of-living escalation clause.

But there is a crucial difference. Having once found it advantageous to bargain for improvements to pensioners' benefits, active workers are not forever thereafter bound to that view or obliged to negotiate in behalf of retirees again. To the contrary, they are free to decide, for example, that current income is preferable to greater certainty in their own retirement benefits or, indeed, to their retirement benefits altogether. By advancing pensioners' interests now, active employees, therefore, have no assurance that they will be the beneficiaries of similar representation when they retire. . . .

We recognize that "classification of bargaining subjects as 'terms [and] conditions of employment' is a matter concerning which the Board has special expertise." Meat Cutters v. Jewel Tea, 381 U.S. 676, 685-686 (1965). The Board's holding in this case, however, depends on the application of law to facts, and the legal standard to be applied is ultimately for the courts to decide and enforce. We think that in holding the "terms and conditions of employment" of active employees to be *vitally* affected by pensioners' benefits, the Board here simply neglected to give the adverb its ordinary meaning. Cf. NLRB v. Brown, 380 U.S. 278, 292 (1965).

IV. The question remains whether the Company committed an unfair labor practice by offering retirees an exchange for their withdrawal from the already negotiated health insurance plan. . . . We need not resolve, however, whether there was a "modification" within the meaning of § 8(d), because we hold that even if there was, a "modification" is a prohibited unfair labor practice only when it changes a term that is a mandatory rather than a permissive subject of bargaining.

Paragraph (4) of § 8(d), of course, requires that a party proposing a modification continue "in full force and effect . . . all the terms and conditions of the existing contract" until its expiration. Viewed in isolation from the rest of the provision, that language would preclude any distinction between contract obligations that are "terms and conditions of employment" and those that are not. But in construing § 8(d), " 'we must not be guided by a single sentence or member of a sentence, but look to the provisions of the whole law, and to its object and policy.' " Mastro Plastics Corp. v. NLRB, 350 U.S. 270, 285 (1956). . . . Seen in that light, § 8(d) embraces only mandatory topics of bargaining. The provision begins by defining "to bargain collectively" as meeting and conferring "with respect to wages, hours, and other terms and conditions of employment." It then goes on to state that "the duty to bargain collectively shall also mean" that mid-term unilateral modifications and terminations are prohibited. Although this part of the section is introduced by a "proviso" clause, . . . it quite plainly is to be construed *in pari materia* with the preceding definition. Accordingly, just as § 8(d) defines the obligation to bargain to be with respect to mandatory terms alone, so it prescribes the duty to maintain only mandatory terms without unilateral modification for the duration of the collective-bargaining agreement. . . .

The structure and language of § 8(d) point to a more specialized purpose than merely promoting general contract compliance. The conditions for a modification or termination set out in paragraphs (1) through (4) plainly are designed to regulate modifications and terminations so as to facilitate agreement in place of economic warfare. . . .

If that is correct, the distinction that we draw between mandatory and permissive terms of bargaining fits the statutory purpose. By once bargaining and agreeing on a permissive subject, the parties, naturally, do not make the subject a mandatory topic of future bargaining. When a proposed modification is to a permissive term, therefore, the purpose of facilitating accord on the proposal is not at all in point, since the parties are not required under the statute to bargain with respect to it. The irrelevance of the purpose is demonstrated by the irrelevance of the procedures themselves of § 8(d). Paragraph (2), for example, requires an offer "to meet and confer with the other party for the purpose of negotiating a new contract or a contract containing the proposed modifications." But such an offer is meaningless if a party is statutorily free to refuse to negotiate on the proposed change to the permissive term. The notification to mediation and conciliation services referred to in paragraph (3) would be equally meaningless, if required at all. We think it would be no less beside the point to read paragraph (4) of § 8(d) as requiring continued adherence to permissive as well as mandatory terms. The remedy for a unilateral mid-term modification to a permissive term lies in an action for breach of contract, . . . not in an unfair-labor-practice proceeding.

As a unilateral mid-term modification of a permissive term such as retirees' benefits does not, therefore, violate § 8(d), the judgment of the Court of Appeals is

Affirmed.

Mr. Justice Douglas dissents.

NOTES

1. Has the Supreme Court foreclosed an employer and a union from converting a permissive bargaining subject into a mandatory one, even for the life of a contract? If so, is this a sound result?

2. Do you understand the Court to be assuming, in Part IV of *Pittsburgh Plate Glass,* that there is an exact correspondence between the kind of subject matter over which an employer must bargain at the request of the union, and the kind of subject matter as to which an employer may not institute unilateral changes without prior bargaining? Is such parallelism logically necessary? Is it desirable?

3. Union-employer bargaining over employee pensions and other benefit plans has been substantially affected by the passage of the Employee Retirement Income Security Act in 1974. *See generally* Fillion & Trebilock, *The Duty to Bargain Under ERISA,* 17 William & Mary L. Rev. 251 (1975).

Order of Railroad Telegraphers v. Chicago & Northwestern Ry., 362 U.S. 330, 80 S. Ct. 761, 4 L. Ed. 2d 774 (1960). An interstate railroad petitioned the public utility commissions of four states for permission to close down certain stations which were little used and wasteful to operate. The union representing the station agents and telegraphers asked the railroad to amend the current labor contract to provide that no existing jobs would be abolished except by agreement of union and carrier. The railroad replied that this request did not constitute a "labor dispute" or raise a bargainable issue under the Railway Labor Act. Subsequently, the railroad sought an injunction in federal district court against the union's striking to enforce its demand. The district court concluded it was without jurisdiction to grant a permanent injunction, but the court of appeals reversed. On certiorari, the Supreme Court held, four justices dissenting, that the district court could not permanently enjoin the strike because § 4 of Norris-La Guardia withdraws jurisdiction from the federal courts to prohibit strikes growing out of a "labor dispute." Section 13(c) of the Act defines "labor dispute" as including "any controversy concerning terms or conditions of employment." Said the Court: "The change desired . . . plainly referred to 'conditions of employment' of the railroad's employees who are represented by the union. The employment of many of these station agents inescapably hangs on the number of railroad stations that will be either completely abandoned or consolidated with other stations. And, in the collective bargaining world today there is nothing strange about agreements that affect the permanency of employment. . . . We cannot agree . . . that the union's effort to negotiate about the job security of its members 'represents an attempt to usurp legitimate managerial prerogative in the exercise of business judgment with respect to the most economical and efficient conduct of its operations.' The Railway Labor Act and the Interstate Commerce Act recognize that stable and fair terms and conditions of railroad employment are essential to a well-functioning national transportation system. The Railway Labor Act safeguards an opportunity for employees to obtain contracts through collective rather than individualistic bargaining."

FIBREBOARD PAPER PRODUCTS CORP. v. NLRB

Supreme Court of the United States
379 U.S. 203, 85 S. Ct. 398, 13 L. Ed. 2d 233 (1964)

MR. CHIEF JUSTICE WARREN delivered the opinion of the Court.

This case involves the obligation of an employer and the representative of his employees under §§ 8(a)(5), 8(d) and 9(a) of the National Labor Relations Act to "confer in good faith with respect to wages, hours, and other terms and conditions of employment." The primary issue is whether the "contracting out" of work being performed by employees in the bargaining unit is a statutory subject of collective bargaining under those sections.

Petitioner, Fibreboard Paper Products Corporation (the Company), has a manufacturing plant in Emeryville, California. Since 1937 the East Bay Union Machinists, Local 1304, United Steelworkers of America, AFL-CIO (the Union) has been the exclusive bargaining representative for a unit of the Company's maintenance employees. In September 1958, the Union and the Company entered the latest of a series of collective bargaining agreements which was to expire on July 31, 1959. The agreement provided for automatic renewal for another year unless one of the contracting parties gave 60 days' notice of a desire to modify or terminate the contract. On May 26, 1959, the Union gave timely notice of its desire to modify the contract and sought to arrange a bargaining session with Company representatives. On June 2, the Company acknowledged receipt of the Union's notice and stated: "We will contact you at a later date regarding a meeting for this purpose." As required by the contract, the Union sent a list of proposed modifications on June 15. Efforts by the Union to schedule a bargaining session met with no success until July 27, four days before the expiration of the contract, when the Company notified the Union of its desire to meet.

The Company, concerned with the high cost of its maintenance operation, had undertaken a study of the possibility of effecting cost savings by engaging an independent contractor to do the maintenance work. At the July 27 meeting, the Company informed the Union that it had determined that substantial savings could be effected by contracting out the work upon expiration of its collective bargaining agreements with the various labor organizations representing its maintenance employees. The Company delivered to the Union representatives a letter which stated in pertinent part:

"For some time we have been seriously considering the question of letting out our Emeryville maintenance work to an independent contractor, and have now reached a definite decision to do so effective August 1, 1959.

"In these circumstances, we are sure you will realize that negotiation of a new contract would be pointless. However, if you have any questions, we will be glad to discuss them with you."

After some discussion of the Company's right to enter a contract with a third party to do the work then being performed by employees in the bargaining unit, the meeting concluded with the understanding that the parties would meet again on July 30.

By July 30, the Company had selected Fluor Maintenance, Inc., to do the maintenance work. Fluor had assured the Company that maintenance costs could be curtailed by reducing the work force, decreasing fringe benefits and overtime payments, and by preplanning and scheduling the services to be performed. The contract provided that Fluor would: "furnish all labor, supervision and office help required for the performance of maintenance work . . . at the Emeryville plant of Owner as Owner shall from time to time assign to Contractor during the period of this contract; and shall also furnish such tools, supplies and equipment in connection therewith as Owner shall order from Contractor, it being understood, however, that Owner shall ordinarily do its own purchasing of tools, supplies and equipment."

The contract further provided that the Company would pay Fluor the costs of the operation plus a fixed fee of $2,250 per month.

At the July 30 meeting, the Company's representative, in explaining the decision to contract out the maintenance work, remarked that during bargaining negotiations in previous years the Company had endeavored to point out through the use of charts and statistical information "just how expensive and costly our maintenance work was and how it was creating quite a terrific burden upon the Emeryville plant." He further stated that unions representing other Company employees "had joined hands with management in an effort to bring about an economical and efficient operation," but "we had not been able to attain that in our discussions with this particular Local." The Company also distributed a letter stating that "since we will have no employees in the bargaining unit covered by our present Agreement, negotiation of a new or renewed Agreement would appear to us to be pointless." On July 31, the employment of the maintenance employees represented by the Union was terminated and Fluor employees took over. That evening the Union established a picket line at the Company's plant.

The Union filed unfair labor practice charges against the Company, alleging violations of §§ 8(a)(1), 8(a)(3) and 8(a)(5). After hearings were held upon a complaint issued by the National Labor Relations Board's Regional Director, the Trial Examiner filed an Intermediate Report recommending dismissal of the complaint. The Board accepted the recommendation and dismissed the complaint. 130 N.L.R.B. 1558.

Petitions for reconsideration, filed by the General Counsel and the Union, were granted. Upon reconsideration, the Board adhered to the Trial Examiner's finding that the Company's motive in contracting out its maintenance work was economic rather than antiunion but found nonetheless that the Company's "failure to negotiate with . . . [the Union] concerning its decision to subcontract its maintenance work constituted a violation of Section 8(a)(5) of the Act." This ruling was based upon the doctrine established in Town & Country Mfg. Co., 136 N.L.R.B. 1022, 1027, enforcement granted, 316 F.2d 846 (5th Cir. 1963), that contracting out work, "albeit for economic reasons, is a matter within the statutory phrase 'other terms and conditions of employment' and is a mandatory subject of collective bargaining within the meaning of Section 8(a)(5) of the Act."

The Board ordered the Company to reinstitute the maintenance operation previously performed by the employees represented by the Union, to reinstate the employees to their former or substantially equivalent positions with back pay computed from the date of the Board's supplemental decision, and to fulfill its statutory obligation to bargain.

On appeal, the Court of Appeals for the District of Columbia Circuit granted the Board's petition for enforcement. 322 F.2d 411. . . .

I. . . . Because of the limited grant of certiorari, we are concerned here only with whether the subject upon which the employer allegedly refused to bargain — contracting out of plant maintenance work previously performed by employees in the bargaining unit, which the employees were capable of continuing to perform — is covered by the phrase "terms and conditions of employment" within the meaning of § 8(d).

The subject matter of the present dispute is well within the literal meaning of the phrase "terms and conditions of employment." See Order of Railroad Telegraphers v. Chicago & N.W.R. Co., 362 U.S. 330 (1960). A stipulation with respect to the contracting out of work performed by members of the bargaining unit might appropriately be called a "condition of employment." The words even more plainly cover termination of employment which, as the facts of this case indicate, necessarily results from the contracting out of work performed by members of the established bargaining unit.

The inclusion of "contracting out" within the statutory scope of collective bargaining also seems well designed to effectuate the purposes of the National Labor Relations Act. One of the primary purposes of the Act is to promote the peaceful settlement of industrial disputes by subjecting labor-management controversies to the mediatory influence of negotiation. The Act was framed with an awareness that refusals to confer and negotiate had been one of the most prolific causes of industrial strife. NLRB v. Jones & Laughlin Steel Corp., 301 U.S. 1, 42-43 (1937). To hold, as the Board has done, that contracting out is a mandatory subject of collective bargaining would promote the fundamental purpose of the Act by bringing a problem of vital concern to labor and management within the framework established by Congress as most conducive to industrial peace.

The conclusion that "contracting out" is a statutory subject of collective bargaining is further reinforced by industrial practices in this country. While not determinative, it is appropriate to look to industrial bargaining practices in appraising the propriety of including a particular subject within the scope of mandatory bargaining. NLRB v. American Nat'l Ins. Co., 343 U.S. 395, 408 (1952). Industrial experience is not only reflective of the interests of labor and management in the subject matter but is also indicative of the amenability of such subjects to the collective bargaining process. Experience illustrates that contracting out in one form or another has been brought, widely and successfully, within the collective bargaining framework.[6] Provisions relating to contracting out exist in numerous collective bargaining agreements,[7] and "[c]ontracting out work is the basis of many grievances; and that type of claim is grist in the mills of the arbitrators." United Steelworkers v. Warrior & Gulf Nav. Co., 363 U.S. 574, 584 (1960).

The situation here is not unlike that presented in Teamsters Union, Local 24 v. Oliver, 358 U.S. 283 (1959), where we held that conditions imposed upon contracting out work to prevent possible curtailment of

---

[6] See Lunden, *Subcontracting Clauses in Major Contracts,* 84 MONTHLY LAB. REV. 579, 715 (1961).

[7] A Department of Labor study analyzed 1,687 collective bargaining agreements, which applied to approximately 7,500,000 workers (about one-half of the estimated work force covered by collective bargaining agreements). Among the agreements studied, approximately one-fourth (378) contained some form of a limitation on subcontracting. Lunden, *supra* at 581.

jobs and the undermining of conditions of employment for members of the bargaining unit constituted a statutory subject of collective bargaining. The issue in that case was whether state antitrust laws could be applied to a provision of a collective bargaining agreement which fixed the minimum rental to be paid by the employer motor carrier who leased vehicles to be driven by their owners rather than the carrier's employees. We held that the agreement was upon a subject matter as to which federal law directed the parties to bargain and hence that state antitrust laws could not be applied to prevent the effectuation of the agreement. . . .

The facts of the present case illustrate the propriety of submitting the dispute to collective negotiation. The Company's decision to contract out the maintenance work did not alter the Company's basic operation. The maintenance work still had to be performed in the plant. No capital investment was contemplated; the Company merely replaced existing employees with those of an independent contractor to do the same work under similar conditions of employment. Therefore, to require the employer to bargain about the matter would not significantly abridge his freedom to manage the business.

The Company was concerned with the high cost of its maintenance operation. It was induced to contract out the work by assurances from independent contractors that economies could be derived by reducing the work force, decreasing fringe benefits, and eliminating overtime payments. These have long been regarded as matters peculiarly suitable for resolution within the collective bargaining framework, and industrial experience demonstrates that collective negotiation has been highly successful in achieving peaceful accommodation of the conflicting interests. Yet, it is contended that when an employer can effect cost savings in these respects by contracting the work out, there is no need to attempt to achieve similar economies through negotiation with existing employees or to provide them with an opportunity to negotiate a mutually acceptable alternative. The short answer is that, although it is not possible to say whether a satisfactory solution could be reached, national labor policy is founded upon the congressional determination that the chances are good enough to warrant subjecting such issues to the process of collective negotiation.

The appropriateness of the collective bargaining process for resolving such issues was apparently recognized by the Company. In explaining its decision to contract out the maintenance work, the Company pointed out that in the same plant other unions "had joined hands with management in an effort to bring about an economical and efficient operation," but "we had not been able to attain that in our discussions with this particular Local." Accordingly, based on past bargaining experience with this union, the Company unilaterally contracted out the work. While "the Act does not encourage a party to engage in fruitless marathon discussions at the expense of frank statement and support of his position," NLRB v. American Nat'l Ins. Co., 343 U.S. 395, 404 (1958), it at least demands that the issue be submitted to the mediatory influence of collective negotiations. As the Court of Appeals pointed out, "it is not necessary that it be likely or probable that the union will yield or supply a feasible solution but rather that the union be afforded an opportunity to meet management's legitimate complaints that its maintenance was unduly costly."

We are thus not expanding the scope of mandatory bargaining to hold, as we do now, that the type of "contracting out" involved in this case — the replacement of employees in the existing bargaining unit with those of an independent contractor to do the same work under similar conditions of employment — is a statutory subject of collective bargaining under § 8(d). Our decision need not and does not encompass other forms of "contracting out" or "subcontracting" which arise daily in our complex economy.[8]

II. The only question remaining is whether, upon a finding that the Company had refused to bargain about a matter which is a statutory subject of collective bargaining, the Board was empowered to order the resumption of maintenance operations and reinstatement with back pay. We believe that it was so empowered. . . .

[Section 10(c)] "charges the Board with the task of devising remedies to effectuate the policies of the Act." NLRB v. Seven-Up Bottling Co., 344 U.S. 344, 346 (1953). The Board's power is a broad discretionary one, subject to limited judicial review. *Ibid.* "[T]he relation of remedy to policy is peculiarly a matter for administrative competence. . . ." Phelps Dodge Corp. v. NLRB, 313 U.S. 177, 194 (1941). "In fashioning remedies to undo the effects of violations of the Act, the Board must draw on enlightenment gained from experience." NLRB v. Seven-Up Bottling Co., 344 U.S. 344, 346 (1953). The Board's order will not be disturbed "unless it can be shown that the order is a patent attempt to achieve ends other than those which can fairly be said to effectuate the policies of the Act." Virginia Elec. & Power Co. v. NLRB, 319 U.S. 533, 540 (1943). Such a showing has not been made in this case.

There has been no showing that the Board's order restoring the status quo ante to insure meaningful bargaining is not well designed to promote the policies of the Act. Nor is there evidence which would justify disturbing the Board's conclusion that the order would not impose an undue or unfair burden on the Company.[10]

_____

[8] As the Solicitor General points out, the terms "contracting out" and "subcontracting" have no precise meaning. They are used to describe a variety of business arrangements altogether different from that involved in this case. For a discussion of the various types of "contracting out" or "subcontracting" arrangements, see Brief for Respondent, pp. 13-17; Brief for Electronic Industries Association as *amicus curiae,* pp. 5-10.

[10] The Board stated: "We do not believe that requirement [restoring the *status quo ante*] imposes an undue or unfair burden on Respondent. The record shows that the maintenance operation is still being performed in much the same manner as it was prior to the subcontracting arrangement. Respondent has a continuing need for the services of maintenance employees; and Respondent's subcontract is terminable at any time upon 60 days' notice." 138 N.L.R.B. at 555, n. 19.

It is argued, nonetheless, that the award exceeds the Board's powers under § 10(c) in that it infringes the provision that "[n]o order of the Board shall require the reinstatement of any individual as an employee who has been suspended or discharged, or the payment to him of any back pay, if such individual was suspended or discharged for cause. . . ." The legislative history of that provision indicates that it was designed to preclude the Board from reinstating an individual who had been discharged because of misconduct. There is no indication, however, that it was designed to curtail the Board's power in fashioning remedies when the loss of employment stems directly from an unfair labor practice as in the case at hand.

The judgment of the Court of Appeals is

Affirmed.

Mr. Justice Goldberg took no part in the consideration or decision of this case.

Mr. Justice Stewart, with whom Mr. Justice Douglas and Mr. Justice Harlan join, concurring.

. . . .

The question posed is whether the particular decision sought to be made unilaterally by the employer in this case is a subject of mandatory collective bargaining within the statutory phrase "terms and conditions of employment." That is all the Court decides. The Court most assuredly does not decide that every managerial decision which necessarily terminates an individual's employment is subject to the duty to bargain. Nor does the Court decide that subcontracting decisions are as a general matter subject to that duty. The Court holds no more than that this employer's decision to subcontract this work, involving "the replacement of employees in the existing bargaining unit with those of an independent contractor to do the same work under similar conditions of employment" is subject to the duty to bargain collectively. Within the narrow limitations implicit in the specific facts of this case, I agree with the Court's decision. . . .

While employment security has thus properly been recognized in various circumstances as a condition of employment, it surely does not follow that every decision which may affect job security is a subject of compulsory collective bargaining. Many decisions made by management affect the job security of employees. Decisions concerning the volume and kind of advertising expenditures, product design, the manner of financing, and of sales, all may bear upon the security of the workers' jobs. Yet it is hardly conceivable that such decisions so involve "conditions of employment" that they must be negotiated with the employees' bargaining representative.

In many of these areas the impact of a particular management decision upon job security may be extremely indirect and uncertain, and this alone may be sufficient reason to conclude that such decisions are not "with respect to . . . conditions of employment." Yet there are other areas where decisions by management may quite clearly imperil job security, or indeed terminate employment entirely. An enterprise may decide to invest in labor-saving machinery. Another may resolve to liquidate its assets and go out of business. Nothing the Court holds today should be understood as imposing a duty to bargain collectively regarding such managerial decisions, which lie at the core of entrepreneurial control. . . .

Applying these concepts to the case at hand, I do not believe that an employer's subcontracting practices are, as a general matter, in themselves conditions of employment. Upon any definition of the statutory terms short of the most expansive, such practices are not conditions — tangible or intangible — of any person's employment. The question remains whether this particular kind of subcontracting decision comes within the employer's duty to bargain. On the facts of this case, I join the Court's judgment, because all that is involved is the substitution of one group of workers for another to perform the same task in the same plant under the ultimate control of the same employer. The question whether the employer may discharge one group of workers and substitute another for them is closely analogous to many other situations within the traditional framework of collective bargaining. Compulsory retirement, layoffs according to seniority, assignment of work among potentially eligible groups within the plant — all involve similar questions of discharge and work assignment, and all have been recognized as subjects of compulsory collective bargaining. . . .

This kind of subcontracting falls short of such larger entrepreneurial questions as what shall be produced, how capital shall be invested in fixed assets, or what the basic scope of the enterprise shall be. In my view, the Court's decision in this case has nothing to do with whether any aspects of those larger issues could under any circumstances be considered subjects of compulsory collective bargaining under the present law. . . .

WESTINGHOUSE ELECTRIC CORP., 150 N.L.R.B. 1574 (1965). For about twenty years, a large manufacturer of electrical appliances had subcontracted maintenance jobs and the manufacture of tools and dies and various components. The company's own employees could have performed most of the maintenance work and could have produced many of the parts and dies. In three separate contract negotiations, the union unsuccessfully sought to have restrictions on subcontracting included in the labor agreement. It then filed charges that the company had refused to bargain by not consulting the union before contracting out operations that could be performed by the company's own employees. The Board found the employer had not violated its statutory obligation by failing to discuss the thousands of individual subcontracting decisions, "bearing in mind particularly that the recurrent contracting out of work here in question was motivated solely by economic considerations; that it comported with the traditional methods by which the Respondent conducted its business operations; that it did not during the period in question vary significantly in kind or degree from what had been customary under past established practice; that it had no demonstrable adverse impact on employees in the unit; and that the Union had the opportunity to bargain about changes in existing subcontracting practices at general negotiating meetings." The Board commented, however, that the subcontracting of unit work is a mandatory subject of bargaining, and that the unilateral contracting out of such work would violate § 8(a)(5) where it "involved a departure from previously established operating practices, effected a change in conditions of employment, or resulted in a significant impairment of job tenure, employment security, or reasonably anticipated work opportunities for those in the bargaining unit."

NLRB v. ADAMS DAIRY, INC., 350 F.2d 108 (8th Cir. 1965), *cert. denied,* 382 U.S. 1011 (1966). A dairy that had distributed its products largely through its own driver-salesmen decided to change to selling all its goods at "dockside" to independent distributors. The routes of these distributors did not correspond to the previous routes of the driver-salesmen, although they covered a similar territory. The independent distributors took title to the products at dockside and had sole responsibility for their sale. The dairy, however, did insist that the distributors maintain certain sanitation and quality standards. No antiunion animus was attributed to the dairy. The court of appeals refused to enforce an NLRB order based on the finding that the employer had violated § 8(a)(5) by neglecting to bargain with the employees' union over the decision to discharge the driver-salesmen and replace them with independent contractors. The court declared: "Contrary to the situation in Fibreboard, then, there is more involved in Adams Dairy than just the substitution of one set of employees for another. In Adams Dairy there is a change in basic operating procedure in that the dairy liquidated that part of its business handling distribution of milk products. Unlike the situation in Fibreboard, there was a change in the capital structure of Adams Dairy. . . . To require Adams to bargain about its decision to close out the distribution end of its business would significantly abridge its freedom to manage its own affairs."

SUMMIT TOOLING CO., 195 N.L.R.B. 479 (1972). An employer closed the manufacturing portion of its operations and terminated the employees without prior notice to the union. Even though the shutdown could be characterized as a partial plant closing, a 2-1 Board majority held that the employer did not violate § 8(a)(5) by its failure to bargain concerning its decision to terminate the manufacturing operation. The decision, said the majority, "involved a major change in the nature of the Respondent's business. . . . The part of the business that remained . . . manufactures nothing, and has little relationship to the work which was performed by [the manufacturing division] nor does it utilize the skills of the employees employed by [the manufacturing division]. In these circumstances, to require Respondent to bargain about its decision to close out its manufacturing operation would significantly abridge Respondent's freedom to manage its own affairs." The employer violated § 8(a)(5), however, by failing to bargain with the union about the *effects* of the closing on the employees.

NOTES

1. Was the NLRB in *Westinghouse,* or the court of appeals in *Adams Dairy* and the Board in *Summit,* more faithful to the Supreme Court's position in the *Railroad Telegraphers* and *Fibreboard* cases? Does *Westinghouse* or *Adams Dairy* and *Summit* represent the sounder balancing of the various interests of employers, employees, and the public? Or is it wrong to assume that there is any inconsistency among these several decisions? *See* Rabin, *Fibreboard and the Termination of Bargaining Unit Work: The Search for Standards in Defining the Scope of Duty to Bargain,* 71 COLUM. L. REV. 803 (1971); Rabin, *The Decline and Fall of Fibreboard,* in N.Y.U. TWENTY-FOURTH ANNUAL CONFERENCE ON LABOR 237 (1972).

2. During the past two decades, the most controversial issue regarding the scope of the duty to bargain has been the extent to which employers must negotiate about managerial decisions that result in a shrinkage of employee job opportunities. The Board for a long time held that in the absence of antiunion animus, management did not have to bargain over decisions to subcontract, relocate operations, or introduce technological improvements, although it did have to bargain about the *effects* of such decisions on the employees displaced. Layoff schedules, severance pay, and transfer rights were thus bargainable, but the basic decision to discontinue an operation was not. *See, e.g.,* Brown-McLaren Mfg. Co., 34 N.L.R.B. 984 (1941); Brown-Dunkin Co., 125 N.L.R.B. 1379 (1959), *enforced,* 287 F.2d 17 (10th Cir. 1961). Under the so-called Kennedy Board, however, a whole range of managerial decisions were reclassified as mandatory subjects of bargaining. These included decisions to terminate a department and subcontract its work, Town & Country Mfg. Co., 136 N.L.R.B. 1022 (1962), *enforced,* 316 F.2d 846 (5th Cir. 1963); to consolidate operations through technological innovations, Renton News Record, 136 N.L.R.B. 1294 (1962); and to close one plant of a multiplant enterprise, Ozark Trailers, Inc., 161 N.L.R.B. 561 (1966). *Contra,* NLRB v. Royal Plating & Polishing Co., 350 F.2d 191 (3d Cir. 1965) (plant shutdown).

Later, as exemplified by *Summit Tooling, supra,* the NLRB seemed to back away from some of the rulings of the Kennedy Board. *See also* General Motors Corp., 191 N.L.R.B. 951 (1971) (sale of dealership; two Board members dissenting), *aff'd sub nom.* UAW Local 864 v. NLRB, 470 F.2d 422 (D.C. Cir. 1972) (one judge dissenting). Under the Kennedy Board as well as its successors, there has been uncertainty about an employer's obligation to bargain over an economically motivated decision to relocate a plant or certain operations. *See* Garwin Corp., 153 N.L.R.B. 664, 665, 680 (1965), *enforced in part,* 374 F.2d 295 (D.C. Cir. 1967), *cert. denied,* 387 U.S. 942 (1967); Cooper Thermometer Co., 160 N.L.R.B. 1902 (1966), *enforced,* 376 F.2d 684 (2d Cir. 1967); Westinghouse Elec. Corp., 174 N.L.R.B. 636 (1969). A critical factor in relocation cases may be the severity of any adverse impact on unit jobs. But apparently there is no duty to bargain about a decision to go completely out of business. *See* Textile Workers v. Darlington Mfg. Co., 380 U.S. 263, 267 n.5 (1965).

For recent decisions holding an employer obligated to bargain, *see* Royal Typewriter Co., 209 N.L.R.B. 1006 (1974), *enforced,* 533 F. 2d 1030 (8th Cir. 1976) (closing one of several plants); Holiday Inn of Benton, 237 N.L.R.B. No. 157, 99 L.R.R.M. 1235 (1978) (converting restaurant to cafeteria); Metromedia, Inc. v. NLRB, 586 F. 2d 1182 (8th Cir. 1978) ("introduction and use" of a "technological innovation," *viz.,* miniature TV cameras). *But cf.* Brockway Motor Trucks v. NLRB, 582 F. 2d 720 (3d Cir. 1978) (closing one of several plants).

3. What remedy should the Board provide when an employer institutes job changes without fulfilling its duty to bargain? Should it always order resumption of the discontinued operations, as in *Fibreboard?* What if this will cause the employer severe financial loss, or prevent it from competing economically in the market? On the other hand, if the status quo ante is not restored, how can the union engage in meaningful bargaining even about the effects of the changes on the employees? For consideration of these questions, see *Renton News Records, supra.* If an employer unlawfully moves a plant without prior bargaining, may the Board order it to bargain at the new location despite the union's lack of a majority status there? How would this affect the rights of the employees at the new plant? *See Garwin Corp., supra.* Where an employer unlawfully failed to bargain over the effects of closing one of its plants, the NLRB ordered it to pay terminated employees their normal wages until (1) the parties bargained to agreement, (2) an impasse occurred, (3) the union failed to request bargaining within a stipulated period, or (4) the union failed to bargain in good faith. No employee was to be paid, however, beyond the date he secured equivalent employment elsewhere or beyond the date the employer went out of business entirely. Royal Plating & Polishing Co., 160 N.L.R.B. 990 (1966).

4. *See generally* Farmer, *Good Faith Bargaining Over Subcontracting,* 51 Geo. L.J. 558 (1963); Goetz, *The Duty to Bargain About Changes in Operations,* 1964 Duke L.J. 1; Platt, *The Duty to Bargain as Applied to Management Decisions,* 19 Lab. L.J. 143 (1968); Smith, *Subcontracting and Union-Management Legal and Contractual Relations,* 17 W. Res. L. Rev. 1278 (1966); Schwartz, *Plant Relocation or Partial Termination — The Duty to Decision-Bargain,* 39 Fordham L. Rev. 81 (1970).

D. THE DURATION OF THE DUTY TO BARGAIN

1. THE EFFECT OF A CHANGE IN THE STATUS OF UNION OR EMPLOYER

BROOKS v. NLRB

Supreme Court of the United States
348 U.S. 96, 75 S. Ct. 176, 99 L. Ed. 125 (1954)

MR. JUSTICE FRANKFURTER delivered the opinion of the Court.

The National Labor Relations Board conducted a representation election in petitioner's Chrysler-Plymouth agency on April 12, 1951. District Lodge No. 727, International Association of Machinists, won by a vote of eight to five, and the Labor Board certified it as the exclusive bargaining representative on April 20. A week after the election and the day before the certification, petitioner received a handwritten letter signed by nine of the 13 employees in the bargaining unit stating: "We, the undersigned majority of the employees ... are not in favor of being represented by Union Local No. 727 as a bargaining agent."

Relying on this letter and the decision of the Court of Appeals for the Sixth Circuit in NLRB v. Vulcan Forging Co., 188 F.2d 927 (6th Cir. 1951), petitioner refused to bargain with the union. The Labor Board found, 98 N.L.R.B. 976, that petitioner had thereby committed an unfair labor practice in violation of §§ 8(a)(1) and 8(a)(5) of the amended National Labor Relations Act, 61 Stat. 140-141, 29 U.S.C. §§ 158(a)(1), (a)(5), and the Court of Appeals for the Ninth Circuit enforced the Board's order to bargain, 204 F.2d 899 (9th Cir. 1953). In view of the conflict between the Circuits, we granted certiorari, 347 U.S. 916 (1954).

The issue before us is the duty of an employer toward a duly certified bargaining agent, if, shortly after the election which resulted in the certification, the union has lost, without the employer's fault, a majority of the employees from its membership.

Under the original Wagner Act, the Labor Board was given the power to certify a union as the exclusive representative of the employees in a bargaining unit when it had determined, by election or "any other suitable method," that the union commanded majority support. Section 9(c), 49 Stat. 453. In exercising this authority the Board evolved a number of working rules of which the following are relevant to our purpose:

(a) A certification, if based on a Board-conducted election, must be honored for a "reasonable" period, ordinarily "one year," in the absence of "unusual circumstances."

(b) "Unusual circumstances" were found in at least three situations: (1) the certified union dissolved or became defunct; (2) as a result of a schism, substantially all the members and officers of the certified union transferred their affiliation to a new local or international; (3) the size of the bargaining unit fluctuated radically within a short time.

(c) Loss of majority support after the "reasonable" period could be questioned in two ways: (1) employer's refusal to bargain, or (2) petition by a rival union for a new election.

(d) If the initial election resulted in a majority for "no union," the election — unlike a certification — did not bar a second election within a year.

The Board uniformly found an unfair labor practice where, during the so-called "certification year," an employer refused to bargain on the ground that the certified union no longer possessed a majority. While the courts in the main enforced the Board's decisions, they did not commit themselves to one year as the determinate content of reasonableness. The Board and the courts proceeded along this line of reasoning:

(a) In the political and business spheres, the choice of the voters in an election binds them for a fixed time. This promotes a sense of responsibility in the electorate and needed coherence in administration. These considerations are equally relevant to healthy labor relations.

(b) Since an election is a solemn and costly occasion, conducted under safeguards to voluntary choice, revocation of authority should occur by a procedure no less solemn than that of the initial designation. A petition or a public meeting — in which those voting for and against unionism are disclosed to management, and in which the influences of mass psychology are present — is not comparable to the privacy and independence of the voting booth.

(c) A union should be given ample time for carrying out its mandate on behalf of its members, and should not be under exigent pressure to produce hot-house results or be turned out.

(d) It is scarcely conducive to bargaining in good faith for an employer to know that, if he dillydallies or subtly undermines, union strength may erode and thereby relieve him of his statutory duties at any time, while if he works conscientiously toward agreement, the rank and file may, at the last moment, repudiate their agent.

(e) In these situations, not wholly rare, where unions are competing, raiding and strife will be minimized if elections are not at the hazard of informal and short-term recall.

Certain aspects of the Labor Board's representation procedures came under scrutiny in the Congress that enacted the Taft-Hartley Act in 1947, 61 Stat. 136. Congress was mindful that, once employees had chosen a union, they could not vote to revoke its authority and refrain from union activities, while if they voted against having a union in the first place, the union could begin at once to agitate for a new election. The National Labor Relations Act was amended to provide that (a) employees could petition the Board for a decertification election, at which they would have an opportunity to choose no longer to be represented by a union, 61 Stat. 144, 29 U.S.C. § 159(c)(1)(A)(ii); (b) an employer, if in doubt as to the majority claimed by a union without formal election or beset by the conflicting claims of rival unions, could likewise petition the Board for an election, 61 Stat. 144, 29 U.S.C. § 159(c)(1)(B); (c) after a valid certification or decertification election had been conducted, the Board could not hold a second election in the same bargaining unit until a year had elapsed, 61 Stat. 144, 29 U.S.C. § 159(c)(3); (d) Board certification could only be granted as the result of an election, 61 Stat. 144, 29 U.S.C. § 159(c)(1), though an employer would presumably still be under a duty to bargain with an uncertified union that had a clear majority, see NLRB v. Kobritz, 193 F.2d 8 (1st Cir. 1951).

The Board continued to apply its "one-year certification" rule after the Taft-Hartley Act came into force, except that even "unusual circumstances" no longer left the Board free to order an election where one had taken place within the preceding 12 months. Conflicting views became manifest in the Court of Appeals when the Board sought to enforce orders based on a refusal to bargain in violation of its rule. Some Circuits sanctioned the Board's position. The Court of Appeals for the Sixth Circuit denied enforcement. The Court of Appeals for the Third Circuit held that a "reasonable" period depended on the facts of the particular case.

The issue is open here. No case touching the problem has directly presented it. In Franks Bros. Co. v. NLRB, 321 U.S. 702 (1944), we held that where a union's majority was dissipated after an employer's unfair labor practice in refusing to bargain, the Board could appropriately find that such conduct had undermined the prestige of the union and require the employer to bargain with it for a reasonable period despite the loss of majority. And in NLRB v. Mexia Textile Mills, Inc., 339 U.S. 563 (1950), we held that a claim of an intervening loss of majority was no defense to a proceeding for enforcement of an order to cease and desist from certain unfair labor practices.

Petitioner contends that whenever an employer is presented with evidence that his employees have deserted their certified union, he may forthwith refuse to bargain. In effect, he seeks to vindicate the rights of his employees to select their bargaining representative. If the employees are dissatisfied with their chosen union, they may submit their own grievance to the Board. If an employer has doubts about his duty to continue bargaining, it is his responsibility to petition the Board for relief, while continuing to bargain in good faith at least until the Board has given some indication that his claim has merit. Although the Board may, if the facts warrant, revoke a certification or agree not to pursue a charge of unfair labor practice, these are matters for the Board; they do not justify the employer self-help or judicial intervention. The underlying purpose of this statute is industrial peace. To allow employers to rely on employees' rights in refusing to bargain with the formally designated union is not conducive to that end, it is inimical to it. Congress has devised a formal mode for selection and rejection of bargaining agents and has fixed the spacing of elections, with a view of furthering industrial stability and with due regard to administrative prudence.

We find wanting the arguments against these controlling considerations. In placing a nonconsenting minority under the bargaining responsibility of an agency selected by a majority of the workers, Congress has discarded common-law doctrines of agency. It is contended that since a bargaining agency may be ascertained by methods less formal than a supervised election, informal repudiation should also be sanctioned where decertification by another election is precluded. This is to make situations that are different appear the same. Finally, it is not within the power of this Court to require the Board, as is suggested, to relieve a small employer, like the one involved in this case, of the duty that may be exacted from an enterprise with many employees.

To be sure, what we have said has special pertinence only to the period during which a second election is impossible. But the Board's view that the one-year period should run from the date of certification rather than the date of election seems within the allowable area of the Board's discretion in carrying out congressional policy. See Phelps Dodge Corp. v. NLRB, 313 U.S. 177, 192-197 (1941); NLRB v. Seven-Up Bottling Co., 344 U.S. 344 (1953). Otherwise, encouragement would be given to management or a rival union to delay certification by spurious objections to the conduct of an election and thereby diminish the duration of the duty to bargain. Furthermore, the Board has ruled that one year after certification the employer can ask for an election or, if he has fair doubts about the union's continuing majority, he may refuse to bargain further with it. This, too, is a matter appropriately determined by the Board's administrative authority.

We conclude that the judgment of the Court of Appeals enforcing the Board's order must be

Affirmed.

NOTE

In Mar-Jac Poultry Co., 136 N.L.R.B. 785 (1962), the Board held that where an employer agrees to bargain in good faith in settlement of a certified union's refusal-to-bargain charge, an election petition by the employer will be denied for twelve months following the settlement agreement. The union was said to be entitled to at least one year of actual bargaining from the date of the settlement.

An uncertified union that has been lawfully recognized on the basis of a "card check" or the settlement of refusal-to-bargain charges is entitled to retain bargaining rights for a "reasonable period of time." The NLRB will not entertain a decertification petition filed during this period, and the filing of such a petition does not constitute sufficient grounds for the employer to refuse to bargain with the union. Universal Gear Serv. Corp., 157 N.L.R.B. 1169 (1966), *enforced,* 394 F.2d 396 (6th Cir. 1968); NLRB v. Montgomery Ward & Co., 399 F.2d 409 (7th Cir. 1968). How long is "reasonable"? What factors should be considered? *Compare* Brennan's Cadillac, Inc., 231 N.L.R.B. No. 34, 96 L.R.R.M. 1004 (1977) (3 months adequate; two members dissenting), *with* Vantran Elec. Corp., 231 N.L.R.B. No. 169, 96 L.R.R.M. 1210 (1977) (4½ months inadequate; one member dissenting), *enforcement denied,* 580 F. 2d 921 (7th Cir. 1978).

An employer is also bound to bargain for the period during which an existing labor contract is a bar to a Board election, despite good-faith doubts about the union's continuing majority. This is so whether the union has been certified, Hexton Furniture Co., 111 N.L.R.B. 342 (1955), or has been recognized voluntarily without an election, Shamrock Dairy, Inc., 119 N.L.R.B. 998 (1957). *See generally* Neary, *The Union's Loss of Majority Status and the Employer's Obligation to Bargain,* 36 TEXAS L. REV. 878 (1958).

STONER RUBBER CO., 123 N.L.R.B. 1440 (1959). A union was certified after winning a representation election by a vote of 32 to 27. Contract negotiations broke down and the union struck. Five months after the strike began and fourteen months after the election, the employer was operating with a complement of eighteen permanent replacements and eighteen former strikers who had abandoned the strike. At this point the employer, believing the union no longer represented a majority of the employees, granted a wage increase without consulting the union. The Board held, 3 to 2, there was no violation of § 8(a)(5). Two members reasoned that after the expiration of the certification year, a certification creates only a presumption of continued majority which may be rebutted by employer evidence sufficient to cast serious doubt on the union's status. Thereafter the NLRB General Counsel, to establish a violation, would have to produce proof that on the refusal to bargain date the union in fact represented a majority of the employees. A third member maintained that an employer should not have to act thus at his peril, and that there should be no violation when an employer takes unilateral action after the certification year, so long as he has a reasonable, good-faith belief the union no longer represents a majority. Two members of the Board, dissenting, argued that after the certification year an employer may withdraw recognition if he has a good-faith doubt of continued majority standing, but that he may not take unilateral action without affording the union an opportunity to protect its established position as bargaining representative.

NOTES

1. The NLRB revised the *Stoner Rubber* rules in Pioneer Flour Mills, 174 N.L.R.B. 1202 (1969), to take account of the 1959 amendment to § 9(c)(3) of the NLRA. Since the amendment provides that replaced economic strikers are entitled to vote in any election conducted within twelve months of the commencement of the strike, the Board held that economic strikers must be counted as members of the bargaining unit for the first twelve months of the strike for the purposes of determining the union's majority status in an 8(a)(5) case. The Board's order was enforced in 427 F.2d 983 (5th Cir. 1970), *cert. denied,* 400 U.S. 942 (1970).

2. The "serious doubt" that is sufficient to rebut the presumption of a union's continuing majority following expiration of the certification year has two components: a reasonable basis in fact, and good faith. Applying this standard, a court of appeals found, contrary to the NLRB, that a company had established the existence of a serious doubt by pointing to a sharp decline in employee checkoff authorizations, and by introducing an intra-union memorandum indicating the loss of majority support. One judge dissented, arguing that the Board could properly infer the employer acted in bad faith since it waited until five months after negotiations began before withdrawing recognition. Machinists Lodges 1746 and 743 v. NLRB, 416 F.2d 809 (D.C. Cir. 1969), *cert. denied,* 396 U.S. 1058 (1970). See also Southern Wipers, Inc., 192 N.L.R.B. 816 (1971).

3. What bearing may the principles of *Gissel, supra* at 237, have on an employer's withdrawal of recognition from a union that he believes no longer commands majority support? See Daisy's Originals, Inc. v. NLRB, 468 F.2d 493 (5th Cir. 1972); Automated Business Systems v. NLRB, 497 F.2d 262 (6th Cir. 1974).

4. In Midwest Piping & Supply Co., 63 N.L.R.B. 1060 (1945), the Board ruled an employer violates § 8(1) (§ 8(a)(1)) of the Act by negotiating a contract with one of two rival unions whose representation petitions are pending before the Board. The *Midwest Piping* doctrine was extended to incumbent unions in Shea Chemical Corp., 121 N.L.R.B. 1027 (1958). The Board declared: "[U]pon presentation of a rival or conflicting claim which raises a real question concerning representation, an employer may not go so far as to bargain collectively with the incumbent (or any other) union unless and until the question concerning representation has been settled by the Board. This is not to say that the employer must give an undue advantage to the rival union by refusing to permit the incumbent union to continue administering its contract or processing grievances through its stewards. . . . However, we wish to make it clear that the *Midwest Piping* doctrine does not apply in situations where, because of contract bar or certification year or inappropriate unit or any other established reason, the rival claim and petition do *not* raise a real representation question." *But cf.* Cleaver-Brooks Mfg. Co. v. NLRB, 264 F.2d 637 (7th Cir. 1959), *cert. denied,* 361 U.S. 817 (1959), where a Board order applying the *Midwest Piping* doctrine was denied enforcement on the ground the union with which the employer executed a contract had a "clear majority" and the other union was "no genuine contender."

AMERICAN SEATING CO.

National Labor Relations Board
106 N.L.R.B. 250 (1953)

. . . .

The facts in the case are undisputed. On September 20, 1949, following an election, the Board certified International Union, Automobile, Aircraft and Agricultural Implement Workers of America (UAW-CIO), and its Local No. 135, herein called the UAW-CIO, as bargaining representative of the Respondent's production and maintenance employees. On July 1, 1950, the Respondent and the UAW-CIO entered into a three-year collective bargaining contract covering all employees in the certified unit. Shortly before the expiration of two years from the date of signing of the contract, Pattern Makers' Association of Grand Rapids, Pattern Makers' League of North America, AFL, herein called the Union, filed a representation petition seeking to sever a craft unit of patternmakers from the existing production and maintenance unit. Both the Respondent and the UAW-CIO opposed the petition, contending that their three-year contract which would not expire until July 1, 1953, was a bar. In a decision issued on September 4, 1952, the Board rejected this contention. It held that, as the contract had been in existence for two years, and as the contracting parties had failed to establish that contracts for three-year terms were customary in the seating industry, the contract was not a bar during the third year of its term. Accordingly, the Board directed an election in a unit of patternmakers, which the Union won.

On October 6, 1952, the Board certified the Union as bargaining representative of the Respondent's patternmakers. Approximately ten days later, the Union submitted to the Respondent a proposed collective bargaining agreement covering terms and conditions of employment for patternmakers to be effective immediately. The Respondent replied that it recognized the Union as bargaining representative of the patternmakers and that it was willing to negotiate or discuss subjects properly open for discussion, but that the existing contract with the UAW-CIO was still in full force and effect and remained binding upon all employees, including patternmakers, until its July 1, 1953, expiration date.

There is no question raised as to the Board's power to direct an election upon its finding that the existing contract between the UAW-CIO and the Respondent was not a bar. The parties differ, however, as to the effect to be given to the new certification resulting from this election. The Respondent contends that the certification of the Pattern Makers merely resulted in the substitution of a new bargaining representative for patternmakers in place of the old representative, with the substantive terms of the contract remaining unchanged. In support of this position, the Respondent argues that the UAW-CIO was the agent of the patternmakers when it entered into the 1950 agreement with that organization, and that the patternmakers, as principals, are bound by that contract to the expiration date thereof, notwithstanding that they have changed their agent. The General Counsel, on the other hand, contends that the certification of the Pattern Makers resulted in making the existing contract with the UAW-CIO inoperative as to the employees in the unit of patternmakers.

The Respondent's principal-agent argument assumes that common-law principles of agency control the relationship of exclusive bargaining representative to employees in an appropriate unit. We think that this assumption is unwarranted and overlooks the unique character of that relationship under the National Labor Relations Act.

Under the common law, agency is a consensual relationship. On the other hand, the status of exclusive bargaining representative is a special one created and governed by statute. "Representatives designated or selected for the purposes of collective bargaining by the majority of the employees in a unit appropriate for such purposes, shall be the exclusive representative of all the employees in such unit for the purposes of collective bargaining. . . ." A duly selected statutory representative is the representative of a shifting group of employees in an appropriate unit which includes not only those employees who approve such relationship, but also those who disapprove and those who have never had an opportunity to express their choice. Under agency principles, a principal has the power to terminate the authority of his agent at any time. Not so in the case of a statutory bargaining representative. Thus, in its most important aspects the relationship of statutory bargaining representative to employees in an appropriate unit resembles a political rather than a private law relationship. In any event, because of the unique character of the statutory representative, a solution for the problem presented in this case must be sought in the light of that special relationship rather than by the device of pinning labels on the various parties involved and applying without change principles of law evolved to govern entirely different situations.

The National Labor Relations Act provides machinery for the selection and change of exclusive bargaining representatives. If after the filing of a petition by employees, a labor organization, or an employer, and the holding of a hearing, the Board is convinced that a question of representation exists, it is directed by statute to conduct an election by secret ballot and certify the results thereof. The Act does not list the situations in which a "question of representation affecting commerce exists." That has been left to the Board to decide. One of the problems in this connection arises from the claim that a collective bargaining contract of fixed term should bar a new election during the entire term of such contract. In solving this problem, the Board has had to balance two separate interests: The interest of employees and society in the stability that is essential to the effective encouragement of collective bargaining, and the sometimes conflicting interest of employees in being free to change their representatives at will. Reconciling these two interests in the early days of the Act, the Board decided that it would not consider a contract of unreasonable duration a bar to an election to determine a new bargaining representative. The Board further decided that a contract of more than one year was of unreasonable duration and that it would direct an election after the first year of the existence of such a contract. In 1947, in the further interest of stability, the Board extended from one to two years the period during which a valid collective bargaining contract would be considered a bar to a new determination of representatives.

. . . If the Respondent's contention is sound, a certified bargaining representative might be deprived of effective statutory power as to the most important subjects of collective bargaining for an unlimited number of years as the result of an agreement negotiated by an unwanted and repudiated bargaining representative. There is no provision in the statute for this kind of emasculated certified bargaining representative. Moreover, the rule urged by the Respondent seems hardly calculated to reduce "industrial strife" by encouraging the "practice and procedure of collective bargaining," the declared purpose of the National Labor Relations Act, as amended.

The purpose of the Board's rule holding a contract of unreasonable duration not a bar to a new determination of representatives is the democratic one of insuring to employees the right at reasonable intervals of reappraising and changing, if they so desire, their union representation. Bargaining representatives are thereby kept responsive to the needs and desires of their constituents; and employees dissatisfied with their representatives know that they will have the opportunity of changing them by peaceful means at an election conducted by an impartial Government agency. Strikes for a change of representatives are thereby reduced and effects of employee dissatisfaction with their representatives are mitigated. But, if a newly chosen representative is to be hobbled in the way proposed by the Respondent, a great part of the benefit to be derived from the no-bar rule will be dissipated. There is little point in selecting a new bargaining representative which is unable to negotiate new terms and conditions of employment for an extended period of time.

We hold that, for the reasons which led the Board to adopt the rule that a contract of unreasonable duration is not a bar to a new determination of representatives, such a contract may not bar full statutory collective bargaining, including the reduction to writing of any agreement reached, as to any group of employees in an appropriate unit covered by such contract, upon the certification of a new collective bargaining representative for them. Accordingly, we find that by refusing on and after October 16, 1952, to bargain with the Pattern Makers concerning wages, hours, and other working conditions for employees in the unit of patternmakers, the Respondent violated §§ 8(a)(5) and (1) of the Act....

NOTE

See Cox, *The Legal Nature of Collective Bargaining Agreements,* 57 MICH. L. REV. 1, 7-14 (1958); Freidin, *The Board, "The Bar," and the Bargain,* 59 COLUM. L. REV. 61, 82 (1959).

Would the newly certified union in the principal case be free to strike for changes in contract terms? Compare § 8(d)(4) of the NLRA.

GARMENT WORKERS LOCAL 57 v. NLRB [GARWIN CORP.], 374 F.2d 295 (D.C. Cir. 1967), *cert. denied,* 387 U.S. 942 (1967). The employer, without consulting the union about its decision, closed its plant in New York City, discharged its employees, and moved its operations to Miami, Florida. The NLRB found the move was motivated by antiunion sentiment, not economic necessity, and held the employer in violation of §§ 8(a)(5), (3), and (1) of the Act. In addition to ordering reinstatement and back pay for the workers, the Board ordered the "runaway" employer to bargain with the union either at the New York plant or the new Florida location, regardless of whether the union had majority status. The court of appeals refused enforcement of the bargaining portion of the Board's order, saying "the remedy fashioned by the Board in this case imposes on the Florida workers a bargaining representative without reference to their choice." Removing the benefits of the employer's wrongdoing, "standing alone and without relationship to redressing grievances of the New York workers, who suffered the violation of their statutory rights," was not enough "to justify infringing fundamental rights of comparable magnitude vested by law in the Florida workers." A dissenting judge stated: "That the Board, in striking a balance between the need to protect a collective bargaining relationship and the interests of new employees in being free to select their own bargaining agent, has determined to give precedence to the former is, in my view, a judgment consistent with its statutory responsibilities." [On remand, the Board ordered bargaining upon proof of a union majority in Florida. 169 N.L.R.B. 1030 (1968), *enforced,* 70 L.R.R.M. 2465 (D.C. Cir. 1969), *cert. denied,* 395 U.S. 980 (1969).]

NOTES

1. The Board's decision in *Garwin Corp.* is noted in 34 GEO. WASH. L. REV. 367 (1965); 79 HARV. L. REV. 855 (1966); 64 MICH. L. REV. 741 (1966); 41 NOTRE DAME LAW. 267 (1965).

2. A widespread phenomenon of recent years, especially in construction, has been the formation by unionized firms of nonunion subsidiaries to permit more competitive bidding for work in the nonunion sector of an industry. What doctrines and policies studied to date are relevant in determining the legal status of these "double-breasted" operations? *Compare* South Prairie Constr. Co. v. Operating Engineers Local 627, 425 U.S. 800 (1976), *with* Appalachian Constr., Inc., 235 N.L.R.B. No. 99, 98 L.R.R.M. 1067 (1978). *See generally* Bornstein, *The Emerging Law of the "Double Breasted" Operation in the Construction Industry,* 28 LAB. L.J. 77 (1977).

3. Special problems arise when one employer succeeds to the status of another, whether by purchase, merger, or otherwise, and the predecessor's employees are represented by a union and covered by an outstanding collective bargaining agreement. The bargaining rights and duties of the successor employer in such circumstances, the propriety of unilateral action on its part, and the possible survival of contractual obligations, will be treated together in section III, *infra* at 721 ff., along with other questions concerning the enforcement of collective agreements.

2. THE EFFECT OF AN EXISTING AGREEMENT

THE JACOBS MANUFACTURING CO.

National Labor Relations Board
94 N.L.R.B. 1214 (1951)

. . . In July 1948, the Respondent and the Union executed a two-year bargaining contract which, by its terms, could be reopened one year after its execution date for discussion of "wage rates." In July, 1949, the Union invoked the reopening clause of the 1948 contract, and thereafter gave the Respondent written notice of its "wage demands." In addition to a request for a wage increase, these demands included a request that the Respondent undertake the entire cost of an existing group insurance program, and another request for the establishment of a pension plan for the Respondent's employees. When the parties met thereafter to consider the Union's demands, the Respondent refused to discuss the Union's pension and insurance requests on the ground that they were not appropriate items of discussion under the reopening clause of the 1948 contract.

The group insurance program to which the Union alluded in its demands was established by the Respondent before 1948. It was underwritten by an insurance company, and provided life, accident, health, surgical, and hospital protection. All the Respondent's employees were eligible to participate in the program, and the employees shared its costs with the Respondent. When the 1948 contract was being negotiated, the Respondent and the Union had discussed changes in this *insurance program,* and had agreed to increase certain of the benefits as well as the costs. However, neither the changes thereby effected, nor the insurance program itself, was mentioned in the 1948 contract.

As indicated by the Union's request, there was no pension plan for the Respondent's employees in existence in 1949. The subject of *pensions,* moreover, had not been discussed during the 1948 negotiations; and, like insurance, that subject is not mentioned in the 1948 contract.

a. For the reasons stated below, Chairman Herzog and Members Huston and Styles agree with the Trial Examiner's conclusion that the Respondent violated § 8(a)(5) of the Act by refusing to discuss the matter of *pensions* with the Union. . . .

We are satisfied . . . that the 1948 contract did not in itself impose on the Respondent any obligation to discuss pensions or insurance. The reopening clause of that contract refers to *wage rates,* and thus its intention appears to have been narrowly limited to matters directly related to the amount and matter of compensation for work. For that reason, a requirement to discuss pensions or insurance cannot be predicated on the language of the contract.

On the other hand, a majority of the Board believes that, regardless of the character of the reopening clause, the Act itself imposed upon the Respondent the duty to discuss *pensions* with the Union during the period in question.

It is now established as a principle of law that the matter of pensions is a subject which falls within the area where the statute requires bargaining. And, as noted above, the 1948 contract between the Respondent and the Union was silent with respect to the subject of pensions; indeed, the matter had never been raised or discussed by the parties. The issue raised, therefore, is whether the Respondent was absolved of the obligation to discuss pensions because of the limitation contained in § 8(d) of the amended Act dealing with the duty to discuss or agree to the modification of an existing bargaining contract. . . .

The crucial point at issue here . . . is the construction to be given the phrase "terms and conditions *contained in* a contract." (Emphasis supplied.) The Board in the *Tide Water* [85 N.L.R.B. 1096] case, concluded that the pertinent portion of § 8(d)

"refers to terms and conditions which have been integrated and embodied into a writing. Conversely it does not have reference to matters relating to wages, hours and other terms and conditions of employment, which have not been reduced to writing. As to the written terms of the contract either party may refuse to bargain further about them, under the limitations set forth in the paragraph, without committing an unfair labor practice. With respect to unwritten terms dealing with wages, hours and other terms and conditions of employment, the obligation remains on both parties to bargain continuously."

Thus, as already construed by this Board in the *Tide Water* case, § 8(d) does not itself license a party to a bargaining contract to refuse, during the life of the contract, to discuss a bargainable subject unless it has been made part of the agreement itself. Applied here, therefore, the *Tide Water* construction of § 8(d) means that the Respondent was obligated to discuss the Union's pension demand.

Members Huston and Styles have carefully re-examined the Board's construction of § 8(d) in the *Tide Water* case, and are persuaded that the view the Board adopted in the *Tide Water* case best effectuates the declared policy of the Act. Chairman Herzog, while joining in the result with respect to the obligation to bargain here concerning pensions — never previously discussed by the parties — joins in the rationale herein *only* to the extent that it is consistent with his views separately recited below, concerning the insurance program.

By making mandatory the discussion of bargainable subjects not already covered by a contract, the parties to the contract are encouraged to arrive at joint decisions with respect to bargainable matters, that, at least to the party requesting discussion, appear at the time to be of some importance. The Act's policy of "encouraging the practice and procedure of collective bargaining" is consequently furthered. A different construction of § 8(d) in the circumstances — one that would permit a party to a bargaining contract to avoid discussion when it was sought on subject matters not contained in the contract — would serve, at its best, only to dissipate whatever the good will that had been engendered by the previous bargaining negotiations that led to the execution of a bargaining contract; at its worst, it could bring about the industrial strife and the production interruptions that the policy of the Act also seeks to avert.

The significance of this point cannot be overemphasized. It goes to the heart of our disagreement with our dissenting colleague, Member Reynolds. His dissent stresses the need for "contract stability," and asserts that the furtherance of sound collective bargaining requires that the collective bargaining agreement be viewed as fixing, for the term of the contract, all aspects of the employer-employee relationship, and as absolving either party of the obligation to discuss, during that term, even those matters which had never been raised, or discussed in the past. We could hardly take issue with the virtue of "contract stability," at least in the abstract, and we would certainly agree that everyone is better off when, in negotiating an agreement, the parties have been able to foresee what all the future problems may be, to discuss those problems, and either to embody a resolution of them in the contract, or to provide that they may not be raised again during the contract. But we are here concerned with the kind of case in which, for one reason or another, this has *not* been done, and the question is what best effectuates the policies of the Act in *such* a case.

In this connection we cannot ignore the fact that to say that a party to an agreement is absolved by § 8(d) of an obligation to discuss a subject not contained in a contract does not mean that the other party is prohibited from taking economic action to compel bargaining on that subject. The portion of § 8(d) we are here considering does no more than provide a *defense* to a charge of a refusal to bargain under § 8(a)(5) or § 8(b)(3) of the Act. It does not render unlawful economic action aimed at securing lawful objectives.[10] That being so, the view urged by Member Reynolds achieves "contract stability" but only at the price of industrial strife, and that is a result which now more than ever we must avoid. The basic policy of this Act to further collective bargaining is founded on the proposition — amply demonstrated by experience — that collective bargaining provides an escape valve for the pressures which otherwise result in industrial strife. With this policy in mind, we are loath to narrow the area of mandatory bargaining, except where the amended statute, in the clearest terms, requires that we do so.

The construction of § 8(d) adopted by the Board in the *Tide Water* case serves also to simplify, and thus to speed, the bargaining process. It eliminates the pressure upon the parties at the time when a contract is being negotiated to raise those subjects that may not then be of controlling importance, but which might in the future assume a more significant status. It also assures to both unions and employers that, if future conditions require some agreement as to matters about which the parties have not sought, or have not been able to obtain agreement, then some discussion of those matters will be forthcoming when necessary.

We cannot believe that Congress was unaware of the foregoing considerations when it amended the Act by inserting § 8(d), or that it sought, by the provision in question, to freeze the bargaining relationship by eliminating any mandatory discussion that might lead to the addition

---

[10] We must note, however, contrary to the assertion of Member Reynolds, that nothing in this decision is to be construed as a determination of the issue of whether a union may strike to compel bargaining on a modification of a contract which seeks to add a matter not contained in the contract without complying with the procedural requirements of § 8(d). Our decision here is limited to a construction of the language "modification of the terms and conditions *contained in* a contract." The issue raised by our dissenting colleague is not before us in this case, and we in no way pass upon it.

of new subject matter to an existing contract. What § 8(d) does do is to reject the pronouncements contained in some pre-1947 Board and court decisions — sometimes *dicta,* sometimes necessary to the holding — to the effect that the duty to bargain continues even as to those matters upon which the parties have reached agreement and which are set forth in the terms of a written contract. But we believe it does no more. Those bargainable issues which have never been discussed by the parties, and which are in no way treated in the contract, remain matters which both the union and the employer are obliged to discuss at any time.

In so holding, we emphasize that under this rule, no less than in any other circumstance, the duty to bargain implies only an obligation to *discuss* the matter in question in good faith with a sincere purpose of reaching some agreement. It does not require that either side agree, or make concessions. And if the parties originally desire to avoid later discussion with respect to matters not specifically covered in the terms of an executed contract, they need only so specify in the terms of the contract itself. Nothing in our construction of § 8(d) precludes such an agreement, entered into in good faith, from foreclosing future discussion of matters not contained in the agreement.[13]

b. Chairman Herzog, for reasons set forth in his separate opinion, believes that — unlike the pensions issue — the Respondent was under no obligation to bargain concerning the *group insurance program.*

However, Members Huston and Styles — a minority of the Board on this issue — are of the further opinion that the considerations discussed above leading to the conclusion that the Respondent was obligated to discuss the matter of pensions, also impel the conclusion that the Respondent was obligated to discuss the Union's group insurance demand. Like pensions, the matter of group insurance benefits is a subject which has been held to be within the area of compulsory bargaining; and like pensions, the Respondent's group insurance program was not mentioned in the terms of the 1948 contract. Members Huston and Styles therefore believe that so far as the controlling facts are concerned the ultimate issues presented by the Union's pension and group insurance demands are identical. . . .

---

[13] For an example of a contract in which such a provision was incorporated, see the contract between United Automobile Workers of America and General Motors Corp., set forth in *Labor Relations Manual* (BNA), vol. 26, p. 63, 91, which states:

(154) The parties acknowledge that during the negotiations which resulted in this agreement, each had the unlimited right and opportunity to make demands and proposals with respect to any subject or matter not removed by law from the area of collective bargaining, and that the understandings and agreements arrived at by the parties after the exercise of that right and opportunity are set forth in this agreement. Therefore, the Corporation and the Union, for the life of this agreement, each voluntarily and unqualifiedly waives the right, and each agrees that the other shall not be obligated, to bargain collectively with respect to any subject or matter not specifically referred to or covered in this agreement, even though such subjects or matter may not have been within the knowledge or contemplation of either or both of the parties at the time that they negotiated or signed this agreement.

Members Huston and Styles believe, moreover, that the view adopted by Chairman Herzog on the insurance issue is subject to the same basic criticism as is the view of Member Reynolds — it exalts "contract stability" over industrial peace; it eliminates mandatory collective bargaining on subjects about which one of the parties *now* wants discussion, and concerning which it may well be willing to take economic action if discussion is denied, solely because the matter has once been discussed in a manner which may warrant an inference that the failure to mention that subject in the contract was part of the bargain. Members Huston and Styles are constrained to reject the view of Chairman Herzog for the further reason that it would establish a rule which is administratively unworkable, and would inject dangerous uncertainty into the process of collective bargaining. Apart from the extremely difficult problems of proof — illustrated in this very case — which would constantly confront the Board in cases of this type, the parties to collective bargaining negotiations would always be faced with this question after a subject has been *discussed* — "Have we really *negotiated,* or are we under an obligation to discuss the subject further if asked to?" To this query the rule of the *Tide Water* case gives a clear and concise answer: "You are obligated to discuss any bargaining subject upon request unless you have reduced your agreement on that subject to writing or unless you have agreed in writing not to bargain about it during the term of the contract." Members Huston and Styles would apply that rule without deviation. . . .

CHAIRMAN HERZOG, concurring in part:

I believe that this Respondent was *not* under a duty to discuss the Union's *group insurance* demand. The individual views which lead me, by a different road, to the result reached on this issue by Members Reynolds and Murdock, are as follows:

Unlike the issue of pensions, concerning which the contract is silent and the parties did not negotiate at all in 1948, the subject of group insurance was fully discussed while the Respondent and the Union were negotiating the agreement. True, that agreement is silent on the subject, so it cannot literally be said that there is a term "contained in" the 1948 contract relating to the group insurance program. The fact remains that during the negotiations which preceded its execution, the issue was consciously explored. The record reveals that the Union expressly requested that the preexisting program be changed so that the Respondent would assume its entire cost, the very proposal that was again made as part of the 1949 midterm demand which gave rise to this case. The Respondent rejected the basic proposal on this first occasion, but agreement was then reached — although outside the written contract — to increase certain benefits under the group insurance program.

In my opinion, it is only reasonable to assume that rejection of the Union's basic proposal, coupled in this particular instance with enhancement of the substantive benefits, constituted a part of the contemporaneous "bargain" which the parties made when they negotiated the entire 1948 contract. In the face of this record as to what the parties discussed and did, I believe that it would be an abuse of this

Board's mandate to throw the weight of Government sanction behind the Union's attempt to disturb, in midterm, a bargain sealed when the original agreement was reached.

To hold otherwise would encourage a labor organization — or, in a § 8(b)(3) case, an employer — to come back, time without number, during the term of a contract, to demand resumed discussion of issues which, although perhaps not always incorporated in the written agreement, the other party had every good reason to believe were put at rest for a definite period. I do not think that the doctrine of the *Tide Water* case was ever intended to go so far as to extend to facts like these, or that it should be so extended. Without regard to the niceties of construing the words of § 8(d) of the amended Act, I am satisfied that it would be both inequitable and unwise to impose a statutory obligation to bargain in situations of this sort. That would serve only to stimulate uncertainty and evasion of commitments at a time when stability should be the order of the day.

MEMBER REYNOLDS, concurring separately and dissenting in part: . . .

[I]t is my opinion that § 8(d) imposes no obligation on either party to a contract to bargain on any matter during the term of the contract except as the express provisions of the contract may demand. This is a result reasonably compatible with the particular § 8(d) language involved, as well as with § 8(d) as a whole. Moreover, not only does the result accord stability and dignity to collective bargaining agreements, but it also gives substance to the practice and procedure of collective bargaining.

It is well established that the function of collective bargaining agreements is to contribute stability, so essential to sound industrial relations. Contractually stabilized industrial relations enable employers, because of fixed labor costs, to engage in sound long-range production planning, and employees, because of fixed wage, seniority, promotion, and grievance provisions, to anticipate secure employment tenure. Hence when an employer and a labor organization have through the processes of collective bargaining negotiated an agreement containing the terms and conditions of employment for a definite period of time, their total rights and obligations emanating from the employer-employee relationship should remain fixed for that time. Stabilized therefore are the rights and obligations of the parties with respect to all bargainable subjects whether the subjects are or are not specifically set forth in the contract. To hold otherwise and prescribe bargaining on unmentioned subjects would result in continued alteration of the total rights and obligations under the contract, thus rendering meaningless the concept of contract stability.

That a collective bargaining agreement stabilizes all rights and conditions of employment is consonant with the generally accepted concept of the nature of such an agreement. The basic terms and conditions of employment existing at the time the collective bargaining agreement is executed, and which are not specifically altered by, or mentioned in, the agreement, are part of the *status quo* which the parties, by implication, consider as being adopted as an essential element of the agreement. This view is termed "reasonable and logical," and its widespread endorsement as sound industrial relations practice makes it a general rule followed in the arbitration of disputes arising during the term of a contract. The reasonableness of the approach is apparent upon an understanding of collective bargaining techniques. Many items are not mentioned in a collective bargaining agreement either because of concessions at the bargaining table or because one of the parties may have considered it propitious to forego raising one subject in the hope of securing a more advantageous deal on another. Subjects traded off or foregone should, under these circumstances, be as irrevocably settled as those specifically covered and settled by the agreement. To require bargaining on such subjects during midterm debases initial contract negotiations. . . .

MEMBER MURDOCK, dissenting in part:

I am unable to agree with my colleagues of the majority that by refusing to discuss pensions and insurance with the Union under the particular circumstances of this case, the Respondent violated § 8(a)(5) of the Act.

Despite the fact that the reopening clause in the contract which the Union here invoked was limited to "wage rates," the Union included insurance and pensions in its demands thereunder in addition to a wage increase. In my view the Respondent properly took the position that the parties were meeting pursuant to the reopening provision of the contract to discuss wage rates and that pensions and insurance were not negotiable thereunder and would not be discussed at that time. . . .

NOTE

The Board majority's position that pensions were a bargainable issue since neither discussed in negotiations nor embodied in the contract received judicial support in NLRB v. Jacobs Mfg. Co., 196 F.2d 680 (2d Cir. 1952). The differences among the Board members in the *Jacobs* case may well have resulted from the critical comments of Professors Cox and Dunlop in *Regulation of Collective Bargaining by the National Labor Relations Board,* 63 HARV. L. REV. 389 (1950), and *The Duty to Bargain Collectively During the Term of an Existing Agreement,* 63 HARV. L. REV. 1097 (1950). For a vigorous defense of the Board, see Findling & Colby, *Regulation of Collective Bargaining by the National Labor Relations Board — Another View,* 51 COLUM. L. REV. 170 (1951).

What must be said during negotiations to give rise to the inference that a particular matter was intended to be left in the employer's hands for the period of the contract? How reliable is the evidence likely to be? *Compare* NLRB v. Nash-Finch Co., 211 F.2d 622 (8th Cir. 1954), *and* Speidel Corp., 120 N.L.R.B. 733 (1958), *with* Beacon Piece Dyeing & Finishing Co., 121 N.L.R.B. 953 (1958), *and* Cloverleaf Div. of Adams Dairy Co., 147 N.L.R.B. 1410 (1964). In Proctor Manufacturing Corp., 131 N.L.R.B. 1166, 1169 (1961), the Board declared: "The Board's rule, applicable to negotiations during the contract term with respect to a subject which has been discussed in precontract negotiations but which has not been specifically covered in the resulting contract, is that the employer violates Section 8(a)(5) if, during the contract term, he refuses to bargain or takes unilateral action with respect to the particular subject, unless it can be said from an evaluation of the prior negotiations that the matter was 'fully discussed' or 'consciously explored' and that the Union 'consciously yielded' or clearly and unmistakably waived its interest in the matter."

Through the use of a "zipper" clause, a union may forego its right to bargain about any employment term not contained in the contract, but such a waiver must be clear and unmistakable. See Tide Water Associated Oil Co., 85 N.L.R.B. 1096 (1949); cf. LeRoy Mach. Co., 147 N.L.R.B. 1431 (1964) (waiver through management functions clause). But cf. Stuart Radiator Core Mfg. Co., 173 N.L.R.B. 125 (1968) (employer violated § 8(a)(5) by rigid insistence in bargaining on broad zipper clause, broad management rights clause, and narrow arbitration clause).

See Nelson & Howard, *The Duty to Bargain During the Term of an Existing Agreement,* 27 LAB. L.J. 573 (1976); Wollett, *The Duty to Bargain over the "Unwritten" Terms and Conditions of Employment,* 36 TEXAS L. REV. 863 (1958); Note, *Mid-Term Modification of Terms and Conditions of Employment,* 1972 DUKE L.J. 813.

NLRB v. LION OIL CO., 352 U.S. 282, 77 S. Ct. 330, 1 L. Ed. 2d 331 (1957). A union and an employer entered into a collective bargaining agreement to remain in effect for one year and thereafter until canceled. The agreement provided that either party could propose amendments by notifying the other party any time after the first ten months of the contract. If agreement could not be reached on amendment of the contract during the 60-day period following this notification, either party could thereafter terminate the agreement by giving a 60-day written notice to the other. At the end of the first ten months, the union duly served notice of its desire to modify the contract. The union never gave the further notice to terminate, and thus the contract remained in effect. Nonetheless, some eight months after its initial modification notice, the union went on strike to back up its demands for amendment. Subsequently, the employer defended against unfair labor practices allegedly committed by it during the strike by asserting that the workers had lost their status as employees under the Act by striking in violation of § 8(d)(4). Section 8(d)(4) provides that a party wishing to modify or terminate a contract must not resort to a strike or lockout "for a period of sixty days after . . . notice is given or until the expiration date of such contract, whichever occurs later." The Supreme Court held that when a contract is subject to reopening in midterm, the phrase "expiration date" as used in § 8(d)(4) should be construed to mean both the final termination date and the first date on which the agreement is subject to amendment. Otherwise, an obvious restriction would be imposed on employees' concerted activities, and long-term bargaining relationships would be discouraged. The Court therefore concluded that the union had fully satisfied the notice and waiting requirements of § 8(d), and the strikers had not lost their status as employees.

NOTE

See Note, *Strike Ban Provisions: Section 8(d) of Taft-Hartley,* 50 Nw. U.L. Rev. 260 (1955); Note, *An Examination of the Sixty-Day Notice Requirement of the Taft-Hartley Act on the Right to Strike,* 44 Geo. L.J. 447 (1956).

The "cooling off" provisions of § 8(d) apply only to strikes to compel a modification or termination of the collective agreement. They do not apply to a strike to protest an employer's unfair labor practice, Mastro Plastics Corp. v. NLRB, 350 U.S. 270 (1956), or to a walkout caused by dangerous working conditions, NLRB v. Knight Morley Corp., 251 F.2d 753 (6th Cir. 1957). It has also been held that the strike-notice provisions of § 8(d) are inapplicable to a strike over an issue not covered by the contract, since this is not a strike to change or end the agreement. Mine Workers, Local 9735 v. NLRB, 258 F.2d 146 (D.C. Cir. 1958).

A union that strikes without complying with the sixty-day notice requirement has been said to "forfeit" its rights as collective bargaining agent, and the strikers lose their status as employees. Boeing Airplane Co. v. NLRB, 174 F.2d 988 (D.C. Cir. 1949). An employer's duty to bargain is also suspended during the period of such a strike. Wholesale Employees District 65, 187 N.L.R.B. 716 (1971).

On § 8(d)(3)'s requirement of a thirty-day notice to mediation agencies, see Retail Clerks, Local 219 v. NLRB, 265 F.2d 814 (D.C. Cir. 1959); Furniture Workers v. NLRB, 336 F.2d 738 (D.C. Cir. 1964), *cert. denied,* 379 U.S. 838 (1964); Note, *Untimely Notice Under Section 8(d)(3) of the Taft-Hartley Act,* 47 Va. L. Rev. 490 (1961).

SECTION II. The Impact of the Antitrust Laws

Although the Sherman Act was passed in 1890 primarily to combat the monopolistic practices of certain business firms, it soon became a major weapon against the organizational activities of labor unions, especially the boycott in all its forms. In recent years, the antitrust laws have been directed much more at the allegedly restrictive provisions that unions have included in collective agreements with employers and groups of employers. To maintain continuity in showing the development of antitrust theory in the labor field, and to take account of the shift in emphasis from organizational to bargaining activities, we have decided to place all the material on unions and the antitrust laws in this section of the Casebook. As will be seen, however, the earlier cases that are presented deal more with union organization than with collective bargaining. The full text of the Sherman Act appears in the *Statutory Appendix,* and should be read at this point.

LOEWE V. LAWLOR ["DANBURY HATTERS"], 208 U.S. 274, 28 S. Ct. 301, 52 L. Ed. 488 (1908). Action for treble damages brought under § 7 of the Sherman Act. Plaintiffs manufactured hats in Danbury, Connecticut. Their complaint alleged: that they did a substantial interstate business; that defendants were members (officers) of the United Hatters of America, which comprised about 9,000 members organized into a large number of subordinate unions, and which was affiliated with the AFL; that defendants were engaged in a combination to force all fur hat manufacturers in the United States, including plaintiffs, to unionize their shops, and had succeeded as to seventy of the eighty-two such manufacturers; that, in pursuance of such object, defendants had called a strike against plaintiffs and had, through the co-operation of the AFL, instituted a nationwide boycott of plaintiffs' products in the hands of wholesalers and dealers; and that as a result plaintiffs had been damaged to the extent of some $80,000. Defendants' demurrer to the complaint was sustained by the trial court. *Held,* demurrer overruled, and case remanded. "If the purposes of the combination were, as alleged, to prevent any interstate transportation at all, the fact that the means operated at one end before physical transportation commenced and at the other end after the physical transportation ended was immaterial."

NOTE

This was the first of several notable boycott cases involving labor decided under the Sherman Act. Final settlement of the case did not occur until several years later. On the trial of the case, plaintiffs obtained a verdict and judgment for $240,000 plus costs, which was affirmed in Lawlor v. Loewe, 235 U.S. 522 (1915). In the summer of 1917, the case was settled for about $234,000, of which the AFL furnished $216,000. *See* E. WITTE, THE GOVERNMENT IN LABOR DISPUTES 134, 135 (1932).

The Court's opinion on the first appeal constituted simply an application to labor activities of the principle of literal construction of the Sherman Act which characterized the earliest period of the Act's application. The statute, said the Court, made *every* combination in restraint of interstate commerce illegal. The Court was not concerned with the kind but rather with the effect of the restraint. This was before the announcement of the famous "rule of reason" in Standard Oil Co. v. United States, 221 U.S. 1 (1911). On the second appeal of the *Hatters* case, the Court thought that the intervening decision in Eastern States Retail Lumber Dealers Ass'n v. United States, 234 U.S. 600 (1914) (which had held a commercial boycott illegal under the Act), made the application of the statute to a labor boycott clear.

On the threshold question of whether the Sherman Act was intended by Congress to apply to labor combinations, see the following: E. BERMAN, LABOR AND THE SHERMAN ACT 3-54 (1930); A. MASON, ORGANIZED LABOR AND THE LAW 122 *et seq.* (1925); Boudin, *The Sherman Act and Labor*

Disputes, 39 COLUM. L. REV. 1283 (1939), 40 COLUM. L. REV. 14 (1940); Emery, *Labor Organizations and the Sherman Law,* 20 J. POL. ECON. 599 (1912); Terborgh, *The Application of the Sherman Act to Trade Union Activities,* 37 J. POL. ECON. 203 (1929). These discussions indicate that there is, at least, very real doubt whether Congress intended any such result. It seems to be conceded that labor counsel were derelict in the early cases in their presentation of this issue to the Court. "It is a sad commentary on the way labor cases are usually argued, that we cannot recall this point to have ever been clearly brought out in any brief submitted on behalf of labor, at least not in the cases argued in the Supreme Court." Boudin, *supra,* 40 COLUM. L. REV. at 20. Berman declares, "An adequate presentation of the *Hatters'* case to the Supreme Court might have greatly changed the history of labor cases since 1908." E. BERMAN, *supra* at 86.

Sections 6 and 20 of the Clayton Act of 1914 are reproduced in the *Statutory Appendix.* They should be read at this point.

DUPLEX PRINTING PRESS CO. v. DEERING, 254 U.S. 443, 41 S. Ct. 172, 65 L. Ed. 349 (1921). This suit, which was tried subsequent to the enactment of the Clayton Act in 1914, was brought in the Southern District of New York against defendants individually and as representatives of two locals of the International Association of Machinists. Complainant manufactured printing presses in Michigan which were sold throughout the United States and abroad. In order to force complainant to unionize its factory, and adopt the eight-hour day and the union wage scale, the IAM called a strike at complainant's factory, which resulted in the withdrawal from work of a small number (14) of complainant's employees, and instituted a nationwide boycott of complainant's product, which was supported by threats of secondary strike and other action against customers, haulers, etc. Defendants invoked the anti-injunction provisions of the Clayton Act. From a decree dismissing the bill complainant appealed. *Held,* reversed and remanded. The Court cited the *Hatters'* cases and the *Eastern States Lumber* case as settling that the restraints involved were within the Sherman Act, whether produced by peaceable persuasion or by force. As to the cited provisions of the Clayton Act it held: First, that § 6 was not intended to legalize the activities of a labor combination which were otherwise unlawful; second, that the restrictive provisions of § 20 applied only to protect "parties standing in proximate relation to a controversy such as is particularly described," and hence could not be invoked by members of a labor organization who were not immediate parties to the dispute; and third, that, in any case, § 20 was not intended to immunize the "secondary boycott" against injunction.

APEX HOSIERY CO. v. LEADER, 310 U.S. 469, 60 S. Ct. 982, 84 L. Ed. 1311 (1940). Apex manufactured hosiery and had a plant in Philadelphia at which it employed 2,500 persons and produced merchandise annually of the value of about $5,000,000. Its principal raw materials were brought in from other states, and it shipped interstate more than eighty percent of its finished product. In April 1937, while the company was operating a nonunion shop, defendant American Federation of Full Fashioned Hosiery Workers made a demand for a closed shop. On May 4, 1937, when only eight of the company's employees were members of the union, it called a strike, and at midday on May 6, while the factory was shut down, members of the union who were employed at other factories in Philadelphia assembled at the plant. When the company again rejected the demand for a closed shop, Leader, the union president, declared a "sit down strike," and the unionists forcibly seized the plant and retained possession until forcibly ejected on June 23, pursuant to an injunction. Manufacture was suspended for more than three months as a result. For damages suffered the company sued and obtained a verdict for $237,310 under the Sherman Act, and judgment was accordingly given for treble this amount. The Third Circuit Court of Appeals reversed on the ground that the effect of defendants' activities on total interstate commerce in hosiery (this plant contributing less than three percent) was not substantial. On certiorari the Supreme Court affirmed.

Stone, J., for the Court, held that while labor organizations are not exempted from the Sherman Act, these particular activities were not within the purview of the statute. The Act was not designed to police violence but looked toward "the prevention of restraints to free competition in business and commercial transactions which tended to restrict production, raise prices or otherwise control the market to the detriment of purchasers or consumers of goods and services. . . ." The Justice stated that "restraints on competition or on the course of trade in the merchandising of articles moving in interstate commerce is not enough, unless the restraint is shown to have or is intended to have an effect upon prices in the market or otherwise to deprive purchasers or consumers of the advantages which they derive from free competition." This case, he said, was not one "of a labor organization being used by combinations of those engaged in an industry as the means or instrument for suppressing competition or fixing prices," and "so far as appears the delay of these shipments [of hosiery] was not intended to have and had no effect on prices of hosiery in the market." He concluded as follows:

"[S]uccessful union activity, as for example consummation of a wage agreement with employers, may have some influence on price competition by eliminating that part of such competition which is based on differences in labor standards. Since, in order to render a labor combination effective it must eliminate the competition from non-union made goods . . . an elimination of price competition based on differences in labor standards is the objective of any national labor organization. But this effect on competition has not been considered to be the kind of curtailment of price competition prohibited by the Sherman Act. . . .

"[A]ctivities of labor organizations not immunized by the Clayton Act are not necessarily violations of the Sherman Act. Underlying and implicit in all of them is recognition that the Sherman Act was not enacted to police interstate transportation, or to afford a remedy for wrongs, which are actionable under state law, and result from combinations and conspiracies which fall short, both in their purpose and effect, of any form of market control of a commodity, such as to 'monopolize the supply, control its price, or discriminate between its would-be purchasers.' These elements of restraint of trade . . . are wholly lacking here. We do not hold that conspiracies to obstruct or prevent transportation in interstate commerce can in no circumstances be violations of the Sherman Act. Apart from the Clayton Act it makes no distinction between labor and nonlabor cases. We only hold now, as we have previously held both in labor and nonlabor cases, that such restraints are not within the Sherman Act unless they are intended to have, or in fact have, the effects on the market on which the Court relied to establish violation in the *Second Coronado* case. . . .

"If, without such effects on the market, we were to hold that a local factory strike, stopping production and shipment of its product interstate, violates the Sherman Law, practically every strike in modern industry would be brought within the jurisdiction of the federal courts, under the Sherman Act, to remedy local law violations. The Act was plainly not intended to reach such a result, its language does not require it, and the course of our decisions precludes it. The maintenance in our federal system of a proper distribution between state and national governments of police authority and of remedies private and public for public wrongs is of far-reaching importance. An intention to disturb the balance is not lightly to be imputed to Congress. The Sherman Act is concerned with the character of the prohibited restraints and with their effect on interstate commerce. It draws no distinction between the restraints effected by violence and those achieved by peaceful but oftentimes quite as effective means. Restraints not within the Act, when achieved by peaceful means, are not brought within its sweep merely because, without other differences, they are attended by violence." 310 U.S. at 503-04, 512-13.

UNITED STATES v. HUTCHESON

Supreme Court of the United States
312 U.S. 219, 61 S. Ct. 463, 85 L. Ed. 788 (1941)

MR. JUSTICE FRANKFURTER delivered the opinion of the Court. . . .

Summarizing the long indictment, these are the facts. Anheuser-Busch, Inc., operating a large plant in St. Louis, contracted with Borsari Tank Corporation for the erection of an additional facility. The Gaylord Container Corporation, a lessee of adjacent property from Anheuser-Busch, made a similar contract for a new building with the Stocker Company. Anheuser-Busch obtained the materials for its brewing and other operations and sold its finished products largely through interstate shipments. The Gaylord Corporation was equally dependent on interstate commerce for marketing its goods, as were the construction companies for their building materials. Among the employees of

Anheuser-Busch were members of the United Brotherhood of Carpenters and Joiners of America and of the International Association of Machinists. The conflicting claims of these two organizations, affiliated with the American Federation of Labor, in regard to the erection and dismantling of machinery had long been a source of controversy between them. Anheuser-Busch had had agreements with both organizations whereby the Machinists were given the disputed jobs and the Carpenters agreed to submit all disputes to arbitration. But in 1939 the president of the Carpenters, their general representative, and two officials of the Carpenters' local organization, the four men under indictment, stood on the claims of the Carpenters for jobs. Rejection by the employer of the Carpenters' demand and the refusal of the latter to submit to arbitration were followed by a strike of the Carpenters, called by the defendants against Anheuser-Busch and the construction companies, a picketing of Anheuser-Busch, its tenant, and a request, through circular letters and the official publication of the Carpenters, that union members, and their friends, refrain from buying Anheuser-Busch beer.

These activities on behalf of the Carpenters formed the charge of the indictment as a criminal combination and conspiracy in violation of the Sherman Law. Demurrers, denying that what was charged constituted a violation of the laws of the United States, were sustained, 32 F. Supp. 600, and the case came here under the Criminal Appeals Act. Act of March 2, 1907. . . .

Section 1 of the Sherman Law on which the indictment rested is as follows: "Every contract, combination in the form of trust or otherwise, or conspiracy, in restraint of trade or commerce among the several states, or with foreign nations, is hereby declared to be illegal." The controversies engendered by its application to trade union activities and the efforts to secure legislative relief from its consequences are familiar history. The Clayton Act of 1914 was the result. . . . Section 20 of that Act . . . withdrew from the general interdict of the Sherman Law specifically enumerated practices of labor unions by prohibiting injunctions against them — since the use of the injunction had been the major source of dissatisfaction — and also relieved such practices of all illegal taint by the catch-all provision, "nor shall any of the acts specified in this paragraph be considered or held to be violations of any law of the United States." The Clayton Act gave rise to new litigation and to renewed controversy in and out of Congress regarding the status of trade unions. By the generality of its terms, the Sherman Law had necessarily compelled the courts to work out its meaning from case to case. It was widely believed that into the Clayton Act courts read the very beliefs which that Act was designed to remove. Specifically, the courts restricted the scope of § 20 to trade union activities directed against an employer by his own employees. Duplex Co. v. Deering, [254 U.S. 443 (1921)]. Such a view, it was urged, both by powerful judicial dissents and informed lay opinion, misconceived the area of economic conflict that had best be left to economic forces and the pressure of public opinion and not subjected to the judgment of courts. *Ibid.,* pp. 485, 486. Agitation again led to legislation and, in 1932, Congress wrote the Norris-La Guardia Act. . . .

The Norris-La Guardia Act removed the fetters upon trade union activities, which, according to judicial construction, § 20 of the Clayton Act had left untouched, by still further narrowing the circumstances under which the federal courts could grant injunctions in labor disputes. More especially, the Act explicitly formulated the "public policy of the United States" in regard to the industrial conflict, and, by its light, established that the allowable area of union activity was not to be restricted, as it had been in the *Duplex* case, to an immediate employer-employee relation. Therefore, whether trade union conduct constitutes a violation of the Sherman Law is to be determined only by reading the Sherman Law and § 20 of the Clayton Act and the Norris-La Guardia Act as a harmonizing text of outlawry of labor conduct.

Were, then, the acts charged against the defendants prohibited or permitted by these three interlacing statutes? If the facts laid in the indictment come within the conduct enumerated in § 20 of the Clayton Act, they do not constitute a crime within the general terms of the Sherman Law because of the explicit command of that section that such conduct shall not be "considered or held to be violations of any law of the United States." So long as a union acts in its self-interest and does not combine with non-labor groups, the licit and the illicit under § 20 are not to be distinguished by any judgment regarding the wisdom or unwisdom, the rightness or wrongness, the selfishness or unselfishness of the end of which the particular union activities are the means. There is nothing remotely within the terms of § 20 that differentiates between trade union conduct directed against an employer because of a controversy arising in the relation between employer and employee, as such, and conduct similarly directed but ultimately due to an internecine struggle between two unions seeking the favor of the same employer. . . .

It is at once apparent that the acts with which the defendants are charged are the kind of acts protected by § 20 of the Clayton Act. The refusal of the Carpenters to work for Anheuser-Busch or on construction work being done for it and its adjoining tenant, and the peaceful attempt to get members of other unions similarly to refuse to work, are plainly within the free scope accorded to workers by § 20 for "terminating any relation of employment," or "ceasing to perform any work or labor," or "recommending, advising or persuading others by peaceful means so to do." The picketing of Anheuser-Busch premises with signs to indicate that Anheuser-Busch was unfair to organized labor, a familiar practice in these situations, comes within the language "attending at any place where any such person or persons may lawfully be, for the purpose of peacefully obtaining or communicating information, or from peacefully persuading any person to work or to abstain from working." Finally, the recommendation to union members and their friends not to buy or use the product of Anheuser-Busch is explicitly covered by "ceasing to patronize . . . any party to such dispute, or from recommending, advising, or persuading others by peaceful and lawful means so to do."

Clearly, then, the facts here charged constitute lawful conduct under the Clayton Act unless the defendants cannot invoke that Act because outsiders to the immediate dispute also shared in the conduct. But we need not determine whether the conduct is legal within the restrictions which *Duplex Co. v. Deering* gave to the immunities of § 20 of the Clayton Act. Congress in the Norris-La Guardia Act has expressed the public policy of the United States and defined its conception of a "labor dispute" in terms that no longer leave room for doubt. . . . Such a dispute, § 13(c), provides, "includes any controversy concerning terms or conditions of employment, or concerning the association or representation of persons in negotiating, fixing, maintaining, changing, or seeking to arrange terms or conditions of employment, regardless of whether or not the disputants stand in the proximate relation of employer and employee." And under § 13(b), a person is "participating or interested in a labor dispute" if he "is engaged in the same industry, trade, craft, or occupation in which such dispute occurs, or has a direct or indirect interest therein, or is a member, officer, or agent of any association composed in whole or in part of employers or employees engaged in such industry, trade, craft or occupation."

To be sure, Congress expressed this national policy and determined the bounds of a labor dispute in an Act explicitly dealing with the further withdrawal of injunctions in labor controversies. But to argue, as it was urged before us, that the *Duplex* case still governs for purposes of a criminal prosecution is to say that that which on the equity side of the court is allowable conduct may in a criminal proceeding become the road to prison. It would be strange indeed that although neither the Government nor Anheuser-Busch could have sought an injunction against the acts here challenged, the elaborate efforts to permit such conduct failed to prevent criminal liability punishable with imprisonment and heavy fines. That is not the way to read the will of Congress, particularly when expressed by a statute which, as we have already indicated, is practically and historically one of a series of enactments touching one of the most sensitive national problems. Such legislation must not be read in a spirit of mutilating narrowness. . . .

The relation of the Norris-La Guardia Act to the Clayton Act is not that of a tightly drawn amendment to a technically phrased tax provision. The underlying aim of the Norris-La Guardia Act was to restore the broad purpose which Congress thought it had formulated in the Clayton Act but which was frustrated, so Congress believed, by unduly restrictive judicial construction. This was authoritatively stated by the House Committee on the Judiciary. "The purpose of the bill is to protect the rights of labor in the same manner the Congress intended when it enacted the Clayton Act, October 15, 1914 (38 Stat. L., 738), which Act, by reason of its construction and application by the Federal courts, is ineffectual to accomplish the congressional intent." H. R. Rep. No. 669, 72d Cong., 1st Sess. 3. The Norris-La Guardia Act was a disapproval of Duplex Printing Press Co. v. Deering, *supra,* and Bedford Cut Stone Co. v. Journeymen Stone Cutters' Ass'n, 274 U.S. 37 (1927), as the authoritative interpretation of § 20 of the Clayton Act, for Congress now placed its own meaning upon that section. The Norris-La Guardia Act reasserted the original purpose of the Clayton Act by infusing into it the immunized trade union activities as redefined by the later Act. In this light § 20 removes all such allowable conduct from the taint of being a "violation of any law of the United States," including the Sherman Law. . . .

Affirmed.

MR. JUSTICE MURPHY took no part in the disposition of this case.

NOTE

Justice Stone wrote a separate concurring opinion arguing that under the previous decisions of the Court, especially the *Apex* case, the activities of the defendants did not bring them under the Sherman Act. He therefore did not find it necessary to resort to the reasoning used by Justice Frankfurter. Justice Roberts wrote a dissenting opinion, in which Chief Justice Hughes joined. As to the impact of the Norris-La Guardia Act, he said: "It is sufficient to say, what a reading of the Act makes letter clear, that the jurisdiction of actions for damages authorized by the Sherman Act, and of the criminal offenses denounced by that Act, are not touched by the Norris-La Guardia Act." He added:

"By a process of construction never, as I think, heretofore indulged by this court, it is now found that, because Congress forbade the issuing of injunctions to restrain conduct, it intended to repeal the provisions of the Sherman Act authorizing actions at law and criminal prosecutions for the commission of torts and crimes defined by the anti-trust laws. The doctrine now announced seems to be that an indication of a change of policy in an Act as respects one specific item in a general field of the law, covered by an earlier Act, justifies this court in spelling out an implied repeal of the whole of the earlier statute as applied to conduct of the sort here involved. I venture to say that no court has ever undertaken so radically to legislate where Congress has refused so to do." 312 U.S. at 245.

For discussions of this case, see Cavers, *And What of the "Apex" Case Now?* 8 U. CHI. L. REV. 516 (1941); Gregory, *The New Sherman-Clayton-Norris-La Guardia Act,* 8 U. CHI. L. REV. 503 (1941); Nathanson & Wirtz, *The Hutcheson Case: Another View,* 36 ILL. L. REV. 41 (1941); Teller, *Federal Intervention in Labor Disputes and Collective Bargaining — The Hutcheson Case,* 40 MICH. L. REV. 24 (1941); Tunks, *A New Federal Charter for Trade Unionism,* 41 COLUM. L. REV. 969 (1941).

ALLEN BRADLEY CO. v. INTERNATIONAL BROTHERHOOD OF ELECTRICAL WORKERS, LOCAL 3

Supreme Court of the United States
325 U.S. 797, 65 S. Ct. 1533, 89 L. Ed. 1939 (1945)

MR. JUSTICE BLACK delivered the opinion of the Court. . . .

Petitioners are manufacturers of electrical equipment. Their places of manufacture are outside of New York City, and most of them are outside of New York state as well. They have brought this action because of their desire to sell their products in New York City, a market area that has been closed to them through the activities of respondents and others.

Respondents are a labor union, its officials, and its members. The union, Local No. 3 of the International Brotherhood of Electrical Workers, has jurisdiction only over the metropolitan area of New York City. It is therefore impossible for the union to enter into a collective bargaining agreement with petitioners. Some of petitioners do have collective bargaining agreements with other unions, and in some cases even with other locals of the IBEW.

Some of the members of respondent union work for manufacturers who produce electrical equipment similar to that made by petitioners; other members of respondent union are employed by contractors and work on the installation of electrical equipment rather than in its production.

The union's consistent aim for many years has been to expand its membership, to obtain shorter hours and increased wages, and to enlarge employment opportunities for its members. To achieve this latter goal — that is, to make more work for its own members — the union realized that local manufacturers, employers of the local members, must have the widest possible outlets for their product. The union therefore waged aggressive campaigns to obtain closed-shop agreements with all local electrical equipment manufacturers and contractors. Using conventional labor union methods, such as strikes and boycotts, it gradually obtained more and more closed-shop agreements in the New York area. Under these agreements, contractors were obligated to purchase equipment from none but local manufacturers who also had closed-shop agreements with Local No. 3; manufacturers obligated themselves to confine their New York City sales to contractors employing the Local's members. In the course of time, this type of individual employer-employee agreement expanded into industry-wide understandings, looking not merely to terms and conditions of employment but also to price and market control. Agencies were set up composed of representatives of all three groups to boycott recalcitrant local contractors and manufacturers and to bar from the area equipment manufactured outside its boundaries. The combination among the three groups, union, contractors, and manufacturers, became highly successful from the standpoint of all of them. The business of New York City manufacturers had a phenomenal growth, thereby multiplying the jobs available for the Local's members. Wages went up, hours were shortened, and the New York electrical equipment prices soared, to the decided financial profit of local contractors and manufacturers. The success is illustrated by the fact that some New York manufacturers sold their goods in the protected city market at one price and sold identical goods outside of New York at a far lower price. All of this took place, as the Circuit Court of Appeals declared, "through the stifling of competition," and because the three groups, in combination as "co-partners," achieved "a complete monopoly which they used to boycott the equipment manufactured by the plaintiffs." Interstate sale of various types of electrical equipment has, by this powerful combination, been wholly suppressed. . . .

[The Court then summarized the historical development of the law dealing with labor under the antitrust statutes.]

The result of all this is that we have two declared congressional policies which it is our responsibility to try to reconcile. The one seeks to preserve a competitive business economy; the other to preserve the rights of labor to organize to better its conditions through the agency of collective bargaining. We must determine here how far Congress intended activities under one of these policies to neutralize the results envisioned by the other.

Aside from the fact that the labor union here acted in combination with the contractors and manufacturers, the means it adopted to contribute to the combination's purpose fall squarely within the "specified acts" declared by § 20 not to be violations of federal law. For the union's contribution to the trade boycott was accomplished through threats that, unless their employers bought their goods from local manufacturers, the union laborers would terminate the "relation of employment" with them and cease to perform "work or labor" for them; and through their "recommending, advising, or persuading others by peaceful and lawful means" not to "patronize" sellers of the boycotted electrical equipment. Consequently, under our holdings in the *Hutcheson* case and other cases which followed it, had there been no union-contractor-manufacturer combination the union's actions here, coming as they did within the exemptions of the Clayton and Norris-La Guardia Acts, would not have been violations of the Sherman Act. We pass to the question of whether unions can, with impunity, aid and abet businessmen who are violating the Act. . . .

. . . Since union members can, without violating the Sherman Act, strike to enforce a union boycott of goods, it is said they may settle the strike by getting their employers to agree to refuse to buy the goods. Employers and the union did here make bargaining agreements in which the employers agreed not to buy goods manufactured by companies which did not employ the members of Local No. 3. We may assume that such an agreement standing alone would not have violated the Sherman Act. But it did not stand alone. It was but one element in a far larger program in which contractors and manufacturers united with one another to monopolize all the business in New York City, to bar all other businessmen from that area, and to charge the public prices above a competitive level. It is true that victory of the union in its disputes, even had the union acted alone, might have added to the costs of goods, or might have resulted in individual refusals of all of their employers to buy electrical equipment not made by Local No. 3. So far as the union might have achieved this result acting alone, it would have been the natural consequence of labor union activities exempted by the Clayton Act from the coverage of the Sherman Act. Apex Hosiery Co. v. Leader, *supra,* 503. But when the unions participated with a combination of businessmen who had complete power to eliminate all competition among themselves and to prevent all competition from others, a situation was created not included within the exemptions of the Clayton and Norris-La Guardia Acts.

Our holding means that the same labor union activities may or may not be in violation of the Sherman Act, dependent upon whether the union acts alone or in combination with business groups. This, it is argued, brings about a wholly undesirable result — one which leaves labor unions free to engage in conduct which restrains trade. But the desirability of such an exemption of labor unions is a question for the determination of Congress. Apex Hosiery Co. v. Leader, *supra.* It is true that many labor union activities do substantially interrupt the course of trade and that these activities, lifted out of the prohibitions of the Sherman Act, include substantially all, if not all, of the normal peaceful activities of labor unions. . . . Congress evidently concluded, however, that the chief objective of antitrust legislation, preservation of business competition, could be accomplished by applying the legislation primarily only to those business groups which are directly interested in destroying competition. The difficulty of drawing legislation primarily aimed at trusts and monopolies so that it could also be applied to labor organizations without impairing the collective bargaining and related rights of those organizations has been emphasized both by congressional and judicial attempts to draw lines between permissible and prohibited union activities. There is, however, one line which we can draw with assurance that we follow the congressional purpose. We know that Congress feared the concentrated power of business organizations to dominate markets and prices. It intended to outlaw business monopolies. A business monopoly is no less such because a union participates, and such participation is a violation of the Act. . . .

Respondents objected to the form of the injunction and specifically requested that it be amended so as to enjoin only those prohibited activities in which the union engaged in combination "with any person, firm or corporation which is a non-labor group. . . ." Without such a limitation, the injunction as issued runs directly counter to the Clayton and the Norris-La Guardia Acts. The district court's refusal so to limit it was error.

The judgment of the Circuit Court of Appeals ordering the action dismissed is accordingly reversed and the cause is remanded to the district court for modification and clarification of the judgment and injunction, consistent with this opinion.

Reversed and remanded. . . .

MR. JUSTICE MURPHY, dissenting. . . .

The union here has not in any true sense "aided" or "abetted" a primary violation of the Act by the employers. In the words of the union, it has been "the dynamic force which has driven the employer-group to enter into agreements" whereby trade has been affected. The fact that the union has expressed its self-interest with the aid of others rather than solely by its own activities should not be decisive of statutory liability. What is legal if done alone should not become illegal if done with the assistance of others with the same purpose in mind. Otherwise a premium of unlawfulness is placed on collective bargaining. . . .

NOTES

1. In Meat & Provision Drivers Local 626 v. United States, 371 U.S. 94 (1962), the Supreme Court held that grease peddlers, who were independent contractors and who joined the union only for the purpose of bringing the union's power to bear in the successful enforcement of an illegal combination of traffic in yellow grease and who had no other economic interrelationship with the other union members, were properly divested of their union membership.

2. For general analyses during this period, see Cox, *Labor and the Antitrust Laws — A Preliminary Analysis,* 104 U. PA. L. REV. 252 (1955); Smith, *Antitrust and Labor,* 53 MICH. L. REV. 1119 (1955); Sovern, *Some Ruminations on Labor, the Antitrust Laws and Allen Bradley,* 13 LAB. L.J. 957 (1962); Winter, *Collective Bargaining and Competition: The Application of Antitrust Standards to Union Activities,* 73 YALE L.J. 14 (1963); *Report of the Attorney General's National Committee to Study the Antitrust Laws* 304-05 (1955).

3. *The place of the Taft-Hartley Act in the antitrust scheme.* Against a background of controversy dealing with the proper place of labor under the antitrust laws, Congress in 1947 considered amendments to the NLRA. The bill passed by the House, the Conference Committee Report notes, "contained a provision amending the Clayton Act so as to withdraw the exemption of labor organizations under the antitrust laws when such organizations engaged in combination or conspiracy in restraint of commerce where one of the purposes or a necessary effect of the combination or conspiracy was to join or combine with any person to fix prices, allocate costs, restrict production, distribution, or competition, or impose restrictions or conditions, upon the purchase, sale, or use of any product, material, machine, or equipment, or to engage in any unlawful concerted activity." 93 CONG. REC. 6380 (1947). Explaining omission of such provisions from the enacted bill, the conference report continued: "Since the matters dealt with in this section have to a large measure been effectuated through the use of boycotts, and since the conference agreement contains effective provisions directly dealing with boycotts themselves, this provision is omitted from the conference agreement." 93 CONG. REC. 6380 (1947).

UNITED MINE WORKERS v. PENNINGTON

Supreme Court of the United States
381 U.S. 657, 85 S. Ct. 1585, 14 L. Ed. 2d 625 (1965)

MR. JUSTICE WHITE delivered the opinion of the Court.

This action began as a suit by the trustees of the United Mine Workers of America Welfare and Retirement Fund against the respondents, individually and as owners of Phillips Brothers Coal Company, a partnership, seeking to recover some $55,000 in royalty payments alleged to be due and payable under the trust provisions of the National Bituminous Coal Wage Agreement of 1950, as amended, September 29, 1952, executed by Phillips and United Mine Workers of America on or about October 1, 1953, and re-executed with amendments on or about September 8, 1955, and October 22, 1956. Phillips filed an answer and a cross-claim against UMW, alleging in both that the trustees, the UMW and certain large coal operators, had conspired to restrain and to monopolize interstate commerce in violation of §§ 1 and 2 of the Sherman Antitrust Act, 15 U.S.C. §§ 1, 2 (1958 ed.). Actual damages in the amount of $100,000 were claimed for the period beginning February 14, 1954, and ending December 31, 1958.

The allegations of the cross-claim were essentially as follows: Prior to the 1950 Wage Agreement between the operators and the union, severe controversy had existed in the industry, particularly over wages, the welfare fund and the union's efforts to control the working time of its members. Since 1950, however, relative peace has existed in the industry, all as the result of the 1950 wage agreement and its amendments and the additional understandings entered into between UMW and the large operators. Allegedly the parties considered over-production to be the critical problem of the coal industry. The agreed solution was to be the elimination of the smaller companies, the larger companies thereby controlling the market. More specifically, the union abandoned its efforts to control the working time of the miners, agreed not to oppose the rapid mechanization of the mines which would substantially reduce mine employment, agreed to help finance such mechanization and agreed to impose the terms of the 1950 agreement on all operators without regard for their ability to pay. The benefit to the union was to be increased wages as productivity increased with mechanization, these increases to be demanded of the smaller companies whether mechanized or not. Royalty payments into the welfare fund were to be increased also, and the union was to have effective control over the Fund's use. The union and large companies agreed upon other steps to exclude the marketing, production, and sale of nonunion coal. Thus the companies agreed not to lease coal lands to nonunion operators, and in 1958 agreed not to sell or buy coal from such companies. The companies and the union jointly and successfully approached the Secretary of Labor to obtain establishment under the Walsh-Healey Act ... of a minimum wage for employees of contractors selling coal to the TVA, such minimum wage being much higher than in other industries and making it difficult for small companies to compete in the TVA term contract market. At a later time, at a meeting attended by both union and company representatives, the TVA was urged to curtail its spot market purchases, a substantial portion of which were exempt from the Walsh-Healey order. Thereafter four of the larger companies waged a destructive and collusive price-cutting campaign in the TVA spot market for coal, two of the companies, West Kentucky Coal Co. and its subsidiary Nashville Coal Co., being those in which the union had large investments and over which it was in position to exercise control.

The complaint survived motions to dismiss and after a five-week trial before a jury, a verdict was returned in favor of Phillips and against the trustees and the union, the damages against the union being fixed in the amount of $90,000, to be trebled under 15 U.S.C. § 15 (1958 ed.). The trial court set aside the verdict against the trustees but overruled the union's motion for judgment notwithstanding the verdict or in the alternative for a new trial. The Court of Appeals affirmed. 325 F.2d 804. It ruled that the union was not exempt from liability under the Sherman Act on the facts of this case, considered the instructions adequate and found the evidence generally sufficient to support the verdict. We granted certiorari. . . . We reverse and remand the case for proceedings consistent with this opinion.

I. We first consider UMW's contention that the trial court erred in denying its motion for directed verdict and for judgment notwithstanding the verdict, since a determination in UMW's favor on this issue would finally resolve the controversy. The question presented by this phase of the case is whether in the circumstances of this case the union is exempt from liability under the antitrust laws. We think the answer is clearly in the negative and that the union's motions were correctly denied.

The antitrust laws do not bar the existence and operation of labor unions as such. Moreover, § 20 of the Clayton Act . . . and § 4 of the Norris-La Guardia Act . . . permit a union, acting alone, to engage in the conduct therein specified without violating the Sherman Act. United States v. Hutcheson, 312 U.S. 219 (1941). . . .

But neither § 20 nor § 4 expressly deals with arrangements or agreements between unions and employers. Neither section tells us whether any or all such arrangements or agreements are barred or permitted by the antitrust laws. Thus *Hutcheson* itself stated:

"So long as a union acts in its self-interest *and does not combine with non-labor groups,* the licit and the illicit under § 20 are not to be distinguished by any judgment regarding the wisdom or unwisdom, the rightness or wrongness, the selfishness or unselfishness of the end of which the particular union activities are the means." 312 U.S. at 232 (Emphasis added.)

And in Allen Bradley v. IBEW Local 3, 325 U.S. 797 (1945), this Court made explicit what had been merely a qualifying expression in *Hutcheson* and held that "when the unions participated with a combination of businessmen who had complete power to eliminate all competition among themselves and to prevent all competition from others, a situation was created not included within the exemptions of the Clayton and Norris-La Guardia Acts." *Id.* at 809. . . .

If the UMW in this case, in order to protect its wage scale by maintaining employer income, had presented a set of prices at which the mine operators would be required to sell their coal, the union and the employers who happened to agree could not successfully defend this contract provision if it were challenged under the antitrust laws by the United States or by some party injured by the arrangement. Cf. Allen Bradley v. IBEW Local 3, 325 U.S. 797 (1945). . . . In such a case, the restraint on the product market is direct and immediate, is of the type characteristically deemed unreasonable under the Sherman Act and the union gets from the promise nothing more concrete than a hope for better wages to come.

Likewise, if as is alleged in this case, the union became a party to a collusive bidding arrangement designed to drive Phillips and others from the TVA spot market, we think any claim to exemption from antitrust liability would be frivolous at best. For this reason alone the motions of the unions were properly denied.

A major part of Phillips' case, however, was that the union entered into a conspiracy with the large operators to impose the agreed upon wage and royalty scales upon the smaller, nonunion operators, regardless of their ability to pay and regardless of whether or not the union represented the employees of these companies, all for the purpose of eliminating them from the industry, limiting production and preempting the market for the large, unionized operators. The UMW urges that since such an agreement concerned wage standards, it is exempt from the antitrust laws.

It is true that wages lie at the very heart of those subjects about which employers and unions must bargain and the law contemplates agreements on wages not only between individual employers and a union but agreements between the union and employers in a multi-employer bargaining unit. NLRB v. Truck Drivers Union, 353 U.S. 87, 94-96 (1957). The union benefit from the wage scale agreed upon is direct and concrete and the effect on the product market, though clearly present, results from the elimination of competition based on wages among the employers in the bargaining unit, which is not the kind of restraint Congress intended the Sherman Act to proscribe. Apex Hosiery v. Leader, 310 U.S. 469, 503-504 (1940). . . . We think it beyond question that a union may conclude a wage agreement for the multi-employer bargaining unit without violating the antitrust laws and that it may as a matter of its own policy, and not by agreement with all or part of the employers of that unit, seek the same wages from other employers.

This is not to say that an agreement resulting from union-employer negotiations is automatically exempt from Sherman Act scrutiny simply because the negotiations involve a compulsory subject of bargaining, regardless of the subject or the form and content of the agreement. Unquestionably the Board's demarcation of the bounds of the duty to bargain has great relevance to any consideration of the sweep of labor's antitrust immunity, for we are concerned here with harmonizing the

Sherman Act with the national policy expressed in the National Labor Relations Act of promoting "the peaceful settlement of industrial disputes by subjecting labor-management controversies to the mediatory influence of negotiation," Fibreboard Paper Prods. Corp. v. NLRB, 379 U.S. 203, 211 (1964). But there are limits to what a union or an employer may offer or extract in the name of wages, and because they must bargain does not mean that the agreement reached may disregard other laws. Teamsters Union v. Oliver, 358 U.S. 283, 296 (1959). . . .

We have said that a union may make wage agreements with a multi-employer bargaining unit and may in pursuance of its own union interests seek to obtain the same terms from other employers. No case under the antitrust laws could be made out on evidence limited to such union behavior.[2] But we think a union forfeits its exemption from the antitrust laws when it is clearly shown that it has agreed with one set of employers to impose a certain wage scale on other bargaining units. One group of employers may not conspire to eliminate competitors from the industry and the union is liable with the employers if it becomes a party to the conspiracy. This is true even though the union's part in the scheme is an undertaking to secure the same wages, hours or other conditions of employment from the remaining employers in the industry.

We do not find anything in the national labor policy that conflicts with this conclusion. This Court has recognized that a legitimate aim of any national labor organization is to obtain uniformity of labor standards and that a consequence of such union activity may be to eliminate competition based on differences in such standards. Apex Hosiery v. Leader, 310 U.S. 469, 503 (1940). But there is nothing in the labor policy indicating that the union and the employers in one bargaining unit are free to bargain about the wages, hours and working conditions of other bargaining units or to attempt to settle these matters for the entire industry. On the contrary, the duty to bargain unit by unit leads to a quite different conclusion. The union's obligation to its members would seem best served if the union retained the ability to respond to each bargaining situation as the individual circumstances might warrant, without being strait-jacketed by some prior agreement with the favored employers.

So far as the employer is concerned it has long been the Board's view that an employer may not condition the signing of a collective agreement on the union's organization of a majority of the industry. American Range Lines, Inc., 13 N.L.R.B. 139, 147 (1939). . . . In such cases the obvious interest of the employer is to ensure that acceptance of the union's wage

_____

[2] Unilaterally, and without agreement with any employer group to do so, a union may adopt a uniform wage policy and seek vigorously to implement it even though it may suspect that some employers cannot effectively compete if they are required to pay the wage scale demanded by the union. The union need not gear its wage demands to those which the weakest units in the industry can afford to pay. Such union conduct is not alone sufficient evidence to maintain a union-employer conspiracy charge under the Sherman Act. There must be additional direct or indirect evidence of the conspiracy. There was of course, other evidence in this case, but we indicate no opinion as to its sufficiency.

demands will not adversely affect his competitive position. . . . Such an employer condition, if upheld, would clearly reduce the extent of collective bargaining. . . . Permitting insistence on an agreement by the union to attempt to impose a similar contract on other employers would likewise seem to impose a restraining influence on the extent of collective bargaining, for the union could avoid impasse only by surrendering its freedom to act in its own interest *vis-à-vis* other employers, something it will be unwilling to do in many instances. Once again, the employer's interest is a competitive interest rather than an interest in regulating its own labor relations, and the effect on the union of such an agreement would be to limit the free exercise of the employees' right to engage in concerted activities according to their own views of their self-interest. In sum, we cannot conclude that the national labor policy provides any support for such agreements.

On the other hand, the policy of the antitrust laws is clearly set against employer-union agreements seeking to prescribe labor standards outside the bargaining unit. One could hardly contend, for example, that one group of employers could lawfully demand that the union impose on other employers wages that were significantly higher than those paid by the requesting employers, or a system of computing wages that, because of differences in methods of production, would be more costly to one set of employers than to another. The anticompetitive potential of such a combination is obvious, but is little more severe than what is alleged to have been the purpose and effect of the conspiracy in this case to establish wages at a level that marginal producers could not pay so that they would be driven from the industry. And if the conspiracy presently under attack were declared exempt it would hardly be possible to deny exemption to such avowedly discriminatory schemes.

From the viewpoint of antitrust policy, moreover, all such agreements between a group of employers and a union that the union will seek specified labor standards outside the bargaining unit suffer from a more basic defect, without regard to predatory intention or effect in the particular case. For the salient characteristic of such agreements is that the union surrenders its freedom of action with respect to its bargaining policy. Prior to the agreement the union might seek uniform standards in its own self-interest but would be required to assess in each case the probable costs and gains of a strike or other collective action to that end and thus might conclude that the objective of uniform standards should temporarily give way. After the agreement the union's interest would be bound in each case to that of the favored employer group. It is just such restraints upon the freedom of economic units to act according to their own choice and discretion that run counter to antitrust policy. . . .

Thus the relevant labor and antitrust policies compel us to conclude that the alleged agreement between UMW and the large operators to secure uniform labor standards throughout the industry, if proved, was not exempt from the antitrust laws.

II. The UMW next contends that the trial court erroneously denied its motion for a new trial based on claimed errors in the admission of evidence.

In Eastern R. Conf. v. Noerr Motors, 365 U.S. 127 (1961), the Court rejected an attempt to base a Sherman Act conspiracy on evidence consisting entirely of activities of competitors seeking to influence public officials. The Sherman Act, it was held, was not intended to bar concerted action of this kind even though the resulting official action damaged other competitors at whom the campaign is aimed. Furthermore, the illegality of the conduct "was not at all affected by any anticompetitive purpose it may have had," *id.* at 140. . . .

We agree with the UMW that both the Court of Appeals and the trial court failed to take proper account of the *Noerr* case. . . .

The jury was instructed that the approach to the Secretary of Labor was legal unless part of a conspiracy to drive small operators out of business and that the approach to the TVA was not a violation of the antitrust laws "unless the parties so urged the TVA to modify its policies in buying coal for the purpose of driving the small operators out of business." If, therefore, the jury determined the requisite anticompetitive purpose to be present, it was free to find an illegal conspiracy based solely on the Walsh-Healey and TVA episodes, or in any event to attribute illegality to these acts as part of a general plan to eliminate Phillips and other distributors similarly situated. Neither finding, however, is permitted by *Noerr* for the reasons stated in that case. . . .

There is another reason for remanding this case for further proceedings in the lower courts. It is clear under *Noerr* that Phillips could not collect any damages under the Sherman Act for any injury which it suffered from the action of the Secretary of Labor. The conduct of the union and the operators did not violate the Act, the action taken to set a minimum wage for government purchases of coal was the act of a public official who is not claimed to be a co-conspirator, and the jury should have been instructed, as UMW requested, to exclude any damages which Phillips may have suffered as a result of the Secretary's Walsh-Healey determinations. . . .

The judgment is reversed and the case remanded for further proceedings consistent with this opinion.

It is so ordered.

MR. JUSTICE DOUGLAS, with whom MR. JUSTICE BLACK and MR. JUSTICE CLARK agree, concurring.

As we read the opinion of the Court, it reaffirms the principles of Allen Bradley Co. v. Union, 325 U.S. 797 (1945), and tells the trial judge:

First. On the new trial the jury should be instructed that if there were an industry-wide collective bargaining agreement whereby employers and the union agreed on a wage scale that exceeded the financial ability of some operators to pay and that if it was made for the purpose of forcing some employers out of business, the union as well as the employers who participate in the arrangement with the union should be found to have violated the antitrust laws.

Second. An industry-wide agreement containing those features is prima facie evidence of a violation. . . .

Congress can design an oligopoly for our society, if it chooses. But business alone cannot do so as long as the antitrust laws are enforced. Nor should business and labor working hand-in-hand be allowed to make that basic change in the design of our so-called free enterprise system. If the allegations in this case are to be believed, organized labor joined hands with organized business to drive marginal operators out of existence. According to those allegations the union used its control over West Kentucky Coal Co. and Nashville Coal Co. to dump coal at such low prices that respondents, who were small operators, had to abandon their business. According to those allegations there was a boycott by the union and the major companies against small companies who needed major companies' coal land on which to operate. According to those allegations, high wage and welfare terms of employment were imposed on the small, marginal companies by the union and the major companies with the knowledge and intent that the small ones would be driven out of business.

The only architect of our economic system is Congress. We are right in adhering to its philosophy of the free enterprise system as expressed in the antitrust laws and as enforced by Allen Bradley v. Union, *supra,* until the Congress delegates to big business and big labor the power to remold our economy in the manner charged here.

MR. JUSTICE GOLDBERG, with whom MR. JUSTICE HARLAN and MR. JUSTICE STEWART join, dissenting from the opinion but concurring in the reversal.*

[The opinion first reviewed the history of labor and antitrust.]

In my view, this history shows a consistent congressional purpose to limit severely judicial intervention in collective bargaining under cover of the wide umbrella of the antitrust laws, and, rather, to deal with what Congress deemed to be specific abuses on the part of labor unions by specific proscriptions in the labor statutes. I believe that the Court should respect this history of congressional purpose and should reaffirm the Court's holdings in *Apex* and *Hutcheson....* Following the sound analysis of *Hutcheson,* the Court should hold that, in order to effectuate congressional intent, collective bargaining activity concerning mandatory subjects of bargaining under the Labor Act is not subject to the antitrust laws. This rule flows directly from the *Hutcheson* holding that a union acting as a union, in the interests of its members, and not acting to fix prices or allocate markets in aid of an employer conspiracy to accomplish these objects, with only indirect union benefits, is not subject to challenge under the antitrust laws. To hold that mandatory collective bargaining is completely protected would effectuate the congressional policies of encouraging free collective bargaining, subject only to specific restrictions contained in the labor laws, and of limiting judicial intervention in labor matters via the antitrust route — an intervention which necessarily under

---

* Mr. Justice Goldberg's single opinion covers both *Pennington* and *Jewel Tea.* We present portions dealing with *Pennington* here; the part dealing with *Jewel Tea* is presented after the other opinions in that case. — [*Eds.*]

the Sherman Act places on judges and juries the determination of "what
public policy in regard to the industrial struggle demands." Duplex
Printing Press Co. v. Deering, 254 U.S. 443, at 485 (1921) (dissenting
opinion of Mr. Justice Brandeis). . . .

Moreover, mandatory subjects of bargaining are issues as to which
strikes may not be enjoined by either federal or state courts. To say that
the union can strike over such issues but that both it and the employer are
subject to possible antitrust penalties for making collective bargaining
agreements concerning them is to assert that Congress intended to permit
the parties to collective bargaining to wage industrial warfare but to
prohibit them from peacefully settling their disputes. . . .

The Court in *Pennington* today ignores this history of the discredited
judicial attempt to apply the antitrust laws to legitimate collective
bargaining activity, and it flouts the clearly expressed congressional intent
that, since "[t]he labor of a human being is not a commodity or article of
commerce," the antitrust laws do not proscribe, and the national labor
policy affirmatively promotes, the "elimination of price competition based
on differences in labor standards," Apex Hosiery Co. v. Leader, *supra* at
503. . . .

Since collective bargaining inevitably involves and requires discussion
of the impact of the wage agreement reached with a particular employer
or group of employers upon competing employers, the effect of the
Court's decision will be to bar a basic element of collective bargaining
from the conference room. If a union and employer are prevented from
discussing and agreeing upon issues which are, in the great majority of
cases, at the central core of bargaining, unilateral force will inevitably be
substituted for rational discussion and agreement. Plainly and simply, the
Court would subject both unions and employers to antitrust sanctions,
criminal as well as civil, if in collective bargaining they concluded a wage
agreement and, as part of the agreement, the union has undertaken to use
its best efforts to have this wage accepted by other employers in the
industry. Indeed, the decision today even goes beyond this. Under settled
antitrust principles which are accepted by the Court as appropriate and
applicable, which were the basis for jury instructions in *Pennington,* and
which will govern it upon remand, there need not be direct evidence of
an express agreement. Rather the existence of such an agreement, express
or implied, may be inferred from the conduct of the parties. . . .

In *Pennington,* central to the alleged conspiracy is the claim that hourly
wage rates and fringe benefits were set at a level designed to eliminate the
competition of the smaller nonunion companies by making the labor cost
too high for them to pay. Indeed, the trial judge charged that there was
no violation of the Sherman Act in the establishing of wages and welfare
payments through the national contract, "provided" the mine workers
and the major coal producers had not agreed to fix "high" rates "in order
to drive the small coal operators out of business." Under such an
instruction, if the jury found the wage scale too "high" it could impute
the unlawful purpose of putting the nonunion operators out of business.
It is clear that the effect of the instruction therefore, was to invite 12

jurymen to become arbiters of the economic desirability of the wage scale in the Nation's coal industry. The Court would sustain the judgment based on this charge and thereby put its stamp of approval on this role for courts and juries. . . .

To allow a jury to infer an illegal "conspiracy" from the agreed-upon wage scale means that the jury must determine at what level the wages could be fixed without impelling the parties into the ambit of the antitrust laws. Is this not another way of saying that, via the antitrust route, a judge or jury may determine, according to its own notions of what is economically sound, the amount of wages that a union can properly ask for or that an employer can pay? It is clear, as experience shows, that judges and juries have neither the aptitude nor possess the criteria for making this kind of judgment. . . .

As I have discussed, the Court's test is not essentially different from the discredited purpose-motive approach. Only rarely will there be direct evidence of an express agreement between a union and an employer to impose a particular wage scale on other employers. In most cases, as was true of *Pennington,* the trial court will instruct the jury that such an illegal agreement may be inferred from the conduct — "indirect evidence" — of the union and employers. To allow a court or a jury to infer an illegal agreement from collective bargaining conduct inevitably requires courts and juries to analyze the terms of collective bargaining agreements and the purposes and motives of unions and employers in agreeing upon them. Moreover, the evidence most often available to sustain antitrust liability under the Court's theory would show, as it did in *Pennington,* simply that the motives of the union and employer coincide — the union seeking high wages and protection from low-wage, nonunion competition and the employer who pays high wages seeking protection from competitors who pay lower wages. When there is this coincidence of motive, does the illegality of the "conspiracy" turn on whether the Union pursued its goal of a uniform wage policy through strikes and not negotiation? As I read the Court's opinion this is precisely what the result turns on and thus unions are forced, in order to show that they have not illegally "agreed" with employers, to pursue their aims through strikes and not negotiations. Yet, it is clear that such a result was precisely what the National Labor Relations Act was designed to prevent. The only alternative to resolution of collective bargaining issues by force available to the parties under the Court's holding is the encouragement of fraud and deceit. An employer will be forced to take a public stand against a union's wage demands, even if he is willing to accept them, lest a too-ready acceptance be used by a jury to infer an agreement between the union and employer that the same wages will be sought from other employers. . . .

Furthermore, I do not understand how an inquiry can be formulated in terms of whether the union action is unilateral or is a consequence of a "conspiracy" with employers independently of the economic terms of the collective bargaining agreement. The agreement must be admitted into evidence and the Court holds that its economic consequences are relevant. In the end, one way or another, the entire panoply of economic fact becomes involved, and judges and juries under the Court's view would then be allowed to speculate about why a union bargained for increased compensation, or any other labor standard within the scope of mandatory bargaining. It is precisely this type of speculation that Congress has rejected. . . .

NOTE

Embry outbid Ross and succeeded it as a supplier of flight-training services to the government. All or most of Ross's employees were to be taken over by Embry. Before this occurred, however, Ross negotiated a labor agreement with a union setting a high wage scale that Embry could not meet without defaulting on its new government contract. Ross thus hoped to recover the work. Is *Pennington* applicable or distinguishable? Note that the union has contracted with only a single employer, Ross, and that only a single bargaining unit is involved. See Embry-Riddle Aeronautical Univ. v. Ross Aviation, Inc., 504 F. 2d 896 (5th Cir. 1974).

AMALGAMATED MEAT CUTTERS & BUTCHER WORKMEN, LOCAL 189 v. JEWEL TEA CO.

Supreme Court of the United States
381 U.S. 676, 85 S. Ct. 1596, 14 L. Ed. 2d 640 (1965)

MR. JUSTICE WHITE announced the judgment of the Court and delivered an opinion, in which THE CHIEF JUSTICE and MR. JUSTICE BRENNAN join.

Like *United Mine Workers v. Pennington,* decided today, this case presents questions regarding the application of §§ 1 and 2 of the Sherman Antitrust Act . . . to activities of labor unions. In particular, it concerns the lawfulness of the following restriction on the operating hours of food store meat departments contained in a collective agreement executed after joint multi-employer, multi-union negotiations:

"Market operating hours shall be 9:00 a.m. to 6:00 p.m. Monday through Saturday, inclusive. No customer shall be served who comes into the market before or after the hours set forth above."

This litigation arose out of the 1957 contract negotiations between the representatives of 9,000 Chicago retailers of fresh meat and the seven union petitioners, who are local affiliates of the Amalgamated Meat Cutters and Butcher Workmen of North America, AFL-CIO, representing virtually all butchers in the Chicago area. During the 1957 bargaining sessions the employer group presented several requests for union consent to a relaxation of the existing contract restriction on marketing hours for fresh meat, which forbade the sale of meat before 9 a.m. and after 6 p.m. in both service and self-service markets. The unions rejected all such suggestions, and their own proposal retaining the marketing-hours restriction was ultimately accepted at the final session by all but two of the employers, National Tea Co. and Jewel Tea Co. (hereinafter "Jewel"). Associated Food Retailers of Greater Chicago, a trade association having about 1,000 individual and independent merchants as members and representing some 300 meat dealers in the negotiations, was among those who accepted. Jewel, however, asked the union negotiators to present to their membership, on behalf of it and National Tea, a counter-offer that included provision for Friday night operations. At the same time Jewel voiced its belief, as it had midway through the negotiations, that any marketing-hours restriction was illegal. On the recommendation of the union negotiators the Jewel offer was rejected by the union membership, and a strike was authorized. Under the duress of the strike vote, Jewel decided to sign the contract previously approved by the rest of the industry.

In July 1958 Jewel brought suit against the unions, certain of their officers, Associated, and Charles H. Bromann, Secretary-Treasurer of Associated, seeking invalidation under §§ 1 and 2 of the Sherman Act of the contract provision that prohibited night meat market operations. The gist of the complaint was that the defendants and others had conspired together to prevent the retail sale of fresh meat before 9 a.m. and after 6 p.m. As evidence of the conspiracy Jewel relied in part on the events during the 1957 contract negotiations — the acceptance by Associated of the marketing-hours restriction and the unions' imposition of the restriction on Jewel through a strike threat. Jewel also alleged that it was a part of the conspiracy that the unions would neither permit their members to work at times other than the hours specified nor allow any grocery firm to sell meat, with or without employment of their members, outside those hours; that the members of Associated, which had joined only one of the 1957 employer proposals for extended marketing hours, had agreed among themselves to insist on the inclusion of the marketing-hours limitation in all collective agreements between the unions and any food store operator; that Associated, its members and officers had agreed with the other defendants that no firm was to be permitted to operate self-service meat markets between 6 p.m. and 9 p.m; and that the unions, their officers and members had acted as the enforcing agent of the conspiracy.

The complaint stated that in recent years the prepackaged, self-service system of marketing meat had come into vogue, that 174 of Jewel's 196 stores were equipped to vend meat in this manner, and that a butcher need not be on duty in a self-service market at the time meat purchases were actually made. The prohibition of night meat marketing, it was alleged, unlawfully impeded Jewel in the use of its property and adversely affected the general public in that many persons find it inconvenient to shop during the day. An injunction, treble damages and attorney's fees were demanded.

The trial judge held the allegations of the complaint sufficient to withstand a motion to dismiss made on the grounds, *inter alia,* that (a) the "alleged restraint [was] within the exclusive regulatory scope of the National Labor Relations Act and [was] therefore outside the jurisdiction of the Court" and (b) the controversy was within the labor exemption to the antitrust laws. That ruling was sustained on appeal. Jewel Tea Co. v.

Meat Cutters, Local 189, 274 F.2d 271 (7th Cir. 1960), *cert. denied,* 362 U.S. 936 (1960). After trial, however, the District Judge ruled the "record was devoid of any evidence to support a finding of a conspiracy" between Associated and the unions to force the restrictive provision on Jewel. Testing the unions' action standing alone, the trial court found that even in self-service markets removal of the limitation on marketing hours either would inaugurate longer hours and night work for the butchers or would result in butchers' work being done by others unskilled in the trade. Thus, the court concluded, the unions had imposed the marketing-hours limitation to serve their own interests respecting conditions of employment, and such action was clearly within the labor exemption of the Sherman Act established by Hunt v. Crumboch, 325 U.S. 821 (1945); United States v. Hutcheson, 312 U.S. 219 (1941); United States v. American Fed. of Musicians, 318 U.S. 741 (1943). Alternatively, the District Court ruled that even if this was not the case, the arrangement did not amount to an unreasonable restraint of trade in violation of the Sherman Act.

The Court of Appeals reversed the dismissal of the complaint as to both the unions and Associated. Without disturbing the District Court's finding that, apart from the contractual provision itself, there was no evidence of conspiracy, the Court of Appeals concluded that a conspiracy in restraint of trade had been shown. The court noted that "the rest of the industry agreed with the defendant local unions to continue the ban on night operations," while plaintiff resisted, and concluded that Associated and the unions "entered into a combination or agreement, which constituted a conspiracy, as charged in the complaint . . . [w]hether it be called an agreement, contract or conspiracy, is immaterial." 331 F.2d 547, 551. . . .

We granted certiorari on the unions' petition . . . and now reverse the Court of Appeals. . . .

I. We must first consider the unions' attack on the appropriateness of the District Court's exercise of jurisdiction, which is encompassed in their contention that this controversy is within the exclusive primary jurisdiction of the National Labor Relations Board. . . .

Thus, the unions contend, Jewel could have filed an unfair labor practice charge with the Board on the ground that the unions had insisted on a nonmandatory subject — the marketing-hours restriction. Obviously, classification of bargaining subjects as "terms or conditions of employment" is a matter concerning which the Board has special expertise. Nevertheless, for the reasons stated below we cannot conclude that this is a proper case for application of the doctrine of primary jurisdiction.

To begin with, courts are themselves not without experience in classifying bargaining subjects as terms or conditions of employment. Just such a determination must be frequently made when a court's jurisdiction to issue an injunction affecting a labor dispute is challenged under the Norris-LaGuardia Act, which defines "labor dispute" as including "any controversy concerning terms or conditions of employment," Norris-LaGuardia Act § 13(c). . . .

Finally, we must reject the unions' primary-jurisdiction contention because of the absence of an available procedure for obtaining a Board determination. The Board does not classify bargaining subjects in the abstract but only in connection with unfair labor practice charges of refusal to bargain. The typical antitrust suit, however, is brought by a stranger to the bargaining relationship, and the complaint is not that the parties have refused to bargain but, quite the contrary, that they have agreed. Jewel's conspiracy allegation in the present case was just such a complaint. Agreement is of course not a refusal to bargain, and in such cases the Board affords no mechanism for obtaining a classification of the subject matter of the agreement. Moreover, even in the few instances when the antitrust action could be framed as a refusal to bargain charge, there is no guarantee of Board action. It is the function of the Board's General Counsel rather than the Board or a private litigant to determine whether an unfair labor practice complaint will ultimately issue. National Labor Relations Act § 3(d). . . . And the six-month limitation period of § 10(b) of the Act . . . would preclude many litigants from even filing a charge with the General Counsel. Indeed, Jewel's complaint in this very case was filed more than six months after it signed the 1957 collective bargaining agreement. . . .

II. Here, as in *United Mine Workers v. Pennington,* the claim is made that the agreement under attack is exempt from the antitrust laws. We agree, but not on the broad grounds urged by the union.

It is well at the outset to emphasize that this case comes to us stripped of any claim of a union-employer conspiracy against Jewel. The trial court found no evidence to sustain Jewel's conspiracy claim and this finding was not disturbed by the Court of Appeals. We therefore have a situation where the unions, having obtained a marketing-hours agreement from one group of employers, have successfully sought the same terms from a single employer, Jewel, not as a result of a bargain between the unions and some employers directed against other employers, but pursuant to what the unions deemed to be in their own labor union interests.

Jewel does not allege that it has been injured by the elimination of competition among the other employers within the unit with respect to marketing hours; Jewel complains only of the union's action in forcing it to accept the same restriction, the union acting not at the behest of any employer but in pursuit of its own policies. It might be argued that absent any union-employer conspiracy against Jewel and absent any agreement between Jewel and any other employer, the Union-Jewel contract cannot be a violation of the Sherman Act. But the issue before us is not the broad substantive one of a violation of the antitrust laws — was there a conspiracy or combination which unreasonably restrained trade or an attempt to monopolize and was Jewel damaged in its business — but whether the agreement is immune from attack by reason of the labor exemption from the antitrust laws. The fact that the parties to the agreement are but a single employer and the unions representing its employees does not compel immunity for the agreement. We must consider the subject matter of the agreement in the light of the national labor policy. . . .

We pointed out in *Pennington* that exemption for union-employer agreements is very much a matter of accommodating the coverage of the Sherman Act to the policy of the labor laws. Employers and unions are required to bargain about wages, hours and working conditions, and this fact weighs heavily in favor of antitrust exemption for agreements on these subjects. But neither party need bargain about other matters and either party commits an unfair labor practice if it conditions its bargaining upon discussions of a nonmandatory subject. NLRB v. Borg-Warner Corp., 356 U.S. 342 (1958). Jewel, for example, need not have bargained about or agreed to a schedule of prices at which its meat would be sold and the union could not legally have insisted that it do so. But if the union had made such a demand, Jewel had agreed and the United States or an injured party had challenged the agreement under the antitrust laws, we seriously doubt that either the union or Jewel could claim immunity by reason of the labor exemption, whatever substantive questions of violation there might be.

Thus the issue in this case is whether the marketing-hours restriction, like wages, and unlike prices, is so intimately related to wages, hours and working conditions that the unions' successful attempt to obtain that provision through bona fide, arms-length bargaining in pursuit of its own labor union policies, and not at the behest of or in combination with nonlabor groups, falls within the protection of the national labor policy and is therefore exempt from the Sherman Act.[5] We think that it is.

The Court of Appeals would classify the marketing hours restriction with the product-pricing provision and place both within the reach of the Sherman Act. In its view, labor has a legitimate interest in the number of hours it must work but no interest in whether the hours fall in the daytime, in the nighttime or on Sundays. "[T]he furnishing of a place and advantageous hours of employment for the butchers to supply meat to customers are the prerogatives of the employer." 331 F.2d 547, 549. That reasoning would invalidate with respect to both service and self-service markets the 1957 provision that "eight hours shall constitute the basic work day, Monday through Saturday; *work to begin at 9:00 a.m. and stop at 6:00 p.m. . . .*" as well as the marketing-hours restriction.

---

[5] The crucial determinant is not the form of the agreement — *e.g.,* prices or wages — but its relative impact on the product market and the interests of union members. Thus in Teamsters v. Oliver, 358 U.S. 283 (1959), we held that federal labor policy precluded application of state antitrust laws to an employer-union agreement that when leased trucks were driven by their owners, such owner-drivers should receive, in addition to the union wage, not less than a prescribed minimum rental. Though in form a scheme fixing prices for the supply of leased vehicles, the agreement was designed "to protect the negotiated wage scale against the possible undermining through diminution of the owner's wages for driving which might result from a rental which did not cover his operating cost." *Id.* at 293-294. As the agreement did not embody a " 'remote and indirect approach to the subject of wages' . . . but a direct frontal attack upon a problem thought to threaten the maintenance of the basic wage structure established by the collective bargaining contract," *id.* at 294, the paramount federal policy of encouraging collective bargaining proscribed application of the state law.

Contrary to the Court of Appeals, we think that the particular hours of the day and the particular days of the week during which employees shall be required to work are subjects well within the realm of "wages, hours, and other terms and conditions of employment" about which employers and unions must bargain. National Labor Relations Act § 8(d); see Timken Roller Bearing Co., 70 N.L.R.B. 500, 504, 515-516, 521 (1964), *rev'd on other grounds,* 161 F.2d 949 (6th Cir. 1947) (employer's unilateral imposition of Sunday work was refusal to bargain); Massey Gin & Machine Works, Inc., 78 N.L.R.B. 189, 195, 199 (same; change in starting and quitting time); Camp & McInnes, Inc., 100 N.L.R.B. 524, 532 (same; reduction of lunch hour and advancement of quitting time). And, although the effect on competition is apparent and real, perhaps more so than in the case of the wage agreement, the concern of union members is immediate and direct. Weighing the respective interests involved, we think the national labor policy expressed in the National Labor Relations Act places beyond the reach of the Sherman Act union-employer agreements on when, as well as how long, employees must work. An agreement on these subjects between the union and the employers in a bargaining unit is not illegal under the Sherman Act, nor is the union's unilateral demand for the same contract of other employers in the industry.

Disposing of the case, as it did, on the broad grounds we have indicated, the Court of Appeals did not deal separately with the marketing-hours provision, as distinguished from hours of work, in connection with either service or self-service markets. The dispute here pertains principally to self-service markets.

The unions argue that since night operations would be impossible without night employment of butchers, or an impairment of the butchers' jurisdiction, or a substantial effect on the butchers' workload, the marketing-hours restriction is either little different in effect from the valid working-hours provision that work shall stop at 6 p.m. or is necessary to protect other concerns of the union members. If the unions' factual premises are true, we think the unions could impose a restriction on night operations without violation of the Sherman Act; for then operating hours, like working hours, would constitute a subject of immediate and legitimate concern to union members.

Jewel alleges on the other hand that the night operation of self-service markets requires no butcher to be in attendance and does not infringe any other legitimate union concern. Customers serve themselves; and if owners want to forego furnishing the services of a butcher to give advice or to make special cuts, this is not the unions' concern since their desire to avoid night work is fully satisfied and no other legitimate interest is being infringed. In short, the connection between working hours and operating hours in the case of the self-service market is said to be so attenuated as to bring the provision within the prohibition of the Sherman Act.

If it were true that self-service markets could actually operate without butchers, at least for a few hours after 6 p.m., that no encroachment on butchers' work would result and that the workload of butchers during normal working hours would not be substantially increased, Jewel's position would have considerable merit. For then the obvious restraint on the product market — the exclusion of self-service stores from the evening market for meat — would stand alone, unmitigated and unjustified by the vital interests of the union butchers which are relied upon in this case. In such event the limitation imposed by the union might well be reduced to nothing but an effort by the union to protect one group of employers from competition by another, which is conduct that is not exempt from the Sherman Act. Whether there would be a violation of §§ 1 and 2 would then depend on whether the elements of a conspiracy in restraint of trade or an attempt to monopolize had been proved.

Thus the dispute between Jewel and the unions essentially concerns a narrow factual question: Are night operations without butchers, and without infringement of butchers' interests, feasible? The District Court resolved this factual dispute in favor of the unions. It found that "in stores where meat is sold at night it is impractical to operate without either butchers or other employees. Someone must arrange, replenish and clean the counters and supply customer services." Operating without butchers would mean that "their work would be done by others unskilled in the trade," and "would involve an increase in workload in preparing for the night work and cleaning the next morning." 215 F. Supp. at 846. Those findings were not disturbed by the Court of Appeals, which, as previously noted, proceeded on a broader ground. Our function is limited to reviewing the record to satisfy ourselves that the trial judge's findings are not clearly erroneous. Fed. Rules Civ. Proc. 52(a).

The trial court had before it evidence concerning the history of the unions' opposition to night work, the development of the provisions respecting night work and night operations, the course of collective negotiations in 1957, 1959, and 1961 with regard to those provisions, and the characteristics of meat marketing insofar as they bore on the feasibility of night operations without butchers.

The unions' opposition to night work has a long history. Prior to 1919 the operating hours of meat markets in Chicago were 7 a.m. to 7 p.m., Monday through Friday; 7 a.m. to 10 p.m. on Saturday, and 7 a.m. to 1 p.m. on Sunday. Butchers worked the full 81-hour, seven-day week. The Chicago butchers' strike of 1919 was much concerned with shortening working hours, and the resulting contract, signed in 1920, set the working day at 8 a.m. to 6 p.m., Monday through Friday, and 8 a.m. to 9 p.m. on Saturday. Various alterations in the hours were made in 1937, 1941, 1945, 1946, and again in 1947, when the present working hours (9 a.m. to 6 p.m., Monday through Saturday) were established. In a mail ballot conducted by the unions in October, 1962, Jewel's meat cutters voted 759 to 28 against night work.

Concomitant with the unions' concern with the working hours of butchers was their interest in the hours during which customers might be served. The 1920 agreement provided that "no customers will be served who come into the market after 6 P.M. and 9 P.M. on Saturdays and on days preceding holidays. . . ." That provision was continued until 1947, when it was superseded by the formulation presently in effect and here claimed to be unlawful. . . .

The unions' evidence with regard to the practicability of night operations without butchers was accurately summarized by the trial judge as follows:

"[I]n most of plaintiff's stores outside Chicago, where night operations exist, meat cutters are on duty whenever a meat department is open after 6 P.M. . . . Even in self-service departments, ostensibly operated without employees on duty after 6 P.M., there was evidence that requisite customer services in connection with meat sales were performed by grocery clerks. In the same vein, defendants adduced evidence that in the sale of delicatessen items, which could be made after 6 P.M. from self-service cases under the contract, 'practically' always during the time the market was open the manager, or other employees, would be rearranging and restocking the cases. There was also evidence that even if it were practical to operate a self-service meat market after 6 P.M. without employees, the night operations would add to the workload in getting the meats prepared for night sales and in putting the counters in order the next day." 215 F. Supp. at 844.

Jewel challenges the unions' evidence on each of these points — arguing, for example, that its preference to have butchers on duty at night, where possible under the union contract, is not probative of the feasibility of not having butchers on duty and that the evidence that grocery clerks performed customer services within the butchers' jurisdiction was based on a single instance resulting from "entrapment" by union agents. But Jewel's argument — when considered against the historical background of union concern with working hours and operating hours and the virtually uniform recognition by employers of the intimate relationship between the two subjects, as manifested by bargaining proposals in 1957, 1959, and 1961 — falls far short of a showing that the trial judge's ultimate findings were clearly erroneous. . . .

Reversed.

MR. JUSTICE DOUGLAS, with whom MR. JUSTICE BLACK and MR. JUSTICE CLARK concur, dissenting.

If we followed Allen Bradley Co. v. Local Union No. 3, 325 U.S. 797 (1945), we would hold with the Court of Appeals that this multi-employer agreement with the union not to sell meat between 6 p.m. and 9 a.m. was not immunized from the antitrust laws and that respondent's evidence made out a prima facie case that it was in fact a violation of the Sherman Act.

If, in the present case, the employers alone agreed not to sell meat from 6 p.m. to 9 a.m., they would be guilty of an anti-competitive practice, barred by the antitrust laws. Absent an agreement or conspiracy, a proprietor can keep his establishment open for such hours as he chooses. . . . That Jewel has been coerced by the unions into respecting this agreement means that Jewel cannot use convenience of shopping hours as a means of competition. . . .

At the conclusion of respondent's case, the District Court dismissed Associated and Bromann from the action, which was tried without a jury, on the ground that there was no evidence of a conspiracy between Associated and the unions. But in the circumstances of this case the collective agreement itself, of which the District Court said there was clear proof, was evidence of a conspiracy among the employers with the unions to impose the marketing-hours restriction on Jewel via a strike threat by the unions. This tended to take from the merchants who agreed among themselves their freedom to work their own hours and to subject all who, like Jewel, wanted to sell meat after 6 p.m. to the coercion of threatened strikes, all of which if done in concert only by businessmen would violate the antitrust laws. See Fashion Guild v. Federal Trade Comm'n, 312 U.S. 457, 465 (1941).

In saying that there was no conspiracy, the District Court failed to give any weight to the collective agreement itself as evidence of a conspiracy and to the context in which it was written. This Court makes the same mistake. . . . Here the contract of the unions with a large number of employers shows it was planned and designed not merely to control but entirely to prohibit "the marketing of goods and services" from 6 p.m. until 9 a.m. the next day. Some merchants relied chiefly on price competition to draw trade; others employed courtesy, quick service, and keeping their doors open long hours to meet the convenience of customers. The unions here induced a large group of merchants to use their collective strength to hurt others who wanted the competitive advantage of selling meat after 6 p.m. Unless *Allen Bradley* is either overruled or greatly impaired, the unions can no more aid a group of businessmen to force their competitors to follow uniform store marketing hours than to force them to sell at fixed prices. Both practices take away the freedom of traders to carry on their business in their own competitive fashion.

My Brother WHITE's conclusion that the concern of the union members over *marketing* hours is "immediate and direct" depends upon there being a necessary connection between marketing hours and working hours. That connection is found in the District Court's finding that "in stores where meat is sold at night it is impractical to operate without either butchers or other employees." It is, however, undisputed that on some nights Jewel does so operate in some of its stores in Indiana, and even in Chicago it sometimes operates without butchers at night in the sale of fresh poultry and sausage, which are exempt from the union ban.

It is said that even if night self-service could be carried on without butchers, still the union interest in store hours would be immediate and direct because competitors would have to stay open too or be put at a disadvantage — and some of these competitors would be non-self-service stores that would have to employ union butchers at night. But *Allen Bradley* forecloses such an expansive view of the labor exemption to the antitrust laws.

MR. JUSTICE GOLDBERG, with whom MR. JUSTICE HARLAN and MR. JUSTICE STEWART join, dissenting from the opinion but concurring in the . . . judgment of the Court. . . .

The judicial expressions in *Jewel Tea* represent another example of the reluctance of judges to give full effect to congressional purpose in this area and the substitution by judges of their views for those of Congress as to how free collective bargaining should operate. In this case the Court of Appeals would have held the Union liable for the Sherman Act's criminal and civil penalties because in the court's social and economic judgment, the determination of the hours at which meat is to be sold is a "proprietary" matter within the exclusive control of management and thus the Union had no legitimate interest in bargaining over it. My Brother DOUGLAS, joined by MR. JUSTICE BLACK and MR. JUSTICE CLARK, would affirm this judgment apparently because the agreement was reached through a multi-employer bargaining unit. But, as I have demonstrated above, there is nothing even remotely illegal about such bargaining. Even if an independent conspiracy test were applicable to the *Jewel Tea* situation, the simple fact is that multi-employer bargaining conducted at arm's length does not constitute union abetment of a business combination. It is often a self-defensive form of employer bargaining designed to match union strength. . . .

[M]y Brother WHITE indicates that he would sustain a judgment here, even absent evidence of union abetment of an independent conspiracy of employers, if the trial court had found "that self-service markets could actually operate without butchers, at least for a few hours after 6 p.m., that no encroachment on butchers' work would result and that the workload of butchers during normal working hours would not be substantially increased. . . ." . . . Such a view seems to me to be unsupportable. It represents a narrow, confining view of what labor unions have a legitimate interest in preserving and thus bargaining about. Even if the self-service markets could operate after 6 p.m., without their butchers and without increasing the work of their butchers at other times, the result of such operation can reasonably be expected to be either that the small, independent, service markets would have to remain open in order to compete, thus requiring their union butchers to work at night, or that the small, independent, service markets would not be able to operate at night and thus would be put at a competitive disadvantage. Since it is clear that the large, automated self-service markets employ less butchers per volume of sales than service markets do, the Union certainly has a legitimate interest in keeping service markets competitive so as to preserve jobs. Job security of this kind has been recognized to be a legitimate subject of union interest. See Telegraphers v. Chicago & N.W.R. Co., 362 U.S. 330 (1960); Teamsters Local 24 v. Oliver, 358 U.S. 283 (1959), 362 U.S. 605 (1960). . . . The direct interest of the union in not working undesirable hours by curtailing all business at those hours is, of course, a far cry from the indirect "interest" in *Allen Bradley* in fixing prices and allocating markets solely to increase the profits of favored employers.

Indeed, if the Union in *Jewel Tea* were attempting to aid the small service butcher shops and thus save total employment against automation, perhaps at a necessarily reduced wage scale, the case would present the exact opposite union philosophy from that of the Mine Workers in

Pennington. Putting the opinion of the Court in *Pennington* together with the opinions of my Brothers DOUGLAS and WHITE in *Jewel Tea,* it would seem that unions are damned if their collective bargaining philosophy involves acceptance of automation *(Pennington)* and are equally damned if their collective bargaining philosophy involves resistance to automation *(Jewel Tea).* Again, the wisdom of a union adopting either philosophy is not for judicial determination. . . .

NOTES

1. *See* Cox, *Labor and the Antitrust Laws: Pennington and Jewel Tea,* 46 B.U.L. REV. 317 (1966); DiCola, *Labor Antitrust: Pennington, Jewel Tea and Subsequent Meandering,* 33 U. PITT. L. REV. 705 (1972); Meltzer, *Labor Unions, Collective Bargaining, and the Antitrust Laws,* 32 U. CHI. L. REV. 659 (1965); St. Antoine, *Collective Bargaining and the Antitrust Laws,* in INDUSTRIAL RELATIONS RESEARCH ASS'N, PROCEEDINGS OF THE 19TH ANNUAL WINTER MEETING 66 (1966).

2. Under *Pennington,* is there a distinction between a union's loss of antitrust immunity and its commission of a substantive violation? If so, what added elements must be shown to establish an offense arising out of an agreement with extra-unit implications?

3. What will be the effect of *Pennington* on "most favored nation" clauses, by which the union agrees to give the signatory employer the benefit of the most favorable terms the union subsequently affords any other employer? *See Dolly Madison Indus., supra* at 558.

4. What other efforts by unions or employers to obtain uniform labor contracts may be placed in question as a result of *Pennington*? For example, what about several unions coordinating bargaining policy with respect to different units of the same business — or several employers coordinating bargaining strategy, in the absence of a multi-employer unit, such as agreeing on a joint lockout in case one employer is struck?

5. A five-to-four majority of the Supreme Court held that the ordinary "preponderance of evidence" standard is applicable to the establishing of substantive violations in civil antitrust actions against labor unions. Only in proving the authority of individual members, officers, or agents of a union to act on its behalf must a "clear proof" test be met. Ramsey v. UMW, 401 U.S. 302 (1971).

6. On remand, the courts held that the small coal operators in *Pennington* and *Ramsey* failed to prove a violation of the antitrust laws. Lewis v. Pennington, 257 F. Supp. 815 (E.D. Tenn. 1966), *aff'd,* 400 F.2d 806 (6th Cir. 1968), *cert. denied sub nom.* Pennington v. UMW, 393 U.S. 983 (1968), *rehearing denied,* 393 U.S. 1045 (1969); Ramsey v. UMW, 344 F. Supp. 1029 (E.D. Tenn. 1972), *aff'd,* 481 F.2d 742 (6th Cir. 1973), *cert. denied,* 94 S. Ct. 576 (1973).

However, other similarly situated coal operators prevailed against the UMW in their treble-damage antitrust suits. Tennessee Consolidated Coal Co. v. UMW, 416 F.2d 1192 (6th Cir. 1969), *cert. denied,* 397 U.S. 964 (1970) (damages of $1,432,500 recovered, plus $150,000 attorneys fees); South-East Coal Co. v. UMW and Consolidation Coal Co., 434 F.2d 767 (6th Cir. 1970), *cert. denied,* 402 U.S. 983 (1971) (damages of $7,231,356, plus $335,000 attorneys fees).

AMERICAN FEDERATION OF MUSICIANS V. CARROLL, 391 U.S. 99, 88 S. Ct. 1562, 20 L. Ed. 2d 460 (1968). Respondents were orchestra "leaders," who booked so-called "club-dates," or one-time engagements, for their groups, and then secured enough "side-men," or supporting instrumentalists, to play at the various events. Usually the leaders performed with their orchestras, sometimes only conducting but often also playing an instrument. Under the rules of petitioners, musicians unions to which the respondents belonged, orchestra leaders had to charge purchasers of music minimum prices prescribed in a "price list." The prices were a total of (a) the minimum wage scales for sidemen, (b) a "leader's fee" which was double the sideman's scale in orchestras of four or more, and (c) an additional eight percent to cover social security, unemployment insurance, and other expenses. Respondents sought an injunction against this price floor and treble damages under the Sherman Act. Relying heavily on *Teamsters Local 24 v. Oliver, supra* at 459, as well as on *Jewel Tea,* the Supreme Court held that the action should be dismissed. Justice Brennan, speaking for the Court, stated that "the price floors, including the minimums for leaders, are simply a means for coping with the job and wage competition of the leaders to protect the wage scales of musicians who respondents concede are employees on club-dates, namely sidemen and subleaders." He added that "the price of the product — here the price for an orchestra for a club-date — represents almost entirely the scale wages of the sidemen and the leader. Unlike most industries, except for the 8% charge, there are no other costs contributing to the price. Therefore, if leaders cut prices, inevitably wages must be cut." Justices White and Black dissented.

NOTE

What are the implications of *Carroll* for a society in which the service industries loom ever more important?

CONNELL CONSTRUCTION CO. v. PLUMBERS LOCAL 100

Supreme Court of the United States
421 U.S. 616, 95 S. Ct. 1830, 44 L. Ed. 2d 418 (1975)

MR. JUSTICE POWELL delivered the opinion of the Court. . . .
I. Local 100 is the bargaining representative for workers in the plumbing and mechanical trades in Dallas. When this litigation began, it was party to a multiemployer bargaining agreement with the Mechanical Contractors Association of Dallas, a group of about 75 mechanical contractors. That contract contained a "most favored nation" clause, by

which the union agreed that if it granted a more favorable contract to any other employer it would extend the same terms to all members of the Association.

'Connell Construction Company is a general building contractor in Dallas. It obtains jobs by competitive bidding and subcontracts all plumbing and mechanical work. Connell has followed a policy of awarding these subcontracts on the basis of competitive bids, and it has done business with both union and nonunion subcontractors. Connell's employees are represented by various building trade unions. Local 100 has never sought to represent them or to bargain with Connell on their behalf.

In November 1970, Local 100 asked Connell to agree that it would subcontract mechanical work only to firms that had a current contract with the union. It demanded that Connell sign the following agreement:

"WHEREAS, the contractor and the union are engaged in the construction industry, and

"WHEREAS, the contractor and the union desire to make an agreement applying in the event of subcontracting in accordance with Section 8(e) of the Labor-Management Relations Act;

"WHEREAS, it is understood that by this agreement the contractor does not grant, nor does the union seek, recognition as the collective bargaining representative of any employees of the signatory contractor; and

"WHEREAS, it is further understood that the subcontracting limitation provided herein applies only to mechanical work which the contractor does not perform with his own employees but uniformly subcontracts to other firms;

"THEREFORE, the contractor and the union mutually agree with respect to work falling within the scope of this agreement that is to be done at the site of the construction, alteration, painting or repair of any building, structure, or other works, that if the contractor should contract or subcontract any of the aforesaid work falling within the normal trade jurisdiction of the union, said contractor shall contract or subcontract such work only to firms that are parties to an executed, current, collective bargaining agreement with Local Union 100 of the United Association of Journeymen and Apprentices of the Plumbing and Pipefitting Industry."

When Connell refused to sign this agreement, Local 100 stationed a single picket at one of Connell's major construction sites. About 150 workers walked off the job, and construction halted. Connell filed suit in state court to enjoin the picketing as a violation of Texas antitrust laws. Local 100 removed the case to federal court. Connell then signed the subcontracting agreement under protest. It amended its complaint to claim that the agreement violated §§ 1 and 2 of the Sherman Act, . . . and was therefore invalid. Connell sought a declaration to this effect and an injunction against any further efforts to force it to sign such an agreement.

By the time the case went to trial, Local 100 had submitted identical agreements to a number of other general contractors in Dallas. Five others had signed, and the union was waging a selective picketing campaign against those who resisted.

The District Court held that the subcontracting agreement was exempt from federal antitrust laws because it was authorized by the construction industry proviso to § 8(e) of the National Labor Relations Act. . . . The court also held that federal labor legislation preempted the State's antitrust laws. . . . The Court of Appeals for the Fifth Circuit affirmed, 483 F. 2d 1154 (5th Cir. 1973), with one judge dissenting. It held that Local 100's goal of organizing nonunion subcontractors was a legitimate union interest and that its efforts toward that goal were therefore exempt from federal antitrust laws. On the second issue, it held that state law was preempted under San Diego Building Trades Council v. Garmon, 359 U.S. 236 (1959). We granted certiorari on Connell's petition. . . . We reverse on the question of federal antitrust immunity and affirm the ruling on state law preemption.

II. The basic sources of organized labor's exemption from federal antitrust laws are §§ 6 and 20 of the Clayton Act, . . . and the Norris-LaGuardia Act. . . . These statutes declare that labor unions are not combinations or conspiracies in restraint of trade, and exempt specific union activities, including secondary picketing and boycotts, from the operation of the antitrust laws. See United States v. Hutcheson, 312 U. S. 219 (1941). They do not exempt concerted action or agreements between unions and nonlabor parties. UMW v. Pennington, 381 U. S. 657, 662 (1965). The Court has recognized, however, that a proper accommodation between the congressional policy favoring collective bargaining under the NLRA and the congressional policy favoring free competition in business markets requires that some union-employer agreements be accorded a limited nonstatutory exemption from antitrust sanctions. Meat Cutters Local 189 v. Jewel Tea Co., 381 U.S. 676 (1965).

The nonstatutory exemption has its source in the strong labor policy favoring the association of employees to eliminate competition over wages and working conditions. Union success in organizing workers and standardizing wages ultimately will affect price competition among employers, but the goals of federal labor law never could be achieved if this effect on business competition were held a violation of the antitrust laws. The Court therefore has acknowledged that labor policy requires tolerance for the lessening of business competition based on differences in wages and working conditions. See UMW v. Pennington, *supra* at 666; Jewel Tea, *supra* at 692-693 (opinion of MR. JUSTICE WHITE). Labor policy clearly does not require, however, that a union have freedom to impose direct restraints on competition among those who employ its members. Thus, while the statutory exemption allows unions to accomplish some restraints by acting unilaterally, *e.g.,* American Federation of Musicians v. Carroll, 391 U. S. 99 (1968), the nonstatutory exemption offers no similar protection when a union and a nonlabor party agree to restrain competition in a business market. See Allen Bradley Co. v. IBEW Local

3, 325 U. S. 797, 806-811 (1945); Cox, Labor and the Antitrust Laws —
A Preliminary Analysis, 104 U. Pa. L. Rev. 252 (1955); Meltzer, Labor
Unions, Collective Bargaining, and the Antitrust Laws, 32 U. Chi. L. Rev.
659 (1965).

In this case Local 100 used direct restraints on the business market to
support its organizing campaign. The agreements with Connell and other
general contractors indiscriminately excluded nonunion subcontractors
from a portion of the market, even if their competitive advantages were
not derived from substandard wages and working conditions but rather
from more efficient operating methods. Curtailment of competition based
on efficiency is neither a goal of federal labor policy nor a necessary effect
of the elimination of competition among workers. Moreover, competition
based on efficiency is a positive value that the antitrust laws strive to
protect.

The multiemployer bargaining agreement between Local 100 and the
Association, though not challenged in this suit, is relevant in determining
the effect that the agreement between Local 100 and Connell would have
on the business market. The "most favored nation" clause in the
multiemployer agreement promised to eliminate competition between
members of the Association and any other subcontractors that Local 100
might organize. By giving members of the Association a contractual right
to insist on terms as favorable as those given any competitor, it guaranteed
that the union would make no agreement that would give an unaffiliated
contractor a competitive advantage over members of the Association.
Subcontractors in the Association thus stood to benefit from any
extension of Local 100's organization, but the method Local 100 chose
also had the effect of sheltering them from outside competition in that
portion of the market covered by subcontracting agreements between
general contractors and Local 100. In that portion of the market, the
restriction on subcontracting would eliminate competition on all subjects
covered by the multiemployer agreement, even on subjects unrelated to
wages, hours and working conditions.

Success in exacting agreements from general contractors would also
give Local 100 power to control access to the market for mechanical
subcontracting work. The agreements with general contractors did not
simply prohibit subcontracting to any nonunion firm; they prohibited
subcontracting to any firm that did not have a contract with Local 100.
The union thus had complete control over subcontract work offered by
general contractors that had signed these agreements. Such control could
result in significant adverse effects on the market and on consumers,
effects unrelated to the union's legitimate goals of organizing workers and
standardizing working conditions. For example, if the union thought the
interests of its members would be served by having fewer subcontractors
competing for the available work, it could refuse to sign collective
bargaining agreements with marginal firms. Cf. *UMW* v. *Pennington*,
supra. Or, since Local 100 has a well-defined geographical jurisdiction, it
could exclude "travelling" subcontractors by refusing to deal with them.
Local 100 thus might be able to create a geographical enclave for local
contractors, similar to the closed market in *Allen Bradley, supra.*

This record contains no evidence that the union's goal was anything other than organizing as many subcontractors as possible. This goal was legal, even though a successful organizing campaign ultimately would reduce the competition that unionized employers face from nonunion firms. But the methods the union chose are not immune from antitrust sanctions simply because the goal is legal. Here Local 100, by agreement with several contractors, made nonunion subcontractors ineligible to compete for a portion of the available work. This kind of direct restraint on the business market has substantial anticompetitive effects, both actual and potential, that would not follow naturally from the elimination of competition over wages and working conditions. It contravenes antitrust policies to a degree not justified by congressional labor policy, and therefore cannot claim a nonstatutory exemption from the antitrust laws.

There can be no argument in this case, whatever its force in other contexts, that a restraint of this magnitude might be entitled to an antitrust exemption if it were included in a lawful collective bargaining agreement. Cf. UMW v. Pennington, *supra* at 664-665; Jewel Tea, *supra* at 689-690 (opinion of MR. JUSTICE WHITE); *id.* at 709-713, 732-733 (opinion of MR. JUSTICE GOLDBERG). In this case, Local 100 had no interest in representing Connell's employees. The federal policy favoring collective bargaining therefore can offer no shelter for the union's coercive action against Connell or its campaign to exclude nonunion firms from the subcontracting market.

III. Local 100 nonetheless contends that the kind of agreement it obtained from Connell is explicitly allowed by the construction industry proviso to § 8(e) and that antitrust policy therefore must defer to the NLRA. The majority in the Court of Appeals declined to decide this issue, holding that it was subject to the "exclusive jurisdiction" of the NLRB. . . . This Court has held, however, that the federal courts may decide labor law questions that emerge as collateral issues in suits brought under independent federal remedies, including the antitrust laws. We conclude that § 8(e) does not allow this type of agreement. . . .

Section 8(e) was part of a legislative program designed to plug technical loopholes in § 8(b)(4)'s general prohibition of secondary activities. In § 8(e) Congress broadly proscribed using contractual agreements to achieve the economic coercion prohibited by § 8(b)(4). See *National Woodwork Manufacturers Assn.,* [386 U. S. 612] at 634. The provisos exempting the construction and garment industries were added by the Conference Committee in an apparent compromise between the House Bill, which prohibited all hot-cargo agreements, and the Senate Bill, which prohibited them only in the trucking industry. Although the garment industry proviso was supported by detailed explanations in both Houses, the construction industry proviso was explained only by bare references to "the pattern of collective bargaining" in the industry. It seems, however, to have been adopted as a partial substitute for an attempt to overrule this Court's decision in NLRB v. Denver Building & Construction Trades Council, 341 U. S. 675 (1951). Discussion of "special problems" in the construction industry, applicable to both the § 8(e) proviso and the attempt to overrule *Denver Building Trades,* focused on the problems of picketing a single nonunion subcontractor on a multiemployer building project, and the close relationship between contractors and subcontractors at the jobsite. Congress limited the construction industry proviso to that single situation, allowing subcontracting agreements only in relation to work done on a jobsite. In contrast to the latitude it provided in the garment industry proviso, Congress did not afford construction unions an exemption from § 8(b)(4)(B) or otherwise indicate that they were free to use subcontracting agreements as a broad organizational weapon. In keeping with these limitations, the Court has interpreted the construction industry proviso as

> "a measure to allow agreements pertaining to certain secondary activities on the construction site because of the close community of interests there, but to ban secondary-objective agreements concerning nonjobsite work, in which respect the construction industry is no different from any other." National Woodwork Manufacturers Assn., *supra* at 638-639 (footnote omitted)....

Local 100 does not suggest that its subcontracting agreement is related to any of these policies. It does not claim to be protecting Connell's employees from having to work alongside nonunion men. The agreement apparently was not designed to protect Local 100's members in that regard, since it was not limited to jobsites on which they were working. Moreover, the subcontracting restriction applied only to the work Local 100's members would perform themselves and allowed free subcontracting of all other work, thus leaving open a possibility that they would be employed alongside nonunion subcontractors. Nor was Local 100 trying to organize a nonunion subcontractor on the building project it picketed. The union admits that it sought the agreement solely as a way of pressuring mechanical subcontractors in the Dallas area to recognize it as the representative of their employees.

If we agree with Local 100 that the construction industry proviso authorizes subcontracting agreements with "stranger" contractors, not limited to any particular jobsite, our ruling would give construction unions an almost unlimited organizational weapon. The unions would be free to enlist any general contractor to bring economic pressure on nonunion subcontractors, as long as the agreement recited that it only covered work to be performed on some jobsite somewhere. The proviso's jobsite restriction then would serve only to prohibit agreements relating to subcontractors that deliver their work complete to the jobsite.

It is highly improbable that Congress intended such a result. One of the major aims of the 1959 Act was to limit "top-down" organizing campaigns, in which unions used economic weapons to force recognition from an employer regardless of the wishes of his employees. Congress accomplished this goal by enacting § 8(b)(7), which restricts primary recognitional picketing, and by further tightening § 8(b)(4)(B), which prohibits the use of most secondary tactics in organizational campaigns. Construction unions are fully covered by these sections. The only special consideration given them in organizational campaigns is § 8(f), which allows "prehire" agreements in the construction industry, but only under careful safeguards preserving workers' rights to decline union representation. The legislative history accompanying § 8(f) also suggests that Congress may not have intended that strikes or picketing could be used to extract prehire agreements from unwilling employers.

These careful limits on the economic pressure unions may use in aid of their organizational campaigns would be undermined seriously if the proviso to § 8(e) were construed to allow unions to seek subcontracting agreements, at large, from any general contractor vulnerable to picketing. Absent a clear indication that Congress intended to leave such a glaring loophole in its restrictions on "top-down" organizing, we are unwilling to read the construction industry proviso as broadly as Local 100 suggests. Instead, we think its authorization extends only to agreements in the context of collective bargaining relationships and, in light of congressional references to the *Denver Building Trades* problem, possibly to common-situs relationships on particular jobsites as well.

Finally, Local 100 contends that even if the subcontracting agreement is not sanctioned by the construction industry proviso and therefore is illegal under § 8(e), it cannot be the basis for antitrust liability because the remedies in the NLRA are exclusive. This argument is grounded in the legislative history of the 1947 Taft-Hartley amendments. Congress rejected attempts to regulate secondary activities by repealing the antitrust exemptions in the Clayton and Norris-LaGuardia Acts, and created special remedies under the labor law instead. It made secondary activities unfair labor practices under § 8(b)(4), and drafted special provisions for preliminary injunctions at the suit of the NLRB and for recovery of actual damages in the district courts. Sections 10(*l*), 303. . . . But whatever significance this legislative choice has for antitrust suits based on those secondary activities prohibited by § 8(b)(4), it has no relevance to the question whether Congress meant to preclude antitrust suits based on the "hot-cargo" agreements that it outlawed in 1959. There is no legislative history in the 1959 Congress suggesting that labor-law remedies for § 8(e) violations were intended to be exclusive, or that Congress thought allowing antitrust remedies in cases like the present one would be inconsistent with the remedial scheme of the NLRA.[16]

---

[16] The dissenting opinion of MR. JUSTICE STEWART argues that § 303 provides the exclusive remedy for violations of § 8(e), thereby precluding recourse to antitrust remedies. For that proposition the dissenting opinion relies upon "considerable evidence in the legislative materials.". . . In our view, these materials are unpersuasive. In the first place, Congress did not amend § 303 expressly to provide a remedy for violations of § 8(e). . . . The House in 1959 did reject proposals by Representatives Hiestand, Alger, and Hoffman to repeal labor's antitrust immunity. . . . Those proposals, however, were much broader than the issue in this case. The Hiestand-Alger proposal would have repealed antitrust immunity for any action in concert by two or more labor organizations. The Hoffman proposal apparently intended to repeal labor's antitrust immunity entirely. That the Congress rejected these extravagant proposals hardly furnishes proof that it intended to extend labor's antitrust immunity to include agreements with nonlabor parties, or that it thought antitrust liability under the existing statutes would be

We therefore hold that this agreement, which is outside the context of a collective bargaining relationship and not restricted to a particular jobsite, but which nonetheless obligates Connell to subcontract work only to firms that have a contract with Local 100, may be the basis of a federal antitrust suit because it has a potential for restraining competition in the business market in ways that would not follow naturally from elimination of competition over wages and working conditions.

IV. Although we hold that the union's agreement with Connell is subject to the federal antitrust laws, it does not follow that state antitrust law may apply as well. The Court has held repeatedly that federal law preempts state remedies that interfere with federal labor policy or with specific provisions of the NLRA. . . . The use of state antitrust law to regulate union activities in aid of organization must also be preempted because it creates a substantial risk of conflict with policies central to federal labor law.

In this area, the accommodation between federal labor and antitrust policy is delicate. Congress and this Court have carefully tailored the antitrust statutes to avoid conflict with the labor policy favoring lawful employee organization, not only by delineating exemptions from antitrust coverage but also by adjusting the scope of the antitrust remedies themselves. See Apex Hosiery Co. v. Leader, 310 U.S. 469 (1940). State antitrust laws generally have not been subjected to this process of accommodation. If they take account of labor goals at all, they may represent a totally different balance between labor and antitrust policies. Permitting state antitrust law to operate in this field could frustrate the basic federal policies favoring employee organization and allowing elimination of competition among wage earners, and interfere with the detailed system Congress has created for regulating organizational techniques.

Because employee organization is central to federal labor policy and regulation of organizational procedures is comprehensive, federal law does not admit the use of state antitrust law to regulate union activity that is closely related to organizational goals. Of course, other agreements between unions and nonlabor parties may yet be subject to state antitrust laws. See Teamsters Local 24 v. Oliver, *supra* at 295-297. The governing factor is the risk of conflict with the NLRA or with federal labor policy.

V. Neither the District Court nor the Court of Appeals decided whether the agreement between Local 100 and Connell, if subject to the antitrust laws, would constitute an agreement that restrains trade within the meaning of the Sherman Act. The issue was not briefed and argued fully in this Court. Accordingly, we remand for consideration whether the agreement violated the Sherman Act.[19]

Reversed in part and remanded.

---

inconsistent with the NLRA. The bill introduced by Senator McClellan two years later provides even less support for that proposition. Like most bills introduced in Congress, it never reached a vote.

[19] In addition to seeking a declaratory judgment that the agreement with Local 100 violated the antitrust laws, Connell sought a permanent injunction against further

Mr. Justice Douglas, dissenting.

While I join the opinion of Mr. Justice Stewart, I write to emphasize what is, for me, the determinative feature of the case. Throughout this litigation, Connell has maintained only that Local 100 coerced it into signing the subcontracting agreement. With the complaint so drawn, I have no difficulty in concluding that the union's conduct is regulated solely by the labor laws. The question of antitrust immunity would be far different, however, if it were alleged that Local 100 had conspired with mechanical subcontractors to force nonunion subcontractors from the market by entering into exclusionary agreements with general contractors like Connell. An arrangement of that character was condemned in Allen Bradley Co. v. Local 3, IBEW, 325 U. S. 797. . . . Were such a conspiracy alleged, the multiemployer bargaining agreement between Local 100 and the mechanical subcontractors would unquestionably be relevant. See United Mine Workers v. Pennington, 381 U. S. 657, 673 (concurring opinion); Meat Cutters v. Jewel Tea Co., 381 U. S. 676, 737 (dissenting opinion). . . .

Mr. Justice Stewart, with whom Mr. Justice Douglas, Mr. Justice Brennan, and Mr. Justice Marshall join, dissenting.

As part of its effort to organize mechanical contractors in the Dallas area, the respondent Local Union No. 100 engaged in peaceful picketing to induce the petitioner Connell Construction Co., a general contractor in the building and construction industry, to agree to subcontract plumbing and mechanical work at the construction site only to firms that had signed a collective bargaining agreement with Local 100. None of Connell's own employees were members of Local 100, and the subcontracting agreement contained the Union's express disavowal of any intent to organize or represent them. The picketing at Connell's construction site was therefore secondary activity, subject to detailed and comprehensive regulation pursuant to § 8(b)(4) of the National Labor Relations Act . . . and § 303 of the Labor Management Relations Act. . . . Similarly, the subcontracting agreement under which Connell agreed to cease doing business with nonunion mechanical contractors is governed

---

picketing to coerce execution of the contract in litigation. Connell obtained a temporary restraining order against the picketing on January 21, 1971, and thereafter executed the contract — under protest — with Local 100 on March 28, 1971. So far as the record in this case reveals, there has been no further picketing at Connell's construction sites. Accordingly, there is no occasion for us to consider whether the Norris-LaGuardia Act forbids such an injunction where the specific agreement sought by the union is illegal, or to determine whether, within the meaning of the Norris-LaGuardia Act, there was a "labor dispute" between these parties. If the Norris-LaGuardia Act were applicable to this picketing, injunctive relief would not be available under the antitrust laws. See United States v. Hutcheson, 312 U. S. 219 (1941). If the agreement in question is held on remand to be invalid under federal antitrust laws, we cannot anticipate that Local 100 will resume picketing to obtain or enforce an illegal agreement.

by the provisions of § 8(e) of the National Labor Relations Act. . . . The relevant legislative history unmistakably demonstrates that in regulating secondary activity and "hot cargo" agreements in 1947 and 1959, Congress selected with great care the sanctions to be imposed if proscribed union activity should occur. In so doing, Congress rejected efforts to give private parties injured by union activity such as that engaged in by Local 100 the right to seek relief under federal antitrust laws. Accordingly, I would affirm the judgment before us. . . .

II. Contrary to the assertion in the Court's opinion, *ante,* . . . the deliberate congressional decision to make § 303 the exclusive private remedy for unlawful secondary activity is clearly relevant to the question of Local 100's antitrust liability in the case before us. The Court is correct, of course, in noting that § 8(e)'s prohibition of "hot cargo" agreements was not added to the Act until 1959, and that § 303 was not then amended to cover § 8(e) violations standing alone. But as part of the 1959 amendments designed to close "technical loopholes" perceived in the Taft-Hartley Act, Congress amended § 8(b)(4) to make it an unfair labor practice for a labor organization to threaten or coerce a neutral employer, either directly or through his employees, where an object of the secondary pressure is to force the employer to enter into an agreement prohibited by § 8(e). At the same time, Congress expanded the scope of the § 303 damage remedy to allow recovery of the actual damages sustained as a result of a union engaging in secondary activity to force an employer to sign an agreement in violation of § 8(e). In short, Congress has provided an employer like Connell with a fully effective private damage remedy for the allegedly unlawful union conduct involved in this case.

The essence of Connell's complaint is that it was coerced by Local 100's picketing into "conspiring" with the union by signing an agreement that limited its ability to subcontract mechanical work on a competitive basis. If, as the Court today holds, the subcontracting agreement is not within the construction industry proviso to § 8(e), then Local 100's picketing to induce Connell to sign the agreement constituted a § 8(b)(4) unfair labor practice, and was therefore also unlawful under § 303(a)[8] . . . .

---

[8] If contrary to the Court's conclusion, see *ante,* at 9-16, Congress intended what it said in the proviso to § 8(e), then the subcontracting agreement is valid and, under the view of the Board and those courts of appeals that have considered the question, Local 100's picketing to obtain the agreement would also be lawful. . . . Connell would therefore have neither a remedy under § 303 nor one with the Board.

It would seem necessarily to follow that conduct specifically authorized by Congress in the National Labor Relations Act could not by itself be the basis for federal antitrust liability, unless the Court intends to return to the era when the judiciary frustrated congressional design by determining for itself "what public policy in regard to the industrial struggle demands." Duplex Printing Press Co. v. Deering, 245 U. S. 443, 485 (Brandeis, J., dissenting). See United States v. Hutcheson, 312 U. S. 219. In my view, however, even if Local 100's conduct was unlawful, Connell may not seek to invoke the sanctions of the antitrust laws. Accordingly, I find it unnecessary to decide in this case whether the subcontracting agreement entered into by Connell and Local 100 is within the ambit of the construction industry proviso to § 8(e), and if it is, whether it was permissible for Local 100 to utilize peaceful picketing to induce Connell to sign the agreement.

Accordingly, Connell has the right to sue Local 100 for damages sustained as a result of Local 100's unlawful secondary activity pursuant to § 303(b). . . . Although "limited to actual, compensatory damages," Local 20, Teamsters v. Morton, 377 U. S. at 260, Connell would be entitled under § 303 to recover all damages to its business that resulted from the union's coercive conduct, including any provable damage caused by Connell's inability to subcontract mechanical work to nonunion firms. Similarly, any nonunion mechanical contractor who believes his business has been harmed by Local 100 having coerced Connell into signing the subcontracting agreement is entitled to sue the union for compensatory damages; for § 303 broadly grants its damage action to "[w]hoever shall be injured in his business or property" by reason of a labor organization engaging in a § 8(b)(4) unfair labor practice.[9]

Moreover, there is considerable evidence in the legislative materials indicating that in expanding the scope of § 303 to include a remedy for secondary pressure designed to force an employer to sign an illegal "hot cargo" clause and in restricting the remedies for violation of § 8(e) itself to those available from the Board, Congress in 1959 made the same deliberate choice to exclude antitrust remedies as was made by the 1947 Congress. . . .

The Landrum-Griffin Bill, H. R. 8400, 86th Cong., 1st Sess., which, as amended, was enacted as the Labor-Management Reporting and Disclosure Act of 1959, by contrast, clearly provided that the new secondary boycott and "hot cargo" provisions were to be enforced solely through the Board and by use of the § 303 damage remedy. See 105 Cong. Rec. 14347-14348; II 1959 Leg. Hist. 1522-1523. Recognizing this important difference, Representative Alger proposed to amend the Landrum-Griffin Bill by adding, as an additional title, the antitrust provisions of H. R. 8003. 105 Cong. Rec. 15532-15533; II 1959 Leg. Hist. 1569. Representative Alger once again stated that his proposed amendment would make it unlawful for an individual local union to "[e]nter into any arrangement — voluntary or coerced — with any employer, groups of employers, or other unions which cause product boycotts, price fixing, or other types of restrictive trade practices." 105 Cong. Rec. 15533; II 1959 Leg. Hist. 1569.

Representative Griffin responded to Representative Alger's proposed amendment by observing that it

---

[9] If Connell and Local 100 had entered into a purely voluntary "hot cargo" agreement in violation of § 8(e), an injured nonunion mechanical subcontractor would have no § 303 remedy because the union would not have engaged in any § 8(b)(4) unfair labor practice. The subcontractor, however, would still be able to seek the full range of Board remedies available for a § 8(e) unfair labor practice. Moreover, if Connell had truly agreed to limit its subcontracting without any coercion whatsoever on the part of Local 100, the affected subcontractor might well have a valid antitrust claim on the ground that Local 100 and Connell were engaged in the type of conspiracy aimed at third parties with which this Court dealt in Allen Bradley Co. v. Local Union No. 3, 325 U. S. 797. . . .

"serves to point out that the substitute [the Landrum-Griffin Bill] is a minimum bill. It might be well at this point to mention some provisions that are not in it.

"There is no antitrust law provision in this bill." . . . 105 Cong. Rec. 15535; II 1959 Leg. Hist. 1571-1572.

The Alger amendment was rejected, as were additional efforts to subject proscribed union activities to the antitrust laws and their sanctions. See, *e.g.,* 105 Cong. Rec. 15853 (amendment offered by Rep. Hoffman); II 1959 Leg. Hist. 1685. The House then adopted the Landrum-Griffin Bill over protests that it "does not go far enough, that it needs more teeth, and that more teeth are going to come in the form of legislation to bring union activities under the antitrust laws." 105 Cong. Rec. 15858 (remarks of Rep. Alger); II 1959 Leg. Hist. 1690. . . .

The judicial imposition of "independent federal remedies" not intended by Congress, no less than the application of state law to union conduct that is either protected or prohibited by federal labor law, threatens "to upset the balance of power between labor and management expressed in our national labor policy." Local 20, Teamsters v. Morton, 377 U. S. at 260. . . .

NOTES

1. Is *Connell* consistent with *Jewel Tea* and earlier cases in the standard it uses for distinguishing between agreements properly concerned with wages, hours, and other components of the labor market, and agreements improperly concerned with the product market? Has the judiciary once again undertaken to weigh the workers' interests in their jobs against the public's interest in a competitive economy? Is such balancing necessarily bad?

2. Would the result have been different in *Connell* if the union's subcontracting clause had been part of a collective bargaining agreement with the employer? If it had been limited to particular job sites? If it had not been limited to one particular union? If two (or all three) of those conditions had been met? How might that have affected the anticompetitive thrust of the clause? *Compare* Larry V. Muko, Inc. v. Southwestern Pennsylvania Building & Constr. Trades Council, 99 L.R.R.M. 2001 (3d Cir. 1978), *with* Carpenters Local 944 (Woelke & Romero Framing), 239 N.L.R.B. No. 40, 99 L.R.R.M. 1580 (1978).

3. *See generally* Conway, *Broadening Labor's Antitrust Liability While Narrowing its Construction Industry Proviso Protection,* 27 CATH. U. L. REV. 305 (1978); Gold, *The "Logic" of the Connell Opinion,* in N.Y.U. TWENTY-NINTH ANNUAL CONFERENCE ON LABOR 25 (1976); Janofsky & Hay, *Connell — Consistent with the Past, Indicative of the Future, id.* at 3; St. Antoine, *Connell: Antitrust Law at the Expense of Labor Law,* 62 VA. L. REV. 603 (1976). *See also* Leslie, *Right to Control: A Study in Secondary Boycotts and Labor Antitrust,* 89 HARV. L. REV. 904 (1976).

SECTION III. The Enforcement of the Collective Agreement

ARCHIBALD COX, LAW AND THE NATIONAL LABOR POLICY 85 (1960)*

Unless the law is once again to fail to meet the needs of men, the principles determining legal rights and duties under collective bargaining agreements should not be imposed by the courts from above because of precepts learned in other contexts; the governing principles must be drawn out of the institutions of labor relations and shaped to their needs.

This is the way in which our commercial law developed. Two and a half centuries ago Lord Mansfield took the customs and practices of the world of commerce — the law merchant — and incorporated them into the common law administered by courts of general jurisdiction. Perhaps a modern Mansfield may again demonstrate the creative talent of the common law by drawing upon industrial jurisprudence.

A. THE LEGAL STATUS OF THE COLLECTIVE AGREEMENT

The expected outcome of the parties' fulfillment of their bargaining obligations is the execution of a collective labor agreement. Today there are an estimated 150,000 labor contracts in existence in the United States. Of these, however, a mere 620 agreements covering units of 2,000 or more employees account for five million out of the approximately eighteen million workers under union contract in the industries surveyed.[1] The national picture thus reflects a mixture of concentration and decentralization in bargaining and contract administration.

Until recent years collective agreements were seldom involved in litigation. About ninety-five percent provide their own grievance and arbitration procedure to resolve disputes over contract interpretation. Court actions have traditionally been regarded as detrimental to healthy labor-management relations in the plant. The paucity of suits for enforcement of collective agreements may be one of the reasons for the delayed and rather sketchy development of theories as to the nature of these instruments.

---

* Copyright © 1960. Reprinted by permission of the University of California, Los Angeles.

[1] U.S. BUREAU OF LABOR STATISTICS, DEP'T OF LABOR, BULL. NO. 1729, CHARACTERISTICS OF AGREEMENTS COVERING 2,000 WORKERS OR MORE 1, 4 (1972). Railroads, airlines, and government were excluded.

Included in the *Statutory Appendix* is a sample collective agreement. Although labor contracts vary so widely according to the nature, size, and complexity of the particular industry or company involved that no single agreement can be called typical, most of them cover relatively standard subjects. The sample agreement should be read thoroughly at this point in order to gain some acquaintance with its contents.

Early common law decisions advanced at least three separate theories to explain the legal nature of the collective agreement:

1. The labor agreement establishes local customs or usages, which are then incorporated into the individual employee's contract of hire. This seems to have been the orthodox view of the American courts, at least prior to the era of the labor relations acts.[2] Under the original form of this theory, the collective agreement itself was not regarded as a contract. It had legal effect only as its terms were absorbed into individual employment contracts.[3] Somewhat similar is the traditional English concept that collective agreements are merely "gentlemen's agreements" or moral obligations not enforceable by the courts.[4] Some American scholars also have voiced an occasional plea that court litigation over collective agreements should be rejected as detrimental to the parties' continuing relationship.[5] Nevertheless, judicial enforcement at the behest of either employers[6] or unions[7] became generally accepted in this country well before the passage of the LMRA in 1947 and was confirmed by that Act.

2. The collective agreement is a contract that is negotiated by the union as the agent for the employees, who become the principals on the agreement.[8] This so-called agency theory was adopted by a few courts that could not rationalize the enforceability of an instrument executed by an unincorporated association lacking juristic personality. Suits between individual employees and employers were maintainable, however, on the theory the union had merely served as the employees' agent in negotiations.

3. The collective agreement is a third party beneficiary contract, with the employer and union the mutual promisors and promisees, and with the employees the beneficiaries.[9] Despite arguable shortcomings (is the

---

[2] See Rice, *Collective Labor Agreements in American Law,* 44 HARV. L. REV. 572, 582 (1931).

[3] *E.g.,* Hudson v. Cincinnati, N.O. & Tex. Pac. Ry., 152 Ky. 711, 154 S.W. 47 (1913); Cross Mountain Coal Co. v. Ault, 157 Tenn. 461, 9 S.W.2d 692 (1928).

[4] Young v. Canadian N. Ry., [1931] A.C. 83 (P.C.); K. WEDDERBURN, THE WORKER AND THE LAW 105-11 (1965).

[5] See Shulman, *Reason, Contract, and Law in Labor Relations,* 68 HARV. L. REV. 999 (1955).

[6] Nederlandsch A.S.M. v. Stevedores' & Longshoremen's Benevolent Soc'y, 265 F. 397 (E.D. La. 1920); Greater City Master Plumbers Ass'n v. Kahme, 6 N.Y.S.2d 589 (Sup. Ct. N.Y. County 1937).

[7] Schlesinger v. Quinto, 201 App. Div. 487, 194 N.Y.S. 401 (1922); Harper v. IBEW Local 520, 48 S.W.2d 1033 (Tex. Civ. App. 1932).

[8] Barnes & Co. v. Berry, 169 F. 225 (6th Cir. 1909); Maisel v. Sigman, 123 Misc. 714, 205 N.Y.S. 807 (Sup. Ct. N.Y. County 1924).

[9] Marranzano v. Riggs Nat'l Bank, 184 F.2d 349 (D.C. Cir. 1950); Yazoo & Mississippi Valley R.R. v. Sideboard, 161 Miss. 4, 133 So. 669 (1931); H. Blum & Co. v. Landau, 23 Ohio App. 426, 155 N.E. 154 (1926).

employer to be left without recourse against the employee beneficiary, who has made no promises?), the third party beneficiary theory became rather widely accepted as the best explanation of the collective agreement in terms of traditional common law concepts.[10]

Today, collective bargaining agreements in industries affecting commerce are enforced as a matter of federal law under § 301 of the LMRA. This means that the Supreme Court's views on the nature of the labor contract are now of primary concern. Two characteristics of the Court's thinking stand out. First, the Court is eclectic in its approach to common law doctrines; it refuses to confine itself to any single theory, but draws upon whatever elements may be helpful in a variety of theories. Second, the Court has emphasized what may be described as the "constitutional" or "governmental" quality of the labor agreement. Thus, the collective agreement has been described as "not an ordinary contract" but rather a "generalized code" for "a system of industrial self-government."[11]

The Supreme Court's eclectic approach to the nature of the labor contract is reflected in the following well-known comments by Mr. Justice Jackson in J. I. Case Co. v. NLRB, 321 U.S. 332, 334-35 (1944): [12]

> Collective bargaining between employer and the representatives of a unit, usually a union, results in an accord as to terms which will govern hiring and work and pay in that unit. The result is not, however, a contract of employment except in rare cases; no one has a job by reason of it and no obligation to any individual ordinarily comes into existence from it alone. The negotiations between union and management result in what often has been called a trade agreement, rather than in a contract of employment. Without pushing the analogy too far, the agreement may be likened to the tariffs established by a carrier, to standard provisions prescribed by supervising authorities for insurance policies, or to utility schedules of rates and rules for service, which do not of themselves establish any relationships but which do govern the terms of the shipper or insurer or customer relationship whenever and with whomever it may be established. . . .
>
> [H]owever engaged, an employee becomes entitled by virtue of the Labor Relations Act somewhat as a third party beneficiary to all benefits of the collective trade agreement, even if on his own he would yield to less favorable terms. The individual hiring contract is subsidiary to the terms of the trade agreement and may not waive any of its benefits, any more than a shipper can contract away the benefit of filed tariffs, the insurer the benefit of standard provisions, or the utility customer the benefit of legally established rates.

---

[10] *See* C. GREGORY, LABOR AND THE LAW 447 (2d rev. ed. 1961).

[11] *See* John Wiley & Sons, Inc. v. Livingston, 376 U.S. 543, 550 (1964); United Steelworkers v. Warrior & Gulf Nav. Co., 363 U.S. 574, 578-80 (1960); Aeronautical Ind. Dist., Lodge 72 v. Campbell, 337 U.S. 521, 528 (1949).

[12] The principal portions of this case are set out in section I, *supra* at 486.

NOTE

Much has been written on the legal nature of the collective agreement, with most commentators noting its unique characteristics and the difficulties and dangers of adopting traditional doctrines developed in other areas of contract law. *See* Chamberlain, *Collective Bargaining and the Concept of Contract,* 48 COLUM. L. REV. 829 (1948); Cox, *The Legal Nature of Collective Bargaining Agreements,* 57 MICH. L. REV. 1 (1958); Feller, *A General Theory of the Collective Bargaining Agreement,* 61 CALIF. L. REV. 663 (1973); Gregory, *The Law of the Collective Agreement,* 57 MICH. L. REV. 635 (1959); Rice, *Collective Labor Agreements in American Law,* 44 HARV. L. REV. 572 (1931); Shulman, *Reason, Contract, and Law in Labor Relations,* 68 HARV. L. REV. 999 (1955); Summers, *Collective Agreements and the Law of Contracts,* 78 YALE L.J. 525 (1969).

B. THE ENFORCEMENT OF THE COLLECTIVE AGREEMENT THROUGH THE GRIEVANCE PROCEDURE AND ARBITRATION

LABOR STUDY GROUP, THE PUBLIC INTEREST IN NATIONAL LABOR POLICY 32 (Committee for Economic Development 1961)

A major achievement of collective bargaining, perhaps its most significant contribution to the American workplace, is the creation of a system of industrial jurisprudence, a system under which employer and employee rights are set forth in contractual form and disputes over the meaning of the contract are settled through a rational grievance process usually ending, in the case of unresolved disputes, with arbitration. The gains from this system are especially noteworthy because of their effect on the recognition and dignity of the individual worker. The system helps prevent arbitrary action on questions of discipline, layoff, promotion, and transfer, and sets up orderly procedures for the handling of grievances. Wildcat strikes and other disorderly means of protest have been curtailed and an effective work discipline generally established. In many situations, cooperative relationships marked by mutual respect between management and labor stand as an example of what can be done.

1. THE GRIEVANCE PROCEDURE

The great mass of day-to-day disputes arising during the term of a collective agreement are settled, in actual practice, through the procedure established and administered by the parties themselves. Where satisfactory industrial relations exist under collective bargaining, only a minute percentage of such disputes will even have to go to arbitration. And of those which do, it is extraordinary for the courts to get involved, either in compelling arbitration or in requiring compliance with awards. Since we will be dealing mostly with these exceptional cases, their relatively small role in the total industrial relations picture should be kept in proper perspective.

The grievance procedure is one of the most universal and important provisions in the collective agreement.[13] Virtually all (ninety-nine percent) of the 1,717 major contracts studied in a national survey included such a procedure.[14] It represents the acceptance in labor-management relations of the fundamental notions of due process, and of the virtues of an orderly method of adjusting disputes. The decisions rendered through the established procedure tend to become the industrial case law for the plant. The use of arbitration as the terminal step in the procedure has produced a mass of decisions through which an "industrial jurisprudence" is developing, outside the established judicial system, much as the rules governing negotiable instruments first evolved as part of the "law merchant," and the principles of unfair competition originated with the medieval merchant guilds. The negotiation and drafting of a procedure for handling grievances in a given plant or enterprise should be undertaken with a full appreciation of the significance of the task.

The principal questions to be decided in the formulation of a grievance procedure are the following:

1. What shall be considered as a "grievance"? Shall the procedure be available only to resolve disputes over the "interpretation or application" of the contract, or shall it be "open" in the sense that an employee or the union may make a complaint about matters not dealt with in the agreement? Shall the procedure be available to handle employer complaints against the union?

2. Shall arbitration be provided for as the terminal point in the procedure? If so, shall the jurisdiction of the arbitrator be restricted, even though the intra-plant phase is to be "open," so that he will be authorized to decide only questions arising under the contract?

3. What shall be the "steps," or appellate stages, in the procedure? The answer, of course, will depend in large part upon the size and complexity of the plant or operation involved.

4. What shall be the "rules" of procedure? Shall there be time limitations on the initial filing of the complaint (in the nature of a "statute of limitations"), on the handling of the complaint by the representative of the other party, or the resort to the next step in the procedure?

5. What shall be the relationship between the union and individual employees, and other in-plant unions, if any, with respect to the presentation and disposition of grievances?

2. VOLUNTARY ARBITRATION

Voluntary arbitration has been defined as a contractual proceeding whereby the parties to any dispute or controversy, in order to obtain a

---

[13] The grievance procedure has been referred to as the "core of the collective bargaining agreement." L. HILL & C. HOOK, MANAGEMENT AT THE BARGAINING TABLE 199 (1945). *See generally* N. CHAMBERLAIN & J. KUHN, COLLECTIVE BARGAINING 141-61 (2d ed. 1965); S. SLICHTER, J. HEALY & E. LIVERNASH, THE IMPACT OF COLLECTIVE BARGAINING ON MANAGEMENT 692-738 (1960).

[14] U.S. BUREAU OF LABOR STATISTICS, DEP'T OF LABOR, BULL. NO. 1425-1, MAJOR COLLECTIVE BARGAINING AGREEMENTS: GRIEVANCE PROCEDURES 1 (1964).

speedy and inexpensive final disposition of the matter involved, select a judge of their own choice and by consent submit their controversy to him for determination.[15] The Supreme Court has observed that while commercial arbitration is a substitute for litigation, labor arbitration is a substitute for industrial strife.[16] The increasing use in recent years of arbitration in the settlement of labor disputes is a strong indication of a higher degree of maturity in industrial relations. Of 1,717 major collective agreements analyzed in a recent study, for example, about ninety-four percent provided for the arbitration of grievances between the parties.[17] Today thousands of disputes are settled in voluntary arbitration proceedings without resort to economic pressure or appeals to the sympathy of the public.[18]

Probably the greatest stimulus toward the use of arbitration to settle industrial grievances was provided by the National War Labor Board during World War II. The Board was given power to settle most types of labor disputes, and it quite regularly ordered the inclusion of arbitration clauses in new contracts whenever the parties were not able to agree upon their grievance procedure. Although less than ten percent of the labor agreements in effect in the early 1930's provided for arbitration, by 1944 the figures had grown to seventy-three percent.[19] It is now agreed by an overwhelming majority of both union and management representatives that the good grievance procedure should have arbitration as the terminal point.[20]

The courts in this country have recognized the rights of employees and unions under collective bargaining agreements, but court procedures are ordinarily ill-adapted to the needs of modern labor-management relations, and in addition are costly, prolonged, and technical.[21] One significant deficiency of litigation as a solution to industrial disputes was described by Professor Harry Shulman in this way: "[L]itigation results in a victory, perhaps, results in a decision in any event, which disposes of the

---

[15] Gates v. Arizona Brewing Co., 54 Ariz. 266, 269, 95 P.2d 49 (1939). *See also* F. ELKOURI & E. ELKOURI, HOW ARBITRATION WORKS 1-2 (3d ed. 1973); C. UPDEGRAFF, ARBITRATION AND LABOR RELATIONS 3 (1971).

[16] United Steelworkers v. Warrior & Gulf Nav. Co., 363 U.S. 574, 578 (1960). For the view that labor arbitration is a substitute for both strikes and litigation ("but in the sense in which a transport airplane is a substitute for a stagecoach"), see Shulman, *Reason, Contract, and Law in Labor Relations,* 68 HARV. L. REV. 999, 1024 (1955).

[17] U.S. BUREAU OF LABOR STATISTICS, DEP'T OF LABOR, BULL. NO. 1425-6, MAJOR COLLECTIVE BARGAINING AGREEMENTS: ARBITRATION PROCEDURES 5 (1966).

[18] R. FLEMING, THE LABOR ARBITRATION PROCESS 27 (1965).

[19] S. SLICHTER, J. HEALY & E. LIVERNASH, THE IMPACT OF COLLECTIVE BARGAINING ON MANAGEMENT 739 (1960).

[20] Jones & Smith, *Management and Labor Appraisals and Criticisms of the Arbitration Process: A Report With Comments,* 62 MICH. L. REV. 1115, 1116-17 (1964).

[21] *E.g.,* F. ELKOURI & E. ELKOURI, HOW ARBITRATION WORKS 8 (3d ed. 1973); Freidin & Ulman, *Arbitration and the National War Labor Board,* 58 HARV. L. REV. 309 (1945).

particular controversy, but which does not affirmatively act to advance the parties' cooperative effort, which does not affirmatively act to affect their attitudes in their relations with one another. Arbitration can be made to do that." [22] Other advantages of arbitration include the saving of time, expense, and trouble. Arbitration permits self-regulation by business and labor, since it is a private rather than a governmental proceeding.

There are two distinct categories of labor-management arbitrations. One is the arbitration of disputes over the substantive terms to be included in a collective agreement. When parties fail to conclude a contract through the usual negotiating sessions, they may agree to break the deadlock by submitting the issues for determination by an arbitrator. This type of arbitration is sometimes called the arbitration of "interests." Today there is a fairly substantial amount of this kind of arbitration, especially by public utilities.[23] Only rarely, however, will unions and employers commit themselves in advance to the arbitration of a new contract by including a provision in their labor agreement that, upon its expiration, arbitration may be invoked to resolve disputes over the terms of a renewal. Less than two percent of the 1,717 major agreements in effect in the early 1960's contained such a provision.[24] This in part reflects a widespread belief that contract terms directed by a third party will often be unworkable or unrealistic, and that agreement of the parties themselves is ordinarily more effective.[25] Furthermore, an absence of definite standards in the arbitration of "interest" disputes is thought to make the arbitral task more difficult. Injudicious use of arbitration in contract negotiation disputes may also impede the development of mature labor-management relationships through collective bargaining. On the other hand, in Great Britain the arbitration of new contract terms is considerably more common than the arbitration of disputes arising under existing contracts.[26] The British apparently feel that outsiders are better equipped to deal with basic wage and hour issues of broad applicability than with individual grievances occurring in a particular local setting.

---

[22] Quoted in F. ELKOURI & E. ELKOURI, HOW ARBITRATION WORKS 7 (rev. ed. 1960).

[23] M. COPELOF, MANAGEMENT-UNION ARBITRATION 10-12 (1948); C. UPDEGRAFF & W. McCOY, ARBITRATION OF LABOR DISPUTES 149-50 (2d ed. 1961).

[24] U.S. BUREAU OF LABOR STATISTICS, *supra* note 17, at 95. "Interest" arbitration, agreed to in advance, received a big boost when the Steelworkers and the major steel producers agreed in 1973 to settle unresolved disputes about the terms of their 1974 contracts through final and binding arbitration. LABOR RELATIONS YEAR BOOK — 1973 pp. 32-37 (1974). *See also* Aksen, *The Impetus to Contract Arbitration in the Public Area,* in N.Y.U. TWENTY-FOURTH ANNUAL CONFERENCE ON LABOR 103 (1972); Feller, *The Impetus to Contract Arbitration in the Private Area,* in N.Y.U. TWENTY-FOURTH ANNUAL CONFERENCE ON LABOR 79 (1972); Fleming, *"Interest" Arbitration Revisited,* 7 U. MICH. J.L. REFORM 1 (1973); McAvoy, *Binding Arbitration of Contract Terms: A New Approach to the Resolution of Disputes in the Public Sector,* 72 COLUM. L. REV. 1192 (1972).

[25] F. ELKOURI & E. ELKOURI, HOW ARBITRATION WORKS 50-54 (3d ed. 1973); Davey, *Hazards in Labor Arbitration,* 1 IND. & LAB. REL. REV. 386, 396 (1948).

[26] I. SHARP, INDUSTRIAL CONCILIATION AND ARBITRATION IN GREAT BRITAIN 444 (1950); Gratch, *Grievance Settlement Machinery in England,* 12 LAB. L.J. 861, 863 (1961).

The task of the arbitrator in an arbitration of interests was well stated by arbitrator Whitley P. McCoy as follows:

> Arbitration of contract terms differs radically from arbitration of grievances. The latter calls for a judicial determination of existing contract rights; the former calls for a determination, upon considerations of policy, fairness, and expediency, of what the contract rights ought to be. In submitting this case to arbitration, the parties have merely extended their negotiations — they have left it to this board to determine what they should, by negotiation, have agreed upon. We take it that the fundamental inquiry, as to each issue, is: What should the parties themselves, as reasonable men, have voluntarily agreed to? [27]

The other main category of labor-management arbitration is that commonly known as "grievance" arbitration, or, in contradistinction to "interest" arbitration, as the arbitration of "rights." This is the type of arbitration that is customarily provided as the terminal point in contract grievance procedures. It deals with disputes arising during the life of an agreement. The function of the arbitrator in the arbitration of "rights" is quasi-judicial. The arbitrator interprets and applies the provisions of the contract; generally he is precluded from adding to or detracting from its terms. Nonetheless, over the years arbitrators have developed somewhat divergent attitudes about the proper approach to the collective agreement. Under a "residual rights" theory the employer retains sole discretion to make managerial decisions affecting employees except as limited, more or less expressly, by the contract.[28] Under an "implied limitations" theory a union may acquire certain rights as a matter of reasonable inference from different clauses or from the instrument as a whole.[29] Views also vary under both theories about the weight the arbitrator should give to past practice and bargaining history between the parties, or to notions of essential justice.[30]

---

[27] Twin City Rapid Transit Co., 7 LAB. ARB. REP. 845, 848 (1947).

[28] M. STONE, MANAGERIAL FREEDOM AND JOB SECURITY 5-7 (1964); Killingsworth, *Standards of Arbitral Decision: Jurisdiction,* in SUMMER INSTITUTE ON INTERNATIONAL AND COMPARATIVE LAW, UNIV. OF MICH. LAW SCHOOL, LECTURES ON THE LAW AND LABOR-MANAGEMENT RELATIONS 228, 230-31 (1951).

[29] *Id.;* Cox, *The Legal Nature of Collective Bargaining Agreements,* 57 MICH. L. REV. 1, 28-36 (1958); Wallen, *The Silent Contract vs. Express Provisions: The Arbitration of Local Working Conditions,* in NATIONAL ACADEMY OF ARBITRATORS, COLLECTIVE BARGAINING AND THE ARBITRATOR'S ROLE, PROCEEDINGS OF THE FIFTEENTH ANNUAL MEETING 117-47 (1962).

[30] *E.g.,* R. FLEMING, THE LABOR ARBITRATION PROCESS 134-98 (1965); Aaron, *The Uses of the Past in Arbitration,* in NATIONAL ACADEMY OF ARBITRATORS, ARBITRATION TODAY, PROCEEDINGS OF THE EIGHTH ANNUAL MEETING 1 (1955); Mittenthal, *Past Practice and the Administration of Collective Bargaining Agreements,* 59 MICH. L. REV. 1017 (1961); Wirtz, *Due Process of Arbitration,* in NATIONAL ACADEMY OF ARBITRATORS, THE ARBITRATOR AND THE PARTIES, PROCEEDINGS OF THE ELEVENTH ANNUAL MEETING 1 (1958).

Arbitration tribunals take several forms: temporary *(ad hoc)* or permanent arbitrators; tripartite boards, boards composed only of neutral or impartial members, or a single arbitrator.[31] Apart from private arrangements made by the parties directly with arbitrators, two important sources of *ad hoc* arbitrators are the American Arbitration Association and the Federal Mediation and Conciliation Service. Both maintain panels of qualified and available arbitrators. The parties then make a selection from lists supplied upon request by the AAA or the FMCS.

As arbitration has matured, it has suffered certain aging pains. Professor Harry T. Edwards has declared that the process has become "too slow and too expensive," with too much "uniformity" and "codification" and an overly "legalistic" approach to day-to-day problems. Thus, a normal case with a one-day hearing costs a union $2200; management will usually pay more. The average time from the filing of a grievance to the issuance of an award runs about two-thirds of a year. These problems may be aggravated by the reluctance of many parties to use new arbitrators. It is estimated that 90% of today's cases are being heard by 10% of the available arbitrators.[32]

3. ARBITRATION UNDER THE RAILWAY LABOR ACT

STATUTORY REFERENCES

RLA §§ 3-9

The Railway Labor Act creates special machinery to deal with the various kinds of labor disputes. The National Mediation Board functions as a mediating agency in what we have described as "interests" disputes, and the National Railroad Adjustment Board handles disputes concerning "rights." The Mediation Board has the responsibility, as to disputes within its cognizance which do not concern representation, first, to use its good offices in an attempt to secure an agreement between the parties, and, second, failing in such attempt, to induce the parties to submit their dispute to arbitration under the procedures of § 7 of the RLA.

Arbitration under § 7 is entirely voluntary, in that both parties must agree to submit an "interests" dispute to a board of arbitration. The board's award, however, is enforceable in federal district court.

Adjudication of grievance disputes or disputes concerning "rights" by the Adjustment Board under § 3 is voluntary in the sense that appeal to the Board is apparently optional. But if either party does refer the case,

---

[31] F. ELKOURI & E. ELKOURI, HOW ARBITRATION WORKS 68-87 (3d ed. 1973).
[32] LABOR RELATIONS YEAR BOOK — 1977 p. 206 (1978).

the Board's jurisdiction attaches and it is directed to dispose of the matter. Upon failure of the carrier to abide by an award an appeal may be made to the appropriate district court where the award will be enforced or set aside. In the district court, "the findings and order of the division of the Adjustment Board shall be conclusive on the parties," except for failure to comply with legal requirements or for fraud or corruption.

In setting up the National Railroad Adjustment Board, Congress proceeded on the basis of fifty years of experience with efforts to provide effective methods for settling labor disputes in the railroad industry. The Board is divided into four jurisdictional divisions, of which two have ten members each, one has eight, and the fourth has six. The members are appointed one-half by the carriers and one-half by the brotherhoods, and are compensated by the parties whom they represent. Because of the even division of members, deadlocks are common. In the event of deadlock, the division may select a referee, but if it fails to do so, the National Mediation Board designates the referee. The referee sits with the division as one of its members and hears the case. The award is written by the referee and must receive a majority vote, including the vote of the referee, for adoption by the division.

The airlines are covered by all the provisions of the Railway Labor Act except § 3. Title II of the Act provides for the establishment of special boards of adjustment and a four-member National Air Transport Adjustment Board to handle grievances and disputes between air carriers and their employees over the interpretation or application of the parties' agreements. The powers and duties of the National Air Transport Adjustment Board are generally similar to those of the National Railroad Adjustment Board.

NOTE

The last three decades have produced a torrent of writing on labor arbitration. Works emphasizing the legal problems of arbitration, including its relationship to the courts and the NLRB, will be cited in the sections to follow which deal with the various questions of law. At this point attention will be paid to books and articles concentrating on the practice and procedure of arbitration itself.

Much valuable material on the operation of voluntary labor arbitration is contained in the *Annual Proceedings* of the National Academy of Arbitrators, published by the Bureau of National Affairs. (The National Academy is the professional association of labor arbitrators.) A useful periodical is the American Arbitration Association's *Arbitration Journal.* Texts of selected arbitration awards are published in BNA's *Labor Arbitration Reports,* CCH's *Labor Arbitration Awards,* and Prentice-Hall's *Labor Arbitration Service,* looseleaf services with bound cumulations. General studies of arbitration include F. ELKOURI & E. ELKOURI, HOW ARBITRATION WORKS (3d ed. 1973); O. FAIRWEATHER, PRACTICE AND PROCEDURE IN LABOR ARBITRATION (1973); R. FLEMING, THE LABOR ARBITRATION PROCESS (1965); P. HAYS, LABOR ARBITRATION: A

DISSENTING VIEW (1966); M. TROTTA, ARBITRATION OF LABOR-MANAGEMENT DISPUTES (1974); C. UPDEGRAFF, ARBITRATION AND LABOR RELATIONS (1971). The developing "substantive law" of arbitral decisions is discussed in W. BAER, DISCIPLINE AND DISCHARGE UNDER THE LABOR AGREEMENT (1972); L. STESSIN, EMPLOYEE DISCIPLINE (1960); M. STONE, LABOR-MANAGEMENT CONTRACTS AT WORK (1961); M. STONE, MANAGERIAL FREEDOM AND JOB SECURITY (1964).

Some of the many notable articles on arbitration are Aaron, *Some Procedural Problems in Arbitration,* 10 VAND. L. REV. 733 (1957); Abrams, *The Integrity of the Arbitral Process,* 76 MICH. L. REV. 231 (1977); Bailer, Lurie & O'Connell, *Arbitration Procedure and Practice,* in N.Y.U. FIFTEENTH ANNUAL CONFERENCE ON LABOR 331, 341, 349 (1962) (three separate papers); Davey, *Arbitration as a Substitute for Other Legal Remedies,* 23 LAB. L.J. 595 (1972); Edwards, *Due Process Considerations in Labor Arbitration,* 25 ARB. J. 141 (1970); Fleming, *Reflections on the Nature of Labor Arbitration,* 61 MICH. L. REV. 1245 (1963); Fuller, *Collective Bargaining and the Arbitrator,* 1963 WIS. L. REV. 1; Jones, *Evidentiary Concepts in Labor Arbitration: Some Modern Variations on Ancient Legal Themes,* 13 U.C.L.A. L. REV. 1241 (1966); Jones & Smith, *Management and Labor Appraisals and Criticisms of the Arbitration Process: A Report With Comments,* 62 MICH. L. REV. 1115 (1964); Roberts, Waldman, Morris & Simon, *Arbitration in a State of Flux,* in N.Y.U. TWENTY-NINTH ANNUAL CONFERENCE ON LABOR 277, 279, 297, 317 (1976) (four separate papers); Seward, *Arbitration and the Functions of Management,* 16 IND. & LAB. REL. REV. 235 (1963).

On the resolution of disputes under the Railway Labor Act, see Kroner, *Minor Disputes Under the Railway Labor Act: A Critical Appraisal,* 37 N.Y.U.L. REV. 41 (1962); Larson, *Collective Bargaining Under the Railway Labor Act,* in SOUTHWESTERN LEGAL FOUNDATION, LABOR LAW DEVELOPMENTS, PROCEEDINGS OF THE ELEVENTH ANNUAL INSTITUTE ON LABOR LAW 179 (1965); Mangum, *Grievance Procedures for Railroad Operating Employees,* 15 IND. & LAB. REL. REV. 474 (1962); C. REHMUS, ED., THE RAILWAY LABOR ACT AT FIFTY: COLLECTIVE BARGAINING IN THE RAILROAD AND AIRLINE INDUSTRIES (1976).

C. JUDICIAL ENFORCEMENT OF THE COLLECTIVE AGREEMENT

1. THE ENFORCEMENT OF VOLUNTARY ARBITRATION AGREEMENTS

(a) At Common Law

In many states voluntary arbitration may be conducted under either statutory or common law rules.[33] Most arbitrations are in fact conducted

---

[33] *See generally* F. ELKOURI & E. ELKOURI, HOW ARBITRATION WORKS 35-41 (3d ed. 1973); C. UPDEGRAFF, ARBITRATION AND LABOR RELATIONS 23-26 (1971). Although it is

outside the statute (if any), with common law principles governing the proceedings. In any event, since state arbitration statutes are often very general in nature, their details must be filled in by resort to the common law. The basic principles of common law arbitration have been summarized by the United States Department of Labor as follows:

> Common law arbitration rests upon the voluntary agreement of the parties to submit their dispute to an outsider. The submission agreement may be oral and may be revoked at any time before the rendering of the award. The tribunal, permanent or temporary, may be composed of any number of arbitrators. They must be free from bias and interest in the subject matter, and may not be related by affinity or consanguinity to either party. The arbitrators need not be sworn. Only existing disputes may be submitted to them. The parties must be given notice of hearings and are entitled to be present when all the evidence is received. The arbitrators have no power to subpoena witnesses or records and need not conform to legal rules of hearing procedure other than to give the parties an opportunity to present all competent evidence. All arbitrators must attend the hearings, consider the evidence jointly and arrive at an award by a unanimous vote. The award may be oral, but if written, all the arbitrators must sign it. It must dispose of every substantial issue submitted to arbitration. An award may be set aside only for fraud, misconduct, gross mistake, or substantial breach of a common law rule. The only method of enforcing the common law award is to file suit upon it and the judgment thus obtained may be enforced as any other judgment.[34]

The common law rule that an agreement to arbitrate future disputes will not be enforced by the courts and is revocable at will by either party was accepted until recently in the majority of American jurisdictions.[35] The National War Labor Board, however, consistently rejected the outmoded common law view that arbitration is to be regarded with hostility as an attempt to supplant the courts. Instead, the Board took the position that agreements for arbitration should be favored and aid given to their enforcement.[36]

---

usually held that the statute supplements and does not abrogate the common law, at least one state, Washington, has declared that its statute completely supersedes the common-law rules. Puget Sound Bridge & Dredging Co. v. Lake Washington Shipyards, 1 Wash. 2d 401, 96 P.2d 257 (1939).

[34] D. ZISKIND, LABOR ARBITRATION UNDER STATE STATUTES 3 (U.S. Dep't of Labor 1943).

[35] Gregory & Orlikoff, *The Enforcement of Labor Arbitration Agreements,* 17 U. CHI. L. REV. 233, 254 (1950).

[36] Freidin & Ulman, *Arbitration and National War Labor Board,* 58 HARV. L. REV. 309, 315 (1945).

(b) State Arbitration Statutes

State arbitration statutes are of three general kinds: (1) general statutes used principally in commercial disputes but often adaptable, with some limitations, to labor disputes; (2) statutes designed specifically for labor disputes, and prescribing the arbitration procedure in some detail; and (3) statutes which merely "promote" arbitration by directing state officials to encourage its use.[37] Massachusetts and Michigan are examples of states having special labor arbitration statutes; New York, on the other hand, simply made its general arbitration statute applicable to labor cases.[38] The usual effect of these statutes is to alter the common law rule by making agreements to arbitrate existing and future disputes valid and enforceable.

In 1955 the Conference of Commissioners on Uniform State Laws promulgated a proposed Uniform Arbitration Act, patterned after the New York Act, which would apply to labor-management agreements to arbitrate. By 1978 twenty-one states had adopted the act, but several excepted collective agreements from its coverage.[39]

The application of federal substantive law under § 301 of the Taft-Hartley Act to union-employer arbitration agreements will make state legislation largely inoperative in industries affecting commerce. State enactments may retain some significance, however, as to procedural matters and as guides in the shaping of the federal law.[40]

(c) Section 301 of the Labor Management Relations Act

TEXTILE WORKERS UNION v. LINCOLN MILLS

Supreme Court of the United States
353 U.S. 448, 77 S. Ct. 912, 1 L. Ed. 2d 972 (1957)

MR. JUSTICE DOUGLAS delivered the opinion of the Court.

Petitioner-union entered into a collective bargaining agreement in 1953 with respondent-employer, the agreement to run one year and from year to year thereafter, unless terminated on specified notices. The agreement

---

[37] D. ZISKIND, LABOR ARBITRATION UNDER STATE STATUTES 2-3 (U.S. Dep't of Labor 1943).

[38] MASS. ANN. LAWS ch. 150C, §§ 1-16 (1976); MICH. COMP. LAWS ANN. § 423.9d (1978); N.Y. CIV. PRAC. LAW § 7501 (McKinney 1963), replacing N.Y. CIV. PRAC. ACT § 1448.

[39] 7 UNIFORM LAWS ANN. 1 (1978).

[40] Smith & Clark, *Reappraisal of the Role of the States in Shaping Labor Relations Law,* 1965 WIS. L. REV. 411, 456. *See also* Comment, *The Applicability of State Arbitration Statutes to Proceedings Subject to LMRA Section 301,* 27 OHIO ST. L.J. 692 (1966).

provided that there would be no strikes or work stoppages and that grievances would be handled pursuant to a specified procedure. The last step in the grievance procedure — a step that could be taken by either party — was arbitration.

This controversy involves several grievances that concern work loads and work assignments. The grievances were processed through the various steps in the grievance procedure and were finally denied by the employer. The union requested arbitration, and the employer refused. Thereupon the union brought this suit in the District Court to compel arbitration.

The District Court concluded that it had jurisdiction and ordered the employer to comply with the grievance arbitration provisions of the collective bargaining agreement. The Court of Appeals reversed by a divided vote. 230 F.2d 81. . . .

The starting point of our inquiry is § 301 of the Labor Management Relations Act of 1947. . . .

There has been considerable litigation involving § 301 and courts have construed it differently. There is one view that § 301(a) merely gives federal district courts jurisdiction in controversies that involve labor organizations in industries affecting commerce, without regard to diversity of citizenship or the amount in controversy. Under that view § 301(a) would not be the source of substantive law; it would neither supply federal law to resolve these controversies nor turn the federal judges to state law for answers to the questions. Other courts — the overwhelming number of them — hold that § 301(a) is more than jurisdictional — that it authorizes federal courts to fashion a body of federal law for the enforcement of these collective bargaining agreements and includes within that federal law specific performance of promises to arbitrate grievances under collective bargaining agreements. Perhaps the leading decision representing that point of view is the one rendered by Judge Wyzanski in Textile Workers Union v. American Thread Co., 113 F. Supp. 137 (1953). That is our construction of § 301(a), which means that the agreement to arbitrate grievance disputes, contained in this collective bargaining agreement, should be specifically enforced.

From the face of the Act it is apparent that § 301(a) and § 301(b) supplement one another. Section 301(b) makes it possible for a labor organization, representing employees in an industry affecting commerce, to sue and be sued as an entity in the federal courts. Section 301(b) in other words provides the procedural remedy lacking at common law. Section 301(a) certainly does something more than that. Plainly, it supplies the basis upon which the federal district courts may take jurisdiction and apply the procedural rule of § 301(b). The question is whether § 301(a) is more than jurisdictional.

The legislative history of § 301 is somewhat cloudy and confusing. But there are a few shafts of light that illuminate our problem.

The bills, as they passed the House and the Senate, contained provisions which would have made the failure to abide by an agreement to arbitrate an unfair labor practice. S. Rep. No. 105, 80th Cong., 1st Sess., pp. 20-21, 23; H.R. Rep. No. 245, 80th Cong., 1st Sess., p. 21. This feature of the law was dropped in Conference. As the Conference Report stated, "Once parties have made a collective bargaining contract, the enforcement of that contract should be left to the usual processes of the law and not to the National Labor Relations Board." H.R. Conf. Rep. No. 510, 80th Cong., 1st Sess., p. 42.

Both the Senate and the House took pains to provide for "the usual processes of the law" by provisions which were the substantial equivalent of § 301(a) in its present form. Both the Senate Report and the House Report indicate a primary concern that unions as well as employees should be bound to collective bargaining contracts. But there was also a broader concern — a concern with a procedure for making such agreements enforceable in the courts by either party. At one point the Senate Report, *supra* at 15, states, "We feel that the aggrieved party should also have a right of action in the Federal courts. Such a policy is completely in accord with the purpose of the Wagner Act which the Supreme Court declared was 'to compel employers to bargain collectively with their employees to the end that an employment contract, binding on both parties, should be made. . . .' "

Congress was also interested in promoting collective bargaining that ended with agreements not to strike. . . .

Thus collective bargaining contracts were made "equally binding and enforceable on both parties." *Id.* at 15. As stated in the House Report, *supra* at 6, the new provision "makes labor organizations equally responsible with employers for contract violations and provides for suit by either against the other in the United States district courts." To repeat, the Senate Report, *supra* at 17, summed up the philosophy of § 301 as follows: "Statutory recognition of the collective agreement as a valid, binding, and enforceable contract is a logical and necessary step. It will promote a higher degree of responsibility upon the parties to such agreements, and will thereby promote industrial peace."

Plainly the agreement to arbitrate grievance disputes is the *quid pro quo* for an agreement not to strike. Viewed in this light, the legislation does more than confer jurisdiction in the federal courts over labor organizations. It expresses a federal policy that federal courts should enforce these agreements on behalf of or against labor organizations and that industrial peace can be best obtained only in that way.

To be sure there is a great medley of ideas reflected in the hearings, reports, and debates on this Act. Yet, to repeat, the entire tenor of the history indicates that the agreement to arbitrate grievance disputes was considered as *quid pro quo* of a no strike agreement. And when in the House the debate narrowed to the question whether § 301 was more than jurisdictional, it became abundantly clear that the purpose of the section was to provide the necessary legal remedies. Section 302 of the House bill, the substantial equivalent of the present § 301, was being described by Mr. Hartley, the sponsor of the bill in the House:

"Mr. Barden. Mr. Chairman, I take this time for the purpose of asking the Chairman a question, and in asking the question I want it understood that it is intended to make a part of the record that may hereafter be referred to as history of the legislation.

"It is my understanding that Section 302, the section dealing with equal responsibility under collective bargaining contracts in strike actions and proceedings in district courts contemplates not only the ordinary lawsuits for damages but also such other remedial proceedings, both legal and equitable, as might be appropriate in the circumstances; in other words, proceedings could, for example, be brought by the employers, the labor organizations, or interested individual employees under the Declaratory Judgments Act in order to secure declarations from the Court of legal rights under the contract.

"Mr. Hartley. The interpretation the gentlemen has just given of that section is absolutely correct." 93 Cong. Rec. 3656-3657.

It seems, therefore, clear to us that Congress adopted a policy which placed sanctions behind agreements to arbitrate grievance disputes,[6] by implication rejecting the common law rule discussed in Red Cross Line v. Atlantic Fruit Co., 264 U.S. 109 (1924), against enforcement of executory agreements to arbitrate. We would undercut the Act and defeat its policy if we read § 301 narrowly as only conferring jurisdiction over labor organizations.

The question then is, what is the substantive law to be applied in suits under § 301(a)? We conclude that the substantive law to apply in suits under § 301(a) is federal law which the courts must fashion from the policy of our national labor laws. See Mendelsohn, Enforceability of Arbitration Agreements Under Taft-Hartley Section 301, 66 Yale L.J. 167. The Labor Management Relations Act expressly furnishes some substantive law. It points out what the parties may or may not do in certain situations. Other problems will lie in the penumbra of express statutory mandates. Some will lack express statutory sanction but will be solved by looking at the policy of the legislation and fashioning a remedy that will effectuate that policy. The range of judicial inventiveness will be determined by the nature of the problem. See Board of Commissioners v. United States, 308 U.S. 343, 351 (1939). Federal interpretation of the federal law will govern, not state law. Cf. Jerome v. United States, 318 U.S. 101, 104 (1943). But state law, if compatible with the purpose of § 301, may be resorted to in order to find the rule that will best effectuate the federal policy. See Board of Commissioners v. United States, *supra* at 351-352. Any state law applied, however, will be absorbed as federal law and will not be an independent source of private rights.

---

[6] Association of Westinghouse Salaried Employees v. Westinghouse Corp., 348 U.S. 437 (1955), is quite a different case. There the union sued to recover unpaid wages on behalf of some 4,000 employees. The basic question concerned the standing of the union to sue and recover on those individual employment contracts. The question here concerns the right of the union to enforce the agreement to arbitrate which it has made with the employer.

It is not uncommon for federal courts to fashion federal law where federal rights are concerned. See Clearfield Trust Co. v. United States, 318 U.S. 363, 366-367 (1943); National Metropolitan Bank v. United States, 323 U.S. 454 (1945). Congress has indicated by § 301(a) the purpose to follow that course here. There is no constitutional difficulty. Article III, § 2 extends the judicial power to cases "arising under . . . the Laws of the United States. . . ." The power of Congress to regulate these labor-management controversies under the Commerce Clause is plain. Houston Texas R. Co. v. United States, 234 U.S. 342 (1914); NLRB v. Jones & Laughlin Corp., 301 U.S. 1 (1936). A case or controversy arising under § 301(a) is, therefore, one within the purview of judicial power as defined in Article III.

The question remains whether jurisdiction to compel arbitration of grievance disputes is withdrawn by the Norris-La Guardia Act. . . . Section 7 of that Act prescribes stiff procedural requirements for issuing an injunction in a labor dispute. The kinds of acts which had given rise to abuse of the power to enjoin are listed in § 4. The failure to arbitrate was not a part and parcel of the abuses against which the Act was aimed. Section 8 of the Norris-La Guardia Act does, indeed, indicate a congressional policy toward settlement of labor disputes by arbitration, for it denies injunctive relief to any person who has failed to make "every reasonable effort" to settle the dispute by negotiation, mediation, or "voluntary arbitration." Though a literal reading might bring the dispute within the terms of the Act (see Cox, Grievance Arbitration in the Federal Courts, 67 Harv. L. Rev. 591, 602-604), we see no justification in policy for restricting § 301(a) to damage suits, leaving specific performance of a contract to arbitrate grievance disputes to the inapposite procedural requirements of that Act. Moreover, we held in Virginian R. Co. v. System Federation, 300 U.S. 515 (1937), and in Graham v. Brotherhood of Firemen, 338 U.S. 232, 237 (1949), that the Norris-La Guardia Act does not deprive Federal courts of jurisdiction to compel compliance with the mandates of the Railway Labor Act. . . . The mandates there involved concerned racial discrimination. Yet those decisions were not based on any peculiarities of the Railway Labor Act. We followed the same course in Syres v. Oil Workers, 350 U.S. 892 (1955), which was governed by the National Labor Relations Act. . . . There an injunction was sought against racial discrimination in application of a collective bargaining agreement; and we allowed the injunction to issue. The congressional policy in favor of the enforcement of agreements to arbitrate grievance disputes being clear, there is no reason to submit them to the requirements of § 7 of the Norris-La Guardia Act. . . .

Reversed.

MR. JUSTICE BLACK took no part in the consideration or decision of this case.

MR. JUSTICE BURTON, whom MR. JUSTICE HARLAN joins, concurring in the result.

This suit was brought in a United States District Court under § 301 of the Labor Management Relations Act of 1947, ... seeking specific enforcement of the arbitration provisions of a collective bargaining contract. The District Court had jurisdiction over the action since it involved an obligation running to a union — a union controversy — and not uniquely personal rights of employees sought to be enforced by a union. Cf. Association of Westinghouse Salaried Employees v. Westinghouse Elec. Corp., 348 U.S. 437 (1955). Having jurisdiction over the suit, the court was not powerless to fashion an appropriate federal remedy. The power to decree specific performance of a collectively bargained agreement to arbitrate finds its source in § 301 itself, and in a Federal District Court's inherent equitable powers, nurtured by a congressional policy to encourage and enforce labor arbitration in industries affecting commerce.

I do not subscribe to the conclusion of the Court that the substantive law to be applied in a suit under § 301 is federal law. At the same time, I agree with Judge Magruder in International Brotherhood v. W. L. Mead, Inc., 230 F.2d 576 (1st Cir. 1956), that some federal rights may necessarily be involved in a § 301 case, and hence that the constitutionality of § 301 can be upheld as a congressional grant to Federal District Courts of what has been called "protective jurisdiction."

[MR. JUSTICE FRANKFURTER dissented in a rather unusual 86-page opinion, including the entire relevant legislative history of § 301 of the Taft-Hartley Act and its predecessor bill, the Case bill, in order to prove the point which he had made in *Westinghouse* — that § 301 did not create substantive rights but was only procedural.]

NOTES

1. In Association of Westinghouse Salaried Employees v. Westinghouse Elec. Corp., 348 U.S. 437 (1955), the Supreme Court avoided the constitutional question reached and decided in *Lincoln Mills* by holding that § 301 was not intended to authorize a union to sue on behalf of employees for accrued wage claims, which were described as "uniquely personal rights." Five years after *Lincoln Mills,* in Smith v. Evening News Ass'n, 371 U.S. 195, 199 (1962), *infra* at 720, the Court declared that *Westinghouse* was "no longer authoritative as a precedent." The lower federal courts have accordingly allowed unions to maintain actions to enforce the rights of employees in a distribution of the assets of a negotiated pension fund, UAW v. Textron, Inc., 312 F.2d 688 (6th Cir. 1963), and to secure for employees wages due under a cost-of-living adjustment clause in a labor contract, Retail Clerks Local 1222 v. Alfred Lewis, Inc., 327 F.2d 442 (9th Cir. 1964). *See* UAW v. Hoosier Cardinal Corp., 383 U.S. 696, 699-700 (1966). In *Hoosier Cardinal* the Supreme Court also held that § 301 suits are governed by state statutes of limitations.

2. The scholarly outpouring generated by *Lincoln Mills* includes Aaron, *On First Looking Into the Lincoln Mills Decision,* in NATIONAL

ACADEMY OF ARBITRATORS, ARBITRATION AND THE LAW, PROCEEDINGS OF THE TWELFTH ANNUAL MEETING 1 (1959); Bickel & Wellington, *Legislative Purpose and the Judicial Process: The Lincoln Mills Case*, 71 HARV. L. REV. 1 (1957); Cox, *Reflections Upon Labor Arbitration*, 72 HARV. L. REV. 1482 (1959); Feinsinger, *Enforcement of Labor Agreements — A New Era in Collective Bargaining*, 43 VA. L. REV. 1261 (1957); Gregory, *The Law of the Collective Agreement*, 57 MICH. L. REV. 635 (1959).

RETAIL CLERKS, LOCALS 128 & 633 v. LION DRY GOODS, INC., 369 U.S. 17, 82 S. Ct. 541, 7 L. Ed. 2d 503 (1962). The union and the employers settled a long strike with a "statement of understanding" in which the union conceded it was not then a majority representative entitled to exclusive recognition. The employers agreed to continue wage schedules and other working conditions in effect, and to arbitrate grievances arising under the statement. Subsequently, the employers refused to abide by arbitration awards disposing of two grievances in favor of the union. The union sued for enforcement under § 301. The employers argued the strike settlement agreement was not a "contract" within the meaning of the statute. On certiorari, the Supreme Court held that the union's action could be maintained under § 301 since "[a] federal forum was provided for actions on other labor contracts besides collective bargaining contracts." Section 301 speaks of "contracts," not collective agreements, the Court observed, and the settlement agreement was a contract, even if not a collective agreement. In addition, the Court held that § 301 was not limited to suits by majority representatives but extended to actions on the legitimate agreements of minority unions.

NOTE

Would § 301 support a suit to enforce an agreement to arbitrate the terms of a new contract? *Compare* Boston Printing Pressmen's Union v. Potter Press, 141 F. Supp. 553 (D. Mass. 1956), *aff'd*, 241 F. 2d 787 (1st Cir. 1957), *cert. denied*, 355 U.S. 817 (1957) ("No"), *with* Builders Ass'n of Kansas City v. Kansas City Laborers, 326 F. 2d 867 (8th Cir. 1964), *cert. denied*, 377 U.S. 917 (1964), *and* Pressmen's Local 50 v. Newspaper Printing Corp., 399 F. Supp. 593 (M.D. Tenn. 1974), *aff'd*, 518 F. 2d 351 (6th Cir. 1975). *See also* Young, *Arbitration of Terms for New Labor Contracts*, 17 W. RES. L. REV. 1302 (1966); Note, *The Enforceability of the No-Strike and Interest Arbitration Provisions of the Experimental Negotiating Agreement in Federal Courts*, 12 VALPARAISO U.L. REV. 57 (1977).

UNITED STEELWORKERS v. WARRIOR & GULF NAVIGATION CO.

Supreme Court of the United States
363 U.S. 574, 80 S. Ct. 1347, 4 L. Ed. 2d 1409 (1960)

MR. JUSTICE DOUGLAS delivered the opinion of the Court.

Respondent transports steel and steel products by barge and maintains a terminal at Chickasaw, Alabama, where it performs maintenance and repair work on its barges. The employees at that terminal constitute a bargaining unit covered by a collective bargaining agreement negotiated by petitioner union. Respondent between 1956 and 1958 laid off some employees, reducing the bargaining unit from 42 to 23 men. This reduction was due in part to respondent contracting maintenance work, previously done by its employees, to other companies. The latter used respondent's supervisors to lay out the work and hired some of the laid-off employees of respondent (at reduced wages). Some were in fact assigned to work on respondent's barges. A number of employees signed a grievance which petitioner presented to respondent, the grievance reading:

"We are hereby protesting the Company's actions, of arbitrarily and unreasonably contracting out work to other concerns, that could and previously has been performed by Company employees.

"This practice becomes unreasonable, unjust and discriminatory in lieu [*sic*] of the fact that at present there are a number of employees that have been laid off for about 1 and ½ years or more for allegedly lack of work.

"Confronted with these facts we charge that the Company is in violation of the contract by inducing a partial lockout, of a number of the employees who would otherwise be working were it not for this unfair practice."

The collective agreement had both a "no strike" and a "no lockout" provision. It also had a grievance procedure which provided in relevant part as follows:

"Issues which conflict with any Federal statute in its application as established by Court procedure or matters which are strictly a function of management shall not be subject to arbitration under this section.

"Should differences arise between the Company and the Union or its members employed by the Company as to the meaning and application of the provisions of this Agreement, or should any local trouble of any kind arise, there shall be no suspension of work on account of such differences but an earnest effort shall be made to settle such differences immediately in the following manner:

"A. For Maintenance Employees:

"First, between the aggrieved employees, and the Foreman involved;

"Second, between a member or members of the Grievance Committee designated by the Union, and the Foreman and Master Mechanic.

. . . .

"Fifth, if agreement has not been reached the matter shall be referred to an impartial umpire for decision. The parties shall meet to decide on an umpire acceptable to both. If no agreement on selection of an umpire is reached, the parties shall jointly petition the United States Conciliation Service for suggestion of a list of umpires from which selection will be made. The decision of the umpire shall be final."

Settlement of this grievance was not had and respondent refused arbitration. This suit was then commenced by the union to compel it.

The District Court granted respondent's motion to dismiss the complaint. 168 F. Supp. 702. It held after hearing evidence, much of which went to the merits of the grievance, that the agreement did not "confide in an arbitrator the right to review the defendant's business judgment in contracting out work." *Id.* at 705. It further held that "the contracting out of repair and maintenance work, as well as construction work, is strictly a function of management not limited in any respect by the labor agreement involved here." *Ibid.* The Court of Appeals affirmed by a divided vote, 269 F.2d 633, the majority holding that the collective agreement had withdrawn from the grievance procedure "matters which are strictly a function of management" and that contracting out fell in that exception. . . .

We held in Textile Workers v. Lincoln Mills, 353 U.S. 448, that a grievance arbitration provision in a collective agreement could be enforced by reason of § 301(a) of the Labor Management Relations Act and that the policy to be applied in enforcing this type of arbitration was that reflected in our national labor laws. *Id.* at 456-457. The present federal policy is to promote industrial stabilization through the collective bargaining agreement. *Id.* at 453-454. A major factor in achieving industrial peace is the inclusion of a provision for arbitration of grievances in the collective bargaining agreement.[4]

Thus the run of arbitration cases, illustrated by Wilko v. Swan, 346 U.S. 427, becomes irrelevant to our problem. There the choice is between the adjudication of cases or controversies in courts with established procedures or even special statutory safeguards on the one hand and the settlement of them in the more informal arbitration tribunal on the other. In the commercial case, arbitration is the substitute for litigation. Here arbitration is the substitute for industrial strife. Since arbitration of labor disputes has quite different functions from arbitration under an ordinary commercial agreement, the hostility evinced by courts toward arbitration of commercial agreements has no place here. For arbitration of labor disputes under collective bargaining agreements is part and parcel of the collective bargaining process itself.

The collective bargaining agreement states the rights and duties of the parties. It is more than a contract; it is a generalized code to govern a myriad of cases which the draftsmen cannot wholly anticipate. See

---

[4] Complete effectuation of the federal policy is achieved when the agreement contains both an arbitration provision for all unresolved grievances and an absolute prohibition of strikes, the arbitration agreement being the *"quid pro quo"* for the agreement not to strike. Textile Workers v. Lincoln Mills, 353 U.S. 448, 455.

Shulman, Reason, Contract, and Law in Labor Relations, 68 Harv. L. Rev. 999, 1004-1005. The collective agreement covers the whole employment relationship. It calls into being a new common law — the common law of a particular industry or of a particular plant. As one observer has put it:[6]

". . . [I]t is not unqualifiedly true that a collective bargaining agreement is simply a document by which the union and employees have imposed upon management limited, express restrictions of its otherwise absolute right to manage the enterprise, so that an employee's claim must fail unless he can point to a specific contract provision upon which the claim is founded. There are too many people, too many problems, too many unforeseeable contingencies to make the words of the contract the exclusive source of rights and duties. One cannot reduce all the rules governing a community like an industrial plant to fifteen or even fifty pages. Within the sphere of collective bargaining, the institutional characteristics and the governmental nature of the collective bargaining process demand a common law of the shop which implements and furnishes the context of the agreement. We must assume that intelligent negotiators acknowledged so plain a need unless they stated a contrary rule in plain words."

A collective bargaining agreement is an effort to erect a system of industrial self-government. When most parties enter into contractual relationship they do so voluntarily, in the sense that there is no real compulsion to deal with one another, as opposed to dealing with other parties. This is not true of the labor agreement. The choice is generally not between entering or refusing to enter into a relationship, for that in all probability preexists the negotiations. Rather it is between having that relationship governed by an agreed-upon rule of law or leaving each and every matter subject to a temporary resolution dependent solely upon the relative strength, at any given moment, of the contending forces. The mature labor agreement may attempt to regulate all aspects of the complicated relationship, from the most crucial to the most minute over an extended period of time. Because of the compulsion to reach agreement and the breadth of the matters covered, as well as the need for a fairly concise and readable instrument, the product of negotiations (the written document) is, in the words of the late Dean Shulman, "a compilation of diverse provisions: some provide objective criteria almost automatically applicable; some provide more or less specific standards which require reason and judgment in their application; and some do little more than leave problems to future consideration with an expression of hope and good faith." Shulman, supra at 1005. Gaps may be left to be filled in by reference to the practices of the particular industry and of the various shops covered by the agreement. Many of the specific practices which underlie the agreement may be unknown, except in hazy form, even to the negotiators. Courts and arbitration in the context of most commercial contracts are resorted to because there has been a breakdown

---

[6] Cox, Reflections Upon Labor Arbitration, 72 Harv. L. Rev. 1482, 1498-1499 (1959).

in the working relationship of the parties; such resort is the unwanted exception. But the grievance machinery under a collective bargaining agreement is at the very heart of the system of industrial self-government. Arbitration is the means of solving the unforeseeable by molding a system of private law for all the problems which may arise and to provide for their solution in a way which will generally accord with the variant needs and desires of the parties. The processing of disputes through the grievance machinery is actually a vehicle by which meaning and content are given to the collective bargaining agreement.

Apart from matters that the parties specifically exclude, all of the questions on which the parties disagree must therefore come within the scope of the grievance and arbitration provisions of the collective agreement. The grievance procedure is, in other words, a part of the continuous collective bargaining process. It, rather than a strike, is the terminal point of a disagreement. . . .

"A proper conception of the arbitrator's function is basic. He is not a public tribunal imposed upon the parties by superior authority which the parties are obliged to accept. He has no general charter to administer justice for a community which transcends the parties. He is rather part of a system of self-government created by and confined to the parties. . . ." Shulman, *supra* at 1016.

The labor arbitrator's source of law is not confined to the express provisions of the contract, as the industrial common law — the practices of the industry and the shop — is equally a part of the collective bargaining agreement although not expressed in it. The labor arbitrator is usually chosen because of the parties' confidence in his knowledge of the common law of the shop and their trust in his personal judgment to bring to bear considerations which are not expressed in the contract as criteria for judgment. The parties expect that his judgment of a particular grievance will reflect not only what the contract says but, insofar as the collective bargaining agreement permits, such factors as the effect upon productivity of a particular result, its consequence to the morale of the shop, his judgment whether tensions will be heightened or diminished. For the parties' objective in using the arbitration process is primarily to further their common goal of uninterrupted production under the agreement, to make the agreement serve their specialized needs. The ablest judge cannot be expected to bring the same experience and competence to bear upon the determination of a grievance, because he cannot be similarly informed.

The Congress, however, has by § 301 of the Labor Management Relations Act, assigned the courts the duty of determining whether the reluctant party has breached his promise to arbitrate. For arbitration is a matter of contract and a party cannot be required to submit to arbitration any dispute which he has not agreed so to submit. Yet, to be consistent with congressional policy in favor of settlement of disputes by the parties through the machinery of arbitration, the judicial inquiry under § 301 must be strictly confined to the question whether the reluctant party did agree to arbitrate the grievance or did agree to give the arbitrator power to make the award he made. An order to arbitrate the particular grievance should not be denied unless it may be said with positive assurance that the arbitration clause is not susceptible of an interpretation that covers the asserted dispute. Doubts should be resolved in favor of coverage.[7]

We do not agree with the lower courts that contracting-out grievances were necessarily excepted from the grievance procedure of this agreement. To be sure, the agreement provides that "matters which are strictly a function of management shall not be subject to arbitration." But it goes on to say that if "differences" arise or if "any local trouble of any kind" arises, the grievance procedure shall be applicable.

Collective bargaining agreements regulate or restrict the exercise of management functions; they do not oust management from the performance of them. Management hires and fires, pays and promotes, supervises and plans. All these are part of its function, and absent a collective bargaining agreement, it may be exercised freely except as limited by public law and by the willingness of employees to work under the particular, unilaterally imposed conditions. A collective bargaining agreement may treat only with certain specific practices, leaving the rest to management but subject to the possibility of work stoppages. When, however, an absolute no-strike clause is included in the agreement, then in a very real sense everything that managment does is subject to the agreement, for either management is prohibited or limited in the action it takes, or if not, it is protected from interference by strikes. This comprehensive reach of the collective bargaining agreement does not mean, however, that the language, "strictly a function of management," has no meaning.

"Strictly a function of management" might be thought to refer to any practice of management in which, under particular circumstances prescribed by the agreement, it is permitted to indulge. But if courts, in order to determine arbitrability, were allowed to determine what is permitted and what is not, the arbitration clause would be swallowed up by the exception. Every grievance in a sense involves a claim that management has violated some provision of the agreement.

Accordingly, "strictly a function of management" must be interpreted as referring only to that over which the contract gives management complete control and unfettered discretion. Respondent claims that the contracting out of work falls within this category. Contracting out work is the basis of many grievances; and that type of claim is grist in the mills of the arbitrators. A specific collective bargaining agreement may exclude contracting out from the grievance procedure. Or a written collateral

---

[7] It is clear that under both the agreement in this case and that involved in American Mfg. Co., *supra* at 564, the question of arbitrability is for the courts to decide. Cf. Cox, Reflections Upon Labor Arbitration, 72 HARV. L. REV. 1482, 1508-1509 (1959). Where the assertion by the claimant is that the parties excluded from court determination not merely the decision of the merits of the grievance but also the question of its arbitrability, vesting power to make both decisions in the arbitrator, the claimant must bear the burden of a clear demonstration of that purpose.

agreement may make clear that contracting out was not a matter for arbitration. In such a case a grievance based solely on contracting out would not be arbitrable. Here, however, there is no such provision. Nor is there any showing that the parties designed the phrase "strictly a function of management" to encompass any and all forms of contracting out. In the absence of any express provision excluding a particular grievance from arbitration, we think only the most forceful evidence of a purpose to exclude the claim from arbitration can prevail, particularly where, as here, the exclusion clause is vague and the arbitration clause quite broad. Since any attempt by a court to infer such a purpose necessarily comprehends the merits, the court should view with suspicion an attempt to persuade it to become entangled in the construction of the substantive provisions of a labor agreement, even through the back door of interpreting the arbitration clause, when the alternative is to utilize the services of an arbitrator.

The grievance alleged that the contracting out was a violation of the collective bargaining agreement. There was, therefore, a dispute "as to the meaning and application of the provisions of this Agreement" which the parties had agreed would be determined by arbitration.

The judiciary sits in these cases to bring into operation an arbitral process which substitutes a regime of peaceful settlement for the older regime of industrial conflict. Whether contracting out in the present case violated the agreement is the question. It is a question for the arbiter, not for the courts.

Reversed.

Mr. Justice Frankfurter concurs in the result.

Mr. Justice Black took no part in the consideration or decision of this case. . . .

Mr. Justice Brennan, with whom Mr. Justice Harlan joins, concurring. . . .

The issue in the *Warrior* case is essentially no different from that in *American* [*infra* at 664], that is, it is whether the company agreed to arbitrate a particular grievance. In contrast to *American,* however, the arbitration promise here excludes a particular area from arbitration — "matters which are strictly a function of management." Because the arbitration promise is different, the scope of the court's inquiry may be broader. Here, a court may be required to examine the substantive provisions of the contract to ascertain whether the parties have provided that contracting out shall be a "function of management." If a court may delve into the merits to the extent of inquiring whether the parties have expressly agreed whether or not contracting out was a "function of management," why was it error for the lower court here to evaluate the evidence of bargaining history for the same purpose? Neat logical distinctions do not provide the answer. The Court rightly concludes that appropriate regard for the national labor policy and the special factors relevant to the labor arbitral process, admonish that judicial inquiry into the merits of this grievance should be limited to the search for an explicit provision which brings the grievance under the cover of the exclusion clause since "the exclusion clause is vague and arbitration clause quite broad." The hazard of going further into the merits is amply demonstrated by what the courts below did. On the basis of inconclusive evidence, those courts found that Warrior was in no way limited by any implied covenants of good faith and fair dealing from contracting out as it pleased — which would necessarily mean that Warrior was free completely to destroy the collective bargaining agreement by contracting out all the work.

The very ambiguity of the *Warrior* exclusion clause suggests that the parties were generally more concerned with having an arbitrator render decisions as to the meaning of the contract than they were in restricting the arbitrator's jurisdiction. The case might of course be otherwise were the arbitration clause very narrow, or the exclusion clause quite specific, for the inference might then be permissible that the parties had manifested a greater interest in confining the arbitrator; the presumption of arbitrability would then not have the same force and the Court would be somewhat freer to examine into the merits.

The Court makes reference to an arbitration clause being the *quid pro quo* for a no-strike clause. I do not understand the Court to mean that the application of the principles announced today depends upon the presence of a no-strike clause in the agreement.

MR. JUSTICE FRANKFURTER joins these observations.

[The dissenting opinion of MR. JUSTICE WHITTAKER is omitted.]

UNITED STEELWORKERS v. AMERICAN MFG. CO., 363 U.S. 564, 80 S. Ct. 1343, 4 L. Ed. 2d 1403 (1960). A collective bargaining agreement contained a "standard" arbitration clause covering "any disputes" between the parties "as to the meaning, interpretation and application of the provisions of this agreement." The union agreed not to strike unless the employer refused to abide by a decision of the arbitrator. The contract reserved to management the power to suspend or discipline any employee "for cause." It also provided that the employer would employ and promote employees on "the principle of seniority . . . where ability and efficiency are equal." An employee left work due to an injury and later settled a workmen's compensation claim against the company on the basis he was permanently partially disabled. Thereafter the union filed a grievance charging that the employee was entitled to return to his job under the seniority provision. The employer refused to arbitrate and the union sued. The Supreme Court held that arbitration should have been ordered. Declared the Court: "The function of the court is very limited when the parties have agreed to submit all questions of contract interpretation to the arbitrator. It is confined to ascertaining whether the party seeking arbitration is making a claim which on its face is governed by the contract. Whether the moving party is right or wrong is a question of contract interpretation for the arbitrator. . . . The courts, therefore, have no business weighing the merits of the grievance. . . . The processing of even frivolous claims may have therapeutic values of which those who are not a part of the plant environment may be quite unaware."

NOTES

1. The two preceding cases, together with *Enterprise Wheel, infra* at 666, are familiarly known as the *Steelworkers Trilogy.* They have evoked a voluminous literature. *See, e.g.,* Aaron, *Arbitration in the Federal Courts: Aftermath of the Trilogy,* 9 U.C.L.A. L. Rev. 360 (1962); Gregory, *Enforcement of Collective Agreements by Arbitration,* 48 Va. L. Rev. 883 (1962); Hays, *The Supreme Court and Labor Law — October Term, 1959,* 60 Colum. L. Rev. 901 (1960); Meltzer, *The Supreme Court, Arbitrability, and Collective Bargaining,* 28 U. Chi. L. Rev. 464 (1961); Smith & Jones, *The Supreme Court and Labor Dispute Arbitration: The Emerging Federal Law,* 63 Mich. L. Rev. 751 (1965); Smith & Jones, *The Impact of the Emerging Federal Law of Grievance Arbitration on Judges, Arbitrators, and Parties,* 52 Va. L. Rev. 831 (1966); Wellington, *Judicial Review of the Promise to Arbitrate,* 37 N.Y.U.L. Rev. 471 (1962); *Symposium — Arbitration and the Courts,* 58 Nw. U.L. Rev. 466, 494, 521, 556 (1963).

2. The lower federal courts appear to be of different minds about the extent to which bargaining history may constitute evidence of an intent to exclude certain claims from arbitration. *Compare* IUE v. General Elec. Co., 332 F.2d 485 (2d Cir. 1964), *with* Communications Workers v. Pacific Northwest Bell Tel. Co., 337 F.2d 455 (9th Cir. 1964). *See also* Lesnick, *Arbitration as a Limit on the Discretion of Management, Union, and NLRB: The Year's Major Developments,* in N.Y.U. Eighteenth Annual Conference on Labor 7, 9-18 (1966).

3. A grievance has been held not arbitrable where specific exclusionary language applied. IUE Local 787 v. Collins Radio Co., 317 F.2d 214 (5th Cir. 1963). May the parties to a collective bargaining agreement nullify the *Warrior* presumption of arbitrability? *See* IUE v. General Elec. Co., 407 F.2d 253, 259 (2d Cir. 1968), *cert. denied,* 395 U.S. 904 (1969).

4. Are the *Trilogy* rules on arbitrability binding on arbitrators as well as courts? If a court orders arbitration, may the arbitrator subsequently make his own independent determination of arbitrability? *See* Smith & Jones, *supra* note 1, 63 Mich. L. Rev. at 761, and 52 Va. L. Rev. at 871-73.

Nolde Bros., Inc. v. Bakery & Confectionery Workers Local 358, 430 U.S. 243, 97 S. Ct. 1067, 51 L. Ed. 2d 300 (1977). A union and an employer had a contract providing that "any grievance" between the parties was subject to binding arbitration. After negotiating for three months for a contract renewal, the union exercised its option to cancel the existing agreement by giving a seven-day termination notice. Negotiations continued for four days past the effective date of the termination. Then the company, faced by a threatened strike, informed the union that it was permanently closing its plant. The company paid the employees their accrued wages and vacation pay but rejected the union's demand for severance pay called for in the labor agreement. The employer also declined to arbitrate the severance pay claims on the ground its duty to arbitrate terminated with the contract. The union sued under § 301 to compel arbitration. The Supreme Court, per Chief Justice Burger, held that the issue was arbitrable. "The dispute. . . , although arising *after* the expiration of the collective bargaining agreement, clearly arises *under* that contract. . . . [N]othing in the arbitration clause . . . expressly excludes . . . a dispute which arises under the contract, but which is based on events that occur after its termination. . . . By their contract the parties clearly expressed their preference for an arbitral, rather than a judicial interpretation of their obligations. . . ." Justices Stewart and Rehnquist dissented, arguing: "The closing of the [plant] necessarily meant that there was no continuing relationship to protect or preserve. . . . And the Union's termination of the contract, thereby releasing it from its obligation not to strike, foreclosed any reason for implying a continuing duty on the part of the employer to arbitrate as a *quid pro quo*. . . ."

NOTE

See generally Goetz, *Arbitration After Termination of a Collective Bargaining Agreement,* 63 VA. L. REV. 693 (1977).

UNITED STEELWORKERS v. ENTERPRISE WHEEL & CAR CORP.

Supreme Court of the United States
363 U.S. 593, 80 S. Ct. 1358, 4 L. Ed. 2d 1424 (1960)

MR. JUSTICE DOUGLAS delivered the opinion of the Court.

Petitioner union and respondent during the period relevant here had a collective bargaining agreement which provided that any differences "as to the meaning and application" of the agreement should be submitted to arbitration and that the arbitrator's decision "shall be final and binding on the parties." Special provisions were included concerning the suspension and discharge of employees. The agreement stated:

"Should it be determined by the Company or by an arbitrator in accordance with the grievance procedure that the employee has been suspended unjustly or discharged in violation of the provisions of this Agreement, the Company shall reinstate the employee and pay full compensation at the employee's regular rate of pay for the time lost."

The agreement also provided:

". . . It is understood and agreed that neither party will institute *civil suits* or *legal proceedings* against the other for alleged violation of any of the provisions of this labor contract; instead all disputes will be settled in the manner outlined in this Article III — Adjustment of Grievances."

A group of employees left their jobs in protest against the discharge of one employee. A union official advised them at once to return to work. An official of respondent at their request gave them permission and then rescinded it. The next day they were told they did not have a job any more "until this thing was settled one way or the other."

A grievance was filed; and when respondent finally refused to arbitrate, this suit was brought for specific enforcement of the arbitration provisions of the agreement. The District Court ordered arbitration. The arbitrator found that the discharge of the men was not justified, though their conduct, he said, was improper. In his view the facts warranted at most a suspension of the men for 10 days each. After their discharge and before the arbitration award the collective bargaining agreement had expired. The union, however, continued to represent the workers at the plant. The arbitrator rejected the contention that expiration of the agreement barred reinstatement of the employees. He held that the provision of the agreement above quoted imposed an unconditional obligation on the employer. He awarded reinstatement with back pay, minus pay for a 10-day suspension and such sums as these employees received from other employment.

Respondent refused to comply with the award. Petitioner moved the District Court for enforcement. The District Court directed respondent to comply. 168 F. Supp. 308. The Court of Appeals, while agreeing that the District Court had jurisdiction to enforce an arbitration award under a collective bargaining agreement, held that the failure of the award to specify the amounts to be deducted from the back pay rendered the award unenforceable. That defect, it agreed, could be remedied by requiring the parties to complete the arbitration. It went on to hold, however, that an award for back pay subsequent to the date of termination of the collective bargaining agreement could not be enforced. It also held that the requirement for reinstatement of the discharged employees was likewise unenforceable because the collective bargaining agreement had expired. 269 F.2d 327. . . .

The refusal of courts to review the merits of an arbitration award is the proper approach to arbitration under collective bargaining agreements. The federal policy of settling labor disputes by arbitration would be undermined if courts had the final say on the merits of the awards. As we stated in United Steelworkers v. Warrior & Gulf Navigation Co., *supra* at 574, decided this day, the arbitrators under these collective agreements are indispensable agencies in a continuous collective bargaining process. They sit to settle disputes at the plant level — disputes that require for their solution knowledge of the custom and practices of a particular factory or of a particular industry as reflected in particular agreements.

When an arbitrator is commissioned to interpret and apply the collective bargaining agreement, he is to bring his informed judgment to bear in order to reach a fair solution of a problem. This is especially true when it comes to formulating remedies. There the need is for flexibility in meeting a wide variety of situations. The draftsmen may never have thought of what specific remedy should be awarded to meet a particular contingency. Nevertheless, an arbitrator is confined to interpretation and application of the collective bargaining agreement; he does not sit to dispense his own brand of industrial justice. He may of course look for guidance from many sources, yet his award is legitimate only so long as it draws its essence from the collective bargaining agreement. When the arbitrator's words manifest an infidelity to this obligation, courts have no choice but to refuse enforcement of the award.

The opinion of the arbitrator in this case, as it bears upon the award of back pay beyond the date of the agreement's expiration and reinstatement, is ambiguous. It may be read as based solely upon the arbitrator's view of the requirements of enacted legislation, which would mean that he exceeded the scope of the submission. Or it may be read as embodying a construction of the agreement itself, perhaps with the arbitrator looking to "the law" for help in determining the sense of the agreement. A mere ambiguity in the opinion accompanying an award, which permits the inference that the arbitrator may have exceeded his authority, is not a reason for refusing to enforce the award. Arbitrators have no obligation to the court to give their reasons for an award. To require opinions free of ambiguity may lead arbitrators to play it safe by writing no supporting opinions. This would be undesirable for a well-reasoned opinion tends to engender confidence in the integrity of the process and aids in clarifying the underlying agreement. Moreover, we see no reason to assume that this arbitrator has abused the trust the parties confided in him and has not stayed within the areas marked out for his consideration. It is not apparent that he went beyond the submission. The Court of Appeals' opinion refusing to enforce the reinstatement and partial back pay portions of the award was not based upon any finding that the arbitrator did not premise his award on his construction of the contract. It merely disagreed with the arbitrator's construction of it.

The collective bargaining agreement could have provided that if any of the employees were wrongfully discharged, the remedy would be reinstatement and back pay up to the date they were returned to work. Respondent's major argument seems to be that by applying correct principles of law to the interpretation of the collective bargaining agreement it can be determined that the agreement did not so provide, and that therefore the arbitrator's decision was not based upon the contract. The acceptance of this view would require courts, even under the standard arbitration clause, to review the merits of every construction of the contract. This plenary review by a court of the merits would make meaningless the provisions that the arbitrator's decision is final, for in reality it would almost never be final. This underlines the fundamental error which we have alluded to in United Steelworkers v. American Manufacturing Co., *supra* at 564, decided this day. As we there emphasized, the question of interpretation of the collective bargaining agreement is a question for the arbitrator. It is the arbitrator's construction which was bargained for; and so far as the arbitrator's decision concerns construction of the contract, the courts have no business overruling him because their interpretation of the contract is different from his.

We agree with the Court of Appeals that the judgment of the District Court should be modified so that the amounts due the employees may be definitely determined by arbitration. In all other respects we think the judgment of the District Court should be affirmed. Accordingly, we reverse the judgment of the Court of Appeals, except for that modification, and remand the case to the District Court for proceedings in conformity with this opinion.

It is so ordered.

MR. JUSTICE FRANKFURTER concurs in the result.

MR. JUSTICE BLACK took no part in the consideration or decision of this case. . . .

MR. JUSTICE WHITTAKER, dissenting. . . .

Once the contract expired, no rights continued to accrue under it to the employees. Thereafter they had no contractual right to demand that the employer continue to employ them, and *a fortiori* the arbitrator did not have power to order the employer to do so; nor did the arbitrator have power to order the employer to pay wages to them after the date of termination of the contract, which was also the effective date of their discharges.

NOTES

1. The first two cases of the *Steelworkers Trilogy* dealt with judicial enforcement of executory agreements to arbitrate; *Enterprise Wheel* dealt with judicial enforcement of an arbitral award. Should a court apply different standards in examining the arbitrator's "jurisdiction" in these two situations? Is there, in any event, a difference between the arbitrator's "jurisdiction" to hear a dispute and his "authority" to render a particular award? The Second Circuit has held that an arbitrator exceeded the scope of the submission when he "added" an implied term to the labor contract on the basis of a past practice which the court found had later been revoked by the employer. Torrington Co. v. Metal Prod. Workers, Local 1645, 362 F.2d 677 (2d Cir. 1966). *Torrington* was criticized in Aaron, *Judicial Intervention in Labor Arbitration,* 20 STAN. L. REV. 41 (1967); Jones, *The Name of the Game is Decision — Some Reflections on "Arbitrability" and "Authority" in Labor Arbitration,* 46 TEXAS L. REV. 865 (1968); Meltzer, *Ruminations About Ideology, Law, and Labor Arbitration,* 34 U. CHI. L. REV. 545 (1967).

2. A court will presumably not enforce an arbitral award that directly violates enacted law (or "public policy"?). How should an arbitrator handle a conflict between "the law" and the parties' contract? For contrasting views, *see* Edwards, *Labor Arbitration at the Crossroads: The "Common Law of the Shop" v. External Law,* 32 ARB. J. 65 (1977); Howlett, *The Arbitrator, the NLRB, and the Courts,* in NATIONAL ACADEMY OF ARBITRATORS, THE ARBITRATOR, THE NLRB, AND THE COURTS, PROCEEDINGS OF THE TWENTIETH ANNUAL MEETING 67 (1967); Meltzer, *supra* note 1 [*id.* at 1]; Mittenthal, *The Role of Law in Arbitration,* in

NATIONAL ACADEMY OF ARBITRATORS, DEVELOPMENTS IN AMERICAN AND FOREIGN ARBITRATION, PROCEEDINGS OF THE TWENTY-FIRST ANNUAL MEETING 42 (1968).

3. Is procedural unfairness a basis for vacating an arbitrator's award? *See* Harvey Aluminum, Inc. v. United Steelworkers, 263 F. Supp. 488 (C.D. Cal. 1967); *cf.* Note, *Labor Arbitration: Appealing the Procedural Decisions of Arbitrators,* 59 MINN. L. REV. 109 (1974).

4. Can an arbitrator fashion a given remedy without express authorization in the contract or submission agreement? Can he reduce a discharge to a suspension if he finds the penalty excessive but not groundless? Can he order back pay as well as reinstatement? *Compare* Teamsters Local 784 v. Ulry-Talbert Co., 330 F.2d 562 (8th Cir. 1964), *and* Textile Workers v. American Thread Co., 291 F.2d 894 (4th Cir. 1961), *with* Machinists Lodge 12 v. Cameron Iron Works, 292 F.2d 112 (5th Cir. 1961), *cert. denied,* 368 U.S. 926 (1961). *See generally* Fleming, *Arbitrators and the Remedy Power,* 48 VA. L. REV. 1199 (1962).

5. Arbitration by an impartial third party is not essential to judicial enforceability under § 301. An award by a joint labor-management committee may be enforced if it is final and binding under the collective bargaining agreement, even though the procedure employed is not styled "arbitration." Teamsters Local 89 v. Riss & Co., 372 U.S. 517 (1963).

6. *See also* Feller, *The Coming End of Arbitration's Golden Age,* in NATIONAL ACADEMY OF ARBITRATORS, ARBITRATION — 1976, PROCEEDINGS OF THE TWENTY-NINTH ANNUAL MEETING 97 (1976); St. Antoine, *Judicial Review of Labor Arbitration Awards: A Second Look at Enterprise Wheel and Its Progeny,* 75 MICH. L. REV. 1137 (1977); Wellington, *Judicial Review of the Promise to Arbitrate,* 37 N.Y.U.L. REV. 471 (1962).

2. THE ENFORCEMENT OF STRIKE BANS AND THE EFFECT OF NORRIS-LA GUARDIA

FELIX FRANKFURTER & NATHAN GREENE, THE LABOR INJUNCTION 36-37, 200-01 (1930)*

The ancient common law action allowed to a master for the forcible taking away of his servant, extended, after the fourteenth century Ordinance and Statute of Labourers to enticement of a servant even without force, was in the middle nineteenth century advanced by an English court to support an action for intentionally inducing breach of a fixed term contract of employment. Eventually, both in America and in England, the traditional limits of "enticement" and of "master and servant" were wholly disregarded in the uses to which the legal categories were put. "Malice" as a requisite of the tort was quickly transformed into a mere word of art; the relationships protected expanded from those based upon a fixed term employment to employments terminable at will. The broad doctrine of "interference with contract relations" has thus been widely invoked in labor controversies. . . .

The restraining order and the preliminary injunction invoked in labor disputes reveal the most crucial points of legal maladjustment. Temporary injunctive relief without notice, or, if upon notice, relying upon dubious affidavits, serves the important function of staying defendant's conduct regardless of the ultimate justification of such restraint. . . . Moreover, the suspension of strike activities, even temporarily, may defeat the strike for practical purposes and foredoom its resumption, even if the injunction is later lifted.

TEAMSTERS, CHAUFFEURS, WAREHOUSEMEN & HELPERS, LOCAL 174 v. LUCAS FLOUR CO.

Supreme Court of the United States
369 U.S. 95, 82 S. Ct. 571, 7 L. Ed. 2d 593 (1962)

MR. JUSTICE STEWART delivered the opinion of the Court.

The petitioner and the respondent (which we shall call the union and the employer) were parties to a collective bargaining contract within the purview of the National Labor Relations Act. The contract contained the following provisions, among others:

"ARTICLE II

"The Employer reserves the right to discharge any man in his employ if his work is not satisfactory. . . .

"ARTICLE XIV

"Should any difference as to the true interpretation of this agreement arise, same shall be submitted to a Board of Arbitration of two members, one representing the firm, and one representing the Union. If said members cannot agree, a third member, who must be a disinterested party shall be selected, and the decision of the said Board of Arbitration shall be binding. It is further agreed by both parties hereto that during such arbitration, there shall be no suspension of work.

"Should any difference arise between the employer and the employee, same shall be submitted to arbitration by both parties. Failing to agree, they shall mutually appoint a third person whose decision shall be final and binding."

In May of 1958, an employee named Welsch was discharged by the employer after he had damaged a new fork lift truck by running it off a loading platform and onto some railroad tracks. When a business agent of the union protested, he was told by a representative of the employer that Welsch had been discharged because of unsatisfactory work. The union thereupon called a strike to force the employer to rehire Welsch. The strike lasted eight days. After the strike was over, the issue of Welsch's discharge was submitted to arbitration. Some five months later the Board of Arbitration rendered a decision, ruling that Welsch's work had been unsatisfactory, that his unsatisfactory work had been the reason for his discharge, and that he was not entitled to reinstatement as an employee.

In the meantime, the employer had brought this suit against the union in the Superior Court of King County, Washington, asking damages for business losses caused by the strike. After a trial that court entered a judgment in favor of the employer in the amount of $6,501.60. On appeal the judgment was affirmed by Department One of the Supreme Court of Washington. 57 Wash.2d 95, 356 P.2d 1 (1960). The reviewing court held that the preemption doctrine of San Diego Bldg. Trades Council v. Garmon, 359 U.S. 236 (1959), did not deprive it of jurisdiction over the controversy. The court further held that § 301 of the Labor Management Relations Act of 1947, 29 U.S.C. § 185, could not "reasonably be interpreted as preempting state jurisdiction, or as affecting it by limiting the substantive law to be applied." 57 Wash. 2d, at 102, 356 P.2d, at 5. Expressly applying principles of state law, the court reasoned that the strike was a violation of the collective bargaining contract, because it was an attempt to coerce the employer to forego his contractual right to discharge an employee for unsatisfactory work. . . .

One of [the] issues — whether § 301(a) of the Labor Management Relations Act of 1947 deprives state courts of jurisdiction over litigation such as this — we have decided this Term in Charles Dowd Box Co. v. Courtney, 368 U.S. 502 (1962).[9] For the reasons stated in our opinion in that case, we hold that the Washington Supreme Court was correct in ruling that it had jurisdiction over this controversy. There remain for consideration two other issues, one of them implicated but not specifically decided in *Dowd Box*. Was the Washington court free, as it thought, to decide this controversy within the limited horizon of its local law? If not, does applicable federal law require a result in this case different from that reached by the state court? . . .

It was apparently the theory of the Washington court that, although Textile Workers v. Lincoln Mills, 353 U.S. 448 (1957), requires the federal courts to fashion, from the policy of our national labor laws, a body of federal law for the enforcement of collective bargaining agreements, nonetheless, the courts of the states remain free to apply individualized local rules when called upon to enforce such agreements. This view cannot be accepted. The dimensions of § 301 require the conclusion that substantive principles of federal labor law must be paramount in the area covered by the statute. Comprehensiveness is inherent in the process by

---

[9] Since this was a suit for violation of a collective bargaining contract within the purview of § 301(a) of the Labor Management Relations Act of 1947, the preemptive doctrine of cases such as San Diego Building Trades Council v. Garmon, 359 U.S. 236 (1959), based upon the exclusive jurisdiction of the National Labor Relations Board, is not relevant. . . . As pointed out in Charles Dowd Box Co. v. Courtney, 368 U.S. at 513, Congress "deliberately chose to leave the enforcement of collective agreements 'to the usual processes of law.' " See also H.R. Conf. Rep. No. 510, 80th Cong., 1st Sess. at 52. It is of course, true that conduct which is a violation of a contractual obligation may also be conduct constituting an unfair labor practice, and what has been said is not to imply that enforcement by a court of a contract obligation affects the jurisdiction of the N.L.R.B. to remedy unfair labor practices, as such. See generally Dunau, Contractual Prohibition of Unfair Labor Practices: Jurisdictional Problems, 57 Colum. L. Rev. 52 (1957).

which the law is to be formulated under the mandate of *Lincoln Mills,* requiring issues raised in suits of a kind covered by § 301 to be decided according to the precepts of federal labor policy.

More important, the subject matter of § 301(a) "is peculiarly one that calls for uniform law." Pennsylvania R. Co. v. Public Service Comm., 250 U.S. 566, 569 (1919). . . . The possibility that individual contract terms might have different meanings under state and federal law would inevitably exert a disruptive influence upon both the negotiation and administration of collective agreements. Because neither party could be certain of the rights which it had obtained or conceded, the process of negotiating an agreement would be made immeasurably more difficult by the necessity of trying to formulate contract provisions in such a way as to contain the same meaning under two or more systems of law which might some day be invoked in enforcing the contract. Once the collective bargain was made, the possibility of conflicting substantive interpretation under competing legal systems would tend to stimulate and prolong disputes as to its interpretation. Indeed, the existence of possibly conflicting legal concepts might substantially impede the parties' willingness to agree to contract terms providing for final arbitral or judicial resolution of disputes.

The importance of the area which would be affected by separate systems of substantive law makes the need for a single body of federal law particularly compelling. The ordering and adjusting of competing interests through a process of free and voluntary collective bargaining is the keystone of the federal scheme to promote industrial peace. State law which frustrates the effort of Congress to stimulate the smooth functioning of that process thus strikes at the very core of federal labor policy. With due regard to the many factors which bear upon competing state and federal interests in this area, . . . we cannot but conclude that in enacting § 301 Congress intended doctrines of federal labor law uniformly to prevail over inconsistent local rules.

Whether, as a matter of federal law, the strike which the union called was a violation of the collective bargaining contract is thus the ultimate issue which this case presents. It is argued that there could be no violation in the absence of a no-strike clause in the contract explicitly covering the subject of the dispute over which the strike was called. We disagree.

The collective bargaining contract expressly imposed upon both parties the duty of submitting the dispute in question to final and binding arbitration. In a consistent course of decisions the Courts of Appeals of at least five Federal Circuits have held that a strike to settle a dispute which a collective bargaining agreement provides shall be settled exclusively and finally by compulsory arbitration constitutes a violation of the agreement. The National Labor Relations Board has reached the same conclusion. W.L. Mead, Inc., 113 N.L.R.B. 1040. We approve that doctrine. To hold otherwise would obviously do violence to accepted principles of traditional contract law. Even more in point, a contrary view would be completely at odds with the basic policy of national labor legislation to promote the arbitral process as a substitute for economic warfare. See United Steelworkers v. Warrior & Gulf Nav. Co., 363 U.S. 574 (1960).

What has been said is not to suggest that a no-strike agreement is to be implied beyond the area which it has been agreed will be exclusively covered by compulsory terminal arbitration. Nor is it to suggest that there may not arise problems in specific cases as to whether compulsory and binding arbitration has been agreed upon, and, if so, as to what disputes have been made arbitrable. But no such problems are present in this case. The grievance over which the union struck was, as it concedes, one which it had expressly agreed to settle by submission to final and binding arbitration proceedings. The strike which it called was a violation of that contractual obligation.

Affirmed.

[The dissenting opinion of MR. JUSTICE BLACK is omitted.]

NOTE

In Charles Dowd Box Co. v. Courtney, 368 U.S. 502 (1962), the Supreme Court held that § 301 of the Taft-Hartley Act did not divest state courts of jurisdiction over a suit for violation of contract between an employer and a labor organization. To the argument that concurrent state court jurisdiction would lead to a disharmony of result incompatible with the *Lincoln Mills* concept of an all-embracing body of federal law, the Court replied: "The legislative history of the enactment nowhere suggests that, contrary to the clear import of the statutory language, Congress intended in enacting § 301(a) to deprive a party to a collective bargaining contract of the right to seek redress for its violation in an appropriate state tribunal. . . . The legislative history makes clear that the basic purpose of § 301(a) was not to limit, but to expand, the availability of forums for the enforcement of contracts made by labor organizations."

Justice Black, dissenting in the principal case, argued that the majority was adding a clause to the contract, on the basis of its own notions of sound policy, that the parties themselves had refused to include. Is there merit in this objection? *See* Wellington, *Freedom of Contract and the Collective Bargaining Agreement,* 112 U. PA. L. REV. 467 (1964). *See generally* Koretz, *The Supreme Court and Labor Arbitration, October Term, 1961,* in N.Y.U. FIFTEENTH ANNUAL CONFERENCE ON LABOR 287 (1962).

BOYS MARKETS, INC. v. RETAIL CLERKS LOCAL 770

Supreme Court of the United States
398 U.S. 235, 90 S. Ct. 1583, 26 L. Ed. 2d 199 (1970)

MR. JUSTICE BRENNAN delivered the opinion of the Court.

In this case we re-examine the holding of Sinclair Refining Co. v. Atkinson, 370 U.S. 195 (1962), that the anti-injunction provisions of the Norris-LaGuardia Act preclude a federal district court from enjoining a strike in breach of a no-strike obligation under a collective bargaining agreement, even though that agreement contains provisions, enforceable under § 301(a) of the Labor-Management Relations Act for binding arbitration of the grievance dispute concerning which the strike was called. The Court of Appeals for the Ninth Circuit, considering itself bound by *Sinclair,* reversed the grant by the District Court for the Central District of California of petitioner's prayer for injunctive relief. 416 F.2d 368 (1969). We granted certiorari. . . . Having concluded that *Sinclair* was erroneously decided and that subsequent events have undermined its continuing validity, we overrule that decision and reverse the judgment of the Court of Appeals.

I. In February 1969, at the time of the incidents that produced this litigation, petitioner and respondent were parties to a collective bargaining agreement which provided, *inter alia,* that all controversies concerning its interpretation or application should be resolved by adjustment and arbitration procedures set forth therein and that, during the life of the contract, there should be "no cessation or stoppage of work, lock-out, picketing or boycotts. . . ." The dispute arose when petitioner's frozen foods supervisor and certain members of his crew who were not members of the bargaining unit began to rearrange merchandise in the frozen food cases of one of petitioner's supermarkets. A union representative insisted that the food cases be stripped of all merchandise and be restocked by union personnel. When petitioner did not accede to the union's demand, a strike was called and the union began to picket petitioner's establishment. Thereupon petitioner demanded that the union cease the work stoppage and picketing and sought to invoke the grievance and arbitration procedures specified in the contract.

The following day, since the strike had not been terminated, petitioner filed a complaint in California Superior Court seeking a temporary restraining order, a preliminary and permanent injunction, and specific performance of the contractual arbitration provision. The state court issued a temporary restraining order forbidding continuation of the strike and also an order to show cause why a preliminary injunction should not be granted. Shortly thereafter, the union removed the case to the federal district court and there made a motion to quash the state court's temporary restraining order. In opposition, petitioner moved for an order compelling arbitration and enjoining continuation of the strike. Concluding that the dispute was subject to arbitration under the collective bargaining agreement and that the strike was in violation of the contract, the District Court ordered the parties to arbitrate the underlying dispute and simultaneously enjoined the strike, all picketing in the vicinity of petitioner's supermarket, and any attempts by the union to induce the employees to strike or to refuse to perform their services.

II. At the outset, we are met with respondent's contention that *Sinclair* ought not to be disturbed because the decision turned on a question of statutory construction which Congress can alter at any time. Since Congress has not modified our conclusions in *Sinclair,* even though it has been urged to do so, respondent argues that principles of *stare decisis* should govern the present case.

We do not agree that the doctrine of *stare decisis* bars a re-examination of *Sinclair* in the circumstances of this case. We fully recognize that important policy considerations militate in favor of continuity and predictability in the law. Nevertheless, as Mr. Justice Frankfurter wrote for the Court, "[S]*tare decisis* is a principle of policy and not a mechanical formula of adherence to the latest decision, however recent and questionable, when such adherence involves collision with a prior doctrine more embracing in its scope, intrinsically sounder, and verified by experience." Helvering v. Hallock, 309 U.S. 106, 119 (1940). . . . It is precisely because *Sinclair* stands as a significant departure from our otherwise consistent emphasis upon the congressional policy to promote the peaceful settlement of labor disputes through arbitration and our efforts to accommodate and harmonize this policy with those underlying the anti-injunction provisions of the Norris-LaGuardia Act that we believe *Sinclair* should be reconsidered. Furthermore, in light of developments subsequent to *Sinclair,* in particular our decision in Avco Corp. v. Aero Lodge 735, 390 U.S. 557 (1968), it has become clear that the *Sinclair* decision does not further but rather frustrates realization of an important goal of our national labor policy.

Nor can we agree that conclusive weight should be accorded to the failure of Congress to respond to *Sinclair* on the theory that congressional silence should be interpreted as acceptance of the decision. The Court has cautioned that "[i]t is at best treacherous to find in congressional silence alone the adoption of a controlling rule of law." Girouard v. United States, 328 U.S. 61, 69 (1946). Therefore, in the absence of any persuasive circumstances evidencing a clear design that congressional inaction be taken as acceptance of *Sinclair,* the mere silence of Congress is not a sufficient reason for refusing to reconsider the decision. *Helvering v. Hallock, supra* at 119-120.

III. From the time Textile Workers Union v. Lincoln Mills, 353 U.S. 448 (1957), was decided, we have frequently found it necessary to consider various substantive and procedural aspects of federal labor contract law and questions concerning its application in both state and federal courts. *Lincoln Mills* held generally that "the substantive law to apply in suits under § 301(a) is federal law, which the courts must fashion from the policy of our national labor laws," 353 U.S. at 456, and more specifically that a union can obtain specific performance of an employer's promise to arbitrate grievances. We rejected the contention that the anti-injunction proscriptions of the Norris-LaGuardia Act prohibited this type of relief, noting that a refusal to arbitrate was not "part and parcel of the abuses against which the Act was aimed," *id.* at 458, and that the Act itself manifests a policy determination that arbitration should be encouraged. See 29 U. S. C. § 108. Subsequently in the *Steelworkers Trilogy* we emphasized the importance of arbitration as an instrument of federal policy for resolving disputes between labor and management and cautioned the lower courts against usurping the functions of the arbitrator.

Serious questions remained, however, concerning the role which state courts are to play in suits involving collective bargaining agreements. Confronted with some of these problems in Charles Dowd Box Co. v. Courtney, 368 U.S. 502 (1962), we held that Congress clearly intended *not* to disturb the pre-existing jurisdiction of the state courts over suits for violations of collective bargaining agreements. We noted that the

> "clear implication of the entire record of the congressional debates in both 1946 and 1947 is that the purpose of conferring jurisdiction upon the federal district courts was not to displace, but to supplement, the thoroughly considered jurisdiction of the courts of the various States over contracts made by labor organizations." *Id.* at 511.

Shortly after the decision in *Dowd Box,* we sustained, in Teamsters Local 174 v. Lucas Flour Co., 369 U.S. 95 (1962), an award of damages by a state court to an employer for a breach by the union of a no-strike provision in their contract. While emphasizing that "in enacting § 301 Congress intended doctrines of federal labor law uniformly to prevail over inconsistent local rules," *id.* at 104, we did not consider the applicability of the Norris-LaGuardia Act to state court proceedings because the employer's prayer for relief sought only damages and not specific performance of a no-strike obligation.

Subsequent to the decision in *Sinclair,* we held in *Avco Corp. v. Aero Lodge No. 735, supra,* that § 301(a) suits initially brought in state courts may be removed to the designated federal forum under the federal question removal jurisdiction delineated in 28 U.S.C. § 1441. In so holding, however, the Court expressly left open the questions whether state courts are bound by the anti-injunction proscriptions of the Norris-LaGuardia Act and whether federal courts, after removal of a § 301(a) action, are required to dissolve any injunctive relief previously granted by the state courts. See generally General Electric Co. v. Local Union 191, 413 F.2d 964 (5th Cir. 1969) (dissolution of state injunction required). Three Justices who concurred expressed the view that *Sinclair* should be reconsidered "upon an appropriate future occasion." 390 U.S. at 562 (STEWART, J., concurring).

The decision in *Avco,* viewed in the context of *Lincoln Mills* and its progeny, has produced an anomalous situation which, in our view, makes urgent the reconsideration of *Sinclair.* The principal practical effect of *Avco* and *Sinclair* taken together is nothing less than to oust state courts of jurisdiction in § 301(a) suits where injunctive relief is sought for breach of a no-strike obligation. Union defendants can, as a matter of course, obtain removal to a federal court, and there is obviously a compelling incentive for them to do so in order to gain the advantage of the strictures upon injunctive relief which *Sinclair* imposes on federal courts. The sanctioning of this practice, however, is wholly inconsistent with our conclusion in *Dowd Box* that the congressional purpose embodied in § 301(a) was to *supplement,* and not to encroach upon, the pre-existing jurisdiction of the state courts. It is ironic indeed that the very provision which Congress clearly intended to provide additional remedies for breach of collective bargaining agreements has been employed to displace previously existing state remedies. We are not at liberty thus to depart from the clearly expressed congressional policy to the contrary.

On the other hand, to the extent that widely disparate remedies theoretically remain available in state, as opposed to federal courts, the federal policy of labor law uniformity elaborated in *Lucas Flour Co.,* is seriously offended. This policy, of course, could hardly require, as a practical matter, that labor law be administered identically in all courts, for undoubtedly a certain diversity exists among the state and federal systems in matters of procedural and remedial detail, a fact which Congress evidently took into account in deciding not to disturb the traditional jurisdiction of the States. The injunction, however, is so important a remedial device, particularly in the arbitration context, that its availability or nonavailability in various courts will not only produce rampant forum-shopping and maneuvering from one court to another but will also greatly frustrate any relative uniformity in the enforcement of arbitration agreements.

Furthermore, the existing scheme, with the injunction remedy technically available in the state courts but rendered inefficacious by the removal device, assigns to removal proceedings a totally unintended function. While the underlying purposes of Congress in providing for federal question removal jurisdiction remain somewhat obscure, there has never been a serious contention that Congress intended that the removal mechanism be utilized to foreclose completely remedies otherwise available in the state courts. Although federal question removal jurisdiction may well have been intended to provide a forum for the protection of federal rights where such protection was deemed necessary or to encourage the development of expertise by the federal courts in the interpretation of federal law, there is no indication that Congress intended by the removal mechanism to effect a wholesale dislocation in the allocation of judicial business between the state and federal courts. . . .

It is undoubtedly true that each of the foregoing objections to *Sinclair-Avco* could be remedied either by overruling *Sinclair* or by extending that decision to the States. While some commentators have suggested that the solution to the present unsatisfactory situation does lie in the extension of the *Sinclair* prohibition to state court proceedings, we agree with Chief Justice Traynor of the California Supreme Court that "whether or not Congress could deprive state courts of the power to give such [injunctive] remedies when enforcing collective bargaining agreements, it has not attempted to do so either in the Norris-LaGuardia Act or section 301." McCarroll v. Los Angeles County Dist. Council of Carpenters, 49 Cal. 2d 45, 61, 315 P.2d 322, 332 (1957), *cert. denied,* 355 U.S. 932 (1958). . . .

An additional reason for not resolving the existing dilemma by extending *Sinclair* to the States is the devastating implications for the enforceability of arbitration agreements and their accompanying no-strike obligations if equitable remedies were not available. As we have previously indicated, a no-strike obligation, express or implied, is the *quid pro quo* for an undertaking by the employer to submit grievance disputes to the process of arbitration. See *Textile Workers Union v. Lincoln Mills, supra* at 455. Any incentive for employers to enter into such an arrangement is necessarily dissipated if the principal and most expeditious method by which the no-strike obligation can be enforced is eliminated. While it is of course true, as respondent contends, that other avenues of redress, such as an action for damages, would remain open to an aggrieved employer, an award of damages after a dispute has been settled is no substitute for an immediate halt to an illegal strike. Furthermore, an action for damages prosecuted during or after a labor dispute would only tend to aggravate industrial strife and delay an early resolution of the difficulties between employer and union.

Even if management is not encouraged by the unavailability of the injunction remedy to resist arbitration agreements, the fact remains that the effectiveness of such agreements would be greatly reduced if injunctive relief were withheld. Indeed, the very purpose of arbitration procedures is to provide a mechanism for the expeditious settlement of industrial disputes without resort to strikes, lock-outs, or other self-help measures. This basic purpose is obviously largely undercut if there is no immediate, effective remedy for those very tactics which arbitration is designed to obviate. Thus, because *Sinclair,* in the aftermath of *Avco,* casts serious doubt upon the effective enforcement of a vital element of stable labor-management relations — arbitration agreements with their attendant no-strike obligations — we conclude that *Sinclair* does not make a viable contribution to federal labor policy.

IV. We have also determined that the dissenting opinion in *Sinclair* states the correct principles concerning the accommodation necessary between the seemingly absolute terms of the Norris-LaGuardia Act and the policy considerations underlying § 301(a). 370 U.S. at 215. Although we need not repeat all that was there said, a few points should be emphasized at this time.

The literal terms of § 4 of the Norris-LaGuardia Act must be accommodated to the subsequently enacted provisions of § 301(a) of the Labor-Management Relations Act and the purposes of arbitration. Statutory interpretation requires more than concentration upon isolated words; rather, consideration must be given to the total corpus of pertinent law and the policies which inspired ostensibly inconsistent provisions. See Richards v. United States, 369 U.S. 1, 11 (1962); Mastro Plastics Corp. v. NLRB, 350 U.S. 270, 285 (1956); United States v. Hutcheson, 312 U.S. 219, 235 (1941).

The Norris-LaGuardia Act was responsive to a situation totally different from that which exists today. In the early part of this century, the federal courts generally were regarded as allies of management in its attempt to prevent the organization and strengthening of labor unions; and in this industrial struggle the injunction became a potent weapon which was wielded against the activities of labor groups. The result was a large number of sweeping decrees, often issued *ex parte,* drawn on an *ad hoc* basis without regard to any systematic elaboration of national labor policy. See Drivers' Union v. Lake Valley Co., 311 U.S. 91, 102 (1940).

In 1932 Congress attempted to bring some order out of the industrial chaos that had developed and to correct the abuses which had resulted from the interjection of the federal judiciary into union-management disputes on the behalf of management. See Declaration of Public Policy, Norris-LaGuardia Act, § 2. . . . Congress, therefore, determined initially to limit severely the power of the federal courts to issue injunctions "in any case involving or growing out of any labor dispute. . . ." § 4. . . . Even as initially enacted, however, the prohibition against federal injunctions was by no means absolute. See Norris-LaGuardia Act, §§ 7, 8, 9. . . . Shortly thereafter Congress passed the Wagner Act, designed to curb various management activities which tended to discourage employee participation in collective action.

As labor organizations grew in strength and developed toward maturity, congressional emphasis shifted from protection of the nascent labor movement to the encouragement of collective bargaining and to administrative techniques for the peaceful resolution of industrial disputes. This shift in emphasis was accomplished, however, without extensive revision of many of the older enactments, including the anti-injunction section of the Norris-LaGuardia Act. Thus it became the task of the courts to accommodate, to reconcile the older statutes with the more recent ones.

A leading example of this accommodation process is Brotherhood of R.R. Trainmen v. Chicago River & Ind. R.R., 353 U.S. 30 (1957). There we were confronted with a peaceful strike which violated the statutory duty to arbitrate imposed by the Railway Labor Act. The Court concluded that a strike in violation of a statutory arbitration duty was not the type of situation to which the Norris-LaGuardia Act was responsive, that an important federal policy was involved in the peaceful settlement of disputes through the statutorily-mandated arbitration procedure, that this important policy was imperiled if equitable remedies were not available to implement it, and hence that Norris-LaGuardia's policy of nonintervention by the federal courts should yield to the overriding interest in the successful implementation of the arbitration process.

The principles elaborated in *Chicago River* are equally applicable to the present case. To be sure, *Chicago River* involved arbitration procedures established by statute. However, we have frequently noted, in such cases as *Lincoln Mills,* the *Steelworkers Trilogy,* and *Lucas Flour,* the importance which Congress has attached generally to the voluntary settlement of labor disputes without resort to self-help and more particularly to arbitration as a means to this end. Indeed, it has been stated that *Lincoln Mills,* in its exposition of § 301(a), "went a long way towards making arbitration the central institution in the administration of collective bargaining contracts."

The *Sinclair* decision, however, seriously undermined the effectiveness of the arbitration technique as a method peacefully to resolve industrial disputes without resort to strikes, lockouts, and similar devices. Clearly employers will be wary of assuming obligations to arbitrate specifically enforceable against them when no similarly efficacious remedy is available to enforce the concomitant undertaking of the union to refrain from striking. On the other hand, the central purpose of the Norris-LaGuardia Act to foster the growth and viability of labor organizations is hardly retarded — if anything, this goal is advanced — by a remedial device which merely enforces the obligation that the union freely undertook under a specifically enforceable agreement to submit disputes to arbitration. We conclude, therefore, that the unavailability of equitable relief in the arbitration context presents a serious impediment to the congressional policy favoring the voluntary establishment of a mechanism for the peaceful resolution of labor disputes, that the core purpose of the Norris-LaGuardia Act is not sacrificed by the limited use of equitable remedies to further this important policy, and consequently that the Norris-LaGuardia Act does not bar the granting of injunctive relief in the circumstances of the instant case.

V. Our holding in the present case is a narrow one. We do not undermine the vitality of the Norris-LaGuardia Act. We deal only with the situation in which a collective bargaining contract contains a mandatory grievance adjustment or arbitration procedure. Nor does it follow from what we have said that injunctive relief is appropriate as a matter of course in every case of a strike over an arbitrable grievance. The dissenting opinion in *Sinclair* suggested the following principles for the guidance of the district courts in determining whether to grant injunctive relief — principles which we now adopt:

"A District Court entertaining an action under § 301 may not grant injunctive relief against concerted activity unless and until it decides that the case is one in which an injunction would be appropriate despite the Norris-LaGuardia Act. When a strike is sought to be enjoined because it is over a grievance which both parties are contractually bound to arbitrate, the District Court may issue no injunctive order until it first holds that the contract *does* have that effect; and the employer should be ordered to arbitrate, as a condition of his obtaining an injunction against the strike. Beyond this, the District Court must, of course, consider whether issuance of an injunction would be warranted under ordinary principles of equity — whether breaches are occurring and will continue, or have been threatened and will be committed; whether they have caused or will cause irreparable injury to the employer; and whether the employer will suffer more from the denial of an injunction than will the union from its issuance." 370 U.S. at 228. (Emphasis in original.)

In the present case there is no dispute that the grievance in question was subject to adjustment and arbitration under the collective bargaining agreement and that the petitioner was ready to proceed with arbitration at the time an injunction against the strike was sought and obtained. The District Court also concluded that, by reason of respondent's violations of its no-strike obligation, petitioner "has suffered irreparable injury and will continue to suffer irreparable injury." Since we now overrule *Sinclair*, the holding of the Court of Appeals in reliance on *Sinclair* must be reversed. Accordingly, we reverse the judgment of the Court of Appeals and remand the case with directions to enter a judgment affirming the order of the District Court.

It is so ordered.

MR. JUSTICE MARSHALL took no part in the decision of this case.

MR. JUSTICE BLACK, dissenting. . . .

Although Congress has been urged to overrule our holding in *Sinclair,* it has steadfastly refused to do so. Nothing in the language or history of the two Acts has changed. Nothing at all has changed, in fact, except the membership of the Court and the personal views of one Justice. I remain of the opinion that *Sinclair* was correctly decided, and, moreover, that the prohibition of the Norris-LaGuardia Act is close to the heart of the entire federal system of labor regulation. In my view *Sinclair* should control the disposition of this case.

Even if the majority were correct, however, in saying that *Sinclair* misinterpreted the Taft-Hartley and Norris-LaGuardia Acts, I should be compelled to dissent. I believe that both the making and the changing of laws which affect the substantial rights of the people are primarily for Congress, not this Court. Most especially is this so when the law involved is the focus of strongly held views of powerful but antagonistic political and economic interests. The Court's function in the application and interpretation of such laws must be carefully limited to avoid encroaching on the power of Congress to determine policies and make laws to carry them out. . . .

[The concurring opinion of MR. JUSTICE STEWART is omitted. MR. JUSTICE WHITE dissented "for the reasons stated in the majority opinion in *Sinclair Refining Co. v. Atkinson.*"]

NOTES

1. What if the contract contains a no-strike clause, but no final and binding arbitration clause? What if it contains a final and binding arbitration clause, but no no-strike clause? *See generally* Axelrod, *The Application of the Boys Markets Decision in the Federal Courts,* 16 B.C. IND. & COM. L. REV. 893 (1975); Gould, *On Labor Injunctions, Unions, and the Judges: the Boys Markets Case,* 1970 SUP. CT. REV. 215; Vladeck, *Boys Markets and National Labor Policy,* 24 VAND. L. REV. 93 (1970).

2. In Gateway Coal Co. v. Mine Workers, 414 U.S. 368 (1974), the Supreme Court held that even a strike against allegedly unsafe conditions could be enjoined, when the union could have arbitrated its grievance that a mining company was retaining foremen who had falsified air flow records. Section 502 of the LMRA, which provides that work stoppages because of abnormally dangerous conditions are not "strikes," does not apply in the absence of "ascertainable, objective evidence" of such unsafe conditions. *See* Atleson, *Threats to Health and Safety: Employee Self-Help Under the NLRA,* 59 MINN. L. REV. 647 (1975).

3. If a state court issues a temporary restraining order against a strike and picketing which would expire by operation of law after 20 days, what is the effect of the union's removing the action to federal court? Does state or federal law govern the continuing validity of the state court restraining order? See Granny Goose Foods, Inc. v. Teamsters Local 70, 415 U.S. 423 (1974).

4. Justice Black wrote the majority opinion in *Sinclair Refining,* which was overruled in *Boys Markets,* and the full force of his legal argument is better understood from the following passage in the earlier decision:

"The language of § 301 itself seems to us almost if not entirely conclusive of this question. It is especially significant that the section contains no language that could by any stretch of the imagination be interpreted to constitute an explicit repeal of the anti-injunction provisions of the Norris-LaGuardia Act in view of the fact that the section does expressly repeal another provision of the Norris-LaGuardia Act dealing with union responsibility for the acts of agents. If Congress had intended that § 301 suits should also not be subject to the anti-injunction provisions of the Norris-LaGuardia Act, it certainly seems likely that it would have made its intent known in this same express manner. That is indeed precisely what Congress did do in §§ 101, amending § 10(h) of the National Labor Relations Act, and 208(b) of the Taft-Hartley Act, by permitting injunctions to be obtained, not by private litigants, but only at the instance of the National Labor Relations Board and the Attorney General, and in § 302(e), by permitting private litigants to obtain injunctions in order to protect the integrity of employees' collective bargaining representatives in carrying out their responsibilities. . . .

"When the inquiry is carried beyond the language of § 301 into its legislative history, whatever small doubts as to the congressional purpose could have survived consideration of the bare language of the section should be wholly dissipated. For the legislative history of § 301 shows that Congress actually considered the advisability of repealing the Norris-LaGuardia Act insofar as suits based upon breach of collective bargaining agreements are concerned and deliberately chose not to do so. . . . The House Conference Report expressly recognized that the House provisions for repeal in contract actions of the anti-injunction prohibitions of the Norris-LaGuardia Act had been eliminated in Conference. . . . And Senator Taft, Chairman of the Conference Committee and one of the authors of this legislation that bore his name, was no less explicit in explaining the results of the Conference to the Senate: 'The conferees . . . rejected the repeal of the Norris-LaGuardia Act.'

"We cannot accept the startling argument made here that even though Congress did not itself want to repeal the Norris-LaGuardia Act, it was willing to confer a power upon the courts to 'accommodate' that Act out of existence whenever they might find it expedient to do so in furtherance of some policy they had fashioned under § 301." 370 U.S. at 204-09.

5. Assume that sound policy supported the result in *Boys Markets,* but assume further (as seems not unlikely) that Norris-LaGuardia had become such a symbolic issue in the eyes of the labor movement that it was politically hazardous for Congress to tamper with it. Would that have cut for or against the Supreme Court's stepping in to do the job Congress could not face up to? For a thoughtful discussion, see Wellington & Albert, *Statutory Interpretation and the Political Process: A Comment Upon Sinclair v. Atkinson,* 72 YALE L.J. 1547 (1963).

6. Should the same standard of presumptive arbitrability applied in the *Steelworkers Trilogy* be used in *Boys Markets* suits? See Comment, *Boys Markets Injunctions Against Employers,* 91 HARV. L. REV. 715 (1978), discussing Lever Bros. v. Chemical Workers Local 217, 554 F. 2d 115 (4th Cir. 1976). It has been held that neither the expiration of a collective bargaining agreement nor the partial liquidation of an employer's business precludes the issuance of *Boys Markets* injunctions against a union or an employer to preserve the status quo. Bituminous Coal Operators Ass'n v. Mine Workers, 585 F. 2d 586 (3d Cir. 1978); Teamsters Local 71 v. Akers Motor Lines, 582 F. 2d 1336 (4th Cir. 1978). *See also* Goya Foods, Inc., 238 N.L.R.B. No. 204, 99 L.R.R.M. 1282 (1978) (no-strike clause "coterminous" with employer's duty to arbitrate under an expired contract, and strikers may be discharged).

7. *Strike Injunctions Under the Railway Labor Act.* In Railroad Trainmen v. Chicago River & Indiana R.R., 353 U.S. 30 (1957), discussed in *Boys Markets,* the Supreme Court held that the Norris-LaGuardia Act does not prevent an injunction against a strike in a so-called "minor dispute," *i.e.,* one involving a grievance under an existing collective agreement which is subject to statutory arbitration before the National Railroad Adjustment Board. On the other hand, the Court declared in Railroad Trainmen Lodge 27 v. Toledo, P. & W. R.R., 321 U.S. 50 (1944), that Norris-LaGuardia does prevent an injunction in a "major dispute" — one concerning future terms of employment. *See generally* Kroner, *Interim Injunctive Relief Under the Railway Labor Act: Some Problems and Suggestions,* in N.Y.U. EIGHTEENTH ANNUAL CONFERENCE ON LABOR 179 (1966).

A federal district court may include conditions in an injunction against a strike in order to protect employees against a harmful change in working conditions while a dispute is pending before the National Railroad Adjustment Board. Locomotive Engineers v. Missouri-Kansas-Texas R.R., 363 U.S. 528 (1960). A union cannot resort to a strike to enforce its interpretation of a money award by the NRAB in favor of an employee; the RLA provides for enforcement by a court suit. A strike in such circumstances can be enjoined, notwithstanding the Norris-LaGuardia Act. Locomotive Engineers v. Louisville & Nashville R.R., 373 U.S. 33 (1963).

BUFFALO FORGE CO. v. UNITED STEELWORKERS

Supreme Court of the United States
428 U.S. 397, 96 S. Ct. 3141, 49 L. Ed. 1022 (1976)

[The Buffalo Forge Company operates three separate plant and office facilities in the Buffalo, New York area. The Steelworkers Union has represented the production and maintenance (P&M) employees at these plants for some years. Other locals of the Steelworkers were certified in 1974 to represent the office clerical-technical (O&T) employees of Buffalo Forge at the same three plants. On November 16, 1974, after several months of negotiations looking toward their first collective bargaining agreement, the O&T employees struck and established picket lines at all three locations. The P&M employees honored the picket lines and stopped work.

The company sued the union under § 301 of the Taft-Hartley Act in Federal District Court for breach of the no-strike clause in the P&M collective agreement, seeking an injunction against the work stoppage. The collective agreement provided for arbitration as follows: "Should differences arise . . . as to the meaning and application of the provisions of this Agreement, or should any trouble of any kind arise in the plant, there shall be no suspension of work on account of such differences, but an earnest effort shall be made to settle such differences immediately. . . . In the event the grievance involves a question as to the meaning and application of this Agreement, and has not been previously satisfactorily adjusted, it may be submitted to arbitration upon written notice of the Union or the Company." The District Court found that the P&M employees had engaged in a sympathy action in support of the O&T employees, but held itself forbidden to enjoin it by the Norris-LaGuardia Act. The Court of Appeals affirmed, and the Supreme Court granted certiorari.]

MR. JUSTICE WHITE delivered the opinion of the Court.

The issue for decision is whether a federal court may enjoin a sympathy strike pending the arbitrator's decision as to whether the strike is forbidden by the express no-strike clause contained in the collective bargaining contract to which the striking union is a party. . . .

. . . .

II. As a preliminary matter, certain elements in this case are not in dispute. The Union has gone on strike not by reason of any dispute it or any of its members has with the employer but in support of other local unions, of the same international organization, that were negotiating a contract with the employer and were out on strike. The parties involved here are bound by a collective bargaining contract containing a no-strike clause which the Union claims does not forbid sympathy strikes. The employer has the other view, its complaint in the District Court asserting that the work stoppage violated the no-strike clause. The contract between the parties also has an arbitration clause broad enough to reach not only disputes between the Union and the employer about other provisions in the contract but also as to the meaning and application of the no-strike clause itself. Whether the sympathy strike the Union called violated the no-strike clause, and the appropriate remedies if it did, are subject to the agreed-upon dispute-settlement procedures of the contract and are ultimately issues for the arbitrator. [Citing the *Steelworkers Trilogy*.] The employer thus was entitled to invoke the arbitral process to determine the legality of the sympathy strike and to obtain a court order requiring the Union to arbitrate if the Union refused to do so. Gateway Coal Co. v. United Mine Workers, 414 U. S. 368 (1974). Furthermore, were the issue arbitrated and the strike found illegal, the relevant federal statutes as construed in our cases would permit an injunction to enforce the arbitral decision. United Steelworkers of America v. Enterprise Wheel & Car Corp. [363 U. S. 593 (1960)].

The issue in this case arises because the employer not only asked for an order directing the Union to arbitrate but prayed that the strike itself be enjoined pending arbitration and the arbitrator's decision whether the strike was permissible under the no-strike clause. . . .

The holding in *Boys Markets* was said to be a "narrow one," dealing only with the situation in which the collective bargaining contract contained mandatory grievance and arbitration procedures. 398 U. S. at 253. "[F]or the guidance of the district courts in determining whether to grant injunctive relief," the Court expressly adopted the principles enunciated in the dissent in Sinclair Refining Co. v. Atkinson, 370 U. S. 195, 228 (1962), including the proposition that:

> " 'When a strike is sought to be enjoined because it is over a grievance which both parties are contractually bound to arbitrate, the District Court may issue no injunctive order until it first holds that the contract *does* have that effect; and the employer should be ordered to arbitrate as condition of his obtaining an injunction against the strike.' " 398 U. S. at 254 (emphasis in *Sinclair*).

The driving force behind *Boys Markets* was to implement the strong congressional preference for the private dispute settlement mechanisms agreed upon by the parties. Only to that extent was it held necessary to accommodate § 4 of the Norris-LaGuardia Act to § 301 of the Labor Management Relations Act and to lift the former's ban against the issuance of injunctions in labor disputes. Striking over an arbitrable dispute would interfere with and frustrate the arbitral processes by which the parties had chosen to settle a dispute. The *quid pro quo* for the employer's promise to arbitrate was the union's obligation not to strike over issues that were subject to the arbitration machinery. Even in the absence of an express no-strike clause, an undertaking not to strike would be implied where the strike was over an otherwise arbitrable dispute. Gateway Coal Co. v. United Mine Workers, *supra;* Teamsters Local v. Lucas Flour Co., 369 U. S. 95 (1962). Otherwise, the employer would be deprived of his bargain and the policy of the labor statutes to implement private resolution of disputes in a manner agreed upon would seriously suffer.

Boys Markets plainly does not control this case. The District Court found, and it is not now disputed, that the strike was not *over* any dispute between the Union and the employer that was even remotely subject to the arbitration provisions of the contract. The strike at issue was a sympathy strike in support of sister unions negotiating with the employer; neither its causes nor the issue underlying it were subject to the settlement procedures provided by the contract between the employer and respondents. The strike had neither the purpose nor the effect of denying or evading an obligation to arbitrate or of depriving the employer of his bargain. Thus, had the contract not contained a no-strike clause or had the clause expressly excluded sympathy strikes, there would have been no possible basis for implying from the existence of an arbitration clause a promise not to strike that could have been violated by the sympathy strike in this case. *Gateway Coal Co. v. Mine Workers, supra* at 382.[10]

Nor was the injunction authorized solely because it was alleged that the sympathy strike called by the Union violated the express no-strike provision of the contract. Section 301 of the Act assigns a major role to the courts in enforcing collective bargaining agreements, but aside from the enforcement of the arbitration provisions of such contracts, within the limits permitted by *Boys Markets,* the Court has never indicated that the courts may enjoin actual or threatened contract violations despite the Norris-LaGuardia Act. In the course of enacting the Taft-Hartley Act, Congress rejected the proposal that the Norris-LaGuardia Act's prohibition against labor-dispute injunctions be lifted to the extent necessary to make injunctive remedies available in federal courts for the purpose of enforcing collective bargaining agreements. . . . The allegation of the complaint that the Union was breaching its obligation not to strike did not in itself warrant an injunction. . . .

The contract here at issue, however, also contained grievance and arbitration provisions for settling disputes over the interpretation and application of the provisions of the contract, including the no-strike clause. That clause, like others, was subject to enforcement in accordance with the procedures set out in the contract. Here the Union struck, and the parties were in dispute whether the sympathy strike violated the Union's no-strike undertaking. Concededly, that issue was arbitrable. It was for the arbitrator to determine whether there was a breach, as well as the remedy for any breach, and the employer was entitled to an order requiring the Union to arbitrate if it refused to do so. But the Union does not deny its duty to arbitrate; in fact, it denies that the employer ever demanded arbitration. However that may be, it does not follow that the District Court was empowered not only to order arbitration but to enjoin the strike pending the decision of the arbitrator, despite the express prohibition of § 4(a) of the Norris-LaGuardia Act against injunctions

---

[10] To the extent that the Court of Appeals, 517 F.2d, at 1211, and other courts . . . have assumed that a mandatory arbitration clause implies a commitment not to engage in sympathy strikes, they are wrong.

prohibiting any person "from ceasing or refusing to perform any work or to remain in any relation of employment." If an injunction could issue against the strike in this case, so in proper circumstances could a court enjoin any other alleged breach of contract pending the exhaustion of the applicable grievance and arbitration provisions even though the injunction would otherwise violate one of the express prohibitions of § 104. The court in such cases would be permitted, if the dispute was arbitrable, to hold hearings, make findings of fact, interpret the applicable provisions of the contract and issue injunctions so as to restore the status quo *ante* or to otherwise regulate the relationship of the parties pending exhaustion of the arbitration process. This would cut deeply into the policy of the Norris-LaGuardia Act and make the courts potential participants in a wide range of arbitrable disputes under the many existing and future collective bargaining contracts, not just for the purpose of enforcing promises to arbitrate, which was the limit of *Boys Markets,* but for the purpose of preliminarily dealing with the merits of the factual and legal issues that are subjects for the arbitrator and of issuing injunctions that would otherwise be forbidden by the Norris-LaGuardia Act.

This is not what the parties have bargained for. Surely it cannot be concluded here, as it was in *Boys Markets,* that such injunctions pending arbitration are essential to carry out promises to arbitrate and to implement the private arrangements for the administration of the contract. As is typical, the agreement in this case outlines the prearbitration settlement procedures and provides that if the grievance "has not been ... satisfactorily adjusted," arbitration may be had. Nowhere does it provide for coercive action of any kind, let alone judicial injunctions, short of the terminal decision of the arbitrator. The parties have agreed to grieve and arbitrate, not to litigate. They have not contracted for a judicial preview of the facts and the law. Had they anticipated additional regulation of their relationships pending arbitration, it seems very doubtful that they would have resorted to litigation rather than to private arrangements. The unmistakable policy of Congress stated in 29 U. S. C. § 173 (d), 61 Stat. 153, is that "Final adjustment by a method agreed upon by the parties is declared to be the desirable method for settlement of grievance disputes arising over the application or interpretation of an existing collective bargaining agreement." *Gateway Coal Co. v. United Mine Workers, supra* at 377. But the parties' agreement to adjust or to arbitrate their differences themselves would be eviscerated if the courts for all practical purposes were to try and decide contractual disputes at the preliminary injunction stage.

The dissent suggests that injunctions should be authorized in cases such as this at least where the violation, in the court's view, is clear and the court is sufficiently sure that the parties seeking the injunction will win before the arbitrator. But this would still involve hearings, findings and judicial interpretations of collective bargaining contracts. It is incredible to believe that the courts would always view the facts and the contract as the arbitrator would; and it is difficult to believe that the arbitrator would not be heavily influenced or wholly preempted by judicial views of the facts and the meaning of contracts if this procedure is to be permitted. Injunctions against strikes, even temporary injunctions, very often permanently settle the issue; and in other contexts time and expense would be discouraging factors to the losing party in court in considering whether to relitigate the issue before the arbitrator.

With these considerations in mind, we are far from concluding that the arbitration process will be frustrated unless the courts have the power to issue interlocutory injunctions pending arbitration in cases such as this or in others in which an arbitrable dispute awaits decision. We agree with the Court of Appeals that there is no necessity here, such as was found to be the case in *Boys Markets,* to accommodate the policies of the Norris-LaGuardia Act to the requirements of § 301 by empowering the District Court to issue the injunction sought by the employer.

The judgment of the Court of Appeals is affirmed.

So ordered.

MR. JUSTICE STEVENS, with whom MR. JUSTICE BRENNAN, MR. JUSTICE MARSHALL, and MR. JUSTICE POWELL join, dissenting. . . .

The Court today holds that only a part of the union's *quid pro quo* is enforceable by injunction.[2] The principal bases for the holding are (1) the Court's literal interpretation of the Norris-LaGuardia Act; and (2) its fear that the federal judiciary would otherwise make a "massive" entry into the business of contract interpretation heretofore reserved for arbitrators. The first argument has been rejected repeatedly in cases in which the central concerns of the Norris-LaGuardia Act were not implicated. The second is wholly unrealistic and was implicitly rejected in *Gateway Coal* when the Court held that "a substantial question of contractual interpretation" was a sufficient basis for federal equity jurisdiction. 414 U. S. at 384. That case held that an employer might enforce a somewhat ambiguous *quid pro quo;* today the Court holds that a portion of the *quid pro quo* is unenforceable no matter how unambiguous it may be. With all respect, I am persuaded that a correct application of the reasoning underlying the landmark decision in Boys Markets, Inc. v. Clerks Union, 398 U. S. 235, requires a different result.

. . . .

[There follows a detailed review of the rationale in *Boys Markets.*]

The *Boys Markets* decision protects the arbitration process. A court is authorized to enjoin a strike over a grievance which the parties are contractually bound to arbitrate, but that authority is conditioned upon

---

[2] The enforceable part of the no-strike agreement is the part relating to a strike "over an arbitrable dispute." In *Gateway Coal,* however, my Brethren held that the district court had properly entered an injunction that not only terminated a strike pending an arbitrator's decision of an underlying safety dispute, but also "prospectively required both parties to abide by his resolution of the controversy." *Id.* at 373. A strike in defiance of an arbitrator's award would not be "over an arbitrable dispute"; nevertheless, the Court today recognizes the propriety of an injunction against such a strike.

a finding that the contract does so provide, that the strike is in violation of the agreement, and further that the issuance of an injunction is warranted by ordinary principles of equity. These conditions plainly stated in *Boys Markets* demonstrate that the interest in protecting the arbitration process is not simply an end in itself which exists at large and apart from other fundamental aspects of our national labor policy.

On the one hand, an absolute precondition of any *Boys Markets* injunction is a contractual obligation. A court may not order arbitration unless the parties have agreed to that process; nor can the court require the parties to accept an arbitrator's decision unless they have agreed to be bound by it. If the union reserves the right to resort to self-help at the conclusion of the arbitration process, that agreement must be respected. The court's power is limited by the contours of the agreement between the parties.[17]

On the other hand, the arbitration procedure is not merely an exercise; it performs the important purpose of determining what the underlying agreement actually means as applied to a specific setting. If the parties have agreed to be bound by the arbitrator's decision, the reasons which justify an injunction against a strike that would impair his ability to reach a decision must equally justify an injunction requiring the parties to abide by a decision that a strike is in violation of the no-strike clause.[18] The arbitration mechanism would hardly retain its respect as a method of resolving disputes if the end product of the process had less significance than the process itself. . . .

In this case, the question whether the sympathy strike violates the no-strike clause is an arbitrable issue. If the court had the benefit of an arbitrator's resolution of the issue in favor of the employer, it could enforce that decision just as it could require the parties to submit the issue to arbitration. And if the agreement were so plainly unambiguous that there could be no bona fide issue to submit to the arbitrator, there must be the same authority to enforce the parties' bargain pending the arbitrator's final decision.

The Union advances three arguments against this conclusion: (1) that interpretation of the collective bargaining agreement is the exclusive province of the arbitrator; (2) that an injunction erroneously entered pending arbitration will effectively deprive the union of the right to strike before the arbitrator can render his decision; and (3) that it is the core purpose of the Norris-LaGuardia Act to eliminate the risk of an injunction against a lawful strike. Although I acknowledge the force of these arguments, I think they are insufficient to take this case outside the rationale of *Boys Markets*.

---

[17] In particular, an implied no-strike clause does not extend to sympathy strikes. See *ante* at n. 10.

[18] The Court recognizes that an injunction may issue to enforce an arbitrator's decision that a strike is in violation of the no-strike clause. . . .

The *Steelworkers Trilogy* establishes that a collective bargaining agreement submitting all questions of contract interpretation to the arbitrator deprives the courts of almost all power to interpret the agreement to prevent submission of a dispute to arbitration or to refuse enforcement of an arbitrator's award. *Boys Markets* itself repeated the warning that it was not for the courts to usurp the functions of the arbitrator. And *Gateway Coal* held that an injunction may issue to protect the arbitration process even if a "substantial question of contractual interpretation" must be answered to determine whether the strike is over an arbitrable grievance. In each of these cases, however, the choice was between interpretation of the agreement by the court or interpretation by the arbitrator; a decision that the dispute was not arbitrable, or not properly arbitrated, would have precluded an interpretation of the agreement according to the contractual grievance procedure. In the present case, an interim determination of the no-strike question by the court neither usurps nor precludes a decision by the arbitrator. By definition, issuance of an injunction pending the arbitrator's decision does not supplant a decision that he otherwise would have made. Indeed, it is the ineffectiveness of the damage remedy for strikes pending arbitration that lends force to the employer's argument for an injunction. The court does not oust the arbitrator of his proper function but fulfills a role that he never served.

The Union's second point, however, is that the arbitrator will rarely render his decision quickly enough to prevent an erroneously issued injunction from effectively depriving the union of its right to strike. The Union relies particularly upon decisions of this Court that recognize that even a temporary injunction can quickly end a strike. But this argument demonstrates only that arbitration, to be effective, must be prompt, not that the federal courts must be deprived entirely of jurisdiction to grant equitable relief. Denial of an injunction when a strike violates the agreement may have effects just as devastating to an employer as the issuance of an injunction may have to the union when the strike does not violate the agreement. Furthermore, a sympathy strike does not directly further the economic interests of the members of the striking local or contribute to the resolution of any dispute between that local, or its members, and the employer. On the contrary, it is the source of a new dispute which, if the strike goes forward, will impose costs on the strikers, the employer, and the public without prospect of any direct benefit to any of these parties. A rule that authorizes postponement of a sympathy strike pending an arbitrator's clarification of the no-strike clause will not critically impair the vital interests of the striking local even if the right to strike is upheld, and will avoid the costs of interrupted production if the arbitrator concludes that the no-strike clause applies.

Finally, the Norris-LaGuardia Act cannot be interpreted to immunize the union from all risk of an erroneously issued injunction. *Boys Markets* itself subjected the union to the risk of an injunction entered upon a judge's erroneous conclusion that the dispute was arbitrable and that the strike was in violation of the no-strike clause. *Gateway Coal* subjected the union to a still greater risk, for the court there entered an injunction to enforce an implied no-strike clause despite the fact that the arbitrability of the dispute, and hence the legality of the strike over the dispute, presented a "substantial question of contractual interpretation." The strict reading that the Union would give the Norris-LaGuardia Act would not have permitted this result.

These considerations, however, do not support the conclusion that a sympathy strike should be temporarily enjoined whenever a collective bargaining agreement contains a no-strike clause and an arbitration clause. The accommodation between the Norris-LaGuardia Act and § 301(a) of the Labor Management Relations Act allows the judge to apply "the usual processes of the law" but not to take the place of the arbitrator. Because of the risk that a federal judge, less expert in labor matters than an arbitrator, may misconstrue general contract language, I would agree that no injunction or temporary restraining order should issue without first giving the union an adequate opportunity to present evidence and argument, particularly upon the proper interpretation of the collective bargaining agreement; the judge should not issue an injunction without convincing evidence that the strike is clearly within the no-strike clause.[27] Furthermore, to protect the efficacy of arbitration, any such injunction should require the parties to submit the issue immediately to the contractual grievance procedure, and if the union so requests, at the last stage and upon an expedited schedule that assures a decision by the arbitrator as soon as practicable. Such stringent conditions would insure that only strikes in violation of the agreement would be enjoined and that the union's access to the arbitration process would not be foreclosed by the combined effect of a temporary injunction and protected grievance procedures. Finally, as in *Boys Markets,* the normal conditions of equitable relief would have to be met.

Like the decision in *Boys Markets,* this opinion reflects, on the one hand, my confidence that experience during the decades since the Norris-LaGuardia Act was passed has dissipated any legitimate concern about the impartiality of federal judges in disputes between labor and management, and on the other, my continued recognition of the fact that judges have less familiarity and expertise than arbitrators and administrators who regularly work in this specialized area. The decision in *Boys Markets* requires an accommodation between the Norris-LaGuardia Act and the Labor Management Relations Act. I would hold only that the terms of that accommodation do not entirely deprive the federal courts of all power to grant any relief to an employer, threatened with irreparable injury from a sympathy strike clearly in violation of a collective bargaining agreement, regardless of the equities of his claim for injunctive relief pending arbitration.

---

[27] Of course, it is possible that an arbitrator would disagree with the court even when the latter finds the strike to be clearly prohibited. But in that case, the arbitrator's determination would govern, provided it withstands the ordinary standard of review for arbitrator's awards. See United Steelworkers of America v. Enterprise Wheel & Car Corp., 363 U. S. 593, 597-599.

Since in my view the Court of Appeals erroneously held that the District Court had no jurisdiction to enjoin the Union's sympathy strike, I would reverse and remand for consideration of the question whether the employer is entitled to an injunction.

NOTES

1. Doesn't *Buffalo Forge* clearly flout the *Boys Markets* policy of substituting arbitration for strikes? On the other hand, if a Justice was uneasy that *Boys Markets* itself may have come close to flouting the congressional policy expressed in Norris-LaGuardia (see Justice Black's majority opinion in *Sinclair Refining,* quoted *supra* at 683), might he not feel more comfortable in limiting federal injunctions so that the enjoinable no-strike *quid* is coextensive with the arbitration *quo*? In any event, how can the Court justify under a strict *Boys Markets-Buffalo Forge* analysis the federal courts' willingness to "specifically enforce" an arbitrator's order that a union cease striking over an issue not itself subject to arbitration? *See, e.g.,* New Orleans S.S. Ass'n v. Longshore Workers Local 1418, 389 F. 2d 369 (5th Cir. 1968), *cert. denied,* 393 U.S. 828 (1968); Pacific Maritime Ass'n v. Longshoremen's Ass'n, 454 F. 2d 262 (9th Cir. 1971).

2. In Cedar Coal Co. v. UMW, 560 F.2d 1153 (4th Cir. 1977), the court ruled that some wildcat sympathy strikes in the coal industry may be subject to injunctive relief, despite the Supreme Court's holding in *Buffalo Forge.* Where "the purpose of the strike of Local [A] was to compel [the company] to concede an arbitrable issue to Local [B], with the same employer, the same collective bargaining agreement, the same bargaining unit, and the cause of Local [B] made its own, the *Buffalo Forge* exception to *Boys Markets* should not apply."

3. *Buffalo Forge* has provided a feast for the law reviews. See, *e.g.,* Gould, *On Labor Injunctions Pending Arbitration: Recasting Buffalo Forge,* 30 STAN. L. REV. 533 (1978); Lowden & Flaherty, *Sympathy Strikes, Arbitration Policy, and the Enforceability of No-Strike Agreements: An Analysis of Buffalo Forge,* 45 GEO. WASH. L. REV. 633 (1977); Smith, *The Supreme Court, Boys Markets Labor Injunctions, and Sympathy Work Stoppages,* 44 U. CHI. L. REV. 321 (1977). The case (or its issue) is noted in 76 COLUM. L. REV. 113 (1976); 29 U. FLA. L. REV. 525 (1977); 53 TEXAS L. REV. 1086 (1975).

ATKINSON v. SINCLAIR REFINING CO.

Supreme Court of the United States
370 U.S. 238, 82 S. Ct. 1318, 8 L. Ed. 2d 462 (1962)

MR. JUSTICE WHITE delivered the opinion of the Court.

The respondent company employs at its refinery in East Chicago, Indiana, approximately 1,700 men, for whom the petitioning international union and its local are bargaining agents, and 24 of whom are also petitioners here. In early February, 1959, the respondent company docked three of its employees at the East Chicago refinery a total of $2.19. On February 13 and 14, 999 of the 1,700 employees participated in a strike or work stoppage, or so the complaint alleges. On March 12, the company filed this suit for damages and an injunction, naming the international and its local as defendants, together with 24 individual union member-employees.

Count I of the complaint, which was in three counts, stated a cause of action under § 301 of the Taft-Hartley Act against the international and its local. . . . The complaint asked for damages in the amount of $12,500 from the international and the local.

Count II of the complaint purported to invoke the diversity jurisdiction of the District Court. It asked judgment in the same amount against 24 individual employees, each of whom was alleged to be a committeeman of the local union and an agent of the international, and responsible for representing the international, the local, and their members. The complaint asserted that on February 13 and 14, the individuals, "contrary to their duty to plaintiff to abide by such contract, and maliciously confederating and conspiring together to cause the plaintiff expense and damage, and to induce breaches of said contract, and to interfere with performance thereof by the said labor organizations, and the affected employees, and to cause breaches thereof, individually and as officers, committeemen and agents of said labor organizations, fomented, assisted and participated in a strike or work stoppage. . . ."

I. We have concluded that Count I should not be dismissed or stayed. Count I properly states a cause of action under § 301 and is to be governed by federal law. Local 174 v. Lucas Flour Co., 369 U.S. 95, 102-104 (1962); Textile Workers v. Lincoln Mills, 353 U.S. 448 (1957). Under our decisions, whether or not the company was bound to arbitrate, as well as what issues it must arbitrate, is a matter to be determined by the Court on the basis of the contract entered into by the parties. . . . We think it unquestionably clear that the contract here involved is not susceptible to a construction that the company was bound to arbitrate its claim for damages against the union for breach of the undertaking not to strike. . . .

Article XXVI [of the parties' contract] imposes the critical limitation. It is provided that local arbitration boards "shall consider only individual or local employee or local committee grievances arising under the application of the currently existing agreement." There is not a word in the grievance and arbitration article providing for the submission of grievances by the company. Instead, there is the express, flat limitation that arbitration boards should consider only employee grievances. Furthermore, the article expressly provides that arbitration may be invoked only at the option of the union. At no place in the contract does the union agree to arbitrate at the behest of the company. The company is to take its claims elsewhere, which it has now done.

The union makes a further argument for a stay. Following the strike, and both before and after the company filed its suit, 14 of the 24 individual defendants filed grievances claiming reimbursement for pay withheld by the employer. The union argues that even though the company need not arbitrate its claim for damages, it is bound to arbitrate these grievances; and the arbitrator, in the process of determining the grievants' right to reimbursement, will consider and determine issues which also underlie the company's claim for damages. Therefore, it is said that a stay of the court action is appropriate.

We are not satisfied from the record now before us, however, that any significant issue in the damage suit will be presented to and decided by an arbitrator. The grievances filed simply claimed reimbursement for pay due employees for time spent at regular work or processing grievances. . . .

For the foregoing reasons, the lower courts properly denied the union's motion to dismiss Count I or stay it pending arbitration of the employer's damage claim.

II. We turn now to Count II of the complaint, which charged 24 individual officers and agents of the union with breach of the collective bargaining contract and tortious interference with contractual relations. The District Court held that under § 301 union officers or members cannot be held personally liable for union actions, and that therefore "suits of the nature alleged in Count II are no longer cognizable in state or federal courts." The Court of Appeals reversed, however, ruling that "Count II stated a cause of action cognizable in the courts of Indiana and, by diversity, maintainable in the District Court."

We are unable to agree with the Court of Appeals, for we are convinced that Count II is controlled by federal law and that it must be dismissed on the merits for failure to state a claim upon which relief can be granted.

Under § 301 a suit for violation of the collective bargaining contract in either a federal or state court is governed by federal law, . . . and Count II on its face charges the individual defendants with a violation of the no-strike clause. After quoting verbatim the no-strike clause, Count II alleges that the 24 individual defendants "contrary to their duty to plaintiff to abide by" the contract fomented and participated in a work stoppage in violation of the no-strike clause. The union itself does not quarrel with the proposition that the relationship of the members of the bargaining unit to the employer is "governed by" the bargaining agreement entered into on their behalf by the union. It is universally accepted that the no-strike clause in a collective agreement at the very least establishes a rule of conduct or condition of employment the violation of which by employees justifies discipline or discharge. . . . The conduct charged in Count II is therefore within the scope of a "violation" of the collective agreement.

As well as charging a violation of the no-strike clause by the individual defendants, Count II necessarily charges a violation of the clause by the union itself. The work stoppage alleged is the identical work stoppage for which the union is sued under Count I and the same damage is alleged as is alleged in Count I. Count II states that the individual defendants acted "as officers, committeemen and agents of said labor organizations" in breaching and inducing others to breach the collective bargaining contract. Count I charges the principal, and Count II charges the agents for acting on behalf of the principal. Whatever individual liability Count II alleges for the 24 individual defendants, it necessarily restates the liability of the union which is charged under Count I, since under § 301(b) the union is liable for the acts of its agents, under familiar principles of the law of agency (see also § 301(e)). Proof of the allegations of Count II in its present form would inevitably prove a violation of the no-strike clause by the union itself. Count II, like Count I, is thus a suit based on the union's breach of its collective bargaining contract with the employer, and therefore comes within § 301(a). When a union breach of contract is alleged, that the plaintiff seeks to hold the agents liable instead of the principal does not bring the action outside the scope of § 301.

Under any theory, therefore, the company's action is governed by the national labor relations law which Congress commanded this Court to fashion under § 301(a). We hold that this law requires the dismissal of Count II for failure to state a claim for which relief can be granted — whether the contract violation charged is that of the union or that of the union plus the union officers and agents.

When Congress passed § 301, it declared its view that only the union was to be made to respond for union wrongs, and that the union members were not to be subject to levy. Section 301(b) has three clauses. One makes unions suable in the courts of the United States. Another makes unions bound by the acts of their agents according to conventional principles of agency law (*cf.* § 301(e)). At the same time, however, the remaining clause exempts agents and members from personal liability for judgments against the union (apparently even when the union is without assets to pay the judgment). The legislative history of § 301(b) makes it clear that this third clause was a deeply felt congressional reaction against the *Danbury Hatters* case (Loewe v. Lawlor, 208 U.S. 274 (1908); Lawlor v. Loewe, 235 U.S. 522 (1915)), and an expression of legislative determination that the aftermath (Loewe v. Savings Bank of Danbury, 236 Fed. 444 (2d Cir. 1916)), of that decision was not to be permitted to recur. In that case, an antitrust treble damage action was brought against a large number of union members, including union officers and agents, to recover from them the employer's losses in a nation-wide, union-directed boycott of his hats. The union was not named as a party, nor was judgment entered against it. A large money judgment was entered, instead, against the individual defendants for participating in the plan "emanating from headquarters" (235 U.S. at 534), by knowingly authorizing and delegating authority to the union officers to do the acts involved. In the debates, Senator Ball, one of the Act's sponsors, declared that § 301, "by providing that the union may sue and be sued as a legal entity, for a violation of contract, and that liability for damages will lie against union assets only, will prevent a repetition of the *Danbury Hatters* case, in which many members lost their homes" (93 Cong. Rec. 5014). See also 93 Cong. Rec. 3839, 6283; S. Rep. No. 105, 80th Cong., 1st Sess. 16.

Consequently, in discharging the duty Congress imposed on us to formulate the federal law to govern § 301(a) suits, we are strongly guided by and do not give a niggardly reading to § 301(b). "We would undercut the Act and defeat its policy if we read § 301 narrowly" (Lincoln Mills, 353 U.S. at 456 (1957)). We have already said in another context that § 301(b) at least evidences "a congressional intention that the union as an entity, like a corporation, should in the absence of agreement be the sole source of recovery for injury inflicted by it" (Lewis v. Benedict Coal Corp., 361 U.S. 459, 470 (1960)). This policy cannot be evaded or truncated by the simple device of suing union agents or members, whether in contract or tort, or both, in a separate count or in a separate action for damages for violation of a collective bargaining contract for which damages the union itself is liable. The national labor policy requires and we hold that when a union is liable for damages for violation of the no-strike clause, its officers and members are not liable for these damages. Here, Count II, as we have said, necessarily alleges union liability but prays for damages from the union agents. Where the union has inflicted the injury it alone must pay, Count II must be dismissed.[7]

The case is remanded to the District Court for further proceedings not inconsistent with this opinion.

It is so ordered.

MR. JUSTICE FRANKFURTER took no part in the consideration or decision of this case.

———————

DRAKE BAKERIES, INC. v. BAKERY WORKERS LOCAL 50, 370 U.S. 254, 82 S. Ct. 1346, 8 L. Ed. 2d 474 (1962). The employer was a large bakery. When Christmas and New Year's fell on Friday, it attempted to maintain a supply of fresh goods by rescheduling production so that employees would not work on the Thursdays before the holidays but would work on the following Saturdays. The union claimed the new schedule violated the labor contract. So few employees reported for work on Saturday, January 2 that the company could not operate. The employer promptly sued the union for damages for breach of the no-strike clause. The union sought a stay of the action pending arbitration, and the Supreme Court held such a stay should be granted. The Court distinguished *Atkinson* on the ground that here the arbitration provision did not exclude claims or complaints of the employer but instead permitted either party to refer a

———————

[7] In reaching this conclusion, we have not ignored the argument that Count II was drafted in order to anticipate the possible union defense under Count I that the work stoppage was unauthorized by the union, and was a wildcat strike led by the 24 individual defendants acting not in behalf of the union but in their personal and nonunion capacity. The language of Count II contradicts the argument, however, and we therefore do not reach the question of whether the count would state a proper § 301(a) claim if it charged unauthorized, individual action.

matter to arbitration. Moreover, the Court observed that the adjustment procedure broadly applied not only to disputes involving "the interpretation or application of any clause or matter" covered by the contract but also to "any act or conduct or relation between the parties." The Court concluded that this "easily reached the employer's claim against the union for damages caused by an alleged strike in violation of the contract.... We can enforce both the no-strike clause and the agreement to arbitrate by granting a stay until the claim for damages is presented to an arbitrator." In response to the employer's argument that the parties could not have intended to arbitrate "so fundamental a matter as a union strike in breach of contract," the Court said: "Arbitration provisions, which themselves have not been repudiated, are meant to survive breaches of contract, in many contexts, even total breach.... We do not decide in this case that in no circumstances would a strike in violation of the no-strike clause contained in this or other contracts entitle the employer to rescind or abandon the entire contract or to declare its promise to arbitrate forever discharged.... [T]here are no circumstances in this record which justify relieving the company of its duty to arbitrate the consequences of this one-day strike, intertwined as it is with the union denials that there was any strike or any breach of contract at all."

PACKING HOUSE WORKERS LOCAL 721 v. NEEDHAM PACKING CO., 376 U.S. 247, 84 S. Ct. 773, 11 L. Ed. 2d 680 (1964). An employer discharged one employee and as a result 190 others walked out. These employees were also discharged when they failed to return to work. About two months later the union filed grievances over the initial and subsequent discharges. The employer refused to arbitrate, declaring its duty to arbitrate was released by the union's alleged breach of a no-strike clause. When the union sued to compel arbitration, the employer counter-claimed for damages caused by the strike. The Supreme Court held that the alleged violation of the no-strike clause "did not release Needham from its duty to arbitrate the union's claim that employees had been wrongfully discharged." *Drake Bakeries* was thought dispositive of the case, even though (1) here the contract did not require the employer to submit its claims to arbitration, and (2) the strike was not merely a one-day work stoppage. The Court went on to say that the employer was not precluded from prosecuting its damage suit on the no-strike clause, but the legal effect of the arbitrator's decision on the court action was left open. The Court also did not decide "whether a fundamental and long-lasting change in the relationship of the parties prior to the demand for arbitration would be a circumstance which, alone or among others, would release an employer from his promise to arbitrate."

NOTES

1. Has the Supreme Court in *Drake* and *Needham* read the "substantial breach" doctrine out of the federal labor contract law being developed

under § 301? See Summers, *Collective Agreements and the Law of Contracts,* 78 YALE L.J. 525 (1969). *Cf.* Steelworkers Local 14055 v. NLRB [Dow Chem. Co.], 530 F.2d 266 (3d Cir. 1976), *cert. denied,* 429 U.S. 807 (1976); *Mastro Plastics Corp. v. NLRB, supra* at 143, and accompanying notes.

2. Some years ago a committee of the American Bar Association echoed a common sentiment when it said, "We feel that damage suits are generally not good medicine for labor relations." *See* Fulda, *The No-Strike Clause,* 21 GEO. WASH. L. REV. 127, 144 (1952) (Report of the Committee on Improvement of Administration of Union-Employer Contracts, ABA Section of Labor Relations Law). Recently, however, there appears to be a trend toward attempting to secure damages for breach of unions' no-strike pledges. *See, e.g.,* Fairweather, *Employer Actions and Options in Response to Strikes in Breach of Contract,* in N.Y.U. EIGHTEENTH ANNUAL CONFERENCE ON LABOR 129 (1966); Stewart, *No-Strike Clauses in the Federal Courts,* 59 MICH. L. REV. 673 (1961). One district court has awarded punitive as well as compensatory damages under § 301 for a strike in breach of contract. Sidney Wanzer & Sons v. Milk Drivers, Local 753, 249 F. Supp. 664 (N.D. Ill. 1966), noted in 80 HARV. L. REV. 903 (1967) and 52 VA. L. REV. 1377 (1966). But a court of appeals has refused to uphold punitive damages under § 301 where an employer violated a contract through a runaway shop. Shoe Workers Local 127 v. Brooks Shoe Mfg. Co., 298 F.2d 277 (3d Cir. 1962). In Teamsters Local 20 v. Morton, 377 U.S. 252 (1964), the Supreme Court held that punitive damages could not be recovered for peaceful secondary activities forbidden by § 303 of the LMRA. Are the language and policy of § 301 and § 303 distinguishable on this issue? *See generally* Brandwen, *Punitive-Exemplary Damages in Labor Relations Litigation,* 29 U. CHI. L. REV. 460 (1962); Ratner, *Damage Actions and the Impact of the Morton Case,* in N.Y.U. EIGHTEENTH ANNUAL CONFERENCE ON LABOR 117 (1966).

3. The Supreme Court in *Atkinson* did not pass on the question of individual employee liability for engaging in an unauthorized or "wildcat" strike in breach of contract. Employer efforts to obtain money damages from individual workers have been extremely rare. One study could find only a single reported case prior to 1958 allowing a recovery against employees for a peaceful strike. *See* Comment, *Liability of Employees Under State Law for Damages Caused by Wildcat Strike,* 59 COLUM. L. REV. 177, 181 (1959), citing Mapstrick v. Ramge, 9 Neb. 390, 2 N.W. 739 (1879). What bearing would the adoption of one or the other of the various legal theories of the labor agreement have on the issue of individual liability? *See* p. 640 *supra.* Are suits against individuals feasible? Are they sound labor relations policy? *See generally* Givens, *Responsibility of Individual Employees for Breaches of No-Strike Clauses,* 14 IND. & LAB. REL. REV. 595 (1961); Gould, *The Status of Unauthorized and "Wildcat" Strikes Under the NLRA,* 52 CORNELL L.Q. 672, 702-04 (1967). For a negative view of § 301 damage actions against individual wildcat strikers, *see* Sinclair Oil Corp. v. Oil Workers, 452 F.2d 49 (7th Cir. 1971), noted in 86 HARV. L. REV. 447 (1972). *But cf.* New York State United Teachers v. Thompson, 99 L.R.R.M. 2751 (N.D.N.Y. 1978) (improper retention of leave pay).

D. THE RELATIONSHIP BETWEEN CONTRACT EN-FORCEMENT AND UNFAIR LABOR PRACTICES

In enacting § 301 of the LMRA, Congress chose not to make breaches of the collective agreement unfair labor practices subject to the jurisdiction of the NLRB; instead, it left the enforcement of the labor contract to "the usual processes of the law." H.R. CONF. REP. No. 510, 80th Cong., 1st Sess. 42 (1947). Nonetheless, the parties to a labor agreement may include a provision paralleling § 8(a)(3) by forbidding discrimination against employees because of union activity. They may provide for arbitration of disputes about the scope of the bargaining unit. At the same time, the Board regards an employer's unilateral change in working conditions, without bargaining, as a violation of § 8(a)(5) — and where a collective agreement is in existence, that agreement is obviously the standard of many if not all working conditions in a unit. Moreover, § 8(d) makes it part of the duty to bargain to refrain from a strike or lockout to "terminate or modify" a contract prior to its expiration date. The inevitable result of all this is the possibility of overlap, or even conflict, between contractual rights and duties and statutory rights and duties.

The practical implications of this overlap may appear in several contexts: (1) before the NLRB, the respondent may claim (a) the allegation in the charge has already been the subject of an arbitral award in the respondent's favor, which the Board should "honor," or (b) the allegation could be the subject of a grievance under the parties' own contract, and the Board should therefore "defer" to arbitration; or (2) before a court (or arbitrator), the defendant may argue the matter involves an unfair labor practice or representational question subject to the exclusive primary jurisdiction of the Labor Board. The materials to follow deal with these various situations. In the leading case of Spielberg Mfg. Co., 112 N.L.R.B. 1080, 1082 (1955), the Board set forth three general conditions under which it would accord "recognition" to an arbitrator's award: "[T]he proceedings appear to have been fair and regular, all parties had agreed to be bound, and the decision of the arbitration panel is not clearly repugnant to the purposes and policies of the Act." The application (and limitations) of this formula will be considered next.

NLRB v. C & C PLYWOOD CORP.

Supreme Court of the United States
385 U.S. 421, 87 S. Ct. 559, 17 L. Ed. 2d 486 (1967)

MR. JUSTICE STEWART delivered the opinion of the Court.

The respondent employer was brought before the National Labor

Relations Board to answer a complaint that its inauguration of a premium pay plan during the term of a collective agreement, without prior consultation with the union representing its employees, violated the duties imposed by §§ 8(a)(5) and (1) of the National Labor Relations Act. The Board issued a cease-and-desist order, rejecting the claim that the respondent's action was authorized by the collective agreement. . . .[2]

In August 1962, the Plywood, Lumber, and Saw Mill Workers Local No. 2405 was certified as the bargaining representative of the respondent's production and maintenance employees. The agreement which resulted from collective bargaining contained the following provision:

"Article XVII

"WAGES

"A. A classified wage scale has been agreed upon by the Employer and Union, and has been signed by the parties and thereby made a part of the written agreement. The Employer reserves the right to pay a premium rate over and above the contractual classified wage rate to reward any particular employee for some special fitness, skill, aptitude or the like. The payment of such a premium rate shall not be considered a permanent increase in the rate of that position and may, at the sole option of the Employer, be reduced to the contractual rate. . . ."

The agreement also stipulated that wages should be "closed" during the period it was effective and that neither party should be obligated to bargain collectively with respect to any matter not specifically referred to in the contract. Grievance machinery was established, but no ultimate arbitration of grievances or other disputes was provided.

Less than three weeks after this agreement was signed, the respondent posted a notice that all members of the "glue spreader" crews would be paid $2.50 per hour if their crews met specified biweekly (and later weekly) production standards, although under the "classified wage scale" referred to in the above quoted Art. XVII of the agreement, the members of these crews were to be paid hourly wages ranging from $2.15 to $2.29, depending upon their function within the crew. When the union learned of this premium pay plan through one of its members, it immediately asked for a conference with the respondent. During the meetings between the parties which followed this request, the employer indicated a willingness to discuss the terms of the plan, but refused to rescind it pending those discussions.

It was this refusal which prompted the union to charge the respondent with an unfair labor practice in violation of §§ 8(a)(5) and (1). The trial examiner found that the respondent had instituted the premium-pay program in good-faith reliance upon the right reserved to it in the collective agreement. He, therefore, dismissed the complaint. The Board

---

[2] The NLRB's order directed respondent to bargain with the union upon the latter's request and similarly to rescind any payment plan which it had unilaterally instituted.

reversed. Giving consideration to the history of negotiations between the parties, as well as the express provisions of the collective agreement, the Board ruled the union had not ceded power to the employer unilaterally to change the wage system as it had. For while the agreement specified different hourly pay for different members of the glue spreader crews and allowed for merit increases for "particular employee[s]," the employer had placed all the members of these crews on the same wage scale and had made it a function of the production output of the crew as a whole.

In refusing to enforce the Board's order, the Court of Appeals did not decide that the premium-pay provision of the labor agreement had been misinterpreted by the Board. Instead, it held the Board did not have jurisdiction to find the respondent had violated § 8(a) of the Labor Act, because the "existence ... of an unfair labor practice [did] not turn entirely upon the provisions of the Act, but arguably upon a good-faith dispute as to the correct meaning of the provisions of the collective bargaining agreement. ..." 351 F.2d at 228.

The respondent does not question the proposition that an employer may not unilaterally institute merit increases during the term of a collective agreement unless some provision of the contract authorizes him to do so. See NLRB v. J.H. Allison & Co., 165 F.2d 766 (6th Cir. 1948), cert. denied, 335 U.S. 814 (1948). Cf. Beacon Piece Dyeing Co., 121 N.L.R.B. 953 (1958). The argument is, rather, that since the contract contained a provision which *might* have allowed the respondent to institute the wage plan in question, the Board was powerless to determine whether that provision *did* authorize the respondent's action, because the question was one for a state or federal court under § 301 of the Act.

In evaluating this contention, it is important first to point out that the collective bargaining agreement contained no arbitration clause.[9] The contract did provide grievance procedures, but the end result of those procedures, if differences between the parties remained unresolved, was economic warfare, not "the therapy of arbitration." Carey v. Westinghouse Corp., 375 U.S. 261, 272 (1964). Thus, the Board's action in this case was in no way inconsistent with its previous recognition of arbitration as "an instrument of national labor policy for composing contractual differences." International Harvester Co., 138 N.L.R.B. 923, 926 (1962), aff'd sub nom., Ramsey v. NLRB, 327 F.2d 784 (7th Cir. 1964), cert. denied, 377 U.S. 1003 (1964).

The respondent's argument rests primarily upon the legislative history of the 1947 amendments to the National Labor Relations Act. It is said that the rejection by Congress of a bill which would have given the Board unfair labor practice jurisdiction over all breaches of collective bargaining agreements shows that the Board is without power to decide any case

---

[9] The Court of Appeals in this case relied upon its previous decision in Square D Co. v. NLRB, 332 F.2d 360 (9th Cir. 1964). But *Square D* involved a collective agreement that provided for arbitration. See Note, Use of an Arbitration Clause, 41 Ind. L.J. 455, 469 (1966).

involving the interpretation of a labor contract. We do not draw that inference from this legislative history.

When Congress determines that the Board should not have general jurisdiction over all alleged violations of collective bargaining agreements and that such matters should be placed within the jurisdiction of the courts, it was acting upon a principle which this Court had already recognized:

"The Railway Labor Act, like the National Labor Relations Act, does not undertake governmental regulation of wages, hours, or working conditions. Instead it seeks to provide a means by which agreement may be reached with respect to them."

Terminal Railroad Ass'n v. Brotherhood of Railroad Trainmen, 318 U.S. 1, 6 (1943). To have conferred upon the National Labor Relations Board generalized power to determine the rights of parties under all collective agreements would have been a step toward governmental regulation of the terms of those agreements. We view Congress' decision not to give the Board that broad power as a refusal to take this step.

But in this case the Board has not construed a labor agreement to determine the extent of the contractual rights which were given the union by the employer. It has not imposed its own view of what the terms and conditions of the labor agreement should be. It has done no more than merely enforce a statutory right which Congress considered necessary to allow labor and management to get on with the process of reaching fair terms and conditions of employment — "to provide a means by which agreement may be reached." The Board's interpretation went only so far as was necessary to determine that the union did not agree to give up these statutory safeguards. Thus, the Board, in necessarily construing a labor agreement to decide this unfair labor practice case, has not exceeded the jurisdiction laid out for it by Congress.

This conclusion is re-enforced by previous judicial recognition that a contractual defense does not divest the Labor Board of jurisdiction. For example, in Mastro Plastics Corp. v. NLRB, 350 U.S. 270 (1956), the legality of an employer's refusal to reinstate strikers was based upon the Board's construction of a "no strike" clause in the labor agreement, which the employer contended allowed him to refuse to take back workers who had walked out in protest over his unfair labor practice. . . .

If the Board in a case like this had no jurisdiction to consider a collective agreement prior to an authoritative construction by the courts, labor organizations would face inordinate delays in obtaining vindication of their statutory rights. Where, as here, the parties have not provided for arbitration, the union would have to institute a court action to determine the applicability of the premium pay provision of the collective bargaining agreement.[15] If it succeeded in court, the union would then have to go

---

[15] The precise nature of the union's case in court is not readily apparent. If damages for breach of contract were sought, the union would have difficulty in establishing the amount of injury caused by respondent's action. For the real injury in this case is to the union's status as bargaining representative, and it would be difficult to translate such damage into dollars and cents. . . .

back to the Labor Board to begin an unfair labor practice proceeding. It is not unlikely that this would add years to the already lengthy period required to gain relief from the Board. Congress cannot have intended to place such obstacles in the way of the Board's effective enforcement of statutory duties. For in the labor field, as in few others, time is crucially important in obtaining relief. . . .

The legislative history of the Labor Act, the precedent interpreting it, and the interest of its efficient administration thus all lead to the conclusion that the Board had jurisdiction to deal with the unfair labor practice charge in this case. We hold that the Court of Appeals was in error in deciding to the contrary.

The remaining question, not reached by the Court of Appeals, is whether the Board was wrong in concluding that the contested provision in the collective agreement gave the respondent no unilateral right to institute its premium pay plan. In reaching this conclusion, the Board relied upon its experience with labor relations and the Act's clear emphasis upon the protection of free collective bargaining. We cannot disapprove of the Board's approach. For the law of labor agreements cannot be based upon abstract definitions unrelated to the context in which the parties bargained and the basic regulatory scheme underlying that context. See Cox, The Legal Nature of Collective Bargaining Agreements, 57 Mich. L. Rev. 1 (1958). Nor can we say that the Board was wrong in holding that the union had not foregone its statutory right to bargain about the pay plan inaugurated by the respondent. For the disputed contract provision referred to increases for "particular employee[s]," not groups of workers. And there was nothing in it to suggest that the carefully worked out wage differentials for various members of the glue spreader crew could be invalidated by the respondent's decision to pay all members of the crew the same wage. . . .

Reversed and remanded.

NOTE

Would the result in the principal case have been different if the collective bargaining agreement had contained a provision for final and binding arbitration? If so, on what theory? Does an arbitration clause constitute an agreement to channel collective bargaining in a particular way, or a waiver of a statutory right to bargain? *See, e.g.,* Timken Roller Bearing Co. v. NLRB, 161 F.2d 949 (6th Cir. 1947); Square D Co. v. NLRB, 332 F.2d 360 (9th Cir. 1964). If so, why wasn't a similar agreement or waiver found in the contract in the principal case, which provided for a grievance procedure and, presumably, permitted a court suit if necessary to resolve disputes? In NLRB v. Huttig Sash & Door Co., 377 F.2d 964 (8th Cir. 1967), a court of appeals, relying on *C & C Plywood,* upheld the Board's jurisdiction to find an employer guilty of an unfair labor practice in unilaterally reducing wages, even though the contract contained an arbitration clause.

Why did the "zipper clause" in the principal case play no significant part in the Court's thinking? Is there a difference between a union's waiver of the right to demand bargaining over a change in working conditions proposed by the union, and a union's waiver of the right to object to, or demand bargaining over, a change in working conditions proposed (or imposed) by the employer? Can the "residual rights" theory of the labor contract (see p. 646 *supra,* text at note 28) be squared with the principal case?

Would C & C Plywood Corp. have avoided violating § 8(a)(5) if it had bargained with the union before instituting the premium pay rates? Would that depend on whether or not the unilateral granting of premium pay was a breach of contract? What if the union had been offered and had rejected an opportunity to bargain? See C & S Industries, Inc., 158 N.L.R.B. 454 (1966), where the Board held an employer's unilateral establishment of an incentive wage system violated § 8(a)(5), even though the union declined to discuss the issue, the labor agreement forbade any change in the method of paying employees without the union's consent, and contract disputes were subject to arbitration.

Although a breach of contract as such is not an unfair labor practice, C & S Industries, Inc., *supra,* the NLRB will direct a party to "honor" a repudiated contract, Hyde's Super Market, 145 N.L.R.B. 1252 (1964), *enforced,* 339 F.2d 568 (9th Cir. 1964); Crescent Bed Co., 157 N.L.R.B. 296 (1966). Remedies have included orders to pay any fringe benefits which would have accrued to employees under a contract the employer unlawfully refused to sign, NLRB v. Strong, 393 U.S. 357 (1969), and to compensate employees for losses incurred because of a unilaterally imposed rider to an insurance policy, Scam Instrument Corp., 163 N.L.R.B. 284 (1967), *enforced,* 394 F.2d 884 (7th Cir. 1968), *cert. denied,* 393 U.S. 980 (1968). Is it still meaningful to say that the enforcement of collective bargaining agreements is a matter for the courts and not for the NLRB? What policy considerations support the enlargement of the Board's role? Can this be reconciled with the congressional decision not to make breaches of contract unfair labor practices but to subject them to court jurisdiction under § 301 of the LMRA?

See generally Bloch, *The · NLRB and Arbitration: Is the Board's Expanding Jurisdiction Justified?* 19 LAB. L.J. 640 (1968); Bond, *The Concurrence Conundrum: The Overlapping Jurisdiction of Arbitration and the NLRB,* 42 S. CAL. L. REV. 4 (1968); Cushman, *Arbitration and the Duty to Bargain,* 1967 WIS. L. REV. 612; Lesnick, *Arbitration as a Limit on the Discretion of Management, Union, and NLRB: The Year's Major Developments,* in N.Y.U. EIGHTEENTH ANNUAL CONFERENCE ON LABOR 7, 22-30 (1966); Wollett, *The Agreement and the National Labor Relations Act: Courts, Arbitrators and the NLRB — Who Decides What?* 14 LAB. L.J. 1041 (1963).

COLLYER INSULATED WIRE

National Labor Relations Board
192 N.L.R.B. 837 (1971)

The complaint alleges and the General Counsel contends that Respondent violated Section 8(a)(5) and (1) of the National Labor Relations Act, as amended, by making assertedly unilateral changes in certain wages and working conditions. Respondent contends that its authority to make those changes was sanctioned by the collective bargaining contract between the parties and their course of dealing under that contract. Respondent further contends that any of its actions in excess of contractual authorization should properly have been remedied by grievance and arbitration proceeding, as provided in the contract. We agree with Respondent's contention that this dispute is essentially a dispute over the terms and meaning of the contract between the Union and the Respondent. For that reason, we find merit in Respondent's exceptions that the dispute should have been resolved pursuant to the contract and we shall dismiss the complaint.

I. The Alleged Unilateral Changes

Respondent manufactures insulated electrical wiring at its plant in Lincoln, Rhode Island. The Union has represented Respondent's production and maintenance employees under successive contracts since 1937. The contract in effect when this dispute arose resulted from lengthy negotiations commencing in December 1968 and concluding with the execution of the contract of September 16, 1969. The contract was made effective from April 1, 1969, until July 2, 1971.

Respondent's production employees have historically been compensated on an incentive basis. The contract provides for a job evaluation plan and for the adjustment of rates, subject to the grievance procedure, during the term of the contract. Throughout the bargaining relationship, Respondent has routinely made adjustments in incentive rates to accommodate new or changed production methods. The contract establishes nonincentive rates for skilled maintenance tradesmen but provides for changes in those rates, also, pursuant to the job evaluation plan, upon changes in or additions to the duties of the classifications. The central issue here is whether these contract provisions permitted certain midcontract wage rate changes which Respondent made in November 1969.

A. *The Rate Increase for Skilled Maintenance Tradesmen:* Since early 1968, Respondent's wage rates for skilled tradesmen have not been sufficiently high to attract and retain the numbers of skilled maintenance mechanics and electricians required for the efficient operation of the plant. The record clearly establishes, and the Trial Examiner found, that other employers in the same region paid "substantially higher rates than those paid by Respondent." In consequence, the number of skilled maintenance workers had declined from about 40 in January 1968 to about 30 in mid-1969, and Respondent had been unable to attract employees to fill the resulting vacancies.

During negotiations, Respondent several times proposed wage raises for maintenance employees over and above those being negotiated for the production and maintenance unit generally. The Union rejected those proposals and the contract did not include any provision for such raises. It is clear, nevertheless, that the matter of the skill factor increase was left open, in *some* measure, for further negotiations after the execution of the agreement. The parties sharply dispute, however, the extent to which the matter remained open and the conditions which were to surround further discussions. The Union asserts, and the Trial Examiner found, that the Union was willing, and made known its willingness, to negotiate further wage adjustments only on a plantwide basis, consistent with the job evaluation system. Respondent insists that it understood the Union's position to be that wage increases for maintenance employees only might still be agreed to by the Union after the signing of the contract, if such increases could be justified under the job evaluation system.

At monthly meetings following conclusion of the contract negotiations, Respondent and the Union continued to discuss the Respondent's desire to raise the rates for maintenance employees. Finally, on November 12, 1969, Respondent informed the Union that five days thence, on November 17, Respondent would institute an upward adjustment of 20 cents per hour. The Union protested and restated its desire for a reevaluation of all jobs in the plant. Respondent's representative agreed to consider such an evaluation on a plantwide basis, upon union agreement to the increase for the skilled tradesmen. The Trial Examiner found that the Union did not agree. The rate increase became effective November 17, 1969.

B. *Reassignment of Job Duties:* One of the production steps, the application of insulating material to conductor, is accomplished through the operation of extruder machines. The insulating material, in bulk, is forced to and through the extruder die by a large worm gear. Each change in the type of insulation used on an extruder requires that the worm gear be removed and cleaned of insulation remaining from the previous production run. The removal, cleaning, and replacement of the worm gear is performed approximately once each week and requires approximately 40 minutes to one hour for each operation. Prior to November 12, 1969, the worm gear removal and cleaning had been performed by a team of two maintenance machinists. On November 12, Respondent directed that future worm gear removals would be performed by a single maintenance machinist with the assistance of the extruder machine operator and helper.

C. *Rate Increases for Extruder Operators:* Respondent's third change, also effective November 17, 1969, produced a rate increase for extruder operators. It had been Respondent's practice to adjust the straight time earnings of extruder operators by a factor representing the amount of time during an eight-hour shift when the extruder was in continuous operation. Under that system, for example, an operator who maintained his machine in continuous operation for eight hours was paid for 10 hours' work. This incentive factor has never been fixed by the contract and Respondent had, in the past, changed the rate for various reasons. This system of compensation operated somewhat to the detriment of first- and third-shift employees in that third-shift employees incurred the non-productive time required to shut down production at the end of each week, and the first-shift employees incurred that required for starting operations each Monday. That perceived inequity had stimulated numerous union requests for adjustment. Respondent sought to obviate this problem by computing the operating time on a weekly basis for each machine, determining the average incentive factor for all three shifts, and computing pay from that average. In making this change, Respondent gave the assurance that no operator would suffer any loss of pay by virtue of the revision. This was accomplished, in part, by raising the previous maximum 10.0 incentive factor to a range of from 10.3 to 10.6 hours' pay for continuous operation.

Another adjustment in computation related to a pair of extruder machines which were equipped with dual extruder heads so that each machine performed a dual insulation function. Respondent had previously paid a 5-percent premium to operators of these machines. On November 17, this premium was adjusted upward to 1-½ percent.

Finally, on February 16, 1970, in response to another complaint by the Union, Respondent restudied the rate on two extruders, pursuant to its contractual duty, and raised the incentive factor for those machines from 10.3 to 10.5 pay hours.

II. Relevant Contract Provisions

The contract now in effect between the parties makes provision for adjustment by Respondent in the wages of its employees during the contract term. Those provisions appear to contemplate changes in rates in both incentive and nonincentive jobs. Thus, article IX, section 2, provides:

"The Corporation agrees to establish rates and differentials of pay for all employees according to their skill, experience and hazards of employment, and to review rates and differentials from time to time. . . . However, no change in the general scale of pay now in existence shall be made during the term of this Agreement. This Article IX is applicable to the general wage scale, but shall not be deemed to prevent adjustments in individual rates from time to time to remove inequalities or for other proper reasons."

Further evidence of the contractual intent to permit Respondent to modify job rates subject to review through the grievance and arbitration procedures is found in article XIII, section 3, paragraph b, covering new or changed jobs. That paragraph provides that the Union shall have seven days to consider any new rating established by the Company and to submit objections. Thereafter, even absent Union agreement, it vests in the Company authority to institute a new pay rate. The Union, if dissatisfied, may then challenge the propriety of the rate by invoking the grievance procedure which culminates in arbitration.

Finally, the breadth of the arbitration provision makes clear that the parties intended to make the grievance and arbitration machinery the exclusive forum for resolving contract disputes. . . .

IV. Discussion

We find merit in Respondent's exceptions that because this dispute in its entirety arises from the contract between the parties, and from the parties' relationship under the contract, it ought to be resolved in the manner which that contract prescribes. We conclude that the Board is vested with authority to withhold its processes in this case, and that the contract here made available a quick and fair means for the resolution of this dispute including, if appropriate, a fully effective remedy for any breach of contract which occurred. We conclude, in sum, that our obligation to advance the purposes of the Act is best discharged by the dismissal of this complaint.

In our view, disputes such as these can better be resolved by arbitrators with special skill and experience in deciding matters arising under established bargaining relationships than by the application by this Board of a particular provision of our statute. The necessity for such special skill and expertise is apparent upon examination of the issues arising from Respondent's actions with respect to the operators' rates, the skill factor increase, and the reassignment of duties relating to the worm gear removal. Those issues include, specifically: (a) the extent to which these actions were intended to be reserved to the management, subject to later adjustment by grievance and arbitration; (b) the extent to which the skill factor increase should properly be construed, under article IX of the agreement, as a "change in the general scale of pay" or, conversely, as "adjustments in individual rates . . . to remove inequalities or for other proper reason"; (c) the extent, if any, to which the procedures of article XIII governing new or changed jobs and job rates should have been made applicable to the skill factor increase here; and (d) the extent to which any of these issues may be affected by the long course of dealing between the parties. . . .

The Board's authority, in its discretion, to defer to the arbitration process has never been questioned by the courts of appeals, or by the Supreme Court. Although Section 10(a) of the Act clearly vests the Board with jurisdiction over conduct which constitutes a violation of the provisions of Section 8, notwithstanding the existence of methods of "adjustment or prevention that might be established by agreement," nothing in the Act intimates that the Board must exercise jurisdiction where such methods exist. On the contrary in Carey v. Westinghouse Electric Corporation, 375 U.S. 261, 271 (1964), the Court indicated that it favors our deference to such agreed methods. . . .

The policy favoring voluntary settlement of labor disputes through arbitral processes finds specific expression in Section 203(d) of the LMRA. . . .

And of course disputes under Section 301 of the LMRA called forth from the Supreme Court the celebrated affirmation of that national policy in the *Steelworkers Trilogy.*

Admittedly neither Section 203 nor Section 301 applies specifically to the Board. However labor law as administered by the Board does not operate in a vacuum isolated from other parts of the Act, or, indeed, from other acts of Congress. In fact the legislative history suggests that at the time the Taft-Hartley amendments were being considered, Congress anticipated that the Board would "develop by rules and regulations, a policy of entertaining under these provisions only such cases . . . as cannot be settled by resort to the machinery established by the contract itself, voluntary arbitration. . . ." [7]

The question whether the Board should withhold its process arises, of course, only when a set of facts may present not only an alleged violation of the Act but also an alleged breach of the collective bargaining agreement subject to arbitration. Thus, this case like each such case compels an accommodation between, on the one hand, the statutory policy favoring the fullest use of collective bargaining and the arbitral process and, on the other, the statutory policy reflected by Congress' grant to the Board of exclusive jurisdiction to prevent unfair labor practices.

We address the accommodations required here with the benefit of the Board's full history of such accommodations in similar cases. From the start the Board has, case by case, both asserted jurisdiction and declined, as the balance was struck on particular facts and at various stages in the long ascent of collective bargaining to its present state of wide acceptance. Those cases reveal that the Board has honored the distinction between two broad but distinct classes of cases, those in which there has been an arbitral award, and those in which there has not.

In the former class of cases the Board has long given hospitable acceptance to the arbitral process. . . . The Board's policy was refined in *Spielberg Manufacturing Company,*[10] where the Board established the now settled rule that it would limit its inquiry, in the presence of an arbitrator's award, to whether the procedures were fair and the result not repugnant to the Act.

In those cases in which no award had issued, the Board's guidelines have been less clear. At times the Board has dealt with the unfair labor practice, and at other times it has left the parties to their contract remedies. . . .

Jos. Schlitz Brewing Company,[12] is the most significant recent case in which the Board has exercised its discretion to defer. The underlying dispute in *Schlitz* was strikingly similar to the one now before us. In *Schlitz* the respondent employer decided to halt its production line during

---

[7] S. Rep. No. 105, 80th Cong., 1st Sess. 23 (1947).

[10] 112 N.L.R.B. 1080, 1082 (1955).

[12] 175 N.L.R.B. No. 23 (1969).

employee breaks. That decision was a departure from an established practice of maintaining extra employees, relief men, to fill in for regular employees during breaktime. The change resulted in, among other things, elimination of the relief man job classification. The change elicited a union protest leading to an unfair labor practice proceeding in which the Board ruled that the case should be "left for resolution within the framework of the agreed upon settlement procedures." The majority there explained its decision in these words:

"Thus, we believe that where, as here, the contract clearly provides for grievance and arbitration machinery, where the unilateral action taken is not designed to undermine the Union and is not patently erroneous but rather is based on a substantial claim of contractual privilege, and it appears that the arbitral interpretation of the contract will resolve both the unfair labor practice issue and the contract interpretation issue in a manner compatible with the purposes of the Act, then the Board should defer to the arbitration clause conceived by the parties. . . ."

The circumstances of this case, no less than those in *Schlitz,* weigh heavily in favor of deferral. Here, as in *Schlitz,* this dispute arises within the confines of a long and productive collective bargaining relationship. The parties before us have, for 35 years, mutually and voluntarily resolved the conflicts which inhere in collective bargaining. Here, as there, no claim is made of enmity by Respondent to employees' exercise of protected rights. Respondent here has credibly asserted its willingness to resort to arbitration under a clause providing for arbitration in a very broad range of disputes and unquestionably broad enough to embrace this dispute.

Finally, here, as in *Schlitz,* the dispute is one eminently well suited to resolution by arbitration. The contract and its meaning in present circumstances lie at the center of this dispute. In contrast, the Act and its policies become involved only if it is determined that the agreement between the parties, examined in the light of its negotiating history and the practices of the parties thereunder, did not sanction Respondent's right to make the disputed changes, subject to review if sought by the Union, under the contractually prescribed procedure. That threshold determination is clearly within the expertise of a mutually agreed-upon arbitrator. In this regard we note especially that here, as in *Schlitz,* the dispute between these parties is the very stuff of labor contract arbitration. The competence of a mutually selected arbitrator to decide the issue and fashion an appropriate remedy, if needed, can no longer be gainsaid.

We find no basis for the assertion of our dissenting colleagues that our decision here modifies the standards established in *Spielberg* for judging the acceptability of an arbitrator's award. . . .

It is true, manifestly, that we cannot judge the regularity or statutory acceptability of the result in an arbitration proceeding which has not occurred. However, we are unwilling to adopt the presumption that such a proceeding will be invalid under *Spielberg* and to exercise our decisional authority at this juncture on the basis of a mere possibility that such a proceeding might be unacceptable under *Spielberg* standards. That risk is far better accommodated, we believe, by the result reached here of retaining jurisdiction against an event which years of experience with labor arbitration have now made clear is a remote hazard.

Member Fanning's dissenting opinion incorrectly characterizes this decision as instituting "compulsory arbitration" and as creating an opportunity for employers and unions to "strip parties of statutory rights."

We are not compelling any party to agree to arbitrate disputes arising during a contract term, but are merely giving full effect to their own voluntary agreements to submit all such disputes to arbitration, rather than permitting such agreements to be sidestepped and permitting the substitution of our processes, a forum not contemplated by their own agreement.

Nor are we "stripping" any party of "statutory rights." The courts have long recognized that an industrial relations dispute may involve conduct which, at least arguably, may contravene both the collective agreement and our statute. When the parties have contractually committed themselves to mutually agreeable procedures for resolving their disputes during the period of the contract, we are of the view that those procedures should be afforded full opportunity to function. The long and successful functioning of grievance and arbitration procedures suggests to us that in the overwhelming majority of cases, the utilization of such means will resolve the underlying dispute and make it unnecessary for either party to follow the more formal, and sometimes lengthy, combination of administrative and judicial litigation provided for under our statute. At the same time, by our reservation of jurisdiction, *infra,* we guarantee that there will be no sacrifice of statutory rights if the parties' own processes fail to function in a manner consistent with the dictates of our law. . . .

V. Remedy

Without prejudice to any party and without deciding the merits of the controversy, we shall order that the complaint herein be dismissed, but we shall retain jurisdiction for a limited purpose. Our decision represents a developmental step in the Board's treatment of these problems and the controversy here arose at a time when the Board decisions may have led the parties to conclude that the Board approved dual litigation of this controversy before the Board and before an arbitrator. We are also aware that the parties herein have not resolved their dispute by the contractual grievance and arbitration procedure and that, therefore, we cannot now inquire whether resolution of the dispute will comport with the standards set forth in *Spielberg, supra.* In order to eliminate the risk of prejudice to any party we shall retain jurisdiction over this dispute solely for the purpose of entertaining an appropriate and timely motion for further consideration upon a proper showing that either (a) the dispute has not, with reasonable promptness after the issuance of this decision, either been resolved by amicable settlement in the grievance procedure or submitted promptly to arbitration, or (b) the grievance or arbitration procedures have not been fair and regular or have reached a result which is repugnant to the Act.

[The concurring opinion of MEMBER BROWN is omitted.]

MEMBER FANNING (dissenting). . . .

I agree with the Trial Examiner that the wage increases for skilled employees only and the related worm gear change were properly subjects for collective bargaining and that Respondent violated Section 8(a)(5) and (1) of the Act by instituting these changes unilaterally. . . .

Clearly . . . the effect of the majority's decision is a direction to the parties to arbitrate a grievance which is no longer contractually arbitrable. The complaint is dismissed, but jurisdiction is retained, presumably to give the Union an opportunity to file a grievance under a time-expired contractual provision, with the implicit threat to the Respondent that the Board will assert jurisdiction, upon a proper motion, if Respondent is unwilling now to submit to arbitration. The majority's insistence that the parties' statutory rights cannot be adjudicated in this case except through the authority of an arbitrator verges on the practice of compulsory arbitration. Historically, in this country voluntarism has been the essence of private arbitration of labor disputes. Neither Congress nor the courts have attempted to coerce the parties in collective bargaining to resolve their grievances through arbitration. Compulsory arbitration has been regarded by some as contrary to a free, democratic society. Collective bargaining agreements, such as the one in the instant case, give aggrieved parties the *right* to file grievances and to present their disputes to an arbitrator. The element of compulsion has been deliberately omitted. To establish the principle, as a matter of labor law, that the parties to a collective bargaining agreement must, in part, surrender their protection under this statute as a consequence of agreeing to a provision for binding arbitration of grievances will, in my view, discourage rather than encourage the arbitral process in this country. Many may decide they cannot afford the luxury of such "voluntary" arbitration. . . .

The effect of the majority's decision in the instant case is clearly a reversal of the established *Spielberg* line of cases. In the future applicable standards for review of arbitration awards will not be followed. Neither the existence of an actual award, the fairness of the arbitrator's opinion or its impingement upon the policies of the Act will be considered by the Board in dismissing complaints of this nature. Under the majority's accommodation theory even consideration of the nature and scope of the alleged unfair labor practices, as set forth in . . . *Joseph Schlitz, supra,* will not receive the Board's attention. The impact of the majority's decision may be said to go beyond compulsory arbitration. For it means that in the future the Board will not concern itself with the *fact* or the *regularity* of the arbitral process, but will strip the parties of statutory rights merely on the *availability* of such a procedure.

The majority does not frame the primary issue in this case in terms calculated to resolve a particular dispute in a particular case. Rather, a new standard for the nonassertion of jurisdiction is announced, embracing a whole class of employers who have entered into contracts with unions containing a grievance-arbitration clause. In the future, complaints based upon such disputes, without regard to the seriousness of the alleged unfair labor practices, may not be litigated before this Board. . . .

Congress has said that arbitration and the voluntary settlement of disputes are the preferred method of dealing with certain kinds of industrial unrest. Congress has also said that the power of this Board to dispose of unfair labor practices is not to be affected by any other method of adjustment. Whatever these two statements mean, they do not mean that this Board can abdicate its authority wholesale. Clearly there is an accommodation to be made. The majority is so anxious to accommodate arbitration that it forgets that the first duty of this Board is to provide a forum for the adjudication of unfair labor practices. We have not been told that arbitration is the only method; it is one method.

We have recently been told by the Supreme Court that preemption in favor of this Board still exists. It is therefore inappropriate, to say the least, for us to cede our jurisdiction in all cases involving arbitration to a tribunal that may, and often does, provide only a partial remedy.

[The dissenting opinion of MEMBER JENKINS is omitted.]

NOTES

1. The *Collyer* deferral doctrine was extended to § 8(a)(3) discrimination cases in National Radio Co., 198 N.L.R.B. 527 (1972), another 3-2 decision. In General American Transp. Corp., 228 N.L.R.B. No. 102, 94 L.R.R.M. 1483 (1977), however, then-Chairman Betty Murphy voted with Members Fanning and Jenkins to trim back *Collyer* to its original 8(a)(5) dimensions and to refuse to defer to arbitration in cases alleging discrimination against individual employees. She reasoned:

"In cases alleging violations of Section 8(a)(5) and 8(b)(3), based upon conduct assertedly in derogation of the contract, the principal issue is whether the complained-of conduct is permitted by the parties' contract. Such issues are eminently suited to the arbitral process, and resolution of the contract issue by an arbitrator will, as a rule, dispose of the unfair labor practice issue. On the other hand, in cases alleging violations of Section 8(a)(1), 8(a)(3), 8(b)(1)(A), and 8(b)(2), although arguably also involving a contract violation, the determinative issue is not whether the conduct is permitted by the contract, but whether the conduct was unlawfully motivated or whether it otherwise interfered with, restrained, or coerced employees in the exercise of the rights guaranteed them by Section 7 of the Act. In these situations, an arbitrator's resolution of the contract issue will not dispose of the unfair labor practice allegation. Nor is the arbitration process suited for resolving employee complaints of discrimination under Section 7. . . ."

Chairman Murphy indicated in *General American* that she would still follow *Spielberg* and honor an arbitration award if the affected employee had voluntarily submitted to arbitration or "even if the award resulted from deferral by our Regional Office under the prevailing *Collyer* policy." She then proceeded to join the two all-out *Collyer* supporters, Members Penello and Walther, in reaffirming the policy of deferral to arbitration where there is alleged unilateral action in violation of § 8(a)(5). Roy Robinson Chevrolet, 228 N.L.R.B. No. 103, 94 L.R.R.M. 1474 (1977).

2. Does *Collyer* reflect a shift in direction from *C & C Plywood?* What factors must be weighed in assessing the deferral policy? *Collyer* touched off a lively, continuing controversy. See, *e.g.*, Atleson, *Disciplinary Discharges, Arbitration, and NLRB Deference,* 20 BUFFALO L. REV. 355 (1971); Christensen, *Private Judges, Public Rights: The Role of Arbitration in the Enforcement of the National Labor Relations Act,* in J. CORREGE, V. HUGHES & M. STONE, EDS., THE FUTURE OF LABOR ARBITRATION IN AMERICA 49 (1976); Getman, *Collyer Insulated Wire: A Case of Misplaced Modesty,* 49 IND. L.J. 57 (1973); Isaacson & Zifchak, *Agency Deferral to Private Arbitration of Employment Disputes,* 73 COLUM. L. REV. 1383 (1973); Nash, Wilder & Banov, *The Development of the Collyer Deferral Doctrine,* 27 VAND. L. REV. 23 (1974); Schatzki, *N.L.R.B. Resolution of Contract Disputes Under 8(a)(5),* 50 TEXAS L. REV. 225 (1972); Zimmer, *Wired for Collyer: Rationalizing NLRB and Arbitration Jurisdiction,* 48 IND. L. J. 141 (1973). The Getman piece was a response to Schatzki and Zimmer; their replies are in 49 IND. L. J. 76, 80 (1973). For judicial approval and qualifications of *Collyer,* see Machinists Lodges 700, 743, 1746 v. NLRB [United Aircraft Corp.], 525 F.2d 237 (2d Cir. 1975); IBEW Local 2188 v. NLRB, 494 F.2d 1087 (D.C. Cir. 1974), *cert. denied,* 419 U.S. 834 (1974).

3. The Board has refused to defer to arbitration, or to honor an award, where the interests of the aggrieved employees were in apparent conflict with the interests of the union as well as of the employer. Kansas Meat Packers, 198 N.L.R.B. 543 (1972); Anaconda Wire and Cable Co., 201 N.L.R.B. 839 (1973); Gateway Transp. Co., 137 N.L.R.B. 1763 (1962) (refusal to honor).

4. Should the NLRB honor an arbitrator's award as a whole, or merely any findings of fact or interpretations of contractual provisions which happen also to be essential parts of the unfair labor practice case? What about an issue that the parties had the opportunity but failed to place before the arbitrator? *Compare* Electronic Reprod. Serv. Corp., 213 N.L.R.B. 758 (1974), *with* Raytheon Co., 140 N.L.R.B. 883 (1963), *enforcement denied on other grounds,* 326 F.2d 471 (1st Cir. 1964), *and* Banyard v. NLRB, 505 F.2d 342 (D.C. Cir. 1974), noted in 88 HARV. L. REV. 804 (1975). Consider also the dispute concerning the propriety of an arbitrator's applying "external law," discussed *supra* at 669 n. 2.

CAREY v. WESTINGHOUSE ELECTRIC CORP.

Supreme Court of the United States
375 U.S. 261, 84 S. Ct. 401, 11 L. Ed. 2d 320 (1964)

MR. JUSTICE DOUGLAS delivered the opinion of the Court.

The petitioner union (IUE) and respondent employer (Westinghouse) entered into a collective bargaining agreement covering workers at several plants including one where the present dispute occurred. The agreement states that Westinghouse recognizes IUE and its locals as exclusive bargaining representatives for each of those units for which IUE or its locals have been certified by the National Labor Relations Board as the exclusive bargaining representative; and the agreement lists among those units for which IUE has been certified a unit of "all production and maintenance employees" at the plant where the controversy arose, "but excluding all salaried technical ... employees." The agreement also contains a grievance procedure for the use of arbitration in case of unresolved disputes, including those involving the "interpretation, application or claimed violation" of the agreement.

IUE filed a grievance asserting that certain employees in the engineering laboratory at the plant in question, represented by another union, Federation, which had been certified as the exclusive bargaining representative for a unit of "all salaried, technical" employees, excluding "all production and maintenance" employees, were performing production and maintenance work. Westinghouse refused to arbitrate on the ground that the controversy presented a representation matter for the National Labor Relations Board. IUE petitioned the Supreme Court of New York for an order compelling arbitration. That court refused. The Appellate Division affirmed, one judge dissenting, 15 App. Div. 2d 7, 221 N.Y.S.2d 303. The Court of Appeals affirmed, one judge dissenting, holding that the matter was within the exclusive jurisdiction of the Board since it involved a definition of bargaining units. 11 N.Y.2d 452, 230 N.Y.S.2d 703. . . .

We have here a so-called "jurisdictional" dispute involving two unions and the employer. But the term "jurisdictional" is not a word of a single meaning. In the setting of the present case this "jurisdictional" dispute could be one of two different, though related, species: either — (1) a controversy as to whether certain work should be performed by workers in one bargaining unit or those in another; or (2) a controversy as to which union should represent the employees doing particular work. If this controversy is considered to be the former, the National Labor Relations Act (61 Stat. 136, 73 Stat. 519, 29 U.S.C. § 151 *et seq.*) does not purport to cover all phases and stages of it. While § 8(b)(4)(D) makes it an unfair labor practice for a union to strike to get an employer to assign work to a particular group of employees rather than to another, the Act does not deal with the controversy anterior to a strike nor provide any machinery for resolving such a dispute absent a strike. The Act and its remedies for "jurisdictional" controversies of that nature come into play only by a strike or a threat of a strike. Such conduct gives the Board authority under § 10(k) to resolve the dispute.

Are we to assume that the regulatory scheme contains an hiatus, allowing no recourse to arbitration over work assignments between two unions but forcing the controversy into the strike stage before a remedy before the Board is available? The Board, as admonished by § 10(k), has often given effect to private agreements to settle disputes of this character; and that is in accord with the purpose as stated even by the minority spokesman in Congress "that full opportunity is given the parties to reach a voluntary accommodation without governmental intervention if they so desire." 93 Cong. Rec. 4035; 2 Leg. Hist., L.M.R.A. 1046 (1947). And see NLRB v. Radio Engineers, 364 U.S. 573, 577.

As Judge Fuld, dissenting below, said: "The underlying objective of the national labor relations laws is to promote collective bargaining agreements and to help give substance to such agreements through the arbitration process." 11 N.Y.2d 452, 458, 230 N.Y.S.2d 703, 706.

Grievance arbitration is one method of settling disputes over work assignments; and it is commonly used, we are told. To be sure, only one of the two unions involved in the controversy has moved the state courts to compel arbitration. So unless the other union intervenes, an adjudication of the arbiter might not put an end to the dispute. Yet the arbitration may as a practical matter end the controversy or put into movement forces that will resolve it. The case in its present posture is analogous to Whitehouse v. Illinois Central R. Co., 349 U.S. 366, where a railroad and two unions were disputing a jurisdictional matter, when the National Railroad Adjustment Board served notice on the railroad and one union of its assumption of jurisdiction. The railroad, not being able to have notice served on the other union, sued in the courts for relief. We adopted a hands-off policy, saying, "Railroad's resort to the courts has preceded any award, and one may be rendered which could occasion no possible injury to it." *Id.* at 373.

Since § 10(k) not only tolerates but actively encourages voluntary settlements of work assignment controversies between unions, we conclude that grievance procedures pursued to arbitration further the policies of the Act.

What we have said so far treats the case as if the grievance involves only a work assignment dispute. If, however, the controversy be a representational one, involving the duty of an employer to bargain collectively with the representative of the employees as provided in § 8(a)(5), further considerations are necessary. Such a charge, made by a union against the employer, would, if proved, be an unfair labor practice, as § 8(a)(5) expressly states. Or the unions instead of filing such a charge might petition the Board under § 9(c)(1) to obtain a clarification of the certificates they already have from the Board; and the employer might do the same. . . .

If this is truly a representation case, either IUE or Westinghouse can move to have the certificate clarified. But the existence of a remedy before the Board for an unfair labor practice does not bar individual employees from seeking damages for breach of a collective bargaining agreement in a state court, as we held in Smith v. Evening News Ass'n, 371 U.S. 195

(1962). We think the same policy considerations are applicable here; and that a suit either in the federal courts, as provided by § 301(a) of the Labor Management Relations Act of 1947 (61 Stat. 156, 29 U.S.C. § 185(a); F.C.A. 29 § 1851(a); Textile Workers v. Lincoln Mills, 353 U.S. 448 (1957)), or before such state tribunals as are authorized to act (Charles Dowd Box Co. v. Courtney, 368 U.S. 502 (1962); Teamsters Local v. Lucas Flour Co., 369 U.S. 95 (1962)) is proper, even though an alternative remedy before the Board is available, which, if invoked by the employer, will protect him.

The policy considerations behind Smith v. Evening News Ass'n, *supra,* are highlighted here by reason of the blurred line that often exists between work assignment disputes and controversies over which of two or more unions is the appropriate bargaining unit. It may be claimed that *A* and *B,* to whom work is assigned as "technical" employees, are in fact "production and maintenance" employees; and if that charge is made and sustained the Board, under the decisions already noted, clarifies the certificate. But IUE may claim that when the work was assigned to *A* and *B,* the collective agreement was violated because "production and maintenance" employees, not "technical" employees, were entitled to it. As noted, the Board clarifies certificates where a certified union seeks to represent additional employees; but it will not entertain a motion to clarify a certificate where the union merely seeks additional work for employees already within its unit. . . .

As the Board's decisions indicate, disputes are often difficult to classify. In the present case the Solicitor General, who appears *amicus,* believes the controversy is essentially a representational one. So does Westinghouse. IUE on the other hand claims it is a work assignment dispute. Even if it is in form a representation problem, in substance it may involve problems of seniority when lay-offs occur (see Sovern, Section 301 and the Primary Jurisdiction of the NLRB, 76 Harv. L. Rev. 529, 574-575 (1963)) or other aspects of work assignment disputes. If that is true, there is work for the arbiter whatever the Board may decide.

If by the time the dispute reaches the Board, arbitration has already taken place, the Board shows deference to the arbitral award, provided the procedure was a fair one and the results were not repugnant to the Act. . . .

Should the Board disagree with the arbiter, by ruling, for example, that the employees involved in the controversy are members of one bargaining unit or another, the Board's ruling would, of course, take precedence; and if the employer's action had been in accord with that ruling, it would not be liable for damages under § 301. But that is not peculiar to the present type of controversy. Arbitral awards construing a seniority provision (Carey v. General Elec. Co., 315 F.2d 499, 509-510 (1963)), or awards concerning unfair labor practices, may later end up in conflict with Board rulings. See International Association of Machinists, 116 N.L.R.B. 645; Monsanto Chem. Co., *supra.* Yet, as we held in Smith v. Evening News Ass'n, *supra,* the possibility of conflict is no barrier to resort to a tribunal other than the Board.

However the dispute be considered — whether one involving work assignment or one concerning representation — we see no barrier to use of the arbitration procedure. If it is a work assignment dispute, arbitration conveniently fills a gap and avoids the necessity of a strike to bring the matter to the Board. If it is a representation matter, resort to arbitration may have a pervasive, curative effect even though one union is not a party.

By allowing the dispute to go to arbitration its fragmentation is avoided to a substantial extent; and those conciliatory measures which Congress deemed vital to "industrial peace" (Textile Workers v. Lincoln Mills, *supra* at 455) and which may be dispositive of the entire dispute, are encouraged. The superior authority of the Board may be invoked at any time. Meanwhile the therapy of arbitration is brought to bear in a complicated and troubled area.

Reversed.

Mr. Justice Goldberg took no part in the consideration or decision of this case.

Mr. Justice Harlan, concurring.

I join the Court's opinion with a brief comment. As is recognized by all, neither position in this case is without its difficulties. Lacking a clear-cut command in the statute itself, the choice in substance lies between a course which would altogether preclude any attempt at resolving disputes of this kind by arbitration, and one which at worst will expose those concerned to the hazard of duplicative proceedings. The undesirable consequences of the first alternative are inevitable, those of the second conjectural. As between the two, I think the Court at this early stage of experience in this area rightly chooses the latter.

Mr. Justice Black, with whom Mr. Justice Clark joins, dissenting. . . .

I agree with the New York court and would affirm its judgment. Stripped of obscurantist arguments, this controversy is a plain, garden-variety jurisdictional dispute between two unions. The Court today holds, however, that the National Labor Relations Act not only permits but compels Westinghouse to arbitrate the dispute with only one of the two warring unions. Such an arbitration could not, of course, bring about the "final and binding arbitration of grievances and disputes" that the Court says contributes to the congressional objectives in passing the Labor Act. Unless all the salutary safeguards of due process of law are to be dissipated and obliterated to further the cause of arbitration, the rights of employees belonging to the Federation should not, for "policy considerations," be sacrificed by an arbitration award in proceedings between IUE and Westinghouse alone. . . .

The result of all this is that the National Labor Relations Board, the agency created by Congress finally to settle labor disputes in the interest of industrial peace, is to be supplanted in part by so-called arbitration which in its very nature cannot achieve a final adjustment of those disputes. One of the main evils it had been hoped the Labor Act would abate was jurisdictional disputes between unions over which union members would do certain work. The Board can make final settlements of such disputes. Arbitration between some but not all the parties cannot. I fear that the Court's recently announced leanings to treat arbitration as an almost sure and certain solvent of all labor troubles has been carried so far in this case as unnecessarily to bring about great confusion and to delay final and binding settlements of jurisdictional disputes by the Labor Board, the agency which I think Congress intended to do that very job.

I would affirm.

NOTE

Arbitration took place following the decision in the principal case. The NLRB subsequently concluded, however, that the ultimate issue of representation could not be decided by the arbitrator through an interpretation of the contract but could be resolved only through the use of Board criteria for unit determinations. While giving "some consideration to the award," the Board proceeded to make a different unit allocation. Westinghouse Elec. Corp., 162 N.L.R.B. 768 (1967). Arbitration awards have been recognized, however, in representation proceedings as well as in unfair labor practice cases. Raley's, Inc., 143 N.L.R.B. 256 (1963).

For a spirited debate on the capacity of an arbitrator to induce (or strongarm) the second union into an arbitration in a *Carey* situation, *see* Bernstein, *Nudging and Shoving All Parties to a Jurisdictional Dispute Into Arbitration: The Dubious Procedure of National Steel,* 78 HARV. L. REV. 784 (1965); Jones, *On Nudging and Shoving the National Steel Arbitration Into a Dubious Procedure,* 79 HARV. L. REV. 327 (1965); Jones, *An Arbitral Answer to a Judicial Dilemma: The Carey Decision and Trilateral Arbitration of Jurisdictional Disputes,* 11 U.C.L.A. L. REV. 327 (1964). *See also* Columbia Broadcasting System v. American Recording & Broadcasting Ass'n, 414 F.2d 1326 (2d Cir. 1969). *Cf.* Bell Aerospace Co. v. UAW Local 516, 500 F.2d 921 (2d Cir. 1974).

Under the Railway Labor Act, the National Railroad Adjustment Board is authorized (and required) to summon the disputing unions before it in order to dispose of all claims to work assignments in a single proceeding. Transportation-Communication Employees Union v. Union Pac. R.R., 385 U.S. 157 (1966), noted by Jones in 15 U.C.L.A. L. REV. 877 (1968).

SMITH V. EVENING NEWS ASS'N, 371 U.S. 195, 83 S. Ct. 267, 9 L. Ed. 2d 246 (1962). Petitioner, a union member, sued his employer in state court for damages, alleging breach of a provision in the collective contract that there would be no discrimination against any employee because of union activity. The state courts dismissed on the ground the subject matter was within the exclusive jurisdiction of the NLRB. The Supreme Court reversed. The Court first declared that the authority of the Board to deal with unfair labor practices which also violate collective agreements "is not exclusive and does not destroy the jurisdiction of the courts in suits under

§ 301." The Court then concluded that an action by an individual employee to collect wages in the form of damages is among those "suits for violation of contracts between an employer and a labor organization" arising under § 301.

NOTES

1. In Arnold Co. v. Carpenters Dist. Council of Jacksonville, 417 U. S. 12 (1974), the Supreme Court held that a state court had jurisdiction to enjoin a union's breach of a no-strike clause, even though the breach arguably involved a violation of § 8(b)(4)(D)'s jurisdictional dispute provisions.

2. *See generally* Dunau, *Contractual Prohibition of Unfair Labor Practices: Jurisdictional Problems,* 57 COLUM. L. REV. 52 (1957); Sovern, *Section 301 and the Primary Jurisdiction of the NLRB,* 76 HARV. L. REV. 529 (1963). The large question of individual employee rights under a labor agreement will be treated in detail in section IV, *infra* at 738 ff.

E. SUCCESSOR EMPLOYERS' CONTRACTUAL AND BARGAINING OBLIGATIONS

JOHN WILEY & SONS, INC. v. LIVINGSTON

Supreme Court of the United States
376 U.S. 543, 84 S. Ct. 909, 11 L. Ed. 2d 898 (1964)

MR. JUSTICE HARLAN delivered the opinion of the Court.

This is an action by a union, pursuant to § 301 of the Labor Management Relations Act, . . . to compel arbitration under a collective bargaining agreement. The major questions presented are (1) whether a corporate employer must arbitrate with a union under a bargaining agreement between the union and another corporation which has merged with the employer, and, if so, (2) whether the courts or the arbitrator is the appropriate body to decide whether procedural prerequisites which, under the bargaining agreement, condition the duty to arbitrate have been met. Because of the importance of both questions to the realization of national labor policy, we granted certiorari . . . to review a judgment of the Court of Appeals directing arbitration (313 F.2d 52), in reversal of the District Court which had refused such relief (203 F. Supp. 171). We affirm the judgment below, but, with respect to the first question above, on grounds which may differ from those of the Court of Appeals, whose answer to that question is unclear.

I. District 65, Retail, Wholesale and Department Store Union, AFL-CIO, entered into a collective bargaining agreement with Interscience Publishers, Inc., a publishing firm, for a term expiring on January 31, 1962. The agreement did not contain an express provision making it binding on successors of Interscience. On October 2, 1961, Interscience merged with the petitioner, John Wiley & Sons, Inc., another publishing firm, and ceased to do business as a separate entity. There is no suggestion that the merger was not for genuine business reasons.

At the time of the merger Interscience had about 80 employees, of whom 40 were represented by this Union. It had a single plant in New York City, and did an annual business of somewhat over $1,000,000. Wiley was a much larger concern, having separate office and warehouse facilities and about 300 employees, and doing an annual business of more than $9,000,000. None of Wiley's employees was represented by a union.

In discussions before and after the merger, the Union and Interscience (later Wiley) were unable to agree on the effect of the merger on the collective bargaining agreement and on the rights under it of those covered employees hired by Wiley. The Union's position was that despite the merger it continued to represent the covered Interscience employees taken over by Wiley, and that Wiley was obligated to recognize certain rights of such employees which had "vested" under the Interscience bargaining agreement. Such rights, more fully described below, concerned matters typically covered by collective bargaining agreements, such as seniority status, severance pay, etc. The Union contended also that Wiley was required to make certain pension fund payments called for under the Interscience bargaining agreement.

Wiley, though recognizing for purposes of its own pension plan the Interscience service of the former Interscience employees, asserted that the merger terminated the bargaining agreement for all purposes. It refused to recognize the Union as bargaining agent or to accede to the Union's claims on behalf of Interscience employees. All such employees, except a few who ended their Wiley employment with severance pay and for whom no rights are asserted here, continued in Wiley's employ.

No satisfactory solution having been reached, the Union, one week before the expiration date of the Interscience bargaining agreement, commenced this action to compel arbitration.

II. The threshold question in this controversy is who shall decide whether the arbitration provisions of the collective bargaining agreement survived the Wiley-Interscience merger, so as to be operative against Wiley. Both parties urge that this question is for the courts. Past cases leave no doubt that this is correct. . . . The duty to arbitrate being of contractual origin, a compulsory submission to arbitration cannot precede judicial determination that the collective bargaining agreement does in fact create such a duty. Thus, just as an employer has no obligation to arbitrate issues which it has not agreed to arbitrate, so a fortiori, it cannot be compelled to arbitrate if an arbitration clause does not bind it at all. . . .

. . . We hold that the disappearance by merger of a corporate employer which has entered into a collective bargaining agreement with a union does not automatically terminate all rights of the employees covered by the agreement, and that, in appropriate circumstances, present here, the successor employer may be required to arbitrate with the union under the agreement.

This Court has in the past recognized the central role of arbitration in effectuating national labor policy. Thus, in Warrior & Gulf Navigation Co., *supra* [363 U.S.] at 578, arbitration was described as "the substitute for industrial strife," and as "part and parcel of the collective bargaining process itself." It would derogate from "the federal policy of settling labor disputes by arbitration," United Steelworkers v. Enterprise Wheel & Car Corp., 363 U.S. 593, 596, if a change in the corporate structure or ownership of a business enterprise had the automatic consequence of removing a duty to arbitrate previously established; this is so as much in cases like the present, where the contracting employer disappears into another by merger, as in those in which one owner replaces another but the business entity remains the same.

Employees, and the union which represents them, ordinarily do not take part in negotiations leading to a change in corporate ownership. The negotiations will ordinarily not concern the well-being of the employees, whose advantage or disadvantage, potentially great, will inevitably be incidental to the main considerations. The objectives of national labor policy, reflected in established principles of federal law, require that the rightful prerogative of owners independently to rearrange their businesses and even eliminate themselves as employers be balanced by some protection to the employees from a sudden change in the employment relationship. The transition from one corporate organization to another will in most cases be eased and industrial strife avoided if employees' claims continue to be resolved by arbitration rather than by "the relative strength . . . of the contending forces," Warrior & Gulf, *supra* at 580.

The preference of national labor policy for arbitration as a substitute for tests of strength between contending forces could be overcome only if other considerations compellingly so demanded. We find none. While the principles of law governing ordinary contracts would not bind to a contract an unconsenting successor to a contracting party,[3] a collective bargaining agreement is not an ordinary contract. ". . . [I]t is a generalized code to govern a myriad of cases which the draftsmen cannot wholly anticipate. . . . The collective agreement covers the whole employment relationship. It calls into being a new common law — the common law of a particular industry or of a particular plant." Warrior & Gulf, *supra* at 578-579 (footnotes omitted). Central to the peculiar status and function of a collective bargaining agreement is the fact, dictated both by circumstance, see *id.* at 580, and by the requirements of the National Labor Relations Act, that it is not in any real sense the simple product of a consensual relationship. Therefore, although the duty to arbitrate, as we have said, *supra* at 546-547, must be founded on a contract, the impressive policy considerations favoring arbitration are not wholly overborne by the fact that Wiley did not sign the contract being construed. This case cannot readily be assimilated to the category of those in which there is no contract whatever, or none which is reasonably related to the party sought to be obligated. There was a contract, and Interscience, Wiley's predecessor,

---

[3] But cf. the general rule that in the case of a merger the corporation which survives is liable for the debts and contracts of the one which disappears. 15 Fletcher, Private Corporations (rev. ed. 1961), § 7121.

was party to it. We thus find Wiley's obligation to arbitrate this dispute in the Interscience contract construed in the context of a national labor policy.

We do not hold that in every case in which the ownership or corporate structure of an enterprise is changed the duty to arbitrate survives. As indicated above, there may be cases in which the lack of any substantial continuity of identity in the business enterprise before and after a change would make a duty to arbitrate something imposed from without, not reasonably to be found in the particular bargaining agreement and the acts of the parties involved. So too, we do not rule out the possibility that a union might abandon its right to arbitration by failing to make its claims known. Neither of these situations is before the Court. . . . In addition, we do not suggest any view on the questions surrounding a certified union's claim to continued representative status following a change in ownership. . . . This Union does not assert that it has any bargaining rights independent of the Interscience agreement; it seeks to arbitrate claims based on that agreement, now expired, not to negotiate a new agreement.[5]

III. Beyond denying its obligation to arbitrate at all, Wiley urges that the Union's grievances are not within the scope of the arbitration clause. . . .

All of the Union's grievances concern conditions of employment typically covered by collective bargaining agreements and submitted to arbitration if other grievance procedures fail. Specific provision for each of them is made in the Interscience agreement. There is thus no question that had a dispute concerning any of these subjects, such as seniority rights or severance pay, arisen between the Union and Interscience prior to the merger, it would have been arbitrable. Wiley argues, however, that the Union's claims are plainly outside the scope of the arbitration clause: first, because the agreement did not embrace post-merger claims, and, second, because the claims relate to a period beyond the limited term of the agreement.

In all probability, the situation created by the merger was one not expressly contemplated by the Union or Interscience when the agreement was made in 1960. Fairly taken, however, the Union's demands collectively raise the question which underlies the whole litigation: What is the effect of the merger on the rights of covered employees? It would be inconsistent with our holding that the obligation to arbitrate survived the merger were we to hold that the fact of the merger, without more, removed claims otherwise plainly arbitrable from the scope of the arbitration clause.

---

[5] The fact that the Union does not represent a majority of an appropriate bargaining unit in Wiley does not prevent it from representing those employees who are covered by the agreement which is in dispute and out of which Wiley's duty to arbitrate arises. Retail Clerks, Locals 128 & 633 v. Lion Dry Goods, Inc., 369 U.S. 17. There is no problem of conflict with another union, cf. L.B. Spear & Co., 106 N.L.R.B. 687, since Wiley had no contract with any union covering the unit of employees which received the former Interscience employees. . . .

It is true that the Union has framed its issues to claim rights not only "now" — after the merger but during the term of the agreement — but also after the agreement expired by its terms. Claimed rights during the term of the agreement, at least, are unquestionably within the arbitration clause; we do not understand Wiley to urge that the Union's claims to all such rights have become moot by reason of the expiration of the agreement. As to claimed rights "after January 30, 1962," it is reasonable to read the claims as based solely on the Union's construction of the Interscience agreement in such a way that, had there been no merger, Interscience would have been required to discharge certain obligations notwithstanding the expiration of the agreement. We see no reason why parties could not if they so chose agree to the accrual of rights during the term of an agreement and their realization after the agreement had expired. Of course, the Union may not use arbitration to acquire new rights against Wiley any more than it could have used arbitration to negotiate a new contract with Interscience, had the existing contract expired and renewal negotiations broken down.

Whether or not the Union's demands have merit will be determined by the arbitrator in light of the fully developed facts. It is sufficient for present purposes that the demands are not so plainly unreasonable that the subject matter of the dispute must be regarded as nonarbitrable because it can be seen in advance that no award to the Union could receive judicial sanction. See Warrior & Gulf, *supra* at 582-583.

IV. Wiley's final objection to arbitration raises the question of so-called "procedural arbitrability." The Interscience agreement provides for arbitration as the third stage of the grievance procedure. "Step 1" provides for "a conference between the affected employee, a Union Steward and the Employer, officer or exempt supervisory person in charge of his department." In "Step 2," the grievance is submitted to "a conference between an officer of the Employer, or the Employer's representative designated for that purpose, the Union Shop Committee and/or a representative of the Union." Arbitration is reached under "Step 3" "in the event that the grievance shall not have been resolved or settled in 'Step 2.' " Wiley argues that since Steps 1 and 2 have not been followed, and since the duty to arbitrate arises only in Step 3, it has no duty to arbitrate this dispute. Specifically, Wiley urges that the question whether "procedural" conditions to arbitration have been met must be decided by the court and not the arbitrator.

We think that labor disputes of the kind involved here cannot be broken down so easily into their "substantive" and "procedural" aspects. Questions concerning the procedural prerequisites to arbitration do not arise in a vacuum; they develop in the context of an actual dispute about the rights of the parties to the contract or those covered by it. In this case, for example, the Union argues that Wiley's consistent refusal to recognize the Union's representative status after the merger made it "utterly futile — and a little bit ridiculous to follow the grievance steps as set forth in the contract." Brief, p. 41. In addition, the Union argues that time limitations in the grievance procedure are not controlling because Wiley's violations of the bargaining agreement were "continuing." These arguments in response to Wiley's "procedural" claim are meaningless unless set in the background of the merger and the negotiations surrounding it.

Doubt whether grievance procedures or some part of them apply to a particular dispute, whether such procedures have been followed or excused, or whether the unexcused failure to follow them avoids the duty to arbitrate cannot ordinarily be answered without consideration of the merits of the dispute which is presented for arbitration. In this case, one's view of the Union's responses to Wiley's "procedural" arguments depends to a large extent on how one answers questions bearing on the basic issue, the effect of the merger; *e.g.*, whether or not the merger was a possibility considered by Interscience and the Union during the negotiation of the contract. It would be a curious rule which required that intertwined issues of "substance" and "procedure" growing out of a single dispute and raising the same questions on the same facts had to be carved up between two different forums, one deciding after the other. Neither logic nor considerations of policy compel such a result.

Once it is determined, as we have, that the parties are obligated to submit the subject matter of a dispute to arbitration, "procedural" questions which grow out of the dispute and bear on its final disposition should be left to the arbitrator. Even under a contrary rule, a court could deny arbitration only if it could confidently be said not only that a claim was strictly "procedural," and therefore within the purview of the court, but also that it should operate to bar arbitration altogether, and not merely limit or qualify an arbitral award. In view of the policies favoring arbitration and the parties' adoption of arbitration as the preferred means of settling disputes, such cases are likely to be rare indeed. In all other cases, those in which arbitration goes forward, the arbitrator would ordinarily remain free to reconsider the ground covered by the court insofar as it bore on the merits of the dispute, using the flexible approaches familiar to arbitration. Reservation of "procedural" issues for the courts would thus not only create the difficult task of separating related issues, but would also produce frequent duplication of effort.

In addition, the opportunities for deliberate delay and the possibility of well-intentioned but no less serious delay created by separation of the "procedural" and "substantive" elements of a dispute are clear. While the courts have the task of determining "substantive arbitrability," there will be cases in which arbitrability of the subject matter is unquestioned but a dispute arises over the procedures to be followed. In all of such cases, acceptance of Wiley's position would produce the delay attendant upon judicial proceedings preliminary to arbitration. . . .

No justification for such a generally undesirable result is to be found in a presumed intention of the parties. Refusal to order arbitration of subjects which the parties have not agreed to arbitrate does not entail the fractionating of disputes about subjects which the parties do wish to have submitted. Although a party may resist arbitration once a grievance has arisen, as does Wiley here, we think it best accords with the usual purposes of an arbitration clause and with the policy behind federal labor law to regard procedural disagreements not as separate disputes but as aspects of the dispute which called the grievance procedures into play. . . .

Affirmed.

MR. JUSTICE GOLDBERG took no part in the consideration or decision of this case.

NOTES

1. An unusually comprehensive study of the problems growing out of *Wiley,* as well as of related successorship issues, is presented by Goldberg, *The Labor Law Obligations of a Successor Employer,* 63 Nw. U.L. REV. 735 (1969). *See also* Barbash, Feller, Jay & Lippman, *The Labor Contract and the Sale, Subcontracting or Termination of Operations,* in N.Y.U. EIGHTEENTH ANNUAL CONFERENCE ON LABOR 255, 259, 277, 293, 315 (1966) (four separate papers); Christensen, *The Developing Law of Arbitrability,* in SOUTHWESTERN LEGAL FOUNDATION, LABOR LAW DEVELOPMENTS, PROCEEDINGS OF THE ELEVENTH ANNUAL INSTITUTE ON LABOR LAW 119 (1965); Platt, *The NLRB and the Arbitrator in Sale and Merger Situations,* in N.Y.U. NINETEENTH ANNUAL CONFERENCE ON LABOR 375 (1967); Shaw & Carter, *Sales, Mergers and Union Contract Relations,* in N.Y.U. NINETEENTH ANNUAL CONFERENCE ON LABOR 357 (1967).

2. *Wiley* is significant not only for its teachings on successorship, but also for its distinction between "substantive" and "procedural" arbitrability. Extending *Wiley,* the Supreme Court has held that whether a union grievance is barred by "laches" is a question for the arbitrator to decide under a broad arbitration agreement applicable to "any difference" not settled by the parties within 48 hours of occurrence, even if the claim of laches is "extrinsic" to the procedures under the agreement. Operating Engineers Local 150 v. Flair Builders, Inc., 406 U.S. 487 (1972).

NLRB v. BURNS INTERNATIONAL SECURITY SERVICES, INC.

Supreme Court of the United States
406 U.S. 272, 92 S. Ct. 1571, 32 L. Ed. 2d 61 (1972)

MR. JUSTICE WHITE delivered the opinion of the Court.

Burns International Security Services, Inc. (Burns), replaced another employer, the Wackenhut Corporation (Wackenhut), which had previously provided plant protection services for the Lockheed Aircraft Service Company (Lockheed) located at the Ontario International Airport in California. When Burns began providing security service, it employed 42 guards; 27 of them had been employed by Wackenhut. Burns refused, however, to bargain with the United Plant Guard Workers of America (the union) which had been certified after an NLRB election as the exclusive bargaining representative of Wackenhut's employees less than four months earlier. The issues presented in this case are whether Burns refused to bargain with a union representing a majority of employees in an appropriate unit and whether the National Labor Relations Board could order Burns to observe the terms of a collective bargaining contract signed by the union and Wackenhut which Burns had not voluntarily assumed. Resolution turns to a great extent on the precise facts involved here.

I. The Wackenhut Corporation provided protection services at the Lockheed plant for five years before Burns took over this task. On February 28, 1967, a few months before the change-over of guard employers, a majority of the Wackenhut guards selected the union as their exclusive bargaining representative in a Board election after Wackenhut and the union had agreed that the Lockheed plant was the appropriate bargaining unit. On March 8, the Regional Director certified the union as the exclusive bargaining representative for these employees, and on April 29, Wackenhut and the union entered into a three-year collective bargaining contract.

Meanwhile, since Wackenhut's one-year service agreement to provide security protection was due to expire on June 30, Lockheed had called for bids from various companies supplying these services, and both Burns and Wackenhut submitted estimates. At a pre-bid conference attended by Burns on May 15, a representative of Lockheed informed the bidders that Wackenhut's guards were represented by the union, that the union had recently won a Board election and been certified, and that there was in existence a collective bargaining contract between Wackenhut and the union. Lockheed then accepted Burns' bid, and on May 31, Wackenhut was notified that Burns would assume responsibility for protection services on July 1. Burns chose to retain 27 of the Wackenhut guards, and it brought in 15 of its own guards from other Burns locations.

During June, when Burns hired the 27 Wackenhut guards, it supplied them with membership cards of the American Federation of Guards (AFG), another union with whom Burns had collective bargaining contracts at other locations, and informed them that they must become AFG members to work for Burns, that they would not receive uniforms otherwise, and that Burns "could not live with" the existing contract between Wackenhut and the union. On June 29, Burns recognized the AFG on the theory that it had obtained a card majority. On July 12, however, the UPG demanded that Burns recognize it as the bargaining representative of Burns' employees at Lockheed and that Burns honor the collective bargaining agreement between it and Wackenhut. When Burns refused, the UPG filed unfair labor practice charges, and Burns responded by challenging the appropriateness of the unit and by denying its obligation to bargain.

The Board, adopting the trial examiner's findings and conclusions, found the Lockheed plant an appropriate unit and held that Burns had violated §§ 8(a)(2) and 8(a)(1) of the Act . . . by unlawfully recognizing and assisting the AFG, a rival of the UPG; that it had violated §§ 8(a)(5) and 8(a)(1) . . . by failing to recognize and bargain with the UPG and by refusing to honor the collective bargaining agreement which had been negotiated between Wackenhut and UPG.

Burns did not challenge the § 8(a)(2) unlawful assistance finding in the Court of Appeals but sought review of the unit determination and the order to bargain and observe the pre-existing collective bargaining contract. The Court of Appeals accepted the Board's unit determination and enforced the Board's order insofar as it related to the finding of unlawful assistance of a rival union and the refusal to bargain, but it held that the Board had exceeded its powers in ordering Burns to honor the contract executed by Wackenhut. Both Burns and the Board petitioned for certiorari, Burns challenging the unit determination and the bargaining order and the Board maintaining its position that Burns was bound by the Wackenhut contract, and we granted both petitions, though we declined to review the propriety of the bargaining unit, a question which was presented in No. 71-198. . . .

II. We address first Burns' alleged duty to bargain with the union. . . . Because the Act itself imposes a duty to bargain with the representative of a majority of the employees in an appropriate unit, the initial issue before the Board was whether the charging union was such a bargaining representative.

The trial examiner first found that the unit designated by the regional director was an appropriate unit for bargaining. The unit found appropriate was defined as "[a]ll full-time and regular part-time employees of [Burns] performing plant protection duties as determined in Section 9(b)(3) of the [National Labor Relations] Act at Lockheed, Ontario International Airport; excluding office clerical employees, professional employees, supervisors, and all other employees as defined in the Act." This determination was affirmed by the Board, accepted by the Court of Appeals, and is not at issue here because pretermitted by our limited grant of certiorari.

The trial examiner then found, *inter alia,* that Burns "had in its employ a majority of Wackenhut's former employees," and that these employees had already expressed their choice of a bargaining representative in an election held a short time before. Burns was therefore held to have a duty to bargain, which arose when it selected as its work force the employees of the previous employer to perform the same tasks at the same place they had worked in the past.

The Board, without revision, accepted the trial examiner's findings and conclusions with respect to the duty to bargain, and we see no basis for setting them aside. In an election held but a few months before, the union had been designated bargaining agent for the employees in the unit and a majority of these employees had been hired by Burns for work in an identical unit. It is undisputed that Burns knew all the relevant facts in this regard and was aware of the certification and of the existence of a collective bargaining contract. In these circumstances, it was not unreasonable for the Board to conclude that the union certified to represent all employees in the unit still represented a majority of the employees and that Burns could not reasonably have entertained a good-faith doubt about that fact. Burns' obligation to bargain with the union over terms and conditions of employment stems from its hiring of

Wackenhut's employees and from the recent election and Board certification. It has been consistently held that a mere change of employers or of ownership in the employing industry is not such an "unusual circumstance" as to affect the force of the Board's certification within the normal operative period if a majority of employees after the change of ownership or management were employed by the preceding employer. . . .

It goes without saying, of course, that Burns was not entitled to upset what it should have accepted as an established union majority by soliciting representation cards for another union and thereby committing the unfair labor practice of which it was found guilty by the Board. That holding was not challenged here and makes it imperative that the situation be viewed as it was when Burns hired its employees for the guard unit, a majority of whom were represented by a Board-certified union. See NLRB v. Gissel Packing Co., 395 U.S. 575, 609, 610-616 (1969).

It would be a wholly different case if the Board had determined that because Burns' operational structure and practices differed from those of Wackenhut, the Lockheed bargaining unit was no longer an appropriate one. Likewise, it would be different if Burns had not hired employees already represented by a union certified as a bargaining agent, and the Board recognized as much at oral argument. But where the bargaining unit remains unchanged and a majority of the employees hired by the new employer are represented by a recently certified bargaining agent there is little basis for faulting the Board's implementation of the express mandates of § 8(a)(5) and § 9(a) by ordering the employer to bargain with the incumbent union. This is the view of several courts of appeal and we agree with those courts. . . .

III. It does not follow, however, from Burns' duty to bargain that it was bound to observe the substantive terms of the collective bargaining contract the union had negotiated with Wackenhut and to which Burns had in no way agreed. Section 8(d) of the Act expressly provides that the existence of such bargaining obligation "does not compel either party to agree to a proposal or require the making of a concession." Congress has consistently declined to interfere with free collective bargaining and has preferred that device, or voluntary arbitration, to the imposition of compulsory terms as a means of avoiding or terminating labor disputes. . . .

This history was reviewed in detail and given controlling effect in H. K. Porter Co. v. NLRB, 397 U.S. 99 (1970). . . .

These considerations, evident from the explicit language and legislative history of the labor laws, underlay the Board's prior decisions which until now have consistently held that although successor employers may be bound to recognize and bargain with the union, they are not bound by the substantive provisions of a collective bargaining contract negotiated by their predecessors but not agreed to or assumed by them. . . .

The Board, however, has now departed from this view and argues that the same policies which mandate a continuity of bargaining obligation also require that successor employers be bound to the terms of a predecessor's collective bargaining contract. It asserts that the stability of labor relations will be jeopardized and that employees will face uncertainty and a gap in the bargained-for terms and conditions of employment, as well as the possible loss of advantages gained by prior negotiations, unless the new employer is held to have assumed, as a matter of federal labor law, the obligations under the contract entered into by the former employer. Recognizing that under normal contract principles a party would not be bound to a contract in the absence of consent, the Board notes that in John Wiley & Sons, Inc. v. Livingston, 376 U.S. 543, 550 (1964), the Court declared that "a collective bargaining agreement is not an ordinary contract" but is rather an outline of the common law of a particular plant or industry. . . . The Board contends that the same factors which the Court emphasized in *Wiley*, the peaceful settlement of industrial conflicts and "protection [of] the employees [against] a sudden change in the employment relationship," *id.* at 549, require that Burns be treated under the collective bargaining contract exactly as Wackenhut would have been if it had continued protecting the Lockheed plant.

We do not find *Wiley* controlling in the circumstances here. *Wiley* arose in the context of a § 301 suit to compel arbitration, not in the context of an unfair labor practice proceeding where the Board is expressly limited by the provisions of § 8(d). That decision emphasized "the preference of national labor policy for arbitration as a substitute for tests of strength between contending forces" and held only that the agreement to arbitrate, "construed in the context of national labor law," survived the merger and left to the arbitrator, subject to judicial review, the ultimate question of the extent to which, if any, the surviving company was bound by other provisions of the contract. *Id.* at 549, 551.

Wiley's limited accommodation between the legislative endorsement of freedom of contract and the judicial preference for peaceful arbitral settlement of labor disputes does not warrant the Board's holding that the employer commits an unfair labor practice unless he honors the substantive terms of the pre-existing contract. The present case does not involve a § 301 suit; nor does it involve the duty to arbitrate. Rather, the claim is that Burns must be held bound by the contract executed by Wackenhut, whether Burns has agreed to it or not and even though Burns made it perfectly clear that it had no intention of assuming that contract. *Wiley* suggests no such open-ended obligation. Its narrower holding dealt with a merger occurring against a background of state law which embodied the general rule that in merger situations the surviving corporation is liable for the obligations of the disappearing corporation. See N.Y. Stock Corporation Law § 90 (1951); 15 W. Fletcher, Private Corporations § 7121 (1961 rev. ed.). Here there was no merger, no sale of assets, no dealings whatsoever between Wackenhut and Burns. On the contrary, they were competitors for the same work, each bidding for the service contract at Lockheed. Burns purchased nothing from Wackenhut and became liable for none of its financial obligations. Burns merely hired enough of Wackenhut's employees to require it to bargain with the union as commanded by § 8(a)(5) and § 9(a). But this consideration is a wholly insufficient basis for implying either in fact or in law that Burns had agreed or must be held to have agreed to honor Wackenhut's collective bargaining contract. . . .

We also agree with the Court of Appeals that holding either the union or the new employer bound to the substantive terms of an old collective bargaining contract may result in serious inequities. A potential employer may be willing to take over a moribund business only if he can make changes in corporate structure, composition of the labor force, work location, task assignment, and nature of supervision. Saddling such an employer with the terms and conditions of employment contained in the old collective bargaining contract may make these changes impossible and may discourage and inhibit the transfer of capital. On the other hand, a union may have made concessions to a small or failing employer that it would be unwilling to make to a large or economically successful firm. The congressional policy manifest in the Act is to enable the parties to negotiate for any protection either deems appropriate, but to allow the balance of bargaining advantage to be set by economic power realities. Strife is bound to occur if the concessions which must be honored do not correspond to the relative economic strength of the parties.

The Board's position would also raise new problems, for the successor employer would be circumscribed in exactly the same way as the predecessor under the collective bargaining contract. It would seemingly follow that employees of the predecessor would be deemed employees of the successor, dischargeable only in accordance with provisions of the contract and subject to the grievance and arbitration provisions thereof. Burns would not have been free to replace Wackenhut's guards with its own except as the contract permitted. Given the continuity of employment relationship, the pre-existing contract's provisions with respect to wages, seniority rights, vacation privileges, pension and retirement fund benefits, job security provisions, work assignments and the like would devolve on the successor. . . .

In many cases, of course, successor employers will find it advantageous not only to recognize and bargain with the union but also to observe the pre-existing contract rather than to face uncertainty and turmoil. Also, in a variety of circumstances involving a merger, stock acquisition, reorganization, or assets purchase, the Board might properly find as a matter of fact that the successor had assumed the obligations under the old contract. *Cf.* Oilfield Maintenance Co., Inc., 142 N.L.R.B. 1384 (1963). Such a duty does not, however, ensue as a matter of law from the mere fact than an employer is doing the same work in the same place with the same employees as his predecessor, as the Board had recognized until its decision in the instant case. . . . We accordingly set aside the Board's finding of a § 8(a)(5) unfair labor practice insofar as it rested on a conclusion that Burns was required to but did not honor the collective bargaining contract executed by Wackenhut.

IV. It therefore follows that the Board's order requiring Burns to "give retroactive effect to all the clauses of said [Wackenhut] contract and, with interest of 6 percent, make whole its employees for any losses suffered by reason of Respondent's [Burns'] refusal to honor, adopt and enforce said contract" must be set aside. We note that the regional director's charge instituting this case asserted that "on or about July 1, 1967, Respondent unilaterally changed existing wage rates, hours of employment, overtime wage rates, differentials for swing shift and graveyard shift and other terms and conditions of employment of the employees in the appropriate unit . . . ," and that the Board's opinion stated that "[t]he obligation to bargain imposed on a successor-employer includes the negative injunction to refrain from unilaterally changing wages and other benefits established by a prior collective bargaining agreement even though that agreement had expired. In this respect the successor-employer's obligations are the same as those imposed upon employers generally during the period between collective bargaining agreements." . . . This statement by the Board is consistent with its prior and subsequent cases which hold that whether or not a successor employer is bound by its predecessor's contract, it must not institute terms and conditions of employment different from those provided in its predecessor's contract, at least without first bargaining with the employees' representative. . . . Thus, if Burns, without bargaining to impasse with the union, had paid its employees on and after July 1 at a rate lower than Wackenhut had paid under its contract or otherwise provided terms and conditions of employment different from those provided in the Wackenhut collective bargaining agreement, under the Board's view, Burns would have committed a § 8(a)(5) unfair labor practice and would be subject to an order to restore to employees what they had lost by this so-called unilateral change. . . .

Although Burns had an obligation to bargain with the union concerning wages and other conditions of employment when the union requested it to do so, this case is not like a § 8(a)(5) violation where an employer unilaterally changes a condition of employment without consulting a bargaining representative. It is difficult to understand how Burns could be said to have *changed* unilaterally any pre-existing term or condition of employment without bargaining when it had no previous relationship whatsoever to the bargaining unit and, prior to July 1, no outstanding terms and conditions of employment from which a change could be inferred. The terms on which Burns hired employees for service after July 1 may have differed from the terms extended by Wackenhut and required by the collective bargaining contract, but it does not follow that Burns changed *its* terms and conditions of employment when it specified the initial basis on which employees were hired on July 1.

Although a successor employer is ordinarily free to set initial terms on which it will hire the employees of a predecessor, there will be instances in which it is perfectly clear that the new employer plans to retain all of the employees in the unit and in which it will be appropriate to have him initially consult with the employees' bargaining representative before he fixes terms. In other situations, however, it may not be clear until the successor employer has hired his full complement of employees that he has a duty to bargain with a union, since it will not be evident until then that the bargaining representative represents a majority of the employees in the union as required by § 9(a) of the Act. . . . Here, for example, Burns' obligation to bargain with the union did not mature until it had selected its force of guards late in June. The Board quite properly found that Burns refused to bargain on July 12 when it rejected the overtures of the union. It is true that the wages it paid when it began protecting the Lockheed plant on July 1 differed from those specified in the Wackenhut collective bargaining agreement, but there is no evidence that Burns ever unilaterally changed the terms and conditions of employment it had offered to potential employees in June after its obligation to bargain with the union became apparent. If the union had made a request to bargain after Burns had completed its hiring and if Burns had negotiated in good faith and had made offers to the union which the union rejected, Burns could have unilaterally initiated such proposals as the opening terms and conditions of employment on July 1 without committing an unfair labor practice. *Cf.* NLRB v. Katz, 369 U.S. 736, 745 n. 12 (1962). . . . The Board's order requiring Burns to make whole its employees for any losses suffered by reason of Burns' refusal to honor and enforce the contract, cannot therefore be sustained on the ground that Burns unilaterally changed existing terms and conditions of employment, thereby committing an unfair labor practice which required monetary restitution in these circumstances.

Affirmed.

MR. JUSTICE REHNQUIST, with whom THE CHIEF JUSTICE, MR. JUSTICE BRENNAN, and MR. JUSTICE POWELL join, concurring in No. 71-123 and dissenting in No. 71-198.

Although the Court studiously avoids using the term "successorship" in concluding that Burns did have a statutory obligation to bargain with the union, it affirms the conclusions of the Board and the Court of Appeals to that effect which were based entirely on the successorship doctrine. Because I believe that the Board and the Court of Appeals stretched that concept beyond the limits of its proper application, I would enforce neither the Board's bargaining order nor its order imposing upon Burns the terms of the contract between the union and Wackenhut. I therefore concur in No. 71-123 and dissent in No. 71-198. . . .

The rigid imposition of a prior-existing labor relations environment on a new employer whose only connection with the old employer is the hiring of some of the latter's employees and the performance of some of the work which was previously performed by the latter, might well tend to produce industrial peace of a sort. But industrial peace in such a case would be produced at a sacrifice of the determination by the Board of the appropriateness of bargaining agents and of the wishes of the majority of the employees which the Act was designed to preserve. These latter principles caution us against extending successorship, under the banner of industrial peace, step by step to a point where the only connection between the two employing entities is a naked transfer of employees. . . .

Burns acquired not a single asset, tangible or intangible, by negotiation or transfer from Wackenhut. It succeeded to the contractual rights and duties of the plant protection service contract with Lockheed not by reason of Wackenhut's assignment or consent, but over Wackenhut's vigorous opposition. I think the only permissible conclusion is that Burns is not a successor to Wackenhut. . . .

To conclude that Burns was a successor to Wackenhut in this situation, with its attendant consequences under the Board's order imposing a duty to bargain with the bargaining representative of Wackenhut's employees, would import unwarranted rigidity into labor-management relations. The fortunes of competing employers inevitably ebb and flow, and an employer who has currently gained production orders at the expense of another may well wish to hire employees away from that other. There is no reason to think that the best interests of the employees, the employers, and ultimately of the free market are not served by such movement. Yet inherent in the expanded doctrine of successorship which the Board urges in this case is the notion that somehow the "labor relations environment" comes with the new employees if the new employer has but obtained orders or business which previously belonged to the old employer. The fact that the employees in the instant case continue to perform their work at the same situs, while not irrelevant to analysis, cannot be deemed controlling. For the rigidity which would follow from the Board's application of successorship to this case would not only affect competition between Wackenhut and Burns, but would also affect Lockheed's operations. In effect, it would be saddled, as against its competitors, with the disadvantageous consequences of a collective bargaining contract unduly favorable to Wackenhut's employees, even though Lockheed's contract with Wackenhut was set to expire at a given time. By the same token, it would be benefited, at the expense of its competitors, as a result of a "sweetheart" contract negotiated between Wackenhut and its employees. From the viewpoint of the recipient of the services, dissatisfaction with the labor relations environment may stimulate a desire for change of contractors. . . . Where the relation between the first employer and the second is as attenuated as it is here, and the reasonable expectations of the employees equally attenuated, the application of the successorship doctrine is not authorized by the Labor Management Relations Act.

This is not to say that Burns would be unilaterally free to mesh into its previously recognized Los Angeles County bargaining unit a group of employees such as were involved here who already have designated a collective bargaining representative in their previous employment. Burns' actions in this regard would be subject to the commands of the Labor Management Relations Act, and to the regulation of the Board under proper application of governing principles. The situation resulting from the addition of a new element of the component work force of an employer has been dealt with by the Board in numerous cases, and various factors are weighed in order to determine whether the new workforce component should be itself a separate bargaining unit, or whether the employees in this component shall be "accreted" to the bargaining unit already in existence. See, *e.g.,* NLRB v. Food Employers Council, Inc., 399 F.2d 501 (9th Cir. 1968); Northwest Galvanizing Co., 168 N.L.R.B. 26 (1967). Had the Board made the appropriate factual inquiry and determinations required by the Act, such inquiry might have justified the conclusion that Burns was obligated to recognize and bargain with the union as a representative for its employees at the Lockheed facility.

But the Board, instead of applying this type of analysis to the union's complaints here, concluded that because Burns was a "successor" it was absolutely bound to the mold which had been fashioned by Wackenhut and its employees at Lockheed. Burns was thereby precluded from challenging the designation of Lockheed as an appropriate bargaining unit for a year after the original certification. 61 Stat. 144, 29 U.S.C. § 159(c)(3).

I am unwilling to follow the Board this far down the successorship road, since I believe to do so would substantially undercut the principle of free choice of bargaining representatives by the employees and designation of the appropriate bargaining unit by the Board which are guaranteed by the Act.

HOWARD JOHNSON CO. v. HOTEL & RESTAURANT EMPLOYEES DETROIT LOCAL JOINT BOARD, 417 U.S. 249, 94 S. Ct. 2236, 41 L. Ed. 2d 46 (1974). The Grissom family operated a restaurant and motor lodge under franchise from Howard Johnson. Howard Johnson purchased the personal property used in the restaurant and motor lodge from the Grissoms, and leased the realty. After hiring only nine of its predecessor's 53 employees, Howard Johnson commenced operation of the establishment with a complement of 45. It refused to recognize the union that had bargained collectively with the Grissoms, and it refused to assume any obligations under the existing labor agreements. The union sued both the Grissoms and Howard Johnson under § 301 to require them to arbitrate the extent of their obligations to the Grissom employees. The Grissoms admitted a duty to arbitrate, but Howard Johnson denied any such duty. The Supreme Court applied *Burns,* even though it dealt with a § 8(a)(5) refusal to bargain charge rather than a § 301 suit for arbitration, and sustained Howard Johnson's refusal to arbitrate. The Court distinguished *Wiley* on the ground it "involved a merger, as a result of which the initial employing entity completely disappeared. . . . Even more important, in *Wiley* the surviving corporation hired *all* of the employees of the disappearing corporation." The Court stressed that "there was plainly no substantial continuity of identity in the work force hired by Howard Johnson with that of the Grissoms, and no express or implied assumption of the agreement to arbitrate." The question of "successorship" was declared "simply not meaningful in the abstract. . . . The answer to this inquiry requires analysis of the interests of the new employer and the employees and of the policies of the labor laws in light of the facts of each case and the particular legal obligation which is at issue, whether it be the duty to recognize and bargain with the union, the duty to remedy unfair labor practices, the duty to arbitrate, etc."

NOTES

1. Do *Burns* and *Howard Johnson* sound the death knell of *Wiley,* or are the three cases genuinely distinguishable? If so, on what basis? Because of the different relationships of the various employers? The differences in the remedies sought by the unions? The differences in the proportions of the predecessor's and the successor's employees involved? If the latter, would it make sense to say that in refusal to bargain cases, the critical factor is the percentage (a majority?) of the successor's employees coming *from* the predecessor, while in suits to compel arbitration of the predecessor's contract, the critical factor is the percentage of the predecessor's employees going *to* the successor? *See* Boeing Co. v. Machinists, 504 F. 2d 307 (5th Cir. 1974), and consider the implications of *Golden State Bottling Co., supra* at 200.

2. A successor employer violates § 8(a)(5) by refusing to bargain with the union that had represented its predecessor's employees, even though the union does not represent a majority of the current work force, if the successor prevented the union from securing a majority by unlawfully discriminating against the predecessor's employees in hiring the new work force. Foodway of El Paso Div. of Kimbell Foods, Inc., 201 N.L.R.B. 933 (1973). *But cf.* NLRB v. Bausch & Lomb, Inc., 526 F. 2d 817 (2d Cir. 1975) (no "successorship" despite unlawful discrimination in hiring if there is insufficient "continuity of identity" in the two businesses).

3. May an employer negate an intention to retain all or substantially all its predecessor's employees, and thus avoid the bargaining obligations of a successor employer (at least regarding the initial terms of employment) by offering the predecessor's employees jobs only on new and less attractive terms? *See* Machinists v. NLRB [Boeing Co.], 98 L.R.R.M. 2787 (D.C. Cir. 1978); *cf.* United Maintenance & Mfg. Co., 214 N.L.R.B. 529 (1974).

4. Prior to *Burns* and *Howard Johnson,* courts of appeals had applied *Wiley* to compel arbitration in non-merger situations, *e.g.,* where the successor was a purchaser. *See* Steelworkers v. Reliance Universal, Inc., 335 F. 2d 891 (3d Cir. 1964); *cf.* Wackenhut Corp. v. Plant Guard Workers, 332 F. 2d 954 (9th Cir. 1964). Are these decisions still supportable? What if the successor has lawfully recognized and contracted with a union different from the one representing the predecessor's employees? *See* McGuire v. Humble Oil & Ref. Co., 355 F. 2d 352 (2d Cir. 1966), noted in 66 COLUM. L. REV. 967 (1966); Machinists v. Howmet Corp., 466 F. 2d 1249 (9th Cir. 1972).

5. Even if logically reconcilable, do *Wiley, Burns,* and *Howard Johnson* vary in their attitudes toward the nature of the collective agreement, and toward the values to be promoted in industrial relations? *See generally* Benetar, *Successorship Liability Under Labor Agreements,* 1973 WIS. L. REV. 1026; Christensen, *Successorships, Unit Changes, and the*

Bargaining Table, in SOUTHWESTERN LEGAL FOUNDATION, LABOR LAW DEVELOPMENTS 1973, PROCEEDINGS OF NINETEENTH ANNUAL INSTITUTE ON LABOR LAW 197 (1973); Morris & Gaus, *Successorship and the Collective Bargaining Agreement: Accommodating Wiley and Burns,* 59 VA. L. REV. 1359 (1973); Severson & Willcoxon, *Successorship Under Howard Johnson: Short Order Justice for Employers,* 64 CALIF. L. REV. 795 (1976); Slicker, *A Reconsideration of the Doctrine of Employer Successorship — A Step Toward a Rational Approach,* 57 MINN. L. REV. 1051 (1973); Comment, *The Bargaining Obligations of Successor Employers,* 88 HARV. L. REV. 759 (1975). *Burns* was noted in 40 U. CHI. L. REV. 617 (1973) and 71 MICH. L. REV. 571 (1973), and *Howard Johnson* in 74 MICH. L. REV. 555 (1976).

SECTION IV. Fair Representation and Individual Contract Rights

CLYDE W. SUMMERS, INDIVIDUAL RIGHTS IN COLLECTIVE AGREEMENTS AND ARBITRATION, 37 N.Y.U.L. REV. 362, 393 (1962)

The individual's interest may more often be vitiated without vindictiveness or deliberate discrimination. Incomplete investigation of the facts, reliance on untested evidence, or colored evaluation of witnesses may lead the union to reject grievances which more objective inquiry would prove meritorious. Union officials burdened with institutional concerns may be willing to barter unrelated grievances or accept wholesale settlements if the total package is advantageous, even though some good grievances are lost. Concern for collective interests and the needs of the enterprise may dull the sense of personal injustice.

ARCHIBALD COX, THE DUTY OF FAIR REPRESENTATION, 2 VILL. L. REV. 151, 167 (1957)

Too strict judicial or administrative supervision through the concept of fair representation would impair the flexibility and adaptability of collective bargaining while substituting governmental decisions for self-determination. Past experience with judicial intervention in labor relations gives little reason to suppose that the judges' decisions would be wiser than negotiated settlements. On the other hand, so long as numerical majorities occasionally yield to selfishness or caprice, there will be somewhat the same need for judicial or administrative checks on majority rule in collective bargaining as there is for judicial review of legislative enactments. Whether courts and agencies steer a safe central course between the opposing dangers will probably depend upon their success in developing standards of "fairness."

A. JUDICIAL ENFORCEMENT OF FAIR REPRESENTATION

STEELE v. LOUISVILLE & NASHVILLE R.R.

Supreme Court of the United States
323 U.S. 192, 65 S. Ct. 226, 89 L. Ed. 173 (1944)

MR. CHIEF JUSTICE STONE delivered the opinion of the Court.

The question is whether the Railway Labor Act . . . imposes on a labor organization, acting by authority of the statute as the exclusive bargaining representative of a craft or class of railway employees, the duty to represent all the employees in the craft without discrimination because of their race, and, if so, whether the courts have jurisdiction to protect the minority of the craft or class from the violation of such obligation.

. . . Petitioner, a Negro, is a locomotive fireman in the employ of respondent railroad, suing on his own behalf and that of his fellow employees who, like petitioner, are Negro firemen employed by the Railroad. Respondent Brotherhood, a labor organization, is as provided under Section 2, Fourth of the Railway Labor Act, the exclusive bargaining representative of the craft of firemen employed by the Railroad and is recognized as such by it and the members of the craft. The majority of the firemen employed by the Railroad are white and are members of the Brotherhood, but a substantial minority are Negroes who, by the constitution and ritual of the Brotherhood, are excluded from its membership. As the membership of the Brotherhood constitutes a majority of all firemen employed on respondent Railroad and as under Section 2, Fourth, the members, because they are the majority, have the right to choose and have chosen the Brotherhood to represent the craft, petitioner and other Negro firemen on the road have been required to accept the Brotherhood as their representative for the purposes of the Act.

On March 28, 1940, the Brotherhood, purporting to act as representative of the entire craft of firemen, without informing the Negro firemen or giving them opportunity to be heard, served a notice on respondent Railroad and on twenty other railroads operating principally in the southeastern part of the United States. The notice announced the Brotherhood's desire to amend the existing collective bargaining agreement in such manner as ultimately to exclude all Negro firemen from the service. By established practice on the several railroads so notified only white firemen can be promoted to serve as engineers, and the notice proposed that only "promotable," *i.e.,* white, men should be employed as firemen or assigned to new runs or jobs or permanent vacancies in established runs or jobs.

On February 18, 1941, the railroads and the Brotherhood, as representative of the craft, entered into a new agreement which provided that not more than 50 percent of the firemen in each class of service in each seniority district of a carrier should be Negroes; that until such percentage should be reached all new runs and all vacancies should be filled by white men; and that the agreement did not sanction the employment of Negroes in any seniority district in which they were not working. . . .

If the Railway Labor Act purports to impose on petitioner and the other Negro members of the craft the legal duty to comply with the terms of a contract whereby the representative has discriminatorily restricted their employment for the benefit and advantage of the Brotherhood's own members, we must decide the constitutional questions which petitioner raises in his pleading.

But we think that Congress, in enacting the Railway Labor Act and authorizing a labor union, chosen by a majority of a craft, to represent the craft, did not intend to confer plenary power upon the union to sacrifice, for the benefit of its members, rights of the minority of the craft, without imposing on it any duty to protect the minority. Since petitioner and the other Negro members of the craft are not members of the Brotherhood or eligible for membership, the authority to act for them is derived not from their action or consent but wholly from the command of the Act. . . .

Section 2, Second, requiring carriers to bargain with the representative so chosen, operates to exclude any other from representing a craft. Virginian Ry. Co. v. System Federation, *supra,* 300 U.S. 545 (1930). The minority members of a craft are thus deprived by the statute of the right, which they would otherwise possess, to choose a representative of their own, and its members cannot bargain individually on behalf of themselves as to matters which are properly the subject of collective bargaining. . . .

The fair interpretation of the statutory language is that the organization chosen to represent a craft is to represent all its members, the majority as well as the minority, and it is to act for and not against those whom it represents. It is a principle of general application that the exercise of a granted power to act in behalf of others involves the assumption toward them of a duty to exercise the power in their interest and behalf, and that such a grant of power will not be deemed to dispense with all duty toward those for whom it is exercised unless so expressed.

We think that the Railway Labor Act imposes upon the statutory representative of a craft at least as exacting a duty to protect equally the interests of the members of the craft as the Constitution imposes upon a legislature to give equal protection to the interests of those for whom it legislates. Congress has seen fit to clothe the bargaining representative with powers comparable to those possessed by a legislative body both to create and restrict the rights of those whom it represents, *cf.* J.I. Case Co. v. NLRB, *supra,* 321 U.S. 335 (1944), but it has also imposed on the representative a corresponding duty. We hold that the language of the Act to which we have referred, read in the light of the purposes of the Act, expresses the aim of Congress to impose on the bargaining representative of a craft or class of employees the duty to exercise fairly the power conferred upon it in behalf of all those for whom it acts, without hostile discrimination against them.

This does not mean that the statutory representative of a craft is barred from making contracts which may have unfavorable effects on some of the members of the craft represented. Variations in the terms of the contract based on differences relevant to the authorized purposes of the contract in conditions to which they are to be applied, such as differences in seniority, the type of work performed, the competence and skill with which it is performed, are within the scope of the bargaining representation of a craft, all of whose members are not identical in their interest or merit. Without attempting to mark the allowable limits of differences in the terms of contracts based on differences of conditions to which they apply, it is enough for present purposes to say that the statutory power to represent a craft and to make contracts as to wages, hours and working conditions does not include the authority to make among members of the craft discriminations not based on such relevant differences. Here the discriminations based on race alone are obviously irrelevant and invidious. Congress plainly did not undertake to authorize the bargaining representative to make such discriminations. . . .

The representative which thus discriminates may be enjoined from so doing, and its members may be enjoined from taking the benefit of such discriminatory action. No more is the Railroad bound by or entitled to take the benefit of a contract which the bargaining representative is prohibited by the statute from making. In both cases the right asserted, which is derived from the duty imposed by the statute on the bargaining representative, is a federal right implied from the statute and the policy which it has adopted. . . .

So long as a labor union assumes to act as the statutory representative of a craft, it cannot rightly refuse to perform the duty, which is inseparable from the power of representation conferred upon it, to represent the entire membership of the craft. While the statute does not deny to such a bargaining labor organization the right to determine eligibility to its membership, it does require the union, in collective bargaining and in making contracts with the carrier, to represent nonunion or minority union members of the craft without hostile discrimination, fairly, impartially, and in good faith. Wherever necessary to that end, the union is required to consider requests of non-union members of the craft and expressions of their views with respect to collective bargaining with the employer and to give to them notice of and opportunity for hearing upon its proposed action. . . .

We conclude that the duty which the statute imposes on a union representative of a craft to represent the interests of all its members stands on no different footing and that the statute contemplates resort to the usual judicial remedies of injunction and award of damages when appropriate for breach of that duty.

The judgment is accordingly reversed and remanded for further proceedings not inconsistent with this opinion.

Reversed.

MR. JUSTICE BLACK concurs in the result.

MR. JUSTICE MURPHY, concurring.

The economic discrimination against Negroes practiced by the Brotherhood and the railroad under color of Congressional authority raises a grave constitutional issue that should be squarely faced. . . .

The constitutional problem inherent in this instance is clear. Congress, through the Railway Labor Act, has conferred upon the union selected by a majority of a craft or class of railway workers the power to represent the entire craft or class in all collective bargaining matters. While such a union is essentially a private organization, its power to represent and bind all members of a class or craft is derived solely from Congress. The Act contains no language which directs the manner in which the bargaining representative shall perform its duties. But it cannot be assumed that Congress meant to authorize the bargaining representative to act so as to ignore rights guaranteed by the Constitution. Otherwise the Act would bear the stigma of unconstitutionality under the Fifth Amendment in this respect. For that reason I am willing to read the statute as not permitting or allowing any action by the bargaining representative in the exercise of its delegated powers which would in effect violate the constitutional rights of individuals.

NOTE

The existence of a duty of fair representation under the NLRA, as well as under the RLA, was established in Syres v. Oil Workers Local 23, 350 U.S. 892 (1955) (per curiam).

On the standard of fairness, the Supreme Court said at a relatively early point in this line of decisions: "Inevitably differences arise in the manner and degree to which the terms of any negotiated agreement affect individual employees and classes of employees. The mere existence of such differences does not make them invalid. The complete satisfaction of all who are represented is hardly to be expected. A wide range of reasonableness must be allowed a statutory bargaining representative in serving the unit it represents, subject always to complete good faith and honesty of purpose in the exercise of its discretion." Ford Motor Co. v. Huffman, 345 U.S. 330, 338 (1953).

Does the duty of fair representation impose on a union the affirmative obligation to seek the elimination of an employer's discriminatory employment practices? If so, how far must a union go to discharge its obligation? Is it sufficient to process a grievance or to raise the question in contract negotiations? Or must the union be prepared to strike to back up its demand? See, e.g., Rubber Workers Local 12 v. NLRB, 368 F.2d 12 (5th Cir. 1966), cert. denied, 389 U.S. 837 (1967); NLRB v. Longshoremen Local 1367, 368 F.2d 1010 (5th Cir. 1966), cert. denied, 389 U.S. 837 (1967), enforcing 148 N.L.R.B. 897 (1964).

For further discussion of the development of the concept of fair representation, see Clark, The Duty of Fair Representation: A Theoretical Structure, 51 TEXAS L. REV. 1119 (1973); Cox, The Duty of Fair Representation, 2 VILL. L. REV. 151 (1957); Murphy, The Duty of Fair

Representation Under Taft-Hartley, 30 Mo. L. Rev. 373 (1965); Sovern, *The National Labor Relations Act and Racial Discrimination,* 62 Colum. L. Rev. 563 (1962); Wellington, *Union Democracy and Fair Representation: Federal Responsibility in a Federal System,* 67 Yale L.J. 1327 (1958).

VACA v. SIPES

Supreme Court of the United States
386 U.S. 171, 87 S. Ct. 903, 17 L. Ed. 2d 842 (1967)

[Owens, a long-time high blood pressure patient, returned from a half-year sick leave to resume his heavy work in a meat-packing plant of Swift & Company. Although Owens' family physician and another outside doctor certified his fitness, the company doctor concluded Owens' blood pressure was too high to permit reinstatement and he was permanently discharged. Owens' union processed a grievance through to the fourth step of the procedure established by the collective bargaining agreement. The union then sent Owens to a new doctor at union expense to "get some better medical evidence so that we could go to arbitration." When this examination did not support Owens' position, the union's executive board voted not to take the grievance to arbitration. Union officers suggested that Owens accept Swift's offer of referral to a rehabilitation center, but Owens declined and demanded arbitration. The union stood by its refusal. Owens thereupon brought a class action in a Missouri state court against petitioners as officers and representatives of the union, alleging that the union had "arbitrarily, [and] capriciously" failed to take his case to arbitration. A jury verdict in his favor was sustained by the Missouri Supreme Court in the amount of $7,000 compensatory and $3,000 punitive damages.]

Mr. Justice White delivered the opinion of the Court.

. . . Although we conclude that state courts have jurisdiction in this type of case, we hold that federal law governs, that the governing federal standards were not applied here, and that the judgment of the Supreme Court of Missouri must accordingly be reversed. . . .

II. Petitioners challenge the jurisdiction of the Missouri courts on the ground that the alleged conduct of the Union was arguably an unfair labor practice and within the exclusive jurisdiction of the NLRB. Petitioners rely on Miranda Fuel Co., 140 N.L.R.B. 181 (1962), enforcement denied, 326 F.2d 172 (2d Cir. 1963), where a sharply divided Board held for the first time that a union's breach of its statutory duty of fair representation violates NLRA § 8(b), as amended. With the NLRB's adoption of *Miranda Fuel,* petitioners argue, the broad pre-emption doctrine defined in San Diego Building Trades Council v. Garmon, 359 U.S. 236 (1959), becomes applicable. For the reasons which follow, we reject this argument.

It is now well established that, as the exclusive bargaining representative of the employees in Owens' bargaining unit, the Union had a statutory duty fairly to represent all of those employees, both in its collective bargaining with Swift, see Ford Motor Co. v. Huffman, 345 U.S. 330 (1953); Syres v. Oil Workers, 350 U.S. 892 (1955), and in its enforcement of the resulting collective bargaining agreement, see Humphrey v. Moore, 375 U.S. 335 (1964). The statutory duty of fair representation was developed over 20 years ago in a series of cases involving alleged racial discrimination by unions certified as exclusive bargaining representatives under the Railway Labor Act, see Steele v. Louisville & N.R.R., 323 U.S. 192 (1944); Tunstall v. Brotherhood of Locomotive Firemen, 323 U.S. 210 (1944), and was soon extended to unions certified under the NLRA, see Ford Motor Co. v. Huffman, *supra.* Under this doctrine, the exclusive agent's statutory authority to represent all members of a designated unit includes a statutory obligation to serve the interests of all members without hostility or discrimination toward any, to exercise its discretion with complete good faith and honesty, and to avoid arbitrary conduct. Humphrey v. Moore, 375 U.S. at 342 (1964). It is obvious that Owens' complaint alleged a breach by the Union of a duty grounded in federal statutes, and that federal law therefore governs his cause of action. *E.g.,* Ford Motor Co. v. Huffman, *supra.*

Although NLRA § 8(b) was enacted in 1947, the NLRB did not until *Miranda Fuel* interpret a breach of a union's duty of fair representation as an unfair labor practice. In *Miranda Fuel,* the Board's majority held that NLRA § 7 gives employees "the right to be free from unfair or irrelevant or invidious treatment by their exclusive bargaining agent in matters affecting their employment," and "that Section 8(b)(1)(A) of the Act accordingly prohibits labor organizations, when acting in a statutory representative capacity, from taking action against any employee upon considerations or classifications which are irrelevant, invidious, or unfair." 140 N.L.R.B. at 185. The Board also held that an employer who "participates" in such arbitrary union conduct violates § 8(a)(1), and that the employer and the union may violate §§ 8(a)(3) and 8(b)(2), respectively, "when, for arbitrary or irrelevant reasons or upon the basis of an unfair classification, the union attempts to cause or does cause an employer to derogate the employment status of an employee." *Id.* at 186. . . .

A. In *Garmon,* this Court recognized that the broad powers conferred by Congress upon the National Labor Relations Board to interpret and to enforce the complex Labor Management Relations Act necessarily imply that potentially conflicting "rules of law, of remedy, and of administration" cannot be permitted to operate. 359 U.S. at 242. . . . Consequently, as a general rule, neither state nor federal courts have jurisdiction over suits directly involving "activity [which] is arguably subject to § 7 or § 8 of the Act." San Diego Building Trades Council v. Garmon, 359 U.S. at 245.

This pre-emption doctrine, however, has never been rigidly applied to cases where it could not fairly be inferred that Congress intended exclusive jurisdiction to lie with the NLRB. . . .

A primary justification for the pre-emption doctrine — the need to avoid conflicting rules of substantive law in the labor relations area and the desirability of leaving the development of such rules to the administrative agency created by Congress for that purpose — is not applicable to cases involving alleged breaches of the union duty of fair representation. The doctrine was judicially developed in *Steele* and its progeny, and suits alleging breach of the duty remained judicially cognizable long after the NLRB was given unfair labor practice jurisdiction over union activities by the LMRA. Moreover, when the Board declared in *Miranda Fuel* that a union's breach of its duty of fair representation would henceforth be treated as an unfair labor practice, the Board adopted and applied the doctrine as it had been developed by the federal courts. Finally, as the dissenting Board members in *Miranda Fuel* have pointed out, fair representation duty suits often require review of the substantive positions taken and policies pursued by a union in its negotiation of a collective bargaining agreement and in its handling of the grievance machinery; as these matters are not normally within the Board's unfair labor practice jurisdiction, it can be doubted whether the Board brings substantially greater expertise to bear on these problems than do the courts, which have been engaged in this type of review since the *Steele* decision.

In addition to the above considerations, the unique interests served by the duty of fair representation doctrine have a profound effect, in our opinion, on the applicability of the pre-emption rule to this class of cases. . . . This Court recognized in *Steele* that the congressional grant of power to a union to act as exclusive collective bargaining representative, with its corresponding reduction in the individual rights of the employees so represented, would raise grave constitutional problems if unions were free to exercise this power to further racial discrimination. . . . Since that landmark decision, the duty of fair representation has stood as a bulwark to prevent arbitrary union conduct against individuals stripped of traditional forms of redress by the provisions of federal labor law. Were we to hold, as petitioners and the government urge, that the courts are pre-empted by the NLRB's *Miranda Fuel* decision of this traditional supervisory jurisdiction, the individual employee injured by arbitrary or discriminatory union conduct could no longer be assured of impartial review of his complaint, since the Board's General Counsel has unreviewable discretion to refuse to institute an unfair labor practice complaint. . . . For these reasons, we cannot assume from the NLRB's tardy assumption of jurisdiction in these cases that Congress, when it enacted NLRA § 8(b) in 1947, intended to oust the courts of their traditional jurisdiction to curb arbitrary conduct by the individual employee's statutory representative.

B. There are also some intensely practical considerations which foreclose pre-emption of judicial cognizance of fair representation duty suits, considerations which emerge from the intricate relationship between the duty of fair representation and the enforcement of collective bargaining contracts. For the fact is that the question of whether a union has breached its duty of fair representation will in many cases be a critical issue in a suit under LMRA § 301 charging an employer with a breach of contract. To illustrate, let us assume a collective bargaining agreement that limits discharges to those for good cause and that contains no grievance, arbitration or other provisions purporting to restrict access to the courts. If an employee is discharged without cause, either the union or the employee may sue the employer under LMRA § 301. Under this section, courts have jurisdiction over suits to enforce collective bargaining agreements even though the conduct of the employer which is challenged as a breach of contract is also arguably an unfair labor practice within the jurisdiction of the NLRB. *Garmon* and like cases have no application to § 301 suits. Smith v. Evening News Ass'n, 371 U.S. 195 (1962).

The rule is the same with regard to pre-emption where the bargaining agreement contains grievance and arbitration provisions which are intended to provide the exclusive remedy for breach of contract claims. If an employee is discharged without cause in violation of such an agreement, that the employer's conduct may be an unfair labor practice does not preclude a suit by the union against the employer to compel arbitration of the employee's grievance; the adjudication of the claim by the arbitrator; or a suit to enforce the resulting arbitration award. See, *e.g.,* Steelworkers v. American Mfg. Co., 363 U.S. 564 (1960).

However, if the wrongfully discharged employee himself resorts to the courts before the grievance procedures have been fully exhausted, the employer may well defend on the ground that the exclusive remedies provided by such a contract have not been exhausted. Since the employee's claim is based upon breach of the collective bargaining agreement, he is bound by terms of that agreement which govern the manner in which contractual rights may be enforced. For this reason, it is settled that the employee must at least attempt to exhaust exclusive grievance and arbitration procedures established by the bargaining agreement. Republic Steel Corp. v. Maddox, 379 U.S. 650 (1965). However, because these contractual remedies have been devised and are often controlled by the union and the employer, they may well prove unsatisfactory or unworkable for the individual grievant. The problem then is to determine under what circumstances the individual employee may obtain judicial review of his breach-of-contract claim despite his failure to secure relief through the contractual remedial procedures. . . .

[W]e think the wrongfully discharged employee may bring an action against his employer in the face of a defense based upon the failure to exhaust contractual remedies, provided the employee can prove that the union as bargaining agent breached its duty of fair representation in its handling of the employee's grievance. We may assume for present purposes that such a breach of duty by the union is an unfair labor practice, as the NLRB and the Fifth Circuit have held. The employee's suit against the employer, however, remains a § 301 suit, and the jurisdiction of the courts is no more destroyed by the fact that the employee, as part and parcel of his § 301 action, finds it necessary to prove an unfair labor practice by the union, than it is by the fact that the suit may involve an unfair labor practice by the employer himself. The court is free to determine whether the employee is barred by the actions of his union representative, and, if not, to proceed with the case. And if, to facilitate his case, the employee joins the union as a defendant, the situation is not substantially changed. The action is still a § 301 suit, and the jurisdiction of the courts is not pre-empted under the *Garmon* principle. This, at the very least, is the holding of *Humphrey v. Moore* with respect to pre-emption, as petitioners recognize in their brief. And, insofar as adjudication of the union's breach of duty is concerned, the result should be no different if the employee, as Owens did here, sues the employer and the union in separate actions. There would be very little to commend a rule which would permit the Missouri courts to adjudicate the Union's conduct in an action against Swift but not in an action against the Union itself.

For the above reasons, it is obvious that the courts will be compelled to pass upon whether there has been a breach of the duty of fair representation in the context of many § 301 breach-of-contract actions. If a breach of duty by the union and a breach of contract by the employer are proven, the court must fashion an appropriate remedy. Presumably, in at least some cases, the union's breach of duty will have enhanced or contributed to the employee's injury. What possible sense could there be in a rule which would permit a court that has litigated the fault of employer and union to fashion a remedy only with respect to the employer? Under such a rule, either the employer would be compelled by the court to pay for the union's wrong — slight deterrence indeed, to future union misconduct — or the injured employee would be forced to go to two tribunals to repair a single injury. Moreover, the Board would be compelled in many cases either to remedy injuries arising out of a breach of contract, a task which Congress has not assigned to it, or to leave the individual employee without remedy for the union's wrong. Given the strong reasons for not pre-empting duty of fair representation suits in general, and the fact that the courts in many § 301 suits must adjudicate whether the union has breached its duty, we conclude that the courts may also fashion remedies for such a breach of duty. . . .

III. Petitioners contend, as they did in their motion for judgment notwithstanding the jury's verdict, that Owens failed to prove that the Union breached its duty of fair representation in its handling of Owens' grievance. Petitioners also argue that the Supreme Court of Missouri, in rejecting this contention, applied a standard that is inconsistent with governing principles of federal law with respect to the Union's duty to an individual employee in its processing of grievances under the collective bargaining agreement with Swift. We agree with both contentions.

A. . . . Quite obviously, the question which the Missouri Supreme Court thought dispositive of the issue of liability was whether the evidence supported Owens' assertion that he had been wrongfully discharged by Swift, regardless of the Union's good faith in reaching a contrary conclusion. This was also the major concern of the plaintiff at trial: the bulk of Owens' evidence was directed at whether he was medically fit at the time of discharge and whether he had performed heavy work after that discharge.

A breach of the statutory duty of fair representation occurs only when a union's conduct toward a member of the collective bargaining unit is arbitrary, discriminatory, or in bad faith. See Humphrey v. Moore, *supra;* Ford Motor Co. v. Huffman, *supra.* There has been considerable debate over the extent of this duty in the context of a union's enforcement of the grievance and arbitration procedures in a collective bargaining agreement. . . . Some have suggested that every individual employee should have the right to have his grievance taken to arbitration. Others have urged that the Union be given substantial discretion (if the collective bargaining agreement so provides) to decide whether a grievance should be taken to arbitration, subject only to the duty to refrain from patently wrongful conduct such as racial discrimination or personal hostility.

Though we accept the proposition that a union may not arbitrarily ignore a meritorious grievance or process it in perfunctory fashion, we do not agree that the individual employee has an absolute right to have his grievance taken to arbitration regardless of the provisions of the applicable collective bargaining agreement. . . . In providing for a grievance and arbitration procedure which gives the union discretion to supervise the grievance machinery and to invoke arbitration, the employer and the union contemplate that each will endeavor in good faith to settle grievances short of arbitration. Through this settlement process, frivolous grievances are ended prior to the most costly and time-consuming step in the grievance procedures. Moreover, both sides are assured that similar complaints will be treated consistently, and major problem areas in the interpretation of the collective bargaining contract can be isolated and perhaps resolved. And finally, the settlement process furthers the interest of the union as statutory agent and as coauthor of the bargaining agreement in representing the employees in the enforcement of that agreement. . . .

For these same reasons, the standard applied here by the Missouri Supreme Court cannot be sustained. For if a union's decision that a particular grievance lacks sufficient merit to justify arbitration would constitute a breach of the duty of fair representation because a judge or jury later found the grievance meritorious, the union's incentive to settle such grievances short of arbitration would be seriously reduced. The dampening effect on the entire grievance procedure of this reduction of the union's freedom to settle claims in good faith would surely be substantial. Since the union's statutory duty of fair representation protects the individual employee from arbitrary abuses of the settlement device by providing him with recourse against both employer (in a § 301 suit) and union, this severe limitation on the power to settle grievances is neither necessary nor desirable. . . .

B. Applying the proper standard of union liability to the facts of this case, we cannot uphold the jury's award, for we conclude that as a matter of federal law the evidence does not support a verdict that the Union breached its duty of fair representation. . . .

In administering the grievance and arbitration machinery as statutory agent of the employees, a union must in good faith and in a nonarbitrary manner, make decisions as to the merits of particular grievances. See Humphrey v. Moore, 375 U.S. 335, 349-350 (1964); Ford Motor Co. v. Huffman, 345 U.S. 330, 337-339 (1953). In a case such as this, when Owens supplied the Union with medical evidence supporting his position, the Union might well have breached its duty had it ignored Owens' complaint or had it processed the grievance in a perfunctory manner. See Cox, Rights under a Labor Agreement, 69 Harv. L. Rev., at 632-634. But here the Union processed the grievance into the fourth step, attempted to gather sufficient evidence to prove Owens' case, attempted to secure for Owens less vigorous work at the plant, and joined in the employer's efforts to have Owens rehabilitated. Only when these efforts all proved unsuccessful did the Union conclude both that arbitration would be fruitless and that the grievance should be dismissed. There was no evidence that any Union officer was personally hostile to Owens or that the Union acted at any time other than in good faith. Having concluded that the individual employee has no absolute right to have his grievance arbitrated under the collective bargaining agreement at issue, and that a breach of the duty of fair representation is not established merely by proof that the underlying grievance was meritorious, we must conclude that that duty was not breached here.

IV. In our opinion, there is another important reason why the judgment of the Missouri Supreme Court cannot stand. Owens' suit against the Union was grounded on his claim that Swift had discharged him in violation of the applicable collective bargaining agreement. . . .

The appropriate remedy for a breach of a union's duty of fair representation must vary with the circumstances of the particular breach. In this case, the employee's complaint was that the Union wrongfully failed to afford him the arbitration remedy against his employer established by the collective bargaining agreement. But the damages sought by Owens were primarily those suffered because of the employer's alleged breach of contract. Assuming for the moment that Owens had been wrongfully discharged, Swift's only defense to a direct action for breach of contract would have been the Union's failure to resort to arbitration, compare Republic Steel Corp. v. Maddox, 379 U.S. 650 (1965), with Smith v. Evening News Ass'n, 371 U.S. 195 (1962), and if that failure was itself a violation of the Union's statutory duty to the employee, there is no reason to exempt the employer from contractual damages which he would otherwise have had to pay. . . . The difficulty lies in fashioning an appropriate scheme of remedies.

Petitioners urge that an employee be restricted in such circumstances to a decree compelling the employer and the union to arbitrate the underlying grievance. It is true that the employee's action is based on the employer's alleged breach of contract plus the union's alleged wrongful failure to afford him his contractual remedy of arbitration. For this reason, an order compelling arbitration should be viewed as one of the available remedies when a breach of the union's duty is proved. But we see no reason inflexibly to require arbitration in all cases. . . .

A more difficult question is, what portion of the employee's damages may be charged to the union: in particular, may an award against a union include, as it did here, damages attributable solely to the employer's breach of contract? We think not. Though the union has violated a statutory duty in failing to press the grievance, it is the employer's unrelated breach of contract which triggered the controversy and which caused this portion of the employee's damages. The employee should have no difficulty recovering these damages from the employer, who cannot, as we have explained, hide behind the union's wrongful failure to act; in fact, the employer may be (and probably should be) joined as a defendant in the fair representation suit, as in Humphrey v. Moore, *supra.* It could be a real hardship on the union to pay these damages, even if the union were given a right of indemnification against the employer. With the employee assured of direct recovery from the employer, we see no merit in requiring the union to pay the employer's share of the damages.

The governing principle, then, is to apportion liability between the employer and the union according to the damage caused by the fault of each. Thus, damages attributable solely to the employer's breach of contract should not be charged to the union, but increases if any in those damages caused by the union's refusal to process the grievance should not be charged to the employer. In this case, even if the Union had breached its duty, all or almost all of Owens' damages would still be attributable to his allegedly wrongful discharge by Swift. For these reasons, even if the Union here had properly been found liable for a breach of duty, it is clear that the damage award was improper.

Reversed.

MR. JUSTICE FORTAS, with whom THE CHIEF JUSTICE and MR. JUSTICE HARLAN join, concurring in the result.

1. In my view, a complaint by an employee that the union has breached its duty of fair representation is subject to the exclusive jurisdiction of the NLRB. It is a charge of unfair labor practice. See Miranda Fuel Co., 140 N.L.R.B. 181 (1962); Rubber Workers Local 12, 150 N.L.R.B. 312, *enforced,* 368 F.2d 12 (5th Cir. 1966). As is the case with most other unfair labor practices, the Board's jurisdiction is pre-emptive. . . . There is no basis for failure to apply the pre-emption principles in the present case, and, as I shall discuss, strong reason for its application. The relationship between the union and the individual employee with respect to the processing of claims to employment rights under the collective bargaining agreement is fundamental to the design and operation of federal labor law. It is not "merely peripheral," as the Court's opinion states. It "presents difficult problems of definition of status, problems which we have held are precisely 'of a kind most wisely entrusted initially to the agency charged with the day-to-day administration of the Act as a whole.'" Iron Workers v. Perko, 373 U.S. at 706. Accordingly, the judgment of the Supreme Court of Missouri should be reversed and the complaint dismissed for this reason and on this basis. I agree, however, that if it were assumed that jurisdiction of the subject matter exists, the judgment would still have to be reversed because of the use by the Missouri court of an improper standard for measuring the union's duty,

and the absence of evidence to establish that the union refused further to process Owens' grievance because of bad faith or arbitrarily.

2. I regret the elaborate discussion in the Court's opinion of problems which are irrelevant. This is not an action by the employee against the employer, and the discussion of the requisites of such an action is, in my judgment, unnecessary. The Court argues that the employee could sue the employer under LMRA § 301; and that to maintain such an action the employee would have to show that he has exhausted his remedies under the collective bargaining agreement, or alternatively that he was prevented from doing so because the union breached its duty to him by failure completely to process his claim. That may be; or maybe all he would have to show to maintain an action against the employer for wrongful discharge is that he demanded that the union process his claim to exhaustion of available remedies, and that it refused to do so. I see no need for the Court to pass upon that question, which is not presented here, and which, with all respect, lends no support to the Court's argument. The Court seems to use its discussion of the employee-employer litigation as somehow analogous to or supportive of its conclusion that the employee may maintain a court action against the union. But I do not believe that this follows. I agree that the NLRB's unfair labor practice jurisdiction does not preclude an action under § 301 against the employer for wrongful discharge from employment. Smith v. Evening News Ass'n, 371 U.S. 195 (1962). Therefore, Owens might maintain an action against his employer in the present case. This would be an action to enforce the collective bargaining agreement, and Congress has authorized the courts to entertain actions of this type. But his claim against the union is quite different in character, as the Court itself recognizes. The Court holds — and I think correctly if the issue is to be reached — that the union could not be required to pay damages measured by the breach of the employment contract, because it was not the union but the employer that breached the contract. I agree; but I suggest that this reveals the point for which I contend: that the employee's claim against the union is not a claim under the collective bargaining agreement, but a claim that the union has breached its statutory duty of fair representation. This claim, I submit, is a claim of unfair labor practice and it is within the exclusive jurisdiction of the NLRB. . . .

3. If we look beyond logic and precedent to the policy of the labor relations design which Congress has provided, court jurisdiction of this type of action seems anomalous and ill-advised. We are not dealing here with the interpretation of a contract or with an alleged breach of an employment agreement. As the Court in effect acknowledges, we are concerned with the subtleties of a union's statutory duty faithfully to represent employees in the unit, including those who may not be members of the union. The Court — regrettably, in my opinion — ventures to state judgments as to the metes and bounds of the reciprocal duties involved in the relationship between the union and the employee. In my opinion, this is precisely and especially the kind of judgment that Congress intended to entrust to the Board and which is well within the pre-emption

doctrine that this Court has prudently stated.... The nuances of union-employee and union-employer relationships are infinite and consequential, particularly when the issue is as amorphous as whether the union was proved guilty of "arbitrary or bad-faith conduct" which the Court states as the standard applicable here. In all reason and in all good judgment, this jurisdiction should be left with the Board and not be placed in the courts, especially with the complex and necessarily confusing guidebook that the Court now publishes....

[The dissenting opinion of MR. JUSTICE BLACK is omitted.]

NOTE

Prior to the principal case, the lower courts had developed at least two main approaches to an individual employee's right to arbitration. Under one line of cases, illustrated by Donnelly v. United Fruit Co., 40 N.J. 61, 190 A.2d 825 (1963), an employee was regarded as having a "statutorily-vested right" under § 9(a) to invoke the grievance procedure, including the final step of arbitration, if the union failed to press his claim. Under a second group of decisions, represented by Black-Clawson Co. v. Machinists Lodge 355, 313 F.2d 179 (2d Cir. 1962), an individual employee could not compel the employer to arbitrate his grievance unless the contract specifically so provided: § 9(a) was deemed merely to permit but not require an employer to hear and adjust employee grievances.

Does the standard of fair representation applied by the Supreme Court appear to be a matter of honesty and subjective good faith, or a matter of "reasonableness"? To what extent should a union, even if acting in accordance with its honest judgment, be allowed to sacrifice individual interests for the sake of the group? Should a union be able to trade off or compromise some claims in order to gain concessions on others? Does it make any difference whether the abandoned grievance involves a discharge, minor discipline, seniority, or wages allegedly accrued and owing? Is it relevant that an arbitration with a single day's hearing may cost a union $2200 and an employer more? See p. 647, supra, text at note 32. Perhaps the most poignant reported instance of conflict between individual and group interests is Union News Co. v. Hildreth, 295 F.2d 658 (6th Cir. 1961). A lunch counter employing twelve persons suffered unexplained losses of food or money and suspected dishonesty among the workers. The employer threatened to fire the entire crew. Rather than have this happen, the union acquiesced in the employer's trial layoff of five employees. Losses dropped, the five employees were permanently discharged, and the union refused to process a grievance on behalf of one protesting worker, even though there was no direct proof of her dishonesty. Did the union act so improperly that a court should intervene? See also Longshoremen's Local 13 v. Pacific Maritime Ass'n, 441 F. 2d 1061 (9th Cir. 1971), cert. denied, 404 U.S. 1016 (1972) ("swapping" of grievance claim for other concessions).

In Ruzicka v. General Motors Corp., 523 F.2d 306 (6th Cir. 1975), rehearing denied, 528 F.2d 912 (1976), the court held that bad faith is not an essential element of a claim of unfair representation. It is enough if the union arbitrarily ignores an employee's grievance and merely allows it to expire out of negligent and perfunctory handling. *See also* Milstead v. Teamsters Local 957, 580 F. 2d 232 (6th Cir. 1978) (inept grievance handling through ignorance of labor contract); Holodnak v. Avco Corp., 381 F. Supp. 191 (D. Conn. 1974), *modified,* 514 F. 2d 285 (2d Cir. 1975), *cert. denied,* 423 U.S. 892 (1975) (attorney "perfunctory").

In Teamsters Local 568 v. NLRB, 379 F.2d 137 (D.C. Cir. 1967), a union's adamant stand against the dovetailing of seniority lists when one company acquired another, and its insistence that one group of merging employees be given priority as a body over the other, was held to violate the duty of fair representation. *See also* Smith v. Hussmann Refrigerator Co., 100 L.R.R.M. 2238 (8th Cir. 1979) (union breached duty by adhering strictly to seniority to exclusion of all other considerations in contesting employer's promotions based on skill and ability).

The Supreme Court elaborated on its *Vaca* rule for calculating damages against a union guilty of unfair representation in Czosek v. O'Mara, 397 U.S. 25 (1970). Said the Court: "Assuming a wrongful discharge by the employer independent of any discriminatory conduct by the union and a subsequent discriminatory refusal by the union to process grievances based on the discharge, damages against the union for loss of employment are unrecoverable except to the extent that its refusal to handle the grievances added to the difficulty and expense of collecting from the employer." *But cf.* IUE Local 485 (Automotive Plating Corp.), 183 N.L.R.B. No. 131, 74 L.R.R.M. 1396 (1970), *enforced in part,* 454 F.2d 17 (2d Cir. 1972).

See generally Blumrosen, *The Worker and Three Phases of Unionism: Administrative and Judicial Control of the Worker-Union Relationship,* 61 MICH. L. REV. 1435 (1963); Cox, *Rights Under a Labor Agreement,* 69 HARV. L. REV. 601 (1956); Feller, *A General Theory of the Collective Bargaining Agreement,* 61 CALIF. L. REV. 663 (1973); Hanslowe, *The Collective Agreement and the Duty of Fair Representation,* 14 LAB. L.J. 1052 (1963); Kirby, *Individual Rights in Industrial Self-Government: A "State Action" Analysis,* 63 NW. U.L. REV. 4 (1968); Summers, *Collective Power and Individual Rights in the Collective Agreement — A Comparison of Swedish and American Law,* 72 YALE L.J. 421 (1963); Lewis, *Fair Representation in Grievance Administration: Vaca v. Sipes,* 1967 SUP. CT. REV. 81.

GLOVER V. ST. LOUIS-SAN FRANCISCO RY., 393 U.S. 324, 89 S. Ct. 548, 21 L. Ed. 2d 519 (1969). Black and white railroad employees sued their union and employer, claiming that racial discrimination practiced by the railroad with the sub rosa agreement of certain union officials kept the plaintiffs from securing higher paying jobs. The defendants moved to dismiss on the ground that the plaintiffs had not exhausted their administrative remedies under the contract grievance procedure, in the union constitution, or before the National Railroad Adjustment Board. Plaintiffs responded that they had tried in vain to present their grievances to union and company officials. The Supreme Court held that since the union and the employer were allegedly scheming together to bar the blacks from promotion, the employees should not be required to pursue further any relief administered by the union, the company, or both. Even though the Railroad Adjustment Board ordinarily has exclusive jurisdiction under § 3 First (i) of the Railway Labor Act to interpret collective bargaining agreements, it too was suspect here since its membership is largely chosen by the railroads and the brotherhoods.

NOTES

1. For further rulings on the need to exhaust administrative remedies before suing, or on the elimination of such a requirement because of futility, see Andrews v. Louisville & N. R.R., 406 U.S. 320 (1972); Steinman v. Spector Freight System, 441 F.2d 599 (2d Cir. 1971). *See generally* Simpson & Berwick, *Exhaustion of Grievance Procedures and the Individual Employee,* 51 TEXAS L. REV. 1179 (1973).

2. Should an employer be able to defend against an employee's § 301 suit on the basis of failure to exhaust internal union remedies? *Compare* Orphan v. Furnco Constr. Co., 466 F. 2d 795 (7th Cir. 1972), *with* Winter v. Teamsters Local 636, 569 F. 2d 146 (10th Cir. 1977). If a union provides an impartial tribunal to review the fairness of its decisions, such as the United Automobile Workers' Public Review Board (see p. 902, *infra*), must a member exhaust this avenue of appeal before he can maintain a § 301 action for unfair representation and breach of contract? *See, e.g.,* Sedlarik v. General Motors Corp., 78 L.R.R.M 2232 (W.D. Mich. 1971).

3. If the collective agreement provides for grievance processing but not arbitration, is an employee precluded from suing upon exhaustion of the grievance procedure? *Compare* Haynes v. U.S. Pipe & Foundry Co., 362 F.2d 414 (5th Cir. 1966), *with* International Bhd. of Telephone Workers v. New England Tel. & Tel. Co., 240 F. Supp. 426 (D. Mass. 1965).

4. May a union and employer write into a contract a clause foreclosing individual actions and restricting the right to maintain suit on employee claims to the union? *Cf.* Elgin, Joliet & Eastern Ry. v. Burley, 325 U.S. 711, 729 (1945) (union cannot, under the RLA, bind employee by grievance settlement of accrued monetary claim without his authorization: "It would be difficult to believe that Congress intended . . . to submerge wholly the individual and minority interest, with all power to act concerning them, in the collective interest and agency, not only in forming the contracts which govern their employment relation, but also in giving effect to them and to all other incidents of that relation"). *But see* Feller, *A General Theory of the Collective Bargaining Agreement,* 61 CALIF. L. REV. 663, 774-92, 835-36 (1973).

5. Certain employee rights, such as the right to vacation pay or retirement benefits, have been held for some time to "vest," or survive the expiration of the labor agreement. *See, e.g., In re* Wil-Low Cafeterias, Inc., 111 F.2d 429 (2d Cir. 1940); Vallejo v. American R.R. of Puerto Rico, 188 F.2d 513 (1st Cir. 1951); Hauser v. Farwell, Ozmun, Kirk & Co., 299 F. Supp. 387 (D. Minn. 1969). *But cf.* Battle v. Clark Equipment Co., 579 F. 2d 1338 (7th Cir. 1978) (supplemental unemployment benefits subject to reduction). Seniority rights have been placed in a different category. They can be cut off by an employer's moving his plant, or by an agreement between employer and union. Oddie v. Ross Gear & Tool Co., 305 F.2d 143 (6th Cir. 1962), *cert. denied,* 371 U.S. 941 (1962); Humphrey v. Moore, 375 U.S. 335 (1964). Is this distinction sound? *See* Aaron, *Reflections on the Legal Nature and Enforceability of Seniority Rights,* 75 HARV. L. REV. 1532 (1962); Blumrosen, *Seniority Rights and Industrial Change: Zdanok v. Glidden Co.,* 47 MINN. L. REV. 505 (1962); Feinberg, Katz & Shaw, *Do Contract Rights Vest?* in NATIONAL ACADEMY OF ARBITRATORS, LABOR ARBITRATION AND INDUSTRIAL CHANGE, PROCEEDINGS OF THE SIXTEENTH ANNUAL MEETING 192, 223, 231 (1963) (three separate papers).

6. Disputes over the right of employees to follow their work have been ruled arbitrable. Piano Workers Local 2549 v. W.W. Kimball Co., 379 U.S. 357 (1964), *rev'g* 333 F.2d 761 (7th Cir. 1964); Warehousemen Local 636 v. American Hardware Supply Co., 329 F.2d 789 (3d Cir. 1964), *cert. denied,* 379 U.S. 829 (1964). In Selb Mfg. Co. v. Machinists District 9, 305 F.2d 177 (8th Cir. 1962), the union was held entitled to enforcement of an arbitration award directing the employer to return his plant to its original location. In the absence of an express ban on employer subcontracting, could a prohibition be inferred from the union recognition and union shop clauses? *See* UAW Local 391 v. Webster Elec. Co., 299 F.2d 195 (7th Cir. 1962).

HINES v. ANCHOR MOTOR FREIGHT, INC.

Supreme Court of the United States
424 U.S. 554, 96 S. Ct. 1048, 47 L. Ed. 2d 231 (1976)

MR. JUSTICE WHITE delivered the opinion of the Court.

The issue here is whether a suit against an employer by employees asserting breach of a collective-bargaining contract was properly dismissed where the accompanying complaint against the Union for breach of duty of fair representation has withstood the Union's motion for summary judgment and remains to be tried.

I. Petitioners, who were formerly employed as truck drivers by respondent Anchor Motor Freight, Inc. (Anchor), were discharged on June 5, 1967. The applicable collective-bargaining contract forbade discharges without just cause. The company charged dishonesty. The practice at Anchor was to reimburse drivers for money spent for lodging while the drivers were on the road overnight. Anchor's assertion was that petitioners had sought reimbursement for motel expenses in excess of the actual charges sustained by them. At a meeting between the company and the union, Local 377, International Brotherhood of Teamsters (the Union), which was also attended by petitioners, Anchor presented motel receipts previously submitted by petitioners which were in excess of the charges shown on the motel's registration cards; a notarized statement of the motel clerk asserting the accuracy of the registration cards; and an affidavit of the motel owner affirming that the registration cards were accurate and that inflated receipts had been furnished petitioners. The Union claimed petitioners were innocent and opposed the discharges. It was then agreed that the matter would be presented to the joint arbitration committee for the area, to which the collective-bargaining contract permitted either party to submit an unresolved grievance.[2] Pending this hearing, petitioners were reinstated. Their suggestion that the motel be investigated was answered by the Union representatives' assurances that "there was nothing to worry about" and that they need not hire their own attorney.

A hearing before the joint area committee was held on July 26, 1967. Anchor presented its case. Both the Union and petitioners were afforded an opportunity to present their case and to be heard. Petitioners denied their dishonesty, but neither they nor the Union presented any other evidence contradicting the documents presented by the company. The committee sustained the discharges. Petitioners then retained an attorney and sought rehearing based on a statement by the motel owner that he had no personal knowledge of the events, but that the discrepancy between the receipts and the registration cards could have been attributable to the motel clerk's recording on the cards less than was actually paid and retaining for himself the difference between the amount receipted and the amount recorded. The committee, after hearing, unanimously denied rehearing "because there was no new evidence presented which would justify reopening this case."

There were later indications that the motel clerk was in fact the culprit; and the present suit was filed in June 1969, against Anchor, the Union and its International. The complaint alleged that the charges of dishonesty made against petitioners by Anchor were false, that there was no just cause for discharge and that the discharges had been in breach of contract. It was also asserted that the falsity of the charges could have been discovered with a minimum of investigation, that the Union had made no effort to

---

[2] The contractual grievance procedure is set out in Art. 7 of the Central Conference Area Supplement to the National Master Agreement. App. 226-233. Grievances were to be taken up by the employee involved and if no settlement was reached, were then to be considered by the business agent of the local union and the employer representative. If the dispute remained unresolved, either party had the right to present the case for decision to the appropriate joint area arbitration committee. These committees are organized on a geographical area basis and hear grievances in panels made up of an equal number of representatives of the parties to the collective-bargaining agreement. Cases that deadlocked before the joint area committee could be taken to a panel of the national joint arbitration committee, composed like the area commitee panels of an equal number of representatives of the parties to the agreement. If unresolved there, they would be resolved by a panel including an impartial arbitrator. The joint arbitration committee for the Detroit area is involved in this case.

ascertain the truth of the charges and that the Union had violated its duty of fair representation by arbitrarily and in bad faith depriving petitioners of their employment and permitting their discharge without sufficient proof.

The Union denied the charges and relied on the decision of the joint area committee. Anchor asserted that petitioners had been properly discharged for just cause. It also defended on the ground that petitioners, diligently and in good faith represented by the Union, had unsuccessfully resorted to the grievance and arbitration machinery provided by the contract and that the adverse decision of the joint arbitration committee was binding upon the Union and petitioners under the contractual provision declaring that "[a] decision by a majority of a Panel of any of the Committees shall be final and binding on all parties, including the employee and/or employees affected." Discovery followed, including a deposition of the motel clerk revealing that he had falsified the records and that it was he who had pocketed the difference between the sums shown on the receipts and the registration cards. Motions for summary judgment filed by Anchor and the Unions were granted by the District Court on the ground that the decision of the arbitration committee was final and binding on the employees and "for failure to show facts comprising bad faith, arbitrariness or perfunctoriness on the part of the Unions." Although indicating that the acts of the Union "may not meet professional standards of competency, and while it might have been advisable for the Union to further investigate the charges ...," the District Court concluded that the facts demonstrated at most bad judgment on the part of the Union, which was insufficient to prove a breach of duty or make out a prima facie case against it. . . .

After reviewing the allegations and the record before it, the Court of Appeals concluded that there were sufficient facts from which bad faith or arbitrary conduct on the part of the local Union could be inferred by the trier of fact and that petitioners should have been afforded an opportunity to prove their charges.[4] To this extent the judgment of the District Court was reversed. The Court of Appeals affirmed the judgment in favor of Anchor and the International. . . .

---

[4] As summarized by the Court of Appeals, the allegations relied on were:

"They consist of the motel clerk's admission, made a year after the discharge was upheld in arbitration, that he, not plaintiffs, pocketed the money; the claim of the union's failure to investigate the motel clerk's original story implicating plaintiffs despite their requests; the account of the union officials' assurances to plaintiffs that 'they had nothing to worry about' and 'that there was no need for them to investigate'; the contention that no exculpatory evidence was presented at the hearing; and the assertion that there existed political antagonism between local union officials and plaintiffs because of a wildcat strike led by some of the plaintiffs and a dispute over the appointment of a steward, resulting in denunciation of plaintiffs as 'hillbillies' by Angelo, the union president." 506 F. 2d 1153, 1156 (CA6 1974).

It is this judgment of the Court of Appeals with respect to Anchor that is now before us on our limited grant of the employees' petition for writ of certiorari. . . . We reverse that judgment. . . .

III. Even though under *Vaca* the employer may not insist on exhaustion of grievance procedures when the union has breached its representation duty, it is urged that when the procedures have been followed and a decision favorable to the employer announced, the employer must be protected from relitigation by the express contractual provision declaring a decision to be final and binding. We disagree. The union's breach of duty relieves the employee of an express or implied requirement that disputes be settled through contractual grievance procedures; if it seriously undermines the integrity of the arbitral process the union's breach also removes the bar of the finality provisions of the contract.

It is true that *Vaca* dealt with a refusal by the union to process a grievance. It is also true that where the union actually utilizes the grievance and arbitration procedures on behalf of the employee, the focus is no longer on the reasons for the union's failure to act but on whether, contrary to the arbitrator's decision, the employer breached the contract and whether there is substantial reason to believe that a union breach of duty contributed to the erroneous outcome of the contractual proceedings. But the judicial remedy in *Humphrey v. Moore* was sought arter the adverse decision of the joint arbitration committee. Our conclusion in that case was not that the committee's decision was unreviewable. On the contrary, we proceeded on the basis that it was reviewable and vulnerable if tainted by breach of duty on the part of the union, even though the employer had not conspired with the union. The joint committee's decision was held binding on the complaining employees only after we determined that the union had not been guilty of malfeasance and that its conduct was within the range of acceptable performance by a collective-bargaining agent, a wholly unnecessary determination if the union's conduct was irrelevant to the finality of the arbitral process. . . .

Anchor would have it that petitioners are foreclosed from judicial relief unless some blameworthy conduct on its part disentitles it to rely on the finality rule. But it was Anchor that originated the discharges for dishonesty. If those charges were in error, Anchor has surely played its part in precipitating this dispute. Of course, both courts below held there were no facts suggesting that Anchor either knowingly or negligently relied on false evidence. As far as the record reveals it also prevailed before the joint committee after presenting its case in accordance with what were ostensibly wholly fair procedures. Nevertheless there remains the question whether the contractual protection against relitigating an arbitral decision binds employees who assert that the process has fundamentally malfunctioned by reason of the bad-faith performance of the union, their statutorily imposed collective-bargaining agent.

Under the rule announced by the Court of Appeals, unless the employer is implicated in the Union's malfeasance or has otherwise caused the arbitral process to err, petitioners would have no remedy against Anchor even though they are successful in proving the Union's bad faith, the falsity of the charges against them and the breach of contract by Anchor by discharging without cause. This rule would apparently govern even in circumstances where it is shown that a union has manufactured the evidence and knows from the start that it is false; or even if, unbeknownst to the employer, the union has corrupted the arbitrator to the detriment of disfavored Union members. As is the case where there has been a failure to exhaust, however, we cannot believe that Congress intended to foreclose the employee from his § 301 remedy otherwise available against the employer if the contractual processes have been seriously flawed by the union's breach of its duty to represent employees honestly and in good faith and without invidious discrimination or arbitrary conduct.

It is urged that the reversal of the Court of Appeals will undermine not only the finality rule but the entire collective-bargaining process. Employers, it is said, will be far less willing to give up their untrammeled right to discharge without cause and to agree to private settlement procedures. But the burden on employees will remain a substantial one, far too heavy in the opinion of some. To prevail against either the company or the Union, petitioners must show not only that their discharge was contrary to the contract but must also carry the burden of demonstrating breach of duty by the Union. As the District Court indicated, this involves more than demonstrating mere errors in judgment.

Petitioners are not entitled to relitigate their discharge merely because they offer newly discovered evidence that the charges against them were false and that in fact they were fired without cause. The grievance processes cannot be expected to be error-free. The finality provision has sufficient force to surmount occasional instances of mistake. But it is quite another matter to suggest that erroneous arbitration decisions must stand even though the employee's representation by the union has been dishonest, in bad faith or discriminatory; for in that event error and injustice of the grossest sort would multiply. The contractual system would then cease to qualify as an adequate mechanism to secure individual redress for damaging failure of the employer to abide by the contract. Congress has put its blessing on private dispute settlement arrangements provided in collective agreements, but it was anticipated, we are sure, that the contractual machinery would operate within some minimum levels of integrity. In our view, enforcement of the finality provision where the arbitrator has erred is conditioned upon the Union's having satisfied its statutory duty fairly to represent the employee in connection with the arbitration proceedings. Wrongfully discharged employees would be left without jobs and without a fair opportunity to secure an adequate remedy.

Except for this case the Courts of Appeals have arrived at similar conclusions. As the Court of Appeals for the Ninth Circuit put it in *Margetta v. Pam Pam Corp.,* 501 F.2d 179, 180 (1974): "To us, it makes little difference whether the union subverts the arbitration process by refusing to proceed as in *Vaca* or follows the arbitration trail to the end, but in doing so subverts the arbitration process by failing to fairly represent the employee. In neither case does the employee receive fair representation."

Petitioners, if they prove an erroneous discharge and the Union's breach of duty tainting the decision of the joint committee, are entitled to an appropriate remedy against the employer as well as the Union. It was error to affirm the District Court's final dismissal of petitioners' action against Anchor. To this extent the judgment of the Court of Appeals is reversed.

So ordered.

MR. JUSTICE STEVENS took no part in the consideration or decision of this case.

[The concurring opinion of MR. JUSTICE STEWART and the dissenting opinion of MR. JUSTICE REHNQUIST, with whom THE CHIEF JUSTICE joined, are omitted.]

NOTES

1. For a thoughtful analysis of the lessons of the major Supreme Court decisions through *Hines,* see Summers, *The Individual Employee's Rights Under the Collective Agreement: What Constitutes Fair Representation?* 126 U. PA. L. REV. 251 (1977). In determining the scope of the duty of fair representation, does it remain relevant that the doctrine may have initially been inferred in *Steele* in order to avoid constitutional questions that would otherwise have arisen from the congressional grant of exclusive recognition to majority bargaining agents?

2. The Supreme Court has held apparently as a blanket rule (5-4), that punitive damages are not available against unions for breach of the duty of fair representation in processing grievances. IBEW v. Foust, 47 U.S.L.W. 4600 (U.S. 1979).

3. *See generally* J. MCKELVEY, ED., THE DUTY OF FAIR REPRESENTATION (1977).

B. UNFAIR REPRESENTATION AS AN UNFAIR LABOR PRACTICE

MIRANDA FUEL CO., 140 N.L.R.B. 181 (1962). During a fuel company's slack season, from April 15 to October 15, employees subject to unsteady employment were entitled under a collective bargaining agreement to a leave of absence without loss of seniority. One employee, Lopuch, obtained the employer's permission to leave at the end of work on April 12, a Friday. Lopuch became ill in mid-October and did not return until October 30. He had a doctor's certificate, however, and the company excused the late return. At the urging of other employees, the union demanded that Lopuch be reduced from the middle to the bottom of the seniority list for violating the contract by his lateness. When the union learned about the excused illness, it changed its claim and relied instead on Lopuch's early departure. The employer reluctantly acquiesced in the seniority reduction even though the contract did not call for it. The Board held (3-2) that the demotion was due to "irrelevant, unfair or invidious reasons," and that it violated the union's duty of fair representation under § 9(a) of the NLRA. Moreover, although Lopuch was a union member himself, the Board majority found that the union had violated §§ 8(b)(1)(A) and 8(b)(2). It reasoned that the union's duty to represent all employees fairly and impartially under § 9(a) is incorporated into employees' § 7 rights "to bargain collectively through representatives of their own choosing." Unfair representation, whether or not influenced by an employee's union activities, violates § 8(b)(1)(A), and attempts to secure employer participation violates § 8(b)(2). Employer complicity is in turn violative of §§ 8(a)(3) and 8(a)(1).

NOTES

1. Enforcement was denied in NLRB v. Miranda Fuel Co., 326 F. 2d 172 (2d Cir. 1963). Judge Medina agreed with the Board's dissenting members that "discrimination for reasons wholly unrelated to 'union membership, loyalty . . . or the performance of union obligations' is not sufficient to support findings of violations of [§ 8] of the Act." Judge Lumbard concurred, finding insufficient evidence of any breach of the union's duty of fair representation, and thus he did not have to consider its status as a possible § 8(b)(1) violation. Judge Friendly dissented, but also avoided the unfair representation issue. He read "discrimination" broadly as any distinction made without a proper basis, and argued that any demonstration of union power causing an employer to discriminate was sufficient "encouragement of union membership" to be grounds for finding violations of §§ 8(b)(2) and 8(a)(3).

2. In Metal Workers Local 1 (Hughes Tool Co.), 147 N.L.R.B. 1573 (1964), the NLRB held that a union's outright rejection of an employee's grievance for racial reasons violated §§ 8(b)(1)(A), 8(b)(2), and 8(b)(3), and that the joint certification issued to a white local and a black local should be rescinded because they had entered into racially discriminatory contracts. Chairman McCulloch and Member Fanning, who had dissented in *Miranda,* concurred in the rescission of the certification and in the finding of a § 8(b)(1)(A) violation, the latter on the narrow ground that the black employee had been discriminated against because he was not a member of the white local. In rejecting once again the concept of unfair representation as an unfair labor practice, McCulloch and Fanning elaborated on the rationale for their *Miranda* dissent:

> Section 7 was part of the Wagner Act which in its unfair labor practice section was aimed only at employer conduct. The Wagner Act also contained the present § 9(a). It hardly seems reasonable to infer, in these circumstances, that § 7 contained a protected implied right to fair representation against the bargaining representative, when the entire Wagner Act did not make any conduct by a labor organization unlawful. Section 7 was continued substantially unchanged in the Taft-Hartley Act except for the addition of the

"right to refrain" clause, which is not material to our problem. Although the Taft-Hartley Act added union unfair labor practices to the list of prohibited conduct, neither the Act nor the legislative history contains any mention of the duty of fair representation, despite the fact that the *Steele* and *Wallace* decisions were well known, having been issued 3 years previously. Again, although in the interval between the dates of the Taft-Hartley and Landrum-Griffin Acts, there were additional court decisions and articles by learned commentators in the law journals dealing with the legal problems of fair representation, Congress made no change in the wording of § 7, and ignored the problem completely in adding a "Bill of Rights" section to the existing statute. If Congress had really intended that violation of the duty of fair representation should be an unfair labor practice, it would seem that the 1959 revision afforded it an opportunity to clear up the uncertainty. Instead it remained silent. We do not believe that realistically this silence can be interpreted as in any way favorable to the contention that the right to fair representation is a protected § 7 right. There are practical reasons for believing that, if there had been any contemporary understanding that the Act had made it an unfair labor practice for a union to fail in its duty of fair representation, the opposition would have been both strong and loud.

There is another and more important reason why the Board should not undertake to police a union's administration of its duties without a clear mandate from Congress. The purpose of the Act is primarily to protect the organizational rights of employees. But apart from the obligation to bargain in good faith, "Congress intended that the parties would have wide latitude in their negotiations, unrestricted by any governmental power to regulate the substantive solution of their differences." Before *Miranda,* it was assumed that contract or grievance decisions by employers and unions were immune from examination by the Board unless they were influenced by union considerations. But, under the underlying reasoning of the *Miranda* majority and that of the present decision, the Board is now constituted a tribunal to which every employee who feels aggrieved by a bargaining representative's action, whether in contract negotiations or in grievance handling, may appeal, regardless of whether the decision has been influenced in whole or in part by considerations of union membership, loyalty, or activity. The Board must determine on such appeal, without statutory standards, whether the representative's decision was motivated by "unfair or irrelevant or invidious" considerations and therefore to be set aside, or was within the "wide range of reasonableness ... allowed a statutory representative in serving the unit it represents ..." and to be sustained. Inevitably, the Board will have to sit in judgment on the substantive matters of collective bargaining, the very thing the Supreme Court has said the Board must not do, and in which it has no special experience or competence.

3. Despite the rebuff by the court of appeals in *Miranda,* the NLRB has persisted in treating unfair representation as an unfair labor practice, and other courts have proved more receptive to this view. In a racial discrimination case, the Fifth Circuit upheld the Board's theory that union unfair representation is a violation of § 8(b)(1)(A) of the NLRA, but did not pass on the Board's contention that it is also a violation of §§ 8(b)(2) and 8(b)(3). Rubber Workers Local 12 v. NLRB, 368 F. 2d 12 (5th Cir. 1966), *cert. denied,* 389 U.S. 837 (1967). *Accord:* Teamsters Local 568 v. NLRB, 379 F. 2d 137 (D.C. Cir. 1967), involving a nonracial situation; NLRB v. Glass Bottle Blowers Local 106, 520 F. 2d 693 (6th Cir. 1975) (sexually segregated locals). *Cf.* NLRB v. Longshoremen Local 1581 [Manchester Terminal Corp.], 489 F. 2d 635 (5th Cir. 1974), *cert. denied,* 419 U.S. 1040 (1974) (§ 8(b)(2) violation for union to discriminate against Mexican citizens in job transfers). Although the Supreme Court has never squarely ruled on the question, its tacit acceptance of the Labor Board's unfair representation doctrine in *Vaca v. Sipes, supra* at 743, has tended to still further debate. *See generally* Albert, *NLRB-FEPC?* 16 VAND. L. REV. 547 (1963); Meltzer, *The National Labor Relations Act and Racial Discrimination: The More Remedies, the Better?* 42 U. CHI. L. REV. 1 (1974); Sherman, *Union's Duty of Fair Representation and the Civil Rights Act of 1964,* 49 MINN. L. REV. 771 (1964); Sovern, *Race Discrimination and the National Labor Relations Act: The Brave New World of Miranda,* in N.Y.U. SIXTEENTH ANNUAL CONFERENCE ON LABOR 3 (1963).

4. Sex discrimination by a union is also unfair representation in violation of §§ 8(b)(1)(A) and 8(b)(2), and a participating employer violates §§ 8(a)(3) and 8(a)(1). Pacific Maritime Ass'n, 209 N.L.R.B. 519 (1974). But an employer's unilateral sex discrimination is not an unfair labor practice. Jubilee Mfg. Co., 202 N.L.R.B. 272 (1973).

5. In an unprecedented decision, a court of appeals held that racial discrimination by an employer acting on his own violates § 8(a)(1) where it has the effect of "producing a docility in its victims which inhibits the exercise of their § 7 rights." Packinghouse Workers v. NLRB [Farmers' Cooperative Compress], 416 F.2d 1126 (D.C. Cir. 1969), *cert. denied,* 396 U.S. 903 (1969). For the case on remand, *see* Farmers' Cooperative Compress, 194 N.L.R.B. No. 3, 78 L.R.R.M. 1465 (1971). *See also* Boyce, *Racial Discrimination and the NLRA,* 65 Nw. U.L. REV. 232 (1970); Leiken, *The Current and Potential Equal Employment Role of the NLRB,* 1971 DUKE L.J. 833.

6. For recent Board findings of union unfair representation in situations not involving race or sex discrimination, *see* Explo, Inc., 235 N.L.R.B. No. 127, 98 L.R.R.M. 1024 (1978) (union business agent appointed his son-in-law and a friend as shop stewards, thereby giving them superseniority); Teamsters Local 860 (The Emporium), 236 N.L.R.B. No. 176, 98 L.R.R.M. 1422 (1978) (union persisted in demanding wage increase it knew would result in termination of employees).

7. When a union has failed to represent employees fairly in grievance handling, it may be required to pay for outside legal counsel to process their case through arbitration. *See* NLRB v. Teamsters Local 396 [United Parcel Serv.], 509 F.2d 1075 (9th Cir. 1975), *cert. denied,* 421 U.S. 976 (1975).

SECTION V. Equal Employment Opportunity

CHRISTOPHER JENCKS ET AL., INEQUALITY: A REASSESSMENT OF THE EFFECT OF FAMILY AND SCHOOLING IN AMERICA 190-91 (1972, 1973) *

In 1962, before the civil rights movement had had any appreciable impact on employment patterns, the average black was in an occupation that ranked 24 points [on the 96-point "Duncan status scale"] below the national average, *i.e.,* below about 84 percent of all whites. This is roughly the difference between a doctor and a schoolteacher, between a schoolteacher and a telephone repairman, between a telephone repairman and a baker, or between a baker and an unskilled laborer.

Many people assumed in 1962, and some still assume today, that blacks were concentrated in low-status occupations primarily because they were the victims of a "vicious circle of poverty." . . . But this does not seem to explain much of the difference between blacks' and whites' occupations. . . .

The cost of being black is perhaps clearest if we look at the fate of men born into the black middle class. If a black man had a father in the same occupation and with as much education as the average white, and a family as small as the average white, he still ended up in an occupation 19 points below the average white — only 5 points above the average black. What this implies is that, so far as white employers in 1962 were concerned, "all blacks looked alike." . . . Having the right parents had been of very little value. Even having additional education had been of limited value.

HARRY T. EDWARDS & BARRY L. ZARETSKY, PREFERENTIAL REMEDIES FOR EMPLOYMENT DISCRIMINATION, 74 MICH. L. REV. 1, 3-5 (1975)**

Despite the Supreme Court's mandate of color blindness in *Brown* and the sweeping civil rights legislation that followed ten years later, statistics demonstrate that Blacks are still far behind white males in the employment market. For example, in 1973 the median income for black families was only $7,269, compared to $12,595 for white families. The ratio of median family income of Blacks to Whites decreased in the period

---

1969-1973 from 0.61 to 0.58, indicating that income differentials actually increased as we entered the seventies. . . . A comparison of unemployment rates further evidences our lack of progress toward equalizing the employment situation of Blacks and Whites. In 1960, the ratio of black unemployed workers to white was 2.1 to 1. By 1970 this ratio had decreased to 1.8 to 1, but by 1973 it was again 2.1 to 1. . . .

Considerable disparity is also evident between the economic status of women and that of white males. In 1972, the median income for full-time female workers was $5,903, compared to $10,202 for males. In 1970, the median income for women was 59.4 per cent of the median income for men, a gap considerably wider than that existing in 1955 when the median income for women was 63.9 per cent of the median income for men. Furthermore, in 1970, 13.5 per cent of full-time male workers earned at least $15,000 per year, while only 1.1 per cent of full-time female workers were in that salary range. . . . [W]omen also tend to lag in earnings when compared to men employed in the same jobs.

A. THE MEANING OF "DISCRIMINATION"

STATUTORY REFERENCES

Civil Rights Act of 1964 § 703
42 U.S.C. §§ 1981—1983

GRIGGS v. DUKE POWER CO.

Supreme Court of the United States
401 U.S. 424, 91 S. Ct. 849, 28 L. Ed. 2d 158 (1971)

MR. CHIEF JUSTICE BURGER delivered the opinion of the Court.

We granted the writ in this case to resolve the question whether an employer is prohibited by the Civil Rights Act of 1964, Title VII, from requiring a high school education or passing of a standardized general intelligence test as a condition of employment in or transfer to jobs when (a) neither standard is shown to be significantly related to successful job performance, (b) both requirements operate to disqualify Negroes at a substantially higher rate than white applicants, and (c) the jobs in question formerly had been filled only by white employees as part of a longstanding practice of giving preference to whites.

Congress provided, in Title VII of the Civil Rights Act of 1964, for class actions for enforcement of provisions of the Act and this proceeding was brought by a group of incumbent Negro employees against Duke Power Company. All the petitioners are employed at the Company's Dan River Steam Station, a power generating facility located at Draper, North Carolina. At the time this action was instituted, the Company had 95 employees at the Dan River Station, 14 of whom were Negroes; 13 of these are petitioners here.

The District Court found that prior to July 2, 1965, the effective date of the Civil Rights Act of 1964, the Company openly discriminated on the basis of race in the hiring and assigning of employees at its Dan River plant. The plant was organized into five operating departments: (1) Labor, (2) Coal Handling, (3) Operations, (4) Maintenance, and (5) Laboratory and Test. Negroes were employed only in the Labor Department where the highest paying jobs paid less than the lowest paying jobs in the other four "operating" departments in which only whites were employed. Promotions were normally made within each department on the basis of job seniority. Transferees into a department usually began in the lowest position.

In 1955 the Company instituted a policy of requiring a high school education for initial assignment to any department except Labor, and for transfer from the Coal Handling to any "inside" department (Operations, Maintenance, or Laboratory). When the Company abandoned its policy of restricting Negroes to the Labor Department in 1965, completion of high school also was made a prerequisite to transfer from Labor to any other department. From the time the high school requirement was instituted to the time of trial, however, white employees hired before the time of the high school education requirement continued to perform satisfactorily and achieve promotions in the "operating" departments. Findings on this score are not challenged.

The Company added a further requirement for new employees on July 2, 1965, the date on which Title VII became effective. To qualify for placement in any but the Labor Department it became necessary to register satisfactory scores on two professionally prepared aptitude tests, as well as to have a high school education. Completion of high school alone continued to render employees eligible for transfer to the four desirable departments from which Negroes had been excluded if the incumbent had been employed prior to the time of the new requirement. In September 1965 the Company began to permit incumbent employees who lacked a high school education to qualify for transfer from Labor or Coal Handling to an "inside" job by passing two tests — the Wonderlic Personnel Test, which purports to measure general intelligence, and the Bennett Mechanical Aptitude Test. Neither was directed or intended to measure the ability to learn to perform a particular job or category of jobs. The requisite scores used for both initial hiring and transfer approximated the national median for high school graduates.

The District Court had found that while the Company previously followed a policy of overt racial discrimination in a period prior to the Act, such conduct had ceased. The District Court also concluded that Title VII was intended to be prospective only and, consequently, the impact of prior inequities was beyond the reach of corrective action authorized by the Act.

The Court of Appeals was confronted with a question of first impression, as are we, concerning the meaning of Title VII. After careful analysis a majority of that court concluded that a subjective test of the employer's intent should govern, particularly in a close case, and that in this case there was no showing of a discriminatory purpose in the adoption of the diploma and test requirements. On this basis, the Court of Appeals concluded there was no violation of the Act.

The Court of Appeals reversed the District Court in part, rejecting the holding that residual discrimination arising from prior employment practices was insulated from remedial action. The Court of Appeals noted, however, that the District Court was correct in its conclusion that there was no finding of a racial purpose of invidious intent in the adoption of the high school diploma requirement or general intelligence test and that these standards had been applied fairly to whites and Negroes alike. It held that, in the absence of a discriminatory purpose, use of such requirements was permitted by the Act. In so doing, the Court of Appeals rejected the claim that because these two requirements operated to render ineligible a markedly disproportionate number of Negroes, they were unlawful under Title VII unless shown to be job-related. We granted the writ on these claims. . . .

The objective of Congress in the enactment of Title VII is plain from the language of the statute. It was to achieve equality of employment opportunities and remove barriers that have operated in the past to favor an identifiable group of white employees over other employees. Under the Act, practices, procedures, or tests neutral on their face, and even neutral in terms of intent, cannot be maintained if they operate to "freeze" the status quo of prior discriminatory employment practices.

The Court of Appeals' opinion, and the partial dissent, agreed that, on the record in the present case, "whites fare far better on the Company's alternative requirements" than Negroes.[6] This consequence would appear to be directly traceable to race. Basic intelligence must have the means of articulation to manifest itself fairly in a testing process. Because they are Negroes, petitioners have long received inferior education in segregated schools and this Court expressly recognized these differences in Gaston County v. United States, 395 U.S. 285 (1969). There, because of the inferior education received by Negroes in North Carolina, this court barred the institution of a literacy test for voter registration on the ground that the test would abridge the right to vote indirectly on account of race. Congress did not intend by Title VII, however, to guarantee a job to every person regardless of qualifications. In short, the Act does not command that any person be hired simply because he was formerly the subject of discrimination, or because he is a member of a minority group. Discriminatory preference for any group, minority or majority, is precisely and only what Congress has proscribed. What is required by Congress is the removal of artificial, arbitrary, and unnecessary barriers to employment when the barriers operate invidiously to discriminate on the basis of racial or other impermissible classification.

---

[6] In North Carolina, 1960 census statistics show that, while 34% of white males had completed high school, only 12% of Negro males had done so. U.S. Bureau of the Census, U.S. Census of Population: 1960, Vol. 1, Part 35, Table 47.

Similarly, with respect to standardized tests, the EEOC in one case found that use of a battery of tests, including the Wonderlic and Bennett tests used by the Company in the instant case, resulted in 58% of whites passing the tests, as compared with only 6% of the blacks. Decision of EEOC, CCH Empl. Prac. Guide ¶17,304.53 (Dec. 2, 1966).

Congress has now provided that tests or criteria for employment or promotion may not provide equality of opportunity only in the sense of the fabled offer of milk to the stork and the fox. On the contrary, Congress has now required that the posture and condition of the job seeker be taken into account. It has — to resort again to the fable — provided that the vessel in which the milk is proffered be one all seekers can use. The Act proscribes not only overt discrimination but also practices that are fair in form, but discriminatory in operation. The touchstone is business necessity. If an employment practice which operates to exclude Negroes cannot be shown to be related to job performance, the practice is prohibited.

On the record before us, neither the high school completion requirement nor the general intelligence test is shown to bear a demonstrable relationship to successful performance of the jobs for which it was used. Both were adopted, as the Court of Appeals noted, without meaningful study of their relationship to job-performance ability. Rather, a vice president of the Company testified, the requirements were instituted on the Company's judgment that they generally would improve the overall quality of the work force.

The evidence, however, shows that employees who have not completed high school or taken the tests have continued to perform satisfactorily and make progress in departments for which the high school and test criteria are now used. The promotion record of present employees who would not be able to meet the new criteria thus suggests the possibility that the requirements may not be needed even for the limited purpose of preserving the avowed policy of advancement within the Company. In the context of this case, it is unnecessary to reach the question whether testing requirements that take into account capability for the next succeeding position or related future promotion might be utilized upon a showing that such long range requirements fulfill a genuine business need. In the present case the Company has made no such showing.

The Court of Appeals held that the Company had adopted the diploma and test requirements without any "intention to discriminate against Negro employees." We do not suggest that either the District Court or the Court of Appeals erred in examining the employer's intent; but good intent or absence of discriminatory intent does not redeem employment procedures or testing mechanisms that operate as "built-in headwinds" for minority groups and are unrelated to measuring job capability.

The Company's lack of discriminatory intent is suggested by special efforts to help the undereducated employees through Company financing of two-thirds the cost of tuition for high school training. But Congress directed the thrust of the Act to the *consequences* of employment practices, not simply the motivation. More than that, Congress has placed on the employer the burden of showing that any given requirement must have a manifest relationship to the employment in question.

The facts of this case demonstrate the inadequacy of broad and general testing devices as well as the infirmity of using diplomas or degrees as fixed measures of capability. History is filled with examples of men and women who rendered highly effective performance without the conventional badges of accomplishment in terms of certificates, diplomas, or degrees. Diplomas and tests are useful servants, but Congress had mandated the common-sense proposition that they are not to become masters of reality.

The Company contends that its general intelligence tests are specifically permitted by § 703(h) of the Act. That section authorizes the use of "any professionally developed ability test" that is not "designed, intended, *or used* to discriminate because of race. . . ." (Emphasis added.)

The Equal Opportunity Commission, having enforcement responsibility, has issued guidelines interpreting § 703(h) to permit only the use of job-related tests. The administrative interpretation of the Act by the enforcing agency is entitled to great deference. . . . Since the Act and its legislative history support the Commission's construction, this affords good reason to treat the Guidelines as expressing the will of Congress.

Section 703(h) was not contained in the House version of the Civil Rights Act but was added in the Senate during extended debate. For a period, debate revolved around claims that the bill as proposed would prohibit all testing and force employers to hire unqualified persons simply because they were part of a group formerly subject to job discrimination. Proponents of Title VII sought throughout the debate to assure the critics that the Act would have no effect on job-related tests. Senators Case of New Jersey and Clark of Pennsylvania, comanagers of the bill on the Senate floor, issued a memorandum explaining that the proposed Title VII "expressly protects the employer's right to insist that any prospective applicant, Negro or white, *must meet the applicable job qualifications.* Indeed, the very purpose of Title VII is to promote hiring on the basis of job qualifications, rather than on the basis of race or color." (Emphasis added.) 110 Cong. Rec. 7247. Despite these assurances, Senator Tower of Texas introduced an amendment authorizing "professionally developed ability tests." Proponents of Title VII opposed the amendment because, as written, it would permit an employer to give any test, "whether it was a good test or not, so long as it was professionally designed. Discrimination could actually exist under the guise of compliance with the statute." 110 Cong. Rec. 13504 (remarks of Sen. Case).

The amendment was defeated and two days later Senator Tower offered a substitute amendment which was adopted verbatim and is now the testing provision of § 703(h). Speaking for the supporters of Title VII, Senator Humphrey, who had vigorously opposed the first amendment, endorsed the substitute amendment, stating: "Senators on both sides of the aisle who were deeply interested in Title VII have examined the text of this amendment and have found it to be in accord with the intent and purpose of that title." 110 Cong. Rec. 13724. The amendment was then adopted. From the sum of the legislative history relevant in this case, the conclusion is inescapable that the EEOC's construction of § 703(h) to require that employment tests be job-related comports with congressional intent.

Nothing in the Act precludes the use of testing or measuring procedures; obviously they are useful. What Congress has forbidden is giving these devices and mechanisms controlling force unless they are demonstrably a reasonable measure of job performance. Congress has not commanded that the less qualified be preferred over the better qualified simply because of minority origins. Far from disparaging job qualifications as such, Congress has made such qualifications the controlling factor, so that race, religion, nationality, and sex become irrelevant. What Congress has commanded is that any tests used must measure the person for the job and not the person in the abstract.

The judgment of the Court of Appeals is, as to that portion of the judgment appealed from, reversed.

MR. JUSTICE BRENNAN took no part in the consideration or decision of this case.

NOTES

1. Does *Griggs* prevent an employer from seeking the "best qualified" job applicants? See United States v. Jacksonville Terminal Co., 451 F. 2d 418 (5th Cir. 1971), *cert. denied,* 406 U.S. 906 (1972).

2. After several years in which they applied differing standards, the four principal federal agencies concerned with enforcing equal employment opportunity (EEOC, the Civil Service Commission, Justice, and Labor) adopted *Uniform Guidelines on Employee Selection Procedures* in 1978. 43 Fed. Reg. 38290 (Aug. 25, 1978). One important provision incorporated a "four-fifths rule of thumb" covering disparate impact. Thus, a selection rate for any race, sex, or ethnic group which is less than 80 percent of the rate for the group with the highest rate will generally be regarded by the federal enforcement agencies as evidence of adverse impact on the part of the selection procedure employed. For amplification of the Supreme Court's views on the use of personnel tests, see *Albemarle Paper Co. v. Moody, infra* at 819.

3. Applying the principles of *Griggs,* the Supreme Court held in Dothard v. Rawlinson, 433 U.S. 321 (1977), that a state's employment practice requiring prison guards to be at least 5'2" tall and 120 pounds weight was prima facie discriminatory against women since it would exclude 44% of U.S. women. The employer made no attempt to show that these requirements were job-related, although the Court suggested that a test for strength might have been appropriate for prison guards. On another point, the Court upheld an Alabama regulation excluding women from "contact" guard positions in all-male prisons. Although noting that the bona fide occupational qualification (BFOQ) provision of § 703(e) of the Civil Rights Act is "an extremely narrow exception" to the general prohibition of discrimination on the basis of sex, the Court found it applicable here, in view of the very real risk of attacks on women guards under the conditions in Alabama prisons which a federal court had stated were characterized by rampant violence and a jungle atmosphere.

4. In Washington v. Davis, 426 U.S. 229 (1976), the Supreme Court held that a personnel test that excludes a disproportionately large number of black applicants for police officer positions with the District of Columbia does not violate the due process clause of the Fifth Amendment by reason solely of its racially disproportionate impact. Title VII of the Civil Rights Act was not applicable to these public employees at the time when this case arose, and the Court of Appeals erred in applying the legal standards applicable to Title VII cases in resolving the constitutional issue before it. For a denial of equal protection, there must be an "invidious discriminatory purpose." *See also* Davis v. County of Los Angeles, 566 F. 2d 1334 (9th Cir. 1977), *vacated as moot,* 99 S. Ct. 1379 (U.S. 1979) (four justices dissenting); Lerner, *Washington v. Davis: Quantity, Quality and Equality in Employment Testing,* 1976 SUP. CT. REV. 263 (1976).

5. The Supreme Court pointed out in Hazelwood School District v. United States, 433 U.S. 299 (1977), that where a job requires special qualifications, the proper procedure in looking to statistical proof of a pattern or practice of discrimination would be to compare the percentage of minority (or women) employees in defendant's work force to the percentage of minority persons (or women) in the *relevant labor market population. Cf.* Sheet Metal Workers Local 638, 15 FEP Cas. 1618 (2d Cir. 1977), where the Second Circuit held that New York City's labor pool is a permissible basis upon which to compute a nonwhite membership goal for a union whose geographic jurisdiction is the city, even though the union draws applicants from a "somewhat wider" residential area. What would be the "relevant labor market population" for faculty prospects for a major state university law school? *See generally* Gastwirth & Haber, *Defining the Labor Market for Equal Employment Standards,* 99 MONTHLY LAB. REV. 32 (March 1976).

6. Members of minority groups are disproportionately subject to arrest and to conviction. May a job application inquire about arrest records? *See* Gregory v. Litton Systems, 472 F. 2d 631 (9th Cir. 1972). What about an absolute bar to the employment of any person convicted of more than a minor traffic offense? *See* Green v. Missouri Pac. R.R., 523 F. 2d 1290 (8th Cir. 1975). How should the seriousness of the offense correlate with the sensitivity of the job? *Compare* Richardson v. Hotel Corp. of America, 332 F. Supp. 519 (E.D. La. 1971), *aff'd,* 468 F. 2d 951 (5th Cir. 1972) (bellhop convicted of theft), *with* Lane v. Inman, 509 F. 2d 184 (5th Cir. 1975) (taxicab driver convicted of smuggling marijuana). *Cf.* New York City Transit Authority v. Beazer, 99 S. Ct. 1355 (U.S. 1979) (transit system may refuse to employ narcotics users, including those receiving methadone maintenance treatment).

7. Males constitute the vast majority of the persons benefited by federal and state laws giving preferences to military veterans in public employment. What result under the Constitution or Title VII? *See* Feeney v. Massachusetts, 47 U.S.L.W. 4650 (U.S. 1979). *See also* Fleming & Shanor, *Veterans' Preferences in Public Employment: Unconstitutional Gender Discrimination?* 26 EMORY L.J. 13 (1977). The problem is noted in 44 GEO. WASH. L. REV. 623 (1976) and 90 HARV. L. REV. 805 (1977).

8. The literature on *Griggs* includes Bernhardt, *Griggs v. Duke Power Co.: The Implications for Private and Public Employers,* 50 TEXAS L. REV.

901 (1972); Blumrosen, *Strangers in Paradise: Griggs v. Duke Power Company and the Concept of Employment Discrimination,* 71 MICH. L. REV. 59 (1972); Wilson, *A Second Look at Griggs v. Duke Power Company: Ruminations on Job Testing, Discrimination, and the Role of the Federal Courts,* 58 VA. L. REV. 844 (1972); Note, *Employment Testing: The Aftermath of Griggs v. Duke Power Company,* 72 COLUM. L. REV. 900 (1972). A comprehensive major study is M. SOVERN, LEGAL RESTRAINTS ON RACIAL DISCRIMINATION IN EMPLOYMENT (1966). For updated overviews, see W. GOULD, BLACK WORKERS IN WHITE UNIONS (1977); Jones, *The Development of the Law under Title VII Since 1965: Implications of the New Law,* 30 RUTGERS L. REV. 1 (1976); Lopatka, *A 1977 Primer on the Federal Regulation of Employment Discrimination,* 1977 U. ILL. L.F. 69. Encyclopedic treatments of the entire subject are A. LARSON, EMPLOYMENT DISCRIMINATION (1975, 1977); B. SCHLEI & P. GROSSMAN, EMPLOYMENT DISCRIMINATION LAW (1976).

INTERNATIONAL BROTHERHOOD OF TEAMSTERS v. UNITED STATES
T.I.M.E.—D.C., INC. v. UNITED STATES

Supreme Court of the United States
431 U.S. 324, 97 S. Ct. 1843, 52 L. Ed. 2d 396 (1977)

MR. JUSTICE STEWART delivered the opinion of the Court.

This litigation brings here several important questions under Title VII of the Civil Rights Act of 1964. . . . The issues grow out of alleged unlawful employment practices engaged in by an employer and a union. The employer is a common carrier of motor freight with nationwide operations, and the union represents a large group of its employees. The District Court and the Court of Appeals held that the employer had violated Title VII by engaging in a pattern and practice of employment discrimination against Negroes and Spanish-surnamed Americans, and that the union had violated the Act by agreeing with the employer to create and maintain a seniority system that perpetuated the effects of past racial and ethnic discrimination. In addition to the basic questions presented by these two rulings, other subsidiary issues must be resolved if violations of Title VII occurred — issues concerning the nature of the relief to which aggrieved individuals may be entitled.

I. . . . The central claim . . . was that the company had engaged in a pattern or practice of discriminating against minorities in hiring so-called line drivers. Those Negroes and Spanish-surnamed persons who had been hired, the Government alleged, were given lower paying, less desirable jobs as servicemen or local city drivers, and were thereafter discriminated against with respect to promotions and transfers.[3] In this connection the

---

[3] *Line drivers,* also known as over-the-road drivers, engage in long-distance hauling between company terminals. They compose a separate bargaining unit at T.I.M.E.-D.C. Other distinct bargaining units include *servicemen,* who service trucks, unhook tractors and trailers, and perform similar tasks; and *city operations,* composed of dockmen,

complaint also challenged the seniority system established by the collective-bargaining agreements between the employer and the union. The Government sought a general injunctive remedy and specific "make whole" relief for all individual discriminatees, which would allow them an opportunity to transfer to line-driver jobs with full company seniority for all purposes.

The cases went to trial and the District Court found that the Government had shown "by a preponderance of the evidence that T.I.M.E.-D.C. and its predecessor companies were engaged in a plan and practice of discrimination in violation of Title VII . . . ." The court further found that the seniority system contained in the collective-bargaining contracts between the company and the union violated Title VII because it "operate[d] to impede the free transfer of minority groups into and within the company." Both the company and the union were enjoined from committing further violations of Title VII.

With respect to individual relief the court accepted the Government's basic contention that the "affected class" of discriminatees included all Negro and Spanish-surnamed incumbent employees who had been hired to fill city operations or serviceman jobs at every terminal that had a line-driver operation. All of these employees, whether hired before or after the effective date of Title VII, thereby became entitled to preference over all other applicants with respect to consideration for future vacancies in line-driver jobs. Finding that members of the affected class had been injured in different degrees, the court created three subclasses. Thirty persons who had produced "the most convincing evidence of discrimination and harm" were found to have suffered "severe injury." The court ordered that they be offered the opportunity to fill line-driver jobs with competitive seniority dating back to July 2, 1965, the effective date of Title VII. A second subclass included four persons who were "very possibly the objects of discrimination" and who "were likely harmed," but as to whom there had been no specific evidence of discrimination and injury. The court decreed that these persons were entitled to fill vacancies in line-driving jobs with competitive seniority as of January 14, 1971, the date on which the Government had filed its system-wide lawsuit. Finally, there were over 300 remaining members of the affected class as to whom there was "no evidence to show that these individuals were either harmed or not harmed individually." The court ordered that they be considered for line-driver jobs ahead of any applicants from the general public but behind the two other subclasses. Those in the third subclass received no retroactive seniority; their competitive seniority as line drivers would begin with the date they were hired as line drivers. The court further decreed that the right of any class member to fill a line-driver vacancy was subject to the prior recall rights of laid-off line drivers, which under the collective-bargaining agreements then in effect extended for three years.

---

hostlers, and city drivers who pick up and deliver freight within the immediate area of a particular terminal. All of these employees were represented by the petitioner International Brotherhood of Teamsters.

The Court of Appeals for the Fifth Circuit agreed with the basic conclusions of the District Court: that the company had engaged in a pattern or practice of employment discrimination and that the seniority system in the collective-bargaining agreements violated Title VII as applied to victims of prior discrimination. United States v. T.I.M.E.-D.C., Inc., 517 F.2d 299. . . . The appellate court held, however, that the relief ordered by the District Court was inadequate. Rejecting the District Court's attempt to trisect the affected class, the Court of Appeals held that all Negro and Spanish-surnamed incumbent employees were entitled to bid for future line-driver jobs on the basis of their company seniority, and that once a class member had filled a job, he could use his full company seniority — even if it predated the effective date of Title VII — for all purposes, including bidding and layoff. This award of retroactive seniority was to be limited only by a "qualification date" formula, under which seniority could not be awarded for periods prior to the date when (1) a line-driving position was vacant, *and* (2) the class member met (or would have met, given the opportunity) the qualifications for employment as a line driver. Finally, the Court of Appeals modified that part of the District Court's decree that had subjected the rights of class members to fill future vacancies to the recall rights of laid-off employees. Holding that the three-year priority in favor of laid-off workers "would unduly impede the eradication of past discrimination," *id.* at 322, the Court of Appeals ordered that class members be allowed to compete for vacancies with laid-off employees on the basis of the class members' retroactive seniority. Laid-off line drivers would retain their prior recall rights with respect only to "purely temporary" vacancies.

The Court of Appeals remanded the case to the District Court to hold the evidentiary hearings necessary to apply these remedial principles. We granted both the company's and the union's petitions for certiorari to consider the significant questions presented under the Civil Rights Act of 1964. . . .

II. In this Court the company and the union contend that their conduct did not violate Title VII in any respect, asserting first that the evidence introduced at trial was insufficient to show that the company engaged in a "pattern or practice" of employment discrimination. The union further contends that the seniority system contained in the collective-bargaining agreements in no way violated Title VII. If these contentions are correct, it is unnecessary, of course, to reach any of the issues concerning remedies that so occupied the attention of the Court of Appeals.

A. Consideration of the question whether the company engaged in a pattern or practice of discriminatory hiring practices involves controlling legal principles that are relatively clear. The Government's theory of discrimination was simply that the company, in violation of § 703(a) of Title VII, regularly and purposefully treated Negroes and Spanish-surnamed Americans less favorably than white persons. The disparity in treatment allegedly involved the refusal to recruit, hire, transfer, or promote minority group members on an equal basis with white people, particularly with respect to line-driving positions. The ultimate factual issues are thus simply whether there was a pattern or practice of such disparate treatment and, if so, whether the differences were "racially premised." McDonnell Douglas Corp. v. Green, 411 U. S. 792, 805 n. 18.[15]

As the plaintiff, the Government bore the initial burden of making out a prima facie case of discrimination. Albemarle Paper Co. v. Moody, 422 U.S. 405, 425; *McDonnell Douglas Corp. v. Green, supra* at 802. And, because it alleged a system-wide pattern or practice of resistance to the full enjoyment of Title VII rights, the Government ultimately had to prove more than the mere occurrence of isolated or "accidental" or sporadic discriminatory acts. It had to establish by a preponderance of the evidence that racial discrimination was the company's standard operating procedure — the regular rather than the unusual practice.

We agree with the District Court and the Court of Appeals that the Government carried its burden of proof. As of March 31, 1971, shortly after the Government filed its complaint alleging systemwide discrimination, the company had 6,472 employees. Of these, 314 (5%) were Negroes and 257 (4%) were Spanish-surnamed Americans. Of the 1,828 line drivers, however, there were only 8 (0.4%) Negroes and 5 (0.3%) Spanish-surnamed persons, and all of the Negroes had been hired after the litigation had commenced. With one exception — a man who worked as a line driver at the Chicago terminal from 1950 to 1959 — the company and its predecessors *did not employ a Negro on a regular basis as a line driver until 1969.* And, as the Government showed, even in 1971 there were terminals in areas of substantial Negro population where all of the companys' line drivers were white. A great majority of the Negroes (83%) and Spanish-surnamed Americans (78%) who did work for the company held the lower-paying city operations and serviceman jobs, whereas only 39% of the non-minority employees held jobs in those categories.

The Government bolstered its statistical evidence with the testimony of individuals who recounted over 40 specific instances of discrimination. Upon the basis of this testimony the District Court found that "[n]umerous qualified black and Spanish-surnamed American applicants who sought line-driving jobs at the company over the years had their

---

[15] "Disparate treatment" such as alleged in the present case is the most easily understood type of discrimination. The employer simply treats some people less favorably than others because of their race, color, religion, sex, or national origin. Proof of discriminatory motive is critical, although it can in some situations be inferred from the mere fact of differences in treatment. . . .

Claims of disparate treatment may be distinguished from claims that stress "disparate impact." The latter involve employment practices that are facially neutral in their treatment of different groups but that in fact fall more harshly on one group than another and cannot be justified by business necessity. . . . Proof of discriminatory motive, we have held, is not required under a disparate impact theory. Compare, *e.g.,* Griggs v. Duke Power Co., 401 U. S. 424, 430-432 . . . with McDonnell Douglas Corp. v. Green, 411 U. S. 792, 802-806. . . .

requests ignored, were given false or misleading information about requirements, opportunities, and application procedures or were not considered and hired on the same basis that whites were considered and hired." Minority employees who wanted to transfer to line-driver jobs met with similar difficulties.

The company's principal response to this evidence is that statistics can never in and of themselves prove the existence of a pattern or practice of discrimination, or even establish a prima facie case shifting to the employer the burden of rebutting the inference raised by the figures. But, as even our brief summary of the evidence shows, this was not a case in which the Government relied on "statistics alone." The individuals who testified about their personal experiences with the company brought the cold numbers convincingly to life.

In any event, our cases make it unmistakably clear that "[s]tatistical analyses have served and will continue to serve an important role" in cases in which the existence of discrimination is a disputed issue. Mayor of Philadelphia v. Educational Equality League, 415 U.S. 605, 620. See also *McDonnell Douglas Corp. v. Green, supra* at 805. Cf. Washington v. Davis, 426 U.S. 229, 241-242. We have repeatedly approved the use of statistical proof, where it reached proportions comparable to those in this case, to establish a prima facie case of racial discrimination in jury selection cases, see, *e.g.,* Turner v. Fouche, 396 U.S. 346; Hernandez v. Texas, 347 U.S. 475; Norris v. Alabama, 294 U.S. 587. Statistics are equally competent in proving employment discrimination. We caution only that statistics are not irrefutable; they come in infinite variety and, like any other kind of evidence, they may be rebutted. In short, their usefulness depends on all of the surrounding facts and circumstances. See, e.g., Hester v. Southern R. Co., 497 F.2d 1374, 1379-1381 (CA5).

In addition to its general protest against the use of statistics in Title VII cases, the company claims that in this case the statistics revealing racial imbalance are misleading because they fail to take into account the company's particular business situation as of the effective date of Title VII. The company concedes that its line drivers were virtually all white in July 1965, but it claims that thereafter business conditions were such that its work force dropped. Its argument is that low personnel turnover, rather than post-Act discrimination, accounts for more recent disparities. It points to substantial minority hiring in later years, especially after 1971, as showing that any pre-Act patterns of discrimination were broken.

The argument would be a forceful one if this were an employer who, at the time of suit, had done virtually no new hiring since the effective date of Title VII. But it is not. Although the company's total number of employees apparently dropped somewhat during the late 1960's, the record shows that many line drivers continued to be hired throughout this period, and that almost all of them were white. . . .

The District Court and the Court of Appeals, on the basis of substantial evidence, held that the Government had proved a prima facie case of systematic and purposeful employment discrimination, continuing well beyond the effective date of Title VII. The company's attempts to rebut that conclusion were held to be inadequate. For the reasons we have summarized, there is no warrant for this Court to disturb the findings of the District Court and the Court of Appeals on this basic issue. . . .

B. The District Court and the Court of Appeals also found that the seniority system contained in the collective-bargaining agreements between the company and the union operated to violate Title VII of the Act.

For purposes of calculating benefits, such as vacations, pensions, and other fringe benefits, an employer's seniority under this system runs from the date he joins the company, and takes into account his total service in all jobs and bargaining units. For competitive purposes, however, such as determining the order in which employees may bid for particular jobs, are laid off, or are recalled from layoff, it is bargaining-unit seniority that controls. Thus, a line driver's seniority, for purposes of bidding for particular runs and protection against layoff, takes into account only the length of time he has been a line driver at a particular terminal. The practical effect is that a city driver or serviceman who transfers to a line-driver job must forfeit all the competitive seniority he has accumulated in his previous bargaining unit and start at the bottom of the line-drivers' "board."

The vice of this arrangement, as found by the District Court and the Court of Appeals, was that it "locked" minority workers into inferior jobs and perpetuated prior discrimination by discouraging transfers to jobs as line drivers. While the disincentive applied to all workers, including whites, it was Negroes and Spanish-surnamed persons who, those courts found, suffered the most because many of them had been denied the equal opportunity to become line drivers when they were initially hired, whereas whites either had not sought or were refused line-driver positions for reasons unrelated to their race or national origin.

The linchpin of the theory embraced by the District Court and the Court of Appeals was that a discriminatee who must forfeit his competitive seniority in order finally to obtain a line-driver job will never be able to "catch up" to the seniority level of his contemporary who was not subject to discrimination.[27] Accordingly, this continued, built-in disadvantage to the prior discriminatee who transfers to a line-driver job was held to constitute a continuing violation of Title VII, for which both the employer and the union who jointly created and maintained the seniority system were liable.

---

[27] An example would be a Negro who was qualified to be a line driver in 1958 but who, because of his race, was assigned instead a job as a city driver, and is allowed to become a line driver only in 1971. Because he loses his competitive seniority when he transfers jobs, he is forever junior to white line drivers hired between 1958 and 1970. The whites, rather than the Negro, will henceforth enjoy the preferable runs and the greater protection against layoff. Although the original discrimination occurred in 1958 — before the effective date of Title VII — the seniority system operates to carry the effects of the earlier discrimination into the present.

The union, while acknowledging that the seniority system may in some sense perpetuate the effects of prior discrimination, asserts that the system is immunized from a finding of illegality by reason of § 703(h) of Title VII . . . .

It argues that the seniority system in this case is "bona fide" within the meaning of § 703(h) when judged in light of its history, intent, application, and all of the circumstances under which it was created and is maintained. More specifically, the union claims that the central purpose of § 703(h), is to ensure that mere perpetuation of *pre-Act* discrimination is not unlawful under Title VII. And, whether or not § 703(h) immunizes the perpetuation of *post-Act* discrimination, the union claims that the seniority system in this case has no such effect. Its position in this Court, as has been its position throughout this litigation, is that the seniority system presents no hurdles to post-Act discriminatees who seek retroactive seniority to the date they would have become line drivers but for the company's discrimination. Indeed, the union asserts that under its collective-bargaining agreements the union will itself take up the cause of the post-Act victim and attempt, through grievance procedures, to gain for him full "make whole" relief, including appropriate seniority.

The Government responds that a seniority system that perpetuates the effects of prior discrimination — pre- or post-Act — can never be "bona fide" under § 703(h); at a minimum Title VII prohibits those applications of a seniority system that perpetuate the effects on incumbent employees of prior discriminatory job assignments.

The issues thus joined are open ones in this Court. [28] We considered § 703(h) in Franks v. Bowman Transportation Co., 424 U.S. 747; but there decided only that § 703(h) does not bar the award of retroactive seniority to job applicants who seek relief from an employer's post-Act hiring discrimination. We stated that "the thrust of [§ 703(h)] is directed toward defining what is and what is not illegal discriminatory practice in instances in which the post-Act operation of a seniority system is challenged as perpetuating the effects of discrimination occurring prior to the effective date of the Act." 424 U.S. at 761. Beyond noting the

---

[28] Concededly, the view that § 703(h) does not immunize seniority systems that perpetuate the effects of prior discrimination has much support. It was apparently first adopted in Quarles v. Phillip Morris, Inc., 279 F. Supp. 505 (ED Va.). The court there held that "a departmental seniority system *that has its genesis in racial discrimination* is not a *bona fide* seniority system." Id. at 517 (first emphasis added). The *Quarles* view has since enjoyed wholesale adoption in the Courts of Appeals. See, e.g., Local 189, United Paperworkers v. United States, 416 F.2d 980, 987-988 (CA5); United States v. Sheet Metal Workers Local 36, 416 F.2d 123, 133-134, n. 20 (CA8); United States v. Bethlehem Steel Corp., 446 F.2d 652, 658-659 (CA2); United States v. Chesapeake & Ohio R. Co., 471 F.2d 582, 587-588 (CA4). Insofar as the results in *Quarles* and in the cases that followed it depended upon findings that the seniority systems were themselves "racially discriminatory" or had their "genesis in racial discrimination," 279 F. Supp. at 517, the decisions can be viewed as resting upon the proposition that a seniority system that perpetuates the effects of pre-Act discrimination cannot be bona fide if an intent to discriminate entered into its very adoption.

general purpose of the statute, however, we did not undertake the task of statutory construction required in this case.

(1) Because the company discriminated both before and after the enactment of Title VII, the seniority system is said to have operated to perpetuate the effects of both pre- and post-Act discrimination. Post-Act discriminatees, however, may obtain full "make whole" relief, including retroactive seniority under *Franks v. Bowman, supra,* without attacking the legality of the seniority system as applied to them. *Franks* made clear and the union acknowledges that retroactive seniority may be awarded as relief from an employer's discriminatory hiring and assignment policies even if the seniority system agreement itself makes no provision for such relief.[29] 424 U.S. at 778-779. Here the Government has proved that the company engaged in a post-Act pattern of discriminatory hiring, assignment, transfer, and promotion policies. Any Negro or Spanish-surnamed American injured by those policies may receive all appropriate relief as a direct remedy for this discrimination.[30]

(2) What remains for review is the judgment that the seniority system unlawfully perpetuated the effects of *pre-Act* discrimination. We must decide, in short, whether § 703(h) validates otherwise bona fide seniority systems that afford no constructive seniority to victims discriminated against prior to the effective date of Title VII, and it is to that issue that we now turn.

The primary purpose of Title VII was "to assure equality of employment opportunities and to eliminate those discriminatory practices and devices which have fostered racially stratified job environments to the disadvantage of minority citizens." *McDonnell Douglas Corp. v. Green, supra* at 800. . . . To achieve this purpose, Congress "proscribe[d] not only overt discrimination but also practices that are fair in form, but

---

[29] Article 38 of the National Master Freight Agreement between T.I.M.E.-D.C. and the International Brotherhood of Teamsters in effect as of the date of the systemwide lawsuit provided:

"The Employer and the Union agree not to discriminate against any individual with respect to his hiring, compensation, terms or conditions of employment because of such individual's race, color, religion, sex, or national origin, nor will they limit, segregate or classify employees in any way to deprive any individual employee of employment opportunities because of his race, color, religion, sex, or national origin."

Any discrimination by the company would apparently be a grievable breach of this provision of the contract.

[30] The legality of the seniority system insofar as it perpetuates post-Act discrimination nonetheless remains at issue in this case, in light of the injunction entered against the union. . . . Our decision today in United Airlines v. Evans . . . is largely dispositive of this issue. *Evans* holds that the operation of a seniority system is not unlawful under Title VII even though it perpetuates post-Act discrimination that has not been the subject of a timely charge by the discriminatee. Here, of course, the Government has sued to remedy the post-Act discrimination directly and there is no claim that any relief would be time-barred. But this is simply an additional reason not to hold the seniority system unlawful, since such a holding would in no way enlarge the relief to be awarded. See Franks v. Bowman, 424 U.S. at 778-779. Section 703(h) on its face immunizes all bona fide seniority systems, and does not distinguish between the perpetuation of pre- and post-Act discrimination.

discriminatory in operation." *Griggs,* 401 U.S. at 431. . . . Thus, the Court has repeatedly held that a prima facie Title VII violation may be established by policies or practices that are neutral on their face and in intent but that nonetheless discriminate in effect against a particular group. . . .

One kind of practice "fair in form, but discriminatory in operation" is that which perpetuates the effects of prior discrimination.[32] As the Court held in *Griggs, supra:* "Under the Act, practices, procedures, or tests neutral on their face, and even neutral in terms of intent, cannot be maintained if they operate to 'freeze' the status quo of prior discriminatory employment practices." 401 U.S. at 430.

Were it not for § 703(h), the seniority system in this case would seem to fall under the *Griggs* rationale. The heart of the system is its allocation of the choicest jobs, the greatest protection against layoffs, and other advantages to those employees who have been line drivers for the longest time. Where, because of the employer's prior intentional discrimination, the line drivers with the longest tenure are without exception white, the advantages of the seniority system flow disproportionately to them and away from Negro and Spanish-surnamed employees who might by now have enjoyed those advantages had not the employer discriminated before the passage of the Act. This disproportionate distribution of advantages does in a very real sense "operate to 'freeze' the status quo of prior discriminatory employment practices." *Ibid.* But both the literal terms of § 703(h) and the legislative history of Title VII demonstrate that Congress considered this very effect of many seniority systems and extended a measure of immunity to them.

Throughout the initial consideration of H. R. 7152, later enacted as the Civil Rights Act of 1964, critics of the bill charged that it would destroy existing seniority rights. The consistent response of Title VII's congressional proponents and of the Justice Department was that seniority rights would not be affected, even where the employer had discriminated prior to the Act. An interpretative memorandum placed in the Congressional Record by Senators Clark and Case stated:

"Title VII would have no effect on established seniority rights. Its effect is prospective and not retrospective. Thus, for example, *if a business has been discriminating in the past and as a result has an all-white working force, when the title comes into effect the employer's obligation would be simply to fill future vacancies on a non-discriminatory basis.* He would not be obliged — or indeed,

---

[32] Asbestos Workers Local 53 v. Vogler, 407 F.2d 1047 (CA5), provides an apt illustration. There a union had a policy of excluding persons not related to present members by blood or marriage. When in 1966 suit was brought to challenge this policy, all of the union's members were white, largely as a result of pre-Act, intentional racial discrimination. The court observed: "While the nepotism requirement is applicable to black and white alike and is not on its face discriminatory, in a completely white union the present effect of its continued application is to forever deny to negroes and Mexican-Americans any real opportunity for membership." 407 F.2d at 1054. . . .

permitted — to fire whites in order to hire Negroes, or to prefer Negroes for future vacancies, or, once Negroes are hired, to give them special seniority rights at the expense of the white workers hired earlier." 110 Cong. Rec. 7213 (1964) (emphasis added).[35]

A Justice Department statement concerning Title VII, placed in the Congressional Record by Senator Clark voiced the same conclusion:

"Title VII would have no effect on seniority rights existing at the time it takes effect. If for example, a collective bargaining contract provides that in the event of layoffs, those who were hired last must be laid off first, such a provision would not be affected in the least by title VII. *This would be true even in the case where owing to discrimination prior to the effective date of the title, white workers had more seniority than Negroes." Id.* at 7207 (emphasis added).[36]

While these statements were made before § 703(h) was added to Title VII, they are authoritative indicators of that section's purpose. Section 703(h) was enacted as part of the Mansfield-Dirksen compromise substitute bill that cleared the way for the passage of Title VII. The drafters of the compromise bill stated that one of its principal goals was to resolve the ambiguities in the House-passed version of H. R. 7152. See, *e. g., id.* at 11935-11937 (remarks of Sen. Dirksen); *id.* at 12707 (remarks of Sen. Humphrey). As the debates indicate, one of those ambiguities concerned Title VII's impact on existing collectively bargained seniority rights. It is apparent that § 703(h) was drafted with an eye toward meeting the earlier criticism on this issue with an explicit provision embodying the understanding and assurances of the Act's proponents: namely, that Title VII would not outlaw such differences in treatment among employees as flowed from a bona fide seniority system that allowed for full exercise of seniority accumulated before the effective date of the Act. It is inconceivable that § 703(h), as part of a compromise bill, was intended

---

[35] Senators Clark and Case were the "bipartisan captains" responsible for Title VII during the Senate debate. Bipartisan captains were selected for each title of the Civil Rights Act by the leading proponents of the Act in both parties. They were responsible for explaining their title in detail, defending it, and leading discussion on it. See 110 Cong. Rec. 6528 (1964) (remarks of Sen. Humphrey); Vass, Title VII: Legislative History, 7 B. C. Ind. & Com. L. Rev. 431, 444-445 (1966).

[36] The full text of the statement is set out in Franks v. Bowman, 424 U.S. at 760 n. 16 . . . . Senator Clark also introduced a set of answers to questions propounded by Senator Dirksen, which included the following exchange:

"Question. Would the same situation prevail in respect to promotions, when the management function is governed by a labor contract calling for promotions on the basis of seniority? What of dismissals? Normally, labor contracts call for 'last hired, first fired.' If the last hired are Negroes, is the employer discriminating if his contract requires they be first fired and the remaining employees are white?

"Answer. Seniority rights are in no way affected by the bill. If under a 'last hired, first fired' agreement a Negro happens to be the 'last hired,' he can still be 'first fired' as long as it is done because of his status as 'last hired' and not because of his race." 110 Cong. Rec. 7217 (1964). See *Franks, supra* at 760 n. 16.

to vitiate the earlier representations of the Act's supporters by increasing Title VII's impact on seniority systems. The statement of Senator Humphrey, noted in *Franks, supra* at 761, . . . confirms that the addition of § 703(h) "merely clarifies [Title VII's] present intent and effect." 110 Cong. Rec. 12723 (1964).

In sum, the unmistakable purpose of § 703(h) was to make clear that the routine application of a bona fide seniority system would not be unlawful under Title VII. As the legislative history shows, this was the intended result even where the employer's pre-Act discrimination resulted in whites having greater existing seniority rights than Negroes. Although a seniority system inevitably tends to perpetuate the effects of pre-Act discrimination in such cases, the congressional judgment was that Title VII should not outlaw the use of existing seniority lists and thereby destroy or water down the vested seniority rights of employees simply because their employer had engaged in discrimination prior to the passage of the Act.

To be sure, § 703(h) does not immunize all seniority systems. It refers only to "bona fide" systems, and a proviso requires that any differences in treatment not be "the result of an intention to discriminate because of race . . . or national origin. . . ." But our reading of the legislative history compels us to reject the Government's broad argument that no seniority system that tends to perpetuate pre-Act discrimination can be "bona fide." To accept the argument would require us to hold that a seniority system becomes illegal simply because it allows the full exercise of the pre-Act seniority rights of employees of a company that discriminated before Title VII was enacted. It would place an affirmative obligation on the parties to the seniority agreement to subordinate those rights in favor of the claims of pre-Act discriminatees without seniority. The consequence would be a perversion of the congressional purpose. We cannot accept the invitation to disembowel § 703(h) by reading the words "bona fide" as the Government would have us do.[38] Accordingly, we hold that an otherwise neutral, legitimate seniority system does not become unlawful under Title VII simply because it may perpetuate pre-Act discrimination. Congress did not intend to make it illegal for employees with vested seniority rights to continue to exercise those rights, even at the expense of pre-Act discriminatees.[39]

---

[38] For the same reason, we reject the contention that the proviso in § 703(h), which bars differences in treatment resulting from "an intention to discriminate," applies to any application of a seniority system that may perpetuate past discrimination. In this regard the language of the Justice Department memorandum introduced at the legislative hearings, see *supra* at 24, is especially pertinent: "It is perfectly clear that when a worker is laid off or denied a chance for promotion because he is 'low man on the totem pole' he is not being discriminated against because of his race. . . . Any differences in treatment based on established seniority rights would not be based on race and would not be forbidden by the title." 110 Cong. Rec. 7207 (1964).

[39] The legislative history of the 1972 amendments to Title VII, summarized and discussed in *Franks, supra,* at 764-765 n. 21, at 796-797 n. 18, in no way points to a different result. As the discussion in *Franks* indicates, that history is itself susceptible of different readings. The few broad references to perpetuation of pre-Act discrimination or

That conclusion is inescapable even in a case, such as this one, where the pre-Act discriminatees are incumbent employees who accumulated seniority in other bargaining units. Although there seems to be no explicit reference in the legislative history to pre-Act discriminatees already employed in less desirable jobs, there can be no rational basis for distinguishing their claims from those of persons initially denied *any* job but hired later with less seniority than they might have had in the absence of pre-Act discrimination.[40] We rejected any such distinction in Franks, finding that it had "no support anywhere in Title VII or its legislative history," 424 U.S. at 768. As discussed above, Congress in 1964 made clear that a seniority system is not unlawful because it honors employees' existing rights, even where the employer has engaged in pre-Act discriminatory hiring or promotion practices. It would be as contrary to that mandate to forbid the exercise of seniority rights with respect to discriminatees who held inferior jobs as with respect to later-hired minority employees who previously were denied any job. If anything, the latter group is the more disadvantaged. As in *Franks,* " '[i]t would indeed be surprising if Congress gave a remedy for the one [group] which it denied for the other.' " *Id.,* quoting Phelps Dodge Corp. v. NLRB, 313 U.S. 177, 187.[41]

"*de facto* segregated job ladders," see, *e.g.,* S. Rep. No. 92-415, pp. 5, 9 (1971); H. R. Rep. No. 92-238, pp. 8, 17 (1971), did not address the specific issue presented by this case. And the assumption of the authors of the Conference Report that "the present case law as developed by the courts would continue to govern the applicability and construction of Title VII," see *Franks, supra* at 765 n. 21, of course does not foreclose our consideration of that issue. More importantly, the section of Title VII that we construe here, § 703(h), was enacted in 1964, not 1972. The views of members of a later Congress, concerning different sections of Title VII, enacted after this litigation was commenced, are entitled to little if any weight. It is the intent of the Congress that enacted § 703(h) in 1964, unmistakable in this case, that controls.

[40] That Title VII did not proscribe the denial of fictional seniority to pre-Act discriminatees who got no job was recognized even in Quarles v. Phillip Morris, Inc., 279 F.Supp. 505 (ED Va.), and its progeny. Quarles stressed the fact that the references in the legislative history were to employment seniority rather than departmental seniority. 279 F.Supp. at 516. In Local 189, United Paperworkers v. United States, 416 F.2d 980 (CA5), another leading case in this area, the court observed: "No doubt, Congress, to prevent 'reverse discrimination' meant to protect certain seniority rights that could not have existed but for previous racial discrimination. For example a Negro who had been rejected by an employer on racial grounds before passage of the Act could not, after being hired, claim to outrank whites who had been hired before him but after his original rejection, even though the Negro might have had senior status but for the past discrimination." 416 F.2d at 944.

[41] In addition, there is no reason to suppose that Congress intended in 1964 to extend less protection to legitimate departmental seniority systems than to plant-wide seniority systems. Then as now, seniority was measured in a number of ways, including length of time with the employer, in a particular plant, in a department, in a job, or in a line of progression. See Aaron, Reflections on the Legal Nature and Enforceability of Seniority Rights, 75 HARV. L. REV. 1532, 1534 (1962); Cooper & Sobol, Seniority and Testing under Fair Employment Laws: A General Approach to Objective Criteria of Hiring and Promotion, 82 HARV. L. REV. 1598, 1602 (1969). The legislative history contains no suggestion that any one system was preferred.

(3) The seniority system in this case is entirely bona fide. It applies equally to all races and ethnic groups. To the extent that it "locks" employees into nonline-driver jobs, it does so for all. The city drivers and servicemen who are discouraged from transferring to line-driver jobs are not all Negroes or Spanish-surnamed Americans; to the contrary, the overwhelming majority are white. The placing of line drivers in a separate bargaining unit from other employees is rational, in accord with the industry practice, and consistent with NLRB precedents.[42] It is conceded that the seniority system did not have its genesis in racial discrimination, and that it was negotiated and has been maintained free from any illegal purpose. In these circumstances, the single fact that the system extends no retroactive seniority to pre-Act discriminatees does not make it unlawful.

Because the seniority system was protected by § 703(h), the union's conduct in agreeing to and maintaining the system did not violate Title VII. On remand, the District Court's injunction against the union must be vacated.

III. Our conclusion that the seniority system does not violate Title VII will necessarily affect the remedy granted to individual employees on remand of this litigation to the District Court. Those employees who suffered only pre-Act discrimination are not entitled to relief, and no person may be given retroactive seniority to a date earlier than the effective date of the Act. Several other questions relating to the appropriate measure of individual relief remain, however, for our consideration. . . .

A. The petitioners' first contention is in substance that the Government's burden of proof in a pattern or practice case must be equivalent to that outlined in *McDonnell Douglas Corp. v. Green, supra.* Since the Government introduced specific evidence of company discrimination against only some 40 employees, they argue that the District Court properly refused to award retroactive seniority to the remainder of the class of minority incumbent employees. . . .

The company and union seize upon the *McDonnell Douglas* pattern as the *only* means of establishing a prima facie case of individual discrimination. Our decision in that case, however, did not purport to create an inflexible formulation. . . . The importance of *McDonnell Douglas* lies not in its specification of the discrete elements of proof there required, but in its recognition of the general principle that any Title VII plaintiff must carry the initial burden of offering evidence adequate to create an inference that an employment decision was based on a discriminatory criterion illegal under the Act.

---

[42] See Georgia Highway Express, 150 NLRB 1649, 1651: "The Board has long held that local drivers and over-the-road drivers constitute separate appropriate units where they are shown to be clearly defined, homogeneous, and functionally distinct groups with separate interests which can effectively be represented separately for bargaining purposes. . . ."

In *Franks v. Bowman Transportation Co.* the Court applied this principle in the context of a class action.... The *Franks* case ... illustrates another means by which a Title VII plaintiff's initial burden of proof can be met. The class there alleged a broad-based policy of employment discrimination; upon proof of that allegation there were reasonable grounds to infer that individual hiring decisions were made in pursuit of the discriminatory policy and to require the employer to come forth with evidence dispelling that inference.

Although not all class actions will necessarily follow the *Franks* model, the nature of a pattern or practice suit brings it squarely within our holding in *Franks.* The plaintiff in a pattern or practice action is the Government, and its initial burden is to demonstrate that unlawful discrimination has been a regular procedure or policy followed by an employer or group of employers.... At the initial, "liability" stage of a pattern or practice suit the Government is not required to offer evidence that each person for whom it will ultimately seek relief was a victim of the employer's discriminatory policy. Its burden is to establish a prima facie case that such a policy existed. The burden then shifts to the employer to defeat the prima facie showing of a pattern or practice by demonstrating that the Government's proof is either inaccurate or insignificant....

When the Government seeks individual relief for the victims of the discriminatory practice, a district court must usually conduct additional proceedings after the liability phase of the trial to determine the scope of individual relief. The petitioners' contention in this case is that if the Government has not, in the course of proving a pattern or practice, already brought forth specific evidence that each individual was discriminatorily denied an employment opportunity, it must carry that burden at the second, "remedial" stage of trial. That basic contention was rejected in the *Franks* case....

The proof of the pattern or practice supports an inference that any particular employment decision, during the period in which the discriminatory policy was in force, was made in pursuit of that policy. The Government need only show that an alleged individual discriminatee unsuccessfully applied for a job and therefore was a potential victim of the proven discrimination. As in *Franks,* the burden then rests on the employer to demonstrate that the individual applicant was denied an employment opportunity for lawful reasons. See 424 U.S. at 773 n. 32....

B. The Court of Appeals' "qualification date" formula for relief did not distinguish between incumbent employees who had applied for line-driver jobs and those who had not. The appellate court held that where there has been a showing of classwide discriminatory practices coupled with a seniority system that perpetuates the effects of that discrimination, an individual member of the class need not show that he unsuccessfully applied for the position from which the class had been excluded. In support of its award of relief to all nonapplicants, the Court suggested that "as a practical matter ... a member of the affected class may well have concluded that an application for transfer to an all [w]hite position such as [line driver] was not worth the candle." 517 F.2d at 320....

The question whether seniority relief may be awarded to nonapplicants was left open by our decision in *Franks,* since the class at issue in that case was limited to "identifiable applicants who were denied employment . . . after the effective date . . . of Title VII." 424 U.S. at 750. . . . We now decide that an incumbent employee's failure to apply for a job is not an inexorable bar to an award of retroactive seniority. Individual nonapplicants must be given an opportunity to undertake their difficult task of proving that they should be treated as applicants and therefore are presumptively entitled to relief accordingly. . . .

(1). . . . [T]he company's assertion that a person who has not actually applied for a job can *never* be awarded seniority relief cannot prevail. The effects of and the injuries suffered from discriminatory employment practices are not always confined to those who were expressly denied a requested employment opportunity. A consistently enforced discriminatory policy can surely deter job applications from those who are aware of it and are unwilling to subject themselves to the humiliation of explicit and certain rejection. . . .

The denial of Title VII relief on the ground that the claimant had not formally applied for the job could exclude from the Act's coverage the victims of the most entrenched forms of discrimination. Victims of gross and pervasive discrimination could be denied relief precisely because the unlawful practices had been so successful as totally to deter job applications from members of minority groups. A *per se* prohibition of relief to nonapplicants could thus put beyond the reach of equity the most invidious effects of employment discrimination — those that extend to the very hope of self-realization. Such a *per se* limitation on the equitable powers granted to courts by Title VII would be manifestly inconsistent with the "historic purpose of equity to 'secur[e] complete justice' " and with the duty of courts in Title VII cases " 'to render a decree which will so far as possible eliminate the discriminatory effects of the past.' " *Albemarle Paper Co. v. Moody, supra* at 418. . . .

(2) To conclude that a person's failure to submit an application for a job does not inevitably and forever foreclose his entitlement to seniority relief under Title VII is a far cry, however, from holding that nonapplicants are always entitled to such relief. A nonapplicant must show that he was a potential victim of unlawful discrimination. Because he is necessarily claiming that he was deterred from applying for the job by the employer's discriminatory practices, his is the not always easy burden of proving that he would have applied for the job had it not been for those practices. Cf. Mt. Healthy City School District Board of Education v. Doyle, 229 U.S. 274. When this burden is met, the nonapplicant is in a position analogous to that of an applicant and is entitled to the presumption discussed in Part III-A, *supra.* . . .

While the scope and duration of the company's discriminatory policy can leave little doubt that the futility of seeking line-driver jobs was communicated to the company's minority employees, that in itself is insufficient. The known prospect of discriminatory rejection shows only that employees who wanted line-driving jobs may have been deterred from applying for them. It does not show which of the nonapplicants actually wanted such jobs, or which possessed the requisite qualifications. There are differences between city and line-driving jobs, for example, but the desirability of the latter is not so self-evident as to warrant a conclusion that all employees would prefer to be line drivers if given a free choice. Indeed, a substantial number of white city drivers who were not subjected to the company's discriminatory practices were apparently content to retain their city jobs. . . .

An employee who transfers into a line-driver unit is normally placed at the bottom of the seniority " board." He is thus in jeopardy of being laid off and must, at best, suffer through an initial period of bidding on only the least desirable runs. . . . Nonapplicants who chose to accept the appellate court's *post hoc* invitation, however, would enter the line-driving unit with retroactive seniority dating from the time they were first qualified. A willingness to accept the job security and bidding power afforded by retroactive seniority says little about what choice an employee would have made had he previously been given the opportunity freely to choose a starting line-driver job. While it may be true that many of the nonapplicant employees desired and would have applied for line-driver jobs but for their knowledge of the company's policy of discrimination, the Government must carry its burden of proof, with respect to each specific individual, at the remedial hearings to be conducted by the District Court on remand.

C. The task remaining for the District Court on remand will not be a simple one. Initially, the court will have to make a substantial number of individual determinations in deciding which of the minority employees were actual victims of the company's discriminatory practices. After the victims have been identified, the court must, as nearly as possible, " 'recreate the conditions and relationships that would have been had there been no' " unlawful discrimination. *Franks, supra,* 424 U.S. at 769. . . . This process of recreating the past will necessarily involve a degree of approximation and imprecision. Because the class of victims may include some who did not apply for line-driver jobs as well as those who did, and because more than one minority employee may have been denied each line-driver vacancy, the court will be required to balance the equities of each minority employee's situation in allocating the limited number of vacancies that were discriminatorily refused to class members.

Moreover, after the victims have been identified and their rightful place determined, the District Court will again be faced with the delicate task of adjusting the remedial interests of discriminatees and the legitimate expectations of other employees innocent of any wrongdoing. . . .

After the evidentiary hearings to be conducted on remand, both the size and the composition of the class of minority employees entitled to relief may be altered substantially. Until those hearings have been conducted and both the number of identifiable victims and the consequent extent of necessary relief have been determined, it is not possible to evaluate abstract claims concerning the equitable balance that should be struck between the statutory rights of victims and the contractual rights of nonvictim employees. That determination is best left, in the first instance, to the sound equitable discretion of the trial court. . . .

For all the reasons we have discussed, the judgment of the Court of Appeals is vacated, and the cases are remanded to the District Court for further proceedings consistent with this opinion.

MR. JUSTICE MARSHALL, with whom MR. JUSTICE BRENNAN joins, concurring in part and dissenting in part. . . .

I do not agree that Title VII permits petitioners to treat non-Anglo line drivers differently from Anglo drivers who were hired by the company at the same time simply because the non-Anglo drivers were prevented by the company from acquiring seniority over the road. I therefore dissent from that aspect of the Court's holding, and from the limitations on the scope of the remedy that follow from it.

As the Court quite properly acknowledges, . . . the seniority provision at issue here clearly would violate Title VII absent § 703(h), . . . which exempts at least some seniority systems from the reach of the Act. . . . "Under the Act, practices, procedures or tests neutral on their face and even neutral in terms of intent, cannot be maintained *if they operate to 'freeze' the status quo of prior discriminatory employment practices.*" Griggs v. Duke Power Co., 401 U.S. 424, 429 (1971) (emphasis added). Petitioners' seniority system does precisely that: it awards the choicest jobs and other benefits to those possessing a credential — seniority — which, due to past discrimination, blacks and Spanish-speaking employees were prevented from acquiring. Consequently, "Every time a Negro worker hired under the old segregated system bids against a white worker in his job slot, the old racial classification reasserts itself, and the Negro suffers anew for his employer's previous bias." Local 189, United Papermakers & Paperworkers v. United States, 416 F.2d 980 (CA5 1969) (Wisdom, J.), *cert. denied,* 397 U.S. 919 (1970).

As the Court also concedes, with a touch of understatement, "the view that § 703(h) does not immunize seniority systems that perpetuate the effects of prior discrimination has much support." . . . Without a single dissent, six courts of appeals have so held in over 30 cases, and two other courts of appeals have indicated their agreement, also without dissent. In an unbroken line of cases, the EEOC has reached the same conclusion. And the overwhelming weight of scholarly opinion is in accord. Yet for the second time this Term, see General Electric Co. v. Gilbert, 429 U.S. 125 (1976), a majority of this Court overturns the unanimous conclusion of the courts of appeals and the EEOC concerning the scope of Title VII. Once again, I respectfully disagree. . . .

II. A. The Court's decision to uphold seniority systems that perpetuate post-Act discrimination — that is, seniority systems that treat non-Anglos who become line drivers as new employees even though, after the effective date of Title VII, these non-Anglos were discriminatorily assigned to city-driver jobs where they accumulated seniority — is explained in a single footnote. Ante, at 174 n. 30. . . . That footnote relies almost entirely on *United Airlines v. Evans.* . . . But like the instant decision, *Evans* is devoid of any analysis of the legislative history of § 703 (h); it simply asserts its conclusion in a single paragraph. For the Court to base its decision here on the strength of *Evans* is sheer bootstrapping.

Had the Court objectively examined the legislative history, it would have been compelled to reach the opposite conclusion. . . . Congress was concerned with seniority expectations that had developed prior to the enactment of Title VII, not with expectations arising thereafter to the extent that those expectations were dependent on whites benefiting from unlawful discrimination. . . .

B. The legislative history of § 703 (h) admittedly affords somewhat stronger support for the Court's conclusion with respect to seniority systems that perpetuate pre-Act discrimination — that is, seniority systems that treat non-Anglos who become line drivers as new employees even though these non-Anglos were discriminatorily assigned to city-driver jobs where they accumulated seniority before the effective date of Title VII. In enacting § 703 (h), Congress intended to extend at least some protection to seniority expectations that had developed prior to the effective date of the Act. But the legislative history is very clear that the only threat to these expectations that Congress was seeking to avert was nonremedial, fictional seniority. Congress did not want minority group members who were hired after the effective date of the Act to be given superseniority simply because they were members of minority groups, nor did it want the use of seniority to be invalidated whenever it had a disparate impact on newly hired minority employees. These are the evils — and the only evils — that the opponents of Title VII raised and that the Clark-Case Interpretive Memorandum addressed. As the Court acknowledges, "there seems to be no explicit reference in the legislative history to pre-Act discriminatees already employed in less desirable jobs." *Ante* at 28. . . .

The Court holds, in essence, that while after 1965 these incumbent employees are entitled to an equal opportunity to advance to more desirable jobs, to take advantage of that opportunity they must pay a price: they must surrender the seniority they have accumulated in their old jobs. For many, the price will be too high, and they will be locked-in to their previous positions. Even those willing to pay the price will have to reconcile themselves to being forever behind subsequently hired whites who were not discriminatorily assigned. Thus equal opportunity will remain a distant dream for all incumbent employees.

I am aware of nothing in the legislative history of the 1964 Civil Rights Act to suggest that if Congress had focused on this fact it nonetheless would have decided to write off an entire generation of minority group employees. Nor can I believe that the Congress that enacted Title VII would have agreed to postpone for one generation the achievement of economic equality. The backers of that Title viewed economic equality as both a practical necessity and a moral imperative. They were well aware of the corrosive impact employment discrimination has on its victims, and on the society generally. They sought, therefore, "to eliminate those discriminatory practices and devices which have fostered racially stratified job environments to the disadvantage of minority citizens"; McDonnell

Douglas Corp. v. Green, 411 U. S. 792, 800 (1973). . . . In short, Congress wanted to enable black workers to assume their rightful place in society. . . .

C. If the legislative history of § 703 (h) leaves any doubt concerning the section's applicability to seniority systems that perpetuate either pre- or post-Act discrimination, that doubt is entirely dispelled by two subsequent developments. The Court all but ignores both developments; I submit they are critical.

First, in more than a score of decisions beginning at least as early as 1969, the Equal Employment Opportunities Commission has consistently held that seniority systems that perpetuate prior discrimination are unlawful. . . . Before I would sweep aside the EEOC's consistent interpretation of the statute it administers, I would require " 'compelling indications that it is wrong.' " Espinoza v. Farah Manufacturing Co., 414 U.S. 86, 94-95 (1973). . . . I find no such indications in the Court's opinion.

Second, in 1972 Congress enacted the Equal Employment Opportunities Act of 1972, . . . amending Title VII. In so doing, Congress made very clear that it approved of the lower court decisions invalidating seniority systems that perpetuate discrimination. That Congress was aware of such cases is evident from the Senate and House Committee reports which cite the two leading decisions, as well as several prominent law review articles. S.Rep. No. 92-415, 92d Cong., 1st Sess., 5 n. 1 (1971); H. R. Rep. No. 92-238, 92d Cong., 1st Sess., 8 n. 2 (1971). Although Congress took action with respect to other lower court opinions with which it was dissatisfied, it made no attempt to overrule the seniority cases. To the contrary, both the Senate and House reports expressed approval of the "perpetuation principle" as applied to seniority systems and invoked the principle to justify the committee's recommendations to extend Title VII's coverage to state and local government employees, and to expand the power of the EEOC. Moreover, the Section-by-Section Analysis of the Conference Committee bill, which was prepared and placed in the Congressional Record by the floor managers of the bill, stated in "language that could hardly be more explicit," Franks v. Bowman Transportation Co., *supra,* 424 U.S. at 765 n. 21, that, "in any areas where a specific contrary intention is not indicated, it was assumed that the present case law . . . would continue to govern the applicability and construction of Title VII." 118 Cong. Rec. 7166, 7564 (1972). And perhaps most important, in explaining the section of the 1972 Act that empowers the EEOC "to prevent any person from engaging in any unlawful employment practice as set forth in section 703 or 704," . . . the Section-by-Section Analysis declared that:

> "The unlawful employment practices encompassed by sections 703 and 704 which were enumerated in 1964 by the original Act, *and as defined and expanded by the Courts* remain in effect." Id. at 7167, 7564 (emphasis added). . . .

NOTES

1. What will prevent a seniority system from being "bona fide"? It is enough that the system was knowingly established or maintained in conjunction with racially segregated jobs or departments, even though "job" or "departmental" seniority in itself is often preferred to "plant" seniority simply as a matter of industrial efficiency? Or must the seniority system have been so structured (or distorted) that it constituted a separate, distinct element in the discriminatory scheme? To what extent does the decision in the principal case leave the lower courts free to infer discriminatory intent in the operation of seniority systems? For consideration of such questions, *see* James v. Stockham Valves & Fittings Co., 559 U.S. 310 (5th Cir. 1977), *cert. denied,* 434 U.S. 1034 (1978). Might a union breach its duty of fair representation by failing to seek the elimination of a facially neutral seniority system that perpetuates the effects of past discrimination?

2. The Civil Rights Act of 1866 (42 U.S.C. § 1981) contains no counterpart to § 703(h) of the CRA of 1964. Does this mean that the seniority system in the principal case could have been successfully attacked in a § 1981 suit? *Compare* Johnson v. Ryder Truck Lines, Inc., 575 F. 2d 471 (4th Cir. 1978), *with* Bolden v. Pennsylvania State Police, 578 F. 2d 912 (3d Cir. 1978). Is it arguable that, despite *Griggs'* "discriminatory impact" theory, "bona fide" seniority systems should not be held discriminatory under Title VII, without regard to § 703(h).

3. The implications of the principal case are analyzed in Jones, *Title VII, Seniority, and the Supreme Court: Clarification or Retreat?* 26 KAN. L. REV. 1 (1977); Zimmer, *Teamsters: Redefinition and Retrenchment of Concepts of Discrimination,* in N.Y.U. THIRTIETH ANNUAL CONFERENCE ON LABOR 51 (1977). Prior to *Teamsters [T.I.M.E. — D.C.],* seniority and related problems were the subject of much academic writing, most of it favorable to the courts of appeals' view that seniority systems perpetuating discriminatory effects were violative of Title VII. See, *e.g.,* Blumrosen, *Seniority and Equal Employment Opportunity: A Glimmer of Hope,* 23 RUTGERS L. REV. 268 (1969); Cooper & Sobol, *Seniority and Testing under Fair Employment Laws: A General Approach to Objective Criteria of Hiring and Promotion, 82 HARV. L. REV. 1598 (1969); Gould, Seniority and the Black Worker: Reflections on Quarles and Its Implications,* 47 TEXAS L. REV. 1039 (1969); Gould, *The Emerging Law against Racial Discrimination in Employment,* 64 NW. U.L. REV. 359 (1969); Kovarsky, *Current Remedies for the Discriminatory Effects of Seniority Agreements,* 24 VAND. L. REV. 683 (1971). Practitioners' perspectives may be found in Kilberg, Moore, Kleiman & Frankel, Ross, Friedman & Katz, Youngdahl, *The Dilemmas of Discrimination, in N.Y.U. TWENTY-EIGHTH ANNUAL CONFERENCE ON LABOR 101, 147, 177, 231, 263, 297 (1975) (six separate papers).*

Reconciling seniority claims and equal employment opportunity is especially vexing in a declining economy. For discussion, see Blumrosen & Blumrosen, *The Duty to Plan for Fair Employment Revisted: Work*

Sharing in Hard Times, 28 RUTGERS L. REV. 1082 (1975); Poplin, *Fair Employment in a Depressed Economy: The Layoff Problem,* 23 U.C.L.A. L. REV. 177 (1975); Stacy, *Title VII Seniority Remedies in a Time of Economic Turndown,* 28 VAND. L. REV. 487 (1975); Summers & Love, *Work Sharing as an Alternative to Layoffs by Seniority: Title VII Remedies in Recession,* 124 U. PA. L. REV. 893 (1976).

UNITED AIR LINES V. EVANS, 431 U.S. 553, 97 S. Ct. 1885, 52 L. Ed. 2d 571 (1977). Carolyn Evans resigned from her flight attendant's job in 1968 under United's rule against married stewardesses. She did not file a charge with the EEOC within the then-required 90 days of her separation, and hence her claim based on that discriminatory act was barred. Meanwhile, the "no-marriage" rule was eliminated and she was rehired on February 16, 1972, but as a new employee without seniority for her past service. She filed charges with EEOC on February 21, 1973 and commenced suit after receiving a "right-to-sue" letter, contending that United was guilty of a present, continuing violation of Title VII. The Supreme Court held, first, that there was no discrimination because certain males hired between Evans's termination in 1968 and her reemployment in 1972 had more seniority despite their lesser total service, since "this disparity is not a consequence of their sex, or of her sex." Second, although the seniority system gave present effect to a past act of discrimination, "a discriminatory act which is not made the basis for a timely charge ... is merely an unfortunate event in history which has no present legal consequences." The "mere continuity" of the seniority system's impact was not enough; "the critical question is whether any present *violation* exists." Justices Marshall and Brennan dissented for the reasons stated in *Teamsters,* concluding that the charge was not time barred because the denial of seniority was a continuing violation.

NOTE

Does the issue in *Evans* differ from that in *Teamsters?* The two cases are noted in 72 NW. U. L. REV. 761 (1977) and 56 TEXAS L. REV. 301 (1978).

McDONALD v. SANTA FE TRAIL TRANSPORTATION CO.

Supreme Court of the United States
427 U.S. 273, 96 S. Ct. 257, 49 L. Ed. 2d 493 (1976)

MR. JUSTICE MARSHALL delivered the opinion of the Court.

Petitioners L. N. McDonald and Raymond L. Laird brought this action in the United States District Court for the Southern District of Texas seeking relief against Santa Fe Trail Transportation Co. (Santa Fe) and International Brotherhood of Teamsters Local 988 (Local 988), which represented Santa Fe's Houston employees, for alleged violations of the

Civil Rights Act of 1866, 42 U. S. C. § 1981, and of Title VII of the Civil Rights Act of 1964, . . . in connection with their discharge from Santa Fe's employment. The District Court dismissed the complaint on the pleadings. The Court of Appeals for the Fifth Circuit affirmed. In determining whether the decisions of these courts were correct, we must decide, first, whether a complaint alleging that white employees charged with misappropriating property from their employer were dismissed from employment, while a black employee [Jackson] similarly charged was not dismissed, states a claim under Title VII. Second, we must decide whether § 1981, which provides that "[a]ll persons . . . shall have the same right . . . to make and enforce contracts . . . as is enjoyed by white citizens . . ." affords protection from racial discrimination in private employment to white persons as well as nonwhites.

I. . . . We reverse.

II. Title VII of the Civil Act of 1964 prohibits the discharge of "any individual" because of "such individual's race," § 703(a)(1). . . . Its terms are not limited to discrimination against members of any particular race. Thus, although we were not there confronted with racial discrimination against whites, we described the Act in Griggs v. Duke Power Co., 401 U. S. 424, 431 (1971), as prohibiting "[d]iscriminatory preference for *any* [racial] group, *minority* or *majority*" (emphasis added). Similarly the EEOC, whose interpretations are entitled to great deference, Griggs v. Duke Power Co., 401 U. S. at 433-434, has consistently interpreted Title VII to proscribe racial discrimination in private employment against whites on the same terms as racial discrimination against nonwhites, holding that to proceed otherwise would

"constitute a dereliction of the Congressional mandate to eliminate all practices which operate to disadvantage the employment opportunities of any group protected by Title VII, including Caucasians." EEOC Decision No. 74-31, 7 FEP 1326, 1238, CCH EEOC Decisions ¶ 6406, p. 4084 (1973).

This conclusion is in accord with uncontradicted legislative history to the effect that Title VII was intended to "cover all white men and white women and all Americans," 110 Cong. Rec. 2579 (remarks of Rep. Celler) (1969), and create an "obligation not to discriminate against whites," *id.* at 7218 (memorandum of Sen. Clark). See also *id.* at 7213 (memorandum of Sens. Clark and Case); *id.* at 8912 (remarks of Sen. Williams). We therefore hold today that Title VII prohibits racial discrimination against the white petitioners in this case upon the same standards as would be applicable were they Negroes and Jackson white.[8]

Respondents contend that, even though generally applicable to white persons, Title VII affords petitioners no protection in this case, because

---

[8] . . . Santa Fe disclaims that the actions challenged here were any part of an affirmative action program, see Brief for Respondent Santa Fe, at 19 n. 5, and we emphasize that we do not consider here the permissibility of such a program, whether judicially required or otherwise prompted. . . .

their dismissal was based upon their commission of a serious criminal offense against their employer. We think this argument is foreclosed by our decision in McDonnell Douglas Corp. v. Green [411 U.S. 792 (1973)]. . . . The Act prohibits *all* racial discrimination in employment, without exception for any group of particular employees, and while crime or other misconduct may be a legitimate basis for discharge, it is hardly one for racial discrimination. Indeed, the Title VII plaintiff in *McDonnell Douglas* had been convicted for a nontrivial offense against his former employer. It may be that theft of property entrusted to an employer for carriage is a more compelling basis for discharge than obstruction of an employer's traffic arteries, but this does not diminish the illogic in retaining guilty employees of one color while discharging those of another color.

At this stage of the litigation the claim against Local 988 must go with the claim against Santa Fe, for in substance the complaint alleges that the Union shirked its duty properly to represent McDonald, but instead "acquiesced and/or joined in" Santa Fe's alleged racial discrimination against him. Local 988 argues that as a matter of law it should not be subject to liability under Title VII in a situation, such as this, where some but not all culpable employees are ultimately discharged on account of joint misconduct, because in representing all the affected employees in their relations with the employer, the Union may necessarily have to compromise by securing retention of only some. We reject the argument. The same reasons which prohibit an employer from discriminating on the basis of race among the culpable employees apply equally to the Union; and whatever factors the mechanisms of compromise may legitimately take into account in mitigating discipline of some employees, under Title VII race may not be among them.

Thus, we conclude that the District Court erred in dismissing both petitioners' Title VII claims against Santa Fe, and petitioner McDonald's Title VII claim against Local 988.

III. Title 42 U. S. C. § 1981 provides in pertinent part: "All persons within the jurisdiction of the United States shall have the same right in every State and Territory to make and enforce contracts . . . as is enjoyed by white citizens . . . ." We have previously held, where discrimination against Negroes was in question, that § 1981 affords a federal remedy against discrimination in private employment on the basis of race, and respondents do not contend otherwise. Johnson v. Railway Express Agency, 421 U. S. 454, 459-460 (1975). See also Runyon v. McCrary, 427 U.S. 160 (1976); Jones v. Alfred H. Mayer Co., 392 U. S. 409 (1968). The question here is whether § 1981 prohibits racial discrimination in private employment against whites as well as nonwhites.

While neither of the courts below elaborated its reasons for not applying § 1981 to racial discrimination against white persons, respondents suggest two lines of argument to support that judgment. First, they argue that by operation of the phrase "as is enjoyed by white citizens," § 1981 unambiguously limits itself to the protection of nonwhite persons against racial discrimination. Second, they contend that such a reading is consistent with the legislative history of the provision, which derives its operative language from § 1 of the Civil Rights Act of 1866. . . . See *Runyon v. McCrary, supra* at 168-170 n. 8; Tillman v. Wheaton-Haven Recreation Assn., 410 U.S. 431, 439 (1973). The 1866 statute, they assert, was concerned predominantly with assuring specified civil rights to the former Negro slaves freed by virtue of the Thirteenth Amendment, and not at all with protecting corresponding civil rights of white persons.

We find neither argument persuasive. Rather, our examination of the language and history of § 1981 convinces us that § 1981 is applicable to racial discrimination in private employment against white persons.

First, we cannot accept the view that the terms of § 1981 exclude its application to racial discrimination against white persons. On the contrary, the statute explicitly applies to "*all* persons" (emphasis added), including white persons. See, *e.g.,* United States v. Wong Kim Ark, 169 U. S. 649, 675-676 (1898). While a mechanical reading of the phrase "as is enjoyed by white citizens" would seem to lend support to respondents' reading of the statute, we have previously described this phrase simply as emphasizing "the racial character of the rights being protected," Georgia v. Rachel, 384 U. S. 780, 791 (1966). In any event, whatever ambiguity there may be in the language of § 1981 . . . is clarified by an examination of the legislative history of § 1981's language as it was originally forged in the Civil Rights Act of 1866.

[The court then made a detailed examination of the legislative history of the 1866 act.]

This cumulative evidence of congressional intent makes clear, we think, that the 1866 statute, designed to protect the "same right . . . to make and enforce contracts" of "citizens of every race and color" was not understood or intended to be reduced by Congressman Wilson's amendment, or any other provision, to the protection solely of nonwhites. Rather, the Act was meant, by its broad terms, to proscribe discrimination in the making or enforcement of contracts against, or in favor of, any race. Unlikely as it might have appeared in 1866 that white citizens would encounter substantial racial discrimination of the sort proscribed under the Act, the statutory structure and legislative history persuades us that the Thirty-ninth Congress was intent upon establishing in the federal law a broader principle than would have been necessary simply to meet the particular and immediate plight of the newly freed Negro slaves. And while the statutory language has been somewhat streamlined in reenactment and codification, there is no indication that § 1981 is intended to provide any less than the Congress enacted in 1866 regarding racial discrimination against white persons. *Runyon v. McCrary.* Thus, we conclude that the District Court erred in dismissing petitioners' claims under § 1981 on the ground that the protections of that provision are unavailable to white persons.

The judgment of the Court of Appeals for the Fifth Circuit is reversed, and the case is remanded for further proceedings consistent with this opinion.

So ordered.

MR. JUSTICE WHITE and MR. JUSTICE REHNQUIST join Parts I and II of the Court's opinion, but for the reasons stated in MR. JUSTICE WHITE'S dissenting opinion in *Runyon v. McCrary, supra* at 192, cannot join Part III since they do not agree that § 1981 is applicable in this case. To that extent they dissent.

NOTE

See generally Larson, *The Development of Section 1981 as a Remedy for Racial Discrimination in Private Employment,* 7 HARV. CIV. RTS.-CIV. LIB. L. REV. 56 (1972); Reiss, *Requiem for an "Independent Remedy": The Civil Rights Act of 1866 and 1871 as Remedies for Employment Discrimination,* 50 SO. CAL. L. REV. 961 (1977).

CONTRACTORS ASS'N OF EASTERN PENNSYLVANIA v. SHULTZ, 442 F.2d 159 (3d Cir. 1971), *cert. denied,* 404 U.S. 854 (1971). On September 23, 1969, the Department of Labor issued its revised "Philadelphia Plan," under which federal contractors in the Philadelphia area would have to make good faith efforts to meet specific percentage "goals" for minority group employment in six construction trades. The goals ranged from 4% to 9% for 1970 up to from 19% to 26% for 1973. They were based on such factors as the availability of minority group persons for employment in each trade, and the impact of the program on the existing labor force. The plan was upheld against constitutional attack on due process and equal protection grounds, and was found to be neither violative of Title VII of the Civil Rights Act nor inconsistent with the NLRA. The court viewed the program as an appropriate requirement of "affirmative action" to eliminate racial discrimination in employment, as called for by Executive Order 11246, and a proper exercise of Presidential authority. To the argument that "a decision to hire any black employee necessarily involves a decision not to hire a qualified white employee," the court replied: "This is pure sophistry. The findings in the September 23, 1969 order disclose that the specific goals may be met, considering normal employee attrition and anticipated growth in the industry, without adverse effects on the existing labor force."

NOTES

1. A state affirmative action plan that was more stringent than a federal "hometown" plan was held applicable to a federally assisted state construction contract in Associated General Contractors v. Altshuler, 490 F.2d 9 (1st Cir. 1973), *cert. denied,* 416 U.S. 957 (1974). In this instance a challenge was based on the supremacy clause as well as the due process and equal protection clauses. The court found that the federal government did not intend to preempt this field.

2. "Affirmative action" programs for the benefit of minorities and women in recruitment, training, hiring, promotion, etc., may have various origins. For example, they may be undertaken voluntarily by unions or employers, or imposed pursuant to Executive Order 11246 as a condition for obtaining a government contract, or mandated by a court order as a remedy for a specific statutory violation. In this last situation, the courts have been prepared to require "quota" hiring or similar numerically oriented action, disposing rather easily of objections of "reverse discrimination" against whites or males. Thus, in Carter v. Gallagher, 452 F. 2d 315 (8th Cir. 1971), *cert. denied,* 406 U.S. 950 (1972), a court of appeals sustained the preferential hiring of minority persons as firefighters on a 1:2 ratio until 20 were employed. *See also* NAACP v. Allen, 493 F. 2d 614 (5th Cir. 1974). And in Rios v. Steamfitters Local 638, 501 F.2d 622 (2d Cir. 1974), the Second Circuit held that a remedy embodying an affirmative action admission program by a union was not prohibited under § 703(j) of Title VII or the equal protection clause of the Federal Constitution. Section 703(j) was only intended to prohibit preferential quota hiring as a means of changing a racial imbalance attributable to causes other than unlawful discrimination.

3. The difficult question is the legality of affirmative action programs not predicated on proven discrimination by a particular party. In Weber v. Kaiser Aluminum & Chem. Corp., 563 F. 2d 216 (5th Cir. 1977), *cert. granted,* 99 S.Ct. 720 (U.S. 1978), the Fifth Circuit struck down as violative of Title VII a provision in a collective bargaining agreement that gave preference to blacks with less seniority than whites for admission on a 1:1 ratio to on-the-job training. Judge Wisdom dissented, arguing that such a ruling would produce an end to voluntary compliance with Title VII, because employers and unions are forced to walk "a high tightrope without a net beneath them." *See also* Detroit Police Officers Ass'n v. Young, 16 FEP Cas. 1005 (E.D. Mich. 1978) (since police department had not engaged in racial discrimination prior to its adoption of an affirmative action program, its preferential promotion plan clearly violated Title VII as an "impermissible racial quota"). On the same day the Supreme Court granted certiorari in *Weber,* EEOC voted to approve *Affirmative Action Guidelines* authorizing employers and unions, on the basis of a self-analysis of their employment practices, to take "appropriate affirmative action," including the use of "goals and timetables . . . which recognize the race, sex, or national origin of applicants or employees." 44 Fed. Reg. 4422 (Jan. 19, 1979). EEOC also invoked its power under § 713 (b) of the CRA to insulate persons complying with these Guidelines from liability under Title VII.

4. Although the Supreme Court has not yet ruled on the legality of affirmative action programs in employment, some inkling of its attitude can be derived from Regents of the University of California v. Bakke, 98 S. Ct. 2733 (U.S. 1978). There the Court held (5-4) that a state medical school's special admissions program, which reserved 16 out of the 100 seats in each entering class for minority applicants, was unlawful, but that race could be taken into account as a factor in admissions decisions. Four justices reasoned that any racially based determination violated Title VI of the 1964 Civil Rights Act, which bars race discrimination in any program receiving federal financial assistance; these justices did not reach any constitutional question. Four other justices would have sustained the California program as it existed against both statutory and constitutional attacks. The swing justice, Justice Powell, held that the total exclusion of non-minority candidates from consideration for a specific percentage of places in a class offended both Title VI and the equal protection clause of the Fourteenth Amendment, but that neither Title VI nor the Federal Constitution precluded treating race as "simply one element — to be weighed fairly against other elements — in the selection process." In the course of his opinion, Justice Powell commented:

> The employment discrimination cases also do not advance [the University's] cause. For example, in Franks v. Bowman Transportation Co., 424 U.S. 747 (1975), we approved a retroactive award of seniority to a class of Negro truck drivers who had been the victims of discrimination — not just by society at large, but by the respondent in that case. While this relief imposed some burdens on other employees, it was held necessary " 'to make [the victims] whole for injuries suffered on account of unlawful employment discrimination.' " Id. at 771, quoting Albemarle Paper Co. v. Moody, 422 U.S. 405, 418 (1975). The courts of appeals have fashioned various types of racial preferences as remedies for constitutional or statutory violations resulting in identified, race-based injuries to individuals held entitled to the preference. *E.g.,* Bridgeport Guardians, Inc. v. Civil Service Commission, 482 F. 2d 1333 (2d Cir. 1973); Carter v. Gallagher, 452 F. 2d 315, *modified on rehearing en banc,* 452 F. 2d 327 (8th Cir. 1972). Such preferences also have been upheld where a legislative or administrative body charged with the responsibility made determinations of past discrimination by the industries affected, and fashioned remedies deemed appropriate to rectify the discrimination. *E.g.,* Contractors Association of Eastern Pennsylvania v. Secretary of Labor, 442 F. 2d 159 (3d Cir.) *cert. denied,* 404 U.S. 854 (1971); Associated General Contractors of Massachusetts, Inc. v. Altschuler, 490 F. 2d 9 (1st Cir. 1973), *cert. denied,* 416 U.S. 957 (1974); *cf.* Katzenbach v. Morgan, 384 U.S. 641 (1966). But we have never approved preferential classifications in the absence of proven constitutional or statutory violations.

After its decision in *Bakke,* the Supreme Court declined without comment to review a 1973 consent decree that required AT&T to promote more blacks and women by granting them an "affirmative action override." The settlement had been challenged by three unions, which charged that their members' contractual rights, as well as their statutory and constitutional rights, had been violated by the preferences accorded classes of persons not all of whom may have been identifiable victims of specific past discrimination. EEOC v. American Telephone & Telegraph Co., 556 F. 2d 167 (3d Cir. 1977), *cert. denied,* 98 S. Ct. 3145 (U.S. 1978).

See also Los Angeles County v. Associated General Contractors, 98 S.Ct. 3132 (U.S. 1978), where the Supreme Court remanded to a lower court with a suggestion of mootness a suit in which a group of California contractors had challenged as "reverse discrimination" a provision of the Federal Public Works Employment Act of 1977 that set aside 10 percent of each grant for minority business firms. The Solicitor General had argued that all the federal contracts had been let and thus there was no further legal controversy for the courts to resolve. For the case below, see Associated General Contractors v. Secretary of Commerce, 441 F. Supp. 955 (C.D. Cal. 1977). On remand, however, the district court reiterated its view that the 10 percent set-aside was unconstitutional. 47 U.S.L.W. 2290 (C.D. Cal. 1978). *Contra,* Fullilove v. Kreps, 584 F. 2d 600 (2d Cir. 1978).

5. The Philadelphia Plan is discussed in Gosseen & Moss, *The Philadelphia Plan: A Critical Analysis,* in N.Y.U. TWENTY-THIRD ANNUAL CONFERENCE ON LABOR 169 (1970); Jones, *The Bugaboo of Employment Quotas,* 1970 WIS. L. REV. 341; Leiken, *Treatment in the Skilled Building Trades: An Analysis of the Philadelphia Plan,* 56 CORNELL L. REV. 84 (1970). Other specific decrees are treated in Gould, *The Seattle Building Trades Order: The First Comprehensive Relief Against Employment Discrimination in the Construction Industry,* 26 STAN. L. REV. 773 (1974); Kilberg, *Current Civil Rights Problems in the Collective Bargaining Process: The Bethlehem and AT&T Experiences,* 27 VAND. L. REV. 81 (1974). More general studies include Blumrosen, *Quotas, Common Sense and Law in Labor Relations: Three Dimensions of Equal Opportunity,* 27 RUTGERS L. REV. 675 (1974); Davidson, *Preferential Treatment and Equal Opportunity,* 55 ORE. L. REV. 53 (1976); Edwards & Zaretsky, *Preferential Remedies for Employment Discrimination,* 74 MICH. L. REV. 1 (1976); N. GLAZER, AFFIRMATIVE DISCRIMINATION 33-66 (1975); St. Antoine, *Affirmative Action: Hypocritical Euphemism or Noble Mandate?* 10 U. MICH. J. L. REF. 28 (1976). For an insider's view, see Nash, *Affirmative Action Under Executive Order 11, 246,* 46 N.Y.U. L. REV. 225 (1971).

CITY OF LOS ANGELES v. MANHART

Supreme Court of the United States
435 U.S. 702, 98 S. Ct. 1370, 55 L. Ed. 2d 657 (1978)

MR. JUSTICE STEVENS delivered the opinion of the Court.

As a class, women live longer than men. For this reason, the Los Angeles Department of Water and Power required its female employees to make larger contributions to its pension fund than its male employees. We granted certiorari to decide whether this practice discriminated against individual female employees because of their sex in violation of § 703 (a)(1) of the Civil Rights Act of 1964, as amended.

For many years the Department has administered retirement, disability, and death benefit programs for its employees. Upon retirement each employee is eligible for a monthly retirement benefit computed as a fraction of his or her salary multiplied by years of service. The monthly benefits for men and women of the same age, seniority, and salary are equal. Benefits are funded entirely by contributions from the employees and the Department, augmented by the income earned on those contributions. No private insurance company is involved in the administration or payment of benefits.

Based on a study of mortality tables and its own experience, the Department determined that its 2,000 female employees, on the average, will live a few years longer than its 10,000 male employees. The cost of a pension for the average retired female is greater than for the average male retiree because more monthly payments must be made to the average woman. The Department therefore required female employees to make monthly contributions to the fund which were 14.84% higher than the contributions required of comparable male employees. Because employee contributions were withheld from pay checks, a female employee took home less pay than a male employee earning the same salary. . . .

The Department and various *amici curiae* contend that: (1) the differential in take-home pay between men and women was not discrimination within the meaning of § 703 (a)(1) because it was offset by a difference in the value of the pension benefits provided to the two classes of employees; (2) the differential was based on a factor "other than sex" within the meaning of the Equal Pay Act and was therefore protected by the so-called Bennett Amendment; (3) the rationale of General Electric Co. v. Gilbert, 429 U. S. 125, requires reversal; and (4) in any event, the retroactive monetary recovery is unjustified. We consider these contentions in turn.

I. There are both real and fictional differences between women and men. It is true that the average man is taller than the average woman; it is not true that the average woman driver is more accident-prone than the average man. Before the Civil Rights Act of 1964 was enacted, an employer could fashion his personnel policies on the basis of assumptions about the differences between men and women, whether or not the assumptions were valid.

It is now well recognized that employment decisions cannot be predicated on mere "stereotyped" impressions about the characteristics of male or females. Myths and purely habitual assumptions about a woman's inability to perform certain kinds of work are no longer acceptable reasons for refusing to employ qualified individuals, or for paying them less. This case does not, however, involve a fictional difference between men and women. It involves a generalization that the parties accept as unquestionably true: women, as a class, do live longer than men. The Department treated its women employees differently from its men employees because the two classes are in fact different. It is equally true, however, that all individuals in the respective classes do not share the characteristic which differentiates the average class representatives. Many women do not live as long as the average man and many men outlive the average woman. The question, therefore, is whether the existence or nonexistence of "discrimination" is to be determined by comparison of class characteristics or individual characteristics. A "stereotyped" answer to that question may not be the same as the answer which the language and purpose of the statute command.

The statute makes it unlawful "to discriminate against any *individual* with respect to his compensation, terms, conditions or privileges of employment, because of such *individual's* race, color, religion, sex, or national origin." 42 U. S. C. § 2000e-2 (a) (1) (emphasis added). The statute's focus on the individual is unambiguous. It precludes treatment of individuals as simply components of a racial, religious, sexual, or national class. If height is required for a job, a tall woman may not be refused employment merely because, on the average, women are too short. Even a true generalization about the class is an insufficient reason for disqualifying an individual to whom the generalization does not apply.

That proposition is of critical importance in this case because there is no assurance that any individual woman working for the Department will actually fit the generalization on which the Department's policy is based. Many of those individuals will not live as long as the average man. While they were working, those individuals received smaller paychecks because of their sex, but they will receive no compensating advantage when they retire.

It is true, of course, that while contributions are being collected from the employees, the Department cannot know which individuals will predecease the average woman. Therefore, unless women as a class are assessed an extra charge, they will be subsidized, to some extent, by the class of male employees. It follows, according to the Department, that fairness to its class of male employees justifies the extra assessment against all of its female employees.

But the question of fairness to various classes affected by the statute is essentially a matter of policy for the legislature to address. Congress has decided that classifications based on sex, like those based on national origin or race, are unlawful. Actuarial studies could unquestionably identify differences in life expectancy based on race or national origin, as well as sex. But a statute which was designed to make race irrelevant in the employment market, see Griggs v. Duke Power Co., 401 U. S. 424, 436, could not reasonably be construed to permit a take-home pay differential based on a racial classification.

Even if the statutory language were less clear, the basic policy of the statute requires that we focus on fairness to individuals rather than fairness to classes. Practices which classify employees in terms of religion, race, or sex tend to preserve traditional assumptions about groups rather than thoughtful scrutiny of individuals. The generalization involved in this case illustrates the point. Separate mortality tables are easily interpreted as reflecting innate differences between the sexes; but a significant part of the longevity differential may be explained by the social fact that men are heavier smokers than women.

Finally, there is no reason to believe that Congress intended a special definition of discrimination in the context of employee group insurance coverage. It is true that insurance is concerned with events that are individually unpredictable, but that is characteristic of many employment decisions. Individual risks, like individual performance, may not be predicted by resort to classifications proscribed by Title VII. Indeed, the fact that this case involves a group insurance program highlights a basic flaw in the department's fairness argument. For when insurance risks are grouped, the better risks always subsidize the poorer risks. Healthy persons subsidize medical benefits for the less healthy; unmarried workers subsidize the pensions of married workers; persons who eat, drink, or smoke to excess may subsidize pension benefits for persons whose habits are more temperate. Treating different classes of risks as though they were the same for purposes of group insurance is a common practice which has never been considered inherently unfair. To insure the flabby and the fit as though they were equivalent risks may be more common than treating men and women alike; but nothing more than habit makes one "subsidy" seem less fair than the other.

An employment practice which requires 2,000 individuals to contribute more money into a fund than 10,000 other employees simply because each of them is a woman, rather than a man, is in direct conflict with both the language and the policy of the Act. Such a practice does not pass the simple test of whether the evidence shows "treatment of a person in a manner which but for the person's sex would be different." It constitutes discrimination and is unlawful unless exempted by the Equal Pay Act or some other affirmative justification.

II. Shortly before the enactment of Title VII in 1964, Senator Bennett proposed an amendment providing that a compensation differential based on sex would not be unlawful if it was authorized by the Equal Pay Act, which had been passed a year earlier. The Equal Pay Act requires employers to pay members of both sexes the same wages for equivalent work, except when the differential is pursuant to one of four specified exceptions. The Department contends that the fourth exception applies here. That exception authorizes a "differential based on any other factor other than sex."

The Department argues that the different contributions exacted from men and women were based on the factor of longevity rather than sex. It is plain, however, that any individual's life expectancy is based on a number of factors, of which sex is only one. The record contains no evidence that any factor other than the employee's sex was taken into account in calculating the 14.84% differential between the respective contributions by men and women. We agree with Judge Duniway's observation that one cannot "say that an actuarial distinction based entirely on sex is 'based on any other factor other than sex'. Sex is exactly what it is based on." 553 F.2d at 588.

We are also unpersuaded by the Department's reliance on a colloquy between Senator Randolph and Senator Humphrey during the debate on the Civil Rights Act of 1964. Commenting on the Bennett Amendment, Senator Humphrey expressed his understanding that it would allow many differences in the treatment of men and women under industrial benefit plans, including earlier retirement options for women. Though he did not address differences in employee contributions based on sex, Senator Humphrey apparently assumed that the 1964 Act would have little, if any, impact on existing pension plans. His statement cannot, however, fairly be made the sole guide to interpreting the Equal Pay Act, which had been adopted a year earlier; and it is the 1963 statute, with its exceptions, on which the Department ultimately relies. We conclude that Senator Humphrey's isolated comment on the Senate floor cannot change the effect of the plain language of the statute itself.

III. The Department argues that reversal is required by General Electric Co. v. Gilbert, 429 U. S. 125. We are satisfied, however, that neither the holding nor the reasoning of *Gilbert* is controlling.

In *Gilbert* the Court held that the exclusion of pregnancy from an employer's disability benefit plan did not constitute sex discrimination within the meaning of Title VII. Relying on the reasoning in Geduldig v. Aiello, 417 U.S. 484, the Court first held that the General Electric plan did not involve "discrimination based upon gender as such." The two groups of potential recipients which that case concerned were pregnant women and nonpregnant persons. "While the first group is exclusively female, the second includes members of both sexes." 429 U. S. at 135. In contrast, each of the two groups of employees involved in this case is composed entirely and exclusively of members of the same sex. On its face, this plan discriminates on the basis of sex whereas the General Electric plan discriminated on the basis of a special physical disability.

In *Gilbert* the Court did note that the plan as actually administered had provided more favorable benefits to women as a class than to men as a class. This evidence supported the conclusion that not only had plaintiffs failed to establish a prima facie case by proving that the plan was discriminatory on its face, but they had also failed to prove any discriminatory effect.

In this case, however, the Department argues that the absence of a discriminatory effect on women as a class justifies an employment practice which, on its face, discriminated against individual employees because of their sex. But even if the Department's actuarial evidence is sufficient to prevent plaintiffs from establishing a prima facie case on the theory that the effect of the practice on women as a class was discriminatory, that evidence does not defeat the claim that the practice, on its face, discriminated against every individual woman employed by the Department.

In essence, the Department is arguing that the prima facie showing of discrimination based on evidence of different contributions for the respective sexes is rebutted by its demonstration that there is a like difference in the cost of providing benefits for the respective classes. That argument might prevail if Title VII contained a cost justification defense comparable to the affirmative defense available in a price discrimination suit. But neither Congress nor the courts have recognized such a defense under Title VII.

Although we conclude that the Department's practice violated Title VII, we do not suggest that the statute was intended to revolutionize the insurance and pension industries. All that is at issue today is a requirement that men and women make unequal contributions to an employee-operated pension fund. Nothing in our holding implies that it would be unlawful for an employer to set aside equal retirement contributions for each employee and let each retiree purchase the largest benefit which his or her accumulated contributions could command in the open market. Nor does it call into question the insurance industry practice of considering the composition of an employer's work force in determining the probable cost of a retirement or death benefit plan. Finally, we recognize that in a case of this kind it may be necessary to take special care in fashioning appropriate relief.

IV. The Department challenges the District Court's award of retroactive relief to the entire class of female employees and retirees. Title VII does not require a district court to grant any retroactive relief. A court that finds unlawful discrimination "may enjoin [the discrimination] and order such affirmative action as may be appropriate, which may include, but is not limited to, reinstatement . . . with or without back pay . . . or any other equitable relief as the court deems appropriate." 42 U. S. C. § 2000e-5(g). To the point of redundancy, the statute stresses that retroactive relief "may" be awarded if it is "appropriate."

In Albemarle Paper Co. v. Moody, 422 U. S. 405, the Court reviewed the scope of a district court's discretion to fashion appropriate remedies for a Title VII violation and concluded that "back pay should be denied only for reasons which, if applied generally, would not frustrate the central statutory purposes of eradicating discrimination throughout the economy and making persons whole for injuries suffered through past discrimination." *Id.* at 421. Applying that standard, the Court ruled that an award of backpay should not be conditioned on a showing of bad faith. *Id.* at 422-423. But the *Albemarle* Court also held that backpay was not to be awarded automatically in every case.

The *Albemarle* presumption in favor of retroactive liability can seldom be overcome, but it does not make meaningless the district courts' duty to determine that such relief is appropriate. For several reasons, we conclude that the District Court gave insufficient attention to the equitable nature of Title VII remedies. Although we now have no doubt about the application of the statute in this case, we must recognize that conscientious and intelligent administrators of pension funds, who did not have the benefit of the extensive briefs and arguments presented to us, may well have assumed that a program like the Department's was entirely lawful. The courts had been silent on the question, and the administrative agencies had conflicting views. The Department's failure to act more swiftly is a sign, not of its recalcitrance, but of the problem's complexity. As commentators have noted, pension administrators could reasonably have thought it unfair — or even illegal — to make male employees shoulder more than their "actuarial share" of the pension burden. There is no reason to believe that the threat of a backpay award is needed to cause other administrators to amend their practices to conform to this decision.

Nor can we ignore the potential impact which changes in rules affecting insurance and pension plans may have on the economy. Fifty million Americans participate in retirement plans other than Social Security. The assets held in trust for these employees are vast and growing — more than $400 billion were reserved for retirement benefits at the end of 1977 and reserves are increasing by almost $50 billion a year. These plans, like other forms of insurance, depend on the accumulation of large sums to cover contingencies. The amounts set aside are determined by a painstaking assessment of the insurer's likely liability. Risks that the insurer foresees will be included in the calculation of liability, and the rates or contributions charged will reflect that calculation. The occurrence of major unforeseen contingencies, however, jeopardizes the insurer's solvency and, ultimately, the insureds' benefits. Drastic changes in the legal rules governing pension and insurance funds, like other unforeseen events, can have this effect. Consequently, the rules that apply to these funds should not be applied retroactively unless the legislature has plainly commanded that result. The EEOC itself has recognized that the administrators of retirement plans must be given time to adjust gradually to Title VII's demands. Courts have also shown sensitivity to the special dangers of retroactive Title VII awards in this field. See Rosen v. Public Serv. Elec. & Gas Co., 328 F. Supp. 454, 466-468 (D.N.J. 1971).

There can be no doubt that the prohibition against sex-differentiated employee contributions represents a marked departure from past practice. Although Title VII was enacted in 1964, this is apparently the first litigation challenging contribution differences based on valid actuarial tables. Retroactive liability could be devastating for a pension fund. The harm would fall in large part on innocent third parties. If, as the courts below apparently contemplated, the plaintiffs' contributions are recovered from the pension fund, the administrators of the fund will be forced to meet unchanged obligations with diminished assets. If the reserve proves inadequate, either the expectations of all retired employees will be disappointed or current employees will be forced to pay not only for their own future security but also for the unanticipated reduction in the contributions of past employees.

Without qualifying the force of the *Albemarle* presumption in favor of retroactive relief, we conclude that it was error to grant such relief in this case. Accordingly, although we agree with the Court of Appeals' analysis of the statute, we vacate its judgment and remand the case for further proceedings consistent with this opinion.

MR. JUSTICE BRENNAN took no part in the consideration or decision of this case.

[The partially concurring and dissenting opinions of MR. JUSTICE MARSHALL and of MR. CHIEF JUSTICE BURGER, in the latter of which MR. JUSTICE REHNQUIST joined, and the partially concurring opinion of MR. JUSTICE BLACKMUN are omitted.]

NOTES

1. The Supreme Court's ruling in General Elec. Co. v. Gilbert, 429 U.S. 125 (1976), that pregnancy could lawfully be excluded from an employer's disability benefit plan, was overturned in 1978 by Pub. L. No. 95-552, which added § 701(k) to the CRA. The definition of sex discrimination was broadened to include discrimination on the basis of "pregnancy, childbirth, or related medical conditions." Even before Congress acted, the Supreme Court in Nashville Gas Co. v. Satty, 434 U.S. 136 (1977), had introduced a distinction between an allowable denial of a benefit to a pregnant worker and the imposition of a substantial burden on her, with the latter being a violation of § 703(a)(2). Thus, an employer could not force an employee who took maternity leave to forfeit her accumulated seniority.

2. In Phillips v. Martin Marietta Corp., 400 U.S. 542 (1971), the Supreme Court indicated that disparate treatment of a subclass of males or females — "sex plus," so called — could violate Title VII. In *Martin Marietta* an employer refused to hire women with pre-school children while hiring men with such children. Similarly, an employer may not terminate female flight attendants upon marriage while retaining married male attendants. Sprogis v. United Air Lines, 444 F. 2d 1194 (7th Cir. 1971), *cert. denied*, 404 U.S. 991 (1971). *See also* Jacobs v. Martin Sweets Co., 550 F. 2d 364 (6th Cir. 1977) (discharge of pregnant unmarried employee violative of Title VII).

Disparate treatment on the basis of "sex plus" will generally violate Title VII only where the "plus" characteristics (1) are "immutable," or (2) involve "fundamental" rights, such as marriage or parenthood, or (3) significantly affect the employment opportunities of one sex in relation to the other. Most courts have therefore upheld employers' sexually differentiated grooming or dress policies. *See, e.g.,* the male "long hair" cases, Fagan v. National Cash Register Co., 481 F. 2d 1115 (D.C. Cir. 1973); Willingham v. Macon Tel. Pub. Co., 507 F. 2d 1084 (5th Cir. 1975) *(en banc);* Earwood v. Continental Southeastern Lines, 539 F. 2d 1349 (4th Cir. 1976); Barker v. Taft Broadcasting Co., 549 F. 2d 400 (6th Cir. 1977). *See also* Carroll v. Talman Federal Sav. & Loan Ass'n, 448 F. Supp. 79 (N.D. Ill. 1978) (female employee suspended for refusing to comply with employer's dress code).

3. Both federal and state courts have consistently struck down as discriminatory under Title VII various state "protective" statutes, which limit the hours women may work or the weights they may lift, or which prohibit them from certain occupations, such as bartending. *See, e.g.,* Rosenfeld v. Southern Pacific Co., 444 F.2d 1219 (9th Cir. 1971); Manning v. UAW, 466 F.2d 812 (6th Cir. 1972); Sail'er Inn, Inc. v. Kirby,

95 Cal. Rptr. 329, 485 P.2d 529 (1971). Where a state law grants a benefit, such as minimum wages or rest periods, to women only, the courts are divided over whether the law should be invalidated or extended to cover men also. *Compare* Hays v. Potlatch Forests, Inc., 465 F. 2d 1081 (8th Cir. 1972), *with* Homemakers, Inc. v. Division of Indus. Welfare, 509 F. 2d 20 (9th Cir. 1974), *cert. denied,* 423 U.S. 1063 (1976). EEOC's *Guidelines on Discrimination Because of Sex* provide that where state laws require a minimum wage and premium pay for overtime be given female employees, employers must grant the same benefits to male employees. 29 C.F.R. § 1604.2(b)(3) (1975).

4. In Diaz v. Pan American World Airways, 442 F.2d 385 (5th Cir. 1971), *cert. denied,* 404 U.S. 950 (1971), a court held that female sex is not a "bona fide occupational qualification" for the job of flight cabin attendant. The preference of airline passengers for female attendants is not determinative. The test is "business necessity," not "business convenience." Discrimination based on sex is permissible only where the essence of the business operation would be undermined by not having members of one sex exclusively in a particular position. Airlines may still consider the ability of individuals to perform nonmechanical functions, but they may not exclude all males merely because most males might not perform adequately. *But cf.* Fesel v. Masonic Home of Delaware, Inc., 447 F. Supp. 1346 (D. Del. 1978), which held that a nursing home for the elderly had established female sex as a BFOQ for a nurse's aide, since many female residents would not consent to intimate personal care by males.

5. Does an employer violate Title VII when a male supervisor retaliates economically against a female employee who has rebuffed his sexual advances? *See* Barnes v. Costle, 561 F. 2d 983 (D.C. Cir. 1977); Tomkins v. Public Serv. Elec. & Gas Co., 568 F. 2d 1044 (3d Cir. 1977).

6. When Congress forbade "sex" discrimination in Title VII, did it mean to include discrimination against employees who are changing sexes? The Ninth Circuit decided that Congress had only traditional notions of "sex" on its mind. Holloway v. Arthur Anderson & Co., 566 F.2d 659 (9th Cir. 1977). Judge Goodwin, dissenting, would interpret the language of the statute to include a transsexual who is discharged for undertaking to change his or her sex.

7. Would it violate the Equal Pay Act's requirement of "equal pay for equal work" if an employer paid male night shift inspectors more than female day shift inspectors? What particular facts might be pertinent to resolving this issue? *See* Corning Glass Works v. Brennan, 417 U.S. 188 (1974). Equal pay violations require a showing that males and females in fact were paid differently for doing essentially the same job. A female who held a unique job could not base an equal pay action on a theory that the employer *would* have paid a greater salary to a male in the same position. Rinkel v. Associated Pipeline Contractors, Inc., 17 FEP Cas. 224 (D. Alaska 1978). The return on a successful Equal Pay Act suit is high—in effect, double back pay.

8. *See generally* Brown, Emerson, Falk & Freedman, *Equal Rights Amendment: A Constitutional Basis for Equal Rights for Women,* 80 YALE L.J. 871, 923 (1971); Edwards, *Sex Discrimination Under Title VII: Some Unresolved Issues,* 24 LAB. L.J. 411 (1973); Hillman, *Sex and Employment Under the Equal Rights Amendment,* 67 Nw. U.L. REV. 789 (1973); Landau & Dunahoo, *Sex Discrimination in Employment: A Survey of State and Federal Remedies,* 20 DRAKE L. REV. 417 (1971); Ross & McDermott, *The Equal Pay Act of 1963: A Decade of Enforcement,* 16 B.C. IND. & COM. L. REV. 1 (1974); Shaman, *Toward Defining and Abolishing the Bona Fide Occupational Qualification Based on Class Status,* 22 LAB. L.J. 332 (1971). As their titles suggest, these articles deal not only with Title VII but also with such other sex discrimination bans as the so-called Equal Pay Act, a 1963 amendment to the Fair Labor Standards Act, 29 U.S.C. § 206(d), and the proposed Equal Rights Amendment to the Federal Constitution.

TRANS WORLD AIRLINES V. HARDISON, 432 U.S. 63, 97 S. Ct. 2264, 53 L. Ed. 2d 113 (1977). Hardison was a member of the Worldwide Church of God, one whose tenets required refraining from work on Saturdays. When Hardison informed his employer of this, the employer agreed that the union steward should seek a job swap or a change of days off; that Hardison would have his religious holidays off whenever possible; and that the employer would try to find Hardison another job more compatible with his religious beliefs. Although the problem was temporarily solved, it reappeared when Hardison bid on a new job in another building, where his low seniority put him in line for Saturday duty. Eventually Hardison was discharged for refusing to work Saturdays. At the time of these events EEOC guidelines required, as § 701(j) of the amended Civil Rights Act requires now, that an employer must "reasonably accommodate" its employees' religious needs, absent "undue hardship" to the business. The Supreme Court held that the employer and the union had satisfied their obligation to make such reasonable accommodation. The Court disagreed with the court of appeals, which had found that the company could have accommodated without undue hardship by (1) permitting Hardison to work a four-day week, utilizing in his place a supervisor or another worker on duty elsewhere, (2) filling Hardison's shift by paying another employee premium overtime pay, or (3) arranging a swap between Hardison and another employee either for another shift or for the Sabbath days. These alternatives would have required the company to bear more than *de minimis* costs, and they would have required a departure from the seniority system under the collective agreement. "[T]he strong congressional policy against discrimination in employment argues against interpreting the statute to require the abrogation of the seniority rights of some employees in order to accommodate the religious needs of others. . . . In *Franks,* we held that once an illegal discriminatory practice occurring after the effective date of the Act is proved, § 703(h) does not bar an award of retroactive seniority status to victims of that discriminatory practice. Here the suggested exception to the TWA-IAM seniority system would not be remedial; the operation of the seniority system itself is said to violate Title VII. In such circumstances, § 703(h) unequivocally mandates that there is no statutory violation in the absence of a discriminatory purpose." Mr. Justice Marshall and Mr. Justice Brennan dissented, arguing that some accommodation could have been found which did not involve "undue hardship."

NOTES

1. Is there more here than meets the eye? Might the Court have feared that a more stringent "accommodation" requirement would have impinged on the First Amendment's bar against an establishment of religion? *See generally* Edwards & Kaplan, *Religious Discrimination and the Role of Arbitration under Title VII,* 69 MICH. L. REV. 599 (1971).

2. In Redmond v. GAF Corp., 574 F. 2d 897 (7th Cir. 1978), the Seventh Circuit ruled that the ban on religious discrimination in Title VII covers all conduct that is "religious motivated" and not merely conduct in which either Sabbatarianism or a practice specifically required or prohibited by a tenet of an employee's religion is involved. It upheld a lower court's decision that an employer violated the Act when it discharged an employee, who was a member of the Jehovah's Witnesses, for leading a Bible study class on Saturdays rather than reporting for overtime work, even though his religion does not proscribe Saturday work.

3. What sort of an accommodation does the law require when an employee refuses because of religious scruples to pay dues or fees under a union shop or agency shop agreement? *See* Yott v. North American Rockwell Corp., 501 F. 2d 398 (9th Cir. 1974); Cooper v. General Dynamics Corp., 533 F. 2d 163 (5th Cir. 1976); McDaniel v. Essex International, Inc., 571 F. 2d 338 (6th Cir. 1978).

4. A less litigated provision of Title VII forbids discrimination on the basis of "national origin." In Espinoza v. Farah Mfg. Co., 414 U.S. 86 (1973), the Supreme Court held this does not prevent an employer from refusing to hire a person because he or she lacks United States citizenship. *But cf.* Sugarman v. Dougall, 413 U.S. 634 (1973) (state law that indiscriminately prohibits employment of aliens in competitive civil service positions violates equal protection clause). *See also* Foley v. Connelie, 98 S. Ct. 1067 (U.S. 1978) (state police may constitutionally be limited to United States citizens; three justices dissented); Ambach v. Norwick, 99 S. Ct. 1589 (U.S. 1979) (certification as public school teacher may constitutionally be denied to aliens who have not manifested intent to become citizens; four justices dissented).

5. Discrimination by employers or unions because of age (from 40 to 70) is forbidden by the Age Discrimination in Employment Act of 1967, as amended, 29 U.S.C. § 621 *et seq.* The Act is enforced by the Wage and

Hour Division of the Department of Labor. For examples of the problems posed, *compare* Usery v. Tamiami Trail Tours, Inc., 531 F. 2d 224 (5th Cir. 1976) (age upheld as BFOQ for intercity bus drivers), *with* Houghton v. McDonnell Douglas Corp., 553 F. 2d 561 (8th Cir. 1977) (age not upheld as BFOQ for test pilots). *See generally* Smith, *Impact of 1978 ADEA Amendments on Collective Bargaining,* 98 LAB. REL. REP. 146, 164 (June 19 & 26, 1978).

B. PROCEDURES; PROOF; REMEDIES

The Equal Employment Opportunity Act of 1972,[1] which extensively amended Title VII of the Civil Rights Act of 1964, is important both for what it did and for what it did not do. Perhaps most significantly, it authorized the Equal Employment Opportunity Commission to bring actions directly against respondents in federal district court when conciliation efforts prove fruitless. Previously, upon the failure of the Commission's conciliation efforts, an aggrieved individual had to pursue the case in the courts on his own. Under the 1972 amendments, the individual complainant still retains the power to sue if he wishes. In addition, the responsibility for bringing actions in cases of a suspected "pattern or practice" of discrimination has been transferred from the Attorney General to EEOC. The Commission was not empowered, however, to issue "cease and desist" orders like the NLRB's.

The Conference Committee removed from the final version of the 1972 Act two restrictive provisions that had been adopted by the House. One would have prevented EEOC from bringing class actions on behalf of groups of complainants. The other would have made EEOC the only federal agency entitled to deal with job discrimination. A complainant is thus left with the option of seeking relief from EEOC, the NLRB, the Office of Federal Contract Compliance Programs under the President's "affirmative action" program, and the courts under the Civil Rights Act of 1866. Furthermore, an individual may utilize a state or local antidiscrimination agency, or a grievance and arbitration procedure under a collective bargaining agreement. Some of the problems arising from the overlapping jurisdiction of this multiplicity of tribunals will be examined in the materials that follow.

In other significant procedural changes made by the 1972 amendments, a complainant's time for filing charges with EEOC was extended from 90 to 180 days following the alleged offense, and the time for filing an individual civil suit after the termination of Commission proceedings was extended from 30 to 90 days. Generally, the courts have avoided highly technical readings of the procedural provisions of Title VII that might bar unwary laypersons from processing their complaints.[2]

---

[1] Pub. L. No. 92-261, 86 Stat. 103. *See generally* Sape & Hart, *Title VII Reconsidered: The Equal Employment Opportunity Act of 1972,* 40 GEO. WASH. L. REV. 824 (1972); Hill, *The Equal Employment Opportunity Acts of 1964 and 1972: A Critical Analysis of the Legislative History and Administration of the Law,* 2 INDUS. REL. L.J. 1 (1977).

[2] *See, e.g.,* Love v. Pullman, 404 U.S. 522 (1972), and cases cited.

The 1972 Act also enlarged the coverage of Title VII to reach smaller employers having at least 15 employees and smaller unions having at least 15 members.

FURNCO CONSTRUCTION CORP. v. WATERS

Supreme Court of the United States
438 U.S. 567, 98 S. Ct. 2943, 57 L. Ed. 2d 957 (1978)

MR. JUSTICE REHNQUIST delivered the opinion of the Court.

Respondents are three black bricklayers who sought employment with petitioner Furnco Construction Corporation. Two of the three were never offered employment. The third was employed only long after he initially applied. Upon adverse findings entered after a bench trial, the District Court for the Northern District of Illinois held that respondents had not proved a claim under either the "disparate treatment" theory of McDonnell Douglas Corp. v. Green, 411 U. S. 792 (1973), or the "disparate impact" theory of Griggs v. Duke Power Co., 401 U. S. 424 (1971). The Court of Appeals for the Seventh Circuit, concluding that under *McDonnell Douglas* respondents had made out a prima facie case which had not been effectively rebutted, reversed the judgment of the District Court. We granted certiorari to consider important questions raised by this case regarding the exact scope of the prima facie case under *McDonnell Douglas* and the nature of the evidence necessary to rebut such a case. . . . Having concluded that the Court of Appeals erred in its treatment of the latter question, we reverse and remand to that court for further proceedings consistent with this opinion.

I. A few facts in this case are not in serious dispute. Petitioner Furnco, an employer within the meaning of §§ 701(b) and (h) of Title VII of the 1964 Civil Rights Act, specializes in refractory installation in steel mills and, more particularly, the rehabilitation or relining of blast furnaces with what is called in the trade "firebrick." Furnco does not, however, maintain a permanent force of bricklayers. Rather, it hires a superintendent for a specific job and then delegates to him the task of securing a competent work force. In August 1971, Furnco contracted with Interlake, Inc., to reline one of its blast furnaces. Joseph Dacies, who had been a job superintendent for Furnco since 1965, was placed in charge of the job and given the attendant hiring responsibilities. He did not accept applications at the jobsite, but instead hired only persons whom he knew to be experienced and competent in this type of work or persons who had been recommended to him as similarly skilled. He hired his first four bricklayers, all of whom were white, on two successive days in August, the 26th and 27th, and two in September, the 7th and 8th. On September 9 he hired the first black bricklayer. By September 13, he had hired eight more bricklayers, one of whom was black; by September 17, seven more had been employed, another of whom was black; and by September 23, 17 more were on the payroll, again with one black included in that number. Between October 12 to 18, he hired six bricklayers, all of whom were black, including respondent Smith, who had worked for Dacies previously and had applied at the jobsite somewhat earlier. Respondents Samuels and Nemhard were not hired, though they were fully qualified and had also attempted to secure employment by appearing at the jobsite gate. Out of the total of 1819 man-days worked on the Interlake job, 242, or 13.3%, were worked by black bricklayers.

Many of the remaining facts found by the District Court and the inferences to be drawn therefrom are in some dispute between the parties, but none was expressly found by the Court of Appeals to be clearly erroneous. The District Court elaborated at some length as to the "critical" necessity of insuring that only experienced and highly qualified fire-bricklayers were employed. Untimely work would result in substantial losses both to Interlake, which was forced to shut down its furnace and lay off employees during the relining job, and to Furnco, which was paid for this work at a fixed price and for a fixed time period. In addition, not only might shoddy work slow this work process down, but it also might necessitate costly future maintenance work with its attendant loss of production and employee layoffs; diminish Furnco's reputation and ability to secure similar work in the future; and perhaps even create serious safety hazards, leading to explosions and the like. . . . These considerations justified Furnco's refusal to engage in on-the-job training or to hire at the gate, a hiring process which would not provide an adequate method of matching qualified applications to job requirements and assuring that the applicants are sufficiently skilled and capable. . . . Furthermore, there was no evidence that these policies and practices were a pretext to exclude black bricklayers or were otherwise illegitimate or had a disproportionate impact, or effect on black bricklayers. . . . From late 1969 through late 1973, 5.7% of the bricklayers in the relevant labor force were minority group members, see 41 CFR § 60-11 *et seq.,* while, as mentioned before, 13.3% of the man-days on Furnco's Interlake job were worked by black bricklayers.

Because of the above considerations and following the established practice in the industry, most of the fire-bricklayers hired by Dacies were persons known by him to be experienced and competent in this type of work. The others were hired after being recommended as skilled in this type of work by his general foreman, an employee (a black), another Furnco superintendent in the area, and Furnco's General Manager John Wright. Wright had not only instructed Dacies to employ, as far as possible, at least 16% black bricklayers, a policy due to Furnco's self-imposed affirmative action plan to insure that black bricklayers were employed by Furnco in Cook County in numbers substantially in excess of their percentage in the local union, but he had also recommended, in an effort to show good faith, that Dacies hire several specific bricklayers, who had previously filed a discrimination suit against Furnco, negotiations for the settlement of which had only recently broken down. . . .

II. A. We agree with the Court of Appeals that the proper approach was the analysis contained in *McDonnell Douglas, supra.*[7] We also think the Court of Appeals was justified in concluding that as a matter of law respondents made out a prima facie case of discrimination under *McDonnell Douglas.* In that case we held that a plaintiff could make out a prima facie claim by showing:

"(i) that he belongs to a racial minority; (ii) that he applied and was qualified for a job for which the employer was seeking applicants; (iii) that, despite his qualifications, he was rejected; and (iv) that, after his rejection, the position remained open and the employer continued to seek applicants from persons of complainant's qualifications." 411 U. S. at 802 (footnote omitted).

This, of course, was not intended to be an inflexible rule, as the Court went on to note that "[t]he facts necessarily will vary in Title VII cases, and the specification . . . of the prima facie proof required from respondent is not necessarily applicable in every respect to differing factual situation." *Id.* at 802 n. 13. See *International Brotherhood of Teamsters v. United States, supra* at 358. But *McDonnell Douglas* did make clear that a Title VII plaintiff carries the initial burden of showing actions taken by the employer from which one can infer, if such actions remain unexplained, that it is more likely than not that such actions were "based on a discriminatory criterion illegal under the Act." *International Brotherhood of Teamsters v. United States, supra* at 358. . . . And here respondents carried that initial burden by proving they were members of a racial minority; they did everything within their power to apply for employment; Furnco has conceded that they were qualified in every respect for the jobs which were about to be open; they were not offered employment, although Smith later was; and the employer continued to seek persons of similar qualifications.

   B. We think the Court of Appeals went awry, however, in apparently equating a prima facie showing under *McDonnell Douglas* with an ultimate finding of fact as to discriminatory refusal to hire under Title VII; the two are quite different and that difference has a direct bearing on the proper resolution of this case. The Court of Appeals, as we read its opinion, thought Furnco's hiring procedures not only must be reasonably related to the achievement of some legitimate purpose, but also must be the method which allows the employer to consider the qualifications of the largest number of minority applicants. We think the imposition of that second requirement simply finds no support either in the nature of the prima facie case or the purpose of Title VII.

   The central focus of the inquiry in a case such as this is always whether

---

[7] This case did not involve employment tests, which we dealt with in *Griggs v. Duke Power Co., supra,* and in *Albemarle Paper Co. v. Moody,* 422 U. S. 405, 412-413 (1975), nor particularized requirements such as the height and weight specifications considered in *Dothard v. Rawlinson,* 433 U. S. 321, 329 (1977), and it was not a "pattern or practice" case like *International Brotherhood of Teamsters v. United States,* 431 U. S. 344, 358 (1977).

the employer is treating "some people less favorably than others because of their race, color, religion, sex, or national origin." *International Brotherhood of Teamsters v. United States, supra* at 335 n. 15. The method suggested in *McDonnell Douglas* for pursuing this inquiry, however, was never intended to be rigid, mechanized, or ritualistic. Rather, it is merely a sensible, orderly way to evaluate the evidence in light of common experience as it bears on the critical question of discrimination. A prima facie case under *McDonnell Douglas* raises an inference of discrimination only because we presume these acts, if otherwise unexplained, are more likely than not based on the consideration of impermissible factors. See *International Brotherhood of Teamsters v. United States, supra* at 358 n. 44. And we are willing to presume this largely because we know from our experience that more often than not people do not act in a totally arbitrary manner, without any underlying reasons, especially in a business setting. Thus, when all legitimate reasons for rejecting an applicant have been eliminated as possible reasons for the employer's actions, it is more likely than not the employer, whom we generally assume acts only with *some* reason, based his decision on an impermissible consideration such as race.

When the prima facie case is understood in the light of the opinion in *McDonnell Douglas,* it is apparent that the burden which shifts to the employer is merely that of proving that he based his employment decision on a legitimate consideration, and not an illegitimate one such as race. To prove that, he need not prove that he pursued the course which would both enable him to achieve his own business goal *and* allow him to consider the *most* employment applications. Title VII forbids him from having as a goal a work force selected by any proscribed discriminatory practice, but it does not impose a duty to adopt a hiring procedure that maximizes hiring of minority employees. To dispel the adverse inference from a prima facie showing under *McDonnell Douglas,* the employer need only "articulate some legitimate nondiscriminatory reason for the employee's rejection." *McDonnell Douglas, supra* at 802.

The dangers of embarking on a course such as that charted by the Court of Appeals here, where the court requires businesses to adopt what it perceives to be the "best" hiring procedures, are nowhere more evident than in the record of this very case. Not only does the record not reveal that the court's suggested hiring procedure would work satisfactorily, but there is nothing in the record to indicate that it would be any less "haphazard, arbitrary, and subjective" than Furnco's method, which the Court of Appeals criticized as deficient for exactly those reasons. Courts are generally less competent than employers to restructure business practices, and unless mandated to do so by Congress they should not attempt it.

This is not to say of course that proof of a justification which is reasonably related to the achievement of some legitimate goal necessarily ends the inquiry. The plaintiff must be given the opportunity to introduce evidence that the proffered justification is merely a pretext for discrimination. And as we noted in *McDonnell Douglas, supra* at 804-805, this evidence might take a variety of forms. But the Court of Appeals, although stating its disagreement with the District Court's conclusion that the employer's hiring practices were a "legitimate, nondiscriminatory reason" for refusing to hire respondents, premised its disagreement on a view which we have discussed and rejected above. It did not conclude that the practices were a pretext for discrimination, but only that different practices would have enabled the employer to at least consider, and perhaps to hire, more minority employees. But courts may not impose such a remedy on an employer at least until a violation of Title VII has been proven, and here none had been under the reasoning of either the District Court or the Court of Appeals.

C. The Court of Appeals was also critical of petitioner's effort to employ statistics in this type of case. While the matter is not free from doubt, it appears the court thought once a *McDonnell Douglas* prima facie showing had been made out, statistics of a racially balanced work force were totally irrelevant to the question of motive.... That would undoubtedly be a correct view of the matter if the *McDonnell Douglas* prima facie showing were the equivalent of an ultimate finding by the trier of fact that the original rejection of the applicant was racially motivated: a racially balanced work force cannot immunize an employer from liability for specific acts of discrimination.... It is clear beyond cavil that the obligation imposed by Title VII is to provide an equal opportunity for *each* applicant regardless of race, without regard to whether members of the applicant's race are already proportionately represented in the work force. See *Griggs v. Duke Power Co., supra* at 430; *McDonald v. Santa Fe Trail Transportation Co.,* 427 U. S. 273, 279 (1976).

A *McDonnell Douglas* prima facie showing is not the equivalent of a factual finding of discrimination, however. Rather, it is simply proof of actions taken by the employer from which we infer discriminatory animus because experience has proved that in the absence of any other explanation it is more likely than not those actions were bottomed on impermissible considerations. When the prima facie showing is understood in this manner, the employer must be allowed some latitude to introduce evidence which bears on his motive. Proof that his work force was racially balanced or that it contained a disproportionately high percentage of minority employees is not wholly irrelevant on the issue of intent when that issue is yet to be decided. We cannot say that such proof would have absolutely no probative value in determining whether the otherwise unexplained rejection of the minority applicants was discriminatorily motivated. Thus, although we agree with the Court of Appeals that in this case such proof neither was nor could have been sufficient to *conclusively* demonstrate that Furnco's actions were not discriminatorily motivated, the District Court was entitled to *consider* the racial mix of the work force when trying to make the determination as to motivation. The Court of Appeals should likewise give similar consideration to the proffered statistical proof in any further proceedings in this case. . . .

MR. JUSTICE MARSHALL, with whom MR. JUSTICE BRENNAN joins, concurring in part and dissenting in part. . . .

The Court of Appeals properly held that respondents had made out a prima facie case of employment discrimination under *McDonnell Douglas.* Once respondents had established their prima facie case, the question for the court was then whether petitioner had carried its burden of proving that respondents were rejected on the basis of legitimate nondiscriminatory considerations. The court, however, failed properly to address that question and instead focused on what other hiring practices petitioner might employ. I therefore agree with the Court that we must remand the case to the Court of Appeals so that it can address, under the appropriate standards, whether petitioner had rebutted respondents' prima facie showing of disparate treatment. I also agree that on remand the Court of Appeals is to address the other theories of liability which respondents have presented. . . .

Where the Title VII claim is that a facially neutral employment practice actually falls more harshly on one racial group, thus having a disparate impact on that group, our cases establish a different way of proving the claim. . . . As set out by the Court in *Griggs v. Duke Power Co., supra,* to establish a prima facie case on a disparate impact claim, a plaintiff need not show that the employer had a discriminatory intent but need only demonstrate that a particular practice in actuality "operates to exclude Negroes." 401 U. S. at 431.

Once the plaintiff has established the disparate impact of the practice, the burden shifts to the employer to show that the practice has "a manifest relationship to the employment in question." *Id.* at 432. The "touchstone is business necessity," *id.* at 431, and the practice "must be shown to be necessary to safe and efficient job performance to survive a Title VII challenge." Dothard v. Rawlinson, 433 U. S. at 332 n. 14. Under this principle, a practice of limiting jobs to those with prior experience working in an industry or for a particular person, or to those who hear about jobs by word of mouth would be invalid if the practice in actuality impacts more harshly on a group protected under Title VII, unless the practice can be justified by business necessity.

There is nothing in today's opinion that is inconsistent with this approach or with our prior decisions. I must dissent, however, from the Court's apparent decision . . . to foreclose on remand further litigation on the *Griggs* question of whether petitioner's hiring practices had a disparate impact. Respondents claim that petitioner's practice of hiring from a list of those who had previously worked for the foreman foreclosed Negroes from consideration for the vast majority of jobs. Although the foreman also hired a considerable number of Negroes through other methods, respondents assert that the use of other methods to augment the representation of Negroes in the work force does not answer whether the primary hiring practice is discriminatory.

It is clear that an employer cannot be relieved of responsibility for past discriminatory practices merely by undertaking affirmative action to obtain proportional representation in his work force. As the Court said in *Teamsters,* and reaffirms today, a "company's later changes in its hiring and promotion policies could be of little comfort to the victims of the earlier . . . discrimination, and could not erase its previous illegal conduct or its obligation to afford relief to those who suffered because of it." *Teamsters,* 431 U. S. at 341-342. . . . Therefore, it is at least an open question whether the hiring of workers primarily from a list of past employees would, under *Griggs,* violate Title VII where the list contains no Negroes but the company uses additional methods of hiring to increase the numbers of Negroes hired.*

The Court today apparently assumes that the Court of Appeals affirmed the District Court's findings that petitioner's hiring practice had no disparate impact. I cannot agree with that assumption. Because the Court of Appeals disposed of this case under the *McDonnell Douglas* analysis, it had no occasion to address those findings of the District Court pertaining to disparate impact. Although the Court of Appeals did discuss *Griggs* in its opinion, 551 F.2d 1085, 1089-1090, as I read that discussion the Court was merely rejecting petitioner's argument that it could defeat respondents' *McDonnell Douglas* claim by showing that the work force had a large percentage of Negro members. I express no view on the issue of whether respondents' claim should prevail on the facts presented here since that question is not presently before us, but I believe that respondents' opportunity to make their claim should not be foreclosed by this Court.

NOTES

1. In a brief per curiam opinion in Trustees of Keene State College v. Sweeney, 99 S.Ct. 295 (U.S. 1978), a majority of the Supreme Court interpreted *McDonnell Douglas* and *Furnco* to mean that after a plaintiff establishes a prima facie case of discrimination, a defendant need only "articulate some legitimate, nondiscriminatory reason" for its action, and need not "prove absence of discriminatory motive." Four justices dissented to the drawing of this distinction.

2. Despite the Supreme Court's three-step analysis of the order of proof in *McDonnell Douglas* and *Furnco* — plaintiff makes prima facie case; defendant shows "justification"; plaintiff shows "pretext" — the lower federal courts have concluded that a "trifurcated" trial was not contemplated. A plaintiff must make a complete presentation in the case in chief or risk dismissal. *See, e.g.,* Sime v. Trustees of California State University & Colleges, 526 F. 2d 1112 (9th Cir. 1975); Peters v. Jefferson Chem. Co., 516 F. 2d 447 (5th Cir. 1975).

---

* Of course, the Court leaves open on remand the issue of whether Furnco's use of the list violated Title VII under a disparate treatment theory. . . .

3. There are only two jurisdictional requirements for a suit by an aggrieved party under Title VII: (1) he (or she) must have filed a timely charge with the Equal Employment Opportunity Commission; and (2) he must sue within the prescribed statutory period (now 90 days) following receipt of notice from EEOC of its inability to secure voluntary compliance. Dent v. St. Louis-San Francisco Ry., 406 F.2d 399 (5th Cir. 1969); Goodman v. City Products Corp., 425 F.2d 702 (6th Cir. 1970); Choate v. Caterpillar Tractor Co., 402 F.2d 357 (7th Cir. 1968). In IUE Local 790 v. Robbins & Meyers, Inc., 429 U.S. 229 (1976), the Supreme Court held that filing a contract grievance against an employer for alleged discrimination does not toll the statute of limitations on filing an EEOC charge under Title VII. The Supreme Court has also held (three justices dissenting) that the timely filing of employment discrimination charges with the EEOC pursuant to § 706 of the Civil Rights Act of 1964 does not toll the running of the limitations period applicable to an action based on the same facts brought under the Civil Rights Act of 1866 (42 U.S.C. § 1981). Johnson v. Railway Express Agency, 421 U.S. 454 (1975). The actions are separate, and an individual need not pursue his remedies under Title VII before instituting suit under 42 U.S.C. § 1981. Long v. Ford Motor Co., 496 F.2d 500 (6th Cir. 1974). Title VII actions brought by EEOC are not subject to any statute of limitations (laches presumably applies). Occidental Life Ins. Co. v. EEOC, 432 U.S. 355 (1977). State limitations govern § 1981 actions.

4. The EEOC can sue for any discrimination stated in a charge or discovered in the course of reasonable investigation of a prior charge as long as the new charge of discrimination is included in the reasonable cause determination and the conciliation process. EEOC v. General Elec. Co., 532 F.2d 359 (4th Cir. 1976). *Compare* EEOC v. Bailey Co., 563 F.2d 439 (6th Cir. 1977), where the court ruled that the EEOC may not sue an employer for religious discrimination that it allegedly uncovered in its investigation of a charge of racial and sex discrimination, since the allegations of religious discrimination exceeded the scope of the investigation reasonably expected to grow out of the prior charge.

There is a conflict among the circuits as to whether EEOC may file an independent action where there is a private suit pending on the same charge, or whether the Commission is limited to permissive intervention even though it seeks litigation on a broader basis. *Compare* EEOC v. North Hills Passavant Hospital, 544 F. 2d 664 (3d Cir. 1976), *with* EEOC v. Missouri Pac. R.R., 493 F. 2d 71 (8th Cir. 1974), *and* EEOC v. Continental Oil Co., 548 F. 2d 884 (10th Cir. 1977).

5. The fourth requirement in *McDonnell* — "after rejection, the position remained open and the employer continued to seek applicants from persons of the complainant's qualifications" — will be ignored in a situation where employees are chosen from a "pool." King v. New Hampshire Dep't of Resources & Econ. Develop., 562 F.2d 80 (1st Cir. 1977).

6. The Supreme Court's views on the use of statistics in making out a prima facie case of discrimination are considerably amplified in Hazelwood School Dist. v. United States, 433 U.S. 299, 311 n. 17 (1977), where it was suggested that "a fluctuation of more than two or three standard deviations would undercut the hypothesis that decisions were being made randomly with respect to race." *See generally* Rosenblum, *The Use of Labor Statistics and Analysis in Title VII Cases: Rios, Chicago and Beyond,* 1 IND. REL. L.J. 685 (1977); Note, *Beyond the Prima Facie Case in Employment Discrimination Law: Statistical Proof and Rebuttal,* 89 HARV. L. REV. 387 (1975); Note, *Employment Discrimination: Statistics and Preferences under Title VII,* 59 VA. L. REV. 463 (1973). *See also* Oaxaca, *Theory and Measurement in the Economics of Discrimination,* in INDUSTRIAL RELATIONS RESEARCH ASS'N, EQUAL RIGHTS AND INDUSTRIAL RELATIONS 1 (1977). For an imaginative overview of *McDonnell, Furnco,* and their offspring, *see* Blumrosen, *Strangers No More: All Workers Are Entitled to "Just Cause" Protection Under Title VII,* 2 IND. REL. L.J. 519 (1978).

ALBEMARLE PAPER CO. v. MOODY

Supreme Court of the United States
422 U.S. 405, 95 S. Ct. 2362, 45 L. Ed. 2d 280 (1975)

MR. JUSTICE STEWART delivered the opinion of the Court.

These consolidated cases raise two important questions under Title VII of the Civil Rights Act of 1964, . . . as amended by the Equal Employment Opportunity Act of 1972. . . . First: When employees or applicants for employment have lost the opportunity to earn wages because an employer has engaged in an unlawful discriminatory employment practice, what standards should a federal district court follow in deciding whether to award or deny backpay? Second: What must an employer show to establish that pre-employment tests racially discriminatory in effect, though not in intent, are sufficiently "job related" to survive challenge under Title VII?

I. The respondents — plaintiffs in the District Court — are a certified class of present and former Negro employees at a paper mill in Roanoke Rapids, North Carolina; the petitioners — defendants in the District Court — are the plant's owner, the Albemarle Paper Company, and the plant employees' labor union, Halifax Local No. 425. In August of 1966, after filing a complaint with the Equal Employment Opportunity Commission (EEOC), and receiving notice of their right to sue, the respondents brought a class action in the United States District Court for the Eastern District of North Carolina, asking permanent injunctive relief against "any policy, practice, custom, or usage" at the plant that violated Title VII. The respondents assured the court that the suit involved no claim for any monetary awards on a class basis, but in June of 1970, after several years of discovery, the respondents moved to add a class demand for backpay. The court ruled that this issue would be considered at trial.

At the trial, in July and August of 1971, the major issues were the plant's seniority system, its program of employment testing, and the question of backpay. In its opinion of November 9, 1971, the court found that the petitioners had "strictly segregated" the plant's departmental "lines of progression" prior to January 1, 1964, reserving the higher paying and more skilled lines for whites. . . . The "racial identifiability" of whole lines of progression persisted until 1968, when the lines were reorganized under a new collective bargaining agreement. The court found, however, that this reorganization left Negro employees "locked in the lower paying job classifications." . . . The formerly "Negro" lines of progression had been merely tacked on to the bottom of the formerly "white" lines, and promotions, demotions, and layoffs continued to be governed — where skills were "relatively equal" — by a system of "job seniority." Because of the plant's previous history of overt segregation, only whites had seniority in the higher job categories. Accordingly, the court ordered the petitioners to implement a system of "plantwide" seniority.

The court refused, however, to award backpay to the plaintiff class for losses suffered under the "job seniority" program. The court explained:

> "In the instant case there was no evidence of bad faith non-compliance with the Act. . . .
> "In addition, an award of back pay is an equitable remedy. . . . The plaintiff's claim for back pay was filed nearly five years after the institution of this action. . . ."

The court also refused to enjoin or limit Albemarle's testing program. Albemarle had required applicants for employment in the skilled lines of progression to have a high school diploma and to pass two tests, the Revised Beta Examination, allegedly a measure of nonverbal intelligence, and the Wonderlic Test (available in alternate Forms A and B), allegedly a measure of verbal facility. . . . [T]he court concluded:

> "The personnel tests administered at the plant have undergone validation studies and have been proven to be job related. . . . However, the high school education requirement used in conjunction with the testing requirement is unlawful in that the personnel tests alone are adequate to measure the mental ability and reading skills required for job classifications. . . ."

A divided Court of Appeals for the Fourth Circuit reversed the judgment of the District Court, ruling that backpay should have been awarded and that use of the tests should have been enjoined, 474 F. 2d 134. . . .

II. Whether a particular member of the plaintiff class should have been awarded any backpay and, if so, how much, are questions not involved in this review. The equities of individual cases were never reached. Though at least some of the members of the plaintiff class obviously suffered a loss of wage opportunities on account of Albemarle's unlawfully discriminatory system of job seniority, the District Court decided that *no* backpay should be awarded to *anyone* in the class. . . . Relying directly on

Newman v. Piggie Park Enterprises, 390 U. S. 400, the Court of Appeals reversed, holding that backpay could be denied only in "special circumstances." The petitioners argue that the Court of Appeals was in error — that a district court has virtually unfettered discretion to award or deny backpay, and that there was no abuse of that discretion in this case.[8]

Piggie Park Enterprises, supra, is not directly in point. The Court held there that attorneys' fees should "ordinarily" be awarded — *i.e.,* in all but "special circumstances" — to plaintiffs successful in obtaining injunctions against discrimination in public accommodations, under Title II of the Civil Rights Act of 1964. . . . There is of course an equally strong public interest in having injunctive actions brought under Title VII, to eradicate discriminatory employment practices. But this interest can be vindicated by applying the *Piggie Park* standard to the *attorneys' fees* provision of Title VII, 42 U. S. C. § 2000e-5(k), see Northcross v. Board of Education, 412 U. S. 427, 428. For guidance as to the granting and denial of *backpay,* one must, therefore, look elsewhere.

The petitioners contend that the statutory scheme provides no guidance, beyond indicating that backpay awards are within the District Court's discretion. We disagree. It is true that backpay is not an automatic or mandatory remedy; like all other remedies under the Act, it is one which the courts "may" invoke. The scheme implicitly recognizes that there may be cases calling for one remedy but not another, and — owing to the structure of the federal judiciary — these choices are of course left in the first instance to the district courts. But such discretionary choices are not left to a court's "inclination, but to its judgment; and its judgment is to be guided by sound legal principles." United States v. Burr, 25 Fed. Cas. 30, 35 (Marshall, C. J.). . . .

The District Court's decision must therefore be measured against the purposes which inform Title VII. As the Court observed in Griggs v. Duke Power Co., *supra,* 401 U. S. at 429-430, the primary objective was a prophylactic one. . . . Backpay has an obvious connection with this purpose. If employers faced only the prospect of an injunctive order, they would have little incentive to shun practices of dubious legality. It is the reasonably certain prospect of a backpay award that "provide[s] the spur or catalyst which causes employers and unions to self-examine and to self-evaluate their employment practices and to endeavor to eliminate, so far as possible, the last vestiges of an unfortunate and ignominious page in this country's history." United States v. N. L. Industries, 479 F.2d 354, 379.

---

[8] The petitioners also contend that no backpay can be awarded to those unnamed parties in the plaintiff class who have not themselves filed charges with the EEOC. We reject this contention. The courts of appeals that have confronted the issue are unanimous in recognizing that backpay may be awarded on a class basis under Title VII without exhaustion of administrative procedures by the unnamed class members. . . . The Congress plainly ratified this construction of the Act in the course of enacting the Equal Employment Opportunity Act of 1972. . . .

It is also the purpose of Title VII to make persons whole for injuries suffered on account of unlawful employment discrimination. This is shown by the very fact that Congress took care to arm the courts with full equitable powers. . . . Title VII deals with legal injuries of an economic character occasioned by racial or other anti-minority discrimination. The terms "complete justice" and "necessary relief" have acquired a clear meaning in such circumstances. Where racial discrimination is concerned, "the [district] court has not merely the power but the duty to render a decree which will so far as possible eliminate the discriminatory effects of the past as well as bar like discrimination in the future." Louisiana v. United States, 380 U. S. 145, 154. And where a legal injury is of an economic character,

> "[t]he general rule is, that when a wrong has been done, and the law gives a remedy, the compensation shall be equal to the injury. The latter is the standard by which the former is to be measured. The injured party is to be placed as near as may be, in the situation he would have occupied if the wrong had not been committed." Wicker v. Hoppock, 6 Wall. 94, at 99.

The "make whole" purpose of Title VII is made evident by the legislative history. The backpay provision was expressly modeled on the backpay provision of the National Labor Relations Act. . . . We may assume that Congress was aware that the Board, since its inception, has awarded backpay as a matter of course — not randomly or in the exercise of a standardless discretion, and not merely where employer violations are peculiarly deliberate, egregious or inexcusable. Furthermore, in passing the Equal Employment Opportunity Act of 1972, Congress considered several bills to limit the judicial power to award backpay. These limiting efforts were rejected, and the backpay provision was re-enacted substantially in its original form. . . . As this makes clear, Congress' purpose in vesting a variety of "discretionary" powers in the courts was not to limit appellate review of trial courts, or to invite inconsistency and caprice, but rather to make possible the "fashion[ing] [of] the most complete relief possible."

It follows that, given a finding of unlawful discrimination, backpay should be denied only for reasons which, if applied generally, would not frustrate the central statutory purposes of eradicating discrimination throughout the economy and making persons whole for injuries suffered through past discrimination. The courts of appeals must maintain a consistent and principled application of the backpay provision, consonant with the twin statutory objectives, while at the same time recognizing that the trial court will often have the keener appreciation of those facts and circumstances peculiar to particular cases.

The District Court's stated grounds for denying backpay in this case must be tested against these standards. The first ground was that Albemarle's breach of Title VII had not been in "bad faith." This is not a sufficient reason for denying backpay. Where an employer *has* shown bad faith — by maintaining a practice which he knew to be illegal or of highly questionable legality — he can make no claims whatsoever on the

Chancellor's conscience. But, under Title VII, the mere absence of bad faith simply opens the door to equity; it does not depress the scales in the employer's favor. If backpay were awardable only upon a showing of bad faith, the remedy would become a punishment for moral turpitude, rather than a compensation for workers' injuries. This would read the "make whole" purpose right out of Title VII, for a worker's injury is not less real simply because his employer did not inflict it in "bad faith." Title VII is not concerned with the employer's "good intent or absence of discriminatory intent" for "Congress directed the thrust of the Act to the *consequences* of employment practices, not simply the motivation." Griggs v. Duke Power Co., *supra,* 401 U. S. at 432. . . . To condition the awarding of backpay on a showing of "bad faith" would be to open an enormous chasm between injunctive and backpay relief under Title VII. There is nothing on the face of the statute or in its legislative history that justifies the creation of drastic and categorical distinctions between those two remedies.

The District Court also grounded its denial of backpay on the fact that the respondents initially disclaimed any interest in backpay, first asserting their claim five years after the complaint was filed. The court concluded that the petitioners had been "prejudiced" by this conduct. . . .

It is true that Title VII contains no legal bar to raising backpay claims after the complaint for injunctive relief has been filed, or indeed after a trial on that complaint has been had. Furthermore, Fed. Rule Civ. Proc. 54(c) directs that

> "every final judgment shall grant the relief to which the party in whose favor it is rendered is entitled, even if the party has not demanded such relief in his pleadings."

But a party may not be "entitled" to relief if its conduct of the cause has improperly and substantially prejudiced the other party. The respondents here were not merely tardy, but also inconsistent, in demanding backpay. To deny backpay because a *particular* cause has been prosecuted in an eccentric fashion, prejudicial to the other party, does not offend the broad purposes of Title VII. This is not to say, however, that the District Court's ruling was necessarily correct. Whether the petitioners were in fact prejudiced, and whether the respondents' trial conduct was excusable, are questions that will be open to review by the Court of Appeals, if the District Court, on remand, decides again to decline to make any award of backpay. But the standard of review will be the familiar one of whether the District Court was "clearly erroneous" in its factual findings and whether it "abused" its traditional discretion to locate "a just result" in light of the circumstances peculiar to the case, Lagnes v. Green, 282 U. S. 531, 541. On these issues of procedural regularity and prejudice, the "broad aims of Title VII" provide no ready solution.

III. In Griggs v. Duke Power Co., 401 U. S. 424, this Court unanimously held that Title VII forbids the use of employment tests that are discriminatory in effect unless the employer meets "the burden of showing that any given requirement [has] . . . a manifest relation to the employment in question." *Id.* at 432. This burden arises, of course, only after the complaining party or class has made out a prima facie case of discrimination — has shown that the tests in question select applicants for hire or promotion in a racial pattern significantly different from that of the pool of applicants. See McDonnell Douglas Corp. v. Green, 411 U. S. 792, 802. If an employer does then meet the burden of proving that its tests are "job related," it remains open to the complaining party to show that other tests or selection devices, without a similarly undesirable racial effect, would also serve the employer's legitimate interest in "efficient and trustworthy workmanship." *Id.* at 801. Such a showing would be evidence that the employer was using its tests merely as a "pretext" for discrimination. *Id.* at 804-805. In the present case, however, we are concerned only with the question whether Albemarle has shown its tests to be job related. . . .

Like the employer in *Griggs,* Albemarle uses two general ability tests, the Beta Examination, to test nonverbal intelligence, and the Wonderlic Test (Forms A and B), the purported measure of general verbal facility which was also involved in the *Griggs* case. Applicants for hire into various skilled lines of progression at the plant are required to score 100 on Beta Exam and 18 on one of the Wonderlic Test's two, alternate forms.

The question of job relatedness must be viewed in the context of the plant's operation and the history of the testing program. The plant, which now employs about 650 persons, converts raw wood into paper products. It is organized into a number of functional departments, each with one or more distinct lines of progression, the theory being that workers can move up the line as they acquire the necessary skills. The number and structure of the lines has varied greatly over time. For many years, certain lines were themselves more skilled and paid higher wages than others, and until 1964 these skilled lines were expressly reserved for white workers. In 1968, many of the unskilled "Negro" lines were "end-tailed" on to skilled "white" lines, but it apparently remains true that at least the top jobs in certain lines require greater skills than the top jobs in other lines. In this sense, at least, it is still possible to speak of relatively skilled and relatively unskilled lines.

In the 1950's while the plant was being modernized with new and more sophisticated equipment, the company introduced a high school diploma requirement for entry into the skilled lines. Though the company soon concluded that this requirement did not improve the quality of the labor force, the requirement was continued until the District Court enjoined its use. In the late 1950's, the company began using the Beta Examination and the Bennett Mechanical Comprehension Test (also involved in the *Griggs* case) to screen applicants for entry into the skilled lines. The Bennett test was dropped several years later, but use of the Beta test continued.

The company added the Wonderlic Tests in 1963, for the skilled lines, on the theory that a certain verbal intelligence was called for by the increasing sophistication of the plant's operations. The company made no attempt to validate the test for job relatedness, and simply adopted the national "norm" score of 18 as a cut-off point for new job applicants. After 1964, when it discontinued overt segregation of the lines of progression, the company allowed Negro workers to transfer to the skilled lines if they could pass the Beta and Wonderlic Tests, but few succeeded in doing so. Incumbents in the skilled lines, some of whom had been hired before adoption of the tests, were not required to pass them to retain their jobs or their promotion rights. The record shows that a number of white incumbents in high ranking jobs groups could not pass the tests.

Because departmental reorganization continued up to the point of trial, and has indeed continued since that point, the details of the testing program are less than clear from the record. The District Court found that, since 1963, the Beta and Wonderlic tests have been used in 13 lines of progression, within eight departments. Albemarle contends that at present the tests are used in only eight lines of progression, within four departments.

Four months before this case went to trial, Albemarle engaged an expert in industrial psychology to "validate" the job relatedness of its testing program. He spent a half day at the plant and devised a "concurrent validation" study, which was conducted by plant officials, without his supervision. The expert then subjected the results to statistical analysis. The study dealt with 10 job groupings, selected from near the top of nine of the lines of progression. Jobs were grouped together solely by their proximity in the line of progression; no attempt was made to analyze jobs in terms of the particular skills they might require. All, or nearly all, employees in the selected groups participated in the study — 105 employees in all, but only four Negroes. Within each job grouping, the study compared the test scores of each employee with an independent "ranking" of the employee, relative to each of his coworkers, made by two of the employee's supervisors. . . .

For each job grouping, the expert computed the "Phi coefficient" of statistical correlation between the test scores and an average of the two supervisorial rankings. Consonant with professional conventions, the expert regarded as "statistically significant" any correlation that could have occurred by chance only five times, or less, in 100 trials. On the basis of these results, the District Court found that "[t]he personnel tests administered at the plant have undergone validation studies and have been proven to be job related." Like the Court of Appeals, we are constrained to disagree.

The EEOC has issued "Guidelines" for employers seeking to determine, through professional validation studies, whether their employment tests are job related. 29 CFR Part 1607 (1974). These Guidelines draw upon and make reference to professional standards of test validation established by the American Psychological Association. The EEOC Guidelines are not administrative "regulations" promulgated pursuant to formal procedures established by the Congress. But, as this Court has heretofore noted, they do constitute "[t]he administrative interpretation of the Act by the enforcing agency," and consequently they are "entitled to great deference." Griggs v. Duke Power Co., *supra,* 401 U.S. at 433-434. . . .

The message of these Guidelines is the same as that of the *Griggs* case — that discriminatory tests are impermissible unless shown, by professionally acceptable methods, to be "predictive of or significantly correlated with important elements of work behavior which comprise or are relevant to the job or jobs for which candidates are being evaluated." 29 CFR § 1607.4(c).

Measured against the Guidelines, Albemarle's validation study is materially defective in several respects:

(1) Even if it had been otherwise adequate, the study would not have "validated" the Beta and Wonderlic test battery for all of the skilled lines of progression for which the two tests are, apparently, now required. The study showed significant correlations for the Beta Exam in only three of the eight lines. Though the Wonderlic Test's Form A and Form B are in theory identical and interchangeable measures of verbal facility, significant correlations for one Form but not for the other were obtained in four job groupings. In two job groupings neither Form showed a significant correlation. Within some of the lines of progression, one Form was found acceptable for some job groupings but not for others. Even if the study were otherwise reliable, this odd patchwork of results would not entitle Albemarle to impose its testing program under the Guidelines. A test may be used in jobs other than those for which it has been professionally validated only if there are "no significant differences" between the studied and unstudied jobs. 29 CFR § 1607.4(c)(2). The study in this case involved no analysis of the attributes of, or the particular skills needed in, the studied job groups. There is accordingly no basis for concluding that "no significant differences" exist among the lines of progression, or among distinct job groupings within the studied lines of progression. Indeed, the study's checkered results appear to compel the opposite conclusion.

(2) The study compared test scores with subjective supervisorial rankings. While they allow the use of supervisorial rankings in test validation, the Guidelines quite plainly contemplate that the rankings will be elicited with far more care than was demonstrated here. Albemarle's supervisors were asked to rank employees by a "standard" that was extremely vague and fatally open to divergent interpretations. Each "job grouping" contained a number of different jobs, and the supervisors were asked, in each grouping, to

> "determine which ones [employees] they felt irrespective of the job that they were actually doing, but in their respective jobs, did a better job than the person they were rating against. . . ."

There is no way of knowing precisely what criteria of job performance the supervisors were considering, whether each of the supervisors was considering the same criteria — or whether, indeed, any of the supervisors actually applied a focused and stable body of criteria of any kind. There is, in short, simply no way to determine whether the criteria *actually* considered were sufficiently related to the Company's legitimate interest in job-specific ability to justify a testing system with a racially discriminatory impact.

(3) The company's study focused, in most cases, on job groups near the top of the various lines of progression. In *Griggs v. Duke Power Co., supra,* the Court left open "the question whether testing requirements that take into account capability for the next succeeding position or related future promotion might be utilized upon a showing that such long-range requirements fulfill a genuine business need." 401 U.S. at 432. The Guidelines take a sensible approach to this issue, and we now endorse it:

> "If job progression structures and seniority provisions are so established that new employees will probably, within a reasonable period of time and in a great majority of cases, progress to a higher level, it may be considered that candidates are being evaluated for jobs at that higher level. However, where job progression is not so nearly automatic, or the time span is such that higher level jobs or employees' potential may be expected to change in significant ways, it shall be considered that candidates are being evaluated for a job at or near the entry level." 29 CFR § 1607.4(c)(1).

The fact that the best of those employees working near the top of a line of progression score well on a test does not necessarily mean that that test, or some particular cutoff score on the test, is a permissible measure of the minimal qualifications of new workers, entering lower level jobs. In drawing any such conclusion, detailed consideration must be given to the normal speed of promotion, to the efficacy of on-the-job training in the scheme of promotion, and to the possible use of testing as a promotion device, rather than as a screen for entry into low-level jobs. The District Court made no findings on these issues. The issues take on special importance in a case, such as this one, where incumbent employees are permitted to work at even high-level jobs without passing the company's test battery. See 29 CFR § 1607.11.

(4) Albemarle's validation study dealt only with job-experienced, white workers; but the tests themselves are given to new job applicants, who are younger, largely inexperienced, and in many instances nonwhite. The Standards of the American Psychological Association state that it is "essential" that

> "[t]he validity of a test should be determined on subjects who are at the age or in the same educational or vocational situation as the persons for whom the test is recommended in practice."

The EEOC Guidelines likewise provide that "[d]ata must be generated and results separately reported for minority or nonminority groups wherever technically feasible." 29 CFR § 1607.5(b)(5). In the present case, such "differential validation" as to racial groups was very likely not "feasible," because years of discrimination at the plant have insured that nearly all of the upper level employees are white. But there has been no clear showing that differential validation was not feasible for lower-level jobs. More importantly, the Guidelines provide:

"If it is not technically feasible to include minority employees in validation studies conducted on the present work force, the conduct of a validation study without minority candidates does not relieve any person of his subsequent obligation for validation when inclusion of minority candidates becomes technically feasible." 29 CFR § 1607.5(b)(1). . . . "[E]vidence of satisfactory validity based on other groups will be regarded as only provisional compliance with the guidelines pending separate validation of the test for the minority groups in question." 29 CFR § 1607.5(b)(5).

For all these reasons, we agree with the Court of Appeals that the District Court erred in concluding that Albemarle had proved the job relatedness of its testing program and that the respondents were consequently not entitled to equitable relief. The outright reversal by the Court of Appeals implied that an injunction should immediately issue against all use of testing at the plant. Because of the particular circumstances of this case, however, it appears that the more prudent course is to leave to the District Court the precise fashioning of the necessary relief in the first instance. During the appellate stages of this litigation, the plant has apparently been amending its departmental organization and the use made of its tests. The appropriate standard of proof for job relatedness has not been clarified until today. Similarly, the respondents have not until today been specifically apprised of their opportunity to present evidence that even validated tests might be a "pretext" for discrimination in light of alternative selection procedures available to the company. We also note that the Guidelines authorize provisional use of tests, pending new validation efforts, in certain very limited circumstances. 29 CFR § 1607.9. Whether such circumstances now obtain is a matter best decided, in the first instance, by the District Court. . . .

Accordingly, the judgment is vacated, and these cases are remanded to the District Court for proceedings consistent with this opinion.

MR. JUSTICE POWELL did not participate in the consideration or decision of these cases.

[The concurring opinions of MR. JUSTICE MARSHALL and MR. JUSTICE REHNQUIST and the partially concurring, partially dissenting opinions of MR. CHIEF JUSTICE BURGER and MR. JUSTICE BLACKMUN are omitted.]

NOTES

1. The court in Patterson v. American Tobacco Co., 535 F.2d 257 (4th Cir. 1976), cert. denied, 429 U.S. 920 (1976), said that in order to carry out the policies of the Albemarle case:

back pay must be allowed an employee from the time he is unlawfully denied a promotion, subject to the applicable statute of limitations, until he actually receives it. Some employees who have been victims of discrimination will be unable to move immediately into jobs to which their seniority and ability entitle them. The back pay award should be fashioned to compensate them until they can obtain a job commensurate with their status. This may be accomplished by allowing back pay for a period commencing at the time an employee was unlawfully denied a position until the date of judgment, subject to the applicable statute of limitations. This compensation should be supplemented by an award equal to the estimated present value of lost earnings that are reasonably likely to occur between the date of judgment and the time when the employee can assume his new position. . . . Alternatively, the court may exercise continuing jurisdiction over the case and make periodic back pay awards until the workers are promoted to the jobs their seniority and qualifications merit.

See also Note, *Front-Pay — Prophylactic Relief Under Title VII,* 26 VAND. L. REV. 211 (1976).

2. Monetary relief, including back pay and attorneys' fees, is an equitable remedy under Title VII, not subject to jury trial. Compensatory and punitive damages are not available under Title VII; they may be available under 42 U.S.C. § 1981, but apparently require a jury trial. EEOC v. Detroit Edison Co., 515 F. 2d 301, 308-10 (6th Cir. 1975); *see* Johnson v. Railway Express Agency, Inc., 421 U.S. 454, 458 (1978). *But cf.* Claiborne v. Illinois Central R.R., 583 F. 2d 143 (5th Cir. 1978)(punitive damages awarded in combined Title VII and § 1981 action, without mention of jury). *See also* Pettway v. American Cast Iron Pipe Co., 494 F. 2d 211 (5th Cir. 1974).

3. In Christianburg Garment Co. v. EEOC, 434 U.S. 412 (1978), the Supreme Court stated that § 706(k) of the 1964 Civil Rights Act, which authorizes the award of attorneys' fees to the prevailing party in a Title VII action, gives a federal district court discretion to award such fees to a prevailing defendant upon a finding that the plaintiff's action was frivolous, unreasonable, or without foundation, even though not brought in subjective bad faith. The general standard for assessing attorneys' fees against EEOC when it loses a Title VII action is not different from the standard applicable to a losing private party, although a court may consider distinctions between EEOC and a private party in determining the reasonableness of the litigation efforts.

4. In East Texas Motor Freight System v. Rodriguez, 431 U.S. 395 (1977), the Supreme Court held it error to certify as a class action a suit brought by three city truck drivers who alleged discrimination by their employer and the Teamsters Union in prohibiting transfer to "over-the-road" (line) jobs, because it was evident that the three named plaintiffs lacked the qualifications to be hired as line drivers and hence were not members of the class they purported to represent. Furthermore, each named plaintiff stipulated that he had not been discriminated against with respect to his initial hire. A black female has also been held an inadequate representative of all blacks (including black males) and all females (including white females) alleging employment discrimination.

Droughn v. FMC Corp., 74 F.R.D. 639 (E.D. Pa. 1977); Colston v. Maryland Cup Co., 18 FEP Cas. 83 (D. Md. 1978). The potentially sweeping impact of a properly grounded class action in a Title VII suit is emphasized, however, by *Albemarle's* footnote 8, indicating that relief may reach unnamed parties who have not personally filed charges with the EEOC.

5. Could an employer lawfully discharge two employees in a unionized firm who resort to the "self help" remedy of picketing to get the employer to hire black workers, without first trying to act through their established collective bargaining representative? What should be the proper accommodation of Title VII rights and NLRA § 7 and § 9 rights in such a situation? *See* NLRB v. Tanner Motor Livery, Ltd., 419 F.2d 216 (9th Cir.1969), *supra* at 142-43. *Cf.* Emporium Capwell Co. v. Western Addition Community Organization, 420 U.S. 50 (1975), *supra* at 489. *See also* Lopatka, *Protection Under the National Labor Relations Act and Title VII of the Civil Rights Act for Employees Who Protest Discrimination in Private Employment,* 50 N.Y.U.L. REV. 1179 (1975). The effect of a union's racial or sexual discrimination upon an employer's duty to bargain was considered, with contrasting results, in NLRB v. Mansion House Corp., 473 F.2d 471 (8th Cir. 1973), *supra* at 229 and in Bell & Howell Co., 230 N.L.R.B. No. 57, 95 L.R.R.M. 1333 (1977), *enforced,* 100 L.R.R.M. 2192 (D.C. Cir. 1979).

6. *See generally* Isaacson & Zifchak, Sape, Barnard, Levitt, Elisburg, *The Second Decade of Title VII: Refinement of the Remedies,* 16 WILLIAM & MARY L. REV. 439, 481, 507, 529, 555 (1975)(five separate papers); Johnson, *Albemarle Paper Company v. Moody: The Aftermath of Griggs and the Death of Employee Testing,* 27 HASTINGS L.J. 1239 (1976).

FRANKS v. BOWMAN TRANSPORTATION CO., INC.

Supreme Court of the United States
424 U.S. 747, 96 S. Ct. 1251, 47 L. Ed. 2d 444 (1976)

MR. JUSTICE BRENNAN delivered the opinion of the Court.

This case presents the question whether identifiable applicants who were denied employment because of race after the effective date and in violation of Title VII of the Civil Rights Act of 1964. . . . may be awarded seniority status retroactive to the dates of their employment applications.[1]

Petitioner Franks brought this class action in the United States District Court for the Northern District of Georgia against his former employer, respondent Bowman Transportation Company, and his unions, the International Union of District 50, Allied and Technical Workers of the United States and Canada and its local, No. 13600, alleging various racially discriminatory employment practices in violation of Title VII. Petitioner Lee intervened on behalf of himself and others similarly situated alleging racially discriminatory hiring and discharge policies

---

[1] Petitioners also alleged an alternative claim for relief for violations of 42 U. S. C. § 1891. In view of our decision we have no occasion to address that claim.

limited to Bowman's employment of over-the-road (OTR) truck drivers. Following trial, the District Court found Bowman had engaged in a pattern of racial discrimination in various company policies, including the hiring, transfer, and discharge of employees, and found further that the discriminatory practices were perpetrated in Bowman's collective-bargaining agreement with the unions. The District Court certified the action as a proper class action under Fed. Rule Civ. Proc. 23(b)(2) and, of import to the issues before this Court, found that petitioner Lee represented all black applicants who sought to be hired or to transfer to OTR driving positions prior to January 1, 1972. In its final order and decree, the District Court subdivided the class represented by petitioner Lee into a class of black nonemployee applicants for OTR positions prior to January 1, 1972 (class 3), and a class of black employees who applied to transfer to OTR positions prior to the same date (class 4).

In its final judgment entered July 14, 1972, the District Court permanently enjoined the respondents from perpetuating the discriminatory practices found to exist, and, in regard to the black applicants for OTR positions, ordered Bowman to notify the members of both subclasses within 30 days of their right to priority consideration for such jobs. The District Court declined, however, to grant to the unnamed members of classes 3 and 4 any other specific relief sought, which included an award of backpay and seniority status retroactive to the date of individual application for an OTR position.

On petitioners' appeal to the Court of Appeals for the Fifth Circuit, raising for the most part claimed inadequacy of the relief ordered respecting unnamed members of the various subclasses involved, the Court of Appeals affirmed in part, reversed in part, and vacated in part. 495 F.2d 398. The Court of Appeals held that the District Court had exercised its discretion under an erroneous view of law insofar as it failed to award backpay to the unnamed class members of both classes 3 and 4, and vacated the judgment in that respect. The judgment was reversed insofar as it failed to award any seniority remedy to the members of class 4 who after the judgment of the District Court sought and obtained priority consideration for transfer to OTR positions. As respects unnamed members of class 3 — nonemployee black applicants who applied for and were denied OTR prior to January 1, 1972 — the Court of Appeals affirmed the District Court's denial of any form of seniority relief. Only this last aspect of the Court of Appeals' judgment is before us for review under our grant of the petition for certiorari. . . .

II. In affirming the District Court's denial of seniority relief to the class 3 group of discriminatees, the Court of Appeals held that the relief was barred by § 703(h) of Title VII. . . . We disagree. . . .

The Court of Appeals reasoned that a discriminatory refusal to hire "does not affect the bona fides of the seniority system. Thus, the differences in the benefits and conditions of employment which a seniority system accords to older and newer employees is protected as 'not an unlawful employment practice' [by § 703(h)]." 495 F.2d, at 417. Significantly, neither Bowman nor the unions undertake to defend the Court of Appeals' judgment on that ground. It is clearly erroneous.

The black applicants for OTR positions composing class 3 are limited to those whose applications were put in evidence at the trial.[10] The underlying legal wrong affecting them is not the alleged operation of a racially discriminatory seniority system but of a racially discriminatory hiring system. Petitioners do not ask modification or elimination of the existing seniority system, but only an award of the seniority status they would have individually enjoyed under the present system but for the illegal discriminatory refusal to hire. It is this context that must shape our determination as to the meaning and effect of § 703 (h).

On its face, § 703(h) appears to be only a definitional provision; as with the other provisions of § 703, subsection (h) delineates which employment practices are illegal and thereby prohibited and which are not. Section 703(h) certainly does not expressly purport to qualify or proscribe relief otherwise appropriate under the remedial provisions of Title VII, § 706(g), 42 U. S. C. § 2000e-5(g), in circumstances where an illegal discriminatory act or practice is found. Further, the legislative history of § 703(h) plainly negates its reading as limiting or qualifying the relief authorized under § 706(g). The initial bill reported by the House Judiciary Committee as H.R. 7152 and passed by the full House on February 10, 1964, did not contain § 703(h). Neither the House bill nor the majority Judiciary Committee Report even mentioned the problem of seniority. That subject thereafter surfaced during the debate of the bill in the Senate. This debate prompted Senators Clark and Case to respond to criticism that Title VII would destroy existing seniority systems by placing an Interpretive Memorandum in the Congressional Record. The Memorandum stated that "Title VII would have no effect on established seniority rights. Its effect is prospective and not retrospective." 110 Cong. Rec. 7213 (1964). Senator Clark also placed in the Congressional Record a Justice Department statement concerning Title VII which stated that "it has been asserted that Title VII would undermine vested rights of seniority. This is not correct. Title VII would have no effect on seniority rights existing at the time it takes effect." 110 Cong. Rec. 7207 (1964). Several weeks thereafter, following several informal conferences among the Senate leadership, the House leadership, the Attorney General and others, . . . a compromise substitute bill prepared by Senators Mansfield and Dirksen, Senate majority and minority leaders respectively, containing § 703(h) was introduced on the Senate floor. Although the Mansfield-Dirksen substitute bill, and hence § 703(h), was not the subject

---

[10] By its terms, the judgment of the District Court runs to all black applicants for OTR positions prior to January 1, 1972, and is not qualified by a limitation that the discriminatory refusal to hire must have taken place after the effective date of the Act. However, only post-Act victims of racial discrimination are members of class 3. Title VII's prohibition on racial discrimination in hiring became effective on July 2, 1965, one year after the date of its enactment. . . . Petitioners sought relief in this case for identifiable applicants for OTR positions "whose applications were put in evidence at the trial." There are 206 unhired black applicants prior to January 1, 1972, whose written applications are summarized in the record and none of the applications relates to years prior to 1970.

of a committee report ... Senator Humphrey, one of the informal conferees, later stated during debate on the substitute that § 703(h) was not designed to alter the meaning of Title VII generally but rather "merely clarifies its present intent and effect." 110 Cong. Rec. 12,723 (1964) (remarks of Sen. Humphrey). Accordingly, whatever the exact meaning and scope of § 703(h) in light of its unusual legislative history and the absence of the usual legislative materials ... it is apparent that the thrust of the section is directed toward defining what is and what is not an illegal discriminatory practice in instances in which the post-Act operation of a seniority system is challenged as perpetuating the effects of discrimination occurring prior to the effective date of the Act. There is no indication in the legislative materials that § 703(h) was intended to modify or restrict relief otherwise appropriate once an illegal discriminatory practice occurring after the effective date of the Act is proved — as in the instant case, a discriminatory refusal to hire.... We therefore hold that the Court of Appeals erred in concluding that, as a matter of law, § 703(h) barred the award of seniority relief to the unnamed class 3 members.

III. There remains the question whether an award of seniority relief is appropriate under the remedial provisions of Title VII, specifically, § 706(g).

We begin by repeating the observation of earlier decisions that in enacting Title VII of the Civil Rights Act of 1964, Congress intended to prohibit all practices in whatever form which create inequality in employment opportunity due to discrimination on the basis of race, religion, sex, or national origin, ... and ordained that its policy of outlawing such discrimination should have the "highest priority," Alexander [v. Gardner-Denver Co., 415 U.S. 36, 47].... Last Term's Albemarle Paper Company v. Moody, 422 U. S. 405 (1975), consistently with the congressional plan, held that one of the central purposes of Title VII is "to make persons whole for injuries suffered on account of unlawful employment discrimination." *Id.* at 418. To effectuate this "make-whole" objective, Congress in § 706(g) vested broad equitable discretion in the federal courts to "order such affirmative action as may be appropriate, which may include, but is not limited to, reinstatement or hiring of employees, with or without backpay ..., or any other relief as the court deems appropriate." *Ibid.* The legislative history supporting the 1972 Amendments of § 706(g) of Title VII affirms the breadth of this discretion. "The provisions of [§ 706(g)] are intended to give the courts wide discretion exercising their equitable powers to fashion the most complete relief possible.... [T]he Act is intended to make the victims of unlawful employment discrimination whole and ... the attainment of this objective ... requires that persons aggrieved by the consequences and effects of the unlawful employment practice be, so far as possible, restored to a position where they would have been were it not for the unlawful discrimination." Section-by-Section Analysis of H. R. 1746, accompanying The Equal Employment Opportunity Act of 1972 — Conference Report, 118 Cong. Rec. 7166, 7168 (1972). This is emphatic confirmation that federal courts are empowered to fashion such relief as the particular circumstances of a case may require to effect restitution, making whole insofar as possible the victims of racial discrimination in hiring. Adequate relief may well be denied in the absence of a seniority remedy slotting the victim in that position in the seniority system that would have been his had he been hired at the time of his application. It can hardly be questioned that ordinarily such relief will be necessary to achieve the "make-whole" purposes of the Act.

Seniority systems and the entitlements conferred by credits earned thereunder are of vast and increasing importance in the economic employment system of this Nation.... Seniority principles are increasingly used to allocate entitlements to scarce benefits among competing employees ("competitive status" seniority) and to compute noncompetitive benefits earned under the contract of employment ("benefit" seniority). ...

Seniority standing in employment with respondent Bowman, computed from the departmental date of hire, determines the order of layoff and recall of employees. Further, job assignments for OTR drivers are posted for competitive bidding and seniority is used to determine the highest bidder. As OTR drivers are paid on a per-mile basis, earnings are therefore to some extent a function of seniority. Additionally, seniority computed from the company date-of-hire determines the length of an employee's vacation and pension benefits. Obviously merely to require Bowman to hire the class 3 victim of discrimination falls far short of a "make-whole" remedy. A concomitant award of the seniority credit he presumptively would have earned but for the wrongful treatment would also seem necessary in the absence of justification for denying that relief. Without an award of seniority dating from the time at which he was discriminatorily refused employment, an individual who applies for and obtains employment as an OTR driver pursuant to the District Court's order will never obtain his rightful place in the hierarchy of seniority according to which these various employment benefits are distributed. He will perpetually remain subordinate to persons who, but for the illegal discrimination, would have been in respect to entitlement to these benefits his inferiors.

The Court of Appeals apparently followed this reasoning in holding that the District Court erred in not granting seniority relief to class 4 Bowman employees who were discriminatorily refused transfer to OTR positions. Yet the class 3 discriminatees in the absence of a comparable seniority award would also remain subordinated in the seniority system to the class 4 discriminatees. The distinction plainly finds no support anywhere in Title VII or its legislative history. Settled law dealing with the related "twin" areas of discriminatory hiring and discharges violative of National Labor Relations Act, ... provides a persuasive analogy. "[I]t would indeed be surprising if Congress gave a remedy for the one which it denied for the other." Phelps Dodge Corp. v. NLRB, 313 U. S. 177, 187 (1941). For courts to differentiate without justification between the classes of discriminatees "would be a differentiation not only without substance but in defiance of that against which the prohibition of discrimination is directed." *Id.* at 188.

Similarly, decisions construing the remedial section of the National Labor Relations Act, § 10(c), ... the model for § 706(g), Albemarle Paper, 422 U. S. at 419,[29] make clear that remedies constituting authorized "affirmative action" include an award of seniority status, for the thrust of "affirmative action" redressing the wrong incurred by an unfair labor practice is to make "the employees whole, and thus restor[e] the economic status quo that would have obtained but for the company's wrongful [act]." NLRB v. J. H. Rutter-Rex Manufacturing Company, 396 U. S. 258, 263 (1969). The task of the NLRB in applying § 10(c) is "to take measures designed to recreate the conditions and relationships that would have been had there been no unfair labor practice." Local 60, United Brotherhood of Carpenters and Joiners of America, AFL-CIO v. NLRB, 365 U. S. 651, 657 (1961) (Harlan, J., concurring). And the NLRB has often required that the hiring of employees who had been discriminatorily refused employment be accompanied by an award of seniority equivalent to that which they would have enjoyed but for the illegal conduct. See, *e.g.,* In re Phelps Dodge Corp., 19 N. L. R. B. 547, 600 & n. 39, 603-604 (1940), modified on other grounds, 313 U. S. 177 (1941) (ordering persons discriminatorily refused employment hired "without prejudice to their other rights and privileges"); In re Nevada Consolidated Copper Corp., 26 N. L. R. B. 1182, 1235 (1940), enforced, 316 U. S. 105 (1942) (ordering persons discriminatorily refused employment hired with "any seniority or other rights and privileges which they would have acquired, had the respondent not unlawfully discriminated against them"). Plainly the "affirmative action" injunction of § 706(g) has no lesser reach in the district courts. "Where racial discrimination is concerned, 'the district court has not merely the power but the duty to render a decree which will so far as possible eliminate the discriminatory effects of the past as well as bar like discrimination in the future.'" *Albemarle Paper, supra* at *418.*

IV. We are not to be understood as holding that an award of seniority status is requisite in all circumstances. The fashioning of appropriate remedies invokes the sound equitable discretion of the district courts. Respondent Bowman attempts to justify the District Court's denial of seniority relief for petitioners as an exercise of equitable discretion, but the record is its own refutation of the argument.

---

[29] To the extent that there is difference in the wording of the respective provisions, § 706(g) grants, if anything, broader discretionary powers than those granted the NLRB. Section 10(c) of the NLRA authorizes "such affirmative action including reinstatement of employees with or without back pay, as will effectuate the policies of this subchapter," ... whereas § 706(g) as amended in 1972 authorizes "such affirmative action as may be appropriate, which may include, *but is not limited to,* reinstatment *or hiring* of employees, with or without back pay ... , *or any other equitable relief as the court deems appropriate."* ... (emphasis added).

Albemarle Paper, supra, at 416, made clear that discretion imports not the Court's "inclination, but . . . its judgment; and its judgment is to be guided by sound legal principles." Discretion is vested not for purposes of "limit[ing] appellate review of trial courts, or . . . invit[ing] inconsistency and caprice," but rather to allow the most complete achievement of the objectives of Title VII that is attainable under the facts and circumstances of the specific case. *Id.* at 421. Accordingly, the District Court's denial of any form of seniority remedy must be reviewed in terms of its effect on the attainment of the Act's objectives under the circumstances presented by this record. No less than with the denial of the remedy of backpay, the denial of seniority relief to victims of illegal racial discrimination in hiring is permissible "only for reasons which, if applied generally, would not frustrate the central statutory purposes of eradicating discrimination throughout the economy and making persons whole for injuries suffered through past discrimination." *Ibid.*

The District Court stated two reasons for its denial of seniority relief for the unnamed class members. The first was that those individuals had not filed administrative charges under the provisions of Title VII with the Equal Employment Opportunity Commission and therefore class relief of this sort was not appropriate. We rejected this justification for denial of class-based relief in the context of backpay awards in *Albemarle Paper,* and for the same reasons reject it here. This justification for denying class-based relief in Title VII suits has been unanimously rejected by the courts of appeals, and Congress ratified that construction by the 1972 Amendments. *Albemarle Paper, supra* at 414 n. 8.

The second reason stated by the District Court was that such claims "presuppose a vacancy, qualification, and performance by every member. There is no evidence on which to base these multiple conclusions." The Court of Appeals rejected this reason insofar as it was the basis of the District Court's denial of backpay, and of its denial of retroactive seniority relief to the unnamed members of class 4. We hold that it is also an improper reason for denying seniority relief to the unnamed members of class 3.

We read the District Court's reference to the lack of evidence regarding a "vacancy, qualification and performance" for every individual member of the class as an expression of concern that some of the unnamed class members (unhired black applicants whose employment applications were summarized in the record) may not in fact have been actual victims of racial discrimination. That factor will become material however only when those persons reapply for OTR positions pursuant to the hiring relief ordered by the District Court. Generalizations concerning such individually applicable evidence cannot serve as a justification for the denial of relief to the entire class. Rather, at such time as individual class members seek positions as OTR drivers, positions for which they are presumptively entitled to priority hiring consideration under the District Court's order,[31] evidence that particular individuals were not in fact

---

[31] The District Court order is silent whether applicants to OTR positions who were previously discriminatorily refused employment must be presently qualified for those positions in order to be eligible for priority hiring under that order. The Court of Appeals, however, made it plain that they must be. 495 F. 2d at 417. We agree.

victims of racial discrimination will be material. But petitioners here have carried their burden of demonstrating the existence of a discriminatory hiring pattern and practice by the respondents and, therefore, the burden will be upon respondents to prove that individuals who reapply were not in fact victims of previous hiring discrimination. Cf. McDonnell Douglas Corp. v. Green, 411 U. S. at 802; Baxter v. Savannah Sugar Refining Corp., 495 F.2d 437, 443-444 (CA5), *cert. denied,* 419 U. S. 1033 (1974). Only if this burden is met may retroactive seniority — if otherwise determined to be an appropriate form of relief under the circumstances of the particular case — be denied individual class members.

Respondent Bowman raises an alternative theory of justification. Bowman argues that an award of retroactive seniority to the class of discriminatees will conflict with the economic interests of other Bowman employees. Accordingly, it is argued, the District Court acted within its discretion in denying this form of relief as an attempt to accommodate the competing interests of the various groups of employees.[33]

We reject this argument for two reasons. First, the District Court made no mention of such considerations in its order denying the seniority relief. As we noted in *Albemarle Paper, supra* at 421 n. 14, if the District Court declines due to the peculiar circumstances of the particular case to award relief generally appropriate under Title VII, "[i]t is necessary . . . that . . . it carefully articulate its reasons" for so doing. Second and more fundamentally, it is apparent that denial of seniority relief to identifiable victims of racial discrimination on the sole ground that such relief diminishes the expectations of other, arguably innocent, employees would if applied generally frustrate the central "make-whole" objective of Title VII. These conflicting interests of other employees will of course always be present in instances where some scarce employment benefit is distributed among employees on the basis of their status in the seniority hierarchy. But, as we have said, there is nothing in the language of Title VII, or in its legislative history, to show that Congress intended generally to bar this form of relief to victims of illegal discrimination, and the experience under its remedial model in the National Labor Relations Act points to the contrary. Accordingly, we find untenable the conclusion that this form of relief may be denied merely because the interests of other employees may thereby be affected. "If relief under Title VII can be denied merely because the majority group of employees, who have not suffered discrimination, will be unhappy about it, there will be little hope

---

[33] Even by its terms, this argument could apply only to the award of retroactive seniority for purposes of "competitive status" benefits. It has no application to a retroactive award for purposes of "benefit" seniority — extent of vacation leave and pension benefits. Indeed, the decision concerning the propriety of this latter type of seniority relief is analogous, if not identical, to the decision concerning an award of backpay to an individual discriminatee hired pursuant to an order redressing previous employment discrimination.

of correcting the wrongs to which the Act is directed." United States v. Bethlehem Steel Corp., 446 F.2d 652, 663 (CA2 1971).

With reference to the problems of fairness or equity respecting the conflicting interests of the various groups of employees, the relief which petitioners seek is only seniority status retroactive to the date of individual application, rather than some form of arguably more complete relief.[36] No claim is asserted that nondiscriminatee employees holding OTR positions they would not have obtained but for the illegal discrimination should be deprived of the seniority status they have earned. It is therefore clear that even if the seniority relief petitioners seek is awarded, most if not all discriminatees who actually obtain OTR jobs under the court order will not truly be restored to the actual seniority that would have existed in the absence of the illegal discrimination. Rather, most discriminatees even under an award of retroactive seniority status will still remain subordinated in the hierarchy to a position inferior to that of a greater total number of employees than would have been the case in the absence of discrimination. Therefore, the relief which petitioners seek, while a more complete form of relief than that which the District Court accorded, in no sense constitutes "complete relief." Rather, the burden of the past discrimination in hiring is with respect to competitive status benefits divided among discriminatee and nondiscriminatee employees under the form of relief sought. The dissent criticizes the Court's result as not sufficiently cognizant that it will "directly implicate the rights and expectations of perfectly innocent employees." *Post,* at 788. We are of the view, however, that the result which we reach today — which, standing alone,[38] establishes that a sharing of the burden of the past discrimination

---

[36] Another countervailing factor in assessing the expected impact on the interests of other employees actually occasioned by an award of the seniority relief sought is that it is not probable in instances of class-based relief that all of the victims of the past racial discrimination in hiring will actually apply for and obtain the prerequisite hiring relief. Indeed, in the instant case, there appear in the record the rejected applications of 166 black applicants who claimed at the time of application to have had the necessary job qualifications. However, the Court was informed at oral argument that only a small number of those individuals have to this date actually been hired pursuant to the District Court's order ("five, six, seven, something in that order"), Tr. of Oral Arg., at 23, although ongoing litigation may ultimately determine more who desire the hiring relief and are eligible for it. *Id.* at 15.

[38] In arguing that an award of the seniority relief established as presumptively necessary does nothing to place the burden of the past discrimination on the wrongdoer in most cases — the employer — the dissent of necessity addresses issues not presently before the Court. Further remedial action by the district courts, having the effect of shifting to the employer the burden of the past discrimination in respect to competitive status benefits, raises such issues as the possibility of an injunctive "hold harmless" remedy respecting all affected employees in a layoff situation, Brief of *Amicus Curiae* for Local 862, United Automobile Workers, the possibility of an award of monetary damages (sometimes designated "front pay") in favor of each employee and discriminatee otherwise bearing some of the burden of the past discrimination, *ibid.;* Brief for the United States and the Equal Employment Opportunity Commission as *Amici Curiae,* and the propriety of such further remedial action in instances wherein the union has been adjudged a participant in the illegal conduct. Such issues are not presented by the record before us, and we intimate no view regarding them.

is presumptively necessary — is entirely consistent with any fair characterization of equity jurisdiction, particularly when considered in light of our traditional view that "[a]ttainment of a great national policy ... must not be confined within narrow canons for equitable relief deemed suitable by chancellors in ordinary private controversies." Phelps Dodge Corp. v. NLRB, 313 U.S. at 188.

Certainly there is no argument that the award of retroactive seniority to the victims of hiring discrimination in any way deprives other employees of indefeasibly vested rights conferred by the employment contract. This Court has long held that employee expectations arising from a seniority system agreement may be modified by statutes furthering a strong public policy interest. Tilton v. Missouri Pacific Railroad Co., 376 U. S. 169 (1964) (construing §§ 9 (c)(1) and 9 (c)(2) of the Universal Military Training and Service Act of 1948, 50 U. S. C. §§ 459 (c)(1)-(2), which provided that a re-employed returning veteran should enjoy the seniority status he would have acquired but for his absence in military service); Fishgold v. Sullivan Drydock & Repair Corp., 328 U. S. 275 (1946) (construing the comparable provision of the Selective Training and Service Act of 1940). The Court has also held that a collective-bargaining agreement may go further, enhancing the seniority status of certain employees for purposes of furthering public policy interests beyond what is required by statute, even though this will to some extent be detrimental to the expectations acquired by other employees under the previous seniority agreement. Ford Motor Company v. Huffman, 345 U. S. 330 (1953). And the ability of the union and employer voluntarily to modify the seniority system to the end of ameliorating the effects of past racial discrimination, a national policy objective of the "highest priority," is certainly no less than in other areas of public policy interests. . . .

V. In holding that class-based seniority relief for identifiable victims of illegal hiring discrimination is a form of relief generally appropriate under § 706(g), we do not in any way modify our previously expressed view that the statutory scheme of Title VII "implicitly recognizes that there may be cases calling for one remedy but not another, and — owing to the structure of the federal judiciary — these choices are of course left in the first instance to the district courts." Albemarle Paper, supra at 416. Circumstances peculiar to the individual case may of course justify the modification or withholding of seniority relief for reasons that would not if applied generally undermine the purposes of Title VII.[41] In the instant

---

[41] Accordingly, to no "significant extent" do we "[strip] the district courts of [their] equitable powers." Rather our holding is that in exercising their equitable powers, district courts should take as their starting point the presumption in favor of rightful place seniority relief, and proceed with further legal analysis from that point; and that such relief may not be denied on the abstract basis of adverse impact upon interests of other employees but rather only on the basis of unusual adverse impact arising from facts and circumstances that would not be generally found in Title VII cases. To hold otherwise would be to shield "inconsisten[t] and capri[cious]" denial of such relief from "thorough appellate review." Albemarle Paper, 422 U. S. at 416, 421.

case it appears that all new hirees establish seniority only upon completion of a 45-day probationary period, although upon completion seniority is retroactive to the date of hire. Certainly any seniority relief ultimately awarded by the district court could properly be cognizant of this fact. Amici and the respondent union point out that there may be circumstances where an award of full seniority should be deferred until completion of a training or apprenticeship program, or other preliminaries required of all new hirees. We do not undertake to delineate all such possible circumstances here. Any enumeration must await particular cases and be determined in light of the trial courts' "keen appreciation" of peculiar facts and circumstances. *Albemarle Paper, supra* at 421-422.

Accordingly, the judgment of the Court of Appeals affirming the District Court's denial of seniority relief to class 3 is reversed, and the case remanded to the District Court for further proceedings consistent with this opinion.

It is so ordered.

MR. JUSTICE STEVENS took no part in the consideration or decision of this case.

MR. CHIEF JUSTICE BURGER, concurring in part and dissenting in part.

I concur in the judgment in part and generally with MR. JUSTICE POWELL, but I would stress that although retroactive benefit-type seniority relief may sometimes be appropriate and equitable, competitive-type seniority relief at the expense of wholly innocent employees can rarely, if ever, be equitable if that term retains traditional meaning. More equitable would be a monetary award to the person suffering the discrimination. An award such as "front pay" could replace the need for competitive-type seniority relief. . . . Such monetary relief would serve the dual purpose of deterring the wrongdoing employer or union — or both — as well as protecting the rights of innocent employees. In every respect an innocent employee is comparable to a "holder-in-due-course" of negotiable paper or a bona fide purchaser of property without notice of any defect in the seller's title. In this setting I cannot join in judicial approval of "robbing Peter to pay Paul."

I would stress that the Court today does not foreclose claims of employees who might be injured by this holding from petitioning the District Court for equitable relief on their own behalf.

MR. JUSTICE POWELL, with whom MR. JUSTICE REHNQUIST joins, concurring in part and dissenting in part. . . .

Although I am in accord with much of the Court's discussion in Parts III and IV, I cannot accept as correct its basic interpretation of § 706(g) as virtually requiring a district court, in determining appropriate equitable relief in a case of this kind, to ignore entirely the equities that may exist in favor of innocent employees. Its holding recognizes no meaningful distinction, in terms of the equitable relief to be granted, between "benefit"-type seniority and "competitive"-type seniority. The Court reaches this result by taking an absolutist view of the "make-whole" objective of Title VII, while rendering largely meaningless the discretionary authority vested in district courts by § 706(g) to weigh the equities of the situation. Accordingly, I dissent from Parts III and IV. . . .

The decision whether to grant competitive-type seniority relief therefore requires a district court to consider and weigh competing equities. In any proper exercise of the balancing process, a court must consider both the claims of the discrimination victims and the claims of incumbent employees who, if competitive seniority rights are awarded retroactively to others, will lose economic advantages earned through satisfactory and often long service. If, as the Court today holds, the district court may not weigh these equities much of the language of § 706(e) is rendered meaningless. We cannot assume that Congress intended either that the statutory language be ignored or that the earned benefits of incumbent employees be wiped out by a presumption created by this Court. . . .

NOTES

1. *Compare* Jersey Cent. Power & Light Co. v. IBEW Locals 327 et al., 508 F. 2d 687 (3d Cir. 1975), *on remand,* 542 F. 2d 8 (3d Cir. 1976). While awarding "front pay" to the victims of a discriminatory seniority system, the Fourth Circuit refused to "bump" incumbent white employees as part of the remedy. Explained the court: "A primary goal of Title VII is to induce voluntary compliance by employers and unions. . . . Demoting employees, especially those who are not responsible for wrongdoing, undoubtedly would encounter more resistance than deferring their future expectancies." The court feared the domino effect could adversely affect not only those who had done no wrong but also those who may have been the victims of discrimination. Patterson v. American Tobacco Co., 535 F.2d 257 (4th Cir. 1976), *cert. denied,* 429 U.S. 920 (1977).

2. *See generally* Edwards, *Race Discrimination in Employment: What Price Equality?* 1976 U. ILL. L.F. 572 (1976); Edwards & Zaretsky, *Preferential Remedies for Employment Discrimination,* 74 MICH. L. REV. 1 (1976).

ALEXANDER v. GARDNER-DENVER CO.

Supreme Court of the United States
415 U.S. 36, 94 S. Ct. 1011, 39 L. Ed. 2d 147 (1974)

MR. JUSTICE POWELL delivered the opinion of the Court.

This case concerns the proper relationship between federal courts and the grievance-arbitration machinery of collective-bargaining agreements in the resolution and enforcement of an individual's rights to equal employment opportunities under Title VII of the Civil Rights Act of 1964. . . . Specifically, we must decide under what circumstances, if any, an employee's statutory right to a trial *de novo* under Title VII may be foreclosed by prior submission of his claim to final arbitration under the nondiscrimination clause of a collective-bargaining agreement.

I. In May 1966, petitioner Harrell Alexander, Sr., a black, was hired by respondent Gardner-Denver Company (the "company") to perform maintenance work at the company's plant in Denver, Colorado. In June 1968, petitioner was awarded a trainee position as a drill operator. He remained at that job until his discharge from employment on September 29, 1969. The company informed petitioner that he was being discharged for producing too many defective or unusable parts that had to be scrapped.

On October 1, 1969, petitioner filed a grievance under the collective-bargaining agreement in force between the company and petitioner's union, Local No. 3029 of the United Steelworkers of America (the "union"). The grievance stated: "I feel I have been unjustly discharged and ask that I be reinstated with full seniority and pay." No explicit claim of racial discrimination was made.

Under Art. 4 of the collective-bargaining agreement, the company retained "the right to hire, suspend or discharge [employees] for proper cause." Art. 5, § 2 provided, however, that "there shall be no discrimination against any employee on account of race, color, religion, sex, national origin, or ancestry," and Art. 23, § 6(a) stated that "[n]o employee will be discharged, suspended or given a written warning notice except for just cause." The agreement also contained a broad arbitration clause covering "differences aris[ing] between the Company and the Union as to the meaning and application of the provisions of this Agreement" and "any trouble aris[ing] in the plant." Disputes were to be submitted to a multi-step grievance procedure, the first four steps of which involved negotiations between the company and the union. If the dispute remained unresolved, it was to be remitted to compulsory arbitration. The company and the union were to select and pay the arbitrator, and his decision was to be "final and binding upon the Company, the Union, and any employee or employees involved." The agreement further provided that "[t]he arbitrator shall not amend, take away, add to, or change any of the provisions of this Agreement, and the arbitrator's decision must be based solely on an interpretation of the provisions of this Agreement." The parties also agreed that there "shall be no suspension of work" over disputes covered by the grievance-arbitration clause.

The union processed petitioner's grievance through the above machinery. In the final prearbitration step, petitioner raised, apparently for the first time, the claim that his discharge resulted from racial discrimination. The company rejected all of petitioner's claims, and the grievance proceeded to arbitration. Prior to the arbitration hearing, however, petitioner filed a charge of racial discrimination with the Colorado Civil Rights Commission, which referred the complaint to the Equal Employment Opportunity Commission on November 5, 1969.

At the arbitration hearing on November 20, 1969, petitioner testified that his discharge was the result of racial discrimination and informed the arbitrator that he had filed a charge with the Colorado Commission because he "could not rely on the union." The union introduced a letter in which petitioner stated that he was "knowledgeable that in the same plant others have scrapped an equal amount and sometimes in excess, but by all logical reasoning I ... have been the target of preferential discriminatory treatment." The union representative also testified that the company's usual practice was to transfer unsatisfactory trainee drill operators back to their former positions.

On December 30, 1969, the arbitrator ruled that petitioner had been "discharged for just cause." He made no reference to petitioner's claim of racial discrimination. The arbitrator stated that the union had failed to produce evidence of a practice of transferring rather than discharging trainee drill operators who accumulated excessive scrap, but he suggested that the company and the union confer on whether such an arrangement was feasible in the present case.

On July 25, 1970, the Equal Employment Opportunity Commission determined that there was not reasonable cause to believe that a violation of Title VII of the Civil Rights Act of 1964, 42 U.S.C. § 2000e *et seq.,* had occurred. The Commission later notified petitioner of his right to institute a civil action in federal court within 30 days. Petitioner then filed the present action in the United States District Court for the District of Colorado, alleging that his discharge resulted from a racially discriminatory employment practice in violation of § 703(a)(1) of the Act. . . .

The District Court granted respondent's motion for summary judgment and dismissed the action. 346 F. Supp. 1012 (1971). The court found that the claim of racial discrimination had been submitted to the arbitrator and resolved adversely to petitioner.[4] It then held that petitioner, having voluntarily elected to pursue his grievance to final arbitration under the nondiscrimination clause of the collective-bargaining agreement, was bound by the arbitral decision and thereby precluded from suing his employer under Title VII. The Court of Appeals for the Tenth Circuit affirmed *per curiam* on the basis of the District Court's opinion. . . .

We granted petitioner's application for certiorari. . . . We reverse.

II. . . . Even in its amended form, . . . Title VII does not provide the Commission with direct powers of enforcement. The Commission cannot adjudicate claims or impose administrative sanctions. Rather, final responsibility for enforcement of Title VII is vested with federal courts. The Act authorizes courts to issue injunctive relief and to order such affirmative action as may be appropriate to remedy the effects of unlawful employment practices. 42 U.S.C. § 2000e-(5)(f) and (g). Courts retain

---

[4] In reaching this conclusion, the District Court relied on petitioner's deposition acknowledging that he had raised the racial discrimination claim during the arbitration hearing. 346 F. Supp. 1012, 1014.

these broad remedial powers despite a Commission finding of no reasonable cause to believe that the Act has been violated. McDonnell Douglas Corp. v. Green, [411 U. S. 792,] 798-799. Taken together, these provisions make plain that federal courts have been assigned plenary powers to secure compliance with Title VII.

In addition to reposing ultimate authority in federal courts, Congress gave private individuals a significant role in the enforcement process of Title VII. Individual grievants usually initiate the Commission's investigatory and conciliatory procedures. And although the 1972 amendment to Title VII empowers the Commission to bring its own actions, the private right of action remains an essential means of obtaining judicial enforcement of Title VII. 42 U.S.C. § 2000e-5(f)(1). In such cases, the private litigant not only redresses his own injury but also vindicates the important congressional policy against discriminatory employment practices. . . .

Pursuant to this statutory scheme, petitioner initiated the present action for judicial consideration of his rights under Title VII. The District Court and the Court of Appeals held, however, that petitioner was bound by the prior arbitral decision and had no right to sue under Title VII. Both courts evidently thought that this result was dictated by notions of election of remedies and waiver and by the federal policy favoring arbitration of labor disputes, as enunciated by this Court in Textile Workers Union v. Lincoln Mills, 353 U. S. 448 (1957), and the *Steelworkers Trilogy*. . . . We disagree.

III. Title VII does not speak expressly to the relationship between federal courts and the grievance-arbitration machinery of collective-bargaining agreements. It does, however, vest federal courts with plenary powers to enforce the statutory requirements; and it specifies with precision the jurisdictional prerequisites that an individual must satisfy before he is entitled to institute a lawsuit. In the present case, these prerequisites were met when petitioner (1) filed timely a charge of employment discrimination with the Commission, and (2) received and acted upon the Commission's statutory notice of the right to sue. 42 U.S.C. §§ 2000e-5(b), (e), and (f). See McDonnell Douglas Corp. v. Green, *supra*, 411 U. S. at 798. There is no suggestion in the statutory scheme that a prior arbitral decision either forecloses an individual's right to sue or divests federal courts of jurisdiction.

In addition, legislative enactments in this area have long evinced a general intent to accord parallel or overlapping remedies against discrimination. In the Civil Rights Act of 1964, . . . Congress indicated that it considered the policy against discrimination to be of the "highest priority." Newman v. Piggie Park Enterprises, Inc., [390 U. S. 400,] 402. Consistent with this view, Title VII provides for consideration of employment-discrimination claims in several forums. See 42 U.S.C. § 2000e-5(b) (EEOC); 42 U.S.C. § 2000e-5(c) (state and local agencies); 42 U.S.C. § 2000e-5(f) (federal courts). And, in general, submission of a claim to one forum does not preclude a later submission to another. Moreover, the legislative history of Title VII manifests a congressional intent to allow an individual to pursue independently his rights under both Title VII and other applicable state and federal statutes. The clear inference is that Title VII was designed to supplement, rather than supplant, existing laws and institutions relating to employment discrimination. In sum, Title VII's purpose and procedures strongly suggest that an individual does not forfeit his private cause of action if he first pursues his grievance to final arbitration under the nondiscrimination clause of a collective-bargaining agreement.

In reaching the opposite conclusion, the District Court relied in part on the doctrine of election of remedies. That doctrine, which refers to situations where an individual pursues remedies that are legally or factually inconsistent, has no application in the present context. In submitting his grievance to arbitration, an employee seeks to vindicate his contractual right under a collective-bargaining agreement. By contrast, in filing a lawsuit under Title VII, an employee asserts independent statutory rights accorded by Congress. The distinctly separate nature of these contractual and statutory rights is not vitiated merely because both were violated as a result of the same factual occurrence. And certainly no inconsistency results from permitting both rights to be enforced in their respectively appropriate forums. The resulting scheme is somewhat analogous to the procedure under the National Labor Relations Act, as amended, where disputed transactions may implicate both contractual and statutory rights. Where the statutory right underlying a particular claim may not be abridged by contractual agreement, the Court has recognized that consideration of the claim by the arbitrator as a contractual dispute under the collective-bargaining agreement does not preclude subsequent consideration of the claim by the National Labor Relations Board as an unfair labor practice charge or as a petition for clarification of the union's representation certificate under the Act. Carey v. Westinghouse Corp., 375 U. S. 261 (1964). Cf. Smith v. Evening News Assn., 371 U. S. 195 (1962). There, as here, the relationship between the forums is complementary since consideration of the claim by both forums may promote the policies underlying each. Thus, the rationale behind the election of remedies doctrine cannot support the decision below.

We are also unable to accept the proposition that petitioner waived his cause of action under Title VII. To begin, we think it clear that there can be no prospective waiver of an employee's rights under Title VII. It is true, of course, that a union may waive certain statutory rights related to collective activity, such as the right to strike. Mastro Plastics Corp. v. NLRB, 350 U. S. 270 (1956); Boys Markets, Inc. v. Retail Clerks Union, 398 U. S. 235 (1970). These rights are conferred on employees collectively to foster the processes of bargaining and properly may be exercised or relinquished by the union as collective-bargaining agent to obtain economic benefits for unit members. Title VII, on the other hand, stands on plainly different ground; it concerns not majoritarian processes, but an individual's right to equal employment opportunities. Title VII's strictures are absolute and represent a congressional command that each employee be free from discriminatory practices. Of necessity, the rights conferred can form no part of the collective-bargaining process since waiver of these rights would defeat the paramount congressional purpose behind Title VII. In these circumstances, an employee's rights under Title VII are not susceptible to prospective waiver. See Wilko v. Swan, 346 U. S. 427 (1953).

The actual submission of petitioner's grievance to arbitration in the present case does not alter the situation. Although presumably an employee may waive his cause of action under Title VII as part of a voluntary settlement, mere resort to the arbitral forum to enforce contractual rights constitutes no such waiver. Since an employee's rights under Title VII may not be waived prospectively, existing contractual rights and remedies against discrimination must result from other concessions already made by the union as part of the economic bargain struck with the employer. It is settled law that no additional concession may be exacted from any employee as the price for enforcing those rights. J. I. Case Co. v. Labor Board, 321 U. S. 332, 338-339 (1944).

Moreover, a contractual right to submit a claim to arbitration is not displaced simply because Congress also has provided a statutory right against discrimination. Both rights have legally independent origins and are equally available to the aggrieved employee. This point becomes apparent through consideration of the role of the arbitrator in the system of industrial self-government. As the proctor of the bargain, the arbitrator's task is to effectuate the intent of the parties. His source of authority is the collective-bargaining agreement, and he must interpret and apply that agreement in accordance with the "industrial common law of the shop" and the various needs and desires of the parties. The arbitrator, however, has no general authority to invoke public laws that conflict with the bargain between the parties. . . . If an arbitral decision is based "solely on the arbitrator's view of the requirements of enacted legislation," rather than on an interpretation of the collective-bargaining agreement, the arbitrator has "exceeded the scope of his submission," and the award will not be enforced. [Steelworkers v. Enterprise Wheel & Car Corp., 363 U. S. 593, 597 (1960).] Thus the arbitrator has authority to resolve only questions of contractual rights, and this authority remains regardless whether certain contractual rights are similar to, or duplicative of, the substantive rights secured by Title VII.

IV. The District Court and the Court of Appeals reasoned that to permit an employee to have his claim considered in both the arbitral and judicial forums would be unfair since this would mean that the employer, but not the employee, was bound by the arbitral award. In the District Court's words, it could not "accept a philosophy which gives the employee two strings to his bow when the employer has only one." . . . This argument mistakes the effect of Title VII. Under the *Steelworkers Trilogy,* an arbitral decision is final and binding on the employer and employee, and judicial review is limited as to both. But in instituting an action under Title VII, the employee is not seeking review of the arbitrator's decision. Rather, he is asserting a statutory right independent of the arbitration process. An employer does not have "two strings to his bow" with respect to an arbitral decision for the simple reason that Title VII does not provide employers with a cause of action against employees. An employer cannot be the victim of discriminatory employment practices. . . .

The District Court and the Court of Appeals also thought that to permit a later resort to the judicial forum would undermine substantially the employer's incentive to arbitrate and would "sound the death knell for arbitration clauses in labor contracts." . . . Again, we disagree. The primary incentive for an employer to enter into an arbitration agreement is the union's reciprocal promise not to strike. As the Court stated in Boys Markets, Inc. v. Retail Clerks Union, 398 U. S. 235, 248 (1970), "a no strike obligation, express or implied is the *quid pro quo* for an undertaking by an employer to submit grievance disputes to the process of arbitration." It is not unreasonable to assume that most employers will regard the benefits derived from a no-strike pledge as outweighing whatever costs may result from according employees an arbitral remedy against discrimination in addition to their judicial remedy under Title VII. Indeed, the severe consequences of a strike may make an arbitration clause almost essential from both the employees' and the employer's perspective. Moreover, the grievance-arbitration machinery of the collective-bargaining agreement remains a relatively inexpensive and expeditious means for resolving a wide range of disputes, including claims of discriminatory employment practices. Where the collective-bargaining agreement contains a nondiscrimination clause similar to Title VII, and where arbitral procedures are fair and regular, arbitration may well produce a settlement satisfactory to both employer and employee. An employer thus has an incentive to make available the conciliatory and therapeutic processes of arbitration which may satisfy an employee's perceived need to resort to the judicial forum, thus saving the employer the expense and aggravation associated with a lawsuit. For similar reasons, the employee also has a strong incentive to arbitrate grievances, and arbitration may often eliminate those misunderstandings or discriminatory practices that might otherwise precipitate resort to the judicial forum.

V. Respondent contends that even if a preclusion rule is not adopted, federal courts should defer to arbitral decisions on discrimination claims where: (i) the claim was before the arbitrator; (ii) the collective-bargaining agreement prohibited the form of discrimination charged in the suit under Title VII; and (iii) the arbitrator has authority to rule on the claim and to fashion a remedy.[17] Under respondent's proposed rule, a court would grant summary judgment and dismiss the employee's action if the above conditions were met. The rule's obvious consequence in the present case would be to deprive the petitioner of his statutory right to attempt to establish his claim in a federal court.

---

[17] Respondent's proposed rule is analogous to the NLRB's policy of deferring to arbitral decisions on statutory issues in certain cases. See Spielberg Manufacturing Co., 112 N.L.R.B. 1080, 1082 (1955).

At the outset, it is apparent that a deferral rule would be subject to many of the objections applicable to a preclusion rule. The purpose and procedures of Title VII indicate that Congress intended federal courts to exercise final responsibility for enforcement of Title VII; deferral to arbitral decisions would be inconsistent with that goal. Furthermore, we have long recognized that "the choice of forums inevitably affects the scope of the substantive right to be vindicated." U. S. Bulk Carriers v. Arguelles, 400 U. S. 358, 359-360 (1971) (Harlan, J., concurring). Respondent's deferral rule is necessarily premised on the assumption that arbitral processes are commensurate with judicial processes and that Congress impliedly intended federal courts to defer to arbitral decisions on Title VII issues. We deem this supposition unlikely.

Arbitral procedures, while well suited to the resolution of contractual disputes, make arbitration a comparatively inappropriate forum for the final resolution of rights created by Title VII. This conclusion rests first on the special role of the arbitrator, whose task is to effectuate the intent of the parties rather than the requirements of enacted legislation. Where the collective-bargaining agreement conflicts with Title VII, the arbitration must follow the agreement. To be sure, the tension between contractual and statutory objectives may be mitigated where a collective-bargaining agreement contains provisions facially similar to those of Title VII. But other facts may still render arbitral processes comparatively inferior to judicial processes in the protection of Title VII rights. Among these is the fact that the specialized competence of arbitrators pertains primarily to the law of the shop, not the law of the land. United Steelworkers of America v. Warrior & Gulf Navigation Co., 363 U. S. 574, 581-583. Parties usually choose an arbitrator because they trust his knowledge and judgment concerning the demands and norms of industrial relations. On the other hand, the resolution of statutory or constitutional issues is a primary responsibility of courts, and judicial construction has proven especially necessary with respect to Title VII, whose broad language frequently can be given meaning only by reference to public law concepts.

Moreover, the fact-finding process in arbitration usually is not equivalent to judicial fact-finding. The record of the arbitration proceedings is not as complete; the usual rules of evidence do not apply; and rights and procedures common to civil trials, such as discovery, compulsory process, cross-examination, and testimony under oath, are often severely limited or unavailable. See Bernhardt v. Polygraphic Co., 350 U. S. 198, 203 (1956); Wilko v. Swan, 346 U. S. 427, 435-437 (1953). And as this Court has recognized, "[a]rbitrators have no obligation to the court to give their reasons for an award." United Steelworkers of America v. Enterprise Wheel & Car Corp., 363 U. S. 593, 598. Indeed, it is the informality of arbitral procedure that enables it to function as an efficient, inexpensive, and expeditious means for dispute resolution. This same characteristic, however, makes arbitration a less appropriate forum for final resolution of Title VII issues than the federal courts.

It is evident that respondents' proposed rule would not allay these concerns. Nor are we convinced that the solution lies in applying a more demanding deferral standard, such as that adopted by the Fifth Circuit in Rios v. Reynolds Metals Co., 467 F.2d 54 (1972). As respondent points out, a standard that adequately insured effectuation of Title VII rights in the arbitral forum would tend to make arbitration a procedurally complex, expensive, and time-consuming process. And judicial enforcement of such a standard would almost require courts to make *de novo* determinations of the employees' claims. It is uncertain whether any minimal savings in judicial time and expense would justify the risk to vindication of Title VII rights.

A deferral rule also might adversely affect the arbitration system as well as the enforcement scheme of Title VII. Fearing that the arbitral forum cannot adequately protect their rights under Title VII, some employees may elect to bypass arbitration and institute a lawsuit. The possibility of voluntary compliance or settlement of Title VII claims would thus be reduced, and the result could well be more litigation, not less.

We think, therefore, that the federal policy favoring arbitration of labor disputes and the federal policy against discriminatory employment practices can best be accommodated by permitting an employee to pursue fully both his remedy under the grievance-arbitration clause of a collective-bargaining agreement and his cause of action under Title VII. The federal court should consider the employee's claim *de novo*. The arbitral decision may be admitted as evidence and accorded such weight as the court deems appropriate.[21]

The judgment of the Court of Appeals is

Reversed.

NOTES

1. On remand, the district court's decision that the discharge was nondiscriminatory was affirmed. Alexander v. Gardner-Denver Co., 519 F. 2d 503 (10th Cir. 1975), *cert. denied,* 423 U.S. 1058 (1976).

2. For pre-*Gardner-Denver* discussions of the multiple forums problem in employment discrimination cases, see Beaird, *Racial Discrimination in*

---

[21] We adopt no standards as to the weight to be accorded an arbitral decision, since this must be determined in the court's discretion with regard to the facts and circumstances of each case. Relevant factors include the existence of provisions in the collective-bargaining agreement that conform substantially with Title VII, the degree of procedural fairness in the arbitral forum, adequacy of the record with respect to the issue of discrimination, and the special competence of particular arbitrators. Where an arbitral determination gives full consideration to an employee's Title VII rights, a court may properly accord it great weight. This is especially true where the issue is solely one of fact, specifically addressed by the parties and decided by the arbitrator on the basis of an adequate record. But courts should ever be mindful that Congress, in enacting Title VII, thought it necessary to provide a judicial forum for the ultimate resolution of discriminatory employment claims. It is the duty of courts to assure the full availability of this forum.

Employment: Rights and Remedies, 6 GA. L. REV. 469 (1972); Gould, *Labor Arbitration of Grievances Involving Racial Discrimination,* 118 U. PA. L. REV. 40 (1969); Meltzer, *Labor Arbitration and Overlapping and Conflicting Remedies for Employment Discrimination,* 39 U. CHI. L. REV. 30 (1971). Postmortems include Cooper, Meltzer, Coulson, *The Arbitration of Title VII Disputes: The Impact of the Gardner-Denver Case,* in N.Y.U. TWENTY-SEVENTH ANNUAL CONFERENCE ON LABOR 183, 189, 201 (1974) (three separate papers); Edwards, *Arbitration of Employment Discrimination Cases: An Empirical Study,* in NATIONAL ACADEMY OF ARBITRATORS, ARBITRATION — 1975, PROCEEDINGS OF THE TWENTY-EIGHTH ANNUAL MEETING 59 (1976); Hill, *The Authority of a Labor Arbitrator to Decide Legal Issues Under a Collective Bargaining Contract: The Situation After Gardner-Denver,* 10 IND. L. REV. 899 (1977); Meltzer, *Labor Arbitration and Discrimination: The Parties' Process and the Public's Purposes,* 43 U. CHI. L. REV. 724 (1976).

3. What does *Gardner-Denver* do to the NLRB's *Collyer* deferral policy? *See* Arnold Co. v. Carpenters Dist. Council of Jacksonville, 417 U.S. 12, 16-17 (1974).

4. An employee who twice accepted back pay and reinstatement in settlement of his grievances against an employer waived his right to sue the employer under the Civil Rights Act of 1866 and Title VII for the same conduct that caused him to file grievances. Strozier v. General Motors Corp., 442 F. Supp. 475 (N.D. Ga. 1977). This is the first reported case in which a court has applied the Supreme Court's suggestion in *Gardner-Denver* that an employee can waive his Title VII claim if he voluntarily and knowingly accepts a settlement that provides him with relief that is "substantially equivalent" to that provided under Title VII.

5. An employee whose claim of discriminatory discharge has been rejected by the NLRB may still be able to litigate a charge of racial discrimination based on the same incidents before EEOC. Tipler v. E. I. duPont de Nemours, 443 F.2d 125 (6th Cir. 1971). Although there is an overlap in the application of the NLRA and the Civil Rights Act, the precisely same issue is not necessarily presented in proceedings under the two statutes.

PART FIVE
INTERNAL UNION AFFAIRS

A. J. MUSTE, FACTIONAL FIGHTS IN TRADE UNIONS, in AMERICAN LABOR DYNAMICS 332-33 (J. Hardman ed. 1928)*

In the first place the trade union seeks to combine within itself two extremely divergent types of social structure, that of an army and that of a democratic town meeting. The union is a fighting instrument and exhibits always more or less definitely a tendency to take on the characteristics of armed forces and warfare in its structure and activities. There are generals, spies, military secrets, battles, armistices, treaties, breaches of diplomatic relations with the enemy and so on. The union seeks to assert in industry and over its actual and potential membership those prerogatives of a sovereign state, the right to conscript and the right to tax.

But the trade-union army elects its own generals, elects them in many instances annually or on the eve of battle. The army votes on the declaration of war and on the terms of armistice and peace. The reports of confidential agents are made to large committees, on which not infrequently the confidential agents of the enemy occupy prominent positions.

Now this situation is bound to continue indefinitely. Whatever be the manner of the warfare, the union must wage war to gain and to maintain tolerable conditions for its membership. It must develop something of the solidarity, discipline, and capacity for swift striking that an army has. On the other hand, the state and other agencies mainly concerned with the maintenance of the status quo in industry will take good care to insist that the union must remain "a purely voluntary agency" and to deprive it of the right to use instruments of coercion such as they themselves employ.

WILLIAM M. LEISERSON, AMERICAN TRADE UNION DEMOCRACY 54, 77, 79 (1959)**

If labor organizations also exercise autocratic powers over their members, then workers may merely be substituting dictatorial rule of union officials for the arbitrary authority of the employer or his managers. Does "industrial democracy" tend to maintain the traditions and liberties of American democratic government, or is it moving in the direction of what in other countries is called "people's democracy"? Increasingly, as organized labor grows in power and influence, questions are being asked as to the kind of democracy that is being furthered by the economic and political programs of union organizations. . . .

In a sense we are betting on the democracy of American labor organizations. The assumption is general that democratic political

* Copyright©1928. Reprinted by permission of Harcourt Brace Jovanovich, Inc.
** Reprinted by permission of Columbia University Press, New York, New York.

institutions can hardly be maintained without free trade unions. Their primary objective, collective bargaining — now established by law as the national labor policy — is considered essential to democracy in industrial relations. If, however, the unions are not the inherently democratic organizations we assume them to be, if industrial democracy must indeed be a one-party system of democracy, then organized labor may be leading to a society marked by more authoritarianism than liberty, while it is being protected and supported as a movement essential to a fuller democracy. . . .

But this is not the whole picture. Democratic traditions are strong in American labor unions, and their strivings for subjecting management to rules of law embodied in working agreements made jointly with representatives of employees are certainly in line with these traditions. Basic democratic rights, such as equal application of laws, equality of opportunity, and individual freedom make it necessary that those who have economic or other power to oppress shall be restrained to enlarge the liberties of those who are disadvantaged. When employers are free to run their industries as they please, employees are not free in their workplaces. Forcing managements to bargain with unions chosen by employees places limits on their freedom in order that workers shall have freedom to a voice in making the shop rules that govern them. Thus is liberty enlarged and balanced. It may well be that the restrictions which union governments impose on the liberties of their members and on nonunionists will work out to provide greater freedom for all employees.

INTRODUCTION

Organizing employees and representing them in collective bargaining have traditionally been the primary functions of labor unions, and unions, as institutions, have been built up around these functions. Like other institutions, however, labor organizations tend to develop both external and internal relationships and problems which, while necessarily colored by their main functions, are nevertheless distinct. These relationships and problems form the subject matter of Part Five. We look here at the union as a "going concern," and our aim is to trace the law applicable to the institutional phases of unionism.

A more or less consistent general pattern of development emerges. In the earlier days of the labor movement the law took a largely "hands-off" position; legislatures were unconcerned, and the courts interfered in union affairs as little as possible. The often iterated dogma were these: the union is not a legal entity and can therefore neither sue nor be sued in its common name; property may not be held by the union as an entity separate from its members; disputes between unions and their members are ordinarily best left to settlement within the union structure; exhaustion of intraunion remedies must precede resort to the courts.

Before long, however, most of these common-law doctrines were well peppered with exceptions, or, in some instances, discarded entirely. The courts began to see that the growth of unions in numbers and power made anomalous a view which would classify them with social and benevolent societies and fraternal organizations, and which would consider their affairs as of little public concern. Then came the labor relations acts, which established the broad right of a union selected by the majority of employees in a bargaining unit to represent all employees in the unit, whether or not they belong to the union. This enlargement of power more than any other circumstance has tended to focus attention upon the subject of union responsibilities and duties.

Pressure for legislation came to a head as the result of the disclosures of the McClellan Committee from 1957 to 1959, and Congress took a long step toward comprehensive regulation of internal union affairs in the enactment of the Labor-Management Reporting and Disclosure Act in 1959. We shall examine this labor reform legislation against the background of the common law and the labor relations acts.

SECTION I. The Legal Status of Unions

A. THE LEGAL BASIS FOR JUDICIAL INTERVENTION IN THE INTERNAL AFFAIRS OF UNIONS

Even though historically labor unions have been considered voluntary associations, theoretically putting them in the same category as churches and fraternal groups, the labor unions of today both in structure and function bear little resemblance to these other voluntary associations. Nevertheless, a traditional reluctance to interfere still remains an underlying attitude in the minds of judges. They have, however, recognized the necessity of judicial intervention in internal union affairs to protect the rights of union members.

The courts show a continuing preoccupation with the legal nature of the action in discipline cases. Over forty years ago Professor Zechariah Chafee analyzed three possibilities and emphasized one as the proper basis of suit: (1) the action sounds in contract, the constitution and bylaws of a union being in effect a contract between the organization and its members; (2) the action is one for the protection of property rights (in union funds, in one's job, etc.); and (3) the one favored by Professor Chafee — a complaint of wrongful discipline is a tort action, and the rights to be protected are the status of the member in the union and his right to work.[1]

Professor Chafee to the contrary notwithstanding, most of the recent cases seem to assume that the action is in contract. A wrongful expulsion or discipline is viewed as a breach of the union's implied promise to maintain the member's standing as long as he respects valid union rules. Illustrative decisions are *Polin v. Kaplan*[2] from New York, *Cason v. Glass Bottle Blowers Ass'n*[3] from California, and *International Printing*

---

[1] Chafee, *The Internal Affairs of Associations Not for Profit*, 43 HARV. L. REV. 993, 1001-07 (1930). *See also* Summers, *Legal Limitations on Union Discipline*, 64 HARV. L. REV. 1049, 1050-58 (1951); Summers, *The Law of Union Discipline: What the Courts Do in Fact*, 70 YALE L.J. 175 (1960).

[2] 257 N.Y. 277, 177 N.E. 833 (1931).

[3] 37 Cal. 2d 134, 231 P.2d 6 (1951).

Pressmen v. Smith[4] from Texas. The last-cited decision, besides going extensively into the reasons why the case sounds in contract, shows that the issue is not without practical importance. Since there had been a lapse of more than two years but less than four in the bringing of the action, the suit would have been barred if classified as a tort action, but not if classified as a contract action based on a written instrument. For an indication that Professor Chafee's tort theory still retains some vitality, however, see *Hurwitz v. Directors Guild* (broad non-Communist oath an unreasonable requirement for continued membership).[5]

In *Machinists v. Gonzales,*[6] the United States Supreme Court had this to say:

> The crux of the claim sustained by the California court was that under California law membership in a labor union constitutes a contract between the member and the union, the terms of which are governed by the constitution and by-laws of the union, and that state law provides, through mandatory reinstatement and damages, a remedy for breach of such contract through wrongful expulsion. This contractual conception of the relation between a member and his union widely prevails in this country and has recently been adopted by the House of Lords in Bonsor v. Musicians' Union, [1956] A.C. 104. It has been the law of California for at least half a century.

The likelihood that state courts will remain the principal adjudicators of members' rights under union constitutions was underscored in *Hotel and Restaurant Employees Local 400 v. Svacek.*[7] There the Ninth Circuit held that a union constitution is not a "contract" within the meaning of § 301 of the LMRA so as to ground jurisdiction in a purely intraunion dispute between a member and his organization.

Leading decisions propounding the property theory of union members' rights include *Heasley v. Operative Plasterers*[8] from Pennsylvania and *Crossen v. Duffy*[9] from Ohio. In *Bires v. Barney,*[10] where the suspension of members and officers of a local union by a parent union did not sever their membership in the union but merely deprived them of the right to visit lodges, the Oregon courts refused to intervene when the suspended members and officers sued for reinstatement, on the ground no property rights were jeopardized.

One of the recommendations of the McClellan Committee in 1958, as the result of its investigations into improper practices involving unions, was that measures should be taken to encourage more "democracy" in internal union affairs. The bill (S. 1555) reported out by the Senate Labor Committee in 1959 contained provisions requiring reporting and disclosure by unions to their members and regulating union elections. However, Senator McClellan introduced an amendment to the committee

---

[4] 145 Tex. 399, 198 S.W.2d 729 (1946).
[5] 364 F.2d 67 (2d Cir. 1966), *cert. denied,* 385 U.S. 971 (1966).
[6] 356 U.S. 617, 618 (1958).
[7] 431 F.2d 705 (9th Cir. 1970).
[8] 324 Pa. 257, 188 A. 206 (1936).
[9] 90 Ohio App. 252, 103 N.E.2d 769 (1951).
[10] 203 Ore. 107, 277 P.2d 751 (1954).

bill providing explicitly a "Bill of Rights" for members of labor organizations, and this was adopted, with modifications, becoming Title I of the Labor-Management Reporting and Disclosure Act of 1959 (reproduced in the *Statutory Appendix*). Most noteworthy in this Act is the emphasis, not upon contract and property rights, but upon the analogy between the rights of union members and the rights of citizens in a political democracy, protected by constitutional freedoms. The dominant idea in the Eighty-Sixth Congress was that labor unions are of such great public importance that legislation to protect union members in the exercise of basic liberties in the democratic process is essential — a far cry indeed from the concept of a labor union as a private voluntary association like a social club.

The various rights guaranteed by Title I of the LMRDA will be treated in detail later in this Part.

B. SUITS BY AND AGAINST UNIONS

STATUTORY REFERENCE
LMRA § 301

Judge-made law — the "pure" common law — holds as a general rule that those unions which are voluntary, unincorporated associations have no legal being apart from their members, and may therefore neither sue nor be sued in their common names.[11] The statutory situation, however, both state and federal, is different. Although limited by its terms to suits by and against unions for violations of collective agreements, § 301 of the LMRA aptly represents the current statutory trend toward recognizing even unincorporated labor unions as legal entities. A further measure of the development of the law in this respect may be gathered from a statement by the National Labor Relations Board: "The common law concept of an unincorporated labor organization as a group of individuals having no separate entity apart from its members has been discarded — to the extent that it was not already outmoded in modern jurisprudence — by the Labor Management Relations Act, 1947. It is clear that the Act treats labor organizations, for all practical purposes, as juridical entities." [12]

The "strict" common-law view on the suability of unions applies both at law [13] and in equity.[14] Nonetheless, many courts have got around the rule by using such devices as the class or representative action to permit

---

[11] The relatively few unions which are incorporated have, of course, the same legal status as other corporations. *See, e.g.,* Faultless Caster Corp. v. UEW-CIO, 119 Ind. App. 330, 86 N.E.2d 703 (1949).

[12] Longshoremen's Union, 79 N.L.R.B. 1487 (1948). *See also* Freight Drivers Local 600 v. Gordon, 576 F. 2d 1285 (8th Cir. 1978) (local union is "person" entitled to file under § 4(a) of the Bankruptcy Act).

[13] *E.g.,* Walker v. Brotherhood of Locomotive Engineers, 186 Ga. 811, 190 S.E. 146 (1938); Pickett v. Walsh, 192 Mass. 572, 78 N.E. 753 (1906). The authorities are gathered in Annot., 27 A.L.R. 786 (1923), and Annot., 149 A.L.R. 508 (1944).

[14] Forest City Mfg. Co. v. ILGWU, Local 104, 233 Mo. App. 935, 111 S.W.2d 934 (1938).

suits in equity by and against unions.[15] An "estoppel" theory has also been invoked to hold a union subject to suit by its members for wrongful expulsion.[16] These roundabout approaches of the state courts were eschewed by the United States Supreme Court in *United Mine Workers v. Coronado Coal Co.*[17] After pointing out the practical acceptance of labor unions as entities separate from their members, and the existence of a considerable body of federal legislation recognizing unions for various legal purposes, the Court met the issue head-on and declared: "In this state of federal legislation, we think that such organizations are suable in the federal courts. . . ." This bold action by the Supreme Court did not affect the states' common law rules, but it did succeed in establishing a different rule for the federal courts.

Apart from § 301 of the LMRA, the federal provision bearing most directly on suability is Rule 17(b) of the Federal Rules of Civil Procedure. "[C]apacity to sue or be sued," this rule provides, "shall be determined by the law of the state in which the district court is held; except that a partnership or other unincorporated association, which has no such capacity by the law of such state, may sue or be sued in its common name for the purpose of enforcing for or against it a substantive right existing under the Constitution or laws of the United States."

State laws on "suability" vary considerably. Some, like New York, permit an action by or against designated officers of an association in their representative capacity.[18] Others — California, for example — provide for suit in the name which an unincorporated association has assumed.[19] A few states, such as Florida, have made unions legal entities, at least for purposes of suit, by express statutory provision.[20]

As has already been seen, § 301 of the LMRA enables unions to sue or be sued as legal entities in the federal courts for breach of union-employer contracts, regardless of diversity of citizenship or the amount in controversy. Section 303 also provides that unions may be sued as entities by persons injured by such conduct as secondary boycotts or jurisdictional strikes. The NLRB is empowered by § 10(c) of the NLRA to require back

---

[15] Smith v. Arkansas Motor Freight Lines, 214 Ark. 553, 217 S.W.2d 249 (1949); Donahue v. Kenney, 327 Mass. 409, 99 N.E.2d 155 (1951). Statutes in about half the states specifically provide for class or representative actions. *See* Sellers, *Suability of Trade Unions as a Legal Entity,* 33 CALIF. L. REV. 444, 447 (1945). On the question whether such statutes permit actions at law for damages, as well as suits in equity, *see* Jackson v. International Operating Engineers, 307 Ky. 485, 211 S.W.2d 138 (1948), and cases cited.

[16] Nissen v. International Bhd. of Teamsters, 229 Iowa 1028, 295 N.W. 858 (1941). *But see* McClees v. International Bhd. of Locomotive Engineers, 59 Ohio App. 477, 18 N.E.2d 812 (1938) (dismissing a suit by a union member against his union on the theory it amounted to a suit against himself).

[17] 259 U.S. 344 (1922). *See also* Dodd, *Dogma and Practice in the Law of Associations,* 42 HARV. L. REV. 977 (1929); Sturges, *Unincorporated Associations as Parties to Actions,* 33 YALE L.J. 383 (1924); Note, *Unions as Juridical Persons,* 66 YALE L.J. 712 (1957).

[18] N.Y. GEN. ASS'NS LAW §§ 12, 13 (McKinney 1942, Supp. 1978).

[19] CAL. CIV. PRO. CODE § 388 (Deering 1972).

[20] Fla. Stat. § 447.11 (1966).

pay of labor organizations responsible for discrimination against individual employees. Another instance of congressional treatment of unions as legal entities is § 102 of the Labor-Management Reporting and Disclosure Act of 1959, which provides for private suits in federal court to enforce the "Bill of Rights" of union members.

Despite the *Coronado* decision, the Supreme Court unanimously held in *United Steelworkers v. R.H. Bouligny, Inc.*,[21] that unions are not entities to the extent of possessing "citizenship" sufficient to support federal diversity jurisdiction, without regard to the citizenship of their members. Lower federal courts have ruled that a union has the citizenship of all its members.[22]

Whether a union can be sued in its common name is only part of the problem of union suability. How is service of process to be effected? From what persons or funds may a money judgment be collected? How is individual or organizational responsibility established? The answers are somewhat analogous to (and as variable as) the answers concerning "suability" — with the common law and the current statutory situation providing the main contrasts, and with the rules of the *Coronado* case falling somewhere in between.

SECTION II. Union Membership

A. THE RIGHT OF ADMISSION

MAYER V. JOURNEYMEN STONECUTTERS' ASS'N, 47 N.J. EQ. 519, 20 A. 492 (1890). This was a suit brought by two journeymen stonecutters and a group of master stonecutters who employed journeymen. Defendant stonecutters' association controlled most employment opportunities in the relevant area. It implemented its position, as the court put it, "by denunciations and persecution applied to the offending workmen," who sought jobs without membership, "and boycotting and strikes applied to the offending employers." Complainants asked the court to require the association to admit to membership the complaining journeymen, as well as all other journeymen in the area. *Held,* relief denied. In so ruling, the court pointed out that there was no showing of a proper request by complainant journeymen for admission. But the court went on to say (47 N.J. Eq. at 523-24):

> But if it were otherwise, has this court power to require the admission of a person to membership in a voluntary association, when it has been denied by the society? These organizations are formed for purposes mutually agreed upon; their right to make

---

[21] 382 U.S. 145 (1965).

[22] Underwood v. Maloney, 256 F.2d 334 (3d Cir. 1958), *cert. denied,* 358 U.S. 864 (1958); Lloyd A. Fry Roofing Co. v. Textile Workers, 152 F. Supp. 19 (E.D. Pa. 1957). *See also* Cohn, *Problems in Establishing Federal Jurisdiction Over an Unincorporated Labor Union,* 47 GEO. L.J. 491, 509 (1959).

by-laws and rules for the admission of members and the transaction
of business is unquestionable. They may require such qualifications
for membership, and such formalities of election, as they choose.
They may restrict membership to the original promoters, or limit the
number to be thereafter admitted. The very idea of such
organizations is association mutually acceptable, or in accordance
with regulations agreed upon. A power to require the admission of
a person in any way objectionable to the society is repugnant to the
scheme of its organization. While courts have interfered to inquire
into and restrain the action of such societies in the attempted
exclusion of persons who have been regularly admitted to
membership, no case can, I think, be found where the power of any
court has been exercised, as sought in this case, to require the
admission of any person to original membership in any such
voluntary association. Courts exist to protect rights, and where the
right has once attached they will interfere to prevent its violation; but
no person has any abstract right to be admitted to such membership.
That depends solely upon the action of the society, exercised in
accordance with its regulations, and, until so admitted, no right exists
which the courts can be called upon to protect or enforce.

NOTE

This represents the orthodox view, predicated on the notion that a
trade union is like any other voluntary association and can thus fix its own
admission standards. In the context of modern developments regarding
the closed and union shop, there are significant judicial and legislative
trends in the direction of requiring an "open" union. Thus, for example,
in James v. Marinship Corp., 25 Cal. 2d 721, 155 P.2d 329 (1944), it was
held in effect that a union could not exercise union shop privileges and
at the same time arbitrarily deny membership or impose "second class
membership." This principle is also embodied (at least as to each
individual employee) in §§ 8(a)(3) and 8(b)(2) of the NLRA and in § 2,
Eleventh of the RLA. *See generally* Summers, *The Right to Join a Union,*
47 COLUM. L. REV. 33 (1947); Blumrosen, *Legal Protection Against
Exclusion From Union Activities,* 22 OHIO ST. L.J. 21 (1961); Lang,
Toward a Right to Union Membership, 12 HARV. CIV. RTS.-CIV. LIB. L.
REV. 31 (1977).

DIRECTORS GUILD OF AMERICA, INC. v. SUPERIOR COURT OF LOS ANGELES
COUNTY, 64 Cal. 2d 42, 409 P.2d 934 (1966). Plaintiff had been assured
employment as an assistant director in a television series. He sought
admission to defendant union, which allegedly controlled production jobs
in the industry through oral agreements with many producers. Although
plaintiff tendered the requisite dues and fees and fulfilled the formal
membership requirements, he was refused admission pursuant to the

union's nepotism policy. The court declined relief on the ground that the "crux" of plaintiff's action was job discrimination, not denial of union membership, and that federal law thus preempted. But a state remedy would have been appropriate if plaintiff had actually been employed and had then been arbitrarily refused membership, thereby making the dispute focus on purely internal union matters. Reasoned the court (64 Cal. 2d at 52-54):

> The decisions of this court thus recognize that membership in the union means more than mere personal or social accommodation. Such membership affords to the employee not only the opportunity to participate in the negotiation of the contract governing his employment but also the chance to engage in the institutional life of the union. Although in the case which involves interstate commerce the union must legally give fair representation to all the appropriate employees, whether or not they are members of the union, the union official, in the nature of political realities, will in all likelihood more diligently represent union members, who can vote him out of office, than employees whom he must serve only as a matter of abstract law.
>
> Our decisions further recognize that the union functions as the medium for the exercise of industrial franchise. As Summers puts it, "The right to join a union involves the right to an economic ballot." (*The Right to Join a Union* (1947) 47 Colum. L. Rev. 33.) Participation in the union's affairs by the workman compares to the participation of the citizen in the affairs of his community. The union, as a kind of public service institution, affords to its members the opportunity to record themselves upon all matters affecting their relationships with the employer; it serves likewise as a vehicle for the expression of the membership's position on political and community issues. The shadowy right to "fair representation" by the union, accorded by the Act, is by no means the same as the hard concrete ability to vote and to participate in the affairs of the union.

> The above grounds for condemnation of arbitrary rejection from membership apply as forcefully to the situation in which the union does not have a union shop contract as to that in which it does. The need of the worker for union participation is not reduced because the union does not enjoy a union shop; the basis for membership lies in the right and desirability of representation, not in the union's economic control of the job.
>
> Our analysis applies, however, only to union membership for those employed in the appropriate craft or industry. To hold that a union must admit *all* persons who seek membership but are not employed in the craft or industry whose employees are represented by the union would raise serious social and economic questions. Any such sweeping ruling would subject the union to an influx of unemployed persons who could distort its function from representation of those working in the relevant craft or industry to purposes alien to such objectives. It would set up for state courts a test as to the scope of the union's obligation of representation which would conflict with the

National Labor Relation Board's counterpart concept of the appropriate bargaining unit. It could gravely affect the basic structure of the union.

NOTE

The California view has not carried the day. In the absence of a statute regulating union membership policies, the following decision still represents the majority position on the issue.

OLIPHANT v. BROTHERHOOD OF LOCOMOTIVE FIREMEN & ENGINEMEN

United States District Court, Northern District of Ohio, Eastern Division
156 F. Supp. 89 (1957)
Aff'd, 262 F.2d 359 (6th Cir. 1958)
Cert. denied, 359 U.S. 935 (1959)

JONES, CHIEF JUDGE. This is an action brought by several Negro firemen employed by various southern railroads seeking an order from this court compelling the Brotherhood of Locomotive Firemen and Enginemen to admit them to membership. The Brotherhood has been certified as exclusive bargaining representative for these men, but the constitution of the Brotherhood forbids the admission of Negroes to membership. . . .

The real question is whether Federal action has deprived these Negro citizens of liberty or property without due process of law. It is the considered judgment of this court, without dealing with the question of whether the alleged right to become a member of a labor organization certified as exclusive bargaining representative is concerned with liberty or property, that sufficient Federal action is not shown to enable the courts to declare the Railway Labor Act, or any part thereof, an unconstitutional deprivation of liberty or property. The purpose of the Act was and is to promote industrial peace. Apparently the Act itself would not have been acceptable to the Congress if Negro membership in the agent had been required. In short, the representatives of all the people could not agree that any control over the membership was essential to the major purpose of the Act. However, expedience does not remove the taint of unconstitutionality, if such there be.

As is mentioned above, the Federal action taken by an agency of the Congress, was the certification of the Brotherhood of Locomotive Firemen and Enginemen as exclusive bargaining representative for the bargaining unit involved, which included persons who were not acceptable to membership under the Constitution of the Brotherhood. Actions by the Brotherhood can be attributed to the Congress only if the act of certification clothes the Brotherhood with some or all of the attributes of a Federal agency. The court is satisfied that this act is not sufficient to change the character of the organization from that of a private association to that of a governmental agency.

The court can feel that a situation is unjust and may need some remedial action, but unless upon sound equitable principles relief can be granted, the remedy does not lie with the courts. . . . To compel by judicial mandate membership in voluntary organizations where the Congress has knowingly and expressly permitted the bargaining agent to prescribe its own qualifications for membership would be usurping the legislative function. . . .

Accordingly, for the reason that there is not sufficient Federal action to render the membership policies of this Brotherhood subject to judicial control, plaintiffs must be denied the relief requested. . . .

NOTES

1. In denying the petition for certiorari in the *Oliphant* case, the Supreme Court said it was making this denial "in view of the abstract context in which the questions sought to be raised are presented by this record." For further discussion of the *Oliphant* case, see Wellington, *The Constitution, the Labor Union, and "Governmental Action,"* 70 YALE L.J. 345 (1961).

2. The National Labor Relations Act does not directly regulate admission to union membership. Section 8(b)(1)(A) states "this paragraph shall not impair the right of a labor organization to prescribe its own rules with respect to the acquisition or retention of membership therein." Section 8(b)(5), however, does prohibit excessive or discriminatory initiation fees by unions having union shop contracts. In addition, a proviso to § 8(a)(3) prevents enforcement of "union security" agreements against employees discriminatorily denied membership.

3. Admission to union membership was not dealt with by the Labor-Management Reporting and Disclosure Act of 1959. Senator McClellan had included the following provision in his original bill (S. 1137, 86th Cong., 1st Sess. (1959)):

"Section 101(2). Eligibility for Membership. — Every person who meets the reasonable qualifications uniformly prescribed by a labor organization for membership therein shall be eligible for and admitted to membership in such organization. . . ."

This provision was not included in the "Bill of Rights" amendment introduced by Senator McClellan and enacted, in modified form, as Title I of the LMRDA. What would have been the practical consequences of such a provision? What reasons could be given for its omission?

4. In Betts v. Easley, 161 Kan. 459, 169 P.2d 831 (1946), black members of a bargaining unit who, under the constitution of the union certified as their bargaining agent, were ineligible for equal membership with whites, sued to enjoin their exclusion and their segregation in separate lodges. In sustaining their cause of action the court stated:

The case here does not, under the allegations, involve denial of seniority rights, as in the *Steele* case, but it does involve a similar issue of racial discrimination. The petition alleges not only that Negro employees are denied the right to take part in such local affairs of the union as the election of officers and the fixing of dues, but are denied the right to participate in determining the position to be taken by the union, as bargaining agent for all employees, as to wages, hours, working conditions, and other such matters vitally affecting their economic welfare. Such denial is repugnant to every American concept of equality under the law. It is abhorrent both to the letter and the spirit of our fundamental charter. Never was it more important than now to reject such racial discrimination and to resist all erosions of individual liberty. The acts complained of are in violation of the Fifth Amendment.

5. Section 703(c) of the Civil Rights Act of 1964, 42 U.S.C. § 2000e-2, forbids any labor organization having 15 or more members "to exclude or to expel from its membership, or otherwise to discriminate against, any individual because of his race, color, religion, sex, or national origin." *See generally* W. GOULD, BLACK WORKERS IN WHITE UNIONS (1977); R. MARSHALL, THE NEGRO AND ORGANIZED LABOR (1965); M. SOVERN, LEGAL RESTRAINTS ON RACIAL DISCRIMINATION IN EMPLOYMENT (1966).

B. COMPULSORY UNIONISM

Unions ordinarily seek to make membership one hundred percent in occupational groups which they represent. To accomplish this, they may employ persuasion or economic pressure. They may also try to obtain so-called "union security" agreements from employers. The most common types of union security agreements are the following:

Closed Shop

From the union point of view, the most effective form of union security provision is the "closed shop." A standard version would read:

"The employer hereby agrees to employ only members in good standing of the Union."

Prior to the enactment of the LMRA in 1947, closed shop agreements were fairly common, especially in such industries as construction, printing, hosiery, clothing, baking, brewing, and trucking, where a majority of the workers covered by collective agreements were under closed shop contracts.

Union Shop

The "union shop" contract does not require the employer to hire only union members, but does require the nonunion employee to become a member of the union within a prescribed period after his initial employment. A typical clause would provide:

"Each employee covered by this agreement shall, as a condition of continued employment, become and remain a member of the Union on and after the thirtieth day following the beginning of his employment or following the effective date of this agreement, whichever is the later."

Next to the closed shop, an agreement of this kind is the most favored by unions as a security device. Since 1947, when the Taft-Hartley Act outlawed the closed shop, the union shop has become the most common form of union security provision. It is now found in about 63 percent of collective agreements.[1]

Agency Shop

In deference to the religious scruples or ethical principles of some employees, or in response to certain state statutes, some labor contracts provide for a so-called "agency shop" instead of the usual union shop. Under an agency shop an employee does not have to become a member of the union, but any employee electing not to join must pay to the union an amount equal to the customary initiation fee and the periodic dues required of members. Agency shop provisions appear in nine percent of contracts.[2]

Maintenance of Membership

"Maintenance of membership" gained wide use as a form of union security during World War II, largely because it was employed by the National War Labor Board as a formula for compromising the demands of unions for the closed shop and the demands of employers for the maintenance of the status quo in their plants during the war. A typical maintenance of membership clause, as directed by the WLB, follows:

"All members who, 15 days after the date of the Directive Order of the National War Labor Board in this case, are members of the Union in good standing in accordance with the constitution and bylaws of the Union, and those employees who may thereafter become members, shall, as a condition of employment, remain members of the Union in good standing during the life of the agreement."

Four percent of today's labor agreements contain maintenance of membership provisions.[3]

Two other kinds of contractual arrangements are often regarded as a form of union security, although they do not necessarily condition employment on union membership or on payments to unions. The first is the "checkoff," under which the employer deducts union dues from the employees' wages and transmits them to the union. Obviously, this is a

---

[1] BNA, LABOR RELATIONS YEARBOOK — 1977 p. 215 (1978). An additional 11 percent of the contracts contain "modified" union shop clauses.

[2] *Ibid.*

[3] *Ibid.*

great aid in keeping members in financial good standing. Sometimes unions have been satisfied with the checkoff as the sole security provision. More often, however, the checkoff has been used together with some type of provision conditioning employment on union membership. (Section 302(c)(4) of the LMRA requires a written authorization from an employee before an employer can check off his dues.)

The second arrangement which plays a role akin to union security is the hiring hall or referral system. Under this arrangement the union registers job applicants and refers them to employers as openings occur. The hiring hall in industries affecting commerce is subject to the NLRA's prohibition of union-caused discrimination, as was seen in Part Two, *supra* at 126.

At common law voluntary closed shop agreements between unions and employers were valid, but strikes to obtain them at first were generally illegal.[4] Later a trend developed toward recognizing the closed shop as a lawful objective of union collective action.[5] Today union security devices are regulated primarily under federal and state statutes.

1. UNION SECURITY UNDER FEDERAL LEGISLATION

STATUTORY REFERENCES

RLA § 2, Fourth, Fifth, and Eleventh
NLRA §§ 8(a)(3), 8(b)(2), 8(b)(5), 8(f), 9(e)

Any agreement that conditions an employee's right to work on membership in a labor organization is a patent interference with his freedom of self-organization and an act of discrimination. In enacting the labor relations act limitations on employer discrimination, Congress and the state legislatures have perforce had to decide whether (1) to equate such interferences with the "yellow-dog" contract and outlaw them altogether, or (2) to exempt them altogether and leave them within the area of collective bargaining, or (3) to regulate their use by imposing conditions and limitations. A fourth alternative was to force employers and employees to accept union security, upon demand of qualified unions, but this was clearly not a practical possibility.[6]

Legislative treatment of the problem has reflected its extremely troublesome nature. In the Railway Labor Act, Congress in the 1934 amendments prohibited all forms of union security arrangements, even including the checkoff, a result the more interesting because the Act of 1926 was supposed to represent the views of both employers and unions in the industry. In the original NLRA, and in the "little Wagner acts" which quickly followed, collective agreements conditioning employment

---

[4] *E.g.,* Colonial Press, Inc. v. Ellis, 321 Mass. 495, 74 N.E.2d 1 (1947), and cases cited.

[5] L. TELLER, LABOR DISPUTES AND COLLECTIVE BARGAINING §§ 97-103 (1940).

[6] This is a possibility that probably could be realized only through a labor-dominated government. It was achieved in Saskatchewan by the Socialist party. *See* SASK. STATS. ch. 98, § 6 (1946), amending the Trade Union Act of 1944.

on union membership were expressly exempted from the prohibition on employer discrimination when such agreements were made with unions having statutory bargaining rights. However, as the pendulum of public opinion, which had swung far toward unionism, began to return, some of the states either banned the closed shop and other forms of union security agreements or imposed various kinds of limiting regulations. Finally Congress, in the LMRA of 1947, adopted a policy of limited approval. Thus, under the amended proviso to § 8(a)(3), the closed shop was outlawed, and union shop agreements were permitted as a form of employer discrimination only if the conditions there specified were met. In 1951 the RLA was amended so as to permit union shop and checkoff agreements subject to conditions approximating those contained in the LMRA. And in 1952 the so-called "Taft-Humphrey" Act liberalized somewhat the restrictions of the LMRA by deleting the requirement of an affirmative vote of the employees before a union could negotiate a union security contract.

NLRB v. GENERAL MOTORS CORP.

Supreme Court of the United States
373 U.S. 734, 83 S. Ct. 1453, 10 L. Ed. 2d 670 (1963)

MR. JUSTICE WHITE delivered the opinion of the Court.

The issue here is whether an employer commits an unfair labor practice, National Labor Relations Act § 8(a)(5), when it refuses to bargain with a certified union over the union's proposal for the adoption of the "agency shop." More narrowly, since the employer is not obliged to bargain over a proposal that he commit an unfair labor practice, the question is whether the agency shop is an unfair labor practice under § 8(a)(3) of the Act or else is exempted from the prohibitions of that section by the proviso thereto. We have concluded that this type of arrangement does not constitute an unfair labor practice and that it is not prohibited by § 8.

Respondent's employees are represented by the United Automobile, Aerospace and Agricultural Implement Workers of America, UAW, in a single, multi-plant, company-wide unit. The 1958 agreement between union and company provides for maintenance of membership and the union shop. These provisions were not operative, however, in such states as Indiana where state law prohibited making union membership a condition of employment.

In June 1959, the Indiana intermediate appellate court held that an agency shop arrangement would not violate the state right-to-work law. Meade Elec. Co. v. Hagberg, 129 Ind. App. 631, 159 N.E.2d 408 (1959). As defined in that opinion, the term "agency shop" applies to an arrangement under which all employees are required as a condition of employment to pay dues to the union and pay the union's initiation fee, but they need not actually become union members. The union thereafter sent respondent a letter proposing the negotiation of a contractual provision covering Indiana plants "generally similar to that set forth" in the *Meade* case. Continued employment in the Indiana plants would be conditioned upon the payment of sums equal to the initiation fee and regular monthly dues paid by the union members. The intent of the proposal, the NLRB concluded, was not to require membership but to make membership available at the employees' option and on nondiscriminatory terms. Employees choosing not to join would make the required payments and, in accordance with union custom, would share in union expenditures for strike benefits, educational and retired member benefits, and union publications and promotional activities, but they would not be entitled to attend union meetings, vote upon ratification of agreements negotiated by the union, or have a voice in the internal affairs of the union. The respondent made no counterproposal, but replied to the union's letter that the proposed agreement would violate the National Labor Relations Act and that respondent must therefore "respectfully decline to comply with your request for a meeting" to bargain over the proposal.

The union thereupon filed a complaint with the NLRB against respondent for its alleged refusal to bargain in good faith. In the Board's view of the record, "the union was not seeking to bargain over a clause requiring nonmember employees to pay sums equal to dues and fees as a condition of employment while at the same time maintaining a closed-union policy with respect to applicants for membership," since the proposal contemplated an arrangement in which "all employees are *given the option* of becoming, or refraining from becoming, members of the union." Proceeding on this basis and putting aside the consequences of a closed-union policy upon the legality of the agency shop, the Board assessed the union's proposal as comporting fully with the congressional declaration of policy in favor of union-security contracts and therefore a mandatory subject as to which the Act obliged respondent to bargain in good faith. At the same time, it stated that it had "no doubt that an agency-shop agreement is a permissible form of union-security within the meaning of §§ 7 and 8(a)(3) of the Act." Accordingly, the Board ruled that respondents had committed an unfair labor practice by refusing to bargain in good faith with the certified bargaining representative of its employees, and it ordered respondent to bargain with the union over the proposed arrangement; no back-pay award is involved in this case. 133 N.L.R.B. 451.

Respondent petitioned for review in the Court of Appeals, and the Board cross-petitioned for enforcement. The Court of Appeals set the order aside on the grounds that the Act tolerates only "an agreement requiring membership in a labor organization as a condition of employment" when such agreements do not violate state right-to-work laws, and that the Act does not authorize agreements requiring payment of membership dues to a union, in lieu of membership, as a condition of employment. It held that the proposed agency shop agreement would violate §§ 7, 8(a)(1), and 8(a)(3) of the Act and that the employer was therefore not obliged to bargain over it. 303 F.2d 428 (6th Cir. 1962). We granted certiorari . . . and now reverse the decision of the Court of Appeals.

Section 8(3) under the Wagner Act was the predecessor to § 8(a)(3) of the present law. Like § 8(a)(3), § 8(3) forbade employers to discriminate against employees to compel them to join a union. Because it was feared that § 8(3) and § 7, if nothing were added to qualify them, might be held to outlaw union-security arrangements such as the closed shop, see 79 Cong. Rec. 7570 (statement of Senator Wagner), 7674 (statement of Senator Walsh); H.R. Rep. No. 972, at 17; H.R. Rep. No. 1147, at 19, the proviso to § 8(3) was added expressly declaring:

"*Provided,* That nothing in this Act . . . or in any other statute of the United States, shall preclude an employer from making an agreement with a labor organization . . . to require as a condition of employment membership therein, if such labor organization is the representative of the employees as provided in section 9(a). . . ."

The prevailing administrative and judicial view under the Wagner Act was or came to be that the proviso to § 8(3) covered both the closed and union shop, as well as less onerous union security arrangements, if they were otherwise legal. The NLRB construed the proviso as shielding from an unfair labor practice charge less severe forms of union-security arrangements than the closed or the union shop, including an arrangement in Public Service Co. of Colorado, 89 N.L.R.B. 418, requiring nonunion members to pay to the union $2 a month "for the support of the bargaining unit." And in Algoma Plywood & Veneer Co. v. Wisconsin Employment Relations Board, 336 U.S. 301, 307 (1949), which involved a maintenance of membership agreement, the Court, in commenting on petitioner's contention that the proviso of § 8(3) affirmatively protected arrangements within its scope, cf. Garner v. Teamsters Union, 346 U.S. 485 (1953), said of its purpose: "The short answer is that § 8(3) merely disclaims a national policy hostile to the closed shop *or other forms of union-security agreement.*" (Emphasis added.)

When Congress enacted the Taft-Hartley Act, it added . . . to the language of the original proviso to § 8(3). . . . These additions were intended to accomplish twin purposes. On the one hand, the most serious abuses of compulsory unionism were eliminated by abolishing the closed shop. On the other hand, Congress recognized that in the absence of a union-security provision "many employees sharing the benefits of what unions are able to accomplish, like collective bargaining, will refuse to pay their share of the cost." S. Rep. No. 105, 80th Cong., 1st Sess., at 6, 1 Leg. Hist. L.M.R.A. 412. Consequently, under the new law "employers would still be permitted to enter into agreements requiring all employees in a given bargaining unit to become members thirty days after being hired" but "expulsion from a union cannot be a ground of compulsory discharge if the worker is not delinquent in paying his initiation fees or dues." S. Rep. No. 105, at 7, 1 Leg. Hist. L.M.R.A. 413. The amendments were intended only to "remedy the most serious abuses of compulsory union membership and yet give employers and unions who feel that such agreements promoted stability by eliminating 'free riders' the right to continue such arrangements." *Ibid.* As far as the federal law was concerned, all employees could be required to pay their way. The bill "abolishes the closed shop but permits voluntary agreements for requiring such forms of compulsory membership as the union shop or maintenance of membership. . . ." S. Rep. No. 105, at 3, 1 Leg. Hist. L.M.R.A. 409.

We find nothing in the legislative history of the Act indicating that Congress intended the amended proviso to § 8(a)(3) to validate only the union shop and simultaneously to abolish, in addition to the closed shop, all other union-security arrangements permissible under state law. There is much to be said for the Board's view that, if Congress desired in the Wagner Act to permit a closed or union shop and in the Taft-Hartley Act the union shop, then it also intended to preserve the status of less vigorous, less compulsory contracts, which demanded less adherence to the union.

Respondent, however, relies upon the express words of the proviso which allow employment to be conditioned upon "membership": since the union's proposal here does not require actual membership but demands only initiation fees and monthly dues it is not saved by the proviso. This position, of course, would reject administrative decisions concerning the scope of § 8(3) of the Wagner Act, *e.g.,* Public Service Co. of Colorado, *supra,* reaffirmed by the Board under the Taft-Hartley amendments, American Seating Co., 98 N.L.R.B. 800. Moreover, the 1947 amendments not only abolished the closed shop but also made significant alterations in the meaning of "membership" for the purposes of union security contracts. Under the second proviso to § 8(a)(3), the burdens of membership upon which employment may be conditioned are expressly limited to the payment of initiation fees and monthly dues. It is permissible to condition employment upon membership, but membership, insofar as it has significance to employment rights, may in turn be conditioned only upon payment of fees and dues. "Membership" as a condition of employment is whittled down to its financial core. This Court has said as much before in Radio Officers' Union v. NLRB, 347 U.S. 17, 41 (1954):

"... This legislative history clearly indicates that Congress intended to prevent utilization of union security agreements for any purpose other than to compel payment of union dues and fees. Thus, Congress recognized the validity of unions' concern about 'free riders,' i.e., employees who receive the benefits of union representation but are unwilling to contribute their fair share of financial support to such union, and gave the unions the power to contract to meet that problem while withholding from unions the power to cause the discharge of employees for any other reason. . . ."

We are therefore confident that the proposal made by the union here conditioned employment upon the practical equivalent of union "membership," as Congress used that term in the proviso to § 8(a)(3). The proposal for requiring the payment of dues and fees imposes no burdens not imposed by a permissible union shop contract and compels the performance of only those duties of membership which are enforceable by discharge under a union shop arrangement. If an employee in a union shop unit refuses to respect any union-imposed obligations other than the duty to pay dues and fees, and membership in the union is therefore denied or terminated, the condition of "membership" for § 8(a)(3) purposes is nevertheless satisfied and the employee may not be discharged for nonmembership even though he is not a formal member. Of course, if the union chooses to extend membership even though the employee will meet only the minimum financial burden, and refuses to support or "join" the union in any other affirmative way, the employee may have to become a "member" under a union shop contract, in the sense that the union may be able to place him on its rolls. The agency shop arrangement proposed here removes that choice from the union and places the option of membership in the employee while still requiring the same monetary support as does the union shop. Such a difference between the union and agency shop may be of great importance in some contexts, but for present purposes it is more formal than real. To the extent that it has any significance at all, it serves rather than violates, the desire of Congress to reduce the evils of compulsory unionism while allowing financial support for the bargaining agent.[12]

In short, the employer categorically refused to bargain with the union over a proposal for an agreement within the proviso to § 8(a)(3) and as such, lawful, for the purposes of this case. By the same token, § 7, and derivatively § 8(a)(1), cannot be deemed to forbid the employer to enter such agreements, since it too is expressly limited by the § 8(a)(3) proviso. We hold that the employer was not excused from his duty to bargain over the proposal on the theory that his acceding to it would necessarily involve him in an unfair labor practice. Whether a different result obtains in States which have declared such arrangements unlawful is an issue still to be resolved in Retail Clerks Union v. Schermerhorn, 373 U.S. 746 (1963), and one which is of no relevance here because Indiana law does not forbid the present contract proposal. In the context of this case, then, the employer cannot justify his refusal to bargain. He violated § 8(a)(5), and the Board properly ordered him to return to the bargaining table.

Reversed and remanded.

MR. JUSTICE GOLDBERG took no part in the consideration or decision of this case.

---

[12] Also wide of the mark is respondent's further suggestion that Congress contemplated the obligation to pay fees and dues to be imposed only in connection with actual membership in the union, so as to insure the enjoyment of all union benefits and rights by those from whom money is extracted. Congress, it is said, had no desire to open the door to compulsory contracts which extract money but exclude the contributing employees from union membership. But, as analyzed by the Board and as the case comes to us, there is no closed-union aspect to the present proposal by the union. Membership remains optional with the employee and the significance of desired, but unavailable, union membership, or the benefits of membership, in terms of permissible § 8(a)(3) security contracts, we leave for another case. . . .

NOTES

1. *Discharge for reasons other than nonpayment of dues.* Is there any
practical difference between the "union shop" and the "agency shop"? In
Union Starch & Ref. Co., 87 N.L.R.B. 779 (1949), *enforced,* 186 F.2d 1008
(7th Cir. 1951), *cert. denied,* 342 U.S. 815 (1951), the Labor Board held
employees could not lawfully be discharged so long as they tendered their
initiation fees and dues, even though they refused to comply with a union
rule requiring all applicants to attend a union meeting and to take a
membership oath. *See also* Hersey Foods Corp., 207 N.L.R.B. 897 (1973).
Similarly, a worker meets the "membership" requirement as long as he
continues to pay union dues, despite his formal resignation from the
union. Marlin Rockwell Corp., 114 N.L.R.B. 553 (1955). Does a union
nonetheless retain a significant practical advantage in being able to write
a union shop clause rather than an agency shop clause into a collective
agreement? The implications of the *Union Starch* doctrine are treated in
Toner, *The Union Shop Under Taft-Hartley,* 5 Lab. L.J. 552 (1954); Note,
52 Mich. L. Rev. 619 (1954).

A union shop provision may not be used to enforce membership
obligations other than dues payments. Thus, for example, a discharge for
failure to pay a union fine is an unfair labor practice. Electric Auto-Lite
Co., 92 N.L.R.B. 1073 (1950), *enforced per curiam,* 196 F.2d 500 (6th Cir.
1952), *cert. denied,* 344 U.S. 823 (1952). Do the present restrictions on
the use of union security agreements unwisely divest unions of effective
power to maintain proper membership standards? Suppose a union
holding a union shop contract decides to purge its ranks of mob elements.
Is the employer precluded from discharging such expelled employees
under any and all circumstances? *Cf.* NLRB v. Kingston Cake Co., 206
F.2d 604 (3d Cir. 1953) (to reinstate a discharged employee who, prior
to his expulsion, refused as a union official to sign a non-Communist
affidavit in order to keep his union off the ballot, would not effectuate the
policies of the Act).

May an employee who has been lawfully suspended or expelled from his
union be required to continue paying dues, on pain of discharge under
a valid union security provision? *Cf.* Steelworkers Local 4186 (McGraw
Edison Co.), 181 N.L.R.B. 992 (1970).

If a union's bylaws set monthly dues at $6.00 but grant a $2.00 refund
for attending monthly meetings, what amount must an employee pay to
satisfy a union shop's requirements? *See* Pulp & Paper Workers Local 171
(Boise Cascade Corp.), 165 N.L.R.B. 971 (1967), *overruling* Leece-Neville
Co., 140 N.L.R.B. 56 (1962). *But cf.* Norris Industries, Thermador Div.,
190 N.L.R.B. 479 (1971).

2. *Belated tender of dues.* Reversing a prior position, the Labor Board
has held that an employee expelled from a union for dues delinquency
may lawfully be discharged even though he makes a belated tender of all
back dues after his discharge is requested but before it actually occurs.
General Motors Corp., Packard Elec. Div., 134 N.L.R.B. 1107 (1961),
overruling Aluminum Workers Local 135 (Metal Ware Corp.), 112
N.L.R.B. 619 (1955).

3. *Duration of obligation.* Could a union and an employer lawfully agree that employees on layoff must continue to pay dues to the union or lose their accrued vacation benefits and their seniority for purposes of recall? *See* Machinists Lodge 1561 (Bendix Corp.), 205 N.L.R.B. 770 (1973). *Cf.* Machinists District 9 (Borg-Warner Corp.), 237 N.L.R.B. No. 207, 99 L.R.R.M. 1133 (1978) (requiring "full and timely notification" to an employee on sick leave).

4. *Statute of limitations.* In Machinists Lodge 1424 v. NLRB, 362 U.S. 411 (1960), the Supreme Court held that the six-months limitation period of § 10(b) of the NLRA barred unfair labor practice proceedings where the only defect in the challenged union security clause was its execution, more than six months earlier, at a time when the union lacked a majority.

5. *Oral arrangements.* An oral union security agreement is enforceable. Both union and employer have a stringent burden of proof, however, in establishing the existence and precise terms of the agreement, and in establishing that affected employees have been fully and unmistakably notified about it. Pacific Iron & Metal Co., 175 N.L.R.B. 604 (1969) (two members dissenting).

6. *Excessive initiation fees.* "In the first such court case to arise under § 8(b)(5) of the Act, which makes it an unlawful practice to 'require of employees covered by an agreement authorized under subsection (a)(3) the payment, as a condition precedent to becoming a member of such organization, of a fee in an amount which the Board finds excessive or discriminatory under all the circumstances,' the Third Circuit in Television and Radio Broadcasting Studio Employees, Local 804 [315 F.2d 398 (3d Cir. 1963)], upheld the Board's finding that a union's increase of its initiation fee from $50 to $500 was excessive, discriminatory, and therefore violative of the Act." NLRB, Twenty-eighth Annual Report 133 (1963). See also Longshoremen Local 1419 (New Orleans S.S. Ass'n), 186 N.L.R.B. 646 (1970) (increase from $500 to $1000).

Could a union lawfully charge members who have become delinquent in their dues payments a "reinstatement fee" in excess of the initiation fee for new members? *See* Boilermakers Local 749 (Sequoia Employers Council), 192 N.L.R.B. 502 (1971). *Cf.* NLRB v. Fishermen Local 33, 448 F.2d 255 (9th Cir. 1971).

7. *Religious accommodation.* As discussed *supra* at 808, Title VII of the 1964 Civil Rights Act requires employers to make a reasonable accommodation to their employees' religious needs, absent "undue hardship." If an employee working under a union shop has religious scruples against paying dues to a union, what must the union and the employer do? Would it be enough for the union to permit an equivalent contribution to a designated charity? Or must the employee be allowed to name his own charity? Or be allowed to pay nothing? *See, e.g.,* Anderson v. General Dynamics Convair Aerospace Div., 17 FEP Cas. 1644 (9th Cir. 1978); Burns v. Southern Pac. Transp. Co., 17 FEP Cas. 1648 (9th Cir. 1978).

8. *See generally* Haggard, *A Clarification of the Types of Union Security Agreements Affirmatively Permitted by Federal Statutes*, 5 RUTGERS CAMDEN L. REV. 418 (1974); Mayer, *Union Security and the Taft-Hartley Act*, 1961 DUKE L.J. 505; Rosenthal, *The National Labor Relations Act and Compulsory Unionism*, 1954 WIS. L. REV. 53. *See also* Lenhoff, *The Problem of Compulsory Unionism in Europe*, 5 AM. J. COMP. L. 18 (1956).

2. STATE "RIGHT-TO-WORK" LEGISLATION

STATUTORY REFERENCE
NLRA § 14(b)

Twenty-one states [7] have "right-to-work" laws, which consist of constitutional or statutory prohibitions of union security arrangements. These laws take a variety of forms. Some merely forbid in terms making union "membership" (or "nonmembership") a condition of employment. (With the exception of the now-repealed Indiana statute,[8] however, such narrowly worded laws have invariably been interpreted by state courts or state attorneys general as reaching the agency shop as well as the union shop.) Other statutes expressly prohibit conditioning employment on the payment of "dues, fees, or other charges of any kind" to a union. Several right-to-work laws go further, proscribing any "employment monopoly," or sanctioning individual bargaining despite the presence of a majority union. Enforcement provisions also vary widely. Most laws allow damages to persons injured by a violation, and many authorize injunctions. About half prescribe criminal penalties.

The constitutionality of state right-to-work laws was upheld by the Supreme Court in *Lincoln Fed. Labor Union 19129 v. Northwestern Iron & Metal Co.*[9] In response to the argument that such laws violate the due process clause of the fourteenth amendment, the Court declared:

> This Court beginning at least as early as 1934, when the *Nebbia* case was decided, has steadily rejected the due process philosophy enunciated in the *Adair-Coppage* line of cases. In doing so, it has consciously returned closer and closer to the earlier constitutional principle that states have power to legislate against what are found to be injurious practices in their internal commercial and business affairs, so long as their laws do not run afoul of some specific federal constitutional prohibition, or of some valid federal law. . . . Under this constitutional doctrine, the due process clause is no longer to be so

---

[7] Alabama, Arizona, Arkansas, Florida, Georgia, Iowa, Kansas, Louisiana, Mississippi, Nebraska, Nevada, New Hampshire, North Carolina, North Dakota, South Carolina, South Dakota, Tennessee, Texas, Utah, Virginia, and Wyoming. 4 LAB. REL. REP. SLL 1:47.

[8] *See* Meade Elec. Co. v. Hagberg, 129 Ind. App. 631, 159 N.E.2d 408 (1959).

[9] 355 U.S. 525 (1949).

broadly construed that the Congress and state legislatures are put in a strait jacket when they attempt to suppress business and industrial conditions which they regard as offensive to the public welfare.

. . . Just as we have held that the due process clause erects no obstacle to block legislative protection of union members, we now hold that legislative protection can be afforded nonunion workers.

RETAIL CLERKS, LOCAL 1625 v. SCHERMERHORN

Supreme Court of the United States
373 U.S. 746, 83 S. Ct. 1461, 10 L. Ed. 2d 678 (1963)

[A collective bargaining agreement provided that employees who chose not to join the union would be required, as a condition of employment, to pay "service fees" to the union equal to the regular initiation fee and membership dues. Four nonunion employees sued to enjoin enforcement of this so-called agency shop clause on the ground it violated Florida's right-to-work law, which forbade denying a person the right to work on account of "membership or nonmembership" in a labor union. The Florida Supreme Court held its state law valid and applicable.]

MR. JUSTICE WHITE delivered the opinion of the Court. . . .

. . . As is immediately apparent from its language, § 14(b) was designed to prevent other sections of the Act from completely extinguishing state power over certain union-security arrangements. And it was the proviso to § 8(a)(3), expressly permitting agreements conditioning employment upon membership in a labor union, which Congress feared might have this result. It was desired to "make certain" that § 8(a)(3) could not "be said to authorize arrangements of this sort in States where such arrangements were contrary to the State policy." H.R. Conf. Rep. No. 510, 80th Cong., 1st Sess. 60, 1 Leg. Hist. L.M.R.A. 564.

The connection between the § 8(a)(3) proviso and § 14(b) is clear. Whether they are perfectly coincident, we need not now decide, but unquestionably they overlap to some extent. At the very least, the agreements requiring "membership" in a labor union which are expressly permitted by the proviso are the same "membership" agreements expressly placed within the reach of state law by § 14(b). It follows that the *General Motors* case rules this one, for we there held that the "agency shop" arrangement involved here — which imposes on employees the only membership obligation enforceable under § 8(a)(3) by discharge, namely, the obligation to pay initiation fees and regular dues — is the "practical equivalent" of an "agreement requiring membership in a labor organization as a condition of employment." Whatever may be the status of less stringent union-security arrangements, the agency shop is within § 14(b). At least to that extent did Congress intend § 8(a)(3) and § 14(b) to coincide.

Petitioners, belatedly, would now distinguish the contract involved here from the agency shop contract dealt with in the *General Motors* case on the basis of allegedly distinctive features which are said to require a different result. Article 19 provides for nonmember payments to the union "for the purpose of aiding the Union in defraying costs in connection with its legal obligations and responsibilities as the exclusive bargaining agent of the employees in the appropriate bargaining unit," a provision which petitioners say confines the use of nonmember payments to collective bargaining purposes alone and forbids their use by the union for institutional purposes unrelated to its exclusive agency functions, all in sharp contrast, it is argued, to the *General Motors* situation where the nonmember contributions are available to the union without restriction.

We are wholly unpersuaded. There is before us little more than a complaint with its exhibits. The agency shop clause of the contract is, at best, ambiguous on its face and it should not, in the present posture of the case, be construed against respondent to raise a substantial difference between this and the *General Motors* case. There is no ironclad restriction imposed upon the use of nonmember fees, for the clause merely describes the payments as being for "the purpose of aiding the Union" in meeting collective bargaining expenses. The alleged restriction would not be breached if the service fee was used for both collective bargaining and other expenses, for the union would be "aided" in meeting its agency obligations, not only by the part spent for bargaining purposes but also by the part spent for institutional items, since an equivalent amount of other union income would thereby be freed to pay the costs of bargaining agency functions.

But even if all collections from nonmembers must be directly committed to paying bargaining costs, this fact is of bookkeeping significance only rather than a matter of real substance. It must be remembered that the service fee is admittedly the exact equal of membership initiation fees and monthly dues, . . . and that, as the union says in its brief, dues collected from members may be used for a "variety of purposes, in addition to meeting the union's costs of collective bargaining." Unions "rather typically" use their membership dues "to do those things which the members authorize the union to do in their interest and on their behalf." If the union's total budget is divided between collective bargaining and institutional expenses and if nonmember payments, equal to those of a member, go entirely for collective bargaining costs, the nonmember will pay more of these expenses than his pro rata share. The member will pay less and to that extent a portion of his fees and dues is available to pay institutional expenses. The union's budget is balanced. By paying a larger share of collective bargaining costs the nonmember subsidizes the union's institutional activities. In over-all effect, economically, and we think for the purposes of § 14(b), the contract here is the same as the *General Motors* agency shop arrangement. Petitioners' argument, if accepted, would lead to the anomalous result of permitting Florida to invalidate the agency shop but forbidding it to ban the present service fee arrangement under which collective bargaining services cost the nonmember more than the member. . . .

NOTES

1. Is the Supreme Court likely to sustain a state's prohibition of a requirement that nonunion employees pay a "service fee" to cover the pro rata share of the union's expenses in negotiating and administering the collective-bargaining agreement? *See* Spielmans, *Bargaining Fee Versus Union Shop,* 10 IND. & LAB. REL. REV. 609 (1957); *cf.* Machinists Local 697 (Canfield Rubber Co.), 223 N.L.R.B. 832 (1976) (costs of grievance handling). What about a fairly apportioned "registration fee" for nonunion job applicants using a lawful hiring hall that serves as employers' exclusive source of employees? *See* Operating Engineers, Local 825 (H. John Homan Co.), 137 N.L.R.B. 1043 (1962); J. J. Hagerty, Inc., 153 N.L.R.B. 1375 (1965), *enforced,* 385 F.2d 874 (2d Cir. 1967), *cert. denied,* 391 U.S. 904 (1968). What about a checkoff? *See* Seapak Div., W. R. Grace Corp. v. NMU, 300 F. Supp. 1197 (S.D. Ga. 1969), *aff'd,* 423 F.2d 1229 (5th Cir. 1970), *aff'd,* 400 U.S. 985 (1971). How should charges against nonmembers for grievance handling or exclusive referrals be treated under the NLRA, with or without a valid union security provision? Do grievance handling and exclusive referrals present different questions?

2. Some right-to-work laws, by their terms or through interpretation, purport to outlaw the exclusive hiring hall. *See, e.g.,* Wyo. Laws c. 39, § 5 (1963); Kaiser v. Price-Fewell, Inc., 235 Ark. 295, 359 S.W.2d 449 (1962), *cert. denied,* 371 U.S. 955 (1963). The NLRB, however, holds that nondiscriminatory hiring halls are not a form of union security subject to state regulation under § 14(b). Houston Chapter, Associated Gen. Contractors, 143 N.L.R.B. 409 (1963), *enforced,* 349 F.2d 449 (5th Cir. 1965).

3. Could a state validly prohibit a majority union from being an exclusive bargaining representative, on the ground this would interfere with dissenters' rights? *Compare* Piegts v. Meat Cutters, Local 437, 228 La. 131, 81 So. 2d 835 (1955), *with* IBEW, Local 415 v. Hansen, 400 P.2d 531 (Wyo. 1965).

4. Does the federal preemption doctrine preclude a state from giving damages under a right-to-work law to a supervisor who was discharged because of his union membership? Consider § 14(a) of the NLRA. *See* Beasley v. Food Fair, Inc., 416 U.S. 653 (1974).

5. In Algoma Plywood & Veneer Co. v. WERB, 336 U.S. 301 (1949), the Supreme Court upheld a state statute which did not absolutely prohibit union security agreements, but which regulated them by requiring a two-thirds employee vote for authorization.

6. Could Texas apply its right-to-work law to invalidate an agency shop clause in a union contract covering seamen who work on the high seas? *See* Oil Workers v. Mobil Oil Corp., 426 U.S. 407 (1976), noted in 55 N.C. L. REV. 685 (1977).

7. *See generally* Henderson, *The Confrontation of Federal Preemption and State Right to Work Laws,* 1967 DUKE L.J. 1079; Hopfl, *The Agency Shop Question,* 49 CORNELL L.Q. 478 (1964).

RETAIL CLERKS, LOCAL 1625 v. SCHERMERHORN, 375 U.S. 96, 84 S. Ct. 219, 11 L. Ed. 2d 179 (1963). On reargument, it was held that § 14(b) allows the states not only to prohibit the execution and application of union security agreements, but also to enforce their laws by appropriate sanctions. "On the other hand, picketing in order to get an employer to execute an agreement to hire all-union labor in violation of a state union-security statute lies exclusively in the federal domain ... because state power, recognized by § 14(b), begins *only with the actual negotiation and execution of the type of agreement described by § 14(b)."* (Emphasis in the original.)

NOTES

1. The dictum quoted from *Schermerhorn II* supplied a rationale for two previous Supreme Court orders, entered with little explication, striking down state court injunctions against union concerted action to secure union security arrangements in violation of right-to-work laws. *See* Construction & Gen. Laborers Local 438 v. Curry, 371 U.S. 542 (1963); IBEW Local 429 v. Farnsworth & Chambers Co., 353 U.S. 969 (1957). Is there any practical justification for letting a state enjoin the execution of a union shop contract but not a strike or picketing to obtain it?

2. An employer does not violate § 8(a)(5) in refusing to bargain over a proposal in conflict with a valid state right-to-work provision. Fort Industry Co., 77 N.L.R.B. 1287 (1948).

3. The right-to-work controversy continues to generate much heat, at both the federal and state levels. Both sides in the dispute traditionally invoke hallowed moral and ethical principles, and act as if weighty economic interests depended on the outcome of the struggle. Yet there is respectable support for the view that right-to-work laws have little real impact in actual operation, and that their existence is more a symptom than a cause of union weakness in the South and parts of the West. *See generally* F. MYERS, "RIGHT TO WORK" IN PRACTICE (1959); P. SULTAN, RIGHT-TO-WORK LAWS (1958); Gordin & Beeson, *State Right-to-Work Laws and Federal Labor Policy,* 52 CALIF. L. REV. 95 (1964); Pollitt, *Right to Work Law Issues: An Evidentiary Approach,* 37 N.C.L. REV. 233 (1959). But cf. Kuhn, *Right-to-Work Laws — Symbols or Substance?* 14 IND. & LAB. REL. REV. 587 (1961).

SECTION III. The Civil Liberties of Members

S. LIPSET, M. TROW & J. COLEMAN, UNION DEMOCRACY: THE INTERNAL POLITICS OF THE INTERNATIONAL TYPOGRAPHICAL UNION 347 (1956, 1962)

It is likely that industrial unions must be dictatorial if they are to survive. The dictator is necessary to arbitrate interest conflicts which can not be settled by simply counting which interest group has more members. . . . [T]he minority crafts in the late-nineteenth-century ITU seceded because they felt that they could not get the ITU to fight their battles. As a general proposition, we may assert that one of the necessary conditions for a sustained democratic political system in an occupational group is that it be so homogeneous that only ideology and not the more potent spur of self-interest divides its members. It is an important property of the ITU's political system that in those "foreign policy" areas where the most important questions are raised, the self-interest of the members is rarely involved, and relatively altruistic ideological commitments dominate political conflict.

ARCHIBALD COX, INTERNAL AFFAIRS OF LABOR UNIONS UNDER THE LABOR REFORM ACT OF 1959, 58 MICH. L. REV. 819, 830 (1960)

An autocratic union may serve the material demands of its members by bargaining effectively for higher wages and increased benefits. It may establish a measure of job security. None except a democratic union, however, can achieve the idealistic aspirations which justify labor organizations. Collective bargaining may limit the employer's power by substituting a negotiated agreement for arbitrary tyranny of the boss, but it scarcely extends the rule of law to substitute an autocratic union. Only in a democratic union can workers, through chosen representatives, participate jointly with management in the government of their industrial lives even as all of us may participate, through elected representatives, in political government.

CLYDE W. SUMMERS, THE IMPACT OF LANDRUM-GRIFFIN IN STATE COURTS, in N.Y.U. THIRTEENTH ANNUAL CONFERENCE ON LABOR 333, 335 (1960)

All of the elaborate arguments that union democracy was unnecessary, unworkable, or even unfortunate have been deliberately rejected. Financial integrity is not enough; the decisions as to dues and expenditures must be democratically made. Officers must be more than honest and responsible; they must be chosen by the members in an open election after free debate. Union members are guaranteed equal rights, freedom of speech and assembly, and due process within the union. Although the statute leaves undefined the exact amount of individual right to be protected, and cannot guarantee the full realization of the democratic process, the policy thrust of the statute is clear and strong. The public has an interest in union democracy.

THE NEW YORK TIMES, August 29, 1966, at 38, col. 4

The Federal Government's chief mediator has predicted that the public can expect more difficult labor disputes in the future. . . .

William E. Simkin, director of the Mediation and Conciliation Service, [stated his belief] . . . in a report on his agency's activities for the fiscal year ended June 30, 1966 . . . that there is major significance in the growth of rank-and-file revolt against contracts negotiated by union leaders.

Mr. Simkin gives "some credence to the fears of union leaders" that Congress, in passing the Landrum-Griffin Act "to restore more democracy to unionism and curb bossism went too far in the other direction of encouraging rebel movements."

As often as not, in Mr. Simkin's opinion, "pure and simple habit" prompts rank-and-file rejection of negotiated contracts because they feel that by turning down offers "they will eventually get something better."

A. THE COMMON LAW AND THE LMRDA

Before Congress passed the Labor-Management Reporting and Disclosure Act of 1959 (the "Landrum-Griffin Act"), state courts relied on such concepts as the contract and property rights of union members to afford them a measure of protection against arbitrary action on the part of their organizations.[1] The principles developed in these common law decisions remain highly significant, since § 603 of the LMRDA makes clear that, unlike the NLRA in the field of labor-management relations, this first major federal intervention in the area of internal union affairs leaves almost entirely intact the body of state law already in existence.[2] In the pages to follow, state and federal safeguards for union members will be treated together. Because Title I (the "Bill of Rights") of the LMRDA provides a convenient and fairly comprehensive catalogue of the principal rights guaranteed union members, the breakdown made by Title I will be observed in the discussion of the various membership rights.

1. GENERAL SCOPE AND COVERAGE OF THE LMRDA

STATUTORY REFERENCES
LMRDA §§ 101-05, 609-10

GRAND LODGE OF MACHINISTS v. KING

United States Court of Appeals, Ninth Circuit }
335 F.2d 340 (1964)
Cert. denied, 379 U.S. 920 (1964)

BROWNING, CIRCUIT JUDGE. Plaintiffs brought suit alleging they were summarily discharged as officers of defendant union because they supported an unsuccessful candidate in a union election. They sought reinstatement and damages. The district court denied defendants' motion to dismiss, and this interlocutory appeal under 28 U.S.C. § 1292 followed.

---

[1] *See generally* Summers, *Legal Limitations on Union Discipline,* 64 HARV. L. REV. 1049 (1951); Summers, *The Law of Union Discipline: What the Courts Do in Fact,* 70 YALE L.J. 175 (1960); Witmer, *Civil Liberties and the Trade Union,* 50 YALE L.J. 621 (1941). For a skeptical appraisal, see Magrath, *Democracy in Overalls: The Futile Quest for Union Democracy,* 12 IND. & LAB. REL. REV. 503 (1959).

[2] *See* Summers, *Pre-emption and the Labor Reform Act — Dual Rights and Remedies,* 22 OHIO ST. L.J. 119 (1961).

I. The district court concluded that plaintiffs' allegation of summary dismissal stated a claim under § 101(a)(5) of the Labor-Management Reporting and Disclosure Act of 1959. . . .

We are satisfied, however, that Congress did not intend § 101(a)(5) to preclude summary removal of a member from union office. While the Act was being considered by Congress, objection was raised to § 101(a)(5) on the ground that it would permit wrong-doing union officials to remain in control while the time consuming "due process" requirements of the section were met. As an alternative it was proposed that the union's power of summary discipline be retained, and that notice and hearing be required after, rather than before, disciplinary action. This solution was rejected; instead, the objection to § 101(a)(5) was met by including limiting language in the legislative history. The Conference Report on the Act stated that § 101(a)(5) "applies only to suspension of membership in the union; it does not refer to suspension of a member's status as an officer in the union." Senator Kennedy, as a Senate conferee, advised the Senate that "this provision does not relate to suspension or removal from a union office. Often this step must be taken summarily to prevent dissipation or misappropriation of funds."

In deference to the "patent legislative intent" it has been held with virtual unanimity [7] that § 101(a)(5) does not apply to removal or suspension from union office.[8] We think these decisions are correct. Furthermore, we think it makes no difference what the reason for the summary removal may have been. Congress's primary concern was that § 101(a)(5) should not bar summary removal of union officials suspected of malfeasance, but the means Congress chose to accomplish its purpose was to wholly exclude suspension or removal from union office from the category of union action to which § 101(a)(5) applied.

II. Plaintiffs also sought to state a claim under §§ 101(a)(1), 101(a)(2), and 609 of the Act. We think they have succeeded, and are therefore authorized by § 102 of the Act to bring a civil action in the district court for appropriate relief.

Plaintiffs allege they were discharged because they actively supported a particular candidate for union office by meeting with other members and expressing views favorable to that candidate. Defendants concede that the right to engage in such intra union political activity is guaranteed to members by §§ 101(a)(1) and 101(a)(2) of the Act, but argue that these and other rights protected by Title I of the Act do not extend to members

---

[7] . . . This does not necessarily mean that an officer-member summarily dismissed has no cause of action under state law. "Violations of the federal statute are actionable in the district courts of the United States. In all other cases improper discipline will give rise to a state cause of action, precisely as in the past. There is no merit to the argument that the federal right is exclusive." Cox, Internal Affairs of Labor Unions Under the Labor Reform Act of 1959, 58 Mich. L. Rev. 819, 838 (1960). . . .

[8] Whether (and, if so, in what circumstances) a member who is also a union official may be "fined, suspended, expelled, or otherwise disciplined," other than by suspension or removal from his union office, without complying with § 101(a)(5), is not before us. . . .

who are also officers of the union. However, §§ 101(a)(1) and (2) apply in terms to "every member," and nothing in the statutory language excludes members who are officers.[11] Nor is there any intimation in the legislative history that Congress intended these guarantees of equal political rights and freedom of speech and assembly to be inapplicable to officer-members.[12] Indeed, the general purpose of the Act points to the contrary. The guarantees of § 101(a)(1) and (2) were adopted to strengthen internal union democracy. To exclude officer-members from their coverage would deny protection to those best equipped to keep union government vigorously and effectively democratic. We therefore conclude that §§ 101(a)(1) and (2) apply to officer-members such as plaintiffs.

Section 102 provides that "[a]ny person whose rights secured by the provisions of this title have been infringed by any violation of this title may bring a civil action in a district court of the United States for such relief (including injunctions) as may be appropriate." We think it follows that plaintiffs' complaint for reinstatement and damages was sufficient to withstand dismissal for failure to state a claim upon which relief could be granted.

In any event, § 609 "makes doubly secure the protection of the members in the exercise of their rights" [16] by making it unlawful for a union "to fine, suspend, expel, or otherwise discipline any of its members for exercising any right to which he is entitled under the provisions of this Act," and by providing explicitly that an action may be brought under § 102 to enforce the specific prohibitions of § 609.

---

[11] This is also true of other sections of Title I. Our conclusion that § 101(a)(5) is inapplicable to the present case is based upon the conclusion that one removed from office is not "otherwise disciplined" within the meaning of § 101(a)(5), rather than upon a reading of the word "member" in that section as excluding officers. See note 8.

[12] Defendants call attention to the fact that as § 101(a)(4) originally passed the Senate it applied to "members or officers," and the words "or officers" were deleted in conference. S. 1555, 86th Cong., 1st Sess. § 101(a)(4) (1959), 1 Leg. His. LMRDA 520; H.R. 8490, 86th Cong., 1st Sess. § 101(a)(4) (1959), 1 Leg. His. LMRDA 877. Defendants argue that this change evidences a congressional understanding that union officers were excluded from the whole of Title I. See Judge Kalodner's opinion in Sheridan v. United Bhd. of Carpenters & Joiners, 306 F.2d 152, 156-157 (3d Cir. 1962).

The language change in § 101(a)(4) was made without comment of any sort. Prior to the change, it was assumed in Senate debate that officers-members were included in § 101(a)(4) (see remarks of Senator Mundt at 105 Cong. Rec. 6478 (1959), 2 Leg. His. LMRDA 1105). Thus, defendants' argument requires the inference that the Conference Committee drastically narrowed the assumed coverage of § 101(a)(4) with no explanation whatever. A more reasonable conclusion is that the Conference Committee recognized that the deleted words "or officers" were surplusage since as a practical matter union officers were also union members, and therefore deleted these words to conform § 101(a)(4) in style with other sections of Title I which used only the inclusive word "members."

[16] Salzhandler v. Caputo, 316 F.2d 445, 449 (2d Cir. 1963).

Defendants argue that the words "otherwise discipline" in § 609 must be read as not including removal from union office, since the same words have that restricted meaning in § 101(a)(5). The argument is a plausible one, for it is natural to suppose that within a single statute the same words will be used with the same meaning. But it is also common experience that identical words may be used in the same statute, or even in the same section of a statute, with quite different meanings. And when they are, it is the duty of the courts to give the words "the meaning which the Legislature intended [they] should have in each instance." Atlantic Cleaners & Dyers, Inc. v. United States, 286 U.S. 427, 433 (1932).

Sections 101(a)(5) and 609 have wholly different purposes, and the difference is such as to satisfy us that although Congress did not intend the words "otherwise discipline" to include removal from union office in § 101(a)(5), it did intend the words to include such action in § 609.

Section 101(a)(5) guarantees to union members, as one of several independent rights conferred upon them by Title I of the Act, that they shall be accorded procedural due process before being subjected to disciplinary action, for whatever reason. Section 609, on the other hand, has no bearing upon the procedures to be followed in disciplining union members. Section 609 appears in Title VI of the Act, a collection of sections having to do with miscellaneous administrative and enforcement matters; § 609 itself is not a source of additional independent rights, but is an enforcement provision, designed, as we have noted, to effectuate rights conferred in other sections of the Act by making it unlawful to punish members who seek to exercise such rights. Punishment for the exercise of these rights is prohibited by § 609 whether inflicted summarily or after a full panoply of procedural protections.

Congress, through the legislative history materials, imposed a limiting gloss upon the words "otherwise discipline" in § 101(a)(5) to preserve union power to summarily remove officer-members suspected of wrongdoing in order to protect unions from continuing depredations while charges are being investigated and resolved. This object is fully accomplished by reading the words "otherwise discipline" in § 101(a)(5) as not including removal from union office. It would not further this purpose in any way to impose the same restriction upon the same words in § 609, since that section has nothing to do with whether or not discipline is summary. There is nothing in the legislative history to indicate that Congress wished to preserve an unrestricted power in the union to discipline officer-members (the subject matter of § 609, when discipline is imposed because of the exercise of rights under the Act), as distinguished from the power to discipline summarily (the subject matter of § 101(a)(5)). Thus, to construe § 609 to exclude from its coverage dismissal from union office would immunize a most effective weapon of reprisal against officer-members for exercising political rights guaranteed by the Act without serving any apparent legislative purpose; and, as we have noted, the members thus exposed to reprisal would be those whose uninhibited exercise of freedom of speech and assembly is most important to effective democracy in union government.[21]

Plaintiffs are appointed officials, and defendants argue that "elected officials of any private or political organization at any level have both the responsibility and the power of their positions, and . . . the burden of the responsibility carries with it the right to appoint subordinate officials to aid in the discharge of that responsibility who are in full and complete accord with the views of the elected officer." Plaintiffs allege they were discharged because they exercised § 101(a)(1) and (2) rights; if defendants dispute this allegation they raise an issue of fact to be resolved at trial. We assume, however, that defendants mean to argue that successful candidates for union office must have the right to discharge appointed union officials who expressed support for their opponents. Realistically, this is simply to argue that members appointed to union office may not actively engage in union political activities while occupying such positions.

Undoubtedly a substantial argument can be made that active, partisan participation by jobholders in intra-organizational politics is a threat to good administration. Congress, in adopting the Hatch Act, endorsed this view with respect to most federal employees. Based upon this precedent, it has been suggested "that the internal political activities of full time union member employees may be regulated to prevent their use for either side in election contests. . . ." [24]

It may well be that the "reasonable rules and regulations" exception of § 101(a)(1) and the similar proviso of § 101(a)(2) would permit a union to adopt the principle of "required political neutrality . . . as a sound element for efficiency," and formulate, and apply without discrimination, regulations imposing reasonable limitations upon the political activity of union jobholders. However, the defendant union has made no effort to implement such a program, and arguments in favor of doing so cannot support defendants' contention that they should be free to discharge particular union employees because they are not their political partisans.

Finally, defendants contend that to extend § 609 to dismissal from union employment would create a potential conflict of jurisdiction between the courts and the National Labor Relations Board since plaintiffs allege conduct which might constitute an unfair labor practice by the union-employer under § 8(a) of the National Labor Relations Act (29 U.S.C. § 158(a)). Congress was aware that the rights conferred by the

---

[21] It has been suggested that the right of union members to remove their officers is itself essential to the democratic self-government. Sheridan v. United Bhd. of Carpenters & Joiners, 306 F.2d 152, 158-159 (3d Cir. 1962). The power of the member-electorate to turn out elected officials for "serious misconduct" is guaranteed by § 401(h) of the Act (73 Stat. 532, 29 U.S.C. § 481 (h)), and is not at issue here. And, as we have said, there is nothing to indicate that Congress believed effective union democracy required that controlling union officials have power to discharge other officers for exercising freedom of speech and assembly in internal union political affairs.

[24] Givens, Federal Protection of Employee Rights Within Trade Unions, 29 Fordham L. Rev. 259, 278 (1960).

Labor-Management Reporting and Disclosure Act of 1959 overlapped those available under state law and other federal legislation, and expressly provided that these rights were to be cumulative.[29]

The Court of Appeals for the Second Circuit has held § 609 applicable to the discharge of a union officer for exercise of § 101(a)(2) rights. There are no decisions to the contrary. We are satisfied that this is the proper construction of the statute. . . .

Affirmed.

NOTES

1. The Fifth Circuit has been more sympathetic to the notion of union "party discipline," and thus readier to sustain the removal from appointive positions of election rivals or persons opposing administration policies. *See, e.g.,* Wambles v. Teamsters, 488 F. 2d 888 (5th Cir. 1974); Sewell v. Machinists Grand Lodge, 455 F. 2d 545 (5th Cir. 1971), *cert. denied,* 404 U.S. 1024 (1972). *Cf.* Retail Clerks Local 770, 208 N.L.R.B. 356 (1974) (no NLRA § 8(a)(3) violation when union acting as employer discharged several office employees openly supporting union president's election opponent). The Ninth Circuit has stood by its position, however, and not without support from other circuits. *See, e.g.,* Cooke v. Orange Belt Dist. Council, 529 F. 2d 815 (9th Cir. 1976); Wood v. Dennis, 489 F. 2d 849 (7th Cir. 1973), *cert. denied,* 415 U.S. 960 (1974). The Supreme Court has drawn a distinction in public employment between policy-making jobs, which are subject to patronage appointments and dismissals, and others that are covered by constitutional protections. Elrod v. Burns, 427 U.S. 347 (1976). Does the analogy fit the union context? *See generally* Note, *Union Officers and Employee Members: Reprisal Discharges as Unlawful Discipline,* 6 GA. L. REV. 564 (1972); Note, *Reprisal Discharges of Union Officials,* 10 U. MICH. J.L. REF. 274 (1977).

2. *Membership under Title I.* Most of the provisions of Title I may be invoked only by union members. Section 3(o) of the LMRDA defines "member" as "any person who has fulfilled the requirements for membership in such organization. . . ." In Hughes v. Iron Workers, Local 11, 287 F.2d 810 (3d Cir. 1961), *cert. denied,* 368 U.S. 829 (1961), an iron worker, who was a member of both his international and his home local union, moved to another area and requested that his membership be transferred to a sister local. The Third Circuit held that the fulfillment of the intraunion membership requirements was all § 3(o) required, even though the plaintiff had not been formally admitted into membership by the sister local. Despite this ruling, however, the Third Circuit held in Ferger v. Iron Workers, Local 483, 356 F.2d 854 (3d Cir. 1966), *cert. denied,* 384 U.S. 908 (1966), that a union under a court order to grant transferees from a sister local "equal rights" in accordance with

---

[29] Section 103. . . .

§ 101(a)(1) was not guilty of contempt in refusing to accept formal transfers of *membership* as such. Section 101(a)(1)'s protection was limited to the specifically listed guarantees of voting, nominating candidates, and participating in meetings.

To be contrasted with *Hughes* is Moynahan v. Pari-Mutuel Employees Guild, 317 F.2d 209 (9th Cir. 1963), *cert. denied,* 375 U.S. 911 (1963). A union arbitrarily denied membership to an individual who had met all the union's requirements except approval by a two-thirds vote of the membership. In holding that the plaintiff was not a "member" within the meaning of § 3(o), the court observed that *Hughes* was inapposite since the requirement in the instant case could "hardly be characterized as a mere formality or ministerial act." Moreover, the court noted, as had the court in *Hughes,* that the "legislative history persuasively demonstrates that Congress did not intend § 3(o) to limit the previously recognized rights of unions to choose their members."

3. *Voting rights.* Section 101(a)(1)'s provision on nominating and voting rights has produced much litigation. The courts have been practically unanimous that this section does not encompass a preelection right to run for union office. *See, e.g.,* Mamula v. Steelworkers, Local 1211, 304 F.2d 108 (3d Cir. 1962), *cert. denied,* 371 U.S. 823 (1962); *cf.* Calhoon v. Harvey, 379 U.S. 134 (1964), *infra* at 929. Much more troublesome have been questions concerning the right to vote itself. Does § 101(a)(1) give federal district courts jurisdiction to supervise union elections? The court in Robins v. Rarback, 325 F.2d 929 (2d Cir. 1963), *cert. denied,* 379 U.S. 974 (1965), said nothing in the legislative history of the Act suggested "that the protection of the right to vote in Title I authorizes the federal courts to enter freely upon the field of supervision of union elections, in total disregard of the limitations imposed on that power by Title IV." On the other hand, in Beckman v. Iron Workers Local 46, 314 F.2d 848 (7th Cir. 1963), the court held that a federal district court had jurisdiction under § 101(a)(1) to grant a preliminary injunction restraining a union from counting ballots where alleged election irregularities, *i.e.,* ballot stuffing, indicated that union members were being deprived of their right to vote in substance, if not in form. *See also* McDonough v. Operating Engineers Local 825, 78 L.R.R.M. 2676, 66 CCH LAB. CAS. ¶ 12,243 (D.N.J. 1971).

In Cleveland Orchestra Comm. v. Cleveland Fed'n of Musicians, 303 F.2d 229 (6th Cir. 1962), § 101(a)(1) was held not to grant symphony musicians an independent right to ratify contracts executed by their union with an orchestra, where the union's constitution and bylaws did not provide for such ratification. *Accord,* Confederated Independent Unions Local 1 v. Rockwell-Standard Co., 465 F.2d 1137 (3d Cir. 1972). But in Arnold v. Meat Cutters, Local 653A, 60 L.R.R.M. 2013, 52 CCH LAB. CAS. ¶ 16,663 (D. Minn. 1965), union members were declared entitled to vote on approving a contract if the question was properly before a membership meeting. Absent voting discrimination, the reasonableness of convention procedure for passing a resolution has been held not subject to general review under § 101(a)(1). Wittstein v. Musicians, 59 L.R.R.M. 2335, 51 CCH LAB. CAS. ¶ 19,684 (S.D.N.Y. 1965).

4. *Remedies.* The courts are divided on whether punitive damages are to be awarded under Title I. *Compare* McCraw v. Plumbers Local 43, 216 F. Supp. 655 (E.D. Tenn. 1963), *aff'd,* 341 F.2d 705 (6th Cir. 1965); Keenan v. Carpenters Dist. Council, 59 L.R.R.M. 2510, 52 CCH Lab. Cas. ¶ 16,571 (E.D. Pa. 1965); Magelssen v. Plasterers Local 518, 240 F. Supp. 259 (W.D. Mo. 1965) ("No"), *with* Boilermakers v. Braswell, 388 F. 2d 193 (5th Cir. 1968), *cert. denied,* 391 U.S. 935 (1968), *and* Morrisey v. NMU, 544 F. 2d 19 (2d Cir. 1976). On the issue of damages for mental anguish, *compare* Simmons v. Textile Workers Local 713, 350 F.2d 1012 (4th Cir. 1965), *with* Boilermakers v. Rafferty, 348 F.2d 307 (9th Cir. 1965). For another important limitation on the relief available under Title I, see Tomko v. Hilbert, 288 F.2d 625, 629 (3d Cir. 1961): "Private misconduct which incidentally may frustrate appellant's rights as a union member does not give rise to an action under the bill-of-rights section." *But cf.* Roganovich v. United States, 318 F.2d 167 (7th Cir. 1963), *cert. denied,* 375 U.S. 911 (1963) (§ 610's criminal sanctions for violent interference with rights under the Act are applicable against individual union members as well as against union officers or agents). *See also Morrisey v. NMU, supra,* holding individual officers liable, "at least" when "acting under the color of union authority."

A union member who vindicates his right of free speech under Title I of the LMRDA renders a substantial service to his union as an institution and to all its members, and thus counsel fees may properly be awarded to a successful plaintiff in a suit brought under § 102 of the Act. Hall v. Cole, 412 U.S. 1 (1973).

5. *Job discrimination.* It has been held that a claim of discrimination in employment because of ouster from union membership is subject to exclusive NLRB jurisdiction and may not be the basis of a Landrum-Griffin action. Spica v. ILGWU, 420 Pa. 427, 218 A.2d 579 (1966); Knox v. UAW, 351 F.2d 72 (6th Cir. 1965); Barunica v. Hatters, Local 55, 321 F.2d 764 (8th Cir. 1963). *But cf.* Figueroa v. NMU, 342 F.2d 400 (2d Cir. 1965); Rekant v. Shochtay-Gasos Union, 320 F.2d 271 (3d Cir. 1963). *See also* Keene v. Operating Engineers Local 624, 569 F.2d 1375 (5th Cir. 1978), where the Fifth Circuit affirmed a ruling that a union and its officers subjected a union member to "other discipline" within the meaning of the Bill of Rights of the Landrum-Griffin Act when the member was denied bona fide assignments to work in retaliation for his political opposition to the officers. *See generally* Arlook, *Federal Preemption and Landrum-Griffin,* in N.Y.U. Thirteenth Annual Conference on Labor 89 (1960).

6. General discussions of the background and effect of the Landrum-Griffin Act are provided by Aaron, *The Labor-Management Reporting and Disclosure Act of 1959,* 73 Harv. L. Rev. 851 (1960); Cox, *Internal Affairs of Labor Unions Under the Labor Reform Act of 1959,* 58 Mich. L. Rev. 819 (1960); Smith, *The Labor-Management Reporting and Disclosure Act of 1959,* 46 Va. L. Rev. 195 (1960); Summers, *American Legislation for Union Democracy,* 25 Mod. L. Rev. 273 (1962). On Title I in particular, see Aaron, *The Union Member's "Bill of Rights":*

First Two Years, 1 IND. REL. 47 (February 1962); Dunau, *Some Comments on the Bill of Rights of Members of Labor Organizations,* in N.Y.U. FOURTEENTH ANNUAL CONFERENCE ON LABOR 77 (1961); Thatcher, *Rights of Individual Union Members Under Title I and Section 610 of the Landrum-Griffin Act,* 52 GEO. L.J. 339 (1964). For contrasting appraisals of the Act after several years in operation, see Murphy, *Major Developments of the Year Under the Landrum-Griffin Act,* in N.Y.U. EIGHTEENTH ANNUAL CONFERENCE ON LABOR 31 (1966); Previant, *Have Titles I-VI of Landrum-Griffin Served the Stated Legislative Purpose?* 14 LAB. L.J. 28 (1963); St. Antoine, *Landrum-Griffin, 1965-1966: A Calculus of Democratic Values,* in N.Y.U. NINETEENTH ANNUAL CONFERENCE ON LABOR 35 (1967). Comparative evaluations of American and foreign legislation are found in Kahn-Freund, *Trade Union Democracy and the Law,* 22 OHIO ST. L.J. 4 (1961); Summers, Aaron, Grunfield, Saratier & Magrez, *Internal Relations Between Unions and Their Members,* 18 RUTGERS L. REV. 236, 279, 343, 375, 394 (1964) (five separate papers). A comprehensive study is Berchem, *Labor Democracy in America,* 13 VILL. L. REV. 1 (1967).

2. FREE SPEECH AND POLITICAL ACTION

SALZHANDLER v. CAPUTO

United States Court of Appeals, Second Circuit
316 F.2d 445 (1963)
Cert. denied, 375 U.S. 946 (1963)

LUMBARD, CHIEF JUDGE. . . . Solomon Salzhandler, a member of Local 442, Brotherhood of Painters, Decorators & Paperhangers of America, brought suit in the district court following the decision of a Trial Board of the union's New York District Council No. 9 that he had untruthfully accused Isadore Webman, the president of the local, of the crime of larceny. The Trial Board found that Salzhandler's "unsupported accusations" violated the union's constitution which prohibited "conduct unbecoming a member . . .," "acts detrimental to . . . interests of the Brotherhood," "libeling, slandering . . . fellow members [or] officers of local unions" and "acts and conduct . . . inconsistent with the duties, obligations and fealty of a member."

Salzhandler's complaint alleged that his charges against Webman were an exercise of his rights as a member of the union and that the action of the Trial Board was in violation of the provisions of the LMRDA under which he was entitled to relief.

The undisputed facts developed during the trial in the district court amply support Salzhandler's claims for relief.

Salzhandler was elected financial secretary of Local 442 in 1953. He was reelected thereafter and at the times in question he was serving a three-year term which was to end June 30, 1962. His weekly compensation as an officer was $35, of which $25 was salary and $10 was for expenses.

The dispute giving rise to this suit was touched off in November 1960 by Salzhandler's distribution to members of Local 442 of a leaflet which accused Webman of mishandling of union funds.

Prior to the audit each July, Salzhandler obtained the checks for the auditor. In going over the union's checks in July 1960 Salzhandler noticed that two checks, one for $800 and one for $375, had been drawn to cover the expenses of Webman and one Max Schneider at two union conventions to which they were elected delegates. The $800 check, drawn on August 21, 1959 to Webman's order, was endorsed by Webman and his wife. The $375 check, drawn on March 4, 1960 to "Cash," was likewise endorsed by Webman and his wife. Schneider's endorsement did not appear on either check. Schneider had died on May 31, 1960.

On July 15, 1960 two checks, each for $6, were drawn as refunds of dues paid by Max Schneider and another deceased member. Such checks were ordinarily mailed to the widows. Webman, however, brought the two checks to Salzhandler and told him to deposit them in a special fund for the benefit of the son of Max Schneider. Salzhandler refused to do this because the checks were not endorsed. Thereafter Sol Feldman and W. Shirpin, who were trustees of the local, each endorsed one of the checks and Salzhandler made the deposit as Webman had requested.

In November 1960 Salzhandler distributed to members of the local a leaflet which accused Webman of improper conduct with regard to union funds and of referring to members of the union by such names as "thieves, scabs, robbers, scabby bosses, bums, pimps, f-bums, [and] jail birds." Attached to the leaflet were photostats of the four checks. With regard to the convention checks, Salzhandler wrote:

"The last convention lasted five days, Monday August 31, to Friday, September 4, 1959. The delegates of 442 presented their credentials Monday, August 31, and on Thursday, September 3, as soon as they got the mileage fare, they disappeared. They were absent at Thursday afternoon session. The most the chairman should have gotten was a week's pay and allowance — $250.00. The auditor's report shows he got $200 in pay and $300 in expenses — $500, or twice what was coming to him, and also $300 as expenses for the Business Agent. The check was made out to *Cash* for $800 (photostat enclosed). So was the voucher. It does not indicate that Max Schneider got any of it. The same goes for a check made out *only* to I. Webman on March 4, 1960 for another convention, where the chairman was to get $250, but got $375. It does not indicate Schneider got his share. Were the checks legal?"

The leaflet also branded Webman as a "petty robber" of the two $6 checks:

"To prove himself most unworthy of any trust, he performed the cheapest petty act ever. Two widows were refunded each $6.00 for overpayment of dues. Two checks were issued to that effect. The petty robber had two of his friends sign their names and the chairman declared these two checks as contributions to the special tax for Michael Schneider — photostats of checks enclosed."

On December 13, 1960, Webman filed charges against Salzhandler with the New York District Council No. 9 of the union, alleging that Salzhandler had violated the union constitution, § 267, by libelling and slandering him in implying that he, Webman, had not reimbursed Max Schneider for convention expenses, and that he had been a "petty robber" in causing the two $6 checks to be deposited in the Michael Schneider fund, rather than being paid over to the two widows. The charge went on to state that Salzhandler was guilty of "acts and conduct inconsistent with the duties, obligations and fealty of a member or officer of the Brotherhood" and that the net effect of the leaflet was untruthfully to accuse an officer of the union of the crime of larceny. For over six hours on the evening of February 23, 1961, Salzhandler was tried by a five-member Trial Board of the District Council. As the union rules permitted, Salzhandler was represented by a union member who was not a lawyer. At the trial, Webman introduced the leaflet. Salzhandler produced the photostats and was questioned by the Trial Board. Webman's witnesses testified that the convention expenditures were approved by the membership. Salzhandler produced three witnesses who testified that Webman had called members names as alleged in the leaflet.

Not until April 2, 1961 did Salzhandler receive notice of the Trial Board's decision and his removal from office and this was from a printed postal card mailed to all members:

"By a decision of the Trial Committee of District Council 9, Sol Saltzhandler [sic] is no longer Financial Secretary of Local Union 442."

Thereafter, on April 4, the District Council mailed to Salzhandler only the final paragraph of its five page "Decision" which read as follows:

"It is our decision that Brother Solomon Salzhandler be prohibited from participating in the affairs of L.U. 442, or of any other Local Union of the Brotherhood, or of District Council 9, for a period of five (5) years. He shall not be permitted during that period to attend meetings of L.U. 442, to vote on any matter, to have the floor at any meeting of any other Local Union affiliated with the District Council, or to be a candidate for any position in any local Union or in the District Council. In all other respects, Brother Salzhandler's rights and obligations as a member of the Brotherhood shall be continued."

Salzhandler did not receive a copy of the full opinion of the Trial Board until after this action was commenced on June 14, 1961. Meanwhile, as the union constitution required appeal within 30 days, Salzhandler filed intraunion appeals with the Secretary-Treasurer of the Council and the General Secretary-Treasurer of the Brotherhood on April 12 and 28. At the time this action was brought, plaintiff had received no word regarding said appeals.

On May 15, 1961, Salzhandler attempted to attend a meeting of the local but was prevented from doing so by Webman. The complaint alleges that Webman assaulted Salzhandler and used violence in removing him.

This action was commenced in the federal court under the Labor-Management Reporting and Disclosure Act of 1959, § 102, requesting a nullification of the order of the Trial Board, reinstatement in the position as financial secretary, and damages.

Judge Wham dismissed the complaint holding that the Trial Board's conclusion that the leaflet was libelous was sufficiently supported by the evidence. He went further, however, and made an independent finding that the statements were, in fact, libelous. The court held, as a matter of law, that "The rights accorded members of labor unions under Title I of the Labor-Management Reporting and Disclosure Act of 1959 . . . do not include the right of a union member to libel or slander officers of the union." We do not agree.

The LMRDA of 1959 was designed to protect the rights of union members to discuss freely and criticize the management of their unions and the conduct of their officers. The legislative history and the extensive hearings which preceded the enactment of the statute abundantly evidence the intention of the Congress to prevent union officials from using their disciplinary powers to silence criticism and punish those who dare to question and complain. The statute is clear and explicit [quoting §§ 101(a)(1), 101(a)(2), 102, and 609].

Appellees argue that just as constitutionally protected speech does not include libelous utterances, Beauharnais v. Illinois, 343 U.S. 250, 266 (1952), the speech protected by the statute likewise does not include libel and slander. The analogy to the First Amendment is not convincing. In Beauharnais, the Supreme Court recognized the possibility that state action might stifle criticism under the guise of punishing libel. However, because it felt that abuses could be prevented by the exercise of judicial authority, 343 U.S. at 263-264, the court sustained a state criminal libel statute. But the union is not a political unit to whose disinterested tribunals an alleged defamer can look for an impartial review of his "crime." It is an economic action group, the success of which depends in large measure on a unity of purpose and sense of solidarity among its members.

The Trial Board in the instant case consisted of union officials, not judges. It was a group to which the delicate problems of truth or falsehood, privilege, and "fair comment" were not familiar. Its procedure is peculiarly unsuited for drawing the fine line between criticism and defamation, yet, were we to adopt the view of the appellees, each charge of libel would be given a trial de novo in the federal court — an impractical result not likely contemplated by Congress, see 105 Cong. Rec. 6026 (daily ed. April 25, 1959) (colloquy between Senator Goldwater and Senator Clark) — and such a Trial Board would be the final arbiter of the extent of the union member's protection under § 101(a)(2).

In a proviso to § 101(a)(2), there are two express exceptions to the broad rule of free expression. One relates to "the responsibility of every member toward the organization as an institution." The other deals with interference with the union's legal and contractual obligations.

While the inclusion of only two exceptions, without more, does not mean that others were intentionally excluded, we believe that the legislative history supports the conclusion that Congress intended only those exceptions which were expressed.[8]

The expression of views by Salzhandler did not come within either exception in the proviso to § 101(a)(2). The leaflet did not interfere in any way with the union's legal or contractual obligations and the union has never claimed that it did. Nor could Salzhandler's charges against Webman be construed as a violation of the "responsibility of every member toward the organization as an institution." Quite the contrary; it would seem clearly in the interest of proper and honest management of union affairs to permit members to question the manner in which the union's officials handle the union's funds and how they treat the union's members. It is that interest which motivated the enactment of the statute and which would be immeasurably frustrated were we to interpret it so as to compel each dissatisfied and questioning member to draw, at the peril of union discipline, the thin and tenuous line between what is libelous and what is not. This is especially so when we consider that the Act was designed largely to curtail such vices as the mismanagement of union funds, criticism of which by union members is always likely to be viewed by union officials as defamatory.

The union argues that there is a public interest in promoting the monolithic character of unions in their dealings with employers. But the Congress weighed this factor and decided that the desirability of protecting the democratic process within the unions outweighs any possible weakening of unions in their dealings with employers which may result from the freer expression of opinions within the unions.

The democratic and free expression of opinion in any group necessarily develops disagreements and divergent opinions. Freedom of expression would be stifled if those in power could claim that any charges against them were libelous and then proceed to discipline those responsible on a finding that the charges were false. That is precisely what Webman and the Trial Board did here when they punished Salzhandler with a five-year ban of silence and stripped him of his office.

So far as union discipline is concerned Salzhandler had a right to speak his mind and spread his opinions regarding the union's officers, regardless of whether his statements were true or false. It was wholly immaterial to Salzhandler's cause of action under the LMRDA whether he spoke truthfully or not, and accordingly Judge Wham's views on whether

---

[8] As initially introduced before the Senate, the freedom of speech section was absolute in form. See 105 Cong. Rec. 5810 (daily ed. April 22, 1959). The section was in fact passed in that form. Id. at 5827. Later the question came to be reconsidered and the free speech section was amended to include the two express exceptions. Id. at 6030 (daily ed. April 25, 1959). In effect, the section as initially passed took away the power of unions to punish for expressions of views. The subsequent amendment restored that power in only two situations.

We are referred to certain statements made during the debate in the Senate which allegedly indicate that "reasonable restraints" on speech were intended. See, e.g., 105 Cong. Rec. 6022 (daily ed. April 25, 1959) (remarks of Senator Kuchel). We find these statements to be ambiguous and we are not persuaded that exceptions other than those specified were intended.

Salzhandler's statements were true are beside the point. Here Salzhandler's charges against Webman related to the handling of union funds; they concerned the way the union was managed. The Congress has decided that it is in the public interest that unions be democratically governed and toward that end that discussion should be free and untrammeled and that reprisals within the union for the expression of views should be prohibited. It follows that although libelous statements may be made the basis of civil suit between those concerned, the union may not subject a member to any disciplinary action on a finding by its governing board that such statements are libelous. The district court erred in dismissing the complaint.

Accordingly, we reverse the judgment of the district court and direct entry of judgment for the plaintiff which, among other things, should assess damages and enjoin the defendants from carrying out any punishment imposed by the District Council Trial Board.

NOTES

1. The principal case was followed in Boilermakers v. Rafferty, 348 F.2d 307 (9th Cir. 1965), which involved the distribution of handbills allegedly containing false statements about another member.

2. In Graham v. Soloner, 220 F. Supp. 711 (E.D. Pa. 1963), § 101(a)(2) was held not to be limited to freedom of expression among union members within the confines of their organization, but to include such public expressions of opinion as picketing union offices with placards critical of the union leadership.

3. The proviso to § 101(a)(2) is generally assumed to cover such matters as the advocacy of a union schism or a wildcat strike. Would urging the nonpayment of dues, in the good faith but mistaken belief they were illegally imposed, violate a member's "responsibility . . . toward the organization as an institution"? Would the proviso apply to criticism of a union administration so severe as to discredit the organization in the eyes of the public or of its membership? *Compare* Farowitz v. Musicians, Local 802, 241 F. Supp. 895 (S.D.N.Y. 1965), *with* Deacon v. Operating Engineers Local 12, 59 L.R.R.M. 2706 (S.D. Cal. 1965). What about active support of the Communist Party? *See* Rosen v. Painters Dist. Council 9, 50 CCH LAB. CAS. ¶ 19,245 (S.D.N.Y. 1964). A union has been enjoined from enforcing a constitutional prohibition of "dishonest or questionable practices to secure the election or defeat of any candidate for office" against members opposing the reelection of incumbent officers, on the ground the provision was so vague that a member would be in peril of violating it whenever he exercised his speech rights under the Act. Semancik v. UMW District 5, 466 F.2d 144 (3d Cir. 1972). Expulsion for advocating dual unionism was upheld in Sawyers v. Machinists Grand Lodge, 57 CCH LAB. CAS. ¶ 12,478 (E.D. Mo. 1967). *But cf.* Machinists Lodge 702 v. Loudermilk, 444 F.2d 719 (5th Cir. 1971) (fine invalid).

4. For a sharp debate on the *Salzhandler* doctrine, *see* Hall, *Freedom of Speech and Union Discipline: The Implications of Salzhandler,* in

N.Y.U. SEVENTEENTH ANNUAL CONFERENCE ON LABOR 349 (1964); Sigal, *Freedom of Speech and Union Discipline: The "Right" of Defamation and Disloyalty, id.* at 367. *See also* Atleson, *A Union Member's Right of Free Speech and Assembly: Institutional Interests and Individual Rights,* 51 MINN. L. REV. 403 (1967); Beaird & Player, *Free Speech and the Landrum-Griffin Act,* 25 ALA. L. REV. 577 (1973).

5. Leading common law decisions by state courts on the right of union members to engage in free speech or political activity without being subjected to reprisals are Mitchell v. Machinists, 196 Cal. App. 2d 796, 16 Cal. Rptr. 813 (1961); De Mille v. American Fed'n of Radio Artists, 31 Cal. 2d 139, 187 P.2d 769 (1947); Crossen v. Duffy, 90 Ohio App. 252, 103 N.E.2d 769 (1951); Madden v. Atkins, 4 N.Y.2d 283, 151 N.E.2d 73 (1958). The first two cases involved public issues outside the union; the latter two dealt with political activity within the union.

3. FINANCIAL EXACTIONS

AMERICAN FED'N OF MUSICIANS V. WITTSTEIN, 379 U.S. 171, 85 S. Ct. 300, 13 L. Ed. 2d 214 (1964). At a national convention, a union approved a dues increase in accordance with its constitutional procedure whereby the votes of the delegates were weighted to reflect the number of members in a local that each delegate represented. Although a roll call showed that the recommendation had carried in terms of a membership count, less than half of the delegates present voted in favor of the proposal. Certain union members challenged the validity of the enactment under § 101(a)(3)(B) of the LMRDA, which provides that the dues of an international union "shall not be increased . . . except . . . by majority vote of the delegates voting at a regular convention." The Supreme Court held that that Act did not prohibit the union's weighted system of voting. The Court pointed out that the literal language of the statute did not foreclose this method, and that the legislative history showed sponsors of the Act favored weighted voting as the most democratic procedure. Added the Court: "Section 101(a)(3)(B), as well as Title IV, authorizes a representative system of government and does not require a town meeting for action by an international or national union."

NOTES

1. Many international constitutions set the dues rate, or a minimum dues rate, for local unions. In light of § 101(a)(3), may a duly constituted international convention increase these rates and put them into effect without submitting the issue to a vote of the locals' members? *See* Ranes v. Office Employees, Local 28, 317 F.2d 915 (7th Cir. 1963) (*Held:* Yes). *Cf.* King v. Randazzo, 346 F.2d 307 (2d Cir. 1965). Could the international effect such an increase through secret ballot votes at a series of duly notified local union membership meetings? *See* Telephone Workers Local 2 v. Telephone Workers, 362 F.2d 891 (1st Cir. 1966), *cert. denied,* 385 U.S. 947 (1966).

2. Must the procedures for setting so-called per capita taxes, payable directly by local unions (rather than by individual members) to their internationals, conform to the requirements of § 101(a)(3)? *Compare* Ranes v. Office Employees Local 28, *supra, with* Telephone Workers, Local 2 v. Telephone Workers, *supra.*

4. THE RIGHT TO SUE; EXHAUSTION OF INTRAUNION REMEDIES

DETROY v. AMERICAN GUILD OF VARIETY ARTISTS

United States Court of Appeals, Second Circuit

286 F.2d 75 (1961)

Cert. denied, 366 U.S. 929 (1961)

LUMBARD, CHIEF JUDGE. The appellant, manager and trainer of a troupe of chimpanzees with which he performs professionally under the name of the "Marquis Family" in theaters, night clubs, circuses, on television, and in motion pictures, instituted this proceeding under § 102 of the Labor-Management Reporting and Disclosure Act of 1959, . . . demanding injunctive relief and damages for an alleged violation of the procedural rights granted union members by § 101(a)(5) of the Act. . . . Upon a motion for summary judgment, the district court dismissed the complaint on the ground that under § 101(a)(4) the plaintiff could bring no court action against a labor union without first exhausting the internal remedies provided by the union, and that in this case the defendant union had established reasonable procedures by its constitution whereby claims against it by members could be heard within the four-month period permitted by the law.

The controversy between the appellant and the American Guild of Variety Artists, a labor union representing variety entertainers in the United States and Canada, arose out of a breach-of-contract claim made against the appellant by a resort hotel in Las Vegas, Nevada. After failing to settle the dispute by negotiation, the AGVA requested the parties to submit it to arbitration, which they did. A panel of three, one selected by each of the parties to the dispute and the third chosen by the two so designated, met in Los Angeles County, California, on January 12, 1960, and decided in favor of the hotel. The union then advised the appellant that if he did not abide by the award, it would place him on the "National Unfair List" appearing in its monthly periodical "AGVA News." The appellant replied that he intended to move to vacate the arbitration award in the California courts, but never began any such proceedings. When the three months provided by California law for vacating arbitration awards had elapsed, the union proceeded to publish the appellant's name in the August 1960 issue of the periodical under a heading which read as follows:

"Notice to Members

"The rules require that you may not work for any employer, agent, booker or third party who is marked 'Unfair' by AGVA. Violation of these rules subjects you to disciplinary action.

"Notice to Agents

".... You are not authorized to book AGVA members in unfair establishments or book performers not in good standing in AGVA. Violation of rules subjects you to revocation of your franchise."

The appellant then began this proceeding in the Southern District of New York, claiming that the listing amounted to disciplinary action within the meaning of § 101(a)(5) of the Labor-Management Reporting and Disclosure Act of 1959, . . . and that he was, therefore, entitled to specific written charges, a reasonable time to defend, and a full and fair hearing before having his name placed on the list.

The appellant did not, however, seek to utilize the procedure made available by Article XX of the Constitution of the AGVA. This article, entitled "Claims of Members," establishes procedures whereby claims asserted against the union are heard and determined by its Board or Executive Committee. Thus, the first issue before us now is whether the proviso in § 101(a)(4), which protects the right of a union member to sue his union, "Provided, That any such member may be required to exhaust reasonable hearing procedures (but not to exceed a four-month lapse of time) within such organization, before instituting legal or administrative proceedings against such organizations or any officer thereof," required of the appellant in this case that he first have recourse to the internal procedures established by the union's constitution. The exhaustion proviso of § 101(a)(4) does not appear in § 102, which grants members who claim that their rights under § 101 have been infringed a federal forum in which to litigate their disputes with the union. It might also appear from the rejection by the House of Representatives of H.R. 8342, the bill originally reported out of the Committee on Education and Labor, which explicitly provided for exhaustion of internal remedies in § 102, that Congress did not mean to have the exhaustion doctrine apply to the rights granted by § 101, except where, as in the case of the right to sue, it was expressly provided. However, the broad language of the proviso in § 101(a)(4) includes suits instituted against labor unions in any court on any claim. Absent a clear directive by Congress, the policy formulated over a course of time by courts reluctant to interfere in the internal affairs of private organizations should not be superseded. We hold, therefore, that the provision in § 101(a)(4) applies, as well, to suits brought in the federal courts for violations of the rights secured by § 101.

Judge Dimock in this case read § 101(a)(4) as imposing upon the union member an absolute duty to exhaust union remedies before applying to the federal courts. The legislative history of the section indicates, however, that Congress had no intention of establishing such a rule.[2]

The statute provides that any member of a labor organization "may be required" to exhaust the internal union remedies, not that he "must" or "is required to" exhaust them. When read in light of the statements made on the floor of Congress by the authors of the statute, it appears clear that the proviso was incorporated in order to preserve the exhaustion doctrine as it had developed and would continue to develop in the courts, lest it otherwise appear to be Congress' intention to have the right to sue secured by § 101 abrogate the requirement of prior resort to internal procedures. In addition, the proviso dictated an outside limit beyond which the judiciary cannot extend the requirement of exhaustion — no remedy which would require proceedings exceeding four months in duration may be demanded. We therefore construe the statute to mean that a member of a labor union who attempts to institute proceedings before a court or an administrative agency may be required *by that court or agency* to exhaust internal remedies of less than four months' duration before invoking outside assistance.

Section 102, under which the appellant instituted his proceeding, provides for enforcement by federal courts of rights secured by federal law. We are not in this case, therefore, bound by the doctrine of exhaustion as developed in the New York, Nevada, or California courts with respect to suits against unions brought in the courts of those states by union members. In enforcing rights guaranteed by the new statute, whether or not similar rights would be enforced under state law by state courts, the federal courts may develop their own principles regarding the time when a union's action taken in violation of § 101 is ripe for judicial intervention. . . . The rules formulated by various state courts may suggest

---

[2] For example, one of the authors of the bill passed by the House, Representative Griffin, expressed a clear opinion on the question. He said:

"The proviso which limits exhaustion of internal remedies is not intended to impose restrictions on a union member which do not otherwise exist, but rather to place a maximum on the length of time which may be required to exhaust such remedies. In other words, existing decisions which require, or do not require, exhaustion of such remedies are not to be affected except as a time limit of 4 months is superimposed. Also, by use of the phrase 'reasonable hearing procedures' in the proviso, it should be clear that no obligation is imposed to exhaust procedures where it would obviously be futile or would place an undue burden on the union member." 105 Daily Cong. Rec. App. A7915 (Sept. 4, 1959).

The statement made by Senator Kennedy, who introduced the original bill to which §§ 101-105 were added as amendments on the Senate floor, is also representative of the attitude taken by those who instituted the legislation. He said:

"Nor is it the intent or purpose of the provision to invalidate the considerable body of State and Federal court decisions of many years standing which require, or do not require, the exhaustion of internal remedies prior to court intervention depending upon the reasonableness of such requirements in terms of the facts and circumstances of a particular case. . . . The doctrine of exhaustion of reasonable internal union remedies for violation of union laws is just as firmly established as the doctrine of exhausting reasonable administrative agency provisions prior to action by courts." 105 Daily Cong. Rec. 16414 (Sept. 3, 1959).

helpful avenues of approach, cf. Textile Workers Union of America v. Lincoln Mills, 1957, 353 U.S. 448, 457, but the authority granted to the federal courts by Congress to secure the rights enumerated in § 101 of the 1959 Act is accompanied by the duty to formulate federal law regarding a union member's obligation to exhaust the internal union remedies before seeking judicial vindication of those rights.

If we look to the substantial body of state law on the subject, we find that the general rule requiring exhaustion before resort to a court has been almost entirely swallowed up by exceptions phrased in broad terms. See Annotation, 168 A.L.R. 1462 (1947); Summers, Legal Limitations on Union Discipline, 64 Harv. L. Rev. 1049, 1086-92 (1951). Rather than decide whether exhaustion is proper by determining whether the union's action can be characterized as "void" (e.g., Tesoriero v. Miller, 1949, 274 App. Div. 670, 88 N.Y.S.2d 87) or as "affecting property rights" (e.g., Sheet Metal Workers, Local 65 v. Nalty, 6 Cir., 1925, 7 F.2d 100), we believe it preferable to consider each case on its own facts.

The congressionally approved policy of first permitting unions to correct their own wrongs is rooted in the desire to stimulate labor organizations to take the initiative and independently to establish honest and democratic procedures. See Cox, The Role of Law in Preserving Union Democracy, 72 Harv. L. Rev. 609, 615 (1959). Other policies, as well, underlie the exhaustion rule. The possibility that corrective action within the union will render a member's complaint moot suggests that, in the interest of conserving judicial resources, no court step in before the union is given its opportunity. Moreover, courts may find valuable the assistance provided by prior consideration of the issues by appellate union tribunals. See Summers, The Law of Union Discipline: What the Courts Do in Fact, 70 Yale L.J. 175, 207 (1960). Congress has provided a safeguard against abuse by a union of the freedom thus granted it by not requiring exhaustion of union remedies if the procedures will exceed four months in duration. But in any case, if the state of facts is such that immediate judicial relief is warranted, Congress' acceptance of the exhaustion doctrine as applied to the generality of cases should not bar an appropriate remedy in proper circumstances.

The affidavits and exhibits submitted in the district court on the motion for summary judgment establish that the only hearing given the appellant before his name was placed on the National Unfair List was that of the arbitration proceeding. The union was not a party to the arbitration, and the issue decided by the arbitrators was not whether the appellant should be disciplined by the union but whether he owed an obligation to an employer with whom he had contracted. It is undisputed that no hearing was held in which the appellant could respond to the union's intention of taking disciplinary action. Quite clearly, a hearing in which some liability between a union member and a third party is determined is not the type of hearing demanded by § 101(a)(5). At no time was the appellant given the opportunity of arguing before the union's hearing board that placing him on the Unfair List exceeded the powers granted to the union by its constitution, nor could he raise other mitigating circumstances in response to an expressed intention to place his name on such a list. The acts on their face, therefore, reveal a violation of the rights guaranteed union members by § 101(a)(5). If the question before us were whether the union's constitution authorized the listing of the appellant's name on an unfair list after a hearing with due procedural safeguards, a union tribunal might provide some insight to aid our decision. But no prior consideration by such a tribunal is necessary or helpful on the question whether the treatment of the appellant violated § 101(a)(5).

In addition, the particular form of the disciplinary action makes it difficult for the union to provide an adequate remedy. The appellant, from the date his name appeared on the list, was virtually barred from employment by those dealing regularly with the AGVA. Since he is an independent contractor whose weekly pay varies according to the terms of the contracts he signs with his employers, the precise extent of damages suffered by the appellant as a result of the listing can never be determined. Even were the union to permit him to present his case before a review board, the board could merely order his name removed from the list and, in order to provide a more satisfactory remedy, award as damages for the period during which he was barred from employment a sum which, at best, could only be an approximation. It appears unlikely that Congress intended that its expressed desire to provide minimum safeguards against arbitrary union discipline be avoided by the union's imposition of a sanction which has its most severe effect within a four-month period, if the consequences of such action cannot be precisely measured in order to assess damages. Early judicial intervention providing an adequate remedy by means of the court's power to enjoin further violations is therefore proper. . . .

Moreover, it is by no means clear that the union's own rules afforded the appellant a remedy within the organization. . . . No provision is made anywhere for any proceeding either before or after the printing of a member's name on the National Unfair List. The union maintains that Article XX of its Constitution, entitled "Claims of Members," provides a means for reviewing the correctness of this sanction. The constitution's separate provision for disciplinary proceedings in Article XVII, however, suggests that Article XX was not intended to provide an alternate procedure for review of a union's sanctions against its members, but merely to grant a forum for other monetary claims against the union. Moreover, after the arbitration award the appellant notified the Western Regional Director of the union by telegram that he intended "appealing to the National Board," and was told in a reply letter that "the decision of the arbitrators is final and . . . you cannot appeal this to the National Board of AGVA." Although this response referred not to the disciplinary measure but to the arbitrators' decision, neither that letter nor the later notification that he was being placed on the National Unfair List notified the appellant that any specific review procedure was available. Thus, an attempt to proceed under Article XX might not have proved futile, but it would have been quite uncertain. When asserting what is clearly a violation of a federal statute, a union member should not be required to first seek out remedies which are dubious. Only resort to those expressly provided in the union's constitution or those clearly called to his attention by the union officials should be demanded of him.

Taking due account of the declared policy favoring self-regulation by unions, we nonetheless hold that where the internal union remedy is uncertain and has not been specifically brought to the attention of the disciplined party, the violation of federal law clear and undisputed, and the injury to the union member immediate and difficult to compensate by means of a subsequent money award, exhaustion of union remedies ought not to be required. The absence of any of these elements might, in light of congressional approval of the exhaustion doctrine, call for a different result. The facts of this case, however, warrant immediate judicial intervention.

Nor can we agree with the union's claim that the listing of the appellant's name did not constitute discipline within the meaning of § 101(a)(5). If a union such as the AGVA undertakes to enforce the contracts made by its members with employers, it does so because such enforcement is to the ultimate benefit of all the members, in that it promotes stability within the industry. A breach of contract or a refusal to abide by an arbitration award, therefore, is not damaging merely to the employer but to the union as well, and the union's listing of those of its members who do violate their contracts is an act of self-protection. In thus furthering its own ends the union must abide by the rules set down for it by Congress in § 101(a)(5), and any member against whom steps are taken by the union in the interest of promoting the welfare of the group is entitled to these guarantees.

In passing on the motions for summary judgment and for a temporary injunction, the district court had before it only the complaint and the affidavits of the appellant and various officers of the union. The undisputed facts of the case require that a temporary injunction issue ordering the union to remove the appellant's name from its Unfair List where it is now retained in apparent violation of § 101(a)(5).

We reverse the order of the district court dismissing the complaint and remand the case with instructions to grant the temporary injunction requested by the appellant.

NOTES

1. Legislative history and early judicial authority can be found to the effect that the four-month limitation in § 101(a)(4) "relates to restrictions imposed by unions rather than the rules of judicial administration or the action of Government agencies." *See, e.g.,* 105 CONG. REC. 17899 (1959) (remarks of Sen. Kennedy); Mamula v. Steelworkers, 414 Pa. 294, 200 A. 2d 306 (1964), *cert. denied,* 379 U.S. 17 (1964). Nonetheless, the *Detroy* analysis has prevailed. In NLRB v. Marine & Shipbuilding Workers, 391 U.S. 418 (1968), the Supreme Court concluded that the proviso to § 101(a)(4) was "not a grant of authority to unions more firmly to police their members but a statement of policy that the public tribunals whose aid is invoked may in their discretion stay their hands for four months, while the aggrieved person seeks relief within the union." *See also* Operating Engineers Local 3 v. Burroughs, 417 F.2d 370 (9th Cir. 1969), *cert. denied,* 397 U.S. 916 (1970).

2. Exhaustion of internal remedies has been dispensed with as a prerequisite to suit where union disciplinary action was "void" because based on an offense not specified in the union constitution, Simmons v. Textile Workers, Local 713, 350 F.2d 1012 (4th Cir. 1965), or where exhaustion was deemed "futile" because of union hostility toward the member, Farowitz v. Musicians, Local 802, 241 F. Supp. 895 (S.D.N.Y. 1965). But the mere fact that a final union decision might not be obtainable within four months does not enable a member to bring suit immediately, where there is no showing the member would be harmed by pursuing an intraunion remedy for the statutory period. Harris v. ILA Local 1291, 321 F.2d 801 (3d Cir. 1963).

3. *See generally* Beaird & Player, *Exhaustion of Intra-Union Remedies and Access to Public Tribunals Under the Landrum-Griffin Act,* 26 ALA. L. REV. 519 (1974); Boyle, *The Labor Bill of Rights and the Doctrine of Exhaustion of Remedies — A Marriage of Convenience,* 16 HASTINGS L.J. 590 (1965); O'Donoghue, *Protection of a Union Member's Right to Sue Under the Landrum-Griffin Act,* 14 CATH. U.L. REV. 215 (1965); Vorenberg, *Exhaustion of Intraunion Remedies as a Condition Precedent to Appeal to the Courts,* 2 LAB. L.J. 487 (1951). Common-law cases are gathered in a comprehensive annotation in 168 A.L.R. 1462 (1947).

4. In UAW v. National Right to Work Legal Defense & Educ. Fndtn., 99 L.R.R.M. 3181 (D.C. Cir. 1978), a court of appeals held that the second proviso in § 101(a)(4) of the LMRDA, which prohibits the financing by "interested" employers of members' suits against their union, does not apply to "the legitimate litigation program of a bona fide, independent legal aid organization, even though the organization receives contributions from interested employers." The financing proviso to § 101(a)(4) has also been read to mean that while employers are forbidden to finance the institution of suits by employees against their union, employers are free to finance a defense or counterclaim by employees. IBEW Local 336 v. Illinois Bell Tel. Co., 496 F.2d 1 (7th Cir. 1974). Would different rulings in these cases have posed substantial constitutional questions?

5. PROCEDURAL DUE PROCESS

(a) Intraunion Safeguards

LEO BROMWICH, UNION CONSTITUTIONS, A REPORT TO THE FUND FOR THE REPUBLIC 29-33 (1959)

In civil society, the phrase "due process" is the summary of an extensive body of law. In briefest form, it states society's determination to give an accused person a fair opportunity to present his defense and is grounded upon the existence of an independent judiciary capable of following its own views in rendering the verdict. How do these conceptions apply to the society of union men and women?

It should already be apparent that the procedural rights of an accused union member are of paramount importance. Given the enormous power of the international president and the many limitations upon rank-and-file control of the union administration, clear and defined rights are essential to any union member who wishes to speak, and criticize, freely. The points that must be examined in determining how the unions handle this problem are fairly obvious. They revolve around the composition of the union tribunals and appellate boards, the time span for appellate procedure, the difference in the regulations regarding the disciplining of an international officer as against a rank-and-file member of a local union. Again, it should be noted that even these important questions are not enough for a full examination of internal union democracy. The presence of good procedure does not guarantee justice, nor is its absence proof of minority control.

A number of unions in our sample have fairly detailed trial procedures indicative of serious concern for due process. These include the International Printing Pressmen, the Mine, Mill and Smelter Workers, and the Upholsterers. In two cases, those of the International Typographical Union and the United Automobile Workers, important constitutional points are spelled out in a way that makes them representative of some of the best of the union trial practices. Although there is considerable variation, even among the better constitutions, an examination of the constitutions of these two unions should give us some idea of the proper type of procedural safeguards.

The constitution of the ITU provides penalties for specific offenses ranging from reprimand or a small fine to expulsion. There is also a category of "violation of laws of the local or international union," "conduct unbecoming a union member," and "malfeasance in office," but the allegations "must be sufficiently specific as to the provisions of union law violated," and the "acts which constitute the basis for the charges" must be cited to permit the defendant to prepare a proper defense. The accusing party must deliver the complaint to the local president within 30 days of the time he became aware of the charge, and the accused has five days in which to answer (though he may waive this right without prejudice to his case).

The charges are discussed at the next meeting of the local. If they are found "cognizable" by the majority of the members present, an investigating committee is appointed by the president of the local. This committee reports at the next regular meeting, and a vote is taken as to whether the case should be prosecuted or dropped. If the vote is to continue the case, the president of the local may appoint a trial committee of three or five members; but if either party to the proceedings objects to the appointment of the committee, its membership is selected by a drawing of lots.

The trial committee is required to notify both parties of the time and place of the hearing. Representation by counsel is permitted, provided that the counsel is a member of the union. After the hearings, the trial committee reports its findings at the next meeting of the local. The members then discuss the verdict, and two-thirds of the members present are required to return a judgment of guilty (voting is by secret ballot). If the accused is found guilty, a vote is then taken on the penalty recommended by the trial committee or, if that is amended, on the heaviest penalty proposed. In order to expel, three-fourths of those present and voting must be in favor. If there is an acquittal, all expenses incurred in connection with the trial are borne by the union (the fees chargeable to counsel should not be in excess of the pay time lost at union scale).

The appeal process in the ITU reflects the same concern for due process. Briefs are filed with the president of the local, time is stipulated for answer and rebuttal, and all documents are forwarded to the international executive council. Unless it is extended by the international president, the maximum time for the filing of documents is 50 days. Appeal from an executive council decision is to the next convention of the international union, but full compliance with the decisions of the lower tribunals is expected pending appeal. A subordinate union, or members not satisfied with the verdict of the convention, may appeal to the courts, but only upon first depositing a bond with the executive council to cover the costs that might be incurred by the international in defending the action. Failure to exhaust these procedural remedies before going into court is punishable by summary expulsion.

In the case of the trial of an international officer, there are somewhat different rules. An international officer of the union may be suspended by the international president or impeached by the executive council. The officer is furnished with a detailed statement of the charges, and the trial board is composed of the presidents of the five largest locals. The decision of this trial board must be rendered within 30 days from the date of suspension, and it can be appealed to the next convention.

There are, of course, some imperfections in this process, but, on the whole, it represents a serious concern for the rights of the members. Thus, the allowance of a "blanket" clause (conduct "unbecoming" a union member, etc.) is, on its face, a violation of the due process requirement of specificity, but then the violation must be fully described. The provision that the accused may select his counsel only among the union members is a limit upon freedom, but in the absence of technical rules of pleading and evidence it will not normally be too serious. The major difficulty is that the trial procedure is placed completely in the hands of officers and union members. Not until the trial and appellate procedures are fully exhausted is there the prospect of judgment by a neutral tribunal.

The United Automobile Workers, whose trial provisions roughly approximate those of the ITU in concern for due process, has addressed itself to this problem of neutral, disinterested judgment. The UAW has a public review board composed of seven "impartial persons of good public repute" who are selected for this service by the international president and approved by the international convention. This board is primarily an appellate body, though it does have original jurisdiction in a few cases. It receives copies of all complaints lodged with the international executive board. If the appellant is dissatisfied with the decision of the executive board, he may then appeal to the public review board. In addition, the board is empowered to act directly on a matter "if it concludes that there is substance to the original complaint and that the action of the International Executive Board does not satisfactorily meet the problem." Thus, a serious attempt is made to keep the judicial decisions of the local and international officers under constant surveillance of a body whose independence cannot be matched by any union tribunal. Yet in the entire labor movement the Upholsterers is the only other union with such independent public review system.[3]

Unfortunately, there are a good number of unions whose procedural rules do not match those of the ITU, the UAW, and the Upholsterers. In the Teamsters, for instance, the executive board of the local is given original jurisdiction in the trial of union members; the general executive board has appellate jurisdiction for the five-year interval between conventions, and charges against international officers are heard by the executive board. The Hod Carriers, the Bakery and Confectionery Workers, and the International Union of Operating Engineers have similar provisions concentrating power in the hands of the local and international executive boards. . . .

MARTIN T. BADURA v. LOCAL 93, UAW

UAW Public Review Board
P.R.B. Case No. 322 (1976)

[Martin Badura, a General Motors' employee, injured his back in a fall in September 1970. The resulting physical disability was estimated by the company's doctor at 20% and by Badura's doctor at 40%. Badura filed a state workmen's compensation claim, and underwent back surgery in 1971. When he returned to work, Badura insisted he was physically unable to perform most of the tasks assigned him, but asserted he could handle other available jobs, such as inspection. The company viewed Badura as simply refusing to work. After successive disciplinary layoffs, he was discharged on February 17, 1972. Badura grieved and shortly thereafter moved to Montana. Badura later testified that he was assured by a union committeeman that his case would be taken to arbitration. The committeeman denied this, pointing out that only the international could authorize arbitration. Badura also maintained that he had always wanted his job back, and that only when pressed had he indicated he would settle for $10,000 plus a year's medical coverage. The union committeeman stated that Badura had told him he wished to quit GM and move to Montana, and had raised the question of the union's getting $10,000 for him. The committeeman said he advised Badura the figure was "impossible."

---

[3] The situation remains essentially unchanged twenty years later. In the intervening period a handful of unions experimented with public review boards, but their efforts were generally abortive. Even the Upholsterers' board has fallen into disuse. — Eds

[On May 23, 1972, the international submitted Badura's grievance to the UAW-GM permanent umpire. On June 5, without further communication with Badura, the UAW settled the case. Badura's discharge was changed to a voluntary quit and he was to receive $500. About the same time he was awarded a 30% disability by the State Workmen's Compensation Bureau. Badura protested the grievance settlement to the membership of the local on November 15-16, 1972. A tie vote of 59-59 was broken by the local president, who voted to sustain the position of the bargaining committee. An additional meeting of the third shift was also held on November 16, where the vote in favor of upholding the decision of the bargaining committee was 11-0. Badura appealed to the International Executive Board (IEB) on December 18, 1972. An IEB appeals committee heard the matter on July 12, 1973 and on December 20 recommended denial of the appeal. The full IEB adopted this recommendation. Badura appealed to the Public Review Board (as an alternative to the UAW Convention Appeals Committee) on January 21, 1974, alleging that the union's settlement with the company constituted collusion, and that the union's handling of the grievance was fraudulent, either actually or constructively.]

The threshold issue presented is our jurisdiction to consider this appeal. In appeals involving the processing of grievances arising under a collective bargaining agreement we are limited to review of those cases involving claims that "fraud, discrimination or collusion with management" affected the disposition of the grievance. Additionally, we must find that one or more of the proscribed elements actually did affect the processing of the grievance before we may assume jurisdiction and dispose of all other facets of the case. . . .

This Public Review Board is a creature of the constitution. The membership has determined to vest ultimate appellate authority in a group of independent persons who are not members of the union and who can deliver an unbiased judgment in disputes arising between members of the organization and those whom they have selected to govern it.

Those who have created this organization necessarily must define the limits of its authority. In exercising that authority we have taken extreme care not to overstep its boundaries as these are described in the constitution. In this case, however, we have been confronted with opposing viewpoints as to the extent of our authority to remedy an alleged breach of the duty of fair representation which appellant Badura claims has been perpetrated by an officer of his local and a staff representative of the international union. The fundamental difference between the position of the two parties in the final analysis has to do with the element of intent. The union maintains that the Public Review Board must find that the union intended to collude, defraud or discriminate against appellant to deprive him of his contractual rights, conduct which it equates with bad faith. Its member, on the other hand, contends that it is not necessary that he prove an intent at all; that it is the duty of the Public Review Board to look at all of the circumstances surrounding the disposition of the grievance and decide whether the Union has represented him fairly. If it concludes that it has not then the member has been defrauded. Such, he declares, is the plain meaning of the term as it is used in article 33, § 8 of the constitution.

It may be useful in the first instance to review briefly the scope of the duty of fair representation and its relation to the authority committed to the PRB by the union's constitution. [The board proceeded with such a review.]

As the union has noted, the constitution does not define our jurisdiction over grievance appeals in terms of a duty of fair representation. Issues of fair representation, however, are obviously involved when the question is raised as to whether the union has acted discriminatorily, fraudulently or in collusion with management in the processing of a grievance. If it has, it has not represented its member fairly or, to use the terminology of the union, it has acted "in bad faith".

But whatever may be the overlap between the union's duty to represent its members fairly on the one hand, and a duty to avoid fraud, collusion and discrimination in grievance handling on the other, the power given to the Public Review Board by the union's constitution is confined to passing upon the latter duty. We hold that our jurisdiction is not the same, or as broad, as the courts'.

In most cases a violation of the union's duty which we enforce will be established by proof of intent to injure or hostile motivation in grievance handling action which prejudices a member's rights under the collective bargaining contract, conduct the union characterizes as "in bad faith". Whether there may be forms of discrimination so clearly invidious or prejudicial in their effects as to come within the reach of our authority even without direct proof of bad faith, or cases where, despite the absence of direct evidence, the inferences of fraud are so compelling as to require us to assert our jurisdiction, we need not here decide. Motive, malice, wilful deceit, all involve elements of intent which most often escape clear proof. If fraud is to have any effective meaning, it too must be subject to the normal evidentiary process. In a proper case the Public Review Board, obviously, has the authority and the duty to infer the requisite intent from the facts. However, this is not such a case. Thus, although the element of bad faith may be the touchstone in most cases, the true test of our jurisdiction which we must apply in each case by reviewing all the circumstances and weighing all the evidence is to determine the presence or absence of fraud, collusion or discrimination.

Applying these standards to the instant appeal, it is clear that we have jurisdiction to decide issues which appellant has raised, for appellant has charged the union with fraudulent representation of his claim. We think it is equally clear, however, that he has not proved his claim.

As heretofore noted, the gravamen of appellant's complaint is that the union settled his grievance without arbitrating it although it had promised him it would do so, without full knowledge of his medical condition, without consulting him first and without timely notifying him of the terms of the settlement.

The proofs, however, fail to establish that anything the union did was fraudulent. The union first investigated appellant's grievance, it then processed it through all of the procedures to and including the umpire's step. Its investigation of the merits, however, convinced it that the case was a weak one primarily because information the union had was that in many instances appellant simply would not attempt to do the job assigned him and would insist that he could not do it by reason of his back condition. While it did not have available the ultimate determination of appellant's disability (30%) it did have appellant's doctor's estimate (40%) and the company doctor's conclusion (20%). It also had the benefit of being able to talk with those who had observed him in the work situation. On the basis of all of this information it decided the best it could do was to protect his record by changing the discharge to a voluntary quit. In addition, it was able to obtain for him a small amount of compensation.

There is, as heretofore noted, no duty on the part of a union to take every case to arbitration, and, although desirable, there is no duty on its part even to consult with the aggrieved respecting a decision not to arbitrate. It is only necessary that it make its settlements in good faith. It was not fraud for it to have settled without obtaining the consent of the aggrieved in the process.

Finally as respects appellant's allegation as to the timeliness of notification, it is apparent that the process of communication was made more difficult by Badura's decision to move out of state without leaving a forwarding address. But in any case appellant is mistaken as respects his notion the settlement could have been set aside at the direction of the membership. It could not, being binding on both the union and the employer. Therefore, he was not prejudiced by the delay in notification. . . .

Affirmed.

[The concurring opinion of MEMBER ARTHURS, joined by MEMBERS McKELVEY and ST. ANTOINE, is omitted.]

NOTES

1. In his concurrence, Member Arthurs argued that recurring claims of unfair representation before the Public Review Board demonstrated that the principal case should be used to provide the union and its members with guidance concerning the board's jurisdiction, beyond that afforded by a case-by-case approach. For Member Arthurs, "fraud" in the UAW constitutional sense would encompass not only "deliberate deceit" but also "acts in violation of trust or confidence," *e.g.,* "where the union cannot show any rational basis for its failure to pursue the member's claim." On the other hand, he would not ordinarily treat incompetent, negligent grievance handling as fraud, requiring instead "proof of the most flagrant incompetence or negligence in order to conclude that fraud had been committed. . . ."

2. For further discussion of the UAW Public Review Board, *see* J. STIEBER, W. OBERER & M. HARRINGTON, DEMOCRACY AND PUBLIC REVIEW,

A REPORT TO THE CENTER FOR THE STUDY OF DEMOCRATIC INSTITUTIONS (1960); Brooks, *Impartial Public Review of Internal Union Disputes: Experiment in Democratic Self-Discipline,* 22 OHIO ST. L.J. 64 (1961); Klein, *UAW Public Review Board Report,* 18 RUTGERS L. REV. 304 (1964). *See also* U.S. BUREAU OF LABOR STATISTICS, DEP'T OF LABOR, BULL. NO. 1350, DISCIPLINARY POWERS AND PROCEDURES IN UNION CONSTITUTIONS (1963); Klein, Linn & Feller, *Public Review Boards: Their Place in the Process of Dispute Resolutions,* in NATIONAL ACADEMY OF ARBITRATORS, ARBITRATION — 1974, PROCEEDINGS OF THE TWENTY-SEVENTH ANNUAL MEETING 189, 205, 221 (1975) (three separate papers).

(b) Legal Safeguards

INTERNATIONAL BROTHERHOOD OF BOILERMAKERS v. HARDEMAN

Supreme Court of the United States
401 U.S. 233, 91 S. Ct. 609, 28 L. Ed. 2d 10 (1971)

MR. JUSTICE BRENNAN delivered the opinion of the Court. . . .

Respondent was expelled from membership in petitioner union and brought this action under § 102 [of the LMRDA] in the District Court for the Southern District of Alabama. He alleged that in expelling him the petitioner violated § 101(a)(5) of the Act. . . .

A jury awarded respondent damages of $152,150. The Court of Appeals for the Fifth Circuit affirmed. 420 F.2d 485 (1969). We granted certiorari limited to the questions whether the subject matter of the suit was preempted because exclusively within the competence of the National Labor Relations Board and, if not preempted, whether the courts below had applied the proper standard of review to the union proceedings. . . . We reverse.

The case arises out of events in the early part of October 1960. Respondent, George Hardeman, is a boilermaker. He was then a member of petitioner's Local Lodge 112. On October 3, he went to the union hiring hall to see Herman Wise, business manager of the Local Lodge and the official responsible for referring workmen for jobs. Hardeman had talked to a friend of his, an employer who had promised to ask for him by name for a job in the vicinity. He sought assurance from Wise that he would be referred for the job. When Wise refused to make a definite commitment, Hardeman threatened violence if no work was forthcoming in the next few days.

On October 4, Hardeman returned to the hiring hall and waited for a referral. None was forthcoming. The next day, in his words, he "went to the hall . . . and waited from the time the hall opened until we had the trouble. I tried to make up my mind what to do, whether to sue the local or Wise or beat hell out of Wise, and then I made up my mind." When Wise came out of his office to go to a local jobsite, as required by his duties as business manager, Hardeman handed him a copy of a telegram asking for Hardeman by name. As Wise was reading the telegram, Hardeman began punching him in the face.

Hardeman was tried for this conduct on charges of creating dissension and working against the interest and harmony of the Local Lodge, and of threatening and using force to restrain an officer of the Local Lodge from properly discharging the duties of his office. The trial committee found him "guilty as charged," and the Local Lodge sustained the finding and voted his expulsion for an indefinite period. Internal union review of this action, instituted by Hardeman, modified neither the verdict nor the penalty. Five years later, Hardeman brought this suit alleging that petitioner violated § 101(a)(5) by denying him a full and fair hearing in the union disciplinary proceedings.

I. We consider first the union's claim that the subject matter of this lawsuit is, in the first instance, within the exclusive competence of the National Labor Relations Board. The union argues that the gravamen of Hardeman's complaint — which did not seek reinstatement, but only damages for wrongful expulsion, consisting of loss of income, loss of pension and insurance rights, mental anguish and punitive damages — is discrimination against him in job referrals; that any such conduct on the part of the union is at the very least arguably an unfair labor practice under §§ 8(b)(1)(A) and 8(b)(2) of the National Labor Relations Act. . . ; and that in such circumstances, "the federal courts must defer to the exclusive competence of the National Labor Relations Board if the danger of . . . interference with national policy is to be averted." San Diego Building Trades Council v. Garmon, 359 U.S. 236, 245 (1959); see Local 100, Journeymen v. Borden, 373 U.S. 690 (1963).

We think the union's argument is misdirected. Hardeman's complaint alleged that his expulsion was unlawful under § 101(a)(5), and sought compensation for the consequences of the claimed wrongful expulsion. The critical issue presented by Hardeman's complaint was whether the union disciplinary proceedings had denied him a full and fair hearing within the meaning of § 101(a)(5)(C). Unless he could establish this claim, Hardeman would be out of court. We hold that this claim was not within the exclusive competence of the National Labor Relations Board. . . .

Those factors suggesting that resort must be had to the administrative process are absent from the present case. The fairness of an internal union disciplinary proceeding is hardly a question beyond "the conventional experience of judges," nor can it be said to raise issues "within the special competence" of the NLRB. See NLRB v. Allis-Chalmers Mfg. Co., 388 U.S. 175, 181, 193-194 (1967). As we noted in that case, the Eighty-Sixth Congress which enacted § 101(a)(5) was "plainly of the view" that the protections embodied therein were new material in the body of federal labor law. 388 U.S. at 194. And that same Congress explicitly referred claims under § 101(a)(5) not to the NLRB, but to the federal district courts. This is made explicit in the opening sentence of § 102. . . .

The union argues that Hardeman's suit should nevertheless have been dismissed because he did not seek an injunction restoring him to membership, and because he did seek damages for loss of employment said to be the consequence of his expulsion from the union. Taken together, these factors are said to shift the primary focus of the action from a review of Hardeman's expulsion to a review of alleged union discrimination against him in job referrals. Since this is a matter normally within the exclusive competence of the NLRB, see Local 100, Journeymen v. Borden, 373 U.S. at 695-696, the union argues that Hardeman's suit was beyond the competence of the district court.

The argument has no merit. To begin with, the language of § 102 does not appear to make the availability of damages turn upon whether an injunction is requested as well. If anything, § 102 contemplates that damages will be the usual, and injunctions the extraordinary form of relief. Requiring that injunctive relief be sought as a precondition to damages would have little effect other than to force plaintiffs, as a matter of course, to add a few words to their complaints seeking an undesired injunction. We see no reason to import into § 102 so trivial a requirement.

Nor are our prior cases authority for such a result. We have repeatedly held, of course, that state law may not regulate conduct either protected or prohibited by the National Labor Relations Act. . . . Where it has not been clear whether particular conduct is protected, prohibited, or left to state regulation by that Act, we have likewise required courts to stay their hand. . . .

The present case, however, implicates none of the principles discussed above. There is no attempt, in this lawsuit, to apply state law to matters preempted by federal authority. Nor is there an attempt to apply federal law of general application, which is limited in the particular circumstances by the National Labor Relations Act. Nor is there an attempt to have the district court enforce the provisions of the National Labor Relations Act itself, without guidance from the NLRB. As we have said, the critical question in this action is whether Hardeman was afforded the rights guaranteed him by § 101(a)(5) of the LMRDA. If he was denied them, Congress has said that he is entitled to damages for the consequences of that denial. Since these questions are irrelevant to the legality of conduct under the National Labor Relations Act, there is no danger of conflicting interpretation of its provisions. And since the law applied is federal law explicitly made applicable to such circumstances by Congress, there is no danger that state law may come in through the back door to regulate conduct that has been removed by Congress from state control. Accordingly, this action was within the competence of the district court.

II. Two charges were brought against Hardeman in the union disciplinary proceedings. He was charged with violation of Article 13, § 1, of the Subordinate Lodge Constitution, which forbids attempting to create dissension or working against the interest and harmony of the union, and carries a penalty of expulsion. He was also charged with violations of Article 12, § 1, of the Subordinate Lodge By-Laws, which forbids the threat or use of force against any officer of the union in order to prevent him from properly discharging the duties of his office; violation may be punished "as warranted by the offense." Hardeman's conviction on both charges was upheld in internal union procedures for review.

The trial judge instructed the jury that "whether or not he [respondent] was rightfully or wrongfully discharged or expelled is a pure question of law for me to determine." He assumed, but did not decide, that the transcript of the union disciplinary hearing contained evidence adequate to support conviction of violating Article 12. He held, however, that there was no evidence at all in the transcript of the union disciplinary proceedings to support the charge of violating Article 13. This holding appears to have been based on the Fifth Circuit's decision in Boilermakers v. Braswell, 388 F.2d 193 (5th Cir. 1968). There the Court of Appeals for the Fifth Circuit had reasoned that "penal provisions in union constitutions must be strictly construed," and that as so construed Article 13 was directed only to "threats to the union as an organization and to the effective carrying out of the union's aims," not to merely personal altercations. 388 F.2d at 199. Since the union tribunals had returned only a general verdict, and since one of the charges was thought to be supported by no evidence whatsoever, the trial judge held that Hardeman had been deprived of the full and fair hearing guaranteed by § 101(a)(5). The Court of Appeals affirmed, simply citing *Braswell.* . . .

We find nothing in either the language or the legislative history of § 101(a)(5) that could justify such a substitution of judicial for union authority to interpret the union's regulations in order to determine the scope of offenses warranting discipline of union members. Section 101(a)(5) began life as a floor amendment to S. 1555, the Kennedy-Ervin Bill, in the Eighty-Sixth Congress. As sponsored by Senator McClellan, and as adopted by the Senate on April 22, 1959, the amendment would have forbidden discipline of union members "except for breach of a published written rule of [the union]." 105 Cong. Rec. 6476, 6492-6493. But this language did not long survive. Two days later, a substitute amendment was offered by Senator Kuchel, who explained that further study of the McClellan amendment had raised "some rather vexing questions." *Id.* at 6720. The Kuchel substitute, adopted the following day, deleted the requirement that charges be based upon a previously published, written union rule; it transformed Senator McClellan's amendment, in relevant part, into the present language of § 101(a)(5). *Id.* at 6720, 6727. As so amended, S. 1555 passed the Senate on April 25. *Id.* at 6745. Identical language was adopted by the House, *id.* at 15884, 15891, and appears in the statute as finally enacted.

The Congress understood that Senator Kuchel's amendment was intended to make substantive changes in Senator McClellan's proposal. Senator Kennedy had specifically objected to the McClellan amendment because

> In the case of . . . the . . . official who bribed a judge, unless there were a specific prohibition against bribery of judicial officers written into the constitution of the union, then no union could take disciplinary action against [an] officer or member guilty of bribery.

. . . .

It seems to me that we can trust union officers to run their affairs better than that. *Id.* at 6491.

Senator Kuchel described his substitute as merely providing "the usual reasonable constitutional basis" for union disciplinary proceedings: union members were to have "constitutionally reasonable notice and a reasonable hearing." *Id.* at 6720. After the Kuchel amendment passed the Senate, Senator Goldwater explained it to the House Committee on Labor and Education as follows:

> "[T]he bill of rights in the Senate bill require[s] that the union member be served with written charges prior to any disciplinary proceedings but it does not require that these charges, to be valid, must be based on activity that the union had proscribed prior to the union member having engaged in such activity." Labor-Management Reform Legislation, Hearings before a Joint Subcommittee of the House Committee on Education and Labor, 86th Cong., 1st Sess. pt. 4, p. 1595 (1959).

And Senator McClellan's testimony was to the same effect. *Id.* pt. 5, 2235-2236, 2251, 2285.

We think that this is sufficient to indicate that § 101(a)(5) was not intended to authorize courts to determine the scope of offenses for which a union may discipline its members. And if a union may discipline its members for offenses not proscribed by written rules at all, it is surely a futile exercise for a court to construe the written rules in order to determine whether particular conduct falls within or without their scope.

Of course, § 101(a)(5)(A) requires that a member subject to discipline be "served with written specific charges." These charges must be, in Senator McClellan's words, "specific enough to inform the accused member of the offense that he has allegedly committed." Where, as here, the union's charges make reference to specific written provisions, § 101(a)(5)(A) obviously empowers the federal courts to examine those provisions and determine whether the union member had been misled or otherwise prejudiced in the presentation of his defense. But it gives courts no warrant to scrutinize the union regulations in order to determine whether particular conduct may be punished at all.

Respondent does not suggest, and we cannot discern, any possibility of prejudice in the present case. Although the notice of charges with which he was served does not appear as such in the record, the transcript of the union hearing indicates that the notice did not confine itself to a mere statement or citation of the written regulations that Hardeman was said to have violated: the notice appears to have contained a detailed statement of the facts relating to the fight which formed the basis for the disciplinary action. Section 101(a)(5) requires no more.

III. There remains only the question whether the evidence in the union disciplinary proceeding was sufficient to support the finding of guilt. Section 101(a)(5)(C) of the LMRDA guarantees union members a "full and fair" disciplinary hearing, and the parties and the lower federal courts are in full agreement that this guarantee requires the charging party to provide some evidence at the disciplinary hearing to support the charges made. This is the proper standard of judicial review. We have repeatedly held that conviction on charges unsupported by any evidence is a denial of due process . . . and we feel that § 101(a)(5)(C) may fairly be said to import a similar requirement into union disciplinary proceedings. Senator Kuchel, who first introduced the provision, characterized it on the Senate floor as requiring the "usual reasonable constitutional basis" for disciplinary action, 105 Cong. Rec. 6720, and any lesser standard would make useless § 101(a)(5)(A)'s requirement of written, specific charges. A stricter standard, on the other hand, would be inconsistent with the apparent congressional intent to allow unions to govern their own affairs, and would require courts to judge the credibility of witnesses on the basis of what would be at best a cold record.

Applying this standard to the present case, we think there is no question that the charges were adequately supported. Respondent was charged with having attacked Wise without warning, and with continuing to beat him for some time. Wise so testified at the disciplinary hearing, and his testimony was fully corroborated by one other witness to the altercation. Even Hardeman, although he claimed he was thereafter held and beaten, admitted having struck the first blow. On such a record there is no question but that the charges were supported by "some evidence."

Reversed.

[The concurring opinion of Mr. Justice White and the dissenting opinion of Mr. Justice Douglas are omitted.]

Parks v. IBEW, 314 F.2d 886, 911-13 (4th Cir. 1963), *cert. denied,* 372 U.S. 976 (1963). In the course of a lengthy opinion sustaining an international union's revocation of a local's charter for engaging in a strike without international authorization, the court of appeals made the following comments on the elements of a "fair hearing" in union disciplinary proceedings:

The common law clearly requires that, to be valid, expulsion of a member or a subordinate body must be rendered after a "fair hearing. . . ." . . . The elements of such a "fair hearing" often resemble constitutional due process requirements and generally encompass full notice and a reasonable opportunity to be heard — including the right to present evidence and the right to confront and cross-examine witnesses. There is also a body of law requiring trial of an accused before an unbiased tribunal. Some commentators seem to think that the courts should play a more active role in reviewing not only specific bias, e.g., prejudgment or use of discipline pretextuously, but also built-in bias, e.g., combined prosecuting and judicial functions and use of "yes men." They have, however, generally recognized either that the courts have not been empowered to do this or that they are unable to reach such bias for it "is an inevitable product of the procedure itself. . . ."

The real basis for the argument that the IP [International President] was biased is that he was, in a sense, both prosecutor and judge. It is quite true that he ordered the charges to be brought and conferred with the International's General Counsel in their formulation as well as in the preparation of the revocation order. But it is also true that the basis for the charges was that the Local had struck in defiance of his repeated admonitions and had rejected his collective bargaining orders. And there can be no doubt that the Constitution vested in the IP these combined prosecuting and judicial functions. . . .

It may well be thought desirable for unions to adopt hearing procedures that keep trial functions separate, but the federal courts are not empowered so to restructure the disciplinary procedures of unions. . . . Some unions, like the United Automobile Workers, have responded to the pressure for fairness in internal trial proceedings by establishing, essentially external to the union orginaization, independent public review boards having the final word in disciplinary matters. Such unions would appear to have gone far to separate prosecuting and ultimate judicial functions. But, in the absence of a clear congressional authorization, it is not for the federal courts to compel such measures. . . .

Separation of functions is not an absolute due process prerequisite to fairness in administrative proceedings, see 2 Davis, Administrative Law Treatise § 13.02; in internal union proceedings it traditionally, and under the LMRDA, has also not been deemed a requirement of fairness. Courts, federal courts expecially, are justified in ruling a union tribunal biased only upon a demonstration that it has been substantially actuated by improper motives — in other words, only upon a showing of specific prejudice.

NOTES

1. Section 101(a)(5)'s guarantee of a "full and fair hearing" was held to include the right to confront and cross-examine opposing witnesses in Anderson v. Carpenters, 53 L.R.R.M. 2793, 47 CCH Lab. Cas. ¶ 18,400 (D. Minn. 1963). But an accused in a union proceeding is not entitled to be represented by legal counsel. Smith v. General Truck Drivers Local 467, 181 F. Supp. 14 (S.D. Cal. 1960). Furthermore, informality or minor departures from prescribed procedures are not fatal defects so long as there is adequate notice of the charges and a full opportunity to be heard. Null v. Carpenters Dist. Council, 239 F. Supp. 809 (S.D. Tex. 1965); Anderson v. Carpenters, 59 L.R.R.M. 2684, 51 CCH Lab. Cas. ¶ 19,747 (D. Minn. 1965). Charges must be drafted with reasonable particularity as to time, place, and circumstances. Failure to comply with this requirement as to each charge on which a finding of guilt is rendered may invalidate the penalty, even though conviction on the other charges only might have

justified it. Gleason v. Hotel & Restaurant Employees Local 11, 422 F.2d 342 (2d Cir. 1970).

2. In Cornelio v. Carpenters Dist. Council, 243 F. Supp. 126 (E.D. Pa. 1965), aff'd, 358 F.2d 728 (3d Cir. 1966), *cert. denied,* 386 U.S. 975 (1967), the court found no cause of action in the allegation that a member's accusers were persons of influence in the union (they were business agents). But it was held a denial of a fair hearing when a union president was suspended from office and from membership by an executive council on which five of the seven members were political opponents who wished to eliminate him as a political force. Needham v. Isbister, 84 L.R.R.M. 2105 (D. Mass. 1973).

3. To what extent should the courts review the findings of fact of union tribunals in disciplinary cases? *See* Vars v. Boilermakers, 320 F.2d 576, 578 (2d Cir. 1963): "Thus, although the courts may be without power to review matters of credibility or of strict weight of the evidence, a close reading of the record is justified to insure that the findings are not without any foundation in the evidence."

4. What constitutes "discipline" under § 101(a)(5)? In Allen v. Armored Car Chauffeurs Local 820, 185 F. Supp. 492 (D.N.J. 1960), it was held that a union's failure to process an employee's grievance was not within the purview of § 101(a)(5). The court stated: "The disciplinary action of which this court is given jurisdiction . . . is not discharge from employment, but the discipline of a member by the Union as to his membership." *Id.* at 494-95. *See also* Seeley v. Painters, 308 F.2d 52 (5th Cir. 1962); Strauss v. Teamsters, 179 F. Supp. 297 (E.D. Pa. 1959). *But cf.* Scovile v. Watson, 338 F.2d 678, 680 (7th Cir. 1964), *cert. denied,* 380 U.S. 963 (1965) ("a refusal by the union . . . to prosecute an arbitration grievance might be considered as a disciplinary measure relating to the employee's membership in the union"); Detroy v. American Guild of Variety Artists, 286 F.2d 75 (2d Cir. 1961), *cert. denied,* 366 U.S. 929 (1961), *supra* at 893. *See generally* Beaird & Player, *Union Discipline of Its Membership Under Section 101(a)(5) of Landrum-Griffin: What is "Discipline" and How Much Process Is Due?* 9 GA. L. REV. 383 (1975); Etelson & Smith, *Union Discipline Under the Landrum-Griffin Act,* 82 HARV. L. REV. 727 (1969).

5. The common-law cases on due process in union proceedings are collected in Annot., 21 A.L.R.2d 1397 (1952).

B. UNION DISCIPLINE UNDER THE NLRA

NLRB. v. ALLIS-CHALMERS MFG. CO.

Supreme Court of the United States
388 U.S. 175, 87 S. Ct. 2001, 18 L. Ed. 2d 1123 (1967)

MR. JUSTICE BRENNAN delivered the opinion of the Court.

The question here is whether a union which threatened and imposed fines [of $20 to $100] and brought suit for their collection, against members who crossed the union's picket line and went to work during an authorized strike against their employer, committed the unfair labor practice under § 8(b)(1)(A) of the National Labor Relations Act of engaging in conduct "to restrain or coerce" employees in the exercise of their right guaranteed by § 7 to "refrain from" concerted activities. . . .

I. . . . It is highly unrealistic to regard § 8(b)(1), and particularly its words "restrain or coerce," as precisely and unambiguously covering the union conduct involved in this case. On its face court enforcement of fines imposed on members for violation of membership obligations is no more conduct to "restrain or coerce" satisfaction of such obligations than court enforcement of penalties imposed on citizens for violation of their obligations as citizens to pay income taxes, or court awards of damages against a contracting party for nonperformance of a contractual obligation voluntarily undertaken. But even if the inherent imprecision of the words "restrain or coerce" may be overlooked, recourse to legislative history to determine the sense in which Congress used the words is not foreclosed. . . .

To say that Congress meant in 1947 by the § 7 amendments and § 8(b)(1)(A) to strip unions of the power to fine members for strikebreaking, however lawful the strike vote, and however fair the disciplinary procedures and penalty, is to say that Congress preceded the Landrum-Griffin amendments with an even more pervasive regulation of the internal affairs of unions. It is also to attribute to Congress an intent at war with the understanding of the union-membership relation which has been at the heart of its effort "to fashion a coherent labor policy" and which has been a predicate underlying action by this Court and the state courts. More importantly, it is to say that Congress limited unions in the powers necessary to the discharge of their role as exclusive statutory bargaining agents by impairing the usefulness of labor's cherished strike weapon. It is no answer that the proviso to § 8(b)(1)(A) preserves to the union the power to expel the offending member. Where the union is strong and membership therefore valuable, to require expulsion of the member visits a far more severe penalty upon the member than a reasonable fine. Where the union is weak, and membership therefore of little value, the union faced with further depletion of its ranks may have no real choice except to condone the member's disobedience. Yet it is just such weak unions for which the power to execute union decisions taken for the benefit of all employees is most critical to effective discharge of its statutory function.

Congressional meaning is of course ordinarily to be discerned in the words Congress uses. But when the literal application of the imprecise words "restrain or coerce" Congress employed in § 8(b)(1)(A) produce the extraordinary results we have mentioned we should determine whether this meaning is confirmed in the legislative history of the section.

II. The explicit wording of § 8(b)(2), which is concerned with union powers to affect a member's employment, is in sharp contrast with the imprecise words of § 8(b)(1)(A). . . . Senator Taft, in answer to protestations by Senator Pepper that § 8(b)(2) would intervene into the union's internal affairs and "deny it the right to protect itself against a man in the union who betrays the objectives of the union . . . ," stated:

"The pending measure does not propose any limitation with respect to the internal affairs of unions. They still will be able to fire any members they wish to fire, *and they still will be able to try any of their members.* All that they will not be able to do, after the enactment of this bill, is this: If they fire a member for some reason other than nonpayment of dues they cannot make his employer discharge him from his job and throw him out of work. That is the only result of the provision under discussion." [13]

. . .

What legislative materials there are dealing with § 8(b)(1)(A) contain not a single word referring to the application of its prohibitions to traditional internal union discipline in general, or disciplinary fines in particular. On the contrary there are a number of assurances by its sponsors that the section was not meant to regulate the internal affairs of unions. . . .

It is true that there are references in the Senate debate on § 8(b)(1)(A) to an intent to impose the same prohibitions on unions that applied to employers as regards restraint and coercion of employees in their exercise of § 7 rights. However apposite this parallel might be when applied to organizational tactics, it clearly is inapplicable to the relationship of a union member to his own union. Union membership allows the member a part in choosing the very course of action to which he refuses to adhere, but he has of course no role in employer conduct, and nonunion employees have no voice in the affairs of the union.

Cogent support for an interpretation of the body of § 8(b)(1) as not reaching the imposition of fines and attempts at court enforcement is the proviso to § 8(b)(1). . . . Senator Holland offered the proviso during debate and Senator Ball immediately accepted it, stating that it was not the intent of the sponsors in any way to regulate the internal affairs of unions. At the very least it can be said that the proviso preserves the rights of unions to impose fines, as a lesser penalty than expulsion, and to impose fines which carry the explicit or implicit threat of expulsion for nonpayment. Therefore, under the proviso the rule in the UAW constitution governing fines is valid and the fines themselves and expulsion for nonpayment would not be an unfair labor practice. Assuming that the proviso cannot also be read to authorize court enforcement of fines, a question we need not reach, the fact remains that to interpret the body of § 8(b)(1) to apply to the imposition and collection of fines would be to impute to Congress a concern with the permissible *means* of enforcement of union fines and to attribute to Congress a narrow and discrete interest in banning court enforcement of such fines. Yet there is not one word of the legislative history evidencing any such

---

[13] 93 Cong. Rec. 4193, II Legislative History of the Labor Management Relations Act of 1947, 1097 (hereafter, Leg. Hist.).

congressional concern. And as we have pointed out, a distinction between court enforcement and expulsion would have been anomalous for several reasons. First, Congress was operating within the context of the "contract theory" of the union-member relationship which widely prevailed at that time. The efficacy of a contract is precisely its legal enforceability. A lawsuit is and has been the ordinary way by which performance of private money obligations is compelled. Second, as we have noted, such a distinction would visit upon the member of a strong union a potentially more severe punishment than court enforcement of fines, while impairing the bargaining facility of the weak union by requiring it either to condone misconduct or deplete its ranks.

There may be concern that court enforcement may permit the collection of unreasonably large fines. However, even were there evidence that Congress shared this concern, this would not justify reading the Act also to bar court enforcement of reasonable fines.

The 1959 Landrum-Griffin amendments, thought to be the first comprehensive regulation by Congress of the conduct of internal union affairs,[33] also negate the reach given § 8(b)(1)(A) by the majority *en banc* below.... In 1959 Congress did seek to protect union members in their relationship to the union by adopting measures to insure the provision of democratic processes in the conduct of union affairs and procedural due process to members subjected to discipline. Even then, some Senators emphasized that "[I]n establishing and enforcing statutory standards great care should be taken not to undermine union self-government or weaken unions in their role as collective-bargaining agents." S. Rep. No. 187, 86th Cong., 1st Sess., 7. The Eighty-sixth Congress was thus plainly of the view that union self-government was not regulated in 1947. Indeed, that Congress expressly recognized that a union member may be "fined, suspended, expelled, or otherwise disciplined," and enacted only procedural requirements to be observed. 29 U.S.C. § 411(a)(5). Moreover, Congress added a proviso to the guarantee of freedom of speech and assembly disclaiming any intent "to impair the right of a labor organization to adopt and enforce reasonable rules as to the responsibility of every member toward the organization as an institution...." 29 U.S.C. § 411(a)(2)....

Thus this history of congressional action does not support a conclusion that the Taft-Hartly prohibitions against restraint or coercion of an employee to refrain from concerted activities included a prohibition against the imposition of fines on members who decline to honor an authorized strike and attempts to collect such fines. Rather, the contrary inference is more justified in light of the repeated refrain throughout the debates on § 8(b)(1)(A) and other sections that Congress did not propose any limitations with respect to the internal affairs of unions, aside from

---

[33] In 1957, in Machinists v. Gonzales, 356 U.S. 617, 620, we said: "[T]he protection of union members in their rights as members from arbitrary conduct by unions and union officers has not been undertaken by federal law, and indeed the assertion of any such power has been expressly denied."

barring enforcement of a union's internal regulations to affect a member's employment status.

III. ... The collective bargaining agreements with the locals incorporate union security clauses. Full union membership is not compelled by the clauses: an employee is required only to become and remain "a member of the union to the extent of paying his monthly dues. ..." The majority *en banc* below nevertheless regarded full membership to be "the result not of individual voluntary choice but of the insertion of [this] union security provision in the contract under which a substantial minority of the employees may have been forced into membership." 358 F.2d at 660. But the relevant inquiry here is not what motivated a member's full membership but whether the Taft-Hartley amendments prohibited disciplinary measures against a full member who crossed his union's picket line. It is clear that the fined employees involved in these cases enjoyed full union membership. Each executed the pledge of allegiance to the UAW constitution and took the oath of full membership. Moreover, the record of the Milwaukee County Court case against Benjamin Natzke discloses that two disciplined employees testified that they had fully participated in the proceedings leading to the strike. They attended the meetings at which the secret strike vote and the renewed strike vote were taken. It was upon this and similar evidence that the Milwaukee County Court found that Natzke "had by his actions become a member of the union for all purposes. ..." Allis-Chalmers offered no evidence in this proceeding that any of the fined employees enjoyed other than full union membership. We will not presume the contrary. Cf. Machinists v. Street, 367 U.S. 740, 774. Indeed, it is and has been Allis-Chalmers' position that the Taft-Hartley prohibitions apply whatever the nature of the membership. Whether those prohibitions would apply if the locals had imposed fines on members whose membership was in fact limited to the obligation of paying monthly dues is a question not before us and upon which we intimate no view.

The judgment of the Court of Appeals is

Reversed.

MR. JUSTICE WHITE, concurring.

It is true that § 8(b)(1)(A) makes it an unfair labor practice for a union to restrain or coerce any employees in the exercise of § 7 rights, but the proviso permits the union to make its own rules with respect to acquisition and retention of membership. Hence, a union may expel to enforce its own internal rules, even though a particular rule limits the § 7 rights of its members and even though expulsion to enforce it would be a clear and serious brand of "coercion" imposed in derogation of those § 7 rights. Such restraint and coercion Congress permitted by adding the proviso to § 8(b)(1)(A). Thus, neither the majority nor the dissent in this case questions the validity of the union rule against its members crossing picket lines during a properly called strike, nor the propriety of expulsion to enforce the rule. Section 8(b)(1)(A), therefore, does not bar *all* restraint and coercion by a union to prevent the exercise by its members of their

§ 7 rights. "Coercive" union rules are enforceable at least by expulsion.

The dissenting opinion in this case, although not questioning the enforceability of coercive rules by expulsion from membership, questions whether fines for violating such rules are enforceable at all, by expulsion or otherwise. The dissent would at least hold court collection of fines to be an unfair labor practice, apparently for the reason that fines collectible in court may be more coercive than fines enforceable by expulsion. My Brother BRENNAN, for the Court, takes a different view, reasoning that since expulsion would in many cases — certainly in this one involving a strong union — be a far more coercive technique for enforcing a union rule and for collecting a reasonable fine than the threat of court enforcement, there is no basis for thinking that Congress, having accepted expulsion as a permissible technique to enforce a rule in derogation of § 7 rights, nevertheless intended to bar enforcement by another method which may be far less coercive.

I do not mean to indicate, and I do not read the majority opinion otherwise, that every conceivable internal union rule which impinges upon the § 7 rights of union members is valid and enforceable by expulsion and court action. There may well be some internal union rules which on their face are wholly invalid and unenforceable. But the Court seems unanimous in upholding the rule against crossing picket lines during a strike and its enforceability by expulsion from membership. On this premises I think the opinion written for the Court is the more persuasive and sensible construction of the statute and I therefore join it, although I am doubtful about the implications of some of its generalized statements.

MR. JUSTICE BLACK, whom MR. JUSTICE DOUGLAS, MR. JUSTICE HARLAN, and MR. JUSTICE STEWART join, dissenting. . . .

I. In determining what the Court here holds, it is helpful to note what it does not hold. Since the union resorted to the courts to enforce its fines instead of relying on its own internal sanctions such as expulsion from membership, the Court correctly assumes that the proviso to § 8(b)(1)(A) cannot be read to authorize its holding. Neither does the Court attempt to sustain its holding by reference to § 7 which gives employees the right to refrain from engaging in concerted activities. To be sure, the Court in characterizing the union-member relationship as "contractual" and in emphasizing that its holding is limited to situations where the employee is a "full member" of the union, implies that by joining a union an employee gives up or waives some of his § 7 rights. But the Court does not say that a union member is without the § 7 right to refrain from participating in such concerted activity as an economic strike called by his union. . . .

With no reliance on the proviso to § 8(b)(1)(A) or on the meaning of § 7, the Court's holding boils down to this: a court-enforced reasonable fine for nonparticipation in a strike does not "restrain or coerce" an employee in the exercise of his right not to participate in the strike. In holding as it does, the Court interprets the words "restrain or coerce" in a way directly opposed to their literal meaning, for the Court admits that fines are as coercive as penalties imposed on citizens for the nonpayment of taxes. Though Senator Taft, in answer to charges that these words were ambiguous, said their meaning "is perfectly clear," 93 Cong. Rec. 4021, II Leg. Hist. 1025, and though any union official with sufficient intelligence and learning to be chosen as such could hardly fail to comprehend the meaning of these plain, simple English words, the Court insists on finding an "inherent imprecision" in these words. And that characterization then allows the Court to resort to "what legislative materials there are."

. . . The real reason for the Court's decision is its policy judgment that unions, especially weak ones, need the power to impose fines on strikebreakers and to enforce those fines in court. It is not enough, says the Court, that the unions have the power to expel those members who refuse to participate in a strike or who fail to pay fines imposed on them for such failure to participate; it is essential that weak unions have the choice between expulsion and court-enforced fines, simply because the latter are more effective in the sense of being more punitive. Though the entire mood of Congress in 1947 was to curtail the power of unions, as it had previously curtailed the power of employers, in order to equalize the power of the two, the Court is unwilling to believe that Congress intended to impair "the usefulness of labor's cherished strike weapon." I cannot agree with this conclusion or subscribe to the Court's unarticulated premise that the Court has power to add a new weapon to the union's economic arsenal whenever the Court believes that the union needs that weapon. That is a job for Congress, not this Court.

II. . . . Contrary to the Court, I am not at all certain that a union's right under the proviso to prescribe rules for the retention of membership includes the right to restrain a member from working by trying him on the vague charge of "conduct unbecoming a union member" and fining him for exercising his § 7 right of refusing to participate in a strike, even though the fine is only enforceable by expulsion from membership. It is one thing to say that Congress did not wish to interfere with the union's power, similar to that of any other kind of voluntary association, to prescribe specific conditions of membership. It is quite another thing to say that Congress intended to leave unions free to exercise a court-like power to try and punish members with a direct economic sanction for exercising their right to work. Just because a union might be free, under the proviso, to expel a member for crossing a picket line does not mean that Congress left unions free to threaten their members with fines. Even though a member may later discover that the threatened fine is only enforceable by expulsion, and in that sense a "lesser penalty," the direct threat of a fine, to a member normally unaware of the method the union might resort to for compelling its payment, would often be more coercive than a threat of expulsion.

Even on the assumption that § 8(a)(1)(A) permits a union to fine a member as long as the fine is only enforceable by expulsion, the fundamental error of the Court's opinion is its failure to recognize the practical and theoretical difference between a court-enforced fine, as here, and a fine enforced by expulsion or less drastic intra-union means. As the Court recognizes, expulsion for nonpayment of a fine may, especially in the case of a strong union, be more severe than judicial collection of the fine. But, if the union membership has little value and if the fine is great, then court-enforcement of the fine may be more effective punishment, and that is precisely why the Court desires to provide weak unions with this alternative to expulsion, an alternative which is similar to a criminal court's power to imprison defendants who fail to pay fines. . . .

The Court disposes of this tremendous practical difference between court-enforced and union-enforced fines by suggesting that Congress was not concerned with "the permissible means of enforcement of union fines" and that court-enforcement of fines is a necessary consequence of the "contract theory" of the union-member relationship. And then the Court cautions that its holding may only apply to court enforcement of "reasonable fines." Apparently the Court believes that these considerations somehow bring reasonable court-enforced fines within the ambit of "internal union affairs." There is no basis either historically or logically for this conclusion or the considerations upon which it is based. First, the Court says that disciplinary fines were commonplace at the time the Taft-Hartley Act was passed, and thus Congress could not have meant to prohibit these "traditional internal discipline" measures without saying so. Yet there is not one word in the authorities cited by the Court that indicates that court enforcement of fines was commonplace or traditional in 1947, and, to the contrary, until recently unions rarely resorted to court enforcement of union fines. Second, Congress' unfamiliarity in 1947 with this recent innovation and consequent failure to make any distinction between union-enforced and court-enforced fines cannot support the conclusion that Congress was unconcerned with the "means" a union uses to enforce its fines. Congress was expressly concerned with enacting "rules of the game" for unions to abide by. 93 Cong. Rec. 4436, II Leg. Hist. 1206. . . .

V. . . . The union here had a union security clause in its contract with Chalmers. That clause made it necessary for all employees, including the ones involved here, to pay dues and fees to the union. But § 8(a)(3) and § 8(b)(2) make it clear that "Congress intended to prevent utilization of union security agreements for any purpose other than to compel payment of union dues and fees." Radio Officers' Union v. Labor Board, 347 U.S. 17, 41. If the union uses the union security clause to compel employees to pay dues, characterizes such employees as members, and then uses such membership as a basis for imposing court-enforced fines upon those employees unwilling to participate in a union strike, then the union security clause is being used for a purpose other than "to compel payment of union dues and fees." It is being used to coerce employees to join in union activity in violation of § 8(b)(2).

The Court suggests that this problem is not present here, because the fined employees failed to prove they enjoyed other than full union membership, that their role in the union was not in fact limited to the obligation of paying dues. For several reasons, I am unable to agree with the Court's approach. Few employees forced to become "members" of the union by virtue of the union security clause will be aware of the fact that they must somehow "limit" their membership to avoid the union's court-enforced fines. Even those who are brash enough to attempt to do so may be unfamiliar with how to do it. Must they refrain from doing anything but paying dues, or will signing the routine union pledge still leave them with less than full membership? And finally, it is clear that what restrains the employee from going to work during a union strike is the union's threat that it will fine him and collect those fines from him in court. How many employees in a union shop whose names appear on the union's membership rolls will be willing to ignore that threat in the hope that they will later be able to convince the Labor Board or the state court that they were not full members of the union? . . .

NOTES

1. If union discipline does not "restrain or coerce" employees within the meaning of § 8(b)(1)(A) in the circumstances of the principal case, does it make any difference *why* the penalty is imposed? In Scofield v. NLRB, 394 U.S. 423 (1969), the Supreme Court found no violation of § 8(b)(1)(A) when a union sued in state court to collect fines levied against members who had breached a union rule forbidding the receipt of pay for production that exceeded a set ceiling. But in NLRB v. Marine & Shipbuilding Workers, 391 U.S. 418 (1968), the Court held that a union violated § 8(b)(1)(A) by expelling a member for filing an unfair labor practice charge with the Board without first having exhausted internal union remedies. Declared the Court: ". . . § 8(b)(1)(A) assures a union freedom of self-regulation where its legitimate internal affairs are concerned. But where a union rule penalizes a member for filing an unfair labor practice charge with the Board other considerations of public policy come into play."

Should a penalty for filing a decertification petition against a member's union be treated any differently from a penalty for filing unfair labor practice charges against it? *See* Tawas Tube Prod., Inc., 151 N.L.R.B. 46 (1965). Since the basis for the union discipline may vary the result, what does this reveal about the meaning of the terms "restrain or coerce" in § 8(b)(1)(A)?

2. Should it make any difference whether a union penalizes a member for filing a decertification petition by fining rather than expelling him? *See* Molders Local 125 (Blackhawk Tanning Co.), 178 N.L.R.B. 208 (1969), *enforced,* 442 F.2d 92 (7th Cir. 1971) (*Held:* Yes, two members dissenting; a fine is punitive and forbidden, while expulsion is defensive and allowable). *Cf.* Tri-Rivers Marine Engineers (U.S. Steel Corp.), 189 N.L.R.B. 838 (1971) (fine and threats of expulsion for soliciting authorization cards on behalf of a rival union).

3. What bearing should an applicable or arguably applicable no-strike clause have on a union's disciplining members for crossing a picket line or refusing to do picket line duty? *Compare* District 50, Local 12419 (National Grinding Wheel Co.), 176 N.L.R.B. 628 (1969), *with* Insurance Workers Local 60 (John Hancock Mut. Life Ins. Co.), 236 N.L.R.B. No. 50, 98 L.R.R.M. 1245 (1978). What if the picket line is unlawful under § 8(b)(4) or § 8(b)(7) of the NLRA? *Compare* NLRB v. Operating Engineers Local 18, 503 F. 2d 780 (6th Cir. 1974), *with* NLRB v. Longshoremen Local 30, 549 F. 2d 698 (9th Cir. 1977), *and* NLRB v. Retail Clerks Local 1179, 526 F. 2d 142 (9th Cir. 1975). How pertinent is the Supreme Court's observation in *Scofield v. NLRB, supra* note 1, at 430: "§ 8(b)(1)(A) leaves a union free to enforce a properly adopted rule which reflects a legitimate union interest, impairs no policy Congress has imbedded in the labor laws, and is reasonably enforced against union members who are free to leave the union and escape the rule."

4. Could a union lawfully charge its members a percentage of their earnings for the right to work behind a picket line set up by the union during an economic strike? *See* National Cash Register Co. v. NLRB, 466 F.2d 945 (6th Cir. 1972).

5. May a union fine supervisor-members for performing rank-and-file work during a strike? For performing only customary supervisory functions, including grievance adjustment? *Compare* Florida Power & Light Co. v. IBEW Local 641, 417 U.S. 790 (1974) ("Yes" to the first question, four justices dissenting), *with* American Broadcasting Cos. v. Writers Guild of America, West, Inc., 437 U.S. 411 (1978) ("No" to the second question, four justices dissenting). Union discipline of members who, as supervisory personnel, displease the union by their administration of the labor contract may violate § 8(b)(1)(B) of the NLRA, since it deprives the employer of the effective representation it is entitled to under the Act. Dallas Mailers Union (Dow Jones Co.), 181 N.L.R.B. 286 (1970), *enforced on other grounds,* 445 F.2d 730 (D.C. Cir. 1971); NLRB v. Lithographers Locals 15-P & 272 [Toledo Blade Co.], 437 F.2d 55 (6th Cir. 1971). What special considerations arise when a union tries to keep its supervisor-members from working during a strike? *See generally* Grissom, *Union Discipline of Supervisor-Members: Drawing the Line After Florida Power,* 27 Ala. L. Rev. 575 (1975).

6. If a union, through its internal disciplinary regulations, unilaterally enforces a maximum-production quota, could it be guilty of an 8(b)(3) refusal to bargain violation? *See* Painters Dist. Council (Westgate Painting & Decorating Corp.), 186 N.L.R.B. 964 (1970), *enforced,* 453 F.2d 783 (2d Cir. 1971), *cert. denied,* 408 U.S. 930 (1972), where a divided Board (3-1) answered "Yes."

7. *See generally* Atleson, *Union Fines and Picket Lines: The NLRA and Union Disciplinary Power,* 17 U.C.L.A. L. Rev. 681 (1970); Gould, *Some Limitations Upon Union Discipline Under the National Labor Relations Act: the Radiations of Allis-Chalmers,* 1970 Duke L.J. 1067; Silard, *Labor Board Regulation of Union Discipline After Allis-Chalmers, Marine Workers, and Scofield,* 38 Geo. Wash. L. Rev. 187 (1969).

NLRB v. BOEING CO.

Supreme Court of the United States
412 U.S. 67, 93 S. Ct. 1952, 36 L. Ed. 2d 752 (1973)

MR. JUSTICE REHNQUIST delivered the opinion of the Court. . . .

From May 16, 1963, through September 15, 1965, Booster Lodge No. 405, International Association of Machinists and Aerospace Workers, AFL-CIO, and The Boeing Company were parties to a collective bargaining agreement. Upon expiration of this agreement the Union called a lawful economic strike at the Company's Michoud plant in New Orleans and at other locations. As of October 2, 1965, the parties signed a new collective bargaining agreement and the strikers thereafter returned to work. Both agreements contained maintenance-of-membership clauses that required Union members to retain their membership during the contract term. New employees were required to notify the Union and the Company within 40 days of accepting employment if they elected not to join the Union.

During the 18-day strike some 143 employees out of 1,900 production and maintenance employees in the bargaining unit at the Michoud plant crossed the picket lines and returned to work. All of these employees were Union members at the time the strike began although some of them tendered their resignations either before or after crossing the picket lines. In late October or early November 1965 the Union notified these employees that charges had been preferred against them for violating the International Union's constitution. The constitution provides penalties for the "improper conduct of a member," which term includes "[a]ccepting employment . . . in an establishment where a strike . . . exists." In accordance with appropriate union procedures, including notice and opportunity for a hearing, all strike-breakers were found guilty, fined $450, and barred from holding Union office for a period of five years. While some of the fines were reduced and some partial payments received by the Union, no member paid the full $450. After warning members to pay their fines or face the consequences, the Union filed suits in state court against nine individual employees to collect the fines. None of these suits has been finally adjudicated.

In February 1966 the Company filed a charge with the Labor Board alleging that the attempted court enforcement of the fines violated § 8(b)(1)(A) of the National Labor Relations Act. . . . [T]he Trial Examiner determined that the fines were impermissibly excessive, but the Board refused to adopt his conclusion. It . . . held that Congress did not intend to give the Board authority to regulate the size of union fines or to establish standards with respect to a fine's reasonableness. . . .

We have previously held that § 8(b)(1)(A) was not intended to give the Board power to regulate internal union affairs, including the imposition of disciplinary fines, with their consequent court enforcement, against members who violate the unions' constitutions and bylaws. NLRB v. Allis-Chalmers Mfg. Co., 388 U.S. 175 (1967); Scofield v. NLRB, 394 U.S. 423 (1969). In *Allis-Chalmers* we held that court enforcement of fines ranging from $20 to $100 for crossing picket lines did not "restrain or coerce" employees within the meaning of the Act. And in *Scofield* we held that the union did not violate the Act in imposing fines of $50 and $100 on members for violating a union rule relating to production ceilings.

In deciding these cases, the Court several times referred to the unions' imposition of "reasonable" fines. In particular, the *Scofield* Court concluded "that the union rule is valid and that its enforcement by *reasonable* fines does not constitute the restraint or coercion proscribed by § 8(b)(1)(A)." 394 U.S. at 436 (emphasis added). The Company contends, not illogically, that the Court's use of the adjective "reasonable" was intended to suggest to the Board that an unreasonable fine would amount to an unfair labor practice.

This interpretation, however, permissible as it may be, is only dicta, since in both *Allis-Chalmers* and in *Scofield* the reasonableness of the fines was assumed. 388 U.S. at 192-193 n. 30; 394 U.S. at 430. Being squarely presented with the issue in this case, we recede from the implications of the dicta in these earlier cases. While "unreasonable" fines may be more coercive than "reasonable" fines, all fines are coercive to a greater or lesser degree. The underlying basis for the holdings of *Allis-Chalmers* and *Scofield* was not that reasonable fines were noncoercive under the language of § 8(b)(1)(A) of the Act, but was instead that those provisions were not intended by Congress to apply to the imposition by the union of fines not affecting the employer-employee relationship and not otherwise prohibited by the Act. The reason for this determination, in turn, was that Congress had not intended by enacting this section to regulate the internal affairs of unions to the extent that would be required in order to base unfair labor practice charges on the levying of such fines. . . .

In *Scofield* we decided that Congress intended to distinguish between the external and the internal enforcement of union rules, and that therefore the Board would have authority to pass on those rules affecting an individual's employment status but not on his union membership status. 394 U.S. at 428-430.

Inquiry by the Board into the multiplicity of factors that the parties and the Court of Appeals correctly thought to have a bearing on the issue of reasonableness would necessarily lead the Board to a substantial involvement in strictly internal union affairs. While the line may not always be clear between those matters that are internal and those that are external, to the extent that the Board was required to examine into such questions as a union's motivation for imposing a fine it would be delving into internal union affairs in a manner which we have previously held Congress did not intend. Given the rationale of *Allis-Chalmers* and *Scofield*, the Board's conclusion that § 8(b)(1)(A) of the Act has nothing to say about union fines of this nature, whatever their size, is correct. Issues as to the reasonableness or unreasonableness of such fines must be decided upon the basis of the law of contracts, voluntary associations, or such other principles of law as may be applied in a forum competent to adjudicate the issue. Under our holding, state courts will be wholly free to apply state law to such issues at the suit of either the union or the member fined.

Our conclusion is also supported by the Board's long-standing administrative construction to the same effect. At least since 1954 it has been the Board's consistent position that it has "not been empowered by Congress . . . to pass judgment on the penalties a union may impose on a member so long as the penalty does not impair the member's status as an employee." Local 283, UAW, 145 N.L.R.B. 1097, 1104 (1964). See also Minneapolis Star and Tribune Company, 109 N.L.R.B. 727, 34 L.R.R.M. 1431 (1954). We have held in analogous situations that such a consistent and contemporaneous construction of a statute by the agency charged with its enforcement is entitled to great deference by the courts. . . .

The Court of Appeals and the Company have suggested several policy reasons why the Board should not leave the determinations of reasonableness entirely to the state courts. Their basic reasons are, first, that more uniformity in the determination of what is reasonable will result if the Board suggests standards and, second, that more expertise in labor matters will be brought to bear if the issue is decided by the Board rather than solely by the courts. Even if we were to concede the relevance of policy factors in determining congressional intent, we are not persuaded that the Board is necessarily the better forum for determining the reasonableness of a fine.

As we noted in *Allis-Chalmers,* court enforcement of union fines is not a recent innovation but has been known at least since 1867. 388 U.S. at 182 n. 9. See also Summers, The Law of Union Discipline: What the Courts Do in Fact, 70 Yale L.J. 175 (1960). The relationship between a member and his union is generally viewed as contractual in nature, International Association of Machinists v. Gonzales, 356 U.S. 617, 618 (1958), . . . and the local law of contracts or voluntary associations usually governs the enforcement of this relationship. NLRB v. Allis-Chalmers Manufacturing Company, 388 U.S. at 182 and 193 n. 32; Scofield v. NLRB, *supra,* at 426 n. 3.

We alluded to state court enforcement of unusually harsh union discipline in *Allis-Chalmers* when we stated that "state courts, in reviewing the imposition of union discipline, find ways to strike down 'discipline [which] involves a severe hardship.' " 388 U.S. at 193 n. 32, quoting Summers, Legal Limitations on Union Discipline, 64 Harv. L. Rev. 1049, 1078 (1951). The Board assumed that in view of this statement, our reference to "reasonable" fines, when reasonableness was not in issue, in *Allis-Chalmers* and in *Scofield,* was merely adverting to the usual standard applied by state courts in deciding whether to enforce union imposed fines. The Board reads these cases, therefore, as encouraging state courts to use a reasonableness standard, not as a directive to the Board.

Our review of state court cases decided both before and after our decisions in *Allis-Chalmers* and *Scofield* reveals that state courts applying state law are quite willing to determine whether disciplinary fines are reasonable in amount. Indeed, the expertise required for a determination of reasonableness may well be more evident in a judicial forum that is called upon to assess reasonableness in varying factual contexts than it is in a specialized agency. In assessing the reasonableness of disciplinary fines, for example, state courts are often able to draw on their experience in areas of the law apart from labor relations.

Nor is it clear, as contended by the Court of Appeals, that the Board's setting of standards of reasonableness will necessarily result in greater uniformity in this area even if uniformity is thought to be a desirable goal. Since state courts will have jurisdiction to determine reasonableness in the enforcement context in any event, the Board's independent determination of reasonableness in an unfair labor practice context might well yield a conflict when the two forums are called upon to review the same fine.

For all of the foregoing reasons we conclude that the Board was warranted in determining that when the union discipline does not interfere with the employee-employer relationship or otherwise violate a policy of the National Labor Relations Act, the Congress did not authorize it "to evaluate the fairness of union discipline meted out to protect a legitimate union interest." The judgment of the Court of Appeals is, therefore,

Reversed.

[The dissenting opinions of MR. CHIEF JUSTICE BURGER, MR. JUSTICE DOUGLAS, and MR. JUSTICE BLACKMUN are omitted.]

NOTES

1. The NLRB has concluded that it is not to assess the fairness of the internal union procedures by which fines are imposed. UE Local 1012 (General Elec. Co.), 187 N.L.R.B. 375 (1970). Procedural due process, said the Board, is irrelevant in determining the legality of fines under the NLRA.

2. In NLRB v. Textile Workers Granite State Joint Board, 409 U.S. 213 (1972), the Supreme Court held that a union violates § 8(b)(1)(A) when it imposes fines collectible by court suit on members who lawfully resigned from the union and thereafter returned to work during a strike. The Court subsequently extended this rule to prevent a union from seeking court enforcement of fines imposed for strikebreaking activities by employees who had resigned from the union, even though the union constitution expressly prohibited members from strikebreaking. Machinists Booster Lodge 405 v. NLRB, 412 U.S. 84 (1973). The Court left open the question of whether the NLRA would preclude any contractual restriction on a member's right to resign.

The NLRB and the courts have continued to avoid the issue of the validity of a clear union rule confining resignations to specified periods or circumstances. *See, e.g.,* UAW Local 1384 (Ex-Cell-O Corp.), 227 N.L.R.B. No. 87, 94 L.R.R.M. 1145 (1977) (end of fiscal year); NLRB v. Machinists Lodge 1871, 575 F. 2d 54 (2d Cir. 1978) (not during strikes).

Could a union bar membership for five years to employees who engaged in strikebreaking after having resigned from the union? *See* NLRB v. Machinists Lodges 99 & 2139 [General Elec. Co.], 489 F.2d 769 (1st Cir. 1974). *Compare* Sheet Metal Workers Local 29, 222 N.L.R.B. No. 183, 91 L.R.R.M. 1390 (1976). *See also* Note, *Union Power to Discipline Members Who Resign,* 86 HARV. L. REV. 1536 (1973).

3. *See generally* Archer, *Allis-Chalmers Recycled: A Current View of a Union's Right to Fine Employees for Crossing a Picket Line,* 7 IND. L. REV. 498 (1974); Craver, *The Boeing Decision: A Blow to Federalism, Individual Rights and Stare Decisis,* 122 U. PA. L. REV. 556 (1974).

SECTION IV. Union Administration

SENATE COMMITTEE ON LABOR AND PUBLIC WELFARE

S. Rep. No. 187 on S. 1555, 86th Cong., 1st Sess. 5-6 (1959)

A strong independent labor movement is a vital part of American institutions. The shocking abuses revealed by recent investigations have been confined to a few unions. The overwhelming majority are honestly and democratically run. In providing remedies for existing evils the Senate should be careful neither to undermine self-government within the labor movement nor to weaken unions in their role as the bargaining representatives of employees.

It is plain that the trade union movement in the United States is facing difficult internal problems and — because of these internal problems — tensions with the surrounding community. The problems of this now large and relatively strong institution are not unlike the difficulties faced by other groups in American society which aspire to live by the same basic principles and values within their group as they hold ideal for the whole community. But equal rights, freedom of choice, honesty, and the highest ethical standards are built into changing institutions only after struggle. Trade unions have grown well beyond their beginnings as relatively small, closely knit associations of workingmen where personal, fraternal relationships were characteristic. Like other American institutions some unions have become large and impersonal; they have acquired bureaucratic tendencies and characteristics; their members like other Americans have sometimes become apathetic in the exercise of their personal responsibility for the conduct of union affairs. In some few cases men who have risen to positions of power and responsibility within unions have abused their power and neglected their responsibilities. In some cases the structure and procedures necessary for trade unions while they were struggling for survival are ill adapted to their new role and to changed conditions; they are not always conducive to efficient, honest, and democratic practices.

Whatever the causes, the problems are recognized by those within as well as those outside the union movement. The action of the American Federation of Labor-Congress of Industrial Organizations in recognizing the importance of adherence to traditional principles of ethical conduct and trade union democracy and in formulating and implementing codes of ethical practices to carry out these established principles, is a dramatic and convincing demonstration of the trade union movement's desire to conduct its internal affairs democratically and in accordance with high standards of trust. Nevertheless, effective measures to stamp out crime and corruption and guarantee internal union democracy, cannot be applied to all unions without the coercive powers of government, nor is the present machinery of the federation demonstrably effective in policing specific abuses at the local level. . . .

The internal problems currently facing our labor unions are bound up with a substantial public interest. Under the National Labor Relations Act and the Railway Labor Act, a labor organization has vast responsibility for economic welfare of the individual members whom it represents. Union members have a vital interest, therefore, in the policies and conduct of union affairs. . . .

NOTES

1. Prior to the passage of the Labor-Management Reporting and Disclosure Act of 1959, the union constitution was usually the primary standard as to substantive rights in suits involving union administration. *See, e.g.,* O'Neill v. Plumbers, 348 Pa. 531, 36 A.2d, 325 (1944) (alleged dictatorial control of local by international). In cases of alleged fraud on the part of officers, courts intervened on the basis of such theories as breach of trust or deprivation of property rights. Collins v. IATSE, 136 N.J. Eq. 395, 42 A.2d 297 (1945), 119 N.J. Eq. 230, 182 A. 37 (1935); Dusing v. Nuzzo, 177 Misc. 35, 29 N.Y.S.2d 882 (Sup. Ct. 1941), *modified and aff'd,* 263 App. Div. 59, 31 N.Y.S.2d 849 (1941). The remedy was often threefold: an accounting; the appointment of a receiver; and an election under the supervision of a court officer. *See, e.g.,* Iron Workers Local 11 v. McKee, 114 N.J. Eq. 555, 169 A. 351 (1933); *cf.* English v. Cunningham, 269 F.2d 517 (D.C. Cir. 1959), *cert. denied,* 361 U.S. 897 (1959). *See generally* Chamberlain, *The Judicial Process in Labor Unions,* 10 Brooklyn L. Rev. 145 (1940).

2. Comprehensive studies of the internal administration of labor organizations include M. Estey, P. Taft & M. Wagner, Eds., Regulating Union Government (1964); J. Grodin, Union Government and the Law (1961); W. Leiserson, American Trade Union Democracy (1959); National Industrial Conference Board, Handbook of Union Government, Structure and Procedure (1955); P. Taft, The Structure and Government of Labor Unions (1962). Perhaps the most penetrating analysis of the government of a single international is S Lipset, M. Trow & J. Coleman, Union Democracy: The International Politics of the International Typographical Union (1956).

A. ELECTION OF OFFICERS

STATUTORY REFERENCES

LMRDA §§ 401-03

CALHOON v. HARVEY

Supreme Court of the United States
379 U.S. 134, 85 S. Ct. 292, 13 L. Ed. 2d 190 (1964)

MR. JUSTICE BLACK delivered the opinion of the Court. . . .

The respondents, three members of District No. 1, National Marine Engineers' Beneficial Association, filed a complaint in Federal District Court against the union, its president and its secretary-treasurer, alleging that certain provisions of the union's bylaws and national constitution violated the Act in that they infringed "the right of members of defendant District No. 1, NMEBA, to nominate candidates in elections of defendant, which right is guaranteed to each member of defendant, and to each plaintiff, by § 101(a)(1) of the LMRDA. . . ." It was alleged that § 102 of Title I of the Act gave the District Court jurisdiction to adjudicate the controversy. The union bylaws complained of deprived a member of the right to nominate anyone for office but himself. The national constitution in turn provided that no member could be eligible for nomination or election to a full-time elective office unless he had been a member of the national union for five years and had served 180 days or more of seatime in each of two of the preceding three years on vessels covered by collective bargaining agreements with the national or its subsidiary bodies. On the basis of these allegations respondents asked that the union be enjoined from preparing for or conducting any election until it revised its system of elections so as to afford each of its members a fair opportunity to nominate any persons "meeting fair and reasonable eligibility requirements for any or all offices to be filled by such election."

The union moved to dismiss the complaint on the grounds that (1) the court lacked jurisdiction over the subject matter, and (2) the complaint failed to state a claim upon which relief could be granted. The District Court dismissed for want of "jurisdiction," holding that the alleged conduct of the union, even if true, failed to show a denial of the equal rights of all members of the union to vote for or nominate candidates guaranteed by § 101(a)(1) of Title I of the Act, so as to give the District Court jurisdiction of the controversy under § 102. The allegations, said the court, showed at most imposition of qualifications of eligibility for nomination and election so restrictive that they might violate § 401(e) of Title IV by denying members a reasonable opportunity to nominate and vote for candidates. The District Court further held that it could not exercise jurisdiction to protect § 401(e) rights because § 402(a) of Title V provides a remedy, declared by § 403 to be "exclusive," authorizing members to vindicate such rights by challenging elections after they have been held, and then only by (1) first exhausting all remedies available with the union, (2) filing a complaint with the Secretary of Labor, who (3) may, after investigating the violation alleged in the complaint, bring suit in a

United States District Court to attack the validity of the election. The Court of Appeals reversed, holding that "the complaint alleged a violation of § 101(a)(1) and that federal jurisdiction existed under § 102." 324 F.2d 486, 487. . . .

I. Jurisdiction of the District Court under § 102 of Title I depends entirely upon whether this complaint showed a violation of rights guaranteed by § 101(a)(1), for we disagree with the Court of Appeals' holding that jurisdiction under § 102 can be upheld by reliance in whole or in part on allegations which in substance charge a breach of Title IV rights. An analysis and understanding of the meaning of § 101(a)(1) and of the charges of the complaint is therefore essential to a determination of this issue. Respondents charge that the bylaws and constitutional provisions referred to above infringed their right guaranteed by § 101(a)(1) to nominate candidates. The result of their allegations here, however, is an attempt to sweep into the ambit of their right to sue in federal court if they are denied an equal opportunity to nominate candidates under § 101(a)(1), a right to sue if they are not allowed to nominate anyone they choose regardless of his eligibility and qualifications under union restrictions. But Title IV, not Title I, sets standards for eligibility and qualifications of candidates and officials and provides its own separate and different administrative and judicial procedure for challenging those standards. And the equal-rights language of § 101(a)(1) would have to be stretched far beyond its normal meaning to hold that it guarantees members not just a right to "nominate candidates," but a right to nominate anyone, without regard to valid union rules. . . .

Plainly, [§ 101(a)(1)] is no more than a command that members and classes of members shall not be discriminated against in their right to nominate and vote. And Congress carefully prescribed that even this right against discrimination is "subject to reasonable rules and regulations" by the union. The complaining union members here have not been discriminated against in any way and have been denied no privilege or right to vote or nominate which the union has granted to others. They have indeed taken full advantage of the uniform rule limiting nomination by nominating themselves for office. It is true that they were denied their request to be candidates, but that denial was not a discrimination against their right to nominate, since the same qualifications were required equally of all members. Whether the eligiblity requirements set by the union's constitution and bylaws were reasonable and valid is a question separate and distinct from whether the right to nominate on an equal basis given by § 101(a)(1) was violated. The District Court therefore was without jurisdiction to grant the relief requested here unless, as the Court of Appeals held, the *"combined* effect of the eligibility requirements and the restriction to self-nomination" are to be considered in determining whether § 101(a)(1) has been violated.

II. We hold that possible violations of Title IV of the Act regarding eligibility are not relevant in determining whether or not a district court has jurisdiction under § 102 of Title I of the Act. Title IV sets up statutory scheme governing the election of union officers, fixing the terms during which they hold office, requiring that elections be by secret ballot, regulating the handling of campaign literature, requiring a reasonable opportunity for the nomination of candidates, authorizing unions to fix "reasonable qualifications uniformly imposed" for candidates, and attempting to guarantee fair union elections in which all the members are allowed to participate. Section 402 of Title IV, as has been pointed out, sets up an exclusive method for protecting Title IV rights, by permitting an individual member to file a complaint with the Secretary of Labor challenging the validity of any election because of violations of Title IV. Upon complaint the Secretary investigates and if he finds probable cause to believe that Title IV has been violated, he may file suit in the appropriate district court. It is apparent that Congress decided to utilize the special knowledge and discretion of the Secretary of Labor in order best to serve the public interest. Cf. San Diego Building Trades Council v. Garmon, 359 U.S. 236, 242 (1959). In so doing Congress, with one exception not here relevant, decided not to permit individuals to block or delay union elections by filing federal-court suits for violations of Title IV. Reliance on the discretion of the Secretary is in harmony with the general congressional policy to allow unions great latitude in resolving their own internal controversies, and, where that fails, to utilize the agencies of government most familiar with union problems to aid in bringing about a settlement through discussion before resort to the courts. Without setting out the lengthy legislative history which preceded the passage of this measure, it is sufficient to say that we are satisfied that the Act itself shows clearly by its structure and language that the disputes here, basically relating as they do to eligibility of candidates for office, fall squarely within Title IV of the Act and are to be resolved by the administrative and judicial procedures set out in that Title.

Accordingly, the judgment of the Court of Appeals is reversed and that of the District Court is affirmed. . . .

MR. JUSTICE DOUGLAS would affirm the judgment of the Court of Appeals for the reasons stated in its opinion as reported in 324 F.2d 486.

MR. JUSTICE STEWART, whom MR. JUSTICE HARLAN joins, concurring.

This case marks the first interpretation by this Court of the significant changes wrought by the Labor-Management Reporting and Disclosure Act of 1959 increasing federal supervision of internal union affairs. At issue are subtle questions concerning the interplay between Title I and Title IV of that Act. In part, both seem to deal with the same subject matter: Title I guarantees "equal rights and privileges . . . to nominate candidates"; Title IV provides that "a reasonable opportunity shall be given for the nomination of candidates." Where the two Titles of the legislation differ most substantially is in the remedies they provide. If a Title I right is at issue, the allegedly aggrieved union member has direct, virtually immediate recourse to a federal court to obtain an adjudication of his claim and an injunction if his complaint has merit. 73 Stat. 523, 29 U.S.C. § 412 (1958 ed., Supp. V). Vindication of claims under Title IV may be much more onerous. Federal court suits can be brought only by the Secretary of Labor, and then, only after the election has been held. . . .

The Court precludes the District Court from asserting jurisdiction over this complaint by focusing on the fact that one of the imposed restrictions speaks in terms of eligibility. And since these are "possible violations of Title IV of the Act regarding eligibility" they "are not relevant in determining whether or not a district court has jurisdiction under § 102 of Title I of the Act." By this reasoning, the Court forecloses early adjudication of claims concerning participation in the election process. But there are occasions when eligibility provisions can infringe upon the right to nominate. Had the NMEBA issued a regulation that only Jesse Calhoon was eligible for office, no one could place great store on the right to self-nomination left to the rest of the membership. This Court long ago recognized the subtle ways by which election rights can be removed through discrimination at a less visible stage of the political process. The decisions in the *Texas Primary Cases* were founded on the belief that the equal right to vote was impaired where discrimination existed in the method of nomination. Smith v. Allwright, 321 U.S. 649 (1944); Nixon v. Herndon, 273 U.S. 536 (1927). See United States v. Classic, 313 U.S. 299 (1941). No less is the equal right to nominate infringed where onerous burdens drastically limit the candidates available for nomination. In scrutinizing devices designed to erode the franchise, the Court has shown impatience with arguments founded in the form of the device. Gomillion v. Lightfoot, 364 U.S. 339, 345 (1960). If Congress has told the courts to protect a union member from infringement of his equal right to nominate, the courts should do so whether such discrimination is sophisticated or simple-minded. Lane v. Wilson, 307 U.S. 268, 275 (1939).

After today, simply by framing its discriminatory rules in terms of eligibility, a union can immunize itself from pre-election attack in a federal court even though it makes deep incursions on the equal right of its members to nominate, to vote, and to participate in the union's internal affairs. . . .

Nonetheless, the Court finds a "general congressional policy" to avoid judicial resolution of internal union disputes. That policy, the Court says, was designed to limit the power of individuals to block and delay elections by seeking injunctive relief. Such an appraisal might have been accurate before the addition of Title I, but it does not explain the emphasis on prompt judicial remedies there provided. In addition to the injunctive relief authorized by § 102 and the savings provisions of § 103, § 101(a)(4) modifies the traditional requirement of exhausting internal remedies before resort to litigation. Even § 403 is not conclusive on the elimination of pre-election remedies. At the least, state-court actions may be brought in advance of an election to "enforce the constitution and bylaws." And as to federal courts, it is certainly arguable that recourse through the Secretary of Labor is the exclusive remedy only after the election has been held. By reading Title I rights so narrowly, and by construing Title IV to foreclose absolutely pre-election litigation in the federal courts, the Court sharply reduces meaningful protection for many of the rights which Congress was so assiduous to create. By so simplifying the tangled provisions of the Act, the Court renders it virtually impossible for the aggrieved union member to gain a hearing when it is most necessary — when there is still an opportunity to make the union's rules comport with the requirements of the Act.

My difference with the Court does not reach to the disposition of this particular case. Whether stated in terms of restrictions on the right to nominate or in terms of limitations on eligibility for union office, I think the rules of a labor organization would operate illegally to curtail the members' equal right to nominate within the meaning of Title I only if those rules effectively distorted the basic democratic process. The line might be a shadowy one in some cases. But I think that in this case the respondents did not allege in their complaint nor demonstrate in their affidavits that this line was crossed. I would therefore remand the case to the District Court with directions to dismiss the complaint for failure to state a claim for relief.

NOTES

1. Is this decision a holding that even *unreasonable* limitations on voting and nominating do not violate § 101(a)(1), so long as the limitations are not discriminatory? *See generally* Topol, *Union Elections Under the LMRDA,* 74 YALE L.J. 1282 (1965).

2. Following the principal case, federal district courts have held that Title IV rather than Title I governs a local's procedure for nominating delegates to an international convention, Paravate v. Insurance Workers Local 13, 59 L.R.R.M. 2169, 51 CCH LAB. CAS. ¶ 19,695 (W.D. Pa. 1965), and an international's action in voiding a local election, Carpenters Local 115 v. Carpenters, 247 F. Supp. 660 (D. Conn. 1965). But Title I jurisdiction has been sustained where "associate members" were allegedly denied the "equal right" to vote and nominate candidates, even though the relief requested included the setting aside of elections already conducted, a remedy within the exclusive domain of Title IV. The court explained that at least some relief would be available under Title I. O'Brien v. Paddock, 246 F. Supp. 809 (S.D.N.Y. 1965). *See also* Beckman v. Iron Workers Local 46, 314 F.2d 848 (7th Cir. 1963) (upholding under § 101(a)(1) a preliminary injunction against counting ballots where voting irregularities were alleged); Schonfeld v. Penza, 477 F.2d 899 (2d Cir. 1973) (removal of union officer and declaration of his future ineligibility are bases for Title I jurisdiction when such actions can fairly be said to form part of scheme to suppress dissent). *But cf.* Robins v. Rarback, 325 F.2d 929 (2d Cir. 1963), *cert. denied,* 379 U.S. 974 (1965). *See also* Note, *Pre-Election Remedies Under the Landrum-Griffin Act,* 74 COLUM. L. REV. 1105 (1974).

3. After an election has been conducted, the Secretary of Labor has exclusive authority to challenge it. But prior to an election, § 403 of the LMRDA expressly recognizes "[e]xisting rights and remedies to enforce the constitution and bylaws of a labor organization with respect to elections." Commentators have argued that the union constitution is to be interpreted as a matter of federal substantive law in preelection suits. *See* Summers, *Preemption and the Labor Reform Act — Dual Rights and Remedies,* 22 OHIO ST. L.J. 119, 136-38 (1961); Note, *Election Remedies Under the Labor-Management Reporting and Disclosure Act,* 78 HARV. L. REV. 1617, 1630 (1965); Note, *Union Elections Under the LMRDA,* 74 YALE L.J. 1282, 1293-94 (1965). The courts, however, have assumed that pre-election actions to enforce a union's electoral rules are governed by state substantive law. Libutti v. DiBrizzi, 343 F.2d 460 (2d Cir. 1965); Wittstein v. Musicians, 59 L.R.R.M. 2335, 51 CCH LAB. CAS. ¶ 19,684 (S.D.N.Y. 1965); McArthy v. Machinists Lodge 9, 61 L.R.R.M. 2652 (E.D. Mo. 1966).

4. Section 401(c) of the LMRDA permits preelection suits by candidates in union elections to enforce certain specified rights, such as the nondiscriminatory use of membership lists to distribute campaign propaganda. Section 601(a) gives the Secretary of Labor investigatory powers to determine whether any person "has violated or is about to violate any provision of this Act (except Title I . . .)." In his bitter (and ultimately fatal) election campaign of 1969 against an entrenched and allegedly corrupt UMW leadership, Joseph Yablonski sought to pursue both these routes. He had limited success in court and was rebuffed by the Secretary of Labor. *See* Yablonski v. UMW, 305 F. Supp. 868, 876 (D.D.C. 1969); *cf.* Hodgson v. United Mine Workers of America, 344 F. Supp. 17 (D.D.C. 1972) (invalidating election). For sharply differing views on the Secretary's proper role, *compare* Rauh, *LMRDA — Enforce It or Repeal It,* 5 GA. L. REV. 643 (1971), *with* Silberman & Driesen, *The Secretary and the Law: Preballoting Investigations Under the Landrum-Griffin Act,* 7 GA. L. REV. 1 (1972).

5. The Secretary of Labor's decision not to file suit to set aside a union election is subject to judicial review under the Administrative Procedure Act, 5 U.S.C. §§ 702 and 704, as "final agency action" for which there is no other adequate judicial remedy. The scope of review is sharply limited, however, and does not encompass a trial-type inquiry into the factual basis of the Secretary's decision. The court must simply determine, after examining the statement of reasons for refusing to file an action that the Secretary is required to furnish both court and complainant, whether the refusal was so irrational as to be arbitrary and capricious. Dunlop v. Bachowski, 421 U.S. 560 (1975). *See also* Hopson, *Judicial Review of the Secretary of Labor's Decision Not to Sue to Set Aside an Election Under Title IV of the LMRDA,* 18 WAYNE L. REV. 1281 (1972).

6. The Supreme Court has ruled that a union member who filed the initial complaint with the Secretary of Labor may intervene in the Secretary's Title IV action to set aside the election. Intervention is confined, however, to the claims of illegality presented by the Secretary's complaint. While agreeing that the Secretary's suit is the exclusive remedy, the Court said: "There is no evidence whatever that Congress was opposed to participation by union members in the litigation, so long as that participation did not interfere with the screening and centralizing functions of the Secretary." Trbovich v. UMW, 404 U.S. 528 (1972), noted in 41 GEO. WASH. L. REV. 560 (1973).

7. If the voting has taken place but the ballots are not yet tallied, has the election been "conducted" so as to preclude a private suit? *Cf.* Jennings v. Carey, 57 L.R.R.M. 2635 (D.D.C. 1964), *on appeal,* 58 L.R.R.M. 2606 (D.C. Cir. 1966).

HODGSON V. STEELWORKERS LOCAL 6799, 403 U.S. 333, 91 S. Ct. 1841, 29 L. Ed. 2d 510 (1971). An unsuccessful candidate for president of a local union protested the election to both the local and the international. He based his protest on several matters, including the use of union facilities to prepare campaign materials for the incumbent president, who was reelected. After failing to obtain relief through internal union procedures, the candidate filed a complaint with the Secretary of Labor under § 402(a) of the LMRDA. The complaint repeated the charge about the use of union facilities. It also raised, for the first time, an additional objection concerning a requirement in the union constitution that candidates for certain local offices must have attended at least one-half of the regular meetings of the local during the thirty-six months immediately preceding the election. Although the attendance requirement had not been challenged in the candidate's internal union protests, the Secretary included it as a basis for setting aside the election in a suit brought in federal district court. The Supreme Court held (7-2) that under these circumstances the Secretary was barred from challenging the attendance rule in a § 402(b) action. The Court reasoned: "The requirement of § 402(a) that a union member first seek redress of alleged election violations within the union before enlisting the aid of the Secretary, was . . . designed to harmonize the need to eliminate election abuses with a desire to avoid unnecessary governmental intervention. . . . To accept [the Secretary's] contention that a union member, who is aware of the facts underlying an alleged violation, need not first protest this violation to his union before complaining to the Secretary, would be needlessly to weaken union self-government."

NOTES

1. In Wirtz v. Laborers Local 125, 389 U.S. 477 (1968), the Supreme Court held that the Secretary of Labor could challenge the validity of a general election of union officers on the basis that ineligible persons had voted, even though the only intra-union protest related to a subsequent runoff election for a single office. Here "respondent union had fair notice from the violation charged by [complainant] in his protest of the runoff election that the same unlawful conduct also occurred at the earlier election." A federal district court has held that the Secretary may litigate alleged Title IV violations discovered during his investigation, despite the complainant's failure to present them directly to the union, under two conditions: (1) the member was ignorant of the facts when he filed his protest, and (2) the alleged violations arose from the same transactions about which the member protested to the union. Hodgson v. Teamsters Local 734, 336 F. Supp. 1243 (N.D. Ill. 1972).

2. If a union holds its next regular election while a challenge to a previous election is still pending, this does not deprive the Secretary of his right to a court order declaring the challenged election void and directing the conduct of a new election under his supervision. Wirtz v. Glass Bottle Blowers Local 153, 389 U.S. 463 (1968).

3. *See generally* Note, *Union Elections and the LMRDA: Thirteen Years of Use and Abuse,* 81 YALE L.J. 407 (1972); Note, *The Enforcement Power of the Secretary of Labor Under Section 402 of the LMRDA,* 1971 U. ILL. L. F. 745.

STEELWORKERS LOCAL 3489 v. USERY

Supreme Court of the United States
429 U.S. 305, 97 S. Ct. 611, 50 L. Ed. 2d 502 (1977)

MR. JUSTICE BRENNAN delivered the opinion of the Court.

The Secretary of Labor brought this action in the District Court for the Southern District of Indiana under § 402(b) of the Labor-Management Reporting and Disclosure Act of 1959 (LMRDA) . . . to invalidate the 1970 election of officers of Local 3489, United Steelworkers of America. The Secretary alleged that a provision of the Steelworkers' International Constitution, binding on the Local, that limits eligibility for local union office to members who have attended at least one-half of the regular meetings of the local for three years previous to the election (unless prevented by union activities or working hours), violated § 401(e) of the LMRDA . . . . The District Court dismissed the complaint, finding no violation of the Act. The Court of Appeals for the Seventh Circuit reversed. 520 F. 2d 516. . . . We affirm.

I. At the time of the challenged election, there were approximately 660 members in good standing of Local 3489. The Court of Appeals found that 96.5% of these members were ineligible to hold office, because of failure to satisfy the meeting-attendance rule. Of the 23 eligible members, nine were incumbent union officers. The Secretary argues, and the Court of Appeals held, that the failure of 96.5% of the local members to satisfy the meeting-attendance requirement, and the rule's effect of requiring potential insurgent candidates to plan their candidacies as early as 18 months in advance of the election when the reasons for their opposition might not have yet emerged, established that the requirement has a substantial antidemocratic effect on local union elections. Petitioners argue that the rule is reasonable because it serves valid union purposes, imposes no very burdensome obligation on the members, and has not proved to be a device that entrenches a particular clique of incumbent officers in the local.

II. The opinions in three cases decided in 1968 have identified the considerations pertinent to the determination whether the attendance rule violates § 401(e). Wirtz v. Hotel Employees, 391 U. S. 492; Wirtz v. Bottle Blowers Assn., 389 U. S. 463; Wirtz v. Laborers' Union, 389 U. S. 477.

The LMRDA does not render unions powerless to restrict candidacies for union office. The injunction in § 401 (e) that "every member in good standing shall be eligible to be a candidate and to hold office" is made expressly "subject to . . . reasonable qualifications uniformly imposed." But "Congress plainly did not intend that the authorization . . . of 'reasonable qualifications . . .' should be given a broad reach. The contrary is implicit in the legislative history of the section and in its wording . . . ." *Wirtz* v. *Hotel Employees, supra* at 499. The basic objective of Title IV of the LMRDA is to guarantee "free and democratic" union elections modeled on "political elections in this country" where "the assumption is that voters will exercise common sense and judgment in casting their ballots." 391 U. S. at 504. Thus, Title IV is not designed merely to protect the right of a union member to run for a particular office in a particular election. "Congress emphatically asserted a vital public interest in assuring free and democratic union elections that transcends the narrower interest of the complaining union member." *Wirtz* v. *Bottle Blowers Assn., supra* at 475; *Wirtz* v. *Laborers' Union, supra* at 483. The goal was to "protect the rights of rank-and-file members to participate fully in the operation of their union through processes of democratic self-government, and, through the election process, to keep the union leadership responsive to the membership." *Wirtz* v. *Hotel Employees, supra* at 497.

Whether a particular qualification is "reasonable" within the meaning of § 401 (e) must therefore "be measured in terms of its consistency with the Act's command to unions to conduct 'free and democratic' union elections." 391 U. S. at 499. Congress was not concerned only with corrupt union leadership. Congress chose the goal of "free and democratic" union elections as a preventive measure "to curb the possibility of abuse by benevolent as well as malevolent entrenched leadership." *Id.* at 503. *Hotel Employees* expressly held that that check was seriously impaired by candidacy qualifications which substantially deplete the ranks of those who might run in opposition to incumbents, and therefore held invalid the candidacy limitation there involved that restricted candidacies for certain positions to members who had previously held union office. "Plainly, given the objective of Title IV, a candidacy limitation which renders 93% of union members ineligible for office can hardly be a 'reasonable qualification.' " *Id.* at 502.

III. Applying these principles to this case, we conclude that here too the antidemocratic effects of the meeting-attendance rule outweigh the interests urged in its support. Like the bylaw in *Hotel Employees,* an attendance requirement that results in the exclusion of 96.5% of the members from candidacy for union office hardly seems to be a "reasonable qualification" consistent with the goal of free and democratic elections. A requirement having that result obviously severely restricts the free choice of the membership in selecting its leaders.

Petitioners argue, however, that the bylaw held violative of § 401 (e) in *Hotel Employees* differs significantly from the attendance rule here. Under the *Hotel Employees* bylaw no member could assure by his own efforts that he would be eligible for union office, since others controlled the criterion for eligibility. Here, on the other hand, a member can assure himself of eligibility for candidacy by attending some 18 brief meetings over a three-year period. In other words, the union would have its rule treated not as excluding a category of member from eligibility, but simply as mandating a procedure to be followed by any member who wishes to be a candidate.

Even examined from this perspective, however, the rule has a restrictive effect on union democracy.[6] In the absence of a permanent "opposition party" within the union, opposition to the incumbent leadership is likely to emerge in response to particular issues at different times, and member interest in changing union leadership is therefore likely to be at its highest only shortly before elections. Thus it is probable that to require that a member decide upon a potential candidacy at least 18 months in advance of an election when no issues exist to prompt that decision may not foster but discourage candidacies and to that extent impair the general membership's freedom to oust incumbents in favor of new leadership.

Nor are we persuaded by petitioners' argument that the Secretary has failed to show an antidemocratic effect because he has not shown that the incumbent leaders of the union became "entrenched" in their offices as a consequence of the operation of the attendance rule. The reasons why leaderships become entrenched are difficult to isolate. The election of the same officers year after year may be a signal that antidemocratic election rules have prevented an effective challenge to the regime, or might well signal only that the members are satisfied with their stewardship; if elections are uncontested, opposition factions may have been denied access to the ballot, or competing interests may have compromised differences before the election to maintain a front of unity. Conversely, turnover in offices may result from an open political process, or from a competition limited to candidates who offer no real opposition to an entrenched establishment. But Congress did not saddle the courts with the duty to search out and remove improperly entrenched union leaderships. Rather, Congress chose to guarantee union democracy by regulating not the results of a union's electoral procedure, but the procedure itself. Congress decided that if the elections are "free and democratic," the members themselves are able to correct abuse of power by entrenched leadership. Procedures that unduly restrict free choice among candidates are forbidden without regard to their success or failure in maintaining corrupt leadership.

Petitioners next argue that the rule is reasonable within § 401 (e) because it encourages attendance at union meetings, and assures more qualified officers by limiting election to those who have demonstrated an

---

[6] Petitioners argue that attendance at 18 relatively short meetings over three years is no very onerous burden on a union member. But this argument misconceives the evil at which the statute aims. We must judge the eligibility rule not by the burden it imposes on the individual candidate, but by its effect on free and democractic processes of union government. Wirtz v. Hotel Employees, 391 U.S. at 499.

interest in union affairs, and are familiar with union problems. But the rule has plainly not served these goals. It has obviously done little to encourage attendance at meetings, which continue to attract only a handful of members.[8] Even as to the more limited goal of encouraging the attendance of potential dissident candidates, very few members, as we have said, are likely to see themselves as such sufficiently far in advance of the election to be spurred to attendance by the rule.

As for assuring the election of knowledgeable and dedicated leaders, the election provisions of the LMRDA express a congressional determination that the best means to this end is to leave the choice of leaders to the membership in open democratic elections, unfettered by arbitrary exclusions. Pursuing this goal by excluding the bulk of the membership from eligibility for office, and thus limiting the possibility of dissident candidacies, runs directly counter to the basic premise of the statute. We therefore conclude that Congress, in guaranteeing every union member the opportunity to hold office, subject only to "reasonable qualifications," disabled unions from establishing eligibility qualifications as sharply restrictive of the openness of the union political process as is petitioners' attendance rule.

IV. Finally, petitioners argue that the absence of a precise statement of what the Secretary of Labor and the courts will regard as reasonable prevents the drafting of a meeting-attendance rule with any assurance that it will be valid under § 401 (e). The Secretary, to whom Congress has assigned a special role in the administration of the Act, see Calhoon v. Harvey, 379 U. S. 134, 140 (1964); Dunlop v. Bachowski, 421 U.S. 560 (1975), has announced the following view:

> "Experience has demonstrated that it is not feasible to establish arbitrary guidelines for judging the reasonableness of [a meeting-attendance eligibility requirement]. Its reasonableness must be gauged in the light of all the circumstances of the particular case, including not only the frequency of meetings, the number of meetings which must be attended and the period of time over which the requirement extends, but also such factors as the nature, availability and extent of excuse provisions, whether all or most members have the opportunity to attend meetings, and the impact of the rule, i. e., the number or percentage of members who would be rendered ineligible by its application." 29 CFR § 452.38 (a) (1976).

Obviously, this standard leads to more uncertainty than would a less flexible rule. But in using the word "reasonable," Congress clearly contemplated exactly such a flexible result. Moreover, on the facts of this case and in light of *Hotel Employees,* petitioners' contention that they had no way of knowing that a rule disqualifying over 90% of a local's members

---

[8] Attendance at Local 3489's meetings averages 47 out of approximately 660 members. There is no indication in the record that this total represents a significant increase over attendance before the institution of the challenged rule.

from office would be regarded as unreasonable in the absence of substantial justification is unpersuasive.[9]

Affirmed.

MR. JUSTICE POWELL, with whom MR. JUSTICE STEWART and MR. JUSTICE REHNQUIST join, dissenting. . . .

As this holding seems to me to be an unwarranted interference with the right of the union to manage its own internal affairs, I dissent.

Stated broadly, the purpose of Title IV of the Act is to insure "free and democratic" elections. But

> "[t]he legislative history [of the Act] shows that Congress weighed how best to legislate against revealed abuses in union elections without departing needlessly from its long-standing policy against unnecessary governmental intrusion into internal union affairs." Wirtz v. Bottle Blowers Assn., 389 U. S. 463, 470-471 (1968); Wirtz v. Hotel Employees, 391 U. S. 492, 496 (1968).

Section 401(e) reflects a congressional intent to accommodate both of these purposes. It provides that a labor organization may set "reasonable qualifications uniformly imposed" for members in good standing who wish to be candidates and to hold office. There is no contention that the attendance rule in question was not "uniformly imposed." Nor does the rule render ineligible for office any member who displays enough interest to attend half of his local's meetings.

The Court nevertheless, relying heavily on *Hotel Employees,* holds that this rule imposes an unreasonable qualification, violative of § 401(e). *Hotel Employees* involved a "prior office" rule that limited candidates for local union office to members who previously had held elective union office. The Court's opinion in that case emphasized that the effect of the prior-office rule was to disqualify 93.1% of the union's membership. In this case, the respondent argues that *Hotel Employees* enunciated a *per se* "effects" rule, requiring invalidation of union elections whenever an eligibility rule disqualifies all but a small percentage of the union's membership. Although the Court today does not in terms adopt a *per se* "effects" analysis, it comes close to doing so. The fact that 96.5% of Local 3489's members chose not to comply with its rule was given controlling weight.

In my view, the Court has extended the reach of *Hotel Employees* far beyond the holding and basic rationale of that case. Indeed, the rule there involved was acknowledged to be a sport — "virtually unique in trade union practice." 391 U. S., at 505. It was a rule deliberately designed, as

---

[9] Also unpersuasive is the argument that a union cannot know in advance how many of its members will be disqualified by a meeting-attendance rule. While the precise number may not be predictable, petitioners must have had some awareness of the general attendance rate at union meetings, and if Local 3489's attendance rate is at all typical (and there is no contention that it is not), it should have been fairly obvious that a rule disqualifying all who had not maintained 50% attendance for three years, admittedly one of the most stringent such rules among labor unions, would have a significant antidemocratic impact.

intimated by the Court's opinion, to entrench union leadership. *Id.* at 499. Moreover, the general effect of the rule in *Hotel Employees* was predictable at the time the rule was adopted. By limiting eligibility to members who held or previously had held elective office, the disqualification of a large proportion of the membership was a purposeful and inevitable effect of the structure of the rule itself. The attendance rule before the Court today has no comparable feature. No member is precluded from establishing eligibility. Nor can the effect of the rule be predicted, as any member who demonstrates the requisite interest in union affairs is eligible to seek office. In short, the only common factor between the prior-office rule in *Hotel Employees* and that before the Court today is the similarity in the percentage of ineligible members. But in one case the effect was predetermined for the purpose of perpetuating control of a few insiders, whereas here the effect resulted from the free choice — perhaps the indifference — of the rank and file membership. . . .

Although the opinion of the Court today discounts the weight to be given these purposes, I agree . . . that at least facially they serve legitimate and meritorious union purposes: (i) encouraging attendance at meetings; (ii) requiring candidates for office to demonstrate a meaningful interest in the union and its affairs; and (iii) assuring that members who seek office have had an opportunity to become informed as to union affairs. One may argue that requiring attendance at 18 of the 36 meetings prior to the election goes beyond what may be necessary to serve these purposes. But this is a "judgment call" best left to the unions themselves absent a stronger showing of potential for abuse than has been made in this case.

The record in this case is instructive. Twenty-three members were eligible to run for office in the 1970 election. These were members who were nominated and who also had complied with the attendance requirement. The record does not show, and indeed no one knows, how many members were eligible under the rule but who were not nominated. Three candidates competed for the office of president, four for the three trustee offices, and six ran unopposed for the remaining offices. Of the 10 officers elected, six were incumbents. Nonincumbents were elected to the offices of vice president, treasurer, recording secretary, and the minor office of guide. There was no history of entrenched leadership and no evidence of restrictive union practices precluding free and democratic elections. Indeed, the record is to the contrary. Five different presidents had been elected during the preceding 10 years, and an estimated 40 changes in officers had occurred in the course of four separate elections. Bernard Frye, who initiated this case by complaint to the Secretary, won the presidency in an election subsequent to 1970 and thereafter lost it.

In the final analysis, respondent, who bears the burden of proving that the rule is "unreasonable," rests his entire case on a facial attack upon the attendance rule itself, an attack supported by a statistical "effects test" that at best is ambiguous and one that could invalidate almost any attendance requirement that served legitimate union purposes. In my view, the respondent has failed to prove that the rule is unreasonable. . . .

NOTES

1. *Eligibility for office.* Prior to the decision in the principal case, a variety of other conditions on eligibility for union office had been found unreasonable and invalid under § 401(e), at least where they had the effect in actual operation of disqualifying a substantial portion of a union's membership. These included: (a) a requirement that monthly or quarterly dues be paid in advance during the entire one-year or two-year period preceding the election, Wirtz v. Operating Engineers Local 406, 254 F. Supp. 962 (E.D. La. 1966) (only 3% of membership eligible); Wirtz v. Operating Engineers Local 9, 254 F. Supp. 980 (D. Colo. 1965), *aff'd,* 366 F.2d 911 (10th Cir. 1966), *vacated as moot,* 387 U.S. 96 (1967) (87% of membership ineligible); Goldberg v. Amarillo Gen. Drivers Local 577, 214 F. Supp. 74 (N.D. Tex. 1963); *but cf.* McDonough v. Johnson, 56 L.R.R.M. 2451, 49 CCH Lab. Cas. ¶ 19,042 (N.D. Ohio 1964); (b) parent local membership as distinguished from branch local membership, where transfer from branch to parent local required payment of initiation fees ranging from $75 to $90, Hodgson v. Operating Eng'rs Local 18, 440 F.2d 485 (6th Cir. 1971) (60% of membership in branches); (c) membership on the union's board of directors for at least six months, Wirtz v. Office Employees Ass'n, 60 L.R.R.M. 2215, 52 CCH Lab. Cas. ¶ 16,629 (N.D. Ind. 1965); (d) a requirement that a member prove his eligibility for an officer's bond of the type prescribed by § 502 of the LMRDA, Wirtz v. Carpenters Local 559, 61 L.R.R.M. 2618, 53 CCH Lab. Cas. ¶ 11,044 (W.D. Ky. 1966); and (e) a requirement that a declaration of candidacy be filed four months prior to the nominating meeting, Wirtz v. Operating Eng'rs Local 30, 242 F. Supp. 631 (S.D.N.Y. 1965), *vacated as moot,* 366 F.2d 438 (2d Cir. 1966). How can one determine whether a given qualification is designed to ensure that candidates will be well-versed and active in a union's affairs, or is designed to deter dissidents and benefit incumbents? Is it best simply to rely on a rule's effects, in terms of the percentage of members disqualified for office? *See generally* Barnard, *Restrictions on the Right to Be a Candidate and Hold Union Office — The "Reasonable Qualifications" Exception in the Labor-Management Reporting and Disclosure Act,* 18 Wayne L. Rev. 1239 (1972); Cohen, *The Secretary of Labor's Court Challenge to the Steelworkers' Meeting Attendance Rule: A Case Study of the Conflict Between Internal Union Self-Government and the Administration of the Landrum-Griffin Act,* N.Y.U. Twenty-sixth Annual Conference on Labor 259 (1974).

2. *Denial of office.* Does § 402(b) confine the Secretary to an action to "set aside" an election, or may he sue to have installed a duly elected candidate who has been illegally denied his office? *Cf.* Wirtz v. Teamsters Local 73, 257 F. Supp. 784 (N.D. Ohio 1966).

3. *Removal from office.* Pursuant to § 401(h) and (i), the Secretary has issued regulations prescribing minimum standards for the procedures which must be made available to enable the removal of an elected local officer guilty of serious misconduct. *See* 29 C.F.R. §§ 417.1-417.25 (1978).

4. *See generally* Beaird, *Union Officer Election Provisions of the Labor-Management Reporting and Disclosure Act of 1959,* 51 VA. L. REV. 1306 (1965). The Secretary of Labor's interpretations of the election provisions of the LMRDA are contained in 29 C.F.R. §§ 452.1-452.138 (1978). For an extensive analysis of state court decisions on union elections, still of major significance in private preelection suits, see Summers, *Judicial Regulation of Union Elections,* 70 YALE L.J. 1221 (1961).

B. FIDUCIARY DUTIES OF OFFICERS

STATUTORY REFERENCE
LMRDA § 501

HIGHWAY TRUCK DRIVERS, LOCAL 107 v. COHEN

United States District Court, Eastern District of Pennsylvania
182 F. Supp. 608 (1960)
Aff'd per curiam, 284 F.2d 162 (3d Cir. 1960)
Cert. denied, 365 U.S. 833 (1961)

CLARY, DISTRICT JUDGE. This is a private suit brought under the recently enacted Labor Management Reporting and Disclosure Act of 1959. . . . That Act establishes a fiduciary responsibility on the part of officers of a labor organization [§ 501(a)], and further provided for a suit in a Federal district court to enforce these responsibilities [§ 501(b)]. The present suit has been brought under § 501(b) to enforce certain of these duties.

The moving parties are nine rank-and-file members of Highway Truck Drivers and Helpers, Local 107, of the International Brotherhood of Teamsters, Chauffeurs, Warehousemen and Helpers of America (hereinafter referred to as "Local 107"), who were given leave by this Court on November 12, 1959 to file a complaint against the defendants, the governing officers of Local 107. The complaint charged the defendants with a continuing mass conspiracy to cheat and defraud the union of large sums of money — the conspiracy alleged to have begun in 1954 and continued to the present time.

The defendants have yet to answer these very serious charges. Having been unsuccessful in first opposing the plaintiffs' petition for leave of this Court to sue, defendants now move to have the complaint dismissed. They are supported in this motion by counsel for Local 107, which has been allowed to intervene as a party defendant. This motion to dismiss is presently before the Court along with the plaintiffs' prayer for a preliminary injunction to prohibit the defendants from using union funds to defray the legal costs and other expenses being incurred by the defendants (and several other members of Local 107) in the defense of civil and criminal actions brought against them in the Courts of Pennsylvania and also the present suit in our own Court. The charges in these cases, in essence, grow out of the alleged activities of the defendants complained of here. The question of the preliminary injunction will be taken up after we resolve the motion to dismiss the complaint. . . .

The defendants' contention that those alleged wrongs which occurred *prior* to the enactment of § 501 can not alone constitute a basis for recovery under that section, must be accepted. Aside from the fact that the plaintiffs have not attempted to meet this contention, the principle that a statute which creates a new substantive right or duty will not, in the absence of clear legislative intent to the contrary, be construed to apply retrospectively, is too well established to admit of argument. . . .

If the only matter before the Court were the motion to dismiss discussed above, the Court might be disposed to grant the motion. However, there is another facet to the case which prevents the dismissal of the action. That facet relates to the motion for a preliminary injunction to prohibit the defendants from using union funds to defray the expense of legal fees in civil and criminal actions which have been brought against them in the Courts of Pennsylvania as well as to defray legal costs of the present action. The charges in those cases, in essence, grow out of alleged misappropriation of funds by the officers, and the plaintiffs maintain that such expenditures are in violation of the fiduciary duties imposed upon officers of a labor union by § 501(a) of the Act, supra, and that unless such expenditures are enjoined the union will suffer irreparable harm thereby.

Shortly after the effective date of the Act and the institution of suits, criminal and civil, in the local Courts against the defendants, the union at a regular monthly meeting, with few dissenting votes, adopted a resolution authorizing the union to bear "Legal costs of such actions [against the officers] which are in reality not directed at our officers but are directed at us, the members of Local 107, our good contracts, our good wages and our good working conditions."

The question, therefore, which faces us is: Does the expenditure of union funds to pay for legal fees in the defense of both criminal and civil actions brought against the various defendant officers for an alleged conspiracy to cheat and defraud their union of large sums of money constitute a breach of that fiduciary duty imposed upon them by § 501(a), supra, notwithstanding the purported authorization of such expenditures by a resolution of the union membership passed at a regular union meeting?

At the hearing on the preliminary injunction, it was brought out that within the limit of some four or five weeks after the adoption of the resolution the union, pursuant to the resolution, paid upwards of $25,000 to the attorneys representing the defendants. It is also clear that counsel for the union has advised the officers that such expenditures are proper. We are, therefore, with the payment of those large sums of money already accomplished and threatened further payments about to occur, in a position factually to pass upon the merits of the plaintiffs' contention. . . .

Section 501, with which we are particularly concerned, is entitled "Fiduciary responsibility of officers of labor organizations." This section . . . attempts to define in the broadest terms possible the duty which the new federal law imposes upon a union official. Congress made no attempt to "codify" the law in this area. It appears evident to us that they intended the federal courts to fashion a new federal labor law in this area, in much the same way that the federal courts have fashioned a new substantive law of collective bargaining contracts under § 301(a) of the Taft-Hartley Act, 29 U.S.C. § 185(a). See Textile Workers Union of America v. Lincoln Mills, 1957, 353 U.S. 448. In undertaking this task the federal courts will necessarily rely heavily upon the common law of the various states. Where that law is lacking or where it in any way conflicts with the policy expressed in our national labor laws, the latter will of course be our guide. . . .

In determining whether or not the expenditures now sought to be enjoined violate the fiduciary responsibility of an officer of a labor organization we must necessarily determine the legal effect of the September 20th Resolution. This goes to the heart of the present problem and appears to be the main ground on which the defendants seek to avoid the injunction.

The plaintiffs assert that the Resolution authorizing such expenditures is encompassed within the express prohibition of § 501(a) against any "general exculpatory resolution." Although not expressly purporting to absolve the defendants of guilt, plaintiffs argue that the Resolution *in effect* does just this. Unfortunately the Act does not define the phrase "general exculpatory resolution."

The defendants take issue with the plaintiffs' interpretation. They maintain that the Resolution should be taken at face value, i.e., as a pledge of the union's faith in their officers and a pledge of financial aid to defend suits which are in reality directed at the union movement. They point to several remarks made in Congress which make it clear that this provision was not intended to restrict in any way the right of the membership to give a grant of authority — which they allege is all that the September 20th Resolution does.

A plain reading of the last sentence in § 501(a) leads me to agree with the defendants, at least in their conclusion. On the other hand, it is not necessary for a resolution to read "The officers are hereby absolved of all responsibility created by the Act" before a court will strike it down as "exculpatory" under § 501(a). Nor must a court accept at face value the stated purpose of a resolution when reason and common sense clearly dictate a different purpose. Nevertheless in my interpretation of § 501(a), the Resolution under discussion is *not* one "purporting to relieve any [officer] of liability for breach of the duties declared by this section. . . ."

We must distinguish between a resolution which purports to *authorize* action which is beyond the power of the union to do and for that reason in violation of § 501(a) when done by an officer (such as the present Resolution) and a resolution which purports to *relieve* an officer of liability for breach of the duties declared in § 501(a). At times this distinction may be a fine one. Very often the result will be the same.

Nevertheless we feel that such a distinction should be made here unless the "exculpatory" provision is to be read as a mere "catchall" phrase.[6]

We turn then to the question of whether the September 20th Resolution is valid, i.e., conforms with the law of Pennsylvania and the Federal Labor laws. See International Union of Operating Engineers, A.F.L.-C.I.O. v. Pierce, Tex. Civ. App., 1959, 321 S.W.2d 914, at page 917-918. If it is inconsistent with either, we think it follows that the present expenditures by the defendants violate that provision in § 501(a) which imposes upon them a strict duty to "expend [union funds] in accordance with its constitution and bylaws and any resolutions of the governing bodies adopted thereunder . . . ." — since we read this sentence to authorize only those expenditures made pursuant to a *lawful* bylaw or resolution. . . .

In answering this question of whether an act is ultra vires, we look first to the Constitution of Local 107. Article I, § 2, sets forth the "objectives" of the organization in broad terms. These objectives might be summed up as an effort to organize workmen, to educate them, to improve their condition and to improve the industry in which they work. The defendants pointed to no more specific provision in the constitution (nor can we find any) which would authorize the type of expenditure dealt with here.

It is true that from the general objectives and purposes of a particular trade union, certain ancillary powers reasonably necessary for their attainment may be implied. In determining whether a particular act falls within this admittedly broad latitude of action, the Court must take into consideration all of the factors surrounding it, i.e., the stated purpose of the action, its immediate effect, its possible future benefit to the union, etc. This is necessary in order to determine whether the union, in light of the authority derived from its constitution, has a sufficient interest in the action to empower it to so act. If it has, a court of law will not interfere regardless of the wisdom or propriety of the act. If it has not, a court of law must intervene at the behest of a single union member. . . .

In passing upon the question of whether a union has sufficient interest in criminal and civil suits brought against various officers for the theft of union funds, to spend large sums of its money on legal fees for those officers, the Court is admittedly without a Pennsylvania case directly on point. There are, however, two interesting English cases which passed upon a similar question and which held that such expenditures were beyond the power of a union to make. Alfin v. Hewlett, 18 T.L.R. 664 (1902); Orman v. Hutt, 1 Ch. 98 (1914) (c.a.). These cases are persuasive.

Furthermore we feel that those cases involving the use of corporate funds to pay for the defense of officers charged with misconduct in office are helpful. Although this question again has not been passed upon in Pennsylvania, several other jurisdictions when faced with the problem have concluded that such expenditures are improper. . . .

---

[6] We might point out in this regard that the original Senate version of the Act (i.e., The Kennedy-Ives Bill, S. Rep. No. 187, 86th Cong., First Session, 1959) contained a somewhat similar prohibition against any exculpatory resolution and *also* contained a clause prohibiting unions from paying the legal fees or fines of any person indicted or convicted of a violation of the Bill.

In light of the foregoing and upon consideration of the situation surrounding the present expenditures, in particular the nature and seriousness of the charges brought against the defendants by the State of Pennsylvania as well as by individual members of their union, the Court feels that such expenditures to pay for the legal expenses incurred by the defendant officers in the criminal and civil suits brought against them individually are expenses to be borne by the officers themselves and are beyond the power of Local 107 to make. Being beyond the powers of the union as derived from its Constitution, it follows that a mere majority vote at a regular union meeting can not authorize such expenditures. . . .

There are undoubtedly situations in which a suit against a union officer would have a direct and injurious effect upon the union itself or would in reality be directed at the union. In such a situation the union would have the power to lend its financial support to such officer. When the question of whether the union has a sufficient interest to spend large sums of money to defend such a suit arises, it must ultimately be resolved by the court. Although a court will allow wide latitude to those in control of the union, it can not, by allowing unlimited latitude, abandon the right of a minority to see that the union spends its monies in accordance with its lawful aims and purposes as expressed in its Constitution and bylaws. Particularly is this true today, when the voice of the individual employee in fixing his own wages, hours and working conditions has necessarily been surrendered to the voice of the collective bargaining unit.

There is a further reason why the present Resolution is no defense here. Aside from its validity under Pennsylvania law, it is inconsistent with the aims and purposes of the Labor Management Reporting and Disclosure Act and violates the spirit of that Act. A stated purpose of the Act is "to *eliminate* . . . improper practices on the part of labor organizations . . . and their officers." (Emphasis added.) To allow a union officer to use the power and wealth of the very union which he is accused of pilfering, to defend himself against such charges, is totally inconsistent with Congress' effort to eliminate the undesirable element which has been uncovered in the labor-management field. To allow even a majority of members in that union to authorize such action, when, if the charges made against these defendants are true, it is these very members whom the officers have deceived, would be equally inconsistent with the Act. If some of those members have not been deceived by the defendants, but because of the immediate gains in their income and working conditions which Local 107 has won for them, they are content to accept as officers anyone who produces immediate results, regardless of what other wrongs those officers may commit in so doing, this Court would still not feel constrained to bow to their will in the light of its duty both to those members of Local 107 who place honesty above material gain as well as to the millions of others in the labor movement whose cause would be seriously injured by such an attitude.

Although we have not attempted to treat defendants' arguments individually, since we feel they are satisfactorily answered in this opinion, something should be said concerning their argument that the plaintiffs are here asking us to do that which Congress specifically refused to do when it failed to adopt subsection 107(b) of the original Senate version of the Labor Bill (The Kennedy-Ives Bill), which specifically prohibited "both unions and employers from directly or indirectly paying or advancing the costs of defense, of any of their officers . . . who [are] indicted for . . . any violation of any provision of the Bill." S. Rep. No. 187, 86th Cong., First Session, 1959, U.S. Code Cong. and Adm. News 1959, at 2318.

We are familiar with this argument in statutory construction. Although the value of such reasoning to discover the "intent" of Congress is often questionable, we can not of course ignore it. . . . Nevertheless there are reasons why we are not persuaded by their argument here.

First, the language contained in the Kennedy-Ives Bill is much broader than our holding in the present case. It is essential to an understanding of our position in this case that this point be made clear. That section quoted above would foreclose financial aid by the union to an officer in suits under the Act, under *any* circumstances. In our case we have expressly limited our holding *to the facts before us.* In the light of all of these facts we do not feel that the several actions brought against the defendants involve any question of sufficient interest to Local 107 to warrant their expending large sums of union money to pay the legal costs of the defendants in these suits. That Congress refused to foreclose the right of a union under *any* circumstances to lend financial aid to an officer when sued under any section of the Kennedy-Ives Bill is not, we feel, a strong argument for the conclusion that under *no* circumstances could a union be prohibited from lending financial aid to an accused officer.

Second, in none of the cases cited by the defendants to support their argument as to the conclusion to be drawn from the omission of § 107(b) were there two distinct bills involved. Here the Act finally passed by Congress (with modification) was the Landrum-Griffin House Bill and not the Kennedy-Ives Senate Bill. Strictly speaking, the Conference Committee did not amend the final Bill as to the provision in question, since it was never contained in it to begin with. Had the Kennedy-Ives Bill ultimately been adopted with § 107(b) deleted, the defendants' argument would be more convincing.

Finally, even assuming that Congress intended to leave a union free to use its funds for the purpose of paying its officers legal expenses in actions brought against them under the new Act, if under the law of Pennsylvania, the state in which the union membership contractual relationship arose, such expenditures are illegal, a union officer could not consistent with his duty to the union (which duties ultimately flow from its Constitution) expend union funds for this purpose. This would follow unless we interpret the omission of this prohibition as creating an affirmative federal right in a union to so spend its funds, which right is intended to supersede any state law to the contrary. We flatly reject such an interpretation of the new Act. . . .

A formal order will be entered enjoining the defendants from expending union funds for the defense of the cases presently pending against the defendants in either the Courts of the Commonwealth of

Pennsylvania or in this Court. This ruling in no way attempts to pass upon the question of whether or not Local 107 may with propriety, by appropriate resolution, reimburse its officers for their legal expenses in the event they are exonerated from any wrongdoing in connection with the handling of union funds involved in the actions presently pending.

NOTES

1. In July 1961 the International Brotherhood of Teamsters amended its constitution to authorize the international and local unions to pay the cost of defending officers and employees in criminal or civil actions. Was this a "general exculpatory provision . . . void as against public policy" under § 501(a)? *See* Highway Truck Drivers Local 107 v. Cohen, 215 F. Supp. 938 (E.D. Pa. 1963), *aff'd,* 334 F.2d 378 (3d Cir. 1964), *cert. denied,* 379 U.S. 921 (1964). *See also* Morrissey v. Curran, 423 F.2d 393 (2d Cir. 1970), *cert. denied,* 399 U.S. 928 (1970).

2. In Gurton v. Arons, 339 F.2d 371, 375 (2d Cir. 1964), the court declared: "A simple reading of [§ 501] . . . shows that it applies to fiduciary responsibility with respect to the money and property of the union and that it is not a catch-all provision under which union officials can be sued on any ground of misconduct with which the plaintiffs choose to charge them." *See also* Yanity v. Benware, 376 F.2d 197 (2d Cir. 1967), *cert. denied,* 389 U.S. 874 (1967). *But cf.* Johnson v. Nelson, 325 F.2d 646, 651 (8th Cir. 1963) (refusal to sign checks approved by the membership; "§ 501 imposes fiduciary responsibility in its broadest application and is not confined in its scope to union officials only in their handling of money and property affairs"); Moschetta v. Cross, 48 L.R.R.M. 2669 (D.D.C. 1961) (refusal to hold special convention previously called in accordance with union's constitution); Sabolsky v. Budzanoski, 457 F.2d 1245 (3d Cir. 1972) (failure to disband nonfunctioning locals as required by union's constitution); Cefalo v. Moffett, 333 F. Supp. 1283 (D.D.C. 1971), *modified in part,* 449 F.2d 1193 (D.C. Cir. 1971) (merger of unions). What factors militate for or against an expansive reading of § 501? *See generally* Clark, *The Fiduciary Duties of Union Officials Under Section 501 of the LMRDA,* 52 MINN. L. REV. 437 (1967); Leslie, *Federal Courts and Union Fiduciaries,* 76 COLUM. L. REV. 1205 (1976); Note, *The Fiduciary Duty Under Section 501 of the LMRDA,* 75 COLUM. L. REV. 1189 (1975).

Section 501 has been held unavailable to union members seeking damages, an accounting, and an injunction against union officers who contributed union funds to partisan political activities and social causes, when the union's constitution and governing resolutions authorized such expenditures. McNamara v. Johnston, 522 F.2d 1157 (7th Cir. 1975), *cert. denied,* 425 U.S. 911 (1976).

Should union officials be held personally liable for unauthorized payments to third parties, when the officials themselves do not profit from the transaction? *Compare* Richardson v. Tyler, 309 F. Supp. 1020 (N.D. Ill. 1970), *with* Morrissey v. Curran, 336 F. Supp. 1107 (S.D.N.Y. 1972).

3. Exhaustion of internal union remedies has been held not a prerequisite to a member's suit under § 501(b), as long as the specific procedural requirements of that section are met. Horner v. Ferron, 362 F.2d 224 (9th Cir. 1966), *cert. denied,* 385 U.S. 958 (1966); Holdeman v. Scheldon, 204 F. Supp. 890 (S.D.N.Y. 1962), *aff'd,* 311 F.2d 2 (2d Cir. 1962). *Contra,* Penuelas v. Moreno, 198 F. Supp. 441 (S.D. Cal. 1961).

4. *Litigation costs.* Should union officers sued under § 501 be entitled to retain counsel paid for by the union? *See* Tucker v. Shaw, 378 F.2d 304 (2d Cir. 1967); Kerr v. Shanks, 466 F.2d 1267 (9th Cir. 1972). What about a union's paying a defendant officer's legal fees after he has been exonerated? *See* Morrisey v. Segal, 526 F. 2d 121 (2d Cir. 1975). *See also* Note, *Counsel Fees for Union Officers Under the Fiduciary Provision of Landrum-Griffin,* 73 YALE L.J. 443 (1964). May successful plaintiffs in § 501 actions be awarded attorneys' fees and other expenses even if there is no monetary recovery? *See* Kerr v. Shanks, *supra;* Bakery Workers v. Ratner, 335 F.2d 691 (D.C. Cir. 1964).

5. *Bonding.* Section 502 of the LMRDA requires the bonding of union personnel handling the organization's funds or property. An analysis of the section as it was originally enacted is contained in Dugan, *To Bond or Not to Bond — Section 502 of the Landrum-Griffin Act,* 12 LAB. L.J. 536 (1961). In 1965 § 502 was amended to allow coverage by a standard "honesty" bond rather than the more expensive "faithful performance" bond formerly required, and to permit the use of a wider range of surety companies.

C. REPORTING AND DISCLOSURE

STATUTORY REFERENCES
LMRDA §§ 201-10, 601

Almost twenty states [1] require labor unions to register or file organizational and financial reports. In addition, the tremendous growth of welfare and pension funds during and after World War II, coupled with legislative investigations revealing loose practice in their administration, led several states to enact laws setting standards for such funds and requiring reporting and disclosure.[2]

Today the most important regulatory and reporting measures in these areas are two federal laws, the Employee Retirement Income Security Act

---

[1] Alabama, Alaska, Arkansas, California, Connecticut, Florida, Hawaii, Kansas, Massachusetts, Michigan, Minnesota, New York, North Carolina, Oregon, South Dakota, Texas, Utah, Virginia, and Wisconsin. 4 LAB. REL. REP. SLL 1:50-51 (1979). *See generally* C. KILLINGSWORTH, STATE LABOR RELATIONS ACTS 99-100 (1948); Aaron & Komaroff, *Statutory Regulation of Internal Union Affairs I,* 44 ILL. L. REV. 425, 460-61 (1949).

[2] Connecticut, Florida, Iowa, Massachusetts, Nevada, New York, Washington, and Wisconsin. 4 LAB. REL. REP. SLL 1:52 (1979).

of 1974 [3] and the Labor-Management Reporting and Disclosure Act of 1959.[4] The former replaced the Welfare and Pension Plans Disclosure Act of 1958,[5] which was primarily a reporting statute, with elaborate regulation of all employee benefit plans maintained by employers and unions in interstate commerce. Pensions, for example, must meet minimum vesting, benefit accrual, and funding requirements. Stiff fiduciary obligations are imposed on all plan trustees and administrators. Enforcement is through civil suit by a plan participant or beneficiary or by the Secretary of Labor. Criminal sanctions apply to willful violations.

As has been seen, the LMRDA as finally passed was much more than a disclosure measure. But reporting provisions remain a central feature of the Act. Title II prescribes five different types of reports: (1) union organizational reports; (2) union financial reports; (3) "conflict of interest" reports by union officers and employees; (4) employer reports on such matters as payments to union representatives and payments to influence employees in the exercise of their collective rights; and (5) reports by labor relations consultants on agreements to so influence employees, or to inform employers about employee or union activities in a labor dispute.[6] The reporting obligations are subject to criminal sanctions and to a civil suit by the Secretary of Labor for an injunction or other appropriate remedy.

The information contained in union organizational and financial reports must be made available to the members of the union.[7] To relieve

---

[3] 88 Stat. 829 (1974), 29 U.S.C. §§ 1001 — 1381. *See generally* Fasser, Levin & Greenberg, *Pension Reform: Its Impact on the Bargaining Scene,* in N.Y.U. TWENTY-EIGHTH ANNUAL CONFERENCE ON LABOR 59, 67, 85 (1976) (three separate papers); Sickles, Donaldson, Gertner, Fillion & Trebilock, *The Employee Retirement Income Security Act of 1974: Labor Law Considerations,* 17 WILLIAM & MARY L. REV. 205, 215, 233, 251 (1975) (four separate papers).

[4] *See generally* Aaron, *The Labor-Management Reporting and Disclosure Act of 1959,* 73 HARV. L. REV. 851, 877-94 (1960); Naumoff, *Reporting Requirements Under the Labor-Management Reporting and Disclosure Act,* in N.Y.U. FOURTEENTH ANNUAL CONFERENCE ON LABOR 129 (1961).

[5] 72 Stat. 997 (1958), as amended, 29 U.S.C. §§ 301-09. *See generally* BNA, FEDERAL-STATE REGULATION OF WELFARE FUNDS (1962).

[6] Labor consultants engaged in "persuader" activities for employer clients must report *all* compensation from all employer clients for labor relations services, whether persuader or nonpersuader. Douglas v. Wirtz, 353 F.2d 30 (4th Cir. 1965), *cert. denied,* 383 U.S. 909 (1966); Price v. Wirtz, 412 F.2d 647 (5th Cir. 1969). *See generally* Beaird, *Reporting Requirements for Employers and Labor Relations Consultants in the Labor-Management Reporting and Disclosure Act of 1959,* 53 GEO. L.J. 267 (1965). On lawyer consultants in particular, see Craver, *The Application of the LMRDA "Labor Consultant" Reporting Requirements to Management Attorneys: Benign Neglect Personified,* 73 NW. U. L. 605 (1978).

[7] Under § 201(c) of the LMRDA a member may sue to inspect a union's books and records to verify its financial reports, but not in order to make an "intelligent vote" on a proposed increase in dues and fees. Flaherty v. Warehousemen Local 334, 574 F. 2d 484 (9th Cir. 1978).

smaller unions of the mountainous paper work involved in detailed financial reporting, the Secretary of Labor, exercising his discretion under § 208, has authorized simplified reports for unions having annual gross receipts of less than $30,000.

The so-called "goldfish bowl" philosophy underlying the union reporting requirements is reflected in the following statement.

HOUSE COMMITTEE ON EDUCATION AND LABOR

H.R. Rep. No. 741 on H.R. 8342,
86th Cong., 1st Sess. 7-9 (1959)

The members of a labor organization are the real owners of the money and property of such organizations and are entitled to a full accounting of all transactions involving such money and property. Because union funds belong to the members they should be expended only in furtherance of their common interest. A union treasury should not be managed as though it were the private property of the union officers, however well intentioned such officers might be, but as a fund governed by fiduciary standards . . .

. . . [T]he rules governing the conduct of the union's business, such as dues and assessments payable by members, membership rights, disciplinary procedures, election of officers, provisions governing the calling of regular and special meetings — all should be known to the members. Without such information freely available it is impossible that labor organizations can be truly responsive to their members.

It is the purpose of this bill to insure that full information concerning the financial and internal administrative practices and procedures of labor organizations shall be, in the first instance available to the members of such organizations. In addition, this information is to be made available to the Government, and through the Secretary of Labor, is to be open to inspection by the general public. By such disclosure, and by relying on voluntary action by members of labor organizations, it is hoped that a deterrent to abuses will be established. . . .

The committee believes that union members armed with adequate information and having the benefit of secret elections, as provided for in title IV of this bill, will be greatly strengthened in their efforts to rid themselves of untrustworthy or corrupt officers. In addition, the exposure to public scrutiny of all vital information concerning the operation of trade unions will help deter repetition of the financial abuses disclosed by the McClellan committee. Where union financial and other practices do not meet reasonable standards, although not willfully dishonest, this bill would have a remedial effect. Under provisions of the committee bill, both labor organizations and their officers are under obligation to make full and accurate reports, subject to criminal penalties.

GOLDBERG v. TRUCK DRIVERS LOCAL 299

United States Court of Appeals, Sixth Circuit
293 F.2d 807 (1961)
Cert. denied, 368 U.S. 938 (1961)

WEICK, CIRCUIT JUDGE. This case involves important questions concerning the right of the Secretary of Labor to secure judicial enforcement of subpoenas duces tecum issued by him and served on union officers in connection with an investigation he was attempting to make under the authority of § 601 of the Labor-Management Reporting and Disclosure Act of 1959. . . .

The union officers appeared in response to the subpoenas, challenged the right of the Secretary to make the investigation and refused to produce the records called for in view of legal questions which the unions and their counsel believed were involved including the constitutionality of certain sections of the Act providing for the issuance of the subpoenas. The union officers had custody of the records subpoenaed and there was no claim of any physical inability on their part to produce them.

The Secretary filed a petition in the District Court for enforcement of the subpoenas, which was denied on the ground that the Secretary had made no showing as to necessity for the investigation and because the subpoenas were too broad.

It appeared on the face of the subpoenas that they were issued in connection with "an investigation by the Bureau of Labor-Management Reports involving a determination whether any person has violated any provision of the Act." The subpoenas called for the production of the following records:

All records for the period from January 1, 1959 to the present date maintained by you or under your control which contain any basic information or data on matters required to be reported from which the organizational report (Form LM-1), and the financial report (Form LM-2) filed with the Secretary of Labor for Local 614, International Brotherhood of Teamsters, Chauffeurs, Warehousemen and Helpers of America may be verified, explained or clarified and checked for accuracy and completeness, in connection with all items referred to or listed in such report and all items omitted or excluded therefrom which are relevant thereto and are required to be included in said reports, such records to include but not be limited to, vouchers, worksheets, ledgers, audit reports, records of receipt of dues, fees, assessments, fines and work permits, accounts receivable, accounts payable, journals, journal vouchers, check register, payroll register and related records and all books of accounts of Local 614, related to the International Brotherhood of Teamsters, Chauffers, Warehousemen and Helpers of America, or other local unions affiliated with said International including all bank statements, cancelled checks, check stubs, audit reports, financial reports, records of loans, records of mortgages, records of ownership of property real and personal, deeds, records of trusts, records of investments, and all correspondence and memoranda pertaining to receipts and disbursements. . . .

In the District Court, the unions contended that it was obligatory on the part of the Secretary to first establish probable cause for the investigation as a condition precedent to obtaining enforcement of the subpoenas by the court.

The District Court, in its opinion denying enforcement, did not expressly use the term "probable cause," but adopted words of like import which imposed a requirement at least as stringent, namely, that the Secretary establish a basis for the investigation. The court said that there must be some "reasonable foundation or valid purpose" rather than merely looking into the records of the union in the hope of turning up something. This, in effect, was a holding that the Secretary had no right merely to investigate, but was required first to establish a probable violation of the Act.

In this Court, the unions contended that as a prerequisite to judicial enforcement of a subpoena duces tecum the Secretary "must show that he has a reasonable belief of necessity [i.e., a reasonable basis] for the investigation."

The statute required the unions to maintain the records which were subpoenaed. . . .

Power was granted to the Secretary to make an investigation [quoting LMRDA § 601]. . . .

The legislative history of the Labor-Management Reporting and Disclosure Act reveals that the original bills introduced in the House and Senate each granted power to the Secretary to make an investigation only when he had probable cause to believe that any person or labor organization had violated any provision of the Act. The probable cause requirement, however, was eliminated from the Act as it was finally passed. The reason for deleting the probable cause requirement is set forth in the minority amendments adopted by the Senate Committee on Labor and Public Welfare. It is as follows: . . .

"As originally worded, this section would have given the Secretary the authority to investigate the books and records of persons reporting under the act only when he had probable cause to believe that a person had violated provisions of the act. On the surface, the term 'probable cause' would appear to give the Secretary all the investigatory power that he needed. But the words 'probable cause' would throw a monkey wrench into the Secretary's investigatory machinery. Probable cause means more than mere suspicion that the act has been violated. To have probable cause, a person must have such evidence as would lead the ordinary prudent man to believe that the act has been violated. Consequently, every time he commenced an investigation the Secretary could be dragged into court until the question of probable cause had been decided. Under nearly every statute requiring the filing of reports, such as the Internal Revenue Act and the Fair Labor Standards Act, the Administrator can conduct 'spot check' investigations unhampered by the 'probable cause' requirement. Our amendment rewrites this section to give the Secretary investigatory power when he believes it necessary in order to determine whether a violation has occurred or is about to occur." U.S. Code Congressional & Administrative News — 86th Congress, 1st Session 1959, at 2395, 2396. . . .

It seems to us that the court ought not to impose a condition, which Congress rejected, on the exercise of the right of the Secretary to investigate. Nor do we see any real difference between the rejected "probable cause" requirement and that of a "reasonable basis" for the investigation adopted by the District Court. While the disclosure sought must not be unreasonable or oppressive (Oklahoma Press Publishing Co. v. Walling, 327 U.S. 186, 208 (1946)), this does not mean that the Secretary is obligated to establish a reasonable basis for his investigation. If the Secretary was in possession of facts establishing a probable violation he might never need to investigate. The purpose of the investigation authorized by Congress was to provide the means of discovery whereby the Secretary could determine whether the Act was being violated, or about to be violated.

All the statute required, in order for the Secretary to investigate, was that he "believe it necessary in order to determine whether any person has violated or is about to violate any provision of this chapter."

In his petition for enforcement filed in the District Court, the Secretary alleged in paragraph six that he believed it was necessary to make the investigation to determine whether any persons violated or were about to violate the law. The unions in their response to the petition (Par. I) admitted the allegations contained in paragraph six and certain other paragraphs of the petition.

In the absence of proof to the contrary, there is a presumption of regularity in the proceedings of a public officer. The burden is upon the party complaining to show otherwise. . . . The trial judge commented on the fact that the Secretary did not offer any evidence to establish the reason or basis for the investigation. In our opinion, the Secretary was not required to do so. The statute was sufficient authority for him to proceed. The purpose of the investigation appeared on the face of the subpoenas. The Secretary could not very well perform his statutory duty and determine whether the Act was being violated or about to be violated without making an investigation. Requiring the Secretary to first establish a probable violation of the Act, as a condition precedent to making an investigation, effectively stripped him of his power to investigate and prevented him from determining whether the Act was being violated or about to be violated. It virtually rendered the enforcement provisions of the Act nugatory.

We believe Oklahoma Press Publishing Co. v. Walling, 327 U.S. 186 (1946) is dispositive of this issue. In upholding enforcement of a subpoena duces tecum issued by the Administrator of the Wage and Hour Division of the Department of Labor, the Court said:

"Congress has made no requirement in terms of any showing of 'probable cause'; and, in view of what has already been said, any possible constitutional requirement of that sort was satisfied by the Administrator's showing in this case, including not only the allegations concerning coverage, but also that he was proceeding with his investigation in accordance with the mandate of Congress and that the records sought were relevant to that purpose. . . .

"The result therefore sustains the Administrator's position that his investigative function, in searching out violations with a view to securing enforcement of the Act, is essentially the same as the grand jury's, or the court's in issuing other pretrial orders for the discovery of evidence, and is governed by the same limitations. These are that he shall not act arbitrarily or in excess of his statutory authority, but this does not mean that his inquiry must be 'limited . . . by . . . forecasts of the probable result of the investigation. . . .' "

. . . In our judgment, the District Court erred in imposing a condition on the exercise of the right granted by Congress to the Secretary to make an investigation.

It is next contended that the subpoenas duces tecum were too broad. In substance, they require production of records containing basic information or data on matters required to be reported from which the organizational reports (Form LM-1) and the financial reports (Form LM-2) filed with the Secretary by the unions may be verified, explained or clarified and checked for accuracy and completeness. These were the records which the statute required the unions to keep and were quasi-public records. Production of the records could not be resisted on the ground of self-incrimination. Shapiro v. United States, 335 U.S. 1 (1948). . . . The unions asserted no such ground. In our opinion, it was not unreasonable to compel production of records which the law required to be kept and from which the reports filed with the Secretary were made. In no other way could the Secretary verify the reports than by examination of the records. These records were relevant to the inquiry because they would throw light on whether the reports filed by the unions with the Secretary spoke the truth. The District Court, however, had the power to impose protective restraints on the conduct of the investigation to relieve against oppression or other illegal conduct. . . . This power was not invoked by the unions. They questioned the right of the Secretary to make the investigation.

Oklahoma Press involved a corporation. It is urged that a different rule should apply to labor unions. We think not. In United States v. White, 322 U.S. 694 (1944), a subpoena duces tecum issued by the District Court requiring a union to produce its records before a Grand Jury was resisted by a union officer on the ground that they might tend to incriminate the union or himself individually or as such officer. The Supreme Court held that this defense was not available. While *White* involved the Fifth Amendment, the opinion of the Court contains language which is pertinent here. The Court said:

"The fact that the state charters corporations and has visitorial powers over them provides a convenient vehicle for justification of governmental investigation of corporate books and records. . . . But the absence of that fact as to a particular type of organization does not lessen the public necessity for making reasonable regulations of its activities effective, nor does it confer upon such an organization the purely personal privilege against self-incrimination. Basically, the power to compel the production of the records of any organization, whether it be incorporated or not, arises out of the inherent and necessary power of the federal and state governments to enforce their laws, with the privilege against self-incrimination being limited to its historic function of protecting only the natural individual from compulsory incrimination through his own testimony or personal records."

The Court concluded:

"The union and its officers acting in their official capacity lack the privilege at all times of insulating the union's books and records against reasonable demands of governmental authorities."

Finally, the unions contend that § 201 of the Act, . . . containing the provisions requiring them to file reports with the Secretary, is unconstitutional in violation of the Commerce Clause, Article I, Section 8. This contention was not passed upon by the District Court. The unions claim that the Secretary's authority to investigate is dependent upon § 201 of the Act, and, therefore, such section is subject to challenge in this case. . . .

In our opinion, § 201 of the Act does not offend against the Commerce Clause.

The judgment of the District Court is reversed and the cause remanded with instructions to grant the petition for enforcement of the subpoenas.

NOTE

The courts have taken a generous view of the Secretary of Labor's investigatory powers under § 601 of the LMRDA. Thus, in accord with the principal case, it has consistently been recognized that the Secretary need not find "probable cause" to believe a violation has occurred before issuing a subpoena. *See, e.g.*, Teamsters v. Wirtz, 346 F.2d 827, 831 (D.C. Cir. 1965); Wirtz v. Teamsters Local 191, 321 F.2d 445 (2d Cir. 1963). Moreover, regardless of the allowable scope of an action by the Secretary under § 402 to invalidate a union election, his investigation of the election under § 601 is not restricted to the items complained about by a member. Operating Engineers Local 57 v. Wirtz, 346 F.2d 552 (1st Cir. 1965); *Wirtz v. Teamsters Local 191, supra.*

A subpoena has even been sustained under § 601 for the purpose of investigating an alleged misuse of union funds in violation of § 501(a), although the latter provision is enforceable by private parties or the Attorney General and not by the Secretary. *Teamsters v. Wirtz, supra.* Similarly, in *Operating Engineers Local 57 v. Wirtz, supra,* the Secretary's power to investigate was held not to be limited to the matters required to be reported by the Act. The Secretary's right of inspection, however, may be subject to other statutory policies against total disclosure in certain circumstances. *See, e.g.,* Teamsters v. Goldberg, 303 F.2d 402 (D.C. Cir. 1962), *cert. denied,* 370 U.S. 938 (1962) (union membership lists).

Are these decisions likely to be affected by the Supreme Court's invalidation of warrantless OSHA inspections in *Marshall v. Barlow's,*

Inc., supra at 44? Many union officials have asserted that the Secretary of Labor's roving commission to investigate under the LMRDA is the most objectionable single feature of the Act. Why might this be?

D. TRUSTEESHIPS; PARENT-LOCAL RELATIONS

STATUTORY REFERENCES

LMRDA §§ 301-06

SECRETARY OF LABOR, UNION TRUSTEESHIPS: REPORT TO THE CONGRESS UPON THE OPERATION OF TITLE III OF THE LABOR-MANAGEMENT REPORTING AND DISCLOSURE ACT 5-11 (1962)*

Background

A trusteeship is any method of supervision or control whereby a labor organization suspends the autonomy otherwise available to a subordinate body under its constitution or bylaws. The practice of imposing trusteeships by unions dates back to the 19th century, but was extremely rare until the development of strong national unions.

During hearings of the McClellan Committee it was disclosed that the power to impose trusteeship was used sometimes for the purpose of "milking" local treasuries or undemocratically controlling votes to perpetuate power. . . .

Provisions covering trusteeships were enacted as title III of the Labor-Management Reporting and Disclosure Act of 1959. . . . This title prescribes conditions under which trusteeships may be established and continued, requires reporting and public disclosure of their stewardship by any labor organization, makes it a crime either to count the votes of delegates of the trusteed union unless democratically elected, or to transfer funds to the supervisory body, and provides redress for the union member or subordinate body either directly in court or through the Secretary of Labor.

The discussions and committee deliberations in Congress recognized that union trusteeships, although sometimes used to control subordinated organizations illegally, most often are used to provide assistance to subordinates in difficulties, to assist in maintenance and stability, and to promote rather than stifle union democracy. . . .

---

* Submitted in September 1962 in accordance with § 305 of the LMRDA; the full report contains much valuable information. — *Eds.*

Conclusions

Operation of the trusteeship provisions of the Labor-Management Reporting and Disclosure Act during the first 2½ years supports the following conclusions:

1. Establishment of trusteeships has never been a widespread practice, except in a few unions. When the Act became effective, trusteeships existed in less than 1 percent of the covered unions. Now, less than half that percentage are involved.

2. The Act has been effective in correcting the malpractices disclosed by the McClellan Committee. Further, a large number of trusteeships, while not corrupt, were unnecessarily continued and have now been terminated.

3. Since enactment of the law, many national union constitutions have been amended to provide greater safeguards against unnecessary suspension of autonomy.

4. Indications are that the Act has not substantially hindered unions from establishing essential trusteeships.

5. The reporting and disclosure of the facts surrounding trusteeships, and the active cooperation of the vast majority of unions and union officers, have resulted in substantial compliance with the law with a minimum need for enforcement.

NOTES

1. At common law, the right of a local union to "secede" from an international, the power of the international to impose a trusteeship to prevent such disaffiliation, and the rights of the respective parties in the assets of the secessionist local, were largely determined as matters of contract law, in accordance with the terms of the particular union constitution insofar as that did not offend public policy. *See, e.g.,* Harker v. McKissock, 7 N.J. 323, 81 A.2d 480 (1951), and cases cited; Comment, *Effects of a Union Split Upon Property Rights,* 1952 Wis. L. Rev. 139.

2. During the late 1940's and the 1950's a number of international unions were expelled from the AFL, the CIO, or the AFL-CIO for Communism or corruption. In several decisions the courts relied on the international's loss of affiliation with the parent federation as a breach of a "material implied condition" or as a "frustration" of the international-local contractual relationship, thus enabling the local to disaffiliate from the international and retain its property. *See, e.g.,* American Bakery Workers Local 240 v. Bakery Workers Local 240, 58 L.R.R.M. 2744, 51 CCH Lab. Cas. ¶ 51,263 (Colo. Dist. Ct. 1965); UE Local 1140 v. UE, 232 Minn. 217, 45 N.W.2d 408 (1950); Crocker v. Weil, 227 Ore. 260, 361 P.2d 1014 (1961). *See also* Summers, *Union Schism in Perspective: Flexible Doctrines, Double Standards, and Projected Answers,* 45 Va. L. Rev. 261 (1959).

3. Common-law rights and remedies regarding parent-local relations, including "trusteeships," remain significant despite the enactment of the

LMRDA. Under § 306 of the Act, federal jurisdiction becomes exclusive only when the Secretary of Labor files a complaint challenging a trusteeship.

UNITED BROTHERHOOD OF CARPENTERS v. BROWN

United States Court of Appeals, Tenth Circuit
343 F.2d 872 (1965)

[The United Brotherhood imposed a trusteeship on Local 201 for failing to comply with the General President's order to affiliate with a union district council and for failing to raise membership dues from $5.80 to $8.00 per month as required by the bylaws of the district council. Individual members of Local 201 sued to have the trusteeship removed.]

HILL, CIRCUIT JUDGE. . . . Appellants contend that the judgment must be reversed and the action dismissed because plaintiffs have not exhausted the administrative remedy available to them under the provisions of § 304(a) of the [LMRDA]. The argument is that plaintiffs were required to first file a complaint with the Secretary of Labor in accordance with § 304(a) and exhaust that remedy before proceeding in court with this lawsuit. There is authority to support that argument. *E.g.,* Cox v. Hutcheson, 204 F. Supp. 442 (S.D. Ind. 1962); . . . Rizzo v. Ammond, 182 F. Supp. 456 (D.N.J. 1960). But, there is also authority supporting the view that a local union member need not exhaust the administrative remedy provided in § 304(a) before bringing suit in the district court under that section. Parks v. International Brotherhood of Electrical Workers, 314 F.2d 886, 923, 924 (4th Cir. 1963), *cert. denied,* 372 U.S. 976 (1963); . . . Executive Board, IBEW, Local 28 v. IBEW, 184 F. Supp. 649 (D. Md. 1960). We believe the latter view is the better rule for the reasons set forth in Judge Watkins' excellent analysis of § 304(a) in the Executive Board case, *supra,* 184 F. Supp. at 655-659. We can add nothing to that discussion and accordingly hold that appellants were not required to exhaust the administrative remedy provided in § 304(a) before instituting this action. . . .

Appellants also contend that the judgment must be reversed and the action dismissed for the reason that the plaintiffs have failed to exhaust the internal remedies afforded by United Brotherhood's Constitution and Laws as required by § 101(a)(4) of the Act. . . . We do not agree. Section 101(a)(4) is applicable only where individual violations of the so-called Bill of Rights provisions are alleged and does not apply where, as here, the validity of a trusteeship is being challenged. As the Supreme Court said in Calhoon v. Harvey, *supra,* 379 U.S. at 138: "Jurisdiction of the district court under § 102 of Title I depends entirely upon whether this complaint showed a violation of rights guaranteed by § 101(a)(1). . . ." In any event, the requirement that internal remedies be exhausted is subject to certain exceptions that are applicable here. . . .

The basic issue in this case is, of course, the validity of the trusteeship imposed upon Local 201 by United Brotherhood. That issue must be determined by reference to § 302 of the Act, . . . which provides that a trusteeship may be established and administered by a labor organization over its subordinate body ". . . only in accordance with the constitution and bylaws of the organization which has assumed trusteeship. . . ." The statute is mandatory in its terms and has nullified or removed whatever inherent power an international union had prior to its enactment to impose such a trusteeship. Unless the constitution and bylaws of the parent organization make provision therefor, such organization has no power to establish a trusteeship over a subordinate body. Flight Engineers Int'l Ass'n v. Continental Air Lines, Inc., 297 F.2d 397 (9th Cir. 1961), *cert. denied,* 369 U.S. 871 (1962). An examination of the constitution and bylaws of United Brotherhood discloses that there is no specific provision authorizing it to impose a trusteeship on any of its subordinate local unions.

It is suggested, however, that United Brotherhood's power to impose the trusteeship in question may be derived from the general authority granted to it in §§ 6B and 6D of its Constitution and Laws, as implemented by the provision in § 10K, which empowers the General Executive Board ". . . to take such action as is necessary and proper for the welfare . . ." of the national union. Appellant's argument is that while its constitution and laws do not specifically grant it the authority to impose trusteeships, such authority may be implied from §§ 6B, 6D and 10K and that implied authority is sufficient. We do not agree. The legislative history of § 302 of the Act clearly discloses an intent on the part of Congress ". . . that there should be a 'limitation on the right of internationals to place local unions in trusteeship' " and one of those limitations was that ". . . the trusteeship must conform to the constitution and bylaws of the labor organization." 2 U.S. Code Cong. & Adm. News, 86th Cong., 1st Sess., 1959, pp. 2333-2334. Obviously, a trusteeship cannot conform to the constitution and bylaws of a labor organization where, as here, the constitution and bylaws make no provision for trusteeships. We think the statute not only contemplates, but requires, more than some vague general reference to the effect that the parent organization shall have power to take such action as is necessary and proper for its welfare. It requires at the very least that the organization's constitution and bylaws set forth the circumstances under which a trusteeship may be established over its local unions and the manner or procedure in which it is to be imposed. It goes without saying, of course, that the constitution and bylaws in that respect must not conflict with applicable provisions of the Act.

A second limitation upon the imposition of trusteeships is that under § 302 it must be for one of the following purposes: (1) To correct corruption or financial malpractice; (2) to assure the performance of collective bargaining agreements or other duties of a bargaining representative; or (3) to restore democratic procedures, or otherwise carry out the legitimate objects of the labor organization. Congress recognized that the use of trusteeships by an international union is a particularly effective device for the maintenance of order within the organization and that "... they have been widely used to prevent corruption, mismanagement of union funds, violation of collective bargaining agreements, infiltration of Communists; in short, to preserve the integrity and stability of the organization itself. ..." But, Congress also recognized that "... in some instances trusteeships have been used as a means of consolidating the power of corrupt union officers, plundering and dissipating the resources of local unions, and preventing the growth of competing political elements within the organization." 2 U.S. Code Cong. & Adm. News, 86th Cong., 1st Sess., 1959, p. 2333. To preserve the legitimate use of trusteeships, Congress in enacting § 302 enumerated the purposes for which a trusteeship could be imposed in language of a broad and general nature. However, in order to prevent their misuse, Congress obviously intended those purposes to have limitations as well and therefore in determining whether a particular case meets the test, the statute must be construed in the light of the various other provisions of the Act.

The purpose of the Act as a whole is not only to stop and prevent outrageous conduct by thugs and gangsters but also to stop lesser forms of objectionable conduct by those in positions of trust and to protect democratic processes within union organizations. ... To accomplish that purpose, a "Bill of Rights of Members of Labor Organizations" was incorporated into the Act. Thus, the rights of individual members of a labor union are protected by federal statute with a view to allowing those members to conduct local matters with a minimum of outside interference. In short, local affairs are to be governed by local members under democratic processes.

With this background in mind we turn to a consideration of the purposes for which the instant trusteeship was imposed. The trial court found, and the evidence confirms, that United Brotherhood established the trusteeship over Local 201 because it would not affiliate with the District Council and would not raise its dues. The court also found, and the evidence shows, that it was not imposed because of "dissension" within the local union. The result is that the trusteeship was established for the purposes of affiliating Local 201 with the District Council and raising the dues of its membership. In determining whether these are proper purposes under § 302, we must remember that a majority of the local membership consistently voted against having anything to do with the District Council and on at least two occasions, by secret ballot, voted against the proposal to raise the monthly dues. We must also remember that the provisions of [§ 101] were designed to afford them protection in that respect. Under these circumstances, we have no hesitancy in holding that the purposes for which this trusteeship was imposed do not fall within any of the categories set forth in § 302. Beyond question, they do not come under the category of correcting corruption or financial malpractice and have nothing whatever to do with collective bargaining. It is also clear to us that the specified purposes are not within the category of restoring democratic processes or otherwise carrying out the legitimate objects of United Brotherhood. To the contrary, the imposition of the trusteeship in question could have no other effect than to stifle democratic processes by, in effect, voiding the results of the properly conducted elections on the issues involved. If we were to hold that the asserted purposes were proper, this court would be placed in the position of allowing a national union to establish a trusteeship over a local union because the members of the local union insisted upon exercising a right granted them by statute. This would in effect nullify and frustrate not only the plain purpose but the express terms of the Act.

It is true that there is a presumption as to the validity of a trusteeship for a period of eighteen months from the date of its establishment. [§ 304(c).] But, it is quite clear from the statute itself and from the legislative history that Congress intended for the presumption of validity to be available only where the trusteeship has been established "... in conformity with the procedural requirements of its [the labor organization's] constitution and bylaws and authorized or ratified after a fair hearing either before the executive board or before such other body as may be provided in accordance with its constitution or bylaws...." [§ 304(c)]; 2 U.S. Code Cong. & Adm. News, 86th Cong., 1st Sess., 1959, p. 2334. Since the trusteeship in this case was not established in conformity with the constitution and bylaws, the presumption is not available to appellants....

NOTES

1. *Compare* Carpenters Local 1302 v. Carpenters, 447 F. 2d 612 (2d Cir. 1973), where the Second Circuit, per Judge Hays, sustained an international's imposition of a trusteeship to prevent a local from disaffiliating from a local Metal Trades Council and seeking separate bargaining rights. The international had concluded that the local's action would have a detrimental effect on well-established collective bargaining. Judge Oakes dissented.

2. The elimination of racial segregation has been held a legitimate basis for imposing a trusteeship aimed at effecting a merger of a white local and a neighboring black local. Musicians Local 10 v. Musicians, 57 L.R.R.M. 2227 (N.D. Ill. 1964); *cf.* Daye v. Tobacco Workers Union, 234 F. Supp. 815 (D.D.C. 1964).

3. What is the effect of a valid trusteeship? In Blassie v. Poole, 58 L.R.R.M. 2359, 51 CCH Lab. Cas. ¶ 19,510 (E.D. Mo. 1965), it was held that an international, having established a legitimate trusteeship, could suspend the local union's constitution and bylaws, remove local officers and employees, and proceed to manage the organization's affairs without calling general membership meetings. Such actions would not violate §§ 101(a)(1), 101(a)(2), 202(a), or 501(a) of the LMRDA.

4. Would an international's revocation of a local's charter and its reissuance to a new organization constitute a "trusteeship" within the meaning of Title III? *See* Parks v. IBEW, 314 F.2d 886 (4th Cir. 1963), *cert. denied,* 372 U.S. 976 (1963). What about the forced merger of several separate locals into one? *Cf.* Brewery Bottlers Local 1345 v.

Teamsters, 202 F. Supp. 464 (E.D.N.Y. 1962). Would it make any difference in classification if a "receivership" was imposed by operation of state law rather than by act of an international? *See* Mills v. Collier, 56 L.R.R.M. 2894, 50 CCH LAB. CAS. ¶ 19,150 (S.D. Ind. 1964).

5. Could a parent union secure an injunction in federal court to *enforce* a trusteeship over a local, in order to prevent an unlawful strike? What would be the basis of jurisdiction? What would be the effect of the Norris-LaGuardia Act? *See* Letter Carriers v. Sombrotto, 449 F.2d 915 (2d Cir. 1971).

6. *See generally* Anderson, *Landrum-Griffin and the Trusteeship Imbroglio,* 71 YALE L.J. 1460 (1962); Beaird, *Union Trusteeship Provisions of the Labor-Management Reporting and Disclosure Act of 1959,* 2 GA. L. REV. 469 (1968); Bellace, *Union Trusteeships: Difficulties in Applying Sections 302 and 304(c) of the Landrum-Griffin Act,* 25 AM. U.L. REV. 337 (1976). Note, *A Fair Hearing Requirement for Union Trusteeships Under the LMRDA,* 40 U. CHI. L. REV. 873 (1973).

SECTION V. Unions and the Public

A. THE REGULATION OF RACKETEERING AND COMMUNIST ACTIVITY

1. BRIBERY AND EXTORTION

STATUTORY REFERENCES

LMRA § 302; LMRDA § 602

ARROYO v. UNITED STATES

Supreme Court of the United States
359 U.S. 419, 79 S. Ct. 864, 3 L. Ed. 2d 915 (1959)

MR. JUSTICE STEWART delivered the opinion of the Court.

The petitioner, a representative of employees in an industry affecting commerce, was convicted in the United States District Court for Puerto Rico of violating § 302(b) of the [LMRA] by receiving $15,000 from two of their employers. . . .

The facts are substantially undisputed. In 1953 the petitioner was president of a union which represented the employees of two affiliated corporations. In that capacity he negotiated a collective bargaining agreement with the employers. This agreement provided for the establishment of a welfare fund, which, it is unquestioned, met the requisite criteria of § 302(c)(5) of the Act. It was agreed that the petitioner would be the union representative on the joint committee which was to administer the fund. After the agreement was signed, the petitioner told the employers' representative that there was to be a union meeting that evening, and that he wanted to exhibit the welfare fund checks to the union members. Accordingly, the petitioner was given two checks for $7,500. Attached vouchers identified the checks as the employers' contributions to the welfare fund.

Instead of subsequently depositing the checks in the existing welfare fund bank account, however, the petitioner used them to open an account in the name of the fund in another bank. A few days thereafter, he gave the bank a purported resolution from the union's board of directors authorizing withdrawals from this account upon his signature alone. As soon as the employers learned what had happened, they attempted to secure performance of the agreement for joint administration of the fund. Over a period of several months, however, the petitioner used the money for his own personal purposes and, after transferring the funds to another account, for nonwelfare union purposes as well.

The Government does not maintain that embezzlement by an employee representative from an employer-financed welfare fund would violate the federal statute under which the petitioner was convicted. It contends, however, that in this case the jury could properly find that the petitioner when he accepted the two checks intended to use the funds for his personal purposes, and that he was therefore guilty not of embezzlement, but of conduct amounting to larceny by trick. We agree that the evidence could properly support an inference that the petitioner's purpose from the outset was to appropriate the two checks for his own use. We cannot agree, however, that this conduct violated § 302(b) of the Act.

Section 302(b) is a reciprocal of § 302(a), applicable to employers. . . . The good faith of the employers in delivering the two checks to the petitioner — their intent that the money go to the welfare fund created by the collective bargaining agreement — was not questioned throughout the trial and is not questioned here. The sole purpose of the delivery of the checks, therefore, was to make a lawful payment. What the petitioner received were checks "paid to a trust fund." The transaction, therefore, was within the precise language of § 302(c), and thus was not a violation of § 302(b).

This is not to say that the statute requires mutuality of guilt for the conviction of either the employer or the representative of employees. An employer might be guilty under subsection (a) if he paid money to a representative of employees even though the latter had no intention of accepting. . . . A representative might be guilty if he coerced payments from an innocent and unwilling employer. . . . Both would be guilty if the payment were ostensibly made for one of the lawful purposes specified in § 302(c) if both knew that such a purpose was merely a sham.

The present case, however, is not an analogue to any of those situations. The checks were drawn by the employers and delivered to the petitioner as payment to a union welfare fund. Their receipt by him, therefore, was not a violation of the federal statute, whether his intent to misappropriate existed at the time of receipt or was formed later. . . .

Throughout the debates in the Seventy-ninth and Eightieth Congresses there was not the slightest indication that § 302 was intended to duplicate state criminal laws. Those members of Congress who supported the amendment were concerned with corruption of collective bargaining through bribery of employee representatives by employers, with extortion by employee representatives, and with the possible abuse by union officers of the power which they might achieve if welfare funds were left to their sole control. Congressional attention was focused particularly upon the latter problem because of the demands which had then recently been made by a large international union for the establishment of a welfare fund to be financed by employers' contributions and administered exclusively by union officials. See United States v. Ryan, 350 U.S. 299.

Congress believed that if welfare funds were established which did not define with specificity the benefits payable thereunder, a substantial danger existed that such funds might be employed to perpetuate control of union officers, for political purposes, or even for personal gain. See 92 Cong. Rec. 4892-4894, 4899, 5181, 5345-5346; S. Rep. No. 105, 80th Cong., 1st Sess., at 52; 93 Cong. Rec. 4678, 4746-4747. To remove these dangers, specific standards were established to assure that welfare funds would be established only for purposes which Congress considered proper and expended only for the purposes for which they were established. See Cox, Some Aspects of the Labor Management Relations Act, 1947, 61 Harv. L. Rev. 274, 290. Continuing compliance with these standards in the administration of welfare funds was made explicitly enforceable in federal district courts by civil proceedings under § 302(e). The legislative history is devoid of any suggestion that defalcating trustees were to be held accountable under federal law, except by way of the injunctive remedy provided in that subsection.

Without doubt the petitioner's conduct was reprehensible and immoral. It can be assumed also that he offended local criminal law. But, for the reasons stated, we hold that he did not criminally violate § 302(b) of the Labor Management Relations Act of 1947.

Reversed.

MR. JUSTICE CLARK, with whom MR. JUSTICE FRANKFURTER, MR. JUSTICE DOUGLAS, and MR. JUSTICE WHITTAKER join, dissenting. . . .

I am sure that the Court agrees that the petitioner's conduct came within the "broad prohibition" of § 302(b). The only question, therefore, is whether he may properly be exculpated by the provisions of subsection (c)(5). . . . Two conclusions, implicitly drawn by the jury, emerge as indisputable when the evidence is compared with this subsection. In the first place, the statutory exception applies only when the money or other thing of value is "paid to a trust fund," and it is clear that insofar as a lawful fund was in existence the checks were not "paid" to it. They were made out payable to the union. Neither the checks nor the money from them ever came near the bona fide trust fund account at the Banco de Ponce. From the moment they were received by petitioner, he had complete control over them.

Secondly, even a casual reading of the subsection shows, as I am sure the Court itself would agree, that the spurious fund established by the petitioner in the National City Bank failed to comply with the statute in almost every respect. Since the checks were deposited in a union account and subject to the control of petitioner, the payments were not held in trust, as required by the subsection. Moreover, the fund which he created by depositing the checks was not subject to the administration of both the employees and the employers, but was subject to the sole control of the petitioner. As the judge instructed the jury, "a plan does not exist, lawfully exist, until it meets all those requirements" of the subsection. Since the sole purpose of the exception as set out in the Act was to permit the creation of a bona fide trust fund, it is obvious that the purposes of the Act were not complied with here because petitioner established no trust fund whatsoever. On the contrary, the checks were made payable to, and deposited in the name of, the union of which the petitioner was the President. His was the only authorized signature permitting withdrawals from the fund. In fact, the receipt of the checks by the petitioner as trust fund moneys was merely a sham. It does not matter what the intent of the employers was in delivering the checks since, as the Court itself says, the statute does not require mutuality of guilt. The petitioner, by receiving the checks from the employers and through artifice and deceit, has deprived the employees of their benefits and stands guilty under § 302(b) of the Act. . . .

NOTES

1. In Walsh v. Schlecht, 429 U.S. 401 (1977), the Supreme Court held that a provision in a construction industry collective agreement between a general contractor and the carpenters' union did not violate § 302(a)(1) of the Taft-Hartley Act but was permitted by § 302(c)(5) and (6). The agreement provided that when the general contractor used signatory carpenter subcontractors, they would be required to pay contributions at an aggregate rate of 96 cents per hour worked by carpenter employees to certain joint-trusteed pension and welfare funds. When he used a non-signatory carpenter subcontractor, he either had to require the sub to be bound by the agreement or else he had to maintain daily records of the subcontractor employees' hours and make the payments into the trust funds himself. The Court's interpretation was that the provision merely required the general contractor to make payments into the trust funds *measured* by the hours of carpentry work performed. If the provision were interpreted to require payments "on behalf of" or "for the benefit of" the employees of non-signatory carpenter employers, it would have run afoul of § 302(a)(1) and it would not have been protected by § 302(a)(5), since the employees of non-signatory employers are ineligible for benefits under such trust funds.

2. Does § 302(c)'s authorization for employer payments to joint union-employer trust funds maintained for certain specified purposes exclude by necessary implication payments to all other types of funds (for example, "industry promotion funds")? *Compare* Plasterers Local 2 v. Paramount Plastering, Inc., 310 F.2d 179 (9th Cir. 1962), *cert. denied,* 372 U.S. 944 (1963), *with* South Louisiana Chapter, Nat'l Elec. Contractors Ass'n v. IBEW Local 130, 177 F. Supp. 432 (E.D. La. 1959).

What about payments to a jointly administered trust fund providing welfare benefits for *retired* employees? Or including union officers and employees along with bargaining unit employees as beneficiaries? *See* Blassie v. Kroger Co., 345 F.2d 58 (8th Cir. 1965). *See also* Goetz, *Employee Benefit Trusts Under Section 302 of the Labor Management Relations Act,* 59 Nw. U.L. Rev. 719 (1965).

Problems of perceived overbreadth in § 302 have been dealt with by amendments adding new individual exceptions to subsection (c), for example, to authorize prepaid legal services plans. Does this seem an appropriate approach or does it suggest a fundamental defect in the structure of § 302? *See generally* Goetz, *Developing Federal Labor Law of Welfare and Pension Funds,* 55 Cornell L. Rev. 911 (1970); Note, *Taft-Hartley Regulation of Employer Payments to Union Representatives: Bribery, Extortion and Welfare Funds Under Section 302,* 67 Yale L.J. 732 (1958).

3. The Hobbs Anti-Racketeering Act, 18 U.S.C. § 1951 subjects anyone who "obstructs . . . commerce . . . by robbery or extortion" to a $10,000 fine and 20 years imprisonment. For definitional issues, *see* United States v. Enmons, 410 U.S. 396 (1973) (violence during lawful strike to secure legitimate bargaining demands); United States v. Green, 350 U.S. 415 (1956) (violence to obtain pay for unwanted and superfluous services).

What is the relationship between the Hobbs Act and the ban on "featherbedding" in § 8(b)(6) of the NLRA? *See* Note, *Labor Violence and the Hobbs Act: A Judicial Dilemma,* 67 Yale L.J. 325 (1957); Note, *Featherbedding and the Federal Anti-Racketeering Act,* 26 U. Chi. L. Rev. 150 (1958).

4. Section 602 of the LMRDA outlaws "extortionate picketing." When the provision was under consideration in 1959, Senator Kennedy explained it as follows:

"There has always been some question as to whether the Hobbs Act applied to cases in which violence did not take place. . . .

"This provision would not weaken or change the Hobbs Act. It would merely provide that when there is any question as to whether the Hobbs Act applies in cases in which violence does not occur — as in the case of shakedown picketing — adequate sanctions are provided." 105 Cong. Rec. 6530 (1959).

See generally Shade, *The Problem of Union Corruption and the Labor-Management Reporting and Disclosure Act of 1959,* 38 Texas L. Rev. 468 (1960). *See also* P. Taft, Corruption and Racketeering in the Labor Movement (1958).

2. RESTRICTIONS ON HOLDING OFFICE

Section 9(h) of the National Labor Relations Act, as added by the Taft-Hartley Act in 1947, required union officers to file non-Communist affidavits before their organizations could have access to the processes of the National Labor Relations Board. The constitutionality of this provision was upheld by the Supreme Court in *American Com-*

munications Ass'n v. Douds.[1] Section 9(h) was repealed in 1959 by the Labor-Management Reporting and Disclosure Act, which replaced the conditional limitation with an outright prohibition. Under § 504(a) of the LMRDA, no person may be a union officer or employee, except as a clerk or custodian, for five years from the time he held membership in the Communist Party, or from the time he was convicted of, or was imprisoned for, any of several specified crimes. Violation of § 504 is declared a criminal offense.

In *United States v. Brown,*[2] the Supreme Court held, with four justices dissenting, that § 504 was unconstitutional as a bill of attainder insofar as it applied to Communist Party members. *Douds* was distinguished in part on the ground it imposed an administrative restraint on the union rather than a criminal penalty on the individual officer. Although the Court made no reference to § 504's similar disqualification of persons convicted of various enumerated offenses, the emphasis on the evils of proscribing anyone simply on the basis of membership in a "political group" suggests that *Brown* would not be dispositive of the constitutionality of the section's anti-convict ban. Furthermore, § 504 would apparently not be vulnerable to attack as *ex post facto* legislation in its application to persons committing crimes prior to the passage of the LMRDA. In *DeVeau v. Braisted,*[3] the Supreme Court upheld a somewhat similar New York law, reasoning that it was designed primarily to safeguard unions against future abuses and not to punish the disqualified officials for past offenses.

In construing § 504's list of disqualifying offenses, the courts have taken a rather broad view toward including both federal and state crimes analogous to those specified.[4] It has also been held that the term "imprisonment" as used in § 504(a) includes any period of parole.[5]

B. UNION POLITICAL ACTION

Statutory Reference

LMRA § 304

Political action has been characteristic of the labor movement since its

---

[1] 339 U.S. 382 (1950).

[2] 380 U.S. 278 (1965). *See generally* D. Saposs, Communism in American Unions (1959).

[3] 363 U.S. 144 (1960).

[4] *E.g.,* Berman v. Teamsters, Local 107, 237 F. Supp. 767 (E.D. Pa. 1964) (conspiracy to cheat and defraud as "grand larceny"); Postma v. Teamsters, Local 294, 229 F. Supp. 655 (N.D.N.Y. 1964), *aff'd per curiam,* 337 F.2d 609 (2d Cir. 1964) (Hobbs Act violation as "extortion").

[5] Serio v. Liss, 300 F.2d 386 (3d Cir. 1961).

earliest days in this country.[6] There are traces of organized political activity on the part of unions as far back as the late 1820's and early 1830's, when workers' parties emerged briefly in Philadelphia, New York, and New England. Toward the end of the nineteenth century, the American Federation of Labor was formed, and, influenced by its first leader, Samuel Gompers, it adopted the political strategy of "rewarding" labor's friends and "punishing" its enemies, regardless of party affiliation. This became the traditional union approach to partisan politics, although in recent times organized labor has increasingly tended to support Democratic candidates.

Today virtually every labor organization — local or international — includes political action among its stated objectives. Unions have many reasons for being interested in politics in general and legislation in particular. They have a stake in wage and hour laws and in the laws governing the work of minorities, women, and children, not only for altruistic reasons but also because unregulated competition from any exploited class poses a constant threat to union standards. Social security in all its forms is one of the greatest desires of working people. Government policies on taxation, spending, and price control are also of vital significance, affecting as they do the distribution and purchasing power of income. And unions are naturally concerned about promoting labor relations legislation that will ensure the right to organize and bargain collectively. Since the merger of the AFL and the CIO in 1955, intensified political activity by the AFL-CIO Committee on Political Education (COPE) has been one of the more substantial accomplishments of the reunited federation.

Five states currently have laws restricting union political contributions or expenditures.[7] In addition, § 304 of the Taft-Hartley Act [8] forbade a labor organization to make a contribution or expenditure "in connection with" any federal election. But the Supreme Court held in *United States v. CIO* [9] that, in order to avoid constitutional questions, § 304 would not be interpreted as prohibiting an endorsement of a political candidate carried in a union newspaper circulated chiefly among the union's own membership. That decision set the pattern for restrictive readings of the statute. Section 304 has since been held inapplicable to political advertising through the commercial press and radio by a small union

---

[6] *See generally* F. DULLES, LABOR IN AMERICA 35-52 (1960); M. KARSON, AMERICAN LABOR UNIONS AND POLITICS, 1900-1918 (1958); J. RAYBACK, A HISTORY OF AMERICAN LABOR 23-36 (1959); C. REHMUS & D. McLAUGHLIN, LABOR AND AMERICAN POLITICS (1967).

[7] Arizona, Indiana, New Hampshire, Pennsylvania, and Texas. 4 LAB. REL. REP. SLL 1:50 (1979). Enactments or proposals in other states have been invalidated by the courts. *See* Alabama State Fed'n of Labor v. McAdory, 246 Ala. 1, 18 So. 2d 810 (1944), *cert. dismissed,* 325 U.S. 450 (1945); AFL v. Reilly, 113 Colo. 90, 155 P.2d 145 (1944); Bowe v. Secretary of Commonwealth, 320 Mass. 230, 69 N.E.2d 115 (1946); AFL v. Bain, 165 Ore. 183, 106 P.2d 544 (1940).

[8] Formerly 18 U.S.C. § 610; reenacted with amendments as 2 U.S.C. § 441(b).

[9] 335 U.S. 106 (1948).

having no newspaper of its own,[10] and to payments to union employees for time spent in political work.[11] In *United States v. UAW*,[12] however, the Supreme Court sustained under § 304 an indictment charging a union with having used union dues to sponsor commercial television broadcasts to influence the electorate in a congressional election. In the *UAW* case the Court refused to deal with the constitutional questions until after a trial.[13]

PIPEFITTERS LOCAL 562 v. UNITED STATES

Supreme Court of the United States
407 U.S. 385, 92 S. Ct. 2247, 33 L. Ed. 2d 11 (1972)

MR. JUSTICE BRENNAN delivered the opinion of the Court.

Petitioners — Pipefitters Local Union No. 562 and three individual officers of the Union — were convicted by a jury in the United States District Court for the Eastern District of Missouri of conspiracy under 18 U. S. C. § 371 to violate 18 U. S. C. § 610. At the time of trial § 610 provided in relevant part:

It is unlawful ... for any corporation whatever, or any labor organization to make a contribution or expenditure in connection with any election at which Presidential and Vice Presidential electors or a Senator or Representative in ... Congress are to be voted for, or in connection with any primary election or political convention or caucus held to select candidates for any of the foregoing offices. . . .

Every corporation or labor organization which makes any contribution or expenditure in violation of this section shall be fined not more than $5,000; and every officer or director of any corporation, or officer of any labor organization, who consents to any contribution or expenditure by the corporation or labor organization, as the case may be, ... in violation of this section, shall be fined not more than $1,000 or imprisoned not more than one year, or both; and if the violation was willful, shall be fined not more than $10,000 or imprisoned not more than two years, or both.

For the purposes of this section "labor organization" means any organization of any kind, or any agency or employee representation committee or plan, in which employees participate and which exist *[sic]* for the purpose, in whole or in part, of dealing with employers concerning grievances, labor disputes, wages, rates of pay, hours of employment, or conditions of work.

---

[10] United States v. Painters Local 481, 172 F.2d 854 (2d Cir. 1949).

[11] United States v. Laborers Local 264, 101 F. Supp. 869 (W.D. Mo. 1951).

[12] 352 U.S. 567 (1957).

[13] On remand to the district court for trial, the jury returned a verdict of not guilty. 41 L.R.R.M. 52 (1958).

The indictment charged, in essence, that petitioners had conspired from 1963 to May 9, 1968, to establish and maintain a fund that (1) would receive regular and systematic payments from Local 562 members and members of other locals working under the Union's jurisdiction; (2) would have the appearance, but not the reality of being an entity separate from the Union; and (3) would conceal contributions and expenditures by the Union in connection with federal elections in violation of § 610.

The evidence tended to show, in addition to disbursements of about $150,000 by the fund to candidates in federal elections, an identity between the fund and the Union and a collection of well over $1 million in contributions to the fund by a method similar to that employed in the collection of dues or assessments. In particular, it was established that from 1949 through 1962 the Union maintained a political fund to which Union members and others working under the Union's jurisdiction were in fact required to contribute and that the fund was then succeeded in 1963 by the present fund, which was, in form, set up as a separate "voluntary" organization. Yet, a principal Union officer assumed the role of director of the present fund with full and unlimited control over its disbursements. The Union's business manager, petitioner Lawler, became the first director of the fund and was later succeeded by petitioner Callanan, whom one Local 562 member described as "the Union" in explaining his influence within the local. Moreover, no significant change was made in the regular and systematic method of collection of contributions at a prescribed rate based on hours worked, and Union agents continued to collect donations at jobsites on Union time. In addition, changes in the rate of contributions were tied to changes in the rate of members' assessments. In 1966, for example, when assessments were increased from 2½% to 3¾% of gross wages, the contribution rate was decreased from $1 to 50¢ per day worked with the result that the change did not cause, in the words of the Union's executive board, "one extra penny cost to members of Local Union 562." At the same time, the contribution rate for nonmembers, who were not required to pay the prescribed travel card fee for working under Local 562's jurisdiction, remained the same at $2 per day worked, approximately matching the total assessment and contribution of members. Finally, in addition to political contributions, the fund used its monies for nonpolitical purposes, such as aid to financially distressed members on strike, and for a period of a few months, upon the vote of its members, even suspended collections in favor of contributions to a separate gift fund for petitioner Callanan. Not surprisingly, various witnesses testified that during the indictment period contributions to the fund were often still referred to as — and actually understood by some to be — assessments, or that they paid their contributions "voluntarily" in the same sense that they paid their dues or other financial obligations.

On the other hand, the evidence also indicated that the political contributions by the fund were made from accounts strictly segregated from Union dues and assessments and that donations to the fund were not, in fact, necessary for employment or Union membership. The fund generally required contributors to sign authorization cards, which contained a statement that their donations were "voluntary . . . [and] no part of the dues or financial obligations of Local Union No. 562 . . .," and the testimony was overwhelming from both those who contributed and those who did not, as well as from the collectors of contributions, that no specific pressure was exerted, and no reprisals were taken, to obtain donations. Significantly, the Union's attorney who had advised on the organization of the fund testified on cross-examination that his advice had been that payments to the fund could not be made a condition of employment or Local 562 membership, but it was immaterial whether contributions appeared compulsory to those solicited.

Under instructions to determine whether on this evidence the fund was in reality a Union fund or the contributors' fund, the jury found each defendant guilty. The jury also found specially that a willful violation of § 610 was not contemplated, and the trial court imposed sentence accordingly. The Union was fined $5,000, while the individual defendants were each sentenced to one year's imprisonment and fined $1,000. . . .

After we heard oral argument, the President on February 7, 1972, signed into law the Federal Election Campaign Act of 1971, which in § 205 amends 18 U. S. C. § 610, see *infra*, at 409-410, effective April 7, 1972. See Federal Election Campaign Act of 1971, § 406, 86 Stat. 20. We, accordingly, requested the parties to file supplemental briefs addressing the impact of that amendment on this prosecution. Having considered those briefs, we now hold that § 205 of the Federal Election Campaign Act merely codifies prior law with one possible exception pertinent to this case; that the change in the law, if in fact made, does not in any event require this prosecution to abate; but that the judgment below must, nevertheless, be reversed because of erroneous jury instructions. This disposition makes decision of the constitutional issues premature, and we therefore do not decide them. . . .

I. We begin with an analysis of § 610.

First. The parties are in agreement that § 610, despite its broad language, does not prohibit a labor organization from making, through the medium of a political fund organized by it, contributions or expenditures in connection with federal elections, so long as the monies expended are in some sense volunteered by those asked to contribute. . . .

The antecedents of § 610 have previously been traced in *United States v. Auto Workers* [352 U.S. 567 (1957)] and *United States v. CIO* [335 U.S. 106 (1948)]. We need recall here only that the prohibition in § 313 of the Federal Corrupt Practices Act of 1925, 43 Stat. 1074, on contributions by corporations in connection with federal elections was extended to labor organizations in the War Labor Disputes Act of 1943, 57 Stat. 163, but only for the duration of the war. As the Court noted in *CIO, supra,* at 115, "It was felt that the influence which labor unions exercised over elections through monetary expenditures should be minimized, and that it was unfair to individual union members to permit the union leadership to make contributions from general union funds to a political party which the individual member might oppose." The prohibition on contributions was then permanently enacted into law in § 304 of the Labor Management Relations Act, 1947, . . . with the addition, however, of a proscription on "expenditures" and an extension of both prohibitions to payments in connection with federal primaries and political conventions as well as federal elections themselves. Yet, neither prohibition applied to payments by union political funds in connection with federal elections so long as the funds were financed in some sense by the voluntary donations of the union membership. Union political funds had come to prominence in the 1944 and 1946 election campaigns and had been extensively studied by special committees of both the House and the Senate. Against the backdrop of the committee findings and recommendations, the Senate debates upon the reach of § 304 attached controlling significance to the voluntary source of financing of the funds. The unequivocal view of the proponents of § 304 was that the contributions and expenditures of voluntarily financed funds did not violate that provision. . . .

Thus, Senator Taft stated:

[I]t seems to me the conditions are exactly parallel, both as to corporations and labor organizations. [An association of manufacturers] receiving corporation funds and using them in an election would violate the law, in my opinion, exactly as the PAC, if it got its fund from labor unions, would violate the law. *If the labor people should desire to set up a political organization and obtain direct contributions for it, there would be nothing unlawful in that.* If the National Association of Manufacturers, we will say, wanted to obtain individual contributions for a series of advertisements, and if it, itself, were not a corporation, then, just as in the case of PAC, it could take an active part in a political campaign. 93 Cong. Rec. 6439 (1947) (emphasis added). . . .

Senator Taft's view that a union cannot violate the law by spending political funds volunteered by its members was consistent with the legislative history of the War Labor Disputes Act and an express interpretation given to that Act by the Attorney General in 1944. His view also reflected concern that a broader application of § 610 might raise constitutional questions of invasion of First Amendment freedoms, and he wished particularly to reassure colleagues who had reservations on that score and whose votes were necessary to override a predictable presidential veto, see 93 Cong. Rec. 7485, of the Labor Management Relations Act. We conclude, accordingly, that his view of the limited reach of § 610, entitled in any event to great weight, is in this instance controlling. . . . We therefore hold that § 610 does not apply to union contributions and expenditures from political funds financed in some sense by the voluntary donations of employees. Cf. United States v. Auto. Workers, 352 U.S. at 592; United States v. CIO, 335 U.S. at 123.

Section 205 of the Federal Election Campaign Act confirms this conclusion by adding at the end of § 610 the following paragraph:

> *As used in this section, the phrase "contribution or expenditure"* shall include any direct or indirect payment, distribution, loan, advance, deposit, or gift of money, or any services, or anything of value (except a loan of money by a national or State Bank made in accordance with the applicable banking laws and regulations and in the ordinary course of business) to any candidate, campaign committee, or political party or organization, in connection with any election to any of the offices referred to in this section; but *shall not include* communications by a corporation to its stockholders and their families or by a labor organization to its members and their families on any subject; nonpartisan registration and get-out-the-vote campaigns by a corporation aimed at its stockholders and their families, or by a labor organization aimed at its members and their families; *the establishment, administration, and solicitation of contributions to a separate segregated fund to be utilized for political purposes by a corporation or labor organization: Provided, That it shall be unlawful for such a fund to make a contribution or expenditure by utilizing money or anything of value secured by physical force, job discrimination, financial reprisals, or the threat of force, job discrimination, or financial reprisal; or by dues, fees, or other monies required as a condition of membership in a labor organization or as a condition of employment,* or by monies obtained in any commercial transaction. 86 Stat. 10 (emphasis added).

This amendment stemmed from a proposal offered by Representative Hansen on the House floor, see 117 Cong. Rec. H 11476, to which the Senate acquiesced in conference. See *id.* at H 12474 (joint conference committee report). Hansen stated that the purpose of his proposal was, with one exception not pertinent here, "to codify the court decisions interpreting [and the legislative history explicating] section 610 . . . and to spell out in more detail what a labor union or corporation can or cannot do in connection with a Federal election." Moreover, there was substantial agreement among his colleagues that the effect of his amendment was, in fact, mere codification and clarification, and even those who disagreed did not dispute that voluntarily financed union political funds are permissible. . . .

Second. Where the litigants part company is in defining precisely when political contributions and expenditures by a union political fund fall outside the ambit of § 610. The Government maintains, first, that a valid fund may not be the alter ego of the sponsoring union in the sense of being dominated by it and serving its purposes, regardless of the fund's source of financing. . . . The requirement that the fund be separate from the sponsoring union eliminates, in the Government's view, "the corroding effect of money employed in elections by aggregated powers," United States v. Auto. Workers, 352 U.S. at 582, which this Court has found to be one of the dual purposes underlying § 610. See *id., passim;* United States v. CIO, 335 U.S. at 113, 115. The Government urges, secondly, that in accordance with the legislative intent to protect minority interests from overbearing union leadership, which we have found to be the other purpose of § 610, see *ibid.,* the fund may not be financed by monies actually required for employment or union membership *or* by payments that are effectively assessed, that is, solicited in circumstances inherently coercive. Petitioners, on the other hand, contend that, to be valid, a political fund need not be distinct from the sponsoring union and, further, that § 610 permits the union to exercise institutional pressure, much as recognized charities do, in soliciting donations. . . .

We think that neither side fully and accurately portrays the attributes of legitimate political funds. We hold that such a fund must be separate from the sponsoring union only in the sense that there must be a strict segregation of its monies from union dues and assessments. We hold, too, that, although solicitation by union officials is permissible, such solicitation must be conducted under circumstances plainly indicating that donations are for a political purpose and that those solicited may decline to contribute without loss of job, union membership, or any other reprisal within the union's institutional power. Thus, we agree with the second half of the Government's position, but reject the first.

As Senator Taft's remarks quoted above indicate, . . . the test of voluntariness under § 610 focuses on whether the contributions solicited for political use are knowing free-choice donations. The dominant concern in requiring that contributions be voluntary was, after all, to protect the dissenting stockholder or union member. Whether the solicitation scheme is designed to inform the individual solicited of the political nature of the fund and his freedom to refuse support is, therefore, determinative.

Nowhere, however, has Congress required that the political organization be formally or functionally independent of union control or that union officials be barred from soliciting contributions or even precluded from determining how the monies raised will be spent. The Government's argument to the contrary in the first half of its position is based on a misunderstanding of the purposes of § 610. When Congress prohibited labor organizations from making contributions or expenditures in connection with federal elections, it was, of course, concerned not only to protect minority interests within the union but to eliminate the effect of aggregated wealth on federal elections. But the aggregated wealth it plainly had in mind was the general union treasury — not the funds donated by union members of their own free and knowing choice. Again, Senator Taft adamantly maintained that labor organizations were not prohibited from expending those monies in connection with federal elections. Indeed, Taft clearly espoused the union political organization merely as an alternative to permissible direct political action by the union itself through publications endorsing candidates in federal elections. The only conditions for that kind of direct electioneering were that the costs of publication be financed through individual subscriptions rather than through union dues and that the newspapers be recognized by the subscribers as political organs that they could refuse to purchase. Neither the absence of even a formally separate organization, the solicitation of subscriptions by the union, nor the method for choosing the candidates to be supported was mentioned as being material. Similarly, the only requirements for permissible political organizations were that they be funded through separate contributions and that they be recognized by the donors as political organizations to which they could refuse support. . . .

This conclusion, too, we find confirmed by § 205 of the Federal Election Campaign Act. . . . Thus, § 205 plainly permits union officials to establish, administer, and solicit contributions for a political fund. The conditions for that activity are that the fund be "separate" and "segregated" and that its contributions and expenditures not be financed through physical force, job discrimination, or financial reprisal or the "threat" thereof, or through "dues, fees, or other monies required as a condition of membership in a labor organization or as a condition of employment." The quoted language is admittedly subject to contrary interpretations. "Separate" could (and normally when juxtaposed to "segregated" would) be read to mean an apartness beyond "segregated"; "threat" could be construed as referring only to the expression of an actual intention to inflict injury; and "dues, fees, or other monies required as a condition of membership in a labor organization or as a condition of employment" could be interpreted to mean only actual dues or assessments. But we think that the legislative history of § 205 establishes that "separate" is synonymous with "segregated"; that "threat" includes the creation of an appearance of an intent to inflict injury even without a design to carry it out; and that "dues, fees, or other monies required as a condition of membership in a labor organization or as a condition of employment" includes contributions effectively assessed even if not actually required for employment or union membership. . . .

Third. Arguably, however, there is one change effected by § 205 material to this case, and that is with regard to the *use* of general union monies for the establishment, administration, and solicitation of contributions for political funds. Section 304 of the Labor Management Relations Act may be interpreted to prohibit such use, while the Hansen amendment plainly permits it. . . .

Thus, § 205 may in one respect have impliedly repealed the substantive law relating to this prosecution. But we need not now decide that question, because even if there has been such an implied repeal, it would not affect this prosecution for reasons to which we now turn. . . .

[The Court concluded that there need be no abatement of the prosecution because of the federal saving statute, 1 U. S. C. § 109.]

III. The Government urges:

The essential charge of the indictment and the theory on which the case was tried was that the [Pipefitters] Fund, although formally set up as an entity independent of Local 562, *was in fact a union fund, controlled by the union,* contributions to which were assessed by the union as part of its dues structure, collected from non-members in lieu of dues, and expended, when deemed necessary, for union purposes and the personal use of the directors of the Fund. Brief for the United States 23 (emphasis added). . . .

This was indeed, as we shall shortly see, the theory on which the indictment was drawn, the jury was instructed, and petitioners' convictions were affirmed. It is also the construction of § 610 that we have rejected in favor of the Government's narrower construction that the prerequisite for a permissible political fund is simply that it not be financed by actual or effective dues or assessments. . . . On the other hand, we find that the indictment may be read to allege not only that the Pipefitters fund was "a union fund, controlled by the union," but that "contributions to [it] were assessed by the union as part of its dues structure, [and were] collected from non-members in lieu of dues . . . ." . . . [H]owever, we do not now construe the indictment as making this essential allegation, but leave that question open for determination on remand. We hold now only that the jury instructions failed to require proof of the essential element for conviction, and hence reverse the judgment below. . . .

Second. The jury instructions embody an interpretation of § 610 that is plainly erroneous. The trial court refused requests by petitioners for instructions that the jury should acquit if it found that contributions to the Pipefitters fund were made voluntarily. Adopting a contrary view, the court instructed the jury, over petitioners' objections, that it should return verdicts of guilty if the fund "was in fact a union fund, . . . the money therein was union money, and . . . the real contributor to the candidates was the union." "In determining whether the Pipefitters Voluntary Fund was a bona fide fund, separate and distinct from the union or a mere artifice or device," the jury was further instructed to "take into consideration all the facts and circumstances in evidence, and in such consideration . . . [to] consider" 19 factors, several of which related to the regularity, rate, method of collection, and segregation from Union monies of payments to the fund. Others concerned the kinds of expenditures the fund made and the Union's control over them. Still others involved whether the payments to the fund were made voluntarily. In the latter regard the court charged (emphasis added):

> A great deal of evidence has been introduced on the question of whether the payments into the Pipefitters Voluntary . . . Fund by members of Local 562 and others working under its jurisdiction were voluntary or involuntary. This evidence is relevant for your consideration, along with all other facts and circumstances in evidence, in determining whether the fund is a union fund. *However, the mere fact that the payments into the fund may have been made voluntarily by some or even all of the contributors thereto does not, of itself, mean that the money so paid into the fund was not union money. . . .*

The instructions, as the Court of Appeals confirmed, clearly permitted the jury to convict without finding that donations to the Pipefitters fund had been actual or effective dues or assessments. This was plain error.

The judgment of the Court of Appeals as to petitioners Callanan and Lawler is vacated, and the case is remanded to the District Court with directions to dismiss the indictment against them. . . . The judgment of the Court of Appeals as to petitioners Local 562 and Seaton is reversed, and the case is remanded to the District Court for proceedings as to them consistent with this opinion.

It is so ordered.

MR. JUSTICE BLACKMUN took no part in the consideration or decision of this case.

MR. JUSTICE POWELL, with whom THE CHIEF JUSTICE joins, dissenting.

The decision of the Court today will have a profound effect upon the role of labor unions and corporations in the political life of this country. The holding, reversing a trend since 1907, opens the way for major participation in politics by the largest aggregations of economic power, the great unions and corporations. This occurs at a time, paradoxically, when public and legislative interest has focused on limiting — rather than enlarging — the influence upon the elective process of concentrations of wealth and power.

I. . . . In its preoccupation with the legislative history, the Court has overlooked the central point involved in this case: that the conviction of petitioners accords with the plain language of the controlling statute. Nor does the majority demonstrate an ambiguity in that statutory language that makes relevant its long journey into the legislative history.

The operative language of § 610 states that: "It is unlawful . . . for any corporation whatever, or any labor organization to make a contribution or expenditure in connection with" any federal election. Despite this unqualified proscription, the majority opinion sustains the right of unions and corporations to make political contributions *directly,* provided only that the funds therefor come voluntarily from members, employees, or stockholders and are maintained separately from the other funds of the union or corporation. . . .

If words are given their normal meaning, the statute and the Court's holding flatly contradict each other. One says that it shall be unlawful for a union to make a political contribution or expenditure. The other says this is perfectly lawful, so long as the funds which the union contributes or expends were donated freely and knowingly. The Court has simply added a qualification, not found in the statutory language, which significantly changes the meaning of this Act of the Congress.

The Court's holding, moreover, directly counters the purposes for which § 610 was enacted. Congress passed this legislation to restrict and minimize the influence corporations and unions might exert on elections. . . .

The two principal motivations for the enactment of § 610, as identified in *CIO,* are (i) the minimizing of influence of labor unions (as well as corporations) on elections "through monetary expenditures"; and (ii) the elimination of the unfairness "to individual union members" of allowing union management to make political contributions from general union funds. It seems self-evident that both of these legislative purposes will be frustrated by the Court's holding that, despite the language of the statute forbidding union contributions, unions may now make political contributions and expenditures, provided only that the source of a fund is voluntary. . . .

II. Accepting, as I think we must, § 610 as written, the issue in this case is whether the political fund of Local 562 was in reality a sham or subterfuge through which the union itself made the contributions forbidden by the statute. The indictment in this case was framed on this basis, and the jury was so instructed. The question properly addressed by the Court of Appeals was "whether the contributions or expenditures were [in fact] made by a labor organization." 434 F. 2d 1116, 1121 (1970). After summarizing the evidence submitted to the jury on this issue, the Court of Appeals concluded:

> There is substantial evidence to support a jury finding that the fund was not a bona fide separate and distinct entity but was in fact a device set up to circumvent the provisions of § 610 and that the fund constituted union money. 434 F. 2d, at 1121.

The majority opinion of this Court does not contest this view. It concludes, rather, that the jury was erroneously instructed, and that accordingly the verdict and judgment must be set aside. If a new trial is held, the jury must be instructed in accordance with the Court's interpretation of § 610 that a union may lawfully make political contributions from a fund it collects and administers so long as the payments into it are voluntary.

It is from this interpretation of § 610 — one which in my view will render the statute largely ineffectual — that I dissent. . . .

NOTES

1. Prior to the decision in the principal case, a federal district court had held that § 304 did not prohibit union contributions or expenditures from that portion of membership dues voluntarily designated for political purposes by individual members. United States v. Teamsters Local 688, 47 L.R.R.M. 2005, 41 CCH Lab. Cas. ¶ 16,601 (E.D. Mo. 1960). Is that ruling still the law? *See* Barber v. Gibbons, 367 F.Supp. 1102 (E.D. Mo. 1973).

2. The implications of *Pipefitters* are probed in Note, *Of Politics, Pipefitters, and Section 610: Union Political Contributions in Modern Context,* 51 Texas L. Rev. 936 (1973). For analyses of earlier developments, *see* Kallenbach, *The Taft-Hartley Act and Union Political Contributions and Expenditures,* 33 Minn. L. Rev. 1 (1948); Ruark, *Labor's Political Spending and Free Speech,* 53 Nw. U.L. Rev. 61 (1958).

3. In Buckley v. Valeo, 424 U.S. 1 (1976), the Supreme Court addressed the constitutionality of the Federal Election Campaign Act of 1971 and 1974. The Court invalidated limitations on individual political campaign expenditures but sustained various limitations on political contributions. Subsequently, in First Nat. Bank of Boston v. Bellotti, 435 U.S. 765

(1978), the Court held that a state statute forbidding expenditures by banks and certain business corporations for the purpose of influencing votes on referendum proposals, other than those affecting the business of the corporation, was an unconstitutional abridgment of free speech. Do *Buckley* and *Bellotti* taken together cast serious doubt on the constitutionality of the anti-expenditure provisions of Taft-Hartley's § 304 (reenacted as 2 U.S.C. § 441(b))? *Buckley* is noted in 76 COLUM. L. REV. 862 (1976); 90 HARV. L. REV. 171 (1976); 75 MICH. L. REV. 627 (1977); 1976 SUP. CT. REV. 1. *See also* Fleishman, *The 1974 Federal Elections Campaign Act Amendments: The Shortcomings of Good Intentions,* 1975 DUKE L.J. 851.

INTERNATIONAL ASS'N OF MACHINISTS v. STREET

Supreme Court of the United States
367 U.S. 740, 81 S. Ct. 1784, 6 L. Ed. 2d 1141 (1961)

MR. JUSTICE BRENNAN delivered the opinion of the Court.

A group of labor organizations, appellants here, and the carriers comprising the Southern Railway System, entered into a union-shop agreement pursuant to the authority of § 2, Eleventh of the Railway Labor Act. The agreement requires each of the appellees, employees of the carriers, as a condition of continued employment, to pay the appellant union representing his particular class or craft the dues, initiation fees and assessments uniformly required as a condition of acquiring or retaining union membership. The appellees, in behalf of themselves and of employees similarly situated, brought this action in the Superior Court of Bibb County, Georgia, alleging that the money each was thus compelled to pay to hold his job was in substantial part used to finance the campaigns of candidates for federal and state offices whom he opposed, and to promote the propagation of political and economic doctrines, concepts and ideologies with which he disagreed. The Superior Court found that the allegations were fully proved and entered a judgment and decree enjoining the enforcement of the union-shop agreement on the ground that § 2, Eleventh violates the Federal Constitution to the extent that it permits such use by the appellants of the funds exacted from employees. The Supreme Court of Georgia affirmed, 215 Ga. 27, 108 S.E.2d 796 (1959)....

I. THE HANSON DECISION. We held in Railway Employees' Dep't v. Hanson, 351 U.S. 225 (1956), that enactment of the provision of § 2, Eleventh authorizing union-shop agreements between interstate railroads and unions of their employees was a valid exercise by Congress of its powers under the Commerce Clause and did not violate the First Amendment or the Due Process Clause of the Fifth Amendment. It is argued that our disposition of the First Amendment claims in *Hanson* disposes of appellees' constitutional claims in this case adversely to their contentions. We disagree. As appears from its history, that case decided only that § 2, Eleventh, in authorizing collective agreements conditioning employees' continued employment on payment of union dues, initiation fees and assessments, did not on its face impinge upon protected rights of association. . . . We clearly passed neither upon forced association in any other aspect nor upon the issue of the use of exacted money for political causes which were opposed by the employees.

The record in this case is adequate squarely to present constitutional questions reserved in *Hanson*. These are questions of the utmost gravity. However, the restraints against unnecessary constitutional decision counsel against their determination unless we must conclude that Congress, in authorizing a union shop under § 2, Eleventh, also meant that the labor organization receiving an employee's money should be free, despite that employee's objection, to spend his money for political causes which he opposes. Federal statutes are to be so construed as to avoid serious doubt of their constitutionality. "When the validity of an Act of the Congress is drawn in question, and even if a serious doubt of constitutionality is raised, it is a cardinal principle that this Court will first ascertain whether a construction of the statute is fairly possible by which the question may be avoided." Crowell v. Benson, 285 U.S. 22, 62 (1932). Each named appellee in this action has made known to the union representing his craft or class his dissent from the use of his money for political causes which he opposes. We have therefore examined the legislative history of § 2, Eleventh in the context of the development of unionism in the railroad industry under the regulatory scheme created by the Railway Labor Act to determine whether a construction is "fairly possible" which denies the authority to a union, over the employee's objection, to spend his money for political causes which he opposes. We conclude that such a construction is not only "fairly possible" but entirely reasonable, and we therefore find it unnecessary to decide the correctness of the constitutional determinations made by the Georgia courts.

II. THE RAIL UNIONS AND UNION SECURITY. The history of union security in the railway industry is marked *first,* by a strong and long-standing tradition of voluntary unionism on the part of the standard rail unions; *second,* by the declaration in 1934 of a congressional policy of complete freedom of choice of employees to join or not to join a union; *third,* by the modification of the firm legislative policy against compulsion, but only as a specific response to the recognition of the expenses and burdens incurred by the unions in the administration of the complex scheme of the Railway Labor Act. . . .

A primary purpose of the major revisions made in 1934 was to strengthen the position of the labor organizations *vis-a-vis* the carriers, to the end of furthering the success of the basic congressional policy of self-adjustment of the industry's labor problems between carrier organizations and effective labor organizations. The unions claimed that the carriers interfered with the employees' freedom of choice of representatives by creating company unions, and otherwise attempting to undermine the employees' participation in the process of collective bargaining. Congress amended § 2, Third to reinforce the prohibitions against interference with the choice of representatives of the employees to select nonemployee representatives. A new § 2, Fourth was added guaranteeing employees the right to organize and bargain collectively, and Congress made it the enforceable duty of the carriers "to treat with" the representatives of the employees, § 2, Ninth. See Virginian Ry. v. System Federation, etc., 300 U.S. 515 (1937). It was made explicit that the representative selected by a majority of any class or craft of employees should be the exclusive bargaining representative of all the employees of that craft or class. . . . In addition to thus strengthening the unions' status in relation to both the carriers and the employees, the 1934 Act created the National Railroad Adjustment Board and provided that the 18 employee representatives were to be chosen by the labor organizations national in scope. § 3. This Board was given jurisdiction to settle what are termed minor disputes in the railroad industry, primarily grievances arising from the application of collective bargaining agreements to particular situations. See Union Pacific R.R. v. Price, 360 U.S. 601 (1959).

In sum, in prescribing collective bargaining as the method of settling railway disputes, in conferring upon the unions the status of exclusive representatives in the negotiation and administration of collective agreements, and in giving them representation on the statutory board to adjudicate grievances, Congress has given the unions a clearly defined and delineated role to play in effectuating the basic congressional policy of stabilizing labor relations in the industry. . . .

Performance of these functions entails the expenditure of considerable funds. Moreover, this Court has held that under the statutory scheme, a union's status as exclusive bargaining representative carries with it the duty fairly and equitably to represent all employees of the craft or class, union and nonunion. Steele v. Louisville & N.R.R., [323 U.S. 192 (1944)]; Tunstall v. Brotherhood of Locomotive Firemen & Enginemen, 323 U.S. 210 (1944). The principal argument made by the unions in 1950 was based on their role in this regulatory framework. They maintained that because of the expense of performing their duties in the congressional scheme, fairness justified the spreading of the costs to all employees who benefited. They thus advanced as their purpose the elimination of the "free riders" — those employees who obtained the benefits of the unions' participation in the machinery of the Act without financially supporting the unions. . . .

This argument was decisive with Congress. The House Committee Report traced the history of previous legislation in the industry and pointed out the duty of the union acting as exclusive bargaining representative to represent equally all members of the class. . . . These considerations overbore the arguments in favor of the earlier policy of complete individual freedom of choice. . . . The conclusion to which this history clearly points is that § 2, Eleventh contemplated compulsory unionism to force employees to share the costs of negotiating and administering collective agreements, and the costs of the adjustment and settlement of disputes. One looks in vain for any suggestion that Congress also meant in § 2, Eleventh to provide the unions with a means for forcing employees, over their objection, to support political causes which they oppose.

III. THE SAFEGUARDING OF RIGHTS OF DISSENT. To the contrary, Congress incorporated safeguards in the statute to protect dissenters' interests. Congress became concerned during the hearings and debates that the union shop might be used to abridge freedom of speech and beliefs. The original proposal for authorization of the union shop was qualified in only one respect. It provided "That no such agreement shall require such condition of employment with respect to employees to whom membership is not available upon the same terms and conditions as are generally applicable to any other member. . . ." This was primarily designed to prevent discharge of employees for nonmembership where the union did not admit the employee to membership on racial grounds. See House Hearings at 68; Senate Hearings at 22-25. But it was strenuously protested that the proposal provided no protection for an employee who disagreed with union policies or leadership. It was argued, for example, that "the right of free speech is at stake. . . . A man could feel that he was no longer able freely to express himself because he could be dismissed on account of criticism of the union. . . ." House Hearings at 115; see also Senate Hearings at 167-169, 320. Objections of this kind led the rail unions to propose an addition to the proviso to § 2, Eleventh to prevent loss of job for nonunion membership "with respect to employees to whom membership was denied or terminated for any reason other than the failure of the employee to tender the periodic dues, fees, and assessments uniformly required as a condition of acquiring or retaining membership." House Hearings at 247. Mr. Harrison presented this text and stated, "It is submitted that this bill with the amendment as suggested in this statement remedies the alleged abuses of compulsory union membership as claimed by the opposing witnesses, yet makes possible the elimination of the 'free rider' and the sharing of the burden of maintenance by all the beneficiaries of union activity." House Hearings at 253. . . .

A congressional concern over possible impingements on the interests of individual dissenters from union policies is therefore discernible. It is true that opponents of the union shop urged that Congress should not allow it without explicitly regulating the amount of dues which might be exacted or prescribing the uses for which the dues might be expended. We may assume that Congress was also fully conversant with the long history of intensive involvement of the railroad unions in political activities. But it does not follow that § 2, Eleventh places no restriction on the use of an employee's money, over his objection, to support political causes he opposes merely because Congress did not enact a comprehensive regulatory scheme governing expenditures. For it is abundantly clear that Congress did not completely abandon the policy of full freedom of choice embodied in the 1934 Act, but rather made inroads on it for the limited purpose of eliminating the problems created by the "free rider." That policy survives in § 2, Eleventh in the safeguards intended to protect freedom of dissent. . . . We respect this congressional purpose when we construe § 2, Eleventh as not vesting the unions with unlimited power to spend exacted money. We are not called upon to delineate the precise limits of that power in this case. We have before us only the question whether the power is restricted to the extent of denying the unions the right, over the employee's objection, to use his money to support political causes which he opposes. Its use to support candidates for public office, and advance political programs, is not a use which helps defray the expenses of the negotiation or administration of collective agreements, or the expenses entailed in the adjustment of grievances and disputes. In other words, it is a use which falls clearly outside the reasons advanced by the unions and accepted by Congress why authority to make union-shop agreements was justified. On the other hand, it is equally clear that it is a use to support activities within the area of dissenters' interests which Congress enacted the proviso to protect. We give § 2, Eleventh the construction which achieves both congressional purposes when we hold, as we do, that § 2, Eleventh is to be construed to deny the unions, over an employee's objection, the power to use his exacted funds to support political causes which he opposes. . . .

IV. THE APPROPRIATE REMEDY. Under our view of the statute, however, the decision of the court below was erroneous and cannot stand. The appellees who have participated in this action have in the course of it made known to their respective unions their objection to the use of their money for the support of political causes. In that circumstance, the respective unions were without power to use payments thereafter tendered by them for such political causes. However, the union-shop agreement itself is not unlawful. *Railway Employees' Dep't v. Hanson, supra.* The appellees therefore remain obliged, as a condition of continued employment, to make the payments to their respective unions called for by the agreement. Their right of action stems not from constitutional limitations on Congress' power to authorize the union shop, but from § 2, Eleventh itself. In other words, appellees' grievance stems from the spending of their funds for purposes not authorized by the Act in the face of their objection, not from the enforcement of the union-shop agreement by the mere collection of funds. If their money were used for purposes contemplated by § 2, Eleventh, the appellees would have no grievance at all. We think that an injunction restraining enforcement of the union-shop agreement is therefore plainly not a remedy appropriate to the violation of the Act's restriction on expenditures. Restraining the collection of all funds from the appellees sweeps too broadly, since their objection is only to the uses to which some of their money is put. Moreover, restraining collection of the funds as the Georgia courts have done might well interfere with the appellant unions' performance of those functions and duties which the Railway Labor Act places upon them to attain its goal of stability in the industry. . . .

Since the case must therefore be remanded to the court below for consideration of a proper remedy, we think that it is appropriate to suggest the limits within which remedial discretion may be exercised consistently with the Railway Labor Act and other relevant public policies. As indicated, an injunction against enforcement of the union shop itself through the collection of funds is unwarranted. We also think that a blanket injunction against all expenditures of funds for the disputed purposes, even one conditioned on cessation of improper expenditures, would not be a proper exercise of equitable discretion. Nor would it be proper to issue an interim or temporary blanket injunction of this character pending a final adjudication. The Norris-La Guardia Act . . . expresses a basic policy against the injunction of activities of labor unions. We have held that the Act does not deprive the federal courts of jurisdiction to enjoin compliance with various mandates of the Railway Labor Act. Virginian R. Co. v. System Federation, 300 U.S. 515 (1937). . . . However, the policy of the Act suggests that the courts should hesitate to fix upon the injunctive remedy for breaches of duty owing under the labor laws unless that remedy alone can effectively guard the plaintiff's right. . . . Moreover, the fact that these expenditures are made for political activities is an additional reason for reluctance to impose such an injunctive remedy. Whatever may be the powers of Congress or the States to forbid unions altogether to make various types of political expenditures, as to which we express no opinion here, many of the expenditures involved in the present case are made for the purpose of disseminating information as to candidates and programs and publicizing the positions of the unions on them. As to such expenditures an injunction would work a restraint on the expression of political ideas which might be offensive to the First Amendment. For the majority also has an interest in stating its views without being silenced by the dissenters. To attain the appropriate reconciliation between majority and dissenting interests in the area of political expression, we think the courts in administering the Act should select remedies which protect both interests to the maximum extent possible without undue impingement of one on the other.

Among possible remedies which would appear appropriate to the injury complained of, two may be enforced with a minimum of administrative difficulty and with little danger of encroachment on the legitimate activities or necessary functions of the unions. Any remedies, however, would properly be granted only to employees who have made known to the union officials that they do not desire their funds to be used for political causes to which they object. The safeguards of § 2, Eleventh were added for the protection of dissenters' interest, but dissent is not to be presumed — it must affirmatively be made known to the union by the dissenting employee. The union receiving money exacted from an employee under a union-shop agreement should not in fairness be subjected to sanctions in favor of an employee who makes no complaint of the use of his money for such activities. . . .

One remedy would be an injunction against expenditure for political causes opposed by the complaining employee of a sum, from those moneys to be spent by the union for political purposes, which is so much of the moneys exacted from him as is the proportion of the union's total expenditures made for such political activities to the union's total budget. The union should not be in a position to make up such sum from money paid by a nondissenter, for this would shift a disproportionate share of the costs of collective bargaining to the dissenter and have the same effect of applying his money to support such political activities. A second remedy would be restitution to an individual employee of that portion of his money which the union expended, despite his notification, for the political causes to which he had advised the union he was opposed. There should be no necessity, however, for the employee to trace his money up to and including its expenditure; if the money goes into general funds and no separate accounts of receipts and expenditures of the funds of individual employees are maintained, the portion of his money the employee would be entitled to recover would be in the same proportion that the expenditures for political purposes which he had advised the union he disapproved bore to the total union budget.

The judgment is reversed and the case is remanded to the court below for proceedings not inconsistent with this opinion.

Reversed and remanded.

[Mr. Justice Douglas concurred.]

Mr. Justice Black, dissenting. . . .

I. Section 2, Eleventh of the Railway Labor Act authorizes unions and railroads to make union-shop agreements notwithstanding any other provision of state or federal law. Such a contract simply means that no person can keep a job with the contracting railroad unless he becomes a member of and pays dues to the contracting union. Neither § 2, Eleventh nor any other part of the Act contains any implication or even a hint that Congress wanted to limit the purposes for which a contracting union's dues should or could be spent. All the parties to this litigation have agreed from its beginning, and still agree, that there is no such limitation in the Act. The Court nevertheless, in order to avoid constitutional questions, interprets the Act itself as barring use of dues for political purposes. In doing this I think the Court is once more "carrying the doctrine of avoiding constitutional questions to a wholly unjustifiable extreme." In fact, I think the Court is actually rewriting § 2, Eleventh to make it mean exactly what Congress refused to make it mean. . . . I must consider this case on the basis of my belief as to the constitutionality of § 2, Eleventh, interpreted so as to authorize compulsion of workers to pay dues to a union for use in advocating causes and political candidates that the protesting workers are against. . . .

III. . . . The Court holds that § 2, Eleventh denies "unions, over an employee's objection, the power to use his exacted funds to support political causes which he opposes." While I do not so construe § 2, Eleventh, I want to make clear that I believe the First Amendment bars use of dues extorted from an employee by law for the promotion of causes, doctrines and laws that unions generally favor to help the unions, as well as any other political purposes. I think workers have as much right to their own views about matters affecting unions as they have to views about other matters in the fields of politics and economics. Indeed, some of their most strongly held views are apt to be precisely on the subject of unions, just as questions of law reform, court procedure, selection of judges and other aspects of the "administration of justice" give rise to some of the deepest and most irreconcilable differences among lawyers. In my view, § 2, Eleventh can constitutionally authorize no more than to make a worker pay dues to a union for the sole purpose of defraying the cost of acting as his bargaining agent. Our Government has no more power to compel individuals to support union programs or union publications than it has to compel the support of political programs, employer programs or church programs. And the First Amendment, fairly construed, deprives the Government of all power to make any person pay out one single penny against his will to be used in any way to advocate doctrines or views he is against, whether economic, scientific, political, religious or any other.

I would therefore hold that § 2, Eleventh of the Railway Labor Act, in authorizing application of the union-shop contract to the named protesting employees who are appellees here, violates the freedom of speech guarantee of the First Amendment. . . .

MR. JUSTICE FRANKFURTER, whom MR. JUSTICE HARLAN joins, dissenting. . . .

I completely defer to the guiding principle that this Court will abstain from entertaining a serious constitutional question when a statute may fairly be construed so as to avoid the issue, but am unable to accept the restrictive interpretation that the Court gives to § 2, Eleventh of the Railway Labor Act. . . . The Court-devised precept against avoidable conflict with Congress through unnecessary constitutional adjudication is not a requirement to distort an enactment in order to escape such adjudication. Respect for the doctrine demands and only permits that we extract an interpretation which shies off constitutional controversy, *provided* such interpretation is consonant with a fair reading of a statute.

And so the question before us is whether § 2, Eleventh of the Railway Labor Act can untorturingly be read to bar activities of railway unions, which have bargained in accordance with federal law for a union shop, whereby they are forbidden to spend union dues for purposes that have uniformly and extensively been so long pursued as to have become commonplace, settled, conventional trade-union practices. No consideration relevant to construction sustains such a restrictive reading.

. . . The aim of the 1951 legislation, clearly stated in the congressional reports, was to eliminate "free riders" in the industry — to make possible "the sharing of the burden of maintenance by all of the beneficiaries of union activity." To suggest that this language covertly meant to encompass any less than the maintenance of those activities normally engaged in by unions is to withdraw life from law and to say that Congress dealt with artificialities and not with railway unions as they were and as they functioned. . . .

For us to hold that these defendant unions may not expend their moneys for political and legislative purposes would be completely to ignore the long history of union conduct and its pervasive acceptance in our political life. American labor's initial role in shaping legislation dates back 130 years. With the coming of the AFL in 1886, labor on a national scale was committed not to act as a class party but to maintain a program of political action in furtherance of its industrial standards. British trade unions were supporting members of the House of Commons as early as 1867. The Canadian Trades Congress in 1894 debated whether political action should be the main objective of the labor force. And in a recent

Australian case, the High Court upheld the right of a union to expel a member who refused to pay a political levy. That Britain, Canada and Australia have no explicit First Amendment is beside the point. For one thing, the freedoms safeguarded in terms in the First Amendment are deeply rooted and respected in the British tradition, and are part of legal presuppositions in Canada and Australia. And in relation to our immediate concern, the British Commonwealth experience establishes the pertinence of political means for realizing basic trade-union interests.

The expenditures revealed by the AFL-CIO Executive Council Reports emphasize that labor's participation in urging legislation and candidacies is a major one. In the last three fiscal years, the Committee on Political Education (COPE) expended a total of $1,681,990.42; the AFL-CIO News cost $756,591.99; the Legislative Department reported total expenses of $741,918.24. Yet the Georgia trial court has found that these funds were not reasonably related to the unions' role as collective bargaining agents. One could scarcely call this a finding of fact by which this Court is bound, or even one of law. It is a baseless dogmatic assertion that flies in the face of fact. It rests on a mere listing of unions' expenditures and an exhibit of labor publications. The passage of the Adamson Act in 1916, establishing the eight-hour day for the railroad industry, affords positive proof that labor may achieve its desired result through legislation after bargaining techniques fail. . . . If higher wages and shorter hours are prime ends of a union in bargaining collectively, these goals may often be more effectively achieved by lobbying and the support of sympathetic candidates. In 1960 there were at least eighteen railway labor organizations registered as congressional lobby groups. . . .

In conclusion, then, we are asked by union members who oppose these expenditures to protect their right to free speech — although they are as free to speak as ever — against governmental action which has permitted a union elected by democratic process to bargain for a union shop and to expend the funds thereby collected for purposes which are controlled by internal union choice. To do so would be to mutilate a scheme designed by Congress for the purpose of equitably sharing the cost of securing the benefits of union exertions; it would greatly embarrass if not frustrate conventional labor activities which have become institutionalized through time. To do so is to give constitutional sanction to doctrinaire views and to grant a minuscule claim constitutional recognition. . . .

[MR. JUSTICE WHITTAKER concurred in part and dissented in part.]

BROTHERHOOD OF RAILWAY & STEAMSHIP CLERKS V. ALLEN, 373 U.S. 113, 83 S. Ct. 1158, 10 L. Ed. 2d 235 (1963). Railroad employees who objected to the use of their dues money for political purposes sued to enjoin the enforcement of the union shop against them. The North Carolina state courts granted the injunction, subject to modification upon a showing by defendant unions of the proportion of expenditures from exacted funds that was reasonably related to collective bargaining. The United States Supreme Court reversed. *Street* controlled and the employees were not entitled to relief until they had complied with their financial obligations under the union shop. But on remand, the unions, not the individual employees, were to bear the burden of proving the proportion of political expenditures (those not "germane to collective bargaining") to total union expenditures. Each employee would then be entitled to a decree ordering (1) the refund of an equivalent portion of the funds exacted from him, and (2) a reduction of future such exactions by the same proportion.

NOTES

1. Can all union spending be classified as either "political" or "germane to collective bargaining"? If not, how should expenditures in the hypothetical third category be treated under the *Allen* formula? *See generally* Wellington, *Machinists v. Street: Statutory Interpretation and the Avoidance of Constitutional Issues,* 1961 SUP. CT. REV. 49.

2. In Reid v. McDonnell Douglas Corp., 443 F.2d 408 (10th Cir. 1971), a court of appeals held that nonunion employees could sue to challenge a union's alleged use of a portion of their agency-shop fees for political purposes opposed by them, and that the preemption doctrine did not require them to take such a complaint to the NLRB. *Cf.* Buckley v. Television & Radio Artists, 496 F.2d 305 (2d Cir. 1974), *cert. denied,* 419 U.S. 1093 (1974), where the court held that two radio and television commentators could constitutionally be required to pay dues and fees to a union, but that other issues concerning compulsory membership and compliance with union regulations fell within the exclusive jurisdiction of the Labor Board. *See also* Seay v. Machinists Lodge 1578 [McDonnell Douglas Corp.], 533 F.2d 1126 (9th Cir. 1976) (dissident entitled to hearing on reasonableness of intraunion procedures for determining amount of dues to be rebated upon protest); *but cf.* Reid v. UAW Dist. Lodge 1093 [McDonnell Douglas Corp.], 479 F.2d 517 (10th Cir. 1973), *cert. denied,* 414 U.S. 1076 (1973) (denying full hearing).

3. In Abood v. Detroit Board of Educ., 431 U.S. 209 (1977), a case arising in the public sector, the Supreme Court finally confronted and resolved the constitutional issue it had taken such pains to avoid in *Street. Abood* sustained the constitutionality of a Michigan statute authorizing the negotiation of "agency shop" agreements under which public employees must pay a service fee to the union, insofar as the service charges are used to finance collective bargaining, contract administration, and grievance adjustment.

On the general issue of the validity of the agency shop for public employees, the Court relied heavily on Railway Employees' Dep't v. Hanson, 351 U.S. 225 (1956), upholding the Railway Labor Act's authorization of agreements requiring financial support of the collective bargaining agent by all employees who receive the benefits of its work. The Court pointed out that, since the Railway Labor Act overrides contrary state laws, the *Hanson* case also presented constitutional questions based on First Amendment claims of freedom of association. "[The State of Michigan] has determined that labor stability will be served by a system of exclusive representation and the permissive use of an agency shop in public employment. . . . There can be no principled basis for according that decision less weight in the constitutional balance than was given in *Hanson* to the congressional judgment reflected in the Railway Labor Act. The only remaining constitutional inquiry evoked by the appellants' argument, therefore, is whether a public employee has a weightier First Amendment interest than a private employee in not being compelled to contribute to the costs of exclusive union representation. We think he does not. . . . The very real differences between exclusive agent collective bargaining in the public and private sectors are not such as to work any greater infringement upon the First Amendment interests of public employees."

On the issue of whether agency shop fees of public employees can validly be used for political or non-collective bargaining purposes, the Court noted that the *Street* decision had been based on a difficult interpretation of the Railway Labor Act precisely to avoid facing the constitutional issue, but that the question now had to be confronted.

"Our decisions establish with unmistakable clarity that the freedom of an individual to associate for the purpose of advancing beliefs and ideas is protected by the First and Fourteenth Amendments . . . . Equally clear is the proposition that a government may not require an individual to relinquish rights guaranteed him by the First Amendment as a condition of public employment. . . . The appellants argue that they fall within the protection of these cases because they have been prohibited not from actively associating, but rather from refusing to associate. They specifically argue that they may constitutionally prevent the union's spending a part of their required service fees to contribute to political candidates and to express political views unrelated to its duties as exclusive bargaining representative. We have concluded that this argument is a meritorious one. . . .

"These principles . . . thus prohibit the appellees from requiring any of the appellants to contribute to the support of an ideological cause he may oppose as a condition of holding a job as a public school teacher.

"There will, of course, be difficult problems in drawing lines between collective bargaining activities, for which contributions may be compelled, and ideological activities unrelated to collective bargaining, for which such compulsion is prohibited. The Court held in *Street,* as a matter of statutory construction, that a similar line must be drawn under the Railway Labor Act, but in the public sector the line may be somewhat hazier. . . . We have no occasion in this case, however, to try to define such a dividing line. . . . All that we decide is that the general allegations in the complaint, if proven, establish a cause of action under the First and Fourteenth Amendments."

As to the remedy, the Supreme Court remanded the case for further proceedings. After reviewing favorably what the Court had said on the question of remedy in *Street* and Brotherhood of Railway & Steamship Clerks v. Allen, 373 U.S. 113 (1963), the Supreme Court indicated that no lesser relief would be justified in the *Abood* case.

Justice Powell, joined by Chief Justice Burger and Justice Blackmun, concurred in the judgment in *Abood,* but asserted that there is no basis for distinguishing "collective bargaining activities" from "political activities" so far as the interests protected by the First Amendment are concerned. Collective bargaining in the public sector is political in any meaningful sense of the word, and the State should have the burden of proving that any union dues or fees that it requires of nonunion employees are needed to serve paramount governmental interests. In Justice Powell's view, the majority's reliance on *Hanson* and *Street* was misplaced, since there is a fundamental distinction between what the Government may permit private employers to do and what it can require of its own employees. "Acting through the Detroit Board of Education, the State has undertaken to compel employees to pay full union dues to the union as a condition of employment."

Appendix

UNITED STEELWORKERS v. WEBER

Supreme Court of the United States
—— U. S. ——, —— S. Ct. ——, —— L.Ed.2d —— (1979)

MR. JUSTICE BRENNAN delivered the opinion of the Court, in which STEWART, WHITE, MARSHALL, and BLACKMUN, JJ., joined.

Challenged here is the legality of an affirmative action plan — collectively bargained by an employer and a union — that reserves for black employees 50% of the openings in an in-plant craft training program until the percentage of black craft workers in the plant is commensurate with the percentage of blacks in the local labor force. The question for decision is whether Congress, in Title VII of the Civil Rights Act of 1964 as amended, 42 U. S. C. § 2000e, left employers and unions in the private sector free to take such race-conscious steps to eliminate manifest racial imbalances in traditionally segregated job categories. We hold that Title VII does not prohibit such race-conscious affirmative action plans.

I. In 1974 petitioner United Steelworkers of America (USWA) and petitioner Kaiser Aluminum & Chemical Corporation (Kaiser) entered into a master collective-bargaining agreement covering terms and conditions of employment at 15 Kaiser plants. The agreement contained, *inter alia,* an affirmative action plan designed to eliminate conspicuous racial imbalances in Kaiser's then almost exclusively white craft work forces. Black craft hiring goals were set for each Kaiser plant equal to the percentage of blacks in the respective local labor forces. To enable plants to meet these goals, on-the-job training programs were established to teach unskilled production workers — black and white — the skills necessary to become craft workers. The plan reserved for black employees 50% of the openings in these newly created in-plant training programs.

This case arose from the operation of the plan at Kaiser's plant in Gramercy, La. Until 1974 Kaiser hired as craft workers for that plant only persons who had had prior craft experience. Because blacks had long been excluded from craft unions,[1] few were able to present such credentials. As a consequence, prior to 1974 only 1.83% (five out of 273) of the skilled craft workers at the Gramercy plant were black, even though the work force in the Gramercy area was approximately 39% black.

---

[1] Judicial findings of exclusion from crafts on racial grounds are so numerous as to make such exclusion a proper subject for judicial notice. See, e.g., United States v. International Union of Elevator Constructors, 538 F. 2d 1012 (3d Cir. 1976). . . . See also United States Commission on Civil Rights, The Challenge Ahead: Equal Opportunity in Referral Unions 58-94 (1976), (summarizing judicial findings of discrimination by craft unions). . . .

Pursuant to the national agreement Kaiser altered its craft hiring practice in the Gramercy plant. Rather than hiring already trained outsiders, Kaiser established a training program to train its production workers to fill craft openings. Selection of craft trainees was made on the basis of seniority, with the proviso that at least 50% of the new trainees were to be black until the percentage of black skilled craft workers in the Gramercy plant approximated the percentage of blacks in the local labor force.

During 1974, the first year of the operation of the Kaiser-USWA affirmative action plan, 13 craft trainees were selected from Gramercy's production work force. Of these, 7 were black and 6 white. The most junior black selected into the program had less seniority than several white production workers whose bids for admission were rejected. Thereafter one of those white production workers, respondent Brian Weber, instituted this class action in the United States District Court for the Eastern District of Louisiana.

The complaint alleged that the filling of craft trainee positions at the Gramercy plant pursuant to the affirmative action program had resulted in junior black employees receiving training in preference to more senior white employees, thus discriminating against respondent and other similarly situated white employees in violation of §§ 703(a) and (d) of Title VII. The District Court held that the plan violated Title VII, entered a judgment in favor of the plaintiff class, and granted a permanent injunction prohibiting Kaiser and the USWA "from denying plaintiffs, Brian F. Weber and all other members of the class, access to on-the-job training programs on the basis of race." A divided panel of the Court of Appeals for the Fifth Circuit affirmed, holding that all employment preferences based upon race, including those preferences incidental to bona fide affirmative action plans, violated Title VII's prohibition against racial discrimination in employment. We granted certiorari. We reverse.

II. We emphasize at the outset the narrowness of our inquiry. Since the Kaiser-USWA plan does not involve state action, this case does not present an alleged violation of the Equal Protection Clause of the Constitution. Further, since the Kaiser-USWA plan was adopted voluntarily, we are not concerned with what Title VII requires or with what a court might order to remedy a past proven violation of the Act. The only question before us is the narrow statutory issue of whether Title VII *forbids* private employers and unions from voluntarily agreeing upon bona fide affirmative action plans that accord racial preferences in the manner and for the purpose provided in the Kaiser-USWA plan. That question was expressly left open in McDonald v. Santa Fe Trail Transt. Co., 427 U. S. 273, 281 n. 8 (1976) which held, in a case not involving affirmative action, that Title VII protects whites as well as blacks from certain forms of racial discrimination.

Respondent argues that Congress intended in Title VII to prohibit all race-conscious affirmative action plans. Respondent's argument rests upon a literal interpretation of §§ 703 (a) and (d) of the Act. Those sections make it unlawful to "discriminate ... because of ... race" in hiring and in the selection of apprentices for training programs. Since, the argument runs, *McDonald v. Santa Fe Trail Transt. Co., supra,* settled that Title VII forbids discrimination against whites as well as blacks, and since the Kaiser-USWA affirmative action plan operates to discriminate against white employees solely because they are white, it follows that the Kaiser-USWA plan violates Title VII.

Respondent's argument is not without force. But it overlooks the significance of the fact that the Kaiser-USWA plan is an affirmative action plan voluntarily adopted by private parties to eliminate traditional patterns of racial segregation. In this context respondent's reliance upon a literal construction of § 703(a) and (d) and upon *McDonald* is misplaced. See *McDonald v. Santa Fe Trail Transt. Co., supra,* at 281 n. 8. It is a "familiar rule, that a thing may be within the letter of the statute and yet not within the statute, because not within its spirit, nor within the intention of its makers." Holy Trinity Church v. United States, 143 U. S. 457, 459 (1892). The prohibition against racial discrimination in §§ 703 (a) and (d) of Title VII must therefore be read against the background of the legislative history of Title VII and the historical context from which the Act arose. . . . Examination of those sources makes clear that an interpretation of the sections that forbade all race-conscious affirmative action would "bring about an end completely at variance with the purpose of the statute" and must be rejected. . . .

Congress' primary concern in enacting the prohibition against racial discrimination in Title VII of the Civil Rights Act of 1964 was with "the plight of the Negro in our economy." 110 Cong. Rec. 6548 (remarks of Sen. Humphrey). Before 1964, blacks were largely relegated to "unskilled and semi-skilled jobs." *Id.,* at 6548 (remarks of Sen. Humphrey); *id.,* at 7204 (remarks of Sen. Clark); *id.,* at 7279-7280 (remarks of Sen. Kennedy). Because of automation the number of such jobs was rapidly decreasing. See 110 Cong. Rec., at 6548 (remarks of Sen. Humphrey); *id.,* at 7204 (remarks of Sen. Clark). As a consequence "the relative position of the Negro worker [was] steadily worsening. In 1947 the non-white unemployment rate was only 64 percent higher than the white rate; in 1962 it was 124 percent higher." *Id.,* at 6547 (remarks of Sen. Humphrey). See also *id.,* at 7204 (remarks of Sen. Clark). Congress considered this a serious social problem. As Senator Clark told the Senate:

> "The rate of Negro unemployment has gone up consistently as compared with white unemployment for the past 15 years. This is a social malaise and a social situation which we should not tolerate. That is one of the principal reasons why this bill should pass." *Id.,* at 7220.

Congress feared that the goals of the Civil Rights Act — the integration of blacks into the mainstream of American society — could not be achieved unless this trend were reversed. And Congress recognized that that would not be possible unless blacks were able to secure jobs "which have a future." *Id.,* at 7204 (remarks to Sen. Clark). See also *id.,* at

7279-7280 (remarks of Sen. Kennedy). As Senator Humphrey explained
to the Senate.

> "What good does it do a Negro to be able to eat in a fine restaurant
> if he cannot afford to pay the bill? What good does it do him to be
> accepted in a hotel that is too expensive for his modest income? How
> can a Negro child be motivated to take full advantage of integrated
> educational facilities if he has no hope of getting a job where he can
> use that education?" *Id.,* at 6547.
>
> . . . .
>
> "Without a job, one cannot afford public convenience and
> accommodations. Income from employment may be necessary to
> further a man's education, or that of his children. If his children have
> no hope of getting a good job, what will motivate them to take
> advantage of educational opportunities." *Id.,* at 6552.

These remarks echoed President Kennedy's original message to Congress
upon the introduction of the Civil Rights Act in 1963.

> "There is little value in a Negro's obtaining the right to be admitted
> to hotels and restaurants if he has no cash in his pocket and no job."
> *Id.,* at 11159.

Accordingly, it was clear to Congress that "the crux of the problem [was]
to open employment opportunities for Negroes in occupations which have
been traditionally closed to them," *id.,* at 6548 (remarks of Sen.
Humphrey), and it was to this problem that Title VII's prohibition against
racial discrimination in employment was primarily addressed.

It plainly appears from the House Report accompanying the Civil Rights
Act that Congress did not intend wholly to prohibit private and voluntary
affirmative action efforts as one method of solving this problem. The
Report provides:

> "No bill can or should lay claim to eliminating all of the causes and
> consequences of racial and other types of discrimination against
> minorities. There is reason to believe, however, that national
> leadership provided by the enactment of Federal legislation dealing
> with the most troublesome problems *will create an atmosphere
> conducive to voluntary or local resolution of other forms of
> discrimination."* H. R. Rep. No. 914, 88th Cong., 1st Sess. (1963), at
> 18. (Emphasis supplied.)

Given this legislative history, we cannot agree with respondent that
Congress intended to prohibit the private sector from taking effective
steps to accomplish the goal that Congress designed Title VII to achieve.
The very statutory words intended as a spur or catalyst to cause
"employers and unions to self-examine and to self-evaluate their
employment practices and to endeavor to eliminate, so far as possible,
the last vestiges of an unfortunate and ignominious page in this country's
history," Albemarle v. Moody, 422 U. S. 405, 418 (1975), cannot be
interpreted as an absolute prohibition against all private, voluntary,

race-conscious affirmative action efforts to hasten the elimination of such vestiges.[4] It would be ironic indeed if a law triggered by a Nation's concern over centuries of racial injustice and intended to improve the lot of those who had "been excluded from the American dream for so long," 110 Cong. Rec., at 6552 (remarks of Sen. Humphrey), constituted the first legislative prohibition of all voluntary, private, race-conscious efforts to abolish traditional patterns of racial segregation and hierarchy.

Our conclusion is further reinforced by examination of the language and legislative history of § 703(j) of Title VII.[5] Opponents of Title VII raised two related arguments against the bill. First, they argued that the Act would be interpreted to *require* employers with racially imbalanced work forces to grant preferential treatment to racial minorities in order to integrate. Second, they argued that employers with racially imbalanced work forces would grant preferential treatment to racial minorities, even if not required to do so by the Act. See 110 Cong. Rec. 8618-8619 (remarks of Sen. Sparkman). Had Congress meant to prohibit all race-conscious affirmative action, as respondent urges, it easily could have answered both objections by providing that Title VII would not require or *permit* racially preferential integration efforts. But Congress did not choose such a course. Rather Congress added § 703 (j) which addresses only the first objection. The section provides that nothing contained in Title VII "shall be interpreted to *require* any employer . . . to grant preferential treatment . . . to any group because of the race . . . of such . . . group on account of" a defacto racial imbalance in the employer's work force. The section does *not* state that "nothing in Title VII shall be interpreted to *permit*" voluntary affirmative efforts to correct racial imbalances. The natural inference is that Congress chose not to forbid all voluntary race-conscious affirmative action.

The reasons for this choice are evident from the legislative record. Title VII could not have been enacted into law without substantial support from legislators in both Houses who traditionally resisted federal regulation of private business. Those legislators demanded as a price for their support that "management prerogatives and union freedoms . . . be left undisturbed to the greatest extent possible." H. R. Rep. No. 914, 88th Cong., 1st Sess., Pt. 2 (1963), at 29. Section 703 (j) was proposed by Senator Dirksen to allay any fears that the Act might be interpreted in such a way as to upset this compromise. The section was designed to prevent § 703 of Title VII from being interpreted in such a way as to lead to undue "Federal Government interference with private businesses because of some Federal employee's ideas about racial balance or imbalance." 110

---

[4] The problem that Congress addressed in 1964 remains with us. In 1962 the nonwhite unemployment rate was 124% higher than the white rate. See 110 Cong. Rec. 6547 (remarks of Sen. Humphrey). In 1978 the black unemployment rate was 129% higher. See Monthly Labor Review, U. S. Department of Labor Bureau of Labor Statistics 78 (Mar. 1979).

[5] Section 703 (j) speaks to substantive liability under Title VII, but it does not preclude courts from considering racial imbalance as evidence of a Title VII violation. See Teamsters v. United States, 431 U. S. 324, 339-340, n. 20 (1977). Remedies for substantive violations are governed by § 706 (g), 42 U. S. C. § 2000e-5 (g).

Cong. Rec., at 14314 (remarks of Sen. Miller).[6] See also *Id.,* at 9881 (remarks of Sen. Allott); *id.,* at 10520 (remarks of Sen. Carlson); *id.,* at 11471 (remarks of Sen. Javits); *Id.,* at 12817 (remarks of Sen. Dirksen). Clearly, a prohibition against all voluntary, race-conscious, affirmative action efforts would disserve these ends. Such a prohibition would augment the powers of the Federal Government and diminish traditional management prerogatives while at the same time impeding attainment of the ultimate statutory goals. In view of this legislative history and in view of Congress' desire to avoid undue federal regulation of private businesses, use of the word "require" rather than the phrase "require or permit" in § 703 (j) fortifies the conclusion that Congress did not intend to limit traditional business freedom to such a degree as to prohibit all voluntary, race-conscious affirmative action.[7]

We therefore hold that Title VII's prohibition in §§ 703 (a) and (d) against racial discrimination does not condemn all private, voluntary, race-conscious affirmative action plans.

---

[6] Title VI of the Civil Rights Act of 1964, considered in University of California Regents v. Bakke, 438 U. S. 265 (1978), contains no provision comparable to § 703 (j). This is because Title VI was an exercise of federal power over a matter in which the Federal Government was already directly involved: the prohibitions against race-based conduct contained in Title VI governed "program[s] or activit[ies] receiving Federal financial assistance." 42 U. S. C. § 2000d. Congress was legislating to assure federal funds would not be used in an improper manner. Title VII, by contrast, was enacted pursuant to the Commerce power to regulate purely private decisionmaking and was not intended to incorporate and particularize the commands of the Fifth and Fourteenth Amendments. Title VII and Title VI, therefore, cannot be read *in pari materia.* See 110 Cong. Rec. 8315 (1964) (remarks of Sen. Cooper). See also *id.,* at 11615 (remarks of Sen. Cooper).

[7] Respondent argues that our construction of § 703 conflicts with various remarks in the legislative record. See, *e.g.,* 110 Cong. Rec. 7213 (Sens. Clark and Case); *id.,* at 7218 (Sens. Clark and Case); *id.,* at 6549 (Sen. Humphrey); *id.,* at 8921 (Sen. Williams). We do not agree. In Senator Humphrey's words, these comments were intended as assurances that Title VII would not allow establishment of systems "to *maintain* racial balance in employment," *id.,* at 11848. They were not addressed to temporary, voluntary, affirmative action measures undertaken to eliminate manifest racial imbalance in traditionally segregated job categories. Moreover, the comments referred to by respondent all preceded the adoption of § 703 (j), 42 U. S. C. § 2000e-2 (j). After § 703 (j) was adopted congressional comments were all to the effect that employers would not be *required* to institute preferential quotas to avoid Title VII liability, see, *e.g., id.,* at 12819 (remarks of Sen. Dirksen); *id.,* at 13079-13080 (remarks of Sen. Clark); *id.,* at 15876 (remarks of Rep. Lindsay). There was no suggestion after the adoption of § 703 (j) that wholly voluntary, race-conscious, affirmative action efforts would in themselves constitute a violation of Title VII. On the contrary, as Representative MacGregor told the House shortly before the final vote on Title VII:

"Important as the scope and extent of this bill is, it is also vitally important that all Americans understand what this bill does not cover.

"Your mail and mine, your contacts and mine with our constituents, indicates a great degree of misunderstanding about this bill. People complain about . . . preferential treatment or quotas in employment. There is a mistaken belief that Congress is legislating in these areas in this bill. When we drafted this bill we excluded these issues largely because the problems raised by these controversial questions are more properly handled at a governmental level closer to the American people and by communities and individuals themselves." 110 Cong. Rec. 15893 (remarks of Rep. MacGregor).

III. We need not today define in detail the line of demarcation between permissible and impermissible affirmative action plans. It suffices to hold that the challenged Kaiser-USWA affirmative action plan falls on the permissible side of the line. The purposes of the plan mirror those of the statute. Both were designed to break down old patterns of racial segregation and hierarchy. Both were structured to "open employment opportunities for Negroes in occupations which have been traditionally closed to them." 110 Cong. Rec. 6548 (remarks of Sen. Humphrey).[8]

At the same time the plan does not unnecessarily trammel the interests of the white employees. The plan does not require the discharge of white workers and their replacement with new black hires. Cf. *McDonald v. Santa Fe Trail Transt. Co., supra.* Nor does the plan create an absolute bar to the advancement of white employees; half of those trained in the program will be white. Moreover, the plan is a temporary measure; it is not intended to maintain racial balance, but simply to eliminate a manifest racial imbalance. Preferential selection of craft trainees at the Gramercy plant will end as soon as the percentage of black skilled craft workers in the Gramercy plant approximates the percentage of blacks in the local labor force.

We conclude, therefore, that the adoption of the Kaiser-USWA plan for the Gramercy plant falls within the area of discretion left by Title VII to the private sector voluntarily to adopt affirmative action plans designed to eliminate conspicuous racial imbalance in traditionally segregated job categories.[9] Accordingly, the judgment of the Court of Appeals for the Fifth Circuit is

Reversed.

MR. JUSTICE POWELL and MR. JUSTICE STEVENS took no part in the consideration or decision of this case.

MR. JUSTICE BLACKMUN, concurring.

While I share some of the misgivings expressed in MR. JUSTICE REHNQUIST's dissent, *post,* concerning the extent to which the legislative history of Title VII clearly supports the result the Court reaches today, I believe that additional considerations, practical and equitable, only partially perceived, if perceived at all, by the 88th Congress, support the conclusion reached by the Court today, and I therefore join its opinion as well as its judgment.

I. In his dissent from the decision of the United States Court of Appeals for the Fifth Circuit, Judge Wisdom pointed out that this case arises from a practical problem in the administration of Title VII. The broad prohibition against discrimination places the employer and the union on

---

.... [8] This is not to suggest that the freedom of an employer to undertake race-conscious affirmative action efforts depends on whether or not his effort is motivated by fear of liability under Title VII.

[9] Our disposition makes unnecessary consideration of petitioners' argument that their plan was justified because they feared that black employees would bring suit under Title VII if they did not adopt an affirmative action plan. Nor need we consider petitioners' contention that their affirmative action plan represented an attempt to comply with Executive Order 11246.

what he accurately described as a "high tightrope without a net beneath them." 563 F. 2d 216, 230. If Title VII is read literally, on the one hand they face liability for past discrimination against blacks, and on the other they face liability to whites for any voluntary preferences adopted to mitigate the effects of prior discrimination against blacks.

In this case, Kaiser denies prior discrimination but concedes that its past hiring practices may be subject to question. Although the labor force in the Gramercy area was approximately 39% black, Kaiser's work force was less than 15% black, and its craft work force was less than 2% black. Kaiser had made some effort to recruit black painters, carpenters, insulators, and other craftsmen, but it continued to insist that those hired have five years prior industrial experience, a requirement that arguably was not sufficiently job-related to justify under Title VII any discriminatory impact it may have had. See Parson v. Kaiser Aluminum & Chemical Corp., 575 F. 2d 1374, 1389 (5th Cir. 1978), *cert. denied,* —— U. S. —— (1979). The parties dispute the extent to which black craftsmen were available in the local labor market. They agree, however, that after critical reviews from the Office of Federal Contract Compliance, Kaiser and the Steelworkers established the training program in question here and modeled it along the lines of a Title VII consent decree later entered for the steel industry. See United States v. Allegheny-Ludlum Industries, Inc., 517 F. 2d 826 (3d Cir. 1976). Yet when they did this, respondent Weber sued, alleging that Title VII prohibited the program because it discriminated against him as a white person and it was not supported by a prior judicial finding of discrimination against blacks.

Respondents' reading of Title VII, endorsed by the Court of Appeals, places voluntary compliance with Title VII in profound jeopardy. The only way for the employer and the union to keep their footing on the "tightrope" it creates would be to eschew all forms of voluntary affirmative action. Even a whisper of emphasis on minority recruiting would be forbidden. Because Congress intended to encourage private efforts to come into compliance with Title VII, see Alexander v. Gardner-Denver Co., 415 U. S. 36, 44 (1974), Judge Wisdom concluded that employers and unions who had committed "arguable violations" of Title VII should be free to take reasonable responses without fear of liability to whites. 563 F.2d, at 230. Preferential hiring along the lines of the Kaiser program is a reasonable response for the employer, whether or not a court, on these facts, could order the same step as a remedy. The company is able to avoid identifying victims of past discrimination, and so avoids claims for backpay that would inevitably follow a response limited to such victims. If past victims should be benefited by the program, however, the company mitigates its liability to those persons. Also, to the extent that Title VII liability is predicated on the "disparate effect" of an employer's past hiring practices, the program makes it less likely that such an effect could be demonstrated. Cf. County of Los Angeles v. Davis, —— U. S. ——, —— (1979) (hiring could moot a past Title VII claim). And the Court has recently held that work force statistics resulting from private affirmative action were probative of benign intent in a "disparate treatment" case. Furnco Construction Corp. v. Waters, 438 U. S. 567, 579-580 (1978).

The "arguable violation" theory has a number of advantages. It responds to a practical problem in the administration of Title VII not anticipated by Congress. It draws predictability from the outline of present law, and closely effectuates the purpose of the Act. Both Kaiser and the United States urge its adoption here. Because I agree that it is the soundest way to approach this case, my preference would be to resolve this litigation by applying it and holding that Kaiser's craft training program meets the requirement that voluntary affirmative action be a reasonable response to an "arguable violation" of Title VII.

II. The Court, however, declines to consider the narrow "arguable violation" approach and adheres instead to an interpretation of Title VII that permits affirmative action by an employer whenever the job category in question is "traditionally segregated." ....

"Traditionally segregated job categories," where they exist, sweep far more broadly than the class of "arguable violations" of Title VII. The Court's expansive approach is somewhat disturbing for me because, as Mr. Justice Rehnquist points out, the Congress that passed Title VII probably thought it was adopting a principle of nondiscrimination that would apply to blacks and whites alike. While setting aside that principle can be justified where necessary to advance statutory policy by encouraging reasonable responses as a form of voluntary compliance that mitigates "arguable violations," discarding the principle of nondiscrimination where no countervailing statutory policy exists appears to be at odds with the bargain struck when Title VII was enacted.

A closer look at the problem, however, reveals that in each of the principal ways in which the Court's "traditionally segregated job categories" approach expands on the "arguable violations" theory, still other considerations point in favor of the broad standard adopted by the Court, and make it possible for me to conclude that the Court's reading of the statute is an acceptable one.

A. The first point at which the Court departs from the "arguable violations" approach is that it measures an individual employer's capacity for affirmative action solely in terms of a statistical disparity. The individual employer need not have engaged in discriminatory practices in the past. While, under Title VII, a mere disparity may provide the basis for a prima facie case against an employer, Dothard v. Rawlinson, 433 U. S. 321, 329-331 (1977), it would not conclusively prove a violation of the Act. Teamsters v. United States, 431 U. S. 324, 339-340, n. 20 (1977); see § 703 (j), 42 U. S. C. § 20003-2 (j). As a practical matter, however, this difference may not be that great. While the "arguable violation" standard is conceptually satisfying, in practice the emphasis would be on "arguable" rather than on "violation." The great difficulty in the District Court was that no one had any incentive to prove that Kaiser had violated the Act. Neither Kaiser nor the Steelworkers wanted to establish a past violation, nor did Weber. The blacks harmed had never sued and so had no established representative. The Equal Employment Opportunity

Commission declined to intervene, and cannot be expected to intervene in every case of this nature. To make the "arguable violation" standard work, it would have to be set low enough to permit the employer to prove it without obligating himself to pay a damage award. The inevitable tendency would be to avoid hairsplitting litigation by simply concluding that a mere disparity between the racial composition of the employer's work force and the composition of the qualified local labor force would be an "arguable violation," even though actual liability could not be established on that basis alone. See Note, 57 N. C. L. Rev. 695, 714-79 (1979).

B. The Court also departs from the "arguable violation" approach by permitting an employer to redress discrimination that lies wholly outside the bounds of Title VII. For example, Title VII provides no remedy for pre-Act discrimination, Hazelwood School District v. United States, 433 U. S. 299, 309-310 (1977); yet the purposeful discrimination that creates a "traditionally segregated job category" may have entirely predated the Act. More subtly, in assessing a prima facie case of Title VII liability, the composition of the employer's work force is compared to the composition of the pool of workers who meet valid job qualifications. Hazelwood, 433 U. S., at 308, and n. 13; Teamsters v. United States, 431 U.S., at 339-340, and n. 20 (1977). When a "job category" is traditionally segregated, however, that pool will reflect the effects of segregation, and the Court's approach goes further and permits a comparison with the composition of the labor force as a whole, in which minorities are more heavily represented.

Strong considerations of equity support an interpretation of Title VII that would permit private affirmative action to reach where Title VII itself does not. The bargain struck in 1964 with the passage of Title VII guaranteed equal opportunity for white and black alike, but where Title VII provides no remedy for blacks, it should not be construed to foreclose private affirmative action from supplying relief. It seems unfair for respondent Weber to argue, as he does, that the asserted scarcity of black craftsmen in Louisiana, the product of historic discrimination, makes Kaiser's training program illegal because it ostensibly absolves Kaiser of all Title VII liability. Absent compelling evidence of legislative intent, I would not interpret Title VII itself as a means of "locking in" the effects of segregation for which Title VII provides no remedy. Such a construction, as the Court points out, would be "ironic," given the broad remedial purposes of Title VII.

The dissent, while it focuses more on what Title VII does not require than on what Title VII forbids, cites several passages that appear to express an intent to "lock in" minorities. In mining the legislative history anew, however, the dissent, in my view, fails to take proper account of our prior cases that have given that history a much more limited reading than that adopted by the dissent. For example, in Griggs v. Duke Power Co., 401 U.S. 424, 434-436 and n. 11 (1971), the Court refused to give controlling weight to the memorandum of Senators Clark and Case which the dissent now finds so persuasive. . . . And in quoting a statement from that memorandum that an employer would not be "permitted . . . to prefer Negroes for future vacancies," . . . the dissent does not point out that the Court's opinion in Teamsters v. United States, 431 U.S. 324, 349-351 (1977), implies that that language is limited to the protection of established seniority systems. Here seniority is not in issue because the craft training program is new and does not involve an abrogation of pre-existing seniority rights. In short, the passages marshaled by the dissent are not so compelling as to merit the whip hand over the obvious equity of permitting employers to ameliorate the effects of past discrimination for which Title VII provides no direct relief.

III. I also think it significant that, while the Court's opinion does not foreclose other forms of affirmative action, the Kaiser program it approves is a moderate one. The opinion notes that the program does not afford an absolute preference for blacks, and that it ends when the racial composition of Kaiser's craft work force matches the racial composition of the local population. It thus operates as a temporary tool for remedying past discrimination without attempting to "maintain" a previously achieved balance. See University of California Regents v. Bakke, 438 U. S. 265, 342 n. 17 (1978) (BRENNAN, WHITE, MARSHALL, and BLACKMUN, JJ.). Because the duration of the program is finite, it perhaps will end even before the "stage of maturity when action along this line is no longer necessary." Id., at 403 (BLACKMUN, J.). And if the Court has misperceived the political will, it has the assurance that because the question is statutory Congress may set a different course if it so chooses.

MR. CHIEF JUSTICE BURGER, dissenting.

The Court reaches a result I would be inclined to vote for were I a Member of Congress considering a proposed amendment of Title VII. I cannot join the Court's judgment, however, because it is contrary to the explicit language of the statute and arrived at by means wholly incompatible with long-established principles of separation of powers. Under the guise of statutory "construction," the Court effectively rewrites Title VII to achieve what it regards as a desirable result. It "amends" the statute to do precisely what both its sponsors and its opponents agreed the statute was *not* intended to do. . . .

The quota embodied in the collective-bargaining agreement between Kaiser and the Steelworkers unquestionably discriminates on the basis of race against individual employees seeking admission to on-the-job training programs. And, under the plain language of § 703 (d), that is "an *unlawful* employment practice."

Oddly, the Court seizes upon the very clarity of the statute almost as a justification for evading the unavoidable impact of its language. The Court blandly tells us that Congress could not really have meant what it said, for a "literal construction" would defeat the "purpose" of the statute — at least the congressional "purpose" as five Justices divine it today. But how are judges supposed to ascertain the *purpose* of a statute except through the words Congress used and the legislative history of the statute's evolution? One need not even resort to the legislative history to recognize what is apparent from the face of Title VII — that it is specious to suggest that § 703(j) contains a negative pregnant that permits employers to do what §§ 703 (a) and (d) unambiguously and unequivocally *forbid* employers from doing. Moreover, as MR. JUSTICE REHNQUIST's opinion — which I join — conclusively demonstrates, the legislative history makes equally clear that the supporters and opponents of Title VII reached an agreement about the statute's intended effect. That agree ment, expressed so clearly in the language of the statute that no one should doubt its meaning, forecloses the reading which the Court gives the statute today.

Arguably, Congress may not have gone far enough in correcting the effects of past discrimination when it enacted Title VII. The gross discrimination against minorities to which the Court adverts — particularly against Negroes in the building trades and craft unions — is one of the dark chapters in the otherwise great history of the American labor movement. And, I do not question the importance of encouraging voluntary compliance with the purposes and policies of Title VII. But that statute was conceived and enacted to make discrimination against *any* individual illegal, and I fail to see how "voluntary compliance" with the no-discrimination principle that is the heart and soul of Title VII as currently written will be achieved by permitting employers to discriminate against some individuals to give preferential treatment to others.

Until today, I had thought the Court was of the unanimous view that "discriminatory preference for any group, minority or majority, is precisely and only what Congress has proscribed" in Title VII. Griggs v. Duke Power Co., 401 U. S. 424, 431 (1971). Had Congress intended otherwise, it very easily could have drafted language allowing what the Court permits today. Far from doing so, Congress expressly *prohibited* in §§ 703(a) and (d) the discrimination against Brian Weber the Court approves now. If "affirmative action" programs such as the one presented in this case are to be permitted, it is for Congress, not this Court, to so direct. . . .

MR. JUSTICE REHNQUIST, with whom THE CHIEF JUSTICE joins, dissenting. . . .

The operative sections of Title VII prohibit racial discrimination in employment *simpliciter*. Taken in its normal meaning, and as understood by all Members of Congress who spoke to the issue during the legislative debates, this language prohibits a covered employee from considering race when making an employment decision, whether the race be black or white. Several years ago, however, a United States District Court held that "the dismissal of white employees charged with misappropriating company property while not dismissing a similarly charged Negro employee does not raise a claim upon which Title VII relief may be granted." McDonald v. Santa Fe Trail Transt. Co., 427 U. S. 273, 278 (1976). This Court unanimously reversed, concluding from the "uncontradicted legislative history" that "Title VII prohibits racial discrimination against the white petitioners in this case upon the same standards as would be applicable were they Negroes . . . ." 427 U. S., at 280.

We have never wavered in our understanding that Title VII "prohibits *all* racial discrimination in employment, without exception for any particular employees." *Id.,* at 283 (emphasis in original). In Griggs v. Duke Power Co., 401 U. S. 424, 429 (1971), our first occasion to interpret Title VII, a unanimous court observed that "[d]iscriminatory preference, for any group, minority or majority, is precisely and only what Congress has proscribed." And in our most recent discussion of the issue, we uttered words seemingly dispositive of this case: "It is clear beyond cavil that the obligation imposed by Title VII is to provide an equal opportunity for *each* applicant regardless of race, without regard to whether members of the applicant's race are already proportionately represented in the work force." Furnco Construction Corp. v. Waters, 438 U. S. 567, — (1978) (emphasis in original).

. . . [T]he Court also seizes upon § 703 (j) of Title VII as an independent, or at least partially independent, basis for its holding. Totally ignoring the wording of that section, which is obviously addressed to those charged with the responsibility of interpreting the law rather than those who are subject to its proscriptions, and totally ignoring the months of legislative debates preceding the section's introduction and passage, which demonstrate clearly that it was enacted to prevent precisely what occurred in this case, the Court infers from § 703 (j) that "Congress chose not to forbid all voluntary race-conscious affirmative action."

Thus, by a *tour de force* reminiscent not of jurists such as Hale, Holmes, and Hughes, but of escape artists such as Houdini, the Court eludes clear statutory language, "uncontradicted" legislative history, and uniform precedent in concluding that employers are, after all, permitted to consider race in making employment decisions. It may be that one or more of the principal sponsors of Title VII would have preferred to see a provision allowing preferential treatment of minorities written into the bill. Such a provision, however, would have to have been expressly or impliedly excepted from Title VII's explicit prohibition on all racial discrimination in employment. There is no such exception in the Act. And a reading of the legislative debates concerning Title VII, in which proponents and opponents alike uniformly denounced discrimination in favor of, as well as discrimination against, Negroes, demonstrates clearly that any legislator harboring an unspoken desire for such a provision could not possibly have succeeded in enacting it into law. . . .

II. Were Congress to act today specifically to prohibit the type of racial discrimination suffered by Weber, it would be hard pressed to draft language better tailored to the task than that found in § 703 (d) of Title VII. . . . Equally suited to the task would be § 703 (a) (2). . . .

Entirely consistent with these two express prohibitions is the language of § 703 (j) of Title VII, which provides that the Act is not to be interpreted "to require any employer . . . to grant preferential treatment to any individual or to any group because of the race . . . of such individual or group" to correct a racial imbalance in the employer's work force.

Seizing on the word "require," the Court infers that Congress must have intended to "permit" this type of racial discrimination. Not only is this reading of § 703 (j) outlandish in the light of the flat prohibitions of §§ 703 (a) and (d), but, as explained in Part III, it is totally belied by the Act's legislative history.

Quite simply, Kaiser's racially discriminatory admission quota is flatly prohibited by the plain language of Title VII. This normally dispositive fact, however, gives the Court only momentary pause. An "interpretation" of the statute upholding Weber's claim would, according to the Court, " 'bring about an end completely at variance with the purpose of the statute.' " . . . . To support this conclusion, the Court calls upon the "spirit" of the Act, which it divines from passages in Title VII's legislative history indicating that enactment of the statute was prompted by Congress' desire "to open employment opportunities for Negroes in occupations which [had] been traditionally closed to them." But the legislative history invoked by the Court to avoid the plain language of §§ 703(a) and (d) simply misses the point. To be sure, the reality of employment discrimination against Negroes provided the primary impetus for passage of Title VII. But this fact by no means supports the proposition that Congress intended to leave employers free to discriminate against white persons. In most cases, "[l]egislative history . . . is more vague than the statute we are called upon to interpret." United States v. Public Utilities Comm'n, 345 U. S. 295, 321 (1954) (Jackson, J., concurring). Here, however, the legislative history of Title VII is as clear as the language of §§ 703 (a) and (d), and it irrefutably demonstrates that Congress meant precisely what it said in §§ 703 (a) and (d) — that *no* racial discrimination in employment is permissible under Title VII, not even preferential treatment of minorities to correct racial imbalance.

III . . . . [There follows an exhaustive, detailed, 22-page summary of the legislative history.]

IV. Reading the language of Title VII, as the Court purports to do, "against the background of [its] legislative history . . . and the historical context from which the Act arose," one is led inescapably to the conclusion that Congress fully understood what it was saying and meant precisely what it said. Opponents of the civil rights bill did not argue that employers would be permitted under Title VII voluntarily to grant preferential treatment to minorities to correct racial imbalance. The plain language of the statute too clearly prohibited such racial discrimination to admit of any doubt. They argued, tirelessly, that Title VII would be interpreted by federal agencies and their agents to require unwilling employers to racially balance their work forces by granting preferential treatment to minorities. Supporters of H. R. 7152 responded, equally tirelessly, that the Act would not be so interpreted because not only does it not require preferential treatment of minorities, it does not *permit* preferential treatment of any race for any reason. It cannot be doubted that the proponents of Title VII understood the meaning of their words, for "[s]eldom has similar legislation been debated with greater consciousness for the need for 'legislative history' or with greater care in the making thereof, to guide the courts in interpreting and applying the law." Title VII: Legislative History, at 444.

To put an end to the dispute, supporters of the civil rights bill drafted and introduced § 703 (j). Specifically addressed to the opposition's charge, § 703 (j) simply enjoins federal agencies and courts from interpreting Title VII to require an employer to prefer certain racial groups to correct imbalances in his work force. The section says nothing about voluntary preferential treatment of minorities because such racial discrimination is plainly proscribed by §§ 703 (a) and (d). Indeed, had Congress intended to except voluntary, race-conscious preferential treatment from the blanket prohibition on racial discrimination in §§ 703 (a) and (d), it surely could have drafted language better suited to the task than § 703 (j). It knew how. Section 703 (i) provides:

> "Nothing contained in [title VII] shall apply to any business or enterprise on or near an Indian reservation with respect to any publicly announced employment practice of such business or enterprise under which a preferential treatment is given to any individual because he is an Indian living on or near a reservation." § 703 (i), 42 U. S. C. § 2000e-2 (i).

V. Our task in this case, like any other case involving the construction of a statute, is to give effect to the intent of Congress. To divine that intent, we traditionally look first to the words of the statute and, if they are unclear, then to the statute's legislative history. Finding the desired result hopelessly foreclosed by these conventional sources, the Court turns to a third source — the "spirit" of the Act. But close examination of what the Court proffers as the spirit of the Act reveals it as the spirit animating the present majority, not the Eighty-eighth Congress. For if the spirit of the Act eludes the cold words of the statute itself, it rings out with unmistakable clarity in the words of the elected representatives who made the Act law. It is *equality.* Senator Dirksen, I think, captured that spirit in a speech delivered on the floor of the Senate just moments before the bill was passed:

> "[T]oday we come to grips finally with a bill that advances the enjoyment of living; but, more than that, it advances the equality of opportunity.
>
> "I do not emphasize the word 'equality' standing by itself. It means equality of opportunity in the field of education. It means equality of opportunity in the field of employment. It means equality of opportunity in the field of participation in the affairs of government . . . .
>
> "That is it.
>
> "Equality of opportunity, if we are going to talk about conscience, is the mass conscience of mankind that speaks in every generation, and it will continue to speak long after we are dead and gone." 110 Cong. Rec. 14510 (1964).

There is perhaps no device more destructive to the notion of equality than the *numerus clausus* — the quota. Whether described as "benign discrimination" or "affirmative action," the racial quota is nonetheless a creator of castes, a two-edged sword that must demean one in order to prefer another. In passing Title VII Congress outlawed *all* racial discrimination, recognizing that no discrimination based on race is benign, that no action disadvantaging a person because of his color is affirmative. With today's holding, the Court introduces into Title VII a tolerance for the very evil that the law was intended to eradicate, without offering even a clue as to what the limits on that tolerance may be. We are told simply that Kaiser's racially discriminatory admission quota "falls on the permissible side of the line." By going not merely *beyond,* but directly *against* Title VII's language and legislative history, the Court has sown the wind. Later courts will face the impossible task of reaping the whirlwind.

Index

References are to page numbers.

B

C

D

Damages,
    punitive, 410-12, 699, 760, 828, 886
    secondary pressure, 410-13
    strikes in breach of contract, 671-74, 693-700
    suits against individual strikers, 693-97, 699-700
    suits by and against unions, 410-13, 436-38, 440-48, 671-74, 693-99, 742-54,
        855-57, 878-99, 906-26, 943-50
    suits in state courts, 436-38, 440-48, 671-74, 742-51, 875
Decertification, 202
Discharge, see also REINSTATEMENT; UNFAIR LABOR PRACTICES
    economic strikers, 150-60
    inducement by labor unions, 126-32, 440-49, 862-76
    "just cause," 122-23
    proof of unfair labor practice, 118-25
    violence and misconduct, 191-97
Discipline, see DISCHARGE; LABOR UNIONS
Discrimination, see EQUAL EMPLOYMENT OPPORTUNITY, RACIAL
DISCRIMINATION; UNFAIR LABOR PRACTICES
Disestablishment, 111-19
Dues and fees, see LABOR UNIONS; UNION SECURITY

E

Economic coercion and inducement, see UNFAIR LABOR PRACTICES
Elections, see LABOR UNIONS; REPRESENTATION ELECTIONS
Emergency disputes,
    alternative proposals, 430-34
    board of inquiry, 426
    eighty-day injunction, 426-29
    Labor Management Relations Act, 426-29
    Railway Labor Act, 429-30
    state legislation, 430
    strike vote, 426
Employees,
    definition under National Labor Relations Act, 50-55
    exclusions, miscellaneous, 54-55
    independent contractors, 50-53
    supervisors, 53-54
Employee Retirement Income Security Act, 564
Employers, see appropriate headings
Equal employment opportunity,
    age discrimination, 43, 809
    discrimination, meaning of, 764-809
    federal legislation, 43-44, 808-09
    national origin discrimination, 807-08
    procedures,
        arbitration, effect of, 839-48
        evidence, 810-27
    race discrimination,
        affirmative action plans, 796-98
        job qualifications, 765-71

S